Instant identification guide

The first 35 pages of Southern African Wildlife (starting opposite) feature a unique, colour-coded instant identification guide, designed to help you identify a species as quickly as possible.

How to use this section

1 Once you've spotted a species you're unable to identify—such as a large antelope—open the colour-coded index at the correct entry, for example 'mammals'.

2 Look for the silhouette bearing the closest resemblance to the animal you've seen, checking its size against the figure of a man shown on each page.

3 Read the main distinguishing marks—shape and colour—accompanying the silhouette, until you spot the description of the animal you've seen.

4 At the end of each description is the name of the species in bold type, together with a page number indicating where the main entry on the animal will be found.

5 Turn to the page indicated (the pages on which the main entries appear are colour-coded to match the index in this section) and use the illustration, distribution map and detailed description to make a positive identification.

All the silhouettes on each page are drawn to the same scale, showing their size in relation to each other and to the drawing of a 1,75 m-tall man, marked in 25 cm horizontal bands. In the case of smaller animals, a hand or thumb, marked in 5 cm bands, has been used.

Well-known animals, such as elephants, giraffes and ostriches, are not featured in this section.

Mammals

- White with black stripes; dewlap under throat; 'gridiron' pattern on top of rump above tail; belly white: **Cape mountain zebra** *page 49*
- White with black stripes, but yellowish or grey 'shadow' stripes between black stripes, particularly on rump; no dewlap on throat; no 'gridiron' pattern; belly normally striped: **Burchell's zebra** *page 49*

- Silvery grey coat; black tail; dark brownish vertical stripes on neck and foreparts; horns curve downwards, then upwards: **blue wildebeest** *page 50*
- Dark brown, black in older males; yellowish-white tail; mane two-tone—yellow at base, black towards tip; horns curve outwards then upwards: **black wildebeest** *page 50*

- Dark brown or black coat; belly pure white; no shaggy neck hair; long, curved, swept-back horns: **sable antelope** *page 51*
- Coat and underparts greyish brown with reddish tinge; shaggy neck and throat hair; long, curving, swept-back horns: **roan antelope** *page 51*
- Pale fawn-grey with dark brown band along each flank separating white belly from fawn-grey back; larger black-white facial markings than roan antelope; straight V-shaped horns; legs black above, white 'stockings' below: **gemsbok** *page 52*

Mammals

- Yellowish tawny coat; yellowish white rump, white extending onto tail base; face yellowish tawny: **Lichtenstein's hartebeest** *page 53*
- Reddish brown coat; yellowish white rump extending to base of tail; black stripe down front of face: **red hartebeest** *page 53*
- Dark, reddish brown coat with purple sheen; no white marks on rump; face dark brown to black: **tsessebe** *page 54*

- Reddish coat, changing abruptly to paler on sides, then abruptly to white on belly; no dark brown stripe on flank, and no white markings on rump and tail; vertical black bands on each side of rump: **impala** *page 54*
- Dark brown stripe on flank separating cinnamon-brown back and white underparts: **springbok** *page 70*

- Reddish brown coat with paler brown (but not white) buttock patch; yellowish lower legs; white facial blaze usually broken between eyes: **blesbok** *page 55*
- Rich dark brown body colour with darker patches on sides of head; flanks and upper limbs have purplish gloss; pure white patch on buttock; white lower legs; white facial blaze usually continuous: **bontebok** *page 55*

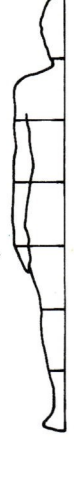

Mammals

- Golden yellow coat; off-white throat and belly; no black bands down front of forelegs: **puku** *page 56*
- Reddish yellow coat; white chin, throat and belly; black bands down front of forelegs; bigger than puku, and with longer horns: **lechwe** *page 56*

- Greyish with white underparts; yellowish head and neck; bushy tail; short horns: **mountain reedbuck** *page 57*
- Greyish brown coat; white underparts; straight horns: **grey rhebok** *page 57*
- Large white circle on rump; greyish brown coat above and below; horns forward-curving: **waterbuck** *page 58*
- Brownish yellow to greyish brown coat; white underparts; wide-set, forward-curved horns; dark brown band on front of legs (unlike mountain reedbuck): **reedbuck** *page 58*

- Drab dark brown, shaggy coat in male; female same as male, but may have four vertical stripes on side; white chevron on top of muzzle: **sitatunga** *page 59*
- Dark brown coat; crest of long white or yellowish hair along spine; no white band on face; variable colour pattern—in north more white lines and spots on sides of body, in south fewer: **bushbuck** *page 60*
- Fawn coat with white spots; conspicuous white patch above eyes; broad white stripe along each flank; males have branched antlers: **fallow deer** *page 74*

- Slate-grey to dark brown coat (male), rich chestnut (female); up to 14 vertical white stripes in young males, reduced to three or four in adulthood; females have up to 18 white stripes throughout life; white chevron on face; two white spots above hooves: **nyala** *page 59*
- Fawn-grey body (females more cinnamon), with 6-10 unevenly spaced vertical white stripes on torso; white chevron on face: **kudu** *page 60*

Mammals

- Grey, sparsely haired coat; crest of long black, brown or yellowish bristly hair from head to tail; prominent tusks and facial warts; tail held erect while running; diurnal: **warthog** *page 61*
- Reddish brown body with lighter mane; pointed ears with hair rising from tips; thick patch of whitish hair on sides of face; tail held down while running; nocturnal: **bushpig** *page 61*

- Spots in rosette shapes on body; no black line on face; heavy body: **leopard** *page 62*
- Slender body; narrow waist; deep chest; small, single (solid) spots; black 'tear' mark on each side of face: **cheetah** *page 63*

- Spotted and barred coat; slim limbs; shortish tail; big rounded ears on small head; back of ear has black band separated from black tip by white band: **serval** *page 63*
- Brindled sandy-brown to brick-red coat; colour darker down mid-back; off-white underparts; long, black ear tufts: **caracal** *page 64*

Mammals

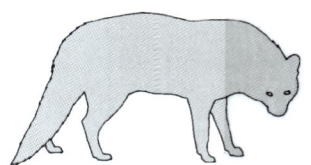

- Black bars, spots and stripes on greyish/whitish background; black 'mask' across and below each eye; lower parts of limbs black; tail black above, but broadly banded below with white: **civet** *page 64*
- Dark to black spots and bars on grey-white background; two black bands from inner ears to shoulders; white-tipped tail banded in black and off-white; black band from behind shoulders along mid-back to base of tail; this can be raised as a crest when under stress: **small-spotted genet** *page 87*
- Very similar to small-spotted genet, but has black-tipped tail; black dorsal crest is not erectile: **large-spotted genet** *page 87*

- Fawn-yellow to dull grey-white body, with dark brown or blackish spots; heavy, high forequarters; slender, lower hindquarters; rounded ears: **spotted hyaena** *page 65*
- Shaggy, medium-to-dark brown coat; prominently lighter 'mantle' on neck and shoulders; black muzzle; pointed ears: **brown hyaena** *page 65*
- Buffy to yellowish white body with several black vertical stripes on flanks; pointed ears; long dorsal crest (raised under stress) on back: **aardwolf** *page 66*

- Reddish brown coat, with black, white-flecked 'saddle' on back; black, bushy tail; pointed ears: **black-backed jackal** *page 67*
- Grey or greyish buff colour; light-and-dark stripe along each flank; broad white tip to tail: **side-striped jackal** *page 67*
- Buff and grey coat; very bushy tail; tawny brown limbs and head: **Cape fox** *page 68*
- Smoky grey or buffy grey upperparts; off-white or buffy underparts; sharp, elongated muzzle; enormous ears; black limbs and black-tipped, bushy tail; black above and brown below: **bat-eared fox** *page 68*

- Yellowish rusty coat; pure white underparts; two whitish blazes on either side of nostrils; small, pale crescent-shaped bands above eyes; almost straight, ridged horns; white rump and white undersurface to tail; upper surface of tail black: **oribi** *page 70*
- Rufous coat; pure white underparts; smooth, pointed, vertical horns; upper surface of tail rufous brown: **steenbok** *page 71*

Mammals

- Greyish buff to reddish yellow coat with white or pale underparts; males have tuft of black hair between base of horns; black blaze on face; front of forelegs dark brown or black; long, narrow ears: **common duiker** *page 71*
- Grey-brown to dark brown coat above, whitish below; hindquarters seem higher than shoulder; ears white in front, grey behind; distinct reddish tinge on front of legs: **blue duiker** *page 72*
- Chestnut-red coat; chestnut and black crest on top of head between short, straight, backward-sloping horns; short ears fringed in black on outside, white on inside: **red duiker** *page 72*
- Reddish brown coat flecked with white hairs; white underparts; black band around leg above each hoof; broad, pink-lined ears: **suni** *page 73*

- Yellow to brown/greyish coat; white underparts, chin and lips; walks on tips of hooves in rocky areas; short, stumpy tail; short muzzle: **klipspringer** *page 74*

- Grey-brown to yellowish grey upperparts; distinctive tuft of long, gingerish hair on forehead, erect when excited; elongated, slightly bulbous nose; short, spikelike horns; tail same colour as body: **Damara dik-dik** *page 73*
- Reddish brown upperparts, abundantly flecked with white hairs; flanks, legs and belly lighter brown; supplementary hooves above fetlocks; short ears and short, vertical horns: **Cape grysbok** *page 75*
- Reddish brown coat flecked with white hairs; horns short, sloping backwards; different range to grysbok; no false hooves: **Sharpe's grysbok** *page 75*

- Long spines, cross-banded in black and white; rounded snout; blackish head with no white band: **porcupine** *page 77*
- Short spines; small, pointed snout; overall brownish, but face blackish with white band across forehead: **Southern African hedgehog** *page 77*

- Fawn to dark brown; black hair covers centrally situated back gland; small rounded ears; no tail: **rock dassie** *page 79*
- Grey to grey-brown coat; off-white hair covers centrally situated back gland; longer body hair: **tree dassie** *page 79*

Mammals

- Greyish coat; very long, black-tipped tail; over 1m long (including tail): **large grey mongoose** *page 80*
- Thickset, uniformly grey coat; no black tip to tail; about 55 to 65 cm long (including tail): **small grey mongoose** *page 81*
- Coat varies geographically from grey, through yellow to reddish; slender body: broad black tip to tail; about 60 cm long (including tail): **slender mongoose** *page 81*
- Tawny yellowish to reddish yellow coat; white-tipped tawny tail; about 40 to 60 cm long (including tail): **yellow mongoose** *page 82*
- Grey-brown with 10 to 12 dark cross-bands; about 55 to 65 cm long (including tail): **banded mongoose** *page 82*
- Uniform dark brown coat; about 35 to 40 cm long (including tail): **dwarf mongoose** *page 83*

- Silvery to brown coat; thin, tapering, dark-tipped tail; black patch around each eye; dark mottling and indistinct barring on upper parts: **suricate** *page 83*

- Dark brown coat (black when wet); light underneath, with white on chest and throat; short-haired, heavy body; no claws on toes: **Cape clawless otter** *page 85*
- Chocolate to reddish brown coat (black when wet); throat and upper chest blotched with white or creamy white; short-haired body and tail; claws on toes: **spotted-necked otter** *page 85*
- Mid-brown to blackish brown coat; shaggy-haired body and tail; smaller than otters; no white on chest: **water mongoose** *page 80*

- Sandy to dark grey coat with darker vertical stripes; reddish brown back to ears; relatively long tail: **African wild cat** *page 86*
- Tawny to cinnamon-buff coat, with distinctive black bars and spots on shoulders and flanks; fawn or cinnamon back to ears; shortish tail: **small spotted cat** *page 86*

- Pale grey coat tinged with brown; long thick woolly tail; small head; large eyes and ears; length (including tail) 70 to 80 cm: **thick-tailed bushbaby** *page 88*
- Pale grey coat tinged with brown; black rings around large, round eyes; slender tail; length (including tail) 40 cm: **southern lesser bushbaby** *page 88*

Mammals

- Cinnamon upperparts, underparts tinged white and buff; single white stripe along each side of body from shoulder to thigh; white rings around eyes; bushy tail; only on ground in arid, open areas: **ground squirrel** page 89
- Brown/grey summer coat with whitish underparts; silvery grey coat in winter; tail dark grey with white fringe; only in south-western Cape: **grey squirrel** page 89
- Pale grey to buff or rust coat with lighter underparts; only in wooded habitats: **tree squirrel** page 90

- Four dark stripes along back: **striped mouse** page 93
- Uniform greyish coat; females with up to 12 pairs of nipples: **multimammate mouse** page 93

- Dark, reddish brown, with an iridescent bronze sheen; flanks lighter than back; underparts lighter, tinged with grey; white cheeks, and white hairs marking ear openings and the positioning of the vestigial (rudimentary) eyes: **Hottentot golden mole** page 95
- Dark brown, with an iridescent bronze sheen; underparts lighter and duller; buff-coloured bands run from the cheeks to the position of the rudimentary eyes: **Cape golden mole** page 95

- Dark brown, sometimes tinged with grey; underparts smoky grey; pale, yellow-brown 'collar' circles the throat; round-tipped wings dark brown, almost black: **Egyptian fruit bat** page 96
- Usually brownish buff, sometimes pale buff; underparts lighter; white patches at base of ears; male has white 'epaulettes' on shoulders: **Peters' epauletted fruit bat** page 96
- Dark sooty brown; underparts also sooty brown or a little lighter; head and neck nearly black; ears large, rounded: **Egyptian free-tailed bat** page 97
- Light (and sometimes irregular) brown; underparts paler; nose-leaf over face between mouth and forehead: **Geoffroy's horseshoe bat** page 97

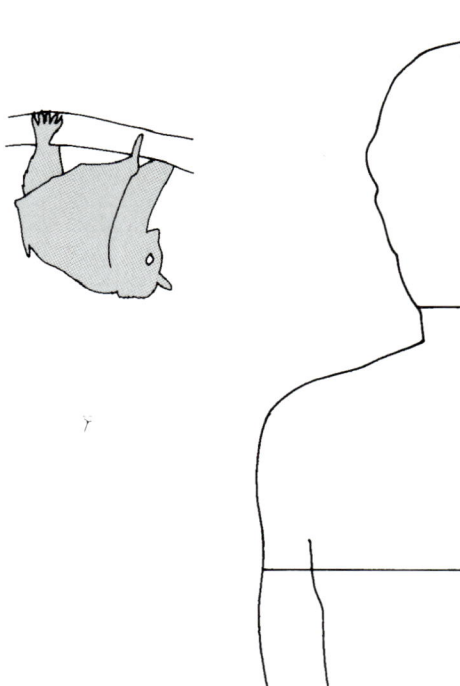

Birds LARGE BIRDS

- Pale grey with black wings, thighs and crest; long, pinkish legs; crest shaggy; bare, bright orange or yellow face; long, stiff tail feathers: **secretarybird** *page 108*
- Elegant and graceful; plain blue-grey; darker on wings; top of head almost white: **blue crane** *page 110*
- Conspicuous yellow crest on black-and-white head; slate grey with large, white wing-patch; drooping yellow plumes over wing at rest; bright red throat wattle; broad, chestnut plumes overlie tail at rest: **grey crowned crane** *page 111*

- Looks like small ostrich; greyish brown above, greyer on neck; belly white; crown black with short crest behind; thick, feathered neck: **Kori bustard** *page 111*
- Brown above with rich chestnut hindneck; below white with foreneck grey in male, light brown in female; crown black above white eyebrow; black-and-white chequerboard pattern on folded wings; legs pale yellow: **Denham's bustard** *page 112*

- Wings broad; face feathered; all white except for black wing tips and trailing edges; bill and legs red: **white stork** *page 105*
- Glossy black with white belly; bill and legs dull grey; bill tip, toes and ankle joints red; bare blue face: **Abdim's stork** *page 106*
- Black above, with greenish gloss; white below; white ruff at base of bare, pinkish neck; huge grey to pinkish bill; legs usually covered with white powder: **marabou stork** *page 106*

Birds

LARGE BIRDS

- Whitish to buffy with black wing tips, trailing edges and tail; underwing shows row of dark spots along border, with black trailing edge; head naked, greyish blue; bare blue patches on either side of crop; iris pale yellow: **Cape vulture** page 148
- Mostly black with white thighs, neck ruff and bar on underwing; breast heavily streaked black and white; head naked, bright pinkish red: **lappet-faced vulture** page 149
- Pale brown to buff; lower back white; underwing buff with dark trailing edge; iris dark brown; head blackish grey: **white-backed vulture** page 149

- Deep, bluish grey; crown, hindneck black, foreneck white; underwing pale in front, dark behind; bill blackish above, paler below: **black-headed heron** page 104
- Back blue-grey; rest of body, including neck, white; black streak above eye and black patch on bend of wing; bill yellow (orange when breeding): **grey heron** page 129
- Slate-grey, with deep chestnut-brown head, neck, belly and wrist-patch; throat white; bill black above, horn below: **Goliath heron** page 129

- Black with variable extent of white from chin to breast; white thigh patches on breeding birds; undersides off-white in immature birds; eyes green: **white-breasted cormorant** page 127
- Plumage black with yellow on throat; bare face bright yellow; bill long and slender; eyes turquoise; bill, legs and feet black: **Cape cormorant** page 127
- Plumage completely black; bill yellow; eyes bright red; underparts whitish on immature and nonbreeding birds: **reed cormorant** page 128
- Mainly black with chestnut foreneck bordered by white stripe: **African darter (breeding male)** page 128
- Brown with pale underparts; bill greenish horn to yellowish brown; iris yellowish, ringed with brown; slender build: **African darter (female** and **nonbreeding male)** page 128

Birds

LARGE BIRDS

- Jet-black, except for white lower back and white V on upper back; feet and base of bill bright yellow; tail somewhat rounded; wings splayed at tips: **Verreaux's eagle** *page 151*
- Back and wings blackish; head whitish, shading to bright yellowish rusty neck and underparts; face mask and bristly beard black: **lammergeier** *page 148*
- Usually light tawny brown, but varies from dark brown to creamy white; feet and base of bill yellow; tail rounded; shaggy feathering on legs: **tawny eagle** *page 151*
- Largest of the eagles; dark brown, except for white belly with dark brown spots; bill black; eyes yellow; feet white: **martial eagle** *page 152*
- Slaty black above; below pale rufous with heavy black barring; underwing in flight deep russet in front, white behind with heavy black bands; tail banded black and white; eyes and feet yellow, *ke-wee ke-wee* calls; found in evergreen forest: **African crowned eagle** *page 152*
- Owl-like face; large yellow eyes; head, breast and upperparts black; underparts and underwing white; underwing banded with black; legs and feet white: **black-chested snake eagle** *page 153*

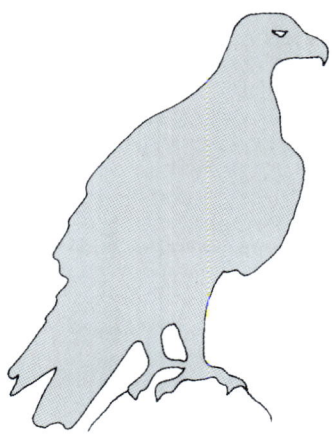

- Head, neck, breast and tail white; wings and back black; belly and underwing deep maroon; legs and feet pale yellow; haunting *whow-kayow-kwow* cry; associated with large inland waters, coastal lagoons and estuaries: **African fish eagle** *page 154*

- Dark glossy green with bronze wing-patch; bare white neck; bill, bare crown and legs bright red: **Southern bald ibis** *page 107*
- Dull dark grey; metallic purple or green reflections on wings; bill and legs dull blackish; red line along top of bill; loud, raucous call: **hadeda ibis** *page 107*

- Plumage reddish brown above, greyish below; dark brown patch around eye and on centre of breast; dark brown collar on neck; undertail bright yellow; legs and feet pinkish red; iris orange, reddish brown or red; bill pinkish red: **Egyptian goose** *page 133*
- Plumage chestnut; head grey; (female has white face); in flight wing shows white with green trailing edge and black tip; bill black; legs black: **South African shelduck** *page 133*
- Dark grey to blackish with pale markings; bill bright yellow with black saddle; wing-patch metallic green, bordered white front and back: **yellow-billed duck** *page 134*

LARGE BIRDS

Birds

- White, except for black wings and back; legs greenish grey; bill bright yellow with red tip to lower jaw; eyes grey: **kelp gull** page 141
- Grey above; white below; head grey when breeding, otherwise white, sometimes with faint grey semicircle behind ear coverts; bill and legs deep red; eyes cream to pale grey: **grey-headed gull** page 142
- White plumage with pale grey back and black wing tips with white spots; bill and legs dark red; eyes dark; breeding birds sometimes have pale grey crescent behind eye: **Hartlaub's gull** page 142
- White with grey back and upper wing; crown black with white forehead; bill light yellow or greenish yellow, slightly drooping; feet black: **swift tern** page 143
- Mostly white; back, wings and rump pale grey; crown black (forehead white in nonbreeding dress); bill black (red with black tip in breeding dress); feet dull red (bright red in breeding dress): **common tern** page 143

- Neck and underparts rich blue-grey; back rusty brown; head black and white; legs yellow; bill yellow at base, black at tip; resonant *kuk-ROW kuk-ka-ROW* call: **blue korhaan** page 112
- Black below and on neck and face, with large white ear-patch and collar on chest; back finely barred black and tawny: **southern black korhaan (male)** page 113
- Similar to above, but neck and breast buff with fine black markings; loud, crowing call which speeds up towards the end—*kraak kraak kraak kraka kraka rak-rak-rak-rak*: **southern black korhaan (female)** page 113

- All white when not breeding; bill yellow; legs dull brownish; breeding birds pinkish buff plumes on crown, back and breast: **cattle egret** page 105
- Slender build; all-white; all-black bill; legs black with yellow feet; feeds exclusively in water: **little egret** page 130
- Black to slaty black; legs and bill black; eyes and feet bright yellow; quiet inland and estuarine waters mainly in tropics and subtropics: **black heron** page 130

Birds

LARGE BIRDS

- Heavy bill; broad wings; black with white collar at back of neck; bill black with white tip; short, fanned tail in flight; high-pitched croak: **white-necked raven** *page 119*
- Glossy black all over; slender bill; bulbous head: **Cape crow** *page 180*
- Glossy black with white breast, belly and collar on hindneck; heavy bill: **pied crow** *page 180*

- Mostly pale grey; belly white with fine pale grey bars; in flight wings largely white, tips black; rump white; base of bill, legs and feet bright red: **southern pale chanting goshawk** *page 155*
- Blue-grey with black wing tips and trailing edges; belly finely barred grey and white; bare face and long, slender legs yellow; tail black with one broad white band: **African harrier hawk** *page 156*

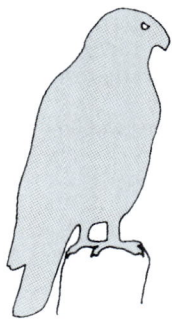

- Above brown, sometimes washed rufous on tail; below white, heavily barred, streaked or mottled with brown; pale band usually visible across breast; underwing whitish with brown leading edge and black trailing edge and tips; likes perching on fence posts and telephone poles: **common buzzard** *page 154*
- Slaty black above and on upper breast; lower breast deep chestnut, sometimes separated from upper breast by narrow white band; belly black with white crossbars; tail rufous; underwing black with broad white band; feet and base of bill yellow; jackal-like cry: **jackal buzzard** *page 155*
- Black; back and tail reddish brown; upperwing grey; very short tail; underwing white with black trailing edge (narrow in female, broad in male); face, base of bill, legs and feet bright red; feet project beyond tail in flight: **bateleur** *page 153*

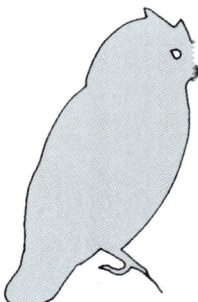

- Dark grey above, spotted with white; below whitish, finely barred with dark grey, and spotted with brown on breast; eyes yellow: **spotted eagle owl** *page 159*
- Grey, finely barred blackish; face paler, boldly outlined with black; eyes dark brown; eyelids pink: **Verreaux's eagle owl** *page 160*

LARGE BIRDS

Birds

- Bright green with blue wings and tail; flight feathers bright red; crest tipped white; white streak above and below eye; bill red: **Knysna turaco** *page 165*
- Body green with dark purplish blue wings and crest; flight feathers crimson; tail glossy greenish black; bill and feet black; eye-ring scarlet: **purple-crested turaco** *page 165*
- Dull grey, darker on wings and tail; bill and feet black; nasal *go'way* call: **grey go-away bird** *page 166*

- Crown, back and tail black; wings boldly mottled black and white; broad white eyebrow; below white, mottled black on breast; bill deep red, rather slender; patch of skin on throat and around eyes pink: **red-billed hornbill** *page 174*
- Crown, back and tail mostly black; broad white eyebrow; wings mottled black and white; eyes yellow; skin on throat and around eyes pink; bill deep yellow, strongly arched on top: **southern yellow-billed hornbill** *page 174*

- Slaty black with white undertail and white streaks on flanks; shield red; bill red with yellow tip; iris red; legs and feet yellowish green: **common moorhen** *page 136*
- Plumage deep blue; back washed green; undertail white; forehead shield, bill and legs bright red: **African purple swamphen** *page 135*
- Plumage black; bill and frontal shield white; knobs above shield dark red; legs and feet dark green to dull slate: **red-knobbed coot** *page 136*
- Body rich chestnut; hindneck black; foreneck white, shading to yellow on breast; bill and frontal shield pale blue: **African jacana** *page 137*

- Reddish brown, faintly streaked with white above; below greyish, finely barred on belly; breast boldly spotted dark brown; head dark with white throat and eyebrow; legs red; bill black; harsh, penetrating call: **crested francolin** *page 108*
- Brown with black streaks; bare throat, eye-patch and lower jaw bright red; upper jaw and legs black; drawn-out, crowing call: **Swainson's spurfowl** *page 109*
- Slate-grey with fine white spots all over; naked head coloured red and blue with yellowish casque (helmet) on top and red-and-blue wattles at base of bill; staccato *kek-kek-kek-krrr* alarm call: **helmeted guineafowl** *page 110*

Birds
LARGE BIRDS

- Brown; face black; bill black above, bluish white below; legs and feet dull red-brown: **speckled mousebird** *page 168*
- Above soft blue-grey; below greyish on chest, shading to sandy yellowish grey on belly; bare face and bill deep red; tip of bill black; legs red; gentle, three-syllable call-note, *ti-wi-wi*: **red-faced mousebird** *page 169*

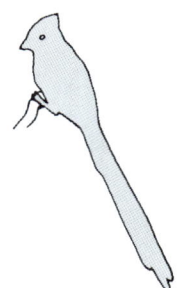

- Above mottled grey and tawny with small black-and-white spots; below white, finely spotted brown; face white, heart-shaped; eyes dark; bill pale; shrill shriek: **barn owl** *page 158*
- Brown above, spotted with white; below white, streaked with brown; eyes yellow: **pearl-spotted owlet** *page 159*
- Rich rufous all over, barred on back with black, and streaked blackish below; large eyes; bill blackish; feet whitish; deep hooting notes: **Pel's fishing owl** *page 169*

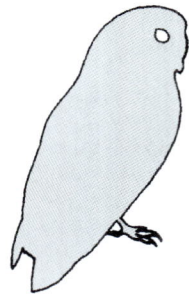

- Back and breast light greyish brown with dark breastband; belly white; crown black with white border; long, bright red legs; bill red with black tip: **crowned lapwing** *page 113*
- Mostly light brown; dark brown breastband separates brown chest from white belly; longish bill; top of head rusty in front, blue-grey behind; eyebrow white; legs white: **Burchell's courser** *page 114*
- Sandy grey above, white below; forehead and eyebrow white; forecrown dark; collar on hindneck white; dark line through eye; tail dark with white outer feathers: **white-fronted plover** *page 138*
- Above brownish grey; face grey; dark crown; white stripe from forehead to hindneck; underparts white; one white and two black breastbands; bill red with black tip: **three-banded plover** *page 138*

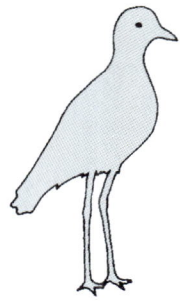

- Plumage black and white; back and wings grey; underparts black from chin to belly; iris red; bill, legs and feet black: **blacksmith lapwing** *page 139*

- Slate-grey above; chest deep rufous; belly barred black and white; bill blackish, yellow at base; eye-ring and feet yellow; *piet-my-vrou* call: **red-chested cuckoo** *page 166*
- Above metallic bronze-green with broad white eyebrow and white spots on wing and outer tail feathers; below white with broad, metallic green bars on flanks; bill black in adults: **diederik cuckoo** *page 167*
- Crown, back and tail black; rump barred with dull white; wings bright rusty; below creamy white; some faint, dusky barring on flanks; northern (tropical) birds have white

eyebrow and white streaks on head and mantle: **Burchell's coucal** *page 167*

SMALLER BIRDS

Birds

- Glossy blue-black all over; rusty-red wings show up clearly in flight: **red-winged starling (male)** *page 122*
- Grey head, breast and mantle, streaked on breast and mantle with black: **red-winged starling (female)** *page 122*
- Iridescent black, faintly spotted with white and buff; wing and tail feathers have brown edges; bill bright yellow; nonbreeding birds more heavily spotted than breeding birds; walks briskly: **common starling** *page 192*
- Head, breast and tail black; rest of body rich brown; wing-patch, tip of tail and undertail white; legs, feet, bill and bare eye-patch bright yellow: **common myna** *page 193*

- Brilliant iridescent purple; belly and outer tail feathers white; eyes yellow: **violet-backed starling (male)** *page 193*
- Brown above, streaked black; below white with heavy blackish streaks; eyes yellow: **violet-backed starling (female)** *page 193*
- Glossy black with bright metallic green reflections; ear coverts glossed purplish; coppery patch on bend of wing; eyes bright orange-yellow: **Cape glossy starling** *page 194*

- Above brown, shading to yellow at edges; below light turquoise blue; throat yellow with narrow black collar; wings, eyebrow and tail green; forehead white; face mask black: **European bee-eater** *page 171*
- Rose-red, pinker below; crown and undertail blue; rump green; face mask black: **southern carmine bee-eater** *page 171*
- Above green; below yellow ochre, tinged orange; throat bright yellow bordered by black collar; wings bright rufous in flight; square (slightly notched) tail: **little bee-eater** *page 172*

- Dull orange, browner on crown and mantle; wings bluish grey; central tail feathers black: **Natal robin-chat** *page 184*
- Greyish brown above; face black with bold white eyebrow; throat and breast light orange; belly grey to whitish; undertail yellowish buff; tail orange with black central feathers: **Cape robin-chat** *page 184*

- Mottled black and white above; below white with one black breastband in female, two in male; broad white eyebrow; bill black: **pied kingfisher** *page 144*
- Above black, spotted with white; below white with chestnut breastband and black-spotted belly in male (reversed in female); large black bill: **giant kingfisher** *page 145*
- Brilliant blue above; crown turquoise; underparts orange-chestnut; white patch on throat and sides of neck; bill and legs scarlet: **malachite kingfisher** *page 145*
- Brilliant light blue on back, wings and tail; large black patch on bend of wing and black line through eye; crown pale grey; underparts white; bill red above, black below: **woodland kingfisher** *page 170*

- Crown dull brown; back blackish in male, brown in female; rump, tail and flight feathers bright blue; below buffy white, washed on breast and flanks with brownish ochre; flanks streaked with black; bill red with blackish tip: **brown-hooded kingfisher** *page 170*

Birds

SMALLER BIRDS

- Long central tail feathers; long, pointed wings; head and breast plain olive-yellow; double breastband of white and maroon; back and wings brownish with pearly grey spots; belly dark brown. Female rich buff, barred and streaked with black: **Namaqua sandgrouse** *page 115*
- Upperparts maroon-brown with white spots; underparts grey; bare eye-patch; legs red; familiar *vukutu-kooo* call: **speckled pigeon** *page 115*
- Above deep slate grey with black collar on hindneck; top of head pale grey; below rich pinkish grey; tip of tail pale grey; eyes red: well known for familiar *KOOku-kuROOkuku* call: **red-eyed dove** *page 161*
- Grey, darker on back; black collar on hindneck; tip of tail feathers white; call is a high-pitched, crooning *kuk-KOORR-ru* repeated several times: **Cape turtle dove** *page 161*
- Above blue-grey and cinnamon; head pinkish grey; breast deep rufous, spotted with black, shading to white belly; tips of tail feathers white: **laughing dove** *page 162*
- Long, tapered tail; upperparts grey with dark purple spots on wing; two dark bands enclose white band on lower back; breast of female grey, shading to white belly; face and breast of male black; bill black in female, yellow in male; wings cinnamon (visible in flight): **Namaqua dove** *page 162*
- Greyish green to yellowish green; thighs yellow; mauve patch on bend of wing; bill red at base, white at tip; feet scarlet: **African green pigeon** *page 163*

- Bright metallic green; yellow tufts at side of chest (usually hidden): **malachite sunbird (male)** *page 195*
- Yellowish grey above; below whitish, washed yellowish grey on breast; throat yellowish; outer tail feathers white: **malachite sunbird (female)** *page 195*
- Bright metallic green on head and upper back; rest of back olive; breast metallic purple; belly bright orange; tail black with long central feathers: **orange-breasted sunbird (male)** *page 196*
- Greenish grey above; below dull yellow; wings and tail dusky: **orange-breasted sunbird (female)** *page 196*
- Bright metallic green on head and back; rump blue; breast bright red with metallic blue collar; belly smoky grey: **southern double-collared sunbird (male)** *page 196*
- Dull grey above, yellowish grey below: **southern double-collared sunbird (female)** *page 196*
- Sooty black with scarlet breast and metallic green throat and crown: **scarlet-chested sunbird (male)** *page 197*
- Brown above; mottled on breast and streaked on belly with brown and yellow; wing feathers edged with white: **scarlet-chested sunbird (female)** *page 197*

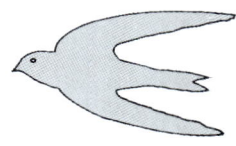

- Mouse-brown with white throat and belly, forming broad brown collar on breast; forked tail; long, sickle-shaped wings: **Alpine swift** *page 116*
- All-black with white throat and broad white band on rump; lives on rock faces and buildings: **little swift** *page 117*
- Uniform light brownish grey; looks silvery at a distance; wings long, slender; tail deeply forked; associated with palm trees: **African palm swift** *page 168*
- Above metallic blue-black; forehead deep rufous; below off-white to buff with rufous throat outlined by broad black collar; tail black, forked, with white 'windows' visible in flight: **barn swallow** *page 177*
- Crown brick-red; back metallic blue-black; rump pale orange; tail black, deeply forked, with white windows; below white, lightly streaked with black: **greater striped swallow** *page 178*
- Upperparts metallic blue-black; rump and underparts white; tail plain black, deeply forked: **common house martin** *page 178*

15

SMALLER BIRDS

Birds

- Body green; head and neck brown; underwing bright yellow (visible in flight only); eyes yellow; emits loud, strident screeches: **brown-headed parrot** *page 163*
- Brown on head and back, with blue rump; breast brown, shading to light green belly; bright yellow patches on crown, bend of wing and thighs; underwing yellow (visible in flight only); eyes red: **Meyer's parrot** *page 164*
- Bright green, paler below; rump blue;

forehead scarlet; face and breast bright pink; bill pale yellowish: **rosy-faced lovebird** *page 164*

- Blue-grey head; underparts bright rusty orange; back mottled brown and rusty; tail orange with black centre: **Cape rock thrush (male)** *page 119*
- Similar to above, but head brown, lightly mottled with white: **Cape rock thrush (female)** *page 119*
- Dark olive-brown above, tinged greyish; throat white, streaked black; breast olive-grey; belly dull orange-yellow, washed olive on flanks; undertail white; bill and legs dull yellow: **olive thrush** *page 183*
- Brownish grey, paler below; ear coverts faintly tinged rusty; rump and tail dull orange; central tail feathers and tips of all tail feathers black, forming black T;

deliberate wing-flicking; familiar around farms: **familiar chat** *page 183*
- Black above, including head and throat; breast and flanks bright chestnut; belly, rump, wing-bar and large patch on each side of neck white: **African stonechat (male)** *page 120*
- Brown above, streaked blackish; breast light, rusty ochre; belly, wing-bar and rump white: **African stonechat (female)** *page 120*

- Above black with white eyebrow, neck-patch and wing-patch; below white with black collar on chest: **African pied wagtail** *page 146*
- Above dull olive-grey; below off-white with grey to blackish collar on breast; outer tail feathers white, conspicuous in flight; very tame in urban areas: **Cape wagtail** *page 147*

- Crown and face blackish; back brown; eyebrow, rump and underparts white; wings and tail dusky, edged with white; breast spotted brown in northern birds: **white-browed sparrowweaver** *page 198*
- Deep buff, mottled black on back; crown deeper brown; black mask on face; sides of belly marked with black arrowheads: **sociable weaver** *page 198*
- Black head with bold semicircle of white on each side; upper back grey; lower back and upper wing bright rusty; wing-bar and underparts white; tail black (female generally duller): **Cape sparrow** *page 199*
- Bright yellow with black face mask ending in point on breast; heavy black mottling on back; eyes red; bill black: **village weaver (breeding male)** *page 199*
- Mottled grey and brown on back; rump

brown; crown olive; throat yellow; rest of underparts white with greyish tinge on breast and flanks; male always has red eyes: **village weaver (female** and **eclipse male)** *page 199*
- Bright yellow, greener on back; face mask black; back faintly streaked; eyes red: **southern masked weaver (male)** *page 200*
- Pale greyish brown above with light streaks; throat yellow shading to buff on breast and white on belly: **southern masked weaver (female** and **nonbreeding male)** *page 200*

Birds

SMALLER BIRDS

- Above black; below white, sometimes washed grey on breast and flanks; white bar on folded wings forms V on upper back; eyebrow white in western birds; chestnut streak on lower flank of female; tail black with white outer feathers: **common fiscal** page 188
- Crown and mantle blue-grey; back and wings russet; tail black with white outer feathers; face mask black; underparts white; female duller in colour with no face mask; tail reddish brown: **red-backed shrike** page 189
- Upperparts slaty black with bold white wing-stripe; below pinkish white with rich rufous wash on flanks and breast; tail black: **southern boubou** page 189
- Above jet-black with conspicuous white wing-stripe; below brilliant crimson: **crimson-breasted shrike** page 190
- Black above, with white markings on wings and fluffy white rump; below white; iris yellow, orange or red; female duller than male with white markings extending onto face: **black-backed puffback** page 190

- Above olive-green with grey crown and nape; tail tipped black and yellow; below yellow with black collar on breast; eyebrow yellow: **bokmakierie** page 191
- Crown to mantle grey; rest of upperparts, including tail, green, tail tipped yellow; forehead and eyebrow yellow; small black mask over eye; below bright yellow with orange wash across breast: **orange-breasted bush shrike** page 191
- Back and tail black with white wing-stripe and white outer tail feathers; crown grey; underparts and forehead white; black stripe on side of neck; legs, feet and large wattle around eye yellow: **white-crested helmetshrike** page 192

- Head and breast bright red, bordered all round by a broad, black collar; back brownish grey; belly pale, dull yellow; heavy black bill: **black-collared barbet** page 175
- Above black, streaked pale yellow; forehead red; large golden wing-patch; underparts pale greenish yellow; monotonous *klink klink* callnotes: **red-fronted tinkerbird** page 175

- Darkish brown above; white below; white crescent around bend of folded wing; clear white eyebrow; bill black: **common sandpiper** page 139
- Above olive-brown with clear white spots; below whitish, faint streaks of grey on breast; eyebrow white; bill black and straight; clear white rump; wings dark; tail barred dark and light; legs dull greenish: **wood sandpiper** page 140
- Above mottled brownish grey; eyebrow, rump and underparts white; white wing-bar in flight; tail dusky: **curlew sandpiper** page 140

- Back greyish brown, streaked with blackish; underparts creamy white; crown deep rufous; tail dull brown, tipped with black and white; bill dusky with pinkish base: **rattling cisticola** page 185
- Dull blue-grey, paler below; crown dull rufous; indistinct buff eye-ring; legs and feet pinkish: **neddicky** page 186

SMALLER BIRDS

Birds

- Black with bright yellow patch on rump and bend of wing: **yellow bishop (breeding male)** *page 122*
- Streaked black on buff above with yellow (male) or olive-yellow (female) patch on wrist; below buff-white, streaked brown on breast and flanks; bright yellow patch on rump: **yellow bishop (female** and **nonbreeding male)** *page 122*
- Black with bright red patch at bend of wing: **fan-tailed widowbird (breeding male)** *page 123*
- Streaked black on buff above with red or rusty patch at bend of wing; below white, streaked brown on breast and flanks; wheezy call: **fan-tailed widowbird (female** and **nonbreeding male)** *page 123*
- All black with scarlet-and-white patch at bend of wing; tail very long and floppy: **long-tailed widowbird (breeding male)** *page 123*
- Streaked black on buff above, brown on whitish below; bend of wing orange; flight feathers black; tail short: **long-tailed widowbird (non-breeding male)** *page 123*

- Similar to above, but smaller; wings brown; no coloured patch on wing; tail short: **long-tailed widowbird (female)** *page 123*
- Greyish brown above, greyer below, with fine blackish bars; bill, eye-patch and centre of belly bright red; undertail black; *ching-ching* callnotes: **common waxbill** *page 124*
- Crown and back brown; face, throat, breast, rump and tail light blue (paler in female); belly buff; male also has blue flanks; double *tsee-seep* callnote: **blue waxbill** *page 201*
- Deep chestnut; forehead and rump bright blue; throat, centre of belly, tail and undertail black; face violet; (female paler than male and lacking black on underparts): **violet-eared waxbill** *page 202*

- Upperparts buff with dark streaks; below white, lightly mottled greyish on breast; breeding male has bright red bill, black or white face mask and pink or yellowish head, neck and upper breast; female has yellow bill: **red-billed quelea** *page 200*
- Deep red below and on rump; centre of belly and undertail blackish; fine white spots on flanks; back brown; crown grey in southern birds, red in northern: **African firefinch (male)** *page 201*
- Light red below, shading to tawny on belly; flanks lightly spotted white; upperparts brown; bill blue-grey: **African firefinch (female)** *page 201*
- Above greyish brown; below barred with buff, white and black; centre of belly buff; head of male bright scarlet; heavy bill pale horn: **red-headed finch** *page 202*
- Head and breast black, with bronze sheen; back and wings grey-brown with green spots on wing; belly white with bold black barring on flanks; bill black above, blue-grey below: **bronze mannikin** *page 203*
- Streaked black and tawny above; head boldly striped black and tawny; below white with buffy breast and blackish streaks on flanks; bill red in male at all times and tail lengthens in breeding season; reddish-brown bill in female: **pin-tailed whydah (female** and **nonbreeding male)** *page 203*
- Black on head, back and long tail; breast brick-red; belly, hindneck yellow: **long-

tailed paradise whydah (breeding male)** *page 204*
- Streaked buff and black above; head boldly striped buff and black; below whitish with buff wash on breast and flanks: **long-tailed paradise whydah (female** and **nonbreeding male)** *page 204*
- Dull green above, with darker streaks; rump and underparts light yellow, shading to greyish on flanks; black eye-stripe and moustache-stripe on yellow face; yellow eyebrows meet across forehead; white tail-tip: **yellow-fronted canary** *page 204*
- Greenish yellow, greener on back and tail; nape and upper back blue-grey: **Cape canary** *page 205*
- Bright yellow below and on rump; upperparts dull greenish, streaked darker; broad yellow eyebrows meet across forehead: **yellow canary (male)** *page 205*
- Greyish brown above, streaked dusky; rump yellow; below dull white, streaked greyish on breast and flanks: **yellow canary (female)** *page 205*

Tortoises

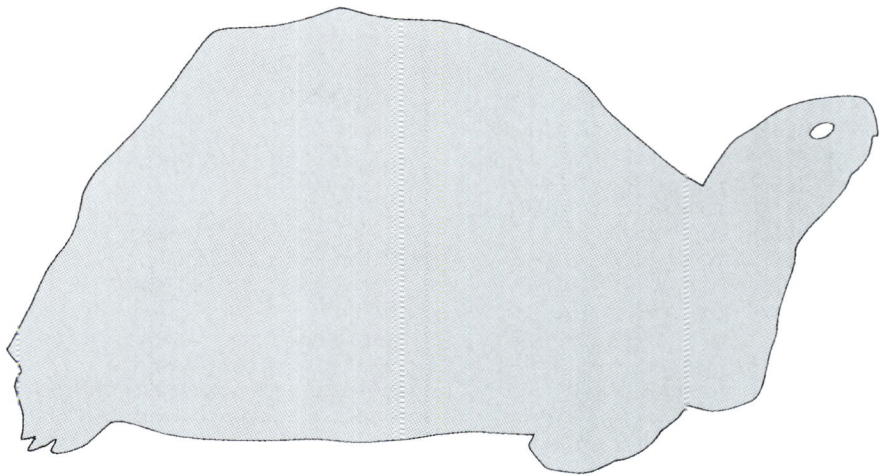

- Rounded, high-domed shell; carapace yellow, flecked with black blotches and streaks when young, darkening often to uniform deep brown with age; two to three horny tubercles on each buttock: **mountain tortoise** *page 209*
- High-domed, rounded carapace yellow to brown or olive-green, each shield patterned with radiating broad black markings; hinge of cartilage across back of shell allows rear of shell to close: **Bell's hinged tortoise** *page 210*

- High-domed, rounded carapace predominantly yellow (usually in old individuals), and dark brown or black (predominantly black in young specimens); circumference of shell distinctively patterned with dark triangles; single (not double) spadelike projection at front of undershell: **angulate tortoise** *page 210*

- High-domed, dark brown or black carapace, with pattern of yellow or orange stripes radiating from centre of each shield; major shields raised into 'tents'; distinctive yellow/white horny spur on each 'buttock': **tent tortoise** *page 211*
- High-domed carapace black with yellow stripes radiating from centre of each pyramidal shield; 'buttocks' yellow with no enlarged scale or horny spur; only in south-western Cape: **geometric tortoise** *page 211*

- Carapace dark brown to black, patterned with yellow-brown stripes radiating from centre of each slightly raised shield; well-developed, spurlike projections on 'buttock'; scales round edge of shell are sharply pointed, especially towards the rear: **Kalahari tent tortoise** *page 212*

- Carapace low, flattened; adult males orange-brown above; females and younger males olive-green or yellowish green above with chestnut centres and dark brown or black margins to shields; four claws to each foot: **Cape padloper** *page 212*
- Low, flattened carapace light brown with black spots and streaks (north of Gariep/Orange), salmon-pink with fine black speckling (south of Gariep/Orange); five toes on each forefoot: **speckled padloper** *page 213*
- Carapace low, flattened; olive-brown to reddish brown above with no markings; five toes on each forefoot: **Karoo padloper** *page 213*

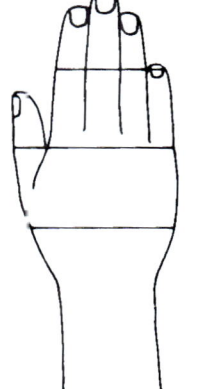

Snakes and lizards

- Triangular head with dark mark on top; grey-brown body with dark brown bars and blotches; average length 3-5 m: **southern African rock python** *page 216*
- Head approximately same width as body; adults uniform black, red-brown, olive or grey-brown; average length 1-2 m: **mole snake** *page 216*
- Head slightly wider than upper body; blackish V-shape on back of head; grey to brown body with 20-30 dark blotches; average length 35-60 cm: **common night adder** *page 230*

- Grass-green above; yellowish green underparts; white lining to mouth; average length 1,5-2,5 m: **green mamba** *page 220*
- From bright green to olive-green (also from light brown to dark brown); large eyes; lives in trees, shrubs; average length 1-1,5 m: **boomslang** *page 220*
- Dull or olive-green, often with a bluish hue; sometimes has black spots over front half of back; underside lighter with white or yellow; lives near reed-lined pans, ponds, rivers and marshes; average length 45-70 cm: **green water snake** *page 221*
- Grey-brown dorsal side flecked with black and pink; green head; lives in trees; average length 1 m: **twig snake** *page 221*
- Olive-green dorsal side, usually finely speckled in white; top of head blue-black; upper lip sometimes reddish; head triangular when threatened; average length 50-75 cm: **herald snake** *page 222*
- Olive-brown to dark, almost blackish brown above; salmon-pink tinge on underparts; always near water; average length 60-75 cm: **common brown water snake** *page 222*
- Light brown to reddish brown above; off-white belly; silver-white line runs through each eye; average length 45 cm-1 m: **brown house snake** *page 223*
- Green or olive above with a continuous or broken narrow orange stripe down middle of back; average length 45-60 cm: **aurora snake** *page 223*
- Juveniles alternately banded in cream and dark brown; adults usually uniform deep grey to black, but can have pairs of dirty white rings; belly yellowish or pink; average length 50-75 cm: **Sundevall's garter snake** *page 224*
- Black head; alternate bands or blotches of black and yellow along body; orange-red stripe along backbone; lives underground; average length 30-50 cm: **spotted harlequin snake** *page 224*
- Light brown to dark brown above, with mottled shades; hard, upturned snout; average length 25 cm: **Sundevall's shovel-snout** *page 225*

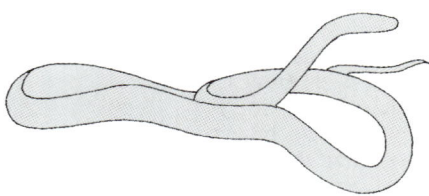

- Grey to greyish brown with blackish zigzag down back; average length 30 cm: **bark snake** *page 225*
- Yellow-brown above with three rows of dark blotches down back; belly yellowish with dark blotches; average length 60-90 cm: **spotted skaapsteker** *page 226*
- Olive to olive-grey dorsal side with brown longitudinal bands; dark-edged, forked markings on top of head; average length 90 cm: **fork-marked sand snake** *page 226*
- Silver-grey dorsal side with a broad brown stripe down middle of back and another along each flank; cream cross-bars on head; average length 60 cm: **cross-marked grass snake** *page 227*
- Black above and below, sometimes with a paler belly; average length 70-90 cm: **Natal black snake** *page 227*
- Uniform brown above with purplish tinge; underparts grey or cream, sometimes with dark blotches; lives underground or in termitaria; average length 45 cm: **southern burrowing asp** *page 228*
- Usually black or dark brown above, sometimes with each scale white-tipped; underparts white or yellowish white speckled with black; average length 30-50 cm: **Cape wolf snake** *page 228*
- Chequerboard pattern of dark brown rhombic spots above (occasionally uniform brown); dark V on top of head; underparts cream; average length 40 cm-1,1 m: **common egg-eater** *page 229*

Snake and lizards

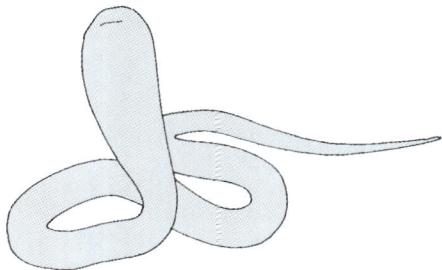

- Yellow-grey to dark brown body, sometimes with 7-10 broad yellowish cross-bands; dark throat band; wide hood; average length 1,5-2 m: **Egyptian cobra** page 217
- Uniform olive-brown to blackish; mouth lining blackish; narrow hood; average length 2,5-3,5 m: **black mamba** page 217
- Dirty yellow through to red-brown or blackish, also speckled brown and yellow; dark throat band in juveniles only; wide hood; average length 1-2 m: **Cape cobra** page 218
- Head and forebody yellow-brown spotted with black, but whole body blackens towards tail; narrow hood; average length 1,5-2 m: **forest cobra** page 218
- Grey to light brown; back darker brown with black-edged scales; pink or yellowish belly; throat banded black; average length 90 cm-1,2 m: **Mozambique spitting cobra** page 219
- Uniform dark brown to black above, but Eastern Cape and Zimbabwe specimens have yellowish and dark brown bands; dark underparts, usually with one or two pale throat bands; wide hood; average length 90 cm-1,2 m: **rinkhals** page 219
- Grey to orange-buff dorsal side with series of dark blotches; head and neck black with pale throat band; black V on back of head; narrow 'hood'; average length 45 cm: **shield-nose snake** page 235

- Reddish brown to olive-brown dorsal side, usually with rows of black dots down backbone; sides grey; average length 30-40 cm: **common slug-eater** page 233
- Grey-brown to red-brown dorsal side; top of head brown-black; black 'collar' around neck; average length 20-30 cm: **Cape centipede-eater** page 234
- Pinkish brown to orange-brown above, with series of dark brown to black cross-bands; average length 75 cm: **eastern tiger snake** page 235

- Back sandy grey to pale brown with three rows of faint dark spots; some have black tail-tips; average length 20-25 cm: **Péringuey's adder** page 230
- Grey-brown to dark brown above with two rows of darker, usually triangular, blotches separated by paler band; average length 35-50 cm: **berg adder** page 231
- Yellowish or brownish with series of black, backward-pointing V-shapes down back; fat and sluggish; average length 70-90 cm: **common puff adder** page 231
- Richly coloured patterns of oblongs and hourglass markings in black, tan, mauve and grey; head buff; underparts yellow; forests only; average length 1,2 m: **Gaboon adder** page 232

- Glossy, dark brown to black overall; head difficult to distinguish; eyes vestigial; looks like bootlace; underground; average length 8-18 cm: **black thread snake** page 233
- Glossy brown to dark olive-brown above; underparts yellowish; head indistinct; barely visible eyes; under soil or stones; average length 35-40 cm: **Bibron's blind snake** page 234
- Yellow-brown to orange-brown body with six black stripes which may be reduced to broken lines or may be lacking altogether; burrowing lizard with no limb vestiges; average length 20-26 cm: **Cape legless skink** page 245

Snakes and lizards

- Yellow to dark brown; sides of head and belly yellow; lives in burrows; average length 35 cm: **sungazer** *page 237*
- Very heavily armoured with spines and projections; yellow-brown; lives in rock crevices; average length 21 cm: **armadillo girdled lizard** *page 238*
- Females dark brown with three cream stripes along back; males have bright blue-green body and head; red-brown tail; very flat lizards; average length 20 cm: **Cape flat lizard** *page 242*
- Females mottled in grey and brown; males have olive- to red-brown colouring with purple throat and blue or greenish

blue head and forelimbs; body plump; head thick, triangular; average length 24-30 cm: **southern rock agama** *page 242*

- Salmon-pink through green and brown to blackish, depending on environment; usually has pale stripe on flanks; scaly crest down middle of throat and along midline of belly; average length 20-35 cm: **flap-neck chameleon** *page 238*
- Usually leaf-green with broad orange stripe on flanks; scaly crest on throat not

extending to belly; average length 13-17 cm: **Cape dwarf chameleon** *page 239*

- Grey or brown with four or five wavy dark bands across back; scattering of white tubercles; vertical pupils; average length 20 cm: **Bibron's gecko** *page 239*
- Yellow-brown with blackish cross-bars or red-brown speckling; banded tail; white belly; lives on semi-desert flats; average length 6-8 cm: **common barking gecko** *page 240*
- Orange to red-brown dorsal side with varied markings; whitish pink underparts; short toes; average length 14-17 cm: **giant ground gecko** *page 240*
- Light brown or greyish dorsal side, speckled with white, black and grey; white

sometimes in cross-bands; white underparts; fat tail; average length 9-13 cm: **Cape gecko** *page 241*
- Semi-transparent in appearance; pinkish upperparts, with darker lines forming irregular rectangles along backbone; blue-grey patch over eyes; pink belly; only in Namibia's coastal desert; average length 10-12 cm: **web-footed gecko** *page 241*

- Pale brown to red-brown dorsal side with light stripes; breeding males yellow on throat and around vent; average length 15-23 cm: **Knox's desert lizard** *page 243*
- Grey-brown body with three light stripes along back; fat-bodied; common, even in suburban gardens; average length 22-27 cm: **Cape skink** *page 243*

- Light glossy brown above, finely speckled in dark brown; thick tail; short legs; average length 15 cm: **Sundevall's writhing skink** *page 244*

- Silver-grey dorsal side, stippled with brown; no forelegs; two tiny hindlegs; average length 12-14 cm: **silvery dwarf burrowing skink** *page 244*
- Olive-brown body with two darker stripes along sides of back; dark, vertical bars on neck; four tiny legs; average length 18-

24 cm: **common long-tailed seps** *page 245*

Frogs and toads

- Heavy, squat body with warty, dry skin, blunt, rounded snout; irregular, asymmetrical dark brown/dark red blotches on lighter brown back; whitish belly, usually with small black spots; warts often bulbous: **Karoo toad** *page 248*
- Body squat with warty, dry skin; blunt rounded snout; usually three to four paired, dark brown blotches down back; belly whitish and never with spots; warts smallish, never large and bulbous: **guttural toad** *page 249*

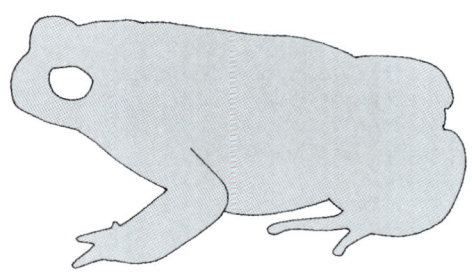

- Bulbous eyes; long, sharp snout; well-developed hindlegs for jumping; green to dark brown, usually with darker blotches; webbing on longest toe does not reach joint of last toe-bone: **Angolan river frog** *page 250*
- Bulbous eyes; long, sharp snout; well-developed hindlegs; green to dark brown with darker blotches; webbing on longest toe almost reaches toe-tip: **Cape river frog** *page 250*
- Bulbous eyes; long, sharp snout; well-developed hindlegs; colour variable but often olive green above with symmetrically arranged brown spots; smaller and more slender than Cape or Angolan river frogs; toes virtually unwebbed: **Gray's frog** *page 251*

- Small, slender; well-developed jumping hindlimbs; upperparts usually translucent green, but can be yellow or light brown; underparts white or pale green; round sucker at tip of each finger and toe: **water lily frog** *page 253*
- Small, slender; well-developed jumping hindlimbs; upperparts variable; in Eastern Cape brown with dark-edged silver spots; from KwaZulu-Natal northwards variable with perhaps black, white, yellow or red spots or stripes; whitish below, but red on undersides of legs and digits; round 'sucker' at tip of each finger and toe: **marbled reed frog** *page 253*

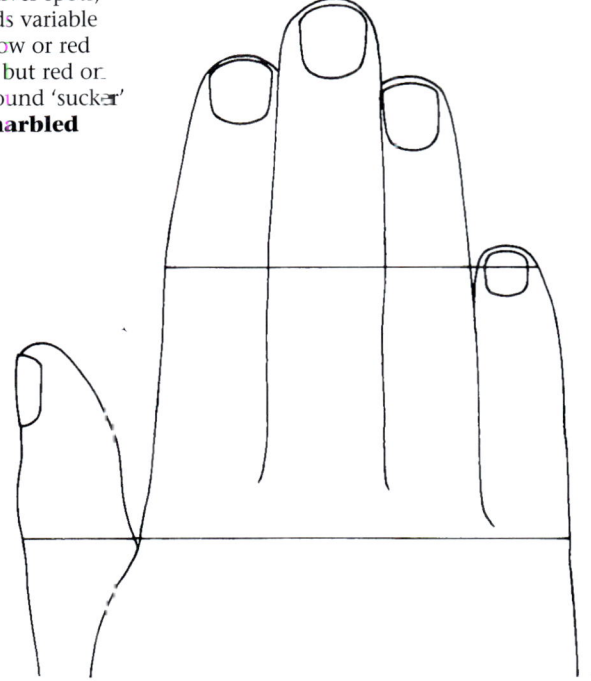

Freshwater fishes

- Silver-olive to bronze-yellow body; belly yellowish silver to yellow; anal fin orange; young fish uniformly silver; large mouth with thick lips; two pairs of short barbels; found only in Gariep-Vaal river system: **largemouth yellowfish** page 256
- Golden olive to yellowish above; below cream to silver; young fish silvery with dark spots or broken vertical bars on flanks; six branched rays in anal fin; thin lips; long, narrow snout; two pairs of barbels; in Berg and Breë river systems: **whitefish** page 257

- Green along back; flanks silver; grey-white belly; often three darkish blotches on each flank; breeding males turn dark bluish black above, whiter on throat and chest, with scarlet-tipped dorsal, anal and tail fins: **Mozambique tilapia** page 258
- Upperparts olive with light-brown edges to scales; dorsal fin has a red margin; throat and belly of adults red; lower half of tail red or yellow, and green on top; juveniles silver: **redbreast tilapia** page 258
- Silver to olive-green body; up to nine vertical stripes of darker green or grey; when breeding, stripes become more intense, horizontal stripes form across snout, and circular stripe runs over forehead. In male dorsal fin and tail become edged with red, and blue-green spots appear on dorsal and anal fins: **banded tilapia** page 259

- Deep-bodied; dorsal surface olive; flanks orange; belly pale olive or orange; younger fish in particular have five dark, vertical bars on flanks; distinctive black flap on upper corner of gill-covers; lower part of gill-cover blue; dorsal and anal fins large; tail fin slightly forked: **bluegill sunfish** page 259

- Silver, shading to olive-brown along back; small black spots over entire body; often pink or red stripe along each flank; slightly forked caudal fin: **rainbow trout** page 262
- Silvery brown, darker on back; back and flanks covered with dark brown spots; a few larger reddish spots, surrounded by bluish rings along each flank; no scales on head; truncated caudal fin: **brown trout** page 262

- Dark olive above, lighter on flanks with a series of dark blotches; juveniles have dark band on flanks; belly white; eyes red; large mouth with bottom jaw extending beyond upper jaw: **largemouth bass** page 261
- Dark olive above, lighter on flanks with faint vertical bars; belly almost white; juveniles have dark bars on tail; pointed snout with thin lips: **smallmouth bass** page 261

Marine fishes

- Uniform grey with white undersides; stocky body; blunt snout; often found in fresh water: **Zambezi shark** page 268

- Dusky upperparts; white belly; streamlined body; distinct interdorsal ridge; pointed snout: **dusky shark** page 268

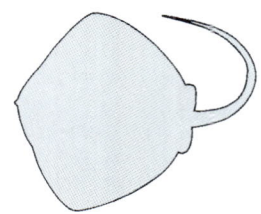

- Disc-shaped body; slightly rounded snout; dorsal surface rich golden brown with blue markings; poisonous spine midway along tail: **blue stingray** page 272
- Diamond-shaped, chocolate-brown body; pale underside; head raised above level of body: **eagleray** page 272
- Diamond-shaped body with sharply pointed snout; dorsal surface grey to brown, occasionally with white spots; white undersides; spines on long tail: **spearnose skate** page 273
- Disc-shaped body chocolate brown, mottled with irregular blotches; short, stocky tail; pale underside; small eyes on top of head: **marbled electric ray** page 273

- Blue-grey body with silver sides; irregular, dark vertical bars on flanks; distinct, wavy lateral line dips between second dorsal fin and tail fin; south and west coast: **king mackerel** page 274
- Elongated, compressed, mainly silver body; grey-blue dorsal surface; underside white; conspicuous, wavy lateral line; prominent dorsal spines in single, long dorsal fin; fins dusky to black; east coast: **snoek** page 275

- Robust body with depressed head; blue-green upper body, sometimes with narrow bronze band along flanks; sharply forked, yellowish tail fin: **Cape yellowtail** page 277
- Large, elongated body; conspicuous lateral line from gill to tail; small scales give a smooth-skinned appearance; ventral surface slopes down to pronounced ventral fin; deeply forked, dusky tail: **garrick** page 278
- Elongated, compressed body; prominent lower jaw; sharp, compressed teeth; bluish green dorsally, silvery below: **elf** page 278

Marine fishes

- Silver-grey body with bronze-blue sheen shading to coppery on head; adults often golden brown; darkens after death; silver scales along lateral line; fins dusky; short, rounded tail: **dusky kob** *page 279*
- Elongated, robust fish; body silvery, but bluish to copper-coloured above; mouth and inner surface of gill-covers yellow; tail fin concave: **geelbek** *page 279*

- Deep-bodied with steep forehead; silvery pink overall, darker above; five to seven darker red vertical bars on sides; numerous dark blotches on body: **red stumpnose** *page 280*
- Orange body; white saddle over middle of back; white bar on gill-covers; shallow forehead; blue line joining eyes: **roman** *page 280*
- Deep-bodied; pinkish red; characteristic black spot at base of dorsal fin; short blue line below each eye: **dageraad** *page 281*
- Very steep forehead; rosy red body, with iridescent blue spots in live specimens;

prominent hump above eyes; blue bar below each eye: **slinger** *page 284*

- Small body; silvery pink overall, belly white; red forehead and pinkish fins; big eyes: **carpenter** *page 281*
- Large, robust body; light red to bronze (some with yellow undersides); fins darker red; slightly extended snout; bony ridge between eyes: **red steenbras** *page 282*
- Moderately elongated body; forehead smoothly convex; upperparts pinkish red with blue sheen; conspicuous black mark on lateral line below fifth and sixth dorsal spines: **seventyfour** *page 282*
- Silvery sheen overall, pinkish above, white below; about five broad, vertical, reddish bars on flanks; bluish sheen on pelvic and anal fins: **santer** *page 284*
- Deep-bodied; rosy pink overall but bluish sheen in freshly caught specimens; six to eight reddish vertical bars on flanks; snout slightly concave; fins pink: **Englishman** *page 285*
- Silvery grey with white underside; may be completely black in muddy regions; sloping

forehead and pointed snout; well-developed spines in dorsal and anal fins: **river bream** *page 290*
- Silvery body with five or more dark, vertical bars; deep forehead and blunt snout; dusky fins: **white stumpnose** *page 296*
- Silvery grey with golden centre to each scale, showing up as longitudinal lines along flanks; fins yellow, fading with age; rounded dorsal profile: **Natal stumpnose** *page 297*

- Robust, oval-shaped body; large head; blunt snout; silvery-grey colour (darkens after death), with faint, longitudinal stripes: **white musselcracker** *page 283*
- Large, fleshy nose in adults; deep-bellied, robust body; sooty grey to black; juveniles greenish brown: **black musselcracker** *page 283*

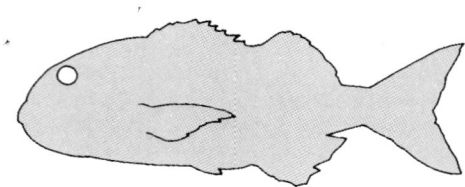

Marine fishes

- Long, sloping forehead and pointed snout; bright silver overall, paler below; irregular rows of small, dark brown spots on upper half of body; larger black blotch on each gill: **spotted grunter** *page 291*
- Long, sloping forehead; piglike snout with small mouth; silvery grey above, white below; mother-of-pearl sheen overall; after death about seven cross-bars visible on flanks: **white steenbras** *page 291*

- Silver-bronze to black; robust and deep-bodied; seven to nine vertical stripes on each flank visible under water; prominent spines on fins; thick lips; pronounced, rounded snout; stout, slightly concave tail fin: **galjoen** *page 294*
- Silvery grey, some specimens with vertical, dark bars on flanks; moderately compressed body; smooth dorsal profile; dusky grey fins; slightly forked tail fin; pointed snout: **stonebream** *page 297*

- Silver, oval-shaped body; pointed snout; distinctive black saddle on caudal peduncle (the narrow section attaching the tail fin to the body); juveniles marked with 8-10 vertical bars: **blacktail** *page 295*
- Oval-shaped, golden-silvery body; five broad, black, vertical bars on each flank; black bar through each eye; fleshy snout; forked tail fin: **zebra** *page 295*

- Body silver, spindle-shaped; dorsal surface bluish and belly white; row of 10-15 dark spots along flanks; fins spineless; tail deeply forked: **South African pilchard** *page 298*
- Elongate body distinctly torpedo-shaped; pointed snout; dorsal colouring brilliant blue-green with black zigzag lines; lower sides silvery white; fins yellowish; wide mouth: **mackerel** *page 299*

Spiders, scorpions and others

- Olive to yellow to blackish; large pincers; long, thin tail: **burrowing scorpion** *page 321*
- Yellowish, often with brown markings; small pincers; large tail: **bark scorpion** *page 321*
- Yellow to dark brown; thick tail; ridges on first two tail segments; largest of all scorpions: **thick-tail scorpion** *page 322*
- Yellowish with black markings on abdomen; large, short sting; thin pincers: **sand-dwelling thick-tail scorpion** *page 322*

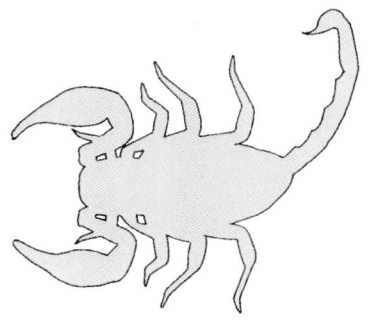

- Light to dark brown; long, fine hairs covering body; huge jaws almost a third of total body length: **sun spider** *page 323*
- Body black and white or grey and white, occasionally brown or brown and white; male more brightly coloured than female; squat body; moves by jumping: **jumping spider** *page 325*

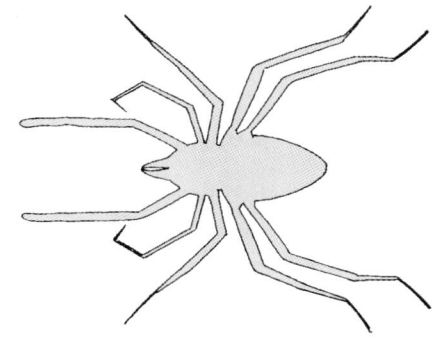

- Vividly striped in variations of yellow, black and silver; intricate 'wagon-wheel' webs; legs held together in pairs so that spider seems to have only four legs: **orb-web spider** *page 324*
- Bright yellowish or white with pink, green or brown markings; can change colour to blend with surroundings; all four legs on each side parallel to one another; always found in flowers; does not construct a web: **crab spider** *page 324*

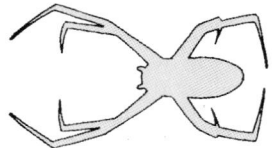

- Generally glossy brown or black, some with dark orange stripes; cylindrical body; many legs tucked neatly under body: **millipede** *page 327*
- Usually dark olive-green, black or dark bluish, sometimes red, yellow or brown; flattened body; legs spread out sideways: **centipede** *page 327*

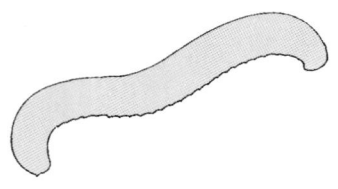

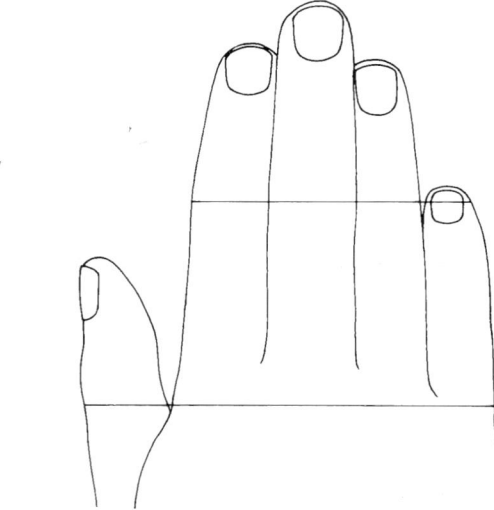

Beetles

BEETLES

- Prominent, sabrelike mouthparts; black, often with white, yellow and red patches on the thorax or elytra (wing-cases); extremely active: **predacious ground beetle** *page 330*
- Dark brown, elongate, segmented body; wingless; tiny head; light-producing organ at tip of abdomen: **female firefly** or **glow-worm** *page 333*
- Squat, globular abdomen, which can make characteristic knocking sound; black or brown; wingless: **toktokkie** *page 334*
- Elongated snout; usually brown or black often with a camouflage pattern of other colours; largest specimens have pink or red spots; 'elbowed' antennae: **weevil** *page 335*

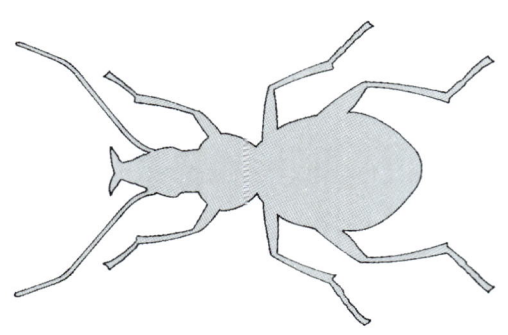

- Oval, stout; black, brown or metallic bronze, blue or green; front legs flat, toothed, used to manipulate dung: **dung beetle** *page 331*
- Flat in shape; brilliantly coloured; one common species is black, with rows of bright yellow patches on the wing-cases; another is green, with yellow bordering the wing-cases: **fruit beetle** *page 332*
- Long abdomen; usually black with bright red, orange or yellow markings; elytra brightly coloured; small thorax: **blister beetle** *page 334*

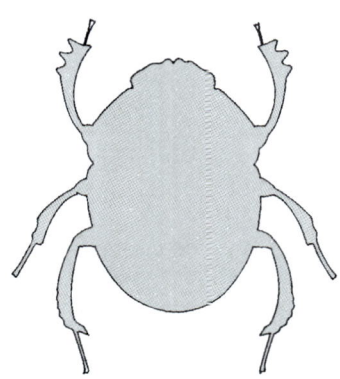

- Smooth, streamlined shape; shiny black or grey, with a paler border to the wing-cases and back in some species; four rearmost legs fringed with bristles; front pair of legs longer than the others; rarely found under water; swims on water surface; eyes divided: **whirligig beetle** *page 330*
- Streamlined, pip-shaped bodies; pale yellow to black, or greenish black with yellow margins; found under water; eyes divided: **water beetle** *page 331*

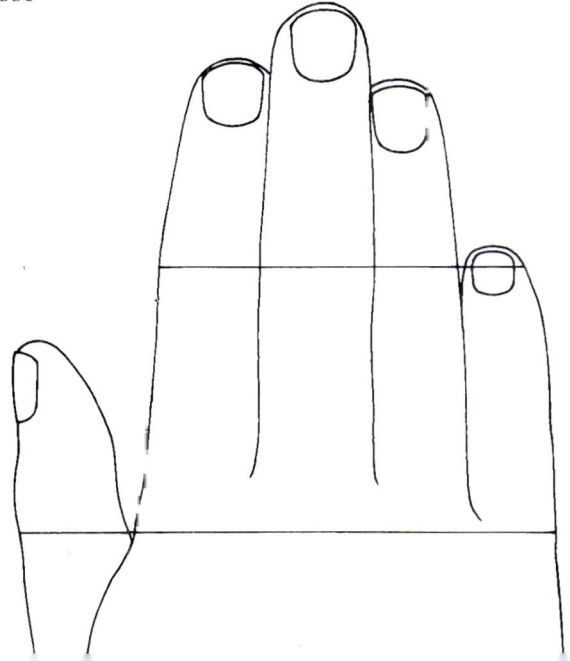

Butterflies

- Cream-yellow wings with greenish tinge and black spot in middle of forewing; wingspan 5,5-6,5 cm: **African migrant** *page 340*
- Black above with white spots and patch on forewing; larger white patch in middle of hindwing extending onto forewing; wingspan 8-8,5 cm: **friar** *page 341*
- Black above with whitish or yellowish spots on forewing and large, yellowish patch on inner half of each hindwing; wingspan 5,5-7,5 cm: **chief** *page 342*
- Male black above with two white patches in forewing and one in hindwing; female orange with black wing borders and white spots in black tip to forewing; wingspan 6-7,5 cm: **diadem** *page 342*
- Orange-brown wings with black border; three or four black spots in orange hindwings; black tip to forewing with white blotches; wingspan 5-7 cm: **southern milkweed** *page 343*
- Mid-brown above, sometimes with reddish tinge; two eye-spots near outer edge of each forewing and (usually) three smaller eye-spots on hindwing; wingspan 4-4,8 cm: **marsh patroller** *page 345*
- White above with black apex to forewing and brownish black border to hindwing; bar in middle of forewing; wingspan 4-4,5 cm: **brown-veined white** *page 349*
- White above with black wing margins and scarlet tip to forewing; hindwing white,

with black-tipped edges; wingspan 4-5 cm: **scarlet-tip** *page 349*
- White above with black dots along outer margins of wings; undersides yellow, shading to orange near wing-bases; wingspan 5-5,5 cm: **dotted border** *page 350*
- Males orange-yellow above with broad black or dark brown margin to wings; small black spot in middle of forewing; yellow edge to inner part of hindwing. Female similar, but orange-yellow is partly obscured by brown; wingspan 3,5-4 cm: **African clouded yellow** *page 350*
- Rich yellow with a broad, blackish brown border to wings; wingspan 3-3,5 cm: **broad-bordered grass-yellow** *page 351*
- Dark brown to black above with several golden, angular spots on both fore- and hindwings; wingspan 2,5-3 cm: **gold-spotted sylph** *page 351*

- Broad black band dotted with orange along outer edges of wings; inner halves of wings orange and brick-red, dotted in places with black; two slender, sharp-pointed tails; wingspan 6,5-8 cm: **koppie charaxes** *page 340*
- Reddish brown outer half of wings, with two rows of yellowish spots on forewings; pearly-white inner half; short tails; wingspan 6,5-8 cm: **pearl charaxes** *page 344*
- Male patterned in yellow and black with broad tail to each hindwing; wingspan 7,5-9 cm: **mocker swallowtail** *page 338*

- Dark brown to black; white band across middle of hindwing; rows of black spots parallel to outer edges of wings; forewing has three white spots near tip, and two white patches in midwing; wingspan 4,2-4,8 cm: **small spotted sailor** *page 341*
- Red or orange-red wings, but outer third of each forewing clear or translucent; red inner part of forewing has two or three small black spots; hindwing has black spots; wingspan 4,5-5,3 cm: **garden acraea** *page 346*

- Pale orange, bordered narrowly in black and evenly covered with small black spots; wingspan 3-3,5 cm: **polka dot** *page 347*
- Orange with black wing margins and wing veins outlined in black; wingspan 2,4-3 cm: **mountain copper** *page 352*

Butterflies

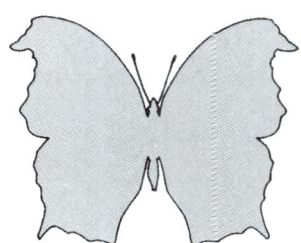

- Whitish green with pearly lustre; wings carry purple, yellow and black eye-spots; tip of forewing bordered in black; hindwings have short tail; wingspan 6,5-8,5 cm: **mother-of-pearl** *page 339*
- Brown above with comma-shaped, black eye-spot (on an orange background) in apex of each forewing; wingspan 6-7 cm: **evening brown** *page 343*
- Orange with black-and-white markings, slightly scalloped margin to wings; wingspan 4-5 cm: **painted lady** *page 346*
- In summer red above with broad black outer margins and black at base of wings; in winter violet-blue dorsal side with black-tipped red spots parallel to outer edges of wings; outer edges of wings scalloped; wingspan 5-6 cm: **gaudy commodore** *page 347*
- Black with orange-yellow patch on each fore- and hindwing, and large, violet-blue spot in centre of each hindwing; wingspan 4-5 cm: **yellow pansy** *page 343*
- Black with large blue spot in each hindwing; broken white band across each forewing; treble white band along outer edge of each hindwing; blue-centred, orange-red eye-spots on each wing; wingspan 4-5 cm: **blue pansy** *page 348*
- Outer halves of male's wings orange-red, with black border to edge of forewing, and black spots; inner halves of wings lustrous, iridescent blue-pink; wingspan 2,3-3 cm: **Thysbe copper** *page 352*

- Black with broken yellow band across each fore- and hindwing; two blue, black and orange eye-spots on each hindwing; wingspan 8-9 cm: **citrus swallowtail** *page 338*
- Dark brown with two (male) or three (female) broken orange bands parallel to outer edge of forewing and another on hindwing, which has mauve eye-spots between outer margin and orange band; wingspan 7-8 cm: **Table Mountain beauty** *page 344*
- Orange above with jagged-edged black patches extending from middle of wings to body; black bar near outer margin of fore- and hindwing; dark wing-veins, wingspan 4-4,8 cm: **joker** *page 345*

- Inner halves of both fore- and hindwings brilliant blue, bordered on outer edges with blackish brown, shading to chestnut brown; brown tail to each hindwing; wingspan 3-3,8 cm: **fig tree blue** *page 353*
- Bright metallic blue above with black border to wings, forming triangular patch at tip of forewing; two red spots at tip of each hindwing; wingspan 3-3,6 cm: **sapphire** *page 353*
- Violet-blue wings with narrow brown outer border, and two small black spots at tip of hindwing; short tail; wingspan 2,5-3,2 cm: **lucerne blue** *page 354*
- Grey-brown with white-edged black spot at rear of each forewing and three to five more along outer margin of each hindwing; whitish tail to each hindwing; wingspan 1,8-2,6 cm: **tailed black-eye** *page 354*

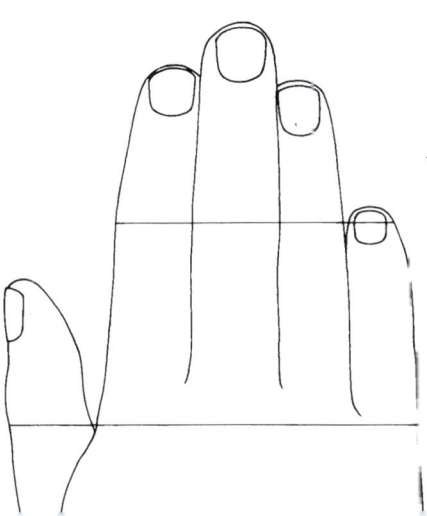

Other insects

- Swift-flying; body brilliantly coloured; wings with dark spot near apex; short antennae: **dragonfly** *page 361*
- Slow-flying; long antennae; transparent wings often vividly patterned in brown, yellow, black and white; active mainly at night: **antlion** *page 372*

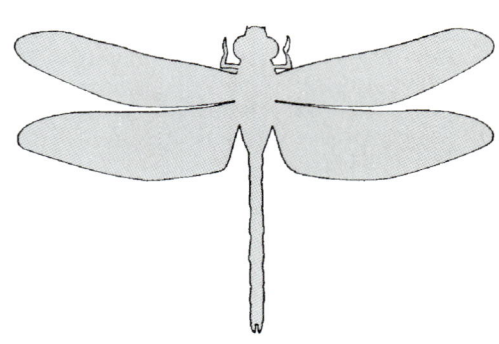

- Spiky plate over neck; dark brown, grey or reddish brown, with two narrow yellow stripes along back of abdomen: **armoured cricket** *page 364*
- Short body, dark brown or black in colour; 'chirping' song: **field cricket** *page 365*
- Forewings translucent and unpigmented; antennae longer than body; swordlike ovipositor; light green or yellow in colour: **tree cricket** *page 365*
- Compact body; digging forelegs flattened with sharp teeth; small wings; golden brown to black: **mole cricket** *page 366*
- Green, sometimes tinged with pink, and often dotted and striped with silver or red; inflated, bladderlike abdomen with dark line along belly: **bladder grasshopper** *page 366*
- Green, brown or black with bright markings; emits foul-smelling foam in response to danger; generally slow-moving: **stink locust** *page 367*
- Generally brown, varying slightly according to species and age; short, thick antennae: **locust** *page 367*

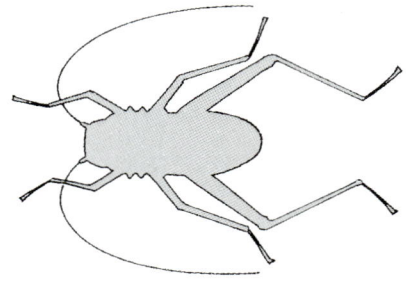

- Black or brown; slender body; female has a long ovipositor; long antennae; most have wings: **ichneumon wasp** *page 377*
- Curled antennae; long hindlegs; body usually black, black and orange or dark brown; wings orange-brown or dark blue; jerky movements when not in flight: **spider wasp** *page 378*
- Brown body with bright markings; builds nests of paper; folds wings longitudinally when at rest; ovipositor concealed under abdomen: **social wasp** *page 378*
- Head, thorax and tip of abdomen black; long waist red; body slender; narrow wings; nests in ground: **sand wasp** *page 379*
- Reddish brown to brown; round body; male has fluffy head and thorax; large wings; often seen in columns: **driver ant** *page 380*

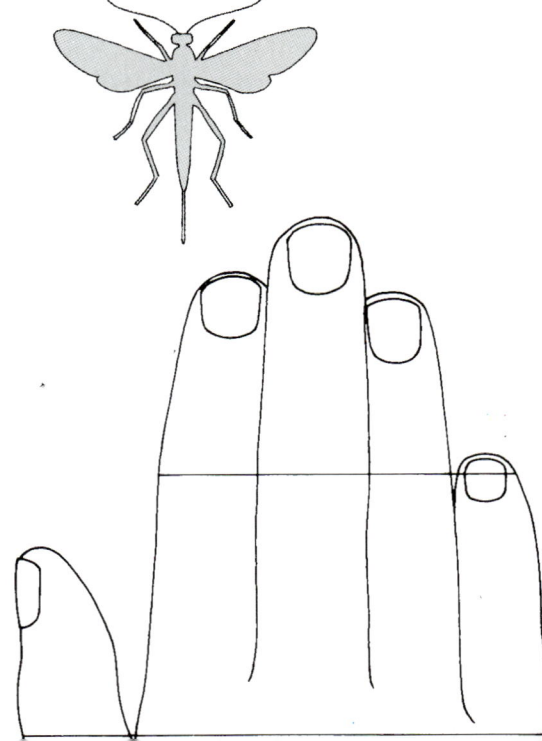

Other insects

- Rounded body; colour varies from brown-grey to reddish brown and pale yellow; head of soldiers large, with huge jaws acting as pincers: **termite** *page 362*
- Slim body; brown, tan, yellow or blackish; two pincers at tail end: **garden earwig** *page 363*

- Usually dark green or black, though sometimes brightly coloured; back legs adapted for jumping; nymphs produce foam or cuckoo-spit nests: **spittle bug** *page 368*
- Green, yellow or black, sometimes with orange or yellow markings; flat bodies; hard forewings; unpleasant smell if held or squashed: **shield bug** *page 369*

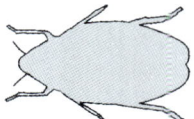

- Short, rounded abdomen; large, iridescent eyes do not meet in middle of head; generally brownish; wings held at sides of body at rest: **horsefly** *page 373*
- Large, compound eyes bulging upwards and separated at top of head by a deep trough; head turns constantly; colour generally brown; very hairy, especially about the face; one pair of wings; stout proboscis: **robber fly** *page 374*
- One pair of wings; colour brown, yellow or black with yellow stripes or spots; body usually stocky; no sting: **hover fly** *page 374*
- Yellow, brown or black with heavily marked wings; two wings held in characteristic drooping fashion when at rest; eyes often iridescent: **fruit fly** *page 375*
- Body brown to black; small, fleshy proboscis beneath head; four dark stripes on thorax; dull wings: **housefly** *page 375*
- Drab yellowish brown; mouthparts project forward and upward from under the head; wings fold across each other when at rest: **tsetse fly** *page 376*
- Body stout; brilliant blue or green; found on meat, carcasses or livestock: **blowfly** *page 376*
- Blackish brown, usually striped with yellow; often seen in swarms; sting present; two pairs of wings; pollen baskets on hindlegs: **honeybee** *page 380*

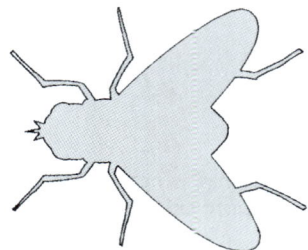

- Shiny blue-black, sometimes with bands of white, yellow or deep orange; pear-shaped abdomen (raised when alarmed); mostly arboreal: **cocktail ant** *page 381*
- Long-limbed; brown or black with whitish yellow abdomen; nests in sand: **sugar ant** *page 381*

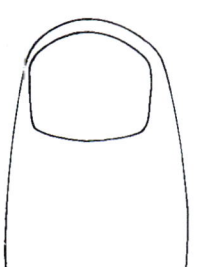

Reader's Digest

SOUTHERN
AFRICAN
WILDLIFE

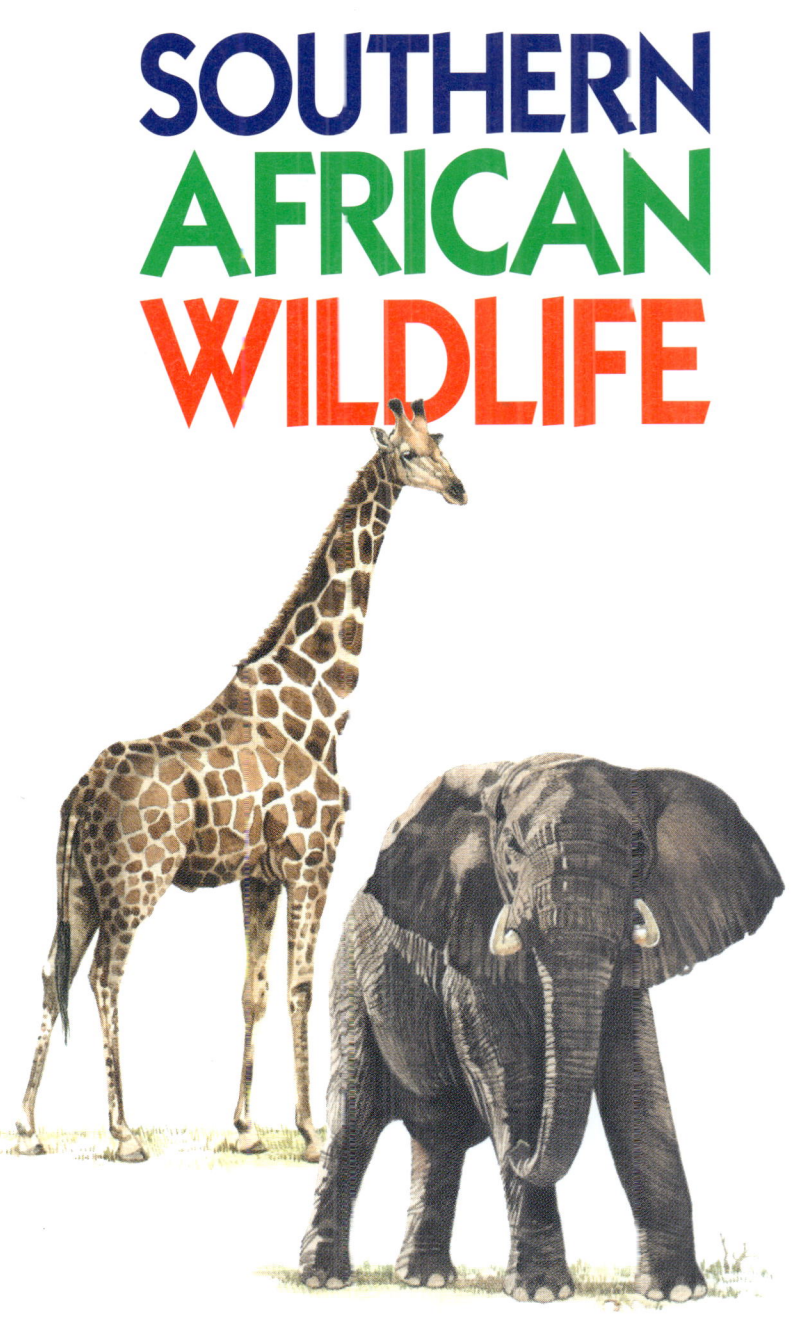

The Reader's Digest Association, Southern Africa

First edition © 1989 The Reader's Digest Association, South Africa (Pty) Ltd
Second edition © 2002 The Reader's Digest Association, Southern Africa, represented by Heritage Publishers (Pty) Limited, 10 Mill Street, Newlands 7708.

Most bird illustrations taken from 'Roberts' Birds of Southern Africa' © Trustees of the John Voelcker Bird Book Fund.

All rights reserved. No part of this book may be reproduced, translated, stored in a retrieval system or transmitted in any form or by any means, electronic, electrostatic, magnetic tape, mechanical, photocopying, recording or otherwise, without permission in writing from the publishers.

Reader's Digest and the Pegasus logo are registered trademarks of the Reader's Digest Association, Inc.

Visit our website at http://www.readersdigest.co.za

Printed in Cape Town
ISBN 1-919750-37-1

SECOND EDITION TEAM:
Editor Judy Beyer
Art director Stuart Nix (Square Edge Design)
Principal writer Jeremy Lawrence
Writers Brian Johnson Barker, Monica Fairall, Dr Marc Griffiths, George Maclay
Proofreaders Anne Wevell, Pat Kramer
Production manager Grant Moore

FIRST EDITION TEAM:
Editor Tim O'Hagan
Art editor Neville Poulter
Research editor Judy Beyer
Project co-ordinator Carol Adams
Principal writer Jeremy Lawrence
Writers Brian Johnson Barker, Monica Fairall, George Maclay
Indexer Ethleen Lastovica

Consultants and contributors

Dr Anthony J Booth, Department of Ichthyology and Fisheries Science, Rhodes University

Antonio J de Freitas, Ph D, Oceanographic Research Institute, Durban

Dr Sheldon Dudley, Natal Sharks Board

Professor Jan Giliomee, Ph D, Department of Entomology and Nematology, University of Stellenbosch

Professor Charles Griffiths, Ph D, Marine Biology Research Institute, University of Cape Town

Dr MH Griffiths, Marine and Coastal Management, Department of Environmental Affairs and Tourism, Cape Town

Henk Geertsema, Ph D, Department of Entomology and Nematology, University of Stellenbosch

Richard Harding, Sea Fisheries Research Institute, Cape Town

Professor Gordon Lindsay Maclean, Ph D, D Sc, Department of Zoology and Entomology, University of Natal

Michael Meyer, Sea Fisheries Research Institute (Marine Mammals), Cape Town

MD Picker, Ph D, Department of Zoology, University of Cape Town

PH Skelton, Ph D, JLB Smith Institute of Ichthyology, Grahamstown

Tony Smith, Jonkershoek Fish Hatchery, Department of Nature and Environmental Conservation, Stellenbosch

Rudy van der Elst, M Sc, Oceanographic Research Institute, Durban

Dr E van Dijk

Professor JH van Wyk, Ph D, Department of Zoology, University of Stellenbosch

John Visser, M Sc

Cheryl Whitmore, M Sc, Department of Entomology and Arachnology, Durban Natural Science Museum

Illustrators

Tobie Beele, Jacque Blaeske, Edward Hayter, René Hermans, John Kramer, Penny Meakin, Sheila Nowers, John Pace, David Thorpe

Contents

Instant identification guide Inside front cover

Introduction 40

How to use this book 41

Mammals 42

Large mammals 46

Smaller mammals 70

Birds 98

Ground birds 104

Waterbirds 125

Birds of prey 148

Tree birds 161

Turtles and tortoises 206

Snakes and lizards 214

Frogs and toads 246

Freshwater fishes 254

Marine fishes 264

Marine mammals 300

Marine invertebrates 304

Spiders, scorpions and others 318

Beetles 328

Butterflies and moths 336

Other insects 358

Families of the wild 382

Highveld 384

Northern savanna 386

Lowveld 388

East coast subtropical forest 390

Eastern Cape and KwaZulu-Natal midlands 392

Drakensberg escarpment 394

Cape fold mountains 396

Southern Cape forest 398

Southwestern Cape fynbos 400

Karoo 402

Namaqualand and Bushmanland 404

Coastal and central Namibia 406

Kalahari 408

Glossary 410

Index 414

Bibliography 431

The wildlife of southern Africa in one volume

Nowhere on Earth is there such an abundance of wildlife as in southern Africa, a land where the tusked giants of the veld rule over a teeming world of animals fascinating in its diversity and seemingly endless in number.

Recognizing and understanding the creatures that inhabit this land is a challenge that few of us can honestly claim to master—even for experts armed with a library of reference books. There are, for example, some 900 different species of birds (one-tenth of the quota of the entire world), 145 snake species, five families of frogs and toads and no fewer than 80 000 different insects. While many of these are extremely rare, hundreds more are regularly seen in nature reserves, forests, farms and even in our own gardens.

It is these animals—the ones you are most likely to see—that this book helps identify. By leaving out the rarer species we've been able to concentrate on the creatures most regularly seen in southern Africa. At the same time, we have also been able to include all the branches of southern Africa's wildlife in one volume, giving you a single, information-packed guide to the creatures that inhabit our natural wonderland.

This second edition has been completely updated to include revised names, both Latin and English. The distribution of certain species has changed, whether due to encroachment by man on their natural habitat or a gradual diminishing or increase in the numbers of a species, and revised maps reflect these current distribution ranges.

Here is a book that takes you into this wildlife domain, as no book has done, introducing you to its more prominent inhabitants, showing you what they look like, how they behave and the intriguing role each animal plays in the wild.

How to use this book

Southern African Wildlife consists of three main sections: an instant identification guide, a field guide and a guide to the natural regions and the animals you'll find there, entitled *Families of the wild*.

Instant identification guide
A unique, colour-coded 'instant identification guide' (see inside the front cover for details on how to use this guide).

Field guide to over 600 species
This section is broken down into easily identifiable groups, each with its own colour code (yellow for mammals, purple for spiders and scorpions, and so on). This colour, which extends in a band across the top of each page, corresponds with the colour-coded index in the 'instant identification guide' at the front of the book. By looking at the book side on, you'll soon become familiar with the colour coding, and be able to turn quickly to the section you need
Each entry in the field guide consists of:
- The name in English, Afrikaans and Latin.
- A concise, italicized identification capsule of vital information about the physical characteristics of the animal: its size, body shape and colour; the animal or animals it could easily be confused with; and the habitats it prefers.
- A description of the animal's habits and the often incredible, sometimes bizarre, effect they have on the lives of other species.
- An illustration of the animal described, with gender symbols (♀ = female; ♂ = male) where appropriate.
- A distribution map, showing where in southern Africa the species is normally found (if you spot a species 'outside' its normal area, you've probably made a wrong identification).

Each major section begins with an overview of the group with easy-to-follow illustrations to help you identify the body parts of the animals in that group.

Families of the wild
This section details the 13 different 'natural regions' or 'environmental zones' of southern Africa, showing how the various animals relate to their particular region. It also lists the animals you're most likely to encounter in each region, with a cross-reference to the main entry.

Glossary
Inevitably, not everyone will be familiar with some of the more technical terms used by naturalists. A full explanation of these begins on page 410.

Index
In order to make it even easier to find a particular species, the index includes all English, Afrikaans and scientific names in one listing.

Mammals

The 340 species of land mammals found in southern Africa are just part of the earth's full complement of around 4 000-4 500 mammal species, and comprise an enormously diverse group of animals, ranging from the bat to the buffalo, the hedgehog to the hippopotamus—the aardvark to the zebra. One feature common to all mammals is the ability to suckle their young; and it is this characteristic from which the name 'mammal' is derived, for the word comes from the Latin *mamma*, meaning a milk-secreting gland or breast.

All mammals share not only the ability to suckle their young—they have other common characteristics too: they nurse their offspring; they are warm-blooded; their skin is protected by fur or hair to a greater or lesser extent; they are vertebrate—in other words, they have a skeleton; and they have four limbs (modified in bats to provide hang-gliderlike wings for flight).

Because of their adaptability and highly developed brains, mammals, including man, represent the dominant group of land animals in southern Africa as they do everywhere else in the world. But, unfortunately, this dominance has not prevented the extinction of numerous mammalian species, brought about by a combination of factors—among them hunting, competition with other species living in the same distribution area, and the destruction or alteration of their natural habitat.

The most recent victims in southern Africa have been the quagga and the blue antelope. Endangered species today include the black (or hook-lipped) rhinoceros, the riverine rabbit and the wild dog.

Most mammals are elusive—a technique for survival—and so are not easy to find. Many antelope, for instance, disappear into the cooling shelter of thick bush during the heat of the day, emerging into the open mostly in the early morning and late afternoon.

Difficult to see at the best of times are the creatures of the night such as the Cape fox, the porcupine, the African wild cat and, of course, the bats (of which there are more than 90 species). Also mainly nocturnal is the largest mammal order of all—the Rodentia—which includes creatures well known to man such as rats, mice and molerats.

Irrespective of their daily rhythms and types of habitat, mammals are difficult to spot because of their often excellent natural camouflage. Brown and grey-brown, the predominant colours of their fur covering, blend with earth shades, with stems and branches, and with sun-baked grass and vegetation. Variations on the colour theme add refinements of disguise. The spots of the leopard, and the giraffe's jigsaw of brown patches, merge with the dappled foliage of these animals' habitat; the vertical stripes of the nyala form part of the mosaic of patterns provided by the vegetation in dry savanna woodlands.

The fur on the underparts of many species—for example, impala—is paler than the upper fur. This two-tone adaptation helps to compensate for any shadow that might make the animal conspicuous against its surroundings. And a distinctive feature of a number of southern African species is that individuals living in the drier west of the subcontinent are paler than those in the east.

So marked can these colour differences be that, in the early days of mammal classification, zoologists would divide what we now regard as a single species into several species on the basis of the variations. Actually the differences, which are often quite subtle across the full distribution range of the species, are simply nature's way of adapting the colour of various species to the predominant colour tones of the natural vegetation.

How to find mammals

An elephant may betray its cover by trumpeting, or a lion by a nocturnal roar, yet mammal sounds are seldom emphatic enough to enable you to find them. Mammals, however, are apt to be extremely sensitive to any sounds that you make—and to the odour that you emit.

Without that keen awareness of their surroundings, they would not be able to survive for long. And, as a game-watcher you, in turn, must develop your own awareness.

Here are some hints to bear in mind when tracking game in the open:

Get up at dawn, or even a little earlier. It is at first light that much of the animal kingdom stirs and unselfconsciously parades itself. Another good time to be on the alert is in the late afternoon and early evening.

Take up your position near a waterhole, for that's where the game will congregate (often in a certain order or precedence, the timid giving priority to the bolder or more aggressive). But before settling down here, or at some other likely observation post, note the direction of the wind and try to stay 'down-wind' of the animals you're watching. Ease the period of waiting by making yourself comfortable; bring along a cushion, a metal-and-canvas folding stool or a shooting stick—if you are lucky enough to acquire one.

Wear clothing in colours that don't stand out sharply against the landscape. Stick to browns, olive greens and similar drab hues—and if the fabric is patterned, so much the better, for the pattern will break up your image so that it becomes less prominent. Avoid shiny material, jewellery and anything else that may catch the light. Also avoid the sort of outfit that rustles as you move—and cameras or other equipment that clanks.

Speak softly or in a whisper. Move quietly too, and slowly, watching where you're going. The crack of a dry twig stepped on becomes a thunderous noise in the silent veld or forest. Make use of bushes and trees to keep yourself out of sight. Get down on your hands and knees, if necessary. Whether you're watching a rhinoceros or a rock dassie, 'freeze' if you think you've been spotted—this may lull the animal into the belief that you're an environmental fixture.

Don't ever smoke. The smell of tobacco signals danger to wild animals. Avoid strong perfumes too. Any smell that savours too strongly of man's urban environment is a drawback. The longer the clothes you wear have been knocking about in the wild, the better.

Finally, never forget for a moment that an animal's instinct for survival can lead to aggression—and that

Mammals

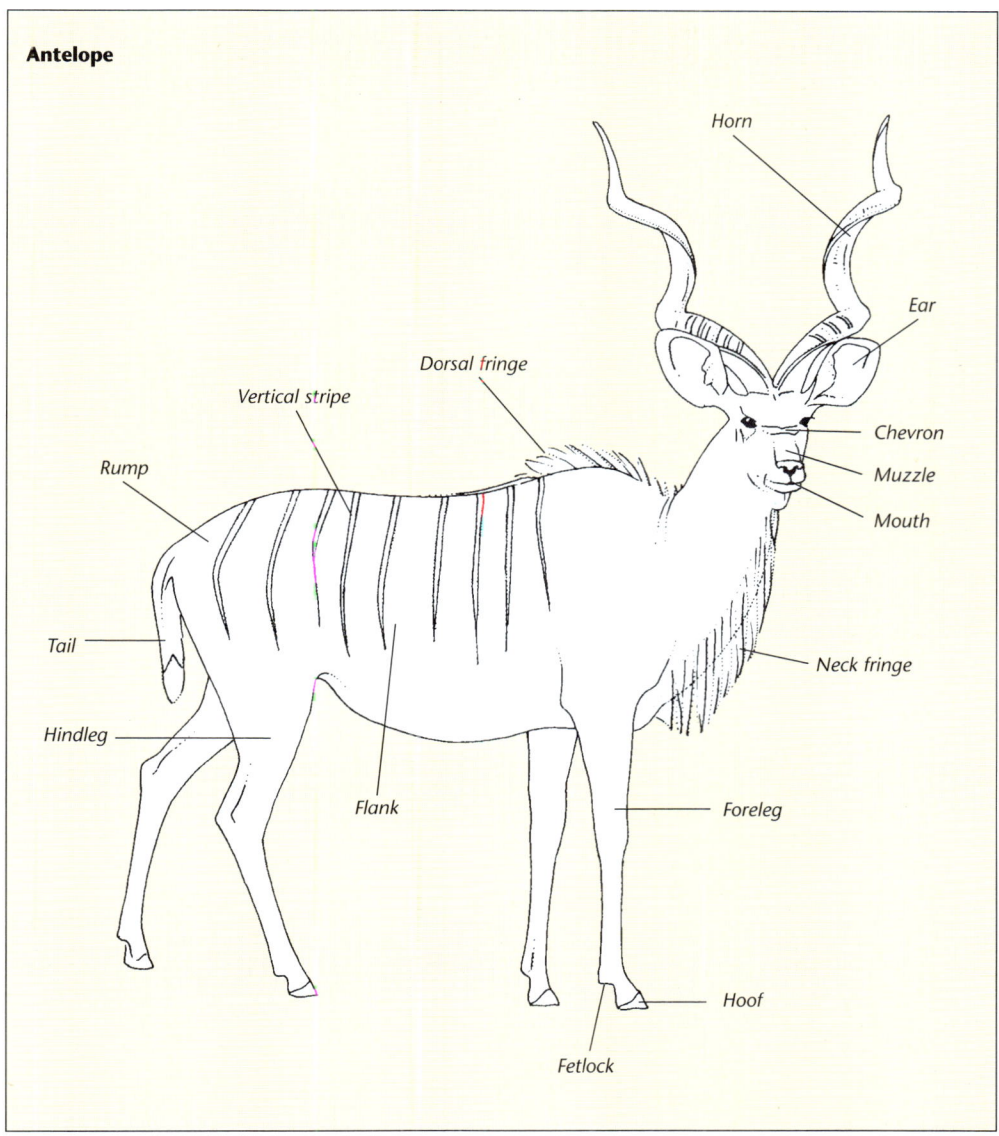

Antelope

there's nothing appealing about being at the receiving end of a charging rhino, lion or elephant. Remember also, that you're visiting an area the animals consider their territory. Put yourself in experienced hands if you're in search of big game and wish to stray from the protection of your vehicle.

Identifying mammals

For the purposes of this book, the mammals of southern Africa are divided into two sections: large mammals and smaller mammals. Within each section, species belonging to the same order (for example, bats), family (antelope) and subfamily (mongooses) are grouped together.

You won't have any problem identifying high-profile members of the animal kingdom such as giraffes and elephants. Not only are their shapes and silhouettes familiar from our kindergarten years, but only a single species of each is indigenous to southern Africa. Other easily recognizable 'single-species' animals include lions, buffalo and hippopotamuses.

For the rest, identifying the correct species is partly a matter of elimination, and here the distribution charts for each species will prove very useful. For example, distribution alone will eliminate any possibility of confusing the Cape mountain zebra (southeast Cape) with Burchell's zebra (north and northeast of the subcontinent) in their natural habitats.

Sometimes, of course, man has introduced a species to a game park or privately owned property far removed from areas where the species occurs naturally in the wild. How, then, do you tell if the formidable monster caught in the sights of your binoculars is a white or black rhinoceros (for, in fact, both animals are grey)? Firstly, refer to the instant identification guide at the beginning of this book; then turn to the detailed description of each species, and in particular the 'Most like' section, where distinguishing traits are listed.

Use this section, too, to decide between other superficial look-alikes such as the leopard and the cheetah, the fox and the jackal, the blesbok and the bontebok, the slender and the yellow mongoose.

Mongoose
Ear
Eye
Muzzle
Total length
Mouth
Foreleg
Tail tip
Claw
Hindleg

Bat
Muzzle
Upper arm
Ear-shield
Ear
Forearm
Eye
Wing claw
Digits
Metacarpal bones
Wing membrane
Hindfoot
Tail
Upper leg
Lower leg

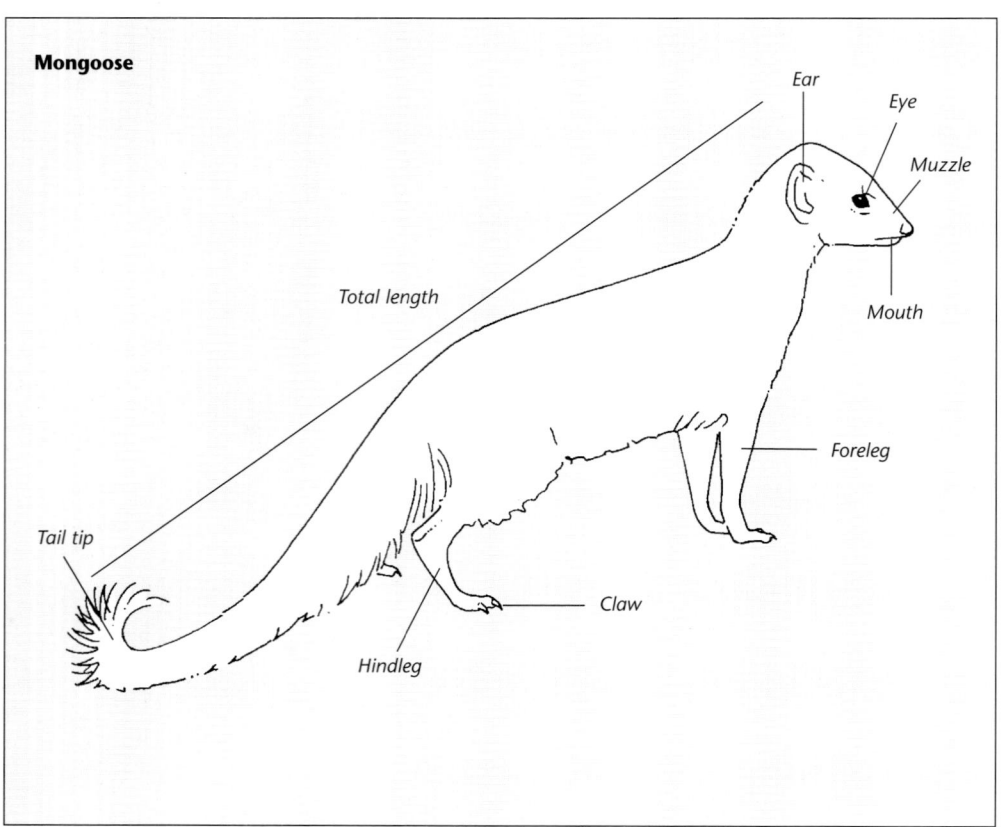

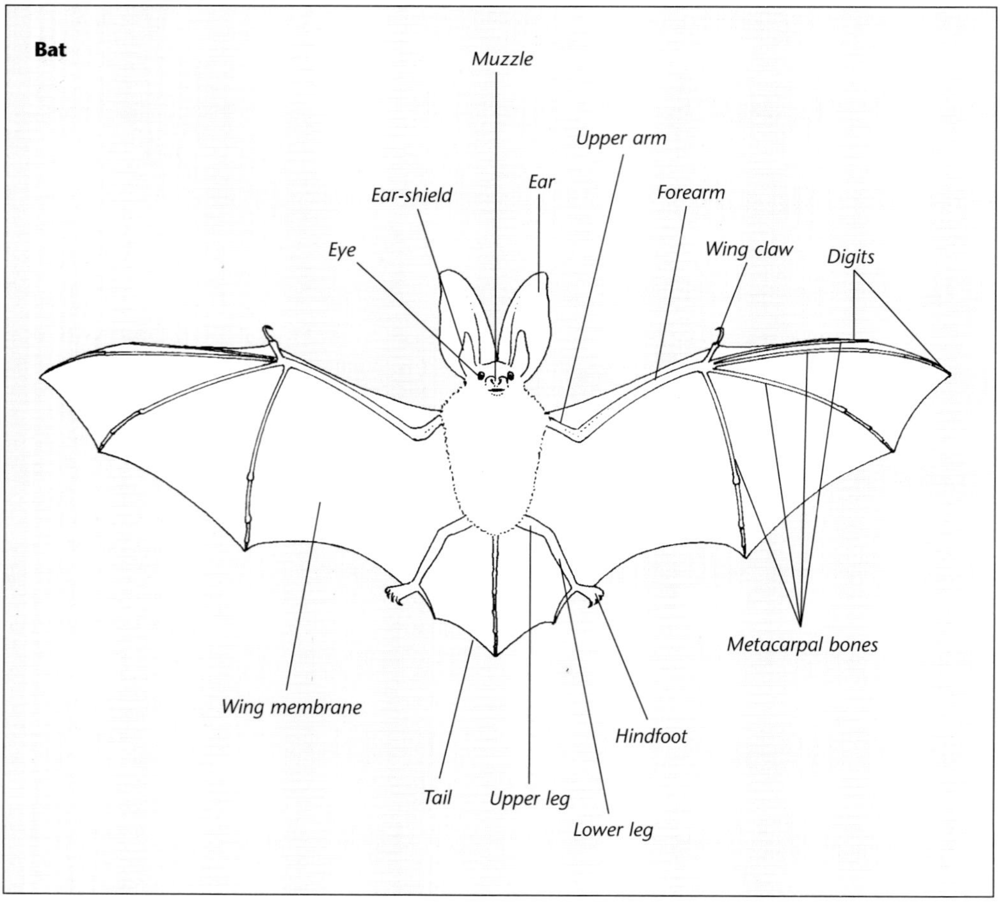

Mammals

First impressions

Buck present problems because there is such a wealth of indigenous species, many of them rather similar even at close quarters. A fleeting glimpse at a distance may be all that you are, in fact, allowed. Try, in those few moments, to retain an impression of the essentials: general shape and size (in relation to shrubs and trees), posture, colour pattern (including belly and tail), length and shape of horns, length of ears.

Movements

How does the buck move? Does it punctuate its flight with the 'pronking', stiff-legged leaps so typical of the springbok? Does it crouch low in retreat, like Sharpe's grysbok? Does it, like the oribi and certain other species, pause characteristically to look for the source of the disturbance? Is it travelling in a herd, a small family group or on its own?

Calls

A few buck species have rather special calls, such as the high-pitched *chee-chee* of the suni, the long-drawn-out barking of the sitatunga, and the whistle of the common reedbuck. You can tune yourself into these calls by listening to recordings of common animal sounds before you go game-watching.

Small mammals—by their very size, and the speed with which they can scuttle to safety—are a challenge for the observer. Sometimes an educated guess may be the best you can do to arrive at the correct species, particularly if the sighting is very brief. With its low legs and long tail, the trim, grey-brown creature scampering into the undergrowth must, you decide, be a mongoose—but of which species? The colour seems wrong for the yellow mongoose, and the area inappropriate for both the large grey and the water mongoose (both of which are usually found near water). It looked too big to be a dwarf mongoose. Finally you settle for the slender mongoose (*Galerella sanguinea*), and you are probably right.

Much more formicable is the identification of bats. Enthusiasts find great satisfaction in studying this most unusual order of mammals; but there are many people who, influenced by the creature's somewhat sinister—if totally unjustified—reputation, would be happy to avoid any confrontation with one at all.

Large mammals

ELEPHANT

Olifant
(*Loxodonta africana*)

Size: Shoulder height (m) 3,2-4 m, (f) 2,5-3,4 m; weight (m) 5 000-6 300 kg, (f) 2 800-3 500 kg.
Colour: Skin greyish, but often assumes the colour of the soil, as elephants cover themselves with dust and mud.
Most like: Cannot be confused with any other animal.
Habitat: Can be as diverse as the northwestern coastal regions of Namibia and the lush woodland of the southern Cape's high rainfall forest, as long as there is sufficient food, water and shelter.

Northern Namibia and ranging eastwards to Botswana, Zimbabwe and western Mozambique. In South Africa confined to reserves in Mpumalanga, Northern Province, KwaZulu-Natal and Eastern Cape. Reintroduced to the St Lucia Park.

The lumbering gait of this towering, tusked monolith of the African veld is one of the truly unforgettable sights in the arena of southern African wildlife. Usually a gentle, mild-mannered vegetarian, the elephant is quite capable of killing other animals such as antelope, and even hippopotamus, in its pursuit of water.

Often tearing out small trees and steamrolling over large ones in its quest for food, an elephant can eat up to 250 kg of leaves, grass, seed pods, wild fruit and bush daily.

An elephant can move about quietly on its tree-trunk legs with their flexible, cushioned feet; and although it can run at a speed of about 40 kilometres per hour, its vast bulk prevents it from jumping even a small ditch. It can swim, though, and sometimes uses its versatile trunk as a snorkel.

The elephant's small eyes see poorly, but its sense of smell is acute. The tusks (the heaviest on record came from an elephant from Kenya—one weighed 97 kg, the other 102,3 kg) are used for digging and fighting, and one tusk wears down more quickly than the other.

Females wield the power in elephant society, and herds are formed around cows and their offspring, which are generally born during the early summer.

Elephants will adopt orphaned calves, help injured elephants and work together.

HIPPOPOTAMUS

Seekoei (*Hippopotamus amphibius*)

Size: Shoulder height (m) 1,5 m, (f) 1,45 m; weight (m) 1 000-2 000 kg, (f) 1 000-1 700 kg.
Colour: Greyish black to brown, with a pinkish tinge around eyes, ears and underparts. Inside of mouth pink. Young paler than adults.
Most like: Unlike any other animal.
Habitat: Any body of water with gently sloping banks bordering grass plains.

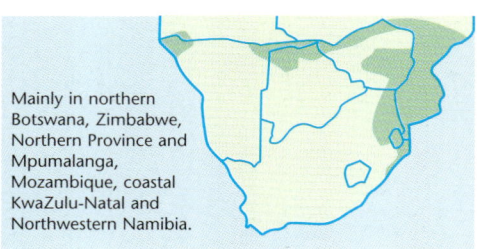

Mainly in northern Botswana, Zimbabwe, Northern Province and Mpumalanga, Mozambique, coastal KwaZulu-Natal and Northwestern Namibia.

Don't be fooled by the comical shape, benign look and sheepish grin of the hippopotamus—this huge amphibious mammal's jaws and curved, tusklike teeth have been known to snap a man in half. Enraged bulls (hippos can live to 40) and cows with calves may storm a boat, so it is best to stay well clear of them at all times.

Hippos may spend part of the day dozing on sandbanks, their hairless skin protected from the blazing sun by the glandular secretion of a reddish fluid. Normally, however, they rest partially submerged in the water, and you may spot the massive head and periscopelike eyes protruding just above the water line, making it easy to see why the ancient Greeks dubbed this animal 'river horse'. When a hippo submerges it closes its slitlike nostrils and disappears; adult males can stay submerged for up to six minutes.

Extremely nimble for their size, hippos move easily on their webbed toes as they walk under water along clearly defined paths on the river bed. On land, they may travel as far as 30 km in a night to search for food.

About 10-15 cows and calves live within a hippo bull's territory—a pear-shaped area about three to eight kilometres long, with the narrow end adjoining water. Mating takes place in the water and, after a gestation period of some eight months, the female gives birth to a single calf weighing 25-55 kilograms. Mother and calf stay together for several months before rejoining the herd. Young bulls are driven out when they reach sexual maturity (at about seven years) and there are fierce clashes between males.

Large mammals

WHITE RHINOCEROS
Witrenoster *(Ceratotherium simum)*

Size: *Shoulder height 1,8 m; weight (m) 2 000-2 300 kg, (f) 1 400-1 500 kg.*
Colour: *Grey, but—like the black, or hook-lipped rhino—taking on the colour of the mud in which the animal performs its ablutions, and of the local soil.*
Most like: *The black rhinoceros, but not as dark. The larger white species is also distinguishable by a hump at the back of the neck, a longer head and a wider, 'square' muzzle.*
Habitat: *Flat, grassy plains, with adequate bush cover and water readily available.*

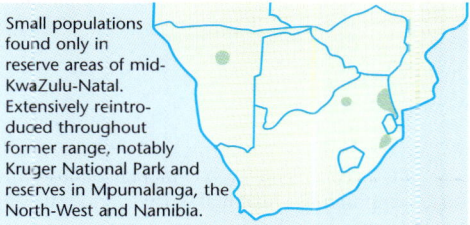

Small populations found only in reserve areas of mid-KwaZulu-Natal. Extensively reintroduced throughout former range, notably Kruger National Park and reserves in Mpumalanga, the North-West and Namibia.

Built like a battle tank, the white rhino—known also as the square-lipped rhino—is the second-largest animal living on land, after the elephant. Yet despite its ugly awesomeness it is basically a placid creature, less irritable and more gregarious than its cousin, the black rhino. It is often found in groups of four to eight, led by a dominant bull.

A grazer, not a browser, it enjoys short grasses which, with its wide, flat mouth, it is able to crop almost to ground level. Its head is usually carried low.

In common with other rhino species, the white rhino has a penchant for mud baths. It's not simply a cosmetic indulgence: the mud traps ticks, and when this dries and falls off, the parasites are shed too.

The rhino's constant companions, the red-billed oxpecker and its rarer cousin, the yellow-billed oxpecker, also help to keep it free of ticks. In addition the birds are the rhino's portable alarm system, their hissing calls warning of approaching danger.

Like the black rhino, the white species is myopic, but makes up for the deficiency with an acute sense of smell and hearing (the ears can be rotated independently). Conversation consists of taciturn grunts and snarls as well as high-pitched squeals.

BLACK RHINOCEROS
Swartrenoster *(Diceros bicornis)*

Size: *Shoulder height (m) 1,6 m; average weight 800-1 100 kg.*
Colour: *Grey, but taking on colour of the mud in which it wallows, and the soil in which it dusts itself.*
Most like: *White, or square-lipped, rhinoceros, but darker. The black rhino is smaller and shorter, without a hump at the back of the neck. It also has the more pointed muzzle, with a distinctive, curved upper lip; and its second horn is longer than the white rhino's.*
Habitat: *Thick bushveld; sometimes grassland with little cover. Must be within reach of water.*

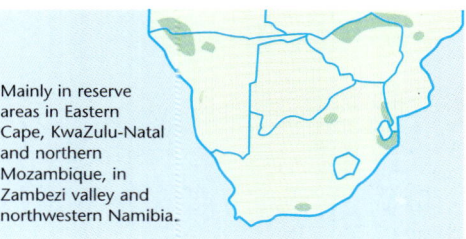

Mainly in reserve areas in Eastern Cape, KwaZulu-Natal and northern Mozambique, in Zambezi valley and northwestern Namibia.

A crusty and unpredictable customer, the black, or hook-lipped, rhino is also unsociable; even an adult male and female enjoy only a fleeting passionate relationship before going their separate ways. The most stable bond is between a female and her calf, which she suckles for about a year—and will reject, sometimes violently, when the next calf is born, usually when her current calf is two to three years old.

The prehensile upper lip that gives this species its alternative name is used to grasp the twigs and shoots on which it browses. If these edible morsels are out of reach, the rhino simply bulldozes the shrub down.

Its two 'horns' are actually composed of tightly compressed hairlike fibres, and they are attached to the skin, not the skull. The well-developed rear horn is usually as long as, or longer than, the front horn. (The medicinal and supposed aphrodisiacal properties associated with these horns have led to many a rhino's wanton slaughter.)

When a black rhino charges, it keeps its head up until the last minute, when the formidable battering ram of its front horn is lowered. A loud shout may be enough to deflect the charge, but it is prudent, however, to give this handsome prima donna a wide berth.

The black rhino once roamed extensively throughout the subregion, but now is regarded as critically endangered, with under 2 000 specimens (about 60 per cent of the world total) in reserve areas.

Large mammals

Giraffe

Kameelperd (*Giraffa camelopardalis*)

Size: Height to top of head (m) 4-5,2 m, (f) 3,7-4,7 m, weight: (m) 970-1 400 kg, (f) 700-950 kg.
Colour: Well-defined, irregularly shaped patches varying from fawn to dark brown, patterned on a paler ground that shades to white on the lower legs. Colouring darkens with age; varies widely geographically.
Most like: Unlike any other animal.
Habitat: From sparsely wooded scrubland to thickly overgrown bush country, especially where there are acacia and other thorn trees to provide the giraffe's staple diet of leaves—and to provide camouflage.

In the savanna of northern Namibia, Botswana and north-western Zimbabwe, in Mpumalanga and south-western Mozambique. Reintroduced to various game reserves, including the Hluhluwe/Umfolozi complex in KwaZulu-Natal.

Nature's skyscraper, the giraffe is the world's tallest animal. Its carotid artery and jugular vein, running down the long neck from head to heart, are equipped with special valves to keep the blood from alternately flooding and evacuating the brain as the head is raised, or lowered to drink water.

The giraffe looks rather as if it were designed by a committee; the ancients' word for it, 'camelopard', shows they saw a resemblance to both the camel and the leopard.

Gregarious and peace-loving, the giraffe's defensive weapon against its main enemy, the lion, is a kick that packs a powerful, hoofed punch. Its gait is ungainly. At full gallop, with the tail twisted over the hindquarters and the neck swinging to and fro in rhythm with the legs, it can achieve a speed of 56 kilometres per hour.

A sleepy giraffe may take 40 winks standing up, with its head supported in the fork of a tree. Even if it lies down it will usually keep its neck upright. If a whole troop of giraffes are resting—as they may do in the heat of the day—they orient themselves in different directions so as to be prepared for danger from whatever quarter.

The female gives birth after a gestation period of about 15 months, its newborn calf weighing in at some 100 kilograms.

Buffalo

Buffalo (*Syncerus caffer*)

Size: Shoulder height 1,4 m; weight (m) 700 kg, (f) 550 kg. Both sexes carry horns.
Colour: Reddish brown to dark brown or black. Males are darker, and both sexes darken with age.
Most like: Black wildebeest, but buffalo has black or dark brown tail and is much larger. The buffalo is also distinctly oxlike in appearance with heavily built limbs.
Habitat: Savanna woodland and bushveld close to water.

Northeastern Namibia, northern Botswana, Zimbabwe and Mozambique. Herds also in KwaZulu-Natal reserves, Eastern Cape's Addo Elephant National Park and Great Fish River Reserve, and the Kruger National Park.

One of the most impressive, and frightening, sights of Africa is the mighty steamroller stampede of a herd of buffalo thundering across the savanna plains. Normally not aggressive, the buffalo is one of the world's most dangerous animals when wounded by its main natural enemies, lions or man. With its menacing, curved horns held high, it will charge, lowering its horns at the last moment to fling its tormentor into the air.

Watchers of the wild are often amazed at the intelligence and cunning of buffalo. An alarmed herd, threatened by a pack of lions, has been seen to go into a defensive semi-circular formation, males on the perimeter facing outwards, protecting the females and calves within.

Unprovoked, a buffalo is inquisitive and placid and will stand and stare at you if you leave it alone. Directly threatened, it may sweep its massive head from side to side in a display of brief bravado, then back off and retreat.

Buffalo are primarily grazers, and like to drink twice a day. Sometimes you will see males cooling down in a mud pool or in the shade of a tree.

A single calf, weighing some 40 kg, is born after a gestation period of almost a year, usually in summer. The calf is able to keep up with the herd just hours after birth.

Large mammals

CAPE MOUNTAIN ZEBRA

Kaapse bergsebra *(Equus zebra zebra)*

Size: Shoulder height 1,3 m; weight 250-260 kg.
Colour: Whitish or cream-coloured coat overlaid by black stripes. White underbody has dark central stripe extending from chest to belly.
Most like: Hartmann's mountain zebra *(Equus zebra hartmannae)*, but slightly smaller in size and weight. Also similar to Burchell's zebra, but lacks Burchell's yellow or grey shadow stripes between the black on the hindquarters.
Habitat: Mountainous areas close to water and suitable grazing. Shelters in ravines or overhangs.

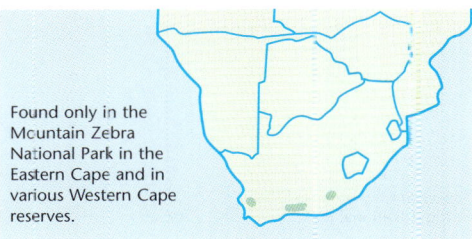

Found only in the Mountain Zebra National Park in the Eastern Cape and in various Western Cape reserves.

One of the world's rarest large mammals—their numbers dwindled to fewer than 100 individuals in 1950—the Cape mountain zebra has come back from the brink of extinction to flourish in selected South African reserves.

The stripes of all zebras, like fingerprints, are never the same on any two individuals, but Cape mountain zebras share habits that are identical. On cold winter mornings they will move, one by one, to the east-facing slopes of their territory and stand at right angles, soaking in the warming rays of the sun.

Young males, preferring the freedom of bachelor life, will team up together at the age of two years and leave the herd, returning when they are old enough to take on a herd, and harem, of their own. The quest for leadership is often a vicious and pugnacious one in which the challenger or challenged may be severely injured.

Cape mountain zebras are found in herds of up to 12 animals, but usually around five or six, consisting of a dominant stallion with mares and foals.

Single foals, born mostly in December, nibble at pellets of their mother's faeces. These contain intestinal micro-organisms which help them digest the grasses that form their staple diet.

BURCHELL'S ZEBRA

Bontsebra *(Equus burchellii)*

Size: Average shoulder height 1,3 m; weight 290-340 kg.
Colour: Whitish or cream coat with black stripes which continue under the belly. Yellow or grey 'shadow stripes' between the black markings on the hindquarters.
Most like: The Cape mountain zebra, but the latter lacks the shadow stripes. Burchell's zebra is bigger than the mountain zebra and the black stripes on its head and body are generally broader and fewer.
Habitat: Open, grassy plains or lightly wooded bushveld, near water.

Widespread throughout northern Namibia, northern Botswana, Zimbabwe, Mozambique, Mpumalanga and northern KwaZulu-Natal.

Herds of Burchell's zebra galloping across the plains, with their magnificent shining coats and rounded bodies rocking in the sun, are one of the truly magnificent spectacles of the subcontinent.

Timid and restless—they invariably bolt from a waterhole after drinking—Burchell's (or plains) zebra are also noisy and very excitable. Their piercing whinny *kwa-ha! kwa-ha!* call is identical to that of the now-extinct quagga.

Under attack from predators, males will put their own safety on the line as they courageously take a protective rearguard position while the rest of the group flees. In very large herds stallions will also form a defensive line along the flanks. In addition, zebra stallions and their mates are fiercely protective of their young: in average breeding herds of three to seven animals, the stallion and his mares will use bared teeth and flailing hooves to attack and maul threatening lions and hyaenas.

The Burchell's habit of keeping close to herds of grazing wildebeest is probably not coincidental: this strategy increases its chances of survival—predators as a rule prefer eating wildebeest. You may also see zebras fraternizing with other species of sociable antelope and ostrich.

A mare will produce a single, 30-35 kg foal after a gestation period of just over a year.

Large mammals

BLUE WILDEBEEST

Blouwildebees *(Connochaetes taurinus)*

Size: Shoulder height (m) 1,5 m, (f) 1,35 m; weight (m) 250 kg, (f) 180 kg. Both sexes carry horns.
Colour: Greyish brown, appearing slate blue in certain lights, with darker vertical stripes on neck and flanks. Black, erect mane and horselike tail.
Most like: The black wildebeest, which is shorter and lighter than the blue wildebeest. The former has a yellowish-white tail that almost reaches the ground.
Habitat: Open savanna, woodland with short grass; open grass plains. Water essential.

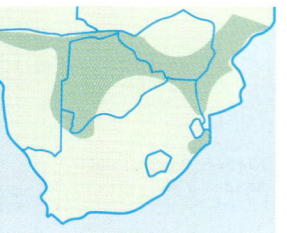

In the plains and open woodlands of northeastern Namibia, Botswana, southern Zimbabwe, Mpumalanga, the Hluhluwe/Umfolozi complex in KwaZulu-Natal, and throughout most of Mozambique.

Driven by their need for water and their partiality for fresh, sprouting grass, blue wildebeest have an amazing ability to track down a rainstorm—even if it is many kilometres away. Sometimes in herds of thousands, they will follow the sound of thunder, or perhaps the sight of rain clouds, until they reach the freshly fallen rain.

Tossing their massive heads about nervously and sniffing the air for the scent of predators, their humped shoulders and sloping backs rolling in a rocking-horse gait, these creatures resemble clumsy clowns of the wild. But their snorts and grunts of alarm are justifiable: they're the favourite prey of lions.

On their immense migrations, the younger, non-territorial bulls are relegated to the perimeter of the herd, often relying on the timidity of accompanying zebra for an early warning if predators are about.

Exceptionally inquisitive, blue wildebeest often stand and stare at an intruder, before suddenly whirling round and galloping off.

Blue wildebeest are tough and, although normally timid, will fight ferociously when cornered.

BLACK WILDEBEEST

Swartwildebees *(Connochaetes gnou)*

Size: Shoulder height 1,2 m; weight 100-180 kg. Both sexes carry horns.
Colour: Very dark brown, appearing black at a distance, the face darker than the body. Mane dark-tipped but lighter at base and erect; fringe of long hair from chest to fore-belly. Long, yellowish-white tail almost reaches the ground.
Most like: Blue wildebeest, but smaller. The blue wildebeest is dark grey, has a blackish tail and has dark, vertical stripes on its neck.
Habitat: Open grassland and bushveld.

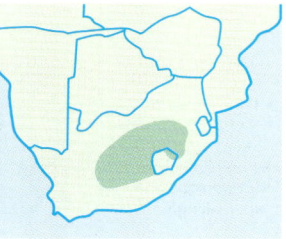

Concentrated in the open grasslands and Karoo bush areas of the Eastern Cape, Free State, western Mpumalanga, Gauteng, North-West Province, Northern and northeastern Western Cape.

The wild-eyed, grumpy black wildebeest probably has the noisiest tail in the animal world. When alarmed, it swishes its long tail back and forth so vigorously that the loud whistling or hissing sound created can be heard from almost a kilometre away.

This is part of a ritual that may include loud snorting, high-kicking with the back legs, and eventually a comical flight in which the herd will gallop off, wheel round, retrace its steps and halt, facing the real or imagined enemy.

Once faced with extinction, these ungainly grazers are now off the danger list.

The early Khoekhoen called the black wildebeest 'gnu' because of its cry: *ge-nu*, which it bellows when alarmed.

The bulls carefully mark their boundaries with urine and piles of faeces and, during the autumn mating season, they will try to keep a number of wandering females in their particular area. If another bull trespasses into this harem, he risks facing an astonishing display of aggression in which the resident wildebeest will thrust his horns into the ground and paw at the soil.

Because there are few predators in their areas nowadays, most wildebeest calves reach adulthood.

Large mammals

SABLE ANTELOPE
Swartwitpens *(Hippotragus niger)*

Size: Shoulder height 1,35 m; weight (m) 235 kg, (f) 210 kg. Both sexes carry the curved horns.

Colour: Upper-body parts dark brown to black, often with a satinlike sheen; males darker than females. Underside and back of thighs white, with white markings on face. Dark, upstanding mane extends along the neck to the shoulders.

Most like: Slightly smaller than the roan antelope, and with a dark brown or black coat, compared with the roan's reddish-grey coat; the roan has shaggy hair on its neck and throat.

Habitat: Open savanna woodland with medium-to-high grass, close to water.

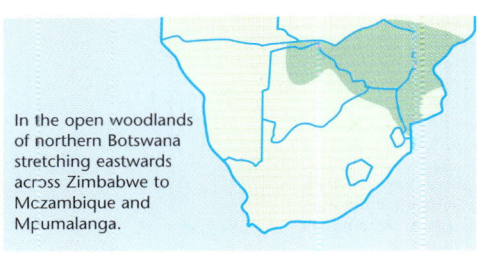

In the open woodlands of northern Botswana stretching eastwards across Zimbabwe to Mozambique and Mpumalanga.

Strikingly coloured and with powerful, scimitarlike horns, the sable is undoubtedly lord of the antelope. Aloof from other species, fearful even to some predators, its approach will encourage other antelope to retire meekly, and even spotted hyaenas, wild dogs, cheetahs and leopards are very reluctant to challenge this courageous, pugnacious and dangerous fighter. Even lions have been known to come off second best—gored to death by those deadly horns.

You will most often see sable in herds of up to 30, although they do form temporary groupings of 50 or more. Adult bulls establish their own territory, and during the mating season aggressively defend it, although serious injuries or fatalities are rare.

Young males know better than to tangle with their elders, and split up into separate bachelor herds until they are old, wise and strong enough to make a successful challenge against a territorial bull.

A breeding herd is led by the territorial bull, but a dominant cow will take the initiative in finding new pastures and water. Single, reddish-brown calves are usually born in January and March when the grass is fairly high, the cow leaving the herd for the birth. Gestation lasts about nine months.

ROAN ANTELOPE
Bastergemsbok *(Hippotragus equinus)*

Size: Shoulder height 1,1-1,5 m; weight (m) 280 kg, (f) 250 kg. Both sexes carry the characteristic, backward-sweeping horns.

Colour: Coat reddish grey, with lighter undersides; the face has a distinctive black-and-white 'mask'.

Most like: The sable antelope which, however, is slightly smaller and black (male) or reddish brown (female) above, unlike the roan's rufous-grey colouring. The roan's horns are shorter and less curved than those of the sable.

Habitat: Medium-to-tall grassland regions, close to trees and water.

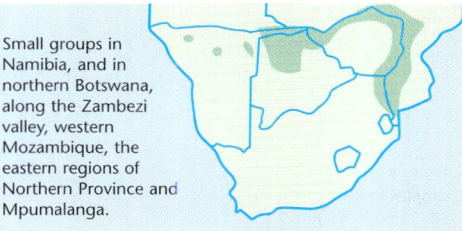

Small groups in Namibia, and in northern Botswana, along the Zambezi valley, western Mozambique, the eastern regions of Northern Province and Mpumalanga.

Second in size only to the eland, the roan, with its horselike face and donkeylike ears with prominent tassles of dark brown hair at the tips, has been known to cause an identity crisis amongst its offspring. More than once, a young calf has broken from cover and dashed after a passing horse, believing it to be its mother.

The roan bull is fiercely protective towards its harem and will ward off the attentions of a stranger by clashing horns with his competitor. During this ritualistic display, both contestants sometimes fall to their knees. Despite lengthy and noisy engagements, serious injuries are rare; as with the sable, the roan's ritualized fighting has evolved to minimize injuries to key members of the population.

Threatened by a predator, the roan may raise its beautifully proportioned body and, hissing and squealing with rage, will bare its teeth and chop at its opponent with flailing hooves and sweeping lunges of its scimitarlike horns.

Roan are fairly gregarious, normally being found in herds of 6-12 animals. They graze in the early morning and late afternoon, resting during the heat of the day.

Cows give birth to one rust-coloured calf at a time, throughout the year, stealing quietly away from the herd and hiding a few days before delivery. The calf will join the herd after about two weeks.

Large mammals

GEMSBOK
Gemsbok *(Oryx gazella)*

Size: Average shoulder height 1,2 m; weight (m) 240 kg, (f) 210 kg. Both sexes carry long, straight horns.
Colour: Pale greyish fawn overall. White face, legs, rump and back carry distinctive dark brown-to-black markings.
Most like: The roan, which also has black-and-white facial markings, but the gemsbok is somewhat smaller, with unmistakeable, straight, rapierlike horns.
Habitat: Arid areas, such as open grassland, Kalahari duneland and bush savanna.

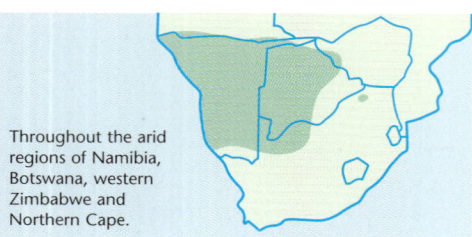

Throughout the arid regions of Namibia, Botswana, western Zimbabwe and Northern Cape.

This powerfully built antelope, easily recognizable by its magnificent, V-shaped pair of horns, can survive in some of the hottest spots on earth without ever drinking water—thanks to a natural air conditioner that keeps its body temperature under control.

During the sizzling heat of the day, the rapid inflow and outflow of air created by the gemsbok's panting passes over a delicate network of blood vessels, cooling the flow of blood to the brain. At the same time, however, the body temperature is allowed to rise—obviating the need to perspire, and thus conserving water. Living in the areas where there is a shortage of drinking water, it obtains moisture from melons, and by unearthing succulent roots and bulbs.

Naturally gregarious, gemsbok lives in herds of 12 or more but break up during the dry season, when food is scarce, into smaller units. The leader of the herd, a territorial male, jealously guards his domain, carefully marking the boundaries with piles of dung pellets to warn off would-be intruder males.

He may reinforce his warning by pawing the ground (his feet are equipped with scent glands) and by thrusting his horns into shrubs and bushes.

If this sabre-rattling doesn't work, the dominant male may challenge the intruder to a duel involving horn-clashing and body-bashing, until one of the gemsbok retreats.

ELAND
Eland *(Taurotragus oryx)*

Size: Shoulder height (m) 1,7 m, (f) 1,5 m; weight (m) 700 kg, (f) 460 kg. Both sexes carry horns.
Colour: Pale reddish fawn coat, tending to a bluish grey in older (particularly male) animals as the skin shows through thinning hair. Males also have a tuft of dark hair on the forehead.
Most like: Unlike any other animal.
Habitat: Open grass plains, scrubland, and woodlands.

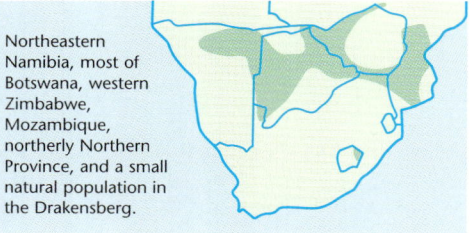

Northeastern Namibia, most of Botswana, western Zimbabwe, Mozambique, northerly Northern Province, and a small natural population in the Drakensberg.

An instant giveaway for eland trying to remain inconspicuous in the wild is the curious, loud clicking sound its knees make when it walks or trots. This huge, oxlike animal, the largest of the African antelope, is shy and timid, but will become very tame in captivity.

Nature has given the mild-mannered eland (Dutch for 'elk'), a resourceful way of coping with extremes of hot and cold. Not only does it rarely drink, but it conserves moisture by not sweating, allowing its body temperature to rise by a few degrees during the day.

In spite of its great size, this gentle giant can walk faster than a man, gallop at great speed for short distances, and leap gracefully over fences up to two metres high. Like gypsies, eland are great roamers and herds, numbering up to a thousand animals, have been seen migrating over long distances in the drier areas of the subcontinent.

Primarily browsers, you will usually find eland in bush country, using their prominent, spiralled horns to break off branches or knock down foliage beyond the reach of their jaws, and their front hooves to dig up roots, melons and tubers.

A single calf is born usually in early summer and, within a few hours, is able to run with its mother. Mothers and calves recognize one another's particular clicks or grunts, and a mother will suckle only her own calf, chasing other calves away by nudging them with her horns.

Large mammals

LICHTENSTEIN'S HARTEBEEST

Lichtenstein se hartbees
(Sigmoceros lichtensteinii)

Size: Average shoulder height 1,25 m; weight (m) 180 kg, (f) 170 kg. Both sexes carry horns.
Colour: Yellowish brown, with off-white rump and lighter flanks. Chin, front of lower legs and tail tuft are black.
Most like: The red hartebeest, but more yellowish overall and with rump less prominently white. Also usually lacking the red hartebeest's dark blaze on the face.
Habitat: Open savanna woodland close to water, and associated flood plain grassland.

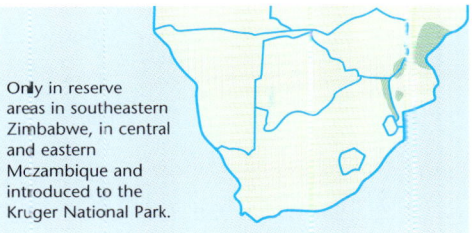

Only in reserve areas in southeastern Zimbabwe, in central and eastern Mozambique and introduced to the Kruger National Park.

RED HARTEBEEST

Rooihartebees *(Alcelaphus buselaphus)*

Size: Average shoulder height 1,25 m; weight (m) 150 kg, (f) 120 kg. Both sexes carry horns.
Colour: Glossy reddish brown, with a black blaze on the face and well-defined, off-white rump and light undersides.
Most like: Lichtenstein's hartebeest, which is more yellowish and lacks the black blaze on the face and the well-defined whitish markings on the rump.
Habitat: Open country, from grassland to semi-desert.

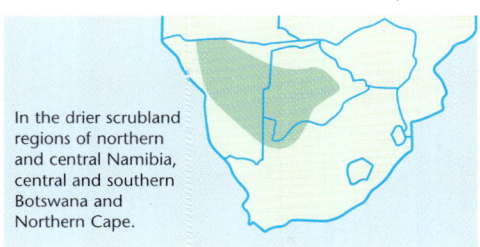

In the drier scrubland regions of northern and central Namibia, central and southern Botswana and Northern Cape.

In times of crisis, the behaviour of the Lichtenstein's territorial bull is gallant and courageous; but such gallantry often costs him his life. Threatened by a hunter or predator, the rest of the herd dashes off, while the bull brings up the rear, stopping every now and then to look back at the danger. Such protective action often earns him a bullet, or sudden death in the jaw of a predator, leaving his widows and orphans to be taken into another harem.

During the mating season, restless bulls leave their own area and earnestly try to entice cows away from other territorial bulls. This leads to noisy confrontations, and prolonged fighting often takes place. Crestfallen bulls, returning empty-handed from their sorties, may find their own harems severely depleted by other raiding bulls. This possibility keeps each bull defensively on his toes. Very protective towards his harem, the bull will stand on an elevated site, such as a termite mound, advertising his dominance and scanning his territory for intruders.

Unlike its keen eyesight, Lichtenstein's hartebeest has a poor sense of smell, and a predator can often approach from downwind without being detected.

This hartebeest is usually found in herds of 8-10 individuals, grazing mostly in the early morning and late evening. A single calf is born in spring after a gestation period of eight months.

The goatlike eyes set in an elongated, ungainly face, make the red hartebeest easily recognizable in the bush. And, when alarmed, the herd tends to mill about in seeming confusion, snorting nervously before running off. Once in its stride, a hartebeest can achieve a speed of 55 kilometres per hour, zigzagging left and right in its characteristic bouncing flight. This, accompanied by its excellent sense of smell, makes it difficult prey for wild dogs and hyaenas.

While red hartebeest are grazing, a territorial bull may climb on top of a termite mound to advertise his presence to other hartebeest, and to keep a watchful eye for lions, cheetahs and leopards.

Like the blue wildebeest, it has an uncanny sense of direction and will find water and fresh grazing after rain has fallen a considerable distance away.

Red hartebeest usually live in herds of about 20 or more individuals; but more than 10 000 animals have been observed on massive migrations across the Kalahari Desert.

Males herd females into their own territories and defend the harem against other trespassing males. Vicious fights often follow, in which rival bulls, their horns interlocked, will drag each other to their knees.

Expectant females leave the herd in early summer and each will give birth to a single calf in a sheltered place. After birth, they lick up their calves' urine and faeces—a ploy to eliminate telltale odours that might attract predators.

Large mammals

Tsessebe

Tsessebe *(Damaliscus lunatus)*

Size: *Average shoulder height 1,2 m; weight (m) 140 kg, (f) 126 kg. Both sexes have horns.*

Colour: *Rufous to dark brown, with purplish sheen. Upperparts of legs darker. Inside hindlegs and the underside yellowish white.*

Most like: *The red hartebeest, but the tsessebe's horns are shorter and its shoulders are not as humped as the hartebeest's. The tsessebe also lacks the clearly defined white marking so evident on the hartebeest's rump.*

Habitat: *Grassland near water and the fringes of woodland.*

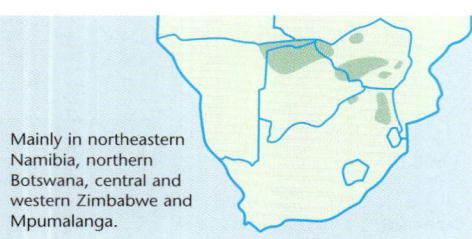

Mainly in northeastern Namibia, northern Botswana, central and western Zimbabwe and Mpumalanga.

This cumbersomely built, rather inquisitive antelope compensates for its awkwardness by being probably the fastest of the southern African buck, capable of maintaining a bouncing gallop of 60 km/h for considerable distances.

Early hunters were amazed at the naivety of tsessebe, which were so overcome by curiosity during a hunt that they stood and stared, while other members of the herd were shot down around them.

When threatened, tsessebe often do no more than canter away to an open vantage point, where they will stop and coolly survey their surroundings before finally breaking into their characteristic easy gallop.

The territorial tsessebe bull ardently defends its harem of cows, and will sometimes climb onto a termite mound or other raised spot in order to keep a lookout for, and warn off, rival bulls.

These antelope are gregarious grazers, sharing their pastures freely. Both males and females mark their territory, using a secretion from glands below their eyes.

Usually born in spring or early summer, calves develop so fast that within a day or two of birth they are strong enough to join the herd. Here they tend to form little nursery groups of their own which are supervised by one or more cows.

Impala

Rooibok *(Aepyceros melampus)*

Size: *Shoulder height (m) 90 cm, (f) 80 cm; weight (m) 50 kg, (f) 40 kg. Only males carry the lyre-shaped horns.*

Colour: *Shining reddish brown coat, with clear division to fawn on the flanks turning paler to pure white undersides. White patch on throat. Bushy tail, with white underside.*

Most like: *Springbok, but lack the latter's dark brown flank stripe separating upperparts from underparts.*

Habitat: *Lightly wooded or bushed country close to water.*

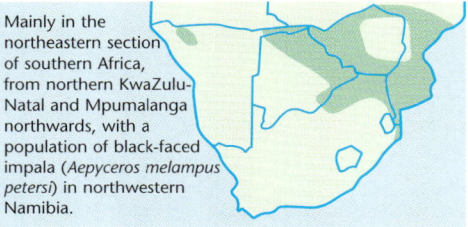

Mainly in the northeastern section of southern Africa, from northern KwaZulu-Natal and Mpumalanga northwards, with a population of black-faced impala *(Aepyceros melampus petersi)* in northwestern Namibia.

This beautiful, bronzed prancer of the wild has the grace of a ballet dancer and the fleet-footed thrust of a high-jump champion—its elegant, bounding leaps clearing heights of three metres and distances of up to 12 m at a time.

Alert and extremely elusive, this gentle, fox-coloured antelope will let out a quick, high-pitched snort when alarmed, taking off with its astonishing leaps over long grass, bushes and small trees.

When it is moving more slowly, you will recognize it easily by its slightly hunched back, and its habit of pressing its tail tightly against its hindquarters. The ears flick busily while it is browsing, and there is frequent, impatient foot-stamping.

Impala are very gregarious, often forming herds of several hundred, especially in winter.

During the mating season from January to May intense rivalry builds up between males and, with loud snorts and grunts, they will resort to threatening displays, horn-thrusting and, occasionally, fatal duels with each other.

Single young, usually born in early summer, are able to join their mothers in the herd within two days of birth, a fact which favours their chances of eluding predators such as lions, leopards, cheetahs, wild dogs and hyaenas.

Large mammals

BLESBOK

Blesbok *(Damaliscus dorcas phillipsi)*

Size: Shoulder height (m) 95 cm, (f) 90 cm; weight (m) 70 kg, (f) 61 kg. Both sexes carry horns.

Colour: Dull reddish brown, with white blaze on the face, usually broken by a narrow brown band just below the eyes. Underside is off-white, and light brownish colour on legs continues to hooves. Tail white on underside with long brown tuft. Horns are straw-coloured.

Most like: The bontebok, but is slightly larger and not as richly coloured; blesbok also lack the bontebok's purple sheen and contrasting white marking on buttocks and lower legs.

Habitat: Open grassland close to shade and water.

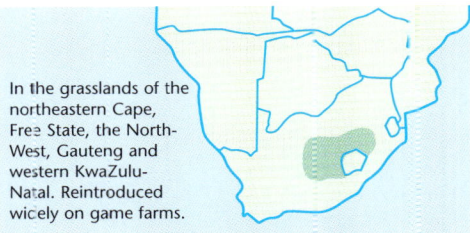

In the grasslands of the northeastern Cape, Free State, the North-West, Gauteng and western KwaZulu-Natal. Reintroduced widely on game farms.

This tireless, nimble-footed athlete of the grasslands—it can run rings around most of the other antelope species—is particularly possessive towards its harem, and performs an impressive ritual of threatening behaviour to warn off rival males. Standing very still, with its head held high and legs straight, the blesbok will resolutely eye its opponent. Then, issuing a menacing volley of snorts, it will lower its head, prod the earth with its horns and hooves and, finally, leap high into the air before clashing horns with its rival. Such fights are usually brief, but rarely fatal.

The blesbok male marks its territory by making dung heaps and also by rubbing scented glands on its face against blades of grass to serve as 'smell beacons' to other males.

Blesbok are primarily grazers, and favour grassland close to water, moving between feeding and resting sites in single file along well-worn paths. During the hottest time of the year they may move deep into shady bushes, resting in small groups.

Expectant mothers stay with the herd to give birth to single calves in early summer. The boundless energy of these calves brings them to their feet within 20-30 minutes of birth, enabling them to run with their mothers.

BONTEBOK

Bontebok *(Damaliscus dorcas dorcas)*

Size: Shoulder height (m) 90 cm, (f) 85 cm; weight (m) 62 kg, (f) 58 kg. Both sexes carry horns.

Colour: Rich, dark brown; darker on flanks and upper limbs, which also have a purple gloss. Unbroken white blaze from forehead to muzzle. Pure white rump, base of tail, underparts and legs from knees downwards.

Most like: The blesbok, which has a duller, more reddish-brown coat, and which lacks the very obvious white patch on the rump.

Habitat: Open fynbos veld with grasses.

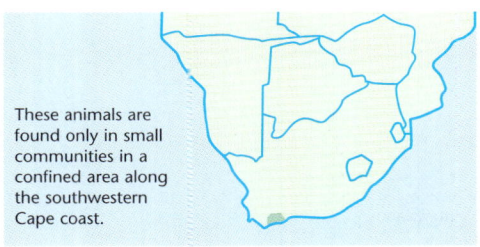

These animals are found only in small communities in a confined area along the southwestern Cape coast.

This handsome, strikingly marked antelope, brought to the brink of extinction by overhunting in the 19th century, has made a significant comeback, thanks to a group of far-sighted farmers who protected a handful of survivors in the Bredasdorp district from the 1830s. Now accommodated in several reserves, including the Bontebok National Park near Swellendam and De Hoop Nature Reserve near Bredasdorp, the bontebok is off the danger list.

During the rut, or mating season, bontebok males entice females into their territories, parading their charms with an extravagant courtship ritual, in which the male bows down his head and lifts his tail over his back. Then, moving in tandem with the female, he rotates in small circles before copulating with her.

Young males and deposed rams dare not be around when this happens; and they have to be content to form celibate bachelor herds, isolated from the mating game.

Fights between bontebok are low-key events, and consist of two males kneeling and perhaps prodding at one another with their horns for just a few seconds, before one of them, usually the intruder, runs off.

Bontebok may be seen during the hot part of the day, standing in groups with their heads held low and facing the sun. The explanation for this behaviour is not clear.

Large mammals

Lechwe
Lechwe *(Kobus leche)*

Size: *Shoulder height (m) 1 m, (f) 90 cm; weight (m) 100 kg, (f) 80 kg. Only males carry the lyre-shaped horns.*
Colour: *Upperparts of body and flanks reddish yellow; underparts and insides of legs white. A white band extends from the white belly to chest and chin. Front of forelegs blackish. Hair long and rough.*
Most like: *Its close relative, the puku, but is slightly larger and the male's horns are larger. The black bands down the front of the forelegs clearly distinguish it from the puku.*
Habitat: *Grassy flood plains and shallow water in seasonal swamps. Rarely found more than a kilometre or two from swamps or rivers with permanent water.*

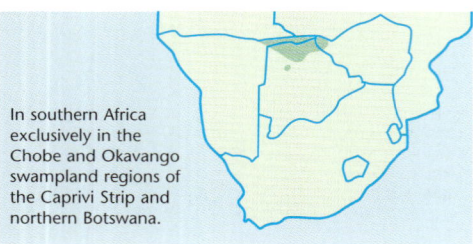

In southern Africa exclusively in the Chobe and Okavango swampland regions of the Caprivi Strip and northern Botswana.

Somewhat clumsy and uncertain on hard ground, the lechwe is a fleet-footed water-lover, skimming across wetlands and swamps with the ease and grace of a gazelle.

Remarkably well adapted to wet conditions, its long hooves splay widely over the soft ground, making it sure-footed and speedy over mud, water and reeds. This robust, long-haired antelope is also a strong swimmer, and will dive into water without hesitation if pursued. The lechwe comes onto dry land only to rest and calve.

Because of its amphibious habits, it is preyed on by a variety of predators, from crocodiles and pythons to lions, leopards, spotted hyaenas and hunting dogs. Like the reedbuck, it sometimes flattens itself on the ground to avoid detection, suddenly taking off in startled leaps and bounds.

Lechwe may congregate in hundreds or thousands, although most herds number about 20-30 individuals.

The ram will defend his own territory with threatening displays, and will fight if an intruder tries to mate with one of his ewes. The clash of horns during these fierce, sometimes fatal, duels may be heard a long distance away.

Cows hide their newborn calves for two or three weeks in the shelter of reeds on an island or other dry spot.

Puku
Poekoe *(Kobus vardonii)*

Size: *Shoulder height (m) 80 cm, (f) 70 cm; weight (m) 74 kg, (f) 62 kg. Only males have the lyre-shaped horns, which are much smaller than those of the lechwe.*
Colour: *Golden brown or brownish orange-yellow with no distinct markings; white or off-white on the undersides and on the throat.*
Most like: *The lechwe, but smaller. The puku is also more brightly coloured, and does not have the lechwe's black markings on its forelegs.*
Habitat: *Open grassy areas near water, but not wide flood plains. Does occur in bushy areas and low woodland very close to water, as long as there is an intervening grassy strip.*

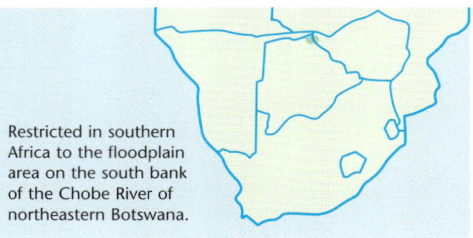

Restricted in southern Africa to the floodplain area on the south bank of the Chobe River of northeastern Botswana.

Puku cows are amongst the worst mothers in the wild. Not only do they often ignore the frantic, high-pitched bleating of their calves, but they rarely defend their young in the face of danger. Calves invariably inherit this offhand attitude, severing their maternal bonds at an early age.

The species is gregarious, occurring in herds averaging six individuals, but sometimes with up to about 30 animals. Occasionally the smaller herds combine, forming large groups of several hundred.

Primarily grazers, puku feed around sunrise and sunset. If danger threatens, they will whistle in alarm, trotting off nervously with their heads held erect. They also respond to the alarm signals of impala, with which they often associate.

Territorial puku males herd their harems into well-defined territories, and although they tend to chase off other males, they sometimes tolerate small bachelor herds, provided their members have no sexual interest in the females. Scrupulous custodians of their own turf, territorial males will challenge and threaten trespassing males. These threats can lead to ritualized horn-clashing, in which the parties are seldom seriously injured.

Large mammals

Mountain reedbuck

Rooiribbok
(*Redunca fulvorufula*)

Size: Shoulder height (m) 80 cm, (f) 70 cm; weight (m) 30 kg, (f) 28 kg. Only males carry the short, ridged, forward-curving horns.

Colour: The soft, woolly coat is reddish grey or grey-fawn. Undersides, including underside of short, brown, bushy tail, are white. Black gland patches under ears.

Most like: Reedbuck, but slightly smaller, much lighter and male has shorter horns. Mountain reedbuck also lack the black or dark brown stripes found on the forelegs of reedbuck.

Habitat: Dry, grassy hill-slopes and lower mountain slopes, usually near water.

In the eastern parts of the subregion, from Northern Province and Mpumalanga to southern Mozambique, Swaziland, KwaZulu-Natal, eastern Free State, Lesotho and Eastern Cape.

Unlike its somewhat antisocial cousin, the reedbuck, the mountain reedbuck is often seen in herd-groups numbering up to a few dozen, sunning itself on the slopes of mountains. Normally, however, you will see it in smaller family parties of three to five individuals.

If alarmed, the mountain reedbuck, like the grey rhebok, will bound away with its tail fanned out. But while the grey rhebok tends to escape upwards to the mountain's higher slopes, the mountain reedbuck, with the same rocking-horse motion, runs across the slope, or obliquely downhill.

Nervous and timid, mountain reedbuck lie closely together when resting, and if danger threatens, one or more of them will utter a shrill whistle of alarm which sends the herd bolting for safety.

Mountain reedbuck have their own answer to bad weather: they merely turn their hindquarters to the direction of heavy wind and rain; alternatively, they lie down on a sheltered slope until the bad weather is over.

Some males occupy the same territory throughout the year, and are particularly on edge when they stray outside its limits. Almost exclusively grazers, mountain reedbuck will never move to areas far from water.

Breeding takes place throughout the year, though mostly in summer. A single calf, weighing about three kilograms, is born after a gestation period of some eight months. To protect themselves, newborn calves instinctively remain hidden for two to three months before joining the rest of the herd.

Grey rhebok

Vaalribbok (*Pelea capreolus*)

Size: Shoulder height (m) 80 cm, (f) 70 cm; weight 20 kg.

Colour: Grey-brown or grey above, but slightly yellowish brown on face and legs. Underparts, including underside of tail, white. Whitish patches around eyes, and on muzzle and chin.

Most like: Mountain reedbuck, but horns are narrower and set vertically, not curved or hooked forward like the mountain reedbuck's. Seen from the front, the grey rhebok's horns are parallel, while the mountain reedbuck's form a V.

Habitat: Rocky hills or mountain slopes, and rocky plains with grass cover.

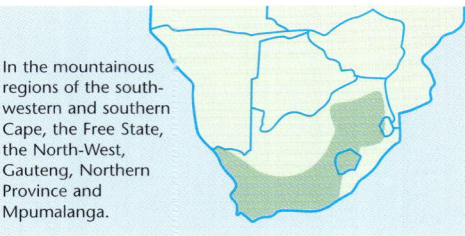

In the mountainous regions of the south-western and southern Cape, the Free State, the North-West, Gauteng, Northern Province and Mpumalanga.

Watch for the stiff-legged, rocking-horse motion of the grey rhebok as it streaks upwards on the upper slopes of mountains, the white underside of its tail flashing distinctively, even from a distance, as it is held above its rump. The strong, bounding leaps and prodigious speed of this small antelope have sent many pursuing predators skulking off empty-handed.

Constantly on the alert for carnivores such as caracals, jackals and eagles, grey rhebok have acquired a reputation in the farming community for attacking and killing small domestic animals. Often greatly exaggerated, this unfortunate belief has led to their being hunted in some areas while, in others, their habitat as well as their allegedly unpalatable flesh have contributed to their survival.

The grey rhebok is mostly a grazer, but unlike the mountain reedbuck, it has little need for water.

It usually lives in family groups of up to 12 animals, headed by a dominant adult ram. The male is strongly territorial, establishing its ownership of land and females by uttering clicking sounds, staging threatening displays and urinating. Although they fight fiercely during the mating season, grey rhebok rarely injure one another.

Single lambs are born in November or December after a gestation period of just under nine months.

Large mammals

WATERBUCK
Waterbok *(Kobus ellipsiprymnus)*

Size: *Shoulder height (m) 1,3 m, (f) 1,2 m; weight (m) 250-270 kg, (f) 200 kg. Only male carries horns.*
Colour: *Grey to greyish brown, coarse, shaggy coat; white ring on rump; white marking around eyes, chin and nose. Legs and abdomen darker; long, dark tuft on tail. Bulls, especially, have a white fringe at the throat.*
Most like: *Reedbuck, but larger. Horns similar but twice as long. White 'target' ring on rump diagnostic, as is coarse and shaggy coat.*
Habitat: *Open plains or woodland close to water.*

In northern Botswana, northern and southern Zimbabwe, northern and central Mozambique and Northern Province. Also in KwaZulu-Natal's Umfolozi/Hluhluwe reserve complex.

The unmistakeable, turpentinelike odour that signals the presence of a waterbuck may be its lifesaver in times of crisis. Threatened on land, this handsome antelope will plunge unflinchingly into crocodile-infested water. Its powerful scent, secreted by glands on its skin, is said to repel even this undiscriminating reptile.

Pursued by predators, a waterbuck may head for water, plunge in up to its nostrils, and do an about-turn, facing its pursuers with its magnificent, thrusting horns.

These horns, found only on the males, are used with chilling effect during fights over females.

A dominant male tries to retain nursery herds of five to ten animals, although you may see larger groups in summer when grazing is more plentiful—their diet consists mainly of grasses, reeds and wild fruits. (In the dry season, however, waterbuck will browse on acacia.)

The dominant male uses a definitive brand of body language to warn off other intruding males. This includes the 'proud' posture in which the bull stands very still and erect, holding his head and curved horns rigidly aloft.

Before giving birth, usually in early or late summer, a cow leaves the herd to seek a well-camouflaged hiding place for its calf. The calf will follow its mother back to the herd after three to four weeks.

REEDBUCK
Rietbok *(Redunca arundinum)*

Size: *Shoulder height (m) 80-90 cm, (f) 80 cm; weight (m) 80 kg, (f) 68 kg. Male carries forward-curving horns.*
Colour: *Dull greyish brown to dark brown coat. Underside, including underside of bushy brown tail, is whitish. Pale patches on the throat, face and around the eyes. Below each ear there is usually a small, round blackish bare patch. The front surface of each foreleg has a vertical black or dark brown stripe.*
Most like: *The mountain reedbuck, but larger and with longer horns. Mountain reedbuck lack the blackish or dark brown foreleg stripes.*
Habitat: *Tall grass or reeds near water.*

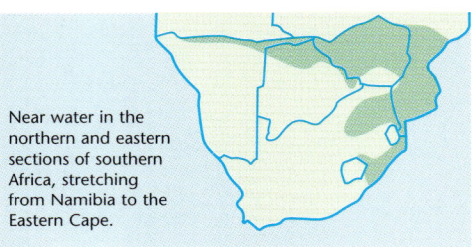

Near water in the northern and eastern sections of southern Africa, stretching from Namibia to the Eastern Cape.

This graceful, whistling antelope of the grasslands, so dependent on water for its existence, is actually very suspicious of it, and even appears to dislike getting its feet wet.

Reedbuck always approach water very cautiously, the cows hanging back as sentries, while the males and young drink first. This suspicious streak is also apparent while they are resting: reedbuck don't lie close together, but spread out, their faces turned cautiously outwards in the direction of any possible danger.

The reedbuck's tawny coat acts as a perfect camouflage among the reeds and long grass, and its ability to 'freeze' when it senses danger often helps it escape the attentions of predators. Once discovered, however, it will jump up in alarm, whistle loudly through its nostrils, and bound away with the same rocking-horse motion used by the rhebok.

Veld fires often sound the death knell for this elegant antelope. Deprived of its natural camouflage, it often doesn't have the ability to outrun its enemies, and is easily brought down by leopards, cheetahs and wild dogs.

A single calf, usually born in summer, is hidden by its mother for two months; she returns each day to suckle it. Both mother and calf join the ram when the offspring is three to four months old.

Large mammals

SITATUNGA
Waterkoedoe *(Tragelaphus spekei)*

Size: Shoulder height (m) 90 cm, (f) 80 cm; weight (m) 115 kg, (f) 80 kg. Only the male sitatunga carries the long, slightly spiralled horns.
Colour: Long-haired, rather shaggy, dark brown or brownish grey coat, more reddish in the female. White markings include patches on the throat, spots on the cheeks and a chevron between the eyes. Tail dark brown above, white below and has dark tuft at the tip.
Most like: The bushbuck, but larger, with shaggier coat and less distinctive white markings.
Habitat: Reed or papyrus swamps, on islands in lakes or rivers.

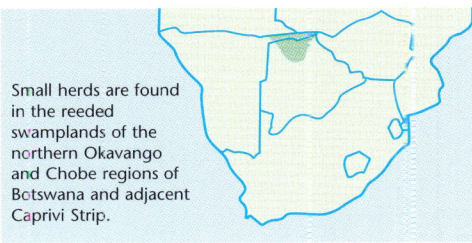

Small herds are found in the reeded swamplands of the northern Okavango and Chobe regions of Botswana and adjacent Caprivi Strip.

Remarkable for their elongated, pointed hooves—up to 18 cm long on the forefeet—sitatunga are powerful swimmers and range easily over soft, swampy surfaces. They are masters of the art of camouflage and sometimes, when wounded by a predator or hunter, will lie up in a dense reed bed, submerging themselves in the water with just their nostrils showing.

Ever alert to the presence of their natural enemies, leopards and lions, sitatunga will walk silently through the water, placing their feet delicately and carefully in the mud of a reed bed. If surprised, however, they will splash through the reeds in great bounds, leap into deeper water, and swim away with only their heads above the water.

Flooding sometimes forces sitatunga from the swamps onto higher ground where they move about somewhat clumsily on the hard surface. Although they do venture out into nearby plains, these buck invariably stay close to their reed beds, leaving a conspicuous V-shaped spoor on the soft ground.

Sitatunga usually move about in herds of up to five animals, feeding mainly on papyrus and other aquatic reeds and grasses.

Single calves are born, usually in midwinter, after a gestation period of seven months. They may instinctively move to higher ground after birth.

NYALA
Njala *(Tragelaphus angasii)*

Size: Shoulder height (m) 1,1 m, (f) 95 cm; weight (m) 108 kg, (f) 62 kg.
Colour: Males shaggy, grey-brown coat; white chevron between eyes; up to 14 faint, narrow vertical stripes on sides. Mane of long, whitish hair from shoulders to rump; bushy tail brown, with a white underside. Lower parts of legs light orange. Females bright orange-brown, with bolder white stripes on their sides; often no chevron; narrow mane of short, bristly black hair from head to tail.
Most like: Males like young kudu bulls, which, however, lack the pronounced chest fringe, the ivory-coloured tips to the horns and the yellow-orange 'socks' on legs. Females unmistakeable with orange coat and vertical white stripes.
Habitat: Dense bush close to water but, where protected, may be seen by day in the open.

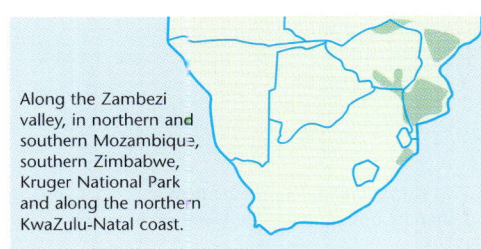

Along the Zambezi valley, in northern and southern Mozambique, southern Zimbabwe, Kruger National Park and along the northern KwaZulu-Natal coast.

Handsome and secretive, these graceful creatures strongly resemble kudu and bushbuck. They are usually silent creatures, but sometimes communicate with some very distinctive sounds: females, for instance, utter a throaty clicking sound when tending their calves; a ram, acting sentry, will let out a resonant, warning bark when danger threatens, sending the rest of the herd fleeing for safety; a calf, separated from its mother, will bleat pitifully.

In spite of the fact that baboons have been known to eat nyala young, these buck often associate with them, picking up the remains of wild fruit, berries and leaves discarded by the baboons on foraging expeditions.

Nyala males are particularly striking in the wild, with their mantles of rich, dark hair, and their impressive lyre-shaped horns held stiffly erect. You may sometimes see older rams browsing among herds of other antelope, especially impala.

Single lambs are born at any time of the year after a gestation period of just over seven months. The lamb remains hidden for two weeks before joining the family group.

Large mammals

Kudu
Koedoe *(Tragelaphus strepsiceros)*

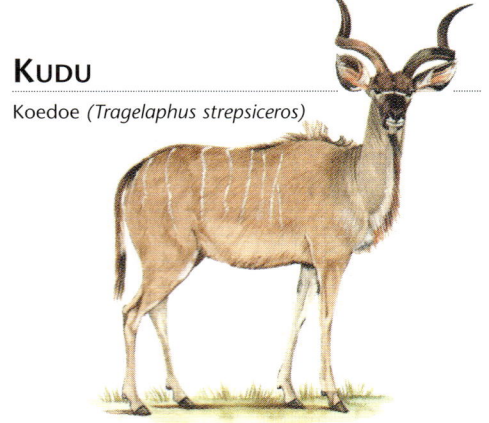

Size: Shoulder height (m) 1,45 m, (f) 1,25 m; weight (m) 250 kg, (f) 180 kg. Only male carries horns.
Colour: Greyish fawn, with narrow, vertical white stripes on sides and rump, a short ridge of white hair along the centre of the back, and a white chevron between the eyes. Males have a brown-and-white fringe from throat to base of neck.
Most like: Nyala, but kudu male's horns more spiralled and there is no heavy fringe of hair hanging below belly.
Habitat: Savanna woodland or scrub, especially close to water and rocky terrain.

Widely distributed throughout Namibia, Botswana, Zimbabwe, Mozambique, Mpumalanga, Northern Province, North-West Province, parts of Western and Eastern Cape, and southern Free State.

Here is the high-jump champion of the animal world—a graceful leaper capable of clearing a 2,5 m fence from a standstill. The male of the species is also immediately identifiable: it sports two magnificent spiral horns.

Despite these awesome armaments, known to reach a length of 1,8 m, the kudu is a gentle animal, preferring flight to fight. However, enraged kudu bulls do engage in fierce combat, sometimes accidentally killing each other by locking their horns together inextricably.

The call of the kudu, the loudest of any antelope, is a penetrating, hoarse bark: *bogh*. Listen for this call at night—it often signals the presence of lions, leopards or other predators nearby. When alarmed, kudu run away, lifting their tails over their rumps and fanning out the white undersurface as a warning signal to others.

The long, arcing leaps of kudu across roads in rural areas pose a real hazard to motorists, especially at night, and their appetite for almost any vegetation, including tobacco and grain crops, tomatoes and lettuce has made them widely hunted by farmers.

Kudu generally occur in herds of three to ten animals, but larger groups (up to 25) have occasionally been seen. These decrease during the mating season when a bull will run with the females.

In summer a cow bears a single calf which it hides in tall grass for a few days until it is strong enough to follow its mother.

Bushbuck
Bosbok *(Tragelaphus scriptus)*

Size: Shoulder height (m) 80 cm, (f) 70 cm; weight (m) 45 kg, (f) 30 kg. Only the males carry horns.
Colour: Dark brown, with two prominent white bands across the chest and throat. White spots and stripes often found on flanks and hindquarters. Bushy tail, brown with white underside. Males have a whitish, bristly mane along the back.
Most like: Nyala, but smaller; bushbuck rams do not have the heavy mane and belly fringe of long hair.
Habitat: Dense vegetation, forests; usually near water. They can survive close to built-up areas if cover is available.

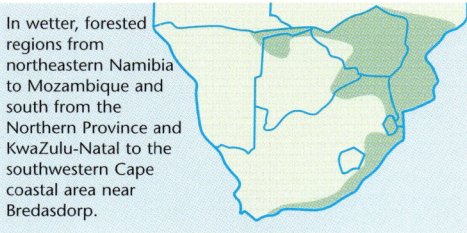

In wetter, forested regions from northeastern Namibia to Mozambique and south from the Northern Province and KwaZulu-Natal to the southwestern Cape coastal area near Bredasdorp.

Don't underestimate the fighting ability of a bushbuck. Normally nervous and shy, a cornered male will turn into a brave and fearsome aggressor, charging its pursuer with its sharp, sturdy horns and a savage will. Leopards, wild dogs and humans have been killed by the repeated thrusting of its slightly spiralled horns which can be up to 52 cm long.

Bushbuck are not only excellent jumpers, but prodigious swimmers: in times of flood they have been known to take to the water and swim for up to three kilometres without apparently tiring.

These solitary, nocturnal creatures are rarely seen, but their fondness for night-time raids into domestic gardens for their favoured food—roses, hydrangeas and fruit—has made them a popular target for irate gardeners.

At night, their hoarse, baboonlike bark can be heard echoing through the dense riverine bush or forest as they challenge other bushbuck or signal the presence of predators.

As long as there is a reliable supply of water nearby, bushbuck will live in the same area for years, wandering further from home only in the wet season. Single young are born after a gestation period of six months, and the calf remains hidden for four months before venturing out with its mother.

Large mammals

WARTHOG

Vlakvark *(Phacochoerus aethiopicus)*

Size: Shoulder height (m) 70 cm, (f) 60 cm; weight (m) 100 kg, (f) 70 kg.

Colour: Dull grey, with smooth skin sparsely covered by dark bristles. A mane of grey, brown or yellowish hair runs from back of head to base of tail, which ends in a blackish tuft.

Most like: The bushpig, which is about the same size, but lighter. The warthog's eyes are set higher, and its ears lack the bushpig's long tuft of hair. The warthog runs with its tail up, the bushpig with its tail down.

Habitat: Open grassland, often near water, avoiding thick bush or forest.

Open grassed areas of northern, central and eastern Namibia, Botswana, Zimbabwe, Northern Province, Mpumalanga, Mozambique and parts of northern coastal KwaZulu-Natal.

Don't be fooled by the comical trot or the short-sighted and nervous disposition of this silent member of the pig family. Behind the tusks and ugly wartlike lumps on its face lies a courageous spirit that has put wild dogs, cheetahs and even formidable leopards to flight.

Easily recognized as it trots through the veld with its tail held erect, the warthog is a gregarious forager that uses the upper surface of its snout as a spade, constantly digging for food in the hardest of soils. Going down on its front knees, which develop large, protective calluses, the warthog keeps its nose to the ground as it walks, rooting out bulbs and tubers.

Home to the warthog is the abandoned burrow of an aardvark, which it uses as a place of refuge when predators are around. Enlarging or modifying the burrow to suit its needs, a sow in season will line its burrow with grass, creating a cosy nest for its litter.

When running for shelter, young warthogs will scamper into their burrow head first, but adults do a remarkable about-turn at the entrance and reverse in, so as to present their formidable tusks to an attacker.

Family groups, numbering between five and ten, avoid other warthogs that may stray into their home ground, and maintain group contact with soft grunts.

BUSHPIG

Bosvark *(Potamochoerus porcus)*

Size: Shoulder height (m) 76 cm, (f) 65 cm; weight (m) 62 kg, (f) 60 kg.

Colour: Reddish to grey-brown coat, with an erectile, off-white crest of bristly hair along the top of the head and neck, and dark tufts at the tips of the ears.

Most like: The heavier warthog, but distinguishable by its long, thin ear tufts, absent in the warthog. Bushpigs are active at night, warthogs by day.

Habitat: Forest, thick bush or reed beds usually near water, but may range great distances in search of food.

In northern Botswana, Zimbabwe, Northern Province, Mpumalanga, Mozambique and along the coast of KwaZulu-Natal and southern Cape.

Seldom seen, but easily identified by its ominous, harsh grunt and piglike appearance, this wily night-time raider with an appetite for domestic crops infuriates farmers with its destructive forages into nearby farmlands.

Aggressive and courageous, bushpigs are positively dangerous to pursuing dogs, the boars often turning on them and slashing at them with their razor-sharp tusks.

Bushpig families numbering as many as 12, but usually four to ten, are gregarious but secretive, avoiding human and predatory interest by sheltering in dense, almost inaccessible undergrowth. Soon after dusk, these abrupt grunters leave their hides, travelling along well-worn paths through the bush in search of food.

The bushpig's probing and sensitive snout will lead it on a gourmet's journey through roots, fruit and vegetables to a variety of insects, eggs, reptiles and carrion. Sometimes, however, it will even kill and eat the young of wild and domestic animals, including chickens and piglets.

Apart from eating there's nothing a bushpig enjoys more than wallowing in mud which cools and protects its skin from insect bites.

The sow burrows into carefully constructed heaps of grass to deliver three to four young. Although staunchly defensive of their offspring, the boar and sow become intolerant of them after about six months, and drive the young pigs out.

Large mammals

LION
Leeu *(Panthera leo)*

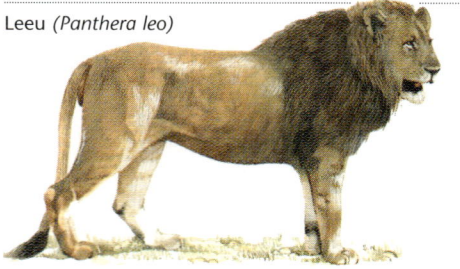

Size: Shoulder height (m) 1,2 m, (f) 1,05 m; weight (m) 150-225 kg, (f) 110-152 kg.
Colour: Tawny, but varies from almost silvery yellow to reddish brown with paler undersides (female belly yellowish to almost white); yellow to black mane. Faint, leopardlike spots on young sometimes retained into adulthood.
Most like: Unlikely to be confused with any other animal.
Habitat: Variety of habitats, from open savanna to semi-desert; never in forests.

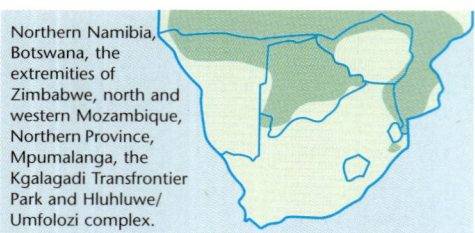

Northern Namibia, Botswana, the extremities of Zimbabwe, north and western Mozambique, Northern Province, Mpumalanga, the Kgalagadi Transfrontier Park and Hluhluwe/Umfolozi complex.

A formidable reputation precedes the king of beasts. And deservedly so. As the largest carnivore on the continent, the lion's strength and stature command respect from the entire animal kingdom. Those creatures foolhardy enough to risk an attack, such as leopards, pythons, hyaenas and wild dogs, grab only at unguarded young.

Lions make it very clear who's the boss: males stake out territory with a deafening roar that can be heard through the African night for up to eight kilometres.

But for all their strength and powerhouse image, lions are lazy. Hanging about as family groups or prides of 3-30 individuals, or as smaller bachelor gangs, they favour the cool and cover of night for hunts, and retire into long grass or the shade of tress when the sun gets too hot. Lolling about in the shade, they spend between 15 and 20 hours of the day inactive, resting on their sides or lying like domesticated kittens on their backs with all four paws dangling in the air.

Indolence is one side of the coin. The other is an intense burst of speed and aggression because, if hungry, not even the noonday sun will deter them from hunting—although another predator's kill will do just as well. Hunting most successfully in groups, the lion menu varies from young hippopotamuses to antelope, zebras and gazelles. Males take little part, leaving the chase and the kill to the females.

Lions have no fixed breeding season. The female gives birth to one to four cubs after a three- to four-month gestation period. Cubs remain with their mother for two or more years before joining the pride.

LEOPARD
Luiperd *(Panthera pardus)*

Size: Shoulder height 70-80 cm; weight (m) 20-90 kg, (f) 17-60 kg.
Colour: Ground colour is off-white to golden, with black spots on the legs, shoulders, head and hindquarters, and irregular, light-centred 'rosettes' scattered profusely over the back and sides.
Most like: The cheetah, but leopard more heavily built and has no tear marks from corner of eye to corner of mouth. Main body markings are rosettes, rather than solid spots.
Habitat: Wide range of habitats includes open savanna, forested terrain, mountains and rocky hills.

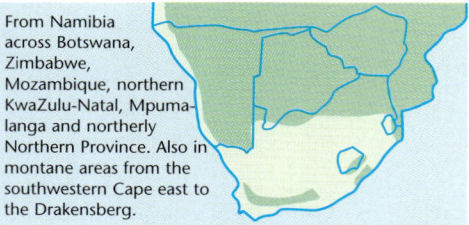

From Namibia across Botswana, Zimbabwe, Mozambique, northern KwaZulu-Natal, Mpumalanga and northerly Northern Province. Also in montane areas from the southwestern Cape east to the Drakensberg.

Although smaller than a lion, the sleuthlike leopard is often more feared. It is fiercer, braver and very intelligent: a perfectly streamlined killing machine with exceptional hearing, good eyesight and sensitive, extra-long whiskers, which help it avoid obstacles in the dark.

The leopard is also a remarkable athlete, capable not only of swimming across rivers, but also of leaping onto rocks up to three metres high, carrying prey as heavy as itself. Its spotted hide is such a perfect camouflage that it has been copied by armed forces for bush warfare.

In 'safe' areas, leopards are active night and day but are otherwise reclusive, nocturnal and solitary. They might be seen basking in early morning sun, and resting places such as caves, trees and rocks double as vantage points over hunting terrain. They retreat from heat, and in semi-desert areas will crawl into disused aardvark burrows for shade.

Males and females mark their territory by spraying urine and by leaving warning claw marks on tree trunks. Normally solitary, males don't mind sharing their space with females, but will fight off other males. Leopard cubs stay with their mothers for almost two years, going on their first hunt at the age of four months.

Leopards will prey on anything from mouse size to a mammal twice their own weight, including wildebeest and young giraffes.

Large mammals

CHEETAH
Jagluiperd *(Acinonyx jubatus)*

Size: Shoulder height 80-85 cm; weight 40-60 kg.
Colour: Sandy yellow coat with solid black spots distributed over entire body and tail. Pale abdomen and chest. Dark tear mark runs from each eye to corner of the mouth.
Most like: The leopard, but cheetah has a slighter build and longer legs. Head is smaller in relation to body, and all its spots are solid; none form 'rosettes'.
Habitat: Open country, from dry savanna to desert.

Most of northern and eastern Namibia, through the Kgalagadi Transfrontier Park and Botswana to Zimbabwe and Mozambique. Also in the Kruger National Park. The cheetah has been reintroduced to KwaZulu-Natal.

Built something like a greyhound with flawless aerodynamics, the cheetah is both the fastest mammal on the earth and one of the most beautiful.

Its long, graceful limbs, reminiscent of the shape of our best human athletes, are made for speed. And the sight of a cheetah chasing prey is breathtaking: keeping its head almost motionless and eyes fixed on its quarry, it can reach the astonishing speed of between 80 and 100 kilometres per hour. Its high, muscular shoulders piston effortlessly over the ground in strides up to seven metres long, and its long tail is used as a balancing mechanism.

But if the prey, such as impala, springbok or steenbok, can keep out of claws' way for long enough, their chances of survival are good—cheetahs don't have much staying power after sprints of about 300 metres.

Active mostly in the morning or late afternoon, cheetahs move either alone, in pairs or in groups, and several adults might collaborate to hunt a larger mammal.

As they are rather peace-loving creatures, cheetahs are often chased from their kills by lions or hyaenas.

Widespread but not common throughout its distribution area, it is estimated that there are between 4000 and 6000 cheetahs in southern Africa. They roam over vast home territories and, although males mark out their turf, they don't go to violent extremes to defend it.

Three cubs usually comprise a cheetah litter, and their mother shifts them from one hiding place to another to avoid hungry predators.

SERVAL
Tierboskat *(Leptailurus serval)*

Size: Shoulder height 60 cm; weight 8-13 kg.
Colour: Pale gold to tawny, with solid black spots which tend to run in bands from back of neck to flanks. Black rings around short tail; back of ears distinctive, with two black bands separated by a white patch.
Most like: The cheetah, which has a similar spotted coat, but a much bigger head, a longer tail and smaller ears which are held back. The serval's ears are proportionally larger and held upright.
Habitat: Open plains, savanna and woodland (sometimes forest). Uses reed beds, long grass and bush for cover.

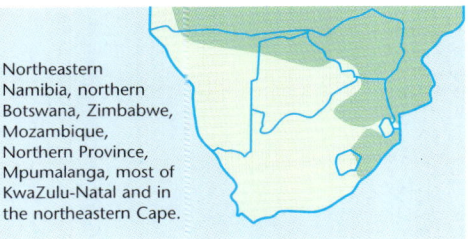

Northeastern Namibia, northern Botswana, Zimbabwe, Mozambique, Northern Province, Mpumalanga, most of KwaZulu-Natal and in the northeastern Cape.

For a wild cat, the serval can be surprisingly bold on human territory. Although its diet usually consists of wild rats, mice and game birds, it has been known to raid domestic stock up to the size of peacocks. When the serval's prey is too large for one meal, it will leave the remains and return for the second course one or two nights later—a habit which makes it most vulnerable to capture.

Catch it in the beam of a car's headlights, however, and this elegant cat will disappear rapidly, its long legs able to carry it speedily for short distances.

The serval can be seen early morning or evening, but is usually nocturnal and solitary. It roams widely in search of food, preferring to use existing roads and paths to reach hunting grounds rather than pick its way across rough terrain.

A thoroughly determined hunter, this cat is capable of catching a bird in flight with a well-timed leap into the air. And not even water will stop it when it's in pursuit of a vlei rat or some other rodent.

With the help of its large ears, a serval will carefully and silently track terrestrial prey and kill it with a downward pounce of its two front paws. If it is not too hungry, it might pause to play with its prey before eating it.

The serval's young are generally born in the summer after a gestation period of nine to ten weeks. The litter consists of up to five kittens, each weighing about 200 grams.

Large mammals

CARACAL
Rooikat *(Caracal caracal)*

Size: Shoulder height 40-45 cm; weight 7-19 kg.
Colour: Coat reddish, varying from pale sandy to brick-red along back with paler, usually spotted, abdomen. The face has black-and-white markings. The pointed ears end in long black tufts.
Most like: The serval, which is roughly the same size but yellow and spotted with black.
Habitat: Open, dry country from semi-desert to savanna. Sleeps in crevices among rocks, stones or fallen trees, dense cover, trees or appropriated burrows.

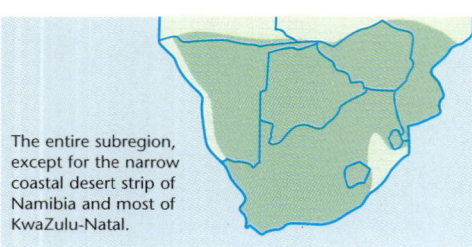

The entire subregion, except for the narrow coastal desert strip of Namibia and most of KwaZulu-Natal.

The caracal's lynxlike head, with its distinctive pointed ears, should be a dead giveaway. But because it is particularly skilled at bush camouflage, lying frozen against the earth and holding its head down when in danger, the caracal is scarcely discernible, even on bare ground.

This savage, graceful cat has all the attributes of a great hunter: speed, lightning reflexes, agility and remarkable stealth that make it capable even of snatching a flying bird out of the air.

Travelling about on short, heavy limbs, the caracal is a fierce killer, with a rasping leopardlike bark. The combination of powerful jaws, long, sharp teeth, and paws with curved, heavy claws make it a fearsome predator, and a dangerous quarry when cornered or wounded.

It has a strong appetite for the meat of sheep and goats, and its nightly raids on stock farms have not endeared it to farmers. In the wild, caracals prey mainly on dassies, birds, lizards and small buck and are competent tree climbers. Prey might be carried into a tree to be eaten, with the caracal preferring to remove fur and feathers from the carcass before tucking in.

Except for brief mating sessions, caracals tend to be largely solitary, moving about silently and secretively on their hunting expeditions at night.

The females produce a litter of one to three in a hollowed tree or disused aardvark hole.

CIVET
Siwet *(Civettictis civetta)*

Size: Shoulder height 40 cm; weight 9-15 kg.
Colour: Wiry, grey coat marked with black spots, rosettes and bars. Grey forehead and conspicuous broad black band across face and around eyes; contrasts with white muzzle, black nose and white upper lip. Throat, chest and lower limbs are distinctively black.
Most like: Large- and small-spotted genets, but much larger. Tail proportionately shorter and not as clearly banded as the genet's. Genet's black facial mask less well developed and not through eyes.
Habitat: Well-watered savanna and woodland; also high grass and reed beds.

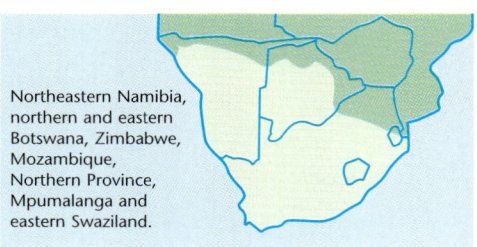

Northeastern Namibia, northern and eastern Botswana, Zimbabwe, Mozambique, Northern Province, Mpumalanga and eastern Swaziland.

This timid creature with the 'Lone Ranger' face mask has been much in demand with the beauty industry—thanks to its habit of marking its territorial range with an anal secretion that retains its smell for up to three months.

Known in the cosmetic trade as 'civet', this strongly scented substance was 'milked' from captive civets and used as a base for perfumes. Fortunately, synthetic substitutes are now largely used instead.

Closely related to mongooses and genets, the civet, with its long body and bushy tail, is almost doglike. Its spoor has clearly visible claw marks. And, like a dog, its ridged mane of long, coarse hair along the spine will rise when threatened. To ensure that the antagonist gets the message, the civet turns sideways, exposing the crest to its fullest extent.

A nocturnal animal that keeps to itself, the civet is usually active for a few hours after sunset. It travels along paths and roads, and can sometimes be spotted in a family group of an adult and two or three youngsters.

The civet's diet consists of grasshoppers, beetles, wild fruit, rats, snakes and millipedes. Civets capture their larger prey with a repertoire of bites, shakes and throws and, as they don't always kill with the first bite, they sometimes have to leap aside to avoid being bitten in return.

Litters of two to four are usually born in summer in dense vegetation, rock crevices or in burrows dug by other animals.

Large mammals

SPOTTED HYAENA

Gevlekte hiëna
(*Crocuta crocuta*)

Size: Shoulder height 85 cm; weight 60-80 kg.
Colour: Drab greyish yellow to rufous body. Feet and face darker brown. Irregular or oval-shaped dark spots are scattered over the body.
Most like: Brown hyaena, but spotted hyaena has rounded ears and short yellowish coat with brown spots. Brown hyaena entirely brown.
Habitat: Semi-desert to moist savanna. Avoids forests, must have drinking water and places to shelter among rocks, in burrows, scrub or tall grass.

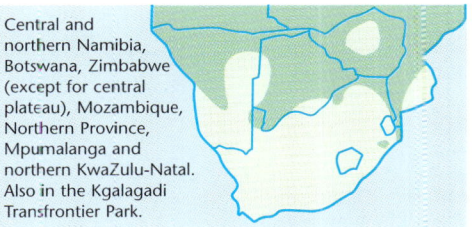

Central and northern Namibia, Botswana, Zimbabwe (except for central plateau), Mozambique, Northern Province, Mpumalanga and northern KwaZulu-Natal. Also in the Kgalagadi Transfrontier Park.

'Nature's garbage remover' is an apt label for the spotted hyaena, which has an astonishing appetite. It consumes its own prey and scavenged carrion with equal gusto and relish, swallowing large chunks of meat noisily and voraciously. Packs of hyaenas have been known to dig up and eat human corpses, and examinations of stomach contents have turned up such bizarre items as the sole of a shoe, nails, elephant skin, rope and a corned beef tin.

The shoulders and sloping back are supported in front by extremely powerful forelegs capable of running fast, knocking down prey and carrying it off for home consumption. Its heavy teeth and jaws can shred tough carcasses in minutes, splintering bones that defeat all other carnivores; its digestive system processes bone, sinew and hide with ease.

The spotted hyaena moves in packs or clans that average 3-30 animals, sometimes up to 80. Each pack marks out its territory with scents from anal glands, glands between its toes, latrines and boundary patrolling.

With strength in numbers, this animal will drive lions and leopards from their kills, attack cattle kraals and even, after dark, solitary humans. With excellent night vision and acute senses of smell and hearing, spotted hyaenas hunt successfully in the dark, flying over the veld like spectral shadows at speeds of up to 50 kilometres per hour.

Hyaenas have no particular breeding season. One to two cubs are born in a burrow where they are protected for several months before joining the pack.

BROWN HYAENA

Strandjut (*Hyaena brunnea*)

Size: Shoulder height 80cm; weight (m) 47kg, (f) 42kg.
Colour: Coat of dark brown, almost black, coarse hair with shaggy mane along spine. Creamy collar around neck; blurred dark cross-stripes on legs.
Most like: The spotted hyaena, but smaller and less powerfully built, and its long, brown coat is distinctive.
Habitat: Semi-desert, open scrub plains and dry savanna.

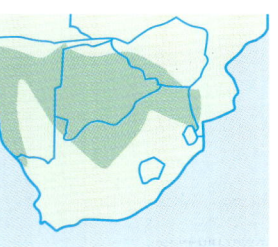

Western and northern Namibia, Botswana (especially in the Kalahari Desert), western Zimbabwe, western Mozambique, Mpumalanga, Northern Province, North-West Province, Free State and Northern Cape.

The brown hyaena's coarse, shaggy mane is not just for looks: it serves to protect it during vicious fights when warring males grab and shake each other violently by the neck, snarling and growling at the same time. In spite of these frenzied fights, brown hyaenas are less aggressive than their spotted cousins.

With its powerful forequarters and relatively small hindquarters, this hyaena travels great distances in small groups, marking out territories as large as 480 square kilometres by saturating bushes, grasses and rocks with a scent from its anal gland.

This gland produces two pastes: one a strong-smelling white paste, the other a less pungent black paste. The two secretions are thought to convey important information relating to the movements of individuals or groups through their own or other hyaenas' territory.

The regularly used latrines along the boundaries serve as 'keep off' signals, and should intruders present any threat, fighting between members of the same sex ensues.

Despite its powerful build and sensitive hearing, the nomadic brown hyaena is not as adept at killing as the spotted hyaena, so it confines itself to preying on small mammals, birds, insects and reptiles; it is, however, predominantly a scavenger.

Travelling males mate with receptive females, who give birth to two to three cubs after a gestation period of three months.

Large mammals

Aardwolf

Aardwolf *(Proteles cristatus)*

Size: Shoulder height: 50 cm; weight 9 kg.
Colour: Sandy to yellow-brown body with four to eight dark brown, vertical stripes. Black feet and tail tip. Thick, distinctive dorsal mane from back of head to base of tail, which is tipped with black.
Most like: Brown hyaena, but aardwolf's body is smaller, its muzzle is pointed and legs are long and slender. Brown hyaena has uniform brown body and no vertical stripes.
Habitat: Open sandy plains and scrubland.

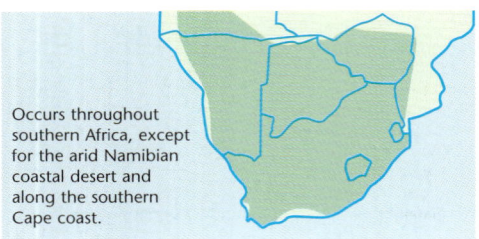

Occurs throughout southern Africa, except for the arid Namibian coastal desert and along the southern Cape coast.

Shy and solitary, the aardwolf keeps such a low profile that it can remain undetected in a particular area for a long time. It is so timid that it will hardly give you a chance to look at it, trotting away with its bushy tail streaming straight out behind. But when it most needs to move out of the way, it doesn't: if caught in the bright beam of car headlights at night, the aardwolf is confused rather than frightened away, and many are killed accidentally by cars.

Although it has a similar frame to the hyaena, with high, muscular forequarters, the aardwolf's facial muscles and jaws are not nearly as powerful. In fact, its tiny teeth are weak and set wide apart, unsuitable for crunching bones and hooves, but adequate for consuming insects.

Termites are the aardwolf's main dish, and it is guided to them by its sharp hearing and keen nose. Using incisor teeth in the lower jaw for excavation, the aardwolf then laps up the termites with a large, relentless tongue covered with sticky saliva.

The aardwolf secretes a musky fluid from two glands just above the anus; it applies this sweet-smelling substance to objects within its home range as a form of communication with other aardwolves.

An angry or frightened aardwolf is quite a spectacle—it lets out an explosively loud roar, and raises its long dorsal mane into a menacing crest.

Young are born in adopted burrows, usually skilfully enlarged by the parents.

Wild dog

Wildehond *(Lycaon pictus)*

Size: Shoulder height 65-80 cm; weight 20-30 kg.
Colour: Irregular blotches of black, white and yellow-brown over whole body. Lower face dark brown with dark stripe down centre of forehead. White tail tip. Large, very distinctive, rounded ears.
Most like: Black-backed and side-striped jackal, but neither of these jackal species has the wild dog's irregularly blotched or spotted coat.
Habitat: Open terrain such as semi-desert, plains and open savanna woodland.

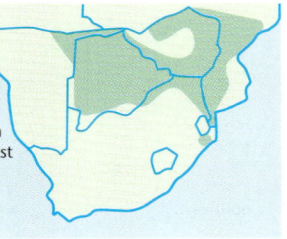

Occurs permanently only in the Kruger National Park. In reserve areas in KwaZulu-Natal, Mpumalanga, Northern Province, the North-West and Botswana. Also in northern and western Mozambique.

For a carnivore about the size of a German shepherd, the wild dog, or Cape hunting dog, has an intimidating reputation, largely because of its ferocious killing style. Living and travelling in nomadic packs, the wild dog hunts early in the morning and evening, when it can see best.

When a pack of wild dogs chooses its prey—in southern Africa mostly blue wildebeest, impala, springbok—an orchestrated battle plan goes into motion. The pack approaches openly and nonchalantly but, when its members start running, they become oblivious of everything but their target. As the leading dogs tire, others take over the relentless chase, reaching speeds of up to 66 kilometres per hour. As the prey flags, the dogs close in. Smaller victims such as duikers or hares are torn to pieces. Larger animals, including wildebeest, have chunks of flesh ripped from their bodies as they run, until they collapse. In contrast with this savagery, the pack's behaviour after a kill is calmly patient: the clearly hungry adults stand back to let juveniles eat their fill.

Young wild dogs (from litters as big as ten) are incessantly pampered by the adults who clean them, guard them and feed them regurgitated meat. The pack, usually numbering 10-15 animals, communicates with calls, body postures and greeting rituals. Wild dogs will drive hyaenas from a kill, and leopards also give way to a pack.

Its numbers greatly reduced by man, the wild dog is the rarest large carnivore in South Africa.

Large mammals

BLACK-BACKED JACKAL

Rooijakkals *(Canis mesomelas)*

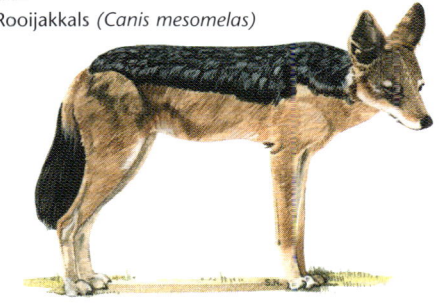

Size: Shoulder height 38 cm; weight 6-10 kg.

Colour: A predominantly black 'saddle', shot through with silver, runs from neck to root of the tail. The long bushy tail is mostly blackish; head, flanks and legs reddish brown. Throat, chest and belly whitish. In the west of the distribution area, male's winter coat develops a particularly rich, reddish colour.

Most like: The side-striped jackal, but has longer ears and sharper muzzle. The side-striped jackal is never reddish, and lacks the black saddle.

Habitat: A wide range of habitats (excluding forests), particularly drier areas and open terrain.

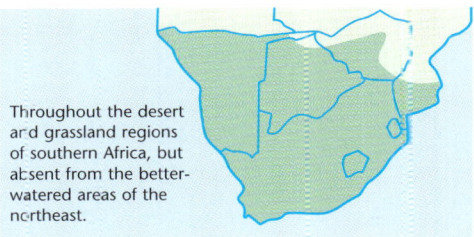

Throughout the desert and grassland regions of southern Africa, but absent from the better-watered areas of the northeast.

The black-backed jackal is a wonderfully resourceful scavenger. On the cheerless beaches of the Namibian coast it will follow fishermen, patiently waiting as they clean the day's catch, then make off with the offal. Better known, however, is the jackal's habit of trailing lions and other large carnivores when a kill is made. Trotting backwards and forwards in slavering anticipation, a temporary aggregation of up to ten jackals will keep a discreet distance until the big predators have had their fill of the carcass, then the jackals dart in to clean up.

They kill for themselves too, as sheep farmers of the Karoo have found to their cost.

It is invariably the defenceless young that the black-backed jackal preys on: lambs, young goats and, in the wild, the helpless newborn offspring of antelope. For the rest, this species of jackal dines on smaller fry such as springhares, mongooses, mice, rats, lizards and insects.

Where they have a free run, as in national parks, black-backed jackals forage by day; but under pressure they are night animals.

The silver-black saddle gives this jackal a sinister appearance, and its call is spine-chilling: a long, drawn-out howl, interrupted by a few sharp barks, heard from sundown till late at night.

SIDE-STRIPED JACKAL

Witkwasjakkals *(Canis adustus)*

Size: Shoulder height 40 cm; weight 8-12 kg.

Colour: Greyish brown, with a whitish stripe fringed with black along each side of the body. Bushy tail mainly black, usually with a white tip. Muzzle, chest and legs are a lighter grey-brown, legs often tinged rufous. Belly off-white.

Most like: The black-backed jackal, but generally greyer and white tip to tail is usually diagnostic. Lacks black-backed jackal's distinctive 'saddle'.

Habitat: Well-watered woodlands, but not forests.

In the well-watered regions of northeastern Namibia, northern Botswana, Zimbabwe, Mozambique, eastern Mpumalanga and northern KwaZulu-Natal.

The side-striped jackal keeps a decidedly low profile. It is shyer and more strictly nocturnal than its close relative, the black-backed jackal, and also much less noisy. Even its voice is low-pitched, articulated as a slow succession of somewhat dispirited yaps. You don't often see this jackal, and when you are lucky enough to do so, it will be on its own or in a small family group, not a pack.

Although it eagerly mops up carrion left by large predators, the side-striped jackal is an accomplished hunter, tracking down a wide range of small mammals, from springhares to mice. It also eats ground-nesting birds, lizards, insects and wild fruit.

This species does not put up a very spirited defence. It is easily overcome by dogs and, if caught live in a trap, is less aggressive than a black-backed jackal.

Side-striped jackals pair for life. The four to six young are born between August and January in holes in the ground that have an alternative exit in case of danger. If sufficiently alarmed, a mother will carry suckling young one by one to another hole. As the cubs grow, both male and female help feed them. Either they bring back food in their mouths or they regurgitate what they have already eaten.

Large mammals

CAPE FOX
Silwerjakkals *(Vulpes chama)*

Size: Shoulder height 35 cm; weight 2,5-4 kg.
Colour: A speckled silvery grey, the underparts being whitish with a buff or reddish tinge to the chest. The hairs of the long, bushy tail are buff-white at their bases, but dark brown or black towards the tip. The head is reddish, but with much white hair on the cheeks, and the throat is buff.
Most like: The two jackal species. The side-striped jackal, however, is much larger, with light-and-dark stripes along each side, and a white tip to the tail. The black-backed jackal is also much larger and has a distinctive black 'saddle' running along its back.
Habitat: Open country, whether a semi-desert, scrub, grassland or fynbos—often in the vicinity of a rocky outcrop.

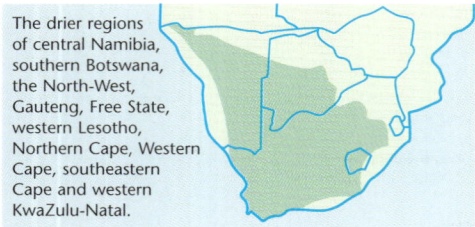

The drier regions of central Namibia, southern Botswana, the North-West, Gauteng, Free State, western Lesotho, Northern Cape, Western Cape, southeastern Cape and western KwaZulu-Natal.

The Cape fox is the only true fox in southern Africa. Shy and nocturnal, this attractive little animal has taken the blame for the slaughter of young lambs and, as a result, some 20 000 were systematically hunted and destroyed in the Free State alone in the 1960s and 1970s. But today experts believe the Cape fox to be largely innocent of the charge. Its staple food consists of much smaller prey—mice, gerbils, lizards, insects and spiders. And in the few cases in which sheep remains have been found in its stomach, the meal could have been taken as carrion, with a black-backed jackal as predator.

During the day the Cape fox's shelter may be of two kinds. Ground-surface cover is provided by thickets, rock crevices and rocky overhangs. Or the fox may choose to rest up in an underground hole, either digging one itself or 'borrowing' one from a springhare or other species.

Keen sight and hearing help it during its nightly foraging. Its contact call with other members of the species is a high-pitched, drawn-out howl ending in two or three yaps. Sometimes these sounds are sustained between two foxes in duet.

Cape fox mothers give birth to one to four pups (usually three) in spring.

BAT-EARED FOX
Bakoorjakkals *(Otocyon megalotis)*

Size: Shoulder height 35 cm; weight 3-5 kg.
Colour: A brindled greyish brown, with underparts a little paler. Both the upper side and the end of bushy tail are black, as are the feet and legs. Muzzle dark brown to black; chin and area around the mouth black; backs of ears brown, and insides of ears white.
Most like: Cape fox, but is less 'foxlike' and has disproportionately large ears. Dark brown to black muzzle and chin can be contrasted with reddish-brown face of Cape fox.
Habitat: Open country with low rainfall: semi-desert scrub, grassland, bushveld.

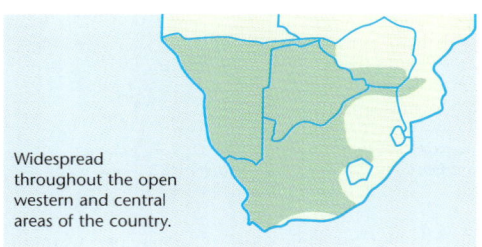

Widespread throughout the open western and central areas of the country.

The huge ears of the bat-eared fox, measuring up to 13 cm in length, are so sensitive that they can pick up the sounds of a beetle in its burrow. Having detected the sound of a subterranean insect, it will approach more closely with head lowered and ears outspread almost parallel to the ground, like a treasure hunter's metal detector. Not until the exact position of the prey has been pinpointed will the animal start digging.

The bat-eared fox is partly diurnal, partly nocturnal. During the heat of the day it takes cover in a burrow, which it may excavate itself or take over one belonging to another species. The burrow system may be elaborate—on more than one level, and with several entrances.

Pair bonding in this species is very strong, possibly for life. The offspring of the constant couple are born in the burrow.

Bat-eared foxes have a genus (*Otocyon*) all to themselves, being neither true foxes nor true jackals, although in build they do resemble a more delicate, scaled-down version of the former.

A colloquial Afrikaans name for this species, *draaijakkals*, alludes to the remarkable way in which, even when travelling at speed, the bat-eared fox can suddenly twist and turn, dodging aside to confuse and shake off a pursuer.

Large mammals

CHACMA (SAVANNA) BABOON
Kaapse bobbejaan
(*Papio cynocephalus ursinus*)

VERVET MONKEY
Blouaap (*Chlorocebus aethiops*)

Size: Length (including tail) (m) 1,2-1,6 m, (f) 1,0-1,2 m; average weight (m) 32 kg, (f) 16 kg.
Colour: Dark yellowish brown, sometimes greyish, coat. Pale chest; dark hair along crown and spine. 'Shepherd's crook' tail dark brown. Pink patches around female rump become scarlet and swollen when she is in season.
Most like: The yellow baboon in the northeast of the subcontinent, but chacma's dark colouring distinctive.
Habitat: Rocky country, savanna (usually with abundant trees) and montane areas. Nearby water essential.

Size: Length (including tail): (m) 1,0-1,3 m, (f) 0,95-1,1 m; average weight (m) 5,5 kg, (f) 4 kg.
Colour: Coarse, brindled grey coat with yellow tinge. Black face, hands, toes and tail-tip. Band of white across forehead continues down sides of face to the chin. Underparts are whitish or white.
Most like: Samango monkey, but vervet is slighter, with paler, shorter coat and black, not brown, face.
Habitat: Riverine and savanna woodland, with cover and fruit-bearing trees

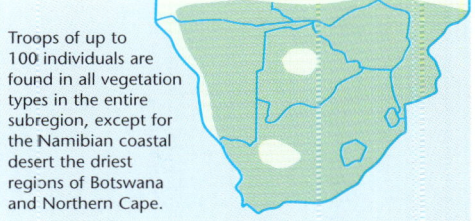

Troops of up to 100 individuals are found in all vegetation types in the entire subregion, except for the Namibian coastal desert the driest regions of Botswana and Northern Cape.

Widespread in the wooded regions of northern Namibia, Botswana, Zimbabwe, Mozambique, Mpumalanga, Northern Province, KwaZulu-Natal, southeastern and southern Cape, the western Free State and the Gariep River valley.

Engagingly humanlike, the chacma, or savanna, baboon wends through forests and rocky hillsides in troops of 15 to 100, with several large males in charge. These males lead the troop movements, initiate mating and defend the troop.

Males also perform guard duty, and at the first sign of danger a sentinel will let out a bisyllabic *wa-hoo* bark, which may send the rest of the troop scurrying for safety. The sight of their arch enemy, the leopard, causes an uproar, and the troop lashes out with a barrage of hysterical shrieks, threatening barks and anxious grunts, often frightening enough to send the leopard slinking away.

Although a showdown with another troop involves more noise and spectacle than anything else, don't write off chacma males as all bombast and show. With their powerful build and large canines, they can fight viciously to the death, and old males can become treacherously bad-tempered

The males' dominance is drilled into the baboons from an early age, and although baboon babies are reared with unswerving devotion, any disobedience or disrespect will often earn the culprit a swift cuff from an admonishing male. Savanna baboons usually forage in the veld for grass, insects, roots and eggs.

Female baboons signal their readiness for mating with bright scarlet skin on their buttocks. After a six-month gestation period, a female gives birth to a single youngster who clings to the underside of its mother for the first few weeks of life.

The vervet monkey is a nervy, excitable creature that turns extremely shy if persecuted. Tamed, however, it can become an entertaining and affectionate pet.

In captivity as in the wild, vervets sleep together in groups of two or three, huddled in rock crevices or on the branches of high trees. Like baboons, they live in tightly knit troops of 15-20 or more, dominated by a mature male. The monkey hierarchy is not as flexible as that of baboons, but authority is still maintained with aggressive threats. Subordinates don't cheek their superiors, but vent their anger on monkeys lower down on the social scale.

The males do sentry duty and defend the troop. Extremely maternal, females will adopt young from other troops; and a bereaved new mother has been known to keep the body of her newly born infant with her for several days.

Energetic and agile, vervets are as much at home on the ground as in trees, where they forage constantly for food. They are largely vegetarian, eating fruit, flowers, seeds and leaves, and even braving the sting of wild velvet beans when food is scarce. Spiders, grubs and locusts also form part of their diet. Their fondness for raiding gardens and croplands has made them unpopular with farmers and home-owners.

The gentle chattering of a vervet often announces its presence; in alarm, this can give way to raucous coughing and agitated screaming.

Smaller mammals

Springbok

Springbok *(Antidorcas marsupialis)*

Size: Shoulder height 75 cm; weight (m) 41 kg, (f) 37 kg. Both sexes carry horns.
Colour: Cinnamon brown, with white underbelly, the white separated from the brown on either flank by a broad, dark brown band. White rump, with dark brown vertical bands on either side; the white tail has a tuft of black hairs at the tip. Backs of forelegs and fronts of hindlegs are white. White throat and face, with a dark brown line from corners of mouth to eyes.
Most like: Impala, but both sexes of springbok carry ridged, lyre-shaped horns. Unlike impala, the springbok has a white face and dark red-brown band along flank.
Habitat: Open, dry grassland, where the grass is low and the terrain flat; other semi-arid regions where ample Karoo-type vegetation exists for feeding.

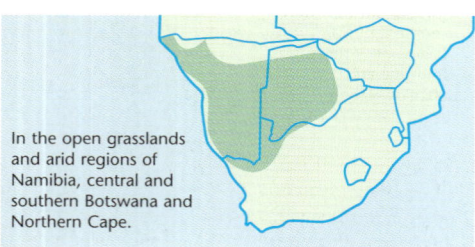

In the open grasslands and arid regions of Namibia, central and southern Botswana and Northern Cape.

When in danger, or through sheer *joie de vivre*, the springbok executes a series of balletic, stiff-legged high leaps—the characteristic 'pronking' or stotting behaviour—during which a crest of white hair on the curved back fans out prominently. A prodigious athlete, the springbok can clear 3,5 metres and at full gallop can reach a speed of almost 90 km/h, and bound 15 metres. Even so, it may be no match for speedy predators such as cheetahs or leopards, its traditional enemies (as are lions).

Springbok are gregarious, roaming in herds of up to 100 in the dry months and several hundreds in the rainy season. They also associate loosely with other game species, including wildebeest, blesbok and ostriches. Both browsers and grazers, they feed on shrubs and grasses, digging out roots and bulbs.

Most springbok lambs are born in the rainy season, when grass is green and food plentiful. The mother hides her newborn offspring in bush or long grass, where for a day or two it remains absolutely still. The newborn lamb soon gains strength and speed, and is able to flee if disturbed or threatened.

Oribi

Oorbietjie *(Ourebia ourebi)*

Size: Shoulder height 60 cm; weight (m) 14 kg, (f) 14,2 kg. Only the males have horns.
Colour: Golden fawn to yellow-orange, with white chin, throat, chest, abdomen and rump. Upper chest golden fawn. Upper surface of bushy tail black or dark brown; under surface white. White blazes around the eyes.
Most like: The steenbok, but the oribi is larger, with a longer and more slender neck. The oribi's black-topped tail distinguishes it from the steenbok, which has a reddish fawn tail.
Habitat: Open grassland, grassed vleis, flood plains. The grass must be short, and water must be in the vicinity.

In isolated areas in the Caprivi Strip, northern Botswana, central and eastern Zimbabwe, central and eastern Mozambique, Mpumalanga, KwaZulu-Natal and Eastern Cape.

When alarmed, the oribi, like an angry referee, resorts to a shrill, snorting whistle and then gallops away smartly. But the gallop soon changes to a different motion: after every few bounds the oribi 'stots' or bounces stiff-legged into the air, enabling it to glance in all directions above the vegetation. After this it may actually halt and walk back towards danger—a foolish form of curiosity apt to lead to its capture or death at the hands of predators or human hunters.

Largest of the small antelope, oribi roam singly, in pairs or in small groups attached to a particular territory. Males mark off their territory by means of a secretion from glands in front of their eyes. (Below the ears of the oribi you can see another scent-secreting gland, in the form of a circle of black skin.)

In common with other buck, the oribi rests during the heat of the day and is active in the morning, late afternoon and evening, as well as on moonlit nights. A grazer, it is particularly partial to the fresh green shoots of grass that spring up after veld fires.

Its predators, like those of the steenbok, are many. Because of this and changing land-use patterns in southern Africa, the oribi has become a fairly rare species here.

Before going off in search of food, the female oribi hides her newborn lamb in thick grass, where it will lie motionless if approached.

Smaller mammals

STEENBOK

Steenbok *(Raphicerus campestris)*

Size: Shoulder height 50 cm; weight 11 kg. Only the ram has horns—usually about 9 cm long.

Colour: Varies above from a rich reddish brown to a lighter reddish fawn. There is a dark patch above the nose, and a dark marking on the forehead. Throat, eyebrows, abdomen, underside of tail and insides of legs are white. Upperside of short tail is reddish fawn.

Most like: The oribi, but smaller, with longer ears and a shorter neck, and with a reddish fawn upper surface to its tail—black in the oribi.

Habitat: Flat, open country, grassy or lightly wooded, and avoids mountain slopes. Cover is essential.

Throughout almost the entire subregion, except coastal Namibia, northern and eastern Zimbabwe, northern Mozambique, southern KwaZulu-Natal and the Transkei region of Eastern Cape.

With its large ears, long slender legs and merest tuft of a tail, the steenbok is unmatched for grace and beauty among the smaller buck. It is usually encountered singly, except when a mother is with her young or when a male and female are courting.

In the morning and evening you may see it demurely feeding at the side of a newly constructed road, where fresh vegetation has sprung, or at some clearing in the grassland—a firebreak, an airstrip or a patch of cultivated land.

A frightened steenbok lies down quietly in the grass but, if flushed from its hideout, darts away with head pressed forward, in an evasive zigzag flight, before stopping to glance back at the danger. It may occasionally go to ground, hiding in an old aardvark hole.

Such tactics are often used, for the steenbok has many natural enemies, ranging from jackals, wild dogs, leopards and cheetahs to martial eagles and pythons. In distress the steenbok emits pitiful screams, but in normal circumstances its conversation is limited to the occasional snort.

It marks its territory carefully with secretions from glands between the hooves on the front and hind feet, a gland between the two halves of the lower jaw, and possibly with glands just in front of the eyes.

COMMON DUIKER

Gewone duiker *(Sylvicapra grimmia)*

Size: Shoulder height (m) 50 cm, (f) 52 cm; weight (m) 18 kg, (f) 21 kg. Only the males carry horns.

Colour: A greyish buff throughout, except for white underparts. Front of forelegs dark brown; dark line runs from the forehead down to the nostrils.

Most like: The steenbok but, although they are of similar height, the common duiker is much heavier. Its greyish coat and whitish underparts are easily distinguished from the orange-brown upperparts and pure white underparts of the more lightly built steenbok.

Habitat: Bush country, although it happily adapts to other types of habitat, with the exception of thick forests and vegetationless desert.

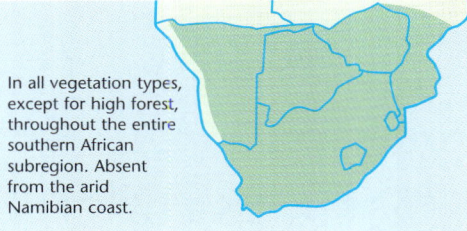

In all vegetation types, except for high forest, throughout the entire southern African subregion. Absent from the arid Namibian coast.

The common, or grey, duiker is a sturdy little survivor, browsing—sometimes on its hindlegs—on an abundant variety of leaves, seeds, flowers, fruit and twigs; digging for roots and tubers; nibbling on bark; and (to the annoyance of farmers) invading crops and even gardens.

That is not all: the common duiker has been known to capture and eat a variety of young birds, from guineafowl to chickens and ducklings. In its turn, however, it is preyed on by numerous enemies, from lions to large owls.

Its name is derived from its habit, when evading pursuit, of disappearing into the bush in a series of plunging jumps (Afrikaans *duik* means to dive). It shares the common compulsion among small buck to stop in order to glance back at the enemy, and this may cause its undoing.

The common duiker is most active in the late afternoon or after dark. It roams singly or in pairs, whisking its little tail as it proceeds. The territory staked out by the male, and marked by a scent-laden secretion from the glands below the front corners of the eyes, is fiercely defended.

Although the common duiker is docile in captivity, the sharp, pointed horns of the ram may nevertheless cause injury.

Smaller mammals

Blue duiker
Blouduiker *(Cephalophus monticola)*

Size: Shoulder height 35 cm; weight (m) 4 kg, (f) 4,5 kg. Both sexes carry horns about 3 cm long.
Colour: Varies from bluish grey to reddish brown. The underparts, including the underside of the tail, are lighter, sometimes white.
Most like: The suni, but slightly smaller and distinguishable by its grey-brown, rather than reddish brown coloration. Blue duiker females have short horns, whereas the suni females are hornless.
Habitat: Dense undergrowth or coastal bush. Water is an essential habitat requirement.

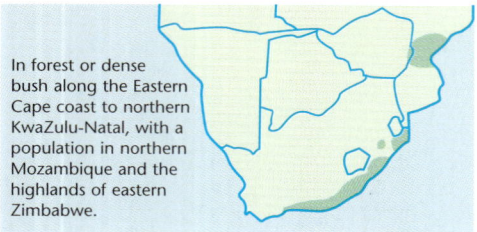

In forest or dense bush along the Eastern Cape coast to northern KwaZulu-Natal, with a population in northern Mozambique and the highlands of eastern Zimbabwe.

Easily the smallest antelope in southern Africa, the blue duiker is also the Garbo of its kind, being extremely shy and difficult to spot, except when it emerges into open glades or onto the open beaches adjoining the thick undergrowth of its natural habitat. It is so short that it can, in fact, move freely below the level of this undergrowth.

For one so timid, the blue duiker incautiously follows well-marked tracks, a habit which enables human hunters to snare the little buck with ease. Among its other enemies are pythons and mambas, large birds and leopards. When pursued, it may take to water and has even been seen swimming in the sea off KwaZulu-Natal.

Blue duikers live on the leaves, shoots and berries of forest shrubs and trees; unlike many kinds of buck, which obtain moisture through their feeding, they are dependent on available water and drink frequently. It is the journey to and from the favourite watering-holes that produces the telltale tracks.

The colouring of the blue duiker provides it with an almost perfect camouflage but, as it moves about in the bushy undergrowth, it constantly flicks its tiny tail, exposing flashes of lighter hair underneath. This can be a giveaway to predators in the vicinity. The newborn lamb is also vulnerable, having a much lighter coat.

Red duiker
Rooiduiker *(Cephalophus natalensis)*

Size: Shoulder height 43 cm; weight 14 kg. Both sexes carry horns, usually about 6 cm long.
Colour: Rich reddish brown, with paler underparts. Chin and throat are whitish, as are the insides of the ears. A tuft of reddish brown and black hairs rises between the short horns. The tail is tipped with white.
Most like: The common duiker, but smaller, and distinguished from it by its reddish colouring. The red duiker also favours a denser bush habitat.
Habitat: Forest and dense bush, whether coastal or mountainous, as long as surface water is available.

In the dense bush and forested areas of KwaZulu-Natal, Swaziland, western Mozambique and Mpumalanga, and in the Kruger National Park. There is a small population in the Soutpansberg Mountains.

The red duiker is a small, shy antelope with a decidedly hunched appearance, the hindlegs seemingly in an almost crouched position—all the better to take flight through the thickets when it senses danger. Once much more widespread in KwaZulu-Natal and the eastern region of the Northern Province, numbers of this little buck have declined in recent decades, and it is now rated as 'low-risk vulnerable' in the International Union for Conservation of Nature and Natural Resources' Red Data Book.

Known also as Natal red duiker, these secretive creatures roam singly, in pairs or in small family groups, browsing, mostly after dark, on the leaves, stems and fruits of low-growing shrubs. Their loud, penetrating cry lies somewhere between a snort and a whistle. Once aware of being observed, they will 'freeze' briefly and then bound away, with the duiker's characteristic 'diving' motion, into the safety of thick undergrowth.

Like other small buck, the red duiker is preyed upon by eagles and pythons, as well as leopards and other forest predators, not to mention man and his traps. In distress its call becomes a deep, throaty cry. This duiker's biggest threat today is the clearing of its natural habitat: forest and bush in many areas untouched for centuries, but now being cleared for agriculture or human habitation.

The young of the red duiker are born reddish black, except for a reddish-brown face.

Smaller mammals

SUNI

Scenie *(Neotragus moschatus)*

Size: Shoulder height 35 cm; weight (m) 5 kg, (f) 5,4 kg. Only the males carry horns.
Colour: Reddish brown, with the hairs tipped a lighter colour, giving a speckled appearance. Underparts and insides of legs white or whitish. Top of the head darker than the rest of the body, and a narrow dark band encircles the legs just above the hooves.
Most like: Blue duiker, but slightly larger and females hornless. The rich, red-brown, white-flecked upperparts of the suni should not be confused with the slate grey to dull brown of the blue duiker. Smaller than Sharpe's grysbok.
Habitat: Dry, densely thicketed bush country or forest.

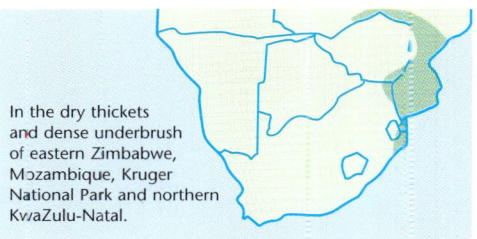

In the dry thickets and dense underbrush of eastern Zimbabwe, Mozambique, Kruger National Park and northern KwaZulu-Natal.

The tiny suni always seems peckish. In fact, its habit of feeding for a short time, then resting and ruminating before once again taking a snack is due to its high metabolic rate and the difficulty it has in digesting the coarser parts of its diet of leaves, shoots and fruits. Nature has, at any rate, supplied it with the ability to acquire its liquid intake from its food: the suni is independent of drinking water.

In the midday heat sunis lie in the shade of bushes or trees, perfectly camouflaged against the fallen leaves but, like the blue duiker, their twitching white-tipped tails may give their presence away. When disturbed, they will 'freeze' at first, but will jump up at the last moment from their hiding places and zigzag away, with a characteristic backward glance to ascertain their safety after they have travelled about 100 metres.

When sensing danger, the suni warns with a distinct, high-pitched, barking cry; if surprised at close quarters, it emits a whistling snort. Its habit of following familiar, well-used tracks makes it particularly vulnerable to human predators.

The courting male suni bleats like a goat when it pursues the female. Their single offspring is born during the summer months between August and February, and has a darker, deep reddish-brown coat.

DAMARA DIK-DIK

Damara dik-dik *(Madoqua kirkii)*

Size: Shoulder height 38 cm; weight 5 kg. Only the males carry spikelike horns, usually about 8 cm long.
Colour: From pale grey-brown to yellowish brown and darker shades of brown, with lighter flecks on the hairs giving the body a grizzled appearance. Underparts and inside of thighs off-white. White rings around eyes.
Most like: The steenbok but much smaller and grey-brown above, rather than rufous brown. The dik-dik also has a distinctive crest of long hair on the forehead, which is lacking in the steenbok.
Habitat: Dry bush or wooded country with thick undergrowth; terrain often stony. On hillsides and in the vicinity of, though not actually on, rocky outcrops.

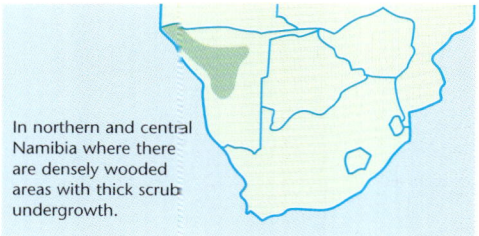

In northern and central Namibia where there are densely wooded areas with thick scrub undergrowth.

With its distinctive, elongated, mobile muzzle the dik-dik searches for its favourite food, standing on its hindlegs if necessary to reach for a succulent shoot, flower or fruit. Foraging is made easier when some larger game animal, such as an elephant or giraffe, has conveniently torn or trampled down the favoured plant.

Dainty and elusive, the Damara dik-dik, also known as Kirk's dik-dik, emits a single, sharp whistle when startled, before racing for cover. Instead of running, it may retreat in a 'stotting' motion—a series of stiff-legged bounds—emitting a further short whistle each time its hooves hit the ground. The name 'dik-dik' is believed to be derived from this series of sounds. The force of the legs hitting the hard terrain is cushioned by the animal's shock absorbers, which are well-developed, rubbery pads at the back of each hoof.

Dik-diks live singly, in pairs or in small family groups. They mark their territories with a secretion from glands in front of the eyes; dung and urine perform the same function.

A single fawn is born in summer after a gestation period of almost six months.

Smaller mammals

KLIPSPRINGER
Klipspringer (*Oreotragus oreotragus*)

Size: Shoulder height (m) 60 cm, (f) 65 cm; weight (m) 10 kg, (f) 13 kg.
Colour: From yellow to grey, speckled with brown; the top of the head darker. Underparts whitish, as are chin and insides of ears. Eyes surrounded by area of light yellow.
Most like: Common duiker, but latter is smaller, rarely found in rocky habitat, and does not have 'proud', erect posture so typical of klipspringer.
Habitat: Rocky locations, including mountains and gorges. Also boulder-strewn river beds. The presence of thick bush, for shelter, is essential.

Namibia, along the Western Cape mountains to the Eastern Cape, in eastern Botswana, Zimbabwe, Northern Province, western Mozambique, northern KwaZulu-Natal, the Hluhluwe/Umfolozi complex and the Drakensberg.

Like a ballet dancer on points, the klipspringer walks on the tips of its hooves, and is often seen poised gracefully like this as it stands sentinel on a high, projecting rock.

Natural adaptation has equipped it superbly for its habitat: the narrow cylindrical, blunt-tipped hooves are the consistency of hard rubber, absorbing the shock as it leaps from rock to rock and enabling it to balance on the narrowest ledge.

The hairs of its coat are coarse, hollow and springy, giving rise to the belief that they served to cushion the klipspringer's body from rock projections. It is now thought that they serve to regulate body temperature. (In times past these hairs were prized for stuffing saddles.) And its salt-and-pepper colouring offers excellent camouflage.

When it senses danger, the klipspringer emits a shrill snort—this warning is often initiated by the male and echoed by the female in a duet. The sounds carry for up to 700 m, alerting any predator to the fact that it has been seen. If need be, the klipspringers will then make their getaway to some inaccessible eyrie. Their enemies include leopards, hyaenas, baboons and large birds of prey.

The klipspringer browses on a wide variety of shrubs and other plants, mostly within the range of its mountainous territory, although occasionally it forages on adjacent flat ground.

FALLOW DEER
Europese takbok (*Cervus dama*)

Size: Average shoulder height 90 cm; weight (m) 95 kg, females slightly smaller.
Colour: In summer, dark brownish yellow ('fallow') with white spots on the flanks, a horizontal white stripe low down on each flank and a nearly vertical white stripe on each thigh. In winter, greyish fawn. Chin, lower jaw and throat are white, and there is a white patch above each eye. Males have a black band running down, extending to the tail; underside of tail is white.
Most like: The bushbuck, which is also dark brown with white spots. Fallow deer, however, never have vertical side stripes, and the male's bony antlers are distinctive.
Habitat: Introduced from Europe to a variety of habitats, from the grassland and oak and pine woodlands on the slopes of Table Mountain, to scrubland in the Eastern Cape.

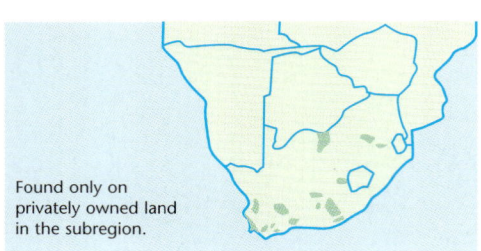

Found only on privately owned land in the subregion.

Most people associate fallow deer, or European fallow deer, with the parks and country estates of northern Europe, but in fact the species originated in the Mediterranean region.

Fallow deer were being kept in the grounds of Newlands House, Cape Town, as early as the 1860s, and in 1897 Cecil Rhodes released specimens on his Groote Schuur estate. Subsequently stocks were introduced to farms in different parts of the country, particularly to wine farms in the Boland, where they are still a part of the landscape today.

As in Europe, the fallow deer is predominantly nocturnal if harassed, but happily browses by day if not disturbed. It eats leaves, berries, nuts and tree bark, and to a lesser extent also grazes. It is not dependent on a water supply.

The magnificent antlers of the fallow deer are carried only by the male. Each November they are shed to make way for a new pair which develop by March in readiness for the autumn rut.

The mating season lasts a month and the (usually single) fawns are born eight months later in midsummer.

Smaller mammals

CAPE GRYSBOK

Grysbok *(Raphicerus melanotis)*

Size: Shoulder height 54 cm; weight 10 kg. Males only bear short, pointed horns.
Colour: Deep reddish brown, speckled with white hairs to give a greyish tinge. Underparts lighter; whitish ring circles the eyes. Large grey-brown ears.
Most like: Sharpe's grysbok and steenbok. Differs from Sharpe's grysbok in that it has a pair of supplementary hooves above the fetlock. Cape grysbok differ from steenbok in having shorter ears and horns, white-speckled upperparts and uniform buffy underparts (steenbok have plain reddish brown upperparts and pure white underparts).
Habitat: Thick fynbos and fringes of coastal forest; sometimes on the lower levels of rocky hillsides adjoining these.

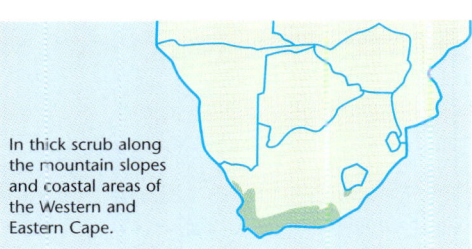

In thick scrub along the mountain slopes and coastal areas of the Western and Eastern Cape.

The secretive, solitary little Cape grysbok is not the wine farmer's best friend, for it is partial to the shoots and leaves of vines, and steals out under cover of darkness to feast on this rich food.

Exclusively South African—it is found from the west coast to the Eastern Cape—this little antelope lacks the grace and proud posture of the steenbok. Its thickset body is mounted on legs that are fragile and disproportionately short, and since the forelegs are a little shorter than the hind ones, its back slopes, much like an ungainly hatchback.

On the plus side, the Cape grysbok is fastidious about its appearance, spending much time washing and grooming its thick, wiry coat.

During the day it lies up, camouflaged by thick scrub bush. If it feels threatened, it may lie flat on the ground and then, with its head held low, speed away as fast as it can, with sudden 'duiker-ish' dives into the refuge of sheltering undergrowth. Its alarm call is a bleating scream.

The Cape grysbok is attached to a particular, not very large territory and you can usually see it on its own or in pairs when mating. The lamb is born with a darker coat than its parents, and it is kept hidden for the first few months, until it can fend for itself.

SHARPE'S GRYSBOK

Sharpe se grysbok *(Raphicerus sharpei)*

Size: Shoulder height 50 cm; weight (m) 7,5 kg, (f) 8 kg.
Colour: A rich reddish brown, speckled with white hairs to give an overall grizzled appearance. Underparts lighter; whitish rings around eyes.
Most like: The Cape grysbok, but smaller and with shorter horns. (Sharpe's grysbok's horn record for southern Africa is 6,35 cm; the Cape grysbok's is 12,38 cm.) Sharpe's grysbok lacks the 'false hooves', which the Cape grysbok has above its fetlocks
Habitat: Dry, sandy areas or rocky terrain where there is low-growing bush and grass cover of medium height.

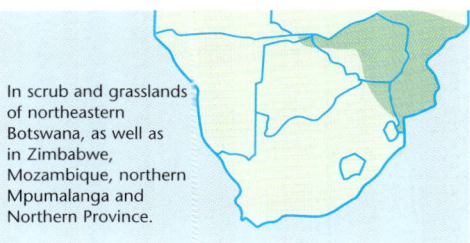

In scrub and grasslands of northeastern Botswana, as well as in Zimbabwe, Mozambique, northern Mpumalanga and Northern Province.

Shy and ever on the alert, the delicate Sharpe's grysbok scuttles unceremoniously away through the thick undergrowth when disturbed, its head held down straight in front like a rabbit, and its body held low, in an almost crouching attitude, to the ground. All you may see as it bolts away for cover is its reddish-brown back above the bush.

Lying quietly in a sheltered spot of its choice, it is so well camouflaged that you are unlikely to see it until almost upon it.

Named after Sir Arthur Sharpe, who came across this species in Malawi, it is smaller than its cousin, the Cape grysbok and the horns of the male are shorter (the ewe carries no horns).

Sharpe's grysbok is apt to be a loner, and the ram generally rests some distance away from the ewe during the heat. It feeds in the cool of the day or at night, nibbling at shrubs and bushes, and sometimes also sampling the tender grasses. Its natural enemies, like those of the steenbok, are many, and include pythons, the larger birds of prey and the normal range of large carnivores, from caracals to lions.

Sharpe's grysbok is found from Mpumalanga north to Malawi and Zambia and as far north as Tanzania—hence its alternative Afrikaans name, *tropiese grysbok*.

Smaller mammals

AARDVARK
Erdvark *(Orycteropus afer)*

Size: Length (including tail) 1,4-1,6 m; weight 40-70 kg.
Colour: Pinkish grey or yellowish grey skin sparsely covered in coarse reddish brown hairs. The skin is apt to be stained darker, depending on the colour of the earth in which the animal burrows.
Most like: Unlike any other animal.
Habitat: Wherever termites and ants are available as food, and where the earth is soft enough for burrowing. The aardvark avoids stony or rocky terrain and high forest, but occurs in open woodland and grassland areas.

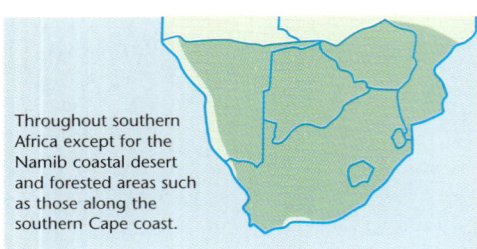

Throughout southern Africa except for the Namib coastal desert and forested areas such as those along the southern Cape coast.

The biologically unique aardvark ('earth-pig') is strictly nocturnal and therefore is seldom seen—a pity because it must be seen to be believed. The fleshy, elongated muzzle and sparsely haired torso are certainly piglike; there is also perhaps a touch of bear in its general appearance (hence its alternative name 'ant bear'). But it has long, rabbitlike ears, a thick, tapering tail, a sticky ribbon of a tongue between 20 and 30 cm long, and sharp claws on the digits of its webbed feet (four digits on the front feet, five on the back ones).

The aardvark is well equipped to forage for its staple diet of ants and termites. Claws burrow into the ant hill, the muzzle is inserted (thick hairs at the end of the muzzle acting as a dust filter), the ears are folded back to exclude dirt, and then the tongue is projected into the maze of passages that make up the ants' home. The ants, their larvae and eggs adhere to the tongue's saliva-laden surface. Virtually the only other food eaten by the aardvark is wild melons—whose hard pips survive the digestive process and germinate in the droppings.

The aardvark is extremely strong and can burrow a shelter in minutes, the entrance being sealed with earth when the animal is in residence. An unoccupied burrow may provide shelter for other fauna, including birds, snakes, pangolin and warthogs.

Aardvark young are born, usually singly, inside the burrow after a gestation period of seven months.

PANGOLIN
Ietermagog *(Manis temminckii)*

Size: Length 70-100 cm; weight 5-15 kg.
Colour: A covering of light brown scales gives this creature an armadillolike appearance. Underparts and sides of face are without scales, the skin dark grey to black.
Most like: Unlike any other animal.
Habitat: Bush country, rocky hills or open flood plains where there is light, sandy soil and an adequate source of the staple food: principally ants, but also termites.

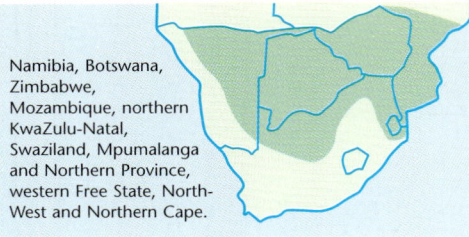

Namibia, Botswana, Zimbabwe, Mozambique, northern KwaZulu-Natal, Swaziland, Mpumalanga and Northern Province, western Free State, North-West and Northern Cape.

Protected by tough, armourlike scales, and a repulsive odour it discharges to chase predators away, the pangolin, or scaly anteater, is indeed a difficult customer to come to grips with. In extreme danger the animal rolls itself into a tight ball, its head tucked underneath its broad scaly tail, a defensive strategy that gave the pangolin its name (*peng-goling* is a Malay word meaning a roller).

If a predator then tries to prise it open, the pangolin has another trick up its sleeve: it slides its broad tail back and forth in a sawing motion capable of seriously injuring (if not severing) the leg of a dog, for example, or a human finger caught between the sharp scales.

Like a rhino's horn, the pangolin's fibrous scales actually consist of compressed hairlike filaments. The newborn youngster's scales do not harden until the second day, after which it may roll itself into a protective ball when alarmed.

Like the aardvark, the pangolin is mostly nocturnal, and it sets about attaining its diet of ants as the aardvark does, burrowing into ant hills with its clawed forefeet and using its long, slender and sticky tongue—a prodigious 40 cm in length—to extract the insects. When not in use, most of the tongue is conveniently packed away into a pouch in the throat.

As a burrower the pangolin is not in the same category as the aardvark. Rather than dig its own burrow, it will shelter in one abandoned by a springhare, aardvark or other animal; or it may bury itself in a heap of debris.

It is normally a slow mover, walking on its hindlegs and balancing on its tail in an almost vertical position should it stop to sniff the wind for signs of danger.

Smaller mammals

Porcupine
Ystervark *(Hystrix africaeaustralis)*

Size: Length 75-100 cm; weight 10-24 kg.
Colour: White, black-ringed quills and spines cover flanks, tail and upper part of body, while the head carries a crest of flexible black spines with white tips. Remainder of body has coarse black hair, shading to brown on older animals.
Most like: Unlike any other animal.
Habitat: A wide variety of habitats including mountains, though not forests or dry desert.

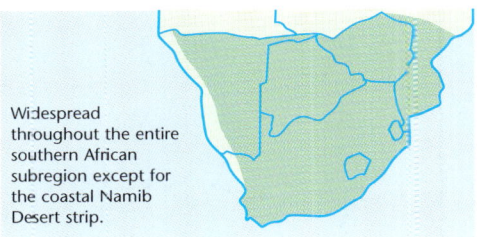

Widespread throughout the entire southern African subregion except for the coastal Namib Desert strip.

This spiky fortress of the wild is a rodent, the largest in southern Africa. When alarmed it becomes the prickliest of customers, erecting its bristling armour of quills and sabre-rattling with its tail: the quills at the end of the tail are hollow and make a loud noise when shaken.

The porcupine fights a tough rearguard action, moving backwards at speed to embed the sharp quills into a soft and vulnerable part of its enemy's anatomy, causing painful, suppurating wounds. Sometimes, fleeing from a predator, it will stop so suddenly that the enemy will be impaled.

Its preferred shelter is a cave or rock crevice, but failing these the porcupine will settle for a hole in the ground such as the disused burrow of an aardvark. Although it is mostly nocturnal, you may be lucky to encounter it by day, sunning itself outside its shelter; but it is very shy and will disappear quickly if disturbed.

It can gnaw through maize stalks with ease, and cause wholesale destruction to root crops and vegetables under cultivation. Bulbs, tubers and wild fruits also form part of its vegetarian diet, and to counteract phosphorus deficiency it gnaws on bones, taking a supply to its shelter.

How do porcupines mate? Very carefully, of course: the female backs up to the expectant male with her spiny tail raised vertically and, thus neutralized, she and her mate enjoy the pangs of passion.

Southern African hedgehog
Suider-Afrikaanse krimpvarkie *(Atelerix frontalis)*

Size: Length 20 cm; weight 350-400 g.
Colour: Brown-and-white spines on upper part of body, including flanks; grey-brown to dark brown hairs on head, limbs and tail, with a band of white hair across the forehead. Underparts vary from off-white to black.
Most like: Occasionally confused with the porcupine, although the hedgehog's brownish colour, small size and short spines easily distinguish it from the much larger, long-spined, black-and-white porcupine.
Habitat: A wide variety of habitats providing dry soil and dry cover for daytime shelter. A plentiful supply of insects, worms and roots is essential.

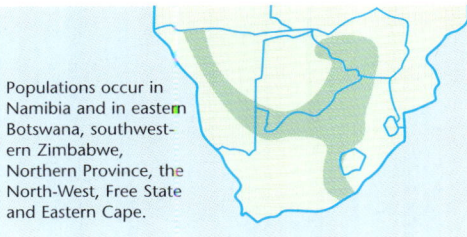

Populations occur in Namibia and in eastern Botswana, southwestern Zimbabwe, Northern Province, the North-West, Free State and Eastern Cape.

When the hedgehog rolls itself up into a tight, protective little ball—the croquet ball of Alice in Wonderland—it is safe from most wild predators, although not from the eagle owl, whose long talons and scaly feet are more than a match for the hedgehog's short, prickly spines.

Like the owl, the hedgehog is nocturnal. After dark it goes in search of food, which it locates by smell and hearing rather than sight. Its appetite is prodigious (it can eat up to one third of its weight every day) and varied: not only worms and insects, but small rodents, frogs, slugs, the eggs and young of ground-nesting birds, and vegetable matter, including roots and fruit. Sometimes after rain you can see hedgehogs foraging for earthworms.

Hedgehogs rest mostly in daylight, curled up cosily under cover of bush, grass or garden rubbish, or in a hole in the ground. Like gypsies, they have no fixed abode and change shelter daily, except in the colder months between May and July when they hibernate, emerging only during warm spells to eat. Before the onset of cold weather, when food supplies are still plentiful, they develop a thick, insulating layer of fat under the skin to protect them in the months ahead.

Grunts and snuffles provide the conversation when two hedgehogs meet. When alarmed their call is quite different, a high-pitched, bloodcurdling cry.

Smaller mammals

SPRINGHARE
Springhaas *(Pedetes capensis)*

Size: Length (including tail) 75-85 cm; weight 2,5-3,8 kg.
Colour: Varies from pale reddish brown to yellowish grey, and with a slightly darker tail broadly black at the tip. The underparts (including tail) and insides of legs white or whitish yellow. Large, dark eyes which shine bright yellow-orange in torchlight.
Most like: Other hares, but distinguished by its excessively developed hindlegs, erect posture and black-tipped tail.
Habitat: Sandy ground covered with scrub, low bush or low grass; this includes the fringes of cultivated land and vleis. Also sandy river banks.

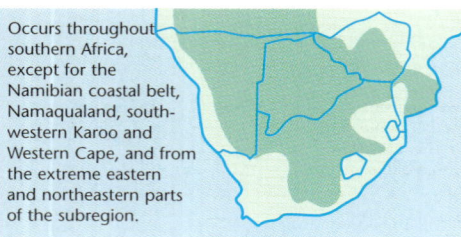

Occurs throughout southern Africa, except for the Namibian coastal belt, Namaqualand, south-western Karoo and Western Cape, and from the extreme eastern and northeastern parts of the subregion.

The springhare's long tail, long and powerful hindlegs and greatly foreshortened forelegs (held together under the chin as if in prayer) give it a kangaroolike appearance. At speed, moving only on its hindlegs, it can cover about two metres at a bound.

It is a rodent, not a hare, and is the only species in its own unique family. In the wild it feeds on grasses, roots and the leaves of low bushes—and on land under cultivation, on such crops as maize, beans, sweet potatoes and groundnuts. Its many enemies include snakes and owls as well as weasels, mongooses and jackals; man is also a major predator. In Zimbabwe and Botswana springhares are sought after as a source of protein; and the San are so fond of them that they eat virtually every part of the anatomy.

Being a night-time wanderer, the springhare is frequently caught on the road in the glare of a car's headlamps, one eye reflecting the dazzle as the animal sits apparently mesmerized.

It shelters in a hole in the ground which, with the strong digging claws of its forelegs, it excavates very quickly. These burrows invariably have more than one exit, providing for a quick getaway from prowling predators, and neighbouring burrows may be linked with one another.

The female springhare gives birth to her single young inside the burrow, where it remains for the first seven weeks of its life, before being weaned onto grass.

CAPE HARE
Vlakhaas *(Lepus capensis)*

Size: Length 45-60 cm; weight 1,4-2,5 kg.
Colour: Grey-brown coat flecked with black, the flanks and legs a more ruddy brown, the abdomen whitish. Pale rings around the eyes. Upperside of tail black, underside white.
Most like: The scrub hare, but has a distinctive yellow-buff chest and white abdomen, while the scrub hare has completely white underparts.
Habitat: Open, dry country, from coastal plains to mountains, with low grass for feeding and grass stands for cover.

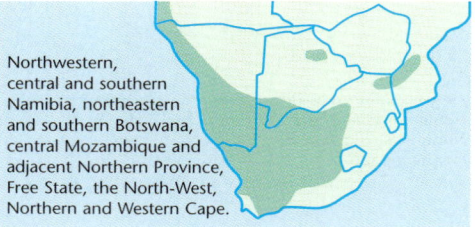

Northwestern, central and southern Namibia, northeastern and southern Botswana, central Mozambique and adjacent Northern Province, Free State, the North-West, Northern and Western Cape.

The Cape hare's recipe for survival is a combination of speed (its hindlegs are powerfully developed) and camouflage: by day it rests, with its long ears folded back, concealed in a shallow depression among vegetation, and will remain there even when approached at close quarters, before springing up and 'haring' away on a zigzag course. Sudden sideways leaps help to throw off pursuing predators such as dogs.

The shallow resting-places are known as 'forms' because the animal's body shapes them. A Cape hare will return to its form day after day, even when some distance away, and will sleep lying in exactly the same position. Under extreme stress it may take alternative refuge in the underground burrow of some other animal.

After dark it emerges to feed on palatable grasses, and sometimes on other plants. Its upper incisors are long and chisel-like in the manner of Bugs Bunny, and they grow throughout the hare's lifetime, making formidable weapons.

When two males fight, as they frequently do when a female is on heat, they stand on their hindlegs and slash at each other with the claws of their forefeet—to such good effect that much fur flies. Behaviour in anger or when threatened includes grinding of teeth, drumming of forefeet and stamping of hindfeet.

The Cape hare's name was chosen by the Swedish biologist Linnaeus, who was sent a specimen from the Cape of Good Hope in the 18th century.

Smaller mammals

ROCK DASSIE

Klipdas *(Procavia capensis)*

Size: *Length 45-60 cm; average weight (m) 3,75 kg, (f) 3,55 kg.*
Colour: *Various shades of brown, from dark brown to yellow-grey, with brindling. Neck and flanks lighter than back. Throat and belly lighter brown, never white. A patch of long black hair covers dorsal gland in centre of back.*
Most like: *Tree dassie, but with shorter hair and black, not white, hair over dorsal gland.*
Habitat: *Rocky outcrops in the form of koppies, kranses and mountain slopes.*

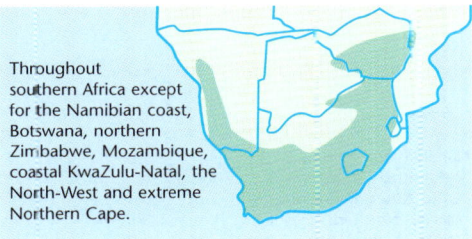

Throughout southern Africa except for the Namibian coast, Botswana, northern Zimbabwe, Mozambique, coastal KwaZulu-Natal, the North-West and extreme Northern Cape.

To the Dutch the dassie, or Cape dassie, looked like a small badger (*dasje*). This comparison is less far-fetched than the somewhat misleading description 'rock-rabbit', for the dassie is more badgerlike than rabbitlike with its very tiny, head-hugging ears and no tail. Oddly enough, it is more closely related to the dugongs and elephants than to either badgers or rabbits.

Thickly padded feet, kept moist by a glandular secretion, help to give dassies remarkable mobility even on steep and smooth rock surfaces.

These sociable animals congregate in colonies of up to 50. They enjoy basking in the sun and seem to spend much of their time idly conserving their energy; in the colder parts of the day and at night they go into a tightly packed huddle together in their dark shelters in order to minimize loss of body heat.

Lions and jackals relish the taste of rock dassies; so do eagles, whose favourite plan of attack is to swoop down out of the morning sun. To combat this blinding attack, nature has equipped the dassie's eyes with a thin, movable membrane that shields the pupil and allows vision directly into the sun. When in the open, a female dassie acts as sentinel and, should she spot danger, her high-pitched warning cry will send the colony scurrying to the shelter of rocky crevices.

Cornered, the dassie is an aggressive little animal, with sharp incisors bared and gnashing. At such times the hair over the dorsal gland rises, in the same way as a dog's hackles. When submitting, the dassie turns his side or rump to the victor.

TREE DASSIE

Boomdas *(Dendrohyrax arboreus)*

Size: *Length 42-52 cm; average weight 2,5-3,5 kg.*
Colour: *From grey to grey-brown, with brindling. Head is slightly darker, throat and belly whitish to pure white. The hair covering dorsal gland in the centre of the back is white or whitish.*
Most like: *The rock dassie, but with longer, more woolly hair. Hair over dorsal gland white, not black. Underparts white or cream, not light brown.*
Habitat: *Evergreen coastal forests and tropical forests.*

Found only in the evergreen forest areas along the Eastern Cape coast, and in southern KwaZulu-Natal; another population exists in central Mozambique.

Tree dassies are extremely noisy at night: when one of them gives a cry, all others in the vicinity follow suit, emitting a cacophony of barks, growls, squeaks and shrieks that rises in a piercing crescendo. The orchestration, which includes a fearsome grinding of teeth, may continue for half an hour and can carry for up to three kilometres. Fear provokes a whistling sound.

Tree dassies are preyed on by large birds of prey such as owls and eagles, pythons and by members of the cat family. When attacked by smaller predators, they protect themselves by biting furiously.

Unlike rock dassies, they are nocturnal by nature, and live in pairs rather than in colonies. By day they shelter in the hollows of trees, among thick foliage or in rock crevices. At nightfall they emerge to forage for plant material and perhaps insects.

A tree dassie marks out its territory by rubbing its dorsal gland against trees. To announce its presence when entering and leaving a tree hole, it calls out. This hole may be high above the ground, for the tree dassie is not an excellent climber but can negotiate the thin, trailing branches festooning its forest habitat with surprising agility and sure-footedness.

Like the rock dassie it is specially equipped to groom its coat: the inside digit of each hindleg has a specialized claw for this purpose.

Smaller mammals

LARGE GREY MONGOOSE

Grootgrysmuishond (*Herpestes ichneumon*)

Size: Length (including tail) 1,0-1,1 m; weight 2,5-4 kg.
Colour: Grey, sometimes with a yellowish tinge; at close quarters appears more brindled. Muzzle and legs a dark greyish brown. Tip of tail characteristically black.
Most like: Small grey mongoose, but is almost twice as long and is distinguishable by the black tip to the tail.
Habitat: Always associated with rivers, lakes, dams, swamps or other wet environments.

In well-watered areas of the Caprivi Strip of northeastern Namibia, northern Botswana, northern Zimbabwe, central and coastal Mozambique, and along the Indian Ocean seaboard to the southwestern Cape.

The large grey, or Egyptian, mongoose is the largest of the mongooses in Africa, and it is found in many other parts of the continent, including West Africa and Egypt's Nile Valley. The ancient Egyptians kept this species as a household pet to catch snakes and rats. It was a sacred animal—itself colloquially known also as 'Pharaoh's rat'—and on its master's death would be killed, embalmed and buried alongside him.

In addition to rodents and snakes, it feeds on lizards, frogs, fish and the eggs and chicks of ground-nesting birds. It gets the better of snakes through sheer agility, and its coarse hair helps to protect it from the venom fangs. Although not averse to hunting for food in shallow water, it steers clear of deep water, unless threatened. It is also not a tree-climber, having the wrong claws for this activity.

The large grey mongoose's natural enemies, apart from snakes, include the larger carnivores and large birds of prey.

When a pair of large grey mongooses, or the two parents and their young, are on the move they proceed head-to-tail in Indian file. Scent glands located near the anus help keep the file, known also as the 'caravan' in formation. But, unlike other mongooses, the large grey mongoose does not seem to make use of the odour from these glands as a defensive weapon if trapped or threatened by man, but uses its high-pitched staccato distress call instead.

The species is more active by day than by night. It sleeps in a sitting position in a burrow of its own, an adopted burrow, a reed or grass thicket, a crevice formed by tree roots, or under an overhanging river bank.

WATER MONGOOSE

Kommetjiegatmuishond (*Atilax paludinosus*)

Size: Length (including tail) 80-100 cm; weight 2,5-5,5 kg.
Colour: Reddish brown to brownish black coat, sometimes grizzled, and with an almost metallic or glossy sheen. The head and underparts may be a little lighter than the back.
Most like: The Cape clawless otter, but only two-thirds as long and a quarter as heavy. Uniform brownish underneath, without silver-white chin, throat and upper chest of clawless otter. Tail bushy brownish black, not short-haired.
Habitat: Well-watered country close to rivers, marshes, vleis and dams; and near reeds, water lilies and other semi-aquatic vegetation.

The Caprivi Strip, northern Botswana, eastern Zimbabwe, Mozambique, Northern Province, Mpumalanga, Swaziland, KwaZulu-Natal, Free State, Eastern and Western Cape, and along the lower reaches of the Gariep River.

The underfur of the water, or marsh, mongoose is woolly and soft, but the 'guard coat' or outer hair looks shaggy and feels coarse—not that there is much opportunity to touch it, for this species is elusive, foraging among the thick vegetation near water. When captured it is almost impossible to tame as a pet, exhibiting symptoms of frenzy if approached.

The water mongoose is a good swimmer. Mostly, though, it needs to do no more than wade into shallow water to acquire its daily food ration, a high proportion of which consists of frogs (and their eggs), crabs, shellfish, rats, mice and insects. It uses the long-clawed digits of its forelegs to gouge the crabs out of their shelters in river banks.

A water mongoose will head for water if pursued and under stress. Having taken shelter in a convenient reed bed, it will remain motionless, totally submerged except for a protruding nose, until it considers the danger is past.

Sometimes, when a marsh or vlei dries up, it switches to a terrestrial diet typical of other species of mongoose—while still remaining in the neighbourhood of the former water source.

The Afrikaans name for the water mongoose is derived from the cuplike sac that surrounds the anus and its glands.

Smaller mammals

SMALL GREY MONGOOSE
Kleingrysmuishond (*Galerella pulverulenta*)

Size: Length (including extended tail) 55-69 cm; weight (m) 900 g, (f) 680 g.
Colour: Speckled dark grey (but lighter grey in dry regions). Underparts are occasionally lighter and less speckled.
Most like: The grey forms of the slender mongoose, but more thickset and with longer, more consistently grey hair. The small grey mongoose also lacks the slender mongoose's black tail-tip.
Habitat: Wide range of habitats, from dry bush country to rocky slopes and forested areas, and from coast to Karoo.

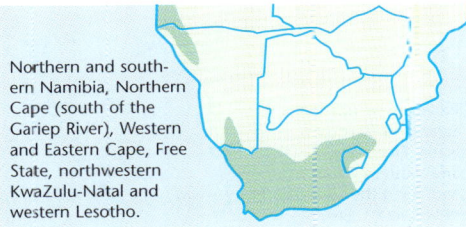

Northern and southern Namibia, Northern Cape (south of the Gariep River), Western and Eastern Cape, Free State, northwestern KwaZulu-Natal and western Lesotho.

You will often see this small, usually solitary, daytime forager crossing a track or country road before darting into the undergrowth. It trots along briskly on short legs, its long tail fully extended close to the ground behind and its head held low, pausing now and then to sniff for insects which it scratches for in the soil. Like other mongoose species, it also eats rats, mice, lizards, snakes, birds' eggs and undefended chicks.

The small grey mongoose, in the manner of all its kind, stalks larger prey rather like a cat, crouching at first, and then dashing out to inflict a bite wherever possible. The victim is then 'worried' before the *coup de grâce*—a head bite—is delivered.

Sometimes these little animals climb trees, either to search for food or escape predators, but the claws of their front feet are not particularly well equipped for either climbing or digging. They may shelter in another animal's burrow (which they adjust to their own use), or else among a pile of rocks or some other natural refuge. Here the young are weaned, emerging only when they can fend for themselves.

This mongoose (also called the Cape grey mongoose as it is largely confined to the Northern, Western and Eastern Cape) has grown so accustomed to man's presence that it may settle on the outskirts of a town or village; while on farms it may make a home under the floorboards of an outbuilding or in another manmade structure such as a barn or shed.

SLENDER MONGOOSE
Swartkwasmuishond (*Galerella sanguinea*)

Size: Length (including tail): 50-65 cm; weight (m) 500-800 g, (f) 370-560 g.
Colour: A wide colour range, from reddish brown to yellowish or dark brown to olive-grey, the body colour being speckled with grey. Underparts less speckled. Tip of tail black or reddish black. Eyes yellow.
Most like: Small grey mongoose, but slightly smaller and more slender, with the characteristic black-tipped tail, lacking in small grey mongoose.
Habitat: From arid areas, but not deserts, to well-watered ones, and from open country to woodland. Absent from dense forests.

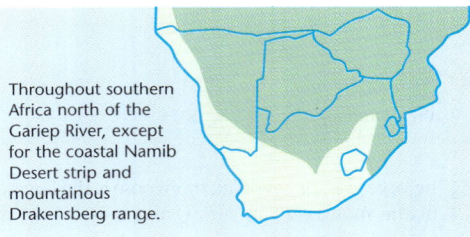

Throughout southern Africa north of the Gariep River, except for the coastal Namib Desert strip and mountainous Drakensberg range.

The squirrel-like mannerisms of the solitary, diurnal slender mongoose make it fairly easy to recognize: curious or alarmed, it will sit up on its hindlegs to look around quizzically, its head held high. Although it can climb trees when being chased or searching for food, it is normally earthbound, making its home in the shelter of rocks or stones, fallen trees and other vegetation, or in the disused burrow of an aardvark.

When running for cover, the slender mongoose, like the small grey mongoose, holds its body flat and its tail horizontal. But, just as it reaches cover, the black-tipped tail flicks up vertically, a sort of last, derisive gesture.

In the course of its daytime wandering, this little creature uses well-worn tracks, a habit that makes it especially vulnerable to birds of prey. Constantly on the alert for an aerial attack, it can actually distinguish between predators such as eagles, and other, harmless birds such as crows, and will often freeze until it has identified the danger.

It is inquisitive, and may actually return after retreating, in a series of small rushes, to take a closer look at you.

The slender mongoose's diet and method of hunting are similar to those of the small grey mongoose. Its predilection for chickens and eggs makes it unpopular among farmers.

Slender mongoose young, usually one or two at a time, are born during the warm, wet months.

Smaller mammals

Yellow mongoose
Witkwasmuishond *(Cynictis penicillata)*

Size: Length (including tail) 40-60cm; weight 450-900g.
Colour: A varied spectrum, from brindled grey in the north of the distribution area (Botswana) to reddish yellow or yellowish brown in the south, with intermediate gradations of colour. Southern specimens have a white-tipped tail; Botswana specimens have uniformly grey tails. The eyes are yellow.
Most like: Grey specimens may be confused with the small grey mongoose, but ranges do not overlap.
Habitat: Open country, from semi-desert scrubland to grassland in the vicinity of vleis. The species avoids deserts, thick bush and forests.

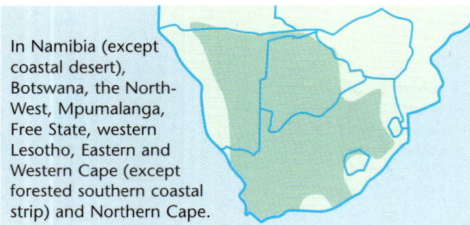

In Namibia (except coastal desert), Botswana, the North-West, Mpumalanga, Free State, western Lesotho, Eastern and Western Cape (except forested southern coastal strip) and Northern Cape.

Share and share alike would seem to be the motto of this gregarious, quick-witted creature. Not only is it an extremely sociable animal, living in colonies of up to 20, but it also happily coexists in underground warrens with ground squirrels and suricates, often taking up residence in their burrows. In this case all the inhabitants will contribute to the housekeeping, helping to maintain the warren, digging extensions to it and adapting it for their particular purposes. It may end up by having as many as 100 entrances.

Insects, for which the yellow mongoose digs, form the bulk of its diet, but it also enjoys mice and thus helps to limit the rodent population. Less admirable from the farmer's point of view, however, is its habit of stealing poultry.

Predators most likely to turn the tables on the yellow mongoose are birds of prey, snakes and jackals.

Members of this species don't all look alike: in the warmer north, 'yellow' mongooses are grey and have shorter hair and shorter tails than their southern counterparts, as well as being somewhat smaller. The northern form also usually lacks the conspicuous white tip to the tail that makes it easy to identify its brother in the south.

Banded mongoose
Gebande muishond *(Mungos mungo)*

Size: Length (including tail) 50-65 cm; weight 1,0-1,6 kg.
Colour: Varies from grey to brownish grey, with 10-12 distinctive, dark brown or black transverse bands from shoulders to root of tail; bands are most noticeable on lower back, and fade away on lower flanks. Tip of tail dark brown, as are legs.
Most like: The suricate, but banding across back more distinct, and suricate is smaller. Banded mongoose's tail is bushy, while suricate's is short-haired.
Habitat: Savanna, usually close to water, and with sufficient undergrowth, fallen logs and other vegetal debris to provide cover.

The savanna woodlands of northeastern Namibia, northwestern Botswana, northwestern and eastern Zimbabwe, Mozambique, Northern Province, Mpumalanga, coastal KwaZulu-Natal and Swaziland.

Industrious and gregarious, banded mongooses live in troops of up to 30, sometimes even more. You can hear them from quite a distance as they march across their territory foraging for food. Giveaway sounds are the rustling of grass and leaf litter, the earth being scratched for insects, and an incessant twittering that serves as the troop's intercom and heightens in pitch as individual animals move further apart from one another.

Danger evokes a harsher chittering. Then the pack will freeze; some will rise on their hindlegs to locate the source of trouble; and then they will all scamper away home, or to temporary shelter if they are far from home. If pressed, the banded mongoose will swim to safety, scale rocks or even climb a tree.

It is a courageous creature: a troop will attack a large, poisonous snake and, if two rival troops clash, fierce fighting ensues. If cornered by a predator, the banded mongoose spits like a cat.

At home, the female dominates the male: banded mongooses live in a matriarchy and it is the female who does the courting.

Like the dwarf mongoose, this little fellow loves birds' eggs, and cracks them by pitching them backwards through its back legs against a rock or stone. They also eat insects, other invertebrates, birds, carrion, reptiles, amphibians and small rodents.

Smaller mammals

Dwarf mongoose

Dwergmuishond *(Helogale parvula)*

Size: Length (including tail) 35-40 cm; weight 230-350 g.
Colour: From reddish brown to dark brown, flecked with grey, the underparts being usually a little lighter.
Most like: The banded mongoose, but is distinctively uniform dark brown and not grey-brown with dark crossbands. It also the smallest of our mongoose species.
Habitat: Savanna and bush country associated with the presence of termite mounds, fallen trees and rocky outcrops.

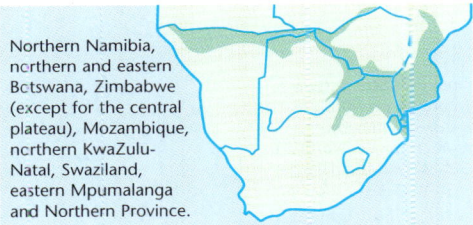

Northern Namibia, northern and eastern Botswana, Zimbabwe (except for the central plateau), Mozambique, northern KwaZulu-Natal, Swaziland, eastern Mpumalanga and Northern Province.

The gregarious dwarf mongoose lives in colonies of between 8-30 members. Social life has the vigour of an animated cartoon as these little animals scuttle about looking for food (or just satisfying their inquisitive instinct), communicating with one another all the time in a wide vocal range of musical twitters, whistles and 'chucks'. Or they may engage in mutual grooming, using incisor teeth to nibble from neck to base of tail.

They are also sun-worshippers and like to lie quietly in the early morning on the ground, or on fallen logs, close to their permanent shelters. These are distinguished by the accumulation of 'scats' or droppings outside them. The permanent shelter may be a burrow excavated deep underground, its entrance often disguised by a rock pile or heap of vegetable refuse. Other, more temporary, shelters are used if the mongoose troop is alerted to danger while out foraging far from home. The alarm call is first given by a male stationed at a vantage point, and then echoed among the troop.

Like other types of mongoose, the dwarf species includes snakes in its diet, the snake being attacked and killed in a communal effort. Birds' eggs too large to be bitten or clawed open are dealt with by inventive means: holding the egg in its forelegs, the mongoose catapults it backwards between its hindlegs onto a rock so that the shell is cracked open.

Suricate

Stokstertmeerkat *(Suricata suricatta)*

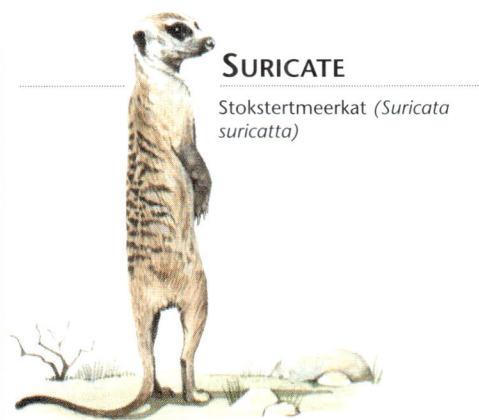

Size: Length (including tail) 45-55 cm; weight 620-960 g.
Colour: Varies from silver-grey to greyish brown, with irregular, often indistinct, brown or black bands across the back, from shoulders to base of tail. Head and throat often whitish, with dark nose, ears and circles around the eyes. The tip of the tail is also dark.
Most like: The banded mongoose, which is also active by day. The suricate is smaller, however, the dark bands across its back are less distinct, and its tail is short-haired and slender, rather than bushy.
Habitat: Arid, open country, including scrub, grassland and fynbos in the southwestern Cape.

Namibia, central and southern Botswana, southern North-West, Free State, western Lesotho, southeastern Cape, northerly Western Cape and Northern Cape.

This attractive little member of the mongoose family is easily distinguishable, and can often be seen in typical pose, perched upright on its haunches in front of its burrow, or on a rock or ant hill. Several suricates may sit together like this, sunning themselves and keeping a watchful eye open for predators. One sharp bark—the alarm call—from any of the pack, and they will all scuttle away to the safety of their cosy burrows.

There's a nuance to that alarm call: to warn off ground predators it is a staccato call, but for an airborne attack the call is long and drawn out. Like ground observers in the Battle of Britain, suricates must constantly survey the sky, and they're able to distinguish harmless birds from lethal ones.

They are gregarious animals, living in colonies of up to 40 individuals and sheltering together in rock crevices or underground burrows. Suricates will often share their burrows with yellow mongooses and ground squirrels, although the suricates may drive the others away. Their favourite food is insects, but they also dig for scorpions, and will take small invertebrates such as lizards and small snakes.

The suricate's alternative name, 'meerkat', is used in Afrikaans for other species of mongoose as well, which can be confusing.

Smaller mammals

STRIPED POLECAT
Stinkmuishond *(Ictonyx striatus)*

Size: Length (including tail) 57-67 cm; weight 0,5-1,4 kg.
Colour: Overall body black with four prominent pure white stripes running from top of head along back and sides to base of tail. Face, legs and underparts black, the face having a white patch above the nose and a larger white patch on each side, between eye and ear. Tail mainly white but black of hair bases shows through.
Most like: The striped weasel. However, the polecat is much larger and stouter, its body hair is longer, and its mainly white tail is bushier.
Habitat: All types of terrain, including arid plains, grassland, bush country, forest, rocky areas, mountains.

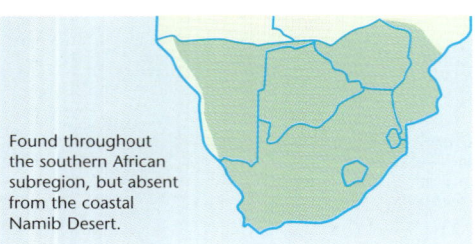

Found throughout the southern African subregion, but absent from the coastal Namib Desert.

HONEY BADGER
Ratel *(Mellivora capensis)*

Size: Length (with tail) 90 cm-1,0 m; weight 8-14 kg.
Colour: Black, except for the broad, white to silver-grey 'saddle' that runs over the whole of the back from above the eyes to the root of the tail. On both sides there is a narrow, slightly whiter border which separates the saddle from the black flanks and underparts.
Most like: Unmistakeable, but could possibly be confused with the civet. The honey badger, however, has no blotches, stripes or spots, its muzzle is shorter and its short ears are little more than ridges of skin.
Habitat: Almost every type of terrain except true desert, and from sea level to at least 1 500 m.

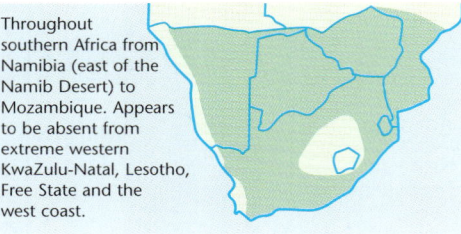

Throughout southern Africa from Namibia (east of the Namib Desert) to Mozambique. Appears to be absent from extreme western KwaZulu-Natal, Lesotho, Free State and the west coast.

No other animal can raise such a stink as the polecat. When angered or in trouble it fluffs out, raises its bushy tail, and straightens its dorsal hairs to form a crest, seemingly increasing the polecat's size. Shrill screams ensue. And then—the masterstroke—the animal presents its rear to its enemy and squirts a nauseating excretion from its anal glands that lingers for days. In the eye, the excretion can even cause blindness. As a last resort, the polecat may sham death until the enemy withdraws.

Although widely distributed in southern Africa, the striped polecat is not commonly encountered because it ventures out for food at dusk and by night. Similar in shape to a mongoose, but with a much fluffier tail, it shares like tastes, foraging for small mammals, insects, spiders, birds' eggs and sometimes a snake. It will also take poultry. Like some mongooses, it will retreat up the nearest tree, if that is the easiest and quickest escape from a predator.

Normally this polecat lives in a burrow, either dug by itself or taken over from another animal, or in a shelter provided by rocks, tree roots or vegetal debris. When it's out foraging, it trots along with its back slightly hunched and its tail held out horizontally.

Polecat young, usually two to three to a litter, are born blind, hairless and pink.

The honey badger's distinctive colouring, like the polecat's, is intended to alert potential adversaries to the risks of incurring its wrath. Few get in its way, for this stocky creature is a fierce fighter, and some of its tactics are decidedly below the belt. It has the muscles of a prize fighter, knifelike claws 3,5 cm long on its front feet, sharp teeth, and a tough, loose skin that enables it to turn around and bite, even when the attacker has it by the scruff of its neck. There are recorded cases of honey badgers tearing out the testicles of buffalo, wildebeest and waterbuck in bushveld confrontations.

This creature's pair of anal glands can emit a profuse, unpleasant secretion, though they are most often used to mark out territory than in combat. Yet another item of the animal's defence mechanism is its thick, coarse 'guard hair'. This and the thick skin are invaluable when the honey badger invades a beehive to feed on both the honey and the grubs.

The honey badger has a legendary relationship with a small bird, the honeyguide, which leads it to stores of honey with an excited, chattering display. The bird benefits when the badger breaks open the hive, enabling it to feast on the tasty grubs and wax.

The honey badger's varied diet also includes scorpions, spiders, insects, mice, lizards, frogs and snakes, which it catches under cover of darkness.

Smaller mammals

Cape clawless otter
Groototter *(Aonyx capensis)*

Size: Length (including tail) 1,1-1,6 m; weight 10-18 kg.
Colour: Light greyish brown to very dark brown, with a silvery sheen. Cheeks, snout, throat and chest are white, and the ears have a whitish edge.
Most like: The spotted-necked otter, which is the only other species of otter in southern Africa. The Cape clawless otter is longer, very much heavier, and lacks the obvious neck spots of its cousin.
Habitat: Grassland, scrub or forest near rivers, streams, lakes, swamps, dams and marine estuaries. Also rock pools along certain parts of the coast.

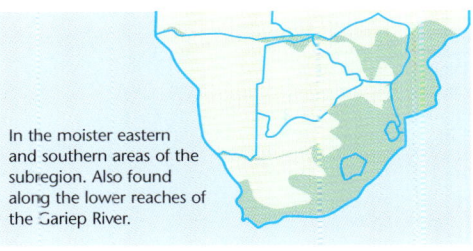

In the moister eastern and southern areas of the subregion. Also found along the lower reaches of the Gariep River.

Cape clawless otters have a great sense of fun. In play they chase one another, indulge in mock fights, fool around with sticks and stones, use smooth rocks as water slides into a pool, and generally frolic about in the water. On land they enjoy sunbathing, sprawling flat on their backs or in some other abandoned position. But to see them off-guard is a privilege, for they are timid, retiring animals.

They are active mostly during the day and, although fond of water, they spend more time out of it than the spotted-necked otter does, lolloping across the countryside in search of new places to feed. They have a taste for crabs and frogs, and less commonly eat fish. The hard shells of the crabs are crushed with their strong cheek teeth, and everything, shell and all, is consumed. These otters also eat birds and insects.

An otter's den is known as a 'holt'. This resting place may be a reed bed, a gully or a hole in the ground adjacent to water. Here the young are born, two or three at a time, and are soon taught by their parents how to swim.

Although they are excellent swimmers, Cape clawless otters have feet that are only marginally webbed. The long tail is flat underneath, and the otter uses it rather like a paddle to propel itself forward.

Spotted-necked otter
Kleinotter *(Lutra maculicollis)*

Size: Length (including tail) 1 m; weight 3-5 kg.
Colour: From rich reddish brown to chocolate brown; throat and upper chest creamy buff, and conspicuously mottled with brown spots.
Most like: The considerably larger Cape clawless otter, but the spotted-necked otter lacks the clawless species' pure white throat and chest, and has well-developed webs between the digits of the feet.
Habitat: Immediate neighbourhood of rivers, lakes and swamps, whether on level ground or in mountains. Numbers are reduced, possibly because of erosion, and this species is considered vulnerable.

Patchy distribution in the Caprivi Strip, the Okavango Swamps, the wetter areas of northern and southern Mozambique, Northern Province, Mpumalanga, Free State, Lesotho, KwaZulu-Natal and the Eastern Cape.

Slender and streamlined, the spotted-necked otter has fully webbed feet and is beautifully equipped in every way for the watery lifestyle in which it revels. The short, sharp claws on its feet are useful for catching fish, which play a more prominent part in its bill of fare than in the Cape clawless otter's. The spotted-necked otter, however, also enjoys eating crabs and frogs, as well as birds and insects.

In the water its dreaded enemy is the crocodile. Ashore one of its principal enemies is man: the otter's dense, soft, rich-coloured hair, which has a lovely sheen, is greatly coveted in the fur trade, where it has considerable value.

This otter seldom strays far from water. And with good reason. On land it is as clumsy as a grounded albatross; in addition it is apt to suffer from the heat. It does, however, emerge from the water to urinate and defecate, and to bask on nearby rocks, where mutual and individual grooming takes place. Shelters (known as 'holts') and breeding places are also near water.

Although otters occur in groups of up to six, they are usually seen alone or as a trio of mother and two young. The best time to catch a glimpse of a spotted-necked otter is in the early morning or at twilight, when it tends to be most active. The male is much heavier and more muscular than the female.

Smaller mammals

African wild cat
Vaalboskat *(Felis sylvestris lybica)*

Size: Length (including the tail) 85 cm-1,0 m; average weight 2,5-6,0 kg.

Colour: Sandy or light grey in drier, western part of sub-continent, ranging to a much darker grey elsewhere, with lighter underparts. Body markings, which are reddish to grey-black, sometimes include a slightly darker spinal stripe; there are always six vertical dark bands on the flanks, as well as horizontal dark bands on the legs, and rings on the tail, which has a black tip.

Most like: The small spotted cat. The African wild cat, however, is bigger, longer-legged and less stocky than the small spotted cat with less-pronounced body markings, and stripes rather than spots.

Habitat: Semi-desert to forest, and from sea level up to about 1 600 m. Cover includes rocks, bushes, tall grasses, crops and disused aardvark burrows.

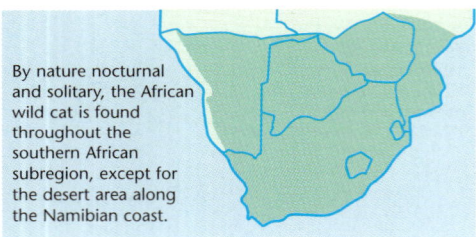

By nature nocturnal and solitary, the African wild cat is found throughout the southern African subregion, except for the desert area along the Namibian coast.

Small spotted cat
Swartpootkat *(Felis nigripes)*

Size: Length (including tail) 50-63 cm; average weight 1,0-2,0 kg.

Colour: Fawn in the northern part of its range, shading to a reddish fawn in the south, with a pattern of dark spots and bands ranging from reddish brown (in the north) to black (in the south), more clearly defined in the southern specimens. The underparts are whitish, the legs horizontally banded, the tail black-tipped.

Most like: The African wild cat, but smaller and with more distinct markings. The backs of the ears are fawn or dark fawn but never rufous like the African wild cat's.

Habitat: Dry, open country with scrub bush or grasses for cover. A water source is not essential.

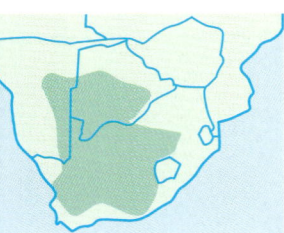

In the dry, open scrubland areas of southeastern Namibia, central and southern Botswana, the North-West, Free State, Northern Cape and the northern reaches of the Western and Eastern Cape.

Larger than a household cat—its legs are proportionally longer—the African wild cat is almost certainly an ancestor of the European domestic cat: in Egypt, where this species is also found, it was tamed for domestic use from as early as 3000 BC. Given an opportunity in the wild, it will interbreed readily with its domestic cousin; indeed in the vicinity of areas of human settlement, pure-bred African wild cats are no longer very easy to find.

They are, in any case, elusive, being shy and mostly nocturnal. The general resemblance to an outsize tabby is strong, except for the African wild cat's longer legs, relatively shorter tail and distinct gait. Also, the backs of the ears are rufous (not the tabby's dark grey).

The African wild cat has typically feline habits: it scales trees with ease, has a predilection for mice and small birds, stalks its prey before pouncing, licks its fur into shape, washes its face with its forepaws, and sharpens its claws on tree trunks. Vocally, too, its repertoire is the same as the domestic cat's, only louder: it mews, purrs, hisses and spits with great gusto.

Pouncing on its prey, the small spotted cat, known also as the black-footed cat, delivers the *coup de grâce* with a bite to the neck, its sharp, bladelike canine teeth severing the spinal column. Stories of the animal killing baby lambs by this means are almost certainly apocryphal, however. Its diet is confined to much smaller mammals such as mice and gerbils, as well as lizards, spiders, insects and birds. Occasionally it eats fresh grass, but perhaps only 'medicinally', in the same way that a domestic cat does.

The small spotted cat is a nocturnal animal, secretive and seldom seen. In daylight hours it retreats to the shelter of bushes or tall grass or, alternatively, to the disused burrow of the aardvark or springhare. It also favours holes in termite mounds, hence the Afrikaans name *miershooptier* ('ant hill tiger') used in the Eastern Cape.

When seen in the wild, the small spotted cat is almost invariably solitary—the original, perhaps, of Kipling's *The Cat that Walked by Himself*—and if caught in a car's headlamps it slinks off to find cover, where it remains well hidden until danger is past. Cornered, it proves ill-tempered and aggressive.

After a gestation period of just over two months, female small spotted cats give birth to one to three kittens during summer.

Smaller mammals

LARGE-SPOTTED GENET
Rooikolmuskejaatkat *(Genetta tigrina)*

Size: Length (including tail) 85 cm-1,1 m; average weight 1,5-3,2 kg.

Colour: Upperparts range from pale grey through yellow to light russet. Along the spine is a dark brown stripe and, on either side of it, rows of large, elongated spots that may be reddish or a much darker rusty brown. The long, whitish tail has about eight dark rings the same colour as the spots, and a broad, black tip. The face is strongly patterned with a whitish chin and whitish bands running from forehead to inner side of each eye.

Most like: The small-spotted genet, which is very similar in size. The large-spotted species has shorter, softer hair, its spots usually being bigger, fewer and more elongated; and the tip of its tail is black, not white. Small-spotted genet has bolder markings on face.

Habitat: Well-watered country, especially in the vicinity of rivers. Favours the cover of high grass, reeds, bushes and trees.

In the well-watered areas of the Caprivi Strip, northern Botswana, Zimbabwe, Mozambique, Northern Province, eastern North-West, Mpumalanga, Swaziland, KwaZulu-Natal, and coastal Eastern and southwestern Cape.

SMALL-SPOTTED GENET
Kleinkolmuskejaatkat *(Genetta genetta)*

Size: Length (including tail) 86 cm-1,0 m; average weight 1,5-2,6 kg.

Colour: Whitish or brownish grey underparts, with a pronounced dark brown spinal stripe and, on either side, smallish, dark brown or blackish spots arranged in rows. The tail has about eight dark rings and usually a white tip. The strongly patterned face has a black chin.

Most like: The large-spotted genet. The small-spotted species, however, raises the hairs of its dark spinal stripe in a prominent crest when it is frightened. Other distinguishing features include the black (not white) chin, bolder facial markings, the white (not black) tip to the tail and the coarse long hair.

Habitat: Open, arid terrain where there is adequate ground cover. Also in well-watered woodland.

Throughout the subregion, except for the Namib Desert, northern and eastern Zimbabwe, northern and coastal Mozambique, KwaZulu-Natal and the Transkei region of Eastern Cape.

The large-spotted, or rusty-spotted, genet has the ability of a cat, indeed, of a squirrel—it easily scales trees when hunting for food or when being pursued, and it may leap from one tree to another across a distance of up to four metres.

Mainly nocturnal in habit, the large-spotted genet holes up during the day in a hollow tree or log, among roots and debris, among rocks, or in the disused burrow of an aardvark or springhare.

Its diet includes insects and rodents (mice and rats), and wild fruit which it often eats in trees. You'd be lucky to spot a large-spotted genet in a tree, as it invariably seeks the shelter of the clumps of foliage, where it will rest in the forks of branches. It is frequently seen near rivers, dams and lakes.

The large-spotted genet's normal gait is more of a slink than a walk, with the head held low. To gain a better look at the surrounding countryside it sometimes sits down in a 'begging' position, its outstretched tail providing balance. If alarmed, it bounds away towards cover.

Two to four young are born in the summer after a gestation period of almost two and a half months.

Tamed by the ancient Egyptians as household pets to kill rodents, these tigerish little animals (unlike large-spotted genets) are found not only in sub-Saharan Africa, but along the north coast of the continent and in Europe. Although popular as pets, they were not regarded as sacred as the large grey mongoose was.

To poultry farmers in southern Africa they are certainly far from sacred, for they can squeeze through the narrowest fault in a fowl run's wire netting, killing far more birds than they can consume. Poultry are at risk unless the run is covered with mesh, for this genet is an adept climber.

The habits of the small-spotted genet are similar to those of its large-spotted cousin. It is nocturnal, scales trees, uses tree-holes, undergrowth or disused burrows as shelter in the day, and likes to eat insects, mice and rats, geckos, frogs, snakes and scorpions. It stalks its prey like a cat. In defence it will arch its back, and the crest of hair down the spine will bristle. At the same time it will emit an unpleasant odour from a secretion in its anal glands.

Two to four young are born during the summer months, usually in the mother's daytime shelter.

Smaller mammals

THICK-TAILED BUSHBABY
Bosnagaap (*Galago crassicaudatus*)

Size: Length (including tail) 70-80 cm; weight 1,0-1,5 kg.
Colour: Grey, tinged with brown; bushy tail usually lighter than body; upper surfaces of feet somewhat darker. Throat and belly are lighter grey.
Most like: The Southern lesser bushbaby, but more than twice as large and eight times heavier; it has a more pointed face and a longer, bushier tail.
Habitat: Forests and woodlands, including eucalyptus and other plantations, from sea level up to 1 800 m.

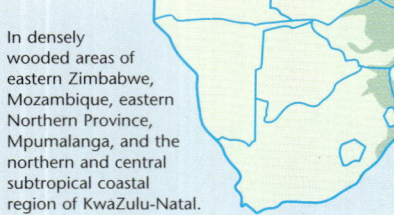

In densely wooded areas of eastern Zimbabwe, Mozambique, eastern Northern Province, Mpumalanga, and the northern and central subtropical coastal region of KwaZulu-Natal.

SOUTHERN LESSER BUSHBABY
Nagapie (*Galago moholi*)

Size: Length (including tail) 30-40 cm; average weight 150 g.
Colour: Grey to grey-brown, with the underparts whitish grey. The forehead is brindled white, the muzzle is white, and there are dark circles around the hazel-brown eyes.
Most like: The thick-tailed bushbaby, but half the size. The lesser bushbaby's tail fluffs out a little towards the tip.
Habitat: Bushveld, in association with acacia, mopane trees and riverine woodland. On the outskirts of forests but not within them.

In forested areas of northern Namibia, northern and eastern Botswana, Zimbabwe, central Mozambique, Northern Province, eastern North-West, Mpumalanga, northern Swaziland and northern KwaZulu-Natal.

Sight, scent and hearing are all well developed in this agile, tree-loving animal, for whom a leap in the dark from branch to branch holds no terrors. Its acute sense of smell is useful for distinguishing tracks and territorial boundaries (marked with a secretion from glands in the middle of the chest). Good hearing not only helps warn this bushbaby of approaching owls and other predators; it also assists the creature to detect the delicate sounds of its own animal prey: reptiles, insects and small birds. The thick-tailed bushbaby's menu, however, is mostly vegetarian and includes fruits, nuts, leaves and the gum of certain trees, especially acacias.

Before setting out at night, bushbabies scrupulously groom themselves, using their lower front teeth for combing, their long thin tongue for preening, and the claw on the second digit of each hindfoot for scratching. Like its cousin, the lesser bushbaby, it 'washes' the soles of its forefeet and hindfeet with urine, a gesture performed to assist it in marking its territory, and to make the feet more adhesive for tree-climbing purposes.

The bushbaby's contact call—a harsh and repetitive wail—somewhat resembles the squalling of a baby in a tantrum. It is this sound that gives the bushbaby its name. In the daytime the bushbaby rests among thick foliage high above the ground—a habit that makes it vulnerable to fires.

With its huge eyes and soft, furry body the lesser bushbaby is an undoubted charmer—a delicate little mammal about the size of a squirrel, whose spectacular leaps it can easily match. Like its close relative the thick-tailed bushbaby, it is strictly nocturnal and spends some time grooming before embarking on the night's activities. But it is much more lively than the thick-tailed bushbaby, and even more confined to its arboreal habitat. It loves foraging in acacias: the gum from these trees is a major item in its diet and is either licked or chewed. It also eats insects, scorpions and small reptiles.

If a convenient tree hole is unavailable, the lesser bushbaby will make itself a flat, treetop nest or appropriate a disused bird's nest. Its sleeping position is the picture of symmetry: ears folded back, forefeet covering the head, and tail curling over the body. When several lesser bushbabies share a nest, they lie at all angles, some upside down, in apparent comfort. They sleep soundly, and take a moment or two to 'come to' when woken. Surprised in this state they can easily be captured.

Like the larger species of bushbaby, the *nagapie* wets the soles of its feet with urine. This helps it mark out its territory—an activity most common among the dominant males. 'Urine-washing' as it is called, is also part of the mating routine.

Females may have two litters a year (in early and late summer), giving birth to one or two young, each weighing a mere nine grams.

Smaller mammals

Ground squirrel

Waaierstertgrondeekhoring *(Xerus inauris)*

Size: *Length (including tail) 40-50 cm; average weight 650 g.*
Colour: *Sandy brown. Underparts and lower legs white; eyes ringed with white; lateral white stripe runs the length of each flank. The bushy tail is a combination of black and white.*
Most like: *The mountain ground squirrel of Namibia and southern Angola, which is virtually identical to the ground squirrel, but lives under rocks, not in burrows.*
Habitat: *Arid, open country, where the soil is sufficiently firm to make burrowing possible.*

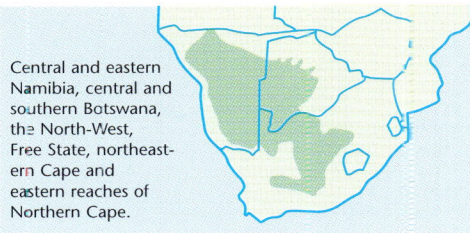

Central and eastern Namibia, central and southern Botswana, the North-West, Free State, northeastern Cape and eastern reaches of Northern Cape.

Grey squirrel

Gryseekhoring *(Sciurus carolinensis)*

Size: *Length (including tail) 50 cm; weight 550-600 g.*
Colour: *Silvery grey, with a sandy coloured dorsal stripe. Tail is a darker grey. The underparts, including underside of tail, are whitish, and the eyes are ringed with white. The upper surfaces of the feet are rufous.*
Most like: *The tree squirrel, but separated geographically, occurring only in the southwestern Cape, while the tree squirrel is found no further south than the savanna woodland of the North-West.*
Habitat: *Oak trees and plantations or stands of various introduced pine, which provide the grey squirrel's staple food. A nearby water source is essential.*

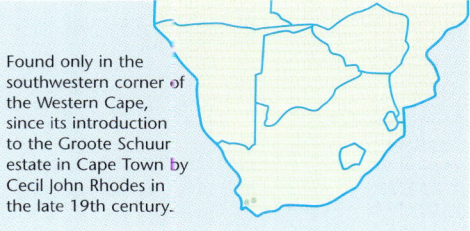

Found only in the southwestern corner of the Western Cape, since its introduction to the Groote Schuur estate in Cape Town by Cecil John Rhodes in the late 19th century.

This resourceful and speedy little creature, known also as the Cape ground squirrel, does not use its tail as a fan (*waaier*), as the Afrikaans name suggests. In fact, the tail serves as a sunshade, held in a bent position over the back when the squirrel is feeding. To signal a warning alarm to the rest of the pack, the squirrel will move its tail up and down and give a long, drawn-out whine.

The ground squirrel confines its activities to the ground (it is a poor climber) and to the daytime. Colonies numbering up to 30 live in a complicated network of interconnecting burrows, often betrayed by a low mound of soil raised by excavations from the warren. Quite often the warren is shared with suricates and yellow mongooses—amicably for the most part, although mongooses have the nasty habit of killing and eating old ground squirrels.

They sunbathe with their bellies to the ground and all four legs stretched out. They 'dustbathe' in the same way, every now and then scratching the sand all over their bodies and then shaking it off.

The social organization of ground squirrels is a feminist's fantasy: small colonies consist of females and their offspring, with the dominant female defending the territory against intruders. Males are accepted into this society only when a female is on heat.

One to three naked young are born after a gestation period of some 45 days. They first emerge from the burrow at the age of six weeks.

In the winter, when it has white fur tufts at the ear tips, a bushier tail and a dense, silver-grey coat, the grey squirrel looks very spruce. But in summer the ear tufts disappear, the coat and tail thin out, and the cute and cuddly Squirrel Nutkin of story-time begins to look rather rattish.

Although the grey squirrel lives chiefly on acorns, pine kernels and other seeds, it will take to more perishable items such as vegetables and deciduous fruits, garden plants and grain crops when the squirrel population explodes and its staple foods are in short supply.

The species is actually a native of North America. Introduced to the south of England in 1876, it is ousting the attractive native British red squirrel. Cecil John Rhodes brought it to the Western Cape at about the same time, releasing specimens on his Groote Schuur estate. Within 20 years grey squirrels had overrun the Peninsula.

It is most active in the early morning and late afternoon, resting in the heat of the day. A squirrel's shelter is called a 'drey'—sometimes a tree-hole, more usually a nest of twigs and leaves built high above the ground in the branches of an oak, pine, bluegum or other tree.

Smaller mammals

TREE SQUIRREL

Boomeekhoring *(Paraxerus cepapi)*

Size: Length (including tail) 35 cm; weight 100-260 g.
Colour: Grizzled coloration varying from pale grey to yellowish grey and rusty grey; upper limbs somewhat more rusty than body. Underparts white, off-white or buffy, and eyes circled by white. Tail flecked with black.
Most like: The ground squirrel, but is always found in association with savanna woodland, and not with open, arid terrain. Lacks ground squirrel's white side-stripe.
Habitat: Savanna woodland, where the trunks and branches of trees offer plentiful holes for shelter.

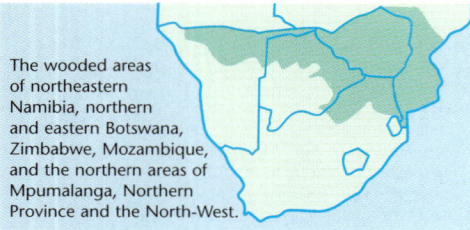

The wooded areas of northeastern Namibia, northern and eastern Botswana, Zimbabwe, Mozambique, and the northern areas of Mpumalanga, Northern Province and the North-West.

A conspicuous feature of tree squirrels' behaviour is 'mobbing', which they sometimes resort to when a predator approaches. All the members of the colony make harsh clicking sounds while flicking their tails. (They sit at a safe distance, of course.) Gradually the mobbers' vocalizing gains momentum and rises to a rattle, as they swish their tails more vigorously in an impressive display of fury.

Alone, a tree squirrel relies on its wits when in danger, always keeping a branch or trunk of a tree between it and the enemy.

Despite its name, this species, also known as the bush squirrel, regularly forages on the ground, looking for roots, grasses and insects such as ants. On open terrain the squirrel is always on the alert—if alarmed, it will flee with great speed, making for the nearest tree where it will lie motionless, flattening itself against a branch.

Home is a hollow tree upholstered with leaves and grass. Here the young are born and, like bird nestlings, remain until they are strong enough to brave the outside world—about three weeks.

Tree squirrels are diurnal. In common with other squirrel species they are also diligent in their grooming. Like purposeful nannies, a mother tree squirrel will hold her offspring down with her forelegs while grooming the little animal with licks, nibbles and her claws.

WOODLAND DORMOUSE

Boswaaierstertmuis *(Graphiurus murinus)*

Size: Length (including tail) 17 cm; weight 28 g.
Colour: Grey to buff-grey, with the underparts lighter to whitish. Lower face, chin and feet are all white or grey-white, and there are slightly darker patches under the eyes. The bushy tail is brownish grey and white-tipped.
Most like: The rock dormouse, but slightly smaller and not found in the rocky habitat favoured by this species. The facial markings of the woodland dormouse are less distinct.
Habitat: Wooded areas, where tree trunks offer holes for shelter in the daytime.

Forests of Namibia, Botswana, Zimbabwe, Mozambique, Swaziland, KwaZulu-Natal, Mpumalanga, Northern Province, Gauteng, the eastern North-West, Free State, Lesotho, Eastern Cape and southern Cape coast.

The woodland dormouse is a swift and sprightly little creature—notwithstanding the storybook image of dormice as incurably lethargic, always apt to fall asleep at a Mad Hatter's tea party. Its ideal refuge is a tree hollow or crevice beneath the bark. But it will settle for just about anything else, including a bird's nest or even a vacant spider's nest. This adopted home will be lined with grasses, feathers and other soft material.

In built-up areas it may shelter under the roof of a house or in an outbuilding, and has been known to appropriate a transformer switch-box, causing a short circuit in the electrical supply.

A unique characteristic of the woodland dormouse is its ability to partially regrow a second tail if it has lost the original one, perhaps in an encounter with an enemy. If only the tip has been severed, a brush of hair grows in its place.

The animal is nocturnal. It is as at home among trees and bushes as it is on the ground, where rocks and debris provide cover. It has a taste for plants and insects, the latter including termites, earwigs and dead bees. Sometimes it may eat eggs and nestlings too.

Little is known about the reproduction of the woodland dormouse, but it appears that litters are born in summer.

Smaller mammals

COMMON VLEI RAT

Vleirot *(Otomys irroratus)*

Size: Length (including the tail) 24 cm; weight (m) 120 g, (f) 115 g.

Colour: A brindled, dark slate-grey body tinged with buff, the flanks, cheeks and underparts being lighter. The upper surface of the tail is dark brown, the under surface buff.

Most like: The five other species of vlei rats in southern Africa. They are best distinguished by habitat preferences and distribution range. The common vlei rat, however, is the most widespread.

Habitat: Lush vegetation growing in the damp soil alongside vleis, swamps, rivers and streams. Also on green hillsides near water.

A small population in eastern Zimbabwe, but mainly found in central Northern Province, the southern North-West, Gauteng, western Mpumalanga, Free State, KwaZulu-Natal, Lesotho, Eastern and Western Cape.

A squat, blunt-muzzled rat with long, shaggy hair and rather a short tail, the common vlei rat, or swamp rat, seldom actually takes to the water unless it is retreating from a predator—when it may dive in precipitately. Owls, eagles, snakes and small carnivores prey on this species.

Sometimes the common vlei rat takes over the burrow of another species (it does not dig its own) but usually it builds a saucer-shaped nest above the high-water level on the banks of streams or rivers, or on the edges of swamplands. Clearly defined runs lead from the nest to the rat's grazing areas; these are marked by piles of chopped grass stems. It feeds by biting through the stem near the base, taking the stem in its mouth and then, like a person tackling a mealie, grasping each end of the stem with one paw before removing and chewing short lengths. It does this sitting upright on its haunches.

There is another eating habit for which the common vlei rat is unlikely to receive an award for etiquette: it eats fresh faeces, that of its colleagues and also its own. This habit supplies newly weaned rats, in particular, with the right bacteria for digesting their food.

The species is most active during the day, and is most often seen either singly or in pairs. Some rural communities regard the common vlei rat as a delicacy for the roasting pot, and lay traps for it.

A litter of one to four young is born at a time (the female may have up to seven litters in a season). The newborn are covered with soft black fur.

BUSHVELD GERBIL

Bosveldnagmuis *(Tatera leucogaster)*

Size: Length 28 cm; weight 70 g.

Colour: Bright and silky, varying from buff to reddish brown; paler in the drier, western parts of southern Africa. Sides of face, chin, throat, remaining underparts and feet all white, and there is a small white patch on the forehead. Dark stripe along upper surface of tail; ears dark brown.

Most like: The Cape gerbil and the Highveld gerbil, but neither of these species has a dark stripe along the upper surface of the tail. Tail-tip never white, unlike some other gerbil species.

Habitat: Mostly in areas of sandy soil suitable for burrowing, with favoured vegetation ranging from open grassland to woodland.

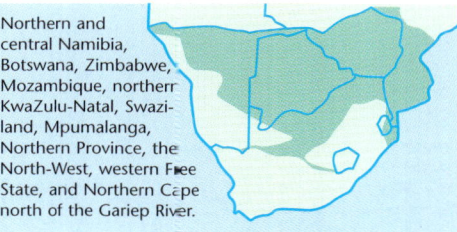

Northern and central Namibia, Botswana, Zimbabwe, Mozambique, northern KwaZulu-Natal, Swaziland, Mpumalanga, Northern Province, the North-West, western Free State, and Northern Cape north of the Gariep River.

You could mistake this rodent for a large mouse, except that its back legs are much longer than its front ones—a 'kangaroolike' construction that enables it to perform impressive leaps.

The typical burrow of a bushveld gerbil has its entrance at the base of a shrub or clump of grass. Each morning you will see a fresh mound of soil at the entrance, for the gerbil conscientiously cleans out its home nightly (it is a nocturnal animal). Warrens consisting of interconnecting burrows have resting chambers lined with vegetable debris. Where the soil is too hard for digging, the gerbil settles in the hole of a termite mound, a crevice among tree roots, or some other natural shelter.

This rodent feeds on the seeds of grasses and other vegetation, and on small bulbs. It also has a taste for insects, including termites.

Like the other *Tatera* gerbils, this species is medically significant as it is one of the rodents which acts as a reservoir of the bubonic plague bacillus. Largely through its presence the disease has spread into the interior of South Africa from ports on the coast. If a colony of bushveld gerbils is infected, the danger to man is at its greatest when the gerbil population suddenly explodes.

Litters of up to nine young are born in the burrows at all times of the year.

Smaller mammals

ROCK ELEPHANT-SHREW

Klipklaasneus *(Elephantulus myurus)*

Size: Length (including tail) 26 cm; weight 60 g.
Colour: Buff-grey body, with flanks a paler grey and underparts white. The eyes are ringed with white. The ears are brown, fringed with white. Reddish brown to brown patches at base of ears.
Most like: The other five species of the genus Elephantulus which are found in southern Africa; all of them are difficult to tell apart.
Habitat: Rocky hillsides and koppies, where crevices exist for shelter; also on flat ground, but in the immediate vicinity of rocky outcrops.

In eastern Botswana, central and eastern Zimbabwe, western Mozambique, Northern Province, the North-West, Gauteng, Mpumalanga, Swaziland, western KwaZulu-Natal, Free State, Lesotho and adjoining Eastern Cape.

The elephant-shrews (there are several species, all confined to Africa) derive their name from the trunklike snout with which the muzzle ends. When the rock elephant-shrew vocalizes, it curls its snout over the top of the muzzle, opens its mouth wide and, with the head held high, emits a sequence of high-pitched squeaks.

At the end of the snout are sensitive nostrils, and the senses of smell, hearing and sight are all acute. Faced with this battery of equipment the elephant-shrew's insect prey hasn't a hope. From the shady cover of a rock or shrub the rock elephant-shrew darts out like a flash of lightning to pounce on its chosen victim and, if the insect is a large one, the shrew then carries it back to the shade to enjoy an unhurried meal.

The species is mostly active by day, particularly in the warmer hours. Normally they travel on all fours, but at speed they leap on their hindlegs.

Shelter is a hole or crevice in a rock. A rocky overhang, or overhanging vegetation, hides the shelter from the attentions of the smaller birds of prey which are among this elephant-shrew's enemies. Sitting motionless on a shaded rock, the animal is well camouflaged and may be mistaken for a stone—its only giveaway being a twitching of the snout and ears.

The natural lifespan of the rock elephant-shrew is only about 13 months, although some elephant-shrews reach the ripe old age of 19 months.

FOREST SHREW

Bosskeerbek *(Myosorex varius)*

Size: Length (including tail) 12 cm; weight 12-16 g.
Colour: Dark grey, with a grizzled fawn or yellow tinge. Underparts light grey, with the same tinge. The tail has a dark brown stripe on top. The feet are light grey.
Most like: Dark-footed forest shrew (Mysorex cafer), which can be distinguished by its dark feet, light brown underparts and uniformly dark brown tail.
Habitat: In dense vegetation associated with moisture (whether along rivers and streams or, in drier areas, with frequent mists).

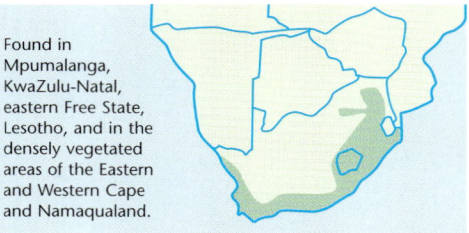

Found in Mpumalanga, KwaZulu-Natal, eastern Free State, Lesotho, and in the densely vegetated areas of the Eastern and Western Cape and Namaqualand.

The forest shrew is one of the more widely distributed of the 18 species of shrew found in southern Africa. It is also one of the most aggressive of these little animals with their tiny eyes and long, pointed snouts. However, the forest shrew is not commonly encountered: firstly, because it prefers dense grass or thick bush and secondly, because it is more active by night than by day.

It is a burrower, though not a very determined one. With its front claws and snout it is content to dig a shallow tunnel under a rock. This tunnel forms part of its nest, which it constructs with soft grass and lines with vegetable debris. Instead of excavating its own tunnel, the forest shrew may be quite content to appropriate the disused burrow of a molerat.

During the day it spends much of its time lying in its nest, venturing out for a few minutes at a time to look for food or to defecate. At night these sorties away from the safety of the nest last an hour or two.

Like all members of the shrew family (Soricidae), forest shrews are essentially insectivorous but, in addition to locusts, grasshoppers, beetles, termites and other insects, they also eat earthworms, snails and slugs. Smaller insects are killed by beheading, but larger prey have their legs twisted off before being devoured. They will also eat their own kind, as well as dead rodents.

When alarmed or fighting a forest shrew utters a sharp little squeak.

The female gives birth to two to four infants during summer, and a nesting pair of forest-shrew parents will chatter intimately to each other as they go about their chores.

Smaller mammals

STRIPED MOUSE
Streepmuis *(Rhabdomys pumilio)*

Size: *Length (including tail) 18-21 cm; weight 30-55 g.*
Colour: *Varies from pale, brindled reddish brown (in the drier, western regions) to dark, brindled greyish buff (in the east). Two distinctive pairs of reddish brown to black stripes run from the back of the neck to the base of the tail. Underparts are white or whitish.*
Most like: *Single-striped mouse, but the four dark stripes along the back of striped mouse are distinctive.*
Habitat: *Wherever there is grass cover, from sea level up to over 1 800 m. Also in dry scrub and savanna woodland.*

Namibia, southern Botswana (with a population around Lake Ngami), Zimbabwe, Northern Province, the North-West, Gauteng, western Mpumalanga, KwaZulu-Natal, Free State, Lesotho, Eastern, Western and Northern Cape.

Unwittingly, the striped mouse acts as an amazing matchmaker for certain species of protea in the southwestern Cape's floral kingdom as it feeds on the succulent bracts and styles on the low-level blooms of some proteas, their pollen clings to its head. Then, when the mouse moves off to feed on other neighbouring flowers of the same species, it carries the pollen with it, thus assisting in the fertilization of these flowers.

Striped mice are predominantly grass-eaters, but they enjoy a wide variety of other vegetable matter and insects too. In captivity they exhibit a more gruesome taste—they eat deceased companions.

In the wild their home is a burrow excavated at the base of a grass thicket, the entrance being well hidden. Like other small burrowing mammals, they line the chambers of their burrows with soft, leafy debris. Alternatively, they construct a ground-level nest, out of sight under cover of dense stands of tall grass.

They forage by day, in the early morning and late afternoon, and can often be seen among the tall grasses growing on the perimeter of cultivated land.

In central Africa, where striped mice are also found, they breed throughout the year, but in the south the breeding season is usually confined to the summer months: September to May. Litters of two to nine are born at a time.

MULTIMAMMATE MOUSE
Vaalveldmuis *(Mastomys coucha)*

Size: *Length (including tail) 24 cm; weight 60-65 g.*
Colour: *Varies from light to dark buffy yellow, the flanks being lighter than the back, and the underparts grey. The upper surfaces of the feet are whitish. In adult females each of the mammae is ringed by white-tipped hairs.*
Most like: *House mouse but larger. The size and extraordinary number of mammae or breasts in the female distinguish the species.*
Habitat: *A wide range of terrain, though not in forests or in the dry west, except in association with rivers.*

In northern Namibia, northern Botswana, Zimbabwe, Mozambique, KwaZulu-Natal, Swaziland, Mpumalanga, Gauteng, Northern Province, North-West, Free State, Lesotho, Eastern Cape and along the Gariep River.

This mouse's name is quite a mouthful: however, it simply indicates that the female has many mammae or breasts—up to 12 pairs of them, which is far more than any other mammal can boast, and quite enough to satisfy the hunger of the average litter of six to ten babies.

It is one of the most common mouse species in southern Africa, being in biologists' parlance 'commensal' with man: that is, living in association with man and sheltering in manmade constructions. However, modern houses are less congenial to it than the type of home with a wooden floor (under which to nest), wooden skirtings to gnaw through, and cracks in the building fabric in which to be concealed.

The mice are a familiar sight on agricultural lands and in kraals. In the wild, they make their homes in the shelter of rocks, fallen leaves, or tree roots; or else they dig their own subterranean burrows, lining them with soft debris.

They are nocturnal. Grass seeds, other seeds, wild fruits and insects make up their menu in the natural state, though in built-up areas they eat just about anything, from cheese to bacon rind.

The female may have her young at any time of the year and, if conditions are right, may do so regularly at intervals of 33 days. This frequently results in population explosions of the mouse in some areas, causing destruction to farmlands and the possibility of disease.

Smaller mammals

GREATER CANE RAT

Grootrietrot *(Thryonomys swinderianus)*

Size: *Average length (including tail) 65-80 cm; average weight (m) 4,5 kg, (f) 3,6 kg.*
Colour: *Dark brown, speckled with yellow. Lips, chin and throat white; remaining underparts whitish to greyish brown.*
Most like: *The lesser cane rat, but 15-20 cm longer, and at least twice as heavy.*
Habitat: *Dense, tall grass or reeds, or other thick undergrowth, always close to water.*

The Caprivi Strip, northern Botswana, Zimbabwe, Mozambique, Northern Province, northern Mpumalanga, Swaziland, KwaZulu-Natal and southwards along the Eastern Cape coast.

COMMON MOLERAT

Vaalmol *(Cryptomys hottentotus)*

Size: *Average length 15 cm; average weight (m) 135 g, (f) 120 g.*
Colour: *Ranges from light yellowish brown to dark slate-grey, with underparts lighter. In the northern part of the distribution area there is usually a white patch on the forehead.*
Most like: *The Cape molerat, but the common molerat is smaller and it lacks the Cape species' white snout and throat and white eye- and ear-patches.*
Habitat: *A wide variety of terrains, whether the soil is loose and sandy, or heavier, stony and more compact—though not heavy clay.*

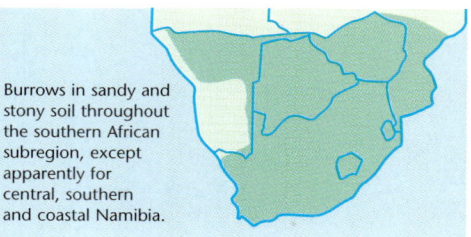

Burrows in sandy and stony soil throughout the southern African subregion, except apparently for central, southern and coastal Namibia.

The greater cane rat, with its powerful, chisel-like incisor teeth, inflicts such damage in sugar cane plantations that farmers go out of their way to protect the python which preys on it.

Among southern African rodents this cane rat is second only in size and mass to the porcupine. Its body is bulky and its head large, while its tail and legs are short; the body hair is rather bristly.

Its name suggests both its habitat and its preferred diet: grasses, rushes, reeds and sugar cane, the stalks of which it bites off at ground level and then cuts up into sections for convenient chewing. The greater cane rat also shows a fondness for cultivated crops such as maize, millet, sweet potatoes, pineapple and groundnuts.

It is mostly a nocturnal animal. From its shelter of flattened reeds or grasses deep within a thicket, well-worn paths lead to foraging sites marked by piles of chopped grass and droppings. Sometimes the journey takes these rats through water.

Alarmed, cane rats give a whistling call and, like rabbits, thump the ground with their hindfeet. They then scurry away, only to 'freeze' a few moments later when they feel they are out of danger.

Pythons, birds of prey, small carnivores and leopards prey on greater cane rats. In some areas, man too hunts them down and savours them as an excellent, protein-rich food; in fact, the greater cane rat appears high on the menus of restaurants in parts of West Africa.

Molerats constitute a family of rodents confined to Africa. Their resemblance to moles is close, both in looks and burrowing habits, but they have formidable projecting incisors that would serve well as a bottle opener. They also have eyes, admittedly functioning very poorly, except in one curious respect: the corneas are very sensitive to air currents. These and the equally sensitive whiskers and bristlelike hairs on the feet alert the molerat when its burrow has been damaged, and the damage is quickly repaired.

Common molerats live in small colonies in burrows which they excavate with their incisors and the long claws of their forefeet. Soil loosened in this process is thrown up in a series of mounds—a great nuisance in gardens and on lawns. After rain, molerats burrow more eagerly than ever, constructing tunnels 15-20 cm below the surface.

Within this labyrinth they build a nesting chamber, and line it with roots and soft vegetable debris. One to five young are born at a time.

Nothing short of flood or famine, or at any rate severe hunger, will drive a molerat from its burrow. In search of a better feeding ground it may travel overland at night, sometimes falling victim to a barn owl.

To the chagrin of many gardeners, its diet consists of fleshy roots and bulbs, which are stored safely in the burrow.

Smaller mammals

Hottentot golden mole

Hottentot gouemol *(Amblysomus hottentotus)*

Size: Length 13 cm; weight 75 g.

Colour: Dark, reddish brown upperparts, with an iridescent bronze sheen, the flanks being a little lighter in colour than the back. Underparts lighter and tinged with grey. Cheeks whitish. White hairs mark the ear openings and the position of the vestigial (rudimentary) eyes.

Most like: Cape golden mole, but Hottentot species is a richer brown. Species are very similar and scientific assistance is needed to differentiate between them.

Habitat: Grassland, with soft, sandy soil in areas of high rainfall; sometimes forest. From sea level up to 3 000 m.

Southern Mozambique, Swaziland, southern Mpumalanga and Northern Province, Gauteng, northeastern Free State, KwaZulu-Natal, northern Lesotho, and along the Eastern and southwestern Cape coast as far west as Cape Town.

Streamlined by nature for its subterranean existence, the Hottentot golden mole survives with surprising cunning and a skill for tunnelling unsurpassed in the animal world. In pushing surplus soil upwards, forming characteristic mounds at regular intervals, the mole never actually breaks the earth's surface. And at the slightest tremor of a footfall or other disturbance it will 'submerge' from the subsurface down to the safer and deeper levels of up to 50 centimetres. At this depth its burrow network may extend in various directions for at least 200 metres.

Golden moles are only distantly related to true moles, which are not found in Africa. The Hottentot species has a compact, cylindrical body, short but sturdy legs, no visible tail, ears represented externally merely by tiny cavities on either side of the head, and no sight.

The rudimentary eyes are entirely covered by fur-covered skin. A horny pad on the nose helps the mole to penetrate through soft soil. Each forepaw has four clawed toes, two of which do the bulk of the digging, the loose earth being pressed back with the hindfeet.

This mole is most at risk after dark when it forages near the surface for earthworms and insects, vegetable matter and snails. When food is scarce it sometimes travels overland in search of new land to colonize—again, at night.

At such moments a hungry owl may swoop down to make a quick killing.

Up to two hairless young are born at a time, in a side tunnel of the burrow system.

Cape golden mole

Kaapse gouemol *(Chrysochloris asiatica)*

Size: Length 11 cm; weight 45 g.

Colour: Dark brown upperparts, with an iridescent bronze-purplish sheen, the underparts being lighter and duller. On either side of the face, buff-coloured bands run from the cheeks to the position of the pale-haired rudimentary eyes.

Most like: Hottentot golden mole, but the face bands are distinctively different, and the Cape species is dark brown rather than reddish brown.

Habitat: Sandy soil, especially cultivated land, including, as every gardener knows, gardens.

Found only in Namaqualand and the southwestern Cape, where sandy soils or ground prepared for cultivation provide ideal conditions for burrowing.

This is the little monster that runs riot just beneath the surface of gardens, loosening seedlings and bulbs in flowerbeds, destroying the immaculate appearance of lawns, and generally upsetting horticultural order.

For many it is little consolation to know that the Cape golden mole (like other moles) performs a service by including garden pests in its diet of insects and worms.

When Swedish botanist Linnaeus first described it in 1758, he recorded it as coming from 'Siberia', and there are western Cape gardeners who dearly wish that Siberia was indeed its natural home.

A raised ridge indicates where a subsurface tunnel has been dug. Where the mole digs deeper, it throws up mounds of fresh earth at intervals. This digging activity is particularly noticeable after rain, when the soil is soft.

The Cape golden mole's leathery snout pad does the preliminary work of 'trail-blazing' and the forepaws, each with three claws of different lengths, then excavate in earnest.

The young of the Cape golden mole are born in winter. In preparation for their arrival the mother lines a special breeding chamber with grasses.

Golden moles are commonly confused with molerats, but are quite unrelated. Molerats are vegetarian rodents and have an obvious pair of incisor teeth at the front of the jaw. Golden moles have small, sharp teeth suitable for an insectivorous diet.

Smaller mammals

Egyptian fruit bat
Egiptiese vrugtevlermuis *(Rousettus aegyptiacus)*

Size: *Length (including tail) 15 cm; wingspan 60 cm; weight 130 g.*

Colour: *Dark brown, in some cases tinged with grey, the underparts being smoky grey. A pale yellow-brown collar circles the throat.*

Most like: *Straw-coloured fruit bat but is smaller, with dark brown, not yellowish, body hair.*

Habitat: *Any terrain offering both tree fruit (wild or cultivated) and caves for daytime shelter.*

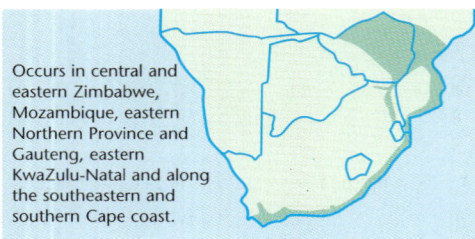

Occurs in central and eastern Zimbabwe, Mozambique, eastern Northern Province and Gauteng, eastern KwaZulu-Natal and along the southeastern and southern Cape coast.

Fruit bats are also known as 'flying foxes'. With their sharp muzzles, large dark eyes and pointed ears, the Egyptian species, like other fruit bats, do look a little foxlike; and they are certainly handsome compared with the Egyptian free-tailed bat or Geoffroy's horseshoe bat.

These bats typically cluster in huge colonies, usually hanging by one foot from the ceiling of a cave, and packing tightly together in the cave's darkest recesses. When they return from their night's foraging just before daybreak, the bats make a great deal of noise as, like a full complement of jumbo jet passengers finding their seats, they jostle for a hanging position in the cave.

The Egyptian fruit bat has extraordinary powers of echolocation which it uses to navigate in darkness. Repeated tongue clicks are bounced back from potential obstacles to their flight path.

Having found a fruit tree, the bats circle it before dispersing to settle on the branches, using their acute sense of smell as well as their eyesight to locate the ripe fruit. Seeds, hard skin and other fibrous matter are discarded; the juicy pulp is either consumed there and then or taken away in special cheek pouches. Wild figs are a favourite fruit, though any pulpy fruit is at the mercy of these creatures, which can devastate a tree in a night.

Peters' epauletted fruit bat
Peters se witkolvrugtevlermuis *(Epomophorus crypturus)*

Size: *Length (including tail) (m) 15 cm, (f) 12 cm; wingspan 56 cm; average weight 80-140 g.*

Colour: *Usually brownish buff, sometimes pale buff or yellowish cream, the underparts being lighter in colour. There are white patches at the base of the ears, and the male has white 'epaulettes' on the shoulders.*

Most like: *Wahlberg's epauletted fruit bat. The only way to separate the two species is to examine their palates. Peters' has two ridges across the palate behind the last molar teeth, while Wahlberg's has only one.*

Habitat: *Evergreen forests and riverine woodland, always in association with fruit-bearing trees.*

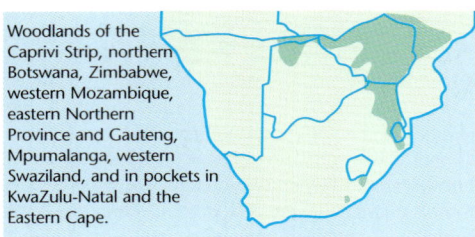

Woodlands of the Caprivi Strip, northern Botswana, Zimbabwe, western Mozambique, eastern Northern Province and Gauteng, Mpumalanga, western Swaziland, and in pockets in KwaZulu-Natal and the Eastern Cape.

Peters' epauletted fruit bats congregate in large colonies and make a great deal of noise together, especially when returning in good spirits after a night's foraging. They hang upside-down from the thinner branches of evergreen trees, whose thick foliage provides cover. As they jockey for position, interfering neighbours are slashed with wings and with the sharp claw at the end of the first digit or thumb on the leading edge of the wing. Eventually they all settle down, slightly spaced out from one another, and silence reigns for the day.

The so-called epaulette on each shoulder of the males is a patch of white hairs covering a sunken glandular pouch. The hairs come into prominence when the pouches are turned outwards—which they do when the animal is under stress, when it vocalizes, and possibly also when it is sexually stimulated.

The male's call is a musical bark, usually uttered as it hangs in its accustomed position.

These bats prefer soft, pulpy fruits. In their raids on cultivated crops, apples and pears will therefore be ignored, but a messy meal is made out of loquats, peaches, figs, guavas and similar juicy fruits.

Smaller mammals

EGYPTIAN FREE-TAILED BAT

Egiptiese losstertvlermuis *(Tadarida aegyptiaca)*

Size: Length (including tail) 11 cm; wingspan up to 30 cm; weight 15 g.
Colour: Dark sooty brown, the underparts being the same colour or a little lighter. Head and neck blackish.
Most like: The other 13 species of free-tailed bat in southern Africa, but lacks the pale neck-yoke present in most other species of free-tailed bats.
Habitat: All types of terrain except forest, although found on the fringes of these.

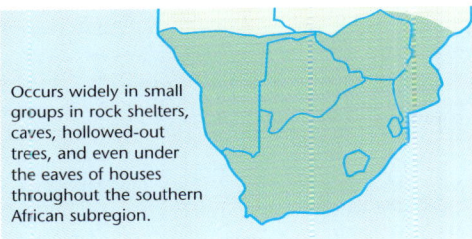

Occurs widely in small groups in rock shelters, caves, hollowed-out trees, and even under the eaves of houses throughout the southern African subregion.

Egyptian free-tailed bats are gregarious, roosting in numbers of up to several hundreds, packing themselves tightly into rock crevices. The caves in which they congregate when resting during the day have an overpowering smell that emanates from their droppings. These bats also shelter in attics and any available crevice in a building.

If this is an unsavoury notion, scientists insist that, despite popular opinion, bats are as clean as cats, regularly grooming themselves.

At night the Egyptian free-tailed bat is primarily a creature of the open spaces, and forages far and wide for insects. It eats nothing else, favouring beetles and other hard-shelled species.

The sonar or echolocation system used by such bats as a navigation tool is far more advanced than anything man has been able to devise. While hunting on the wing, the bat emits anything up to 250 little 'beeps' a second at frequencies usually much higher than the highest tones audible to man. These sounds bounce off surrounding obstacles in their flight path, helping the bat to fly freely.

The female of the species gives birth to a single offspring in the summer, and 'maternity colonies', consisting entirely of females, are sometimes formed.

This bat is also widespread in the Nile Valley and East Africa. It was named after a specimen found in Egypt by the famous French biologist, Geoffroy, who served under Napoleon.

GEOFFROY'S HORSESHOE BAT

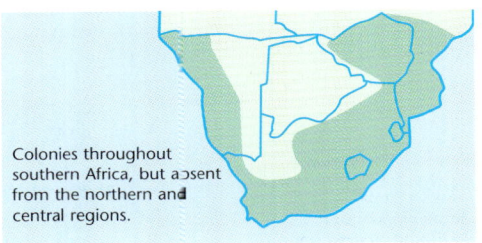

Geoffroy se saalneusvlermuis *(Rhinolophus clivosus)*

Size: Length (including tail) 9,6 cm; wingspan 32 cm; weight (m) 16 g, (f) 17 g.
Colour: Light (and sometimes irregular) brown, with underparts paler.
Most like: The other nine species of horseshoe bat found in southern Africa, but Geoffroy's is one of the larger species.
Habitat: Across a wide range of country, from desert to the fringes of forests, but predominantly savanna woodland. The presence of caves or rock crevices for shelter is essential.

Colonies throughout southern Africa, but absent from the northern and central regions.

In close-up the horseshoe bat is no oil painting, yet the feature that gives the species its name—a delicate, horseshoe-shaped 'leaf' on top of the muzzle—is a remarkable piece of equipment. It forms part of the nostrils and is essential to the highly evolved system of echolocation by which these bats find their way in the dark.

Sounds emitted at a high pitch through the nostrils are amplified, it is thought, by the 'horseshoe', which acts partly as a megaphone, but essentially as a means of focusing the sound into beams that can be swept from side to side like a searchlight. The large, pointed ears then gather the echoes of the nasal signals bounced back from objects in the bat's path, and relay them to the brain for interpretation. Although horseshoe bats can see, it is on this echolocation that they rely on for orientation at night.

Geoffroy's horseshoe bats (named after a French biologist who studied bats in Egypt at the beginning of the 19th century) set out from their caves soon after sunset in search of food, exclusively insects, and return before dawn.

While feeding they hang themselves in rows on tree branches, or maybe from the trelliswork of a verandah. In the hanging position, they wrap their wings around the front of their bodies, but with the tail section folded back over the rump. This forms a channel for rainwater to run down and ensures that the fur stays dry.

Like other bats, Geoffroy's horseshoe bat bears live young, usually singly, which are suckled.

Birds

Bird-watching is one of the fastest-growing recreational pursuits in southern Africa today. With an avian population of more than 900 different species, including seabirds, a fascinating and remarkably varied world of birds awaits discovery virtually at your doorstep. Birds have a special appeal for everyone; they are attractive to look at, their habits are interesting, and their voices are not only delightful to hear, but are useful for identification.

Like mammals, birds are vertebrates: they have a 'back-bone' made up of elements called vertebrae. All birds have feathers (their one unique feature), a toothless beak or bill, and a skeleton which is adapted primarily for flight, even though the power of flight may have been lost in the course of evolution. Even the ancestor of the ostrich once flew, and you can see the legacy of this in the ostrich's skeleton to this day.

The ancestors of birds were lizardlike reptiles that took to the trees, developed grasping hindfeet for holding onto branches, claws on their forelimbs for climbing, and feathers to keep their body heat in. With time these feathers became modified in several ways, not only to insulate the body against the elements and the environment, but later also to provide expanded surfaces for flight (the tail and wing feathers), colours for camouflage, species recognition and display and warning behaviour. The feathers also provided plumes for sexual recognition and to enhance already existing displays.

Undoubtedly, these were truly remarkable products of evolution.

How birds are classified

Of the 900 species of birds in southern Africa three-quarters are resident; the rest consist of breeding migrants that spend winter in tropical Africa (50-60 species), non-breeding migrants from tropical Africa or from Eurasia that visit us only in our summer (about 120 species), and about 70 species that are rare vagrants to the region, having been recorded only once or a very few times.

Birds are classified into families, such as the bustard family (Otididae), the swifts (Apodidae) or the bulbuls (Pycnonotidae), and the families are grouped into orders. Southern Africa has 26 orders of birds, the largest of which is the order Passeriformes, comprising just over 430 species—not quite half of all southern African birds. These are known as the 'passerines'. All other birds are non-passerines.

This is a convenient division, though perhaps not all that simple for the beginner to grasp at first. Put most simply, most tree-dwelling (arboreal) birds are passerine and are to be found in the second half of this section. Most non-passerines, on the other hand, are waterbirds and will be found in the first half of this section.

However, quite a large number of non-passerines are also tree-dwelling, such as doves, parrots, woodhoopoes, bee-eaters and kingfishers, and they are most conveniently called 'near-passerines' because they fall between the obvious non-passerines of the aquatic habitats and the obvious passerines of the arboreal habitats. The birds in these three divisions are shown on the opposite page.

Bird-watching for all

Bird-watching gets people into the great outdoors where they can enjoy clean air, beautiful surroundings and a healthy walk.

Identifying birds is not only pleasurable—it presents enough of a challenge to make any outing exciting and rewarding. Bird-watching, alone or in a group, is fun.

No matter where you are, you can see birds. On top of the Drakensberg, at the seaside, in a Free State mealie field or at your local sewerage works, birds are there, going about their business, freely available for you to appreciate.

Even if you are waiting at an airport for a plane, you can enjoy the sight of house sparrows, Cape sparrows, Cape wagtails and other birds that have adopted man's environment, as they hop or walk about the lawns or tarmac, or look for bread crumbs at a canteen door.

Equipment

You really need only four pieces of equipment to take up watching birds: a good field guide, a pair of binoculars, a pocket notebook and a pen.

Be discriminating when you choose binoculars. The best sizes are 7x35, 8x40 and 10x25. The first number in each case is the magnification, and the second number the diameter in millimetres of the objective (the lens in front, away from your eyes). The objective diameter indicates the size of the field of view and how much light your binoculars let in. The bigger the better. Whether you go for the conventional Porro prism binoculars (named for Italian physicist Ignatio Porro, who invented the prism system used in these binoculars), which are bulky, but cheaper, or the more advanced roof-prism type (more compact and expensive) depends mainly on your pocket. Check out some reputable makes at a good camera shop and choose a pair in your price range that has good definition (a sharp image) and true colour resolution. You can get excellent roof-prism binoculars for under R500.

The notebook and pen are for making lists of the birds you see and notes and diagrams of unknown species before they fly away. Once you have your notes and diagrams, you can go to your field guide at your leisure, without having to worry that the birds will disappear before you can identify them.

An additional tool in your arsenal of equipment is a good set of recordings of bird voices. Several cassette tapes and CDs of southern African bird calls are available—one featuring the calls of more than 500 different species. These recordings are both entertaining and educational.

Listen carefully to the recordings and match the sounds to the descriptions of the individual species in the following pages. This will be especially helpful if you are going bird-watching in a forest or in dense bush, because the birds will be hard to see, yet highly vocal, so you can do most of your identification by sound alone (though it is a good idea to see the bird too, if you are a beginner and not yet fully conversant with bird calls).

It is an exciting challenge in the outdoors to try to get a glimpse of the bird to confirm your initial decision, but it requires a great deal of patience.

Birds

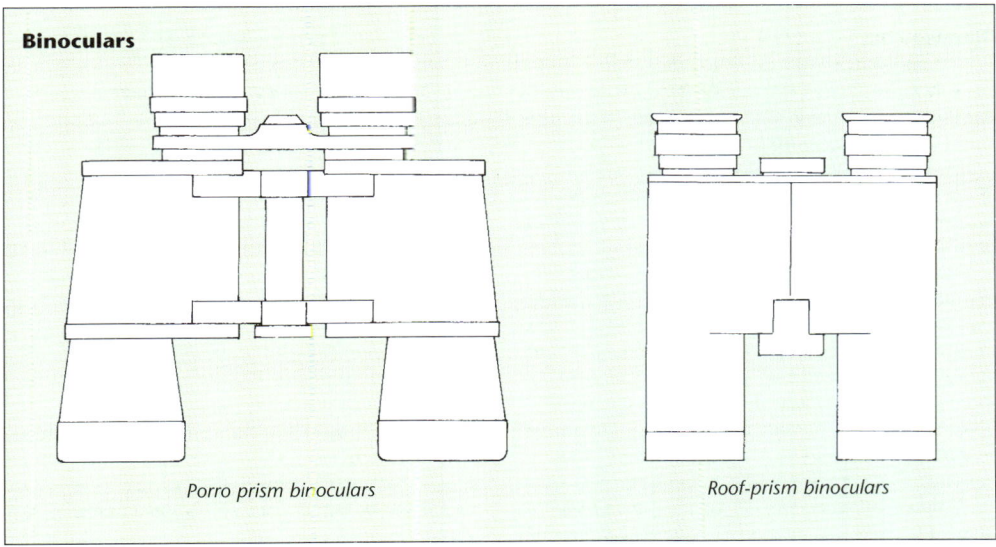

Porro prism binoculars

Roof-prism binoculars

Recordings can also be used in order to lure birds out from their hiding places, but do this judiciously and sparingly, otherwise you may seriously affect the behaviour of the birds. If a bird does not respond to two or three playbacks, then cease trying and move on; once a bird has emerged in response to your recorded playback, don't repeat the performance immediately.

The three major groups of southern African bird families

Non-passerines

Ostriches
Penguins
Grebes
Albatrosses, petrels
Tropicbirds
Pelicans, flamingos
Gannets, boobies, frigatebirds
Cormorants, darters
Herons, egrets, bitterns
Hamerkops
Storks, ibises, spoonbills
Ducks, geese
Secretarybirds
Vultures, diurnal birds of prey
Ospreys
Guineafowl, francolins, quails
Buttonquails
Rails, crakes, moorhens, coots
Finfeet
Cranes
Bustards, korhaans
Jacanas
Painted snipes
Oystercatchers
Plovers, crab plovers
Snipes, sandpipers
Avocets, stilts
Dikkops/thick-knees
Coursers, pratincoles
Gulls, skuas, terns
Skimmers
Sandgrouse

Near-passerines

Doves and pigeons
Parrots
Louries/turacos
Cuckoos, coucals
Owls
Nightjars
Swifts
Mousebirds
Trogons
Kingfishers
Bee-eaters
Rollers
Hoopoes
Woodhoopoes
Hornbills
Barbets
Honeyguides
Woodpeckers
Wrynecks
Sunbirds

Passerines

Broadbills
Pittas
Larks
Swallows
Cuckooshrikes
Drongos
Orioles
Crows, ravens
Tits
Penduline tits
Creepers
Babblers
Bulbuls
Thrushes, robins, chats
Warblers
Flycatchers
Wagtails, pipits, longclaws
Shrikes
Bush shrikes
Helmetshrikes
Starlings
Oxpeckers
Sugarbirds
White-eyes
Weavers, sparrows, bishops,
   widowbirds
Waxbills
Whydahs
Canaries, buntings

Birds

Starting out

The best time of day for bird-watching is early morning, because birds tend to quieten down towards mid-morning and you will see fewer and fewer as the day wears on.

If you are a real beginner, start bird-watching at a place where birds are easy to see and likely to be easy to identify, such as at a dam or pond. Sewage ponds are excellent for this purpose.

Select a comfortable spot from where you can scan the water and let the birds come to you. You can use this technique in any habitat. As a bird appears, watch it carefully through your binoculars and note down any features that look distinctive. Just enjoy the novelty of the new pastime, and don't worry too much about not being able to identify—or incorrectly identifying— the species.

If you know of a local expert, go out birding with him or her; in this way you can learn more quickly about the birds and how to identify them. Finding experts and capitalizing on their knowledge is just one advantage of joining a bird club and going on organized outings with competent leaders. There are, of course, also the fellowship and pleasure of like-minded company.

When you are in the field, move carefully and quietly. Avoid sudden gestures, loud noises (however excited you may get) and brightly coloured clothing, especially white.

Don't be too concerned if your initial success rate is low. You will be surprised at how quickly your skill and knowledge grows with some practice.

Identifying birds

When trying to identify a bird, first identify its habitat.

Then look at the illustration of birds for that habitat and select those that most clearly match your unknown species. Where two birds are featured in one illustration the gender symbols ♂ male and ♀ female will tell you which is which. Having narrowed down the possibilities by a combination of habitat and the pictures, check the distribution map to see if the likely bird occurs where you have seen it. If it does, pursue your investigations step by step according to all possible criteria, and remember to use the text as well as the illustrations!

In the text you will find a section on identification, which refers to the body parts of a bird—some of the terms used may be unfamiliar to you. For example, the 'front' of a bird is the forehead, not the breast. The diagram featured below will help you to learn the names which apply to the different parts of a bird's external structure.

Size

Size is also an important factor in identifying birds. Generally speaking, the smaller birds are passerines and the larger birds are non-passerines. Compare the size of your bird with that of a bird familiar to you: perhaps a domestic pigeon or fowl, a common (or Indian) myna or house sparrow. Make a note of it in your pocket notebook.

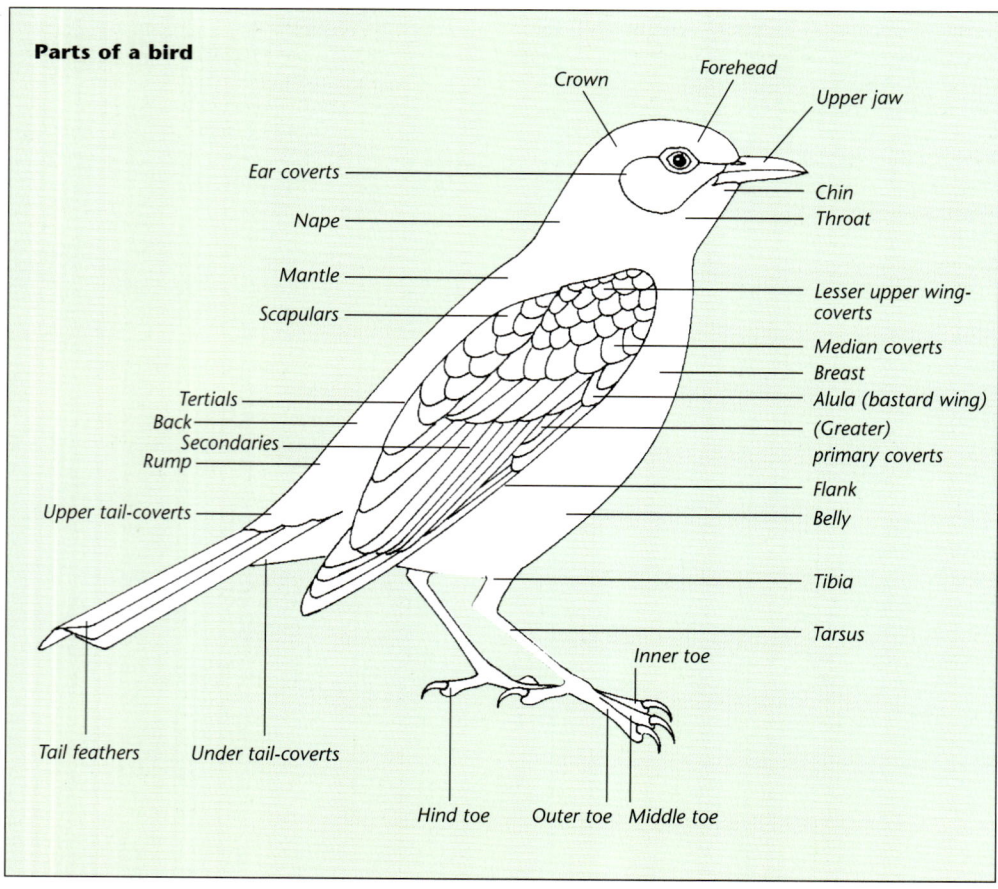

Birds

Then note the proportions of the bird: build (stout or slender), relative length of neck and legs, shape and length of bill, and so on.

Bill

The bill of a bird is a very useful aid to identification; various bill shapes are shown on page 102, from which it will be clear to you that bills are extremely variable in both their length and shape.

For example, among the passerines you can distinguish two main bill shapes: conical and slender. Passerines with conical bills are the seed-eaters, such as sparrows, weavers, waxbills, whydahs, canaries and buntings. The rest all have bills that are not conical, though the shape varies from stout and hooked in the shrikes, to slim and decurved (downward-sloping) in the sunbirds. Most bill shapes among the passerines are intermediate and adapted to feeding on insects.

Among the near-passerines are many familiar kinds of birds with characteristic proportions and bill shapes. For example, there are the kingfishers, with their large, straight bills, big heads and rather short tails; and there are the woodhoopoes and bee-eaters with their long, slender, downcurved bills; owls and parrots have stoutly hooked bills; and hornbills have huge, curved bills often topped by a swelling called a casque that has a characteristic shape for each species and often also for the different sexes.

The rest of the non-passerines have bills of highly varied design, but each family or order of birds tends to have a fairly constant bill shape that makes recognition easy. For example, all birds of prey have robust, hooked bills for tearing their prey apart; the herons have sharply pointed, straight bills for spearing water animals; ducks have flattened bills for filtering fine particles out of the mud and water; ibises have long, curved bills ideally suited to probing into soil or ooze.

One family that is rather variable with regard to bill shape is the sandpiper family, which includes the snipes, godwits, curlews, stints and phalaropes.

General impressions

Look at the illustrations of birds in this section, and familiarize yourself with the general appearance of the different bird families. Birders call this general appearance the 'jizz' of a bird, a term derived from wartime pilots who learned to recognize different kinds of aircraft without seeing their insignia.

The tail

The length and shape of the tail will help you identify birds. Refer to page 103 for the main kinds, and for some of the definitions used in describing tails. Note particularly the differences between the rounded, square, graduated, wedge-shaped and forked tails.

You don't have to see every feature of a bird to identify it with certainty, but try to record as many features as you can. Add to those already mentioned such things as flight pattern (fast or slow, floppy or with whirring wingbeats, direct or undulating), the way it moves on the ground (hopping, walking, running in short bursts), foraging methods (pecking at the ground, gleaning from bark and leaves, plucking fruit, probing in the soil) and anything else you believe may be characteristic.

And don't forget the voice.

Bird calls

Since bird calls are difficult to describe in words, a tape or CD of bird calls is a very useful adjunct to learning them. Quite often, especially in the case of small, hard-to-identify birds (known as LBJs, or Little Brown Jobs), voice is the surest means of identification, such as in cisticolas, larks, pipits and sandpipers. Even birds of prey can be identified by voice, so it is worth becoming familiar with bird vocalizations.

Another way of identifying birds through sound is by means of sonagrams—pictorial images of bird vocalizations—which indicate the pitch, duration and loudness of particular calls.

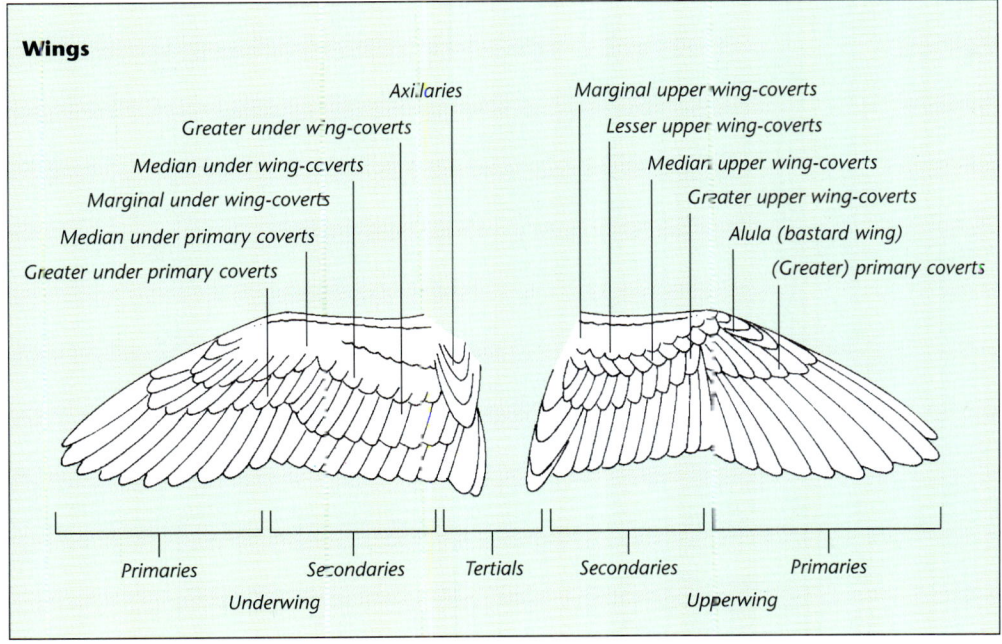

Birds

Types of bill

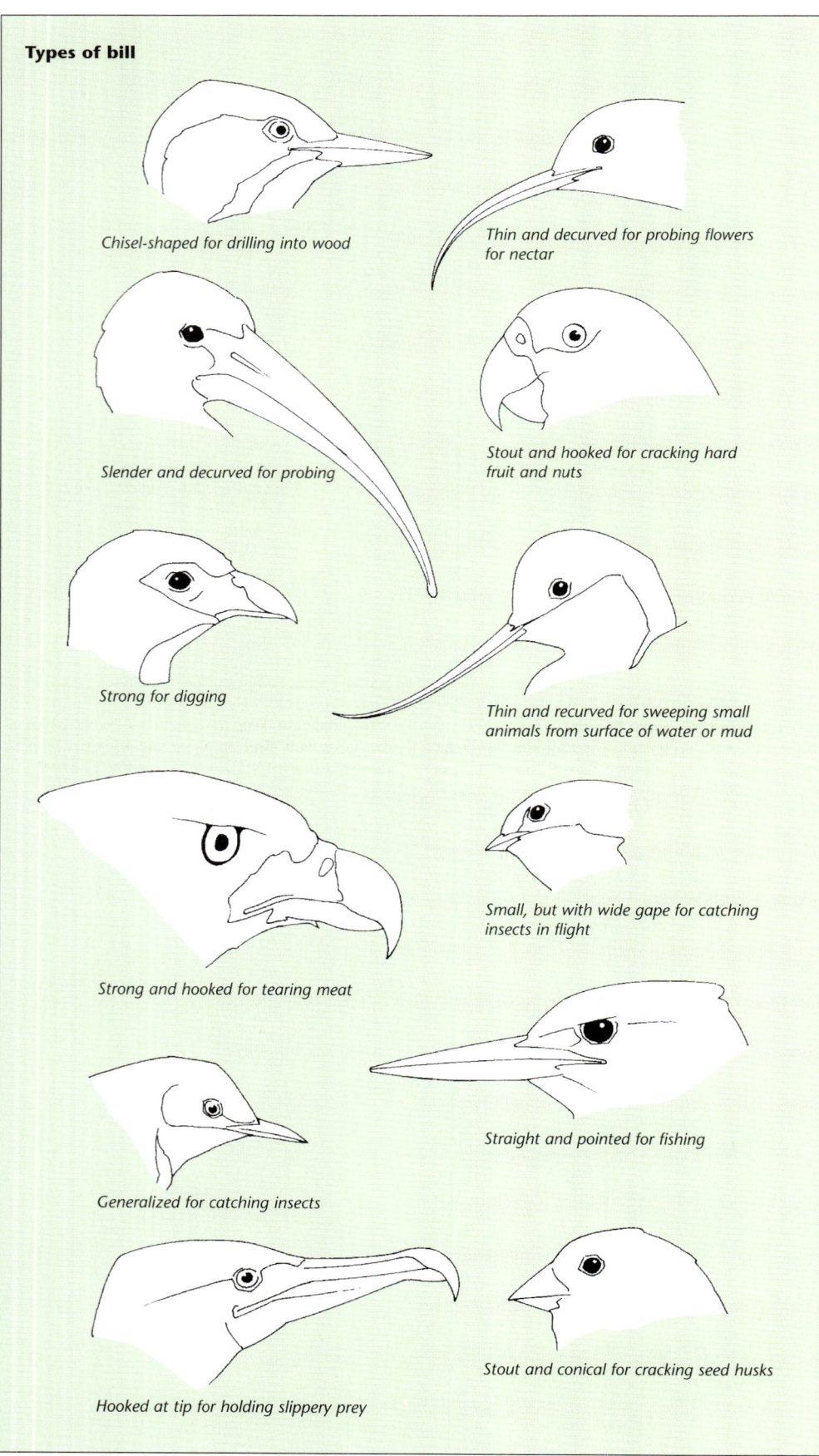

Birds

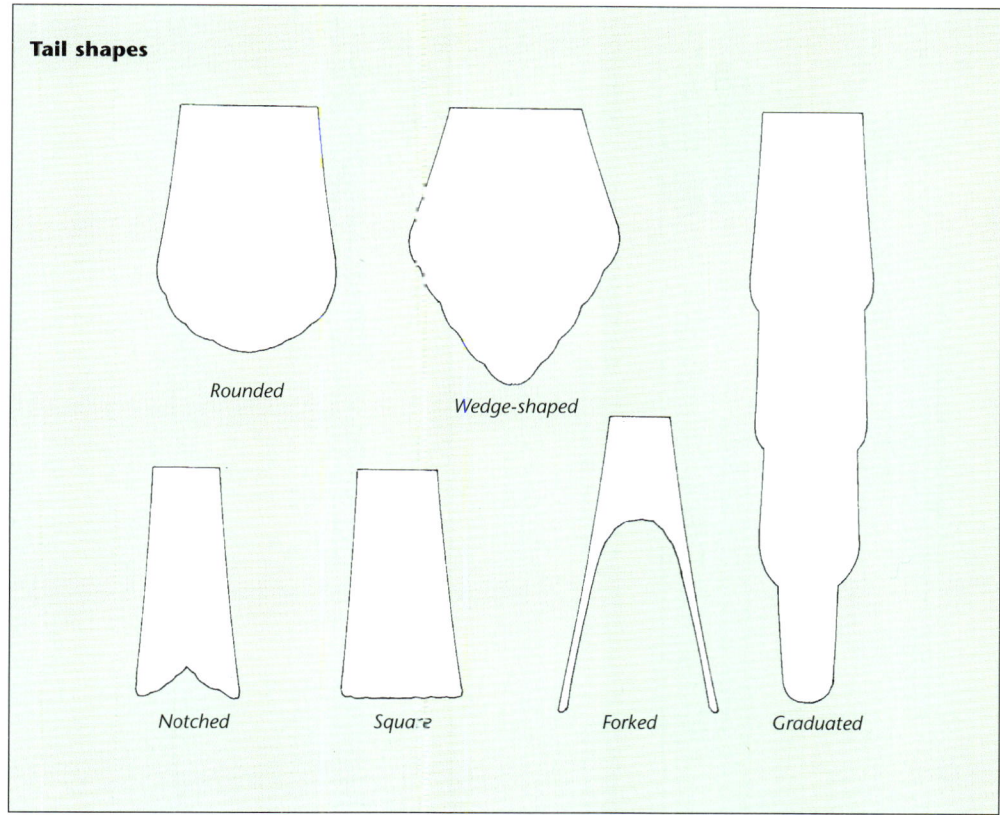

Tail shapes: Rounded, Wedge-shaped, Notched, Square, Forked, Graduated

Putting your knowledge to work

Once you have acquired a reasonable working knowledge of the bird species in this guide to southern African wildlife, you may want to extend your activities and obtain a more comprehensive handbook or field guide. Later on you may acquire some more general works of bird biology to find out how birds live. The pleasures and rewards of natural history are endless.

Apart from being purely recreational, bird identification and making lists can be put to good use if you join the Southern African Ornithological Society (SAOS) or one of its branches and then participate in the Southern African Bird Atlas Project (SABAP), designed to map more accurately the distribution of birds in southern Africa. Write to PO Box 87234, Houghton, South Africa 2041.

You could also keep nest record cards (NRCs) for all the nests you find in your excursions; the NRC scheme is housed in the Percy Fitzpatrick Institute for African Ornithology at the University of Cape Town and forms a most useful source of information for research workers in the field of breeding biology.

Interesting observations of any kind can be sent into your local bird-club newsletter for the information of your fellow birders; and of course you too will derive considerable information and entertainment from reading the newsletter yourself. This is a further incentive to join a bird club; everyone benefits from each new member, since your subscription pays for the newsletters, journals, research projects and conservation projects which are undertaken by your club or society.

Ground birds

OSTRICH

Volstruis *(Struthio camelus)*

Size: *Height 2 m; weight 82 kg.*
Colour: *Male black with white plumes in wing, buff plumes in tail; legs and neck grey, naked; front of legs of male bright red in breeding season; female mostly brownish grey, including wing and tail plumes.*
Most like: *Unlike any other bird.*
Habitat: *Bushveld to desert, but usually open country.*

Found in various types of terrain throughout Namibia, Botswana, central and western Zimbabwe, southwestern Mozambique, Northern Province and the drier northern regions of Northern Cape.

The ostrich is the biggest bird alive today. Its deep booming calls sound like the distant roar of a lion and carry for several kilometres—*boo boo booooh*. Ostriches may occur singly or in pairs, but at times gather into flocks of up to 600. Smaller flocks of 30-40 birds are quite common and may keep company with herds of antelope, such as springbok, gemsbok or wildebeest; because of their height and sharp vision, they keep a lookout for enemies such as lions, cheetahs and man.

Ostriches can be dangerous when disturbed near their nest or young, the males displaying their spectacular white wing feathers to distract intruders. They may even attack, kicking with a formidable claw that can kill a man or a dog.

Ostriches can run at up to 70 kilometres per hour. They feed on many kinds of plant food and some insects, eating about 3,5 kg of food a day. They can survive almost indefinitely without water, but will drink if water is available. In the Namib Desert they get water by feeding on wind-blown chaff that has absorbed fog from the Atlantic Ocean.

A breeding male will have one to three females in a harem, each female laying three to eight eggs in a communal nest scrape on the ground, until a clutch of 15-20 eggs has accumulated. Up to 43 eggs have been recorded in a single nest. Each egg weighs around 1,5 kg and contains the volume of 24 chicken eggs. Only the 'chief wife' incubates for six to seven weeks. The chicks run with their parents within three days of hatching.

BLACK-HEADED HERON

Swartkopreier *(Ardea melanocephala)*

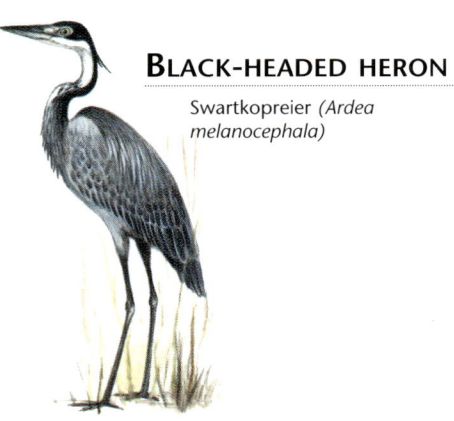

Size: *Length about 1m; weight 700 g-1,5 kg.*
Colour: *Mostly deep bluish grey; crown and hindneck black, foreneck white; underwing pale in front, dark behind; bill blackish above, paler below.*
Most like: *Grey heron, but black head, dark bill and half-dark, half-light underwing distinctive. Goliath heron has all dark chestnut neck and is much bigger.*
Habitat: *Open grassveld, fallow lands and edges of inland waters.*

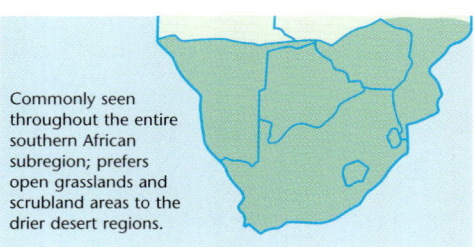

Commonly seen throughout the entire southern African subregion; prefers open grasslands and scrubland areas to the drier desert regions.

Most people associate herons with the waterside, but the black-headed heron spends most of its feeding time in the veld or on farmlands, hunting for rodents, nestling birds, reptiles and insects. It eats mostly insects and rodents, but will even swallow a small puff adder after softening it up with its bill. It hunts for larger prey by the stand-and-wait method, but probably stalks for insects.

For most of its life the black-headed heron is silent. However, it has the typical heron repertoire of loud croaks and squawks which it gives mainly at its breeding sites. Though it feeds in the veld, it follows its ancestral inclination by roosting and breeding in trees.

In flight it displays paired white 'landing lights' at the front edge of each wing as it flaps slowly homeward.

Nesting black-headed herons congregate to form large colonies, often in company with other herons, egrets, ibises and other waterbirds. They build large nests of sticks in the forks of trees, the males carrying the material and the females building it into the nest structure. Members of a mated pair display with stretched necks, and with raised crests and wings at the nest site.

The female lays three pale blue eggs which are incubated by both parents for 23-27 days.

Ground birds

CATTLE EGRET
Veereier *(Bubulcus ibis)*

Size: *Length 54 cm; weight 350 g.*
Colour: *White with yellow bill and dull brownish legs; breeding birds have pinkish buff plumes on crown, back and breast, orange bill and dull yellow to red legs.*
Most like: *Yellow-billed egret, but neck shorter and legs not black; buff plumes distinctive in summer; little egret has black bill; yellow-billed and little egrets feed in water.*
Habitat: *Grassland, lawns, pastures, savanna, often where large game or stock mammals are present.*

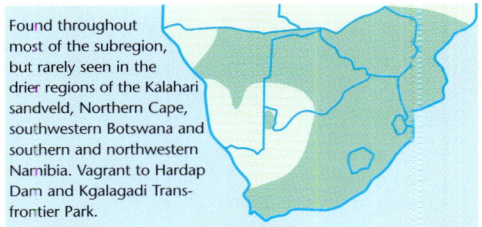

Found throughout most of the subregion, but rarely seen in the drier regions of the Kalahari sandveld, Northern Cape, southwestern Botswana and southern and northwestern Namibia. Vagrant to Hardap Dam and Kgalagadi Transfrontier Park.

The cattle egret is the 'tickbird' so familiar to all who live in Africa, though tickbird is not really an appropriate name, since the birds follow mammals to catch the insects disturbed by them and not to take ticks off them. They also eat worms, frogs and lizards, and have taken to following ploughs in farmlands to catch insect larvae in the newly turned soil.

At night cattle egrets roost in large numbers in trees, often near water. By day they fly out to neighbouring farmlands or playing fields to forage, returning again in small groups or in long, V-shaped squadrons to their roosting trees, where they may also nest during the summer.

Cattle egrets breed in dense colonies, building flimsy platforms in trees or reed beds. These heronries become very noisy and smelly; sometimes the trees will die from the effects of the birds' droppings.

Two to four pale blue eggs are laid and incubated for 24 days by both parents, which feed the young for a further 45 days. The young can fly at about 30 days. Many die after falling to the ground or getting caught by the neck in the fork of a tree.

Today these birds are as familiar a part of the landscape of North and South America, the Mediterranean region, southern Asia and tropical regions of Australia as they are in Africa, having spread to these parts within the past 50 years or so.

WHITE STORK
Witooievaar *(Ciconic ciconia)*

Size: *Length 1,2 m; wingspan 1,6 m; weight 3,5 kg.*
Colour: *All white except for black wing tips and trailing edges; bill and legs red.*
Most like: *Yellow-billed stork, but white stork's bill red and face feathered; herons have black or yellow bills and dark legs.*
Habitat: *Usually high grassveld; also vleis, cultivated lands and Karoo.*

Mainly in open grassland and cultivated areas throughout the subregion, except for the drier desert areas of southern Namibia and the northwestern Northern Cape.

White storks are prodigious long-distance fliers, travelling between 11 000 and 12 000 km every year on migration routes from their breeding places in Europe and Asia to southern Africa. Their broad wings carry them to such great heights over the Alps that they can cross the Mediterranean—generally over the eastern and western extremes of the sea—in almost a single glide. They arrive in November and head north again in March.

A few white storks have stayed on to breed in South Africa in the Bredasdorp and Mossel Bay areas where they build huge stick platforms in trees.

Flocks of several hundred may gather where insects are plentiful, though their numbers have been dwindling in recent years, possibly because of collisions with powerlines, hail storms, hunting, or poisoning from pesticides used to combat plagues of locusts.

Apart from insects, white storks eat small vertebrates, including the nestlings of small ground birds; they walk slowly over the veld, picking up food as they go, and are unlikely to overlook small reptiles, frogs and even molluscs. Between feeds they fly to water to rest on the shoreline, then head for trees to roost at night.

White storks are voiceless and display to each other with clattering bills. Usually two to four chalky white eggs are laid, and they are incubated by both parents for 34 days. The nestlings can fly at the age of 60 days.

Ground birds

Abdim's stork

Kleinswartooievaar
(*Ciconia abdimii*)

Size: Length 76 cm; weight 1-1,5 kg.
Colour: Glossy, purplish black with white belly; bill grey-green with red bill tip; legs dull grey; toes and ankle joints red; bare blue face.
Most like: Black stork, but latter is larger, with bright red bill and legs.
Habitat: Mainly highveld grassland; also Kalahari sandveld, savanna and cultivated fields.

East of the coastal desert in Namibia, throughout Botswana, Zimbabwe, Mozambique, eastern KwaZulu-Natal, Swaziland, Mpumalanga, Northern Province, Gauteng, North-West Province, central and northern Free State and Northern Cape.

Abdim's storks are strong and graceful fliers: towards evening you may see long lines of them heading for their favourite groves of trees (often eucalyptus) in order to roost, arriving like clockwork at the same time each day.

In warm weather the birds may soar high in the sky on rising thermals, then descend with dramatic swoops to search for food. This descent produces a powerful whooshing sound as the air rushes through the wings.

The storks are highly gregarious. You can often see loose groups of dozens or hundreds of them around temporary pans and pools after good rains in the interior of southern Africa. For most of each day the flocks stalk the open veld for large insects. They may also take frogs, lizards, mice, fishes and crabs.

Like most storks, Abdim's storks are almost voiceless, though at the nest they clatter their bills loudly in display.

This species does not breed in southern Africa, but migrates here in October and leaves again in April. It nests mainly in East and West Africa.

Congregating in colonies of 20-40 pairs in trees or on cliffs, Abdim's storks may even build a nest on the roof of a hut in the middle of an African village. The platform of sticks may be used year after year as long as it stays intact and the site remains undisturbed. The two to three white eggs hatch after 30-31 days into pale grey, downy chicks that are initially fed by regurgitation. Two months later they are ready to fly and will travel up to 7 000 km to South Africa for the southern summer.

Marabou stork

Maraboe (*Leptoptilos crumeniferus*)

Size: Length 1,5 cm; wingspan 2,5; weight 7 kg.
Colour: Black above, glossed greenish; white below; white ruff at base of bare, pinkish neck; huge grey to yellowish or pinkish bill; legs usually covered with white powder.
Most like: Some other storks, but bill dull-coloured and very large; neck naked and pinkish (black or white in other storks).
Habitat: Bushveld, woodland, lake shores, rubbish dumps (especially near abattoirs).

Mainly in game reserves, but is often spotted throughout southern Africa, except for the arid Namib Desert and the dry Kalahari sandveld, where it is thinly distributed.

The marabou is the largest of our storks. Like the vulture, its bare neck and strong bill are designed for easy feeding on carrion, and for easy cleaning afterwards. Not that the marabou usually looks clean; indeed it often looks very soiled, except for its spotless white ruff and belly. At a carcass it lords it over even the biggest of the vultures, which are no match for its powerful bill. Apart from carrion, marabou eat small water animals (crocodiles, frogs and fishes) as well as the occasional snake or lizard.

Despite its huge size and ungainly appearance on the ground, the marabou stork flies well and soars beautifully for hours on hot days, and may be seen doing aerobatics when descending from great height.

At rest it may stand solemnly on one leg, its head tucked into its shoulders. The marabou's legs are in fact black, but it urinates onto them in hot weather in order to cool them. As the urine dries, a deposit of fine, white, uric acid crystals remains, giving the legs their white appearance.

During courtship the male marabou inflates a hanging neck sac and clatters his bill loudly. In a large stick nest the female lays two to three chalky white eggs that hatch after 30 days. The young, which are fed by both parents, stay in the nest for more than 100 days before they can fly.

Ground birds

SOUTHERN BALD IBIS

Kalkoenibis (*Geronticus calvus*)

Size: *Length 80 cm; weight 1,3 kg.*
Colour: *Dark glossy green with bronze wing-patch, bare white neck; bill, bare crown and legs bright red.*
Most like: *Hadeda ibis, but darker and glossier with red head, bill and legs; not at all noisy like hadeda ibis.*
Habitat: *Mostly high grassveld, also cultivated fields and heavily grazed pastures.*

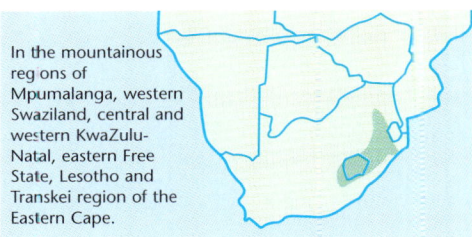

In the mountainous regions of Mpumalanga, western Swaziland, central and western KwaZulu-Natal, eastern Free State, Lesotho and Transkei region of the Eastern Cape.

Formerly seriously threatened with extinction, this beautiful bird is now out of danger because of increased conservation awareness that has led to a better protection of its breeding sites. If you drive through the northeastern Free State or the uplands of KwaZulu-Natal you may see a flock of 20-30 southern bald ibises foraging peacefully in the open veld, walking along in loose array, probing for insects, snails, worms and other animals, including the occasional small bird or mammal. The long, slender bill is used for turning over leaves and dung in the search for food.

In the late afternoon flocks fly in long V-shaped lines to their roosting cliffs in the valleys of major rivers, such as the Tugela, Mooi and Wilge. More roosting and breeding colonies are being established on South African farms as their numbers increase.

Unlike the hadeda ibis, this ibis is silent, only occasionally giving a few grunts and groans at the nest—a stick platform on a ledge or in a pothole, sometimes on the face or sides of a waterfall. The nests may be so crowded together as to touch each other.

The one to three eggs are pale blue with red spots. Both parents incubate the eggs for about 30 days, and feed the young until they can fly at the age of 40-45 days. The young have greyish, feathered necks and a patch of red on the forehead, and are dependent on their parents for about two months after leaving the nest.

HADEDA IBIS

Hadeda (*Bostrychia hagedash*)

Size: *Length 76 cm; weight 1,3 kg.*
Colour: *Dull dark grey, with metallic purple or green reflections on wing in good light; red line along top of the bill.*
Most like: *Southern bald ibis, but head and neck grey and feathered; bill and legs dull blackish; greyer and stockier than glossy ibis; rather like hamerkop in flight, but larger, and bill long and decurved.*
Habitat: *Lawns, playing fields, airfields, grassveld, forest.*

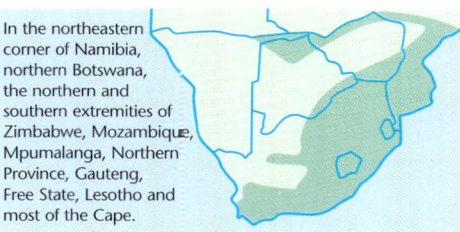

In the northeastern corner of Namibia, northern Botswana, the northern and southern extremities of Zimbabwe, Mozambique, Mpumalanga, Northern Province, Gauteng, Free State, Lesotho and most of the Cape.

The hadeda ibis must have the loudest voice of any bird in the world; and there cannot be many South Africans who have not heard its raucous, sometimes startling, *ha-ha-hadeda* call as it flies overhead.

Its flight is buoyant, but looks laboured because of the jerky, irregular beats of its broad wings.

You are likely to see the hadeda ibis in towns and suburban gardens—particularly in the eastern parts of southern Africa—walking about probing for worms and insects, sticking its long decurved bill up to half its length into the soil.

Flocks of 20 or more birds (up to 100 when they're not breeding) gather at water to drink after feeding, frequently just before going to their roosting trees in the evening. They become active at daybreak, and you can hear them flying to their feeding grounds even in thick mist. During the day, they perch on treetops or power pylons to rest between feeds.

Hadedas build their nests in trees, particularly along rivers and streams, or leaning out from cliff faces. An occupied nest is often surrounded by a colony of Cape weaver nests, their smaller occupants going about their noisy business while the ibis sits quietly on its three olive-green, brown-smudged eggs.

An incubation period of 28 days is followed by a nestling period of 36 days, during which time the chicks take their juicy sustenance directly from their parents' stomachs by plunging their heads and bills into the parents' throats.

Ground birds

SECRETARYBIRD
Sekretarisvoël (*Sagittarius serpentarius*)

Size: Length up to 1,5 m; weight 4 kg.
Colour: Pale grey with black wings, thighs and crest; bare, bright orange or yellow face; long pinkish legs.
Most like: Blue crane, but distinguished by black in plumage (including thighs), long, stiff tail feathers and shaggy crest.
Habitat: Open country from woodland to grassland and semi-desert.

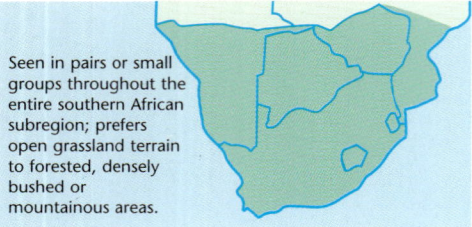

Seen in pairs or small groups throughout the entire southern African subregion; prefers open grassland terrain to forested, densely bushed or mountainous areas.

The secretarybird is one of the best known and most loved of all African veld birds because of its large size, regal appearance and reputation for killing snakes. In fact it very seldom eats snakes, though it can kill them easily when it encounters them. Its main food is insects and small vertebrates such as frogs, lizards, rodents and birds. It will even eat birds' eggs.

Secretarybirds stride in measured steps across the veld—usually in pairs—at a speed of about three kilometres per hour, stopping now and then to catch an insect or kill a rodent, which they do by first immobilizing it with their bills and then stamping on it with their feet to kill it and soften it up for swallowing whole. They treat snakes in the same way.

Undigested parts (fur, bones, teeth, hard parts of insects) are regurgitated later as firm pellets.

Outstanding fliers, secretarybirds commonly run before take-off, flap strongly to gain lift, and then soar on thermals like storks or vultures. They can also take off from a standing start. On landing again, they run for several paces before folding their wings.

Breeding occurs in any month, but mostly from August to December in South Africa. A huge stick nest is built on top of a large bush and lined with grass, dung and regurgitated pellets. The two large white eggs (rarely three) hatch after 42-46 days. The young fly at about 80-100 days. Rarely is more than one chick reared, though the cause of death of the sibling is unknown.

CRESTED FRANCOLIN
Bospatrys (*Peliperdix sephaena*)

Size: Length 33 cm; weight 225-350 g.
Colour: Mostly reddish brown above, faintly streaked white; below greyish, finely barred on belly; breast boldly streaked dark brown; head dark with white throat and eyebrow; legs reddish; bill black.
Most like: Other francolins, but striped appearance of head and finely barred belly distinctive; combination of black bill and red legs unique.
Habitat: Bushveld, woodland, savanna.

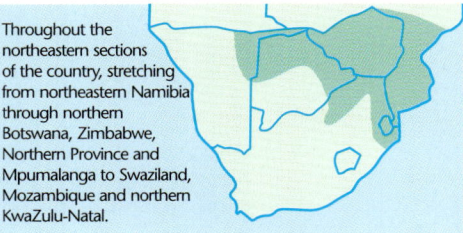

Throughout the northeastern sections of the country, stretching from northeastern Namibia through northern Botswana, Zimbabwe, Northern Province and Mpumalanga to Swaziland, Mozambique and northern KwaZulu-Natal.

The crested francolin's harsh, penetrating call, somewhat fancifully described as *beer-and-cognac*, is commonly heard in the game reserves of the lowveld. In the morning and evening these crowing notes are repeated in bursts of several phrases at a time by the male, often from a perch in a tree. The birds are usually concealed in bushes or woodland, but may come out of cover onto roads or clearings; if disturbed, they run away quickly with cocked-up tails, looking rather like plump bantams.

A patient observer may sit and watch a family of crested francolins (the crest is a feature only when the birds are alarmed) scratching and digging in soft soil for bulbs, seeds and insects. They may feed in company with Swainson's spurfowl, but seldom venture far from the cover of trees.

The birds fly reluctantly but well, reaching an impressive speed on their rounded, whirring wings, and showing a conspicuous black tail.

The crested francolin nests on the ground in a scrape lined with a little grass, placed most often under cover of a rank grass tuft or thorny shrub. It lays between four and nine pale cream eggs.

Surprisingly little is known about the breeding habits of our francolins, though the incubation period of this one is said to be about 20 days. Incubating francolins sit tightly on the nest, so that the camouflaged parent conceals the eggs from predators. The nestlings are able to fly at eight weeks.

Ground birds

SWAINSON'S SPURFOWL

Bosveldfisant (*Pternistes swainsonii*)

Size: Length 38 cm; weight (m) 700 g, (f) 500 g.
Colour: Brown with black streaks; bare throat, eye-patch and lower jaw bright red; upper bill and legs are black.
Most like: Other francolins, but no white in plumage; combination of red on bill and black legs unique.
Habitat: Very variable; bushveld, woodland, savanna, open grassveld, cultivated lands, rocky hillsides.

In northeastern Namibia, northern and eastern Botswana, Zimbabwe, western Mozambique, western KwaZulu-Natal, Swaziland, Mpumalanga, Northern Province, North-West Province, northern Free State, northern Lesotho and the extreme northeastern Cape.

Swainson's spurfowl has the widest choice of habitat of any land bird in southern Africa, and it is abundant wherever it occurs, from subtropical bushveld to high sandstone ridges in the eastern Free State and open veld in North-West Province.

It has a harsh, drawn-out crowing call which gains in volume and then dies away before stopping abruptly. Where protected, it is quite tame and will call in full view from the top of a termite mound or rock. In game reserves, you are likely to see it coming out of the grass verges to scratch for its food of seeds, berries and insects on open roads. Although usually spotted alone or in pairs, coveys of up to eight birds (probably a family group) may be seen together; keep a lookout near water in the mornings and evenings when it comes to drink. If you disturb the bird, it slinks into cover and disappears; if chased it will fly with surprising agility between the trees. In farming areas—particularly where it is hunted—it becomes shy and wary.

Swainson's spurfowl, also known as Swainson's francolin, roosts in trees or bushes at night, though it nests on the ground like other members of the francolin family. The nest scrape is lined with dry grass and set under a tuft or among brushwood. The average clutch is six eggs, but as many as 12 may be laid in one nest; the eggs are buff or cream in colour with fine, white pores.

Eggs and young are heavily preyed on by monitor lizards, mongooses, snakes and baboons, while adults are taken by larger birds of prey, cats and genets.

COMMON QUAIL

Afrikaanse kwartel (*Coturnix coturnix*)

Size: Length 17 cm; weight 100 g.
Colour: Brown above, streaked white and mottled darker; underparts pale buff; male has bold brown-and-white facial pattern and black streak down centre of throat; female has dark streaks on breast.
Most like: Harlequin quail female, but less rusty below, and lacks brown collar on throat. Similar to button-quails, but chest not bright rufous.
Habitat: Grassveld, croplands, Karoo, Kalahari sandveld.

Absent from the arid regions of western and northeastern Namibia, Botswana, western Zimbabwe, and the northern and western extremities of the Northern Cape.

The piercing *whit-WHITtit, whit-WHITtit* calls of the common quail in the lush days of summer are well known in the moister eastern parts of southern Africa. If you're walking through the grassy uplands of KwaZulu-Natal or Mpumalanga, a plump form on whirring wings may fly up at your feet with a trilling *skree, skree*—and drop suddenly back into the grass after a low, quick flight.

The common quail is a favourite with sportsmen as it presents a challenging shot on the wing and is said to make a fine meal. Sensible hunting laws have, however, been introduced to ensure the survival of this quail.

Some common quail populations migrate northwards to Angola and the Democratic Republic of the Congo after breeding, while others stay on in southern Africa. Some of the migrating birds have been seen well out to sea.

The birds' diet includes seeds, tubers, flowers, snails, insects and arthropods. They roost on the ground at night in small coveys. During the September-April breeding season you may hear the males calling throughout the night if there's a bright moon out. The nest is well-hidden in dense grass, shrubs or cultivated crops—a scrape in the soil, lined with dry grass and small roots.

The clutch of eggs numbers five to seven as a rule; they are light yellowish, heavily blotched or speckled with dark brown. The female incubates for 17 days and cares for the chicks by herself until they are fully able to fly at about 21 days. The young are able to make short flights from as early as nine days old.

Ground birds

Helmeted guineafowl
Gewone tarentaal
(*Numida meleagris*)

Size: Length 55 cm; weight 1,3 kg.
Colour: Slate-grey with fine white spots all over; naked head coloured red and blue with yellowish casque (helmet) on top and red-and-blue wattles at base of bill.
Most like: Francolins, but small, bare, coloured head with horny crown distinctive.
Habitat: Mostly open country; grassveld, vlei, Karoo, savanna and croplands.

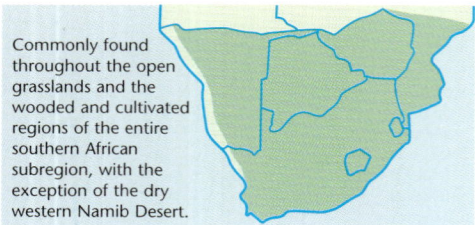

Commonly found throughout the open grasslands and the wooded and cultivated regions of the entire southern African subregion, with the exception of the dry western Namib Desert.

Blue crane
Bloukraanvoël
(*Anthropoides paradisea*)

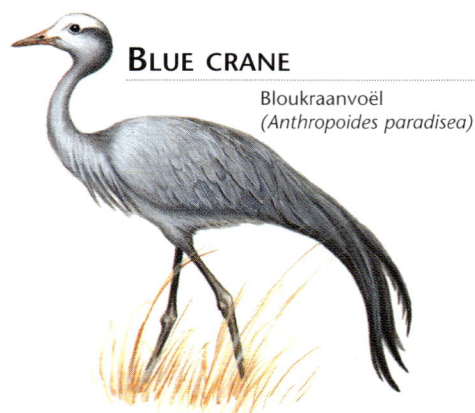

Size: Length 1,05 m; weight (m) 5,6 kg, (f) 3,6 kg.
Colour: Plain blue-grey, darker on wings; top of head almost white.
Most like: Secretarybird, but has no black in plumage and no crest on head; similar to wattled and grey crowned cranes, but lacks white on neck and in wing.
Habitat: Karoo, high grasslands, cultivated fields.

The Karoo and Eastern Cape, central and eastern Free State, Lesotho, western KwaZulu-Natal and southern Mpumalanga and Gauteng, with isolated groups in Northern Province and Namibia.

Guineafowls look like fussy ladies holding their skirts up out of the dust as they run with their wings raised to form a characteristic arch over the back, a posture exaggerated in displays between members of a flock.

When pursued, they can run very fast, giving their staccato *kek-kek-kek-krrr* alarm call. If pressed harder, the birds take off with rapidly whirring wings, gliding intermittently until they are out of danger. They then glide to the ground, run a little further, and gather into a tight flock.

If danger is close by, the birds may land in a tree from where they scold the intruder noisily. Guineafowls also roost in trees, using the same sites for years if not disturbed.

The helmeted guineafowl—one of the best known of all southern Africa's veld birds—is abundant on farmlands and in game reserves where you can see it in flocks of a dozen to several hundred, searching for seeds, bulbs, fruit and grain.

It has many natural enemies, as well as man: large eagles, cats, genets, pythons and many others. Flocking may help the birds to detect predators more easily, bur during the breeding season the birds pair off and the flocks break up. The female selects a nest site in dense vegetation and lays up to 19 eggs in a grass-lined hollow on the ground.

The cream-coloured eggs are very hard-shelled, pitted, flattened at the thick end and pointed at the thin end. They hatch in about 26 days.

The chicks can fly a little at only 14 days old, but do not fledge fully until about two weeks later.

Admired for its startling grace and beauty, the blue crane is equipped with superb powers of flight, its elegant wings taking it so high that it is barely visible to the naked eye.

Magnificent to watch on the ground and easily identified by its evocative calls, this bird occurs in flocks of up to 400 in the eastern Karoo. More often, however, you will see the birds in pairs or groups of 10-20, feeding in open grasslands or fields on insects, small vertebrates (frogs, fishes, reptiles), fallen grain and green plants.

Blue cranes are well known in captivity and as South Africa's national bird. Because they occasionally pull up sprouting grain, some farmers regard them as pests, but on the whole they do far more good than harm.

When they have finished feeding, blue cranes gather around a dam or pan to drink, loaf and preen; they may also roost standing in water. The long plumes that droop to the ground when the birds are at rest are not the tail feathers as they appear to be, but rather the innermost wing feathers which stream out behind them in flight.

The blue crane lays its two camouflaged eggs on the bare ground in open country where visibility is good, so that it can see any disturbance a long way off, and sneak away. After a month of incubation by both sexes, two downy, grey chicks with ginger heads hatch out. They are fed by the female for about six weeks, after which they pick up their own food. The chicks, however, do not fly until about 12 weeks old.

Ground birds

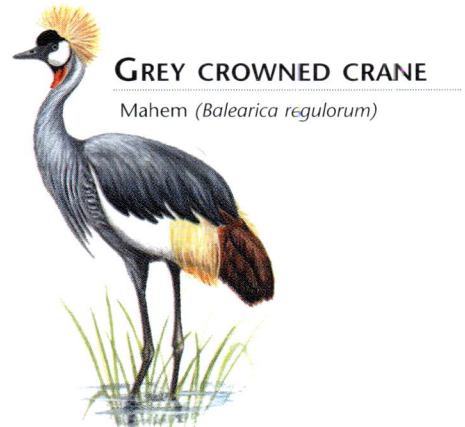

Grey crowned crane
Mahem *(Balearica regulorum)*

Size: *Length 1,05 m; weight 3,6 kg.*
Colour: *Mainly slate-grey with large white wing-patch; drooping yellow plumes overlie part of wing at rest; conspicuous yellow crest on black-and-white head with bright red throat wattle; broad chestnut plumes overlie tail at rest.*
Most like: *Other cranes, but wattle crane has white neck; blue crane lacks coloured patches in grey plumage; only grey crowned crane has crested head.*
Habitat: *Marshes, vleis, open moist grassland and cultivated lands.*

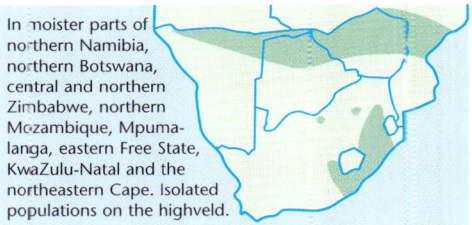

In moister parts of northern Namibia, northern Botswana, central and northern Zimbabwe, northern Mozambique, Mpumalanga, eastern Free State, KwaZulu-Natal and the northeastern Cape. Isolated populations on the highveld.

Kori bustard
Gompou *(Ardeotis kori)*

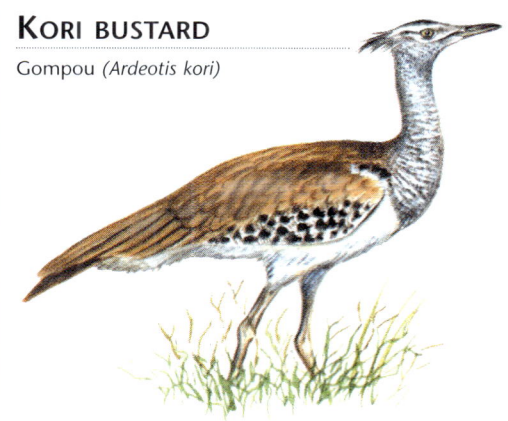

Size: *Length 1,35 m; weight 16,5 kg.*
Colour: *Greyish brown above, greyer on neck; belly white; neck and breast finely barred; crown black with short crest behind.*
Most like: *Denham's and Ludwig's bustards, but larger and without chestnut coloration on hindneck; looks rather like small ostrich, but with thick, feathered neck.*
Habitat: *Karoo, semi-desert and thornveld.*

Found in Namibia, Botswana, central and western Zimbabwe, southern Mozambique, Northern Province, North-West Province, western Free State and the central and northern parts of the Cape.

This beautiful crane is happily still common throughout most of its range in southern Africa. Its striking plumage and large size are singularly attractive and have made the bird a great favourite in captivity. There are few sights to compare with that of a pair of grey crowned cranes, or perhaps a small flock of them, in an African marsh, whether it be in the KwaZulu-Natal midlands or the Okavango swamps.

The Afrikaans name *mahem* is derived from the bird's two-note trumpeting call, often heard in flight, the second note louder and higher than the first. More rarely, you may hear a pair of courting cranes let out a deep, booming call. The pair also displays with dancing and posturing, accompanied by wing-spreading. This dancing may trigger off other members of a flock to do likewise until an entire ballet of birds is performing all at once.

Flocks of crowned cranes seldom number more than 20 or 30 birds, though rarely one may see up to 150 of them together. They forage in marshland and grassveld, picking up almost any small animals and fallen grain. They roost on the ground or, occasionally, in trees.

The nest is a large mound of reeds and grass in a marsh, usually well hidden in tall vegetation. The two to three eggs are unusual among cranes, being a plain pale blue.

Both sexes incubate for a month, and the fluffy chicks stay with their parents for about ten months.

Imagine a bird big enough to reach the weight of the normal baggage allowance on an aeroplane. This will give you some idea of the size of the kori bustard, one of the heaviest birds capable of flight.

This bustard spends most of its time walking sedately about looking for food—insects, small vertebrates and seeds. It holds its elegant bill up at a slight angle, which gives it a somewhat superior look.

When breeding, these shy and silent birds may be seen alone or in pairs; otherwise they flock together in groups of up to 40 or more birds. One reason for its shyness is its popularity as a game bird, not only among humans but also among predators such as jackals and martial eagles.

When disturbed the kori bustard flies well, usually with a short run before take-off, though it is quite capable of taking off from a standing position. Once in flight, it seldom lands again before disappearing over the nearest hill or dune, sometimes several kilometres away.

The male kori bustard has a magnificent courtship display in which he inflates his neck, raises his tail and droops his wings until the tips touch the ground; then he may tilt his head back to touch the tip of his tail.

The female makes no nest, laying two dull green, brown-flecked eggs on the bare ground. She does all the incubation while the male sometimes stands guard in the vicinity. The eggs hatch in four to five weeks.

Ground birds

Denham's Bustard
Veldpou *(Neotis denhami)*

Size: Length (m) 1,1 m, (f) 87 cm; weight (m) 9 kg, (f) 4 kg.
Colour: Brown above with rich chestnut hindneck; below, white with foreneck grey in male, light brown in female; crown black above white eyebrow; black-and-white checkerboard pattern on folded wing; legs pale yellow.
Most like: Ludwig's bustard, but foreneck grey or pale brown (not dark brown); there is much more white in the folded wing, and the legs are yellowish (not grey). Kori bustard lacks chestnut on hindneck.
Habitat: Open grassveld, Karoo, lightly wooded savanna, ploughed fields.

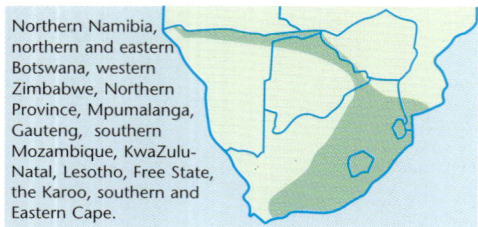

Northern Namibia, northern and eastern Botswana, western Zimbabwe, Northern Province, Mpumalanga, Gauteng, southern Mozambique, KwaZulu-Natal, Lesotho, Free State, the Karoo, southern and Eastern Cape.

Blue Korhaan
Bloukorhaan *(Eupodotis caerulescens)*

Size: Length 55 cm; weight 1,5 kg.
Colour: Neck and underparts rich blue-grey; back rusty brown; head black and white; legs yellow; bill blackish, yellow at base.
Most like: Southern white-bellied korhaan, but lacks white on belly and is tawny on the hindneck.
Habitat: Open, short grassveld, Karoo scrub and lands under cultivation.

Concentrated in the open grasslands and scrubland highveld regions of the Karoo, northeastern Cape, Free State, western Lesotho, western KwaZulu-Natal, southern North-West Province and Gauteng.

Although you may find Denham's and Ludwig's bustards in similar habitats in the eastern Karoo, Denham's is more a bird of the moister eastern parts of southern Africa, Ludwig's more of the drier west. You can see Denham's bustard in the high, lush grasslands of the Drakensberg foothills, the northeastern Cape, the eastern Free State and the highveld. Pairs of these magnificent birds can be seen walking slowly over the veld, occasionally stopping to peck at an insect or other small animal (even a lizard or rodent); they will also eat seeds, flowers and other plant parts.

Denham's bustard is shy and wary and, like the other large bustards, is usually silent. However, in display the male makes a throaty bark or resonant booming sound as he puffs out his white breast feathers and struts about with head pressed back.

The nesting female is excessively wary. She lays one or two blotched, greenish-brown eggs on the bare ground, usually among rocks or concealing grass tufts. She takes care of all the parental duties, since the male is polygamous and unavailable for such tasks.

According to the 2000 International Union for Conservation of Nature and Natural Resources' Red Data List, Denham's bustard is an endangered species.

The handsome blue korhaan—the common korhaan of the eastern Free State highveld—has a marvellous, resonant croaking call, *kuk-ka-ROW kuk-ka-ROW*, which you can hear repeatedly in the early morning and late afternoon, especially in summer.

If you're travelling along any of the major roads through the northern regions of the Eastern Cape, Free State, southern North-West Province and Gauteng, you are likely to see these birds; they are also quite common in the Karoo's irrigated lucerne fields, near towns such as Middelburg and Colesberg.

The blue korhaan usually occurs in groups of three to four and, more rarely, in flocks of up to 11, especially near water or on burnt veld where food is easily found. The birds walk slowly, picking insects and plant material from the ground and shrubs.

When alarmed, they run with their heads lowered until they are a safe distance away. If harder pressed, they take off and fly strongly, sometimes for a kilometre or more, before landing in a safe place and displaying to each other with rapidly bobbing movements of their conspicuously puffed-out heads.

Very shy when breeding, blue korhaans do not easily reveal the whereabouts of their nests; the two olive-green eggs, camouflaged with brown and grey streaks, are among the hardest to find of any veld bird, being laid in a mere scrape on the ground where the grass is short enough to give the bird good visibility all round. The female incubates the eggs for about 27 days. The young are very vulnerable to predators such as mongooses and wild cats, but one of the brood usually manages to survive and can fly at about five weeks.

Ground birds

SOUTHERN BLACK KORHAAN

Swartvlerkkorhaan
(*Eupodotis afra*)

Size: Length 50 cm; weight 700 g.
Colour: Male black below and on neck and face, with large white ear-patch and collar on chest; back finely barred black and tawny; bill orange; legs bright yellow. Female similar, but has buff neck and breast with fine black markings.
Most like: Black-bellied bustard, but smaller and stockier; neck all black; female black-bellied bustard has no black on belly. Male red-crested korhaan has buff neck, but back marked with chevrons, not bars.
Habitat: Drier grassveld, Karoo, semi-desert and scrubland.

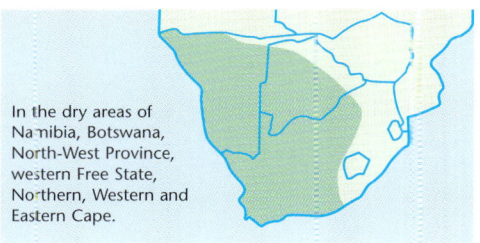

In the dry areas of Namibia, Botswana, North-West Province, western Free State, Northern, Western and Eastern Cape.

The southern black korhaan—the most common korhaan over most of southern Africa—is well known for its noisy and conspicuous behaviour. The male has a loud, crowing call which speeds up towards the end—*krak krak krraka krraka kraka kraka*. It may call from the ground, but more often does so in display flight in which it flies up to a height of about 20 m, calling as it goes, then slowly drops vertically in fluttering flight with dangling yellow legs. On landing, it often runs a short way before coming to a stop.

Although the male southern black korhaan is so conspicuous, the female is very seldom seen. She spends most of the time on the ground, hiding among shrubs or grass tufts.

This species feeds on insects, seeds and other plant material. The conspicuous behaviour and coloration of the male are associated with unpalatable flesh, which is described as 'rather tough and strong in flavour'; its bold colours (known as aposematic or warning coloration) are common in dangerous, poisonous or poor-tasting animals, many of which are black and white. Southern black korhaans owe their relative abundance to this distasteful flesh of theirs, but their eggs and young nestlings often fall prey to snakes and mongooses.

Only one egg is laid as a rule, on the bare ground. It is almost round and coloured deep khaki or olive-brown. The female alone bears the responsibility of incubating and caring for her chick, which is able to fly after about 75 days.

CROWNED LAPWING

Kroonkiewiet (*Vanellus coronatus*)

Size: Length 30 cm; weight 170 g.
Colour: Back and breast light greyish brown with dark breastband; belly white; crown black with white border; long, orange-red legs; bill red with black tip.
Most like: Black-winged lapwing, but red legs and black-and-white crown diagnostic; African wattled lapwing has streaked breast and yellow legs; Burchell's courser has white legs.
Habitat: Short grassveld, semi-desert, open savanna, playing fields, parks.

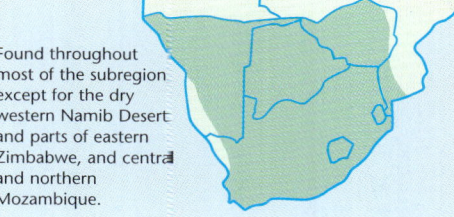

Found throughout most of the subregion except for the dry western Namib Desert and parts of eastern Zimbabwe, and central and northern Mozambique.

Who has not walked with a dog across a winter field and been dive-bombed by a screaming pair of crowned lapwings, or kiewiets, whose nest or chicks are lying invisibly in the grass nearby? These excitable birds, with their sealing wax legs and strident calls, occur almost throughout southern Africa, avoiding only the extremely dry Namib and the extremely wet northeastern parts. You can see them on islands in the centre of highways in Gauteng or on the broad plains of Savuti Marsh in Botswana.

Crowned lapwings are quite sociable for most of the year, even when nesting, though adjacent pairs are somewhat territorial and will threaten and screech at one another at their common boundaries.

These birds feed mainly on ants and termites, running in short bursts and stabbing at their prey with a sharp forward bow.

The crowned lapwing (also known as the crowned plover) has the typical black-and-white wing pattern of the larger lapwings, so called because of their heavy flapping flight. This pattern shows up strikingly in flight and in display, when, for example, a pair of nesting lapwings tries to lure a dog from their eggs by spreading their wings and pretending to be injured.

The nest is a shallow scrape on the ground and contains two to three khaki, black-spotted eggs. The young run with their parents within hours of hatching, and are cared for by both parents for approximately three months.

Ground birds

SPOTTED THICK-KNEE

Gewone dikkop
(Burhinus capensis)

Size: Length 44 cm; weight 450 g.
Colour: Rich buff, spotted with black on back; underparts white, washed cinnamon on breast and streaked with black; large eye and long legs bright yellow; bill mainly black, with basal third yellow.
Most like: Water thick-knee, but spotted, not streaked; the spotted thick-knee has no wing bars, is seldom seen near water, and has yellow, not greenish, legs.
Habitat: Grassland near trees and bushes, savanna, semi-desert, lawns, playing fields, golf courses and parks.

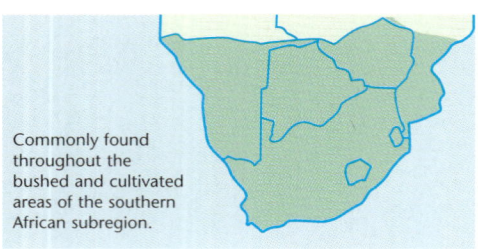

Commonly found throughout the bushed and cultivated areas of the southern African subregion.

The rather eerie, but beautifully melodious cries of the spotted thick-knee (also called the Cape dikkop) in the rain-wet softness of a spring night are among the most evocative sounds of southern Africa. The piping notes rise in pitch and volume, then slowly die away.

Thick-knees are quite common in towns and suburbs with open grassy fields, and may nest in full view of passers-by, relying on their superb camouflage to remain undetected. They will feed on insects attracted to street lights, and are also fond of grass seeds, small frogs, crustaceans and molluscs.

During the day spotted thick-knees stand motionless in the shade of a bush or tree, singly or in pairs, more rarely in small groups. In winter they form larger flocks, sometimes numbering between 40 and 50 birds which hide among tall weeds on stony ground. If disturbed, they run away on their long legs or fly like large moths on black-and-white wings.

The female lays two well-camouflaged eggs on the bare ground, often among stones or small grass tufts. An incubating thick-knee may sit tight or may sneak quietly away, leaving the eggs looking like two stones on the ground. The incubation period lasts about 24 days.

Like other ground-nesting birds they are preyed on by a variety of creatures, including genets, mongooses, cats and snakes. The adults bravely defend their eggs and young, and are even known to drive a herd of grazing cattle away by spreading their boldly patterned wings and making growling noises.

BURCHELL'S COURSER

Bloukopdrawwertjie
(Cursorius rufus)

Size: Length 23 cm; weight 75 g.
Colour: Mostly light brown; dark brown breastband separates brown chest from white belly; top of head rusty in front, blue-grey behind, with white eyebrow; legs greyish white.
Most like: Temminck's courser, but blue hindcrown distinctive; white legs separate it from crowned lapwing; spotted, immature bird looks like double-banded courser, but lacks breastbands.
Habitat: Dry grassveld, especially where overgrazed or burnt; also Karoo and Namib flats.

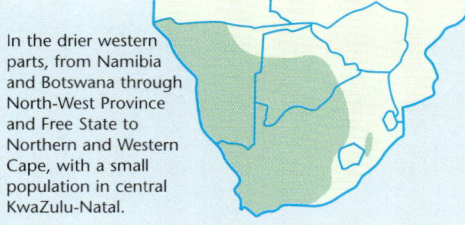

In the drier western parts, from Namibia and Botswana through North-West Province and Free State to Northern and Western Cape, with a small population in central KwaZulu-Natal.

Burchell's courser is an elegant, ploverlike runner of the open veld; between runs it stops to peck at food on the ground or to rock its body anxiously up and down while keeping the head quite still. It digs with its longish bill in soft sand at the base of shrubs or inside a grass tuft to get insect larvae and possibly seeds. When it takes off it shows a white flash in the wing (absent in Temminck's courser) and sometimes gives a harsh, grunting *chuk* call.

Burchell's courser is often quite sociable, gathering into flocks of up to 15 birds. When a flock is disturbed the birds run quickly away and stand still, usually behind a shrub or mound from where they can still keep an eye on the intruder. With their big eyes they are active at night, especially when the moon is bright.

This busy little bird makes no nest, but lays two eggs on the bare ground, usually among sun-darkened antelope droppings; the eggs themselves are almost black because of the dense black speckling and streaking on a pale background, and closely resemble the droppings. The newly hatched chicks are camouflaged in buff and black, which makes them extremely hard to see when they crouch on the ground after being warned by their parents of the presence of snakes, mongooses or man.

Ground birds

Namaqua sandgrouse

Kelkiewyn *(Pterocles namaqua)*

Size: Length 26 cm; weight 175 g.
Colour: Head and breast plain olive-yellow; double breastband of white and maroon; back and wings brownish with pearly grey spots; belly dark brown. Female rich buff, barred and streaked with black.
Most like: Other sandgrouse, but long central tail feathers distinctive; looks pigeonlike, but long tail feathers, long pointed wings and bold plumage markings diagnostic.
Habitat: Desert, semi-desert, Kalahari sandveld, Karoo, usually where stony and/or shrubby.

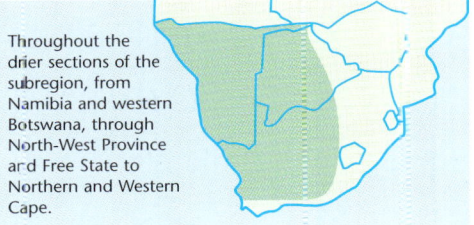

Throughout the drier sections of the subregion, from Namibia and western Botswana, through North-West Province and Free State to Northern and Western Cape.

Visit a waterhole in the Kalahari or Namib an hour or two after sunrise and you will hear the melancholy three-note *kelkiewyn* calls of approaching flocks of Namaqua sandgrouse as they fly in for their daily drink. The flocks may number ten birds or several hundred, which may gather in thousands a short distance from the water before flying or running down to drink. About the size of a Cape turtle dove and similar in shape, sandgrouse are dovelike in habits too, feeding on small dry seeds on the ground and having to drink water regularly.

Sandgrouse drink quickly, then take to the air on rapid, clattering wings. They scatter to their feeding grounds again and rest during the heat of the day under the shade of bushes. Unlike doves, sandgrouse cannot perch, because the hind toe is a mere vestige. The three front toes are short and robust for walking and running on the ground.

The Namaqua sandgrouse nests mainly in winter, laying three greenish, greyish or pinkish stone-coloured eggs in a thinly-protected scrape on the ground. The female incubates by day and the male by night for about 28 days. The downy chicks also feed on dry seeds and therefore need regular supplies of water. This is brought to them by the male, who carries it in his belly feathers, which he soaks during his first morning drink. The female keeps her feathers dry so as to be able to brood the chicks during the icy-cold winter spells.

Speckled pigeon

Kransduif *(Columba guinea)*

Size: Length 33 cm; weight 350 g.
Colour: Upperparts maroon-brown with white spots; underparts grey; bare eye-patch and legs.
Most like: African olive pigeon but greyer below and lacking bright yellow eye-patch and legs; African olive pigeon mostly confined to evergreen forest. Somewhat like common rock dove, but distinguished by dull red eye-patch and white spots.
Habitat: Mountains, cliffs, rocky gorges, buildings.

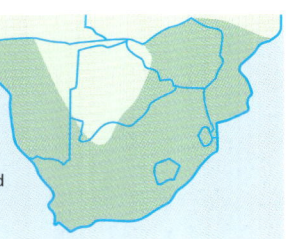

Common in rocky mountains, cliffs and cities of the entire subregion, except for northeastern Namibia, most of Botswana, western Zimbabwe and the extreme northerly Northern Cape.

The familiar *vuku-u-kooo* notes of courting speckled pigeons, as well as the male's deep-throated territorial *doo-doo-doo*, which rises in volume before dying away, may be heard throughout the year. Many southern African children grow up hearing these evocative sounds outside their classrooms. Every now and then a male speckled pigeon will take off from a ledge with bursts of wing-clapping, circle around and glide back again—apparently an advertising display.

An indigenous species, the speckled pigeon has managed to exist side-by-side with the introduced rock dove for perhaps 200 years or more without serious competition between the two. You can see both species on the roofs and window ledges of buildings in towns and cities almost throughout southern Africa.

Speckled, or rock, pigeons are also found in rural areas, including cultivated lands, where they pick up fallen grain after the harvest. Although flocks usually number no more than about 20, many hundreds may congregate where seed supplies are plentiful.

The typical stick-platform nest is built on a ledge at any time of the year. The male brings the sticks, while the female stays at the site and builds them into shape. She lays two pure white eggs which hatch after about 15 days into blind, thinly clad chicks called squabs. Both parents feed them a mixture of seeds, water and 'pigeon's milk'—a nutritious secretion from the lining of the crop. The young fly at about 26 days.

Ground birds

FIERY-NECKED NIGHTJAR

Afrikaanse naguil (*Caprimulgus pectoralis*)

Size: Length 24 cm; weight 37-66 g.
Colour: Intricately mottled, marbled and barred with grey, rust, black and white to give a highly camouflaged effect; large white patch on foreneck; bright rufous collar around neck; white spots in spread wing, outer tail feathers tipped white.
Most like: Other nightjar species; not easily separable in the field by sight alone; best identified by song (see below).
Habitat: Woodland, plantations, savanna, bushveld.

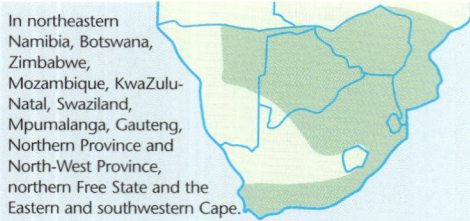

In northeastern Namibia, Botswana, Zimbabwe, Mozambique, KwaZulu-Natal, Swaziland, Mpumalanga, Gauteng, Northern Province and North-West Province, northern Free State and the Eastern and southwestern Cape.

ALPINE SWIFT

Witpenswindswael (*Tachymarptis melba*)

Size: Length 22 cm; weight 67-91 g.
Colour: Mouse-brown with white throat and belly, forming broad brown breastband.
Most like: Other swifts but white belly, forked tail and large size diagnostic. Somewhat similar to banded martin, but forked tail and all-dark underwing distinctive.
Habitat: Mostly mountains and gorges with high cliffs, but forages anywhere.

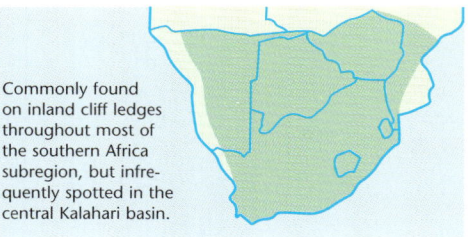

Commonly found on inland cliff ledges throughout most of the southern Africa subregion, but infrequently spotted in the central Kalahari basin.

The melodious *good-lord-deliver-us* call of the fiery-necked nightjar is a song most people recognize instantly, although few know the author of the sound. From this call comes the nickname 'litanybird'; you can hear it in the bushveld at any time of the year, but usually only in winter and spring in higher country. Its excellent camouflage makes it very difficult to find as it nestles on leaf litter by day, usually under a shady bush or tree. It will remain quite still, allowing you to walk within a metre of it before taking off.

The wings of all nightjars are long and pointed, giving these aerial predators a light, buoyant flight which is all but soundless. They catch their insect food in flight mainly at dusk and early dawn, or during bright, moonlit nights. A nightjar will spot a passing beetle, one of its favourite snacks, from a perch, snap it up in the air, and then return to its perch. Large eyes and a wide gape are adaptations to this kind of hunting.

From August to December fiery-necked nightjars lay their two pinkish-cream eggs on the leaf litter, sometimes clearing a small scrape on the ground in a spot sheltered by trees. The female incubates by day and the male by night; after about 18 days the helpless, downy chicks hatch and have to be fed for about 40 days before they become independent of the parents.

Propelled by long, sickle-shaped wings, swifts spend most of their lives on the wing, catching flying insects and small, floating spiders. Their flight is rapid and direct, unlike the more fluttering flight of the swallow family, and their aerial acrobatics as they swoop up to their nesting crevices on cliffs are a breathtaking spectacle.

The largest of our swifts, the Alpine swift is so named because it was first described from the mountains of central Europe, but it occurs throughout Africa, Madagascar and southern Asia to Sri Lanka. You can see it circling about the cliffs and over the veld around its breeding sites, often in the company of other species of swift.

Because they are extremely fast and powerful fliers, Alpine swifts are able to travel hundreds of kilometres every day and will feed far from mountains. Before a storm they can be seen foraging low over the ground; they are attracted to veld fires, where they catch the insects flushed out by the flames and smoke.

The nest site of the Alpine swift is a deep, vertical crack high on a cliff face; there the bird builds a half cup of feathers, gluing them together with its own saliva. The Alpine swift collects feathers for the nest in flight, snapping them up easily as they float in the wind. The female lays one or two white eggs which take about three weeks to hatch, and her young may stay in the nest for as long as nine weeks before they are able to fly properly.

Because of a common food supply and hunting method, swifts and swallows have evolved along very similar lines and consequently are similarly structured.

Ground birds

Little swift
Kleinwindswael *(Apus affinis)*

Size: Length 13 cm; weight 19–34 g.
Colour: All black with white throat and broad white band on rump.
Most like: White-rumped and Horus swifts, but square tail and broad white rump diagnostic. Böhm's and mottled spinetails also have square tails and white rumps, but are birds of forest and woodland.
Habitat: Cliffs, gorges, mountains and urban areas.

Found on high buildings, bridges or steep inland cliff ledges throughout the subregion, but rarely sighted in the central Kalahari basin where these features are absent.

Southern ground hornbill
Bromvoël *(Bucorvus leadbeateri)*

Size: Length 1,1 m; weight 3,5 kg.
Colour: All black, except for white flight feathers (visible in flight only) and bare, bright red skin, throat and wattles.
Most like: Domestic turkey. Not like any other indigenous southern African bird.
Habitat: Grassland, savanna, woodland.

Found throughout the well-watered regions of northern Namibia, northern Botswana, Zimbabwe, Mozambique, Swaziland, Mpumalanga, central and eastern KwaZulu-Natal and the Eastern Cape.

As with Alpine swifts, little swifts are included among ground birds because they live on rock faces and buildings.

Telltale signs of their presence around the lower parts of cliffs and on larger buildings in cities are the untidy clusters of nests which are glued securely together under overhanging ledges, and an accumulation of droppings scattered on the ground below.

You can often hear screaming parties of little swifts in the mornings and evenings around their home sites, since the birds use their nests throughout the year to roost in.

During the breeding season, little swifts fly up to their nests with twittering screams, barely touching the nest before dropping away again and flying off in a circle to return and repeat the performance. This is probably some kind of advertising display, possibly by males to show females which nests are suitable for breeding in and which males are ready for pairing off.

The nest is a rounded bowl of grass and feathers glued with saliva in the angle of an overhang; adjacent nests touch each other and may share a common entrance. From one to three white eggs are laid. Incubation takes about 21 days and the young fly at about 40 days but, because the availability of the aerial food of swifts is highly dependent on weather conditions, nestling periods vary considerably, taking far longer in wet weather than in fine.

You won't easily forget the deep, booming *du-du-dudududu* duet of the southern ground hornbill—one of the most unforgettable and stirring sounds of the eastern and more tropical parts of southern Africa. No less striking than this magnificent, reverberating voice is this ground hornbill's appearance—jet black with red accessories. When it flies, the visual effect of the white primary wing feathers is truly breathtaking.

Groups of three to eight birds pad solemnly about on the ground, looking for any kind of animal small enough to swallow whole (tortoises, snakes, frogs, insects and mammals). Sometimes they use their huge bills like picks to excavate food from the soil.

Despite their large size and mainly terrestrial feeding habits, small groups of southern ground hornbills roost in trees, well out on the end of a stout branch, their heads tucked into their shoulders and their bills pointing skywards like a row of scimitars. The groups are territorial and defend their boundaries by chasing each other in aerial pursuit—quite a sight, considering the size and apparent ungainliness of the bird.

Like all hornbills, this species nests in a hole, usually in a tree, but at times in a cliff or in the side of a deep donga. Unlike other hornbills, however, the female doesn't seal herself into the nest. She lays one or two white eggs and incubates them on her own for about 40 days, during which time she is fed by her mate and various other, immature members of her group. These nonbreeding 'helpers' benefit in the long run by gaining experience in parental care.

Ground birds

Rufous-naped lark
Rooineklewerik (*Mirafra africana*)

Size: Length 17 cm; weight 45 g.
Colour: Above mottled dark and light brown; flight feathers edged rufous with bold breast streaks; rufous nape visible only when crest is raised during singing. Light eye-stripe.
Most like: Some other larks, but large size, chunky shape, robust bill and generally rusty appearance diagnostic; rufous wings separate rufous-naped lark from other large lark species; voice very distinctive.
Habitat: Open grassland with perches (bushes, fence posts, termite mounds), acacia savanna, cultivated fields.

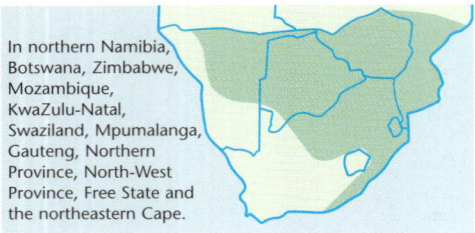

In northern Namibia, Botswana, Zimbabwe, Mozambique, KwaZulu-Natal, Swaziland, Mpumalanga, Gauteng, Northern Province, North-West Province, Free State and the northeastern Cape.

Rock martin
Kransswael (*Hirundo fuligula*)

Size: Length 13 cm; weight 23 g.
Colour: Smoky brown above, pale ochre-brown or pinkish cinnamon below; square brown tail shows small, rounded white windows when spread in flight.
Most like: Brown-throated martin, but square tail with white windows, and pale brown (not white) belly distinctive.
Habitat: Rocky cliffs, gorges, mountains, buildings.

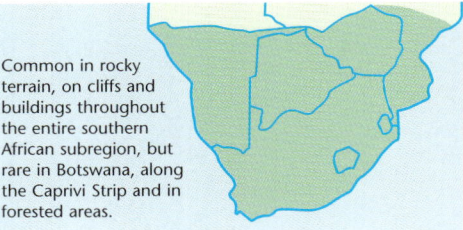

Common in rocky terrain, on cliffs and buildings throughout the entire southern African subregion, but rare in Botswana, along the Caprivi Strip and in forested areas.

Larks are usually hard to identify, but there's no mistaking the cheerful, whistled *tiree-tiroo* of the rufous-naped lark in summer when the males are in song. You will hear this simple song—interspersed with an occasional brief wing-rattle—coming from the lark's perch on a telephone wire, a termite mound or even a rooftop.

While cruising several metres above the ground, the males also whistle a flight song which imitates the calls of other lark species.

Rufous-naped larks are common and widespread, and you will find them even in suburban areas where some open grassveld still exists.

The bird usually betrays its presence by jumping up in front of you, flying a short way on its rusty wings, then dropping suddenly into the grass again, often with a twist in its flight path. It runs like a rodent between the tufts and disappears.

The bird builds its shallow, domed nest on the ground against a grass tuft, often with the living grass woven into the roof. Two or three speckled eggs are laid. Near the nest you may see the parents perform a wing-snapping distraction flight as they bounce in the air, but the nest itself won't be easy to find.

The rufous-naped lark feeds mainly on insects, but also enjoys a meal of spiders, earthworms, millipedes and seeds when these are available.

Although it looks like a slow flier, the rock martin has been timed cruising effortlessly at speeds of up to 80 kilometres per hour. Because it flies so well it is able to forage far afield, especially outside the breeding season which falls mostly between August and April. It is the only all-brown swallow in southern Africa and is distributed throughout the region wherever a suitable habitat is available. (Swallows and martins belong to the same family; martins are usually brown, swallows metallic blue, but this is a not fixed rule.)

Rock martins are well camouflaged in their natural habitat of brown rocks, where they often rest on cliff ledges or in potholes in between bouts of foraging for flying insects. You may see them foraging with other kinds of swallows and swifts, usually singly or in pairs, seldom far from cliffs or taller buildings. As with many cliff-dwellers, rock martins have taken to buildings as substitutes for cliffs; in very flat country they even choose farmhouses or road culverts as roosting and nesting sites. The provision of manmade structures away from mountains has led to a spread of this bird in southern Africa.

For a nest both the male and female rock martin build a half cup of mud pellets against a vertical wall or rock face under a protective overhang, usually two metres or more above the ground. The clutch numbers two to three white eggs (rarely up to six in a good season) which hatch in 16-17 days. The young are fed in the nest for up to a month before they can fly.

Ground birds

WHITE-NECKED RAVEN

Withalskraai *(Corvus albicollis)*

Size: Length 52 cm; weight 600 g.
Colour: Black with white collar at back of neck; bill black with white tip.
Most like: Pied crow, but without white on belly; Cape crow is all black with slender bill; white-necked raven has very heavy bill, broad wings and relatively short, fanned tail in flight.
Habitat: Mountains, gorges and cliffs.

Occurs in central and eastern Zimbabwe, northern and southern Mozambique, KwaZulu-Natal, Lesotho, the eastern Free State, the Eastern Cape and southwestern Cape.

CAPE ROCK THRUSH

Kaapse klipsyter *(Monticola rupestris)*

Size: Length 22 cm; weight 60-63 g.
Colour: Male has blue-grey head; underparts bright rusty orange; back mottled dark brown and rusty; tail orange with black centre. Female similar, but head brown, lightly mottled with white.
Most like: Sentinel and short-toed rock thrushes, but sentinel male has whole breast and back blue-grey; short-toed male has white crown. Sentinel female has underparts mottled brown and white; short-toed female is plain brown above with white throat.
Habitat: Rocky gorges, cliffs and mountainsides, usually with scattered bushes.

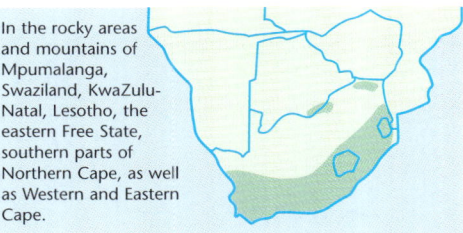

In the rocky areas and mountains of Mpumalanga, Swaziland, KwaZulu-Natal, Lesotho, the eastern Free State, southern parts of Northern Cape, as well as Western and Eastern Cape.

White-necked ravens, like speckled pigeons, love wild, steep mountains where inaccessible cliffs and strong winds create ideal conditions for soaring. You will often hear the raven's high-pitched croaking in mountainous regions, particularly in Lesotho and the Drakensberg. They are great scavengers, and their strong bills make easy work of picking away at the tough meat and skin of carrion, which they particularly enjoy. They also feed on tortoises, which they scoop up and drop from a height to break the shell. Indeed, ravens will eat almost anything, and they don't smell too good either.

Usually occurring singly or in pairs, white-necked ravens sometimes congregate in flocks of up to 150 at a rich source, such as a carcass, but they give way to the larger Cape vultures when they arrive on the scene. Ravens are wily birds, however, and, given the chance, will sneak in between the vultures to snatch titbits of meat and entrails.

Farmers don't care much for white-necked ravens because they sometimes injure lambs or calves during birth. However, the pied crow is far more prone to such macabre behaviour than the raven.

The raven's nest, built on an inaccessible cliff ledge, consists of a large bowl of sticks which it lines with soft material, such as wool, grass, hair or rags. Four eggs, coloured light green with grey, brown and olive streaks, are laid and incubated for about 20 days. The nestling period is about 40 days. Like most black-and-white birds, ravens have few natural enemies.

The clear notes of the Cape rock thrush echo beautifully among the rocks and gorges it inhabits, which is not surprising because rock thrushes are among South Africa's finest singers. The Cape rock thrush's song consists of short, sweet, whistled phrases interspersed with short pauses, uttered from the top of a rock or bush.

Several species of rock-dwelling birds have rust and blue-grey colour patterns, possibly for camouflage among the lichen-covered rocks. These include the rock thrushes, some of the buntings (Cape and rock), the female red-winged starling, the rockrunner of Namibia, the rockjumpers, the speckled pigeon and the rock kestrel. The Cape rock thrush is one of the commonest and most widespread species of the group in southern Africa and can be seen from the coast to the Drakensberg. It generally prefers steeper and more rugged places than does the sentinel rock thrush.

Cape rock thrushes feed on almost any kind of insect, as well as on spiders, small frogs and even nectar and fruit.

They nest in spring and summer in a crevice or on a ledge, making a large mass of grass and soil with a neat cup-shaped hollow at the top, in which three pale blue eggs are laid. The eggs hatch after about 14 days.

Ground birds

African stonechat
Gewone bontrokkie (*Saxicola torquata*)

Size: Length 14 cm; weight 12-18 g.
Colour: Male black above, including head and throat; breast and flanks bright chestnut; belly, rump, wing bar and large patch on each side of neck white. Female brown above, streaked blackish; breast light, rusty ochre; belly, wing bar and rump white.
Most like: Black-headed canary, but chestnut and black coloration on body feathers reversed. White rump distinguishes both sexes of stonechat from all other birds of similar size and coloration.
Habitat: Lush grasslands, vleis, canefields, irrigated lands, riverine scrub.

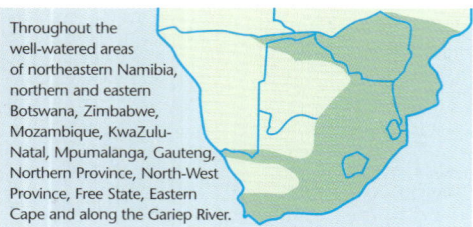

Throughout the well-watered areas of northeastern Namibia, northern and eastern Botswana, Zimbabwe, Mozambique, KwaZulu-Natal, Mpumalanga, Gauteng, Northern Province, North-West Province, Free State, Eastern Cape and along the Gariep River.

The scientific name of the stonechat means 'collared rock-dweller', but this is not entirely true. The male's white neck patches may resemble a collar, but the bird is not confined to rocky places in southern Africa or anywhere else.

It is included among the ground birds here, because it catches most of its food on the ground, but it spends most of its time perched perkily on top of a weed, bush or telephone wire, from which it scans the ground for insects.

In flight, stonechats show a bright white rump that is concealed at rest, though 'rest' is something that these smart little birds never seem to do. Even when perched, they flick their tails and wings nervously, especially when alarmed. The repeated *seep-chak-chak* alarm call notes are often a sign that the adults have eggs or young nearby. The juveniles have spotted buff and blackish plumage.

Some stonechats seem to migrate between Zimbabwe and South Africa. However, most of those living in mountainous areas, such as the Drakensberg and in Lesotho, migrate down to KwaZulu-Natal and the Free State in winter, then move back into the mountains to breed from about September. Their nest is perhaps the hardest of all ground-nesting birds to find. A small grassy cup is deeply concealed under a grass tuft, often on a sloping hillside or on a low bank. Only the female incubates the three to four bright, blue-green eggs, but both parents feed the young.

Cape rockjumper
Kaapse berglyster (*Chaetops frenatus*)

Size: Length 24 cm.
Colour: Male grey on back, streaked with black; throat and breast black, sharply outlined at sides with white stripe; eyebrow and wing bar white; belly and rump bright chestnut, tail black with white tip. Female less brightly coloured; throat and breast greyish.
Most like: Drakensberg rockjumper, but belly always chestnut in both sexes, not light rusty orange.
Habitat: Rocky slopes from sea level to high mountains.

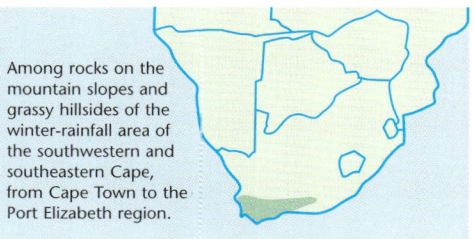

Among rocks on the mountain slopes and grassy hillsides of the winter-rainfall area of the southwestern and southeastern Cape, from Cape Town to the Port Elizabeth region.

Rockjumpers are highly specialized babblers, adapted to bounding about steep, rock-strewn habitats on their long, strong legs. They use their wings only if the rocks are far apart, flying in long glides with bursts of wingbeats in between, the longish, white-tipped tail fanned out behind.

The Cape rockjumper is a delight to see and hear because of its cheerful postures and ringing calls. It runs about, seeking out insects and lizards on the ground and in low vegetation, often holding its conspicuous tail cocked up at an angle, rather like a small roadrunner.

For a nest it builds a bulky bowl of grass on the ground against a rock, usually hidden under a grass tuft, and lines it with fine roots and hair. The eggs— usually two—are white. This is unusual among ground-nesting birds, but may indicate that, like doves' eggs, they don't taste good and should be left alone by potential predators. After the chicks hatch, both parents feed them until they are old enough to run about foraging for themselves.

The Cape and Drakensberg rockjumpers used to be considered geographical races of one species, but they have now been separated, the Cape rockjumper occurring in the winter-rainfall region of the southwestern Cape, and the orange-breasted rockjumper in the summer-rainfall region further east.

Ground birds

AFRICAN PIPIT

Gewone koester *(Anthus cinnamomeus)*

Size: Length 17 cm; weight 20-28 g.
Colour: Above light brown, streaked dark brown; below buffy to whitish, streaked dark brown on breast; tail dark with white outer feathers.
Most like: Mountain pipit, but mainly in lowlands; very like most other pipits and not easily distinguished by sight alone; outer tail feathers buff to greyish in mountain, long-billed, plain-backed and buffy pipits.
Habitat: Grassveld, savanna, airfields, playing fields, city parks.

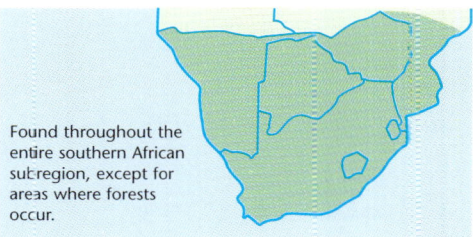

Found throughout the entire southern African subregion, except for areas where forests occur.

The commonest pipit in southern Africa, the African pipit—also called Richard's or grassveld pipit—is the ultimate LBJ (Little Brown Job). Almost any southern African pipit away from rocky habitats and mountains is likely to be the African pipit, especially if it has white outer tail feathers.

You can see this species on grassy sidewalks or road islands in built-up areas, where it runs about feeding on insects and grass seeds. Pipits characteristically dip their tails two or three times after landing, thereby distinguishing themselves from the otherwise similar larks.

In spring and summer the African pipit has a distinctive display flight in which the male rises from the ground in a series of upward loops, getting ever higher and giving a short series of *tree-tree-tree* notes at each loop. At a height of 30-40 m the bird suddenly dives straight to the ground, uttering an unbroken series of call notes as it goes. It may end its display by landing on the ground or perching on a fence, a termite mound or low bush.

When disturbed on the ground, the African pipit flies off with a repeated two-note *chissik* call.

Like all other pipits, this species nests on the ground in dense grass, concealing its cup of rootlets and grass under a tuft or weed. The female lays three light grey- and brown-speckled eggs which hatch at about two weeks. An incubating pipit often leaves its nest with an injury-feigning display and wheezy calls to distract a predator.

CAPE LONGCLAW

Oranjekeelkalkoentjie
(Macronyx capensis)

Size: Length 20 cm; weight 41-49 g.
Colour: Above deep buffy brown, streaked and spotted with dark brown; throat brightly orange, bordered by broad black collar; belly and eyebrow deep mango-yellow; tail dark with white tips; female slightly less brightly coloured than male.
Most like: Yellow-throated longclaw, but throat orange; belly deeper, duller yellow; voice very different.
Habitat: Moist grassland and vlei areas, usually without trees.

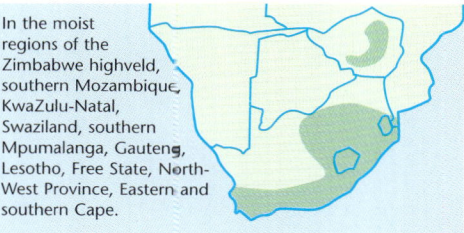

In the moist regions of the Zimbabwe highveld, southern Mozambique, KwaZulu-Natal, Swaziland, southern Mpumalanga, Gauteng, Lesotho, Free State, North-West Province, Eastern and southern Cape.

Few wildlife experiences can match the first good view of a Cape (also known as orange-throated) longclaw with its underparts exposed, transforming a drab, well-camouflaged pipitlike bird into a bright, colourful one as if by magic. The name 'longclaw' refers to the very long toes and claws that enable these birds to walk easily over the tussocky grass of their chosen habitat. In fact, a longclaw perched on a fence will be seen to have almost ungainly feet.

Put to flight, the Cape longclaw makes a catlike mewing, sometimes interspersed with sharp *deewit, deewit* calls, quite unlike the mellow whistles of the yellow-throated longclaw with which it sometimes overlaps. As it flies it shows the white tips of the spread tail feathers; then it suddenly dives into the grass and disappears from view.

It may perch on a termite mound or fence to sing or look around, but it spends most of its day foraging on the ground for its insect food. It may even follow a plough to see what it can find in the newly turned soil.

Cape longclaws breed from August to April, but mainly in midsummer (November to January) when the grass is green and dense. A bowl of coarse grass, lined with fine rootlets, is placed in a scrape at the base of a grass tuft, usually well hidden from above. Three white, grey- or brown-spotted eggs are laid, which are incubated for about two weeks.

Ground birds

RED-WINGED STARLING

Rooivlerkspreeu *(Onychognathus morio)*

Size: Length 28 cm; weight 115-148 g.
Colour: Glossy blue-black all over, except for rusty-red wings which show up clearly in flight. Female has grey head, breast and mantle, streaked on breast and mantle with black.
Most like: Pale-winged starling, but red-winged starling has dark rusty wings, not pale creamy orange, and eyes dark, not bright orange.
Habitat: Mountains, cliffs, buildings; also coastal bush and fruiting trees.

In central and northern Zimbabwe, western Mozambique, KwaZulu-Natal, Mpumalanga, Gauteng, parts of Northern Province, Lesotho, central and eastern Free State, the Karoo, and the southwestern and Eastern Cape.

Red-winged starlings keep in touch with each other by means of a series of melodious whistles, whether they are foraging or flying high to their roosting cliffs. They spend most of their lives on cliffs or buildings, coming to feed on the ground only when suitable food, such as termites, is available there. Otherwise they forage in trees for fruit and insects, or take nectar from aloes, daubing their faces a bright orange with pollen. Like their close relatives, the oxpeckers, red-winged starlings may ride on the backs of larger game mammals and domestic stock to feed on ticks and other parasites.

Gregarious except when breeding, flocks of these starlings number from about a dozen birds to several hundred, even up to 3 000, depending on the concentration of the food supply.

Alarmed by a cat or a snake, they let out a harsh *skharrr* alarm call, especially if they are nesting. When there are young in the nest the aggressive male may even dive-bomb and strike a person walking by.

Redwings nest in holes or crevices of cliffs, caves or buildings, making a large bowl of plant material which they bind with mud and line with finer fibres such as hair or pine needles. The female usually lays three bright blue-green eggs which she incubates for about 16 days. Both parents feed the chicks for about a month before they can fly.

Having adapted from cliffs to buildings, red-winged starlings regularly take up residence in some southern African towns and cities. You can attract them to your garden by growing suitable fruit trees.

YELLOW BISHOP

Kaapse flap *(Euplectes capensis)*

Size: Length averages (m) 14 cm, (f) 12,5 cm; weight (m) 21 g, (f) 17 g.
Colour: Breeding male black with bright yellow patch on rump and bend of wing. Female and nonbreeding male streaked black on buff above with yellow (male) or olive-yellow (female) patch on wrist; below buff-white, streaked brown on breast and flanks; male has bright yellow rump in all plumages.
Most like: Other female and nonbreeding male widows and bishops, but yellowish patch on wrist distinguishes it, as does the yellow rump of male. Breeding male similar to yellow-backed and white-winged widowbirds, but rump yellow, not black, no white in wing and no yellow on upper back of yellow bishop.
Habitat: Lush grasslands, marshes, vleis, often with bushes, usually in hilly country.

In eastern Caprivi, central and eastern Zimbabwe, Mozambique, KwaZulu-Natal, Mpumalanga, Gauteng, eastern Free State and Lesotho, and along the southeastern and southern Cape coast.

Yellow bishop males look like giant black-and-yellow bees as they buzz around with puffed-out plumage, nasal zipping *zimp zitit zeemp* song and wing-rattling. The drab females are either on their nests or bringing food to hungry young and are less often noticed.

Although it used to be called the Cape bishop (its other alternative name is yellow-rumped widow), this bird is by no means confined to the Cape—it occurs as far north as Ethiopia and Nigeria. It is generally found in small groups or in the company of up to 20 birds, often with other *Euplectes* species, foraging for seeds and insects.

Almost any marshy place in the eastern mountains and the southern fynbos region of southern Africa will have its breeding group of yellow bishops, usually a male with two to three females. Two or more such groups may inhabit such a marsh if it is big enough.

The breeding male weaves a framework of green grass in dense, low vegetation, forming an oval with a side entrance near the top. The female then lines this with dry grass and lays three blotched, greenish or bluish eggs inside. She performs all the parental duties, although the male may help feed the young at times.

Ground birds

FAN-TAILED WIDOWBIRD

Kortstertflap *(Euplectes axillaris)*

Size: Length averages (m) 18 cm, (f) 14 cm; weight (m) 30 g, (f) 22 g.

Colour: Breeding male black with bright red patch at bend of wing (may be concealed when perched). Female and nonbreeding male streaked black on buff above with red or rusty patch at bend of wing; below white, streaked brown on breast and flanks.

Most like: Other widowbirds and bishops in nonbreeding plumage, but distinguished by reddish patch on wrist; breeding male unmistakeable.

Habitat: Open, moist grassland, vleis, marshes, edges of sugar cane fields.

Along the east coast from the southeastern Cape, through KwaZulu-Natal and Swaziland to the Mozambique coast, with populations also occurring in the Okavango Delta system of Botswana.

Floppy display flights, accompanied by wheezy calls, are characteristic of the breeding male of this species, one of the commonest grassland birds in the eastern lowlands of southern Africa.

The fan-tailed (also known as the red-shouldered) widowbird has adapted well to human farming practices in KwaZulu-Natal, and is particularly partial to fields of sugar cane and lush pastures which resemble its ancestral marshy habitat.

Like other widowbirds, this conspicuously coloured breeding male has a harem of two to four females in his territory which he patrols regularly.

Unless it is in flight or actively displaying, the male's red epaulettes are often concealed, so the bird looks completely black, except for its bluish-grey bill.

Outside of the breeding season, you can distinguish the males in nonbreeding plumage from the females because they retain their black flight feathers.

Mixed flocks of males and females of one or more widowbird species gather in winter, often in hundreds, to forage for seeds on the ground.

Males build the nests in lush grass and the females line them, each female laying two to four greenish, grey-clouded eggs in the oval nest with its side-top entrance.

Only the female participates in parental care, incubating the eggs for 12-13 days and feeding the chicks (mainly on insects) for 15-16 days.

LONG-TAILED WIDOWBIRD

Langstertflap *(Euplectes progne)*

Size: Breeding (m) 58 cm, nonbreeding (m) 23 cm, (f) 19 cm; weight (m) 42 g, (f) 32 g.

Colour: Breeding male all black with scarlet-and-white patch at bend of wing; tail very long and floppy; nonbreeding male streaked black on buff above, brown on whitish below; bend of wing orange; flight feathers black; bill blue-grey. Female similar to nonbreeding male, but smaller, wings brown; no coloured patch on wing.

Most like: Larger widowbirds, but tail short and floppy in female and nonbreeding male; wings broad, flight heavy. Breeding male much larger than fan-tailed widowbird (which has shorter tail) and red-collared widowbird (which lacks coloured wing patches).

Habitat: Open grassland and vleis.

Found in the well-watered grassy areas of the Gauteng and Mpumalanga highveld, inland KwaZulu-Natal, Lesotho, eastern Free State and Eastern Cape.

The long-tailed widowbird or *sakabula* is common in the highveld where you can see the breeding males flying laboriously across the grass, their long tails—measuring up to 50 cm—streaming out behind them. Looking rather like slow, black rockets, the birds fly quite high as a rule, coming down to roost in reeds beds in the evening.

This gregarious bird forages mainly on the ground, walking with short steps as it keeps a close watch for seeds and insects.

In display the males depress their tails to produce an elegantly bowed effect with which they advertise their territories at intervals throughout the day. When danger threatens, the male flies about, giving *zik-zik* warning notes which send the females fleeing from their nests in the grass.

The nest, built low down in a grass tuft, consists of a woven framework filled with a ball of dry grass with a wide side entrance.

Here the female lays three dull greenish eggs with brown and grey smudges. She incubates for 14 days and takes care of the chicks without any help from the male. The young can fly at about 17 days.

Although it has been said that the males cannot fly when their tails get waterlogged, this is not so because the feathers shed water quite easily.

Ground birds

COMMON WAXBILL

Rooibeksysie *(Estrilda astrild)*

Size: Length 12 cm; weight 10 g.
Colour: Greyish brown above, greyer below, with fine blackish bars; bill, eye-patch and centre of belly bright red; undertail black.
Most like: Some other waxbills, but red bill and belly diagnostic in adults. Not easily confused with any other small seed-eating bird in southern Africa.
Habitat: Rank grass and weeds, often near water or in marshy country; also in gardens and around cultivated lands.

Found throughout the damp, long-grassed and river-fed parts of the southern African subregion, but absent from the dry central Kalahari Desert area.

You can hear the common waxbill's familiar *ching-ching-ching* notes in the open veld or at a feeding tray in a garden. A favourite cage bird in South Africa, it prefers feeding on the ground, picking up seeds and husking them with sharp movements of its strong bill, but it will also take green grass seeds off standing stalks.

Common waxbills move about the countryside searching for food in flocks of up to 30 or more birds. As they land in the grass they flick their longish tails from side to side, showing the black undertail feathers; then they work their way down the grass stems to the ground, or up the stems to the seeding tops. Many hundreds may roost together at night in rows in reed beds.

Towards spring and early summer the flocks of waxbills break up as the birds pair off to breed.

The nest is built on the ground—an oval of dry grass with a tubular entrance facing onto a small bare earth 'courtyard'. Between three and nine tiny white eggs are laid, each weighing less than a gram. Both parents incubate for about 12 days and feed the chicks for a further 20 days. The common waxbill is the favoured host of the pin-tailed whydah, and raises its own chicks along with those of the whydah in apparent harmony.

The common waxbill has been introduced to many oceanic islands and to Brazil, but its home is Africa south of the Sahara.

CAPE BUNTING

Rooivlerkstreepkoppie *(Emberiza capensis)*

Size: Length 16 cm; weight 17-24 g.
Colour: Mainly grey, streaked on back with black; head boldly striped black and white; wings bright rusty.
Most like: Cinnamon-breasted and golden-breasted buntings, but grey underparts distinctive.
Habitat: Rocky mountains, gorges and hillsides.

In the drier regions of western Namibia, central Zimbabwe, the highlands of Mpumalanga, Gauteng and North-West Province, western KwaZulu-Natal, Lesotho, Free State, and throughout most of Northern, Western and Eastern Cape.

The clear *weetypee-weetypee* call notes of the Cape bunting make it easy to identify in the rocky terrain where it is most commonly found, from the arid Namib to the high Drakensberg. You will most likely see it perched on top of a rock or stone, partly camouflaged by its grey and rusty colours.

This usually tame little bird learns quickly to come to food put out for it, such as seeds or a crust of bread. It also eats soft-bodied insects and spiders, which it feeds to its young as a source of protein and water. It comes singly or in pairs to drink at pools, especially in the drier parts of southern Africa. When foraging on the ground, it walks or shuffles with small steps, but hops when it wants to move more quickly. It flies with a bouncing rhythm and lands on top of rocks—often doing a quick about-face. The Afrikaans name *rooivlerkstreepkoppie* draws attention to two highly distinctive features—the reddish wing and the striped head—by which you can easily identify it.

Cape buntings breed mainly during the rainy season, so they start in winter in the Cape, and in January or February further north.

The nest is a small cup of grass and rootlets on the ground or low down in a dense bush next to a rock. The spotted white, bluish or pale green eggs, usually two to three in a clutch, are probably incubated largely or entirely by the female, but parental care in this species has not been well studied.

As with so many other southern African birds, the Cape bunting's distribution ranges from high, cold mountainous regions to hot, dry lowlands in the west.

Waterbirds

African penguin

Brlpikkewyn *(Spheniscus demersus)*

Size: *Length 60 cm; weight 2,1-3,6 kg.*
Colour: *Above black; below white with narrow black band across chest down flanks to legs; broad white eyebrow continuous with white upper breast; face patch black; pink patch above each eye; bill and feet black.*
Most like: *Some other small penguins, but black band on white underparts distinctive; other penguin species very rare on southern African coasts.*
Habitat: *Open sea and offshore islands; occurs rarely on mainland.*

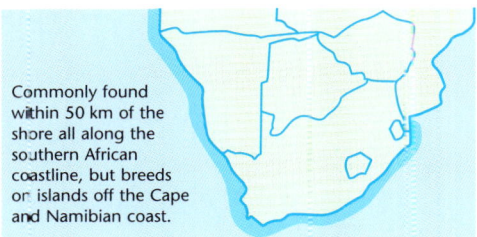

Commonly found within 50 km of the shore all along the southern African coastline, but breeds on islands off the Cape and Namibian coast.

According to the 2000 International Union for Conservation of Nature and Natural Resources' Red Data Book, the African penguin (previously called the jackass penguin) is a vulnerable species, which means it is of great conservation concern and must be carefully protected if it is not to become extinct. Since this is our only endemic southern African penguin, its loss would be a tragedy.

Once seen in vast numbers on southern African shores, this species has suffered from over-exploitation by man, as well as from oil pollution.

African penguins leave their roosting islands at dawn to forage at sea, seldom travelling more than 12 km from land. They have a taste for anchovies, gobies, squid and octopuses, on which they feed around midday. They return to their islands again at dusk. These penguins pursue prey under water, propelled by their flippers which are modified wings; they use their feet only as a rudder. The hook at the tip of the bill and the pointed protrusions on the tongue and palate help the birds hold slippery prey.

They make a loud, donkeylike braying when at their breeding grounds—the source of their previous 'jackass' nomenclature. Honks and growls also form part of their vocal repertoire, although the penguins are usually silent when actually in the sea.

The individual nests consist of a pad of feathers and grass in a shallow burrow in the ground, and occur in fairly dense colonies. Two white eggs form the clutch. After an incubation period of about 38 days, the parents feed the nestlings for a further 80 days or more before they can forage for themselves.

Little grebe

Kleindobbertjie *(Tachybaptus ruficollis)*

Size: *Length 20 cm; weight 119-197 g.*
Colour: *Blackish brown above; pale rusty below; sides of neck rich chestnut; pale cream-coloured swelling at base of bill.*
Most like: *White-backed duck, but back plain; bill relatively small and pointed; fluffy 'tail-less' posterior distinguishes little grebe from all ducks; black-necked grebe has no pale swelling at base of bill and has pure white belly.*
Habitat: *Any inland waters, including slow-flowing rivers and streams.*

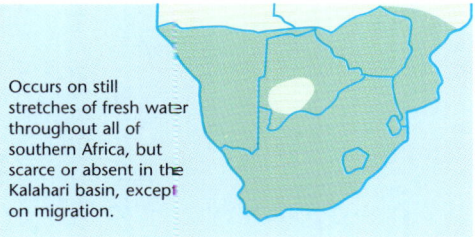

Occurs on still stretches of fresh water throughout all of southern Africa, but scarce or absent in the Kalahari basin, except on migration.

Previously called the dabchick, from the ancient English words 'dab', to dive, and 'chick', an abbreviated form of chicken, this fluffy little diving bird is one of the most adaptable of all small aquatic birds—it occurs from the smallest dams and ponds to larger pans and marshes.

The little grebe announces its presence with a shrill ascending then descending trill. Often, however, the only initial evidence of this species' presence might be a gently fading series of concentric ripples on the water. The bird may pop up later a short way off, or surface silently among the emergent plants at the water's edge and remain so still and well camouflaged as to be almost undetectable.

As it dives, it may kick up its large, lobed feet with a splash, though it can submerge with hardly a ripple. It can remain underwater as long as 50 seconds and travel up to 30 metres. Its plumage remains perfectly dry because of its water-repellency.

The little grebe's legs are set so far back on its body that it can hardly walk on land, so it builds a floating nest on the water. Made of water plants, the nest is anchored to branches and stems.

The clutch consists of three to five white eggs that soon become stained brown. When the sitting parent leaves the nest it covers the eggs with a billful of loose nest material to conceal them and make the nest look like flood debris. Incubation takes 18-25 days and the young learn to fly at about 50 days.

Waterbirds

Great white pelican
Witpelikaan
(*Pelecanus onocrotalus*)

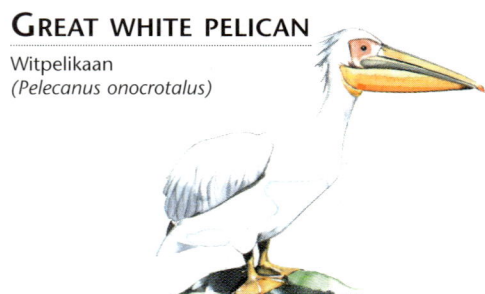

Size: Length 1,4-1,78 m; weight (m) 9-15 kg, (f) 5,4-9 kg.
Colour: Mostly white, tinged pink when breeding; edges and tips of wings black; large greyish to yellowish bill, legs and feet yellow or pink.
Most like: Pink-backed pelican, but whiter; wings show highly contrasting black-and-white pattern (generally greyer and more uniform in pink-backed pelican); yellow bill usually distinctive (greyer in pink-backed pelican).
Habitat: Sheltered marine bays and large expanses of inland waters.

Along the coast from Cape Town to northern Namibia, Botswana and western Zimbabwe. Also along the east coast from Mozambique to Transkei region of the Eastern Cape, inland KwaZulu-Natal and Mpumalanga.

One of the most splendid sights in the arena of southern African wildlife is a long skein of great white pelicans in flight over a large body of water, whether it be Durban Harbour or Etosha Pan. These huge birds with their three-metre wingspan glide and soar with seemingly effortless grace, rising at times to heights of 1000m or more, before re-forming into a V-shaped squadron and flying to their feeding grounds.

Great white pelicans have a taste for fish—usually up to around 100g in weight, though they may swallow fish up to four kilograms at times. A group of pelicans may fish cooperatively; swimming abreast, they dip their heads and partly raise their wings in unison, as if in a ballet. As they close in on a shoal, the water foams with frantic fishes, and the pelicans plunge their heads faster and faster into the water, scooping their prey up in their large bill pouches.

Crustaceans are another sought-after delicacy.

Great white pelicans breed in large colonies on offshore islands as well as on islands and shorelines of large bodies of water. The nest is a mere scrape on the ground, lined with grass, sticks and feathers collected by the male from nearby plants, or pilfered from other pelicans' nests. The female arranges the material in the scrape and then lays two chalky white eggs which both parents incubate for about 40 days. Because the first-hatched chick kills the second, only one is raised at the time. The survivor leaves the nest after about two-and-a-half months.

Cape gannet
Witmalgas (*Morus capensis*)

Size: Length 84-94 cm; weight (m) 2,3-3 kg, (f) 2,2-3,2 kg.
Colour: White; tail, wing tips and rear edge of wing black; head washed with golden yellow; bill pale blue-grey.
Most like: Some albatrosses, but pale greyish, pointed bill and yellow head distinctive; flight flapping with little gliding (albatrosses mostly glide).
Habitat: Open sea and offshore islands.

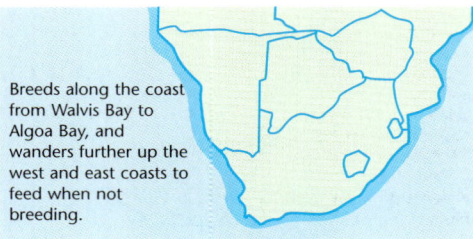

Breeds along the coast from Walvis Bay to Algoa Bay, and wanders further up the west and east coasts to feed when not breeding.

The magnificent spectacle of Cape gannets diving *en masse* onto shoals of fish—such as the KwaZulu-Natal sardine run—is one of nature's truly unforgettable shows. Hundreds of these large, white birds fill the sky with their wheeling shapes as others plunge rocketlike into the sea, sending up columns of white foam as they hit the water. Each dive is aimed at a particular fish. As the fish is caught, the Cape gannet swallows it and then takes off again to resume its glide-and-plunge foraging—each bird eats some 300g of food per day.

You will see feeding flocks of Cape gannets at their real home on the cold west coast of southern Africa, but not in such concentrations as those which follow the sardine run. These great birds once fed mainly on pilchards, but heavy competition from commercial trawlers forced them to turn to anchovies for the bulk of their food. Indeed, pilchards are barely obtainable any more, and numbers of these birds have declined significantly as a result. Given a respite from trawling, pilchard and gannet populations may well increase.

Despite a reduction in their numbers, Cape gannets are still common on the islands of the west coast. Each evening they return in long, loose flocks to these roosting islands, which are also used as nesting places. Dense colonies of thousands of gannets congregate to build their rough bowls of seaweed, guano and sticks on the ground. Each female lays only one chalky bluish-white egg which both parents take turns to incubate by covering it with their large, webbed feet. The egg hatches in approximately 42 days, and the chicks leave the nest after three months.

Waterbirds

WHITE-BREASTED CORMORANT

Witborsduiker
(Phalacrocorax carbo lucidus)

Size: Length 90 cm; weight 1-2,2 kg.
Colour: Black with greenish gloss; variable extent of white from chin to breast; breeding birds have white thigh patches; immature birds have whole underside off-white.
Most like: Immature and nonbreeding reed cormorant, but much larger; eyes green (red in reed cormorant).
Habitat: Inland waters and inshore seas and bays.

Inhabits freshwater and coastal areas throughout the southern African subregion, including rocky islands off the Western Cape coast. Absent from the waterless Kalahari basin.

The white-breasted cormorant, like other cormorants, perches with its wings spread after a fishing expedition, as if holding them out to dry. One apparent reason for this is to expose an area of short, black down on its back to the warming rays of the sun, thus restoring vital body heat lost to the water. Once its body temperature is above normal, it dives again to 'offload' the excess heat and catch more food.

Cormorants lose heat easily because their plumage is not waterproof (unlike that of ducks and most waterbirds), and the water gets to the skin. This reduces the bird's buoyancy and therefore the amount of energy it needs to remain submerged, a useful adaptation when it is pursuing underwater prey.

This species is the largest of our cormorants and has an almost worldwide distribution, including most of Africa south of the Sahara, Europe, central and southern Asia, Australasia and eastern North America. Although found on almost any inland waters, it prefers bigger dams and pans where it pursues fishes and frogs underwater, swimming with its large webbed feet.

The white-breasted cormorant may forage alone or gregariously, but it invariably nests in colonies of several to many pairs. It builds a large stick nest on the ground of a protected island, or in a tree standing in a dam. The clutch usually consists of three greenish-blue and white eggs which both sexes incubate for about 28 days. The parents feed the chicks on regurgitated food for about 50 days. However, if disturbed, the young will leave the nest before they can fly.

CAPE CORMORANT

Trekduiker *(Phalacrocorax capensis)*

Size: Length 61-64 cm; weight 1,1-1,3 kg.
Colour: Black all over; bare facial skin bright yellow, iris turquoise.
Most like: Bank cormorant, but yellow face and rather long, slender bill distinctive; more heavily built than crowned cormorant and tail proportionately shorter.
Habitat: Inshore coastal waters and some estuaries.

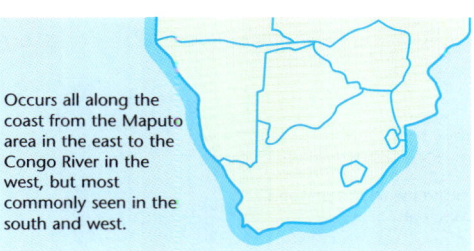

Occurs all along the coast from the Maputo area in the east to the Congo River in the west, but most commonly seen in the south and west.

Stand anywhere on the shoreline of the Cape Peninsula in the mornings and evenings and you may see long skeins of black birds flying low over the sea as they head homeward to their roosts or out to sea to their fishing grounds. From time to time the line of birds may disappear from sight behind a large swell, only to rise again in a wavy line beyond, cruising steadily at a speed of about 75 kilometres an hour. These are flocks of Cape cormorants, among the most abundant of all the seabirds off the west coast of southern Africa.

Cape cormorants are gregarious at all times. Flocks fly together, feed together, roost together and breed in large colonies. They fish by pursuing their prey under water, remaining submerged for up to 30 seconds. Nature has endowed the Cape cormorant with a hook at the tip of its bill—designed to hold the slippery prey before swallowing it at the surface. Most of the fishes eaten are quite small and consist of the common cold-water species such as anchovies and maasbankers, although pilchards are preferred if they are available.

Breeding colonies assemble on offshore islands or artificially constructed guano platforms from Algoa Bay to Namibia. Nests often touch each other and consist of a shallow bowl of seaweed or sticks. The clutch usually consists of two or three white eggs, which both sexes incubate alternately for about 22 days. The chicks fly at about nine weeks, although they remain dependent on their parents for food for some weeks afterwards.

Waterbirds

Reed cormorant
Rietduiker
(Phalacrocorax africanus)

Size: Length 60 cm; weight (m) 570-685 g, (f) 425-570 g.
Colour: All black with yellow bill and bright red eyes; immature and nonbreeding birds have whitish underparts.
Most like: Crowned cormorant, but entirely freshwater in distribution; somewhat similar to white-breasted cormorant, but much smaller; underparts never pure white; distinguished from African darter by much shorter neck, hook at tip of bill and lack of white streaks on back.
Habitat: Any inland waters.

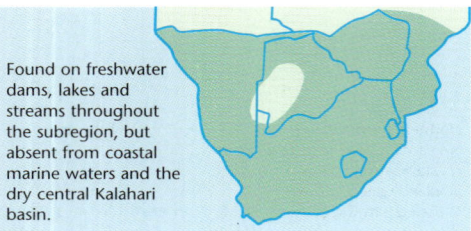

Found on freshwater dams, lakes and streams throughout the subregion, but absent from coastal marine waters and the dry central Kalahari basin.

African darter
Slanghalsvoël *(Anhinga rufa)*

Size: Length 80 cm; weight 948 g-1,8 kg.
Colour: Male mainly black with chestnut foreneck bordered by white stripe; female and nonbreeding male browner with pale underparts.
Most like: Reed cormorant, but bigger, with longer neck and tail, and more slender build; bill pointed (hooked at tip in all cormorants).
Habitat: Quiet inland waters; rarely on estuaries and coastal lagoons.

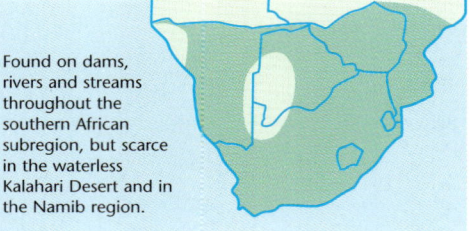

Found on dams, rivers and streams throughout the southern African subregion, but scarce in the waterless Kalahari Desert and in the Namib region.

When the high-flying reed cormorant travels with swiftly beating wings from one body of water to another, its long neck, body, tail and 90 cm wingspan give it a symmetrical, crosslike appearance.

This bird is the smallest and most widespread of our cormorants, and is usually solitary, except when breeding. You can see it on even the smallest ponds or farm dams because its main diet is frogs, which are ubiquitous. Reed cormorants also eat tiny fishes, as well as insects, crustaceans and even small birds. Such a wide diet ensures the success of the species. Much of what has been said of fishing adaptations in the white-breasted cormorant and the African darter applies also to the reed cormorant.

Usually silent, reed cormorants bleat, hiss and cackle at the nesting colony much as other cormorants do. And, like most other cormorants, this species breeds in the company of other cormorants or with herons, egrets and ibises.

Their stick nests are crowded together and may even touch each other. Nesting sites may be anywhere—some in reeds or on trees near water, others far from water on rocky cliff ledges.

The clutch of two to five (usually three or four) chalky bluish or greenish eggs hatches out in about 24 days and the parents feed their young by regurgitating food into their mouths for a further 35 days in the nest. Chicks may fall prey to water monitors, and only about 60 per cent of them survive the nestling period.

You will easily recognize the African darter by its long, kinked, snakelike neck (hence *slanghalsvoël*), its habit of swimming low in the water with just the neck showing, and the way it perches with its wings spread wide to dry, much as cormorants do (*see* white-breasted cormorant).

It swiftly pursues fishes and frogs under water, paddling with both feet simultaneously for maximum thrust; when swimming on the surface, it paddles its feet alternately like a duck. The African darter uses its pointed bill to spear prey and then brings it to the surface. Here it shakes the victim free, catches it in the air and swallows it head-first.

Because its plumage absorbs water, the darter uses little energy to stay submerged, but it does get heavier as a result and takes off with difficulty from the water. Once it has splashed its way into the air, it flies easily on quickly beating wings and may soar if conditions are right.

African darters become gregarious when breeding or roosting in partly submerged trees or reed beds. The nest is a rough platform of sticks or reeds, about 40-45 cm in diameter, a few metres above the water. The male collects most of the material and the female builds the nest. She then lays three to five chalky eggs which both sexes incubate for three to four weeks. The young take about six weeks to reach flying age, but will clamber out of the nest earlier if disturbed.

The darter has a wide distribution from Africa south of the Sahara to tropical Asia and Australia.

Waterbirds

GREY HERON
Bloureier *(Ardea cinerea)*

Size: Length 1 m; weight 1-1,8 kg.
Colour: Back grey; rest of body, including neck, white; black streak above eye and black patch on bend of wing; bill yellow (orange when breeding).
Most like: Black-headed heron, but whole neck white with few black streaks in front; yellow bill diagnostic (black in black-headed heron); underwing plain grey (contrasting black and white in black-headed heron).
Habitat: Inland waters; sometimes rocky coastlines.

Commonly spotted around both freshwater and saltwater sources throughout the southern African subregion, but rarely seen in the low-rainfall desert areas.

Almost any dam, river or sewage pond will serve at some time or another as the grey heron's hunting ground.

Though not as common as the black-headed heron, the grey heron is just as widespread, occurring throughout Africa, Europe and Asia. It is far more strictly tied to watery habitats than other herons for its food of frogs, fishes and other aquatic animals. It may eat fishes of up to 110g in weight, but seems to prefer something smaller—around 10-20 grams. It is typically a stand-and-wait fisher and you will most likely see it standing, sometimes belly-deep, in water—waiting motionless for food to swim by. It may swim in deeper water, but is not well designed for this type of travel.

When put to flight, the grey heron may utter two or three loud, strident croaks as it beats its way into the air. Once airborne, it folds its neck into a tight S-shape against its chest and then gives the impression of being quite buoyant.

Grey herons nest in trees or cliff ledges, usually in colonies and often in company with other herons and egrets. The nest is a large stick platform lined with grass or reeds, in which two to three pale blue eggs are laid. Both parents incubate for 26 days and then feed the nestlings on regurgitated food for about a month in the nest. Then the young clamber about the nesting area for 20 days or so before they can fly. They are dependent on their parents for food for a further three weeks.

GOLIATH HERON
Reuse-reier *(Ardea goliath)*

Size: Length 1,4 m; weight 4,3 kg.
Colour: Large, slate-grey body with deep chestnut-brown head, neck, belly and wrist-patch; throat white.
Most like: Purple heron, but bill dark above, horn below (not yellow), and much bigger. Lack of extensive white or black in plumage distinguishes Goliath from other big herons.
Habitat: Large, shallow inland waters (rivers, dams, pans, lakes) and wide estuaries.

In moister regions of Namibia, Botswana, Zimbabwe, Mozambique, Mpumalanga, Gauteng, Northern Province, the North-West, Free State, coastal KwaZulu-Natal and at inland waters and estuaries in the Eastern Cape.

Standing at least a metre tall, the elegant Goliath heron is one of our largest flying birds, though not among the heaviest. It is also one of the most solitary of the avian species. You can usually see it standing statuelike in shallow water, waiting for a fish or frog to swim by. When one does, the heron's huge, dagger-shaped bill streaks down like lightning, tosses the victim into the air, catches it and swallows it. Also included in this bird's diet are small reptiles, mammals and crabs.

A slow, ponderous flier, the Goliath heron often touches water with the tips of its down-curved wings on take-off. Until it is fully airborne, the bird's legs tend to hang below the horizontal, but once aloft, it brings its legs up under its tail for better streamlining.

The larger rivers of Africa, especially in the tropics, are the favoured feeding grounds of the Goliath heron, especially where wide stretches of shallow water are interlaced with sand bars. This heron also occurs on larger inland pans, such as Barberspan in North-West Province, and on the biggest dams.

During the summer the Goliath heron becomes more sociable, joining other species of herons, ibises and wading birds in waterside trees or reed beds to build its large nest of sticks. In the absence of trees it will also nest on a rock or on the ground, building hardly any nest at all. It lays two to four pale, blue-green eggs up to 70 mm long. Both parents incubate them for about 30 days, then feed the nestlings for 8-11 weeks.

Waterbirds

Little egret
Kleinwitreier *(Egretta garzetta)*

Size: *Length 64 cm; weight 280-614 g.*
Colour: *Pure white; the bill is black and slender; the legs black with yellow feet.*
Most like: *Yellow-billed, great (or great white) and cattle egrets, but black bill and yellow feet distinguish it from all three. Immature cattle egret also has black bill, but feet are dark and neck is short.*
Habitat: *Shores of inland and marine waters.*

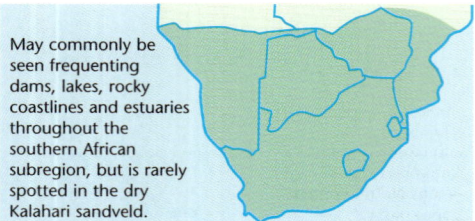

May commonly be seen frequenting dams, lakes, rocky coastlines and estuaries throughout the southern African subregion, but is rarely spotted in the dry Kalahari sandveld.

The little egret may turn up anywhere it can find water with an adequate supply of fishes, frogs and other aquatic organisms. It feeds alone in shallows as a rule, but larger flocks may gather at a rich food source. It hunts either by the stand-and-wait method or by the dart-and-stab method in which it runs about in the water, thrusting here and there with its sharp bill as it goes. The bird may stir the mud with its foot or flash its wings open to drive prey into open water. As it stalks through the water it steps high, showing its bright yellow feet.

Little egrets may perform seasonal migrations in southern Africa. One bird ringed in the southwestern Cape was caught in the vicinity of the Limpopo River, some 1840 km away. Only further ringing and recoveries of ringed birds will help us to unravel the secrets of the little egret's movements.

At the beginning of the breeding season little egrets acquire two to three long, slender white plumes on the head, and their legs may turn bright orange to red. This red colour is lost soon after courtship, when the legs return to black again.

Once the pair bond has been established, the birds build a nest in a colony with other wading birds, either in bushes, trees or reed beds. The clutch consists of two to four pale, greenish-blue eggs, which both parents incubate for 21 to 27 days. About 30 days later the chicks leave the nest, but cannot fly until they are 40-50 days old.

Black heron
Swartreier *(Egretta ardesiaca)*

Size: *Length 66 cm; weight 270-390 g.*
Colour: *Black or slaty black; legs and bill black; eyes and feet bright yellow.*
Most like: *Slaty egret, but black legs with yellow feet diagnostic. Slaty egret has yellow legs, small rufous patch on throat and its plumage is rather greyer than in black heron.*
Habitat: *Quiet inland and estuarine waters, mainly in tropics and subtropics.*

Common in the well-watered parts of northern Namibia, northern and eastern Botswana, Zimbabwe, Mozambique, Mpumalanga, Gauteng, Northern Province, the North-West, KwaZulu-Natal, northern Free State and the southeastern Cape coast.

If you see what looks like a black umbrella floating on a pond, wait a few seconds and it will miraculously fold up and turn into a black heron. This posture, known as 'canopying' in which the bird quickly opens its wings over its lowered head, seems to be designed either to improve the bird's vision by cutting out glare, or to attract small fishes to the shade of the canopy. Of course it could serve both functions. A remarkable spectacle is a whole group of black herons canopying in unison.

While its wings are spread, the bird may stir the mud with a foot, then use its bill to stab quickly at the prey it has disturbed (fishes, crustaceans and other water animals).

After feeding, the birds may take off with quickly flapping wings, and fly in V-formation to a new pond or a communal roosting site in waterside trees. In flight the bright yellow feet trail conspicuously behind the sooty black body. The slaty egret of the Okavango Delta system never canopies, though it looks very similar.

Black herons breed mostly in the summer months, building their stick-and-twig platforms on branches overhanging water or in thick stands of reeds growing in water, usually in a small colony, sometimes in company with other herons and egrets. Two to four blue or greenish-blue eggs form the clutch. Nothing is known of the incubation or nestling periods. The eggs are preyed on by crows and man, and nesting success seems on the whole to be rather poor, though the species is quite common over most of its range.

Waterbirds

HAMERKOP

Hamerkop *(Scopus umbretta)*

Size: Length 56 cm; weight 415-430 g.
Colour: Plain dark brown; bill, legs and feet black; large bill and crest give hammerhead effect (hence hamerkop name).
Most Like: Hadeda ibis in flight, but bill stout and straight; on ground the hammer-shaped head is unmistakeable.
Habitat: Almost any inland water, even small rainwater puddles; rarely on seashore.

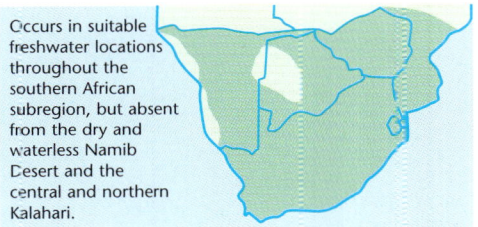

Occurs in suitable freshwater locations throughout the southern African subregion, but absent from the dry and waterless Namib Desert and the central and northern Kalahari.

The hamerkop must be one of Africa's best known waterbirds. Its comically wise appearance, hammerlike head and weird cries immediately set it apart from any other bird.

For centuries some rural black communities in Africa have regarded it with superstition—a fact which has guaranteed it some protection from persecution. However, apart from a vague reputation for being rather clever, the hamerkop does not seem to be a major object of fear.

A foraging hamerkop wades about in water, rapidly darting to and fro to catch tadpoles and small fishes, or it will stir the bottom mud with a foot to disturb water animals. If the water is too deep for wading, and the shoreline too steep for walking on, the hamerkop will hunt on the wing, catching frogs (especially platannas) as they come to the surface to take a floating insect or a gulp of air.

The hamerkop's nest is legendary—a huge, domed structure of sticks, grass and other plant material up to two metres in diameter and weighing anything from 25-50 kilograms. An entrance hole low down on one side, about 13-18 cm in diameter, leads through a mud-lined passage into a larger chamber, also lined with mud. The walls and roof of the nest can support the weight of a full-grown man. The nest, which can take from as little as three weeks to six months to build, is sometimes usurped by other birds, mammals, snakes or bees. The one to seven white eggs are incubated for about 30 days and the nestlings are able to leave the nest after about seven weeks.

AFRICAN SACRED IBIS

Skoorsteenveër *(Threskiornis aethiopicus)*

Size: Length 90 cm; weight 1-1,7 kg.
Colour: Body and wings white; head, neck, bill, legs black, as are the plumelike feathers on the back when wings are folded.
Most like: Some storks and egrets, but black, decurved (downward-pointing) bill and bare black head and neck distinctive; storks and egrets have straight bills.
Habitat: Edges of inland waters, but also flooded grasslands, playing fields, farmyards, rubbish dumps, coastal lagoons and offshore islands.

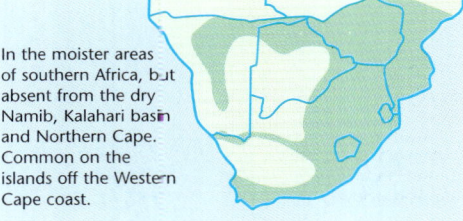

In the moister areas of southern Africa, but absent from the dry Namib, Kalahari basin and Northern Cape. Common on the islands off the Western Cape coast.

The name *skoorsteenveër* (chimney sweep) aptly describes the African sacred ibis' sooty black head and fluffy, black, brushlike feathers on its lower back when the wings are folded, looking like chimney brushes. The English name derives from its religious association with ancient Egyptian culture, specifically with the god Thoth, who was depicted with the head of an ibis. The bird has not occurred in Egypt since about 1850, however.

The African sacred ibis has one of the most varied diets of any bird, reflecting its wide habitat. You can often see it feeding around piggeries and sewage ponds, as well as in the places mentioned above. It probes in mud for live prey such as molluscs, worms and crustaceans; and also takes carrion, birds' eggs and chicks, and many terrestrial invertebrates such as insects and millipedes. It swallows large amounts of refuse from dung heaps where it may also find beetle larvae by probing with its long bill.

This is a gregarious species, and flocks of hundreds of ibises may gather at a good food supply or in waterside trees to roost at night. They build their stick-platform nests in large colonies in trees, reed beds or on islands.

The female lays two to three white eggs with sparse reddish-brown spots. Both parents incubate the eggs for 28-29 days and feed the young for up to seven weeks.

Waterbirds

AFRICAN SPOONBILL

Lepelaar *(Platalea alba)*

Size: Length 90 cm; weight 1,5-1,7 kg.
Colour: Pure white with reddish bill, face, legs and feet.
Most like: Larger white egret, but red, spoon-shaped bill distinctive. Great egret and yellow-billed egret have blackish legs and yellow, pointed bills.
Habitat: Shallow inland waters.

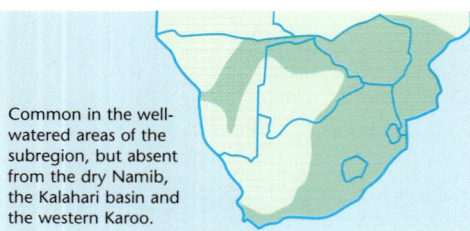

Common in the well-watered areas of the subregion, but absent from the dry Namib, the Kalahari basin and the western Karoo.

The building of farm dams in southern Africa has enabled many waterbirds to expand their ranges and increase their population; the African spoonbill is no exception. You can see this handsome white bird feeding singly or in small groups around the shorelines of even quite small dams. Wading through the water, it sweeps its long bill from side to side, the sensitive tip submerged and ready to snap up a tasty meal in the form of a small fish or aquatic invertebrate whose movement it detects.

Resting groups of spoonbills stand on the shoreline with their bills tucked into their feathers and one leg usually folded up into the belly plumage. They are rather silent—except in their nesting colonies of up to 250 pairs of birds—and quite shy, flying readily with shallow wingbeats, usually in V-formation. Roosting flocks will join ibises and herons in waterside trees or reed beds at night; they also use these sites for breeding from early winter to early spring, before water levels are likely to rise and flood the nests.

The nest is the usual platform of sticks built by most wading birds; the male collects the material and the female builds it in. The clutch consists mostly of three eggs, white spotted with brown and grey, which are incubated for between 25 and 29 days. The chicks are fed by both parents on regurgitated food, mainly in the mornings and evenings, the chick placing its head in the parent's mouth to receive the soupy meal. After 28 days the young can fly, but they remain dependent on the adults until nearly 50 days after hatching.

LESSER FLAMINGO

Kleinflamink
(Phoenicopterus minor)

Size: Length 1,2 m; weight 1,6-1,78 kg.
Colour: Mostly white, lightly washed pale pink; wings mottled bright red; bill dark red with black tip (looks all black at a distance); legs red.
Most like: Greater flamingo, but darker bill diagnostic (pale pink in greater flamingo); usually smaller and pinker in colour than greater flamingo.
Habitat: Large bodies of brackish or saline water.

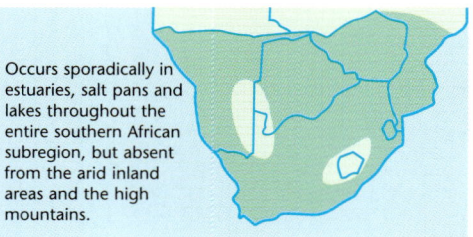

Occurs sporadically in estuaries, salt pans and lakes throughout the entire southern African subregion, but absent from the arid inland areas and the high mountains.

Proportionally, the flamingo has the longest neck and legs of all our birds. Its front toes are webbed like those of a duck, so that it can feed even in water too deep to wade in. Its long neck enables its head to reach the bottom when the bird is standing upright; in this position its head is upside down, which accounts for the curious bent shape of a flamingo's bill. With its head so positioned, the tip of the bill is horizontal with the surface of the water or mud.

Like all flamingos, the lesser flamingo is a filter feeder. The tongue acts as a plunger to draw water into its mouth and force it out sideways through fine, comblike 'teeth' (or *lamellae*) which trap the microscopic plants on which it feeds. The lower jaw (which is on top in the feeding position) consists of light spongy bone with air-filled spaces that give it buoyancy.

Lesser flamingos are the most gregarious of all waterbirds, though flocks in southern Africa seldom number more than a few hundred. Dense breeding colonies occur on mud flats at places like Etosha Pan. The nest is a low cone of mud about 30 cm tall, with a hollow on top to hold the single white egg.

Incubation takes about 28 days. The parents feed the chick in the nest for the first six days or so, after which it leaves to join huge crèches of thousands of other chicks. The parents find their chick by voice and feed it until it can fly at 65-75 days.

Waterbirds

Egyptian goose
Kolgans *(Alopochen aegyptiacus)*

Size: Length 63-73 cm; weight (m) 2,5 kg, (f) 1,9 kg.
Colour: Above deep reddish brown; below light greyish with brown patch on centre of breast (hence the name kolgans); eye-patch and collar brown; bill and legs pinkish red; in flight wing shows white area with green trailing edge and broad, black tip.
Most like: South African shelduck, but Egyptian goose's grey underparts and red bill and legs diagnostic.
Habitat: Any inland waters.

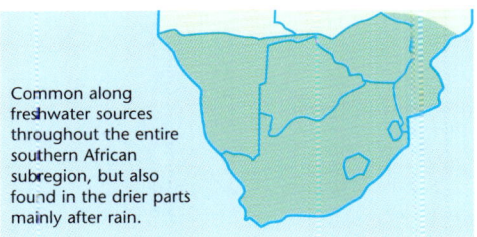

Common along freshwater sources throughout the entire southern African subregion, but also found in the drier parts mainly after rain.

The Egyptian goose, so-called because of its resemblance to a goose, is really a species of shelduck, immediately recognizable by its handsome coloration and hoarse calls. You will usually see these geese in pairs, but sometimes they form family groups and, out of the breeding season, congregate in large flocks.

Almost any farm dam has its pair of Egyptian geese; they are also common on rivers and marshes. Like the true geese, they graze in grassland or cultivated fields, sometimes pulling up young cereal plants. They feed mainly at night, spending the day at the water's edge or floating lazily about on the surface in a characteristically high-tailed posture, like old sailing ships.

Egyptian geese have flourished so well partly because they eat almost any plant material: grass, leaves, seeds and bulbs. They are even known to breed in towns; a pair once nested in the tower of the Grahamstown cathedral, successfully hatching a brood above the city.

In general, however, Egyptian geese nest in concealed places on the ground, although they are also known to nest in old crows' nests or on cliff ledges, from which the young have to jump just six hours after they have all hatched. Five to ten creamy eggs are laid and incubated by the female for a month. As soon as the hatchlings leave the nest, the parents lead them to the water where they guard them for almost two months until they are able to fend for themselves.

South African shelduck
Kopereend *(Tadorna cana)*

Size: Length 61-64 cm; average weight (m) 1,4 kg, (f) 1,1 kg.
Colour: Body bright chestnut; head grey; female has white face; in flight wing shows much white with green trailing edge and broad black tip; bill and legs black.
Most like: White-faced duck and Egyptian goose, but white-faced duck has dark brown body, barred flanks and upright stance on land; Egyptian goose has pinkish bill and legs (black in South African shelduck).
Habitat: Inland waters, especially brackish pans, large dams, rivers and estuaries.

On inland waters in the drier regions of central Namibia, southeastern Botswana, western Zimbabwe, Northern, Western and Eastern Cape, eastern North-West Province, Free State, Lesotho and inland KwaZulu-Natal.

The shelducks, including the similar Egyptian goose, are a distinctive group of waterfowl found in Africa, Eurasia and Australasia. Most of them nest in burrows and have striking plumage, usually brighter in the female.

The beautiful South African shelduck is common in its distributional range, especially in the highveld of the Free State where flocks may number several thousands after the breeding season.

You will usually see shelducks in pairs, sometimes with a brood of young in the late winter. Their striking plumage and evocative, honking calls—impressively amplified when the birds are in large flocks—make them easily recognizable. They feed by dabbling near the shoreline for algae and crustaceans, or by flying to nearby lands to pick up fallen grain after the harvest.

The female shelduck takes the initiative in courtship—an unusual situation among birds. The mating pair breeds in winter, seeking out a large burrow, such as that of a porcupine or aardvark. In a subterranean chamber, the female makes a scrape. This she lines thickly with grey down from her belly, and lays eight to ten eggs, which she incubates for a month or so. Later, the parents lead the ducklings to the nearest water, up to two kilometres away. Both parents care for the young until they're able to fly—at about 70 days.

Waterbirds

YELLOW-BILLED DUCK
Geelbekeend *(Anas undulata)*

Size: Length 51-63 cm; weight (m) 533 g-1,3 kg, (f) 660 g-1,2 kg.
Colour: Dark grey to blackish with pale, scaly markings; bill bright yellow with black saddle; wing-patch (speculum) metallic green, bordered white front and back.
Most like: African black duck, but yellow bill diagnostic; feet black (African black duck has a black bill, yellow legs and feet, and a blotchier appearance).
Habitat: Any inland water; rarely also estuaries.

On open water in Namibia, northern and eastern Botswana, western Zimbabwe, southern Northern Province, the North-West, Gauteng, Mpumalanga, Swaziland, southern Mozambique, KwaZulu-Natal, Free State and Eastern, Western and Northern Cape.

The yellow-billed duck is the most familiar of the indigenous waterfowl over much of southern Africa because it is abundant, widespread and occurs on small bodies of water, such as dams, vleis, small streams and temporarily flooded grassland. It is about the size of a domestic duck and has a very similar quacking voice. Yellow-billed ducks are usually seen in pairs when breeding, which may be at any time of the year, but they gather into nonbreeding flocks numbering scores or even hundreds of birds. They prefer fresh waters, avoiding those that are saline or highly acidic. They feed by dabbling in shallow water, or by up-ending in deeper water. You may see them foraging on land, grazing or picking up fallen grain in farmlands. Their aquatic diet includes seeds, leaves, stems, tubers and insects. For most of the day, the ducks relax at the water's edge.

If you see a yellow-billed duck get up at your feet and flop into the water with churning wings and anxious quacks, you can be fairly sure that it has just left a nest or a brood of young. Ducklings will scatter and be very hard to find, but you can locate a nest by parting the vegetation where you first saw the bird, and exposing the clutch of 4-12 creamy, yellowish eggs nestled in a thick bed of dark brown down. The nest is usually close to water. Incubation takes a month and the brood flies at about 70 days; the young will stay with the female for a further six weeks before venturing abroad on their own.

RED-BILLED TEAL
Rooibekeend *(Anas erythrorhyncha)*

Size: Length 46 cm; weight 570 g.
Colour: Above brown with buff, scaly markings; below buff with dark brown spots; head dark brown above, buff below, giving two-toned appearance; bill pinkish red; wing-patch (speculum) creamy beige.
Most like: Hottentot teal, but bill red, not blue; beige wing-patch diagnostic in flight (deep metallic green in Hottentot teal). Red-billed teal larger.
Habitat: Inland waters, especially larger, shallow bodies.

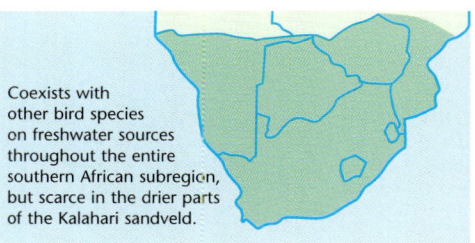

Coexists with other bird species on freshwater sources throughout the entire southern African subregion, but scarce in the drier parts of the Kalahari sandveld.

Red-billed teal are restless nomads, moving about southern Africa in search of water conditions which suit them. Such is their range that ringed birds have been recovered 2 000 km or more from their original tagging site. South African birds, for example, have been recovered as far afield as Angola, Zambia, Namibia and Zimbabwe, and birds from Barberspan in the North-West Province have been sighted in Cape Town. Whether these movements are regular migrations still has to be established, but it is clear that redbills disperse widely after rains to temporary waters. As these dry up, the birds once again fly in to more permanent bodies of water.

Their preference for shallow, temporary waters means that redbills are commoner in the central and western parts of southern Africa than in the east. Flocks are usually quite small, but hundreds or even thousands of redbills may congregate in the dry season.

They feed on fruits and other parts of water plants, as well as on some aquatic animals such as insects and crustaceans. They obtain their food by dabbling or up-ending, depending on the depth of the water.

You will find the red-billed teal's nest in dense, waterside vegetation; a down-lined hollow in the ground containing 5-12 buffy eggs. The female incubates alone for up to 28 days and usually tends the young without the help of the male for a further eight weeks.

Waterbirds

SPUR-WINGED GOOSE

Wildemakou *(Plectropterus gambensis)*

Size: Length (m) 1 m, (f) 90 cm; weight (m) 5,4-10 kg, (f) 4,1-5,4 kg.
Colour: Mostly black with variable amount of white on belly; male usually has some white on face; bill, facial skin and legs pinkish red.
Most like: No other southern African bird; large size, pied plumage and red bare parts are unmistakeable.
Habitat: Larger inland waters.

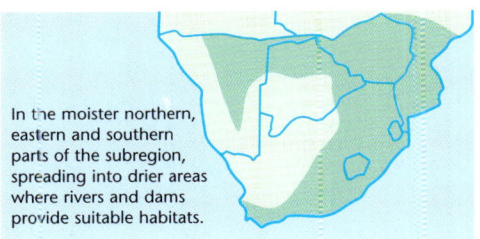

In the moister northern, eastern and southern parts of the subregion, spreading into drier areas where rivers and dams provide suitable habitats.

The spur-winged goose is not the type of bird you could mistake for anything else: its striking appearance, large size and feeble, wheezy high-pitched *chewit chewit* callnotes make it very conspicuous. In fact, this bird is not a goose, but a larger and widespread species of perching duck that South Africans know well.

Large flocks gather at suitable localities, especially when they moult. At this time, like other waterfowl, the birds drop their flight feathers and are flightless for a month or so. The shorelines of their favourite lakes and dams become littered with piles of huge black feathers blown in or washed up by waves.

Spur-winged geese are shy birds, and if disturbed will either take off or swim out to the relative safety of open water. They are mostly night feeders, flying in flocks to flooded grasslands or fallow fields to feed on grass, fallen grain and other material. In large numbers they may severely damage crops. By day the flocks return to water, landing with a great *whoosh* and shaking their wings as they settle.

The nest is a grass-lined hollow filled with a little white down; it may be on the ground in dense vegetation, on a cliff ledge or on top of the larger stick nest of a bird of prey or hamerkop. The clutch usually consists of 6-12 cream or light brown eggs. The female incubates for about 35 days until the yellow-and-brown ducklings hatch out. They remain flightless for three months or so.

AFRICAN PURPLE SWAMPHEN

Grootkoningriethaan
(Porphyrio porphyrio madagascariensis)

Size: Length 40-46 cm; weight 320-780 g.
Colour: Mostly deep blue, washed green on back; undertail white; forehead shield, bill bright red; legs pinkish red.
Most like: Allen's (lesser) gallinule, but much bigger; forehead shield red (not blue or green as in Allen's gallinule).
Habitat: Marshes and swamps, dams and estuaries fringed with bulrushes, sedges or reeds.

Found among reeds and grassy wetlands throughout most of the subregion, but absent from the extremely dry central and western parts, except as vagrants.

The shy African purple swamphen (previously called the purple gallinule) is a cryptic denizen of the reed beds. As it walks along on its long, red legs, it constantly flicks its tail to show off the white 'powderpuff' under it. Stalking slowly about among the emergent plants or in shallow water, it lifts a foot high at each step. It will fly only if hard pressed, and then does so unwillingly and with dangling legs.

The purple swamphen's wide diet of plant and animal food includes birds' eggs and young, and the soft stems of bulrush stalks, which it bites to pieces with its strong bill. A reed bed inhabited by this species often echoes to its weird vocalization— groans, screams, cackles and grunts, like the background music to a horror movie.

For its nest, the purple swamphen builds a substantial bowl of reeds or rushes on a floating pad of vegetation or in standing plants up to a metre above the water. Two to six pinkish-buff eggs with dark spots form the clutch. They hatch out in about 24 days into jet-black, downy chicks that leave the nest immediately to accompany their parents about the marsh for the next eight weeks or so. Both parents feed and brood the young until they become independent. Breeding occurs in almost any month. One of the best places to see purple swamphens is at the Rondebult Bird Sanctuary near Germiston in Gauteng; here the birds are used to people, and you can sit in the comfort of a hide and view them at close range.

Waterbirds

COMMON MOORHEN
Grootwaterhoender *(Gallinula chloropus)*

Size: Length 30-36 cm; weight 175-340 g.
Colour: Mainly black; undertail and streaks in flanks white; forehead shield and bill bright red, tip yellow; legs yellowish green with red garter at top.
Most like: Lesser moorhen, but bill red at base (not all yellow), red garter on upper leg and body about a third bigger; similar to red-knobbed coot, but common moorhen's red bill and frontal shield diagnostic.
Habitat: Reed beds, marshes and reed-fringed edges of most inland waters.

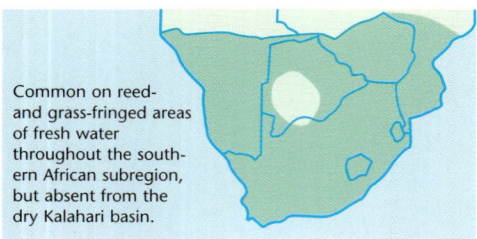

Common on reed- and grass-fringed areas of fresh water throughout the southern African subregion, but absent from the dry Kalahari basin.

RED-KNOBBED COOT
Bleshoender *(Fulica cristata)*

Size: Length 43 cm; weight 460 g-1,2 kg.
Colour: Plain black; bill and broad forehead shield white; two dark red knobs on top of forehead shield.
Most like: Common moorhen, but white bill and frontal shield diagnostic (red in moorhen); no white in plumage.
Habitat: Inland waters, especially with submerged or floating vegetation; occurs rarely on estuaries and coastal lagoons.

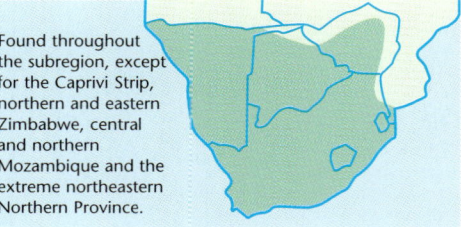

Found throughout the subregion, except for the Caprivi Strip, northern and eastern Zimbabwe, central and northern Mozambique and the extreme northeastern Northern Province.

The common moorhen's feet are designed to cope with almost any condition; they can walk about on floating plants or mud, or clamber about the reeds and rushes of their preferred habitat with ease and grace.

You will very likely see a moorhen or two where there is water with emergent plants. Sewage ponds form ideal manmade habitats, even in desert towns such as Swakopmund and Walvis Bay. Though they have long, slender toes, moorhens usually swim about on open water, sometimes far from cover. They dive readily for food, but pick up much of it from the water's surface and even on land.

The common moorhen's vocal repertoire is wide and resonant, ranging from high-pitched croaks and clucks to nasal toots and squawks. Its food is equally variable: seeds, fruits, snails, worms, insects, tadpoles and even carrion. As with many other omnivorous birds, it owes its success partly to its wide diet.

Moorhens nest during almost any month of the year, but mostly in summer. The pair builds a bowl of plant stems in a concealed site among the water plants, well above flood level. The four to nine eggs are buff with spots of brown and grey. The female incubates by day and the male by night, for about three weeks. The black, downy chicks follow their parents out of the nest as soon as they are dry, and are tended for 8-13 weeks, although they can fly at six to seven weeks.

You could mistake the red-knobbed coot for a duck. However, its white frontal shield—from which comes the familiar saying 'as bald as a coot'—is quite distinctive. Moreover, if you could get a close look at a coot on land, you would see quite clearly that, unlike a duck, its toes are lobed, not webbed.

Red-knobbed coots are mostly vegetarian. Before they submerge to harvest underwater stems and leaves they give a pronounced jump; then bob up to the surface again like a cork. Many small dams have a resident pair of coots, though bigger flocks (sometimes several hundred birds) may occur on larger bodies of water where there is a good food supply.

A quiet bird, the coot emits some nasal *klukuk* or *vvvvm* callnotes. Dominant individuals often chase subordinates about the water, pattering along with their feet as they flap wildly without quite taking off. They land again on their breasts, never on their feet as ducks do.

Coots build a large, floating, bowl-shaped nest of water plants, sometimes concealed in vegetation, but more often right out in the open. This nest is carefully and firmly anchored to submerged stems.

Three to nine pinkish-buff-coloured eggs with purplish-brown spots form the average clutch. The parents share the incubation duties for a period of between 18 and 25 days. Newly hatched chicks are black with yellow down on their necks and bare, blue-and-red skin on their heads. Both parents care for them until they are able to fly at the age of about 60 days.

Waterbirds

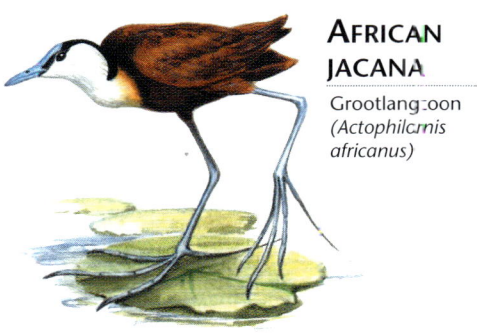

African Jacana
Grootlangtoon
(*Actophilornis africanus*)

Size: Length 25-30 cm; weight (m) 115-160 g, (f) 176-270 g.
Colour: Body rich chestnut-brown; hindneck black; forehead white, shading to yellow on breast; bill and frontal shield pale blue.
Most like: No other African bird; immature jacana similar to lesser jacana, except for larger size, paler brown back and lack of white in wings.
Habitat: Inland waters with floating plants, mainly tropical regions.

Northern Namibia, northern and eastern Botswana, Zimbabwe, Mozambique, Northern Province, Mpumalanga, Swaziland, KwaZulu-Natal and coastal Transkei region of Eastern Province. Vagrant in Free State, Northern Cape and Namibia.

Conspicuous by virtue of their white forehead and bright chestnut bodies, African jacanas often draw attention to themselves with noisy *kreep-kreep-kreep* calls as they chase each other in flight across the water. In the air the birds trail their long legs and toes behind their tails; on landing they hold their wings momentarily aloft before folding them and running nimbly over the water weeds.

The very long toes distribute the bird's weight over floating plants that otherwise would not support it. If a jacana is let down by a flimsy patch of vegetation, it will fly or swim to the nearest firm foothold. Jacanas, like ducks, lose all their flight feathers when moulting and have to swim to get about; they can also dive with ease, if necessary.

Jacanas feed on water animals and seeds.

Their breeding is also closely associated with water. The large female takes the initiative in courtship and may have in her territory two to four males who build a nest of floating vegetation and plant stems in which she lays a clutch of four shiny, coffee-brown eggs scrolled with black. Their wet look camouflages them well in their watery environment. The male incubates alone for about 23 days and cares for the chicks until they can fly at about 40 days. When the chicks are small the male carries them under his wings, two on each side, either to keep them warm or to remove them from danger.

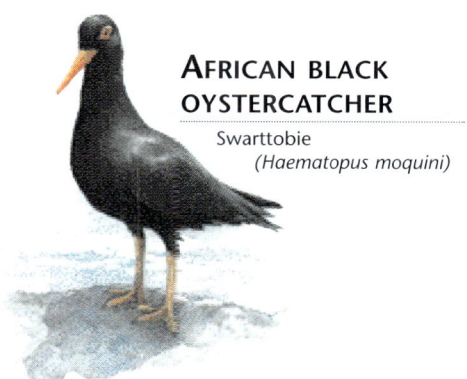

African Black Oystercatcher
Swarttobie
(*Haematopus moquini*)

Size: Length 41 cm; weight (m) 580-735 g, (f) 650-830 g.
Colour: Sooty black with red bill and eyes; legs and feet purplish pink.
Most like: No other southern African bird; the rare Eurasian oystercatcher is similar but has white belly and wing bar, and is smaller in size.
Habitat: Rocky and sandy beaches on mainland and offshore islands. Sometimes at coastal lagoons and vleis.

Found on the rocky shores, estuaries and offshore islands of southern Africa, from northern Namibia to the Transkei region of Eastern Cape. It also occurs as a vagrant on the KwaZulu-Natal coast.

Along the west coast of southern Africa the wild, piping *klee-weep, klee-weep*, or *tsa-pee, tsa-pee* calls of the African black oystercatcher join with the wind off the sea to make evocative music.

This bird uses its remarkably flattened, bladelike bill to prise shellfish from the rocks and to open mussels and oysters by cutting the muscle that holds the two halves of the shell together. They also eat other marine invertebrates such as worms, crustaceans, sea anemones and sea squirts, which they probe for in rock pools or on sandy beaches.

Although usually seen in pairs, African black oystercatchers may form flocks of over 100 outside the breeding season, which lasts from October to March. The birds frequently display to each other with bowed heads, downward-pointing bills and loud calls. This display may occur in groups or 'piping parties'.

The conspicuous black plumage of the African black oystercatcher may seem to be a poor adaptation for life on a white sandy beach, but the colour becomes a wonderful camouflage when the birds are nesting among dried fronds of blackened kelp or on rocks.

An incubating oystercatcher, when spotting an intruder in the distance, will sneak away from its eggs and try to deflect the stranger from her nest by pretending to be feeding at the water's edge. Her eggs, usually two to a clutch, are greenish to buffy putty-coloured, with large, scrolled markings of black and grey. These make them quite hard to see in their simple nest scrape in the sand. Incubation takes about 32 days, and the young are able to fly some 40 days after hatching.

Waterbirds

WHITE-FRONTED PLOVER
Vaalstrandkiewiet *(Charadrius marginatus)*

Size: *Length 18 cm; weight 38-59 g.*
Colour: *Above light sandy grey; below white; forehead white; bordered behind by dark band; eyebrow and hindneck white; dark line through eye; bill and legs black.*
Most like: *Kittlitz's plover, but white eyebrow complete; black line through eye does not extend down sides of neck; breast usually white; almost plain, pale upperparts and lack of breastband distinctive.*
Habitat: *Marine shores, sandbanks of larger rivers and some larger inland pans.*

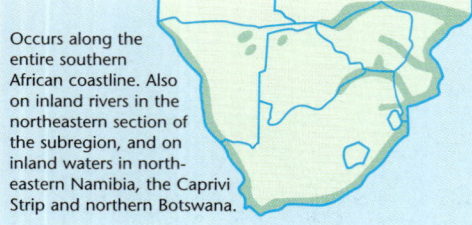

Occurs along the entire southern African coastline. Also on inland rivers in the northeastern section of the subregion, and on inland waters in northeastern Namibia, the Caprivi Strip and northern Botswana.

Like a wisp of sand blowing along the beach, the white-fronted plover runs on legs that move so fast as to seem invisible. In a somewhat hunched posture the little birds, usually in pairs, will keep a safe distance from you, running and stopping in turn, until finally they take off with gentle *wit* notes and fly over the breakers back to their territory, their dark wings showing a white bar.

White-fronted plovers forage among the kelp and jetsam on the beach or at the water's edge, sometimes even probing in wet sand for their food of insects, crustaceans and other invertebrate animals. Because they take in some salt water with their food, they are equipped with a gland above each eye to remove the excess salt from the blood and conserve water; this allows them even to drink seawater if need be.

Outside the main summer breeding season white-fronted plovers can gather in flocks of up to 100 birds, but when breeding they are usually in pairs.

The nest is a mere scrape in the sand, usually next to a piece of driftwood or seaweed, and sometimes lined with small pieces of shell. The parent may partly cover the eggs (usually two) with sand if it is disturbed; even so, the eggs are very hard to see, being sandy coloured with fine, black speckles. Incubation takes 30 days, during which time many eggs fall prey to mongooses and other mammalian predators. The chicks run with the parents as soon as they are dry and can fly at around 36 days.

THREE-BANDED PLOVER
Driebandstrandkiewiet *(Charadrius tricollaris)*

Size: *Length 18 cm; weight: 25-45 g.*
Colour: *Above brownish grey; below white with two black breastbands; white stripe from forehead over eye to hindneck; eye-ring and bill bright red, tip black; legs pinkish grey.*
Most like: *Common ringed plover, but two black breastbands diagnostic; common ringed plover has single broad band and yellow bill and legs.*
Habitat: *Shorelines of inland waters and rivers; less often on rocky seashore.*

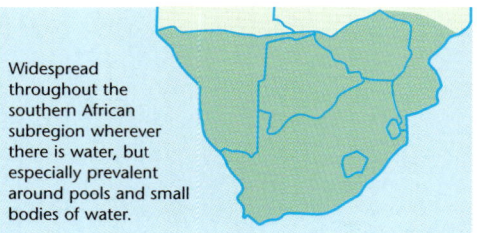

Widespread throughout the southern African subregion wherever there is water, but especially prevalent around pools and small bodies of water.

The three-banded plover is the commonest and most widespread plover in southern Africa. It frequents small bodies of water, including flooded quarries, sewage ponds and tiny spring-fed pools in desert watercourses. Its ability to find such small, isolated waters is a reflection of its highly nomadic lifestyle, though how it finds them is a mystery. It prefers waters with a firm shoreline, but will also take to muddy shores with seepage water where there is a plentiful food supply.

The three-banded plover feeds restlessly by darting forward in short bursts of small, tripping steps, stopping to probe with rapid stabs in the mud between runs. Because of its short bill it cannot probe deeply, but successfully harvests tiny water animals such as insects, worms, molluscs and crustaceans.

You will see these plovers mostly in pairs, less often in loose flocks of 20-30 birds. Their high, piping callnotes are most often heard when they're flying. Like many plovers, this species is partly nocturnal and you can hear it passing overhead at night.

Because it is extremely wary when breeding, this plover's nest is difficult to find. Two dark, stone-coloured eggs are laid in a pebble-lined scrape on a shoreline or on a gravel patch far from water. Both parents share incubation for about a month and care for their downy young for about 40 days, when they're able to fly.

Waterbirds

BLACKSMITH LAPWING

Bontkiewiet *(Vanellus armatus)*

Size: *Length 30 cm; weight 110-220 g.*
Colour: *Boldly pied black and white; forecrown, hindneck and lower belly white; wings and saddle across back pale grey; hindcrown, lower back and rest of underparts to chin black; bill and legs black.*
Most like: *Pied avocet, but bill short and straight; underparts largely black; long-toed lapwing has plain brown back, white face and bill and legs.*
Habitat: *Shorelines of inland waters; also moist grassland, large lawns and playing fields.*

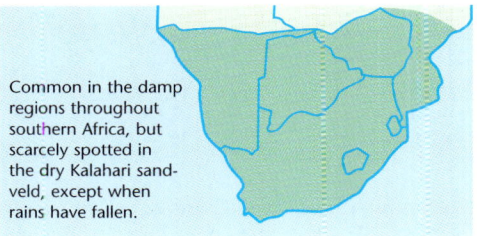

Common in the damp regions throughout southern Africa, but scarcely spotted in the dry Kalahari sandveld, except when rains have fallen.

COMMON SANDPIPER

Gewone ruiter *(Actitis hypoleucos)*

Size: *Length 19 cm; weight 34-56 g.*
Colour: *Darkish bronzy brown above (faint barring on wings and tail visible in good light); below white, washed brown on breast; white of belly comes up around bend of folded wing as crescent (diagnostic); clear white eyebrow; bill black, straight, about as long as head; legs greenish grey.*
Most like: *Wood and green sandpipers, but without white spots on brown underparts or white rump; in flight white wing bar is distinctive (the wings are all dark in the wood and green sandpipers); a plain brown back is quite uncommon among sandpipers.*
Habitat: *Any shoreline, from high montane rivers and streams to estuaries and seashore.*

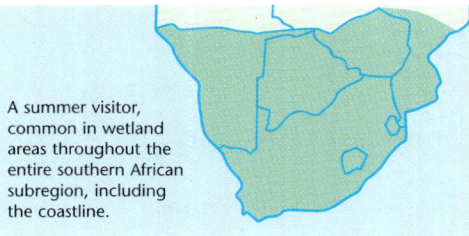

A summer visitor, common in wetland areas throughout the entire southern African subregion, including the coastline.

The blacksmith lapwing is an emotional bird at any time of the year. If you walk through its territory, it will immediately let out its characteristic *klink-klink-klink* calls, closely resembling the sound of a hammer on an anvil (hence the bird's name). When really agitated, it flies about with strident screams, especially if it has chicks nearby. Blacksmith lapwings (previously called blacksmith plovers) are almost always solitary or in pairs. Outside the breeding season—normally between July and October—the birds become more sociable until flocks of 20 or more may gather in suitable habitats. They eat insects and other invertebrates, sometimes probing for them in the mud.

The birds' conspicuous coloration indicates that they are probably not good to eat; in fact, it has been shown that their flesh is unpalatable and that birds of prey tend to avoid attacking them (black-and-white coloration is a widely used warning signal in nature).

Blacksmith lapwings are rather wary when nesting. They make a shallow scrape on an open shoreline, lining it with bits of plant material, soil and small stones. The incubating bird sneaks away from the nest as soon as it sees danger approaching, leaving the four yellow-ochre, black-spotted eggs to the protection of their own camouflage. Both parents incubate the eggs for about a month and the young fledge in about 40 days.

The characteristic frantic bobbing of the common sandpiper's body as it walks distinguishes it from most other sandpipers and the lapwing family. Its quick, jerky movements and forward-tilting carriage make it a lively subject to watch.

This restless little bird is usually solitary, although it roosts in small groups of up to 30 birds. It forages by pecking at small water animals on the surface or by probing for them in the mud with its longish bill. It may also feed away from the water on grassy shorelines, finding insects in animal dung. It has been said to pick leeches off the skin of hippos, to the mutual benefit of both.

As it flies, usually low over the water, the common sandpiper's wings beat in short; rapid bursts below its body, revealing a conspicuous white wing stripe. When it lands, it bobs its body even more wildly than usual, before setting off again with its body tilted forward.

The common sandpiper breeds only in the northern hemisphere, arriving in southern Africa in about August as a nonbreeding visitor. It stays for about eight months before returning in April to breed, mostly in Europe.

Waterbirds

WOOD SANDPIPER
Bosruiter *(Tringa glareola)*

Size: Length 20 cm; weight 34-89 g.
Colour: Above olive-brown with clear white spots; underparts whitish, faintly streaked grey on breast; eyebrow white; bill black, straight, about as long as head; clear white rump visible in flight; wing all dark; tail barred dark and light; legs usually dull greenish.
Most like: Green sandpiper, but underwing pale in flight; common sandpiper has plain brown back and white wing bar (no wing bar in wood sandpiper).
Habitat: Inland and estuarine waters with a preference for marshy shorelines.

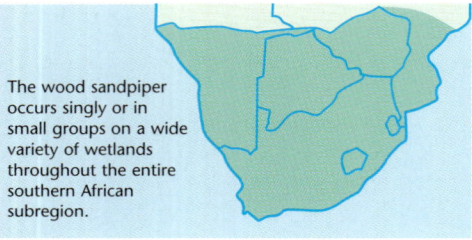

The wood sandpiper occurs singly or in small groups on a wide variety of wetlands throughout the entire southern African subregion.

A typical wader, the wood sandpiper comes to southern Africa from August to March as a nonbreeding migrant from northern Europe and Asia where it breeds. Because it likes soggy shorelines, you will find this bird on sewage ponds and small, weedy dams in southern Africa.

In common with most other sandpipers, it probes in soft ooze and mud for molluscs, crustaceans, worms and insects, foraging either alone or in loose groups of 5-20 birds. Although not particularly shy, the common sandpiper seldom lets you approach it. Sometimes, however, it may stay in one place as you come near, camouflaged by its spotted upperparts against a background of spangled, sunlit water; at the last moment it will jump up at your feet, making its piping *twee-twee-twee* call of three to six notes.

The wood sandpiper is one of the most widespread of all northern hemisphere waders in the southern African summer months. The similar, but much rarer, green sandpiper is unlikely to be seen by the average birdwatcher.

Wood sandpipers usually nest on the ground like most other waders, but have the curious habit of sometimes nesting up in a tree in the old nest of a thrush or shrike. Presumably such a site is safer than one on the ground, but the chicks have to jump to the ground after hatching.

CURLEW SANDPIPER
Krombekstrandloper *(Calidris ferruginea)*

Size: Length 20 cm; weight 54-75 g.
Colour: Above mottled brownish grey; eyebrow, rump and underparts white, lightly streaked on breast; white wing bar in flight; tail dusky; underparts deep rusty in breeding plumage, rarely seen in southern Africa.
Most like: Dunlin, but rump lacks dark centre line of most *Calidris* sandpipers; distinguished from other small sandpipers by downcurved bill tip.
Habitat: Shorelines of sea, pans, dams and vleis.

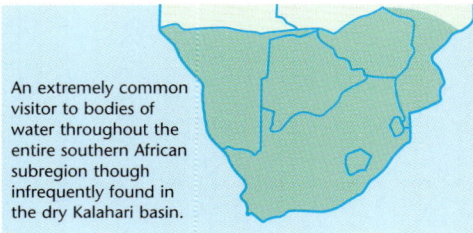

An extremely common visitor to bodies of water throughout the entire southern African subregion though infrequently found in the dry Kalahari basin.

The curlew sandpiper is one of the most common waders on the southern African coastline, especially in the west. Many individuals spend winter here—mostly sexually immature birds hatched the previous season in the northern hemisphere. They arrive in August and leave in April, by which time a few may have begun to acquire their rusty breeding dress. Ringing has shown that many come to us from Russia, a distance of up to 14 000 kilometres.

The curlew sandpiper nests in the tundra and heads south as soon as its young are on the wing. The journey takes the birds about a month to six weeks, involving travel of about 300 km a day. But for these excellent fliers, this is no difficult task.

Once in their southern quarters the sandpipers concentrate at tidal mudflats and other rich sources of food, often in flocks of hundreds or thousands of birds that dip and wheel in flight with incredible precision, showing first their dark backs, then their white bellies.

They also feed in groups, probing in the mud with their long, curved bills for worms, molluscs, insects and crustaceans. Their numbers fluctuate in a three-year cycle which has been shown to correlate with populations of foxes and lemmings on their tundra nesting grounds. When the lemmings are abundant, foxes prefer to feed on them and the birds have a higher survival rate.

Waterbirds

PIED AVOCET

Bontelsie *(Recurvirostra avosetta)*

Size: *Length 43-46 cm; weight 258-390 g.*
Colour: *Boldly pied black and white above, below white; bill thin, black and curved upwards at tip; legs long, whitish grey.*
Most like: *Black-winged stilt, but head black on top; legs white (not red); blacksmith lapwing has short, straight bill, mostly black underparts and black legs; upcurved bill of pied avocet is unique.*
Habitat: *Shallow waters, inland and coastal, usually brackish or saline.*

Found on lakes, vleis and estuaries throughout most of the southern African subregion, but highly nomadic. Absent from Lesotho, the Transkei region of Eastern Cape and southern KwaZulu-Natal.

The remarkable upturned bill of the pied avocet is designed for feeding on tiny water creatures (insects, crustaceans and small fishes) at the surface of the water or in the mud under water. It gathers its food by sweeping its bill from side to side. When it lowers its head to feed, the bill tip is horizontal to the feeding surface—perfectly positioned for this type of foraging.

The bird's long legs enable it to wade in fairly deep water, where it may submerge its head entirely to reach the muddy bottom. If the water gets deeper than the length of its legs, it can swim with its partly webbed feet. The webs also help to support the bird on soft mud, acting rather like snowshoes.

Because it likes brackish water, the pied avocet often frequents small bodies of temporary water left by heavy rains, especially in Namibia, where roadside excavations provide suitable feeding places until the water dries up. Pied avocets may even breed at such unlikely sites, placing their nests on small, emerging islands left by receding water.

The nest is a collection of twigs, grass and mud pellets in a shallow scrape on the ground. The clutch consists of four ochre-coloured eggs with bold black spots. Both sexes incubate for 22-24 days. When the chicks hatch they have short, straight bills that grow and curve upwards by the time they are fully fledged, a period of 26-28 days.

KELP GULL

Swartrugmeeu *(Larus dominicanus)*

Size: *Length 56-60 cm; average weight (m) 1,08 kg, (f) 920 g.*
Colour: *White, except for black wings and back; legs greenish grey; bill bright yellow with red tip to lower jaw; eyes grey.*
Most like: *Lesser black-backed gull, but greyish legs and eyes distinguish it (both yellowish in lesser black-backed gull).*
Habitat: *Marine shores.*

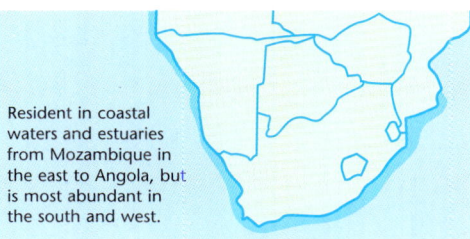

Resident in coastal waters and estuaries from Mozambique in the east to Angola, but is most abundant in the south and west.

The kelp gull is a large, handsome, aggressive and noisy bird, giving vent to the familiar, loud *meew* screams and guttural choking sounds. A flock around a source of carrion is an unruly mass of fighting, fluttering bills and wings, birds chasing each other or tugging at opposite ends of the same piece of food, and voicing loud protests.

Widespread around the entire southern African coastline, the kelp gull is a scavenger and you may see it picking up scraps and offal at rubbish dumps or following trawlers returning from fishing trips. These gulls also take live food such as insects, birds' eggs and shellfish. They pick mussels off the rocks or the beach and drop them from a height to break the shells. Not all drops succeed and the mussels often land on sand, requiring the pick-up-and-drop procedure to be repeated.

Although they are mostly inshore birds, kelp gulls follow ships up to 200 km out to sea—which is probably the reason they can also be found in South America and on Marion and other sub-Antarctic islands.

Kelp gulls build their nests on the ground. These consist of a shallow bowl of plants, feathers and twigs. The female lays one to three eggs, varying in colour from green to turquoise or brown, with darker blotches. After an incubation period of about 28 days, the downy young hatch; they stay in the nest unless disturbed and are able to fly at six to seven weeks.

Waterbirds

GREY-HEADED GULL

Gryskopmeeu *(Larus cirrocephalus)*

Size: *Length 42 cm; weight 211-377 g.*
Colour: *Grey above, white below; head grey when breeding, otherwise white, sometimes with faint grey semicircle behind ear coverts; bill and legs deep red; eye cream to pale grey; white spots on black wing tip.*
Most like: *Hartlaub's gull, but red bill and legs and pale eye diagnostic; Hartlaub's gull has dark eyes and much darker bill and legs, looking almost black at a distance.*
Habitat: *Seashore and larger inland and coastal waters.*

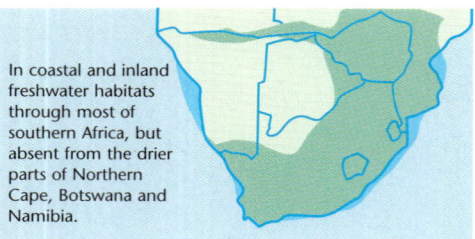

In coastal and inland freshwater habitats through most of southern Africa, but absent from the drier parts of Northern Cape, Botswana and Namibia.

HARTLAUB'S GULL

Hartlaub se meeu *(Larus hartlaubii)*

Size: *Length 36-38 cm; weight 235-340 g.*
Colour: *White, except for pale grey back and black wing tips with white spots; bill and legs dark red, looking blackish at a distance; eyes dark; sometimes pale grey crescent behind eye in breeding plumage.*
Most like: *Grey-headed gull, but head never grey all over; bill and legs much darker; dark eye distinguishes it.*
Habitat: *Marine shores, coastal towns and cities, farmlands.*

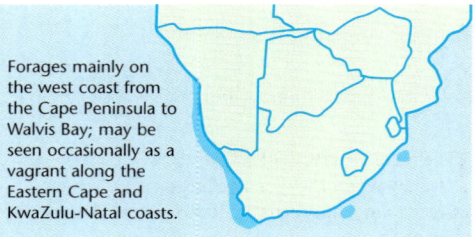

Forages mainly on the west coast from the Cape Peninsula to Walvis Bay; may be seen occasionally as a vagrant along the Eastern Cape and KwaZulu-Natal coasts.

Some people are surprised when they see gulls away from the sea, mainly because they mistakenly believe them to be 'seagulls'. This term, however, is inaccurate, and many species of gull are in fact freshwater birds. The grey-headed gull is highly versatile and has adapted to both marine and freshwater environments. It is abundant in parts of its distribution area, descending in large numbers to scavenge for scraps and offal at rubbish dumps. It also eats fishes, insects and the eggs and young of other birds.

Grey-headed gulls are not only gregarious, but also highly vocal, screaming *kraaa* loudly as they fly about over the water, behind a plough or at some other food source. They may land on the water to pick up food, to bathe or simply to rest, floating lightly and gracefully, and paddling with their delicately webbed feet. Breeding colonies, which may number hundreds of birds, are especially noisy, as neighbouring birds scream their territorial rights.

Nesting colonies are established on islands or protected shorelines and, more rarely, on floating water plants. The nest is a bowl of plant material, either in the open or against a shrub or grass tuft. The eggs, generally two to three in a clutch, are beautifully coloured in bluish green to olive-green or brown, with rich blotches of brown and grey.

The incubation period is not known, but the young leave the nest to wander about the colony within a day or so of hatching.

Hartlaub's gull is the common small gull of the west coast of southern Africa, although you may also see the grey-headed gull in the same vicinity. A well-established resident of Cape Town, Hartlaub's gull can be seen bathing in the fountains, walking about on park lawns and standing solemnly on the heads of statues. It has adapted well to man, and its light and buoyant flight brings it to the open windows of parked cars and hotel diningrooms for scraps of food that it catches deftly in the air. It also follows farm ploughs, presumably to pick up the insect larvae exposed in the newly turned soil.

Like most gulls, it follows ships for scraps dropped overboard. It looks for live food by wading in shallow water, and catches insects in the light of streetlamps at night.

The natural roosting and breeding places of Hartlaub's gull are offshore islands, but today the rooftops and ledges of buildings commonly serve both purposes. The nest is like that of most gulls—a bowl of plant material and shells, placed on the ground or on a rooftop, usually in a colony. The clutch usually consists of one to three dull greenish to brownish eggs with darker blotches of brown and grey. Incubation by both sexes takes about 25 days and the young can fly at about 40 days.

A colony of Hartlaub's gulls may number from 10-100 pairs and may also include a few grey-headed gulls. Hybrids between the two species are known but are very rare.

Waterbirds

SWIFT TERN

Geelbeksterretjie *(Sterna bergii)*

Size: *Length 46-50 cm; weight 325-350 g.*
Colour: *White with grey back and upper wing; crown black with white forehead; bill light yellow or greenish yellow, slightly drooping; legs and feet black.*
Most like: *Lesser crested tern, but bill yellow (not orange) and forehead white (not black); size large.*
Habitat: *Marine shores and estuaries.*

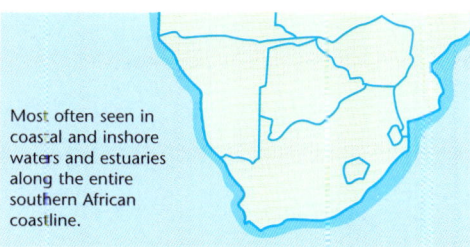

Most often seen in coastal and inshore waters and estuaries along the entire southern African coastline.

Their great powers of flight allow terns to travel widely when they are not breeding and they may wander many hundreds or thousands of kilometres in a season.

The swift tern, so named for its fast flight on quickly beating wings, is particularly common on the west coast of southern Africa and you can often see it together with other tern species, resting on rocky shores. It is a graceful flier, with long, pointed, narrow wings.

The tern uses its long, pointed bill to catch food, either by plunging it into water, or by plucking edible dainties from the water's surface. It favours fishes, but will also take squid, crustaceans and insects. Prey may weigh as much as 30 g, but is usually substantially less.

Although often solitary, the swift tern is gregarious, and may be found in flocks of 40-50 birds, sometimes in the company of gulls or other tern species.

Nonbreeding swift terns can be identified by their white-speckled crowns. Apart from occurring in southern Africa, they are also found throughout the Indian Ocean to Australasia and the western Pacific, although the exact movement of the species over this vast region has not been mapped. They appear to reside in southern Africa.

Swift terns breed in colonies on offshore marine islands, as well as on smaller islands in coastal pans and vleis. A scrape on flat, exposed ground serves as the nest. The one or two eggs vary in colour, from buff, pink and turquoise to white, with patches and streaks of brown and grey. It is not known how long it takes for them to hatch, but the young are able to fly at 35-40 days. Many fall prey to kelp gulls and sacred ibises.

COMMON TERN

Gewone sterretjie *(Sterna hirundo)*

Size: *Length 32-38 cm; weight 93-155 g.*
Colour: *Mostly white; back, wings and rump pale grey; crown black (forehead white in nonbreeding dress); bill black (red with black tip in breeding dress); feet dull red (bright red in breeding dress).*
Most like: *Arctic tern, but grey rump diagnostic (white in Arctic tern); wing tips project to or beyond tail at rest (tail projects beyond wing tips in resting roseate and Arctic terns).*
Habitat: *Seashore and estuaries.*

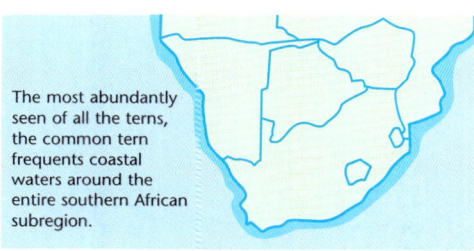

The most abundantly seen of all the terns, the common tern frequents coastal waters around the entire southern African subregion.

Because common and Arctic terns are so hard to tell apart, many people refer to any smallish, white, marine tern as a 'comic' tern. Arctic and common terns are both also very similar to roseate terns, but look for the common tern's distinctive grey rump and smudgy black wing tip.

Common terns, as their name implies, are among the most abundant of marine terns in the southern summer. You will find them in flocks of hundreds of birds resting on rocky shores, estuarine sandbanks, boats and buoys, all facing upwind. When disturbed the flock rises like papers in the breeze, then settles again as the danger passes. Such flocks often consist of more than one species of tern, so look carefully for detailed field marks.

Common terns forage out at sea and inshore by diving or dipping into the water for small fishes and other water animals. Their flight is light and gracefully swallowlike on long, pointed wings.

This tern species migrates to southern Africa from the northern hemisphere where they breed. Southern African birds have been trapped with rings on their legs from Britain, Scandinavia and Germany, so they fly many thousands of kilometres each year, migrating at an average rate of about 100 km per day.

Waterbirds

African Skimmer
Waterploeër (*Rynchops flavirostris*)

Size: Length 36-40 cm; weight 111-204 g.
Colour: Black above; white below; long bill bright red with yellow tip; legs and feet bright red.
Most like: Some terns, but no inland tern is black above; skimmer's bill is diagnostic because lower jaw is longer than the upper one; terns all have pointed bills.
Habitat: Tropical rivers, lakes and coastal lagoons.

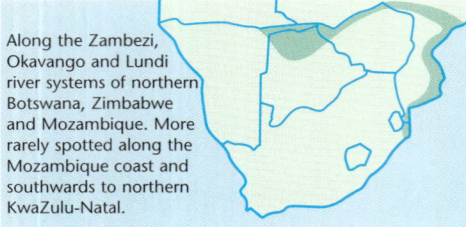

Along the Zambezi, Okavango and Lundi river systems of northern Botswana, Zimbabwe and Mozambique. More rarely spotted along the Mozambique coast and southwards to northern KwaZulu-Natal.

The African skimmer, one of only three species worldwide, is among nature's most curious evolutionary products. The unique structure of its bill—the lower jaw is much longer than the upper—is closely linked with the way it feeds. Flying low with its bill wide open, about two-thirds of the long, bladelike lower jaw slices through the water like a keel. As the blade strikes a small fish, the bill snaps shut, the head is drawn momentarily downwards, the fish is swallowed, and skimming continues with scarcely a pause.

In this way a skimmer catches fishes up to eight centimetres long. The bird's wings, spanning just over a metre, are ideally suited to prolonged flight, as is the forked tail. Although they are known to forage both during the day and night, for most of the day African skimmers stand around on sandbanks in flocks, facing into the wind.

There are few suitable habitats for skimmers in South Africa, but the African skimmer has occurred as far south as northern KwaZulu-Natal, and has even nested there in the past. Today, you can find skimmers in significant numbers only on the Zambezi and Okavango rivers.

Breeding is colonial on sandbanks. The nest is a deepish scrape in the sand and contains one to four eggs, buff with black blotches, and well camouflaged. The eggs are laid in late winter or early spring, and are incubated for 21 days, during which time both parents cool them on hot days with soaked belly feathers. Small fishes are brought to the chicks until they're able to fly at the age of five to six weeks.

Pied Kingfisher
Bontvisvanger (*Ceryle rudis*)

Size: Length 25-29 cm; weight 70-90 g.
Colour: Mottled black-and-white coloration above; below white with one black breastband in female, two in male; broad white eyebrow; bill black.
Most like: Giant kingfisher, but smaller and without chestnut on underparts; broad white eyebrow diagnostic.
Habitat: Inland and coastal waters.

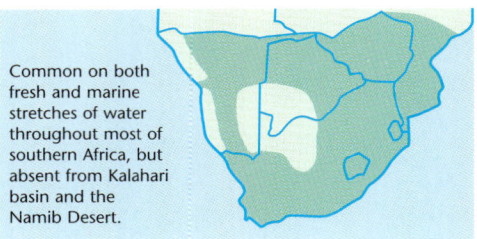

Common on both fresh and marine stretches of water throughout most of southern Africa, but absent from Kalahari basin and the Namib Desert.

In some areas pied kingfishers follow the movements of the Cape clawless otter as it hunts, because the mammal disturbs water animals that kingfishers would otherwise not detect on their own.

Invariably you will find pied kingfishers in pairs, sometimes in small groups, sitting quietly on a perch scanning the water below. Sometimes they hover with their bodies almost vertical, and dive onto their prey, hitting the water with a loud splash. Not every dive is successful, but if it is, the bird takes its prey to a perch, beats it soundly and swallows it. Beating immobilizes fishes that might otherwise erect sharp spines in their fins, thus injuring the bird. The kingfisher's menu includes tiny fishes (weighing one to two grams), crustaceans and insects.

You will find these birds on almost any sizeable body of water from the highveld to the sea, but particularly in the more subtropical parts of southern Africa. If you are in their territory you will probably hear their high-pitched twittering calls and squeaks as they chase each other from perch to perch.

Pied kingfishers are tame and you can observe them easily from a boat or from the shore.

The nest is a burrow up to two metres long in a vertical bank at the water's edge. At the end of this burrow is a small chamber in which the female lays two to six white eggs (four eggs form the usual clutch). Nothing is known of the incubation or nestling periods of this common bird, but both parents, sometimes assisted by one to four helpers, feed the offspring.

Waterbirds

Giant kingfisher

Reuse visvanger (*Megaceryle maxima*)

Size: Length 43-46 cm; weight 338-375 g.
Colour: Above black, spotted with white; below white with broad chestnut breastband and black-spotted belly in male; belly colours reversed in female (black-and-white mottled breastband, belly and undertail chestnut); large black bill.
Most like: Pied kingfisher, but much bigger and darker; chestnut on underparts diagnostic; no white eyebrow.
Habitat: Streams, rivers, estuaries, lakes and ponds; less commonly seashore.

In northern Namibia, northern Botswana, Zimbabwe, Mozambique, and southwest to the Northern and Western Cape.

The giant kingfisher's large bill equips it well to deal with its favourite food of crabs, which it catches by diving into water, sometimes quite shallow. Bits of shell and limbs of crabs lie scattered under the birds' favourite perches on streamside rocks or trees. Regurgitated fish scales also lie scattered around these sites—evidence that the giant kingfisher has a taste for fishes too. The fish is taken to a perch, beaten against the perch until it is immobilized, and then swallowed head-first.

Although the giant kingfisher is such a large bird, you will see it on quite small streams, usually where there is some forest or bushy vegetation. It hunts mostly from a perch over water, but over the sea it will hover and drop onto its prey from the air. The unmistakeable, loud *wak-wak-wak* calls of the giant kingfisher, usually uttered as the bird flies low over the water, can be heard from far off. It spends long periods motionless on a perch and you could quite easily overlook it, despite its size.

This kingfisher's nesting burrow is excavated about a metre from the top of a vertical bank. In it is dug a tunnel, normally about two metres long (sometimes up to eight metres!), which ends in a chamber about 30 cm in diameter. Here the female lays three to five white, rounded eggs. The incubation period is unknown, but the chicks hatch after 37 days, and are fed by both parents.

Malachite kingfisher

Kuifkopvisvanger (*Alcedo cristata*)

Size: Length 14 cm; weight 13-21 g.
Colour: Above deep brilliant blue; crown turquoise; orange-chestnut underparts; white patch on throat and sides of neck; bill and legs scarlet.
Most like: African pygmy kingfisher, but malachite kingfisher lacks chestnut eyebrow and mauve patch behind ear coverts; habitat entirely waterside (pygmy kingfisher mainly forest); half-collared kingfisher has black bill like immature malachite, but is plain bright blue above; immature malachite kingfisher is dark blue above with bright blue spots.
Habitat: Inland waters and rivers with marginal, emergent vegetation.

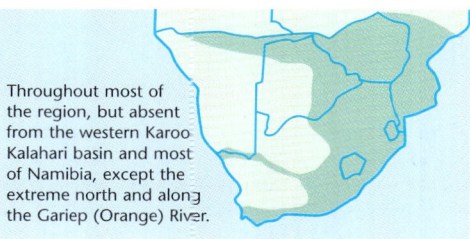

Throughout most of the region, but absent from the western Karoo, Kalahari basin and most of Namibia, except the extreme north and along the Gariep (Orange) River.

The malachite kingfisher is the jewel of the African waterside. To see it reflected, blue and russet, in a tranquil backwater of the Zambezi River, or streaking down a stream bed in the highveld is an unforgettable experience. It is normally a silent bird; and for one so brightly coloured, it is also rather unobtrusive as it sits on a perch looking for fishes, tadpoles or dragonflies to eat.

Because of the malachite kingfisher's shy nature, you will seldom be able to approach it closely. But you will be able to see it dive for its food at lightning speed from a twig or reed stem, to which it usually returns after a successful strike. The bird swallows its prey head-first in one quick gulp. It may dive again from the same perch or may fly to another lookout point nearby.

The malachite kingfisher begins to excavate its nesting tunnel by repeatedly flying against the vertical bank of a stream or river, using the tip of its bill as a pick. Once it has made a small niche in the bank, it continues excavating from the perch, pecking the soil loose with its bill and pushing it out backwards with its feet until it has dug a tunnel 30-90 cm long, with a small chamber at the end of it. Here it lays three to six shiny white eggs. Incubation takes 14-16 days.

Waterbirds

LESSER SWAMP WARBLER

Kaapse rietsanger *(Acrocephalus gracilirostris)*

Size: Length 17-18 cm; weight 13-22 g.
Colour: Above medium brown with whitish eyebrow; below buffy white with rufous wash on flanks.
Most like: Other swamp, reed, marsh and sedge warblers, but rusty wash on flanks distinctive; eyebrow clearer than in African marsh warbler.
Habitat: Reeds, rushes and sedges in marshes, estuaries, lagoons, pans and dams.

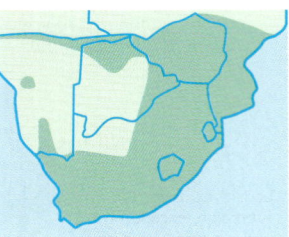

Found in marshy, reeded areas throughout the entire subregion, but absent from the drier areas of central Namibia, central and southern Botswana and the northerly reaches of Northern Cape.

Of all the bird songs you may hear at the waterside in Africa, the most beautiful is that of the lesser swamp warbler. Its rich, flutelike notes interspersed with mellow trills are a delightful experience, though the phrase is not sustained as in most other warblers. Short bursts of song are followed by intervals of silence, during which only the movements of the reeds betray the bird's presence as it hops about looking for its insect food. Occasionally it takes small frogs.

The lesser swamp warbler (also known as the Cape reed warbler) is a solitary bird which spends much of its time low down in the reeds near the water level. Even if you don't get a good look at the bird, its song immediately identifies it. It is quite different from the harsh and sustained singing of the commoner African reed warbler, which lives in the same habitat. It's fortunate for birdwatchers that these small brown birds have such distinctive songs—identifying them by sight alone could be very difficult.

The nest of the lesser swamp warbler is a masterpiece of woven basketry, a cone-shaped cup tied to upright stems of reeds or bulrushes, or into the inflorescence of a sedge. Two or three white to greenish eggs with dull grey and brown spots are laid. The incubation and nestling periods appear to be unknown, but male and female participate almost equally in both stages of the breeding cycle.

The lesser swamp warbler is an inquisitive bird, and will respond to a playback of its song by emerging from its hiding place to perch on top of a reed and look around.

AFRICAN PIED WAGTAIL

Bontkwikkie *(Motacilla aguimp)*

Size: Length 20 cm; weight 27-30 g.
Colour: Above black with white eyebrow, neck and wing-patch; below white with black collar on chest.
Most like: Cape and mountain wagtails, but black instead of grey above; white neck patches distinctive; immature specimens may be confused with Cape wagtail because black parts are dull grey.
Habitat: Larger rivers, sewage ponds, mown grassy areas.

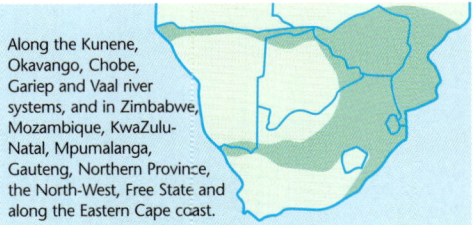

Along the Kunene, Okavango, Chobe, Gariep and Vaal river systems, and in Zimbabwe, Mozambique, KwaZulu-Natal, Mpumalanga, Gauteng, Northern Province, the North-West, Free State and along the Eastern Cape coast.

The handsome African pied wagtail, like most wagtails, has adapted to man quite well, and you may see it at your kitchen door or at a campsite, scavenging for breadcrumbs and porridge—although its usual diet is small insects. Less common than the Cape wagtail, this bird is very conspicuous, and utters loud piping notes as it walks about on the shoreline or grass looking for food.

Although you will be more likely to see African pied wagtails in pairs, they do form flocks of up to 30 or 40, especially when the birds are not nesting. They usually pick their food up on the ground, but occasionally intercept flying insects in the air.

The wagtail's enchanting habit of wagging its black tail up and down as it walks is enhanced by the contrasting white outer tail feathers, which also show up well when the tail is spread in flight.

The bird's territorial song is a series of loud, piping notes repeated in groups of two or three of the same notes following each other quickly.

Its nest is a large accumulation of rags and plant material, with a neat cup in the top, lined with fine grass and straw. It is made in a building, a cavity in a river bank, a rocky overhang or some other protected site near water; sometimes a nest is built in a boat that is not being used.

The female lays three or four whitish, cloudy eggs which take 13 days to hatch. The young stay in the nest for about 16 days and then accompany their parents on foraging trips until they are quite independent.

Waterbirds

CAPE WAGTAIL

Gewone kwikkie *(Motacilla capensis)*

Size: Length 18-20 cm; weight 17-25 g.
Colour: Above dull olive-grey; below off-white with grey to blackish collar on breast; outer tail feathers white, conspicuous in flight.
Most like: Immature African pied wagtail, but smaller and more slender, and with no white wing-stripe; mountain wagtail is bright blue-grey above.
Habitat: Shorelines of inland waters, parks, gardens, playing fields, sewage works.

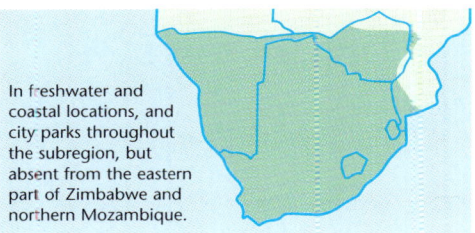

In freshwater and coastal locations, and city parks throughout the subregion, but absent from the eastern part of Zimbabwe and northern Mozambique.

Why does a wagtail wag its tail? It is possibly designed to act as a recognition signal to tell other wagtails some distance away what species it is. Wagtails wag their tails at different rates and the extent of the wagging conveys information about the bird's emotional state; an anxious bird wags its tail very exaggeratedly. Cape wagtails also draw attention to themselves by calling frequently as they walk about feeding.

The Cape wagtail has become very tame in urban areas and sometimes will barely move out of your way on a sidewalk. Although it often forages at the edge of water, it also catches its insect food in short grass and among grazing cattle that disturb insects as they move. It also feeds on beaches and seaside rocks where you can hear its piercing calls above the sound of the breakers.

Cape wagtails often nest on or around buildings, using a hole in a wall, a creeper or a hanging flowerpot; they will also use boats, trailers and jetties as nesting sites. The most common natural site, however, is among vegetation overhanging the bank of a stream, even in open veld.

The nest is a neat cup of grass, rootlets and hair set into a bulky foundation of coarse plant material. The clutch is usually three eggs, dull yellowish or greyish with cloudy markings. After an incubation period of 14 days, the chicks hatch out and are fed by both parents for another 14 days before leaving the nest.

SOUTHERN RED BISHOP

Rooivink *(Euplectes orix)*

Size: Length 12-13 cm; weight (m) 15-26 g, (f) 13-25 g.
Colour: Breeding male scarlet above with black face and brown wings; below black with scarlet chest and undertail; bill black; legs pinkish. Female and eclipse male brown above, streaked darker; below buffy with brown streaks on breast and flanks; wings and tail dark brown; bill pinkish brown.
Most like: Black-winged (or fire-crowned) bishop; but wings and tail brown (not black); female and eclipse male robustly built with short tail; no distinctive colour at bend of wing as in some other bishop species.
Habitat: Reed beds, gardens, orchards when breeding; otherwise open grassveld, fallow lands.

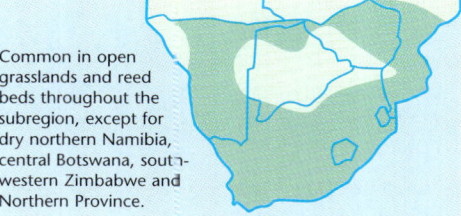

Common in open grasslands and reed beds throughout the subregion, except for dry northern Namibia, central Botswana, south-western Zimbabwe and Northern Province.

Most southern Africans are familiar with the brilliant breeding plumage of male red bishops in summer as they chase each other about their territories with puffed-out feathers and wheezy *tsarippy-tsarippy-tsarippy* songs. The inconspicuous females, on the other hand, simply go about their business with a minimum of fuss.

Gregarious at all times, southern red bishops form large flocks in winter often along with other species of bishops or widowbirds. These flocks forage in grasslands or farmlands for seeds and grain. In summer the birds also eat insects, especially larvae.

You are most likely to see them in gardens and fruit trees; they also often frequent feeding trays.

Nesting colonies are established in waterside grass, reeds, rushes or sedges, or in the tops of low trees in gardens. The nest is an oval of finely woven grass with an entrance at the top on one side, sheltered by a roofed porch. Three blue-green eggs form the clutch which the female incubates for 12-13 days. She feeds the young on her own until they can fly at the age of about two weeks.

The southern red bishop's territory overlaps with that of the similar black-winged, or fire-crowned, bishop only in the extreme northeastern corner of southern Africa.

Birds of prey

BEARDED VULTURE/ LAMMERGEIER

Baardaasvoël (*Gypaetus barbatus*)

Size: Length 1,1 m; weight 5,2-6,2 kg.
Colour: Back and wings blackish; head whitish, shading to bright yellowish rusty neck and underparts; face mask and bristly beard black.
Most like: White-backed vulture, but underwing all dark; wedge-shaped tail diagnostic at all times, especially in flight; wings tend to be pointed.
Habitat: Drakensberg and neighbouring mountain ranges.

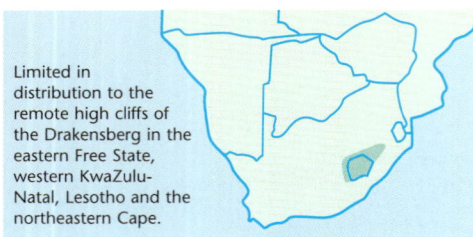

Limited in distribution to the remote high cliffs of the Drakensberg in the eastern Free State, western KwaZulu-Natal, Lesotho and the northeastern Cape.

If you're in bearded vulture territory, look for one or more flat slabs of rock with scattered fragments of bone lying around them. These slabs are called ossuaries, and the bearded vultures use them as bone-breaking sites; any piece of bone too big to swallow is taken aloft and dropped with remarkable accuracy on the ossuary to break it. The bearded vulture may have to repeat this bone-dropping performance several times before the bone fragments are small enough to swallow. This extraordinary behaviour indicates how important bone is in the diet of this magnificent bird, which is listed as 'rare' in the 2000 International Union for Conservation of Nature and Natural Resources' Red Data Book.

Once quite widespread in South Africa and Lesotho, the bearded vulture's range has shrunk since 1940, probably because of increasingly sophisticated farming practices which include the removal of carcasses for burial. The birds now depend for food on more primitive farming regions such as those found in Lesotho.

The bearded vulture roosts and nests on inaccessible ledges or potholes in high cliffs. A platform of sticks, lined with rags, grass, dung, skin and other debris, is built to contain the one or two large eggs, which are white with mottled markings of brown and grey. After an incubation period of about 57 days, mostly by the female, the downy greyish chicks hatch, but never more than one survives. Both parents feed the young bird for about four months in the nest and for a further 60 days after it has flown.

CAPE VULTURE

Kransaasvoël (*Gyps coprotheres*)

Size: Length 1,0-1,2 m; weight 7,3-10 kg.
Colour: Whitish to buffy with black wing tips, trailing edges and tail; underwing shows row of dark spots along border, with black trailing edge; head naked, greyish blue; bare blue patches on either side of crop; iris pale yellow.
Most like: White-backed vulture, but lacks white patch on rump; pale eye diagnostic at close quarters; usually paler than white-backed vulture.
Habitat: Usually around mountains; sometimes over savanna or semi-desert.

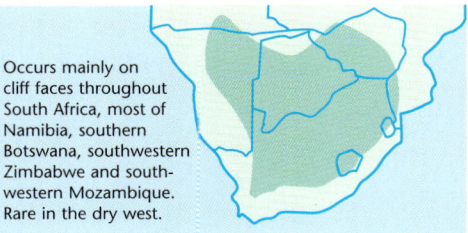

Occurs mainly on cliff faces throughout South Africa, most of Namibia, southern Botswana, southwestern Zimbabwe and south-western Mozambique. Rare in the dry west.

Conserving the Cape vulture has become a priority in southern Africa. Listed as 'vulnerable' in the 2000 International Union for Conservation of Nature and Natural Resources' Red Data Book, the Cape vulture's numbers have dwindled dangerously as a result of man's indiscriminate use of poisons, the erection of powerlines on which the birds were electrocuted (a problem now largely solved by fitting safe perches to electricity pylons), and the burial of dead stock animals which served as the bird's main source of carrion after the disappearance of natural herds of game.

The largest species of vulture in southern Africa, the Cape vulture now needs special protection to prevent a further deterioration in its numbers that could lead to its extinction. Only about 10 000 birds are estimated to be left in southern Africa today.

Cape vultures are gregarious both at their roosts on high cliffs and on the ground at a carcass. Many sandstone cliffs in the eastern Free State are whitewashed with the droppings of these great birds.

The vultures breed on inaccessible ledges, and although they sometimes build a substantial platform of sticks, usually there is hardly any nest at all. Both parents incubate the single white egg for about 57 days. They then feed the chick for just over seven months after hatching.

Birds of prey

WHITE-BACKED VULTURE

Witrugaasvoël *(Gyps africanus)*

Size: *Length 90-98 cm; weight 4,4-6,6 kg.*
Colour: *Mostly pale brown to buff; lower back white; underwing buff with dark trailing edge; iris dark brown; head blackish grey.*
Most like: *Cape vulture, but darker; white lower back distinctive (visible in flight); dark eye visible at close quarters.*
Habitat: *Savanna and bushveld.*

In bushveld areas of most of Namibia, Botswana, Zimbabwe, Mozambique, northern KwaZulu-Natal, eastern Swaziland, Northern Province, North-West Province and the Northern Cape.

Watching a feeding flock of white-backed vultures is a truly memorable experience. This seething mass of hissing, squealing birds makes quick work of a carcass in the veld, ravenously ripping away at meat, skin and entrails. Fifty of these birds have been known to devour a 23 kg impala carcass in ten minutes!

The most common and most widespread vulture in southern Africa, the white-backed vulture occurs in the larger subtropical game reserves.

Individuals cruise at approximately 60 km per hour, scanning the terrain below for clues which may lead to a carcass. Other scavengers, such as crows, bateleurs or hyaenas, often serve as beacons leading white-backed vultures to carrion. Once a carcass has been sighted, the birds swoop down to it at great speed—sometimes exceeding 100 km per hour

After feeding, the birds may proceed to a nearby waterhole to drink and bathe, sometimes until they are so full or so waterlogged that they cannot take off. Unlike Cape vultures, whitebacks roost in trees, many of them sharing a perch.

They build large stick nests on the topmost branches of tallish trees, usually acacias. The centre of the hollow platform is lined with grass or green leaves and contains a single white egg which weighs about 215 grams. The incubation period is 56-58 days.

The nestling is dependent on the parents for food for up to 130 days, and after leaving the nest has to be fed by them for a further four months or so.

LAPPET-FACED VULTURE

Swartaasvoël *(Torgos tracheliotus)*

Size: *Length 98 cm-1,0 m; weight 5,9-7,9 kg.*
Colour: *Mostly black with white thighs, neck ruff and bar on underwing; breast heavily streaked black and white; head naked, bright pinkish red.*
Most like: *Other dark vultures, but combination of large size, bright reddish head, white bar on leading edge of underwing and striped breast distinctive.*
Habitat: *Savanna to desert with thorn trees.*

Throughout southern Africa in the drier regions north of the Gariep, Limpopo and Tugela rivers. Also found in the thornveld regions of the lowveld.

This large vulture, one of southern Africa's biggest flying land birds, is an impressive sight at a carcass where it dominates the smaller vulture species. As the morning sun warms the African soil, thermals form which enable this heavy bird, with its 2,6 m wingspan, to soar effortlessly so high in the sky as to become almost invisible. In the absence of thermals it flies with difficulty.

When the lappet-faced vulture sees a carcass it glides down to land near it. Then it bounds in, scattering lesser birds before it, and feeds until it is full, tearing easily into the tough carcasses with its large, hooked bill. After the meal it will probably sit quietly on the ground nearby until it is ready to take off.

Surprisingly, this vulture sometimes depends for food on quite small animals and is known to kill small mammals, fishes and nestling flamingos.

It is not as gregarious as the smaller vulture species and is usually found alone or in pairs.

The lappet-faced vulture builds an enormous stick platform on top of a low tree or large thorn bush. It lines the nest with grass and lays a single white, brown-blotched egg. Both sexes incubate for 56 days and feed the chick for up to five months before it leaves the nest, though it depends on its parents for food for a further six months or so.

Birds of prey

BLACK KITE/YELLOW-BILLED KITE

Swartwou *(Milvus migrans)*/Geelbekwou *(Milvus migrans aegyptius)*

Size: Length about 55 cm; average weight (m) 650 g, (f) 750 g.
Colour: Dark brown all over; head paler in black kite; bill yellow (yellow-billed kite) or black (black kite).
Most like: No other southern African raptor, because forked tail diagnostic; yellow bill of yellow-billed kite distinctive in adults only.
Habitat: Woodland, villages, suburbs, savanna.

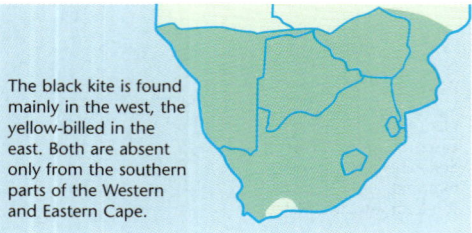

The black kite is found mainly in the west, the yellow-billed in the east. Both are absent only from the southern parts of the Western and Eastern Cape.

These large, dark brown kites glide and soar magnificently on their long, angled wings, and you will see them frequently over highways, searching for animals killed on the road. If a dead animal is small enough, the kite will simply pluck it from the surface of the road and fly off with it, but larger carcasses require the kite to land and feed on the road surface, where it runs the risk of being struck by a passing vehicle.

Kites also catch their own live prey in the form of insects, small vertebrates and even snails. After rain in the semi-arid western parts of southern Africa, black kites gather in flocks of hundreds, forming great, funnel-shaped pillars that soar across the sky. Yellow-billed kites are less gregarious, being found usually in pairs. This is a reflection of the fact that the black kite is a nonbreeding migrant from Eurasia, while the yellow-billed kite arrives from equatorial Africa to breed in southern Africa from about September.

The kite's nest consists of a 50-80 cm-diameter platform of sticks in a tree, lined with grass, dung and rags. The female lays two or three white eggs which both parents incubate for 35 days. The chicks stay in the nest for up to 45 days and the female feeds them food brought by the male. Adults at the nest are extremely shy, but quite vocal, giving a quavering *quillllerrr* cry that betrays their presence immediately.

Although previously considered to be geographical variations of a single species, the yellow-billed/black complex of kites is now regarded as separate species with very similar habits.

BLACK-SHOULDERED KITE

Blouvalk *(Elanus caeruleus)*

Size: Length 30 cm; average weight (m) 240 g, (f) 260 g.
Colour: Pale grey above; white below; patch on bend of wing and at wing tip black; eye bright cherry red; bill black; feet yellow.
Most like: Some small goshawks, but never barred on belly; shape dumpy and wings pointed.
Habitat: Very variable; mostly open grassland with scattered trees or telephone poles.

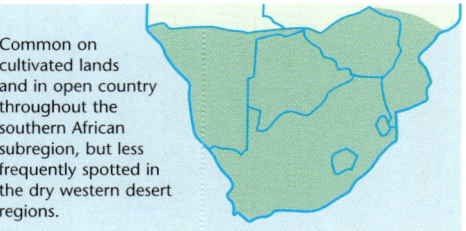

Common on cultivated lands and in open country throughout the southern African subregion, but less frequently spotted in the dry western desert regions.

The black-shouldered kite is the greatest rodent catcher of all the southern African birds of prey. You will see it flying buoyantly and rather gull-like in its pale grey-and-white plumage, suddenly stopping in the air to hover as it scans the ground below for an unwary rat or mouse. When it spots prey it drops from the sky like a large butterfly, its legs outstretched to grasp the unfortunate animal; then takes the rodent to a perch to skin and gut it before tearing it apart to eat.

This beautiful little kite also hunts from a perch and may spend long periods on top of a pole or tree, either resting or looking for mice. Rarely it may take a small bird or reptile if mammals are scarce.

When agitated it wags its tail up and down and may give a wheezy *peeeu* call as it does so.

By day you will usually see a black-shouldered kite by itself, though occasionally two birds will keep company together. Less often you may be lucky to see a communal roost of 100 or more birds in trees at night.

The peak of breeding activity starts in the winter and early spring in the Western Cape, moves into summer in the Eastern Cape, and falls in the autumn further north.

The black-shouldered kite builds a rather scanty stick nest in a tree, and the female lays three or four white eggs with heavy brown markings. Incubation and nestling periods are each about a month. The female does most of the incubation and nearly all the feeding of the young, though the male brings the food.

Birds of prey

Verreaux's eagle

Witruisarend *(Aquila verreauxii)*

Size: Length 84 cm; weight 3,0-5,8 kg.
Colour: Jet black, except for white lower back and white V on upper back; feet, skin around eyes and base of bill are bright yellow.
Most like: Lammergeier when seen silhouetted against the sky, but tail somewhat rounded, not wedge-shaped; wings splayed at tips, not pointed.
Habitat: Rocky cliffs of mountains, gorges and hills.

Montane and hilly regions of Namibia, eastern Botswana, Zimbabwe, western Mozambique, KwaZulu-Natal, Mpumalanga, Northern Province, Gauteng, the North-West, Free State, Lesotho, Eastern, Western and Northern Cape.

Verreaux's eagle, also called the black eagle, is the best known and most widespread of all the large southern African eagles. Once you've seen it in flight, you won't easily forget its magnificent colouring and superb powers of gliding and soaring. It has recently become the farmer's friend because of its habit of catching great numbers of dassies for food. Large dassie populations are a threat to grazing lands, and the black eagle is one of the main forms of natural control.

Apart from dassies, which form about 90 per cent of its diet, the black eagle also kills hares, monkeys, small antelope and other mammals, as well as the larger game birds such as guineafowl and francolins. It seldom takes reptiles, and even more rarely domestic stock such as lambs.

Although its numbers have declined under persecution by man, changed attitudes have led to its acceptance in the natural scheme of things, and farmers generally welcome a pair of black eagles on their farms.

Before the egg-laying season from April to June, the black eagle builds a huge stick nest on a rocky ledge, high above the foot of a cliff. This is often an old nest, refurbished with grass, and lined with green leaves broken off nearby trees. On this fresh bed the female lays two large white eggs which she incubates for 45 days. Although both eggs usually hatch, the older chick invariably kills the younger one and receives all the food. The chick leaves the nest after 90-98 days.

Tawny eagle

Roofarend *(Aquila rapax)*

Size: Length 65-72 cm; average weight (m) 1,9 kg, (f) 1,5-2,4 kg.
Colour: Usually light tawny brown, but varies from dark brown to creamy white; feet and base of bill yellow.
Most like: Steppe eagle, but not migratory (therefore present in winter also); feathering of legs much shaggier than in the lesser spotted eagle; tail rounded (square in Wahlberg's eagle).
Habitat: Bushveld, savanna, semi-arid acacia thornveld.

Most of southern Africa, but absent from dry southwestern Namibia, Western and Eastern Cape, the Free State and Gauteng highveld, and coastal and southern KwaZulu-Natal.

If you see an untidy, quite large brown eagle with scruffy, feathered 'trousers' on its legs, it will probably be a tawny eagle—though it could easily be confused with the lesser spotted eagle (a European breeding species) in summer in the lowveld. Quite a solitary bird, the tawny eagle most often perches on the top of a tree, often on a dead branch, from which it swoops when its eye lands on suitable prey.

Its usual diet consists of small mammals, but it will eat almost anything that moves and is small enough to kill. The tawny eagle is also partial to carrion. After rain, when flying termites emerge from their holes, tawny eagles walk about picking them up as they mill about on the ground before trying to fly away.

The great colour variation in this eagle makes identification difficult at times, but the very darkest and lightest colour variants are uncommon, and you can be sure that, in winter at least, you cannot confuse it with any of the migrants from the northern hemisphere.

Tawny eagles nest mainly in winter. They build a smallish platform of sticks in a tree, and then line it with green leaves before the female lays the eggs. Usually two white eggs form the clutch, which is incubated mostly by the female for about 40 days.

The first chick to hatch kills the unfortunate younger one. The survivor is ready to leave the nest after 12 weeks, but depends on the parents for food for a further two months before fending for itself.

Birds of prey

MARTIAL EAGLE

Breëkoparend *(Polemaetus bellicosus)*

Size: *Length 78-83cm; average weight (m) 5kg, (f) 6kg.*
Colour: *Dark brown, except for white belly with dark brown spots; bill black; eyes yellow; feet greenish or bluish white.*
Most like: *Black-chested snake eagle, but underwing all dark in flight; dark spots on white belly diagnostic at closer range.*
Habitat: *Almost any countryside with trees.*

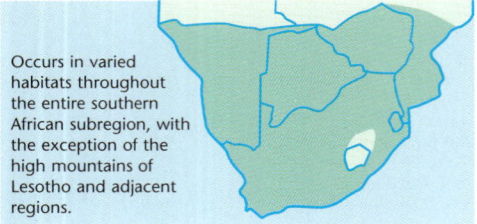

Occurs in varied habitats throughout the entire southern African subregion, with the exception of the high mountains of Lesotho and adjacent regions.

The impressive martial eagle, the largest of the true eagles of southern Africa, is a great soarer over open country. It swoops down from the air or from high perches onto its prey of game birds, small mammals and larger reptiles, and can kill animals up to the size of a stork or a duiker. It is wisely shy of man.

You can recognize eagles proper by their feathered legs, giving them a trousered look. Martial eagles are increasingly rare and are now listed in the Red Data Book as 'vulnerable', which means that they are in need of stringent conservation measures to prevent their numbers from declining to a dangerously low level. An increasing awareness among the people of southern Africa, farmers in particular, of the value of the large birds of prey in nature, as well as an awareness of their aesthetic value, seems to have turned the tide of opinion in the eagles' favour and now raises hopes for their future survival.

The martial eagle's nest is an enormous structure of sticks, up to two metres wide, built in a tall tree or on a power pylon. The bowl in the centre is lined with green leaves during the breeding period, which starts mainly in the autumn and winter. The female lays only one egg and incubates it for 50 days. She alone feeds the young bird, although the male provides most of the food. After about 97 days the young eagle is able to leave the nest, but it remains dependent on its parents for up to eight months after its first flight.

AFRICAN CROWNED EAGLE

Kroonarend *(Stephanoaetus coronatus)*

Size: *Length 80-90cm; weight 3,4-4,1 kg.*
Colour: *Slaty black above; below pale rufous with heavy black barring; underwing in flight deep russet in front, white behind with heavy black bands; tail banded black and white; eyes and feet yellow.*
Most like: *Some other large eagles, but forest habitat, conspicuous underwing pattern and heavy barring on belly and breast diagnostic.*
Habitat: *Evergreen forest, including riverine forest.*

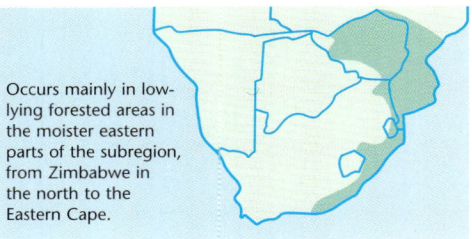

Occurs mainly in low-lying forested areas in the moister eastern parts of the subregion, from Zimbabwe in the north to the Eastern Cape.

High over the canopy of an evergreen forest a large eagle swoops and dives, giving its pulsating *kewee-kewee-kewee* calls that ring out clearly in the African air. This is the African crowned eagle. Seen from below, its powerful, banded wings, backlighted by the bright sky, reveal a checkerboard pattern formed by the flight feathers.

The bird has a very broad appearance, enhanced by its relatively short wings. These have been adapted to flying vertically upward in a closed forest, enabling the eagle to carry such heavy prey as a vervet monkey or blue duiker. Dassies are also regularly taken.

Crowned eagles are happily still quite common, because they can live in small patches of forest and may hunt well away from the forest in open country. They usually hunt by keeping a lookout for prey from a hidden perch, then descending on the unfortunate victim in a lightning dash. They seldom hunt in flight.

A mass of sticks in a stout fork is built by a breeding pair, usually in the late winter or early spring; or the birds may simply re-line an already existing nest. Normally two eggs are laid, but only one chick survives after hatching. The nestling period is about 110 days, but the fledgling may remain with its parents for nearly a year after it first leaves the nest, so that most adults breed only every two years.

Birds of prey

BLACK-CHESTED SNAKE EAGLE

Swartborsslangarend *(Circaetus pectoralis)*

Size: Length 63-68 cm; weight 1,2-2,2 kg.

Colour: Head, breast and upperparts black; underparts and underwing white; underwing boldly banded with black; legs and feet white; eyes bright yellow.

Most like: Martial eagle, but smaller and with white underwing; no dark spots on white belly; legs bare, white; large yellow eyes in owl-like face characteristic.

Habitat: Light woodland, savanna, semi-desert, highveld with scattered trees.

Frequents varied habitats throughout the southern African subregion, with the exception of the Drakensberg area, KwaZulu-Natal, the southern and Eastern Cape and southwestern Namibia.

Snake eagles have short toes adapted to grasping their relatively narrow prey of snakes and lizards. The black-chested snake eagle can kill snakes up to two metres long, including the highly poisonous cobras, mambas and adders. Smaller snakes are swallowed whole in flight, larger ones are dismembered on the ground and eaten piecemeal.

When the eagle grabs the snake, it seems to try to immobilize it by breaking its back. During this strike, it holds its wings wide open, exposing a large area at which the snake can strike harmlessly.

While black-chested snake eagles have a particular taste for snakes, they also catch and eat mammals, birds, frogs, fishes and insects. They hunt from soaring flight, parachuting down onto their prey to pick it up. If food is plentiful, several may hunt together, but usually you will see a black-chested snake eagle soaring alone.

The nest is a smallish platform of sticks with a shallow, leaf-lined bowl on top. The clutch consists of one egg which the female incubates for 51 days. Both parents feed the nestling for about 90 days and continue to care for it for up to six months after it can fly. This may be in order to enable the young snake eagle to perfect its snake-hunting skills without risking starvation.

BATELEUR

Berghaan *(Terathopius ecaudatus)*

Size: Length 55-70 cm; weight 1,8-2,9 kg.

Colour: Black; back and tail reddish brown; upperwing grey; underwing white with black trailing edge (narrow in female, broad in male); face, base of bill, legs and feet red.

Most like: No other bird of prey; short tail distinctive; wings broad at base, narrower at tips and unmistakably black and white below; feet project beyond tail in flight.

Habitat: Bushveld, savanna and Kalahari thornveld.

Prevalent in the drier regions of northeastern Namibia, Botswana, most of Zimbabwe, Mozambique, northern KwaZulu-Natal, eastern Swaziland, the lowveld and the extreme Northern Cape.

The sight of a bateleur against the blue African sky must be one of the most familiar sights in almost any game reserve. But it's a spectacle that's becoming increasingly rare—because of man's indiscriminate use of poisons, the bateleur has become the most vulnerable of southern Africa's eagles.

The bird's name comes from the French word for a slapstick comedian or a juggler and is said to refer to the bird's habit of tilting from side to side in flight in much the same way that a tightrope walker does in a circus. This characteristic may result from instability because of the bird's short tail.

Although usually alone, bateleurs may gather in loose groups of up to 40 birds. They spend most of each day gliding and soaring high above the ground at speeds of 60-80 km/h, hardly needing to flap their wings at all.

When it spots prey, a bateleur may make a high-speed swoop or may parachute gently down. Its menu includes insects, game birds, small antelope weighing up to four kilograms, and carrion.

Bateleurs nest during any month of the year, but mostly in February and March. The nest is a platform of sticks in the horizontal fork of a large tree, sometimes right in the canopy. The female lays only one white egg which is incubated for about 55 days. The nestling period is about 111 days. Both parents feed the young bird in the nest and for about 100 days after it leaves the nest.

Birds of prey

AFRICAN FISH EAGLE
Visarend (*Haliaeetus vocifer*)

Size: Length 63-73 cm; weight (m) 2,0-2,5 kg, (f) 3,1-3,6 kg.
Colour: Head, neck, breast and tail white; wings and back black; belly and underwing maroon; legs and feet yellow.
Most like: Palmnut and Egyptian vultures, but body and underwing all dark; tail does not have black tip in adult.
Habitat: Larger inland waters, coastal lagoons and estuaries with big trees.

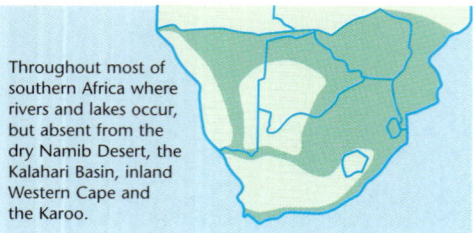

Throughout most of southern Africa where rivers and lakes occur, but absent from the dry Namib Desert, the Kalahari Basin, inland Western Cape and the Karoo.

Most southern Africans are familiar with the haunting, ringing cry of the magnificent African fish eagle, one of the most plentiful birds of prey in Africa—in spite of its large size and specialized habits. If you haven't come across it in a game reserve or along a large river, the chances are you've seen it on a television programme featuring the Okavango Delta or the Pongolo flood plain, both regions where the bird is found in large numbers. It is becoming increasingly common too on quite small bodies of water, such as farm dams and sewage disposal ponds.

The fish eagle spends most of each day perched on top of a tall tree. From here it scans the water or shoreline for the telltale movement of a fish; then, taking off in a long, shallow glide towards the water, it suddenly brings its feet forward for the final strike and usually catches the fish in one graceful swoop, flying on without more than a momentary check. If the prey is fairly deep, however, the eagle may submerge completely. Its unfeathered legs and roughened feet are specially designed to help the bird slip through water easily and get a good grasp on their prey.

African fish eagles lay their eggs mostly in midwinter in a large stick nest that may be used year after year, sometimes reaching a depth of 1,2 metres. The bowl is lined with grass, leaves and reeds. The female usually lays two white eggs which are incubated by both sexes. After 75 days the young are ready to fly, but will stay with the parents for a further two months.

COMMON BUZZARD
Bruinjakkalsvoël (*Buteo buteo*)

Size: Length 45-50 cm; weight 700-925 g.
Colour: Above brown, sometimes washed rufous on tail; below white, more or less heavily barred, streaked or mottled with brown; pale band usually visible across breast; underwing largely whitish with brown leading edge and black trailing edge and tips.
Most like: Forest buzzard: not safely distinguishable by plumage, but prefers open country; forest buzzard usually associated with mountains and/or forest.
Habitat: Open grassveld, farmland, savanna.

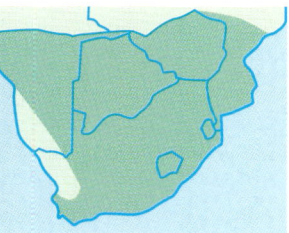

Found in open country throughout the entire southern African subregion, but absent from the arid parts of southern Namibia and the northwestern and Northern Cape coast.

If you're travelling across country in summer keep an eye out for common buzzards on their favourite perches—telephone poles along the roadside. These poles, and fence posts on farmlands, provide ideal observation points when searching for food, although these striking birds do occasionally hover to detect prey on the ground. They're also known for their dramatic dive-bombing aerobatic displays.

Common, or steppe, buzzards mainly eat insects and perform a service to farmers by eradicating pests in agricultural parts of southern Africa. They also take birds, mammals and lizards.

Unlike small migratory birds, they migrate during the daylight hours, usually in large flocks of hundreds of birds. These flocks use thermals or updrafts of air along mountain ranges to gain height as they fly, thereby saving energy. For this reason they will not cross any large body of water, because no thermals can develop over water, nor do they form at night when the ground cools down. It takes the birds about a month to travel the 10 000-12 000 km from Europe to southern Africa.

The bird gets the name 'steppe buzzard' from the open steppes that it inhabits in Europe and Asia, where it breeds during our winter. In southern Africa it also prefers steppe country, but does not breed here.

Birds of prey

JACKAL BUZZARD

Rooiborsjakkalsvoël
(*Buteo rufofuscus*)

Size: Length 44-53 cm; weight (m) 865 g-1,08 kg, (f) 1,1-1,7 kg.
Colour: Slaty black above and on upper breast; lower breast chestnut, sometimes separated from upper breast by white band; belly black with white crossbars; tail rufous; underwing black with broad white band; feet and base of bill yellow.
Most like: Augur buzzard, but dark underwing and underparts distinctive; bateleur is all black below with bright red face and feet.
Habitat: Mostly mountains, valleys and broken country.

In southern Namibia, Western, Eastern and most of Northern Cape (except the extreme north), Free State, Lesotho, Gauteng, the eastern North-West, Northern Province, Mpumalanga, Swaziland and KwaZulu-Natal.

SOUTHERN PALE CHANTING GOSHAWK

Bleeksingvalk
(*Melierax canorus*)

Size: Length 46-54 cm; weight 493 g-1,2 kg.
Colour: Mostly pale grey; belly white with fine, pale grey bars; in flight wings largely white, tips black; rump white; base of bill, legs and feet bright red.
Most like: Dark chanting goshawk, but paler overall with pure white rump and much white in wings; African harrier hawk (gymnogene) has yellow bare parts, not red, and only one white band on tail.
Habitat: Desert to semi-desert and dry Karoo.

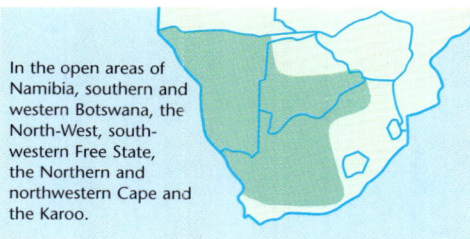

In the open areas of Namibia, southern and western Botswana, the North-West, south-western Free State, the Northern and northwestern Cape and the Karoo.

The jackal buzzard, so named for its jackal-like cry, is a familiar sight among the rocky hills and scarps of many parts of South Africa. You can see it soaring lazily on thermals or gliding along a ridge on the uplift generated by wind against the steep ground. When it perches on a roadside telephone pole (a habit that most buzzards have) you can get a close look at its coloration and see the tips of the long wings projecting beyond the tail at rest.

Many people mistake the jackal buzzard for the bateleur (*see page 153*) because of its black-and-white underwings and dark underparts, but the bateleur's more tropical distribution and savanna habitat make it unlikely that the two species overlap more than occasionally. Jackal buzzards are common in the southern parts of their range, where they are regarded as useful predators of rodents and insects; they also take birds and snakes from time to time and will come to feed on road-killed carrion.

The nest of the jackal buzzard is usually on an inaccessible precipice, less often in the stout fork of a tree. The nest is a pile of sticks with a leaf-lined hollow in the top, in which two white eggs with reddish brown blotches are laid. The eggs hatch out after 40 days and the parents care for the nestlings for a further 50 days before they can fly.

When you drive through the dry, western parts of southern Africa, say from Kimberley to Windhoek, you will become very familiar with the pale chanting goshawks that sit on telephone poles along the roadside. The bird's name derives from its melodious, repeated song of piping notes *WIP-pi-pi-pi-pi-pi-pip* that increase in volume and pitch and then die away. It may sing either in flight or from its perch.

This bird has developed an interesting association with the honey badger and slender mongoose, following them and catching small rodents that the small mammals disturb. Up to six goshawks will walk behind the badger or mongoose in a way that shows that the relationship is quite deliberate. They will forage on the ground even in the absence of honey badgers, though, mainly for insects and lizards.

But the southern pale chanting goshawk can also be quite a ferocious predator, attacking birds up to the size of a korhaan (about its own weight), mammals as big as a hare and even snakes.

The nesting season is mainly in spring when the pale chanting goshawk builds its nest, often in a thorn tree. The female lays one or two greenish-white eggs. After an incubation period of 37 days the grey-and-white chicks hatch out and are fed in the nest for seven to eight weeks. For a further two months the family stays together until the young goshawks leave to fend for themselves.

Birds of prey

AFRICAN MARSH HARRIER

Afrikaanse vleivalk *(Circus ranivorus)*

Size: Length 44-49 cm; weight 380-590 g.
Colour: Brown, obscurely mottled with whitish; belly and thighs more rufous; leading edge of wing whitish; underwing boldly barred black and white.
Most like: Other harriers, but boldly barred underwing diagnostic; pale leading edge of dark brown wing characteristic.
Habitat: Open moist grassland, vlei and marsh, but will hunt over other habitats at times.

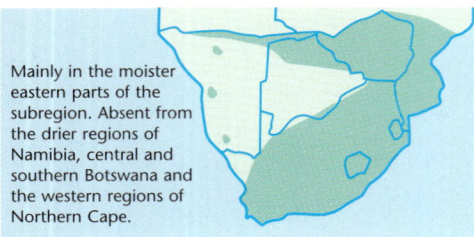

Mainly in the moister eastern parts of the subregion. Absent from the drier regions of Namibia, central and southern Botswana and the western regions of Northern Cape.

Gliding slowly over the veld or marshland on its long, upswept wings, so typical of harriers, the African marsh harrier is a graceful sight. As it glides it scans the ground below for small animals, mainly rodents and birds, and may catch anything up to the size of a small duck. As its scientific name implies, though, it also eats frogs, and it is not above taking birds' eggs and carrion too.

When it spots prey, the harrier checks its flight and drops onto its victim with its long legs outstretched. Evidence of its kills can be found at the harrier's roosting place, which is always littered with regurgitated remains of feathers, bones and fur in the form of pellets.

Marsh harriers roost on the ground or in reed beds, sometimes in groups outside the breeding season, though otherwise in pairs. When not actually hunting, the birds may rest on a perch or soar high in the sky.

Breeding takes place in almost any month, but mainly in winter when the danger of flooding is small. The nest is a platform of sticks or dry grass built in a marsh, sometimes right at water level, or on the ground in tallish grassland or standing crops some distance from water. The bowl is lined with dry grass and contains three to four white eggs that the female incubates on her own for 31-34 days. The female also feeds the young, but the male brings the food for the family. After about 40 days the young leave the nest and can fly fairly well.

AFRICAN HARRIER HAWK

Kaalwangvalk *(Polyboroides typus)*

Size: Length 60-66 cm; weight 640-950 g.
Colour: Blue-grey body with black wing tips and trailing edges; belly finely barred grey and white; bare face and long slender legs yellow; tail black with one broad white band.
Most like: Chanting goshawks, but yellow face and legs diagnostic (red in chanting goshawks); goshawks and harriers' wings black at tip only; distinguished from pallid and Montagu's harriers by black trailing edge to wings and by black tail with white band.
Habitat: Forest, wooded gorges, suburban areas with trees.

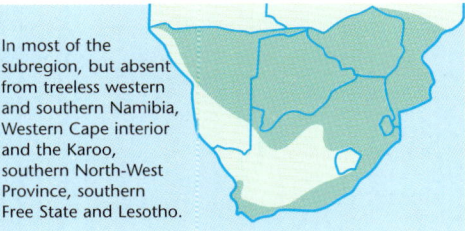

In most of the subregion, but absent from treeless western and southern Namibia, Western Cape interior and the Karoo, southern North-West Province, southern Free State and Lesotho.

If you see a large, broad-winged hawk with a broad white band on its black tail soaring over the treetops, it will certainly be a African harrier hawk, or gymnogene, a name which comes from the Greek words for bare-cheeked (echoed in the Afrikaans name, too). Usually the bare face is light yellow, but when two gymnogenes greet each other at the nest or elsewhere, the faces blush to deep orange.

The African harrier hawk has a unique way of extracting small animals from deep crevices in trees or rock faces; its ankle joint can bend forwards, allowing its foot to probe down a vertical crack. This is why you may see this harrier hawk hanging onto a tree trunk and flapping to keep its balance while it investigates a likely hole with one foot.

The African harrier hawk's plumage undergoes a bewildering variety of changes from juvenile to adult, starting off uniform chocolate brown, passing through mottled lighter brown and buff with whitish underparts, and finally ending up as the blue-grey adult. But the slender body, small head and long legs help in identification.

The nest is the usual platform of sticks built on a ledge, or in a tree or bush. The clutch normally consists of two eggs which hatch after 35 days. Sometimes one chick will eat the other—a phenomenon known as Cainism.

Birds of prey

Lanner falcon
Edelvalk *(Falco biarmicus)*

Size: *Length 35-40cm; average weight (m) 530g, (f) 750g.*

Colour: *Deep bluish grey upperparts, barred blackish; below creamy white, sometimes with some black spots on sides of belly; forehead, eye-stripe and line below eye black; crown bright rufous; bill horn, bluish at tip; legs and feet yellow.*

Most like: *Peregrine falcon, but rufous crown diagnostic; larger than most other similar falcons or kestrels and with almost plain underparts in adult.*

Habitat: *Any kind of country, especially with cliffs or scattered trees.*

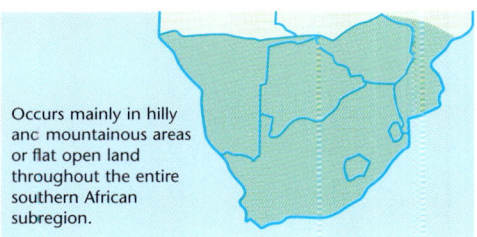

Occurs mainly in hilly and mountainous areas or flat open land throughout the entire southern African subregion.

Common kestrel
Kransvalk *(Falco tinnunculus)*

Size: *Length 30-33cm; average weight (m) 180g, (f) 220g.*

Colour: *Rich russet all over, lightly spotted with black; head blue-grey (duller in female); tail blue-grey, barred with black and tipped white; underwing white in flight.*

Most like: *Male lesser kestrel, but darker below; lesser kestrel has blue band on upperwing and no spots on its back.*

Habitat: *Mainly rocky outcrops in highveld, but also in savanna and semi-desert.*

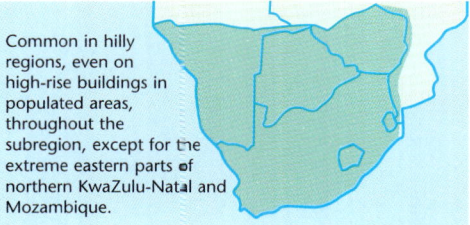

Common in hilly regions, even on high-rise buildings in populated areas, throughout the subregion, except for the extreme eastern parts of northern KwaZulu-Natal and Mozambique.

The commonest and most widespread falcon in southern Africa, the lanner has also the most catholic taste in places to live. You can see it perched in a dead tree in the Kalahari or Namib, soaring over mountains or forests in the green, rolling country of KwaZulu-Natal, or dashing along the gorges of the Zambezi River below Victoria Falls. It is a spectacular flier, adapted to hunting birds on the wing, either while in flight or by launching from a perch.

A favourite hunting area is around a waterhole in dry country where doves and sandgrouse come to drink. The lanner may make several passes over the waterhole, putting the quarry to flight, until one frightened dove will freeze on the ground; the lanner then circles quickly back again, swoops down, grasps the unfortunate bird with its foot, and takes it to a perch to tear apart. Lanners may also hunt cooperatively, one falcon putting the birds to flight, another taking a dove or sandgrouse in the air by coming in at right angles to its path

Lanner falcons build no nests—they use the old nests of other birds, or simply a scrape on the ledge of a cliff. About three to four eggs are laid; they are cream with heavy markings of brick red and rust. Both sexes incubate for 32 days. The male brings food for the young, which the female feeds to them After about 45 days the young can fly, but they remain in the nest area for a further month before they are completely independent.

The common, or rock, kestrel is best known for its habit of hovering on rapidly fluttering wings as it scans the ground below for prey. Once it has sighted a likely quarry, it descends in a series of parachuting drops, until it drops firmly onto the animal. This kestrel has a taste for small mammals, reptiles and insects, though it is quite capable of catching small birds in open flight.

Common kestrels spend a lot of time perched high on top of a dead tree, telephone pole or rocky promontory. Like many birds of rocky places, their colour scheme of rust and grey provides them with excellent camouflage (see also the account of the Cape rock thrush on page 119).

They are a solitary, resident species, unlike the gregarious, migratory, lesser kestrel which comes to southern Africa only in our summer. They also tend to be rather silent, except near the nest when they give vent to excited *kee-kee-kee* callnotes that echo among the kranses.

The common kestrel nests in the old nest of another bird in a tree or in a pothole in a cliff face, less often on the ledge of a building or bridge. Usually four reddish-brown eggs are laid, each weighing about 20 grams. The incubation period lasts for 30 days and the nestling period about 34 days, after which the fledglings stay in the parental territory for another month or so before going off to earn their living.

Birds of prey

Pygmy falcon

Dwergvalk *(Polihierax semitorquatus)*

Size: *Length 19,5 cm; weight 60-67 g.*
Colour: *Grey above; white below; female has chestnut upper back; wings and tail black with white spots; rump white; blue-grey bill with black tip.*
Most like: *Large shrike, but orange cere (swelling at base of upper bill) and eye-ring diagnostic; pygmy falcon's white-spotted feathers conspicuous in flight.*
Habitat: *Semi-desert and acacia sandveld.*

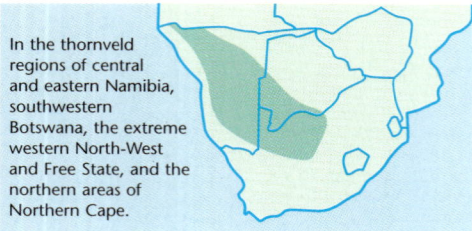

In the thornveld regions of central and eastern Namibia, southwestern Botswana, the extreme western North-West and Free State, and the northern areas of Northern Cape.

This smallest of all African birds of prey has such a close association with the sociable weaver that the distributions of the two species coincide exactly. The pygmy falcon uses the sociable weaver's communal nest masses for roosting and nesting, usually taking over two or three chambers and leaving the rest of the colony undisturbed. This is not to say that the falcons won't catch and eat a sociable weaver, but obviously this is rare, because the falcon must not overexploit its host. Pygmy falcons also roost in nests of white-browed sparrowweavers.

Pygmy falcons feed mostly on insects and lizards. Usually you will see them in pairs; the male and female communicate with each other by means of sharp, rather twittering callnotes and greet each other by bobbing their heads and wagging their tails, especially near the nest.

A telltale sign that a sociable weaver's nest is occupied by a pair of pygmy falcons is the presence of a white deposit of droppings on the threshold of the chambers in which the falcons have taken up residence. In the spring and early summer, the female falcon uses one of the chambers as a breeding nest, laying three white eggs inside. She adds no material to the chamber because, like all falcons, she does not do any nest building. After a month, the white, downy chicks hatch out and spend a further month in the nest. You can recognize immatures by the rufous wash on their plumage. They appear to depend on their parents for about two months after leaving the nest.

Barn owl

Nonnetjie-uil *(Tyto alba)*

Size: *Length 30-33 cm; weight 220-470 g.*
Colour: *Above mottled grey and tawny with small black-and-white spots; below white, finely spotted brown; face heart-shaped, white; eyes dark; bill pale.*
Most like: *African grass owl, but much paler upperparts and more distinctly spotted below; marsh owl also dark, but has larger, dark rings around eyes.*
Habitat: *Variable woodland, open country near buildings or cliffs for roosting.*

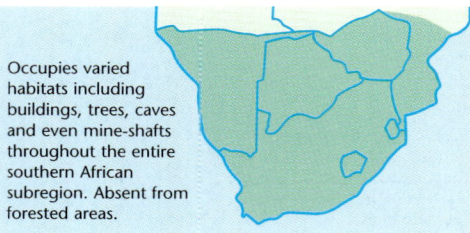

Occupies varied habitats including buildings, trees, caves and even mine-shafts throughout the entire southern African subregion. Absent from forested areas.

You have probably heard the shrill night-time shriek of a barn owl, calling in flight or from a perch, possibly even the roof of a house, without realizing what it was.

This owl hunts only at night, and is able to detect prey entirely by sound in total darkness. The merest rustling of a leaf or the tiniest squeak of a mouse is enough to draw the owl's attention to the spot. Its main prey is indeed rodents (it is the nocturnal counterpart of the black-shouldered kite), though in certain areas, such as towns, it may rely on small birds for most of its food.

Barn owls are seldom far from a suitable roosting site, whether it be a tree or building, a well or mine-shaft. During the day the birds adopt a sleeked-down posture, their eyes, barely open, forming slanting slits, and their legs looking very long and slender.

The barn owl's nest is the bare ledge of a building or any other concealed place. Up to nine white eggs form the clutch, though usually only four to five are laid. Incubation starts with the first egg, so the entire brood does not hatch at the same time. The young take 50-55 days to reach flying age, but possibly less if food is really abundant. In years of rodent plagues the clutch may go up to 13 eggs, and the first egg of the next clutch may be laid before the young of the current brood have left the nest.

Birds of prey

Pearl-spotted owlet

Witkoluil *(Glaucidium perlatum)*

Size: Length 17-21 cm; average weight (m) 61 g, (f) 87-116 g.
Colour: Brown above, spotted with white; below white, streaked with brown; eyes yellow; bill pale green to dull yellow; feet dull yellow.
Most like: African barred owlet, but spotted (not barred) above, and streaked (not barred or spotted) below; African scops and southern white-faced scops owl have 'ear tufts' and grey plumage.
Habitat: Almost any kind of woodland.

In thornveld areas of Namibia, Botswana, Zimbabwe, Mozambique, northern KwaZulu-Natal, Mpumalanga, Northern Province, the North-West, Northern Cape. Isolated population in Eastern Cape. Absent from desert regions.

You can often see this delightful little owl during the day, either when it is hunting, or when it is being mobbed by a group of other small birds. Otherwise it is very difficult to spot among the dappled light and shade of a leafy bush or tree where it is roosting, even if it is staring at you with its bright yellow eyes. At dusk and just before daybreak it starts to utter its loud and penetrating *tiu-tiu-tiu-tiu* whistled calls, rising and falling in pitch and volume.

An interesting feature of the pearl-spotted owlet is the 'false face' on the back of its head, formed by the colour pattern of the feathers that look like two large eyes. Whether this is a real adaptation or merely coincidence has not yet been established.

The diet of this little owl consists mainly of insects, but it takes small vertebrates also. It hunts from a perch, dropping onto its prey, though it is said to be able to catch bats in flight—quite a remarkable feat in view of bats' extraordinary navigational ability.

Its flight is undulating, like that of a woodpecker, the dips interspersed with bursts of quick wingbeats.

Pearl-spotted owlets nest mainly in spring and summer, using a hole in a tree, either a natural one or one excavated by a barbet or woodpecker. Three white eggs form the usual clutch that takes 29 days to hatch. The male brings food to the nest and the female feeds it to the chicks for the 30 days it takes them to become airborne.

Spotted eagle owl

Gevlekte ooruil *(Bubo africanus)*

Size: Length 43-47 cm; weight 450-990 g.
Colour: Dark grey above, spotted with white; below whitish, finely barred with dark grey and spotted with brown on breast; eyes yellow.
Most like: Cape eagle owl, but eyes yellow (not orange) and underparts finely barred (not heavily blotched); Verreaux's eagle owl has dark eyes and no blotching or spotting below.
Habitat: Variable: rocky places, dongas, woodland, semi-desert, towns and savanna regions.

The most common of the large owls, the spotted eagle owl frequents bushy country or open lands throughout the entire southern African subregion.

This is the most common large owl in most parts of southern Africa. Despite its rather large size, its main diet is insects, but it also takes birds, reptiles, mammals and other prey. In fact, this opportunistic eater will take whatever is available at the time.

Like most of the bigger owls, it is found usually in pairs that roost close to each other by day, either in a leafy tree or on the ledge of a gully. The birds rely on their camouflage to avoid detection, taking flight only at the very last moment with silent wingbeats.

At night spotted eagle owls become quite vocal, calling in a duet, each bird giving a two-note hoot, the second note lower than the first. They also start to hunt at dusk, dropping onto prey from a perch.

You will often see a spotted eagle owl sitting on a fence post or telephone pole at the roadside, using the road as a convenient hunting area that provides good visibility. This has an unfortunate consequence—these birds are frequently struck by passing cars as they fly down to the road surface.

The female lays two to three white eggs on a ledge of earth or in the old stick nest of another bird; the owl may even use a window box as a nest if it is undisturbed. The female incubates all on her own for just over 30 days. The nestlings leave the nest after about 40 days and stay with the parents for at least five weeks until they are independent.

Birds of prey

Verreaux's eagle owl

Reuse-ooruil
(*Bubo lacteus*)

Size: *Length 58-65 cm; weight 680g-3,0 kg.*
Colour: *Light grey, finely barred blackish; face paler, boldly outlined with black; eyes dark brown; eyelids pink.*
Most like: *Spotted eagle owl, but lacks any bold blotching; dark eyes, light-coloured bill and pink eyelids diagnostic (eyes yellow in other eagle owls).*
Habitat: *Woodland and savanna.*

Rarely seen, but widespread throughout southern Africa north of the Gariep River, Lesotho and northern KwaZulu-Natal. Isolated populations in the Western and Eastern Cape.

The usually solitary Verreaux's (or giant) eagle owl perches by day on the branch of a tree, mostly in the shade, where its grey plumage camouflages it well. If you get a good look at the bird, you will see it blink its big brown eyes slowly, showing its pink eyelids that look as if they have make-up on them. At dusk this owl becomes bolder and will perch in the open on an exposed snag.

Verreaux's eagle owl hunts from a perch, diving onto its prey with a sudden swoop. It feeds on almost any vertebrate small enough to overpower, and is able to take animals as big as a monkey, korhaan and other large owl species. Its regurgitated pellets often contain bones of mongooses, and it has been known to attack vultures and hawks too. Its favourite food seems to be hedgehogs.

Verreaux's eagle owls may be quite vocal just before dawn, giving vent to gruff hoots from the top of a tall tree. Otherwise they are fairly silent birds, unless disturbed, when they signal their distress with a resonant, agitated *ooo-aau-au*.

The nest site is usually the old nest of a raptor, the top of a hamerkop nest, the roof of a sociable weaver nest or, less often, a hollow in a tree.

One or two white, rounded eggs form the clutch which the female incubates for 39 days, sometimes assisted by the male. Seldom is more than a single chick reared; the nestling period is about two months and the young one stays with the parents until the following breeding season.

Pel's fishing owl

Visuil (*Scotopelia peli*)

Size: *Length 63 cm; weight 2,0-2,2 kg.*
Colour: *Rich rufous all over, barred on back with black and streaked blackish below; eyes large and dark; bill blackish; feet whitish.*
Most like: *No other southern African bird; other large owls have grey plumage and conspicuous 'ear tufts'.*
Habitat: *Larger tree-lined rivers and swamps in the subtropics.*

Along the larger rivers, from the Zambezi in the north, southwards through Mozambique, eastern Zimbabwe and the Limpopo River to the Mpumalanga lowveld and northern KwaZulu-Natal.

The deep hooting notes of Pel's fishing owl carry up to three kilometres in parts of the Okavango Delta where it is a fairly common species, although not always easy to see. The calls are often in the form of a hoot-grunt duet between male and female. At the start of the breeding season just after the peak of the summer floods, the female begs for food from the male with a drawn-out howl—quite the most spine-chilling voice of any African bird.

This huge owl spends most of each day concealed in the thick foliage of a dark-leaved riverine tree. At night it emerges to hunt fishes along the waterways, perching a metre or two above the water and diving down to grasp a fish with its huge feet. Its legs are bare, unlike those of other owls, and the feet have especially long toes and claws, and spiny soles for holding the slippery prey which may weigh up to two kilograms.

The fishing owl augments its diet with crabs, frogs and other water animals at times, even taking young crocodiles when these are available.

The female lays one or two white eggs in a large, natural tree-hole or on a broad fork, usually within 100 m of water. She incubates the eggs for about 35 days. Only one chick is usually reared, even if two hatch, and it takes about 70 days for it to reach flying age. The chick then stays with its parents for several months after leaving the nest, learning in the meantime how to fish for itself.

Tree birds

RED-EYED DOVE
Rooioogtortelduif (*Streptopelia semitorquata*)

Size: Length 33-36 cm; weight (m) 207-326 g, (f) 211-260 g.
Colour: Above deep slate-grey with broadish black collar on hind neck; top of head pale grey; below rich pinkish grey; tip of tail pale grey.
Most like: Cape turtle dove, but darker, bigger and pinker below, with contrasting pale head; African mourning dove has pale yellow eyes surrounded by bare red skin; grey tail tip diagnostic (white in all other collared doves).
Habitat: Big trees in thornveld, woodland, plantations, suburbs and farmyards.

In the forested regions of the northern, eastern and southern parts of southern Africa, but absent from the dry western regions and most of the Karoo.

Red-eyed doves, well known for their familiar, repetitive *KOOkukooROOkuku* call, commonly inhabit large trees in the moister parts of southern Africa. They spend most of their time pecking at berries and fruit high in the leafy treetops unless they are feeding on the ground. They come readily to seed put out at feeding stations, but are unwilling to perch on a feeding tray for any length of time.

The most nervous of all the 'collared' doves, always wary and suspicious, the red-eyed dove is also, as a rule, less gregarious than other doves. They will, however, feed in company with Cape turtle doves and laughing doves.

These birds are heavy but strong fliers, looking rather like miniature jumbo jets as they come into land. As they fly away, the grey tips to the tail feathers immediately distinguish them from other grey doves of similar size.

Like most doves, the red-eyed dove nests at any time of the year. The female sits at the nest site while the male collects sticks and roots, which he presents to her for building. The small platform that results contains a clutch of two white eggs. Both sexes incubate for about 17 days and then feed the chicks for 20 days or so before they are able to fly. The young birds differ from their parents in that they have buff edges to their feathers, and no black collar.

CAPE TURTLE DOVE
Gewone tortelduif (*Streptopelia capicola*)

Size: Length 26-28 cm; weight 92 g-2,0 kg.
Colour: Grey, darker on back; black collar on hindneck; tip of tail-feathers white.
Most like: Red-eyed dove, but lacks tinge to underparts and purplish tinge to back; head not noticeably paler than back; differs from African mourning dove in having dark eye without red eye-ring.
Habitat: Almost anywhere with trees, from bushveld to semi-desert and savanna, including towns, cities and farmyards.

Found wherever trees occur throughout the entire southern African subregion.

The lazy *where's father* song of the Cape turtledove is the most familiar animal sound of Africa. Whether you are in the bush or in the city, this is the call you will hear throughout the day and even on moonlit nights. Another familiar sound is the high, crooning *kirrr kirr* trills that this dove makes as it comes in to land on a branch.

Males now and then take off from a perch with stiff wingbeats, and then glide back to the same or a different perch in a display called 'towering'. This is probably a territorial advertisement.

In the more arid parts of southern Africa large numbers may gather at a feeding place or waterhole. Just after sunrise each morning the birds begin to arrive to drink and it is then that birds of prey tend to hunt them. This dove's diet consists mostly of seeds, but it relishes flying termites, which emerge after rain.

Nests are built throughout the year—the usual stick platform so characteristic of the doves—in the fork of a branch, at any height from the ground, depending on the available bushes or trees.

The female lays two white eggs, which take about 15 days to hatch; the male incubates most of the day and the female at night. In less than two weeks the young are able to leave the nest and the adults are ready to breed again within a week or less.

Tree birds

LAUGHING DOVE

Rooiborsduifie *(Streptopelia senegalensis)*

Size: Length 25 cm; weight 74-118 g.
Colour: Mottled blue-grey and cinnamon above; head pinkish grey; breast deep rufous, spotted with black, shading to white belly; tips of tail feathers white.
Most like: Cape turtle dove, but lacks black collar on hindneck; black-spotted rufous breast and blue-and-cinnamon wings are diagnostic.
Habitat: Almost any woodland (but uncommon in arid country), gardens, farmyards, city centres.

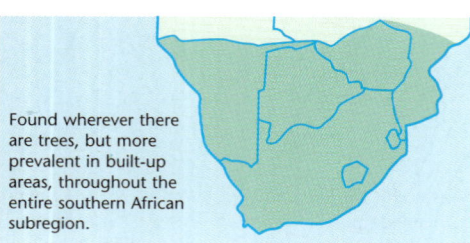

Found wherever there are trees, but more prevalent in built-up areas, throughout the entire southern African subregion.

In parts of southern Africa the laughing dove is the common urban dove, replacing the Cape turtle dove in this role. They're abundant at feeding stations and spend much time chasing one another from the food. Laughing doves do not seem to have to work too hard for a living; they rise and go to bed early, apparently finding plenty of food during their short active period.

The call of the laughing dove is a bubbling series of six to eight notes falling a little in pitch towards the end and sounding somewhat like gentle laughter, hence the bird's name. It is a restful sound on a lazy summer day, but you can hear it at any time of the year throughout the daylight hours.

Laughing doves walk about with small, delicate steps and nodding heads as they search the ground for seeds. Now and then a male approaches a female in courtship, his reddish chest puffed out and the black spots showing handsomely. The usual response seems to be for the female to fly away but, judging by the numbers of laughing doves everywhere, courtship must be highly successful.

Breeding takes place throughout the year. The nest, often one used previously, is a flimsy platform of twigs on a branch; sometimes you can see the two white eggs from below. Incubation by both sexes usually takes 12-17 days. In 11-14 days the young have grown to flying age and a week later they strike out to face life on their own.

NAMAQUA DOVE

Namakwaduifie *(Oena capensis)*

Size: Length 24-27 cm; weight 29-48 g.
Colour: Upperparts grey with dark purple spots on wing; two dark bands enclose white band on lower back; breast of female grey, shading to white belly; face and breast of male black; bill black in female, yellow in male; wings cinnamon (visible in flight).
Most like: Some other small doves, but long, tapered tail diagnostic in both sexes; black face and chest and yellow bill diagnostic in male.
Habitat: Dry bushveld, scrub, Karoo, highveld farmyards.

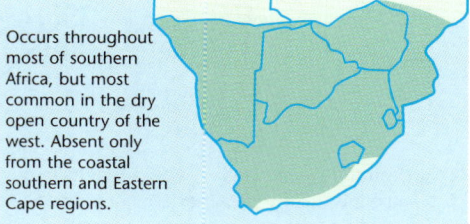

Occurs throughout most of southern Africa, but most common in the dry open country of the west. Absent only from the coastal southern and Eastern Cape regions.

The Namaqua dove is a tame little bird which flies away from danger only at the very last moment, a habit that's often fatal if the danger happens to be a falcon looking for lunch. It is one of the most appealing birds, with its delicate colouring and long tail, which it lifts slowly after alighting on the ground or on a branch.

Its flight has a clattering quality, especially at take-off, and is fast and direct, with the body turning from side to side at intervals.

This dove eats seeds, which it finds by walking along with minute steps in a hunched posture, pecking at the ground. Look out for them at waterholes in dry areas, such as in the Kalahari, where their coming and going is like a railway station at rush hour.

The Namaqua dove's nest must be one of the most casual of any bird's: a tiny platform of rootlets and twigs on the fork of a branch, often within centimetres of the ground, and sometimes on the ground itself. The two eggs are yellowish buff in colour and take about 14 days to hatch. Both parents feed the young for 15-16 days, at which time they have a plumage that is boldly spotted and barred with buff and black, making them look quite different from the adult birds.

Although widespread throughout southern Africa, the Namaqua dove prefers the dry, western areas of the subcontinent.

Tree birds

AFRICAN GREEN PIGEON

Papegaaiduif *(Treron calva)*

Size: Length 28-30 cm; weight 250 g.
Colour: Greyish green to yellowish green; thighs yellow; mauve patch on bend of wing; bill red at base and bluish white at tip; upper legs and lower belly yellow; feet scarlet.
Most like: Some parrots, but red feet and red-and-white bill distinctive; gentle voice very different from strident shrieks of the parrot family.
Habitat: Riverine fig forest, woodland, and the perimeters of evergreen forest.

In central and northern Namibia, northern and eastern Botswana, Zimbabwe, Mozambique, Swaziland, Mpumalanga, Northern Province, northern North-West, KwaZulu-Natal lowlands and the Eastern Cape coast.

The beautiful green pigeon is unusual in its family because it is exclusively a fruit-eater. It is especially fond of wild figs and you can be sure to see flocks of green pigeons in the fig forest along any lowveld river, such as in the Kruger National Park or KwaZulu-Natal's Ndumu Game Reserve. While feeding, the birds make a lot of noise with their wings as they flap to keep balance when reaching for fruit on the outermost branches; they also call a lot, giving a soft whistling twitter interspersed with some gentle growling notes.

If it were not for the noise they make, green pigeons would be hard to see because their plumage camouflages them almost perfectly in the leafy canopy of their favourite trees. When alarmed or wary, however, they freeze, blending into the foliage and becoming almost invisible.

Their flight is remarkably parrotlike: swift and straight, with quick wingbeats. The bright yellow tail tip shows up as the birds take off and immediately distinguishes them from parrots.

Although they usually feed high up, green pigeons may nest in quite small trees, sometimes as low as two metres above the ground. The nest is the usual slight platform of twigs, so characteristic of doves in general, built on the horizontal fork of a bough, or in a small clump of mistletoe to give it a firm base. The female lays two white eggs, which are incubated by both sexes for about 14 days; when on the nest the incubating bird sits very tightly and seems unusually tame. The chicks leave the nest within 11-13 days. Sometimes breeding occurs in loose groups of birds, almost forming a colony.

BROWN-HEADED PARROT

Bruinkoppapegaai *(Poicephalus cryptoxanthus)*

Size: Length 22-24 cm; weight 123-156 g.
Colour: Body green; head and neck brown; underwing bright yellow (visible in flight only); eye greenish yellow.
Most like: Meyer's parrot, but lacks yellow and blue patches; Cape parrot, but lacks scarlet patches on forehead and bend of wing.
Habitat: Woodland, riverine trees.

In the extreme eastern lowveld regions, from Mozambique southwards through Mpumalanga and eastern Swaziland to northern KwaZulu-Natal.

Listen for the loud, strident screeches of the brown-headed parrot, then follow its movements through the treetops of its habitat; in flight its yellow underwing is immediately conspicuous (hence the scientific name of *cryptoxanthus*, which means 'hidden yellow', a reference to the concealment of this yellow patch when the bird is at rest). The brown-headed parrot is the most common parrot in the Kruger National Park and can be seen in small groups or in flocks of up to 50 birds.

Because it is green and brown, the brown-headed parrot is not always easy to see as it clambers about feeding on fruit and seeds in the treetops, often hanging upside down as it opens a particularly recalcitrant seed pod. In the flowering season of certain plants, these parrots will tear the flowers open for the nectar at their base. When disturbed they screech and fly off like bullets.

Brown-headed and Meyer's parrots may hybridize where their territories overlap, indicating a close relationship, though they do not overlap in southern Africa to any great extent outside Mozambique.

The brown-headed species nest in holes in trees, up to ten metres above the ground. The female incubates the clutch of three glossy, white eggs for about 30 days, the male bringing her food on the nest during this time. In captivity one brood of young left the nest after 84 days, a surprisingly long nesting period for a bird this size. Other similar parrots (such as Meyer's and Rüppell's) have nesting periods of approximately 60 days.

Tree birds

MEYER'S PARROT

Bosveldpapegaai *(Poicephalus meyeri)*

Size: Length 21-23 cm; weight 118 g.
Colour: Brown on head, back and wings, with blue rump; breast brown, shading to light green belly; bright yellow patches on crown, bend of wing and thighs; underwing yellow (visible in flight only); eye red-orange.
Most like: Brown-headed parrot, but yellow patches on head and wing distinctive; distinguished from Rüppell's parrot by green belly and yellow patch on crown.
Habitat: Bushveld, savanna, woodland, riverine trees.

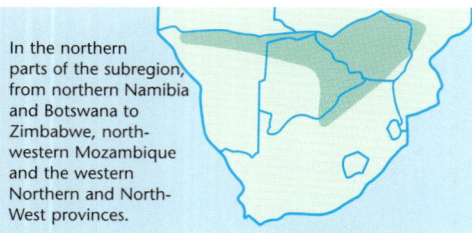

In the northern parts of the subregion, from northern Namibia and Botswana to Zimbabwe, north-western Mozambique and the western Northern and North-West provinces.

A noisy shriek and a rapidly disappearing flutter of wings are all you may experience of a Meyer's parrot in the bush. It is shy and wary, taking flight at the slightest disturbance. It forages in the tops of tall trees for fruits, seeds and nuts, cracking open even the hardest kernels. It also takes nectar from flowers such as those of the boerboon, and has a great liking for standing crops of grain. In Botswana and elsewhere some farmers position helpers or family members in the shelters adjacent to the fields of ripening grain to chase the parrots away, because of the considerable damage they can cause.

Meyer's parrot flies so high and fast that you are unlikely to get a close look at it, though sometimes it will perch on an exposed branch to sun itself on a winter's morning; then you will have a clear view of its beautiful turquoise-green belly and bright yellow wing- and head-patches (though the head-patch may sometimes be absent). The parrots fly about in pairs or small parties and roost at night in holes in trees.

They also nest in tree holes, without adding any nest material; the parrots may also make their nests in a tangle of creepers—if it is dense enough. The usual clutch is three white eggs that the female incubates for a month. After about 56 days the chicks are ready to leave the nest, at which stage they lack the yellow patches on the crown, wings and thighs.

ROSY-FACED LOVEBIRD

Rooiwangparkiet *(Agapornis roseicollis)*

Size: Length 15-18 cm; weight 48-60 g.
Colour: Bright green, paler below; rump blue; forehead scarlet; face and breast bright pink; bill pale yellowish.
Most like: Lilian's lovebird, but bill yellowish (not red); blue rump diagnostic; face pink (not reddish).
Habitat: Arid to semi-arid woodland, riverine trees, and rocky hillsides with bushes.

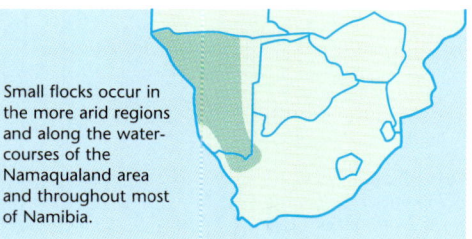

Small flocks occur in the more arid regions and along the water-courses of the Namaqualand area and throughout most of Namibia.

Many people are probably not aware that the rosy-faced lovebird—a favourite pet with a loud voice—is a southern African species. Its brightly coloured plumage has made it popular among bird-keepers for many years; it takes kindly to captivity, thriving and breeding freely.

However, there is nothing to compare with the sight of a flock of these beautiful lovebirds in the wild places of Namibia where they can still be seen in quite large numbers. Flocks of up to 20 birds (rarely 100 or more) fly shrieking noisily from tree to tree, searching for seeds and flowers. Although they also raid grain crops, they usually occur well away from agricultural areas, so they do not constitute a major nuisance.

Man is more of a threat to the birds than the other way round, since the cage-bird trade attracts many unscrupulous people to its ranks, and the rosy-faced lovebird needs to be strictly protected.

The breeding habits of these lovebirds are very interesting. Pairs usually form bonds when still immature, and mate for life. Groups of lovebirds usually nest in a colony. The nest site is a hole in a rock face or building, or in the chamber of a sociable weaver nest. Inside the cavity the female builds a cup-shaped nest of grass and leaves, which she carries stuck into the feathers of her rump and not in her bill as most birds do. From four to six white eggs form the clutch, which the female incubates for 23 days. Both parents feed the young for 42-43 days and look after them for a further two weeks after they leave the nest.

Tree birds

KNYSNA TURACO

Knysnaloerie (*Tauraco corythaix*)

Size: Length 45-47 cm; weight 262-380 g.
Colour: Bright green with dark metallic-green wings and tail; bright red flight feathers conspicuous in flight: green crest tipped white; white streak above and below eye; bill red.
Most like: Purple-crested turaco, but red bill, white-tipped crest and white marks around eye distinctive.
Habitat: Mostly evergreen forest and riverine woodland; sometimes also mature deciduous woodland.

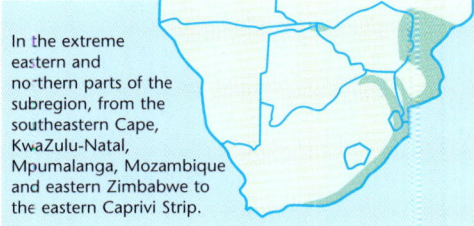

In the extreme eastern and northern parts of the subregion, from the southeastern Cape, KwaZulu-Natal, Mpumalanga, Mozambique and eastern Zimbabwe to the eastern Caprivi Strip.

The growling calls of the Knysna turaco, known to many as the Knysna lourie, is usually the first clue you will have to its presence. Then you may be lucky enough to see one launch into the air, showing its crimson wings, which contrast vividly with its brilliant green body. This magnificent bird is quite common in the eastern forests of southern Africa, where it bounds about the stouter branches of trees in search of fruit and insects. Southern birds have a fan-shaped crest, while those in the north have a tall, pointed crest.

This bird's ability to run along branches has to be seen to be believed; for this purpose it can turn its outermost toe forwards or backwards to allow it a firm grasp. It spends most of its time high in the canopy of taller trees, where it is difficult to see until it spreads its wings. Groups of as many as ten birds may forage together, but you will usually see only a pair at a time. As one bird calls, another may respond vocally until several are growling together.

The birds breed in winter in the southeastern Cape and in spring or summer elsewhere, so their breeding habits seem to be tied in with rainfall and, probably, the availability of fruit and insect food. The nest, a rather dovelike platform of sticks, is built in a leafy tree or creeper. Both parents incubate the two white eggs for about 25 days, sometimes sitting together on the nest. They feed the nestlings for a little over three weeks, regurgitating food into their mouths.

PURPLE-CRESTED TURACO

Bloukuifloerie (*Musophaga porphyreolopha*)

Size: Length 41-42 cm; weight 218-328 g.
Colour: Body green with dark purplish blue wings and crest; flight feathers crimson; tail glossy greenish black; bill and feet black; eye-ring scarlet.
Most like: Knysna turaco, but black bill and purple crest diagnostic. Much more rapid calls than Knysna turaco's deliberate series of notes.
Habitat: Dense woodland, thornveld and savanna, evergreen thickets, riverine forest.

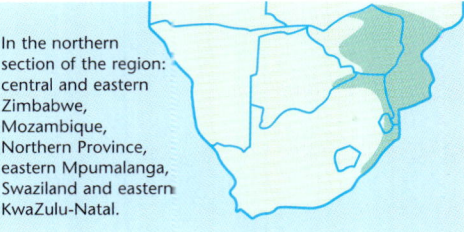

In the northern section of the region: central and eastern Zimbabwe, Mozambique, Northern Province, eastern Mpumalanga, Swaziland and eastern KwaZulu-Natal.

The fruit-loving purple-crested turaco is particularly partial to figs, a taste that is well-catered for as there is seldom a time when at least one or two fig trees are not in fruit in the evergreen forests along the east coast of southern Africa. The young are also fed insects and molluscs, probably for their higher protein content.

Purple-crested turacos, or louries, prefer rather drier country than Knysna turacos do; though on the KwaZulu-Natal south coast you can see both species feeding together.

The brilliant red wings of the purple-crested turaco can be seen to best advantage as the bird takes off against the sun; the bird is also breathtaking to watch from a high vantage point as it flies over the tops of trees. Its flight is heavy with alternating flapping and gliding. Its voice carries as far as that of the Knysna turaco, but the notes are faster and have a more staccato quality.

Pairs or small groups of these birds travel about the woodlands in search of food, keeping mostly to the tops of the trees, where they agilely leap from branch to branch. When purple-crested turacos come down to drink, they usually perch on a tree that has fallen into the water.

Purple-crested turacos breed in the summer months from August to January. The nest is a frail platform of twigs well hidden in foliage. Two or three glossy white eggs form the clutch, which both parents incubate for 22-25 days. Nestlings may leave the nest at 25 days to clamber about the branches, but they cannot fly properly until they are nearly 40 days old.

Tree birds

Grey go-away bird

Kwêvoël *(Corythaixoides concolor)*

Size: Length 47-50 cm; weight 200-340 g.
Colour: Dull grey, darker on wing and tail feathers; bill and feet black.
Most like: Great spotted cuckoo but lacks any markings and is uniformly grey underneath.
Habitat: Bushveld and savanna regions, and riverine trees along arid watercourses.

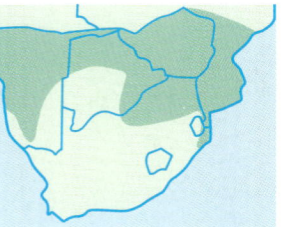

In drier bushland areas of central and northern Namibia, northern and eastern Botswana, Zimbabwe, Mozambique, northern KwaZulu-Natal, eastern Swaziland, Northern Province, Gauteng and the North-West.

The grey go-away bird's call must be one of the most evocative sounds in the lowveld game reserves. Its nasal *go'way* and other chattering and yelping noises are familiar to anyone who has visited the Kruger National Park or Etosha Game Reserve. Alert and inquisitive, groups of two to 20 birds will come to investigate any unusual presence, their crests flopping to and fro as they balance on thin branches in the treetops.

Their agility in the trees is astounding, but their flight is rather laboured, with floppy wingbeats and heavy tail.

The grey go-away bird lives in the driest country of any southern African turaco, even in the arid southern parts of Namibia where thorn trees line the dry river beds. It has become quite a common bird in some Johannesburg suburbs where suitable garden trees have been planted. Its main food is fruit, but it also eats flowers and leaves, including cabbage, lettuce and other garden vegetables, which does not endear it to hard-working gardeners. It is also known to come to the ground to feed on harvester termites, and may even take nesting birds.

Grey go-away birds usually build their nests in thorny acacia trees, without trying to conceal them; the stick platform is usually 3-10 m above the ground. The female lays three white eggs, which are incubated for about 28 days. The chicks can climb out of the nest at the age of only two or three weeks, but they cannot fly properly until they are about six weeks old. Both parents feed them and are sometimes assisted by a third bird, known as a helper. The breeding season is poorly defined, but nesting reaches a peak from September to October in Zimbabwe.

Red-chested cuckoo

Piet-my-vrou *(Cuculus solitarius)*

Size: Length 28-30 cm; weight 66-80 g.
Colour: Slate grey above; chest deep rufous; belly barred black and white; bill blackish, yellow at base; eye-ring and feet yellow.
Most like: European and African cuckoos, but rufous chest and voice diagnostic.
Habitat: Forest, woodland, trees in gardens and farmyards.

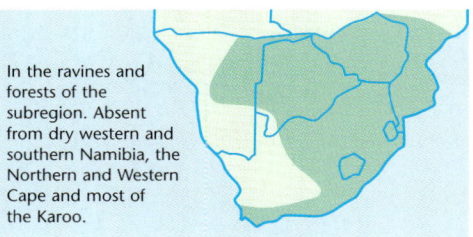

In the ravines and forests of the subregion. Absent from dry western and southern Namibia, the Northern and Western Cape and most of the Karoo.

This is the author of the familiar *piet-my-vrou* call that you will hear in summer throughout much of southern Africa, wherever there are big trees. The red-chested cuckoo has even taken to plantations of exotic trees such as wattle and gum. The calling bird sits high in the canopy, usually well concealed by leaves, though occasionally it will perch on a leafless branch to sing.

You will hear the male's rather monotonous but mellow voice mostly in the mornings and evenings and even on moonlit nights from about September to December, tailing off towards the end of summer and finally ceasing in February.

The male establishes a territory in a suitable habitat where its robin and wagtail hosts' nests are likely to occur. Females pass through to mate, lay eggs and move on. Other less common hosts of this handsome cuckoo include chats, thrushes and flycatchers. Only one egg per host nest is laid as a rule, the usual colour being a plain, deep olive green or chocolate brown, not matching the host's eggs at all.

When the young cuckoo hatches out, it gets under the host's eggs and/or chicks and, using its hollow back and holding its little wings up as a prop, it hoists them up and over the side of the nest. The host ignores the eggs or young out of the nest and will simply allow them to die there. The young cuckoo remains the sole occupant, receiving undivided attention and food from its foster parents, and grows to flying age in about three weeks.

Tree birds

Diederik cuckoo
Diederikkie *(Chrysococcyx caprius)*

Size: Length 18-20 cm; weight (m) 23-39 g, (f) 28-43 g.

Colour: Above metallic bronze-green with broad white eyebrow and white spots on wing and outer tail feathers; below white with broad, metallic-green bars on flanks; bill black in adult, coral red in juvenile.

Most like: Klaas's cuckoo, but barred on flanks; Klaas's cuckoo has outer tail feathers all white; female Klaas's and emerald cuckoos have white outer tail feathers, barred brown-and-green upperparts and fully barred underparts; male emerald cuckoo has bright yellow belly and no white eyebrow.

Habitat: Almost any woodland, including Kalahari thornveld; also farmyards and exotic plantations.

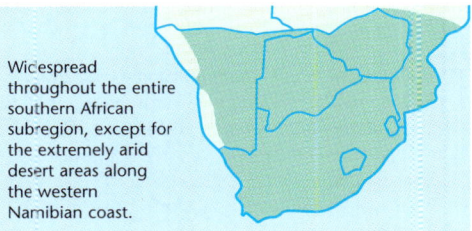

Widespread throughout the entire southern African subregion, except for the extremely arid desert areas along the western Namibian coast.

Few sounds herald the arrival of spring as sweetly as the *dee-dee-deederik* of this cuckoo, which gets its name from its call. It means that October has finally arrived and that the weavers, sparrows and wagtails had better guard their nests carefully or be landed with a foster child to bring up in the shape of a young diederik cuckoo.

When a male cuckoo sees a female in his established territory he sings loudly and tries to win her heart with offerings of hairy caterpillars. The pair bond is apparently short-lived, the female laying her eggs in a suitable host nest and then going off to find another territorial male.

Each female diederik parasitizes only one species of host bird, usually a member of the weaver family, but also sometimes a Cape wagtail. She lays an egg that matches those of the host so that the host is misled into believing it to be her own. The cuckoo's egg hatches in only 10-12 days, and its chicks eject any eggs or chicks of the host that may be in the nest. After 20-21 days the young cuckoo leaves the nest, but continues to beg from the foster parents for another month.

Burchell's coucal
Gewone vleiloerie *(Centropus burchellii)*

Size: Length 38-44 cm; weight (m) 130-210 g, (f) 153-210 g.

Colour: Crown, back and tail black; rump barred with dull white; wings bright rusty; below creamy white; some faint, dusky barring on flanks; northern (tropical) birds have white eyebrow and white streaks on head and mantle.

Most like: Senegal and coppery-tailed coucals; no barring on rump of Senegal coucal; no barring on flanks of any other coucal; Senegal coucal has rusty upper back.

Habitat: Dense bush along watercourses, coastal bush, marshes, gardens and parks.

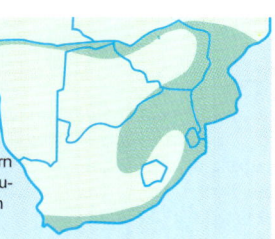

Northern Namibia, northern and south-eastern Botswana, northern and eastern Zimbabwe, Mozambique, Mpumalanga, Gauteng, Northern Province, northern Free State, eastern KwaZulu-Natal and the southeastern and southern Cape coast.

Familiarly known as the 'rain bird', Burchell's coucal has a beautiful song that sounds like the deep bubbling of water running out of a bottle. Though you may hear it even on moonlit nights, this song usually heralds drizzly or rainy weather. More often seen than heard, Burchell's coucal is fairly common in the moister regions of southern Africa.

A dense creeper in your garden may well attract a pair of Burchell's coucals to nest there, though all you will see of them as a rule is a flash of bright russet as they pass in floppy flight across an open space from one thicket to the next.

Burchell's coucals usually occur in pairs. They skulk in the undergrowth looking for food in the form of nestling birds, snails, frogs, lizards and almost anything that moves. They run well on the ground and clamber agilely through the bushes.

Their nest is an untidy ball of twigs and leaves, measuring up to 50 cm in diameter, and placed in a creeper or bush about two metres above the ground. Through the side entrance you will see three to four eggs lying on a grassy lining. These are incubated for 14-18 days. The downy nestlings look a bit like hedgehogs at first, but develop their proper plumage when they leave the nest after about 20 days.

Tree birds

African Palm Swift
Palmwindswael
(*Cypsiurus parvus*)

Size: *Length 14-17 cm; weight 10-18 g.*
Colour: *Uniform light brownish grey, appearing silvery from a distance.*
Most like: *Some other swifts, but distinguished by its very long, slender build, plain grey colour (no black or white in plumage) and its association with palm trees.*
Habitat: *Palm trees in wetter parts of southern Africa, usually at lower elevations.*

Northern Namibia, northern and eastern Botswana, Zimbabwe, Mozambique, Northern Province, the North-West, Mpumalanga, Swaziland, KwaZulu-Natal and the extreme northeastern corner of the Northern Cape.

Speckled Mousebird
Gevlekte muisvoël
(*Colius striatus*)

Size: *Length 27-36 cm; weight 32-70 g.*
Colour: *Plumage brown; face black; bill black above, bluish white tinge below; iris brown; dull red-brown to purple-brown legs and feet.*
Most like: *Other mousebirds, but without red on face or white on back.*
Habitat: *Woodland, thickets, riverine bush, the edges of dense vegetation, gardens.*

Found in eastern Zimbabwe, Mozambique, eastern Northern Province, Mpumalanga, Gauteng, Swaziland, KwaZulu-Natal, southern and eastern Free State, the Karoo and in the Eastern and southwestern Cape.

The elegant shape and buoyant flight of the African palm swift immediately distinguishes it from swallows and from other species of swift. Its wings are especially long and slender, as is its deeply forked tail. In the Okavango Delta, where ilala palms grow in profusion, you can see these birds wheeling about the treetops at almost any time of the day. They may also sometimes be seen in the company of other species of swift and swallow where aerial insects are particularly abundant.

Although swifts are well known for their screaming parties, usually in the mornings and evenings, the palm swift must rank as one of the more silent species. It also screams, but less often and far more faintly than the other species of swift do.

Also unusual is the fact that it is associated with trees rather than cliffs or buildings like most other swifts. Palm swifts cannot perch, but use their sharply clawed feet to hang onto the surface of the palm leaves on which they build their nests. Each nest is a small pad of feathers which the bird glues with its own saliva to the flat, vertical surface of a drooping frond. The lower edge of the pad is formed into a shallow lip, which supports the two white eggs as well as the incubating bird.

So precarious is the site, though, that the eggs are also glued to the nest pad with saliva. Incubation takes about 20 days. The nestling is fed in the nest by its parents for about 30 days, before its wings are strong enough to take to the air.

Although called 'speckled', this bird always looks a rather uniform dull brown, but at close quarters you may be able to see the fine barring on the belly. It is the most common of the mousebirds in the eastern parts of southern Africa and seems to be replacing the white-backed mousebird in Johannesburg, probably because the planting of greenery makes the habitat more like that of the lowveld than of the highveld to which the white-backed mousebird is better adapted.

Speckled mousebirds usually move about in flocks of five to ten, but bigger flocks may gather where fruit is abundant. They are particularly fond of the red or orange berries of firethorn and cotoneaster, but will also eat leaves, seeds and nectar. They can cause considerable damage to fruit trees, and also raid vegetable gardens to eat cabbages, lettuces and other produce.

These birds characteristically fly fast and straight, their stiff, long tails making them look like small brown rockets shooting across the sky. A flock of mousebirds will invariably dash into a nearby bush with great haste, apparently unconcerned about finding a suitable perch.

When evening falls, speckled mousebirds close ranks and roost together in tightly packed bunches, their tails all pointing downwards.

They breed at almost any time of the year, building a rough bowl of plant material in a bush or tree. In this the female lays two to four eggs, although it is not uncommon for two females to lie in the same nest, producing a combined clutch of up to eight eggs. The females incubate these for a period of about 14 days. After the chicks hatch, they take about 18 days to reach flying age.

Tree birds

RED-FACED MOUSEBIRD
Rooiwangmuisvoël
(*Urocolius indicus*)

Size: Length 30-37 cm; weight 33-78 g.

Colour: Above soft blue-grey; below greyish on chest, shading to sandy, yellowish grey on belly; bare face and bill deep red; tip of bill black; legs red.

Most like: Other species of mousebird, but red face and all-grey back distinctive.

Habitat: Savanna, riverine bush, gardens and parks.

Occurs throughout the entire southern African subregion, but absent from the arid desert region along the southern Namibian coastline, and from the Drakensberg area.

The red-faced mousebird is the most widespread mousebird species in southern Africa, though not always the most abundant. You will recognize it immediately by its red face and gentle three-syllable *ti-wi-wi* callnote, which led to its Zulu name of *umtshivovo*.

This species travels in flocks of about six birds, flying fast, straight and quite high compared with other mousebirds. Like other species, they don't perch on a branch, but hang below it. This habit, their somewhat hairlike plumage and their grey colour give them their mousebird name. Their long, stiff tails probably add to the mouselike impression. All members of the mousebird family have easily identifiable, perky crests.

Red-faced mousebirds are less raucous than the other species. They also seem to be less tame, taking flight at the least sign of danger.

Like the speckled mousebird, its red-faced cousin will damage fruit trees and vegetables that are left unprotected. Both species may gather in fair numbers at fruiting trees, and in the Johannesburg area you can even see white-backed mousebirds in their company. Fruit trees of any kind are sure to attract red-faced and other mousebirds to your garden.

In the southwestern Cape the breeding season is from June to February; further north from July to February.

Nesting takes place in most months, but seldom in autumn. The nest is a bowl of plant stems and twigs, with a softer lining, sometimes of wool. The female lays between two and four eggs, which are white or cream with reddish-brown markings. Incubation takes about two weeks, as does the nestling period.

NARINA TROGON
Bosloerie (*Apaloderma narina*)

Size: Length 29-34 cm; weight 60-70 g.

Colour: Brilliant metallic green above and on breast, with golden tinge on head and mantle; belly bright red; outer tail feathers white; bill yellow; female duller below, with rusty pink throat and pink belly.

Most like: No other southern African bird.

Habitat: Evergreen and riverine forest, plantations, dense woodland, bushveld.

In the wooded areas of northern Namibia, northern Botswana, northern and eastern Zimbabwe, Mozambique, Mpumalanga, eastern KwaZulu-Natal and the southeastern and southwestern Cape coast.

Every new birder wants to see a Narina trogon, perhaps more than any other species of bird in southern Africa. This is no surprise—the bird is extremely beautiful, but frustratingly elusive. But, although it may be hard to see, the Narina trogon is not that uncommon if you look in the right places. It is plentiful in the Oribi Gorge Nature Reserve in KwaZulu-Natal, for example. It is also common in patches of indigenous forest in the Eastern Cape and along the KwaZulu-Natal coast.

More surprising is its presence in wattle plantations in the Drakensberg foothills, although it is only a temporary visitor here because of the lack of nest sites. The Narina trogon is a tame bird and you can track it down by following the male's hooting song in summer. The double gruff *hroo-hoo* notes may be difficult to pinpoint, but they are unmistakeable and can be imitated easily.

The bird often sits for long periods on a branch, its vivid green plumage merging into the dark green of the forest trees. Until it moves, or unless it has its bright red belly facing towards you, you may easily overlook it.

Although Narina trogons are plump-looking birds, they are light and agile fliers, quite capable of catching flying insects in the air or taking them in flight off the bark of a tree trunk.

Nesting occurs in summer. The female lays two to three eggs in a hole in a tree, and incubates for about 16 days.

Tree birds

WOODLAND KINGFISHER

Bosveldvisvanger *(Halcyon senegalensis)*

Size: Length 22-24 cm; weight 55-80 g.
Colour: Brilliant light blue on back, wings and tail; large black patch on bend of wing and black line through eye; crown pale grey; underparts white; bill red above, black below.
Most like: Mangrove kingfisher, but black line through eye, and half-red, half-black bill diagnostic (bill all red in mangrove kingfisher); other kingfishers found in woodland habitat are much duller.
Habitat: Woodland, dense savanna, riverine bush.

In the grasslands, woodlands and riverine forests of extreme northern Namibia, northern and eastern Botswana, Zimbabwe, Mozambique, northern KwaZulu-Natal, northern Swaziland and Northern Province.

The blue coloration of kingfishers is not a blue pigment, but a structural effect known as Tyndall scattering, in which fine airspaces in the feather material scatter short wavelengths of light, giving rise to the intense blue effect. If you were to look at a kingfisher feather with the light shining through it, instead of reflected off it, it would be brown. The brown pigment, called melanin, absorbs all other wavelengths of light to intensify the blueness.

The woodland kingfisher is the most radiant blue of any woodland bird and its *krit-trrrrrrr* call is as cheerful as the colour of its blue back. It comes to southern Africa to breed from October to April, departing after that for more tropical latitudes. Because these birds migrate mainly at night, they sometimes collide with unexpected obstacles or lighted windows, killing or injuring themselves.

These kingfishers feed mainly on insects and reptiles; they seldom occur near water and rarely dive for fish.

Members of a pair display by gyrating from side to side and flashing their blue-black wings as they sing their inimitable song.

The nest is either a natural hole in a tree or one excavated by a woodpecker or barbet. Woodland kingfishers may even build their nests under the eaves of houses. Here the female lays her three glossy white eggs, which hatch out in 13-14 days. Both parents feed the nestlings for two to three weeks.

BROWN-HOODED KINGFISHER

Bruinkopvisvanger *(Halcyon albiventris)*

Size: Length 22-24 cm; weight 45-80 g.
Colour: Crown dull brown; back blackish in male, brown in female; rump, tail and flight feathers bright blue; below buffy white, washed on breast and flanks with brownish ochre; flanks streaked with black; bill red with blackish tip.
Most like: Grey-hooded kingfisher, but brown head and streaked flanks diagnostic. Striped kingfisher has white cheeks and top half of bill black.
Habitat: Woodland with thickets, dense savanna, forest edge, riverine bush, gardens.

In Caprivi Strip, northern and eastern Botswana, Zimbabwe, Mozambique, Northern Province, Mpumalanga, Gauteng, North-West, northern Free State, north-eastern, southeastern and southwestern Cape.

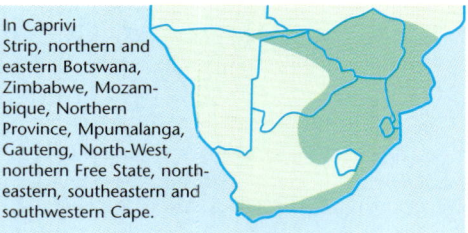

The brown-hooded kingfisher is the best known of the woodland-dwelling kingfishers in southern Africa because it is so widespread and occurs in gardens in many southern and eastern towns and cities such as Port Elizabeth, Pietermaritzburg and Durban. It is also fairly often seen on the highveld. Even if you can't spot the birds you will recognize their shrill, descending *KI-ti-ti-ti, KI-ti-ti-ti* song.

In duet the birds can be very noisy indeed, making a great racket with their sharp calls. Perching on a branch or post as they duet, they bob and pivot their bodies and flash their wings open and closed.

Brown-hooded kingfishers are usually solitary, though you may often see members of a pair in close proximity. From their lookout post on an exposed branch, telephone wire or post, sometimes over a roadway, they scan the ground below for food in the form of insects and lizards.

They also eat snakes up to 25 cm long, small rodents and birds the size of waxbills and sunbirds.

The nest is a burrow excavated in a bank, mostly from September to December, but sometimes late into the autumn in KwaZulu-Natal. The tunnel is seldom more than a metre or two above ground level, and ends in a chamber in which the two to five white eggs are laid. The chicks are born after about two weeks, and are fed by both parents. It is not known when they leave the nest.

Tree birds

EUROPEAN BEE-EATER

Europese byvreter *(Merops apiaster)*

Size: Length 25-29 cm; weight 47-64 g.
Colour: Above brown, shading to yellow at edges: below light turquoise blue; throat yellow with narrow black collar; wings, eyebrow and tail green; forehead white; face mask black, iris red; bill black.
Most like: Other bee-eaters with long central tail feathers, but yellow throat and brown back diagnostic; tail square, rounded or forked in little, white-fronted and swallow-tailed bee-eaters respectively.
Habitat: Woodland, savanna, scrub, semi-desert.

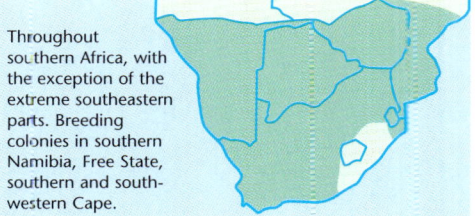

Throughout southern Africa, with the exception of the extreme southeastern parts. Breeding colonies in southern Namibia, Free State, southern and south-western Cape.

SOUTHERN CARMINE BEE-EATER

Rooiborsbyvreter *(Merops nubicoides)*

Size: Length 33-38 cm; weight 51-75 g.
Colour: Rose-red body, pinker below; crown and undertail blue; rump green; face mask black.
Most like: Other bee-eaters with long central tail feathers, but southern carmine bee-eater's large size and generally pink or red colour distinctive.
Habitat: Savanna, marshes, woodland and riverine bush, especially in lowveld.

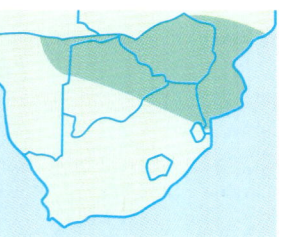

Colonies found from northern Namibia and the Caprivi Strip, northern and eastern Botswana to Mozambique. Nonbreeding birds move south to Northern Province and Mpumalanga.

Although called the 'European' bee-eater this species actually has two breeding populations, one in Eurasia and the other in southern Africa. This almost unique arrangement probably arose when part of the population, which migrates to southern Africa as a nonbreeding species in our summer, stayed over one southern winter and began to breed here the following summer.

Birds that breed in southern Africa don't travel to Europe any more—they migrate northwards in the southern winter as far as the Northern Province and Rwanda. Any European bee-eaters which you may see in southern Africa between mid-April and mid-September are likely to be from this group. Eurasian birds and southern birds occur together between the months of September and April and cannot be told apart.

You can hear the mellow callnotes of these beautiful birds in many parts of southern Africa, except the extreme southeast.

The birds fly fairly high, hawking bees, wasps and other insects in the air. Between hunting forays they perch on branches, posts and telephone wires to rest.

European bee-eaters nest from about September to January, depending on the region. Small colonies make their nesting tunnels (up to two metres long) in earth banks; at the end of the tunnels they dig a chamber, then line the floor with the regurgitated remains of their insect prey. They lay two to six white eggs which hatch after about three weeks. The nestlings are able to fly after a further month.

In Botswana's Chobe National Park southern carmine bee-eaters ride on the backs of kori bustards as they stride out across the open grassveld in order to catch insects disturbed by the bustards. No sooner does a bustard leave the shade of a bush than a carmine bee-eater lands on its back, staying there until the patient bustard takes to the cool shade again. This extends the bee-eaters foraging range beyond the rather scattered bushes and trees from which they usually hawk their flying prey. In different parts of Africa southern carmine bee-eaters can be seen on the backs of ostriches, storks, herons, cranes and ibises.

You can also see carmine bee-eaters perched on fence posts and low, leafless shrubs, waiting for an insect to fly past. As it does so, the bee-eater launches from its perch, snaps the insect in the air and returns to the perch to beat it before swallowing. This species also hunts while cruising on the wing and it may soar high in the thermals like a small falcon. Like many aerial predators, they are attracted to grass fires and to herds of large game mammals to catch the insects they disturb.

The sheer beauty of this species makes them very popular with visitors to the Kruger National Park in the second half of summer.

Colonies of southern carmine bee-eaters, sometimes in flocks of hundreds of birds, excavate nesting tunnels in vertical river banks. Here the female lays a clutch of two to five eggs in a chamber at the end of a straight tunnel about two metres long. The nestlings take about 30 days to reach flying age.

Tree birds

LITTLE BEE-EATER
Kleinbyvreter *(Merops pusillus)*

Size: *Length 17-18 cm; weight 11-18 g.*
Colour: *Above green; below yellow-ochre, tinged orange; throat bright yellow bordered by black collar; wings bright rufous in flight.*
Most like: *Some other bee-eaters, but small size, square (slightly notched) tail and orange-ochre belly diagnostic; the tails of other bee-eaters are rounded, forked or have long central feathers.*
Habitat: *Savanna, reed beds, riverine vegetation, and bushveld, usually near water.*

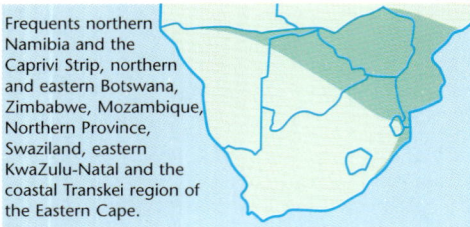

Frequents northern Namibia and the Caprivi Strip, northern and eastern Botswana, Zimbabwe, Mozambique, Northern Province, Swaziland, eastern KwaZulu-Natal and the coastal Transkei region of the Eastern Cape.

One of the most charming sights in nature is a row of up to 15 little bee-eaters perched tightly together on a branch at roosting time. Although solitary during the day, small groups gather towards evening to roost with their bodies touching, probably to keep each other warm.

The little bee-eater is one of the few members of its family which is not gregarious at all times. You may see one perched on top of a bush or tall weed, then suddenly it will fly off, snap up an insect in flight and land on another perch. It may do this several times in quick succession, sometimes accompanying its manoeuvres with little piping *kreee-kree* calls, especially if its mate is nearby.

Its food consists mainly of bees, ants, wasps and flies; though other kinds of insects are also eaten.

You can see little bee-eaters at the same perches day after day. A mated pair roosts in the nest burrow during the breeding season. The nest is a solitary tunnel in a bank or in the roof of an aardvark burrow, rarely on flat ground. The tunnel, which is between 50 cm and a metre long, ends in a small chamber, the floor of which becomes covered with regurgitated remains of insects.

The female usually lays four eggs. These are white, as is the case with most hole-nesters, and take about 20 days to hatch out. Both parents feed and care for the young for a further 26 days or so.

LILAC-BREASTED ROLLER
Gewone troupant *(Coracias caudata)*

Size: *Length 35-36 cm; weight 97-107 g.*
Colour: *Crown light green; back light brown; rump and tail blue; breast mauve, streaked white; belly blue; edges of wings bright deep blue.*
Most like: *Other rollers, but forked tail, green crown and lilac breast diagnostic; no rackets on lilac-breasted roller's tail as in racket-tail roller.*
Habitat: *Savanna, open woodland, bushveld.*

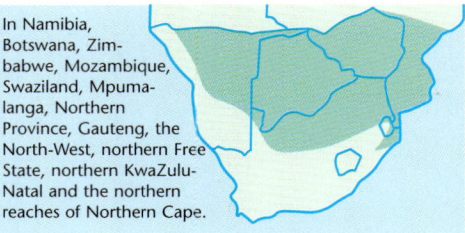

In Namibia, Botswana, Zimbabwe, Mozambique, Swaziland, Mpumalanga, Northern Province, Gauteng, the North-West, northern Free State, northern KwaZulu-Natal and the northern reaches of Northern Cape.

The lilac-breasted roller is the most beautiful—and the most common—roller in southern Africa. You can see it in any woodland in the more subtropical parts where it perches on telephone poles and conspicuous treetops or bushes, often returning to the same perch day after day.

Some people incorrectly call this bird a 'blue jay', but it is not a jay at all.

Usually solitary, this roller shows its beautiful blue wings as it flies down to the ground to catch an insect or other small animal. You can also see these clearly when the bird is displaying in the air, looping up and over, and falling with almost closed wings as it gives its harsh calls. The roller gets its name from these aerial manoeuvres, which are used when rival males stand up to each other and, probably, as part of the courtship ritual; they are also performed to distract possible predators at the nest.

Apart from large insects, lilac-breasted rollers feed on lizards, small snakes, frogs, small birds and rodents. Their strong bills are adapted to handling tough beetles and scaly reptiles; they beat their prey against a perch to immobilize it before swallowing.

Lilac-breasted rollers choose natural tree holes for their nests. The female lays two to four white eggs, which both parents incubate for 17-18 days. The chicks are able to leave the nest after 20 days. The nest has an unpleasant smell, which probably repels potential predators.

Tree birds

AFRICAN HOOPOE

Hoephoep *(Upupa africana)*

Size: Length 25-27 cm; weight 46-67 g.
Colour: Body rufous with bold black-and-white bars on wing; tail black with white base; crest rufous with black spots near feather tips.
Most like: No other bird; coloration, conspicuous crest, long thin bill and short legs distinctive.
Habitat: Woodland, savanna, parks, gardens, lawns.

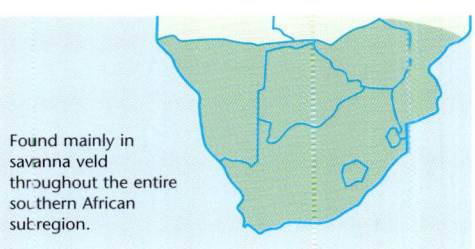

Found mainly in savanna veld throughout the entire southern African subregion.

The African hoopoe must be one of the best-loved birds in southern Africa. Its habit of raising its fan-shaped crest now and then gives it an air of comic appeal and its short, delicate footsteps and nodding head make it look a bit like a fussy old lady on a shopping expedition.

The hoopoe gets its name from its two-to-three-syllable *hoop-hoop-hoop* call which you can hear mostly in the late winter and early spring when the birds are establishing territories and trying to attract mates.

It uses its long, thin bill to probe in the soil for insect larvae and worms. As it walks along it pushes the bill into the ground like a sewing machine needle, every now and then extracting a tasty morsel.

Such a conspicuous bird might seem vulnerable to cats and other predators but, if you watch your cat in the presence of a hoopoe, though it may show initial interest, it will soon abandon the hunt because hoopoes taste bad and smell very pungent; the black-and-white colouring is a warning device to indicate the unpleasant flavour to would-be predators. This is why hoopoes can nest in holes in the ground in the presence of snakes, rodents and mongooses, without coming to harm. The unlined nest hole smells foul, so it is no wonder that other animals find these birds and their nesting cavities distasteful.

Nest sites also include tree holes and holes under the eaves of buildings. Between July and December the female lays two to six white-pored, greenish-blue eggs, and incubates them for about 17 days. Two or three broods may be reared each season. Both sexes then feed the young for about 30 days after hatching.

GREEN WOODHOOPOE

Rooibekkakelaar *(Phoeniculus purpureus)*

Size: Length 30-36 cm; weight 61-75 g.
Colour: Metallic greenish black with bright red bill and feet; white spots on wings and tail visible in flight.
Most like: Violet woodhoopoe, but gloss is green, not purple, and tail is not as long; red bill and feet distinguish it from common scimitarbill.
Habitat: Forest, woodland, savanna, plantations and gardens.

Northern Namibia, northern Botswana, Zimbabwe, Mozambique, KwaZulu-Natal, Swaziland, Mpumalanga Northern Province, the North-West, Gauteng, central and northern Free State, and along the Eastern Cape coast.

The loud, cackling calls of the green (also called the red-billed) woodhoopoe have been likened by the Zulu and Xhosa people to the laughter of women, hence the name they use for this bird, *inhlekabafazi*. The birds usually move about in groups of three to ten, often flying from tree to tree, scrambling about on the trunk and branches and probing and chiselling for insects and lizards.

You may see them hacking away at loose bark, sending chips of it flying. As they forage, their long tails swing about in a clownish fashion. Every now and then a pair or the entire group stops feeding to indulge in a bout of calling and displaying, rocking to and fro on the perch as they cackle like clockwork toys. Then the flock takes off for the next tree, flying in untidy formation. In winter the birds may feed on the nectar of the flowers of erythrina trees and aloes.

As with other hoopoes, green woodhoopoes have a pungent, musky odour.

They nest in tree holes almost any time of the year, sometimes taking over the hole made in a previous season by a barbet or woodpecker. There are usually three greenish eggs to a clutch, which the female incubates on her own for about 18 days. During this time her mate and possibly one male helper feed her. After the young hatch both parents feed them, often assisted by other adults and perhaps juveniles from previous broods. The help given by these nonbreeding adults and young helpers stands them in good stead when they too become breeders.

Tree birds

RED-BILLED HORNBILL
Rooibekneushoringvoël *(Tockus erythrorhynchus)*

Size: Length 42-50 cm; weight 125-134 g.
Colour: Crown, back and tail black; wings boldly mottled black and white; broad white eyebrow; below white, mottled black on breast; bill deep red, rather slender; patch of skin on throat and around eye pink.
Most like: Southern yellow-billed hornbill, but slender red bill diagnostic; African grey hornbill more uniformly grey on wings; remaining species of hornbill lack white eyebrow.
Habitat: Mopane woodland, savanna, bushveld.

Savanna woodlands of northern Namibia, northern and eastern Botswana, most of Zimbabwe, northern and southern Mozambique, Northern Province, eastern Swaziland and northern KwaZulu-Natal.

The female red-billed hornbill has her own way of ensuring privacy and isolation at nesting time—she seals herself in her nest hole, using cement made of mud, droppings and fruit pulp. She plasters this cement on the sides of the entrance hole with her bill, leaving a narrow slit through which the male can pass food. The cement hardens and keeps out intruders, allowing the female to undergo a complete feather moult in her protected cavity.

In suitable habitats you will see hundreds of red-billed hornbills fly up from the roadside as you pass, often in company with southern yellow-billed hornbills. They feed mainly on the ground, digging with their picklike bills in soil and cattle dung for insects, seeds, scorpions and small reptiles.

Red-billed hornbills display to each other with an exaggerated nodding of the head as they give their rhythmic *kawak-kawak-kawak* calls.

Although fairly gregarious out of the breeding season, you will usually see them in pairs from October to December in the eastern parts of southern Africa and later than this in the west.

After laying her three to five white, pitted eggs, the female incubates them for 25 days. About three weeks later, she breaks her way out of the nest and helps the male feed the young. The young reseal the nest themselves and break out at the age of about 45 days when they can fly.

SOUTHERN YELLOW-BILLED HORNBILL
Geelbekneushoringvoël *(Tockus leucomelas)*

Size: Length 48-60 cm; average weight (m) 2,1 kg, (f) 1,6 kg.
Colour: Crown, back and tail mostly black; broad white eyebrow; wings mottled black and white; eyes yellow; skin on throat and around eye dark pink; bill deep yellow with black along cutting edges, strongly arched on top.
Most like: Red-billed hornbill, but yellow bill diagnostic; iris always yellow (may be brown in red-billed hornbill); African grey hornbill more uniformly grey on wing; remaining hornbill species lack white eyebrow.
Habitat: Bushveld, woodland, thornveld.

In central and northern Namibia, Botswana, southern and far northern Zimbabwe, southern Mozambique, northern KwaZulu-Natal, Swaziland, Northern Province and the extreme Northern Cape.

Of all the southern African hornbills, the southern yellow-billed is probably the most familiar because it is so common in game reserves, from the Kruger National Park to the Kgalagadi Transfrontier Park and Etosha National Park in Namibia. It is very similar to the red-billed hornbill, with which it often associates, foraging on the ground where it runs about on its short legs like a wind-up toy.

The southern yellow-billed hornbill digs far less than its red-billed cousin, preferring to pick up its food from the surface of the soil. It also chases and swoops upon moving prey. In the dry season it likes to eat ants and termites; in the wet season it feeds more on other kinds of insects, as well as on centipedes, scorpions and seeds.

In a territory of about 17 ha, a pair of yellow-billed hornbills seeks out a suitable tree in which to nest. They line the floor with dry grass, leaves and bark, and the female seals herself into the hole in the manner described for the red-billed hornbill (*see left*). She then lays three to four white eggs, which take about 24 days to hatch.

The male feeds the incubating female through a slit in the sealed nest entrance until she breaks out about three weeks after the chicks hatch. Both parents then feed the growing family for a further 25 days.

Tree birds

BLACK-COLLARED BARBET

Rooikophoutkapper *(Lybius torquatus)*

Size: Length 19-20 cm; weight 47-70 g.
Colour: Head and breast bright red, bordered all round by a broad, black collar; back brownish grey; belly pale, dull yellow; wings and tail edged with yellow; heavy black bill.
Most like: Other barbets, but red head distinctive.
Habitat: Forest edge, coastal bush, woodland, gardens.

The Caprivi Strip, northern and eastern Botswana, Zimbabwe, Mozambique, Mpumalanga, Northern Province, the North-West, Gauteng, northern Free State, KwaZulu-Natal, Swaziland and the Eastern Cape coast.

The wonderful duet of a pair of black-collared barbets is so perfectly synchronized that it is hard to believe that two birds are making the familiar *two-puddly, two-puddly* call. The birds start their song with a harsh, swizzling call and then break into the full duet, the first bird calling *two* and the second replying *puddly*; the *puddly* may be three to four syllables instead of just two. As they call the two birds bob up and down in front of each other on a branch, spreading their wings slightly as they rise.

Black-collared barbets form small parties of up to about ten birds, though their groups usually number only three or four. These may constitute a family of birds. At night up to 11 birds may roost in a single nest hole but, again, the usual group size is seldom more than four birds.

From the round entrance the excavation goes down into the heart of the branch for 30-40 cm, ending in a floor covered with wood chips. A favourite nest site is a length of dried agave (a member of the sisal family) pole tied to a tree.

Both parents incubate the three to five white eggs for about 19 days, and feed the young for up to 35 days, sometimes with the aid of one or two helpers.

People often ask why the black-collared barbet is not called 'red-headed', since the red head is its most conspicuous feature. True, but in other parts of the world there are already a red-headed, a scarlet-hooded, a crimson-throated and red-faced barbet, so this obvious characteristic has already been used to the full—hence black-collared!

RED-FRONTED TINKERBIRD

Rooiblestinker *(Pogoniulus pusillus)*

Size: Length 12 cm; weight 10 g.
Colour: Above black, streaked with pale yellow; forehead red; large, golden wing-patch; underparts pale greenish yellow.
Most like: Yellow-fronted tinkerbird, but golden patch on wing diagnostic (wing streaked with pale narrow bars in yellow-fronted tinkerbird); forehead red (yellow or orange in yellow-fronted tinkerbird).
Habitat: Coastal and riverine bush, evergreen forest, dense thornveld, wooded gorges.

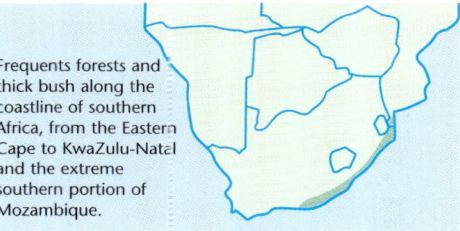

Frequents forests and thick bush along the coastline of southern Africa, from the Eastern Cape to KwaZulu-Natal and the extreme southern portion of Mozambique.

The monotonous *tink-tink* callnotes of the red-fronted tinkerbird, from which it gets its name, ring throughout most of the daylight hours, especially in summer when the birds are breeding. The notes are uttered rather faster than those of the related yellow-fronted tinkerbird and serve as a means of identification. Calling may continue uninterrupted for three minutes or more and can be singularly distracting if you are trying to concentrate your thoughts on something else.

In its restricted southern African range the red-fronted tinkerbird is a common little bird, especially in the Eastern Cape. In upcountry KwaZulu-Natal you may hear it in the hot, tangled bush along the Tugela River. It is not always easy to get a clear view of this pretty tinkerbird, which generally perches in the treetops, but you can call it out by imitating its song.

It forages rather like a warbler does, searching through vegetation with diligent little jerks of the head, darting out after an insect now and then and picking the fruits off mistletoe clumps. It regurgitates the sticky seeds of mistletoe and wipes them on a branch. Here they adhere, germinate and parasitize a new host plant.

The nest hole is excavated in a dead bough. The entrance, no more than two centimetres across, may be only a metre or so above the ground. The female lays up to four tiny, white eggs on the floor of the excavation, but nothing is known of incubation or nestling periods.

Tree birds

CRESTED BARBET
Kuifkophoutkapper
(*Trachyphonus vaillantii*)

Size: Length 23-24 cm; weight 58-83 g.
Colour: Head and face yellow with red scallops and small black crest; rest of upperparts black with white spots and scallops; rump red; belly yellow with red streaks; broad black collar on breast, scalloped with white; bill pale greenish ivory with grey tip.
Most like: Some woodpeckers, but bill stubby and not straight and pointed, plumage looks untidy and not neatly 'laddered' like that of most woodpeckers.
Habitat: Woodland thickets, riverine bush, gardens.

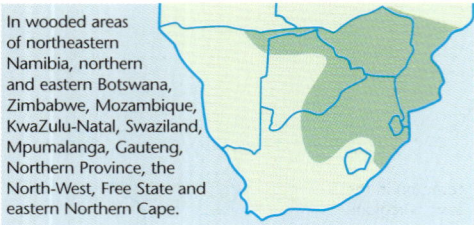

In wooded areas of northeastern Namibia, northern and eastern Botswana, Zimbabwe, Mozambique, KwaZulu-Natal, Swaziland, Mpumalanga, Gauteng, Northern Province, the North-West, Free State and eastern Northern Cape.

GREATER HONEYGUIDE
Grootheuningwyser
(*Indicator indicator*)

Size: Length 19-20 cm; weight 28-62 g.
Colour: Grey, darker above, paler below; light golden-yellow patch at bend of wing; flanks lightly streaked dusky; male has black throat and large white ear-patch; bill of female blackish, of male pale pink; tail blackish with white outer feathers (conspicuous in flight).
Most like: Other larger honeyguides, but yellow wrist-patch in both sexes, and black throat and white ear-patch of male distinctive; throat and forehead not mottled as in scaly-throated honeyguide; back not greenish as in lesser honeyguide. Voice of male distinctive.
Habitat: Woodland, savanna, riverine bush, plantations of exotics, farmyards.

In thornveld and open woodlands throughout the subregion, except for the drier western parts—Namibia, western Botswana, the Northern Cape, Namaqualand and the Karoo.

The penetrating, unmusical trilling of the crested barbet, which sounds like the ringing of an alarm clock without a bell, may last unbroken for up to 30 seconds. Occasionally you may hear two birds calling together in a ragged duet that lacks the close synchronization of the black-collared barbets' vocal performance.

Crested barbets call to maintain contact with one another, express aggression, advertise territory and attract a mate. A calling bird doesn't try to conceal itself in the branches, and you can see crested barbets perched right out in the open.

The crested barbet both looks and behaves like a clown, especially when feeding on the ground, as it hops about with its extended crest looking like a clown's conical hat. Crested barbets forage for fruit and insects in bushes and trees, and can be tempted to a feeding tray by pawpaw and the pulp from squeezed oranges. Suet put into a mesh bag and hung from a branch is also a favourite food.

In order to attract a pair of crested barbets to nest in your garden, tie a 60 cm length of dried sisal or agave pole to a tree, with the start of a nest entrance near the top of the pole. Soon the birds will excavate a nest hole in the pole and will lay their two to four white eggs on the floor at the bottom. Incubation takes 17 days and the nestlings leave the nest in a month or slightly less. The crested barbet may rear up to four broods in one season.

All honeyguides have white outer tail feathers, but only the greater and scaly-throated honeyguides lead man to beehives. The story that the greater honeyguide guides the honey badger or any other mammal has not been substantiated. Its habit of guiding man is, nevertheless, a remarkable one because it is instinctive.

A greater honeyguide leads you to a hive by fluttering in front of your face, bouncing its body and flirting with its tail, at the same time giving a distinctive rattling call, rather like matches being shaken in a box. When it reaches the site of the hive it perches nearby and waits for the hive to be opened. It then feeds on the adult bees, bee larvae and beeswax.

Like all honeyguides, the greater is a brood parasite. In the breeding season the male sits high in a treetop, singing his *WHIT-prrrr* phrase repeatedly for hours. A female in breeding condition will respond by mating with him and finding a suitable home—the hole-nest of host species such as the kingfisher, bee-eater, hoopoe, swallows—in which to lay her egg, usually only one per nest. Each female lays four to eight eggs in a season and often breaks a host egg for each one she lays.

When the nestling is born, it ensures its survival by killing the host young with hooks on its bill which it loses after two weeks. Some 30 days later the young honeyguide is ready to leave the nest.

Tree birds

CARDINAL WOODPECKER

Kardinaalspeg (*Dendropicos fuscescens*)

Size: Length 14-16 cm; weight 20-38 g.

Colour: Forecrown coffee brown; hindcrown black in female, red in male; upperparts barred olive and off-white; underparts white, boldly streaked black; face white with black moustache stripe at side of throat.

Most like: Other woodpeckers, but brown forecrown combined with dark, streaked belly and black moustache stripe diagnostic.

Habitat: Woodland to semi-arid savanna, forest edges, parks, gardens, plantations, riverine bush.

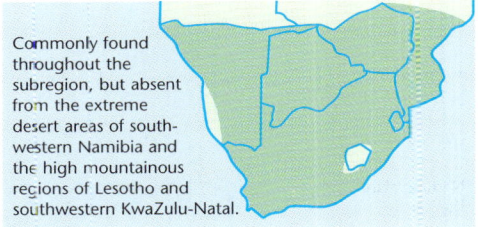

Commonly found throughout the subregion, but absent from the extreme desert areas of south-western Namibia and the high mountainous regions of Lesotho and southwestern KwaZulu-Natal.

BARN SWALLOW

Europese swael (*Hirundo rustica*)

Size: Length 20 cm; weight 14-22 g.

Colour: Metallic blue-black above; forehead deep rufous; below off-white with rufous throat outlined by broad black collar; tail black, forked with white 'windows' visible when spread in flight.

Most like: White-throated swallow, but the throat rufous (not white); South African cliff swallow, but tail forked (not square) and rump metallic blue-black like back (not orange).

Habitat: Highly variable, but not in forest; mostly open grassland and over water.

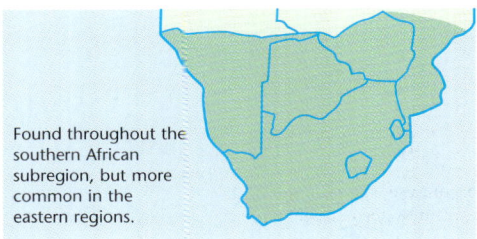

Found throughout the southern African subregion, but more common in the eastern regions.

Cardinal woodpeckers drill into wood for insect larvae (mainly boring beetles) and will even perch on dry maize stalks to extract these succulent morsels. They are equipped with specialized feet, having two toes pointing forward and two back, as well as a set of stiffened tail feathers to act as a prop against the vertical trunk of a tree or the underside of a horizontal branch.

The rapidly rolling call of this woodpecker is usually the first sign of its presence, as it is an unobtrusive little bird, although it taps vigorously and audibly on a branch while foraging, usually working from the bottom of the tree to the top. Like most woodpeckers it also has a drumming display in which it taps rapidly on dead wood with its bill, producing a resonating rattle that is part of its courtship and territorial behaviour.

Cardinal woodpeckers are the most common members of the woodpecker group in almost any habitat where there are trees. They occur usually in pairs and may join up with other species to form a foraging 'bird party'.

They nest in almost any month of the year, but the peak of breeding is from August to October. Both sexes excavate a hole in a dead tree trunk or stoutish branch. The female lays one to five (usually two) white eggs on a bed of wood chips at the bottom of the hole. These take 12-13 days to hatch, and the nestlings are fed by both parents for about 28 days.

Huge flocks of barn (or European) swallows gathered on telephone and power lines in autumn before they migrate back to the northern hemisphere are a common sight along roadsides in southern Africa.

The swallows arrive here around September and you can watch them spiralling gracefully in the air every evening before descending to their roosting places in reed beds. Here they may number tens of thousands of birds—even millions.

The swallows feed on the wing, catching small flying insects by plunging towards the ground with quick, swooping aerobatics. Around a barn or stable you can hear their bills snap as they catch flies.

Flocks of barn swallows commonly mix with other species of swallow and swifts where airborne insect food is plentiful.

Like other migrants from the northern hemisphere, barn swallows don't breed in southern Africa. Most of the birds seen here come from Britain and western Russia, though some come from as far afield as Siberia, making a round trip of some 25 000 km every year.

Although less common in the dry west than in the east, there is no part of southern Africa where you won't see barn swallows at some stage during the summer.

Tree birds

GREATER STRIPED SWALLOW
Grootstreepswael *(Hirundo cucullata)*

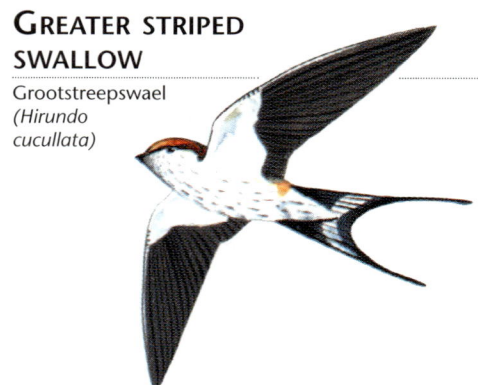

Size: Length 18-20 cm; weight 19-35 g.
Colour: Crown chestnut; metallic blue-black back; pale orange rump; tail black, deeply forked, with white windows; below white, lightly streaked with black, up to and including ear coverts.
Most like: Lesser striped swallow, but ear coverts not red like crown; streaks on underparts much fainter (very heavy in lesser striped swallow).
Habitat: Open grassland near rocky outcrops, farmyards, towns, mountain slopes.

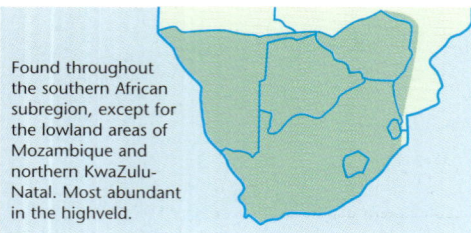

Found throughout the southern African subregion, except for the lowland areas of Mozambique and northern KwaZulu-Natal. Most abundant in the highveld.

COMMON HOUSE MARTIN
Huisswael *(Delichon urbica)*

Size: Length 14-15 cm; weight 18-19 g.
Colour: Metallic blue-black upperparts; rump and underparts white; tail plain black, deeply forked.
Most like: Pearl-breasted swallow, but white rump diagnostic; white-throated swallow, but no black collar on throat, no white in tail and no rufous on forehead.
Habitat: Open grassland, cultivated fields; often around tall buildings, dam walls and rocky hillsides.

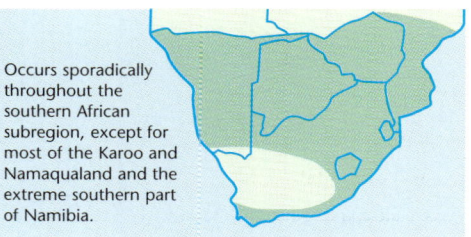

Occurs sporadically throughout the southern African subregion, except for most of the Karoo and Namaqualand and the extreme southern part of Namibia.

Greater striped swallows are gentle birds with mellow voices that twitter, chuckle and gargle. Their flight is slow and leisurely, and far more sedate than the quick, darting flight of most other members of the swallow family.

If you live in the highveld, these birds will probably be quite familiar to you. Although they are included here among the tree birds, they perch in trees only if telephone wires are not available. You will see them most often sitting along the roadside on the wires or on a fence. Around farm buildings they perch on rooftops and on railings, often coming right inside a building to nest.

These swallows are also common among the cave-sandstone formations of the Northern Cape, Free State and KwaZulu-Natal. In their natural environment, where wires are absent, they perch on the leafless twigs of bushes and small trees, or on the ledges of the rocky overhangs under which they nest. The tunnel-and-bowl nests of these birds are also a familiar sight under verandahs and eaves. Built of mud pellets strengthened with saliva, the nests can last for many years if vandals don't break them down, and the swallows will return year after year to the same site to lay their eggs.

The bowl of the nest is lined with grass and feathers and the female incubates the three speckled eggs for 18 days. Both parents feed the young, which take about a month to reach flying age.

You may have seen great numbers of house martins without even realizing what they are. Abundant in some parts of the country, these migrants from Europe and Russia gather in their thousands on telephone wires, leafless trees and even on dry sunflower tops before migrating in the autumn. Although most house martins are nonbreeding birds, some have bred in southern Africa at scattered localities such as Cape Town, Somerset West, Otjiwarongo, Keiskammahoek and Kokstad. What prompts the species to breed here is a mystery.

House martins forage over open country with a quick, fluttering flight. They roost in various sites, including reed beds, much as the barn (European) swallow does, but in smaller flocks. In the eastern parts of southern Africa house martins occur sporadically, preferring higher areas as a rule, although they have been seen at sea level.

After a cold snap, many thousands of birds may die of a combination of cold and starvation, because their aerial insect prey becomes scarce in bad weather and the birds cannot find enough to eat.

The house martin's nest is a rounded ball of mud pellets, placed against the angle of a roof and a wall, with a rounded side entrance near the top. The female lays three to four white eggs, which hatch out in about 14 days, and both sexes feed the young for about a month before they can fly properly.

Tree birds

FORK-TAILED DRONGO

Mikstertbyvanger
(*Dicrurus adsimilis*)

Size: Length 25 cm; weight 38-58 g.
Colour: Black with slight sheen; wings palely translucent in flight.
Most like: Southern black flycatcher, but more robustly built, tail deeply notched (hence 'fork-tailed'), and bill deep at base and sloping up to forehead; southern black flycatcher's forehead more rounded, rising steeply from base of rather slender bill. Square-tailed drongo smaller with almost square tail and evergreen-forest habitat. Black cuckooshrike male has rounded tail and yellow gape.
Habitat: Savanna, woodland, forest edge, gardens, riverine bush, plantations.

Commonly seen in a variety of habitats throughout the southern African subregion, but absent from Namaqualand, the Karoo, southern Free State and Lesotho.

You can usually see fork-tailed drongos perched conspicuously in the open on a fence post or dead branch. They also take up posts on the backs of large game mammals to catch prey disturbed by them as they graze.

Most people who live in the eastern parts of southern Africa know the fork-tailed drongo well as a garden bird, and a very aggressive one at that. It dive-bombs people, dogs and cats if disturbed while nesting, usually with startling effect.

Its creaking and twanging voice is a familiar sound in regions where it is common; it becomes scarcer towards the west, but can still be found in dry country as long as there are some trees in which it can perch and nest.

It hunts from a perch, sallying out to catch an insect in flight, or gliding to the ground to pick up a spider, scorpion or other crawling animal. Fork-tailed drongos also catch small birds and will dive into water for fishes.

In the summer months the fork-tailed drongo builds a nest in the shape of a shallow hammock, slung in a horizontal fork far from the main trunk of a tree. The female lays three spotted or plain eggs, which are white to pink in colour. Incubation lasts 16-17 days and the young take about 18 days to reach flying age.

BLACK-HEADED ORIOLE

Swartkopwielewaal (*Oriolus larvatus*)

Size: Length 24-25 cm; weight 59-72 g.
Colour: Head and upper breast glossy black; back moss green; underparts and collar on hindneck brilliant yellow; flight feathers black with white edges; bill reddish pink.
Most like: Other orioles which, however, lack glossy black head; some male weavers, but much larger and with heavy flight (weavers fly straight and fast).
Habitat: Woodland, forest edge, dense coastal and riverine bush, plantations, gardens.

Wooded areas of northern Namibia, northern Zimbabwe, Mozambique, Mpumalanga, Northern Province, eastern North-West Province, KwaZulu-Natal, Swaziland and the Eastern and southeastern Cape coast.

As with most treetop birds, it is the black-headed orioles call—a lovely, mellow, liquid sound—that first attracts your attention. To see the bird itself requires patience, because it spends its time in the foliage of the tree's canopy and emerges only briefly to fly rather heavily on broad wings from tree to tree. Then you can appreciate its vivid yellow belly, greenish back and black head.

Sometimes you may be lucky enough to see the bird briefly exposed on a branch in the open, but it is usually shy and reluctant to be examined for too long.

Black-headed orioles feed on fruit—they are particularly fond of figs—and insects, gleaning these from branches of taller trees. In winter you can also see them collecting nectar from aloe flowers, getting their foreheads thoroughly dusted with orange pollen in the process. This is the best time to get a close view of these otherwise elusive birds.

The nest is a masterpiece of construction: a deep cup of woven plant fibres and spider web, suspended in a horizontal fork, high in a tree. The clutch consists of two to three eggs, beautifully marked with brown and grey on a pinkish background. The incubation period is about 14 days. Nestlings take 15-18 days to reach flying age, and then accompany their parents for a while longer until they are completely independent. Immatures have distinctive, heavy black streaks on the yellow belly.

Tree birds

CAPE CROW
Swartkraai *(Corvus capensis)*

Size: Length 48-53 cm.
Colour: Glossy black all over.
Most like: Pied crow, but no white in plumage; bill much more slender and head rather bulbous (pied crow has heavier bill and more slender head).
Habitat: Open grassland, cultivated fields, mountain slopes, semi-desert, plantations, farmyards.

Common in the open grasslands and agricultural areas of the subregion, but absent from eastern Namibia, most of Botswana, western and eastern Zimbabwe, Mozambique and northern KwaZulu-Natal.

The Cape, or black, crow is the clown of the crow family, fluffing out its rounded head and hackled neck as it makes its gulping, bubbling and growling calls. It often bows its head and spreads its wings too as it calls, comically resembling a gowned professor trying to make an especially important point to a group of uninterested students.

One of the commonly used Afrikaans names for this bird is *koringlandkraai*, which aptly describes its predilection for fallow fields where it comes to feed on the fallen grain after the harvest.

Cape crows spend much of their resting time on telephone poles along the road in the more settled parts of southern Africa. They also use perches to seek out road-killed animals on which to feed. In remoter areas, they perch on trees and bushes. Apart from grain and carrion, they eat almost any kind of animal or plant food, such as insects, frogs and fruit, but they do not harm farm animals as the pied crow sometimes does.

Cape crows usually nest in summer, but may start as early as July. They build a large bowl of sticks high in the smaller branches of a tall tree (rarely in a big bush), and line it with soft materials such as wool, cloth, hair and feathers. In the absence of a tree, a telephone pole will do as well. The female lays four or five beautiful pink, red-spotted eggs. Incubation takes 18-19 days and the chicks grow up in about six weeks. The family stays together for several months after the young fly for the first time.

PIED CROW
Witborskraai *(Corvus albus)*

Size: Length 46-52 cm; weight 420-610 g.
Colour: Glossy black with white breast, belly and collar on hindneck; bill black.
Most like: White-necked raven, but white belly and breast diagnostic, bill heavier than that of Cape crow, which lacks white markings on plumage.
Habitat: Almost anywhere, except forest, high mountains and Kalahari sandveld.

Throughout the subregion, except for the Kalahari basin of Eastern Namibia, southern Botswana, North-West Province, extreme Northern Cape and the mountains of Lesotho.

Pied crows are familiar birds because of their habit of coming down to feed on road-killed carrion, as Cape crows sometimes do. Farmers don't like them because they are known to injure newborn calves and lambs. On the whole, however, they probably do more good than harm because of all the insects they eat, although most of their food consists of seeds and other plant material. They're also able to catch small birds when in flight.

Pied crows are the best known of the crow family in southern Africa and, for most of the year, also the most gregarious. Flocks numbering up to 300 gather to roost in tall trees, especially outside the breeding season. They favour eucalyptus trees in urban areas and perform wonderful aerobatics before coming in to roost in the evening.

These crows can be quite noisy birds, cawing harshly at times, but they are seldom as vocal as Cape crows. They make marvellous pets and can learn to talk well.

You can usually see pied crows in rather open country, though they prefer wooded surroundings. They scavenge at picnic sites along the major roads of southern Africa, where they get quite tame.

The nest, a bowl of sticks lined with fur, dung and other soft materials, is built in the stout fork of a tree, or on a telephone pole or the platform of a windmill. The clutch of four to five eggs is pale green with blotches of olive and grey. The female does most of the incubation, but the male helps out at times for the 19-day period. The young stay in the nest for 35-45 days and are fed by both parents.

Tree birds

SOUTHERN BLACK TIT
Gewone swartmees *(Parus niger)*

Size: Length 15-16 cm; weight 17-26 g.
Colour: Black, shading to greyish black on belly; wing bar white; undertail coverts edged white; narrow white tip to tail; female generally less jet black than male, especially on face and underparts.
Most like: Carp's tit, but wing bar narrower; white on undertail coverts diagnostic.
Habitat: Woodland, forest, dense savanna, plantations of exotics, gardens.

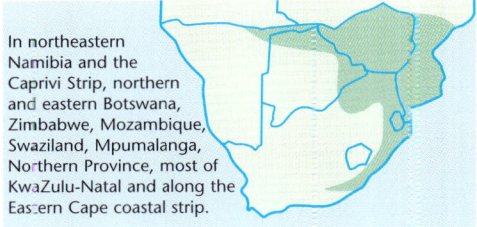

In northeastern Namibia and the Caprivi Strip, northern and eastern Botswana, Zimbabwe, Mozambique, Swaziland, Mpumalanga, Northern Province, most of KwaZulu-Natal and along the Eastern Cape coastal strip.

The southern black tit performs some astonishing acrobatics in its quest for food, and sometimes you will even see it hanging upside down to examine the underside of a branch for tasty morsels. On its menu are adult insects and larvae which it extracts from tough seed pods by holding the pod in its foot and hammering it open with its small, strong bill.

In North America the tits are called 'chickadees' because of their calls, and the southern black tit makes the same harsh *chickadee-dee-dee* call as it forages for delicacies.

These birds usually move about in pairs or small parties, maintaining contact by calling intermittently. You will often see them forming large parties with other species, apparently to benefit from the insects disturbed by all the movement. Their flight is bouncy, the birds looking as if they are on wire springs.

The birds breed mainly in September and October. Each group consists of a male and a female and one to four adult male helpers which feed the incubating female and her young after hatching. The clutch consists of four to five white eggs, speckled with red, brown and grey, laid on a soft pad of lichen, hair and grass at the bottom of a deep hole in the trunk of a tree.

The female incubates her clutch for about 15 days, after which her nestlings stay in the nest for 24 days. While on the nest the female defends herself by hissing like a snake and pecking at any intruder—a most effective deterrent.

ARROW-MARKED BABBLER
Pylvlekkatlagter *(Turdoides jardineii)*

Size: Length 23-25 cm; weight 56-80 g.
Colour: Greyish brown, paler below, with white arrowhead markings on underparts and indistinct whitish markings on upper back; tail plain dark brown; eye bright orange; bill and legs black.
Most like: Hartlaub's and black-faced babblers, but lacks white rump; white arrowhead markings diagnostic.
Habitat: Thickets in woodland and reed beds along watercourses.

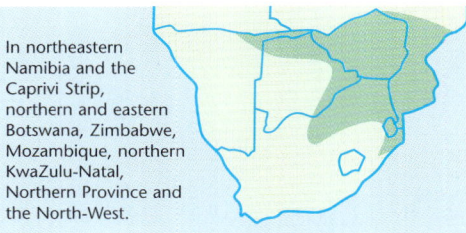

In northeastern Namibia and the Caprivi Strip, northern and eastern Botswana, Zimbabwe, Mozambique, northern KwaZulu-Natal, Northern Province and the North-West.

Noisy throngs of arrow-marked babblers are very much a feature of the lowveld regions and drier midlands of southern Africa, as well as the denser woodlands of the interior, especially in river valleys. Moving in groups of five to ten birds, they keep contact with each other with ratchetlike calls that build up to a peak and then die away.

The birds spend a lot of time on the ground looking for food, though they also forage in low bushes and brushwood, bounding from branch to branch and clambering about the vegetation. They eat mostly insects, but also take spiders, snails, small reptiles and some fruit.

Arrow-marked babblers may feed in company with Hartlaub's babblers where the two species overlap in range, such as in the campsites of northern Botswana. They fly directly, alternately fluttering and gliding, often landing on a fence or other conspicuous perch before dropping to the ground again to continue foraging.

Nesting takes place throughout the year in the warmer parts of the region, but only in summer further south. The nest is a bulky bowl of grass and twigs lined with finer material and placed in dense cover, usually quite low down. There are three plain, blue-green eggs in a clutch and the breeding pair and some adult helpers incubate these. Up to five helpers also help feed the chicks, but the periods of incubation and nestling have not been recorded. The arrow-marked babbler is sometimes host to the striped cuckoo.

Tree birds

Dark-capped bulbul

Swartoogtiptol *(Pycnonotus tricolor)*

Size: Length 20-22 cm; weight (m) 26-49 g, (f) 29-45 g.
Colour: Head black with low pointed crest; back and breast greyish brown; belly dull whitish; undertail light yellow; tail dark brown.
Most like: Cape and African red-eyed bulbuls, but eye-ring black (white in Cape bulbul, red in African red-eyed bulbul).
Habitat: Woodland, forest edge, dense growth along watercourses, gardens, plantations, parks.

In Northern Namibia, Botswana, most of Zimbabwe, Mozambique, Mpumalanga, Gauteng, Northern Province, eastern North-West, northeastern Free State, KwaZulu-Natal and the Eastern Cape.

In some Afrikaans-speaking circles the dark-capped, or black-eyed, bulbul was called *bottergat* because of its yellow undertail. It was also known as *geelgat* for many years, until prudery gained the upper hand and the popular, more onomatopoeic name *tiptol* was substituted. English-speaking people now generally call the dark-capped bulbul 'toppie'—a name derived from its cheerful vocalizations heard in gardens throughout southern Africa, since the Cape and African red-eyed bulbuls have similar calls.

Dark-capped bulbuls are among the first birds to be heard at dawn. Presumably they call mostly to establish territory, since you usually see the species in pairs or singly, indicating that territories are probably held all year round.

This bird eats mainly fruit, but will also eat insects, nectar and even small vertebrates such as lizards. It forages in trees and bushes, seldom coming to the ground, though it will do so readily to pick up cutworms from lawns or scraps from picnic sites. It also visits feeding trays if these have suitable food in the form of fruit or mealie pap.

The nest is a thin-walled but strong cup of dry plant stems, lined with hair, and placed in the fork of a bush or tree at any height from the ground, often way out on a limb.

The female lays three pink, purple-spotted eggs, which take 12-14 days to hatch. The female does most of the incubation but both the parents feed the young for the 10-17 days it takes them to reach flying age.

Sombre greenbul

Gewone willie *(Andropadus importunus)*

Size: Length 19-23 cm; weight (m) 26-40 g, (f) 24-30 g.
Colour: Uniform dull greyish green, somewhat paler below; sometimes with yellowish tinge; eye white.
Most like: Stripe-cheeked, yellow-bellied and yellow-streaked bulbuls, but white eye always diagnostic; duller below than yellow-bellied and stripe-cheeked; head not greyish as in yellow-streaked; call highly distinctive.
Habitat: Evergreen forest; thickets; coastal and riverine bush; also gardens.

From eastern Zambezi valley to Mozambique, the Mpumalanga and Northern Province lowveld, eastern Swaziland, eastern KwaZulu-Natal and along the Eastern and southwestern Cape coast to Cape Town.

The bright *willy* call of the sombre greenbul, usually camouflaged in the canopy of a forest, invariably betrays its presence. If you hear it, be patient and you will probably see the bird appear briefly on an exposed branch. The song of the sombre greenbul, like its call, is equally unmistakeable: it is a set phrase that sounds like a quickly uttered *willy-come-have-a-fight, scaaared*, the final note drawn out plaintively and falling in pitch. This can also be sung *willy come-and-play-with-me, pleeease*.

As it flies jerkily from one bush to another, watch where it disappears and follow the movement of the branches and leaves until the bird appears at the top of the bush. A 'spishing' noise, which you can create by saying *psssh psssh* through your teeth several times loudly, will often bring the bird right into the open if it is reluctant to expose itself completely.

The sombre greenbul spends most of its time in the treetops searching for its food of fruit and insects. It is almost always solitary, and rarely seen in pairs.

Sombre greenbuls (previously called sombre bulbuls) breed from September until the late summer. The nest is a smallish cup of plant material, built on a thin branch fairly low down and quite well hidden. Two eggs usually form the clutch; they are dull white with spots of olive green and grey. The female incubates alone for about 16 days. The chicks stay in the nest for about two weeks.

Tree birds

OLIVE THRUSH

Olyflyster *(Turdus olivaceus)*

Size: Length 24 cm; weight 60-80 g.
Colour: Above dark olive-brown, tinged greyish; throat white, streaked black; breast olive-grey; belly dull orange-yellow, washed olive on flanks; undertail white; bill and legs dull yellow.
Most like: Kurrichane thrush, but no dark line down sides of throat and no white in centre of belly or throat; bill yellow, not orange.
Habitat: Evergreen forest in KwaZulu-Natal and more easterly parts of range; elsewhere riverine bush, plantations, gardens, parks.

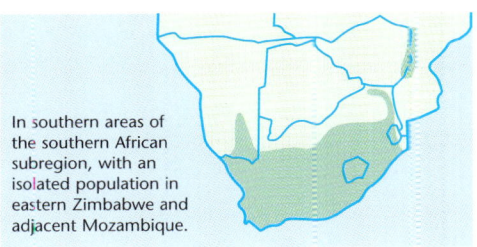

In southern areas of the southern African subregion, with an isolated population in eastern Zimbabwe and adjacent Mozambique.

In the highveld you can see the olive thrush in almost any garden or city park, and it is particularly common in Johannesburg and Bloemfontein. In the Karoo and drier western parts it comes to farmyards and other places where exotic trees provide cover and a suitable feeding habitat.

The olive thrush spends much of its time running along the ground in short bursts, stopping now and then to probe for a worm or to toss some leaves aside for insects, spiders or snails. When these are scarce it will also eat fruit and seeds; sometimes it may also tackle a lizard, chameleon or nestling bird.

When disturbed this bird gives a thin *tseep* call as it takes off, taking refuge in the security of a tree until the intruder goes away.

Its song is a series of trilled, melodious phrases, each separated by a short pause, characteristic of the thrush family.

Nesting is usually in summer, but in the Western Cape may take place all year round, with the olive thrush constructing a bowl-shaped nest of coarse plant material high up on a stout branch or in a fork.

The female lays two eggs which are bright blue-green, thickly spotted and blotched with rich brown and grey. She incubates the eggs for 14 days, and both parents feed the young for 16 days. When the young leave the nest they have a distinctively spotted plumage, quite unlike that of the adult.

FAMILIAR CHAT

Gewone spekvreter *(Cercomela familiaris)*

Size: Length 15 cm; weight 19-28 g.
Colour: Brownish grey, paler below; ear coverts faintly tinged rusty; rump and tail dull orange; central tail feathers and tips of all tail feathers black, forming black T.
Most like: Other smaller chats, but rump and tail deeper orange than any other chat's; black T on tail distinctive; deliberate wing-flicking highly characteristic (flicks wings outwards rather than upwards as in sickle-winged chat); *peep-chak-chak* callnote also diagnostic.
Habitat: Rocky outcrops, buildings in towns and on farms, dongas, riverine woodland in dry country.

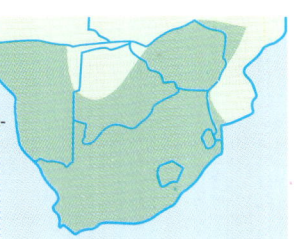

Commonly found throughout the southern African subregion, with the exception of northeastern Namibia and the Caprivi Strip, northern Botswana and the lowlands of Mozambique.

The familiar chat's association with man has made it quite literally a familiar sight around farms. Its Afrikaans name *spekvreter* refers to its liking for animal fat, which it used to obtain from the greased wheels of ox-wagons.

It flicks its wings two or three times whenever it stops, whether hopping on the ground or landing on a perch. Even if you can't see its orange rump or the tail with its distinctive black T-shaped pattern, this wing-flicking will identify it for you.

Familiar chats are usually in pairs and forage on the ground by hopping along and picking up insects and scraps of human food at kitchen doors or picnic sites.

During summer, or after rain at any time of the year in semi-desert country, the familiar chat seeks out a nesting hole, whether it be a shallow depression in the ground, an old burrow in the wall of a donga, a crevice in a stone wall, a disused chamber in the nest of a sociable weaver, or the steel framework of a farm implement.

For its nest the bird builds a foundation of small stones and bits of earth, on top of which it sets a neat, soft cup of animal fur or plant down. The two to four (usually three) bright blue-green eggs with red speckles are incubated for about 14 days.

Both parents feed the hatchlings, which leave the nest after about 16 days.

Tree birds

NATAL ROBIN-CHAT

Nataljanfrederik (*Cossypha natalensis*)

Size: Length 17,5-20 cm; weight 25-40 g.
Colour: Dull orange, browner on crown and mantle; bluish grey on wings; central tail feathers black.
Most like: Chorister robin-chat, but face orange, not black; white-browed robin-chat, but lacks white eyebrow.
Habitat: Evergreen forest, riverine thickets in woodland, lush parks and gardens.

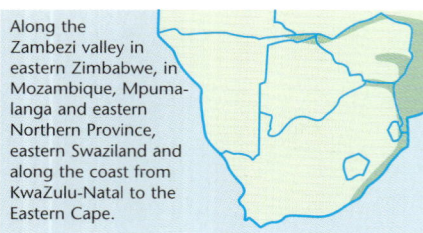

Along the Zambezi valley in eastern Zimbabwe, in Mozambique, Mpumalanga and eastern Northern Province, eastern Swaziland and along the coast from KwaZulu-Natal to the Eastern Cape.

Natal robin-chats are very good at imitating the songs of other birds and human whistles. If you hear a fish eagle in an unusual place, or a nightjar during the day, you can be sure that you are listening to a Natal robin-chat playing some of its adroit vocal tricks.

However, while its repertoire of songs is rich and varied, its callnote is monotonous and rather froglike—*preep-prrup*—repeated over and over again.

Like all the southern African *Cossypha* robins, the Natal robin-chat (also called the red-capped robin-chat) has an orange tail with a black centre, but its almost completely orange body without any white or black in the plumage is easy to recognize.

This elusive, usually solitary bird keeps to the undergrowth of the darker parts of forest and bush, and is common on the KwaZulu-Natal South Coast where it lives in the coastal dune forest among the banana palms (*Strelitzia nicolai*) within earshot of the breakers. A rustling in the undergrowth may be all that alerts you to this robin-chat's presence, though it may sit quite still on a low perch for long periods.

At dusk it drops to the ground to look for its favourite meal of insects, spiders and centipedes, sometimes taking insects disturbed by molerats. In winter it will feed on fruit.

The nest of this bird is a neat cup of dead leaves and moss, lined with fine fibres, well hidden in a dense creeper or hollow stump. In it the female lays three chocolate-brown eggs, though sometimes they may be green with brown and olive spots. Incubation is by the female only and takes about 14 days. Both parents feed the chicks for some 12 days until they leave the nest for the first time in their young spotty plumage.

CAPE ROBIN-CHAT

Gewone Janfrederik (*Cossypha caffra*)

Size: Length 16-18 cm; weight 22-40 g.
Colour: Above greyish brown; face black with bold white eyebrow; throat and breast light orange; belly grey, shading to whitish; undertail yellowish buff; tail orange with black central feathers.
Most like: White-browed and white-throated robin-chats, but contrasting orange breast and grey belly distinctive.
Habitat: Riverine bush and scrub, evergreen forest, wooded gulleys, gardens, parks.

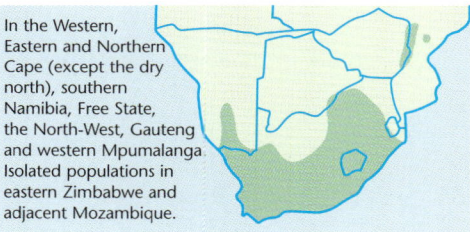

In the Western, Eastern and Northern Cape (except the dry north), southern Namibia, Free State, the North-West, Gauteng and western Mpumalanga. Isolated populations in eastern Zimbabwe and adjacent Mozambique.

The Cape robin-chat is one of the best known and best loved of all the garden birds in South Africa. Its sweet song is a familiar sound at dawn and dusk in almost every part of the country, as well as in the southern parts of Namibia along the better-wooded watercourses. There is also an isolated population in eastern Zimbabwe.

This song has been likened to someone reading a shopping list; each phrase starts with the same note and ends with a varied jumble of notes, sometimes incorporating imitations of other bird calls. Alarmed, the Cape robin-chat flies into the undergrowth, showing its orange-and-black tail, and gives its two- or three-note *WAdeda* alarm call.

Cape robin-chats are tame around homes and may come to feed from the family dog's food bowl. Their usual food, though, is insects, spiders, lizards, worms and fruit.

They nest mostly in summer, though in midwinter in the winter-rainfall regions. The nest is a mess of decaying plant material which is built in a hole in a wall, a creeper, a tuft of grass on a stream bank or on the ground.

The female lays two to three pale green or pinkish, rusty-speckled eggs and incubates them for 14-18 days. The spotted young leave the nest after about 16 days, unless the nest has been parasitized by a red-chested cuckoo, in which case the eggs or young are thrown out by the cuckoo chick.

Tree birds

BAR-THROATED APALIS

Bandkeelkleinjantjie *(Apalis thoracica)*

Size: *Length 12-13 cm; weight 8-12 g.*
Colour: *Crown grey; back yellowish olive; throat white bordered by black collar; rest of underparts pale yellow; tail dark grey with white edges; iris white to cream.*
Most like: *Rudd's apalis, but lacks white eyebrow and distinguished by whitish eye (brown in Rudd's apalis).*
Habitat: *Forest edge, dense savanna, valley bushveld, wooded kloofs, gardens.*

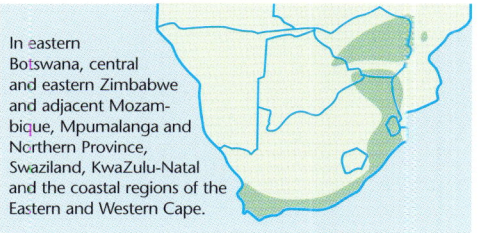

In eastern Botswana, central and eastern Zimbabwe and adjacent Mozambique, Mpumalanga and Northern Province, Swaziland, KwaZulu-Natal and the coastal regions of the Eastern and Western Cape.

The tiny bar-throated apalis, camouflaged in the foliage of its woodland or forest habitat, gives itself away with its penetrating *tlip, tlip, tlip* call. It is a handsome little warbler with its black collar and white throat, but can be quite hard to see among the leaves. With patience, however, you can watch it working its way from branch to branch and leaf to leaf until it comes to an open space where you can get a better view. Its longish tail and white iris give it a particularly perky look.

The bar-throated apalis gleans most of its insect food from the surface of vegetation, specializing in small, soft caterpillars. It moves restlessly about, though it is not really shy and will join bird parties readily. Although it spends most of its active hours high in the treetops, it comes down into the undergrowth from time to time to forage and also to nest. You may even see it foraging on the ground between lichen-covered rocks.

The nest is an oval purse of plant material held together with cobwebs, decorated on the outside with bits of green moss, and lined with soft plant material. It has a round side entrance and is built in a leafy bush or creeper, between 30 cm and three metres above the ground. Another favourite nest site is a hanging tangle of tree roots at the edge of an erosion gully. The clutch of three eggs, spotted with brown and grey on a pale pinkish or greenish background, is incubated for about 17 days and the chicks take a similar length of time to become fully feathered. Breeding starts early, around August, and ends in late summer or autumn.

RATTLING CISTICOLA

Bosveldtinktinkie *(Cisticola chinianus)*

Size: *Length (m) 14-16 cm; (f) 12-13 cm; weight (m) 13-21 g, (f) 11-21 g.*
Colour: *Crown deep rufous; back greyish brown with blackish streaks; underparts creamy white; tail dull brown, tipped black and white; bill dusky with pinkish base; legs and feet pinkish brown.*
Most like: *Tinkling cisticola, but less rufous, especially on tail; no russet eye-ring or ear coverts and no distinct pale eyebrow. Separated from most other similar cisticolas by habitat.*
Habitat: *Thornveld, savanna, bushveld, coastal scrub.*

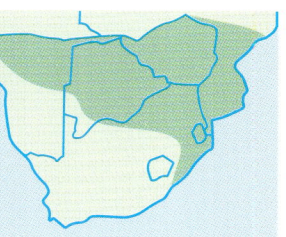

Northeastern Namibia, most of Botswana, Zimbabwe, Mozambique, Mpumalanga, Northern Province, Gauteng, North-West Province, northern Free State, KwaZulu-Natal and coastal Eastern Cape.

Chee chee t-r-r-r-r-r from the treetops advertises the territory of the rattling cisticola and gives it its unusual name. As long as cisticolas are singing (which happens mostly in summer when they're breeding) you cannot mistake them, since the song of each species is so easily recognizable.

The rattling cisticola also has a loud, complaining *cheeeee* alarm call by which you can identify it at any time of the year. In fact, it is one of the easier of the 'little brown jobs' to identify because it is one of the few cisticolas living in a woodland habitat.

This highly vocal bird usually occurs in pairs. Look for the black inside of the male's mouth when he is singing or calling during the breeding season. His song is one of the most commonly heard sounds in the reserves of northern KwaZulu-Natal and Mpumalanga; it is also common in the northern parts of Botswana and Namibia.

Nesting occurs from October to March or April, when the grass is well grown under the trees. An oval of dry, grey grass blades, stuck together with spider web, is built in a tall tuft of grass or in the fork of an acacia sapling where the grass has grown up to conceal it. Through the round side-top entrance you can see the three to four pale, speckled eggs lying on a lining of soft plant down. Only the female incubates the clutch, but the duration is not known. The nestlings stay in the nest for about two weeks.

Tree birds

NEDDICKY

Neddikkie *(Cisticola fulvicapillus)*

Size: Length 10-11 cm; weight 7-9 g.
Colour: Dull blue-grey body, paler below; crown dull rufous; indistinct buff eye-ring; legs and feet pinkish.
Most like: Lazy cisticola, but smaller and with shorter tail; voice quite different.
Habitat: Shrubby undergrowth in woodland, savanna and plantations, rank vegetation along streams and roadsides, low shrubby growth on rocky hillsides, gardens.

In the northern and eastern parts of the subregion. Absent from the dry west.

You can always recognize the neddicky by its rattling alarm call, which resembles the sound made by a fingernail drawn unmusically across the teeth of a comb. In summer, when the birds are territorial and breeding, the characteristic song can also be heard—a monotonous *weep-weep-weep* or *teep-teep-teep* that goes on for several seconds and is sung from a conspicuous perch at the top of a tree, bush or weed stem.

The variable habitat of this tiny cisticola reflects its adaptability, and therefore its success. It is also widespread and is a friendly inhabitant of gardens with low shrubs that provide suitable feeding and nesting places.

As the bird moves about, particularly when it is alarmed, it flicks its tail rapidly sideways as it disappears into the undergrowth. Unlike the rather similar lazy cisticola, it seldom cocks its tail over its back.

In the spring, while the male advertises his territory from a high perch on a treetop, telephone wire or tall bush, the female builds a ball-shaped nest of dry grass blades stuck together with spider web, low down in a mixture of grass and shrub (often thorny). A side entrance gives access to a softly lined interior where the female lays a clutch of four speckled eggs. The eggs vary in colour from white to pale pink or blue, and have a thin covering of reddish markings. Incubation and nestling periods are each about 13 days.

The neddicky, whose name is a corruption of the Xhosa and Zulu word *incede*, may be parasitized by the brown-backed honeybird (also known as the sharp-billed honeyguide) in the more easterly parts of its range.

KAROO PRINIA

Karoolangstertjie *(Prinia maculosa)*

Prinia maculosa hypoxantha

Size: Length 13-15 cm; weight 8-11 g.
Colour: Above brown; eyebrow and throat white; rest of underparts pale yellow, streaked black.
Most like: Other prinias, but streaked underparts diagnostic in all plumages.
Habitat: Montane and coastal scrub, Karoo, fynbos, tangled thickets along watercourses and roads, scrub around edges of vleis, gardens.

In southern Namibia, Western, Eastern and Northern Cape (except the drier northern parts), southern and eastern Free State, and the uplands of Mpumalanga, Swaziland, KwaZulu-Natal and Lesotho.

The Karoo prinia, also known as the spotted prinia, can become very tame and will build its nest less than two metres from you if you sit quietly and avoid making sudden movements. Listen for its rasping *krrrt-krrrt* callnotes as it skulks in the bushes and grass, or in the trees where it forages for insects on leaves and twigs.

Prinias all have longish tails that they often hold cocked up over their backs like wrens, hence the older name of 'wren warbler'. The Karoo prinia is the common species of high and dry country, being replaced in the east by the tawny-flanked prinia (*P. subflava*), and in the semi-desert and grassveld by the black-chested prinia (*P. flavicans*).

If you disturb a pair of Karoo prinias (especially when breeding) the birds will go to the top of a tall shrub or weed and perch there, giving their alarm calls as they flick their long tails about. They will then dive back into the vegetation and move off.

Nesting starts mainly in the spring in the summer-rainfall regions, but as early as July in the Western Cape, and continues until the end of summer. The oval nest is woven of fine grass blades and has an entrance at the side near the top. A lining of soft plant down completes the architecture and the female lays four pale blue eggs, with spots or blotches of brown or chestnut and grey. Both parents add lining throughout the 14-day incubation period and both feed their chicks during their two weeks in the nest.

The young birds, with lighter-coloured plumage than their parents, leave the nest when their tails are less than half the length of their adult counterparts.

Tree birds

African dusky flycatcher

Donkervlieëvanger *(Muscicapa adusta)*

Size: Length 13 cm; weight 12 g.

Colour: Above dark grey; below dull white, indistinctly streaked grey on breast and flanks; whitish eye-ring visible at close quarters.

Most like: Spotted flycatcher, but greyer and less distinctly streaked on underparts, and not spotted on forehead; somewhat similar to brown-backed honeybird, but lacks white outer tail feathers and grey wash on flanks.

Habitat: Evergreen and riverine forest, thickets in woodland, plantations, parks, gardens.

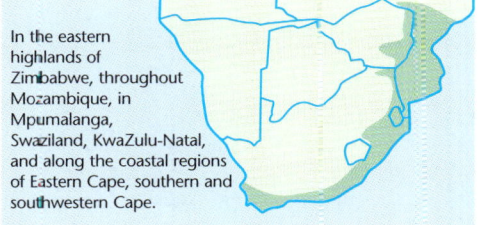

In the eastern highlands of Zimbabwe, throughout Mozambique, in Mpumalanga, Swaziland, KwaZulu-Natal, and along the coastal regions of Eastern Cape, southern and southwestern Cape.

The dusky flycatcher is one of southern Africa's least conspicuous little birds. It is overlooked very easily because of its dull coloration and unobtrusive ways. But once you have identified its two most frequent calls—one a thin, descending whistle and the other a sharp little *tsip-tsip-tsirrrt*—you will have no trouble locating and identifying it.

It has a habit of sallying out from a perch, snapping an insect in the air and returning to the perch this immediately identifies it as a flycatcher. Study the bird and try to make out the faintly streaked breast and pale eye-ring.

It doesn't catch all its food on the wing, but takes much of it from the surface of vegetation, as a warbler does. However, its habit of flicking its wings on landing will tell you immediately that it is not one of the warblers. Apart from insects, it occasionally eats small fruit.

African dusky flycatchers breed in spring and summer. They build small, cup-shaped nests of plant fibres mixed with moss and lichen in a concealed niche in a bank, tree or dense creeper, or in a fern basket hanging on an outside verandah or in a greenhouse. The clutch of three spotted eggs usually takes 14-15 days to hatch, and the nestling period is about 15 days. The fledglings are heavily spotted buff on grey when they eventually leave the nest and look quite different from the adults.

Chinspot batis

Witliesbosbontrokkie *(Batis molitor)*

Size: Length 12-13 cm; weight 8-14 g.

Colour: Above grey with black-and-white wing bars; face mask black, topped by narrow white eyebrow; below white with chestnut breastband and throat patch in female, black chest band in male; tail black with white outer feathers; eye yellow; bill, legs and feet black.

Most like: Other batises; flanks and wing with chestnut in Cape batis; back more mottled black and grey in male pale (Mozambique) batis, and breastband narrower; black markings on flanks of male pririt batis; female of Woodwards' and pririt batises have ochre, rather than chestnut, markings on throat and breast; female Woodwards' batis has rufous breastband.

Habitat: Savanna, open woodland, bushveld.

Northern Namibia, northern and eastern Botswana, Zimbabwe, most of Mozambique, Mpumalanga, Northern Province, Gauteng, KwaZulu-Natal and along the southeastern Cape coast to the Port Elizabeth region.

The male chinspot batis has a three-note song that sounds a bit like the opening notes of the nursery rhyme *Three Blind Mice*, though descending by only half a tone rather than a full tone. It also has a sandpapery alarm call, especially near its nest.

Chinspot batises are usually solitary or in pairs, foraging among the twigs and leaves of trees for small insects and spiders. They spend most of their time in the canopy, flying out every now and then to snap an insect in the air. The breeding male also snaps his wings in a territorial display flight over the treetops.

The nest of the chinspot batis is a tiny cup of plant material bound together and cemented with spider web to a horizontal branch or small fork, and decorated on the outside with flakes of lichen for camouflage. The female lays two pale, heavily blotched eggs which she incubates for 16-17 days during which time the male feeds her. Both parents feed the nestlings for about 17 days. After leaving the nest in their first mottled plumage, they accompany the parents for a further two weeks or so before becoming completely independent.

Tree birds

African paradise flycatcher
Paradysvlieëvanger
(*Terpsiphone viridis*)

Size: Length (including long tail) (m) 23-40 cm, (f) 16-18 cm; weight 11-17 g.
Colour: Back and tail (long in male) bright rusty red; crested head greenish black, shading to grey on breast and upper belly; lower belly white; bill and eye-ring bright blue to greenish blue.
Most like: Blue-mantled and white-tailed flycatchers, but rusty back and tail diagnostic.
Habitat: Forest edge, riverine bush, thickets in savanna and woodland, parks, gardens, exotic plantations.

Northern Namibia, northern and eastern Botswana, Mozambique, Mpumalanga, Swaziland, Gauteng, Northern Province, the North-West, KwaZulu-Natal, Free State, Eastern Cape and coastal southern and southwestern Cape.

African paradise flycatchers are firm favourites with everyone. These birds—particularly the males with their spectacular streaming tails—look like orange-red rockets as they swoop out from their perches to catch passing insects. Their beauty and tameness endear them to all, even those who know little about birds.

Usually solitary or in pairs, paradise flycatchers keep contact with *zweet-zwayt* callnotes that also serve as alarm calls when danger threatens. Their song is a delightful tripping *tzzee switty sweety-tsweep* phrase, fitting for so graceful a bird.

It is a restless bird, always on the move, darting about, landing and shooting off again to some other urgent business. It bathes by plunging into water from a perch, flying back up again, preening and shaking vigorously and then plunging again.

Both members of the pair select the nest site—usually a slender drooping branch, often over a stream—with much excited twittering, and both build the exquisite cup-shaped nest of roots, bark and other material, bound with spider web and decorated on the outside with lichens that camouflage it perfectly. In it the female lays two to three pink eggs with brick-red spots. They take about 14 days to hatch, and are incubated by both parents; the sitting male's tail droops over the edge of the nest in an arc.

Both parents feed the young for about 12 days.

Common fiscal
Fiskaallaksman (*Lanius collaris*)

Size: Length 21-23 cm; weight 34-58 g.
Colour: Above black; below white, sometimes washed grey on flanks and breast; white bar on folded wing forms V on upper back; eyebrow white in western birds; female has chestnut streak on lower flank; tail black with white outer feathers.
Most like: Fiscal flycatcher, but tail longish, slender and lacks white rectangular patches; wing bar on wing coverts, not on flight feathers; bill of common fiscal heavy and hooked.
Habitat: Almost any open country with trees, bushes or perches such as fence posts and telephone wires.

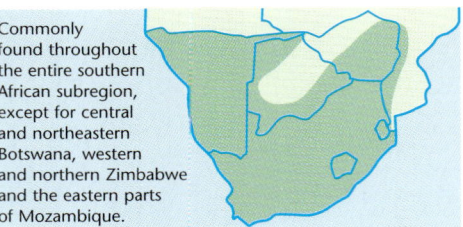

Commonly found throughout the entire southern African subregion, except for central and northeastern Botswana, western and northern Zimbabwe and the eastern parts of Mozambique.

Like most successful birds, the common fiscal (or fiscal shrike) has a wide choice of habitats and has adapted well to man's presence. It must be one of the best known birds of Africa outside of the forests, and you have probably seen one or a pair along the roadside, perched conspicuously on a wire or a tree. Its slim tail is often held at a slight angle to its body.

Well known for their harsh callnotes, common fiscals are disliked by many people, because they kill and eat small birds from time to time. However, this behaviour is natural and birds are not a staple ingredient in their diet. You should, in fact, welcome fiscals to your garden, where they will catch unwary insects, spiders and scorpions. These handsome birds also scan the ground below their perches for other delicacies—lizards or frogs. If a fiscal sees a foraging longclaw, it may take cover and wait to steal a large grasshopper from it as it emerges from a grass tuft; this behaviour is called kleptoparasitism, and is literally food-stealing.

The common fiscal builds a bulky, bowl-shaped nest of coarse plant material in a bush or tree, often unconcealed. In it the female lays three to four whitish eggs with cloudy yellowish olive markings which she incubates for about 16 days. She takes the greater share of feeding the young, though the male helps too. The fledglings leave the nest after about three weeks.

Tree birds

RED-BACKED SHRIKE

Rooiruglaksman
(Lanius collurio)

Size: *Length 17-18 cm; weight 21-46 g.*
Colour: *Male: blue-grey crown and mantle; russet back and wings; tail black with white outer feathers; face mask black; underparts white. Female: similar to male but less brightly coloured; underparts barred at sides; tail reddish brown; no face mask.*
Most like: *Souza's shrike, but lacks white bar; lesser grey shrike, but rufous colour on back diagnostic; heavy, hooked bill distinguishes shrikes from flycatchers.*
Habitat: *The red-backed shrike favours savanna, drier woodland, bushveld and farmland.*

Throughout the southern African subregion, except for the mountainous regions of KwaZulu-Natal and Lesotho, and the southeastern Cape, Western Cape and southern parts of the Northern Cape.

From Namibia to KwaZulu-Natal you can expect to see red-backed shrikes in summer wherever scrubby woodland occurs. Although not very common, the species is widespread in southern Africa from about October to April, coming to us from its breeding grounds in Europe and western Asia. It does a round trip of about 22 000 km every year on its migrations.

The red-backed shrike is a solitary bird and you can usually see it perched on a fence or the lower outer branches of a tree or bush, waiting to pounce on its prey of insects or small reptiles. Like most shrikes, it will also take nestling birds if they are available. This shrike impales its animal prey on thorns (a habit shared with common fiscals) and eats the impaled victims when food is scarce.

The different populations in Europe and Asia overlap during their southern African stay. Plumage differences show that red-backed shrikes from western Europe and western Siberia occur, together with those from southern Russia and the Crimea, right across from central Namibia to KwaZulu-Natal and Swaziland, while shrikes from central Russia and the more easterly parts of Siberia visit mainly the arid interior and western regions of southern Africa.

When red-backed shrikes return in the southern autumn they segregate again and go to their ancestral homes to nest.

SOUTHERN BOUBOU

Suidelike waterfiskaal *(Laniarius ferrugineus)*

Size: *Length 21-23 cm; weight 44-68 g.*
Colour: *Upperparts slaty black with bold white wing-stripe; below pinkish white with rich rufous wash on flanks and breast; tail black.*
Most like: *Tropical boubou, but distinguished by rufous wash below and somewhat smaller size; swamp boubou pure white below; tropical and swamp boubous glossy black (not dull slaty) above.*
Habitat: *Dense coastal and riverine bush, thickets, and bushy hillsides, forest edges, overgrown gardens.*

In southeastern Zimbabwe, southern Mozambique, Swaziland, Northern Province, Mpumalanga, Gauteng, North-West, northeastern Free State, KwaZulu-Natal, Eastern Cape, and coastal southern and southwestern Cape.

The southern boubou (pronounced *boo-boo*, and named after one of its many calls) has a confusing array of mellow and harsh calls and songs, usually performed in duet, with each bird ringing out the varied calls and notes alternately.

Birds which live in dense vegetation often have loud calls to compensate for the poor visibility. Some sing alone, others together, but almost any duet you hear in the denser bush of the southern Cape, KwaZulu-Natal and further north is likely to be made by a pair of southern boubous keeping contact with each other. They communicate with an almost endless variety of ringing, tooting and rasping notes; one bird will utter a series of calls and another will answer it with a different series, until the two may be singing in a delightful synchronized duet.

These boubous, endemic to southern Africa, are members of the bush-shrike family, a group not particularly closely related to the true shrikes, and found only in Africa south of the Sahara. They feed on a great variety of small animals, from insects to snakes and nestling birds, and will even take seeds, fruit and household scraps at times.

They breed in spring and summer, making a well-hidden, shallow bowl of roots and twigs one to four metres above the ground in a dense bush or creeper. The female lays two to three speckled eggs, which are incubated for 16 days by both parents. The young take about the same time to leave their nest, and accompany their parents for almost three months before gaining complete independence.

Tree birds

CRIMSON-BREASTED SHRIKE
Rooiborslaksman *(Laniarius atrococcineus)*

Size: Length 23 cm; weight 40-55 g.
Colour: Above jet black with conspicuous white wing-stripe; below brilliant crimson.
Most like: The boubous, except for crimson underparts.
Habitat: Semi-arid scrub and thornveld, lighter bushveld.

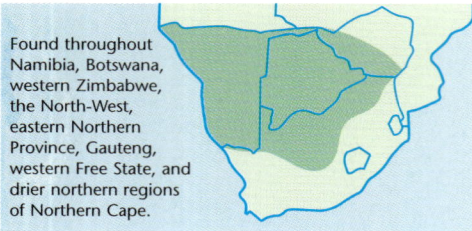

Found throughout Namibia, Botswana, western Zimbabwe, the North-West, eastern Northern Province, Gauteng, western Free State, and drier northern regions of Northern Cape.

Arguably the most beautiful bird in southern Africa, the crimson-breasted shrike never fails to elicit wonder from those who see it. Its combination of black, white and crimson—the colours of the flag of the old German Reich—have lead to its being called *Reichsvogel* or *Kaiservogel* by German-speakers in Namibia.

Although fairly shy at times, it will venture into the open, especially around rest camps in game reserves such as the Kgalagadi Transfrontier and Etosha national parks, where it has grown used to people.

It feeds on the ground, rather like a thrush, hopping and running in short bursts, stopping to pick up an item of food, and then running on again. This bird's menu consists mainly of insects, although it may occasionally take a meal of other small animals.

Almost always seen in pairs, crimson-breasted shrikes keep contact with each other by means of loud, sharp calls, sometimes almost in the form of a duet, that carry great distances. Ringing, tearing, zipping noises make up the song of this magnificent bird.

The nest, a bowl of bark strips lined with rootlets and grass, is placed on a stout branch or in the fork of a low tree, seldom higher than three metres above the ground. The birds breed in spring and summer when insects are most abundant. The clutch consists of two to three greenish eggs with brown and grey speckles. Both sexes incubate for 16 days and both feed the nestlings for 19 days. When they leave the nest, the fledglings are barred black-and-buff on the underparts, with just a dash of crimson under the tail.

BLACK-BACKED PUFFBACK
Sneeubal *(Dryoscopus cubla)*

Size: Length 17-18 cm; weight 20-36 g.
Colour: Black above, with white markings on wings and fluffy white rump; iris bright yellow, orange or red; female duller than male, with white extending onto face; legs and feet grey.
Most like: Brubru, but lacks white eyebrow and chestnut streak on flank. Smaller than common fiscal, shorter-tailed and with different habitat and habits.
Habitat: Canopy of trees in woodland, riverine and lowland forest; exotic plantations.

Northern Namibia, Botswana, Zimbabwe, Mozambique, Mpumalanga, Gauteng, Northern Province, the North-West, northeastern Free State, KwaZulu-Natal, extreme Northern Cape and along the southeastern Cape coast to Port Elizabeth.

Because it keeps very much to the top of trees, you will probably hear a black-backed puffback before you see it—its sharp whistling, rasping and clicking calls ringing intermittently through the foliage as the birds forage for insects on the leaves and branches. These birds, almost invariably found in pairs, usually communicate with a two-syllabled *click-weeu*, repeated several times.

In display the male has a habit of raising the feathers of his white rump so that they produce a beautiful powder-puff effect—hence its English and Afrikaans names. You won't see this display too often, but it's certainly well worth waiting for, so keep a close watch on a pair if you're lucky enough to spot them. Puffbacks are not shy and you can get a fairly good look at them if you are prepared to wait until they come out onto an open branch.

Their flight is bouncy, with loud wingbeats.

In summer the males establish their territories and the females build their beautiful cup-shaped nests high in the trees. The nest is small and neatly made of plant fibres felted together with spider web, which also binds the nest to the site—a thin, upright fork. The female lays two or three spotted and streaked eggs. Both parents incubate for 13 days and the nestlings take 17 days to reach flying age. Once they have learned to fly, they stay with their parents to form a close family unit until the beginning of the next breeding season.

Tree birds

BOKMAKIERIE

Bokmakierie *(Telophorus zeylonus)*

Size: Length 22-24 cm; weight 57-76 g.

Colour: Olive-green back with grey crown and nape; tail tipped black and yellow; below bright yellow with broad black collar on breast; eyebrow yellow.

Most like: Gorgeous bush shrike, but throat yellow, not red; habitat quite different; differs from other bush shrikes in having black collar.

Habitat: Scrub or bushy thickets on hillside, valley slopes, watercourses, open grassland; also in gardens, parks, fynbos and farmyards.

Western and southern Namibia, Northern, Western and Eastern Cape, Free State, the North-West, Gauteng, Mpumalanga, and KwaZulu-Natal highlands. Also in eastern Zimbabwe and adjacent Mozambique.

The bokmakierie is one of South Africa's favourite birds. Most people who live in the highveld know it for its cheerful song heard throughout the year: a ringing duet that echoes in mountainous regions, adds to the domestic sounds on a Free State farm, or breaks the silence in the vast spaces of the Namib Desert, where the only cover is the shrubby vegetation along dry watercourses.

Not only is the bokmakierie a superb vocalist but it is also beautiful to look at. When it sings it perches high on a bush, rock or fence, lifts its bill skyward and really looks as if it is thoroughly enjoying itself. The bird's name derives from one of its calls, but it has a variety of the most marvellous bell-like notes, augmented by ascending or descending trills and some harsh rolling notes.

Bokmakieries forage on the ground for insects, small reptiles and frogs; they also take nestling birds and domestic scraps. When disturbed they fly up into a bush, showing their brilliant yellow tail tips as they go. Once sheltered by cover, they are difficult to see because of their green backs.

From midwinter to autumn these birds build their bowl-shaped nests in dense bush or trees. The three eggs in the clutch are vivid turquoise blue with red spots; they take 15-16 days to hatch. Both parents feed the young for about 18 days.

ORANGE-BREASTED BUSH SHRIKE

Oranjeborslaksman *(Telophorus sulfureopectus)*

Size: Length 18-19 cm; weight 20-32 g.

Colour: Crown to mantle grey; rest of upperparts, including tail, green; tail tipped yellow; forehead and eyebrow yellow; small black mask over eye; below bright yellow with bright orange wash across breast.

Most like: Grey-headed bush shrike, but bill less heavy, and black face mask distinctive; black-fronted bush shrike, but yellow eyebrow distinctive; olive phase of olive bush shrike, but black face mask does not extend to neck, yellow eyebrow extends to forehead, head grey, tail green.

Habitat: Valley bushveld, thickets in thornveld.

In the moister regions of Northern Namibia, northern and eastern Botswana, Zimbabwe, Mozambique, Northern Province and the lowlands of KwaZulu-Natal and the Eastern Cape.

Like most bush shrikes, the orange-breasted species skulks in dense vegetation, but you can call it out easily with a whistled imitation or a playback of a recording of its melodious song. It also responds to a 'spishing' sound, but be ready with your binoculars before you call it up as it only ventures out into the open for a short while.

This lovely bird is a real gem of the bushveld and fortunately it is quite common. It spends most of its time high in the bushes and trees, snapping up insects on leaves and branches.

Although usually solitary, the orange-breasted bush shrike often joins mixed bird parties or loose flocks of different species. Together the birds move through the bush, all benefiting from the insects disturbed by each other's movements.

The orange-breasted bush shrike nests in summer, building a shallow and rather flimsy saucer of twigs, scantily lined with rootlets. Oddly enough, although the adults are so shy, the nest may not be at all well hidden. Two eggs, dull greenish with cloudy markings of brown and grey, form the clutch.

The incubation habits of this bird haven't been recorded, but the nestling period is only about 12 days. The young birds, which are fed by both parents, have dull plumage, with blackish bars above and below.

Tree birds

WHITE-CRESTED HELMETSHRIKE

Withelmlaksman
(*Prionops plumatus*)

Size: Length 19-20 cm; weight 25-39 g.
Colour: Crown grey; slightly bushy white crest on forehead; back and tail black with white wing-stripe and white outer tail feathers; underparts and forehead white; black stripe on side of neck; legs, feet and large wattle around eye yellow.
Most like: Lesser grey shrike, but white forehead and yellow eye-wattle of the white-crested helmetshrike is diagnostic (forehead black in lesser grey shrike).
Habitat: Occurs in deciduous woodland, bushveld, acacia savanna.

In northern Namibia and the Caprivi Strip, Botswana (except the dry southwestern parts), Zimbabwe, Mozambique, Northern Province, eastern Swaziland and the northern parts of KwaZulu-Natal.

The sight and sound of a chattering throng of white-crested helmetshrikes in the African bush is always refreshing. Like big black-and-white butterflies the birds flutter from bush to bush in groups of about ten, sometimes as many as twenty. Although rather noisy when feeding, they fly silently and arrive quite suddenly and unexpectedly. They roost communally in a huddled row on a branch.

You can see these birds foraging in trees and bushes, as well as on the ground, keeping contact with their ratchety callnotes, sometimes calling as a group.

Their big yellow eye-rings make them look somewhat startled, and their habit of raising their bushy white frontal crests accentuates the look of innocent surprise.

White-crested helmetshrikes feed mostly on insects and spiders, but also take small vertebrates at times. Quite tame around human settlements, they are often seen at bushveld campsites. The flocks consist of a nucleus of two or more adults and several young from previous broods.

When breeding, these family groups form co-operatives, because the nonbreeding members help the breeding adults with nesting duties. The nest is a neat cup of felted plant fibres and spider web placed on a horizontal branch a few metres from the ground. Up to nine spotted and blotched eggs form a clutch if more than one adult female is present in the group, but one female alone seldom produces more than four eggs. All members of the group help to incubate the eggs (17 days) and feed the nestlings (20 days).

COMMON STARLING

Europese spreeu (*Sturnus vulgaris*)

Size: Length 19-22 cm; weight 55-96 g.
Colour: Iridescent black with violet-green sheen, faintly spotted with white and buff; wing and tail feathers have brown edges; bill bright yellow; nonbreeding birds are more heavily spotted than breeding birds.
Most like: Common myna, but starling is black below (not brown) and lacks the yellow eye-patch and white wing-patch.
Habitat: Cities, towns, farmyards.

Throughout Namaqualand, the Western Cape, most of the Eastern Cape and eastwards into southern KwaZulu-Natal.

The common, or European, starling's quick flight and brisk walk give it a jaunty air. One of the smaller starlings in southern Africa, it was introduced to Cape Town by Cecil Rhodes in 1899. Since then it has spread eastwards into KwaZulu-Natal and northwards as far as the Gariep (Orange) River, always along manmade routes to human settlements. It owes its success to its catholic diet of all kinds of animal and plant foods (insects, snails, worms, seeds, fruit and so on), and to the way it has adapted to man's environment, especially to his agricultural practices.

This bird has become a pest in the fruit orchards and vineyards of the Western Cape, but it probably also does quite a lot of good by eating large numbers of insects on lawns and in cultivated fields. It feeds mostly by probing into the grass with its bill closed, opening the bill to expand the hole, and then extracting the insect or worm from inside the cavity.

Common starlings roost in thousands on buildings and in tall trees where they nest. In the early summer, the female lays three to six pale blue eggs in a bowl lined with plant material, feathers and other soft fibres, and incubates them for 12-13 days. Both parents feed the nestlings for about three weeks; this long nestling period is typical of hole-nesting birds.

As the starlings expand their territory eastwards, they encounter common mynas with increasing frequency. It will be interesting to see how the two species compete with each other for the manmade niche they have both adopted.

Tree birds

COMMON MYNA

Indiese spreeu *(Acridotheres tristis)*

Size: Length 21-25 cm; weight 82-138 g.
Colour: Head, breast and tail black; rest of body rich brown; wing-patch, tip of tail and undertail white; legs, feet, bill and bare eye-patch bright yellow.
Most like: Common starling, but brown body, white wing-patch and yellow eye-patch diagnostic.
Habitat: Human settlements (cities, towns, villages).

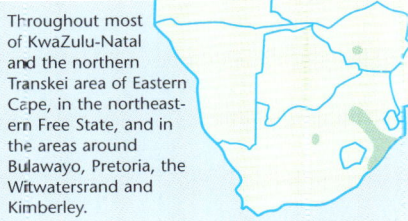

Throughout most of KwaZulu-Natal and the northern Transkei area of Eastern Cape, in the northeastern Free State, and in the areas around Bulawayo, Pretoria, the Witwatersrand and Kimberley.

Like common starlings, common mynas were introduced into South Africa in the late 19th century via Durban. Nearly 40 years later they were encountered on the Witwatersrand, having spread naturally or been introduced there. Since then they have been recorded throughout KwaZulu-Natal and have reached the Transkei area of the Eastern Cape, Kimberley, Pretoria and Bulawayo in Zimbabwe.

Lines of expansion lie along roads and railways, the birds moving from one set of buildings to another. No sooner is a suburban housing scheme started, than the mynas are already prospecting the houses under construction for suitable nesting and roosting sites. Their capitalistic ways have had tremendous success in ensuring the expansion of the species, but the fear that they drive our indigenous birds away is probably unfounded, for the myna fills an urban niche that few of our indigenous birds have taken to in any significant way.

Common mynas roost in thousands in large trees, especially in winter when they are not breeding. If every occupant of every building in the bird's range were to block every possible nesting site, the myna 'problem' would almost disappear in a short time, because the bird would simply be unable to breed.

They build their untidy bowl-shaped nests in holes or crevices in buildings. Up to five turquoise eggs form the clutch, which takes about 18 days to hatch. Both parents feed the chicks for about 23 days in the nest; they continue to beg for food for several weeks after flying.

VIOLET-BACKED STARLING

Witborsspreeu *(Cinnyricinclus leucogaster)*

Size: Length 17,5-19 cm; weight 33-55 g.
Colour: Male is brilliant iridescent purple; belly and outer tail feathers white; female is brown above, streaked black; below white with heavy blackish streaks; eye yellow in both sexes; bill, legs and feet black.
Most like: Male looks like no other southern African bird; female somewhat similar to female thick-billed weaver, but bill slender and all black.
Habitat: Bushveld, savanna, woodland, gallery forest along watercourses.

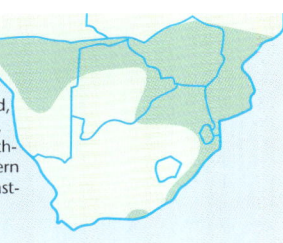

Northern Namibia, northern and eastern Botswana, Zimbabwe, Mozambique, Swaziland, Gauteng, Mpumalanga, Northern Province, north-eastern Free State, eastern KwaZulu-Natal, northeastern Cape and the area around Port Elizabeth.

One of southern Africa's most beautiful birds, the male violet-backed starling has a metallic-looking plumage that shines black, purple, red or rose, depending on how the sunlight falls on it, and it is offset by the brilliant white belly. The female is sometimes difficult to identify because she is so unlike the male and bears equally little resemblance to other starlings, but her heavily streaked plumage is a good clue.

Violet-backed starlings (also called plum-coloured or amethyst starlings) move about in small flocks when they are not breeding. They spend most of their day foraging in trees, especially among the upper branches. Their food is mostly fruit and insects.

An interesting and characteristic habit of these birds is to flick their wings after landing in a tree. Their flight is fast and straight, fairly typical of the smaller starlings.

You can see this handsome bird only from October to April in southern Africa, after which it leaves for more northerly parts, such as Zambia, Angola and even further afield.

The nest is typically that of a starling: a pad of grass, hair and dry dung placed in a hole in a tree. The pad is then lined with fresh green leaves throughout the incubation period of about 12 days. The female incubates the two to four greenish blue eggs with brown and purple spots. Both parents feed the young for three weeks until they leave the nest.

Tree birds

CAPE GLOSSY STARLING

Kleinglansspreeu (*Lamprotornis nitens*)

Size: Length 22-23 cm; weight 78-104 g.
Colour: Glossy black with bright metallic green reflections; ear coverts glossed purplish; coppery patch on bend of wing; bright orange-yellow eye.
Most like: Greater and lesser blue-eared starlings, and black-bellied starling; glossier than black-bellied, especially underparts; less silky-lustrous than blue-eared starlings, and with less contrasting ear coverts; voice diagnostic.
Habitat: Woodland, savanna, semi-arid scrub, riverine bush, farmyards, gardens.

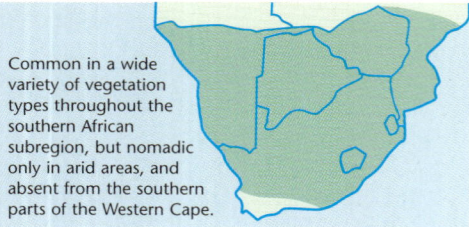

Common in a wide variety of vegetation types throughout the southern African subregion, but nomadic only in arid areas, and absent from the southern parts of the Western Cape.

If you see one of the metallic green starlings, listen for the distinctive *turr-rreeu* callnote of the Cape glossy starling before deciding on its identification. It lacks the whining quality of the calls of the greater blue-eared starling and the harshness of those of the lesser blue-eared starling. Otherwise the three species appear very similar, though their differences show up clearly if you see them together.

Cape glossy starlings tolerate many different habitats and can be found in the most inhospitable parts of southern Namibia, as well as around forest edges on the KwaZulu-Natal south coast. They forage on the ground, running in bursts and then stopping to look around or pick up insects. They also take fruit and nectar, especially that of aloes.

As they take off, the wings of Cape glossy starlings make a characteristic zipping noise caused by the shape of the flight feathers. They are wary birds, but not especially shy, and spend long periods singing their warbling song from a perch in a tree.

The female nests in summer, in a hole in a tree or building, a hollow fence post or on a ledge in a chimney. Here she builds a pad of grass, paper and other fibres, and lays three greenish blue eggs with rusty speckles. The nestlings hatch after an incubation period of about two weeks, and the parents feed them for nearly three weeks.

RED-BILLED OXPECKER

Rooibekrenostervoël (*Buphagus erythrorhynchus*)

Size: Length 20-22 cm; weight 42-59 g.
Colour: Head, breast and upperparts brown; rest of underparts creamy white; bill and eye red; bright yellow ring around the eye.
Most like: Yellow-billed oxpecker, but bill all red (red at tip only in yellow-billed) and upperparts almost uniform brown (rump very pale in yellow-billed).
Habitat: Bushveld, savanna, woodland.

In northern Namibia, northern and eastern Botswana, Zimbabwe (except the central and eastern highlands), Mozambique, Gauteng, Northern Province and North-West lowveld, eastern Swaziland and northern KwaZulu-Natal.

Red-billed oxpeckers have a marvellous relationship with game mammals in which the two different groups live together for each other's mutual benefit. The oxpeckers get their food of ticks and horseflies from the mammals, as well as nesting material in the form of hair. In return, the mammals benefit in two ways: the oxpeckers rid them of parasites, and warn them of approaching danger.

If you visit the Kruger National Park or one of the game reserves in KwaZulu-Natal, you will probably see small groups of red-billed oxpeckers clambering on the bodies the bigger game mammals, from impalas and the larger antelopes to white rhinoceros, giraffes and zebras. In farming areas these brown birds with red bills have adopted cattle and horses as hosts but, because domestic stock is dipped to rid them of ticks and other parasites, oxpeckers have become rare outside game reserves; not only has the dip eliminated an important food source for them, but it has also poisoned them.

Red-billed oxpeckers give 'chittering' and hissing calls when alarmed and when flying, mainly to keep contact with one another, but also as alarm calls. They roost at night, usually in palm trees or reed beds, but sometimes in tree holes or stone walls.

They breed in tree holes and line the floor of their nests with grass and hair. Both parents incubate the clutch of two or three pinkish-white, speckled eggs for 13 days. Both parents and up to three helpers feed the chicks until they are ready to leave the nest after about a month.

Tree birds

Cape sugarbird

Kaapse suikervoël
(*Promerops cafer*)

Size: Length (m) 37-44 cm, including tail, (f) 24-29 cm; weight 26-39 g.

Colour: Upperparts and long, floppy tail brown, streaked blackish; underparts white, washed rufous on breast; undertail bright yellow; black stripe on each side of white throat.

Most like: Gurney's sugarbird but tail much longer and breast less brightly russet.

Habitat: Fynbos with proteas in winter-rainfall region.

This species is limited in its distribution to the extreme southwestern and southern Cape, extending as far as the Grahamstown area.

Sugarbirds are the only family of birds unique to southern Africa. There are only two species in the family, with the Cape sugarbird of the Western and southern Cape being the more spectacular because of its longer tail. Sugarbirds have long, curved bills for probing deep into tubular flowers for nectar. You will see them perched on indigenous proteas, red-hot pokers, watsonias and heaths, and also on the flowers of introduced agave and eucalyptus. Apart from nectar, these birds also eat insects which they find in the flowers or catch in the air.

Cape sugarbirds are usually solitary, though they may gather in groups of up to a dozen birds where nectar-bearing flowers are abundant.

The male displays with his long, graduated tail which he flicks up and down when flying over his territory. The tail also blows about in the strong winds of the Western Cape when the bird perches on a protea bush to sing—its song is a noisy creaking, chipping and twanging jumble of phrases. Its rasping alarm call has been likened to the sound made by a rusty metal hinge.

Nesting is closely tied to proteas, both for nest sites and for food during the flowering season, which is mainly in winter. The cup-shaped nest of twigs and grass built in the fork of a protea bush, or some other bush or tree, is lined with protea down. The female lays two eggs—cream or pink with black, brown and grey markings—and incubates them for 17 days. Both parents feed the chicks until they leave the nest at the age of about 20 days.

Malachite sunbird

Jangroentjie (*Nectarinia famosa*)

Size: Length (m) 24-26 cm, including tail, (f) 15 cm; weight (m) 15-21 g, (f) 12-17 g.

Colour: Male: bright metallic malachite green; yellow tufts at sides of chest rarely shown in display; female: yellowish grey above; below whitish, washed yellowish grey on breast; throat yellowish; outer tail feathers white.

Most like: Male resembles male bronze sunbird, but is greener; female similar to some other female sunbirds, but large size, long bill and white tail feathers diagnostic.

Habitat: Montane grasslands and scrub, riverine bush, fynbos, succulent semi-desert, gardens.

In Namaqualand, the Karoo, Western Cape, southeastern Cape, eastern Free State, Lesotho, inland KwaZulu-Natal, Gauteng and Mpumalanga highveld and the highlands of Zimbabwe and adjacent Mozambique.

The brilliant green male malachite sunbird, with his cheerful, piping calls, is a familiar and beautiful sight in the highveld, the Western Cape or Namaqualand. He is a lively character, always on the move, darting from flower to flower, his long central tail feathers streaming out behind his vivid body. He often perches right on top of a bush to display and sing; when he sees a female, he may raise his tail and expose his yellow pectoral tufts as he shivers his wings and sings quietly.

The female is quieter and her colour much more subdued, since she doesn't have to advertise herself or her territory. Members of a mated pair are seldom seen together, except when the male is chasing the female in wild flight, snapping at her tail. This is all part of the courtship display and pair-bonding.

The long bill is used to probe into flowers for nectar and insects, though many insects are also caught in flight with a loud snapping of the bill.

The female builds the beautiful oval nest of grass and leaves and binds it all together with spider web. She fixes the nest to a drooping branch, often overhanging a road, stream or steep bank, and lays inside it two cloudy grey eggs which she incubates for 13 days. The nestlings take nearly three weeks to leave the nest.

Tree birds

ORANGE-BREASTED SUNBIRD
Oranjeborssuikerbekkie
(*Anthobaphes violacea*)

Size: Length (m) 17 cm, (f) 13 cm; weight (m) 9-11 g, (f) 8-9,7 g.
Colour: Male bright metallic green on head and upper back; rest of back olive; breast metallic purple; belly bright orange; tail black with long central feathers; the female is greenish grey above; dull yellow below; the wings and tail are dusky.
Most like: Male quite distinctive (the only southern African sunbird with orange belly); female similar to female southern double-collared sunbird, but yellower.
Habitat: Fynbos in winter-rainfall region.

Limited in distribution to the winter-rainfall regions of the extreme southwestern and southern Cape.

SOUTHERN DOUBLE-COLLARED SUNBIRD
Klein-rooibandsuikerbekkie (*Cinnyris chalybea*)

Size: Length 11-13 cm; weight (m) 6-10 g, (f) 6-9,5 g.
Colour: Male bright metallic green on head and back; rump blue; breast bright red topped by metallic blue collar; belly grey; female dull grey above, yellowish grey below.
Most like: Greater double-collared sunbird, but male's red breast narrower (only 8mm wide); bill shorter; miombo double-collared sunbird, but no grey on rump; Neergaard's sunbird, but belly grey, not black; female not safely distinguishable from females of miombo double-collared and Neergaard's sunbirds.
Habitat: Evergreen forest and bush, lush gardens, riverine bush, succulent semi-desert.

Along the Drakensberg and Soutpansberg escarpment, in western Swaziland, central KwaZulu-Natal, along the Eastern and Western Cape coastal belt, and into Namaqualand and adjacent southern Namibia.

The orange-breasted sunbird is one of the prettiest of all the bird species unique to the South African winter-rainfall region. The brilliantly coloured male is a jewel, and is often accompanied on his foraging trips by the sombre, neat female in her yellowish grey suit.

You can see orange-breasted sunbirds in great numbers in the Western Cape's Kirstenbosch Botanic Gardens, along with other local specials such as Cape sugarbirds, feeding on the abundance of nectar-bearing plants such as proteas and ericas. They are tame little birds and fly fearlessly within a few centimetres of you. As many as 50 or 60 may occur together at a good food supply.

Like all sunbirds, the orange-breasted catches insects in flight in between probing for nectar. You will often see it darting about, twittering loudly, especially at the start of the breeding season in winter.

The female builds a purse-shaped nest of twigs and grass, held together with spider web and tucked into a low shrub, usually less than a metre above ground. She lines the inside with soft down from proteas and lays two lightly blotched eggs, which she incubates for a fortnight. The chicks take 20 days to reach flying age. The family stays together for up to two weeks after the youngsters first leave the nest.

It is difficult to predict where you will see a southern (or lesser) double-collared sunbird—in spite of its limited range it enjoys a wide range of habitats. However, if you do happen to see one, be sure to take a careful look at its bill (which should be relatively short) and its red breastband (which should be narrower than ten millimetres); otherwise you may well be looking at a greater double-collared sunbird.

The voice of this little sunbird, raised in a rapid twittering song of rather sharp notes, is so high-pitched it is sometimes almost inaudible.

Its diet consists of the nectar of both indigenous and exotic flowers, the juice of overripe figs, as well as insects and spiders, which it catches by hovering in front of the webs and picking them out with the tip of its bill.

The nesting time varies according to the time of the rainy season; in the Western Cape and Namaqualand it takes place mainly in winter, in the east mainly in summer. The typical sunbird nest, an oval with an entrance at the side near the top, is suspended from a branch or vine low down near the ground. The female builds and incubates on her own. The clutch of two eggs takes 13 days to hatch and the chicks leave the nest after about 17 days.

Tree birds

SCARLET-CHESTED SUNBIRD

Rooiborssuikerbekkie *(Chalcomitra senegalensis)*

Size: *Length 13-15 cm; weight (m) 15-16 g, (f) 10,2-15,3 g.*

Colour: *Male sooty black with scarlet breast and metallic green throat and crown; female brown above; below mottled on breast and streaked on belly with brown and pale yellow; wing feathers edged with white.*

Most like: *Male unmistakeable; female like female amethyst sunbird, but yellower below and without black throat-patch or distinct black streaks on breast.*

Habitat: *Woodland, savanna, gardens.*

In Namibia (except the extreme dry south and west), northern Botswana, Zimbabwe, Mozambique, Swaziland, Northern Province and Mpumalanga lowveld, and through lowland KwaZulu-Natal to the Eastern Cape.

The belligerent nature of the scarlet-chested sunbird is clearly shown by its frequent habit of fighting its reflection in windows or the hubcaps of cars. Like most sunbirds, it is aggressive and noisy, giving loud, piercing chirps and whistles from a conspicuous perch in a tree. The magnificent male that behaves like this is one of the most handsome birds of subtropical Africa, and can be seen in the Kruger National Park.

Scarlet-chested sunbirds are usually solitary, though you can see pairs in the breeding season. Because they appear and disappear seasonally in some areas, particularly in the south of their range, they may have some kind of regular migration, but it is not known for certain where they go.

Despite their aggressiveness, these sunbirds may forage with other species of sunbirds at rich sources of nectar, such as flowering aloes and erythrinas. They take nectar by probing into the flowers with their long bills, either perching on the flower stalks or hovering in front of them. Their diet also includes spiders and insects.

The oval nest of leaves, grass, paper and other material is hung from a branch quite high above the ground. The female lays two cloudy grey eggs and incubates them on her own for about 14 days. The male may help her feed the young for 17 days or so, until they leave the nest.

CAPE WHITE-EYE

Kaapse glasogie *(Zosterops pallidus)*

Size: *Length 10-13 cm; weight 7,7-14,6 g.*

Colour: *Above greyish green; below grey, greenish, whitish or rufous, with yellow throat and undertail; eye-ring conspicuously white.*

Most like: *African yellow white-eye, but never uniformly bright yellow below; upperparts greener, without yellow wash. Similar to some small warblers, but eye-ring of Cape white-eye always diagnostic.*

Habitat: *Forest, woodland, riverine bush, gardens, parks.*

In central and southern Namibia, most of South Africa (except the extreme Northern Cape). Also in southeastern Botswana, adjacent Zimbabwe, southwestern Mozambique, Swaziland and Lesotho.

Most South Africans are familiar with the Cape white-eye, a favourite, friendly garden bird found as far afield as the Namib Desert where it inhabits trees and bushes along watercourses. White-eyes come readily to birdbaths and feeding trays supplied with fruit. They usually appear in bands of up to a dozen birds, flitting from leaf to twig, busily gleaning insects from the surfaces of trees and other plants; as they do so they perform all kinds of acrobatics, hanging sideways and even upside down as they diligently search for food. Occasionally you can see bigger flocks of up to 100 birds in winter.

The flocks often come down to drink, and sometimes bathe, at pools or birdbaths. They then fly up to the branches of nearby trees to shake and preen until dry. As they move restlessly about, the birds keep contact with each other with musical chirrups and twitters.

The Cape white-eye's song, which you can hear in early summer, is a loud set of sweet piping notes, often incorporating imitations of other birds' calls and songs.

Its nest, a beautiful, sometimes translucent, little cup made of fine plant fibres, grass and strips of lichen and bark, bound together with spider web, is suspended in a small horizontal fork. In it the female lays two or three white or pale blue eggs. Both sexes share incubation for about 11 days and feed the chicks for a further 12 days. The parents guard their nests carefully and will give loud alarm calls if you approach too closely.

Tree birds

WHITE-BROWED SPARROWWEAVER
Koringvoël *(Plocepasser mahali)*

Size: *Length 16-18 cm; weight (m) 43-53 g, (f) 40-54 g.*
Colour: *Crown and face blackish; back brown; eyebrow, rump and underparts white; wings and tail dusky, edged white; breast spotted brown in northern birds (Zimbabwe and Mozambique); eye reddish brown.*
Most like: *Some male sparrows, but larger, with no rufous in plumage; white rump distinctive.*
Habitat: *Drier woodland and savanna, farmyards.*

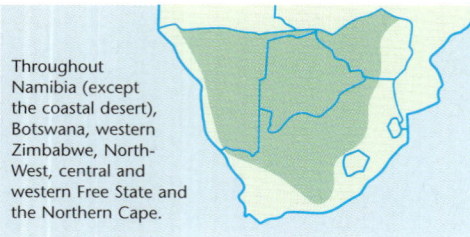

Throughout Namibia (except the coastal desert), Botswana, western Zimbabwe, North-West, central and western Free State and the Northern Cape.

Conspicuous groups of straw nests—usually ten or a dozen, sometimes many more—in the trees are a sure sign that white-browed sparrowweavers are around. A colony of these birds, usually numbering four to five, but sometimes as many as nine, will build their nests close together in one or two adjacent trees. Each group consists of a mated pair of birds and one or more helpers. Group sizes tend to be bigger in Zimbabwe than in South Africa.

The next thing that will attract your attention to these handsome birds is their loud, sometimes musical, calls and songs consisting of full-bodied, rolling notes. When you finally see them you will be struck by their bold plumage and white rump that is so conspicuous in flight.

Seldom far from their nest tree, white-browed sparrowweavers feed on the ground, mainly on seeds, though they take enough insects to make them independent of drinking water. They roost in their nests at night. Each nest has two entrances, so a bird can make a quick getaway.

At the start of the breeding season, one of the nests is modified by blocking one of the entrances to make an egg chamber. In it the female lays one to three pale pink or white eggs with beautiful pink, brown and grey markings that form clouds and spots. The chicks take 14 days to hatch and are incubated only by the breeding female. However, all members of the colony feed the young, which leave the nest after 22 days.

SOCIABLE WEAVER
Versamelvoël *(Philetairus socius)*

Size: *Length 14 cm; weight 20,8-32 g.*
Colour: *Mostly deep buff, mottled on the back with black; deeper brown on top of head; black face mask; sides of belly marked with black arrowheads.*
Most like: *Some of the true weavers (southern masked, village), but never bright yellow.*
Habitat: *Kalahari acacia woodland, tree-lined watercourses in Namibia and rocky, semi-desert regions with kokerboom.*

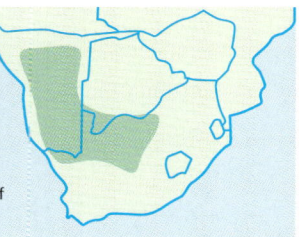

Common in the drier areas of central and southern Namibia, southern Botswana, western North-West, western Free State, northern Namaqualand and northernmost areas of the Northern Cape.

With the ingenuity of accomplished architects, sociable weavers build huge, co-operative apartment houses in the thorn trees and kokerbooms of the Northern Cape and Namibia. These huge grass nests, looking more like the thatched roofs of rondavels than massive tenement blocks, are a unique sight. A single colony of sociable weavers may number as many as 300 birds (rarely fewer than ten), and all the birds jointly maintain the nest throughout the year.

The nest mass contains of many chambers, each about as big as a man's fist, leading to the outside via a vertical tube about 20 cm long. The grass straws in this tube are arranged with their sharp, nipped-off ends pointing down and inward—a natural deterrent to predators trying to get into the nest. Only snakes, mainly Cape cobras, can effectively bypass this gauntlet to enter the nest chambers in search of eggs and young.

Like many birds of semi-desert regions, the sociable weaver breeds only after rain when the insects on which it feeds become plentiful. The full clutch varies from two to six eggs, each taking 14 days to hatch. The young leave the nest about three weeks later and then help their parents to feed the next brood. Because sociable weavers feed predominantly on insects, they do not need to drink water.

Tree birds

CAPE SPARROW

Gewone mossie
(Passer melanurus)

Size: Length 14-16 cm; weight 20-38 g.
Colour: Male has black head with bold semicircle of white on each side; upper back grey; lower back and upper wing bright rusty; wing bar and underparts white; tail black; eye dark brown; female similar to male, but grey where male black, and generally duller.
Most like: Southern grey-headed sparrow, but the pale semicircle on the sides of the head is diagnostic; the male is unmistakeable; rusty rump distinguishes all African sparrows from introduced house sparrow.
Habitat: Savanna, semi-desert, riverine bush, farmland, plantations, gardens, parks, urban areas.

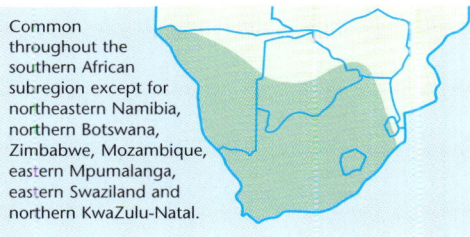

Common throughout the southern African subregion except for northeastern Namibia, northern Botswana, Zimbabwe, Mozambique, eastern Mpumalanga, eastern Swaziland and northern KwaZulu-Natal.

The mellow, cheerful song of the Cape sparrow is a typical sound of daybreak, and can be heard throughout southern Africa, with the exception of the lowveld areas.

This bird is familiar to most people because of its adoption of manmade environments. It often feeds alongside the house sparrow in city streets, railway yards and farmyards where it picks up fallen grain and scraps. Cape sparrows also come readily to feeding trays in gardens.

While adult birds only occasionally eat insects, youngsters are fed mainly on insect larvae, especially caterpillars.

Cape sparrows are very common in the arid and semi-arid parts of southern Africa, sometimes occurring in flocks of hundreds when food is plentiful.

The untidy nest is a familiar sight in the highveld, whether it is in a tree or bush, on a telephone pole or in the brackets of a traffic light. The chamber inside the mass of grass and weeds is lined thickly with feathers and other soft materials. The usual clutch is three to four greenish eggs, thickly clouded and spotted with grey and brown. The female does most of the incubation for the 14 days it takes the eggs to hatch; though the male assists by day. Both parents feed the young in the nest for about three weeks, and out of the nest for a further week or two.

VILLAGE WEAVER

Bontrugwewer *(Ploceus cucullatus)*

Size: Length 15-17 cm; weight (m) 25-45 g, (f) 26-43 g.
Colour: Breeding male brilliant yellow with black face mask ending in point on breast (head all black in northern birds); heavy black mottling on back; bill black; female and eclipse male mottled grey and brown on back; rump brown; crown olive; throat yellow; rest of underparts white with greyish tinge on breast and flanks; male always has red eyes.
Most like: Southern masked weaver, but heavily mottled back and yellow forehead (southern birds) or all-black head (northern birds) distinctive; mask of lesser masked weaver is rounded below; female and eclipse male not safely separable from other female and eclipse male weavers.
Habitat: Woodland, savanna, riverine bush, parks, gardens, forest edge.

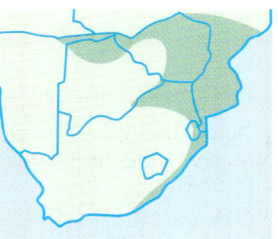

In Caprivi Strip, northern and south-eastern Botswana, most of Zimbabwe, Mozambique, Northern Province, eastern Swaziland, eastern KwaZulu-Natal and along the Eastern Cape coast.

People often confuse the village (or spotted-backed) and southern masked weavers, but the former prefer more subtropical locations. They are noisy and vigorous, best known for their conspicuous nesting colonies in towns and also for their habit of stripping the leaves from the branches of plane and palm trees on which they build their nests.

The leaf-stripping does not harm the tree and has probably evolved to make the nest more conspicuous for display purposes, and less accessible to predators.

Their call is a lovely, rolling *cheee cheee shrrrr* song, punctuated at the end by an unusual wheezing sound; in flight, their call is a staccato *chip chip*.

The village weaver's diet consists of seeds, insects and household scraps, as well as nectar.

Several males share a nesting tree, and each breeding male will attract a number of females to his part of the territory. The nests form part of their courtship and you can see the males displaying beneath them, hanging upside down and fluttering their wings as they pivot from side to side. A paired female lays a clutch of two or three eggs which vary in colour and markings. She incubates for about 12 days and the chicks take nearly three weeks to fly.

Tree birds

Southern masked weaver
Swartkeelgeelvink *(Ploceus velatus)*

Size: Length 15-16 cm; weight (m) 17-40 g, (f) 17-36 g.
Colour: Breeding male bright yellow, greener on back; face mask black, ending in point on throat and extending onto forehead; back faintly streaked; eye red; female and nonbreeding male pale greyish brown above with light streaks; throat yellow, shading to buff on breast and white on belly.
Most like: Village weaver male, but back faintly streaked (not heavily mottled) and forehead black, contrasting with yellow crown; lesser masked weaver male, but eye red (not pale yellow) and face mask ends in point below (rounded in lesser masked weaver); female southern masked weaver not safely distinguishable from other female weavers.
Habitat: Very variable, but mostly relatively open country with scattered trees, usually near water.

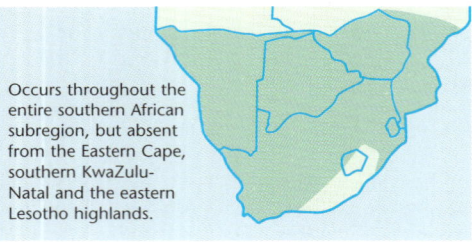

Occurs throughout the entire southern African subregion, but absent from the Eastern Cape, southern KwaZulu-Natal and the eastern Lesotho highlands.

Of the three weavers in southern Africa that have black face masks, the southern masked weaver is the only one seen in the highveld and in semi-desert areas. Its groups of neat hanging nests are commonly found in waterside willow trees. These masked weavers have also taken to building their nests in roadside trees, so that you can see them even far out in the veld, away from water at picnic sites and small clumps of thorn trees.

Many highveld farmyards buzz throughout the summer to the rasping *zzzzrrr chik chik chik zzzrrr* calls of the males as they display at their nests. They visit sheds and barns to pick up fallen meal and grain, and patronize fowl runs for the same purpose. They also eat large numbers of insect larvae and grasshoppers.

Southern masked weavers nest mostly from midwinter onwards, but in the Kalahari and other dry regions will breed at any time of the year after good rains, even though the males may not acquire their breeding plumage. The females line the nests and each lays a clutch of two to three eggs that vary in colour and markings. Incubation and nestling times are unrecorded, but the female is the only parent to feed her young.

Red-billed quelea
Rooibekkwelea *(Quelea quelea)*

Size: Length 12 cm; weight (m) 20 g, (f) 19 g.
Colour: Upperparts streaked blackish on buff; below white, lightly mottled greyish on breast; breeding male has bright red bill, black or white face mask and pink or yellowish head, neck and upper breast; female has yellow bill.
Most like: Nonbreeding pin-tailed whydah, but build chunkier, tail shorter and head not boldly streaked; widows and bishops never have red or yellow bills; other female queleas have horn-coloured bills at all times.
Habitat: Savanna, bushveld, cultivated fields.

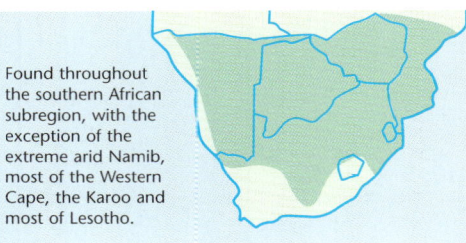

Found throughout the southern African subregion, with the exception of the extreme arid Namib, most of the Western Cape, the Karoo and most of Lesotho.

Imagine a swarm of small birds numbering tens of thousands, swirling about in the sky, wheeling back and forth, the flock changing from light to dark as the birds turn from side to side. This is what a flock of red-billed queleas look like in flight, the co-ordination of the birds being so perfect that they move as one. Wonderful as the sight may be, it is one that strikes fear into the hearts of farmers the length and breadth of Africa, because red-billed queleas regard standing cereal crops as a good source of food. A large flock is capable of doing as much damage as an equivalent swarm of locusts.

In parts of Africa the birds occur in hundreds of thousands or even millions. When they come to drink they may weigh down the branches of waterside trees to such an extent that many birds drown. A nesting colony may extend for a kilometre or more, each tree containing hundreds of nests. The noise can be quite deafening as all the birds chatter and twitter in chorus.

The nest is a small woven purse of grass strips with little or no lining. The clutch of two to four pale green eggs can be seen through the fabric of the nest. Both sexes incubate for about 10-11 days and feed the young for 11-13 days until they can fly.

Tree birds

AFRICAN FIREFINCH

Kaapse vuurvinkie *(Lagonosticta rubricata)*

Size: Length 11-12 cm; weight 8-13 g.

Colour: Male deep red below and on rump; centre of belly and undertail blackish; fine white spots on flanks; back brown; crown grey in southern birds, red in northern; female light red below, shading to tawny on belly; flanks lightly spotted white; upperparts brown; blue-grey bill.

Most like: Jameson's firefinch, but African firefinch has browner back (less reddish) and no brown in centre of crown; red parts deeper in tone, less pinkish.

Habitat: Forest and plantation edges, bushveld, dense savanna, weedy tangles along streams and roadsides.

Frequents the highlands of eastern Zimbabwe and adjacent Mozambique, Swaziland, Mpumalanga and Gauteng, northeastern Free State, most of KwaZulu-Natal and the Eastern Cape.

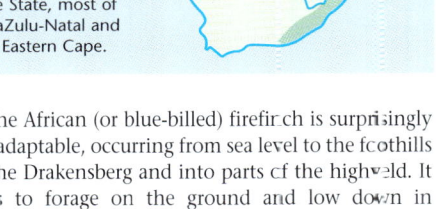

The African (or blue-billed) firefinch is surprisingly adaptable, occurring from sea level to the foothills of the Drakensberg and into parts of the highveld. It likes to forage on the ground and low down in thickets and tangles, hopping about and keeping contact with its mate or other members of a small party with tinkling callnotes.

When disturbed the birds fly out from one patch of cover to the next, showing their plum-red rumps as they go. They seldom perch in the open.

These birds eat mainly small seeds and insects.

In early summer the African firefinch builds a ball of loosely assembled dry grass in a low bush or clump of brushwood. A side entrance leads to a chamber within and is so thickly lined with feathers that you can seldom see the three to five white eggs inside. The chicks hatch after an incubation period of only 11 days, and are fed for a further 15-16 days until they are ready to leave the nest.

The African firefinch is host to the black widowfinch, one of the highly specialized brood parasites that deposits its eggs in the firefinch's nest for the firefinch to hatch out and rear along with its own young. The widowfinch's chicks match those of the firefinch very closely, even to the colour of the mouth spots.

BLUE WAXBILL

Gewone blousysie *(Uraeginthus angolensis)*

Size: Length 12-13 cm; weight 6,3-13 g.

Colour: Crown and back brown; face, throat, breast, rump and tail light blue (paler in female): underparts pinkish buff; male also has blue flanks.

Most like: No other southern African bird; highly distinctive coloration.

Habitat: Woodland, savanna, bushveld, edges of cultivated fields, gardens.

In northern Namibia, northern and southeastern Botswana, Zimbabwe, Northern Province, Mpumalanga, Gauteng, northern Free State, Swaziland, most of KwaZulu-Natal and parts of the Transkei coast.

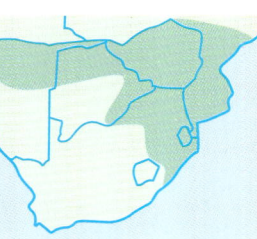

The double *tsee-seep* callnote of the blue waxbill must be among the most characteristic sounds of eastern and northern Botswana and of most of Zimbabwe where this species is abundant. It forages on the ground in pairs or flocks of up to about 50 birds that fly up to the nearest tree or bush when disturbed. If you wait a few moments, the birds are likely to come back to their feeding place and you can watch them at your leisure. Their little blue rumps are easy to see in flight and immediately identify the species.

Blue waxbills are tame and quickly get used to your presence, but in the more remote parts of the bush where they are not used to people they can be quite skittish at first. An easy place to watch for them is at a birdbath where they come to drink frequently throughout the day. Their need to drink is a result of their main food being dry seeds, but they will also take insects.

Because of their lovely colours, blue waxbills have long been favourite cage birds.

These birds breed at almost any time of the year, especially in the more subtropical parts of southern Africa. The nest is the usual waxbill-type of a grass ball with a side entrance, placed in a tree or bush, and softly lined with finer material. The clutch consists of four to five white eggs that hatch in 11-12 days. Both parents feed the chicks, which take nearly three weeks to leave the nest.

Tree birds

VIOLET-EARED WAXBILL
Koningblousysie *(Uraeginthus granatina)*

Size: *Length 14-15 cm; weight 8,6-15 g.*
Colour: *Male deep chestnut; forehead and rump bright blue; throat, centre of belly, tail and undertail black; face violet; female paler than male and lacking black on underparts.*
Most like: *No other southern African bird.*
Habitat: *Dry thornveld and woodland.*

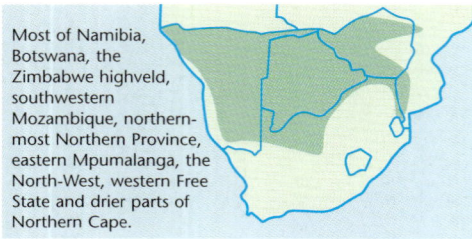

Most of Namibia, Botswana, the Zimbabwe highveld, southwestern Mozambique, northernmost Northern Province, eastern Mpumalanga, the North-West, western Free State and drier parts of Northern Cape.

Every bird photographer who visits the drier parts of southern Africa dreams of photographing a violet-eared waxbill, one of the most beautiful small birds in the region. The best place to see them is at a waterhole where, like most waxbills, they come to drink, usually in pairs, on and off throughout the day.

Violet-ears may form flocks with blue waxbills, and have the same habit of flying up from the ground when disturbed, and perching in the nearest bush or tree. They feed on insects and small seeds on the ground, and prefer to have cover nearby. Flocks seldom number more than ten birds.

Although violet-ears are great favourites among birdlovers because of their beautiful colours, they never look as good in a cage as they do in the bush. These avian gems are a most surprising and delightful sight in the hot, dry Kalahari where most of the birds tend to be rather drab.

The nest—a ball of dry grasses with a feather-lined chamber—is built in a thorn bush in late summer. The clutch consists of four to five tiny white eggs that hatch out in only 12-13 days. The nestling period is 16 days and both parents care for the young.

Immature violet-eared waxbills are confusing because they lack violet on the face altogether, and have only a tinge of blue on the rump.

The violet-eared waxbill is host to the parasitic shaft-tailed whydah, a handsome member of this interesting brood-parasitic family, all of which parasitize waxbills of one species or another.

RED-HEADED FINCH
Rooikopvink *(Amadina erythrocephala)*

Size: *Length 14 cm; weight 19-30 g.*
Colour: *Above greyish brown; below barred with buff, white and black; centre of belly plain buff; head of male bright scarlet; bill whitish horn, very heavy; rounded tail tipped white.*
Most like: *Cut-throat finch, but not barred above except on rump; red head of male diagnostic (cut-throat finch has red band on throat only).*
Habitat: *Clumps of trees and farmyards in open grassveld, dry savanna and thornveld.*

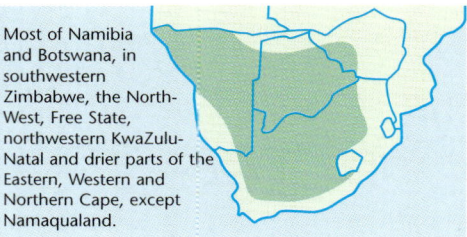

Most of Namibia and Botswana, in southwestern Zimbabwe, the North-West, Free State, northwestern KwaZulu-Natal and drier parts of the Eastern, Western and Northern Cape, except Namaqualand.

In the Kalahari sandveld red-headed finches can be very plentiful, sometimes occurring in flocks of a hundred birds or more. They come to water readily, drink very quickly and fly away again with their typical chinking callnotes. The speed at which they drink indicates how dangerous waterholes are for birds: many predators have learned that birds concentrate at such places, so the hunting is relatively easy. The main predators are likely to be small birds of prey such as kestrels, falcons and sparrowhawks, all of which are also quite capable of catching a finch in full flight.

Red-headed finches eat mainly dry seeds, as do most waxbill species, but they feed their young largely on insects. The birds pick up most of their food on the ground and fly to the nearest perch when disturbed. The movements of the birds in a flock are so well synchronized that they suggest instantaneous communication between them.

Red-headed finches do not build their own nests, but line the old nest of a sparrow or weaver, or perhaps a hole in a wall or tree, with feathers and grass. Up to seven white eggs form the clutch, which both parents incubate for about two weeks.

The breeding season of red-headed finches falls when most other birds are not nesting, so that vacant, used nests are freely available.

Tree birds

BRONZE MANNIKIN

Gewone fret *(Lonchura cucullata)*

Size: Length 9-10 cm; weight 7-12 g.

Colour: Head and breast black, with slight bronze sheen; grey-brown back and wings with metallic green spots on wing; belly white with bold black barring on flanks; bill black above, blue-grey below.

Most like: Other mannikins, but back chestnut in red-backed mannikin and barred in magpie mannikin; flanks mottled black and buff in magpie mannikin; barred undertail of bronze mannikin distinctive.

Habitat: Thickets in woodland and savanna, near water in cultivated fields, parks, gardens and farmyards.

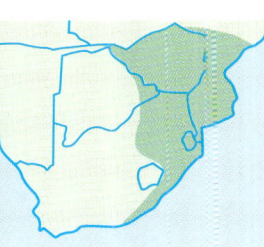

Throughout the moister parts of extreme eastern Botswana, Zimbabwe, Mozambique, Northern Province, Gauteng, Mpumalanga, Swaziland, eastern Free State, most of KwaZulu-Natal and the Eastern Cape coast.

When young bronze mannikins are being fed they turn their heads upside down so that the parents can regurgitate food into their eager, gaping mouths. This typically waxbill behaviour pattern distinguishes them from the weaver family, most of which also have stout, conical bills for husking seeds. The adult mannikins prefer to feed on the ground and may gather in parties of 30 or more birds where fallen grain has accumulated. They also eat insects.

Very common in gardens in the eastern parts of southern Africa, these little birds come to feeding trays in parties, the adults accompanied by several plain greyish buff young that frequently utter chittering begging calls. When disturbed, they fly off into the nearest tree, their wings making a tiny whirring sound.

Mannikins are highly sociable little birds, often perching in a tight row on a branch. They seem to enjoy physical contact with one another, and roost communally at night either on a branch or in nests built for the purpose.

The breeding nest, which is similar to the roosting nest, is a ball of dry grass, sometimes quite high up in a tree. A side entrance gives access to a chamber lined with soft grass flowers and contains the clutch of three to six tiny white eggs. These take about 15 days to hatch. The chicks stay in the nest for about three weeks, being fed by both parents, after which they accompany the parents for at least two weeks.

PIN-TAILED WHYDAH

Koningrooibekkie *(Vidua macroura)*

Size: Length (m) 26-34 cm (tail about 50 cm in nonbreeding male and 163-260 cm in breeding male), (f) 12-13 cm; weight (m) 12,5-18 g, (f) 10-16 g.

Colour: Breeding male pied black and white with long black tail and bright red bill; female and nonbreeding male streaked black and tawny above; head striped black and tawny; below white with buffy breast and dark streaks on flanks; bill red in male at all times, reddish brown in female.

Most like: Other female and nonbreeding male whydahs and widowfinches, but combination of striped head and red bill diagnostic, except for nonbreeding male village indigobird (steel-blue widowfinch), but bigger; breeding male quite distinctive.

Habitat: Farmlands, gardens, open savanna.

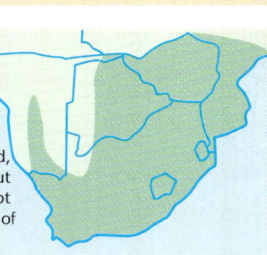

In southern and central Namibia, eastern Botswana, Zimbabwe and Mozambique, Swaziland, Lesotho, and throughout all of South Africa except the arid northerly parts of the Northern Cape.

The male pin-tailed whydah is polygamous, having two or more wives in the breeding season—hence his alternative name 'king-of-six'. Most people dislike him because of his aggressive nature, which causes him to chase other birds from feeding trays, but he is a handsome fellow and should be welcomed to the bird-tray fraternity.

Like so many common and widespread birds, the pin-tailed whydah is successful because it can adapt to a wide variety of habitats, including environments modified by man such as agricultural lands, farms and gardens. It is a brood parasite like all the whydahs and widowfinches but, unlike the others, it is not confined to only one species of waxbill as a host. It parasitizes at least five waxbill species, as well as some of the smaller warblers.

The main host of the pin-tailed whydah is the common waxbill in whose nest each female lays one or two eggs. The incubation period is 11 days and the young of the two species grow up together in the nest, leaving after about 20 days.

Tree birds

LONG-TAILED PARADISE WHYDAH

Gewone paradysvink
(Vidua paradisaea)

Size: Length (breeding m) 33-38 cm, (f) 15 cm; weight 19-22 g.

Colour: Breeding male black on head, back and long tail; breast brick red; belly and hindneck straw yellow; female and nonbreeding male streaked buff and black above; head boldly striped buff and black; below whitish with buffy wash on breast and flanks.

Most like: Other female and nonbreeding male whydahs and widowfinches and probably not easily separable in the field; male similar to broad-tailed paradise whydahs, but tail narrow and pointed.

Habitat: Thornveld, open woodland, cultivated lands.

In northern Namibia, most of Botswana, Zimbabwe, Mozambique, Swaziland, Mpumalanga, Gauteng, Northern Province, the North-West, extreme northern section of the Free State and northern KwaZulu-Natal.

A displaying male long-tailed paradise whydah is a spectacular sight in summer as he bounces upwards in flight to a height of nearly 100 m, raising his central broad tail feathers like a bustle, and then descending in a dive to his perch. As he flies his long tail makes a rustling sound. He displays like this all day long, stopping only in the evening to feed on the ground with his females and some immature males.

These birds feed mostly on open patches, such as roadways and paths in the bush. Towards dusk the males from neighbouring territories gather on the tops of bushes before roosting time. You will usually see long-tailed paradise whydahs in small flocks; though territorial males do perch alone on top of a bush or on a telephone wire during the day.

The host of this whydah species is the melba finch, a pretty waxbill of similar habitat. The male has several females in his entourage, each of which lays between one and three white eggs in each host nest. Each female can lay up to 22 eggs in a single breeding season, which lasts from January to June. Incubation is 12-13 days and nestling about 16 days; the nestlings of host and parasite grow up amicably together and the paradise whydah's young become independent after about a month.

YELLOW-FRONTED CANARY

Geeloogkanarie *(Serinus mozambicus)*

Size: Length 12 cm; weight 12 g.

Colour: Dull green above, streaked darker; rump and underparts light yellow, shading to greyish on flanks; distinctive black eye-stripe and moustache-stripe on yellow face; broad yellow eyebrows meet across forehead; tip of tail white.

Most like: Other yellow canaries, but greyish flanks, yellow rump and white-tipped tail diagnostic; yellow canary has all-yellow underparts and no white tail tip; brimstone canary has green forehead, indistinct facial markings and greenish wash across breast; Cape canary has blue-grey nape.

Habitat: Savanna, woodland, gardens, plantations.

In northern Namibia and along the Caprivi Strip, northern and eastern Botswana, Zimbabwe, Mozambique, Swaziland, Mpumalanga, Gauteng, Northen Province, northern Free State, KwaZulu-Natal and the Eastern Cape.

Only two southern African canaries have yellow rumps and white-tipped tails: the yellow-fronted (or yellow-eyed) and the black-throated. Clearly these two species are closely related, the yellow-fronted being the eastern representative of the pair. (The black-throated inhabits higher and drier country.) Even their song is very similar.

The yellow-fronted canary is an endearing little bird, common in gardens, though reluctant to come to feeding trays. It feeds mostly on the ground, though it will perch on seeding grass heads to feed too. The species' main food is grass seeds, but they sometimes take insects, nectar and flowers.

They sing well and, when danger threatens, will take to the air with a little whistling *tswirri* callnote to alert the rest of the group.

The yellow-fronted canary nests throughout the summer, building a neat, cup-shaped nest in a bush or tree, up to six metres above the ground. The clutch is usually three to four eggs, white or pale blue, plain or speckled. The female incubates for 14 days and the nestlings, which are fed by both parents, leave the nest after 16-20 days.

Tree birds

CAPE CANARY

Kaapse kanarie *(Serinus canicollis)*

Size: Length 13-14 cm; weight 11-19,5 g.
Colour: Greenish yellow, greener on back and tail; nape and upper back blue-grey.
Most like: Other yellow canaries, but blue-grey nape diagnostic; no distinct facial markings; yellow deeper and greener than in yellow-fronted and yellow canaries.
Habitat: Mountains, open grassveld, bushy hillsides, plantations, gardens, parks, seed crops.

Southern and Eastern Cape, Lesotho, eastern Free State, most of KwaZulu-Natal and the highveld escarpment. Also frequents the highlands of Zimbabwe and adjacent Mozambique.

Because the Cape canary is one of the best singers in southern Africa, it has been a popular cage bird for years. Its song is much sweeter than that of the brimstone or yellow canary, and is certainly more sustained than those of yellow-fronted or black-throated canaries. This very common species moves round according to the season. You may see them in certain parts of the country in winter, but not in those same places in summer.

In winter nonbreeding flocks, numbering several to hundreds of birds, move about from one food supply to the next, their bouncing flight clearly exposing their notched tails. Cape canaries feed on the ground or on standing crops of seeds, whether grass or grain, and are especially fond of the fluffy seeds of some kinds of daisies that grow as weeds in disturbed ground. They also eat buds of the sagewood, as well as fruit and flowers.

As August approaches the flocks break up into mated pairs that begin to breed, probably rearing several broods until midsummer or later. The nest is a neat, compact cup of plant stems, roots, moss and other materials, including cotton and wool, placed in a bush or tree, sometimes quite high up. The female lays three or four whitish or greenish eggs with black or brown markings, and incubates them for two weeks. Both parents feed the young in the nest for 16-18 days after which they form flocks with the adults as they move from place to place to find food.

YELLOW CANARY

Geelkanarie *(Serinus flaviventris)*

Size: Length 13-14 cm; weight (m) 14,7-19,9 g, (f) 14,7-18,7 g.
Colour: Male bright yellow below and on rump; upperparts dull greenish, streaked darker; broad yellow eyebrows meet across forehead; female greyish brown above, streaked darker; rump yellow; below dull white, streaked greyish on breast and flanks.
Most like: Other 'yellow' canaries, but underparts completely clear yellow; no white tip to tail; forehead green in brimstone canary; female resembles white-throated canary, but off-white, dusky-streaked underparts diagnostic; black-throated canary has black throat and white tip to tail.
Habitat: Montane shrub, open grassland, arid scrub, desert and semi-desert, fynbos, gardens, farmyards.

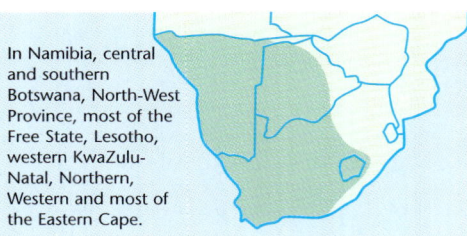

In Namibia, central and southern Botswana, North-West Province, most of the Free State, Lesotho, western KwaZulu-Natal, Northern, Western and most of the Eastern Cape.

The yellow canary male is probably the most handsome of all the 'yellow' canaries and a good singer too. This species underscores the fact that birds adapted to high mountains are also adapted to arid country, since it occurs from the very top of the Drakensberg escarpment at 3000 m to the Namib desert on the Atlantic coast.

Usually tame, it has adapted to man and nests commonly in gardens throughout the western parts of southern Africa. A nesting female may even allow you to touch her as she sits on her eggs.

Yellow canaries eat seeds on the ground, flowers and buds when these are available, and sometimes nectar and insects or small crustaceans. In arid regions, such as the Kalahari, succulent foods such as flower bases are valuable sources of water; when there is no succulent food the birds have to fly to waterholes to drink.

This canary's nest is typical of the family—a small cup of plant stems, lined with softer material and placed in a low bush or small tree. The female lays three to four white, pale blue or pale green spotted eggs, which she incubates alone for about 12 days. Both parents feed the chicks until they can fly at the age of 14 days.

Turtles and tortoises

Turtles and tortoises make up the reptilian order Chelonia. In their presence we are, as it were, in direct touch with prehistory, for they are the oldest form of living reptiles, and species very similar to today's existed 200 million years ago. There's something uniquely fascinating about an animal that, so literally, 'carries its house on its back'. The general appearance of these reptiles is so distinctive that you couldn't possibly mistake them for any other creature.

The boxlike shell that encases chelonians is one of nature's most cunning protective adaptations. The upper shell, usually domed and often attractively patterned, is known as the carapace; the one shielding the animal's soft underbelly is called the plastron. They are joined together by 'bridges' on either side, between the fore- and hindlegs—leaving apertures at the front and back for the withdrawal of head, limbs and tail when danger threatens. Some species have actually improved on this basic design by evolving a hinged carapace, part of which can be moved, rather like a drawbridge, to close the rear aperture (in the hingeback land tortoises), or a hinged plastron which closes the front aperture (in the hinged terrapins).

The typical chelonian carapace is made up of two layers. The inner one consists of bony plates, to which the ribs are fused. The outer layer is an interconnecting jigsaw of horny scales or shields that don't correspond with the plates underneath. As the hatchling grows into an adult, each of these shields increases in size, spreading out from the central portion or areola. The shields give the carapace its characteristic patterning.

The giant leatherback turtle is exceptional in that its carapace lacks a horny outer layer; the carapace is relatively thin, is not fused to the skeleton, and consists of numerous bones set in a leathery skin.

Note that in southern African usage 'turtle' refers to marine species (with feet in the form of flippers) and 'tortoise' to the land-dwelling species, with clawed feet. 'Water tortoises' or 'terrapins' inhabit fresh water, although in fact they are quite at home on land too; they have webs to their feet, are excellent swimmers and can stay under water for very long periods.

How does a tortoise breathe, constricted as it is by its bony straitjacket? By contracting abdominal muscles near the hindlegs it is able to enlarge the lung cavity to take in air; air is expelled by the action of other abdominal muscles that force the viscera up against the lungs, deflating them. All this may sound a struggle but the action is, of course, as effortless and involuntary as our own breathing.

Sea turtles are just as dependent on a regular air supply as their land-dwelling relatives, and they must surface at intervals to take in a new supply of oxygen.

Unlike other reptiles, chelonians have no teeth to their jaws; but cutting edges of keratin or horn adequately equip them to process their chosen meal, whether it be vegetable (as among most land tortoises) or of animal origin (as among terrapins). Helmeted terrapins have been known to seize unsuspecting waterbirds resting on the surface of a pond or vlei, drag them under to drown them, and then consume them. Handle tortoises with care, for their toothless jaws can inflict an unpleasant bite.

Female turtles and tortoises lay eggs. These are deposited in a hole in the ground which is then filled in and tamped down—not always safe from such predators as meerkats or leguaans, which have an uncanny knack of finding the nests and digging out the eggs. The buried clutch is left by the mother, and the sun speeds up incubation.

For the female sea turtle, egg-laying is a particular ordeal. Not only are her flippers ill-equipped to manoeuvre her huge frame over the beach once she has emerged from the sea, but she also finds breathing much more difficult on land, and gives audible sighs indicating her discomfort. The tears shed by Lewis Carroll's Mock Turtle were no mere invention either, though in nature they are not tears of distress but serve a precise function: as the female turtle digs a nesting hole with her flippers she throws up a flurry of sand, and the lubricating tears rid her eyes of it.

Are tortoises as long-lived as they are rumoured to be? Stories of living specimens that existed in Shakespeare's time are certainly grossly exaggerated; but a lifespan of up to 150 years seems possible among the captive giant tortoises of the Seychelles.

Some 12 species of land tortoise and eight terrapins are indigenous to southern Africa. Although five species of marine turtle are found in our offshore waters, only two breed here, the loggerhead and the leatherback.

Identifying turtles and tortoises

Colour

The colour pattern of the carapace provides an excellent clue to the identification of many species. Watch out for the spots and speckles of the speckled padloper of Namaqualand, the leopardlike black spots and blotches of the mountain or leopard tortoise, and the red plastron of the Western Cape form of the angulate tortoise. Almost identical markings—yellow stripes (on a black background) radiating from each areola in a star pattern—are the remarkable feature shared by three small species: the geometric, tent and Kalahari tortoises. But their distribution areas do not overlap (except in a small area north of the Gariep, or Orange, River for the latter two species), and in fact one species (the geometric) is now so rare that it is virtually unknown outside a group of small nature reserves in the southwestern Cape. Once thought to be extinct, it now has the unenviable distinction of being officially listed as an 'endangered species'.

Shape

The carapaces of water tortoises are appropriately smooth and streamlined for their habits and habitat. Among land tortoises the 'padlopers'—so-called because all species have a liking for following the beaten track—have relatively flattened carapaces. Nothing could contrast more with this low silhouette than that of the very conspicuous, high-domed mountain tortoise, which is by far the largest species of the subregion.

Carapace shape is an especially valuable indicator when you are uncertain whether the specimen before

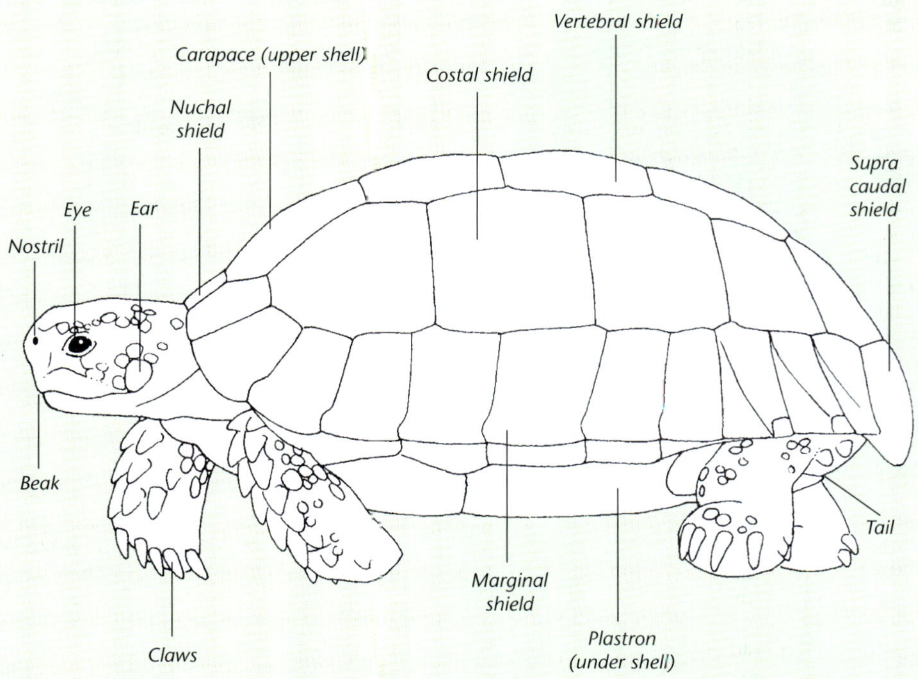

Turtles and tortoises

Tortoise

(Labels: Nostril, Eye, Ear, Beak, Claws, Nuchal shield, Carapace (upper shell), Costal shield, Vertebral shield, Supra caudal shield, Tail, Plastron (under shell), Marginal shield)

you is a fully grown member of one species or a juvenile of another. In one species, the angulate tortoise, the shape of the plastron provides easy identification, for it projects at the front, beneath the head, into a ram (used by the males to overturn rivals competing for a female).

Head
When a terrapin is disturbed, it withdraws its head into its shell, the neck is bent sideways, and one beady eye glares balefully at the intruder. Land tortoises pull their heads directly back; the mobile neck forming a vertical S shape. Watch out for the distinctively shaped snout that gives the parrot-beaked tortoise its name.

Legs and feet
Both land and water tortoises have clawed feet but water tortoises have, in addition, webs to their feet. The legs of turtles are very large and powerful (especially the forelimbs) and have been modified into broad, oarlike flippers; they carry no claws. Terrapins have five toes to each hindfoot, and the Cape padloper and the greater padloper have only four toes to each forefoot.

Eggs
The mountain tortoise and all turtles lay white, circular eggs, shaped like ping-pong balls; but the eggs of the smaller land tortoises and the water tortoises are oval. Since all chelonians bury their eggs and then smooth the soil to disguise the whereabouts of the clutch, you are unlikely to come across them unless they have already been unearthed by some natural predator.

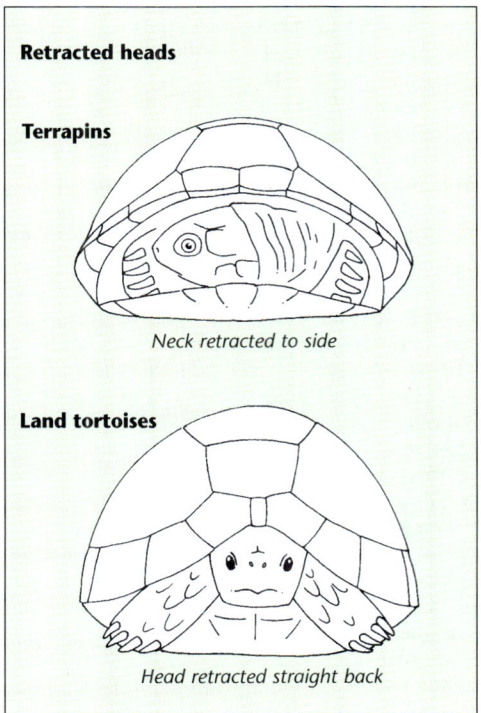

Retracted heads

Terrapins

Neck retracted to side

Land tortoises

Head retracted straight back

Turtles and tortoises

LEATHERBACK TURTLE

Leerrug/Reuse-seeskilpad *(Dermochelys coriacea)*

Size: Length 1,3-1,7 m; average weight 400 kg.
Colour: Shiny black carapace (upper shell), spotted with pale grey or blue; head and upper surfaces of skin black, spotted with pale grey or blue; head has a pink or reddish mark on top. Tail black. Under surfaces white and pink.
Most like: Loggerhead turtle, but bigger and with a distinctive carapace which carries seven clear, longitudinal ridges from front to back.
Habitat: From tropical to temperate, and sometimes colder, ocean waters. Nesting takes place on tropical beaches with an unobstructed approach from the sea.

Inhabits surface waters of tropical, subtropical and temperate oceans and can be found all around the southern African coast.

The leatherback turtle is the heaviest living reptile: the largest specimen found in southern African waters weighed 646 kg, while giants of up to 865 kg (and 2,5 m long) have been recorded in the Pacific Ocean. For all its size, however, this impressive sea creature is a bit of a milksop. It has no teeth, and the adult turtle feeds almost exclusively on jellyfish; horny spines in its throat help it to take hold of and retain this slithery diet.

It is also given to copious tears. Biologists believe that by weeping the leatherback turtle is able to rid itself of excess salt taken in when it swallows seawater. For the female turtle, laying her eggs on the beach, the tears serve another purpose: they help free her eyes of the sand whipped up by her massive flippers as she digs a nest.

Nesting is an arduous exercise for her—after dragging herself across the beach to dry sand, she has to dig a hollow deep enough to take perhaps as many as 120 white, spherical eggs. Having laid the eggs, she covers up the hollow to conceal them.

Some two-and-a-half months later the hatchlings emerge from their shells, dig themselves to the surface, and instinctively make for the sea—occasionally having to run the gauntlet of gulls, crabs and other predators.

The leatherback turtle has been listed as an endangered species.

LOGGERHEAD TURTLE

Karet/Grootkop-seeskilpad *(Caretta caretta)*

Size: Length 1 m; average weight 135 kg.
Colour: Reddish-brown carapace, streaked with lighter or darker brown. Upper surfaces of the skin are brown. Under surfaces range from dirty white to pinkish yellow or plain yellow; throat, neck and sides of head are usually yellow.
Most like: Leatherback turtle, but the loggerhead is smaller, has a more chunky head and a flat, not ridged, carapace. It has clearly defined shields on its carapace, unlike the smooth-shelled leatherback.
Habitat: From tropical to temperate seas. Nesting takes place on beaches flanking subtropical waters and often adjacent to rocky outcrops or inshore reefs.

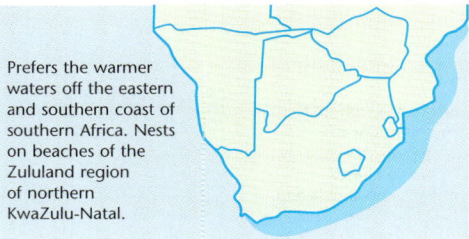

Prefers the warmer waters off the eastern and southern coast of southern Africa. Nests on beaches of the Zululand region of northern KwaZulu-Natal.

Although listed as endangered, this is the most common species of turtle found off the east coast of southern Africa. It is a formidable animal with a slightly tapering carapace, a large wide head, a somewhat hooked 'beak', and powerful jaws capable of crushing the shells of crabs, molluscs and sea urchins, the adult turtle's major source of food. (Juveniles feed on floating organisms such as jellyfish, bluebottles and sponges.)

Although turtles are almost entirely aquatic, they have to come to the surface of the sea regularly to breathe, raising their heads as they do so to take in air through their nostrils, which are situated just above their beaks.

The reproductive cycle of the loggerhead resembles that of the even larger leatherback turtle. At dusk the female drags herself ashore and excavates a nest above the high-water mark in which she lays about 100 eggs. Then she fills in the hole and camouflages its site by flinging loose sand about.

The eggs are white and spherical, rather like billiard balls. Considered a delicacy by man, they are also sought after by predators such as leguaans and jackals. The hatchlings emerge from their shells after three months and dig themselves out of their burrows. They then scuttle seawards, risking predation by gulls.

Turtles and tortoises

HELMETED TERRAPIN

Helm-/Moeras-waterskilpad *(Pelomedusa subrufa)*

Size: *Length 22-32 cm.*

Colour: *The carapace (upper shell) varies from greyish brown to olive-brown or blackish, while the plastron (under shell) can be blackish or more usually has symmetrical yellow and reddish or dark brown markings. In young specimens the outer edge of the carapace is marked with yellow.*

Most like: *Hinged water tortoise, but the carapace of the helmeted terrapin is much flatter, and the forepart of the plastron cannot be raised to hide the head and forelimbs as the serrated hinged terrapin's can.*

Habitat: *In or near ponds and vleis throughout southern Africa, even if this water is only seasonal.*

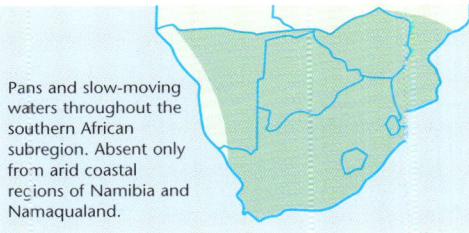

Pans and slow-moving waters throughout the southern African subregion. Absent only from arid coastal regions of Namibia and Namaqualand.

Although the helmeted, or Cape, terrapin is a strong swimmer and very much at home in the water, you will often see it on terra firma. It enjoys basking on a mud bank, and can travel across land at quite a brisk pace. It reacts to danger in such circumstances by emitting an offensive odour from stink glands on the flanks at the base of each leg; the smell is, quite literally, enough to frighten horses, which are said to associate it with the smell of lions.

This species is omnivorous. Its catholic diet includes such aquatic fauna as frogs and tadpoles, crabs and fish. It may also make a meal of a duckling or other small waterbird, seizing its prey by a leg and dragging it underwater to drown it. With the sharp claws of its forelegs it can rip the victim apart.

Like sea turtles, female helmeted terrapins come ashore to excavate a hole in which to lay their eggs. To soften the hard soil the female urinates copiously and 'bulldozes' the resultant mud into a nest with the front of her plastron or under shell. Her oval eggs, usually 20-25 in a clutch, have soft shells that later harden. The clutch is covered over with mud and other debris, and it takes about three months for the hatchlings to emerge.

MOUNTAIN TORTOISE

Bergskilpad *(Geochelone pardalis)*

Size: *Length 30-60 cm; weight 8-20 kg.*

Colour: *Background colour of carapace yellow, blotched and streaked in black, most vividly in younger specimens; older animals may appear almost uniform deep brown. The plastron is straw-coloured with irregular black markings.*

Most like: *Unmistakeable when mature as no other southern African tortoise can match this species for size. Younger specimens, however, could be confused with Bell's hinged tortoise, although they have no sign of a hinge.*

Habitat: *A wide range of habitats, from dry bushveld to moister coastal plains.*

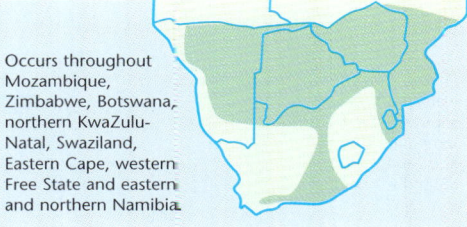

Occurs throughout Mozambique, Zimbabwe, Botswana, northern KwaZulu-Natal, Swaziland, Eastern Cape, western Free State and eastern and northern Namibia.

The mountain, or leopard, tortoise is the most widely distributed and also the biggest of the 12 species of land tortoise found in southern Africa. It is believed to take its name 'mountain' tortoise from its size rather than its habitat. (The alternative name of 'leopard' tortoise comes from the black-and-yellow blotched patterns on its high-domed carapace.)

Though not averse to gnawing on an old bone, the mountain tortoise is mostly vegetarian, feeding on a variety of plant matter, including grass shoots, succulents such as cotyledons, fungi and fruit.

When mating time approaches in spring, males become increasingly aggressive in competing for the favours of a female; two rivals will butt each other until the loser is overturned.

As with other tortoise species, the female lays her 5-20 hard-shelled eggs in a hole she has dug; then she fills it in and, in a clumsy but effective stamping manoeuvre with her hindlegs, flattens the soil all around the clutch. The incubation period varies from 8-14 months.

Not only are the eggs at risk from ants and other insects, but also from such predators as rats, jackals, meerkats and mongooses. The hatchlings provide a delicacy for many small and medium-sized carnivores and a host of birds.

Adults usually weigh from 10-15 kg, but some specimens of over 40 kg have been recorded in the Eastern Cape.

Turtles and tortoises

BELL'S HINGED TORTOISE

Bell se skarnierskilpad *(Kinixys belliana)*

Size: Length 14-18 cm.
Colour: The base colour of the carapace ranges from pale yellow to brown or olive-green, each shield patterned with radiating broad black markings. The plastron is straw-yellow with symmetrical brown markings.
Most like: Tortoises of the genus Homopus, including the Cape padloper (Homopus areolatus), but the carapace of Bell's hinged tortoise is less flattened, the hinge is much larger, and there are five claws on each forefoot.
Habitat: Coastal lowland savanna and dune forest to highveld and bushveld.

Found in the bushveld and savanna of northern KwaZulu-Natal, Mozambique, Swaziland, Mpumalanga, Northern Province, eastern North-West Province, eastern Botswana and Zimbabwe.

Evolution has supplied this tortoise with an ingenious addition to its protective armoury: the rear third of its upper shell (carapace) is hinged on either side and can be lowered, when danger threatens, so as to meet the under shell (plastron). In this way the hindlegs and the tail end of the animal are completely enclosed and protected. The reflex action is often accompanied by an angry hiss as the tortoise discharges air from its lungs.

Bell's hinged tortoise has omnivorous tastes. It supplements its vegetarian diet of grasses, succulents, fruits and fungi with snails and millipedes; it also has a taste for carrion—the dead bodies of small rodents and frogs. This wide tolerance of different foods has helped it to survive in a variety of habitats.

In common with other tortoise (and sea turtle) species, the female hinged tortoise deposits her eggs in a hole in the ground that she subsequently fills in and camouflages. Throughout the summer she is able to lay eggs at intervals of 40 days. Each clutch is small—between one and eight eggs—and, as usual for tortoises, the hard-shelled eggs are oval. The hatchlings that eventually break the surface of the soil are only three to four centimetres long.

At the start of the cold, dry winter this tortoise burrows a compartment for itself in soft earth embankments and hibernates until spring.

ANGULATE TORTOISE

Rooipens *(Chersina angulata)*

Size: Length 15-28 cm.
Colour: The carapace is predominantly yellow (usually in old individuals), and dark brown or black (predominantly black in young specimens), its circumference being distinctively patterned with dark triangles. The under shell (plastron) is yellow, strongly tinged with light orange to dark red in west coast specimens.
Most like: Bell's hinged tortoise, which can have a very similar yellow-and-black pattern, but has the distinctive hinge on the carapace and two short shields at the front end of the plastron, not the single, spadelike shield of the angulate tortoise.
Habitat: Coastal sandveld, valley bushveld, Karoo veld.

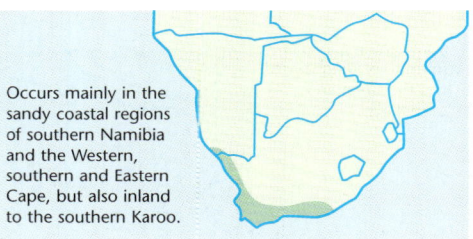

Occurs mainly in the sandy coastal regions of southern Namibia and the Western, southern and Eastern Cape, but also inland to the southern Karoo.

Nature has endowed the angulate tortoise with a sturdy throat shield which is used both in combat and self-defence. The shield, or 'bowsprit', projects at the front of the under shell, and is used in much the same way as a battering ram: to dislodge and overpower rivals. This bowsprit, combined with the relatively small opening of the carapace in front, also protects the angulate tortoise's head when it is withdrawn.

During territorial or mating skirmishes, a duelling male angulate tortoise achieves ultimate success when he manages to tip a male rival over onto his back. This is an undignified position for any tortoise—though not a permanent one, for with some agitated thrashing of his four legs and with a rocking motion of his body, the creature is eventually able to right himself.

Although angulate tortoises are vegetarians—specimens in captivity are particularly partial to young beans—they are thought to supplement their diet in the wild by feeding occasionally on carrion. They will certainly not refuse meat in captivity.

The female lays a single, oval egg at a time, burying it in a 10 cm-deep hole burrowed in a sandy and well-drained locality. She repeats the process regularly over the course of several weeks. The incubation period varies from three to seven months.

Turtles and tortoises

TENT TORTOISE

Knoppiesdopskilpad *(Psammobates tentorius)*

Size: Length (m) 10 cm, (f) 13,5 cm.
Colour: Carapace dark brown or black, with a pattern of yellow or orange stripes radiating from the centre of each domed shield making up the carapace.
Most like: Geometric tortoise, Psammobates geometricus, but the tent tortoise has a distinctive spurlike white or yellowish projection on each buttock.
Habitat: Dry, semi-desert regions.

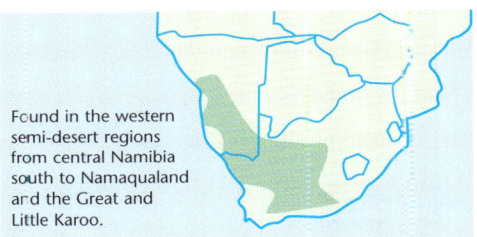

Found in the western semi-desert regions from central Namibia south to Namaqualand and the Great and Little Karoo.

GEOMETRIC TORTOISE

Suurpootjieskilpad *(Psammobates geometricus)*

Size: Length (m) 12,5 cm, (f) 14,5 cm.
Colour: Black carapace, with yellow stripes radiating from the yellow centre of each pyramidal shield.
Most like: Tent tortoise, but the geometric tortoise doesn't have the tent tortoise's projecting 'horn' on the middle of each convex buttock.
Habitat: The flat coastal renosterveld of the south-western Cape.

Confined to the surviving patches of coastal renosterveld in the southwestern Cape, from Gordon's Bay north to Piketberg and inland to Ceres and Worcester.

The tent tortoise has a beautiful geometric pattern of 'Bedouin tents' on its upper shell, and this is appropriate, for this attractive specimen is quite at home in the semi-desert—the sparse conditions of Namibia, Namaqualand, Bushmanland and the Karoo. Unfortunately, in the past, this species and its close cousin, the geometric tortoise, have been sought and sold by pet traders, with the resultant loss of large numbers from their natural habitat. It is doubtful if many specimens survived in captivity for long: they depend on a very specialized diet including assorted Karoo bushes, mesembryanthemums and other South African succulents.

In addition, their desert-adapted constitutions are not suited to moister climates and they tend to succumb to lung, nasal and eye infections when removed from the dry interior of southern Africa.

The colouring and size of this little tortoise vary greatly, particularly from one area to another, but also within a single 'population'. Three subspecies are recognized by biologists. Of these, *Psammobates tentorius trimeni*, found on the Namaqualand coast, boasts the boldest markings, the brightest colours and well-developed 'tents'. Subspecies *verroxii*, found in the driest parts of the Karoo, has underdeveloped 'tents', while subspecies *tentorius*, from the Eastern Cape, has the best-developed 'tents' of all.

The female tent tortoise lays a clutch of one to three eggs, and buries them in the sand as all other tortoises do. The young emerge in late summer or early autumn.

The geometric tortoise's main defensive weapon, apart from its strong carapace, is actually its distinctive patterning. Bold as this often is, the black-and-yellow, raylike markings provide an efficient camouflage in the tortoise's natural environment.

It's estimated that only 2 000-3 000 geometric tortoises exist, and you will find these in a handful of nature reserves in the southwestern Cape. Concerted efforts are being made to ensure the survival of this delightful little tortoise.

Renosterveld, the geometric tortoise's natural habitat, once stretched at least 160 km northwards from Cape Town along the west coast, and the distribution of the species matched this spread. However, man's demand for agricultural land for wheat and vines has reduced the renosterveld drastically, and with it the tortoise population. Pet-hunters, particularly, have taken their toll of the species; so too have its natural enemies which include baboons, jackals, mongooses, crows and secretarybirds.

Mating takes place in spring and the female's clutch of up to four eggs, which she buries in the soil, hatch in autumn.

Psammobates geometricus is the only one of southern Africa's 12 species of land tortoise to be threatened with extinction. As it happens, all tortoise species in South Africa are protected by law.

Turtles and tortoises

KALAHARI TENT TORTOISE

Kalahari-tentskilpad *(Psammobates oculiferus)*

Size: Length 9-12 cm.
Colour: The dark brown to black carapace is patterned with yellow-brown stripes radiating from the centre of each slightly raised shield or 'scute'.
Most like: Tent and geometric tortoises, but the shields of the Kalahari tent tortoise are not elevated into prominent 'tents' or pyramids like those of the other two species, and are only fractionally raised. Also, each of the last four small shields on each side of the carapace ends in a unique, deeply serrated edge.
Habitat: Dry savanna and scrub desert.

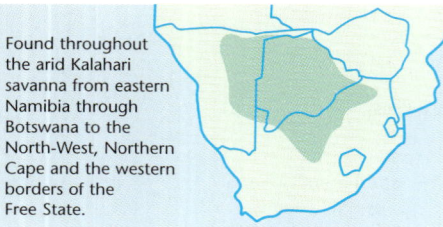

Found throughout the arid Kalahari savanna from eastern Namibia through Botswana to the North-West, Northern Cape and the western borders of the Free State.

In its beautiful patterning this species closely resembles the endangered geometric tortoise and the tent tortoise. All three are members of the genus *Psammobates*, which means 'sand-walker' in Greek, and of the three, the Kalahari tortoise best lives up to its name in its dry, sandy environment. In addition to the small succulents and grasses provided by this Spartan habitat, it sometimes eats the droppings of sheep, hyaenas and game, a diet which is rich in calcium. Ironically, the hyaena is one of the predators of this species.

For shelter the tortoise burrows into the soft, loose soil at the base of the meagre scrub and bush, or uses the abandoned subterranean home of one of the small, burrowing mammals. The female lays her clutch of one or two eggs in a hole she digs in spring or summer. The young emerge at the end of summer or in early autumn.

Before legal restrictions were imposed, the pet and tourist trades made heavy inroads into the Kalahari tent tortoise population (and into those of its relatives, the tent and geometric tortoises, too). The creatures were either sold alive, or they were slaughtered and their attractive shells offered for sale.

The San have a taste for Kalahari tent tortoises; they also decorate the shells, and use them as powder-holders or buchu pouches.

CAPE PADLOPER

Kaapse padloper *(Homopus areolatus)*

Size: Length (m) 10 cm, (f) 11,5 cm.
Colour: Each shield of the carapace is olive-green or yellowish green, with a reddish brown centre and a narrow dark brown or black border. Sometimes the carapace of adult males shades to an almost uniform orange-brown.
Most like: Greater padloper, which is the only other southern African tortoise with four toes on all four feet; the latter, however, is 2-3 cm longer and is uniform olive-brown to reddish brown above.
Habitat: From coastal fynbos to drier grassy habitats.

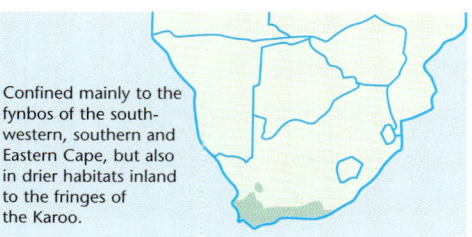

Confined mainly to the fynbos of the south-western, southern and Eastern Cape, but also in drier habitats inland to the fringes of the Karoo.

This tiny tortoise has earned its name, padloper or road-walker: it has a habit of taking to the road when it goes for a stroll, oblivious of the fact that by doing so it dices with death. Fortunately, the species is not so rare that its wanderings into the highways and byways will lead to its extinction; in fact it is relatively common in the southern coastal areas of the Western and Eastern Cape.

The upper jaw of the Cape padloper ends in a hooked beak, especially noticeable in males, and rather like a parrot's, hence one of its alternative names: parrot-beaked tortoise. The beak is used for foraging and fighting. Another name, 'areolated tortoise', refers to the distinctive patterning of the shields, which form three rows of 'areolas' or greenish circles on the carapace.

Finally, the generic name *Homopus* derives from the Greek for 'same-footed', a reference to the fact that the tortoise has four claws on each of its four feet, unlike nearly all tortoises, which have five claws on the front feet and four on the back feet.

The Cape padloper gives no trouble to farmers or home gardeners, for it feeds almost exclusively on indigenous vegetation.

Two to four hard-shelled, oval eggs are laid by the female at intervals during her reproductive period. The eggs, buried and concealed in the usual tortoise way, take about five to seven months to incubate.

Turtles and tortoises

SPECKLED PADLOPER

Gespikkelde padloper *(Homopus signatus)*

Size: Length 8-10 cm.
Colour: The carapace of the subspecies Homopus signatus signatus *(found in southern Namibia and Namaqualand)* is light brown, with black spots or streaks; the carapace of the subspecies Homopus signatus cafer *(Piketberg to Calvinia)* is orange-red to pink, with black speckles.
Most like: The Karoo padloper, which is about the same size, also lives in rocky terrain, but never has black markings.
Habitat: Ranges mainly from semi-desert and succulent Karoo to fynbos.

Found only in Namaqualand, from the Gariep River south to Graafwater and Citrusdal, and inland to Calvinia.

The speckled padloper, the world's smallest tortoise, would fit very easily into the breast-pocket of a jacket, as its carapace has only the shallowest of curves. The serrated edges at the rear end of the carapace of the subspecies *H. s. signatus* might, however, prove a snag; and anyway the exercise is not one to be recommended, for tortoises are inclined to urinate when frightened.

You are most likely to come across a speckled padloper early in the morning, when it is out and about foraging for a meal of succulents among the rocks. Later in the day it will shelter under a rock slab, often in the company of others of its kind.

For a creature so small, it is really quite bold. Yet its defences are relatively insignificant, and predators are mostly undeterred by the shell, which is not as stout as those of most other tortoises. A jackal can easily crunch through to the delicate flesh below; a bird of prey can use its beak to peck out the padloper's tasty meat, leaving the shell behind; a secretarybird may swallow the creature whole, and let the digestive process deal with the rest.

In summer, the female speckled padloper digs a hole, lays a single egg, and then buries it.

The speckled species is one of five 'padlopers' found in southern Africa, all of which belong to the genus *Homopus*. The speckled padloper is classified as a vulnerable species.

KAROO PADLOPER

Karoo-padloper/Donderweerskilpad *(Homopus boulengeri)*

Size: Length 10-11 cm.
Colour: Uniform reddish brown carapace, occasionally olive-brown
Most like: Nama padloper, which is also reddish brown above but usually has dark edges to the scales.
Habitat: Dry, stony terrain.

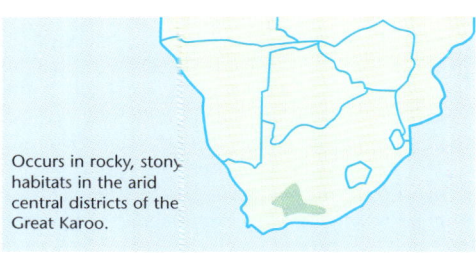

Occurs in rocky, stony habitats in the arid central districts of the Great Karoo.

The alternative Afrikaans name for this little creature—*donder-weerskilpad* or 'thundery weather tortoise'—is one of several others on the same theme: *onweerskilpad* ('bad weather tortoise'), *reënskilpad* ('rain tortoise'), *swaarweerskilpad* ('heavy weather tortoise'). The allusion in each case is to a belief in the Karoo, the sole habitat of the species, that this secretive tortoise is usually seen only shortly before a thunderstorm, when it emerges from its shelter and briskly takes a walk in the open veld. It is welcomed as a forecaster of rain.

The Karoo padloper is one of five diminutive tortoises belonging to the genus *Homopus*, four of which are virtually restricted to the Western and Eastern Cape. Despite the generic name, derived from Greek and indicating that there are the same number of claws (four) on all four feet, the Karoo species has the more normal tortoise complement of five claws on the front feet and four on the rear ones.

The tortoise's carapace is flattened and not high-domed, which equips it well to wedge itself under rocks for protection as well as to make progress over stony terrain without overbalancing and 'turning turtle', though if it is unlucky enough to do just this, it manages to get back on all fours.

The species is seldom found far from some rocky outcrop as it prefers to seek shelter beneath an overhang rather than in a bush. Its enemies include predatory birds such as crows, which easily crush the relatively soft carapace. It feeds on succulent Karoo plants and their flowers. The female deposits one to three eggs in a hole which she then conceals with soil. Incubation may take from five to seven months.

Snakes and lizards

Snakes (suborder Serpentes) and lizards (suborder Sauria) both belong to the reptilian order Squamata, 'the scaly ones', and have a great deal in common. In fact, from the evolutionary point of view, snakes are no more than specialized lizards. Certain lizards—such as dwarf burrowing skinks, with their elongated bodies and rudimentary limbs, or no limbs at all—are snakelike in appearance. And though you would be unlikely to mistake a snake for anything else, some snakes, such as the python, retain the trace of ancestral hindlimbs in the form of a pair of clawlike spurs near the anal vent.

Snakes have no eyelids and no external ear openings. Most lizards have both. Snakes cannot grow a new tail should the original one be lost, whereas many lizards have this ability.

There is another, more significant distinction. The two parts of a snake's lower jaw, which are connected at the front only by an elastic ligament, can separate widely and function independently. This, and the jaw's leverlike connection to the cranium, enable the snake to swallow prey several times its own diameter.

Lizards must settle for smaller prey, for the two halves of their lower jaw are fused together (articulated) at the front and the mouth cannot be opened widely.

Snakes

In the process of evolution snakes have acquired an impressive number of vertebrae, in some species exceeding 300, and an equally impressive number of ribs. Their body surface is covered in closely fitting scales that form a complete skin.

The external streamlining is matched by an internal economy of vital organs. For instance, there is usually only one functioning lung, greatly elongated to at least a third of the snake's body length.

The snake's unblinking, hypnotic stare is attributable to the fact that it has no eyelids. What were once lids have fused into a transparent film (or 'spectacle') over the eye, like a contact lens. When a snake sloughs its skin—as it must frequently do in the early part of its life as it literally 'grows out of' its existing skin—the film over each eye is discarded too, and replaced by another.

Though snakes have no external ears, they are very sensitive to vibrations picked up from the ground. Tree snakes, at any rate when perched on a branch, clearly cannot pick up such vibrations, and so it may be possible for you to get close to a boomslang without betraying your presence. But be careful, its bite can be fatal.

The snake's most important sensory organ is its deeply forked tongue, which can be extruded through a groove at the front of the mouth even when the mouth is closed. This tongue flicks in and out of the mouth, picking up scented particles in the air and transferring them to a specialized organ in the roof of the mouth which can identify the scents; it therefore acts as a 'nose' to smell out food.

By the formation of their sharp, backward-curving teeth, snakes can be divided into three broad categories. Harmless, or nonvenomous, species have only solid teeth; these may be in the upper jaw only (blind snakes), the lower jaw only (thread snakes) or both jaws (the brown house snake and the common brown water snake).

A second category not only has solid teeth, but one or more pairs of grooved fangs—longer teeth for conveying venom—towards the back of the upper jaw. Most of these 'back-fanged' snakes, such as the skaapsteker, are only moderately poisonous to man. But the bite of the boomslang and the twig snake can be fatal.

The third category consists of the front-fanged snakes (cobras, mambas and adders), their long poison fangs being near, or at, the front of the upper jaws, where they can be swivelled forwards for maximum effect.

Snake venom is of different kinds, which have varied effects. 'Neurotoxic' venom (most cobras, mambas and berg adders) attacks the central nervous

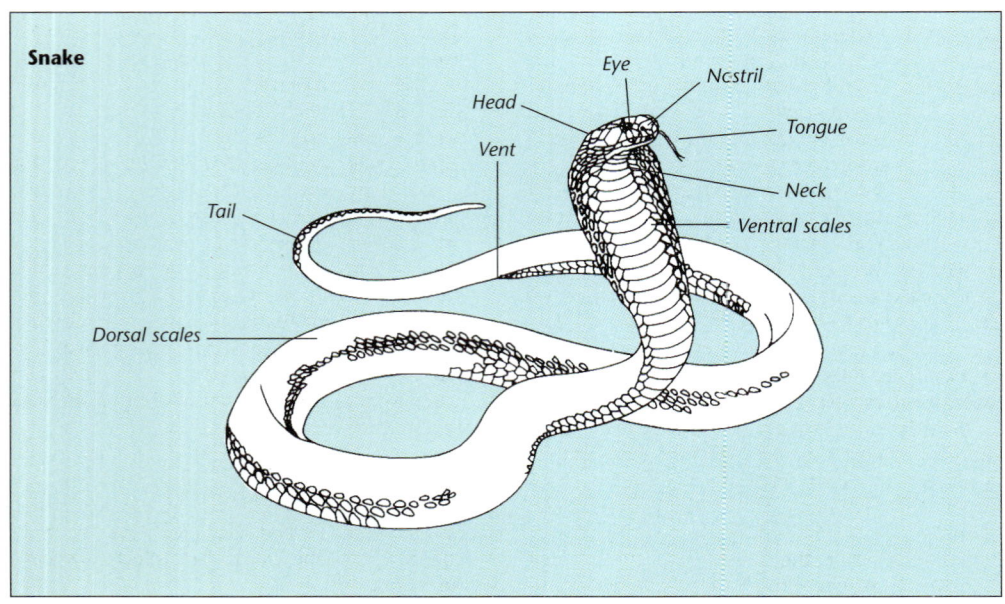

Snake

Snakes and lizards

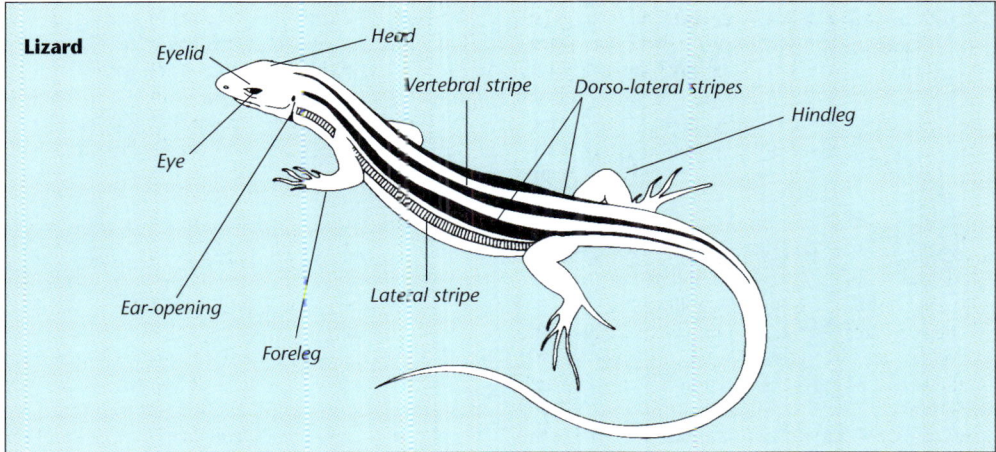

system, affecting movement, breathing, swallowing, speech and sight. 'Haematoxic' venom (boomslangs and twig snakes) affects the blood, using up the clotting factors so that it no longer coagulates, causing extensive blood loss into the tissues.

'Cytotoxic' venom (adders, spitting cobras and rinkhals) attacks the body cells or tissues, and a bite is extremely painful, with much swelling and marked symptoms of shock.

'Myotoxic' venom (yellow-bellied sea snakes) attacks the muscles and in some cases can lead to death from kidney and heart failure.

Snake venom acts fast, and a victim must be treated without delay. Acquaint yourself thoroughly with first-aid measures before setting out on an expedition in which you may encounter a dangerous snake. Also be sure to wear suitably protective clothing, preferably boots and long trousers. In the event of a snakebite, immediately try to identify the snake that delivered the bite and be sure to pass the information on to the doctor or hospital that ultimately treats the victim.

Identifying snakes

More than 2 500 species of snake have been recorded worldwide. While only some 130 of these are indigenous to southern Africa, as many as 35 of them are highly poisonous. They include a sinister quintet: the puff adder, the Egyptian cobra, the Cape cobra, the black mamba and the green mamba.

Unfortunately nature has not gone out of her way to distinguish the harmless species from the venomous ones. There are a lot of 'look-alikes'.

When you see a snake, carefully observe its colour, length, the shape of its head, and its posture. Does it rear up, like the rinkhals, cobra and coral snake, the neck flattening to form a 'hood'? Is it more inclined to strike than to slink away? Does it move forward in a straight line (like pythons and most adders) or, as is more usual, in a series of side-to-side undulations?

Man, like other primates, seems to have an inbuilt horror of snakes in general, but the temptation to slaughter every snake should be avoided.

Lizards

Lizards represent the largest and most varied suborder of reptiles, with about 230 different species indigenous to southern Africa. To most people the 'typical' species is probably the little rock lizard that spends much of its time basking in the sun—an agile creature with an alert, inquisitive snout, well-developed feet and claws, and a long, thin tail. But the suborder includes a diverse range of forms, from delicate arboreal chameleons to powerful leguaans or monitors up to 1,5 m long; and it includes glossy, limbless species as well as heavily armoured ones.

Most lizards can do no worse than nip your finger, although leguaans, with their strong jaw and claws, are more formidable; they can also deliver a nasty blow with their tail. No indigenous lizards, however, are venomous.

Identifying lizards

Most of the groups into which lizard species are divided are quite distinctive.

By their size alone, leguaans, of which there are only two indigenous species, are easy to identify. Chameleons, likewise, are unmistakeable, with their jerky locomotion, and their hands, feet and prehensile tail adapted mostly for an arboreal existence.

Geckos usually have splayed, round-ended, adhesive discs on the tips of their toes, which enable them to walk up a vertical surface or even upside down across a ceiling. However, some terrestrial species lack this ability, and some have tiny claws to their toes. There is also a web-footed species; its webs help it to walk over fine sand. Geckos lack moveable eyelids; they are fused to form a transparent 'spectacle' over the eye; and their wide-eyed look sets them apart from other lizards.

Skinks are lizards possessing smooth-scaled, cylindrical bodies. They range from species that conform to 'typical' lizard appearance, to those which are snakelike, with degenerate limbs or none at all.

Agamas should be quite easy to identify: they have broad, toadlike heads, flattened, wide bodies and long, thin tails.

Nile crocodile

For convenience, the Nile crocodile is described in this section of the book although it belongs to an order of reptiles, the Crocodylia, distinct from snakes and lizards.

Snakes and lizards

SOUTHERN AFRICAN ROCK PYTHON

Gewone luislang *(Python sebae natalensis)*

Size: Length 3-5 m.
Colour: Light brown ground colour with a pattern of dark brown, including a forward-pointing, spear-shaped marking on the head.
Most like: Anchieta's dwarf python, which is limited to northern Namibia and southern Angola and is seldom longer than 1,5 m.
Habitat: Open savanna, but particularly fond of thick bush bordering forest, along rivers and cliffs. Never far from permanent water.

Mainly in the open savanna woodland and riverine bush of northern Namibia, southeastern and northern Botswana, Zimbabwe, Mozambique, Northern Province, Mpumalanga, Swaziland and southern KwaZulu-Natal.

The tough, handsome skin of this whopper, Africa's largest snake, has always been much in demand in the leather trade, but legislation now protects the species. Farmers should be grateful, for the python includes harmful rodents in its eclectic diet.

Moving through the bush it presents an awe-inspiring sight. It hunts by ambush, lying along a game trail or submerged in water at a waterhole, patiently awaiting the arrival of a suitably sized animal. Then it lunges from its concealed cover and strikes, with its mouth wide open. When the python's long, curved-back teeth hit the prey, it throws its coil around the unfortunate animal and starts asphyxiating it. The struggle is usually over within two or three minutes. Every time the prey exhales, the python constricts a little more, so that inhalation becomes increasingly difficult. The sheer panic of the victim often accelerates the end.

Contrary to popular belief, death is usually caused by suffocation alone, and not by crushing, although ribs may puncture essential organs.

Pythons eat anything from guineafowl to bushbuck; the larger the animal, the longer the swallowing process. Though nonvenomous, pythons can be dangerous to man, inflicting lacerating wounds with their bite—and there is the obvious danger to breathing if the snake coils around your chest.

MOLE SNAKE

Molslang *(Pseudaspis cana)*

Size: Length 1-2 m.
Colour: Black in the western parts of the Western Cape, but usually brown or reddish brown in the Eastern Cape, KwaZulu-Natal, highveld and rest of this snake's distribution area. Young specimens are light or dark brown, with a regular series of darker blotches along the back.
Most like: Rufous-beaked snake, in the northern part of the mole snake's range, but the mole snake lacks the beaked snake's distinctive hooked snout.
Habitat: Sandy areas where rodents such as molerats, striped mice and gerbils are common.

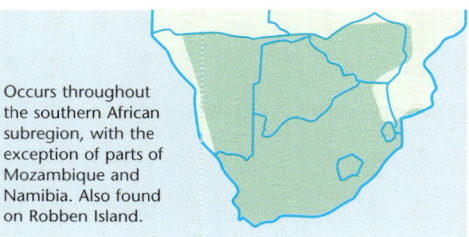

Occurs throughout the southern African subregion, with the exception of parts of Mozambique and Namibia. Also found on Robben Island.

This large, thick, glossy snake is often bludgeoned to death in the mistaken belief that it is a Cape cobra, yet it is not poisonous, does not rear up and does not spread a hood in cobra fashion. Likewise, the mole snake's spotted young are confused with the rhombic skaapsteker or the African egg-eater (the former mildly venomous, the latter not). Although the mole snake itself is nonvenomous, catching a large specimen is tricky, for it puts up a show of ferocity and can, with little provocation, inflict a lacerating bite.

Mole snakes burrow into sandy soil waiting to pounce on mammals with similar habits, especially molerats and golden moles. They have relatively small, pointed heads (even a large mole snake's head is just some three centimetres wide), and the fact that it can swallow a Cape dune mole (sometimes as large as a rabbit) is eloquent testimony to the stretching powers of its lower jaw.

Young mole snakes feed on small rodents and lizards, but the adults take only warm-blooded prey which they kill by constriction.

For shelter, mole snakes often retreat into the burrows of molerats or gerbils. They adapt to captivity quite well and make interesting pets, provided each snake is accommodated in a large enclosure.

Snakes and lizards

Black mamba

Swartmamba *(Dendroaspis polylepis)*

Size: Length 2,5 m-3,5 m.
Colour: Greyish green, olive-green, grey-brown or gunmetal grey (especially in humid coastal regions), but seldom black. The underside is pale grey or grey-green. The inside of the mouth is blackish.
Most like: Grey-brown to blackish forms of the Egyptian cobra, particularly Anchieta's cobra, but the latter spreads a typically cobralike hood when threatened (larger than the mamba's hood), and has a dark brown and black band across its throat.
Habitat: Subtropical and tropical open bush country.

Central and northern Namibia, eastern Botswana, Zimbabwe, Mozambique, the North-West, Northern Province, Mpumalanga, Swaziland, eastern KwaZulu-Natal and the Transkei region of the Eastern Cape.

The mere mention of the name black mamba, the largest venomous snake in Africa, is guaranteed to strike fear into most people. This snake's fast-acting neurotoxic and cardiotoxic venom is so potent that, without immediate first-aid, it can kill a person in under seven hours. Most bites are accidental, however, as mambas do not attack unless molested, and are far more inclined to flee. However, they do react quickly to what they perceive to be an invasion of their privacy. Because they rear up to strike, their bite is apt to be on the upper body or head.

These snakes often enter houses and outbuildings and are then particularly dangerous

Black mambas live either in a hole in the ground—perhaps an abandoned termite mound, or the burrow of one of the small mammals—or in a hollow tree or rock crevice.

They are usually up and about at first light, hunting for rats, dassies, squirrels or small game birds, then ascending large, leafy trees to sunbathe. During the heat of midday the black mamba will retreat into the shady recesses of the tree.

When hunting, mambas course through the grass with the forepart of the body raised in a graceful curve. They can travel at a maximum speed of 15 km per hour.

The female lays her eggs in midsummer. The hatchlings are retiring, nervous and as poisonous as adults.

Egyptian cobra

Egiptiese kobra *(Naja annulifera)*

Size: Length 1,5-2 m.
Colour: Yellowish brown to bluish black above, and yellow below, usually spotted or blotched with brown. There is also a banded form, with 7-10 yellow bands on the black body and two on the tail. Most specimens have a distinctive dark band across the throat.
Most like: Black specimens lacking yellow bands could be confused with the forest cobra, where the ranges of the two species overlap. The forest cobra, however, has brown front half to body and a shiny black rear half.
Habitat: Bushveld. Large wood piles, holes at the bases of disused termite mounds, fallen trees and rodent burrows are used as shelter.

In the bushveld regions of north-eastern Namibia, northern and eastern Botswana, Zimbabwe, Mozambique, the North-West, Northern Province, Mpumalanga, Swaziland and northern KwaZulu-Natal.

This is the most widespread cobra species in Africa—a formidable snake that, in anger, raises the first third of its body and spreads a large, saucer-shaped hood up to 12 cm in diameter.

Although not normally aggressive, the Egyptian cobra will attack if disturbed or flushed out of its hiding place. Its venom attacks the nervous system, and can have potentially lethal results; in fact this species and the black mamba are responsible for most snakebite deaths in northern KwaZulu-Natal, Mpumalanga, Northern Province, North-West Province, Zimbabwe and Namibia.

The Egyptian cobra often enters homesteads and outbuildings and, like other cobra species, will live quite happily close to man. It will be particularly attracted to old piles of wood in the garden, discarded building material or neglected grounds. These usually provide protection from the elements, not only for the snake but for its prey. Here the cobra will stay until forcibly dislodged. In the wild it will continue to use the same shelter for years.

Included in the Egyptian cobra's diet are toads, rodents, lizards, birds and their eggs, and other snakes. It hunts mostly at night, and will return repeatedly to raid poultry-runs. Like the rinkhals, this species may sham death when caught. Eggs are laid, 8-20 at a time in a sheltered hole in the ground, or in trees. The hatchlings measure 23-34 cm in length.

Snakes and lizards

Cape cobra

Kaapse kobra (Naja nivea)

Size: Length 1-2 m.
Colour: A wide range, from various shades of yellow and brown (sometimes with speckles) to purplish black. Whatever the colour, the snake has a glossy appearance. The young usually have a dark band at the neck.
Most like: Small specimens may be confused with a variety of harmless species, such as the mole snake, but the cobra's habit of rearing up with hood splayed identifies it.
Habitat: Usually arid, sandy areas where there is a good rodent population.

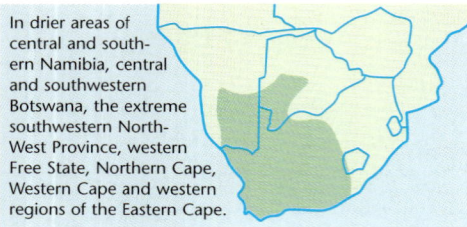

In drier areas of central and southern Namibia, central and southwestern Botswana, the extreme southwestern North-West Province, western Free State, Northern Cape, Western Cape and western regions of the Eastern Cape.

The Cape cobra has a curiously disconcerting habit that could quite literally scare the pants off you: it slithers indoors in search of water, sometimes seeking refuge under the rim of a toilet seat!

This has been known to happen within the environs of Cape Town, where the snakes come down into the gardens on the slopes of the Twelve Apostles. Their quest for water often ends at a fish pond or dripping tap but, in the absence of these, the snakes sometimes find their way into a house where they may slake their thirst in a toilet bowl.

Always treat a Cape cobra with the greatest respect. Not only is it very common, but its venom is also the most potent of all the African cobras. If no easy escape route is available it will rear up and may charge its opponent. Its venom is rapidly absorbed by the body, paralysing the motor nerves. Without immediate treatment, death may follow within six to eight hours.

The numerous colour varieties of this species have given rise to an array of common names. Although it is known also as the yellow cobra and the speckled cobra, Cape cobra remains the most suitable name because it is essentially a Cape species. However, it also occurs in southern Namibia and Botswana, and southern North-West Province.

These cobras eat rodents, lizards, toads and other snakes. They shelter in rodent or other burrows, and also under rubble in the vicinity of built-up areas.

Forest cobra

Boskobra (Naja melanoleuca)

Size: Length 1,5-2 m.
Colour: Front half of body yellow-brown, flecked with black; back half shiny black.
Most like: Black specimens of the Egyptian cobra, but the forest cobra has a more slender body and spreads a much narrower hood.
Habitat: Natural forest and plantations in northern KwaZulu-Natal, north of the Tugela river, and in Mozambique and the eastern areas of Zimbabwe.

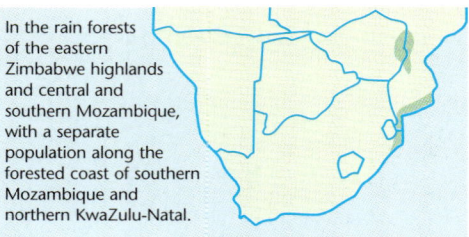

In the rain forests of the eastern Zimbabwe highlands and central and southern Mozambique, with a separate population along the forested coast of southern Mozambique and northern KwaZulu-Natal.

A forest cobra kept in captivity will respond to food with astonishing speed, often giving its keeper some hair-raising moments as it charges out of its cage towards the offered meal. In the wild, however, this is a distinctly shy species that will try to avoid contact with human beings at all costs.

Nevertheless, beware—the venom of the forest cobra is neurotoxic, and potentially lethal to man. If pursued, it will not hesitate to attack, and generally does so very effectively, being one of the few snakes to exhibit seemingly 'intelligent' and calculating behaviour. It will launch its attack just at the right moment: when the pursuer is a little off balance, momentarily too close or at some other disadvantage. However, this cobra is not a 'spitting' snake, but injects its venom with a bite.

The forest cobra is widely distributed in Africa and is associated with rain-forests. Yet it will invade single-crop plantations and is common among the eucalyptus trees at Mtubatuba in northern KwaZulu-Natal. It is always found near permanent water and, besides taking mammalian prey, toads, frogs, lizards and other snakes, it is an adept predator of fish. Needless to say, it is an excellent swimmer.

Although a nocturnal terrestrial species, the forest cobra readily takes to climbing trees to escape a pursuer. Like other cobra species, it will not hesitate to live in close association with man, and is quick to exploit a source of small stock.

Female forest cobras have been known to lay up to 26 eggs at a time under logs, or in other suitable sites such as holes in trees.

Snakes and lizards

MOZAMBIQUE SPITTING COBRA
Mosambiekse spoegkobra
(*Naja mossambica*)

RINKHALS
Rinkhals (*Hemachatus haemachatus*)

Size: Length 90 cm-1,2 m.

Colour: The shiny back varies from grey and light brown to darker shades of brown, each scale usually being edged in black. The belly is pink or yellowish, and the throat has both narrow and wide black bars across it.

Most like: The brown phase of the Egyptian cobra which, however, has only one dark throat-band.

Habitat: Hills, rocky outcrops and rodent holes near rivers and vleis in savanna country.

From the coastal districts of southern KwaZulu-Natal, through Swaziland, Mpumalanga, North-West, Northern Province, Mozambique and Zimbabwe, and westwards through Botswana to northern Namibia.

Size: Length 90 cm-1,2 m.

Colour: Black or brown, either uniform or with spots or variegations. A banded form has a black head and alternate bands of brownish black and yellow or orange along the back. Underparts dark brown or black with one or two (occasionally three) broad white bands across the throat, visible when the rinkhals rears up and spreads its hood.

Most like: Uniform brown form resembles mole snake, which does not, however, rear up and spread a hood. Brown and black forms resemble Egyptian cobra, but latter usually has yellowish underparts and black band under neck. Banded form resembles Namibian subspecies of black-necked spitting cobra, but latter has yellowish underparts and a wide black throat band.

Habitat: Grassland, where it lives in rodent burrows or old termite mounds when not sunning itself.

Mainly in the Western and Eastern Cape, Lesotho, Free State, Gauteng, Mpumalanga and western Swaziland, with a small population in the Inyanga region of Zimbabwe.

This common species has the disconcerting habit of spitting its venom in defence, which it does with little encouragement and great accuracy. It may even do so without rearing up, simply turning back, 'snarling' to spit and then continuing on its way. It may also bite with little or no provocation; there are regular instances of its biting sleeping victims indoors after dark.

The snake's venom is cytotoxic (tissue-destroying) and not neurotoxic (attacking the motor nerves) like that of other cobra species. A bite will lead to some initial swelling and slight discoloration; in due course the entire area down to the muscle layer may slough away, not at the bite but sometimes at sites remote from it. Venom spat into the eyes is very painful and causes inflammation, but will have less serious effects provided that it is washed out immediately with water; a scratchy feeling may persist for an hour or two, but permanent damage to the eye is unlikely.

It is not true, as often claimed, that the snake instinctively spits at the eyes. It aims for the area of the body where there is greatest movement—invariably the upper part of the body. An adult spitting cobra can direct its venom accurately to a distance of three metres.

The Mozambique spitting cobra preys on a wide variety of animals, including toads, lizards, other snakes, rodents, birds and insects.

The rinkhals, the Mozambique spitting cobra and the black-necked spitting cobra are the only snake species in southern Africa that 'spit' venom. The rinkhals is the least effective of the three, even though it seems to hurl the poison forwards, the reared part of its body often hitting the ground with an audible thud during the exercise. Its range is up to 2,5 metres. Venom that enters the eyes should be washed out immediately to prevent damage.

The rinkhals may also bite. Its venom is neurotoxic (causing nervous dysfunction), and death—although rare—can result from respiratory paralysis. Antivenom is effective against the toxin, however.

As a last resort when cornered, a rinkhals will feign death and go completely limp, but with one wary eye open. The 'revived' snake may suddenly make a getaway, or give a nasty bite.

Mainly nocturnal, though sometimes seen on cloudy days, the rinkhals feeds mostly on small vertebrates, and is particularly partial to toads.

The rinkhals is closely related to the cobras but its scales have a prominent central ridge or keel and are not smooth.

Snakes and lizards

GREEN MAMBA

Groenmamba
(Dendroaspis angusticeps)

Size: Length 1,5-2,5 m.

Colour: Bright grass-green back and yellowish green underneath; the mouth lining is white.

Most like: The green form of the boomslang, and the green snake; the mamba, however, has smooth body scales while the boomslang's are 'keeled' or ridged, and rough to the touch. The mamba's eye is much smaller proportionately than that of the boomslang.

Habitat: Tropical or subtropical forest and coastal bush.

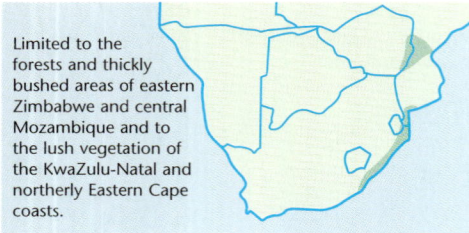

Limited to the forests and thickly bushed areas of eastern Zimbabwe and central Mozambique and to the lush vegetation of the KwaZulu-Natal and northerly Eastern Cape coasts.

During the mating season, you may be fortunate enough to see two male green mambas thrashing each other with their bodies and hurling their coils with such force that a slapping noise is created. No real harm is done, for this is all part of ritualized fighting—or what is known as 'combat dancing'.

Because many people confuse green mambas with other green snakes—they are generally believed to be widespread in KwaZulu-Natal. However, they are found only along a narrow coastal strip (except in the vicinity of rivers), and are becoming increasingly threatened as the rampant commercial and agricultural development of the KwaZulu-Natal coast destroys the last vestiges of coastal bush. In the north of the subregion green mambas are found much further inland: for example, along the eastern border of Zimbabwe and right across Mozambique.

Unlike the black mamba, the green mamba is entirely arboreal. Though elusive, like the black mamba, it is less excitable, and instances of snakebite are rarer. While its neurotoxic venom is less toxic, too, this difference is academic as far as the human victim is concerned: the bite should be taken seriously and the relevant treatment given immediately.

The female lays her eggs either in a tree hollow or on the ground, among plant debris. The babies hatch in about two-and-a-half months and are olive green, but within days the baby green mamba assumes the beautiful grass-green hue of the adult.

BOOMSLANG

Boomslang *(Dispholidus typus)*

Size: Length 1-1,5 m.

Colour: A wide colour range, from light brown to dark brown and from bright green to olive-green, the underside being lighter—greenish white, brown or yellow. There is also a black form, with yellow underneath, the yellow scales being edged with black. The large eyes are grey or brown. Young snakes are usually ash-grey with blue flecks and a greenish yellow throat.

Most like: Green mamba, black mamba, green snake, but has a disproportionately large eye and is more arboreal than these three species.

Habitat: Trees and shrubs where birds and other arboreal prey are common.

Throughout the subregion, except for the Namib Desert, southern Namibia, southwestern Botswana, the Northern and north-western Cape and high-lying regions to the east.

Boomslangs are retiring snakes and generally only rough handling induces them to bite. If cornered, and this takes some doing as these snakes move with lightning speed through the trees, an aggravated boomslang will inflate its neck or even the front two-thirds of its body to more than twice its usual diameter. It will certainly try to bite if molestation continues. When it does so, it holds on and chews away at the site of the bite. The only way to remove it is to rip it away boldly.

Boomslang venom is slow-acting but extremely potent and mostly haemotoxic, preventing clotting and causing severe bleeding. Characteristic symptoms—headache, nausea and the formation of discoloured areas on the body or limbs, representing internal bleeding—may take 24-48 hours to show.

The boomslang's colouring and its ability to remain immobile for long periods provide it with ideal camouflage as it lies in wait for its prey: tree-dwelling chameleons, lizards and birds. It will also forage on the ground, but if disturbed will immediately make for the nearest tree; it will also take any prey into a tree before consuming it. In common with many other snakes it will head for water if necessary and is a strong swimmer.

Snakes and lizards

GREEN WATER SNAKE

Groen waterslang *(Philothamnus hoplogaster)*

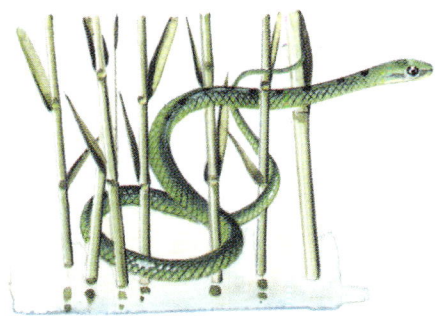

Size: Length 45-70 cm.
Colour: Dull or olive green, often with a bluish hue and sometimes with black spots over the front half of the back. Bright grass-green body after sloughing (shedding of the skin). The underside is lighter and tinged with white or yellow.
Most like: Green mamba (especially after the water snake has sloughed), and boomslang, but smaller than these. Mamba, however, never has black spots on front half of back.
Habitat: Reed-lined pans, ponds, rivers and marshes.

Near water throughout most of Zimbabwe, Mozambique, Swaziland, Mpumalanga, Northern Province, northern and coastal KwaZulu-Natal, and along the Transkei and southeastern Cape coast.

This snake is nonvenomous, tames readily, and even when captured does not thrash around and bite. However, on the KwaZulu-Natal coastal belt there is always the risk of confusing this species with a young green mamba, and inexperienced collectors should proceed with caution.

As its name implies, the green water snake is usually found near water, on coastal plains, inland grasslands or high mountain forest. Apart from fish and lizards its favourite food is frogs and it will search for these from the water's bank. Having caught its prey, it swims back to the shore with the victim in its mouth, and consumes it at leisure.

Interestingly, because so few southern African snakes are known to feed on invertebrates, young green water snakes will readily make a meal of grasshoppers, beetles and other insects.

Though an adept swimmer and diver, this species is equally at home on the ground and in trees. It is a nimble little snake that is most active during the day.

The green water snake is one of five species belonging to the genus *Philothamnus* found in southern Africa. Four of them are known as 'green snakes' and are closely associated with water; the fifth, also green, but usually spotted or barred with black, is the arboreal spotted bush snake. None of these snakes is poisonous.

TWIG SNAKE

Takslang *(Thelotornis capensis)*

Size: Length 1 m.
Colour: Shades of grey, mottled with pinkish and black flecks to resemble light bark. Top of head green, with or without black markings.
Most like: The very young resemble the bark snake, but larger twig snakes are quite unlike any other species.
Habitat: Woodland ranging from coastal forest to bushveld savanna.

Found in northern Namibia, northern and southeastern Botswana, Zimbabwe, Mozambique, eastern KwaZulu-Natal, Swaziland, Gauteng, Northern Province and eastern North-West Province.

Known also as the vine snake or bird snake, this species has three claims to fame. The first is its external appearance: its camouflage is nearly perfect, and you need to look very carefully to distinguish it from a dry branch or twig. Secondly, it is one of the few snakes that appears to be able to identify stationary prey, even at a distance. If you encountered, say, a cobra in the veld and it reared up and faced you, it would soon drop its hood and move off again if you stood perfectly still; by remaining motionless you would have 'disappeared' into the background. But the twig snake is not so easily fooled. It has, in fact, a strong preference for chameleons, which spend much of their time quite motionless.

Its third claim to fame is that its haemotoxic venom is extremely toxic. Like the boomslang (whose venom works in a similar way to cause haemorrhaging), it is one of the few back-fanged species with a bite that can be lethal to man. When the twig snake decides to bite, it remains dedicated to the idea and may follow up an unsuccessful strike. And, like the boomslang, it may grossly inflate the throat area and sometimes the whole front of its body when threatened.

Twig snakes don't seem to do much active hunting, spending much of their time lying in wait for prey. The female lays between four and 13 eggs during the summer. The banded markings on the hatchlings are exactly the same as those of their parents.

Three subspecies exist: the southern twig snake (*Thelotornis capensis capensis*), Oates's twig snake (*T.c. oatesii*) and eastern twig snake (*T.c. mossambicanus*).

Snakes and lizards

HERALD SNAKE

Rooilipslang *(Crotaphopeltis hotamboeia)*

Size: Length 50-75 cm.
Colour: Olive-green back, either uniform or with tiny white flecks. Underside white or cream. Upper lip usually bright orange or red, sometimes white or yellow. Top of head iridescent purplish black.
Most like: May be mistaken for a night adder or small cobra, not because it looks similar but because of its similar nocturnal habits and threat display, which involves flattening the head, to give it a triangular, adderlike appearance.
Habitat: Prefers damp, marshy areas in fynbos, grassland and savanna. Often finds shelter in gardens and near houses and outbuildings.

 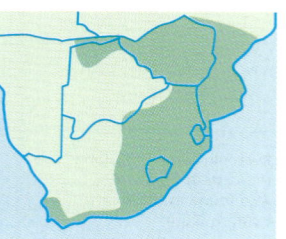

In moist regions of northern Botswana, Zimbabwe, Mozambique, Swaziland, Mpumalanga, Gauteng, Northern Province, the North-West, Free State, Lesotho, KwaZulu-Natal, Eastern Cape, southern and southwestern Cape.

This is surely the only snake to bear the name of a newspaper. Despite having been known to science since 1768, it remained without a generally accepted common name until it was found in the Eastern Cape by JM Leslie, who named it in honour of the *Eastern Province Herald*; the ensuing publicity given to it in this Port Elizabeth newspaper led to its common name being widely adopted.

A nocturnal species, it is fond of wet areas and feeds almost exclusively on amphibians: when these are not available it will, however, resort to lizards and small rodents.

An annoyed or startled herald snake will immediately draw its head back over its body coils, flatten it and strike out with wide-open mouth. This aggressive threat display often results in the species being mistaken for an adder, thought of as highly venomous and summarily bludgeoned to death. When it bites it has the unpleasant habit of keeping its fangs embedded and chewing the flesh of its victim. The venom causes immediate pain followed by a local stinging sensation but is otherwise harmless to man.

This back-fanged snake is commonly found in gardens, particularly near fishponds or other water features inhabited by frogs and toads.

COMMON BROWN WATER SNAKE

Bruin waterslang *(Lycodonomorphus rufulus)*

Size: Length 60-75 cm.
Colour: Olive-brown to dark brown, or glossy black in some older specimens. Upper lip and underside pale yellow or pink. Pink tongue.
Most like: Dusky-bellied water snake, but the common water snake is shorter and lacks the blackish band running the length of the dusky-bellied water snake's underside.
Habitat: The vicinity of streams and vleis; under debris and rocks during the day, and on reeds and in water at night.

In moister regions of eastern Zimbabwe, southern Mozambique, Swaziland, Mpumalanga, Gauteng, eastern North-West, KwaZulu-Natal, Lesotho, Free State, Eastern Cape and coastal southern and Western Cape.

Frogs, tree and reed frogs in particular, have a strong aversion to water snakes, which have the habit of killing them by constriction, and then swallowing them head-first. These snakes also have an appetite for tadpoles and small fish, which they expertly capture in the water and take ashore to eat.

The water snake doesn't have things all its own way, however. When it encounters a full-grown Cape river frog (*Rana fuscigula*) the tables may be turned and the frog-eater often ends up as a meal itself. To escape the attentions of river frogs and other small carnivorous animals, a water snake may shelter underwater beneath a rock where it can remain submerged for a considerable time.

This snake is much feared by the Zulu people, and it is thought their fear may be based on the fact that the water snake looks like the black mamba which is common along KwaZulu-Natal's rivers. The brown water snake, however, is nonvenomous and seldom tries to bite when caught, though it may thrash about a little when handled for the first time.

Unlike many snake species, it is able to tolerate and be active at quite low temperatures.

Water snakes go frog-hunting at night, slithering through reeds, and up them, looking for victims. They are unwelcome guests around fish hatcheries.

Snakes and lizards

Brown house snake

Bruin huisslang *(Lamprophis fuliginosus)*

Size: Length 45cm-1m.
Colour: Light brown to reddish brown above, or dark brown in old specimens. Underparts off-white. On each side of the head is a prominent, horizontal, silvery line running from the tip of the snout through the eye. These lines may rarely extend along the front half of the body, especially in young snakes.
Most like: Young Egyptian or Cape cobra, but the house snake's twin silver head streaks are distinctive, and its underparts are uniform off-white, without a dark throat-band.
Habitat: Under debris near human habitation; under stones in rocky areas.

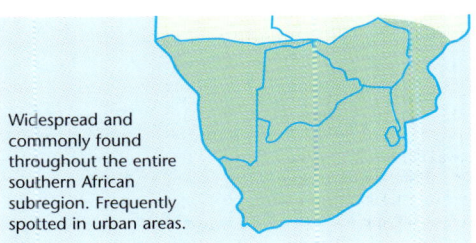

Widespread and commonly found throughout the entire southern African subregion. Frequently spotted in urban areas.

Brown house snakes are among the most common, and perhaps the most useful, snakes in southern Africa: attracted to areas of human habitation, they readily consume those other, less desirable, cohabitants of man—mice and rats. They are nonvenomous and quite harmless to man.

House snakes are powerful constrictors. Large specimens have no trouble killing a rat, which is first seized in the jaws before the coils are thrown around it. When the rat is dead, the snake's asphyxiating grip is relaxed and the prey eaten head-first. If the snake's favoured diet is unavailable it will eat frogs, lizards, birds and eggs. The young feed on lizards.

Because of their useful role in eliminating vermin, brown house snakes deserve to be spared, not slaughtered. Their own predators include larger snakes and birds of prey, particularly owls, which hunt them when they're out and about at night.

In captivity adult house snakes and their young initially put up a ferocious display, striking and biting; but, except for the occasional intractable individual, they soon settle down in captivity to become quite tame. The female lays her eggs in early summer among vegetable debris, compost or similar decaying matter, and the hatchlings emerge two to three months later.

Aurora snake

Aurora huisslang *(Lamprophis aurora)*

Size: Length 45-60cm.
Colour: A shiny olive-green or serpentine green, with a yellow or orange beaded stripe over the head and running down the length of the back to the tip of the tail. Underside yellowish or greenish white. Young specimens are slightly darker than adults.
Most like: Striped harlequin snake (Homoroselaps dorsalis), which also has a yellow vertebral stripe, but the Aurora house snake is never as dark as the harlequin snake, which is black rather than green.
Habitat: Moist areas generally, usually in grassland or coastal bush (or fynbos in the southwestern Cape). Sometimes found in drier, rocky country where there are vleis and seasonal small streams.

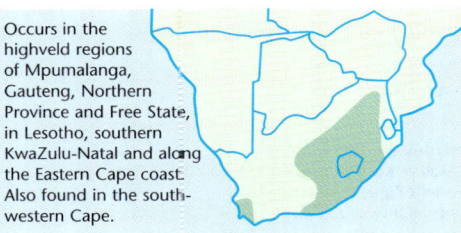

Occurs in the highveld regions of Mpumalanga, Gauteng, Northern Province and Free State, in Lesotho, southern KwaZulu-Natal and along the Eastern Cape coast. Also found in the southwestern Cape.

This harmless, attractive-looking snake derives its name from the small village of Aurora in the southwestern Cape. Rare in comparison with other house snakes, it preys on smaller rodents and, occasionally, lizards, killing by constriction as it has no venom glands.

Like other house snakes it lives in association with man because of man's rodent 'commensals': the mice and rats that thrive around human habitation. Though occasionally it may be seen sunning itself in the early morning or late afternoon, the Aurora house snakes is mostly a nocturnal creature and so is not often encountered. Its daytime shelter is typically a pile of logs or heap of rocks.

Although this snake is found in many areas of South Africa and in Lesotho, it is very unevenly distributed over this range. Its popularity as a pet (a discouraged pastime) and the fact that many are killed on the roads at night as urbanization spreads, have considerably reduced the number of the species.

The female lays 8-12 oval eggs, each about 20x 35mm, between late October and early November. The first hatchlings appear in December, and each of the tiny snakes is about 20cm long and darker than its parents.

Snakes and lizards

Sundevall's garter snake

Sundevall se kousbandslang *(Elapsoidea sundevallii)*

Size: Length 75 cm.
Colour: Slate-grey to black back, with a reddish or purplish iridescence. Pairs of dirty white rings occur along the length of the body. Each pair of rings marks the limits of a buff band that is very distinct in young snakes but darkens in adults; young garter snakes have 21-38 of these bands. Underside yellowish or pinkish buff.
Most like: Other garter snake species, particularly Boulenger's garter snake which, however, has a grey-to-black belly and only 12-17 light bands or pairs of bands.
Habitat: Grassland, coastal forest and sandy savanna.

Nocturnal and rarely seen, it occurs on the grasslands of Namibia and Botswana, the Northern Province, Mpumalanga, Gauteng and Free State highveld, in southern Mozambique, eastern KwaZulu-Natal and Swaziland.

Always treat Sundevall's garter snake with respect. Although it has a quiet disposition and can generally be handled freely, it may, almost as an afterthought, suddenly cease its contented crawling over its keeper's arm to inflict a sharp and painful bite.

What follows is a generalized allergic reaction, with stuffiness in the nose and itching all over the body. The bite area swells and discolours within a few hours, the result of bleeding. Without antivenom the effects take three to five days to subside.

Garter snakes are front-fanged and belong to the same family (Elapidae) as cobras and mambas. Although they do not rear and spread hoods, an agitated snake will flatten its neck and make sideways lunges in attempting to bite.

Sundevall's garter snake has five recognized subspecies in southern Africa, distinguished by their differing scale counts. They are not commonly seen, being nocturnal and sheltering underground, often in disused termite mounds. Furthermore they appear to be active only during the summer rains. If flushed out of their burrows by rain, they may take refuge under a pile of logs.

The diet of Sundevall's garter snake consists of lizards' eggs, snakes, rain frogs, rodents and moles.

The female lays up to ten eggs at a time, each measuring about 20 x 8 millimetres.

Spotted harlequin snake

Gevlekte kousbandjie *(Homoroselaps lacteus)*

Size: Length 30-50 cm.
Colour: Black head, with alternate black and yellow bands or blotches all down the body, and a bright orange or red vertebral stripe running from the top of the head to the tail. Or (in the more northern areas of this snake's distribution) all black, except for the bright orange or red vertebral stripe, and with each black scale bearing a yellow dot.
Most like: The coral snake which has a broader body and is more regularly transversely banded, with alternate black and coral-red to orange cross-bands.
Habitat: In disused termite mounds, or under stones or debris in sandy areas in coastal bush.

Along the Western and southern Cape coast, in the Eastern Cape, southern KwaZulu-Natal, Lesotho, the Free State, eastern North-West, Gauteng and along the Mpumalanga escarpment.

The name 'harlequin' aptly describes this snake's bright, multicoloured appearance. If disturbed, it does not strike but is quick to wriggle away, giving an impression of flashing colours on the move. It objects to being handled and will wriggle strenuously when caught. Although it is inoffensive and does not often bite, it may do so quite unexpectedly. Fortunately its small mouth normally prevents it from taking a full bite, and its venom is comparatively mild; but that is no reason to be careless when dealing with this snake.

The species, known also as the spotted dwarf garter snake, is nocturnal and given to prowling in and out of grass tufts, where its favourite prey, legless lizards of the genus *Scelotes*, reside. It also preys on small snakes, including burrowing snakes such as blind snakes and thread snakes. In pursuit of these two, it spends much time underground.

The captive life of the spotted harlequin snake is usually short—either because the collector is unable to keep it supplied with suitable food or because it escapes. It is quite a Houdini, finding and taking the tiniest gap to freedom that exists in any cage, often squeezing through the door frame or a chink at the side of the lid.

The female lays her small eggs, usually some six at a time, during the middle of summer.

Snakes and lizards

SUNDEVALL'S SHOVEL-SNOUT

Sundevall se graafneusslang *(Prosymna sundevallii)*

Size: Length 25 cm.

Colour: Ranges from yellowish to reddish or greyish brown, with two (sometimes four) rows of dark spots down the back and tail. Usually a yellow patch on top of the head. Underparts yellowish white.

Most like: Fisk's house snake which is also nocturnal and also lives partly underground. The latter, however, has a normal rounded snout and yellow head with brown cross-bars.

Habitat: Under stones or in old termite mounds, in dry, sandy soils.

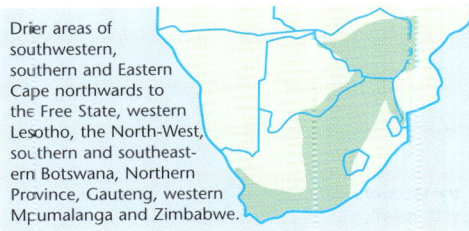

Drier areas of southwestern, southern and Eastern Cape northwards to the Free State, western Lesotho, the North-West, southern and southeastern Botswana, Northern Province, Gauteng, western Mpumalanga and Zimbabwe.

The favourite dish of Sundevall's shovel-snout consists of the eggs of other reptiles, whether lizards or snakes. With the strangely flattened, rather bladelike teeth at the back of its upper jaw it slits open soft-shelled eggs before swallowing them. But it will swallow a hard-shelled gecko egg whole—the digestive juices then break down the shell, and the contents are absorbed.

You have to examine this snake in profile to notice the distinctive shape of the snout, with its sharp and slightly upturned cutting edge.

You will rarely encounter Sundevall's shovel-snout in the open; it will only venture out on warm, humid nights. Although it lives underground, using its sharp snout to facilitate burrowing in soft soil, it does not have the poor eyesight associated with specialized burrowers such as worm snakes. Its eyes are, in fact, quite large and well developed to assist it in its nocturnal above-ground forays for food.

The shovel-snout may be harmless to man, but it puts up an intimidating display when threatened. First it coils its body from head to tail in a wide circle; then straightens out in a flash to form a circle on the other side. The action is repeated rapidly and erratically, which could deter and frighten anyone who isn't familiar with the defence mechanism of these snakes.

BARK SNAKE

Basslang *(Hemirhagerrhis nototaenia)*

Size: Length 30 cm.

Colour: Grey to greyish brown, with distinctive blackish zigzag pattern down back formed by two rows of spots on either side of a central stripe; this patterning grows lighter towards the tail, the end third of which is usually yellow or salmon-pink. Sides of head and neck have a reddish tinge; underparts off-white, mottled with grey.

Most like: Young twig snake but black zigzag pattern down back should identify bark snake; the twig snake has widely spaced cross-bands of light and dark blotches.

Habitat: Under loose bark of trees, especially that of mopane trees in savanna woodland.

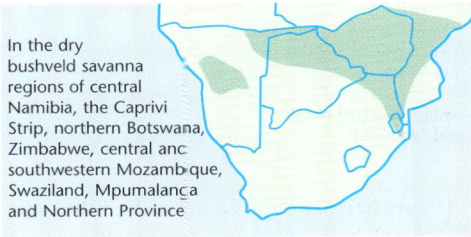

In the dry bushveld savanna regions of central Namibia, the Caprivi Strip, northern Botswana, Zimbabwe, central and southwestern Mozambique, Swaziland, Mpumalanga and Northern Province

Living under loose bark, this species likes to have its meal at its doorstep as it were, for the small geckos and skinks it feeds on share the same savanna habitat. Frogs, especially the little reed or tree frogs of the genus *Hyperolius*, also feature in its diet.

The record size for a bark snake in southern Africa is 43,2 centimetres. Known also as the mopane snake, this species is widely distributed over the eastern half of the African continent as far north as southern Sudan and Somalia (where it makes its home in trees other than the mopane).

In some respects it is a singularly unsnakelike little snake: an inoffensive reptile that is very seldom inclined to bite, even when caught and handled. You could keep a specimen as a pet, but of course you would have to ensure that there was a steady supply of small geckos.

The female egg lays between four and eight extremely elongated eggs at a time, each of which measures about 24 x 6 mm in size.

Two subspecies, the eastern bark snake and the western bark snake, are recognized in southern Africa. The latter's dorsal markings are similar to those of the eastern subspecies, although its dorsal spots are generally larger and are not connected to the central dorsal stripe.

Snakes and lizards

SPOTTED SKAAPSTEKER

Gevlekte skaapsteker *(Psammophylax rhombeatus)*

Size: *Length 60 cm in the south, but 90 cm in the Eastern Cape and to the north.*

Colour: *Greyish to yellowish brown or olive-brown, with three (sometimes four) rows of dark, rhomboid spots down the back. In the Eastern Cape and to the north, colouring darker and spots join to form continuous bands. Underparts yellowish white, with darker markings. The top of the head is a uniform brown.*

Most like: *Common egg-eater, but latter has a forward-pointing, dark brown V-shape on top of head, and strongly keeled scales compared with the skaapsteker's smooth scales.*

Habitat: *Open grassland and fynbos, from sea level to mountains. Often under rock debris.*

Found in the southern areas of Northern Province, in Gauteng, western Mpumalanga, Free State, Lesotho, KwaZulu-Natal, Eastern and Western Cape. Relict populations in Northern Cape and Namibia.

The name 'skaapsteker' is derived from the belief that this snake bites and kills sheep—but in fact it is incapable of killing anything so large, or even of sinking its fangs into the skin of a sheep and injecting a lethal dose of venom. The confusion arises because the species is often found in grazing areas; but where a sheep dies from snakebite, the culprit is likely to be a cobra, rinkhals or adder.

Skaapstekers are active snakes and make off at great speed if uncovered. They are diurnal and will hunt small creatures such as frogs, lizards, mice and shrews.

Other than pythons, the skaapsteker is one of the few species to incubate its clutch of eggs. When a female lays the eggs in a pile among dead leaves or in a hole, they are only partly incubated and she remains with the clutch for a further five to six weeks until the eggs hatch. Up to 30 eggs may be laid at a time; these hatch out some five to six weeks later.

The venom of spotted skaapstekers is largely neurotoxic, but is not dangerous to humans because of the small quantity that can be injected. Also, the species is not at all aggressive and is unlikely to attack.

Predators of this snake include birds, small carnivores and other snakes.

FORK-MARKED SAND SNAKE

Vurkmerksandslang *(Psammophis leightoni)*

Size: *Length 80 cm.*

Colour: *Ranges from olive to light brown, reddish brown or dark brown, with a white or yellowish vertebral stripe and a similar pale stripe on either side of the body. The top of the head is marked with white stripes in a forklike pattern (subspecies* trinasalis*), or spotted or barred (subspecies* leightoni *and* namibensis*). Under-parts white or yellowish, with a greyish median band.*

Most like: *Stripe-bellied sand snake which, however, does not have a light vertebral stripe.*

Habitat: *Dry, open sandveld and grassland.*

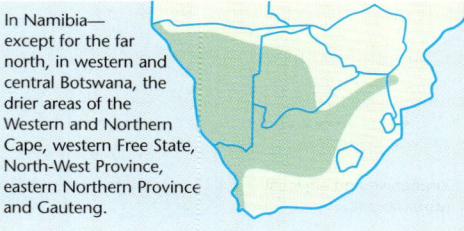

In Namibia—except for the far north, in western and central Botswana, the drier areas of the Western and Northern Cape, western Free State, North-West Province, eastern Northern Province and Gauteng.

Would-be snake collectors will find the fork-marked sand snake something of a Houdini. Sometimes in open country it will head for a bush, where it will remain immobile at the base of the plant in the hope of escaping attention. Should you get close to it, it is likely to travel upwards into the bush itself and, aided by its clever camouflage, somehow simply disappear.

Like most sand snakes, the fork-marked sand snake does not like being handled, and it will thrash about and bite, often hanging on and chewing away at the site of the bite. The venom is not dangerous to man.

Sand snakes are quick-moving, diurnal animals. They mainly eat sand lizards, although they will also consume mice and small snakes. Sometimes they themselves fall victim to snake eagles. You may see one of these birds swallowing a sand snake while perched on a telephone pole—or else see it as it flies to its nest, with the snake clutched in the talons of one foot.

Of the nine species of sand and grass snakes of the genus *Psammophis* occurring in southern Africa, the fork-marked sand snake has the widest distribution. The largest recorded specimen was a 1,37 m Namib sand snake captured in the Namib Desert.

Snakes and lizards

CROSS-MARKED GRASS SNAKE

Kruismerkgrasslang *(Psammophis crucifer)*

Size: Length 60 cm.

Colour: A black-edged, brown, vertebral band runs the length of the body and tail with, on either side, a silvery grey (or pale tan) stripe and then another brown stripe. In Cape specimens there is a single, and sometimes double, dark cross-band on the nape, this cross usually absent in specimens elsewhere. Underparts yellow or orange-yellow, bordered with a dark streak or row of blackish dots on each side.

Most like: Stripe-bellied sand snake, but the brown vertical stripe of the latter is flanked on each side by a cream to yellowish, not silver grey, stripe.

Habitat: Highveld and montane grassland, fynbos and sandy scrub in coastal areas.

In Namaqualand, Western and Eastern Cape, Free State, Lesotho, North-West, Gauteng, Mpumalanga and KwaZulu-Natal. Relict population in eastern Zimbabwe and adjacent Mozambique.

One of the smallest of our sand and grass snakes, the cross-marked grass snake is less gracefully built than others of the genus *Psammophis*, being somewhat chunky. But despite this it is quick off the mark and disappears as swiftly as its relatives when disturbed.

It is an inoffensive little snake and, although it struggles wildly when caught, very rarely attempts to bite. Technically it is venomous, with small poison-glands associated with its back fangs, but its venom is not at all dangerous to man. This, and the fact that it settles down quickly in captivity, make it a popular pet.

Like other grass snakes, it is strictly diurnal. Its natural enemies include other snakes, birds of prey and bullfrogs. Its diet consists mainly of small lizards, especially geckos, but this species also eats frogs.

Although essentially a South African species, the cross-marked grass snake is also found in the eastern highlands of Zimbabwe and neighbouring regions of Mozambique. This northern population is considered to be an isolated relic of a once continuous distribution.

The largest recorded specimen was a female of 70,9 cm found in the Free State.

Females lay clutches of up to 13 eggs.

NATAL BLACK SNAKE

Natalse swartslang *(Macrelaps microlepidotus)*

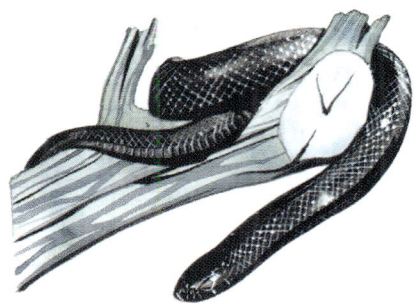

Size: Length 70-90 cm.

Colour: Glossy charcoal black to jet black, sometimes becoming lighter underneath.

Most like: Purple-glossed snake, but differs from latter in having a single, not a double, row of scales growing on the underside of the tail.

Habitat: Under logs and stones in marshy areas and along rivers in the coastal bush of KwaZulu-Natal and the Eastern Cape.

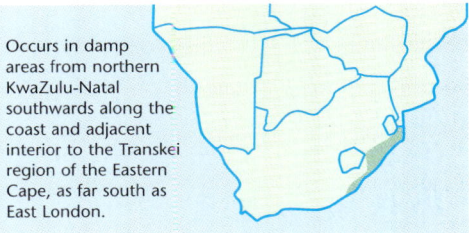

Occurs in damp areas from northern KwaZulu-Natal southwards along the coast and adjacent interior to the Transkei region of the Eastern Cape, as far south as East London.

The venom of this back-fanged snake has an unusual and disconcerting effect: it causes a temporary loss of consciousness and collapse (usually associated with neurotoxic poisoning), but no other symptoms. It is not known whether the effect, which may last for up to 30 minutes, is in fact due to a nerve poison or to a venom component causing a drop in blood pressure.

Natal black snakes love damp situations, particularly on woodland floors, and are said to be very good swimmers. When a captive specimen is kept in dry conditions its glossy skin desiccates.

The species is a burrower (in moist soil rich in leaf-litter), and is strictly nocturnal, having a strong aversion to light. It is also rather sluggish and placid by nature.

You are most likely to encounter one of these snakes in summer after a night rain. They are particularly prevalent after dark on the roads around East London. Adult snakes in captivity readily take mice, and sometimes legless lizards and birds as well. Rain frogs also form part of the snake's natural diet. The Natal black snake will eat these creatures even if they have been dead for some days. Live prey is quickly seized in the mouth, wrapped in the snake's coils and chewed to inject the venom.

The female lays from three to ten large eggs in midsummer, the newly emerged young measuring up to 29 centimetres.

The genus *Macrelaps* is represented by this single, endemic species.

Snakes and lizards

Southern burrowing asp

Suidelike grawende aspis *(Atractaspis bibronii)*

Size: Length 45 cm.
Colour: A glossy purplish brown to black. Underparts usually cream or yellowish, but sometimes blotched brown to dark brown.
Most like: Natal black snake, purple-glossed snake, eastern white-lipped snake, Cape wolf snake.
Habitat: Underground in grassland, semi-desert, bushveld and coastal forest environments.

In northern and eastern Namibia, Botswana, Zimbabwe, Mozambique, KwaZulu-Natal, Swaziland, Mpumalanga, Northern Province, North-West, western Free State and northerly Northern Cape.

The southern burrowing asp is one of those rare species that will bite the instant it is touched. If you try to hold the snake behind the head, it will simply twist and jab a fang into your finger.

Its bite is inflicted in an unusual and highly effective way. Because the bones of the head have fused as an adaptation to the snake's burrowing lifestyle, the long, backward-facing poison fangs cannot be rotated forwards; instead the snake sticks its fangs out of the side of its mouth. To engage the fang, it swings its body sideways and jerks backwards the moment the fang makes contact with the victim. It manages all this in a flash.

The southern burrowing asp usually inflicts its bite at night after rain in summer, particularly to bare feet. The venom is mildly neurotoxic but also has an extremely painful local cytotoxic effect (that is, it attacks the body's cells).

Swelling can be extensive and may spread to the whole hand and part of the arm, or the foot and part of the leg. In areas not well endowed with tissue, such as fingers and toes, cell death may occur and cause deformity.

The species preys on a variety of other snakes, limbless lizards and rats and mice, usually attacking these in their own burrows.

Because amateur collectors easily misidentify this dangerous little snake (known also as the southern mole viper or burrowing adder), there are many people walking around with a deformed, if not missing, fingertip.

Cape wolf snake

Kaapse wolfslang *(Lycopnidion capense capense)*

Size: Length 30-50 cm.
Colour: Ranges from light brown through reddish or purplish brown to jet black; shiny, and often with a speckled white effect towards the sides. Underparts white to yellowish white but occasionally grey or black.
Most like: Burrowing asp, but wolf snake's head is much flatter, and often the white speckling is distinctive.
Habitat: Savanna and grassland under stones, logs or vegetable debris, or in disused termite mounds.

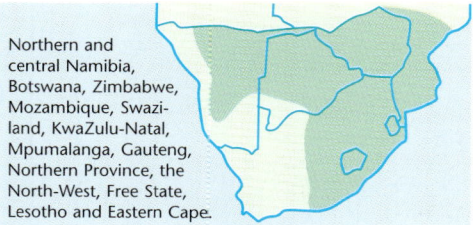

Northern and central Namibia, Botswana, Zimbabwe, Mozambique, Swaziland, KwaZulu-Natal, Mpumalanga, Gauteng, Northern Province, the North-West, Free State, Lesotho and Eastern Cape.

The long, curved-back teeth of both upper and lower jaws have earned this species its common name. This needle-sharp dentition has evolved to penetrate the hard, smooth scales of the lizards of the skink family that are its major prey. It also feeds on other lizards and occasionally small snakes. Once it has bitten into the body of its victim (usually at the back of the neck), it moves in for the kill by throwing its coils around the prey and constricting. It then swallows its dinner head-first.

The Cape species is the most widely dispersed of four wolf snakes found in southern Africa. It is mainly nocturnal and terrestrial, although specimens have been found high up in trees, presumably hunting for lizards. In winter these snakes commonly hibernate in old termite mounds, which they share with other species such as house snakes and egg-eaters.

The Cape wolf snake is somewhat sluggish and submits to handling without much fuss. But its specialized way of life and diet make it unsuitable as a captive.

The female lays three to nine eggs during early summer.

The species is entirely restricted to the eastern half of South Africa, except for an isolated finding near Mossel Bay. In northern Namibia a distinct subspecies, *multimaculatum*, occurs, while another subspecies, *vermiculatum*, is found in eastern Zimbabwe and the central parts of Mozambique.

Snakes and lizards

CAPE FILE SNAKE

Kaapse vylslang *(Mehelya capensis capensis)*

Size: Length 1-1,2 m.
Colour: Ranges from grey to olive and purplish brown, with a prominent white or yellowish stripe down the ridge of the back, from head to tip of tail. Underparts white or yellowish.
Most like: Appropriate colour forms of mole snake but file snake's triangular cross-section and whitish backbone stripe distinctive.
Habitat: Warm bushveld and coastal forest.

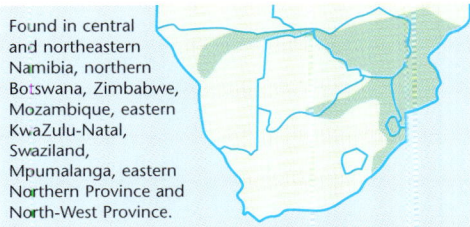

Found in central and northeastern Namibia, northern Botswana, Zimbabwe, Mozambique, eastern KwaZulu-Natal, Swaziland, Mpumalanga, eastern Northern Province and North-West Province.

The Cape file snake is probably the most distinctive snake in southern Africa. It has a white vertebral stripe, large spade-shaped head and a backbone that projects upwards under the enlarged row of scales running down the centre of the body, giving it a triangular, filelike appearance. Although it looks fearsome, it is harmless and is not the highly venomous snake many think it to be.

This snake is best known for its snake-eating tendencies. Seemingly immune to the venom of other snakes, it does not hesitate to attack and consume them, whether or not they are poisonous. Although its victim may put up a spirited defence by biting and coiling round it, the file snake carries on chewing. Also included in its diet are toads, frogs, lizards and rodents.

Although they are not particularly common, you may be lucky enough to encounter several of these nocturnal snakes crossing a few kilometres of tarred road. They enjoy prowling about on warm summer nights after rain, in forest or bushveld terrain.

The file snake is popular with collectors because of its placid nature and its readiness to settle down in captivity. When you encounter it in the wild it doesn't dart off, but continues slowly on its way.

A relative of the Cape species, the Nyasa or black file snake, is found in Mpumalanga and KwaZulu-Natal, and in parts of Botswana and Namibia.

COMMON EGG-EATER

Gewone eievreter *(Dasypeltis scabra)*

Size: Length 40 cm-1,1 m.
Colour: On the highveld this snake is occasionally uniformly brown above. Elsewhere, it has a 'chequer-board' pattern consisting of a vertebral series of dark brown, squarish or rhomboid spots, alternating with grey-brown; on either side of this is another series of dark brown spots or bars alternating with light brown. Dark patch behind head is normally V-shaped, with apex of V towards the head. Underparts cream to yellow.
Most like: Common night adder which it mimics in its pattern of dark, rhombic vertebral spots or blotches. The night adder, however, has much bolder V on back of head, and far fewer blotches along back.
Habitat: Rock crevices, old termite mounds, where birds nest in numbers.

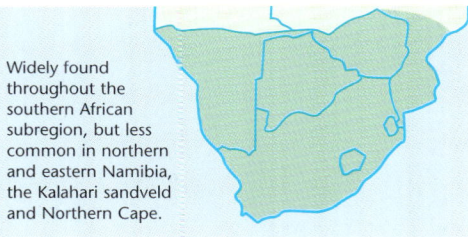

Widely found throughout the southern African subregion, but less common in northern and eastern Namibia, the Kalahari sandveld and Northern Cape.

The common egg-eater can quite easily swallow a bird's egg four-and-a-half times the diameter of its own head—an achievement made possible because of the enormous degree to which the two halves of its lower jaw can separate and drop down. In all snakes the two halves of the lower jaw are connected at the front by an elastic ligament, and at the back are not joined to the upper jaws directly but via the 'quadrate' bone which is attached to a projection at the back of the skull and which acts as a double-jointed hinge. When the egg-eater swallows, the two halves of the lower jaw are stretched sideways and downwards to the limit, both at the front and back.

Once swallowed, the egg is forced by the snake's throat muscles against the neck vertebrae which protrude into the throat during feeding and puncture the shell. The contents of the egg are consumed and the shell, squashed and neatly packaged like a banana, is regurgitated. In another adaptation to its diet, the species has a special 'valve' that keeps the liquid egg contents down while the shell comes up.

The female lays up to 20 eggs during summer.

Snakes and lizards

COMMON NIGHT ADDER

Gewone nagadder *(Causus rhombeatus)*

Size: *Length 35-60 cm.*
Colour: *Ranges from grey to olive-green and light brown, with dark markings consisting of a distinctive V over the head (its apex pointing to the mouth), and a series of rhomboid spots down the back and tail. Often these dark markings are edged with white. Underparts grey to yellowish.*
Most like: *Common egg-eater, but much thicker, and with a more clear-cut, boldly black or dark brown V on top of the head.*
Habitat: *Moist areas near small streams, often in the vicinity of old termite mounds, piles of stones or plant refuse, in which the snake can seek shelter.*

Caprivi Strip, northern Botswana, central and eastern Zimbabwe, coastal Mozambique, Mpumalanga, Northern Province, Gauteng, Swaziland, KwaZulu-Natal, southern Free State, south-eastern and southern Cape.

Despite its name this species is not entirely nocturnal, for it enjoys sunning itself in the early morning and late afternoon. Toads and frogs are its chief prey and, although the snake is generally rather sluggish in its movements, the presence of one of these amphibians will galvanize it into action. Not only does it move extremely quickly in pursuit, but it searches frantically if it loses sight of its quarry.

In getting the better of its victim the night adder doesn't resort to constriction. It simply bites and holds on; and even though a large toad may buffet it about, at every opportunity the adder moves its hold to nearer the toad's head. Then, whether or not its venom has immobilized the struggling prey, the adder starts swallowing. Sometimes the prey will continue resisting convulsively inside the snake.

Although the common night adder has very long poison glands, the amount of venom produced is not exceptional, and it is feeble in its action on human beings. The usual consequences of a bite are limited pain, swelling and discoloration at the site of the bite, and later tenderness in the joint and affected limbs.

PÉRINGUEY'S ADDER

Namib-duinadder *(Bitis peringueyi)*

Size: *Length 20-25 cm.*
Colour: *Sandy grey to pale brown, with three rows of small, blackish and white spots down the body. End of tail sometimes black. Underparts whitish, often spotted with brown.*
Most like: *Namaqua dwarf adder, which occurs in the southern coastal areas of Namibia and the Northern Cape.*
Habitat: *The sand valleys of the Namib Desert.*

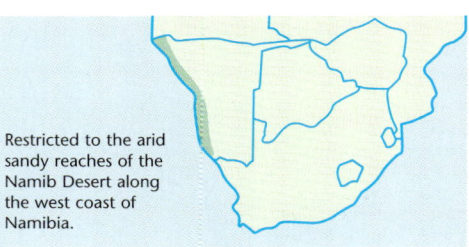

Restricted to the arid sandy reaches of the Namib Desert along the west coast of Namibia.

Lying semi-submerged beneath the sands of the Namib Desert, Péringuey's (or sidewinding) adder retains a wide-angle view of the world around it, for its eyes—uniquely among the snakes of southern Africa—are on top of its head. This is how it waits in ambush, often with the black tip of its tail also exposed and stirring, as a decoy. Should a desert or sand lizard approach too close, the adder explodes out of the sand to bite, holding on until the lizard collapses from the effect of the venom. At night, web-footed geckos suffer the same sudden fate.

To cope with the soft, unconsolidated sand of the desert this little snake 'sidewinds', moving by stretching out the front part of its body while the rear remains stationary, and then bringing the rear forward and to one side. As it rapidly repeats this series of movements it seems to float over the surface.

It takes some expertise to find this adder. One of the best means is to follow its distinctive tracks (parallel grooves in the sand) and to look for it on misty, windless days, moving along the surface of the desert sands. At other times, it will submerge itself, with only the top of its head exposed; and it will burrow down further if it becomes too hot, flattening its body and twisting from side to side. Total submersion can take less than 20 seconds.

Sand-surfing is a popular pastime in parts of Namibia, and this activity regularly uncovers Péringuey's adders.

Snakes and lizards

BERG ADDER
Bergadder *(Bitis atropos)*

Size: *Length 35-50 cm.*

Colour: *Olive to dark brown above, with an elaborate pattern of black markings: two rows of large triangular or semi-circular spots down the back, normally with a complete or broken white line on the lower side of these and then, on either side, a further row of spots. Chin and throat pink or creamy, spotted with black; belly ranges from dirty white to dark grey.*

Most like: *Horned adder which, however, has three rows of dark spots, one down the middle of the back. It also has the distinctive pair of 'horns' above the eyes.*

Habitat: *Mountain plateaus in moist grassland, but also in the southern Cape down to sea level in fynbos vegetation.*

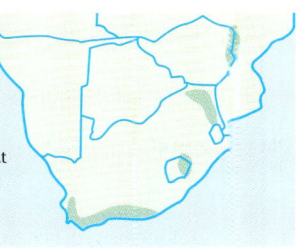

At higher altitudes in eastern Zimbabwe, eastern Northern Province, Mpumalanga, the Lesotho Drakensberg and southern Cape. At sea level in the southern Cape west to the Cape Peninsula.

The berg adder, or Cape mountain adder, is a very ill-tempered little snake and is quick to hiss and strike at anything much larger than its usual prey of small rodents, amphibians and ground-nesting birds. In fact, strolling through berg adder country and listening for the creature's rapid hisses is one of the standard collecting techniques for this species.

When a berg adder bites, it injects its victim with a neurotoxic venom that often affects the ocular nerves: there may be temporary blindness lasting usually from four to five days, but up to three weeks in extreme cases. The stages of blindness include double vision, dilation of the pupils and an inability to focus, followed by complete paralysis of the eyelids. Unlike the neurotoxic venoms of the cobras, the adder's poison has no direct effect on breathing. Eyesight returns to normal without any permanent after-effects.

Though the species is generally considered a rare find, there are areas in Mpumalanga and Northern Province where these snakes occur in large numbers. Much of the 'rarity' elsewhere may be attributed to the difficulty of seeing the snake in the low, thick vegetation of mountain slopes and plateaus.

Between 8-15 live young are produced at a time.

COMMON PUFF ADDER
Pofadder *(Bitis arietans)*

Size: *Length 70-90 cm.*

Colour: *Ranges from straw-yellow to light brown or orange-brown, with a series of pale-edged, black, backward-pointing chevrons (V-shaped markings) along the back and tail. Specimens from the western part of the distribution area tend to be lighter in colour.*

Most like: *Berg adder or gaboon adder, but the puff adder's distinctive backward-pointing, pale-edged black chevrons make it easily distinguishable.*

Habitat: *A wide variety of habitats, from dry savanna to high-rainfall areas.*

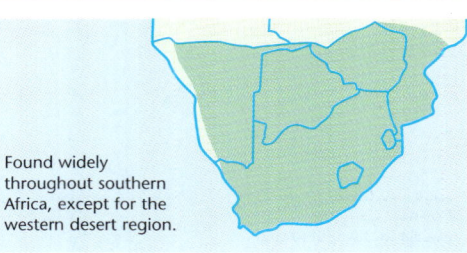

Found widely throughout southern Africa, except for the western desert region.

The common puff adder, which inflates itself with air when disturbed (hence its name), is the most widespread poisonous snake in Africa. Couple this with its proximity to humans in built-up areas, and its reluctance to give man the right of way—and you have a recipe for snakebite. With few exceptions, adders do not make themselves scarce when a person approaches, relying on immobility to escape attention. The well-camouflaged puff adder takes this habit to the extreme. By the time you notice its presence you are within striking distance (if, indeed, you have not actually stepped on it).

The strike is rapid and the fangs, which may be 18mm long in larger specimens, penetrate deeply. Symptoms include instant excruciating pain, increasing swelling that may reach huge proportions and may include part of the trunk, and the loss of blood from general circulation into tissue. The last of these symptoms is particularly dangerous and can lead to collapse and even death if blood transfusions are not administered. Later, huge blisters and tissue-death at the site of the bite arise, with the possibility of permanent disability.

Newly laid eggs contain fully formed young, which emerge within minutes—already capable of killing.

Snakes and lizards

Gaboon adder
Gaboenadder *(Bitis gabonica)*

Size: Length 1,2 m.

Colour: A rich geometric pattern of colours, including a vertebral series of buff oblongs alternating with characteristic 'hourglass' markings of black, grey, tan and mauve and, on either side of the body, a series of large two-tone brown spots of roughly diamond shape, bordered with paler and darker stripes. The broad, flattened head, resembling the spade depicted on playing cards, is light buff, the underparts yellowish buff, blotched with grey or brown.

Most like: Quite distinctive and unlike any other snake found in Africa. It is large and fat like most adders, and its light buff-coloured head and striking pastel geometric patterning along the length of its body are not found in any other snake species.

Habitat: Occurs in the low undergrowth of tropical and subtropical forests.

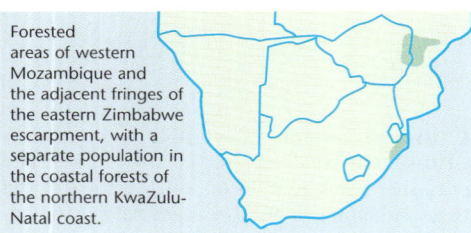

Forested areas of western Mozambique and the adjacent fringes of the eastern Zimbabwe escarpment, with a separate population in the coastal forests of the northern KwaZulu-Natal coast.

The largest of the African adders (it can attain a length of 1,8 m) the Gaboon adder is also the most colourful. Yet on the rich, leafy floor of its forest habitat this sinister harlequin is beautifully camouflaged. Immobile among the leaf litter or under a small shrub, it watches for ground birds, rodents and amphibians. Some Gaboon adders are said to lie in the same spot for several weeks, patiently waiting for prey. The lightning strike is made without any warning sign, and the struggle is over in less than a minute, not only because of the toxicity of the venom but also from mechanical injury to the prey's organs, inflicted by the snake's massive fangs (of up to 40 millimetres).

Fortunately these large snakes are much more placid than puff adders. Some collectors go so far as to pick them up, without being bitten. Such bravado, however, is for the unintelligent, because during a bite a vast quantity of venom is injected deeply into the tissue, and its volume and potency cause a rapid drop in blood pressure. Collapse occurs within a matter of minutes and cardiac arrest is quick to follow; survival without good primary care is unlikely after 30 minutes.

During late summer, once every two or three years, the females give birth to some 10-13 live young.

Yellow-bellied sea snake
Swart-en-geel seeslang *(Pelamis platurus)*

Size: Length 60-75 cm.

Colour: Top half of body black or dark brown, with yellow underparts. The vertically flattened tail is yellow, blotched with black.

Most like: Could be mistaken for an eel, but the scales of the sea snake are much larger, the colour pattern is unique and the laterally flattened, paddle-shaped tail is distinctive. Unlike eels, sea snakes have to surface regularly to breathe.

Habitat: Warm surface waters of the Indian Ocean, sometimes occurring as far west (with the Agulhas Current) as the Cape Peninsula.

Widely distributed, this sea snake has been recorded all along the coastline from Mozambique in the north to False Bay in the Western Cape.

The only time you are likely to see this snake is after a storm, when a specimen is cast up on the beach or finds itself stranded in a tidal pool along the southern African coast. Beware, for the sea snake is front-fanged and related to cobras and mambas. However, although the yellow-bellied sea snake is venomous, its reputation as a poisonous killer has been exaggerated, according to South African herpetologist Bill Branch. He believes its bad reputation has been unjustly transferred from the genuinely venomous sea snake of the East Indies.

Like other sea snakes, this species swims through the water by using the same lateral undulations that terrestrial snakes employ to travel over land. It can put on short bursts of speed, either forwards or backwards, but for long-distance travel it depends on the ocean currents, and when they sweep it too close to the shore it may find itself in trouble. Washed up on the beach, it is unable to head for the sea again. Its body is somewhat flattened in cross-section, so that any movement simply topples it over on one side or the other.

The species lives entirely on small fish, which are instantly paralysed after being bitten.

In common with other sea snakes, *Pelamis platurus* gives birth at sea to live young—from three to eight in a batch—each of which is about 25 cm long. The young are able to fend for themselves immediately.

Snakes and lizards

COMMON SLUG-EATER

Gewone slakvreter *(Duberria lutrix)*

Size: *Length 30-40 cm.*
Colour: *Ranges from reddish brown to olive above, sometimes with a row of black spots along the spine from head to tail; the sides are usually grey, and a line of black specks separates this colour from the back. The underparts are off-white or yellowish.*
Most like: *Brown house snake which, however, is much larger, has two pale yellow streaks on the sides of the head, passing through the eyes, and does not have the slug-eater's grey lateral bands.*
Habitat: *Damp situations, under stones, rotting wood, leaf litter.*

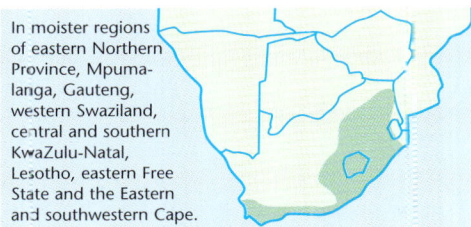

In moister regions of eastern Northern Province, Mpumalanga, Gauteng, western Swaziland, central and southern KwaZulu-Natal, Lesotho, eastern Free State and the Eastern and southwestern Cape.

This inoffensive gardener's friend has a appetite for snails that often proves fatal, for many a slug-eater has been suffocated, its head firmly wedged within the shell of the snail it has tried unsuccessfully to extract, or poisoned by the bait set out to kill the snails.

The slug-eater—slugs join snails as favourite items on its menu—is exceptionally abundant in areas it favours; in parts of the Cape Peninsula, for example, a knowledgeable collector could collect a bucketful or two of slug-eaters during the course of a day.

This species, also known as the russet garden snake, has never been reported to bite. Even if it did, its small teeth would probably not cause any pain, and it possesses no venom. If stressed in any way, it is quick to curl up like a roll of tobacco, behaviour that has earned it its common Afrikaans name, 'tabakrolletjie'. It meets real threat with a less appetizing response: the snake simply empties the contents of its lower intestine.

The female gives birth to her 6-12 live young from early to late summer.

The common slug-eater thrives in captivity, provided the leaf litter in which it is kept is constantly sprayed to keep it damp, and provided, of course, that there is a ready supply of poison-free snails and slugs. In the Cape, this innocuous snake is often battered to death in the belief that it is a baby Cape cobra.

BLACK THREAD SNAKE

Swart draadslang *(Leptotyphlops nigricans)*

Size: *Length 8-18 cm.*
Colour: *Uniformly dark brown to black above and below, with a high gloss.*
Most like: *The other eight species of thread snakes, such as the Cape thread snake and the slender thread snake; the thread snakes, however, are difficult to distinguish from one another without recourse to scale counts.*
Habitat: *In termite mounds, among leaf and vegetable debris, and under stones or rotting logs in fynbos and grassland habitats.*

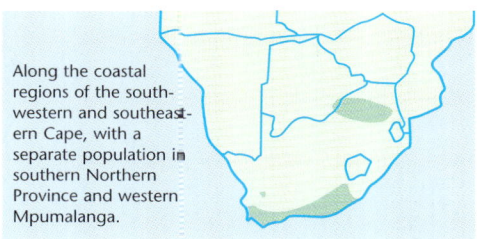

Along the coastal regions of the southwestern and southeastern Cape, with a separate population in southern Northern Province and western Mpumalanga.

Snakes evolved from a lizard stock, and the thread snake, like blind snakes and most pythons and boas, shows this evolutionary origin in that it still possesses the traces of a pelvis. To all appearances, however, it looks very much like a worm or a black bootlace: the head, neck, body and tail of this creature are all the same width, and its vestigial eyes lie beneath large scales. The scales covering the body fit snugly and are gleaming black in colour.

The black thread snake's movements on its occasional travels above ground are not at all graceful: it proceeds along in a series of squiggles. When molested, it wriggles violently—so violently, often, that it makes little forward progress. If it is constantly stimulated or threatened, it will feign death and go completely limp, not moving even when picked up.

Black thread snakes (known also as black worm snakes) eat termites and their eggs (as well as ant eggs). They feed rapidly, apparently sucking in the eggs rather than grasping them in the mouth and swallowing them; as for the termites, their abdomens are first punctured and then sucked out.

These tiny snakes are seldom seen above the ground, except when heavy rain flushes them out from under stones and debris. Little is known about their reproductive habits; the tiny eggs resemble rice grains, and there are five to seven eggs in a clutch.

The black thread snake is one of nine species of thread snake found in southern Africa. A very similar species found in KwaZulu-Natal is often branded 'baby black mamba'. Because of their food requirements, these snakes do not flourish in captivity.

Snakes and lizards

BIBRON'S BLIND SNAKE

Bibron se blindeslang *(Typhlops bibronii)*

Size: Length 35-40 cm.
Colour: *Glossy brown to dark olive-brown above, with underparts yellowish, yellowish brown or almost as dark as the upper parts.*
Most like: *Southern burrowing asp, but the blind snake is more wormlike in appearance, with a stubby, nontapering tail, and its eyes are very small.*
Habitat: *Under logs or stones, in termite mounds or in loose soil in highveld and coastal grassland.*

North-West Province, Northern Province, Gauteng, Mpumalanga, Swaziland, KwaZulu-Natal and Eastern Cape. Also in the eastern Free State and Lesotho, with a separate population in Zimbabwe's eastern highlands.

Bibron's blind snake has a tiny, sharp spike at the end of its tail without which it probably would not survive. It depends largely on this spike for locomotion, inserting it vertically into the soil to obtain purchase and then thrusting its body forward. Should the surface be too smooth to make use of the spike, the snake wriggles about aimlessly. The spike, which is hard and sharp, is also used in defence, and can hurt if jabbed into the flesh.

Superficially, blind snakes are larger and fatter versions of thread snakes. They are diggers, and many of the seven species found in southern Africa (including Bibron's) have wedge-shaped snouts.

Bibron's blind snake, the most common blind snake in its distribution area, is found nearer the surface of the soil after good rains, when its retreat has been flooded, and it is often uncovered during ploughing.

As with thread snakes, the mouth is underslung and tiny, and not in a position to do damage to a human hand even though the snake may try to bite if roughly handled.

Its diet includes mainly termites and their eggs, as well as worms and soft-bodied insects and their larvae. The female lays her clutches of 5-12 eggs in late summer, and the hatchlings emerge within a week. An unusual biological fact is that the females of both blind snakes and thread snakes have dispensed with the left oviduct, no doubt in the interests of internal economy, in the same way as many snakes have either a very reduced right lung, or none at all.

CAPE CENTIPEDE-EATER

Kaapse honderdpootvreter *(Aparallactus capensis)*

Size: Length 20-30 cm.
Colour: *Grey-brown, yellowish brown or reddish brown, the top of the head being black or brown; there is a distinctive black collar around the neck which is sometimes joined to the black of the head. Underparts white or yellowish.*
Most like: *Herald snake which, however, has an olive-green back; herald snake's black head has a purplish-blue iridescence.*
Habitat: *Open bush country and montane grassland, in termite mounds, under stones or logs, and among the roots of shrubs and grasses.*

Eastern Caprivi Strip, eastern Botswana, Zimbabwe, northern and southern Mozambique, Swaziland, KwaZulu-Natal, Mpumalanga, Gauteng, Northern Province, North-West, the Free State, Lesotho and Eastern Cape.

Like the common slug-eater, the Cape centipede-eater belongs to that small minority of snakes in southern Africa that feeds exclusively on invertebrate prey. Centipedes make a formidable diet. Some specimens are half as long as, and twice the diameter of, their reptilian predator; many are venomous, with substantial jaws. In the showdown between the snake and its victim, a dramatic struggle often takes place, but should the snake be bitten it simply releases the centipede and then immediately seizes it again, aiming always to get a hold behind the centipede's head. Once it succeeds in this, the battle is over, and the still-struggling prey is swallowed.

Centipede-eaters are back-fanged venomous snakes. To man, however, they are quite harmless, for their teeth are too small to pierce the skin.

The species is commonly found in disused termite mounds, which provide refuge from the winter's cold, and which also provide a haven for centipedes, except when a centipede-eater is in residence! Large numbers of them are sometimes found together when such a mound is dug up. When caught, individual specimens behave differently, some remaining placid while others struggle and fight to free themselves, attempting to bite.

The 'blackhead', as this snake is often called, is one of four species of the centipede-eater found in southern Africa. The female lays between two and four eggs at a time, with the hatchlings measuring some ten centimetres in length.

Snakes and lizards

SHIELD-NOSE SNAKE

Skildneusslang *(Aspidelaps scutatus)*

Size: Length 45 cm.

Colour: From greyish brown to reddish brown, with a series of dark brown blotches running down back and tail. Back of head marked with a broad black V, and behind this are more black markings that usually encircle the neck, the chin and throat between these rings being pale grey. Underparts white or yellowish.

Most like: Coral snake but latter has reddish head marked with black cross-bands down the length of the back, not dark blotches.

Habitat: Usually in arid, sandy and stony country in open bushveld savanna.

In central and northeastern Namibia, the Caprivi Strip, throughout most of Botswana, in southern Zimbabwe, central and southern Mozambique, Northern Province and Mpumalanga.

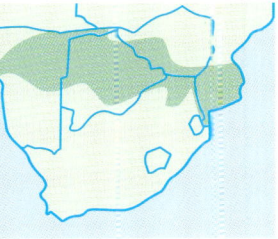

This snake uses its large, squared-off nose-scale or 'rostral shield' to plough through loose sand in search of the lizards, other snakes, toads and rodents that make up its diet. It is very aggressive and, when molested, rears up immediately like a cobra and flattens its neck (although it does not actually spread a hood). As it prepares to strike it will also take in air and emit low, sinister hisses, like a puff adder. In desperate straits it feigns death—and here its behaviour resembles that of a rinkhals.

A bite from one of these snakes will produce symptoms resembling poisoning by cobra venom, including general muscular weakness and impaired breathing. Collectors regard them as something of a find, and look for them in summer after rain, when wet conditions have persuaded them to take up temporary residence under rocks or logs.

Three distinct populations, or subspecies, of the snake are recognized. The common shield-snake, *Aspidelaps scutatus scutatus*, occurs over the northern two-thirds of Namibia, all of Botswana and western Zimbabwe, Northern Province, the North-West, Gauteng and Mpumalanga. The intermediate subspecies, *A.s. intermedius*, is confined mainly to the lowveld of Mpumalanga. And the pale buff-coloured eastern subspecies, *A.s fulafula*, is found in the south-eastern part of Zimbabwe and in Mozambique.

EASTERN TIGER SNAKE

Oostelike tierslang *(Telescopus semiannulatus)*

Size: Length 75 cm.

Colour: Ranges from pinkish brown to yellow-brown (according to the locality), with a series of dark brown or black bands across top of back. Underparts yellowish to orange with a pink flush.

Most like: Coral snake, but the dark cross-bands of this species are narrower, and each one encircles the body.

Habitat: Bushveld, predominately on the ground or in trees and rock crevices.

Central and northern Namibia, Botswana, Zimbabwe, Mozambique, northern KwaZulu-Natal, Swaziland, Mpumalanga, Northern Province, the North-West and the northernmost Northern Cape.

The striking colour pattern of the tiger snake serves as a warning and, indeed, this back-fanged snake with its bulbous orange eyes can produce a convincing display of ferocity, flattening its head in irritation and quickly flicking its pink tongue in and out. It may also inflate its body with air like a puff adder, and then expel the air in hisses.

Irascible and quick to bite it may be, but the eastern tiger snake is a slow mover and, fortunately, its venom has a comparatively mild effect on human beings: a bit of pain and some local swelling are temporary symptoms.

It is undoubtedly a snake of character, and therefore a most desirable pet for the snake-collecting fanatic. The trouble is that a captive specimen is inclined to attack any other snake within range.

Chief prey of the eastern tiger snake are nocturnal lizards, such as geckos, and small rodents and bats; it also feeds on chameleons and on small, sleeping birds, as well as their eggs. Having bitten its victim, the eastern tiger snake will not release it until the venom has taken its lethal effect.

Though mainly terrestrial, it is quite at home in shrubs and trees, being an excellent climber. The female lays a clutch of anything from 6-20 eggs at a time during summer.

This rather sluggish and slow-moving snake may grow to just over a metre long. One other species of tiger snake, the Namib tiger snake, is found in southern Namibia and the Karoo.

Snakes and lizards

Nile crocodile
Nylkrokodil *(Crocodylus niloticus)*

Size: Length 3,6-3,9 m; weight 450-600 kg.
Colour: *Green or greenish yellow (with black markings), darkening progressively with age to grey or black. Throat and underparts cream or pale yellow.*
Most like: *Unlike any other animal.*
Habitat: *Rivers, lakes and waterholes.*

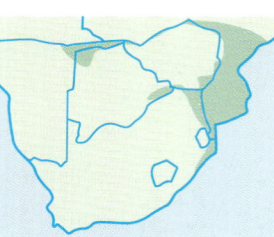

Found in the Kunene, Okavango and Zambezi rivers in the north of the subregion, south through Mozambique to Northern Province and Mpumalanga, and south to the Tugela River in KwaZulu-Natal.

The Nile crocodile, the only species of crocodile found in southern Africa, is a heavily armoured reptile with a fearsome reputation as a man-eater, and possibly the original of that scaly monster, the leviathan, so fancifully described in the Book of Job. The largest specimen killed locally (in 1968 in the Okavango Swamps) measured 5,86 m and weighed an estimated 800 kilograms.

Like all crocodiles, this species is amphibious. For much of the day it basks lazily in the sun, but spends the night partially submerged in the water, with only its eyes, nostrils and ear-openings above water level. It can remain completely submerged for about four minutes, during which time valves seal off its long nasal passages. Another large valve closes the throat, so that the reptile can survive under water even with its jaws open—as they are when it captures its prey and drags it under the surface to drown.

The drowned, or drowning, prey is disposed of in a particularly nasty, if effective, way. Holding the victim in its powerful jaws, the crocodile spins round in the water, jerking it vigorously from side to side until a bite-sized chunk of flesh breaks loose.

The Nile crocodile's menu includes mammals ranging from small antelope to large buffalo. However, it also has a taste for carrion, fish and nestling birds which may be swept from their riverside perch by a swift flick of the cunning croc's hefty tail.

The female deposits layers of 15-80 white, double-skinned eggs in a 40 cm-deep 'nest' scraped in the sand of a river bank. She covers the nest and waits nearby until her live young have hatched. These eggs are much sought after by water leguaans, mongooses and hyaenas.

Water leguaan
Waterlikkewaan *(Varanus niloticus)*

Size: Length 1,3-2 m.
Colour: *Juveniles black with bold yellow spots and cross-stripes; adults grey-brown to olive-brown with darker markings and scattered yellow spots. Underparts yellowish, with grey-black transverse markings.*
Most like: *Rock leguaan, but longer and slimmer.*
Habitat: *In or near rivers, dams, waterholes, lakes.*

Rivers, lakes and pans in the Northern and Eastern Cape, KwaZulu-Natal, Swaziland, Free State, the North-West, Northern Province, Gauteng, Mpumalanga, Mozambique, Zimbabwe and northern Botswana.

With its giant curved claws and muscular tail the water leguaan, or Nile monitor, is perfectly capable of climbing trees, but it is happiest in the vicinity of water. It is a strong, swift swimmer and, like the crocodile, uses its tail as a kind of paddle to propel itself through the water. The tail is also its chief defensive weapon, thrashed viciously from side to side. When molested, this outsize lizard also arches its neck and emits loud, deep hisses, creating an awesome and somewhat prehistoric spectacle. As a last resort it will feign death, sometimes for hours on end. However, these leguaans do prefer to avoid confrontation, and will run away from danger if possible.

Water leguaans spend a large part of the day basking in the sun at the water's edge. Their diet consists of fish, frogs and other small creatures, crabs and mussels (which their large, rounded, peglike teeth can easily crack). Crocodile eggs and the young which hatch from them are also a delicacy.

The female water leguaan lays her own eggs deep within a hole she excavates in a termite mound, a location which ensures a constant temperature and humidity for the year-long incubation period. Anxious to repair the damage, the termites set to work, enclosing the eggs safely from the sight of predators. Ungratefully, the hatchlings make a meal of their host termites and other insects, before heading instinctively for the nearest water.

An attractive leather can be made from the skin of the water leguaan and it was formerly exploited extensively for the fashion trade. However, it is now a protected animal in South Africa.

Snakes and lizards

Rock leguaan

Veldlikkewaan *(Varanus exanthematicus)*

Size: Length 70 cm–1,25 m.
Colour: Dark greyish brown, with grey or yellow spots arranged in five or six transverse rows, and a dark streak running from the eye to a position above the foreleg. Underparts dull white to yellowish white. Throat grey or white extending up side of neck to dark stripe behind the eye; tail banded alternately with yellowish white and dark brown to black rings. Legs spotted above with yellowish white.
Most like: Water leguaan, but more compact and sturdy.
Habitat: Rocky grassland and open bush or forest country, often far from water.

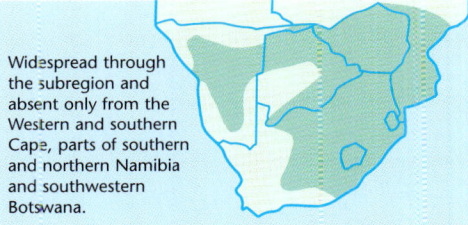

Widespread through the subregion and absent only from the Western and southern Cape, parts of southern and northern Namibia and southwestern Botswana.

This outsize lizard looks rather like a sad sack that, under threat, will puff itself out, thrash its striped tail and hiss menacingly. Unlike its cousin the water leguaan, the rock leguaan is by no means at home in water, although it will take a dip to cool off in hot, dry weather.

A great wanderer, this leguaan sleeps in tree hollows, in a hole in the ground or in a burrow dug under rock overhangs. In severe winters it may actually hibernate buried in its underground retreat—to be dug up, if unlucky, by a ratel or other predator. It may feign death to escape the attentions of a predator. (It may do so with one hindleg firmly grasped in its mouth; in this contorted position it would make an awkward meal for a python.) Birds of prey are amongst its natural enemies, though not many come off best when taking on this awesome foe.

The rock leguaan feeds on small mammals, other reptiles, birds and their eggs, snails and various insects. The prey is swallowed whole and may take a long time to digest if it is large. There is a popular but completely erroneous, belief that the species sucks milk from cows and other livestock. In fact it drinks liquid by lapping with its long blue-and-yellow tongue which darts in and out of its mouth much in the manner of a snake.

The female normally lays her 8-37 eggs in holes she digs to a depth of about 20 cm in soft soil, then covers them up and leaves them untended.

Sungazer

Sonkyker *(Cordylus giganteus)*

Size: Length 35 cm.
Colour: Pale yellow-brown to dark brown, with yellow-brown sides and straw-yellow underparts.
Most like: Armadillo girdled lizard, but latter is only found in the Western Cape, while the sungazer occurs only in the Free State, western KwaZulu-Natal and southern Mpumalanga. The sungazer is nearly twice the size of the armadillo girdled lizard.
Habitat: Flat or gently sloping grassland.

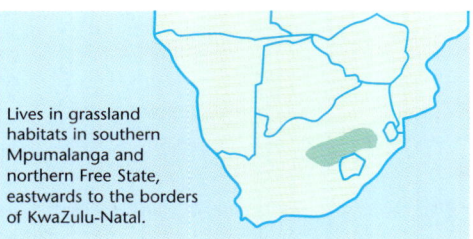

Lives in grassland habitats in southern Mpumalanga and northern Free State, eastwards to the borders of KwaZulu-Natal.

There is something decidedly prehistoric about the appearance of the sungazer as it takes up its characteristic pose—staring, without benefit of dark glasses, directly at the afternoon sun from the vantage-point of a mound of earth, termite mound or stones. With its head and torso raised well above the ground, the sungazer remains motionless for some minutes, as if time were suspended.

This well-armoured reptile, known also as the giant girdled lizard, is covered in horny scales, each of which carries a needle-sharp spine, especially on the tail. To an enemy the tail can deliver a stunning blow.

Girdled, or 'girdle-tailed', lizards are so named because of the whorls of scales that encircle the bodies and tails of all species in the family. The sungazer is the largest of the group. It is a formidable creature, but even it has a weak spot—its soft underbelly. That is why it will strongly resist any attempt to be turned upside down. As a last resort it may lie rigidly on its belly with both sets of limbs pressed back firmly against its body.

Sungazers live colonially in underground burrows which they dig in soft, fine soil. These may be up to half a metre deep and 1,8 m long and are sloped towards the surface to avoid flooding.

These large lizards are mainly insectivorous, but will include small rodents in their diet. The female sungazer gives birth to live young, usually not more than two at a time.

Snakes and lizards

Armadillo girdled lizard
Blinkogie *(Cordylus cataphractus)*

Size: Length 21 cm.
Colour: Yellowish brown, either uniform or occasionally with irregular, dark brown markings.
Most like: Sungazer, which is almost twice as long and has 22-25 transverse rows of back scales to the 15-17 of the armadillo girdled lizard.
Habitat: Dry, rocky country.

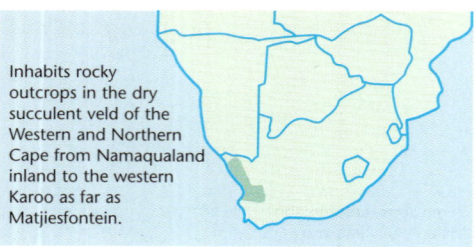

Inhabits rocky outcrops in the dry succulent veld of the Western and Northern Cape from Namaqualand inland to the western Karoo as far as Matjiesfontein.

The armadillo girdled lizard, like the American armadillo, is equipped with a protective covering of horn-covered bony plates, but has spines for additional protection. At the slightest threat it disappears into the deepest available crevice and jams its spines against the walls to prevent itself being dislodged. Surprised in the open it will roll on its back, then, curling its tail over its soft belly, will seize its tail in its jaw and remain locked in that position, a virtually impregnable little hoop. You can even roll it around without it uncurling.

This reptile is one of the girdled, or girdle-tailed, lizards confined mainly to southern Africa, with about 19 different local species.

The armadillo girdled lizard has a flattened, spiny, club-like tail and if by any chance this should be lost, another (inferior) one will grow in its place. Its entire body is somewhat flat, allowing it to wriggle into narrow rock crevices, where it habitually shelters.

A particular rock cleft or crevice may be shared by a colony or family group of up to ten lizards, for this is a gregarious species. Once they have found a suitable home they are likely to use it for a long time.

They are most active in the day, feeding on a wide range of insects and spiders. The termites that appear in large numbers after spring rains are eagerly consumed. Because they are slow movers, the lizards are exposed to predators such as mongooses and may easily be caught by hand.

The young develop into fully formed lizards inside their mother's body, and the one to three newborn, miniature versions of their parents, break out of their soft membranous shells the moment they are born.

Flap-neck chameleon
Flapnek-verkleurmannetjie *(Chamaeleo dilepis)*

Size: Length (with tail unrolled) 20-35 cm.
Colour: From salmon-pink through greens and browns to almost black, depending on the environment and the level of excitement or fear. Usually has a pale strip on either side of the body and, above each shoulder, a whitish spot, often with another one behind it.
Most like: Namaqua chameleon which, however, has a distinctive crest of knoblike tubercles all along the spine.
Habitat: Bush country and open savanna woodland.

Widespread in savanna woodland in northern and eastern Namibia, Botswana, Zimbabwe, Mozambique, coastal KwaZulu-Natal, Mpumalanga, Northern Province, the North-West and the Northern Cape.

When angered or disturbed, the male flap-neck chameleon inflates itself to what seems like bursting point, so that its throat skin shows bright orange between the scales. At the same time the mouth is held agape, revealing the red-orange lining inside, and the characteristic neck flaps are raised—all this being accompanied by a loud hiss. The combined impression is most fearsome, and yet it is also rather comical, for these theatrical effects represent the full extent of this chameleon's ability to defend itself. It is, in fact, perfectly harmless, with neither teeth nor claws. Still, the inhabitants of many rural communities in southern Africa regard the creature with such extreme awe that they cannot be induced to touch it.

This chameleon is the largest of ten species of chameleon found in South Africa, and preys on a variety of flying insects, such as beetles and grasshoppers, as well as spiders, snails and centipedes. While foraging it is assisted by its highly mobile eyes (capable of independent motion) and its extraordinarily long tongue, tipped with a sticky pad. The chameleon shoots its tongue out with great speed and accuracy to more than its body length in order to capture prey, and then folds it back compactly in its mouth with the victim still attached.

The female lays about 40 eggs at a time, digging a hole in the earth for them in late summer, and then covering them with soil.

Snakes and lizards

CAPE DWARF CHAMELEON
Kaapse dwergverkleurmannetjie *(Bradypodion pumilum)*

Size: Length (with tail unrolled) 13-17 cm.
Colour: Variable, but basically leaf-green with a broad orange stripe along each side of the body and orange markings on the head.
Most like: The other 12 recognized species of dwarf chameleon in southern Africa, each of which has its own separate geographical location, and all of which are similar in shape and colour.
Habitat: Small bushes and reeds, in open or scrub-covered country; often in urban gardens.

Found only in the southwestern Cape, although closely related species occur from Mpumalanga and KwaZulu-Natal to the Eastern and southern Cape, the Karoo and Namaqualand.

Bradypodion, the generic name of this species, is the Greek for 'slow foot' and refers to the hesitant 'stop-go' pace so characteristic of the chameleons you sometimes find in your garden, prowling stealthily along a leafy branch. This irregular movement, like the chameleon's well-known ability to change colour, is all part of the animal's natural camouflage, and blends in with the uneven stirring of foliage blown by the breeze.

Camouflage serves two purposes: it enables the chameleon to stalk its prey unseen, and also protects it from predators, against which it has no effective defence except a display of aggression, which includes a sinister hiss.

The Cape dwarf chameleon is one of the largest of the 13 species of dwarf chameleon in southern Africa. In males the tail is slightly longer than the head and body combined; in the female it is slightly shorter. Down the cranium, and along the back and the front two-thirds of the tail, runs a crest consisting of small nodules or tubercles; a more prominent crest hangs from the throat.

The species feeds mostly on small grasshoppers and other flying insects.

The female gives birth to live young, from 5-12 in a litter. Each little chameleon, about 40 mm long, arrives in a sticky bag that the mother fixes to a twig. Within a minute or two the hatchling wriggles itself out of the envelope and is immediately independent.

BIBRON'S GECKO
Bibron se geitjie *(Pachydactylus bibronii)*

Size: Length 20 cm.
Colour: Grey or purplish grey to brown, with four or five wavy, dark brown bands across the back, and scattered white tubercles which extend onto the legs. The tail has a series of nine or ten dark bands which fade as the gecko grows older. Underparts cream or dull white.
Most like: The Cape gecko, which also has a wide distribution throughout southern Africa but, at 9-13 cm, is smaller and has less well-developed tubercles on its back.
Habitat: In rock crevices, cracks in walls, loose stones and tree bark, thatched roofs, termite mounds, piles of leaves.

Throughout southern Africa but absent from coastal Mozambique, western Mpumalanga and Gauteng, most of the Free State, Lesotho and KwaZulu-Natal, and parts of the Eastern and Western Cape.

Adhesive discs at the tips of the Bibron's gecko's splayed toes enable it to travel not only across vertical surfaces but even upside down, across ceilings—a trick characteristic of the gecko family but denied to other lizard groups.

Bibron's gecko is one of the largest of the 64 different species of gecko in southern Africa. While they're all perfectly harmless, this species can administer a nasty little nip if it is molested and chooses not to scuttle away. It hangs on stubbornly with its tiny teeth and can even draw blood. In protest against being handled it may utter a series of high-pitched squeaks.

This gecko is a gregarious creature: 20 or more of them may share the same shelter, departing from it at night to feed on insects. Occasionally it comes out in the early morning or late evening, and sometimes even in the middle of the day. You may have seen one chasing after its prey on an outhouse wall.

Geckos are egg-layers. The female Bibron's gecko leaves her two eggs in any convenient sheltered crevice or hole, often in the communal nest.

If attacked by a bird or other predator, the gecko sheds its tail, which snaps off with disconcerting ease and continues to wriggle, diverting the predator's attention so that the gecko can escape. A new tail will eventually replace the original one.

Snakes and lizards

COMMON BARKING GECKO

Gewone blafgeitjie *(Ptenopus garrulus)*

Size: *Length 6-8 cm.*
Colour: *Yellowish brown, either speckled in reddish brown or with irregular blackish cross-bars which also extend onto the tail. The tail is banded. The throat of the male carries a bright gold heart-shaped mark. Underparts white.*
Most like: *Carp's barking gecko which, however, is creamy white in colour with brown speckling and dark brown cross-bars over the back, and Kock's barking gecko which is reddish brown with dark speckling, and has no dark bars on the back.*
Habitat: *Among small shrubs and bushes, or tufts of grass, in dry, sandy flats.*

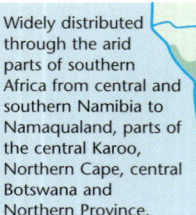

Widely distributed through the arid parts of southern Africa from central and southern Namibia to Namaqualand, parts of the central Karoo, Northern Cape, central Botswana and Northern Province.

Geckos are unique among lizards in that they can make a sound louder than an elementary hiss. The word 'gecko' itself is onomatopoeic, imitating the creature's call, and of all species, the barking gecko boasts by far the loudest voice. Just before sunset the male geckos stand at the entrance to their burrows and start chirping—a loud, persistent *whick-whick* or clicking cry that can be imitated by striking two pebbles together. Although it is thought to be a love song, this cry may also serve to define male territories. When produced simultaneously by a large congregation of these geckos, the noise can be almost deafening.

As darkness falls the calling usually stops, and there is complete silence. The common barking gecko then emerges from its shelter and sets about hunting for its supper: termites, ants, small beetles, bees and wasps.

Most geckos have soft, splayed toes with scales; minute hairs on the scales catch in small cracks, enabling the geckos to walk on vertical surfaces. The barking gecko's toes, however, are different: they are sharply clawed, and long scales at the edges prevent the animal from sinking into sandy soil.

The claws help it to dig a steeply angled burrow about 30 cm deep. The entrance is carefully disguised, being under a bush or tuft of grass.

GIANT GROUND GECKO

Grootgrondgeitjie *(Chondrodactylus angulifer)*

Size: *Length 14-17 cm.*
Colour: *Yellowish to reddish brown, with four or five dark-edged, pale cross-bands across the back, each ending in a pale spot on each side. The tail has dark cross-bars. Underparts white, flushed with pink.*
Most like: *The three species of barking gecko which also live in the western desert regions, but the giant ground gecko is much bigger.*
Habitat: *Dry river beds and sandy and gravel plains in desert regions.*

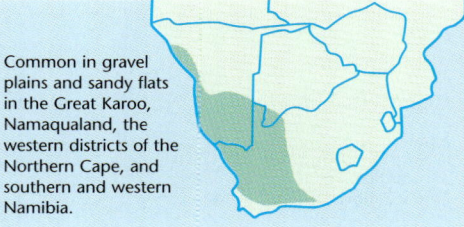

Common in gravel plains and sandy flats in the Great Karoo, Namaqualand, the western districts of the Northern Cape, and southern and western Namibia.

Standing motionless on long, slender legs, with its tail curled upwards well above the ground, the giant ground gecko looks a little absurd as it waits for its prey to pass by. It is a plucky animal which, when molested, puts up an aggressive display, loudly hissing and sometimes launching itself right off the ground as it makes for the cause of the disturbance. But, like most other geckos, its movements are normally sluggish and it can quite easily be caught. With luck you will capture a complete specimen, for this species is less apt than some others to shed its tail (an involuntary defence mechanism designed to divert the predator's attention).

The giant ground gecko has a rather large head and long, slender legs tipped with stubby-toed feet that are marginally reminiscent of the human hand. The undersides of the toes do not have the adhesive pads of rock-living geckos, and are covered with small, spiny scales. These feet are particularly well suited to digging. With them the gecko shovels out quantities of sand to make a burrow up to 90 cm long—a habit it shares with the barking geckos. Alternatively, it appropriates and enlarges the disused hole of a scorpion. And in such a shelter, or beneath loose stones, it remains during the day, usually coming out only after dark to forage. It eats termites, small ground-dwelling beetles and spiders.

In summer the female lays two hard-shelled, sticky eggs, which are quite undetectable in the sand.

Snakes and lizards

CAPE GECKO

Kaapse geitjie *(Pachydactylus capensis)*

Size: Length 9-13 cm.
Colour: From light grey to greyish brown above, with separate white and dark brown flecks and spots. Underparts greyish white.
Most like: The ocellated gecko which, however, is usually smaller at 8 cm, and whose spots are whitish with dark edges.
Habitat: Rock crevices, rotten logs and termite mounds, or under stones, rubble, loose tree bark and undergrowth in grassland, Karoo and dry savanna.

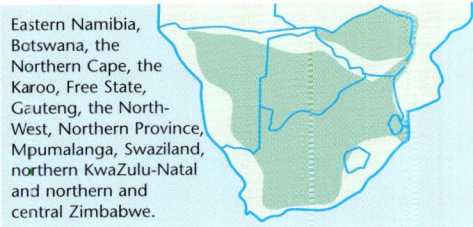

Eastern Namibia, Botswana, the Northern Cape, the Karoo, Free State, Gauteng, the North-West, Northern Province, Mpumalanga, Swaziland, northern KwaZulu-Natal and northern and central Zimbabwe.

Though shy, like all geckos, the Cape gecko takes up residence in houses, and you may see one cautiously proceeding across a wall (or upside down on a ceiling) as it searches for moths and other insects.

Its feet, which have splayed toes with adhesive pads underneath them, look like flowers with radiating petals, hence the Afrikaans name *blommetjie* sometimes given to these geckos.

In typical gecko fashion this species readily sheds its tail if threatened or touched, and makes its escape while the aggressor's attention is diverted by the twisting and turning of the self-amputated tail. In fact, few adults still have their original tails intact. A secondary, boneless tail replaces the first one and, should only part of the original be lost, the new growth will give the gecko a two-tailed appearance.

As with other gecko species, the common Cape species sheds its skin frequently; even the skin over the eye is sloughed. The gecko then generally eats its discarded covering.

There are no movable lids over the gecko's eyes; consequently its unblinking stare is somewhat snakelike, helping to account for the genuine awe in which many people hold this innocuous creature. The pupil of the eye is vertical, reducing to a mere slit in the strong light of day but widening out during the night, when the Cape gecko is at its most active.

The female lays her oval eggs in pairs, often at right angles to each other, under loose stones or in a rock crevice or some other form of shelter. The newborn offspring are about three to five centimetres long.

WEB-FOOTED GECKO

Webvoetgeitjie *(Palmatogecko rangei)*

Size: Length 10-12 cm.
Colour: Flesh pink to pale pinkish brown, with indistinct darker cross-bars. Belly and lower sides white, but rest of undersides, including tail, uniform pink.
Most like: Giant ground gecko but smaller and lacking the latter's white spots.
Habitat: Desert sands.

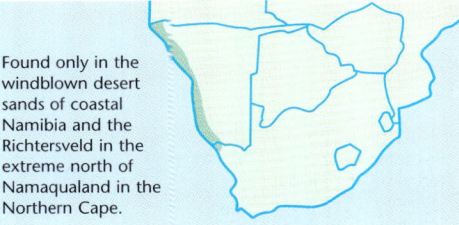

Found only in the windblown desert sands of coastal Namibia and the Richtersveld in the extreme north of Namaqualand in the Northern Cape.

Like some other animal species that have carved a niche for themselves in the harsh Namib Desert, the resourceful web-footed gecko drinks dew that condenses on stones during the night from the coastal fogs that roll in from the sea; it also uses its long tongue to collect the fine beads of water that form on the top of its head and on its body.

Unique to the species, known also as the palmate desert gecko, are its webbed feet. They serve a dual purpose: most importantly they act like snowshoes, enabling it to travel across the desert sands without sinking in. This gecko moves rapidly over the hot dunes, keeping its body well clear of the sand and leaving little trace of its progress. The webs are also useful for burrowing into the sand, whether to hide from a predator or from the remorseless heat of the sun. One of the creature's main predators is thought to be the large dune spider.

Burrows are usually made in the shelter of an overhanging rock or small bush. When digging, the gecko uses a forefoot to dig and the corresponding hindfoot to shovel the soil away; when these feet are tired, it switches to the feet on the other side of the body. At night it lies in its burrow with its head facing the entrance, ready to pounce on any insect, especially a beetle or cricket, that innocently passes by.

The semi-transparent skin of the web-footed gecko allows the delicate vertebral column and internal organs to show through to some extent, and the beautiful eyes, with their cream vertical irises, appear as bloodshot, bluish shadows in the head.

Snakes and lizards

SOUTHERN ROCK AGAMA
Suidelike rotskoggelmander *(Agama atra)*

Size: *Length 24-30 cm.*
Colour: *Females and nonbreeding males blotched and mottled above in shades of brown and cream, with red flecks on sides and a whitish streak running from neck to base of tail; belly off-white; bluish lines on throat. Breeding males have blue or blue-green head and forelimbs, and a vivid purplish-blue throat; back olive-green to reddish brown with pale spots and blackish mottling.*
Most like: *Ground agama, the males of which have less bright blue colouring on head and three parallel blackish lines on sides of throat.*
Habitat: *Rocky outcrops and boulders, ranging from sea level to mountain tops.*

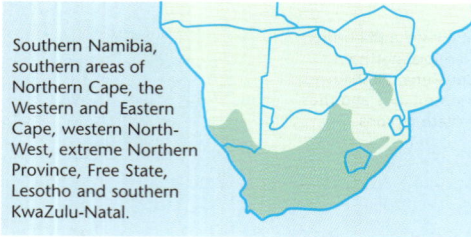

Southern Namibia, southern areas of Northern Cape, the Western and Eastern Cape, western North-West, extreme Northern Province, Free State, Lesotho and southern KwaZulu-Natal.

One of the popular Afrikaans names for this lizard—*koggelmannetjie* (little mimicking man)—derives from the male's habit, when displaying to other males, of rapidly bobbing and turning his head, for all the world like an inquisitive, crotchety human being. If threatened, he may try to camouflage himself by fading the colours on his head and pressing himself down against a rock. If this fails, he scampers away at an astonishing speed, scaling perpendicular surfaces and jumping agilely from rock to rock before disappearing into a crevice. When running at full speed the rock agama uses its hindlegs only, the forelegs being raised clear off the ground.

One of the best known of nine species of *koggelmannetjie* found in southern Africa, the rock agama enjoys basking in the sun. It takes time off from this pleasure to scuttle after the insects that provide its diet: mostly ants and termites.

The female rock agama deposits her 6-12 eggs in a hole in a sunny but protected position near a rock. After recovering from her efforts she scrapes soil over the eggs, then leaves them to hatch. After three months or so the hatchlings dig themselves out and can fend for themselves.

CAPE FLAT LIZARD
Kaapse platakkedis *(Platysaurus capensis)*

Size: *Length 20 cm.*
Colour: *In males, the head, throat and front two-thirds of the back are a bright metallic blue or blue-green, the rest of the back and tail being orange-brown or greyish brown. Sides of body and tail are reddish orange. The chest is navy blue, continuing as black along the centre of the belly. Females and juveniles are greyish brown or olive-brown above, with three paler streaks from head to tail; the tail is paler than the body, and the underparts are white, with an elongated black patch up the middle.*
Most like: *The other eight species of southern African flat lizards, but the Cape flat lizard is the only one in the lower Gariep (Orange) River valley.*
Habitat: *Rocky slopes often near water or dry watercourses, in succulent veld.*

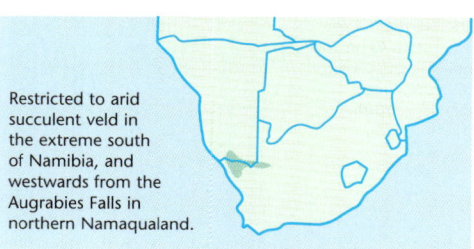

Restricted to arid succulent veld in the extreme south of Namibia, and westwards from the Augrabies Falls in northern Namaqualand.

The bright coloration of the Cape flat (also known as the red-tailed) lizard makes this foppish species a memorable sight for visitors to the Augrabies Falls on the Gariep (Orange) River, where these lizards scamper about on the granite rocks at the water's edge. Like the other eight species of 'flat lizards' (that is what the Greek *platysaurus* means) in southern Africa, their slenderness enables them to make homes in the narrowest of rock crevices.

They move quickly and are very agile. All flat lizards are gregarious, living in colonies of hundreds. They prey on small beetles, caterpillars and an assortment of flying insects, including bees.

In the mating season the male Cape flat lizard flaunts its bright blue head and throat ostentatiously by standing with its forelegs straightened and the forepart of its body raised. The drab female is suitably impressed, and in the spring or early summer she lays two eggs in a nest lined with damp leaf mould and wedged into a vertical fissure in the rock.

In a colony of these lizards the dominant males fiercely defend their harem of females against intruding males, especially in the breeding season.

Snakes and lizards

KNOX'S DESERT LIZARD

Knox se woestynakkedis *(Meroles knoxii)*

Size: Length 15-23 cm.
Colour: Pale brown-grey in the western coastal area; further inland the background colour is more reddish brown or purplish brown; rows of eyelike spots, dark with a light centre, run down the back and sides. Underparts whitish or pale blue-grey. Breeding males have bright yellow on the chin, throat and around the vent.
Most like: Spotted desert lizard which does not occur on the Namaqualand coast, except in the north towards the mouth of the Gariep (Orange) River. Only experts can tell the difference between the two.
Habitat: Found in sandy succulent scrub and coastal sand dunes.

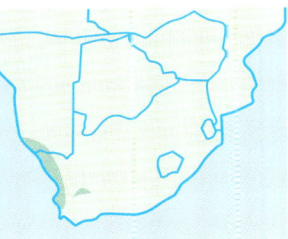

Inhabits sandveld along the Western and Northern Cape coast from Cape Town north to the Gariep (Orange) River, extending further north into southern Namibia and inland to the Karoo.

CAPE SKINK

Kaapse skink *(Mabuya capensis)*

Size: Length 22-27 cm.
Colour: Light brown to grey-brown or olive-brown, with three yellowish or off-white stripes running down the back, the central stripe being the widest and most distinct. Underparts grey or yellowish white.
Most like: Striped skink which has a pale stripe on each side but lacks the Cape skink's central back stripe.
Habitat: A wide range of habitats, from mangrove swamps at sea level to montane grassland, but sandy savanna in particular. Also near human habitation in rural areas.

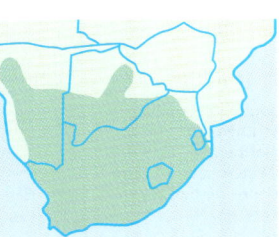

Throughout most of the subregion, with the exception of coastal and northern Namibia, northern Botswana, Zimbabwe, Mozambique and the eastern regions of Mpumalanga and Northern Province.

The colouring of this active, quick-moving, diurnal lizard provides it with good camouflage in its sandy habitat—and just as well, for it is less well-protected by scales than the skinks are. If it senses real danger it relies first on speed to escape but, if pursued closely, will burrow under the sand. As a last resort it may also cast off its tail to provide a wriggling distraction to any predator.

Knox's desert lizard, also known as the ocellated sand lizard, shelters in a burrow that it digs in firm soil beneath a shrub or plant detritus. Emerging to forage, it will dart from one tuft of grass to another in search of beetles, flies and other insects.

The female lays a clutch of two to six eggs, each of which measures 7-13 mm in length.

'Ocellate'—meaning eyelike—refers to the characteristic markings of this species, one of six species of desert lizard of the genus *Meroles*. All are found in the dry western, mainly coastal regions of southern Africa, and all have well-developed feet adapted for rapid burrowing. The toes of Knox's desert lizard are slightly fringed, a further aid to digging.

Though this lizard is distributed mainly along the coast, from the southwestern Cape to southern Namibia, you may come across it as far inland as Matjiesfontein.

Skinks are a large and very common family of lizards, with 59 species and numerous subspecies in southern Africa. Many are plump and all have smooth, shiny scales that fit closely to their bodies. This natural 'streamlining' equips them well for burrowing in the soil and wedging into rock crevices with ease.

The well-known Cape or three-striped skink is a somewhat sluggish species. Its natural home is under the shelter of loose stones or in a hole excavated beneath a small bush or tuft of grass. To catch the warmth of the late-afternoon sun it may actually climb into the bush. It feeds mostly on insects: beetles, crickets, grasshoppers, but also on other small creatures such as spiders and worms.

The female may take up to a week to produce all of her offspring, of which there may be 8-18 per brood. Each is born in a thin, membranous bag (or 'shell') that the active, newborn skink breaks and wriggles out of within seconds—although sometimes the mother gives some assistance, with a vigorous tug of her mouth. The newborn lizards measure five to seven centimetres.

If you come across one of these skinks in your garden and ensure that it remains unmolested, it can grow quite tame. In fact its presence is worth encouraging, for its diet includes common garden pests such as crickets, rose-beetles and moths.

Snakes and lizards

SILVERY DWARF BURROWING SKINK
Silwergrys dwerg-grawende skink *(Scelotes bipes)*

Size: Length 12-14 cm.
Colour: Shiny silvery grey, often tinged with buff, and with a faintly streaked or stippled appearance caused by the dark brown centres to the scales.
Most like: The other 13 species of burrowing skink in southern Africa, but especially the lowveld dwarf burrowing skink, which also lacks forelimbs but has a pale stripe along each side of the body.
Habitat: Under stones or in sandy ground, often among the roots of shrubs or clumps of grass.

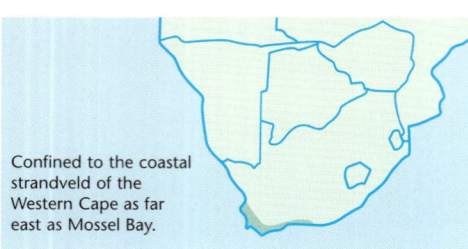

Confined to the coastal strandveld of the Western Cape as far east as Mossel Bay.

To the casual eye, all that distinguishes the silvery dwarf burrowing skink from a small snake or large worm is its two absurdly small hindlegs, each bearing two tiny clawed toes, one of which is twice the length of the other. As with many other related skink species, these limbs have degenerated during the course of evolution, and the front pair of legs has disappeared altogether.

This beautifully coloured little creature, also known as the silver sand lizard, is totally at home in its sandy environment. Despite the absence of forelimbs, it burrows easily and speedily, and maintains a mostly underground existence. The flattened head, small, smooth scales, scaly lower eyelids and minute ear-openings are adaptations to this way of life. Above ground it wriggles along, bearing a remarkable resemblance to a snake. Its tail, like those of several other skinks with reduced legs (or no legs at all) is shorter than its body.

This dwarf burrowing lizard feeds on slugs, worms and an assortment of small insects including the larvae of termites and beetles. The female produces live young, not eggs, and her 'litter' consists of no more than two babies, born at the end of summer and each measuring some 60-65 mm in length.

Scelotes bipes is one of 14 dwarf burrowing skinks in southern Africa. All have undergone some degree of limb loss during the evolutionary process; some have no external limbs at all, some have all four, and some have lost the forelegs and certain toes of the hindlegs.

SUNDEVALL'S WRITHING SKINK
Sundevall se wriemelskink *(Lygosoma sundevallii)*

Size: Length 15 cm.
Colour: Ranges from olive-brown to orange-brown, with a faint iridescent sheen; each scale has a dark spot, giving this lizard a finely speckled appearance. Underparts yellowish or creamy white, sometimes speckled with brown on the undersides of the tail.
Most like: Cape legless skink and the common long-tailed seps, but the former has no legs, and the latter has a much longer tail.
Habitat: Sandy savanna and open bushveld, often under stones, plant refuse or manure heaps, or in old termite mounds. Disused campsites are also favoured.

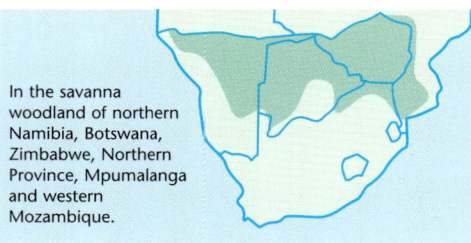

In the savanna woodland of northern Namibia, Botswana, Zimbabwe, Northern Province, Mpumalanga and western Mozambique.

With its short and sturdy limbs this snakelike skink seems neither quite one thing nor the other. It manoeuvres its plump, muscular little body across the ground in a rapid serpentine wriggle; yet its legs play a part in locomotion too, slowly moving to and fro.

The Sundevall's writhing skink's streamlined body can travel reasonably fast through soft loose soil or litter. A burrowing species, it lives largely underground but comes to the surface to forage for insects (and their larvae), including beetles, termites, grasshoppers and crickets. It also eats spiders, woodlice and soft snails. When such favoured food is readily available, Sundevall's writhing skink is apt to remain at the same site for a long time.

The female lays her white, oval eggs, usually four at a time, in summer. She often lays them in a termite mound, or may create her own subterranean nest.

You may have difficulty capturing one of these lizards, simply because its body is so smooth and slippery. There is also a danger that it may lose its tail, which is very brittle. In fact, very few adult specimens still retain their original tail; when this is lost, a substitute, slightly deformed one grows in its place.

Snakes and lizards

CAPE LEGLESS SKINK

Kaapse pootlose skink *(Acontias meleagris)*

Size: Length 20-26 cm.
Colour: Ranges from greyish brown to golden-amber and dark liver-brown, the underparts being yellowish.
Most like: The other six species of legless skink of the genus Acontias. They are, however, separated geographically to a certain extent—the Cape legless skink is the dominant species in the Western and southeastern Cape.
Habitat: Dry, sandy soil under sparse vegetation. Often found under stones and logs.

Common in sandy soils in the Western and southeastern Cape extending inland to the southern parts of the Karoo.

Ingeniously, nature has given the Cape legless skink, or golden sand lizard, translucent lower eyelids, enabling it to detect light when it is burrowing underground with its lids closed. It also has a hard, pointed nose that can push its way through quite firm soil, and a hard-tipped tail which the lizard uses as a hook to pull itself into reverse.

Like other members of the genus *Acontias*, these lizards cannot boast the vestige of a limb—even an X-ray will reveal no more than a reduced pelvic girdle. It is difficult for the layman to appreciate the fact that these reptiles are lizards and not snakes.

The Cape legless skink is one of 12 species of such legless, stubby-tailed skinks found in southern Africa. Like the others, its habitat is mostly underground and, with its long, cylindrical body closely covered in small, hard, shiny scales, it is well adapted to burrow beneath the surface.

On the surface these legless skinks undulate along like a snake, but the motion is slow and they are not difficult to capture, except that they are extremely slippery and apt to writhe. They are quite harmless.

They feed on such small creatures as they can find beneath the soil: mainly worms and insect larvae. During the latter part of summer the female gives birth to three or four live young.

Two subspecies exist. *A.m meleagris* is found in the Western and southern Cape, and *A m. orientalis* is a native of the Eastern Cape.

COMMON LONG-TAILED SEPS

Gewone langstertseps *(Tetradactylus tetradactylus)*

Size: Length 18-24 cm.
Colour: Olive, with two dark brown stripes along the back and tail, and short, vertical dark brown or black bars on the lower head and neck. Underparts paler olive.
Most like: African long-tailed seps which, however, has only a single toe (not four) on each of its limbs; sometimes it may have no forelimbs.
Habitat: Open fynbos or grassy mountain slopes.

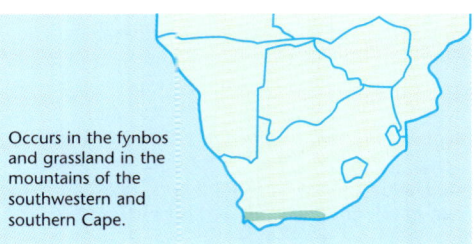

Occurs in the fynbos and grassland in the mountains of the southwestern and southern Cape.

Known also as the Cape snake-lizard, the common long-tailed seps is a member of the same family as the sungazer and the armadillo girdled lizard. It has four tiny, clawed toes at each of its four spindly legs. These limbs support the lizard when it is stationary and help it, when the need arises, to make small movements in long vegetation; but they are non-functional when the creature moves at speed, for then it undulates, or 'swims' along much as a snake does, and at a distance it could very easily be mistaken for one.

The tail of this species is three times as long as its body and the lizard uses it to propel itself along. To catch one of these slithery and extremely swift animals is very difficult. Should you manage to grab one by its tail, the tail may come off in your hand, as is common among most species of lizard, allowing the threatened reptile to escape. A tail is essential to its survival, however, and another one grows quickly in place of the original.

This snake-lizard feeds on grasshoppers, flies and other insects. A diurnal species, it seeks shelter at night among stones or tufts of grass. A captive specimen was seen to sleep on its back on many occasions—unusual behaviour for a lizard; it is not known whether the species adopts the same posture in the wild.

Biologists recognize two subspecies: *T.t. tetradactylus*, which is found among the mountains of the southwestern and southern Cape, and the rarer *T.t. bilineatus* of the Eastern Cape.

Frogs and toads

Frogs and toads are the only true amphibians—members of the class Amphibia—in southern Africa, and lead 'double' lives, in that most species are equally at home in fresh water as they are on land. As a group they are known either as the Anura—a reference to the absence of a tail in all the members of this order—or as the Salientia, a word which means they can leap or jump. Because frogs and toads rely on water for survival they are much less common in the drier parts of the subregion than they are in the wetter parts, where their variety is greater too.

The way in which the aquatic, fishlike tadpole, breathing through a pair of external gills, is transformed into a lung-breathing frog, is one of nature's most remarkable achievements. The speed of this metamorphosis varies according to species and also to such variables such as the prevailing local temperature. Although the common river frog's tadpole, for example, may take anything from nine months to two years to metamorphose, those of the bullfrog and dainty frog, which have adapted to living in arid areas, can complete this phase of development in a mere 16 to 18 days. These two species take advantage of rare local thunderstorms to breed, and their offspring have to complete the egg/tadpole/frog cycle before their pan or puddle dries up completely.

How do you tell the difference between a frog and a toad? The distinction is clear in England where these terms originated, because only two types of frog exist there. The English members of the genus *Rana* are sharp-nosed, smooth-skinned water 'frogs' with prodigious jumping skills, while members of the genus *Bufo*—the toads—are blunt-nosed, warty-skinned terrestrial species, which visit water only to breed, and which move in short hops, not huge leaps.

In southern Africa this distinction between frog and toad is not as clear, because instead of two families with one genus each, we have five families, with a total of 25 genera. True, toads of the genus *Bufo* do occur here, but in company with other blunt-snouted, short-legged, dry and warty-skinned species quite unrelated to the toads, the rain frogs.

It is quite untrue, incidentally, that by touching a toad you can acquire warts. The worst that might befall you from contact with certain species, such as the guttural toad or the common rain frog, (which secrete a toxic substance in their skin glands) is a skin irritation. To be on the safe side, keep your hands away from your mouth and eyes immediately after handling frogs, and wash your hands well. Of the well over 100 species indigenous to southern Africa, not one is even potentially dangerous to humans. However, one species—the bullfrog, with three blunt, toothlike projections in its lower jaw—can administer a painful bite.

When froggy goes a-wooing, he usually takes to the water. Among most species copulation—true coupling—does not take place, for the sex act consists of the male fertilizing the eggs with his sperm immediately *after* they have been laid (usually in the water) by the female. Each egg is coated in a transparent gelatinous material that protects the inner embryo. Most frogs lay their eggs in clumps, true toads in long strings. Huge numbers of eggs are produced by many species—but the eggs are extremely vulnerable to a wide variety of aquatic predators, from fish to water beetles.

Adult frogs and toads have many natural enemies too, including snakes, lizards, tortoises, crocodiles and birds such as cranes and herons. There is no reason why man should add his name to the list: amphibians play a valuable role by consuming insect pests, including mosquitoes, and they have voracious appetites. (But they will eat only living, moving prey, a fact to be considered by anyone contemplating keeping a frog as a pet.)

The gravest charge we can lay against frogs and toads is that their call is sometimes loud, monotonously persistent and unpleasant to our ears. (Although the call may keep you awake at night, it can also be as melodious as birdsong, as cheerful as a cricket's chirp.)

Most species are nocturnal, and it is at night that the chorus rings out. It is only the males that make any noise; it is their mating call. Where thousands of males are gathered together, as often happens in ponds, vleis and marshes after rain has fallen, the combined contribution of rival songsters may indeed be deafening.

To an expert, the 'song' of each species is quite distinctive and usually enables easy identification.

Identifying frogs and toads

Shape and size

Frogs come in all shapes and sizes, from the endangered micro frog of the southwestern Cape, which is only 1,5 cm long, to the bullfrog, which can achieve 20 cm or more. Look at their hindfeet to determine their lifestyle: the completely aquatic platanna has fully webbed toes, while the common rain frog is independent of standing water and has no webbing on its feet. River frogs are always associated with water and have well-webbed toes, while our various toad species visit standing water only to breed, and have poorly developed webbing.

Rain frogs and bullfrogs dig burrows into friable soils where they avoid predation and desiccation by the sun during daylight hours. Their hindfeet carry a hard, spadelike flange used in digging; this flange is often present, if less clearly defined, in toads, which also require underground shelter. Aquatic frogs do not possess hindfoot flanges.

Look also at the length of a frog's hindlegs. Long-legged species escape predators by jumping and swimming (for example, river frogs, stream frogs, reed frogs and the foam nest frog); species with moderately developed hindlegs, such as toads, rely on camouflage or poison glands to escape predation. Species with abnormally short legs (rain frogs) live mostly underground and also produce toxins as a defensive measure; when threatened, they inflate themselves and resemble nothing so much as a golf ball on four stubby legs. The comical-looking long-legged species progress by hopping; medium and short-legged species 'walk'.

Certain frogs in southern Africa, such as the foam nest frog, water lily frog and reed frogs have lifestyles

Frogs and toads

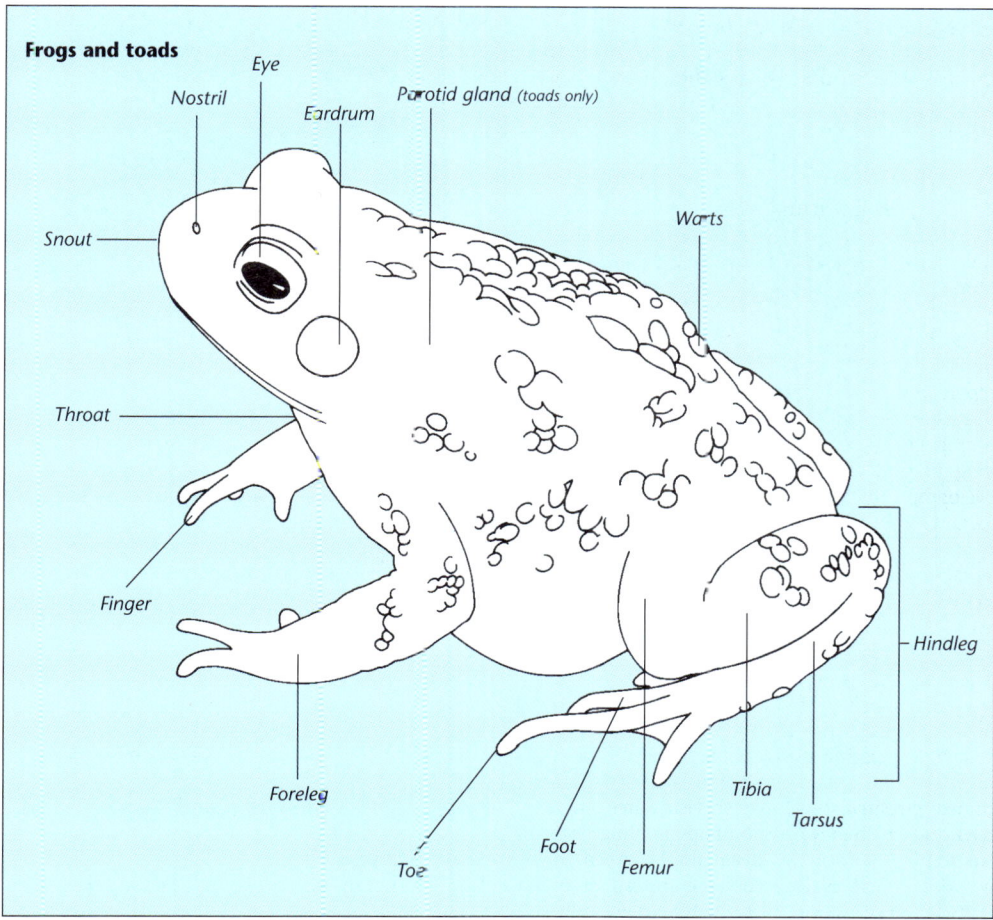

Frogs and toads: Snout, Nostril, Eye, Eardrum, Parotid gland (toads only), Warts, Throat, Finger, Foreleg, Toe, Foot, Femur, Tibia, Tarsus, Hindleg

which involve climbing reed stems or other smooth surfaces. Such species are equipped with 'suckers' (flat terminal discs) at the tips of their fingers and toes, which provide adhesion to smooth surfaces.

The more aquatic the species, the damper its skin. The platanna is well supplied with mucus and is slippery and almost impossible to hold in one hand. Toads, however, have dry, warty skins and possess a pair of well-developed, oblong 'parotid' glands on the top of the head behind the eyes. The reed frogs and river frogs strike a happy medium and are damp and smooth-skinned, but not at all slimy.

Colour

Frogs and toads can be very colourful but remember that most species can change colour quickly, depending on temperature, light intensity or possibly even the background colour. The water lily frog, however, is always green; toads are usually patterned in various shades of brown, the running frog is usually silvery gold with three dark brown to blackish vertebral stripes, and the adult bullfrog is usually olive-green above with orange patches around the armpits. The marbled reed frog is one of the most variable of all frogs, with many colour forms.

When to look

The best time to look for most frogs is on damp nights. Use a torch, or drive along slowly, using the car's headlights to pick up frogs in the road. In the winter-rainfall region of the Western Cape, the frogs mostly breed in winter; the reverse is true of the summer-rainfall areas. In arid areas, frogs and toads take advantage of any shower of rain, regardless of when it falls.

Calls

The best way to find and identify frogs is to listen carefully to their calls. Each frog and toad has its own distinctive call, emitted by the male to attract females and to maintain his territory against rivals. These vary from the high-pitched whistle of the painted reed frog to the liquid *quoip* of the running frog and the low-pitched, cowlike *whoop* of the bullfrog. Recordings of frog calls are available commercially, or you can learn to distinguish the calls yourself by watching frogs in action.

Frogs and toads

Common platanna

Gewone platanna (*Xenopus laevis*)

Size: Length up to 12 cm.
Colour: Pale grey-green to almost black upperparts. Underparts usually off-white or pale yellow-grey, sometimes with black spots or blotches.
Most like: Cape platanna and tropical platanna, but Cape species has a yellow-mottled ('sago-belly') abdomen and is vary rare in the southwestern Cape. Tropical platanna has a long, obvious 'tentacle' projecting from below each eye, absent in the common platanna.
Habitat: Ponds, dams and vleis. Seldom found in running water.

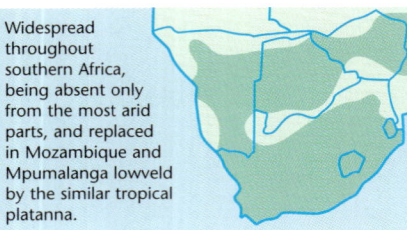

Widespread throughout southern Africa, being absent only from the most arid parts, and replaced in Mozambique and Mpumalanga lowveld by the similar tropical platanna.

This slippery customer is completely aquatic in its habits, more so than any other African amphibian. Feeding and breeding under water, it has a number of special characteristics that equip it for its totally aquatic lifestyle. Its smooth skin and streamlined body enable it to slide easily through water, and its extremely muscular back legs, with their large, fully webbed feet, enable it to swim as quickly and skilfully as a fish. Like all frogs and toads the platanna breathes air, and it can also absorb oxygen from the water through the pores of its skin.

The short but conspicuous black claws that protrude from three of the toes on each of its hindfeet are probably used to stir up mud at the bottom of the pond—either to flush out small prey or create a protective screen of murky water.

It eats underwater insects, small fish and tadpoles—including those of its own species. Because it hunts under water it doesn't need the long, sticky tongue common to most other frogs and toads; in fact, it doesn't have a tongue at all, and uses its relatively weak forelimbs to help push food into its mouth.

The male common platanna is a singer of sorts, producing a soft underwater buzzing. How it makes this sound is not clear, since it does so without releasing air or making any visible movement.

Karoo toad

Karooskurwepadda (*Bufo gariepensis*)

Size: Body length up to 9,5 cm.
Colour: Upperparts pinkish brown or olive-grey, with irregular asymmetrical dark red or dark brown patches. Underparts off-white to pale yellow, usually with small black spots, especially in younger specimens.
Most like: Guttural toad and raucous toad; the Karoo toad, however, is the only one of the three to have spots on its belly; the dark blotches on its back are asymmetrical, not paired as in the other two.
Habitat: Sandy ground covered by grass or low scrub, usually in arid areas.

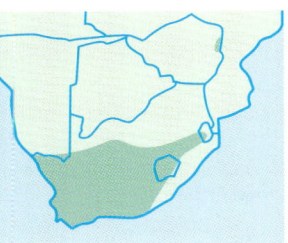

Occurs widely in the Western, Northern and Eastern Cape, Free State, Lesotho, northwestern KwaZulu-Natal and western Swaziland. A relict population occurs in Zimbabwe's eastern highlands.

You could mistake the shrill cry of a frightened or angry Karoo toad for that of a human baby—an unnerving experience if you're out alone in the Karoo at night. Its usual, more reassuring, night time call, however, consists of a loud, rasping *kwaa* which the male repeats at roughly one-second intervals at breeding ponds or pools.

Although frogs and toads are normally associated with water, this toad is an exception to the rule, as it inhabits dry, sandy countryside. During the day it shelters from the sun in a hole in the ground or a crevice among the rocks, leaving this hiding place in the evening to hunt for insects, beetles and other small creatures.

Unlike other large toads, which tend to hop by pushing off with both hindfeet at once, the Karoo toad usually prefers to walk on all four legs independently and progress in an ungainly waddle.

Like other members of the toad family it has to shed its skin periodically as it grows larger. Typically the old, outer skin first tears along the back; then the animal laboriously works itself free.

Another characteristic that the Karoo toad shares with many of its relatives is a pair of elongated skin glands, set just behind the eyes, which secrete a milky white fluid. Poisons in this fluid act on the heart muscles and can be fatal to small animals.

Frogs and toads

GUTTURAL TOAD
Gutturale skurwepadda *(Bufo gutturalis)*

Size: Length 8-11 cm.
Colour: Varies from pale yellow to dark olive-brown. Large brown or yellow blotches on the back, usually paired; underparts generally pale grey, but males have dark throats; usually has irregular reddish patches on the thighs.
Most like: Raucous toad which, however, never has red spots or blotches on thighs. The dark brown blotches on the top of the raucous toad's head between eyes are usually joined, not separate as in guttural toad.
Habitat: Open grassveld or bush country.

In western Northern Cape, Free State, Lesotho, extreme Eastern Cape, KwaZulu-Natal, Swaziland, Mpumalanga, Gauteng, the North-West, Northern Province, Mozambique, Zimbabwe, and northern Botswana and Namibia.

The guttural toad is a great, noisy guzzler that tucks into its favoured meal of flying ants with such enthusiasm that its belly becomes distended to the point that it can scarcely move. In the mating season the male adds to the image of obesity by producing an amphibian roar during which it inflates its throat to such a size that it looks like a balloon.

You can hear the loud, snorelike croak of the guttural toad at almost any time of the year, but particularly after wet weather. A good spell of rain brings these toads out in force, especially at night, leading to a deafening chorus of guttural creativity.

During the day guttural toads conceal themselves from the prying rays of the sun, seeking refuge under logs, beneath thick vegetation, or tucked away in shallow holes which they excavate with their hindlegs. As soon as darkness falls, they emerge to gorge on insects, worms, snails or flying ants. They are unafraid of man, and often approach houses to prey upon insects attracted to the outside lights. The living is so easy here that they will often set up home within a metre or so of the verandah.

An old European superstition credits the toad with the power of inflicting warts. One reason for this is perhaps that its own skin is covered with wartlike glands, which exude a sticky white substance whenever the animal becomes angry or frightened.

BUSHVELD RAIN FROG
Bosveldblaasop *(Breviceps adspersus)*

Size: Length 3-6 cm.
Colour: Upperparts usually yellow-brown to mid-brown with blotches of darker brown and yellow-orange. Underparts white, but throat dark brown in males.
Most like: Most other rain frog species which are all very similar. The bushveld rain frog's range overlaps with that of the plaintive rain frog; the call of the latter, however, is a drawn-out, mournful whistle, not a short, sharp chirp like that of the former.
Habitat: Underground in loose, sandy soil in lightly wooded savanna areas.

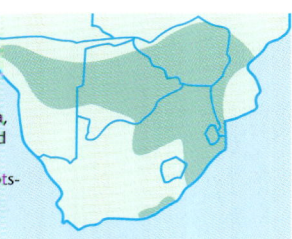

Found in KwaZulu-Natal, northern Free State, the North-West, Gauteng, Northern Province, Mpumalanga, Swaziland, western and central Mozambique, Zimbabwe, most of Botswana, central Namibia and Eastern Cape.

The rain frog's most common Afrikaans name, *blaasop*, meaning 'blow up', comes from its ability to inflate its body with air whenever it becomes frightened or angry. When fully distended it is scarcely recognizable as a frog, resembling rather more closely a jelly balloon, with two blinking black eyes, and four tiny limbs sticking out.

Many South Africans have numbers of rain frogs in their gardens without ever having seen one. These frogs live mostly underground, surfacing at night before, during or after rain. However, while they are seldom seen, they are certainly heard. The male's night-time call during the breeding season is a high-pitched, musical clicking sound, reminiscent of an insect's chirruping.

These rain frogs are so well adapted to their subterranean existence that they need never venture out in search of streams or pools of water. They eat insects and worms and other invertebrates which they encounter on their nocturnal travels, but they shelter underground and mate underground. The female lays her eggs in a special 10-12 cm chamber which she constructs—also underground.

The eggs are enclosed in jellylike capsules that serve as reservoirs of moisture. When the eggs hatch, the tadpoles continue to live and grow in this jelly within the capsule, and dig their way out after five weeks as fully formed young frogs.

Frogs and toads

ANGOLAN RIVER FROG

Angolese rivierpadda *(Rana angolensis)*

Size: *Length up to 8 cm.*
Colour: *Green or greenish brown, varying to dark brown, usually with darker markings, spots or blotches. Often a pale central stripe extends along the length of the head and the back. Underparts creamy white and throat sometimes mottled in brown or grey; back legs have dark bands across them.*
Most like: *Cape river frog, but usually not as large. Angolan river frog more streamlined, with a more pointed snout and slightly longer legs.*
Habitat: *River banks, streams and the marshy fringes of vleis and dams.*

In moist habitats of the Eastern Cape, KwaZulu-Natal, Lesotho, Free State, Swaziland, Mpumalanga, Gauteng, Northern Province, the North-West, Northern Cape, northern Mozambique and central and eastern Zimbabwe.

This is the most commonly encountered frog in southern Africa. The male's distinctive croak, an oft-repeated *krik-krik* sometimes ending with a long, drawn-out *kraak-eeeow*, is a constant presence along most South Africans streams and river banks—day and night, and through all seasons of the year.

If you are walking along or near the river bank the croaking will grow steadily louder as you approach the frog; then, when the frog becomes aware of your presence, it will suddenly stop. Walk even closer and the frog will leap from its hiding place and land with a 'plop' in the water; the powerful muscles of its hindlegs can propel it up to four metres in a single jump. Once in the water it may swim under the surface to a sheltering mass of vegetation, or it may simply hide in the sludge on the bottom. It can stay under water for more than half an hour.

The female lays thousands of eggs at a time, usually in summer, depositing them in a cluster in shallow water. Each egg is surrounded by a spherical capsule of transparent jelly, from which the tadpoles emerge about a week after being laid.

The tadpoles grow to a surprisingly large size before metamorphosing into adult frogs. Depending on the food available, a tadpole may take from nine months to two years to complete its change into a frog. If food is scarce, this process may take even longer.

CAPE RIVER FROG

Kaapse rivierpadda *(Rana fuscigula)*

Size: *Length up to 12,5 cm.*
Colour: *Varies from grey-green to dark olive-brown, sometimes with blotches of darker brown. Usually a yellow central stripe runs the length of head and back. Underparts usually whitish; throat (and sometimes belly) mottled with dark brown marks.*
Most like: *Angolan river frog, but the Cape river frog is larger, has a more rounded snout and slightly shorter legs. Its croak is harsher than the Angolan river frog's.*
Habitat: *River banks, streams and marshy areas.*

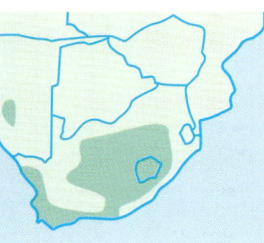

In moister areas of the Northern, Western and Eastern Cape, Lesotho, the Transkei region of the Eastern Cape, western KwaZulu-Natal, Free State, southern Gauteng and the North-West. A relict population occurs in central Namibia.

The Cape river frog has a prodigious and varied appetite, gobbling up insects, beetles, worms, small fish, tadpoles and even smaller frogs. A large specimen won't even think twice about taking on an unwary mouse. Some frog-keepers feed their Cape river frogs little pieces of meat, which they dangle temptingly in front of their noses from long sticks. These frogs have an undiscriminating palate and not even their own species—including their offspring—are spared the ravages of their enormous appetite. In fact, one of the greatest threats to a small Cape river frog's survival is a large Cape river frog.

The scientific name *fuscigula* means simply 'dark throat'; formerly it was thought that this served to distinguish the Cape river frog from the Angolan (or common) river frog but, in fact, the latter often has an equally mottled jaw and throat. The two species are very difficult to separate, and experts find that the call of the male is the best guide. The Cape river frog gives vent to a short, strangled grunt, or a series of tapping sounds; the Angolan river frog gives a brief croak, as well as a sharp rattling call ending with a mournful *kraak-eeeoww*.

The female may lay as many as 15 000 eggs at a time, each contained in a sphere of jelly. She deposits these usually in gently running water, and the tadpoles emerge after a week or so. Complete metamorphosis may take up to three years.

Frogs and toads

Gray's frog
Gray se padda (*Strongylopus grayii*)

Size: Length up to 6 cm.
Colour: Pale olive-green or grey upperparts with a symmetrical arrangement of chocolate-brown or almost black spots or blotches. Often a narrow central stripe of white or pale yellow runs the length of the back and head. Underparts white, becoming yellow on the throat in breeding males.
Most like: The striped grass frog, also known as the long-toed frog or the striped rana. However, the latter has no spots and is golden yellow with three pairs of dark brown stripes running the length of its back and sides; it also has extremely elongated toes.
Habitat: Open grassy verges near streams and pools; moist kloofs and forests.

Occurs in the Western and Eastern Cape, Lesotho, the eastern Free State, western and southern KwaZulu-Natal and Mpumalanga escarpment; also in Zimbabwe's eastern highlands.

Although Gray's frog may lay its eggs in shallow water, it sometimes lays them out of water, on moist moss or mud. In the latter case, the newly hatched tadpoles face a special challenge: how to get out of their capsules of jelly and into the water.

Without rain, this is impossible, so during long, dry spells they remain enclosed in their jelly capsules in a state of suspended animation for up to two months. When it does rain the jelly softens and the eggs are moistened. The tadpoles spring to life, break out of the jelly and wriggle down enthusiastically through the rainwater to a nearby stream or pool.

The female tries to make this journey as short as possible for her tadpoles by depositing the sticky mass of a few hundred eggs 20-30 cm from the water's edge.

Once in the water the tadpoles live off the water plants for three or four months, then metamorphose into small adult frogs.

In a warm climate the eggs will hatch within five days and the tadpoles are ready to swim in the water.

Gray's frog has a distinctive clicking call (hence its alternative name, clicking grass frog) which it repeats monotonously, with short intervals between each click, or sometimes in rapid succession.

Foam nest frog
Skuimnespadda (*Chiromantis xerampelina*)

Size: Length up to 8.5 cm.
Colour: Upperparts vary from pale mottled grey to tan and almost black, and blend in amazingly well with the bark of a tree. The frog can change colour, growing lighter or darker to suit its surroundings. Underparts pinkish pale grey, with darker freckling towards the throat.
Most like: Unlike any other amphibian found in southern Africa, and easily distinguished by its large size, the large 'suckers' or the tips of all its fingers and toes, its grey colouring and the fact that it lives on the branches of trees.
Habitat: Trees in open, subtropical woodland. Needs access to pans, dams or slow-moving rivers to breed.

Found in savanna woodlands in northern KwaZulu-Natal, Mozambique, Swaziland, Mpumalanga, Northern Province, North-West Province, eastern Botswana and Zimbabwe.

The tree-climbing foam nest frog ensures the survival of its offspring in a unique and ingenious way: the female is mated on a tree branch overhanging water; as she lays her eggs there, she and her mate beat the mass of jelly into a froth with their hindlegs; this done, the frogs sit back and let nature take over.

The jelly-froth sticks to the branch on which it has been deposited in a mass about the size of an ostrich egg, and during the following days the sun dries the outer surface into a glittering white, protective crust—while the inside remains moist. The eggs hatch after three or four days into small white tadpoles which sink to the bottom of the nest and, after another two days, break the bottom crust and fall into the water below. There they swim about and develop eventually into frogs in the usual tadpole manner.

What makes the whole cycle so remarkable is that the frogs unerringly select a branch or rock that hangs over water—even though it may be as much as 15 m above the surface of a seasonal pond.

The eggs may be laid at any time during the summer rainy season, and there are usually about 150 eggs in each foamy nest. Their call, a concert of squeaks and gurgles, may also be heard at this time.

Frogs and toads

BULLFROG

Brulpadda *(Pyxicephalus adspersus)*

Size: *Length up to 22 cm.*
Colour: *Upperparts vary from olive-green to brown, with dark brown spots or blotches. Underparts generally yellow, turning to brown on the throat in males and bright orange around the armpits. Young adults bright green with a pale green or yellowish stripe down centre of back.*
Most like: *Any one of the seven species of larger toad in southern Africa, but the bullfrog is distinguished by its large size, greenish coloration, orange armpits and by the series of skin-fold ridges along its back.*
Habitat: *Grass-covered and bushy countryside, ideally with shallow pans or puddles.*

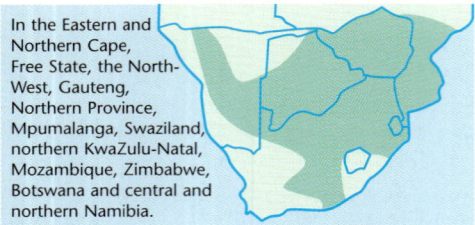

In the Eastern and Northern Cape, Free State, the North-West, Gauteng, Northern Province, Mpumalanga, Swaziland, northern KwaZulu-Natal, Mozambique, Zimbabwe, Botswana and central and northern Namibia.

When a bullfrog becomes angry or agitated it inflates itself with air like a rain frog. And don't think this formidable inflation is all just show—it can inflict a powerful bite. The large mouth and two bony 'teeth' in the lower jaw are powerful enough to leave their mark in a wooden broom handle.

As if this is not enough to intimidate the faint-hearted, an adult male bullfrog makes an extremely loud noise during the mating season—something like the bellow of an agitated bull.

By far the largest frog in southern Africa the bullfrog, like the rain frog, has a hard spadelike growth on each hindfoot which it uses to burrow backwards into the ground. It spends much of its time in the burrow, but emerges when hungry to feast on insects, mice, small birds, lizards and other frogs.

During the summer rainy season large numbers of both sexes collect in shallow pans to breed. The males make a lot of noise as they tussle for a good position, and at times like these they are particularly fierce and fearless.

Each female lays a batch of three to four thousand eggs in the shallow water, and after two days these hatch into tadpoles. Within three weeks of the egg-laying, huge numbers of tiny bullfrogs are ready to leave the water.

SENEGAL KASSINA

Senegalese kassina *(Kassina senegalensis)*

Size: *Length up to 4,5 cm.*
Colour: *Upperparts pale grey or silver to beige, with three dark brown to blackish stripes down the back. Central stripe is the most pronounced and is never broken; the others are sometimes broken into elongated patches. Underparts white or pale yellow, but throat dark grey-brown in males.*
Most like: *Rattling kassina, but the Senegal kassina usually grows much larger. The latter's hands and feet are whitish, while the rattling kassina's hands and feet are yellow.*
Habitat: *Open grass-covered countryside, with access to streams and vleis.*

In grassland savanna in the Eastern Cape, Lesotho, KwaZulu-Natal, Free State, Gauteng, the North-West, Northern Province, Mpumalanga, Swaziland, Mozambique, Zimbabwe, northern Botswana and Namibia.

As its alternative name 'running frog' implies, this species differs from most other frogs in that it runs on all four legs when hunting prey, while other frogs are content simply to hop along using both hindfeet at once.

You are unlikely to see it very often as it spends the days hidden in dense clusters of grass or reeds, emerging at night to track down small insects.

While making its distinctive, far-carrying call—a loud, melodious *quoip*, resembling the popping of a champagne cork—the frog's throat inflates to form an elongated balloon. Because the sides of the throat inflate more than the base, the balloon appears to have two halves, roped in at the middle.

Most studies made of the Senegal, or bubbling, kassina have focused on its unusual tadpole form. The adult female lays up to 400 eggs under water, which become attached a few at a time to the leaves and stalks of water plants. After five or six days these eggs hatch into tadpoles that look a lot like little fishes.

The tadpole's tail fins are deep and long, reaching along the body on both the upper and lower surfaces but taper off to end in a whiplike point. Often the tadpoles grow larger than the adult frogs, and they are brightly coloured, with the tail containing patches of red, gold, brown and dark blue.

Frogs and toads

WATER LILY FROG

Waterleliepadda *(Hyperolius pusillus)*

Size: *Length up to 2 cm.*
Colour: *Upperparts of body usually a translucent pale green, but sometimes yellow or light brown, occasionally small black spots on head and back. Underparts white or pale green, and often so translucent that internal organs can be seen. Eyes golden with horizontal black pupils.*
Most like: *Marbled reed frog. However, water lily frog is usually green and never as colourfully marked as the marbled reed frog. It never has red on the undersurfaces of its limbs or on its digits and webbing; the marbled reed frog is always red on these parts.*
Habitat: *Ponds and vleis, especially those in which water lilies or other floating plants grow.*

Occurs in the wetter parts of southern Africa from the coastal districts of the Eastern Cape and KwaZulu-Natal to eastern Swaziland, Mpumalanga and Mozambique.

This pretty little frog is seldom seen, simply because it is active only at night. During the day a lily-covered pond might seem to harbour no members of this species at all, although if you look closely at reeds and leaves you may see one sitting motionless, beautifully camouflaged and safe from predation, holding onto the smooth surfaces of a leaf with the suckerlike discs at the tip of each toe.

The same pond at night could be an amphibian circus, with hundreds of these energetic little frogs jumping about on the lily leaves, calling loudly with a harsh *chick-chick chereek*, catching small insects and jostling each other aggressively.

To establish whether water lily frogs live in your pond, inspect the broad lily leaves in summer to see if any of them are stuck together—the female lays her eggs in small clusters between overlapping leaves. The eggs are encased in tiny jelly capsules and these have the effect of gluing the leaves together.

The eggs are tiny and green and, after roughly five days, small green tadpoles hatch out and wriggle away into the water. About six weeks later the tadpoles will have metamorphosed into a new generation of little green frogs. The breeding season lasts from the start to finish of summer.

MARBLED REED FROG

Marmerrietpadda *(Hyperolius marmoratus)*

Size: *Length up to 3 cm.*
Colour: *Black, white, yellow and red stripes running the full length of the body in specimens from northern KwaZulu-Natal northwards, but some individuals are blotched or spotted, others uniform yellow-brown throughout. In southern KwaZulu-Natal and Eastern Cape the dominant pattern is brown with dark-edged silver spots. Underparts usually white or cream but bright pink under belly and red on inner surface of legs.*
Most like: *Water lily frog, but marbled reed frog distinguished by its more varied colouring and the distinctive red colour of the inner sufaces of thighs, digits and webbing.*
Habitat: *Near pools and vleis, especially those fringed with reed beds.*

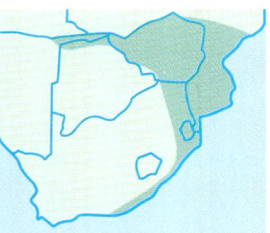

Common in the coastal districts of Eastern Cape, north through KwaZulu-Natal and Swaziland to Mpumalanga, Mozambique, Zimbabwe, the Caprivi Strip and extreme northern Botswana.

When several hundred marbled reed frogs call out in unison from the reeds or floating plants of a small pond, the chorus is quite deafening, and observers report having actually experienced pain from the noise.

The males are responsible for the shrill, whistlelike *weep-weep* calls which they give vent to on summer nights. When calling the skin under the frog's throat inflates into a balloon that is monstrously big for a creature so small.

These brightly coloured frogs exist in large numbers in suitable areas with permanent shallow water and readily take up residence in gardens with ponds, particularly in the summer-rainfall areas of the eastern half of the subcontinent. During the day you may see them clinging upright to the stalks of reeds—often some distance from the nearest stretch of water.

On summer nights they become extremely active, catching small insects and jumping aggressively.

Marbled reed frogs are particularly visible after rain when they come to windows and doors, either attracted by the light or by insects drawn to the light.

You may find this frog difficult to identify because its coloration varies considerably.

Freshwater fishes

Southern Africa's irregular network of rivers, lakes, swamps, vleis and dams supports about 250 species of freshwater fishes, the largest variety belonging to the tropical and subtropical water systems of the north and northeast. A much smaller variety of indigenous fishes populates the many waterways arising in the mountains of the south and southwestern Cape. Further east, in the Eastern Cape Province, there is only a single true indigenous freshwater species.

Interestingly, similarities between widely spaced fish—for example, those of the Gariep (Orange) River and of the Olifants River of the southwestern Cape—indicate that freshwater links probably once existed where today there are none. And fish fossils unearthed among Karoo sediments conjure up images of a prehistoric southern Africa unrecognizably different from today's.

Compared with the profusion of fishes indigenous to equatorial Africa, the number of species in southern Africa is modest. What is more, several of them, including tench, carp, rainbow trout, brown trout, bluegill sunfish, largemouth bass and smallmouth bass, are exotic imports from Europe and America. They were introduced for the benefit of anglers, sometimes with scant regard to the sensitive balance between food supply and the competition for it, and the effect their presence would have on our indigenous fish. (The smallmouth bass, for example, has proved a particularly voracious alien predator of indigenous species.)

Most freshwater fish are unable to tolerate salt water. However, a few species, including the Mozambique tilapia, freshwater eels and the exotic trout can adjust readily to gradual changes in salinity. In fact, eels are born at sea, and the young migrate up our rivers to live and grow for approximately 10-15 years, during which a female can reach a weight of 18 kilograms. When the time is right, the mature eels then migrate back to the sea to breed, and supposedly die, for these adults are never seen again. Conversely, trout in their native countries normally live in the sea and migrate up rivers to breed.

In the coastal lagoons of the southern Cape, KwaZulu-Natal and Mozambique, freshwater and marine fish are found together. Freshwater fish run a particular hazard in the estuaries of large rivers, into which formidable marine predators such as the Zambezi shark and the smalltooth sawfish, both of which tolerate salinity changes, venture on foraging expeditions.

Freshwater fish are often restricted by geographical and climatic factors. In many parts of southern Africa the flow of rivers is seasonal; a fish trapped in a stagnant pool is likely to fall prey to predators and diseases, even if it is able to survive on a rarefied oxygen supply until the next rains.

A waterfall may prove so effective a barrier that the fish fauna upstream of it differ markedly from the fauna below it; for example, the Victoria Falls on the Zambezi River and the Augrabies Falls on the Gariep (Orange) River. Waterfalls and rapids may also prove to be insurmountable obstacles to seasonal migration, and so may artificial barriers such as dam and weir walls. Small fish that are forced to mass in their thousands against these walls in their annual spawning migrations are not only prevented from reaching their breeding grounds, but also fall easy victims to birds, crocodiles and other predators. The South African National Parks Board has erected fish 'ladders'—shallow stepped aqueducts—alongside dam walls within its jurisdiction, to allow migrating fish to overcome the manmade impasse and breed successfully.

Like land animals, freshwater fish species have distinct habitats in which they grow, develop and forage. Some thrive in fast-flowing streams; others prefer placid open waters.

Habitat and diet are closely related: there are surface feeders, and species such as carp that scavenge on the bottom of the water. Some fishes—trout and tench, for example—flourish only in cold waters, whereas tigerfish and tilapia are among the warm-water species that may die in their hundreds if a particularly cold spell causes water temperature to plummet.

Man has destroyed natural habitats not only by building dams but by canalizing rivers, by polluting them with industrial effluents and by allowing alien vegetation and eroded soil to choke water-courses. Today, fortunately, there is a greater awareness of the need for conservation. Fish-farming and artificial propagation programmes by conservation authorities are means by which the stocks of certain species are being replenished. Although dam building creates new areas for freshwater fishes, this favours the exotic species such as bass and carp, to the detriment of indigenous fishes.

Unlike marine fishes, freshwater species are generally far too few in number to support a thriving, large-scale commercial industry. They do however, supplement the diet of some rural communities—and also offer sport and recreation to numerous anglers.

Identifying freshwater fishes

Body shape
This is often the starting point in identification. The fish 'profile' ranges from sleek and streamlined (trout, yellowfish) to deep-bodied (bream, bluegill). Carp are distinguished by a high-curving back and a flat belly; eels are long and ribbonlike; sharks have distinctive fins.

Note that in descriptions of fish species 'length' is measured from the tip of the snout to the end of the longest part of the tail fin.

Colour
Watch out for any colour clues in the species name itself—'rainbow' trout, 'bluegill' sunfish, 'redbreast' tilapia—although these are sometimes misleading: the whitefish is actually a bronzy green.

The colour of a species may vary to some extent with the watery environment, depending on whether this is clear or muddy or dark with vegetation. The males of some species, such as the Mozambique tilapia, rainbow trout and many minnow species, take on bright colours in the breeding season.

Freshwater fishes

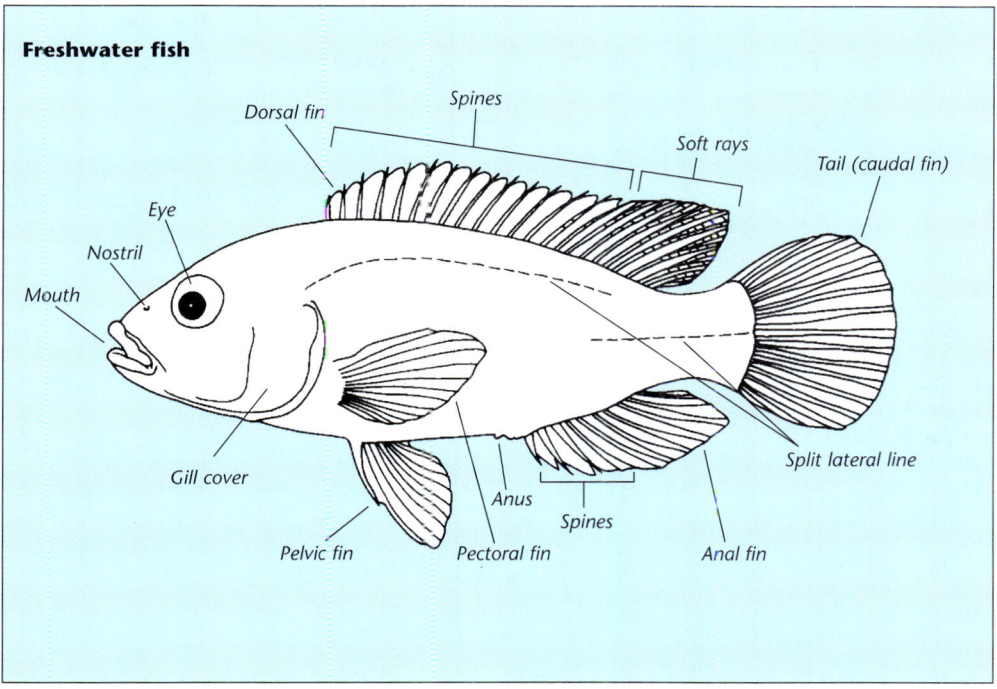

Fins
Check the number, shape, position and size of these against the illustrations. They comprise a back or dorsal fin (a few freshwater fishes, such as the vundu, have two); a tail or caudal fin; an anal fin, at the rear of the underbody; a pair of pectoral fins, on each flank behind the head; and a pair of pelvic fins between the pectorals and the anal fin. Not all freshwater species have a full complement of fins (eels have no pelvic fins). Fins are made up of spines (hard, sharp) or rays (softer, single or branched), or they may be merely fatty appendages known as adipose fins.

Head
Are the lips thick or thin? Does the lower jaw recede or protrude? Are the eyes large or small, situated high or low on the head? Again, verify such details by referring to the species illustrations. Prominent 'barbels'—slender appendages around the mouth that act as sensory organs—are a feature of certain species, including the barbel itself and the sharptooth catfish.

Teeth
Jaw-teeth are absent altogether from members of the Cyprinid family, which includes carp, yellowfish and minnows. Large, sharp teeth are a feature of predators, such as the tigerfish (a relative of the South American piranha), while plant-grazers such as the redbreast tilapia have small, close-set teeth.

Scales
The scales of some fish have an evenly curved border ('cycloid' scales) and are smooth to the touch. Others have comblike scales with tiny serrations on the free edge ('ctenoid' scales); these give the fish a rough feel. Scales also vary considerably in size; and catfish are without scales altogether. A feature common to all scaled freshwater fishes is the so-called 'lateral line' along either flank, each scale in the line being pitted so that a sensory organ is in direct contact with the water, enabling the fish to pick up vibrations in the water. Species such as the yellowfish have particularly prominent lateral lines; others, such as tilapia species, have two distinct lateral line series on each flank.

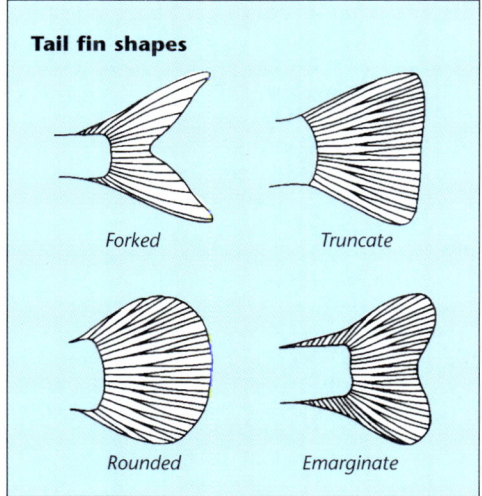

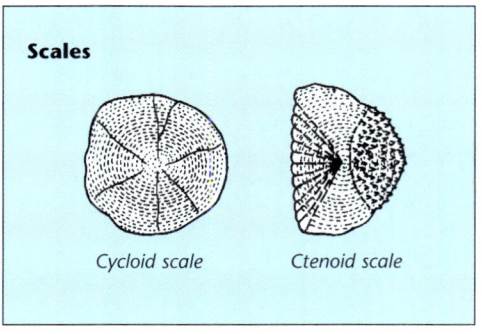

Freshwater fishes

Sharptooth catfish

Skerptand-baber *(Clarias gariepinus)*

Size: Weight averages 1,5 kg, but can reach 29 kg.
Colour: Uniform grey to olive-yellow flanks, with dark slate or greenish brown back, and white underparts; or pale olive, mottled irregularly with dark brownish green; or uniformly silvery olive. Colour variations are related to the clarity of the water.
Most like: Blunt-tooth catfish (Clarias ngamensis), but the latter has a short, fleshy fin at the base of the tail, absent in the sharptooth catfish.
Habitat: Rivers, lakes and swamps. Shallow waters during the breeding season.

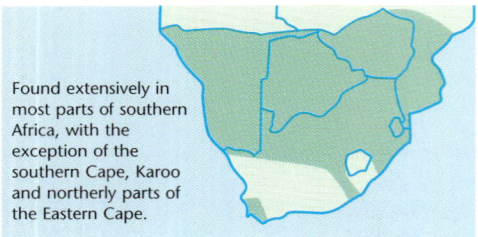

Found extensively in most parts of southern Africa, with the exception of the southern Cape, Karoo and northerly parts of the Eastern Cape.

This is one of the largest freshwater fishes in southern Africa, second only in size to the vundu of Zambezian waters. The name 'catfish' derives from the four pairs of long, trailing sensory organs (barbels) around its mouth which give the fish a bewhiskered, catlike appearance.

The scaleless body of the sharptooth catfish is elongated, with long, low dorsal and anal fins and a smoothly rounded tail fin.

The flat, bony head has small eyes set far forward. At the back of the head above the gills is a subsidiary breathing organ that allows the fish to take in oxygen directly from the air. By doing so the catfish can survive even in shallow, poorly oxygenated pools—and has been known to travel some distance overland, wriggling through dew-wet grass to reach stretches of water that are otherwise inaccessible to it. The fish's strong, small pectoral fin (immediately in front of the anal one) has a serrated spine that helps it to 'walk'.

This species is an omnivorous scavenger; it forages, mostly at night, on anything from fish, crabs, frogs, snails and insects to young birds, snakes and even plants and fruits. Large specimens are often cannibalistic, feeding on the young of their own species.

Breeding takes place in very shallow, weedy waters, usually after heavy summer rains, when the fish have migrated upstream, sometimes into the shallows of lakes. The tiny fertilized eggs attach to plants and debris and hatch out within a day and a half.

Largemouth yellowfish

Grootbek-geelvis *(Barbus kimberleyensis)*

Size: Weight averages 2,5 kg, but can reach 21 kg.
Colour: Silver olive to bronze yellow, the belly being lighter and ranging from silver with just a touch of yellow, to uniformly yellow. Anal fin orange. Young specimens of this species are silver all over.
Most like: Smallmouth yellowfish (Barbus aeneus), but Barbus kimberleyensis has a larger mouth, a flatter head and smaller, more deeply set eyes. The largemouth also reaches a larger size.
Habitat: Rapidly flowing waters in the mainstream of large rivers, shallow waters of dams, where the fish feed.

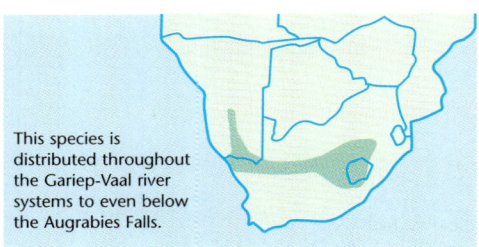

This species is distributed throughout the Gariep-Vaal river systems to even below the Augrabies Falls.

With its moderately thick-lipped mouth and high, deep-set eyes the largemouth yellowfish has an unusual profile, lacking the more conventional smooth-lined elegance of the smallmouth species. From either side of the deeply underslung mouth hangs a pair of short barbels. There are no jaw teeth inside the mouth—prey is swallowed whole and chewed in the throat.

The largemouth's body is streamlined and the fins are well developed. The tail fin is deeply forked; the dorsal fin has a strong, bony spine.

This species is the largest scale-bearing freshwater fish in the subregion, and can attain a weight of some 21 kilograms. The fish is a strong swimmer and has always been very popular among anglers.

Unfortunately the largemouth's numbers are declining, partly because dam building on the Vaal River has altered the flow of waters that once formed their natural habitat, and partly because industrial effluents have polluted the rivers.

Mature specimens of largemouth yellowfish caught in the wild are being used in captivity for artificial breeding. This is a long-term process, as specimens reach sexual maturity only after seven or eight years.

This species is only found in the Gariep-Vaal river system and is restricted to the mainstream environments and larger tributaries because of its preference for strongly flowing currents.

Freshwater fishes

CHUBBYHEAD MINNOW

Dikkop-ghieliemientjie *(Barbus anoplus)*

Size: Weight averages 3 g, but can reach 5 g.
Colour: Silvery, with olive-green back and white belly. There is a small dark spot on each flank at the base of the tail, and sometimes a broad, darkish band along each flank. In the breeding season (throughout summer) the males become a brilliant golden colour on their flanks and belly, and the fins are yellow.
Most like: Other minnow species, but the chubbyhead's blunt, rounded snout is distinctive.
Habitat: A wide range, from small streams and marshy pools to large dams, at altitudes of up to 2 000 m. Usually found near vegetation (where breeding takes place) but occasionally in open, deep water.

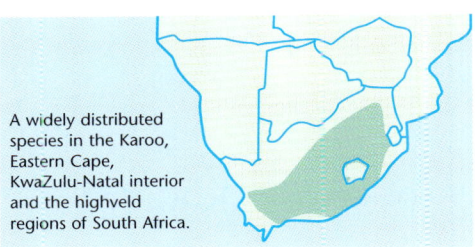

A widely distributed species in the Karoo, Eastern Cape, KwaZulu-Natal interior and the highveld regions of South Africa.

Despite its diminutive size, the chubbyhead minnow (or chubbyhead barb, as it is sometimes called) manages to ascend rapids and overcome other river obstacles in a series of determined jumps. It is an opportunist: in a wet year it will take advantage of spring rains to colonize new waters. This fish is the most widely dispersed of indigenous southern African species and occupies a wide range of habitats, from small streams to large impoundments. It has been used as a fodder fish for bass and trout in some areas.

Chubbyhead minnows are found in small shoals from the Karoo to the highveld and the Drakensberg foothills, though they are absent from the coastal rivers of the southern and Western Cape.

In profile the chubbyhead looks rather like a sardine (as do other minnows), with a spindle-shaped body and large, forked tail fin. The dorsal fin is smooth and slender, and has no hard spine: all fin rays are soft and flexible, hence the species name *anoplus*, meaning 'unarmed'. The eyes are large and round. On either side of the small mouth is usually only a single, short barbel.

This species feeds mainly on insect larvae (mostly midges) and small flying insects, though it occasionally eats vegetable matter too.

Spawning takes place during spring and summer. Young chubbyhead minnows reach sexual maturity at about four centimetres.

WHITEFISH

Witvis *(Barbus andrewi)*

Size: Weight averages 1,5 kg but can reach 5,2 kg.
Colour: Golden olive to yellowish above, cream to silver below. Young specimens are silvery, with irregular dark spots or broken vertical bars on the flanks.
Most like: Sawfin (Barbus serra), but the spine of the latter's dorsal fin is stouter and more markedly serrated than that of the whitefish. The whitefish occurs in the Berg and Breë rivers; the sawfin is confined to the Olifants river system.
Habitat: Clear waters. However, in the early summer breeding season, the more turbulent, well-aerated water below rapids and low waterfalls is favoured.

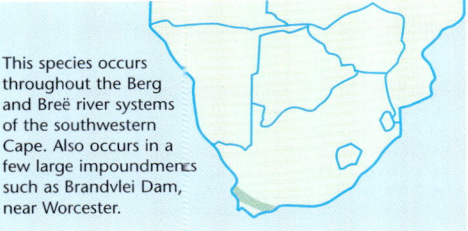

This species occurs throughout the Berg and Breë river systems of the southwestern Cape. Also occurs in a few large impoundments such as Brandvlei Dam, near Worcester.

To call this denizen of the southwestern Cape's Breë River 'white' is erroneous, for its colour is far from that. Yet silvery white glints do flash as it twists and turns in the water, and that is probably how the fish acquired its name.

A fish with large, radially streaked scales, the whitefish has a long, narrow snout and a pair of barbels hanging down each corner of the thin-lipped mouth. Like other members of the genus *Barbus*, it has no jaw teeth and swallows its prey, consisting mostly of insects, whole. The dorsal fin is wedge-shaped and the largest spine is serrated. The large tail fin is strongly forked.

Great shoals of whitefish assemble below low waterfalls in the spawning season. The fertilized eggs fall through the water, to lodge among the stones of the river bed; and here, well protected, they hatch within a week, the fry (young fish) remaining in this locality until they are strong enough to swim freely.

The largest recorded whitefish weighed 5,2 kg, though few specimens reach this size.

The destruction of the whitefish's natural habitat, and predation by introduced species such as bass, have led to a substantial decline in its numbers in southern Africa. In an attempt to restore these depleted numbers, the fish were, for a period, bred artificially at the Western Cape Nature Conservation Board's hatchery at Jonkershoek. However, the whitefish is still classified as vulnerable on the 2000 IUCN (International Union for Conservation of Nature and Natural Resources) Red List of Threatened Species.

Freshwater fishes

Mozambique Tilapia

Blou-kurper *(Oreochromis mossambicus)*

Size: Weight averages 1 kg, but can reach 3,4 kg.
Colour: Green along the back, silver flanks and grey-white belly. There are often three darkish blotches on each flank. At breeding time the colouring of the males becomes dark bluish black above and whiter on the throat and chest, and the edges of the dorsal, anal and tail fins are often scarlet.
Most like: Redbreast tilapia (Tilapia rendalli) and banded tilapia (Tilapia sparrmanii), *but the Mozambique tilapia lacks the former's red chest and the latter's vertical bars.*
Habitat: Lakes and slow-flowing rivers and estuaries.

Found naturally from the lower Zambezi southwards down to the Bushmans River in the Eastern Cape. It occurs almost throughout the Limpopo River system, and has been introduced to the southern and southwestern Cape and Namibia.

The Mozambique tilapia, known also as blue bream or blue kurper, is of particular interest to scientists due to the fact that it is a 'mouth-brooder' and can tolerate a wide range of salinity. At breeding time the male scoops out a shallow 'nest' in the bed of the lake or pool. The female lays her eggs in this depression and the male fertilizes them; then the female sucks them up into her mouth. For several days she holds them here, directing a flow of water over them with gentle movements of her mouth. Even after the young fish hatch they stay close to their mother, and a sudden movement will send a shoal of week-old fingerlings scurrying for safety into their mother's mouth.

This species is indigenous to the warmer waters of southeastern Africa, its natural home reaching south along the east coast as far as the Bushmans River in the Eastern Cape. It is now widely distributed, even to the southwestern Cape. Although classified as a freshwater fish, it can live in waters that are even saltier than the sea, presumably in adaptation to coastal estuaries where varying degrees of salinity occur. Mozambique tilapia has considerable commercial value. They multiply rapidly and their flesh is sought after for human consumption. Their own varied diet includes algae, plants, insect larvae and worms, which means that a given stretch of water can support more Mozambique tilapia than most other species.

Redbreast tilapia

Rooibors-kurper *(Tilapia rendalli)*

Size: Weight averages 1 kg, but can reach 2,2 kg.
Colour: Upper surface olive with light brown edges to the scales; dorsal fin has a red margin, and in adults the throat and belly are also red; lower half of tail red or yellow and green on top. Juveniles silver.
Most like: Banded tilapia, *but the latter has 8-9 vertical stripes, while the redbreast tilapia has 5-6 vertical stripes. Banded tilapia lacks the red throat and belly of the redbreast tilapia.*
Habitat: Perennial rivers, lakes and quiet pools.

This fish occurs throughout tropical Africa, as far south as the lower Phongolo River in the east and the Kunene River in the west. Has been introduced to many parts of KwaZulu-Natal by man.

Like its cousin, the Mozambique tilapia, this species is a fine fighting fish that always gives anglers a good run for their money.

It isn't a fussy eater and will be quite content to feed on algae, small crustaceans, worms and larvae, although it tends to be more of a vegetarian than the Mozambique tilapia, preferring still waters with a thick growth of weeds, where it will nibble on the soft tissues of aquatic plants.

Because of its healthy appetite for water plants in particular, it has been introduced into many dams to check the growth of weeds. Its weed-eating habits and rapid breeding rate make it a reasonably successful commercial species, particularly in the warmer, subtropical parts of southern Africa.

Redbreast tilapia differ from Mozambique tilapia in that they are not 'mouth-brooders'. The male clears out a saucerlike hollow, or nest, in a patch of vegetation near the margins of a body of water, and burrows a series of 'pockets' into the nest. The female lays her eggs and the male fertilizes them in the pockets, often on plant roots. Often the parents then move the eggs to one or more similar depressions nearby, after which both of them 'stand guard' over the eggs until the young fry hatch out and are able to swim away freely.

Freshwater fishes

BANDED TILAPIA
Vlei-tilapia *(Tilapia sparrmanii)*

Size: Weight averages 60 g, but can reach 150 g.
Colour: Ranges from silver to olive-green, with up to nine vertical stripes of a darker green or grey. During summer breeding season both sexes become more colourful. Vertical stripes become darker, two dark horizontal stripes develop across snout, and a circular stripe runs through eyes and over forehead. In males dorsal fin and tail become edged with red, and blue-green spots appear on dorsal and anal fins.
Most like: Redbreast tilapia, but banded tilapia easily distinguished by its vertical stripes and its light grey, not red, breast.
Habitat: Rivers and gently flowing streams, especially where there is a lot of aquatic plant growth.

Found extensively in the Zambezi, Okavango, Kunene and Gariep rivers and in the east coast river systems down to the Tugela. Also introduced widely to most systems in the Western and Eastern Cape.

The banded tilapia, or Sparrman's tilapia, is a distinctly smaller fish than either the Mozambique tilapia or the redbreast tilapia, and offers the fisherman little sport. It is, however, a particularly attractive fish, especially during the breeding months from November to March.

Although it does not quite qualify as a 'mouthbrooder', the banded tilapia displays a similar degree of dedicated parental care. As the water warms up with the advent of summer, and the fish begin to develop their breeding colours, the male selects a spawning site and hollows out a saucerlike 'nest' at the base of a rock or an underwater plant. Here he displays in front of the female, luring her to lay her eggs in the hollow he has made.

This accomplished, the male fertilizes the eggs, and both parents then 'stand guard' over them, fanning water over them with their fins. Often one of the parents will pick the eggs up in its mouth, but only to move them gently to another nearby hollow in the river bed.

The parents continue to guard their offspring after they hatch, maintaining a close proximity to their young ones as they swim about in a silvery shoal, feeding on microscopic organisms.

BLUEGILL SUNFISH
Blouwang-sonvis *(Lepomis macrochirus)*

Size: Weight averages 190 g, but can reach 1 kg.
Colour: An attractive green-bronze, darkening on the back. The younger fish in particular have five dark bars running vertically down the whole body. There is a distinct black projection on the upper corner of the gill-covers. The lower part of the gill-cover ranges from black to bright blue—hence the fish's name.
Most like: Tilapia, but the bluegill sunfish has distinctly rounded edges to its dorsal and anal fins, and it has four nostrils, unlike tilapia which have two.
Habitat: Rivers, lakes and dams.

This exotic fish occurs widely in the Western and Eastern Cape. It occurs fairly frequently in KwaZulu-Natal but has not penetrated much of the Free State or further north.

The petite and dainty looking bluegill derives its name from the iridescent blue 'collar' around its throat. In spite of its beguiling appearance, the bluegill is a predator that relishes insect larvae, small fish and fish eggs.

This fish is also a prolific breeder, entering shallow waters in great numbers to breed. During the summer spawning season female bluegills lay up to 20 000 eggs in their underwater nests, small hollows in the bed of a lake or dam which are 'guarded' by the males.

Members of the Centrarchidae family, bluegills are native to North America and were originally brought to South Africa as food for largemouth bass, which were imported at the same time. Because of their breeding prowess, the bluegill population not only outstripped that of the bass, but damaged the bass's breeding sites and ate their eggs and young. The result is that many of the dams originally stocked with both bass and bluegills now contain only a few bass and large numbers of bluegills.

From the angler's point of view the bluegill is a determined fighter, but unfortunately seldom grows large enough to make much of a trophy.

What's more, in waters where bluegill have become well established and exist in large numbers, competition for food results in stunted growth, presenting the angler with huge numbers of disappointingly small fish.

Freshwater fishes

Cape kurper

Kaapse kurper *(Sandelia capensis)*

Size: Average weight 40 g, but can reach 155 g.
Colour: Olive brown, with a patchwork of dark brown markings. Darker along the dorsal side and yellow on the belly. Three dark stripes run backwards from each eye. Fin rays are brown.
Most like: May be confused with tilapia, but can be distinguished by its long, slightly rounded anal fin with six to eight spines. The tilapia has a slightly forked anal fin with a total of 16 spines.
Habitat: Rivers and lakes.

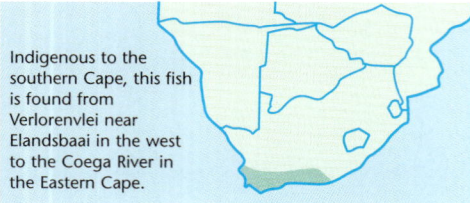

Indigenous to the southern Cape, this fish is found from Verlorenvlei near Elandsbaai in the west to the Coega River in the Eastern Cape.

The Cape kurper is related to the famous tree-climbing perch of India, and has similar special air-breathing organs that supplement its gills, enabling it to breathe out of water. Many fishermen, attempting to wash an apparently 'dead' kurper, have been amazed to see the 'dead' fish spring to life and swim away.

This species is a predator, living on insect larvae, crustaceans and smaller fish. It breeds in shallow, still water during spring and early summer, and its spawning has been described as a 'whirling embrace' during which the female releases her eggs and the male fertilizes them. The eggs sink to the bottom, sticking to any underwater object they touch, and the male remains in the vicinity to guard over them.

Indigenous to the southern and southeastern Cape, the Cape kurper was given the scientific name *Sandelia* after the Gaika chief Sandile (at one time spelt Sandeli). It is closely related to the multi-spined climbing perch (*Ctenopoma multispinis*), from the upper Congo and Zambezi systems and the Okavango Swamps, and also to the rocky (*Sandelia bainsii*), which is found in the Kowie, Buffalo and Nahoon rivers in the Eastern Cape. Imported largemouth and smallmouth bass have reduced the numbers of kurper in many Cape waters, but the kurper have resisted the intruders more successfully than many of the *Barbus* species. Being a relatively small fish it offers little sport to anglers, but is very tasty.

Carp

Karp *(Cyprinus carpio)*

Size: Weight averages 1,5 kg, but can reach 24 kg.
Colour: Back olive-brown; flanks yellow-green or bronze; underparts cream or pale yellow. Fins greenish brown, sometimes tinted pinkish red.
Most like: Tench, but the carp can be distinguished by the fact that it has a pair of barbels on each side of its mouth, while the tench has only one on each side.
Habitat: Still waters with a muddy bottom and an ample supply of aquatic vegetation.

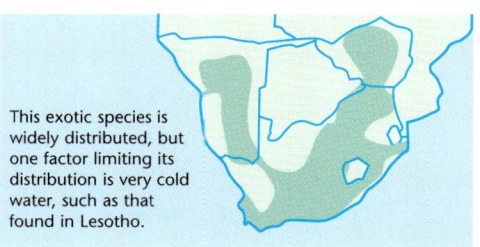

This exotic species is widely distributed, but one factor limiting its distribution is very cold water, such as that found in Lesotho.

Carp, which are related to domestic goldfish, have an amazing talent for reproduction: a large female is quite capable of laying more than half a million eggs at a time. The transparent eggs hatch in three to six days. This enables immigrant carp to fully populate a new stretch of water within a short period of time.

Despite their reproduction ability and their prolific numbers, however, carp are not easy to catch, and it takes patience and skill to hook one.

Carp are omnivorous, eating insect larvae and worms as well as plant matter. Because they don't have teeth in their mouth (they only have teeth set further back in the throat), carp secure much of their diet by sucking up mouthfuls of mud from the bottom of the pond, lake, dam or river bed. This often causes the water to be so muddy that other fish cannot live in the vicinity.

A general complaint against the carp's culinary appeal is that its flesh has a 'muddy' flavour. However, experts contend that this can be eliminated if the fish is prepared and cooked correctly. In many parts of central and eastern Europe carp ranks as one of the most highly prized items on the menu, and often features as the main dish for Christmas dinner.

There is a good deal of variety in the scales of a carp. Some varieties have evenly sized scales (fullscale carp), some have only a double row of greatly enlarged scales (mirror carp), and others have no scales at all (leather carp).

Carp originated in China, and were introduced to the Cape in the 18th and 19th centuries.

Freshwater fishes

LARGEMOUTH BASS

Grootbek-baars *(Micropterus salmoides)*

Size: Weight averages 1,8 kg, but can reach 4,2 kg.
Colour: Olive, becoming darker along the back, and paling almost to white on the belly. Dark blotches are often found on flanks.
Most like: Smallmouth bass, but the largemouth, as its name suggests, has a larger mouth. It also has larger scales.
Habitat: Rivers, lakes and dams.

Widespread in the Western and Eastern Cape as well as large parts of KwaZulu-Natal, Gauteng, Mpumalanga and Northern Province. Also found in parts of the Free State and Namibia.

Although fish feature high up on the menu of largemouth bass, frogs, snakes, rats, or even birds swimming on the surface of lakes and dams should also beware, for these bass are known to glide up invisibly from the depths to make quick meal of such unsuspecting prey. Even swallows swooping above the water have been taken by these fish. Because of their fondness for smaller fish, many conservationists regard these aliens as a pest because they are believed to have been responsible for the near extermination of several indigenous species. This fish's voracious appetite often leads to its own demise: death by suffocation takes place when the bass takes on a bluegill sunfish that is too large to swallow, and the victim's spines become stuck in its throat.

The silvery grey juveniles, which have a horizontal dark stripe down the flanks, change colour as they grow older, gradually turning an olive colour.

Bass belong to the sunfish family Centrarchidae which originated in North America, and whose members were subsequently distributed widely to provide sport for freshwater fishermen.

South Africa's largemouth bass were imported from Holland in 1928 and were first bred at the Jonkershoek hatchery outside Stellenbosch in the Western Cape. From here they have been introduced into many dams and rivers throughout the country, and in general they have adapted to local conditions extremely successfully.

Apart from being regarded by anglers as fine sporting fish, both the largemouth and the smallmouth bass are good to eat.

SMALLMOUTH BASS

Kleinbek-baars *(Micropterus dolomieu)*

Size: Weight averages 1,5 kg, but can reach 2,8 kg.
Colour: Olive. Colour darker along back, paling almost to white on belly. Back and flanks flecked with black or grey. The smallmouth bass and largemouth bass cannot be readily distinguished by colour, except in the case of small specimens when the dark bars on the tail of smallmouth bass are characteristic.
Most like: Largemouth bass but, as its name suggests, the smallmouth has a smaller mouth, which ends in front of the eye. The smallmouth also has smaller scales than the largemouth, and a less deeply notched dorsal fin.
Habitat: Chiefly rocky habitats in rivers.

Has become established in river systems throughout the southwestern, southern and Eastern Cape, as well as parts of KwaZulu-Natal, Gauteng, Mpumalanga and Northern Province.

Primarily a riverine species, the male smallmouth bass is a considerate and attentive parent: after constructing a 'nest' or shallow hollow in a gravel riverbed and fertilizing the eggs the female lays there, he stands guard over them, fanning them gently with his fins to prevent a build up of sediment. If any other fish ventures too close, the angry smallmouth is quick to charge, sending the trespasser swimming away.

Like the largemouth, the smallmouth is an active predator, feeding on crustaceans, smaller fish, snails, frogs and aquatic insect larvae. The smallmouth will also take a wide variety of artificial lures, poppers, spinners and artificial worms and frogs—making it a much sought-after sporting fish for anglers.

South Africa's stocks of smallmouth bass are descended from a consignment imported from Maryland in the United States of America in 1937. The initial stock was cared for at the Jonkershoek hatchery near Stellenbosch in the Western Cape, then released into various local waters and into the Umtata River in the Eastern Cape. The descendants of these first few have thrived, and there are now substantial populations of smallmouth bass throughout the Berg, Breë and Olifants river systems of the Cape.

Just as they have thrived, so must they take their full share of the blame, along with largemouth bass, for depleting the stocks of indigenous fish in these areas.

Freshwater fishes

RAINBOW TROUT
Reënboogforel (*Oncorhynchus mykiss*)

Size: Weight averages 1 kg, but can reach 5,5 kg in dams.

Colour: Silver, shading to olive-brown along the back, with small black spots over entire body, and often a pink or red stripe running along each flank, hence the 'rainbow' in the name.

Most like: Brown trout, but the rainbow trout is distinguished by the pink-red stripe along each flank, its smaller spots and the fact that none of them is red.

Habitat: Rivers and dams where the water remains cool throughout the year.

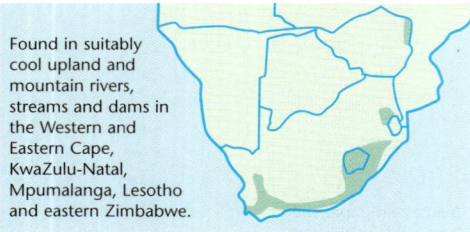

Found in suitably cool upland and mountain rivers, streams and dams in the Western and Eastern Cape, KwaZulu-Natal, Mpumalanga, Lesotho and eastern Zimbabwe.

To appreciate all the colours of the rainbow trout you must see it alive, or freshly caught, for death robs it of its pink-red lustre, and the colours fade rapidly. The colours are at their brightest during the breeding season (May and June).

Like all members of the salmon and trout family (Salmonidae), rainbow trout are prodigious travellers, capable of migrating great distances downstream to the sea, returning to their home streams for spawning.

Incredibly, they can adapt without difficulty from freshwater to a saline, marine environment.

This marine existence actually changes the colour of rainbow trout from olive-brown to blue-green, and gives them a more silvery appearance overall.

From an early age rainbow trout are voracious predators with a diet that changes as they mature. The fingerlings devour large numbers of insect larvae. As they grow older they feed on water fleas and any winged insects that venture too near the surface of the water. The larger trout tend to feed more on tadpoles, crabs and small fish, including smaller rainbow trout.

Indigenous to North America, rainbow trout were brought to South Africa in 1897 for the benefit of local fishermen, and they thrived in those parts of the country where the water temperature remains relatively cold throughout the year: the mountain streams of Mpumalanga, the Drakensberg in KwaZulu-Natal and Lesotho and the Eastern and southwestern Cape.

BROWN TROUT
Bruinforel (*Salmo trutta*)

Size: Weight averages 1,5 kg, but can reach 5,4 kg.

Colour: Silvery brown, darkening along the back. The back and sides are covered with dark brown spots; there are usually a few larger reddish spots, surrounded by bluish rings, along each flank. There are no scales on the head.

Most like: Rainbow trout, but the brown trout can be distinguished by the dark reddish spots on its flanks, absent in the rainbow. The brown trout lacks the rainbow's bright pink-red stripe along the flank.

Habitat: High-altitude streams and dams where the water remains cool throughout the year.

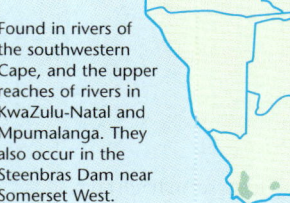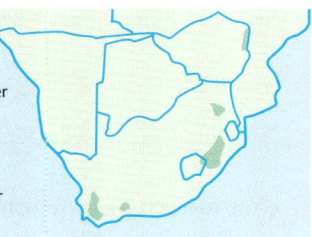

Found in rivers of the southwestern Cape, and the upper reaches of rivers in KwaZulu-Natal and Mpumalanga. They also occur in the Steenbras Dam near Somerset West.

To the irrepressible fly-fishermen who venture deep into the mountains in search of their silvery quarry, the brown trout ranks as the noblest trout of all. A cunning and cautious fish, with an elongated body, large mouth and pointed teeth, this species is said to be a far more difficult quarry to land than its cousin, the rainbow trout.

Not only is it difficult to catch, but its preference for the colder waters found high up in mountain streams and dams makes it considerably less accessible than the rainbow trout. The fact that it is a deep-water fish that feeds at night also contributes to its elusiveness.

Spawning generally occurs during autumn in upstream running water, the female making a hollow in the gravelly shallows with her tail. The male fertilizes her eggs, and the fry hatch after 40 days.

Although it's called 'brown', this trout often appears silver, because its colour changes markedly in different environments. In the crystal-clear streams of the Drakensberg, for example, where brown trout swim over glittering beds of bright pebbles, they generally develop a silvery colouring. The same fish living in cloudy river water will have a yellow-brown hue.

Like the rainbow, the brown trout is an alien in South African waters. It is less commercially viable than the rainbow trout because it is less prolific and grows more slowly. The original stock was imported from England.

Freshwater fishes

TIGERFISH

Tiervis *(Hydrocynus vittatus)*

Size: Weight averages 4 kg, but can reach 15,5 kg.
Colour: Flanks and undersides silver, back blue; fins often bright red or orange. A series of black stripes run along body from head to tail.
Most like: Unlikely to be confused with any other fish.
Habitat: Well-aerated rivers and lakes.

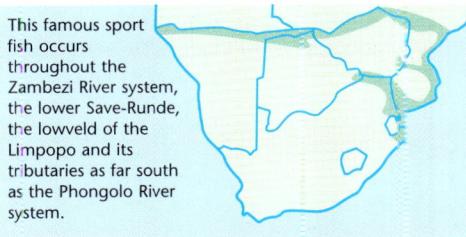

This famous sport fish occurs throughout the Zambezi River system, the lower Save-Runde, the lowveld of the Limpopo and its tributaries as far south as the Phongolo River system.

With large, sharp teeth set in hard, bony jaws, the tigerfish has a menacing appearance that fully justifies its scientific name: 'striped water-dog'. This fish is related to the notorious piranha of South America and, like the piranha, it is an energetic predator.

When tiny, tigerfish live on minute water creatures, but by the time they are ten centimetres long they are swift and efficient predators of other fish. They swallow their prey whole, and will readily devour fish as much as a third of their own size or more.

A fully-grown tigerfish has only three major enemies: crocodiles, otters and man—and all three need a certain amount of luck to catch one. In fact, more devastating to tigerfish populations is badly aerated and cold water. The construction of dams, which prevent the spawning migration of tigerfish, has also significantly affected the fish's numbers.

Among freshwater fish, tigerfish have no peers when it comes to fighting ability: once hooked, they twist and turn violently, leaping out of the water in an attempt to throw the hook. If you catch a tigerfish, watch out for the razor-sharp teeth: many an angler has lost a finger trying to remove a hook from one.

Tigerfish flesh is edible, but must be eaten soon after the fish is caught. However, the flesh contains large numbers of small, sharply pointed bones.

This species is widely distributed on the African continent, occurring from the Nile River in the north, through west and east Africa, down to the Phongolo River and its tributaries in the south.

MOGGEL

Moggel *(Labeo umbratus)*

Size: Weight averages 1,2 kg, but can reach 2,8 kg.
Colour: Pale grey with darker grey mottling, becoming almost white on the belly. Sometimes there is a pinkish hue in the mottling.
Most like: Clanwilliam sandfish (Labeo seeberi), but the latter has considerably smaller scales and a single barbel under its mouth, while the moggel has two barbels.
Habitat: The moggel is found in freshwater rivers, lakes and dams. It thrives in shallow waters and the pools that form in seasonal rivers.

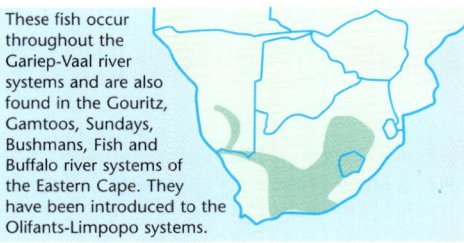

These fish occur throughout the Gariep-Vaal river systems and are also found in the Gouritz, Gamtoos, Sundays, Bushmans, Fish and Buffalo river systems of the Eastern Cape. They have been introduced to the Olifants-Limpopo systems.

The moggel, also known as the mud mullet, is not the best-looking inhabitant of the freshwater fish world: it has a large suckerlike mouth with thick, fleshy lips and two small barbels trailing underneath them. These fleshy protuberances aren't much to look at, but they are ideal for vacuuming algae off underwater surfaces.

This indigenous fish has several close relatives distributed throughout southern Africa, most of them very similar in appearance and habits.

It is omnivorous, and will take worms, small crustaceans and insect larvae, but its staple diet consists of minute forms of algae, moss and weeds that grow on underwater stones, dead trees and on the muddy river bed.

In many South African rivers and vleis moggel account for the bulk of the fish population in terms of total mass. Sometimes they migrate upstream when rivers are in flood and you can see them jumping low waterfalls and racing up through rapids. In parts of the country the flooding of rivers coincides with the summer breeding season.

The moggel spawn in the flooded upper reaches of rivers, laying their eggs on vegetation in shallow water. Both adults and young then travel downstream as the floodwater subsides. Often large numbers of fish are trapped in isolated pools and die off when the pools dry up, but the fish breed so prolifically that the overall moggel population is hardly affected.

Unfortunately, moggel are not ideal table fish because they have a lot of bones but, if carefully de-boned, they can be turned into tasty fish cakes.

Marine fishes

The waters around southern Africa support an extraordinarily rich variety of marine life, including some 2 200 different fish species. Probably as many as 14 per cent of these species are to be found nowhere else in the world; for fishes, like terrestrial animals, are restricted by their habitat and cannot swim at will from one ocean to the next if the conditions for their survival are lacking.

The most important barrier to the free movement of our fishes is sea temperature. Southern Africa's coastal waters can be divided into three temperature zones. Along the west coast, cold green sub-Antarctic waters are swept northwards by the Benguela Current; these mineral-rich polar and sub-polar seas are full of tiny organisms that provide nutritious food for the local fish population. In this zone the number of species is quite limited, but pelagic fish such as pilchards, mackerel and maasbankers gather in vast shoals, to the delight of local fishermen.

East coast waters, by contrast, are warmed by the southward-sweeping Mozambique Current. Though it cools in the southern latitudes (where it is known as the Agulhas Current), it is still noticeably warmer than the Benguela. That is why, off the Cape Peninsula, the waters of False Bay may differ in temperature from those of Table Bay by as much as eight degrees Celsius.

From Cape Town to the vicinity of East London lies a zone of temperate waters supporting many popular angling fish as well as such commercially exploited species as stockfish or hake, *Merluccius capensis* and *Merluccius paradoxus*. The great Agulhas Bank, abounding in fish, lies within this zone. Northeast of East London, coastal waters grow appreciably warmer, and the great variety of fish inhabiting this zone is apt to be more colourful and more typically 'tropical', like the seashells found on the adjoining beaches.

A few species, such as the various forms of kob (kabeljou), can adapt to temperature changes and survive the transition from cold to temperate zones.

Another important limitation on the free movement of marine fish is the salinity of the water.

A marine fish's body fluids are themselves salty, but less so than the surrounding sea; excess salt is removed from the blood by a special process and eliminated through the gills.

Despite their natural ability to get rid of surplus salt, most marine fish off the coast are unable to tolerate much more than a one per cent change in the sea's salinity. They will temporarily move away from the inland coastal waters of the east coast, for instance, when rivers coming down in flood dilute the sea's saltiness.

However, certain species, such as river bream, mullet and Zambezi sharks, are able to adjust to extremely low salt levels and happily frequent river estuaries, where they will do much of their foraging. In other species it is only the young that have this tolerance; they grow up in the shelter of river-bank nurseries, venturing into deeper sea as young adults.

'Pelagic' fish—so named from the Greek word for sea, *pelagos*—are those that live in the clear surface waters, or middle depths, of the open sea. They represent the majority of the ocean's fish fauna. They are usually darkly coloured on top, with lighter, often silvery, underparts—so that, seen from above or below, they are camouflaged against the background.

Fish that prefer coastal waters have a choice of habitats. Some frequent estuaries; others (galjoen, zebra, blacktail) enjoy the rough and tumble of surf breaking on rocky shores or rushing into rock gullies. Some of the most beautiful and delicate species, such as powder-blue surgeon, butterflyfish and angelfish, lead tranquil lives in the warm waters that swathe coral reefs. And there are species (including stingrays and guitarfishes) that prefer a sandy habitat, where

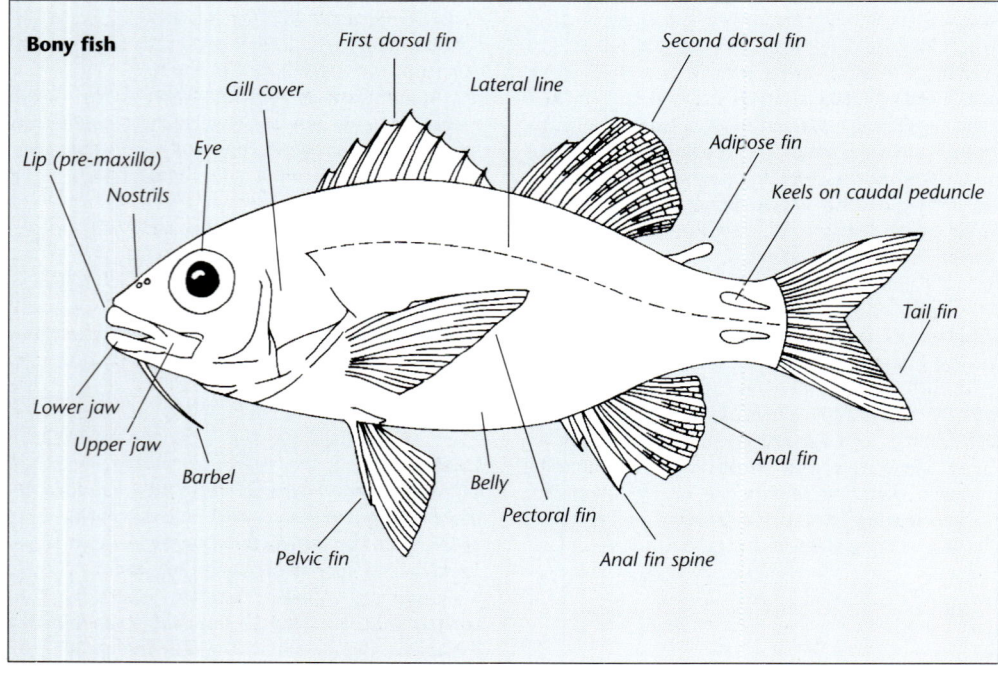

Marine fishes

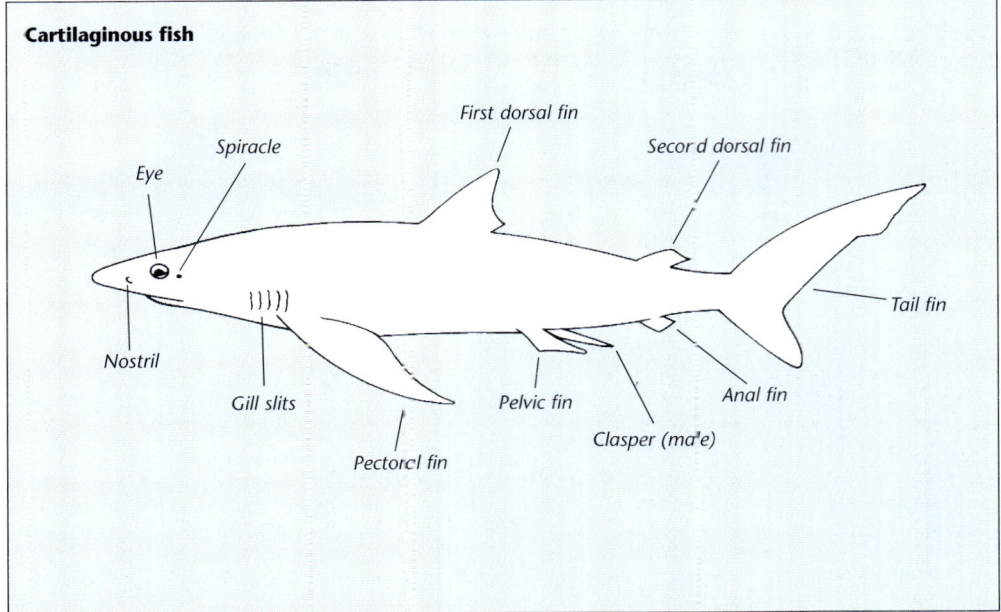

Cartilaginous fish

they can lurk in ambush, sometimes half buried on the sea bed, for their prey. A prized game fish, the white steenbras is another species that favours the waters adjoining sandy beaches.

A primary distinction among marine fish species is between 'bony fish'—comprising the vast majority—and 'cartilaginous fish', consisting of sharks, skates, rays, guitarfish and sawfish. This second group lacks a boned skeleton (although bone is present in the teeth and in the spines of the dorsal fins).

Identifying marine fishes

Body shape
The shape of a particular fish alone may be sufficient to enable you to identify it, or the group to which it belongs, if you study the illustrations in this section of the book.

Marine fishes may be long and ribbonlike (eels, for example), streamlined and torpedo-shaped (pilchards, mackerel) or thick-set and sturdy (galjoen, bream, kob); they may be compressed vertically (moonfish) or compressed horizontally (sole). When alarmed, the thorny-skinned blaasop puffs itself up until it is almost globular. (The blaasop, incidentally, is one of the very few local species whose flesh is toxic, and under no circumstances should it be eaten.) Among cartilaginous species, guitarfish (shaped like the musical instrument) and rays (a flat disc with a whiplike tail) are particularly distinctive.

Colour
The most brightly coloured species are apt to live among coral reefs, where their distinctive patterning blends well with the striking marine vegetation. Bear in mind that descriptions of colour in the entries for each species refer to the live fish. After death a specimen may lose its lustre, and its colours may either fade or darken. Where this change is particularly noticeable, the entry draws attention to it.

Fins
Check the number of fins, and their position and shape, against the sample illustrations of 'likely' species. A full complement consists of a tail fin (or 'caudal' fin); one, two or three dorsal fins (on the ridge of the back), an anal fin (on the underside, towards the rear); two pectoral fins (one on each flank, behind the gill); and two pelvic fins (on the underside, usually towards the front). Rigid, unsegmented fin supports are known as spines; flexible, segmented ones are known as rays. The number of spines and rays in the dorsal and anal fins may be a clue to species identification. The fins of sharks and other cartilaginous fish are quite different from those of bony fish, being strengthened by fibrous tissue and not by spines or rays.

Mouth and teeth
Watch out for mouth shapes—whether thick- or thin-lipped, and whether at the tip of the snout (typical of vegetarian 'nibblers') or wide-mouthed (the natural asset of a predator). In some species the under lip protrudes, in others it recedes under the top lip. Trailing from the sides of the mouth there may be whiskerlike barbels, sensory organs to locate food; the catfish has no less than four pairs of barbels.

Teeth give an indication of eating habits. Musselcrackers are equipped with strong, rounded molars for crushing, as well as grinding teeth in the pharynx (upper gullet). Predacious species such as snoek seize their victims with sharp canines. Herrings and pilchards, which filter plankton from the sea, lack teeth altogether.

Scales
The scales of most marine fish species overlap, like roof tiles; but occasionally (for example, in triggerfish) they are spaced out, paving-stone fashion, without overlapping. Sharks have no scales; their skin owes its sandpapery texture to innumerable tiny projections that resemble teeth and are covered in an enamel-like substance.

Marine fishes

Whale shark
Walvishaai *(Rhincodon typus)*

Size: *Length averages 10-12 m, but may reach 18 m.*
Colour: *Upper surface dark, gunmetal grey or brown, extensively covered with white chequerboard markings.*
Most like: *The much rarer basking shark, which attains a similar size, but the basking shark has an underslung mouth, a pointed snout, much larger gill slits and a notched tail; it also lacks the ridges along the length of the back and the distinctive chequerboard pattern.*
Habitat: *Whale sharks are widespread in tropical and subtropical waters, but off southern Africa are particularly common off beaches of KwaZulu-Natal, where aerial surveys have revealed between 49 and 95 whale sharks at a time in shallow water.*

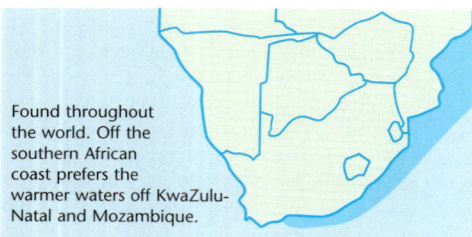

Found throughout the world. Off the southern African coast prefers the warmer waters off KwaZulu-Natal and Mozambique.

This leviathan of the sea is the largest fish on earth—yet despite its formidable appearance, it is a true gentle giant, completely harmless and very easily approached under water. Intrepid scuba divers have been known to take impromptu rides on the back of whale sharks swimming close to the surface, although this practice is not encouraged by conservation authorities. The sharks are commonly accompanied by remoras and also large game fish, such as prodigal son and queenfish.

The enormous, robust body is characterized by three distinct ridges along each flank, large first dorsal and tail fins, and a very wide mouth that is set almost terminally on a broad, blunt snout, not on the underside as in other shark species.

Like the larger whales, this is a filter-feeding species, capable of sucking in water through the wide mouth, straining it through special sievelike gill structures, and passing it out through the large gill slits. This filtering process traps enormous quantities of plankton, squid and small bait fish, which are then swallowed.

The whale shark bears live young—a pregnant female caught off Taiwan in 1996 had 300 embryos of between 42 and 63 cm in its uteri. The young have occasionally been netted, together with tuna shoals.

Little else is known about migrations and other behaviour of this giant shark. The species is thought to be highly migratory, despite scant evidence, and satellite-tracking devices have been attached to a number of sharks in an attempt to gather information.

Great white shark
Witdoodshaai *(Carcharodon carcharias)*

Size: *Length averages 3 m, but can reach about 7 m.*
Colour: *Upper body dark grey or metallic blue-grey with the underside distinctly white. The lower margins of the pectoral fins are dusky and tips are black.*
Most like: *The mako shark, which can be distinguished by its non-serrated, spear-shaped (lanceolate) teeth.*
Habitat: *Throughout the world's temperate and tropical seas, often in proximity to seal colonies. Prefers cooler regions. In South Africa many are seen near the islands off the southern Cape coast between False Bay and Algoa Bay.*

In southern Africa this magnificent predator inhabits coastal waters from Namibia to Mozambique. Recorded mainly in the shallower waters of the continental shelf, though it does occur in oceanic waters.

People don't call this shark 'the white death' for nothing. It is probably the most feared animal on earth, a giant and fierce predator that commonly attacks and consumes marine mammals such as seals and dolphins and, very occasionally, man himself. The shark has also been known to ram and bite small boats, batter diving cages and send shaken spearfishermen swimming for the shore after 'charging' them or their speared fish underwater. Nevertheless, most shark attacks are due to chance rather than active 'man-eating' intent—and most of the great white's natural diet consists of other sharks, large rays, bony fish, seals and small dolphins.

This feared denizen of the deep is well adapted to its lifestyle, having serrated, razor-sharp triangular teeth set in a huge mouth. These teeth can slice through large prey with ease. Having selected its meal the great white, propelled by its large tail with lateral keels, moves at an astonishing speed, thrusting its snout upwards and its jaws out to seize the unfortunate victim.

Great whites are among the shark species that lift their heads clear of the water to inspect the surface. They also have an acute sense of smell, and will swim into the current to locate the source of a smell.

Great white sharks are live-bearers, with the embryos being nourished with egg yolk. In southern African waters, great white sharks tagged off the southwestern Cape have been recovered off KwaZulu-Natal, a distance of over 1 400 kilometres.

Marine fishes

TIGER SHARK

Tierhaai *(Galeocerdo cuvier)*

Size: Length averages 2,5 m, but can reach 5,5 m.
Colour: Brownish grey above, with vertical dark grey bars on sides of the body and across dorsal fin. Stripes particularly conspicuous in younger specimens. Underside is pale.
Most like: Distinctive body markings and cockscomb-shaped teeth make the tiger shark unlike any other shark.
Habitat: Warmer coastal waters, in shallow lagoons and at the mouths of rivers in flood. Often near offshore islands and coral reefs. Equally at home in clear and turbid seas. May be seen following ships at sea.

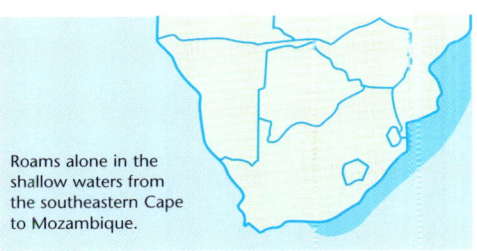

Roams alone in the shallow waters from the southeastern Cape to Mozambique.

With its strongly serrated teeth set in very wide jaws, this handsome but aggressive and dangerous shark has a fearsome reputation, justifiably earned through being responsible for more confirmed attacks in tropical waters than any other shark species.

An amazing variety of food features on the tiger shark's menu, which includes fish, other sharks, rays, seals, turtles, sea snakes, birds, lobsters and crabs.

Many unusual items have also been recorded in the shark's stomach, such as tin cans, plastic bags, shells, wood, polystyrene, metal and even a barrel.

This common predator-scavenger is usually solitary, although it does sometimes form feeding aggregations. It is often found near the mouths of rivers in flood where it easily eats the remains of cattle, sheep and occasionally human beings. It seems to feed mostly at night.

While most tiger sharks have been recorded close to land, they also cruise along isolated coral atolls, confirming their ability to migrate across oceans.

The tiger's large, patterned body has a rather broad head with a blunt snout, and the narrow tail section has a 'keel' or longitudinal ridge on either side.

Like the ragged-tooth shark, the tiger shark can cruise quite slowly because of its ability to pump water over its gills for respiration.

Females produce anything between 10 and 82 pups in a litter, each pup measuring between 51 and 76 cm in length. The largest recorded adult tiger shark is a 5,5 m specimen caught off Cuba.

SPOTTED RAGGED-TOOTH SHARK

Spikkel-skeurtandhaai *(Carcharias taurus)*

Size: Length averages 1,8 m, but can reach 3,2 m.
Colour: Light brown, sometimes khaki-coloured, with a distinct paler underside. Large, irregularly spaced darker brown spots usually cover the body, though they may fade to some extent with age.
Most like: Not easily confused with any other shark, with the possible exception of the rare bumpytail ragged-tooth shark (or smalltooth sand tiger), in which the first dorsal fin is larger than the second dorsal and anal fins.
Habitat: Shallow coastal waters throughout southern Africa. Widespread throughout subtropical to cool temperate seas of the Atlantic, Indian and western Pacific oceans.

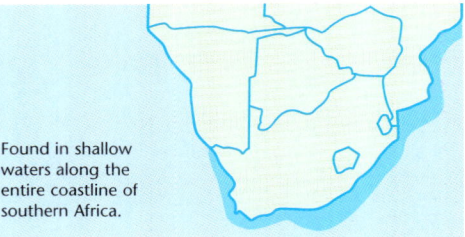

Found in shallow waters along the entire coastline of southern Africa.

This big, rather plump-bodied shark presents a formidable appearance with its large, thickset fins (the first and second dorsal fins and anal fin being all of similar size), its sharp snout, a conspicuous array of slender, pointed teeth set unevenly in the mouth, and small eyes located far forward. But the ragged-tooth shark, known also as the grey nurse shark (in Australia) or sand tiger shark (in America), is not normally dangerous unless provoked, and you may even approach it underwater, if careful.

In the second half of the year male and female spotted ragged-tooth sharks migrate northwards from Cape waters to KwaZulu-Natal, where they mate. They congregate over shallow reefs at known localities such as the Aliwal Shoal where they form a major attraction for sport divers. In summer many pregnant females move further north to congregate at places such as the reefs near Leven Point in the St Lucia Marine Reserve. They then migrate southwards and, six to nine months later, in waters off the Eastern Cape, give birth to two pups each.

Reproduction is remarkable because the many embryos occupying each uterus are free-swimming and cannibalistic: they feed on one another until only the strongest pup survives in each uterus. The surviving pups then feed on a supply of unfertilized eggs produced by the mother. After birth these pups often enter estuary mouths such as that of the Keiskamma River at Hamburg.

This relatively common shark feeds on a variety of small fish and other sharks, often lying in ambush for them; its teeth are equipped for grasping, not cutting, and so the prey is swallowed whole.

Marine fishes

ZAMBEZI SHARK

Zambesihaai/bulhaai *(Carcharhinus leucas)*

Size: Length averages 2 m, but can reach 3,5 m.
Colour: Predominantly dark grey above with a creamy white underside. The fins are not conspicuously marked, though in young Zambezi sharks the tips may be darker.
Most like: Other sharks of the genus Carcharhinus, especially the Java shark, C. amboinensis. The second dorsal fin of the Zambezi is higher than the Java shark's, in proportion to the first dorsal fin.
Habitat: Shallow coastal waters, including turbid regions near river mouths. Common in larger estuaries and rivers, sometimes great distances from the sea. Widespread throughout the world's tropical and subtropical seas.

Found in rivers, coastal waters and estuaries, where it bears its young in summer, from the southern Cape northwards to Mozambique.

Anyone who knows about sharks and shark attacks will regard the Zambezi (known also as the bull shark) with great respect: its sharply serrated, broad-based upper teeth and more pointed, thinner lower teeth, set in massive jaws, have often found their mark in human flesh, and it is commonly regarded as one of the sharks most dangerous to bathers.

It has a short, bluntly rounded snout and small eyes which are set far forward in the head.

Large and stocky, the Zambezi shark is a truly remarkable fish in that it can tolerate completely fresh water for extended periods; it has been found as far upstream in the Zambezi River as the entrance to the Kariba Gorge, some 1 000 km from the sea. (Now, of course, that journey is interrupted by the Cahora Basa dam wall.) During these inland migrations it feeds on freshwater fishes and land mammals, including duiker, that venture into shallow water to drink or cool themselves.

The shark's normal marine diet is highly varied and includes other sharks, fishes, dolphins and turtles. Its ability to attack large prey is facilitated by the sharp and efficient teeth that cut through flesh like butter.

The sharks become sexually mature when they reach the length of about 2,25 metres. Litters of up to 12 pups are born during summer following a gestation period of 10-11 months. These young often spend the early part of their lives within estuaries, especially at St Lucia.

DUSKY SHARK

Donkerhaai *(Carcharhinus obscurus)*

Size: Length averages 1,2 m, but can reach 3,77 m.
Colour: Upper body surface plain grey, underside pale cream. Fin tips usually dusky.
Most like: Several species of the genus Carcharhinus, common in southern African waters. Zambezi and Java sharks are stockier and lack the ridge between the dorsal fins. Copper sharks (or bronze whalers) usually have no ridge and bear bent, narrower teeth. Blacktip and spinner sharks also have no ridge and have sharper snouts and more distinctive black tips to some of the fins. The sandbar shark has a ridge, but a much taller first dorsal fin further forward on the body.
Habitat: Adults live some distance from shore, near the edge of the continental shelf, where packs may be seen following ships; newborn young common along beaches and rocky points of KwaZulu-Natal and Eastern Cape.

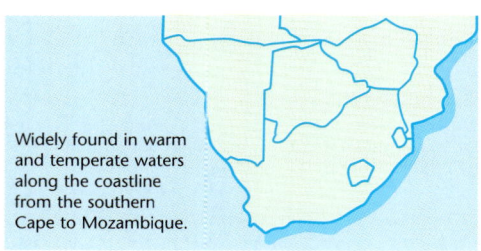

Widely found in warm and temperate waters along the coastline from the southern Cape to Mozambique.

This is the species most often caught in the protective shark nets off the KwaZulu-Natal coast. Known also as the ridgeback grey shark, this formidably large predator has a relatively slender body, rounded snout, well-developed fins, and a distinctive low ridge running along the back between the two dorsal fins.

During autumn, following a gestation period that may last up to two years, pregnant females move close inshore to give birth to about ten pups each. These infants then forage in packs close to shore, well away from their parents, apparently to avoid the possibility of cannibalism. Some young duskies undertake lengthy migrations from KwaZulu-Natal waters to the southern Cape, with tagged animals being captured up to 1 200 km from where they were tagged. Some have been known to travel 1 000 km in 40 days.

Catches of juvenile duskies taken in KwaZulu-Natal shore-angling competitions increased steadily from the 1960s to the early 1990s, then fell markedly. Originally attributed to the shark nets, which prevented large sharks, normally predators of smaller sharks, entering shallower waters, it's now thought that angling itself may have played a role in changes in the ecosystem.

Duskies prey on virtually all types of bony fish (including sharks, even young duskies), rays, crustaceans and cuttlefish. Adults include dolphins in their diet. Their sharply serrated, triangular teeth allow them to cut up large prey, and the adults are potentially dangerous to victims of shipwrecks.

Marine fishes

GREAT HAMMERHEAD SHARK

Groot hamerkop (*Sphyrna mokarran*)

Size: Length averages 3 m, but can reach 6 m.
Colour: Upper body surfaces grey brown; underside paler. No obvious fin markings.
Most like: The two other hammerhead species in southern African waters, the scalloped hammerhead and the smooth hammerhead, but the latter two are smaller and have curved 'hammers', while that of the great hammerhead is straight.
Habitat: Surface waters, ranging from shallow inshore waters, no more than a metre or two deep, to oceans, but mostly in coastal waters. Off southern Africa, occurs from KwaZulu-Natal northwards.

Found in tropical seas throughout the world; in southern Africa it inhabits coastal waters off northern KwaZulu-Natal and Mozambique.

The extraordinary hammer-shaped head may make you think nature's plan for this bizarre creature had gone awry but, in reality, this strange appendage, which has a large eye at each end of the hammer, is thought to have a number of functions. The widely spaced eyes and nostrils seem to enhance the shark's sensory capabilities, and it is thought the head probably functions as a hydrofoil, helping to provide lift as the shark swims. The great hammerhead has also been observed using its head to pin down prey.

This species' wide-angle vision makes it easier to prey on a wide variety of squid, crustaceans, bony fish, rays and small sharks. However, the mouth of the great hammerhead is too small to consume very large prey, and it probably does not constitute a serious threat to bathers. Nevertheless, a number of shark attacks globally have been attributed to these hammerhead sharks. Indeed, an approaching great hammerhead, with its high dorsal fin breaking the surface, looks formidable and should be treated with respect.

The female produces between 13 and 42 young in a litter.

Hammerheads may be migratory, mostly moving to higher latitudes during summer. This shark is sometimes caught by ski-boat fishermen off the northern KwaZulu-Natal coast.

BROADNOSE SEVENGILL SHARK

Platneus-sewekiefhaai (*Notorynchus cepedianus*)

Size: Length averages 1,2 m, but can reach 2,9 m.
Colour: Upper body ranges from pale grey to russet, closely speckled with dark spots, underside unmarked and much paler. Fins speckled like the upper body.
Most like: The three other species of cowshark, but the broadnose sevengill is distinguished by the shape of its nose from the sharpnose sevengill, and by the number of its gill slits from the sixgill and the bigeye sixgill. None of the other species is speckled.
Habitat: Common throughout cooler waters of the world, including those off the Cape and Namibian coasts, where it lives close to the bottom, from great depths to shallow bays.

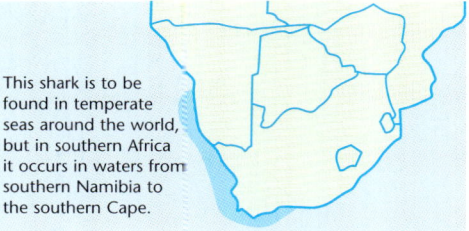

This shark is to be found in temperate seas around the world, but in southern Africa it occurs in waters from southern Namibia to the southern Cape.

Despite its apparent cowlike lethargy, this shark is a potent and powerful predator, not only of other sharks, rays and fish but also of carrion and seals. In California it has been known to attack bathers, and in captivity will also attack humans.

Like other cowsharks, this large, rather podgy species has a single dorsal fin, a long tail fin without a lower lobe, and rows of curious, sawlike teeth in the lower jaw, capable of biting larger fish in half.

The broadnose sevengill belongs to the family Hexanchidae, one of the most primitive of all shark families. It is very sluggish, spending most of its time near the sea bed in search of prey.

The shark is ovoviviparous: that is, the young develop from egg-cases within the female body, and are expelled by her as soon as they hatch. The mother bears up to 82 small pups each season. Most are born in shallow water, where they remain until they reach adolescence before migrating to deeper water—ranging from 100-600 metres.

The broadnose sevengill shark is very popular with fishermen throughout the world, often being hooked from the shore when it ventures into shallow waters in search of food. It puts up a good fight when caught. There is a commercial demand for the broadnose sevengill as a source of food. Its oil is rich in vitamin A, and its skin is sought after for use as fine-quality leather.

This shark is particularly common in the waters off the Cape coast.

Marine fishes

STRIPED CATSHARK

Streep-kathaai *(Poroderma africanum)*

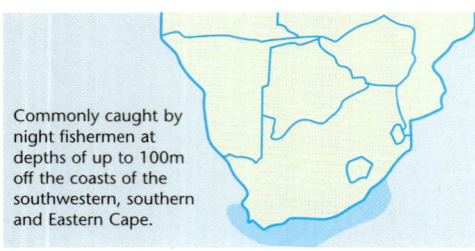

Size: Length averages 70 cm, but can reach 95 cm.
Colour: Creamy brown, slightly paler below, with dark brown, longitudinal stripes that tend to break into blotches towards the tail and undersides.
Most like: Several other catshark species, such as the leopard catshark (Poroderma pantherinum), which have much the same silhouette and arrangement of fins—but the dark brown, longitudinal stripes on the back of this species are quite distinctive.
Habitat: The rocky bottom of shallow waters. Seldom found deeper than 100 m.

Commonly caught by night fishermen at depths of up to 100m off the coasts of the southwestern, southern and Eastern Cape.

The longitudinal stripes of this sleepy looking predator give it an unmistakeable 'pyjama-ed' appearance, hence its alternative name, pyjama shark. One of the largest members of the catshark family, it has a distinct air of malevolence about it. Several rows of thin, three-pointed teeth are set in the small mouth that is located directly below the blunt snout. The nasal barbels—fleshy projections that act as organs of touch and taste—reach halfway down to the mouth.

The shark's pectoral fins are broad, but other fins are quite small; and, significantly, the two rather soft dorsal fins are set far back on the body. This indicates that it leads a sluggish, bottom-dwelling life, without the need for rapid changes of direction; by contrast, fast-swimming sharks use their large, rigid, forward-set dorsal fins as rudders in predatory manoeuvres.

The striped catshark is primarily a nocturnal creature and spends much of the daylight hours sheltering in gullies or caves. During the night, however, it stirs to life in catlike fashion and feeds on a variety of crabs, lobsters, squid and certain bony fish.

Female striped catsharks become mature at about 70cm and usually produce only two egg-cases each season. These 10cm leathery, brownish 'mermaid's purses' (as the egg-cases are called) have sticky tendrils which attach themselves to plants, corals and other submerged vegetation. The young, each measuring some 15cm in length, hatch about six months later.

HARDNOSED SMOOTH-HOUND

Hardeneus-hondhaai *(Mustelus mosis)*

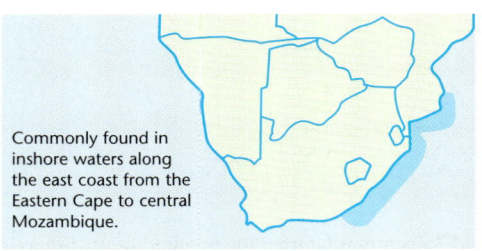

Size: Length averages 70 cm, but can reach 1,5 m.
Colour: Drab grey-brown above, occasionally with black spots, and with paler underside. Trailing edges of first dorsal fin and tail fin pale; tips of second dorsal and tail fin dark. Eyes often green.
Most like: The two other smooth-hound species found in local waters: Mustelus mustelus, which is uniformly greyish, and Mustelus palumbes, which is spotted white. The smooth-hound also resembles various houndshark and dogfish shark species, but is distinguished by its smooth, bluntly rounded teeth and absence of spines and dorsal fins.
Habitat: Eastern coastal waters, ranging from the surf zone to depths of at least 150 m. Prefers sandy bottoms and may also be encountered in quite turbid water.

Commonly found in inshore waters along the east coast from the Eastern Cape to central Mozambique.

Smooth-hounds (like houndsharks and dogfish) are said to have doglike 'muzzles', though it may take imagination to see this. There's little of the dog about the smooth-hound's pavement of small, flat molar teeth—numerous rows of them in each jaw. However, the teeth are well suited to the job of crushing crabs, lobsters and the other crustaceans that form much of the shark's diet (along with squid and small fish).

The cartilage at the tip of the hardnosed species' long, rounded snout is calcified.

Two dorsal fins, prominent and triangular, are spaced well apart, with an inconspicuous ridge between them. The tail fin trails horizontally behind the body, rather than standing up at an oblique angle in typical sharklike fashion.

Adults tend to cruise sluggishly over the sea bed in search of food, but newly born sharks are often found in the surf; many will remain in shallow water during their early years. The young develop from embryos within the female and are born in the summer, about ten to a litter, each about 27 cm long.

Smooth-hounds are edible, and in some countries they commonly make up a proportion of the 'fish' sold in fish-and-chip shops.

Marine fishes

SMALLTOOTH SAWFISH

Kleintand saagvis *(Pristis microdon)*

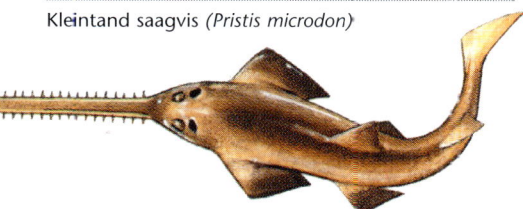

Size: Length averages 2 m, but can reach at least 4.6 m.
Colour: Uniform pale brown to khaki above, pale cream on the underside.
Most like: The closely related, but rarer, largetooth sawfish (Pristis pectinata), which has 24-34 pairs of teeth on its sawlike snout as opposed to the 17-22 pairs present in the smalltooth sawfish.
Habitat: Large estuaries, such as St Lucia and Richards Bay, and offshore muddy banks, as at the mouth of the Tugela River. Prefers shallow, turbid water.

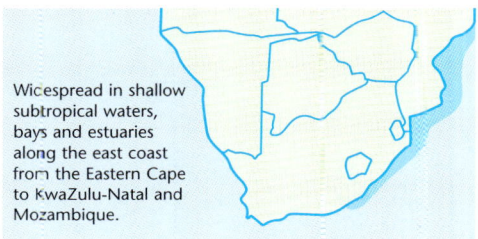

Widespread in shallow subtropical waters, bays and estuaries along the east coast from the Eastern Cape to KwaZulu-Natal and Mozambique.

Carpentry is far from the mind of the sawfish as it cruises shallow water in search of supper. It uses its 'saw', the long, toothed rostrum or snout that is almost half its body length, not to cut with but to dig up the muddy sea bed. Here it finds shellfish, which it crushes between the pavement of small, blunt teeth set in transverse rows in each jaw. In addition, the sawfish can make powerful and effective use of the saw to slash into a shoal of fish, causing mayhem.

The snout is actually an extension of the skull and is made of calcified cartilage, not bone, for the sawfish is a cartilaginous species. The saw-teeth are true teeth in that they are composed of dentine and enamel; their front cutting edges are blunt, while the rear edges are sharp.

The elongated body and arrangement of fins are sharklike, except that the large pectoral fins expand forward onto the sides of the head. They are of great help as the sawfish stealthily manoeuvres its way near the sea bottom. On top of the head, immediately behind the eyes, is a pair of large breathing openings or spiracles.

Enormous pregnant females are known to enter lower estuaries in order to give birth to 15-20 pups each season. Each pup is born with a special covering over the 'saw' to protect the mother as they emerge. The young remain within the estuary for several years before moving out to sea to join the adult community.

The smalltooth sawfish is very tasty, although it is not exploited commercially.

LESSER GUITARFISH

Kleiner sandkruiper *(Rhinobatos annulatus)*

Size: Length averages 80 cm, but can reach 1,4 m.
Colour: Upper surface ranges from a pale toffee colour to much darker brown, with numerous spots that may either be plain dark brown (specimens from KwaZulu-Natal waters) or ringed and eyelike (Cape waters). Underside pale.
Most like: Greyspot guitarfish, but the greyspot is distinguished by its pale bluish-grey spots.
Habitat: Surf zone of sandy, muddy coastal waters, seldom deeper than 50 m, and only rarely in estuaries.

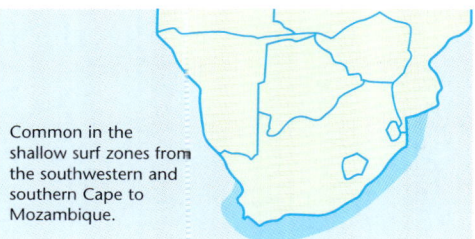

Common in the shallow surf zones from the southwestern and southern Cape to Mozambique.

The lesser guitarfish, so named because its outline bears a resemblance to the musical instrument's, is excellently camouflaged on the sandy sea bottom, where it sometimes actually buries itself with only its small spiracles (breathing holes) protruding.

Should you accidentally tread on a specimen in the surf zone it will slither from under your feet without doing any harm. Its fine, pavementlike teeth cannot inflict a serious bite, and the worst you'll suffer is a nasty fright.

The guitarfish, known also as the lesser sandshark, looks rather like a cross between a shark and a ray. In fact, it is in evolutionary transition between the two, displaying important features of both. Its flattened, wedge-shaped body is eminently well adapted to its sluggish life on the sandy bottom. The mouth is on the underside of the head but the spiracles face upwards and are situated just behind the eyes. This means that the fish can take in clean water from above while grovelling in the mud for food. It has a taste for small crabs, prawns, shellfish, sea lice and assorted small fish.

Lesser guitarfish are among the relatively few marine fish that are able to adjust successfully to changes in sea temperature: tagging has shown that this species may undertake extensive seasonal migrations between the waters of the east and west coast.

Breeding time is in summer. The female reaches sexual maturity at about 60 cm, and bears live young in litters of three to eight.

Marine fishes

BLUE STINGRAY

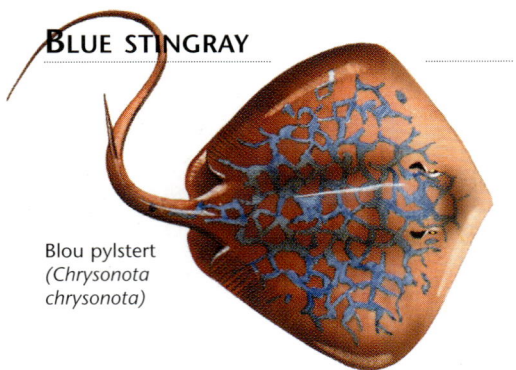

Blou pylstert
(*Chrysonota chrysonota*)

Size: *Disc width averages 50 cm, but can reach 75 cm.*
Colour: *Upper surface golden brown, patterned with blue mottlings that give a beautiful, marblelike effect; underside pale and unmarked.*
Most like: *Blue-spotted stingray or blue-spotted ribbon-tailray, but the blue markings of these are in the form of distinct spots, not blotches as in the blue stingray.*
Habitat: *Sandy coastal waters, ranging from the surf zone to depths of 50 m.*

Widespread along most of the southern African coastline from Namibia to KwaZulu-Natal.

Strictly speaking, stingrays live a lie for they have no sting. What the blue stingray does have, midway along its long, slender, whiplike tail, is a serrated spine like a modified tooth. It is stout and sharp and covered with a mucous substance; if this enters your skin it can cause an unpleasant sore that may take several weeks to clear up. If the spine breaks off in your flesh it will probably have to be cut out.

You can recognize stingrays instantly by their flattened, disc-shaped bodies that consist primarily of large pectoral fins fused to the head. The tail is usually long, while the pelvic and dorsal fins are either absent or very small. The eyes and spiracles (breathing holes) are located on the upper side, clearly an advantage when the ray is lying on the bottom, or lying camouflaged below a thin layer of sand.

Like many of its relatives, the blue stingray feeds on a variety of bottom-living marine organisms such as crabs, prawns, worms and small fish. Most of these are eaten whole or crushed by the strong pavement-like teeth.

This species is particularly common along the shallow, sandy beaches of the Cape and southern KwaZulu-Natal. It migrates seasonally between various regions within its distribution range. The females produce small litters of one to four pups each season.

Blue stingrays (like many other rays) fall prey to large sharks—such as the Zambezi—but the shark may be left with 'battle scars' when the sharp tail spine penetrates the flesh on its snout.

EAGLERAY

Arendrog
(*Myliobatus aquila*)

Size: *Disc width averages 50-70 cm, but can reach 1,5 m.*
Colour: *Upper body surface plain chocolate-brown to blackish; underside pale creamy.*
Most like: *Bullray, Pteromylaeus bovinus, but the eagleray's snout is blunt and short, not pointed, and lacks the crossbars of the bullray. Rays are similar in appearance to mantas, but lack the manta's pair of hornlike fins projecting from the head.*
Habitat: *Shallow coastal waters, especially along sandy beaches or within deeper estuaries.*

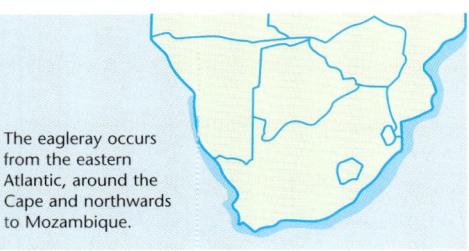

The eagleray occurs from the eastern Atlantic, around the Cape and northwards to Mozambique.

The eagleray derives its name from the winglike pectoral fins that enable it to swim in mid-water with long, graceful strokes, reminiscent of an eagle in flight. At certain times eaglerays congregate in small shoals near the surface and can be seen leaping into the air in an apparent attempt to shake off parasites.

The flat, diamond-shaped body is about 1,7 times wider than it is long and ends in a whiplike tail twice its body length. At the base of this tail, just behind the tiny dorsal fin, are one or two sharply serrated spines that are effectively used to discourage predators (and can lacerate careless hands). The seven rows of teeth of eaglerays are fused, forming two massive, pavementlike plates able to crush the mussels and other shellfish on which they feed. (They can also crush fingers and toes.)

Like other eaglerays, the head is raised above the level of the body—a feature that sets it apart from the stingrays. Eyes (with breathing holes just behind them) are on either side of the head, providing wide lateral vision.

Sexual maturity is reached at about 50 cm disc width, and after a one-year gestation the females give birth to three to seven young, each measuring 20-25 cm across.

Though eaglerays are edible, few anglers will kill these beautiful creatures.

Marine fishes

SPEARNOSE SKATE

Spiesneus-rog *(Raja alba)*

Size: Disc width averages 1 m, but can reach 1,8 m.
Colour: Upper surface greyish brown, often scattered with small white spots; underside cream to white.
Most like: Other skate species, of which more than 20 are found in southern African waters. The spearnose is the largest and is distinguished by the combination of pointed snout, undulating front profile, rows of thorns on body and tail, and colour pattern on its dorsal surface.
Habitat: Sandy and muddy offshore banks of cooler waters, often to depths of 400 m but not infrequently in the shallows.

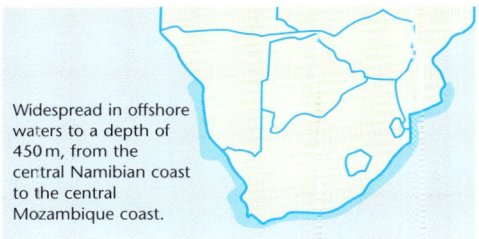

Widespread in offshore waters to a depth of 450 m, from the central Namibian coast to the central Mozambique coast.

Like other skates, the spearnose spends much of its time reclining on the sea bed, where it is well camouflaged. But let a small fish venture too close and the clumsy-looking skate springs to life, pouncing on its prey and smothering it with huge 'wings' before seizing the fish in its jaws. (A skate has to pounce because its mouth, on the underside of its flat body, is ill-placed for a more direct assault.)

Skates are cartilaginous fishes, lacking true bony skeletons. Greatly enlarged pectoral fins—the 'wings'—are fused with the head and trunk to form a flattened, flexible, diamond-shaped body. The pectoral fins end at the back in two distinct lobes.

The spearnose skate's protective armour is the assortment of tiny thorns from the tip of its projecting snout to the end of its tail. But the tail is not armed, like a ray's, with poisoned spines.

Despite their prodigious pectoral fins, skates are poor swimmers. When they move it is merely to glide, spectral and sinister, just above the sea bed.

The spearnose eats small fish, burrowing molluscs and prawns.

Females grow considerably larger than males. They produce two or more four-sided egg-cases with a horn at each corner—the so-called 'mermaids' purses' that cling to submerged objects. The young develop within the cases before hatching out as tiny replicas of the adult.

MARBLED ELECTRIC RAY

Marmer-drilvis
(Torpedo sinuspersici)

Size: Disc width averages 50 cm, but can reach 1,3 m.
Colour: Upper surface chocolate-brown patterned all over with irregular, light-coloured markings. Can radically change colour to blend in with the paler, sandy bottom. Undersides always pale.
Most like: Atlantic electric ray, Torpedo nobiliana, but the latter is a uniform brown, not 'marbled' with lighter markings.
Habitat: Muddy and sandy bottoms, occasionally in estuaries, and ranging from shallow beaches to depths of 200 m.

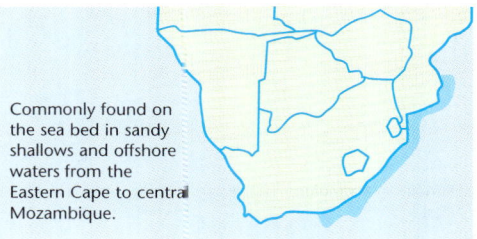

Commonly found on the sea bed in sandy shallows and offshore waters from the Eastern Cape to central Mozambique.

The marbled electric ray is a solitary species capable of delivering a remarkably powerful electric shock to repel would-be aggressors or stun its prey, mostly slow-swimming fish and prawns. The 75-volt output is derived from specially modified paired organs located on the upper body, which convert nervous energy to electricity. Though not dangerous to human beings, the shock could temporarily stun an unwary bather or diver.

This ray is an expert at camouflage and usually lies buried beneath a few centimetres of sand with only the eyes and spiracles (breathing holes) protruding. Many of these rays frequent the edges of shallow reefs in the St Lucia Marine Reserve.

The flattened body is very smooth-skinned. Together with the large, fleshy pectoral fins, it has the form of a disc but with a narrower extension at the back to which the pelvic fins are attached. There is a short, stocky tail with a rounded tail fin and, just in front of it, two small dorsal fins. The marbled electric ray has several rows of fine pointed teeth.

This ray reaches sexual maturity at about 40 cm disc width, and in summer the female gives birth to 9-22 live young after they have hatched from egg-cases inside her.

The generic name *Torpedo* is the Latin word for 'numbness', the effect that electric shock produces on the ray's victims.

Marine fishes

BLACK MARLIN

Swart marlyn *(Makaira indica)*

Size: *Length averages 2,2 m, but can reach 4,5 m.*
Colour: *Metallic blue-black above; white below. Colour changes to an overall dull black after death.*
Most like: *Blue marlin and striped marlin, but the black marlin lacks the lighter vertical bars of the other two species, and its pectoral fins, projecting at right angles to the body, cannot be folded back.*
Habitat: *Warm and temperate waters; usually open water over the continental shelf, but also far away from landmasses.*

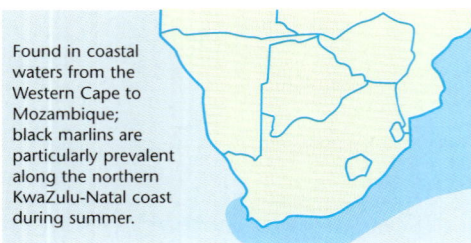

Found in coastal waters from the Western Cape to Mozambique; black marlins are particularly prevalent along the northern KwaZulu-Natal coast during summer.

Marlins are instantly recognizable by the large, rigid, sickle-shaped tail, and by the greatly extended upper jaw that forms a spearlike snout. It is this 'bill' that gives marlin their name, from its supposed resemblance to a marlinspike, a tool used for splicing rope.

The fins are without spines, and most of them can be neatly folded away into grooves, streamlining the body for high speeds through the water—although the black marlin's pectoral fins always remain extended. The thornlike scales are deeply embedded in the tough skin, further enhancing the fish's fast-swimming capabilities. The eyes are large and round.

The black marlin is a powerful and usually solitary predator, often using its bill to slash at and injure its prey, which consists primarily of other smaller game fish such as tuna, yellowtail and bonito. Though the mouth is large, the teeth inside it are small and rasplike, and therefore the black marlin has to swallow its prey whole.

This giant game fish, probably the most common marlin species in southern African waters, is known to undertake extensive trans-oceanic migrations.

Females grow much larger than males. The eggs are fertilized externally and the large quantities of minute young are distributed far and wide by ocean currents. Newly hatched young lack the marlin's characteristic bill.

This is a prized game fish—the largest recorded weight is 708 kg, though the largest specimen caught in southern African waters weighed 503 kilograms.

KING MACKEREL

Katonkel *(Scomberomorus commerson)*

Size: *Length averages 80 cm-1 m, but can reach 2,2 m. Maximum recorded weight 50 kg.*
Colour: *The bright metallic silvery-blue sides and upper surface are conspicuously patterned with darker wavy vertical bars. The lateral line forms a distinct wavy black stripe along each flank.*
Most like: *The closely related queen mackerel (Natal snoek) but, unlike the king mackerel, it has rows of spots arranged longitudinally along its body.*
Habitat: *Widespread throughout the Indo-Pacific, in warm oceanic water, usually close to landmasses. In South Africa most occur off KwaZulu-Natal in clear water.*

Hunts along rocky shores and in the deeper waters of northern KwaZulu-Natal in the winter, moving southwards towards the Eastern Cape in summer.

This most powerful of mackerels has a sleek body with fins that are either reduced or can be folded away during high speed. The tail is large and forked—typical of game fish—as are the jaws, being set with rows of razor-sharp triangular teeth. This dentition is used to great effect when tackling prey, which are rapidly cut up and swallowed. Much of its food consists of small tuna, lizardfishes, a variety of bait fish and squid, though it also eats prawns and mantis shrimps occasionally when they are in abundance.

King mackerel usually move in shoals, but become more solitary as they grow larger.

During winter king mackerel, known also as couta or cuda, migrate in shoals from tropical Mozambique to northern KwaZulu-Natal, while during the summer months they may reach as far south as East London. Spawning occurs primarily off Mozambique and the fish reach sexual maturity at a length of one metre, which corresponds to an age of three to four years.

The female produces hundreds of eggs, which are released and fertilized in the water. However, where the 'young-of-the-year' go to is not known. This swift game fish is particularly sought after by fishermen, not only because it is good to eat, but also because it is such a tenacious fighter in the water.

The body cavity of the king mackerel is infested with parasites such as roundworms and tapeworm larvae, which are harmless to both the fish and humans, but contaminate their marine predators.

Marine fishes

LONGFIN TUNA

Albakoor *(Thunnus alalunga)*

Size: Length averages 90 cm, but can reach 1,27 m.
Colour: Deep blue above with lighter metallic flanks and a white belly. After death the blue fades to a dull blue-grey. The dorsal fin may be yellowish.
Most like: Bluefin, yellowfin and bigeye tuna, but none has the combination of a long pectoral fin and grey-coloured dorsal and anal finlets.
Habitat: Circumglobal in all oceans but especially prevalent at oceanic fronts, where cool and warm water meet, such as off Cape Point. These tuna prefer clear water, often far away from land. Though present all year, most catches are made off the Cape during the late summer months, after which shoals migrate up the west coast towards Tripp Sea Mount and northward.

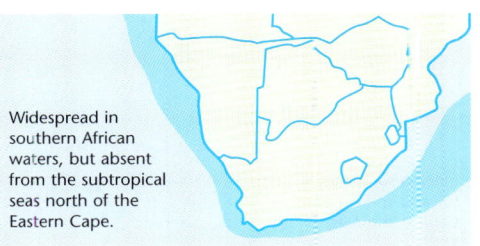

Widespread in southern African waters, but absent from the subtropical seas north of the Eastern Cape.

This highly evolved, torpedo-shaped game fish is perfectly designed for its oceanic and pelagic lifestyle. It has very well-developed and rigid fins that greatly facilitate its swimming power. The particularly large pectoral fins are most distinctive, especially when you look down onto the fish from a vessel at sea. There are numerous small, detached finlets on the upper and lower hind regions and, like other tuna, the longfin, or albacore, can fold its fins away in special torso grooves so as to streamline the body. Its strong, robust, spineless tail is typically that of a game fish, while its large eyes facilitate vision in the deeper low-light regions of the ocean.

The longfin tuna may feed either on the surface of the ocean, or at considerable depths. Its diet consists of a variety of small organisms, such as anchovies, squid, crab larvae, krill and other crustaceans. Most of this food is trapped by the long gill rakers before being swallowed.

Longfin tuna are well known for their spectacular trans-oceanic migrations, tagged specimens having been recaptured up to 8 500 km away within a year. These migrations are made possible by a special block of warm-blooded red muscles in the centre of the body, which is maintained at a temperature 3-4°C higher than the surrounding water.

SNOEK

Snoek *(Thyrsites atun)*

Size: Length averages 1 m, but can reach 1,5 m.
Colour: Unmarked, strikingly silver body with a dark blue or blue-grey dorsal surface and white belly. The wavy lateral line is most conspicuous.
Most like: Black snoek (Thyrsitoides marleyi), but the latter's general colour is blackish brown, not silver.
Habitat: This is an open-water pelagic species, generally confined to the continental shelf, but ranging from the surface to depths exceeding 200 m. Its distribution is confined to the cooler waters surrounding the tips of continents in the southern hemisphere.

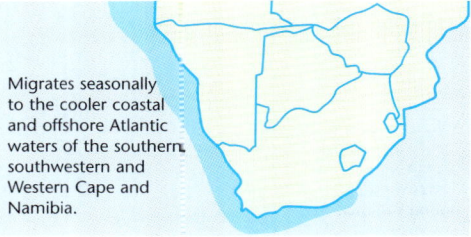

Migrates seasonally to the cooler coastal and offshore Atlantic waters of the southern, southwestern and Western Cape and Namibia.

Surely one of South Africa's best known and popular fish, this swift and powerful predator moves in large shoals—often in hot pursuit of its prey, which consists of anchovies, krill and squid. Snoek and their relatives have very elongated, compressed bodies, with a long, pronounced dorsal fin, several finlets and large mouths set with fearsome triangular teeth.

Anglers have learned to handle live snoek with great care: a bite from the sharp teeth can be extremely painful and cause profuse bleeding. A number of line fishermen have lost a finger or two to the snapping teeth of a freshly caught snoek.

The scales of a snoek are so minute and arranged in such a compact way that the fish appears almost scaleless. The powerful tail is forked, but lacks the lateral keels found in tuna and mackerels.

Snoek migrate extensively each year, and between November and April huge shoals are found in the coastal and offshore waters off the west coast to Walvis Bay. From April through to August they are caught in the waters of the southwestern Cape—even providing good catches as far east as Hermanus.

It is well known among fishermen that the condition of snoek deteriorates rapidly just after spawning. Young-of-the-year snoek may be found in sheltered bays, such as False Bay, where they grow up in relatively calm and nutrient-rich areas.

The largest snoek recorded weighed in at an impressive 8,6 kilograms.

Marine fishes

DORADO
Dorade *(Coryphaena hippurus)*

Size: *Average length 80 cm-1 m, but may attain 2 m. Maximum recorded weight is 40 kg.*
Colour: *Vivid metallic blue-green body flecked with golden-orange spots and tinged bright yellow on the underside. Fins dusky, but anal fin sometimes golden.*
Most like: *The deeper-bodied and slightly smaller pompano dorado—a much rarer species.*
Habitat: *All oceans, often far away from landmasses, and most commonly in warm waters*

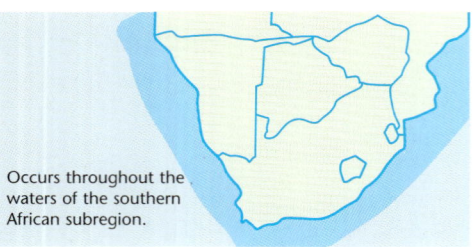

Occurs throughout the waters of the southern African subregion.

The dorado, or dolphinfish, is unquestionably one of the most beautiful of marine fish, and yet death, as in some sinister tale of retribution, deprives it of all its rainbowed brilliance.

In outline it combines sleek elegance with a rather academic mien, for the 'forehead' is extremely steep, and grows more so with age, especially in males.

The highly compressed body is covered with minute scales and has a deeply forked tail fin. The spineless dorsal fin starts at the top of the forehead and sweeps along the entire back, decreasing gradually in height; one to three small spines precede the long, spineless anal fin.

Despite its predatory habits, the dorado does not have large teeth and depends on prey that it can swallow whole. It excels at this, pouncing on the small fishes that shelter below drifting objects at sea. Included in its diet are juvenile triggerfish, boxfish, crab larvae, nautiluses and many other organisms that are captured when dorados patrol the oceans, moving from flotsam to flotsam.

Dorados often live in pairs; the male and female are thought to form a permanent bond. Spawning occurs throughout the year, with the females producing large quantities of eggs. The abundant larvae form part of the drifting organisms collectively known as plankton, and they are widely dispersed by surface ocean currents. Their growth is extremely rapid: within one year this fish may attain a weight of five kilograms.

GREAT BARRACUDA
Groot barrakuda *(Sphyraena barracuda)*

Size: *Length averages 1 m, but can reach 1,65 m.*
Colour: *Silvery grey, darker above and with irregular, inky-black blotches on rear flanks; belly silvery white. Some specimens have about 20 faint crossbars on flanks. Fins dusky. Rays have pale tips.*
Most like: *The nine other barracuda species in the southern African waters; though this species is distinguished by its inky blotches. The common pickhandle barracuda has 20 prominent vertical crossbars.*
Habitat: *Widespread throughout the world's tropical seas, usually patrolling the outer edges of coral reefs, but also in coastal lagoons and off sandy beaches.*

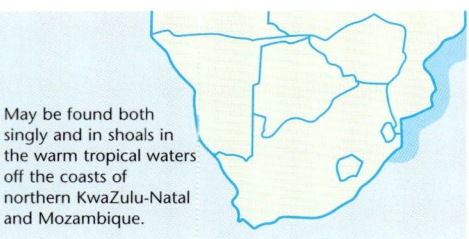

May be found both singly and in shoals in the warm tropical waters off the coasts of northern KwaZulu-Natal and Mozambique.

No prizes for guessing that the great barracuda is a formidable predator: in the pointed snout the wide, fearsome jaws are studded with an array of sharp teeth, and the beady eyes seem to glower malevolently. The way the lower jaw juts out beyond the upper one adds to the general impression of thrusting aggressiveness.

This is a rather unpredictable customer. Great barracuda have been positively implicated in attacks on human beings and, though the real danger may sometimes be overstated, these bold fish often circle divers in close proximity.

The body is almost cylindrical in cross-section. It is densely covered with rows of small but tough scales. Fins include two small and widely separated dorsals, short pectorals and pelvics, and a single, smallish anal fin; the tail fin is broad and has a wavy trailing edge.

The diet of this barracuda species consists primarily of fish. Young specimens feed on small surface-shoaling species, while adults prefer the larger reef-dwelling ones.

Spawning occurs in the open ocean, usually during the summer months in the tropics. The juveniles shelter in shallow, mangrove-edged bays before joining the adults a year or two later.

Popular with anglers and spearfishermen, the barracuda is of moderate eating value.

Marine fishes

CAPE YELLOWTAIL
Kaapse geelstert *(Seriola lalandi)*

Size: *Average 80 cm, but can attain 1,5 m.*
Colour: *Metallic blue-green above, with silvery flanks and a white belly. A striking yellow or bronze band stretches from the snout to the yellow tail fin.*
Most like: *Greater yellowtail and longfin yellowtail, but only the Cape species has the bright yellow tail fin.*
Habitat: *Temperate seas, in open water but usually in association with offshore banks or prominent headlands. Ranges freely from surface water to depths of 50 m or more; occasionally pursues prey into shallow surf.*

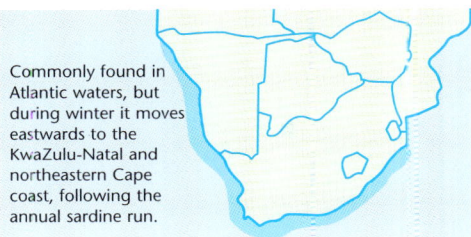

Commonly found in Atlantic waters, but during winter it moves eastwards to the KwaZulu-Natal and northeastern Cape coast, following the annual sardine run.

The yellowtail is built for speed, as any angler who has hooked one will tell you. Its body is torpedo-shaped and covered in very fine scales and, while the tail fin is large and deeply forked, the other fins are reduced or streamlined, with dorsal spines folding away sleekly into dorsal grooves. Just in front of the tail fin, in the area known as the 'peduncle', there is a small lateral ridge or 'keel' on either side of the body—hydrodynamic extras that are typical of swiftly swimming game fish.

This is one of South Africa's best-known and most esteemed game fish, both with shore-anglers and spearfishermen. It is highly seasonal in appearance, for it undertakes lengthy migrations, being able to adapt from the cold Atlantic zone to the warmer seas of the east coast. Great numbers follow the spring 'sardine run', the mass migration of pilchards north-eastwards into northeastern Cape and KwaZulu-Natal waters, and at times huge shoals congregate in offshore shallows to a depth of about 50 metres.

The Cape yellowtail feeds on a wide variety of marine organisms, all of which are swallowed whole as the yellowtail has in each jaw several rows of extremely fine, ineffective teeth. Included in its diet are small bait fish, squid, mantis shrimps and crabs.

Spawning occurs along the east coast, but eggs and larvae are transported westwards by the ocean currents so that the young grow to maturity in southern Cape waters. The breeding ground of the Cape yellowtail is believed to be far more extensive than was originally thought.

GIANT KINGFISH
Reuse koningvis *(Caranx ignobilis)*

Size: *Average length 60 cm, but can attain 1,65 m.*
Colour: *Olive-green overall, but darker above and white below; often lightly speckled with black spots on upper flanks. Older fish, especially males, are considerably darker, sometimes even dark grey. Fins pigmented grey to black, or sometimes yellowish.*
Most like: *Other kingfish species in southern African waters (there are at least 20), but this species is by far the largest and most robust. Fine scales cover almost the entire chest region, which is partially naked in many other species.*
Habitat: *Warmer waters of the Indo-Pacific region and westwards to Port Elizabeth. These fish occur singly or in small groups along the outer edges of reefs, off rocky points and around oceanic islands. They hunt mostly quite close inshore, often in very shallow water or even estuaries; sometimes to depths of 50 m.*

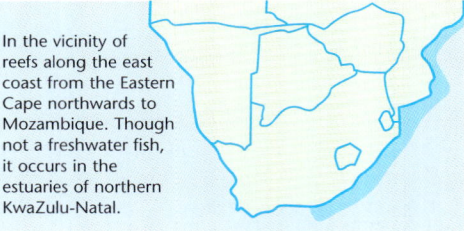

In the vicinity of reefs along the east coast from the Eastern Cape northwards to Mozambique. Though not a freshwater fish, it occurs in the estuaries of northern KwaZulu-Natal.

Among the fishing fraternity this robust, deep-bodied species separates the men from the boys, for once hooked it becomes a fighting fury to test the strength, and the tackle, of the most seasoned angler.

The giant kingfish has a large and powerful, deeply forked tail set on a very narrow tail stock—a feature typical of all game fish. All other fins are well developed, especially the long, sickle-shaped pectorals, which arch back well beyond the mid-body, and indicate a high degree of manoeuvrability.

The eyes are set high up in the steeply sloping head; the rear half of each eye is covered by a thick layer of fatty tissue. Inside the large mouth the jaws are equipped with strong, conical teeth, enabling the kingfish to feed on a wide variety of fish, as well as squid, shrimps and occasionally crabs. A fierce predator, it hunts both day and night and often pursues its prey very close inshore, moving swiftly from reef to reef.

Spawning takes place in summer in the warmer tropical zones, and groups of young giant kingfish are often encountered in estuaries.

Marine fishes

Garrick

Leervis *(Lichia amia)*

Size: Length averages 1 m, but can reach 1,8 m.
Colour: Back and upper flanks brownish to blue-grey, lower flanks silvery, belly white. A conspicuous, wavy lateral line runs from gill to tail on each flank. Fins mostly dusky. Juveniles less than 10 cm are strikingly different, having a bright orange-yellow body with numerous black crossbars.
Most like: Talang queenfish *(Scomberoides commersonnianus)*, but this lacks the obvious lateral line and has 5-8 large blotches on each flank.
Habitat: Surf zone of inshore waters, often in very turbulent and shallow water. Juveniles may be found in coastal bays and estuaries.

In the wave zone of waters off the southern Mozambique and KwaZulu-Natal coasts in winter, migrating to Western and Northern Cape and Namibian waters in summer.

Anglers know this large and powerful predator for its cunning, and there is a suggestion that the species was named after the great English actor David Garrick—for he, like the crafty fish hooked at the end of a line, was the finest of 'players'! Be that as it may, the fish's alternative name, leervis, is easily accounted for. The sleek body is covered with scales so minute that the tough skin resembles leather (Afrikaans *leer*).

The head is rather pointed, while the rear half of the body tapers noticeably, ending in a powerful, deeply forked tail. Despite its fierce nature, the garrick lacks any formidable teeth (the teeth are very fine), and hence its diet is confined to fish that can be swallowed whole—for example, grunters, pilchards and elf.

Garrick usually move in small groups: they hunt together, trapping shoals of smaller bait fish in gullies and then systematically devouring them.

This species migrates from Cape waters in winter to spawn in the warmer waters of KwaZulu-Natal. The Agulhas Current then transports the eggs and larvae back to the Cape, where juveniles spend their first few years before joining the adult populations.

Garrick is highly sought after by both anglers and spearfishermen (although it is not generally regarded as good eating).

Elf

Elf *(Pomatomus saltatrix)*

Size: Length averages 40 cm, but can reach 1,2 m.
Colour: Silvery, with a sea-green upper surface and white belly. Larger fish might be bluish.
Most like: Some kingfish, queenfish, yellowtail and mackerel bear a general resemblance, but elf has no lateral line of scutes (bony scales) along each flank, no detached finlets and no lateral keels (ridges) in front of the tail fin.
Habitat: In cooler coastal surface waters, mostly close to shore, but occasionally ranging some distance offshore and sometimes descending to depths of 50 m over offshore banks. Elf frequently congregate in medium-sized shoals at prominent rocky outcrops or breakwaters on long, sandy stretches of coastline.

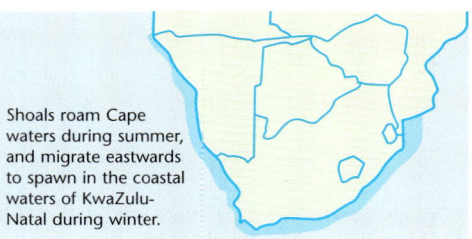

Shoals roam Cape waters during summer, and migrate eastwards to spawn in the coastal waters of KwaZulu-Natal during winter.

The set, underhung lower jaw and downward-sloping mouth give the elf, or shad, a look of Churchillian pugnacity, and indeed this species puts up a very game fight when hooked. It may jump repeatedly out of the water, behaviour that gives the fish its species name *saltatrix* (Latin for 'dancing girl').

The elf's body is streamlined and covered with minute scales. All the fins are well developed, especially the long and moderately forked tail fin. This fish is a fierce predator with razor-sharp teeth that can shred quite large fish within seconds; the teeth are also capable of inflicting a nasty bite to an unwary angler's hand. Confronted by a shoal of smaller fish such as pilchards and anchovies, a hungry elf will attack with a ravenous frenzy and gorge itself. It will then regurgitate its meal, and frenetically start all over again.

Each winter elf migrate from Cape waters to those off KwaZulu-Natal where spawning takes place in spring. After spawning, the adult fish migrate back to the Cape for summer. The fertilized eggs and larvae follow the adults' course, drifting purposefully south-westwards with the Agulhas Current back to the shallow, sandy shores of the Cape. In these waters the young fishes spend from two to three years growing to maturity.

Marine fishes

Dusky kob

Silwer kabeljou (*Argyrosomus japonicus*)

Size: Weight 45-60 kg, maximum recorded 75 kg.
Colour: Silvery-grey body, with bronzy-blue sheer, sometimes coppery on head; silver scales along flanks. Adults often golden brown, particularly after death.
Most like: The two other species of true kob in South African waters: squaretail (*A. thorpei*) and silver kob (*A. inodorus*). Externally all very similar; but dusky kob tends to be darker in colour, particularly after death.
Habitat: Widely distributed in the warm-temperate Indian and Western Pacific Oceans. In southern African waters, it prefers the warmer waters of the east coast.

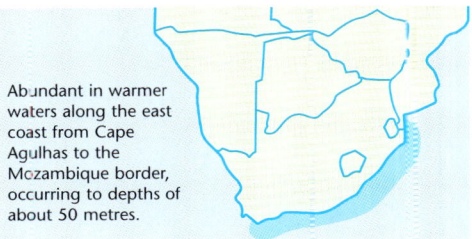

Abundant in warmer waters along the east coast from Cape Agulhas to the Mozambique border, occurring to depths of about 50 metres.

Dutch settlers arriving at the Cape in the 1600s mistook the kob for the cod of the northern hemisphere, thus naming it *kabeljauw* (of which kob or cob is a derivative). Kob are, in fact, not related to cod at all but belong to a family of fishes (Sciaenidae) commonly known as croakers or drums because of the sounds they produce using specialized drumming muscles attached to a large, gas-filled swim-bladder which acts as an amplifier. The sounds are used for communication and during courtship and mating.

Dusky kob, as suggested by their large mouths and teeth, are voracious predators, and will happily eat crabs, prawns, other fish and octopuses. Larger specimens even take small sharks. Equipped with a large swim-bladder and ear bones, and a well-developed lateral-line sensory system, this kob can home in on vibrations produced by its prey, and successfully hunts at night or in the murky water it is so fond of.

The adults of this prized angling species are known as 'dagga salmon' in KwaZulu-Natal and 'boer kabeljou' in the Cape. Dusky kob mature at around six years of age and a weight of 13 kg, and live to at least 42 years. Spawning takes place in the sea at depths of 10-50 metres. The offspring remain in the ocean for about four weeks before heading for murky estuaries.

Owing to their estuarine/surf-zone nursery, late age at maturity and longevity, the dusky kob is particularly vulnerable to overfishing, and it's estimated that the South African population has been reduced to 2,3 per cent of original numbers. This is because most fish are caught before they have a chance to spawn. Stringent bag and size limits will soon be implemented to remedy this situation.

Geelbek

Geelbek (*Atractoscion aequidens*)

Size: Length averages 80 cm, but can reach 1,3 m.
Colour: Silvery, but bluish or coppery above and white below. Fins dusky or translucent. Interior of mouth and gill chambers bright yellow-orange.
Most like: Various kob species (there are nine in southern African waters) but the geelbek is distinguished by the bright yellow interior of its mouth and the concave trailing edge of its large tail fin, which is rounded or straight in a kob.
Habitat: Temperate coastal waters, ranging from the surface to depths of at least 100 m. Shoals are frequently found close to the bottom, near pinnacles or in the vicinity of shipwrecks. Clear water is preferred; estuaries are avoided.

Common in deep waters off the west coast during summer; during winter they spawn in the warmer waters of the KwaZulu-Natal coast.

A shoal of surface-feeding geelbek in hot pursuit of their prey is a spectacle to behold, for this is a fierce and voracious predator and a powerful swimmer. The streamlined body, covered with small scales, has well-developed fins, the pectoral and slightly concave tail fin being noticeably large. The mouth has a wide gape and is set with several rows of fine, very sharp teeth.

Geelbek take squid occasionally but prefer anchovies, maasbanker, mackerel and pilchards which they follow each season on their migration to KwaZulu-Natal.

This migration also coincides with their reproductive season. Large shoals of spawning geelbek congregate in deep water off southern KwaZulu-Natal and the northeastern Cape during spring; the fertilized eggs soon disperse southwestwards with the Agulhas Current.

Despite the popular name 'Cape salmon', or simply 'salmon', common in KwaZulu-Natal, the species is unrelated to the true, northern hemisphere salmon. Geelbek are, nevertheless, highly sought after as table fish and also to make the traditional dish of pickled fish (*ingelegde vis*).

Geelbek are particularly susceptible to changes in sea temperature and therefore their migratory habits are not entirely predictable. For this reason catches fluctuate widely from year to year.

Marine fishes

RED STUMPNOSE

Rooistompneus *(Chrysoblephus gibbiceps)*

Size: Length averages 35 cm, but can reach 75 cm.
Colour: Striking silvery pink, somewhat darker above, with five to seven darker red, vertical bars running down each side. Numerous black blotches and speckles occur irregularly on the upper flanks. Fins are reddish.
Most like: Dageraad, which has a similar shape and shares the same distribution but lacks the stumpnose's vertical bars and black blotches.
Habitat: Rocky reefs and offshore banks to a depth of 150 m. Occasionally caught from the shore. Prefers clear waters.

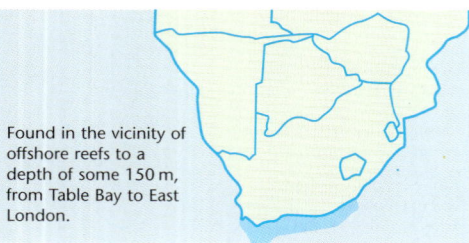

Found in the vicinity of offshore reefs to a depth of some 150 m, from Table Bay to East London.

The red stumpnose's high forehead suggests intelligence, and in its foraging around flattish reefs this bottom-dweller does, in fact, display ingenuity. If it suspects that an octopus is lurking inside a rock cleft it will patiently cruise in the vicinity, or remain still for long periods, until the octopus emerges, and then strike. Sand-dwellers such as crabs are 'blown' out of hiding as the stumpnose forcefully ejects a jet of water from its mouth into the mud.

Also known as Miss Lucy in the Port Elizabeth area, this fish has four to five rows of strong molars and an outer row of canine teeth to cope with its assorted prey, which includes a wide variety of invertebrate organisms such as redbait, worms, sea urchins, octopuses and occasionally small fish.

Brilliant colouring makes up for what the red stumpnose may lack in graceful physique. This is a robust, deep-bodied fish with a smallish, thick-lipped mouth at the end of a rather pointed snout. The dorsal fins have strong spines typical of the seabream family, to which this species belongs. But its most noticeable feature is the steep forehead that is slightly concave below the eyes. As the males grow older, they develop a large, white, bulbous projection on the upper forehead, which tends to become increasingly pitted and spongelike.

Spawning occurs in the late spring and early summer.

ROMAN

Roman *(Chrysoblephus laticeps)*

Size: Length averages 30 cm, but can reach 50 cm.
Colour: Reddish orange, with a distinctive white saddle over the middle of the back, and a white bar on the gill covers. Fins dusky red, except the pectorals, which are bright orange, especially when alive. There is a blue line between the eyes and occasionally a series of blue spots along the top of the head.
Most like: Natal Dane, but the roman's white saddle are distinctive and should serve to prevent confusion.
Habitat: Among rocks and submerged reefs, to depths of 100 m. Seldom occurs close to the shore, and avoids discoloured water.

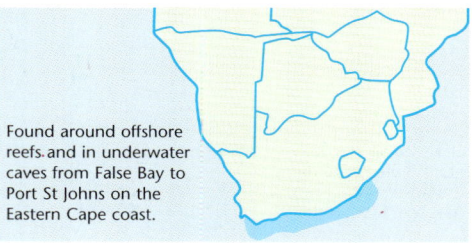

Found around offshore reefs and in underwater caves from False Bay to Port St Johns on the Eastern Cape coast.

This beautifully coloured fish is subject to sex reversal, a common phenomenon among the seabream (Sparidae) family. All roman are born female, reaching maturity at about 20 cm and then, after one or two summer spawning seasons, changing to the male gender. Consequently all fish larger than 35 cm are certain to be males.

The seabream's sex reversal is accompanied by a distinctive change in behaviour: smaller, gregarious females form shoals over open, rocky reefs, but larger males adopt a more solitary, cave-dwelling existence, often remaining permanent residents of these sheltered homes.

Roman are small, plump fish with well-developed, spinous dorsal and anal fins, long pectoral fins and a moderately forked tail fin. Tough scales cover the body, while the jaws are set with several rows of strong molars and an outer row of canine teeth—a crushing apparatus which is particularly suited to coping with the roman's diet of hard-shelled organisms such as sea urchins, crabs and feather-stars.

The roman is an important food fish of the Cape, and is popular with both commercial and recreational fishermen. Sometimes it is referred to as 'red roman', but the adjective is superfluous since roman is a corruption of the Afrikaans *rooi man* ('red man').

Marine fishes

DAGERAAD

Dageraad *(Chrysoblephus cristiceps)*

Size: Average length 35 cm, but can reach 75 cm. Maximum weight 9 kg.

Colour: Pinkish red all over. Living specimens display beautifully iridescent shades of gold, orange and blue when removed from the water. There is a black blotch just behind the dorsal fin. Fins dusky pink. Juveniles have extensive black body markings.

Most like: Other seabreams such as the slinger and red stumpnose, but the dageraad's black blotch is distinctive and its body is deeper.

Habitat: Flat reefs between depths of 20 m and 100 m; seldom found close to the shore.

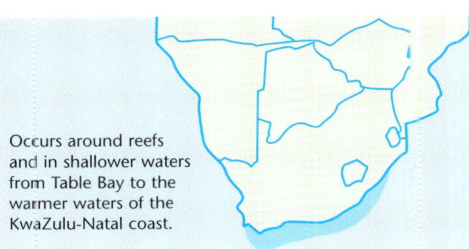

Occurs around reefs and in shallower waters from Table Bay to the warmer waters of the KwaZulu-Natal coast.

The rainbow of colours—a sort of visual swansong—displayed by this fish in its last living moments give it its name, which derives from a Dutch word meaning 'dawn'. It is a close relative of the red stumpnose, but more beautiful both in colouring and in appearance, for its forehead is less steep than the stumpnose's and not humped.

The body is deep, the fins spinous and well developed; pectoral fins reach back as far as the anal fin. The moderate-sized mouth at the end of the pointed snout bears at least three rows of formidable molar teeth, as well as an outer row of canines, an array well-suited to cope with this species' diet of crabs, tube worms, squid and small fish.

Dageraad are shoaling fish, and foraging shoals may be seen moving across a reef in the early morning, systematically feeding on all available food items. Later the shoal may rise to mid-water and 'rest' for part of the day.

Spawning occurs mostly during summer, but the whereabouts of larvae and juveniles remain unknown. The young, however, are all born female, and undergo a sex change to become males at about 40 centimetres.

The dageraad, in some areas also known as 'daggerhead', a corruption of the name, is very popular with line fishermen.

CARPENTER

Kapenaar *(Argyrozona argyrozona)*

Size: Averages 45 cm, but can reach 90 cm. Maximum recorded weight is 2,5 kg.

Colour: Silvery, but there is pinkish hue all over, especially on the carpenter's upper surface. The fins are pinkish translucent and, in some specimens, there may be as many as seven rows of iridescent blue spots.

Most like: Easily confused with several other seabreams, especially the panga and red tjor-tjor. However, it has a more elongate body and prominent canines.

Habitat: This is a deep-water fish, found as deep as 200 m and seldom, if ever, close to the shore. Large shoals congregate over offshore banks and at the edges of reefs. It is endemic to Cape waters, especially over the Agulhas Bank.

Ranges in both shallow and deep offshore waters from Saldanha Bay on the west coast to Port St Johns.

Bunches of carpenter, known as 'doppies', used to be a valuable source of income to Malay fishermen touting their catches at wharfsides in the southwestern Cape a few decades ago. Today these fish (their name is a corruption of the Dutch word *Kapenaar*, meaning 'of the Cape') are still caught in large quantities, but they are not as abundant as they used to be.

Known also as silverfish, carpenter are handsome, elongate fish with large, quizzical eyes, a wide mouth with long, flaring canines and small molars, and well-developed spinous fins. Their bodies are completely covered with tough scales and there is a distinct lateral line running down each flank.

These fish are strictly carnivorous, preying on a variety of squid, crabs, worms and other reef-dwelling organisms. They reach sexual maturity at about 20 cm, and spawning takes place in spring or summer, mostly over the Agulhas Bank; from there, the fertilized eggs and larvae are widely distributed by ocean currents.

Little is known about the exact movements of these fish, although they are believed to undergo seasonal migrations, possibly reaching as far as the west coast.

Marine fishes

RED STEENBRAS
Rooisteenbras *(Petrus rupestris)*

Size: *Length averages 75 cm–1 m, but can attain 2 m.*
Colour: *Reddish, with a beautiful bronze hue on the upper flanks and occasionally yellow underneath. Sometimes has a darker patch just behind the dorsal fin. Bodies of very large males acquire other irregular black patches. Fins dark red. The brilliance of this fish's colouring fades soon after death.*
Most like: *Other members of the seabream family, but the red steenbras is distinguished by being the largest, with only 11 dorsal fin spines (the others have 12) and no molar teeth.*
Habitat: *Large reefs to a depth of 100 m, although occasional specimens venture close to shore and into deep estuaries.*

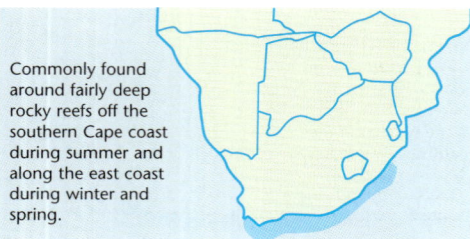

Commonly found around fairly deep rocky reefs off the southern Cape coast during summer and along the east coast during winter and spring.

Few other fish rival the aggressive nature of this very powerful predator—to anglers an almost legendary species, esteemed for its rare fighting prowess. Its robust body has a large head with an extended snout and a big mouth set with powerful canines that can cause serious wounds, even sever a finger. To make matters worse, the mucus on the teeth contains an anti-coagulant.

The red steenbras's dorsal and anal fins are spinous, and the strong tail fin is moderately forked.

The life cycle of this fish involves sex reversal: smaller specimens are mostly female, while the very large fish captured or seen off the east coast are invariably males. Large solitary males may become territorial and often dominate considerable areas of reef, where they prey on a variety of other reef fishes, including fingerfins (Family Cheilodactylidae) and Frans madames (*Boopsoidea inornata*), as well as squid and octopus.

Red steenbras migrate in spring, when large shoals of adults congregate off the Eastern Cape and KwaZulu-Natal coasts in a spawning condition. The young are more common towards Cape Agulhas, suggesting that the fry are carried southwestwards with the current.

The liver of this feisty fish, which can reach 30 years of age, is poisonous: it contains toxic levels of vitamin A.

SEVENTYFOUR
Vier-en-sewentig *(Polysteganus undulosus)*

Size: *Length averages 50 cm, but can reach 1 m.*
Colour: *Pinkish, with four to six lines of iridescent blue spots along each side, a white belly and a conspicuous black mark overlying the lateral line on each upper flank. Adult males may display a black patch on the chin.*
Most like: *Other larger seabream such as the Scotsman, but the seventyfour's black mark on each flank is distinctive.*
Habitat: *Deeper reefs; large shoals of mature fish often congregate around sea-bed pinnacles, ranging to depths of 200 m. Never found very close to shore.*

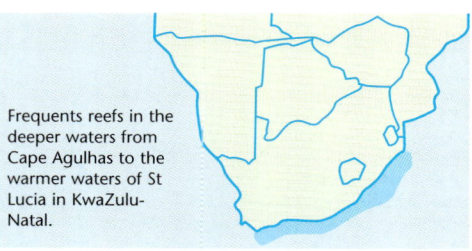

Frequents reefs in the deeper waters from Cape Agulhas to the warmer waters of St Lucia in KwaZulu-Natal.

Though this attractive species is named after a man-o'-war (the old 'seventy-four' sailing ship, whose formidable array of gun ports was arranged in rows like the fish's iridescent dots), it is not known for its aggression. In fact, it is very vulnerable to capture by man at the spawning stage, and has become relatively scarce as a result.

In silhouette the body is smoothly convex above, with a long, spiny dorsal fin. The shorter anal fin is spiny too, while the large, prominent tail fin is slightly forked. Inside the small mouth are rows of canines and, behind them, many finer, hairlike teeth. Seventyfour prey on a variety of smaller organisms that live in association with reefs, including fish, squid, mantis shrimps and pteropods (planktonic molluscs).

Unlike many other seabreams, the seventyfour does not undergo sex reversal. It generally undertakes extensive migrations that result in large congregations of spawning fish at certain reefs, such as the Illovo and Protea banks off the southern KwaZulu-Natal coasts. Eggs and larvae are distributed southwards by the Agulhas Current, and juvenile seventyfour occur commonly on reefs between East London and Knysna.

This sought-after species is considered to be one of the finest table fish in southern Africa, and commands high market prices accordingly.

Marine fishes

WHITE MUSSELCRACKER
Witbiskop *(Sparodon durbanensis)*

Size: Length up to 1,2 m.
Colour: Silvery to grey, with bluish tinge above. Fins grey. The young have six to seven narrow horizontal brown stripes on the flanks, and orange fins. Colouring of adults darkens soon after death.
Most like: Black musselcracker or black steenbras, but the latter is sooty grey to black while the white musselcracker is silvery to grey.
Habitat: Inshore coastal waters, especially where there are rocks, but not where the water is too turbulent.

Found along inshore coastal waters from Saldanha Bay on the west coast to Durban, where it is more common in winter.

The white musselcracker has the broad, heavy head of a prizefighter, and indeed this robust fish is renowned and respected among rock anglers as a tough customer. The array of teeth inside the thick-lipped mouth is formidable: a 'pavement' of crushing molars of several sizes and, at the front of each strong jaw, four prominent incisors. Each central pair of incisors is enlarged and curved, the upper pair projecting over the lip and clearly visible.

The primary victims of this display are black mussels, whose tough shells are no match for the gluttonous white musselcracker. The fish's diet also includes sand mussels, molluscs, redbait, crabs, lobsters and small fish.

This is normally an unsociable species which swims singly or in pairs, except when spawning takes place in winter and spring; then musselcracker are found in shoals, and are vulnerable to over-fishing.

Adults of this species can darken or lighten their colouring to blend in with their immediate surroundings, whether sandy sea bed or mussel-strewn rock reefs. The brightly coloured young often shelter in tidal rock pools.

Known as 'white musselcracker' in the Western Cape, and 'brusher' in KwaZulu-Natal, the species is also referred to as 'musselcrusher', 'white biskop' and 'silver (or white) steenbras'. Its flesh is tasty, though inclined to be tough in large specimens. Some people regard the head as a particular delicacy.

BLACK MUSSELCRACKER
Poenskop *(Cymatoceps nasutus)*

Size: Length averages 75 cm, but can reach 1,3 m.
Colour: Large specimens sooty grey or black above and on flanks; belly pale. Medium-sized black musselcracker are lighter and may have several cross-bars down each flank. Juveniles are greenish brown with numerous paler blotches.
Most like: White musselcracker (Sparodon durbanensis), but the black musselcracker is darker, heavier and rather more full-bodied.
Habitat: Rocky reefs, ranging from the shoreline to depths of 100 m, often in caves or below overhanging ledges. Dislikes discoloured water and sensitive to temperature changes, avoiding cold currents.

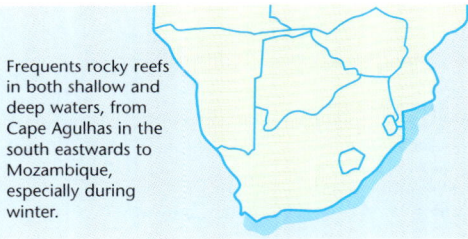

Frequents rocky reefs in both shallow and deep waters, from Cape Agulhas in the south eastwards to Mozambique, especially during winter.

The black musselcracker looks a tough customer, and so it is, for though not speedy it will fight doggedly at the end of a fishing line, thumping its ungainly head back and forth in an attempt to break free. It is a popular angling fish of many aliases, among them 'black steenbras', 'biskop', 'musselcrusher' and 'blue musselcracker'—depending on where they occur on the southern African coastline.

This is one of the larger seabreams, with a very robust body and well-developed, spinous fins. The powerful jaws are set with both conical teeth and rounded molars, and the mouth is surrounded by thick, fleshy lips. With age, the snout develops into a large fleshy projection or 'nose' that extends forward over the mouth.

The black musselcracker is a solitary and aggressive species that feeds mostly on invertebrate reef organisms. Its strong teeth are prefectly able to cope with large, tough, shelled animals such as crabs, lobsters and sea urchins.

This musselcracker becomes increasingly abundant along the east coast during winter—a time that coincides with its spawning period. Juveniles are quite plentiful in subtidal pools and gullies of the Eastern Cape.

Unfortunately the numbers of this great fighting fish have diminished considerably along the southern African coast over the years.

Marine fishes

SLINGER

Slinger *(Chrysoblephus puniceus)*

Size: Length 30-85 cm, specimens at the lower end of this range being much more common.

Colour: Rose-red, spotted with iridescent blue, and with a narrow, blue bar just below each eye. Fins translucent pink, the tail fin with an orange tinge.

Most like: Could be confused with immature specimens of the dageraad, *Chrysoblephus cristiceps*, but has fewer scales and more rakers on the gills.

Habitat: Rocky sea beds, from 20-100 m deep, and the seas immediately above them.

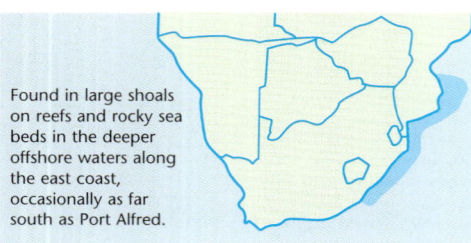

Found in large shoals on reefs and rocky sea beds in the deeper offshore waters along the east coast, occasionally as far south as Port Alfred.

The attractively coloured slinger is an important food fish in KwaZulu-Natal and southern Mozambique: one that is in danger of over-exploitation by deep-sea anglers equipped with sophisticated equipment such as echo-sounding devices to detect shoals. The very word 'slinger' (a name used worldwide for this species) refers to the action by which these fish are thrown into boats in large numbers.

Because of the inroads commercial fishing has made on this fish's numbers, marine reserves have been established in some of its breeding grounds in an effort to stabilize dwindling populations.

Slingers are deep-bodied fish with a high, steep 'forehead' and a little hump immediately above the eyes (prominent in older specimens). A single, spiny dorsal fin runs the length of the back, the anal fin is about half as long, and the large tail fin is deeply forked. The rather small mouth has both canine teeth and molars. The wide diet of this species is taken both from the sea bed (shrimps, crabs, squid, mussels and other bivalves) and from mid-water (tiny planktonic organisms sifted from the water with the help of the gill-rakers).

These fish form large, straggling shoals sometimes found among reefs on rocky sea beds in association with santer (*Cheimerius nufar*). Spawning takes place in summer, when slingers are most abundant and catches reach a peak.

The slinger is an excellent table fish.

SANTER

Santer *(Cheimerius nufar)*

Size: Length up to 75 cm.

Colour: Bright silver but pinkish above and white below. On each flank, four to five broad, vertical, reddish bars that are very evident in young specimens but faint in adults. Irregular dark specks on the back. Fins pink, the anal and pelvic fins having a bluish sheen.

Most like: Two other species of santer found along the west coast, *C. gibbosus* and *C. barnardi*, but *C. nufar* can be distinguished from the former because it lacks the small black dot at the rear of the dorsal base, and it doesn't have the dark red blotch present at the base of *C. barnardi's* dorsal rays.

Habitat: Rock and coral reefs, to a depth of 80 m.

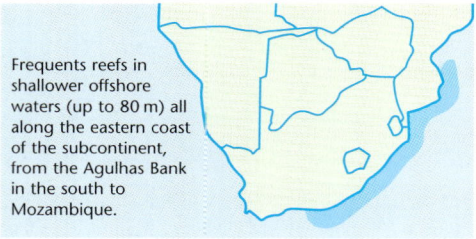

Frequents reefs in shallower offshore waters (up to 80 m) all along the eastern coast of the subcontinent, from the Agulhas Bank in the south to Mozambique.

A supposed resemblance to the colourful army uniforms of times past has given this striped species its alternative name, soldier. However, when this fish dies, it rapidly fades to almost white, and this accounts for the name *witvis* used for it in the Cape. There is something gruffly sergeant-majorish in the appearance of the santer, with its low-slung, tight-lipped, pointed mouth and enormous, glaring eyes, which are set in a steep profile.

The silhouette of the santer is almost oval, but with a flattened underside. The long, single dorsal fin has high spines in front; the largish tail fin is slightly forked. The jaws are set with canine teeth and several rows of other, cone-shaped teeth.

Santer parade in loose shoals in the vicinity of reefs, sometimes in the company of slinger (*Chrysoblephus puniceus*), foraging for fish, squid and small crustaceans.

Adults rarely venture close inshore, except when there is stormy weather at sea. However, the young are well known for their habit of sheltering in estuaries and other protected inshore waters where they grow to adulthood. Spawning occurs in summer.

The santer is an excellent table fish. It is caught mainly in the deep sea, rarely from the shore.

Marine fishes

ENGLISHMAN

Engelsman *(Chrysoblephus anglicus)*

Size: *Length up to 80cm (and occasionally up to 1m in warmer, northern waters of the distribution area).*

Colour: *Pink to reddish, with a bluish sheen caused by the blue spot on each scale of the upper flanks. Belly paler than upper body. There are six to eight red, vertical bars on each flank. Fins pink.*

Most like: *Two species of soldier bream, Argyrops filamentosus and Argyrops spinifer, but the dorsal spines of the Englishman are much shorter.*

Habitat: *Warm offshore coastal waters ranging in depth from 20m to 100m.*

In shallow and deeper offshore waters along the east coast, sometimes ranging as far south as Port Elizabeth. Abundant off the KwaZulu-Natal coast during summer.

The flushed, choleric looks of John Bull, the English stereotype, are said to be reflected in the appearance of this species. Quite apart from its colour, the almost vertical head (with its large, glowering, golden eyes) and high-arched back are certainly distinctive and give this fish its own particular character.

Conforming, perhaps, to the stereotype implied in its name, the Englishman is not particularly gregarious although it may forage in small groups, or else singly. Spawning takes place in summer, and it is at this time that the species is most plentiful.

Though it occasionally strays as far south as Port Elizabeth, the Englishman is better known in the warmer waters of KwaZulu-Natal and Mozambique; even so, it is unfamiliar to rock anglers and spearfishermen because of its relatively deep-water habitat. It is regularly caught by line fishermen, however, and its flesh is considered very good to eat.

There is a long, single, spiny dorsal fin, a shorter anal one and a largish, forked tail fin. The rather small mouth is equipped with canine teeth and several rows of molars.

The Englishman's diet consists of shrimps, crabs, molluscs, squid and sometimes small fish. It can reach a weight of six kilograms.

YELLOWBELLY ROCKCOD

Geelpens-klipkabeljou *(Epinephelus marginatus)*

Size: *Can reach 1,5m in length.*

Colour: *Greyish to dark brown, with irregular white blotches on back and flanks, as well as on dorsal fin. Underparts and chin deep yellow to whitish. Fins may be edged in yellow or orange.*

Most like: *The brown-barred rockcod, but the latter is much smaller, has dark, vertical bands down each flank and does not have the yellowbelly's white blotches.*

Habitat: *Coastal waters off rocky shores, from very shallow water to a depth of 200m.*

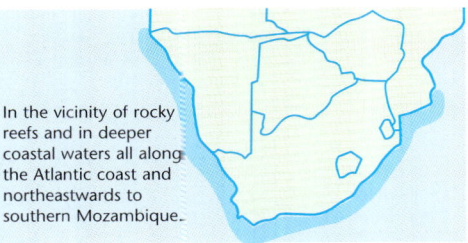

In the vicinity of rocky reefs and in deeper coastal waters all along the Atlantic coast and northeastwards to southern Mozambique.

The yellowbelly rockcod is a robust fish with a discerning appetite: it likes nothing better than a lobster, which it swallows whole. Powerful acid secretions in the stomach soften the shell and enable digestion to take place.

This is one of the largest, and probably the best known, rockcod species found in local waters, and is eagerly sought after by anglers and spearfishermen. It is both aggressive and tough: a specimen hooked and landed will stay alive for hours unless summarily finished off with a knife.

The forepart of the single dorsal fin is prominently spined; the rayed rear part is symmetrically matched by the anal fin. The tail fin is rounded and brushlike. Gill-covers are equipped with extremely sharp, bristly rakers that should be avoided, for an injury is painful and could cause blood-poisoning. The mouth has large canines at the front and rows of fine teeth that can be depressed, folding backwards

Lobsters are the most important of the crustaceans eaten by the yellowbelly rockcod, which also preys on fish that cruise the bottom of the sea; the rockcod's typical foraging technique is to wait in ambush, darting out from the cover of a rock cave or mass of seaweed, among which it is well camouflaged.

Spawning takes place in winter, a time when the species is most abundant. The young shelter in tidal rock pools, their 'nurseries'.

Marine fishes

LIMESPOT BUTTERFLYFISH

Eenkol-vlindervis *(Chaetodon unimaculatus)*

Size: Length up to 20 cm.
Colour: Lime-yellow, with a circular black spot (extending downwards to become tear-shaped in older specimens) on either side of the body, just below the long, spiny dorsal fin. A black vertical bar runs down either side of the head, passing through the eye; a thinner black stripe borders the trailing edges of the dorsal and anal fins.
Most like: Zanzibar butterflyfish which is similar in size and colour, but lacks the black stripe on the tail and anal fins, and has a white or bluish band around the dorsal spot.
Habitat: Coral reefs in coastal, tropical waters from 5 to 25 m deep. In summer, on rocky reefs in subtropical waters as far south as Port Alfred.

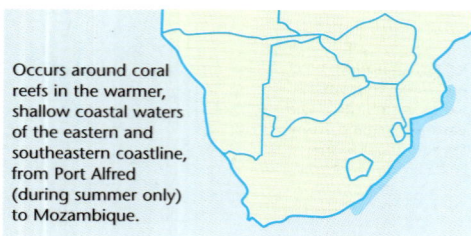

Occurs around coral reefs in the warmer, shallow coastal waters of the eastern and southeastern coastline, from Port Alfred (during summer only) to Mozambique.

There is indeed something of the delicate butterfly about this beautiful, round-bodied fish as it flits among the reefs in search of a meal: plankton, algae, small crustaceans and soft coral polyps. As it does so, it probes with its well-defined snout, which is able to extract food from crevices in the coral or among the rocks. The mouth is small but the teeth of both jaws are long, thin and bristlelike (the generic name *Chaetodon* means 'hair tooth').

Viewed head-on, the impression of this fish's fragility is heightened by its narrowness. In silhouette it is almost circular, except for the protruding triangle of its head, its tail fin and the little five-rayed pelvic fin.

Pairs of limespot butterflyfish (also known as teardrop butterflyfish) often forage together in the reefs. Gregarious by nature, the male and female of this species are apt to form a bond for life.

The limespot butterflyfish is among 20 species of *Chaetodon* found in southern African coastal waters, and among more than 90 species found worldwide. It is widely distributed in other oceans, where it is apt to be paler in colour, sometimes mostly white.

OLD WOMAN

Ou vrou *(Pomacanthus striatus)*

Size: Length up to 46 cm.
Colour: Adults mostly grey-brown, with the rear third of the body a paler blue-grey. Fins and tail are dark. Young specimens brown or black, with up to 20 narrow, vertical, blue-white stripes running the full width of the body.
Most like: Semicircle angelfish, but the latter's body is greenish brown, flecked with dark blue spots.
Habitat: Shallow coastal waters, among coral reefs or adjacent to rocky shores. Young are frequently found in intertidal rock pools.

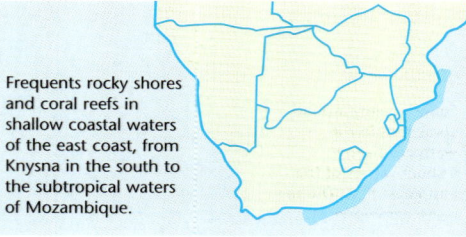

Frequents rocky shores and coral reefs in shallow coastal waters of the east coast, from Knysna in the south to the subtropical waters of Mozambique.

It seems bad luck that the species should bear such an unflattering popular name—derived from the drab colours paraded by adult specimens—when the young are decked in attractively striped finery. The stripes gradually fade away as the fish grows beyond a length of some ten centimetres. Such marked colour variation between young and old is a feature of other angelfish species too.

The old woman's body has a trim, compressed symmetry: oval, with matching dorsal and anal fins (quite large, spiny and soft) above and below the large, brushlike tail fin. A noticeable hump over the head tends to develop with age. The generous gill openings on either side of the head seem almost an extension of the small mouth, giving the illusion of a broad grin.

Like the limespot butterflyfish the old woman has slender, hairlike teeth that serve it well as it browses on the miniature marine life associated with coral and rock reefs: sea squirts, crabs, worms, sponges, the coral polyps themselves, plankton and other organisms.

Adult angelfish are gregarious, and in certain localities quite abundant, though the juveniles encountered in rock pools are extremely shy and dart for shelter at the first sign of danger. Like butterflyfish, they are popular recruits to aquariums. They are also caught for the table, for they make good eating.

Marine fishes

POWDER-BLUE SURGEON
Poeierblou-doktervis (*Acanthurus leucosternon*)

Size: Length up to 23 cm.
Colour: Light blue, with black head, white 'chin' or 'chest', bright yellow dorsal fin and white anal fin. Black tail, with vertical white panel. A short, bright yellow horizontal stripe just in front of the tail marks the position of the spine or 'knife' on either side.
Most like: The elongate surgeon, which is larger and has a darker yellow dorsal fin and a brown body, not blue as in the powder-blue surgeon.
Habitat: Coral reefs in shallow, tropical and subtropical coastal waters.

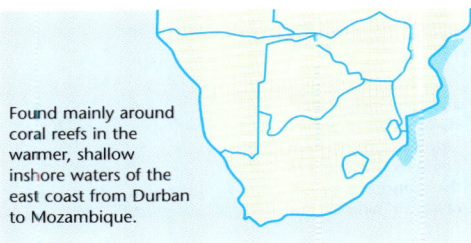

Found mainly around coral reefs in the warmer, shallow inshore waters of the east coast from Durban to Mozambique.

This bright and beautiful little fish, a prized specimen for the aquarium, harbours an unpleasant secret, the two knife-sharp spines hidden near its tail: these are its surgeon's lancets. Their hinged action is rather like that of a pocket knife. Normally they are sheathed in grooves, but under provocation they can be raised, and as the fish lashes its tail from side to side they can draw blood from a predator or from a human hand.

Surgeonfish (of which there are 19 species in southern African waters) have compressed oval bodies and thick skin covered in very small scales. The single, well-developed dorsal fin runs the full length of the back. The mouth is small, with close-set teeth in a single row in each jaw.

The powder-blue surgeon's diet includes assorted seaweeds as well as molluscs and crustaceans scraped off the inshore reefs the fish frequents.

This species, also called the painted surgeon, is apt to be solitary but, when breeding, shoals gather preparatory to pairing off and mating. Newly hatched fish are at the mercy of ocean currents, which may waft them long distances.

Powder-blue surgeons are wary of intruders and are quick to make themselves scarce in rock crevices or among the coral; but if escape is barred, the knives are out and predators must beware.

SERGEANT-MAJOR
Sersant-majoor (*Abudefduf vaigiensis*)

Size: Length up to 20 cm.
Colour: Body colour varies from white to pale blue or bluish grey, often with bright yellow upper flanks; five dark, vertical bars on each flank are normally present. Fins darkish and translucent.
Most like: Fourbar damsel which, however, has four, not five dark, vertical bars on its body and lacks the yellowish dorsal colouring of the sergeant-major.
Habitat: Inshore reefs, especially in the more turbulent waters of their upper reaches; also in the vicinity of harbour piers. Young specimens are found in tidal pools.

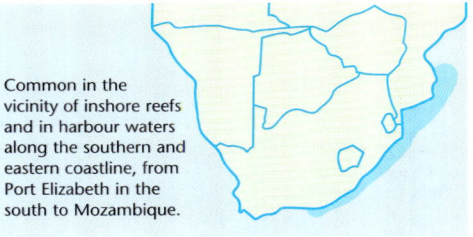

Common in the vicinity of inshore reefs and in harbour waters along the southern and eastern coastline, from Port Elizabeth in the south to Mozambique.

The military-style 'stripes' of this species give it its common name—but there is something sergeant-majorish, too, in the aggressive way the fish bullies its neighbours in an aquarium tank. It's a tough, sturdy, coarse-scaled little creature, often assembling in small shoals, and enjoying a wide range of foods, including crustaceans and seaweed, for which it forages by day only. Characteristic features of its appearance, in addition to its stripes, are the short, blunt, full-lipped snout and large, deeply forked tail fin.

The species is territorial in that a sergeant-major will have a particular home range and nesting area. Young specimens drift along the oceans in the company of an assortment of flotsam, under which they shelter. Marine life that attaches itself to such floating objects provides food for the juvenile sergeant-majors until such time as the convoy approaches a coral reef; then the fish leave the convoy to start their own colony.

The sergeant-major is one of about 45 species of damselfish found in southern African waters. Members of this abundant family are not fished commercially and, although the sergeant-major can be eaten, it is not highly regarded locally. It is, however, collected for aquariums despite its somewhat hostile nature.

The generic name *Abudefduf* is Arabic.

Marine fishes

BRIDLE TRIGGERFISH

Toom-snellervis *(Sufflamen fraenatus)*

Size: Length up to 50 cm.
Colour: Brown, paler underneath than on flanks. A pinkish yellow ring around mouth, and on either side a yellow stripe (the 'bridle') from corner of mouth almost as far as base of pectoral fin. Fins dark brown.
Most like: Black triggerfish, but lighter in colour and has the characteristic bridle marking on its head.
Habitat: Coral reefs and rock reefs to a depth of 100 m, in coastal waters on the east of the subcontinent, as far south as Port Shepstone.

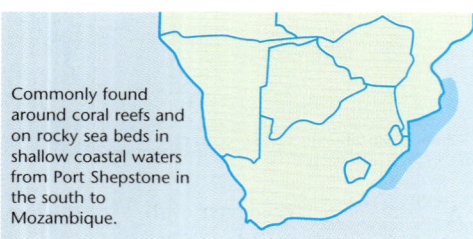

Commonly found around coral reefs and on rocky sea beds in shallow coastal waters from Port Shepstone in the south to Mozambique.

Tiny eyes, set behind grooves in an almost rhomboid-shaped brown body, don't enhance the appearance of the bridle triggerfish. But one feature of this species (and of other triggerfish) is particularly interesting: its front, three-spined dorsal fin. Normally this is folded back flat in a sheath; but when the fish is alarmed the fin is erected in a formidable spike, the whole apparatus held stiffly in place by the 'trigger' action of the second spine in its vertical position.

The sharp weapon is enough to deter most predators from venturing too close. At any hint of danger the triggerfish may head swiftly for a rock crevice, where the raised front dorsal fin also serves to wedge it firmly in its place of refuge.

The rear dorsal fin, and the anal one symmetrically placed below it, are soft and are rapidly waved from side to side by the fish to propel itself forward. The large, brushlike tail fin serves only as a rudder.

Within the small, pursed mouth are strong, white teeth that are used to good effect on the coral to scrape off seaweeds, crustaceans and coral polyps.

The bridle triggerfish is not regarded as edible (although it is not poisonous, as is the flesh of certain triggerfish species). It takes well to life in an aquarium.

Spawning takes place in summer and juveniles are often found amongst seaweeds.

GOLDBAR WRASSE

Goudstaaf-lipvis *(Thalassoma hebraicum)*

Size: Length up to 25 cm.
Colour: Background of torso green or blue, with two narrow, semicircular violet or darker blue stripes radiating back from the eye. A distinct white or pale yellow bar (known as the 'collar') runs down each flank from a position at the front of the dorsal fin to a position on the belly behind base of pectoral fin. Fins are generally the same colour as the body. The striking coloration of this species is less noticeable in fish that have died.
Most like: Crescent-tail wrasse, but the latter lacks yellow or white 'collar' and has a distinctive, red-edged, crescent-shaped tail fin. Goldbar wrasse has blue bands on face, and crescent-tail wrasse has pink-to-red bands.
Habitat: Coral and rock reefs of inshore waters; shallow tidal pools. Young specimens often found in such rock pools.

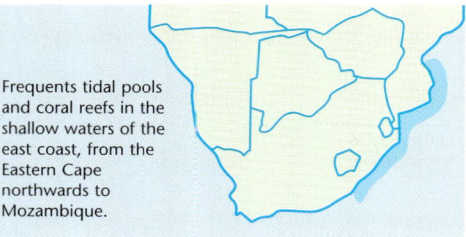

Frequents tidal pools and coral reefs in the shallow waters of the east coast, from the Eastern Cape northwards to Mozambique.

This handsome fish swims by moving its pectoral fins rhythmically up and down in the manner of wings, while its broad tail fin serves as a rudder directing it in and out among the rocks. The top and bottom rays of the tail fin are noticeably long, trailing behind the fish like a pair of underwater aerials.

The goldbar wrasse's diet consists largely of sea urchins, molluscs, corals and other tough or tough-shelled marine organisms. It is well equipped to cope with this assortment: inside its small mouth are strong teeth and, behind them in the gullet, grinding plates for crushing unwanted shell parts. All the discarded detritus is ejected back into the sea through the wrasse's gill openings.

This wrasse is found in large numbers among some reefs, probably being one of the most common wrasse species of the region. It shows strong territorial behaviour and will hostilely repulse intruders of the same species.

Young goldbar wrasse are regularly found in sheltered rock pools, and it is thought that these are used as spawning areas.

Wrasse are bony fish and, though edible, they are seldom caught for consumption. They do find their way into aquariums, however.

Marine fishes

BLACKSADDLE GOATFISH

Swartsaal-bokvis *(Parupeneus rubescens)*

Size: Length up to 45 cm.

Colour: Greenish to bronze, tinged with pink, and with translucent pink fins. A purplish band runs from eyes to snout; there is usually a black 'saddle' in front of the tail, and in front of this a light pinkish patch. Once dead the fish reddens all over. The young are silvery, without markings.

Most like: The Indian goatfish, but the latter has a blotch on its back and a number of bluish lines on its head, absent in the blacksaddle goatfish.

Habitat: Coastal waters, especially near reefs, to a depth of 80 m. Goatfish live at the sea bottom.

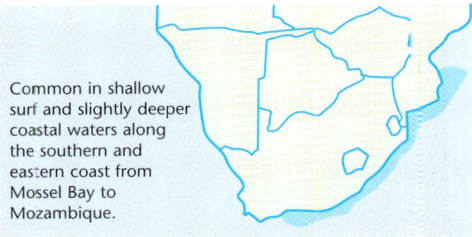

Common in shallow surf and slightly deeper coastal waters along the southern and eastern coast from Mossel Bay to Mozambique.

Two long barbels projecting from the chin, rather like a goat's beard, give the fish its name. They are sensors used to rake the sea bed, probing the mud in search of food: crabs, shrimps and other tiny crustaceans, as well as larval fish. During courtship the male and female goatfish face each other head-on, intertwining their barbels. When the barbels are not in use, they are neatly tucked back under the chin.

Some 16 species of goatfish, of which the blacksaddle is the most common, have been recorded in southern African waters. They all have prominent barbels, are often brightly coloured, and live close to the sea bed. Characteristic features include two dorsal fins, a deeply forked tail fin, a flattened underside, rather large eyes and fleshy lips. Each jaw is equipped with a single row of fine teeth. The underslung mouth is quick to scoop up any suitable prey discovered by the barbels while foraging.

The blacksaddle goatfish is not regarded as a true sport fish, but its taste is highly esteemed and it can be hooked with light bait. In the Far East, where it is an important source of nourishment, the species is fished commercially by means of traps and trawls.

Juveniles are known to swim beneath floating objects at sea and are therefore distributed far and wide by the ocean currents.

HONEYCOMB MORAY EEL

Heuningkoek-bontpaling *(Gymnothorax favagineus)*

Size: Length up to 1,5 m in southern African waters (up to 2,5 m in other areas).

Colour: Irregular dark brown spots separated by a network of yellow or white lines in a honeycomb pattern. This pattern continues into the mouth.

Most like: Reticulated moray eel, but the latter is much shorter and its dark brown blotches are bigger.

Habitat: In coastal waters, deep among coral and rock reefs.

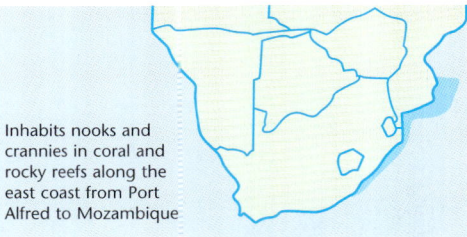

Inhabits nooks and crannies in coral and rocky reefs along the east coast from Port Alfred to Mozambique.

An unexpected encounter with a pugnacious honeycomb moray eel can be unnerving for a diver: if it cannot escape or feels its 'territory' invaded, the eel will attack, and its powerful bite (though not poisonous) may be deep and painful. In addition to sharp, prominent teeth on the jaws, it is armed with fangs along the middle of the palate.

Eels are indeed fish but the modifications to the 'normal' fishlike physique are extreme. The moray eel has large jaws in a small head, with a small pair of eyes set far forward. Tiny, circular gill openings are much further back, behind the mouth. The thick, cylindrical body, tapering at the tail, is smooth and scaleless, and covered in mucus.

What seems like a continuous fin (actually the dorsal and anal fins connected at the rear by a flap) runs, ribbonlike, from just behind the head to the tail and then back again underneath as far as the anal vent, which is positioned far forward on the body.

With its cryptic colouring the honeycomb moray lurks well camouflaged in reef caves and crevices, darting out to prey on octopuses (its preferred food) and assorted fishes. By consuming octopuses it is incidentally doing lobsters—high up on the octopus's own diet—a favour.

In its growth the young eel of this species may spend anything up to a year in a transparent larval stage before taking on the characteristic honeycomb patterning and coloration.

Unappetizing as it may appear, the honeycomb moray eel can, in fact, be eaten.

Marine fishes

River bream

Slimjannie *(Acanthopagrus berda)*

Size: Length up to 75 cm (90 cm in tropical waters), but usually no more than 30 cm.
Colour: Various shades of silvery grey or olive, depending on the habitat: in muddy waters, sometimes even black. Belly often lighter than upperparts.
Most like: Twobar seabream, but river bream lacks two vertical bars on face and black edges on dorsal and tail fin. The river bream is also larger.
Habitat: River estuaries and brackish waters.

Frequents inshore waters and estuaries along the east coast, from Mozambique down to Knysna.

A well-known, popular angling fish, the river bream earns its Afrikaans name *slimjannie* because of its cunning way with bait offered to tempt it: it usually resists bait in clear waters in broad daylight, or at any rate will treat it with the utmost caution, approaching with mouselike stealth. But it will be less cautious towards dusk and, if baited, will fight bravely to get off the hook.

River bream tolerate water that is only slightly salty, and specimens (especially young ones) have even been recorded in freshwater reaches some distance from the sea. Because this species is also partial to the turbid waters of estuaries, it is sometimes given the name 'mud bream'. (A third name, black porgy, is of American origin.)

River bream feed on a wide diet that includes shrimps, crabs, sea urchins, marine worms and molluscs; they have also been known to scavenge for dead or dying organic matter.

The species has a distinctive silhouette. The underside is flattened, the back steeply arched, the profile low and the snout pointed; the large tail fin is forked, although not deeply so. Both the long dorsal fin and smaller anal fin are prominently spined (the generic name *Acanthopagrus* means 'thorned bream').

Spawning occurs in winter near estuaries, where the young return soon after hatching.

The flesh of the river bream makes good eating.

River snapper

Rivier-snapper *(Lutjanus argentimaculatus)*

Size: Length 1-1,5 m.
Colour: Coppery red, but paler underneath and generally greenish brown on the back; the strong body scales have dark centres and white edges, giving a mottled look. After death the colour changes to deeper red. Young fish (those not more than 15 cm long) are paler than adults, with whitish horizontal bars on the flanks.
Most like: The twinspot snapper, which is purple-red to brown, and darker above. The latter also has a yellowish blotch on its gill-covers, absent in the river snapper.
Habitat: Younger specimens are generally found in small estuaries. The adults only occur over offshore coral and rock reefs, to a depth of 80 m.

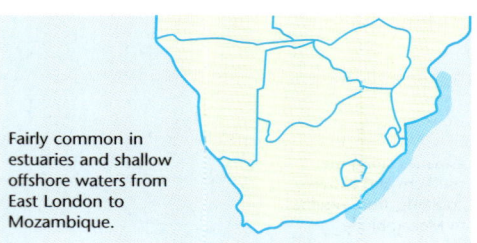

Fairly common in estuaries and shallow offshore waters from East London to Mozambique.

The word 'snapper' manages to describe this colourful fish's predatory appearance as well as its typical movement when hunting for food. The top of its head recedes sharply, and its large, wide mouth is arrayed with bands of strong, sharp teeth, those on the outer band being larger than the inner teeth. It is prepared to wait in ambush for long periods at a time, deep in the shadowy recesses of a rocky reef or river bank, and only when the unsuspecting victim (fish, lobster or crab) is nicely in position will it dart out to claim its dinner.

Known also as river roman, this fish is large, powerful and long-bodied, with a big, brushlike tail and spiny dorsal and anal fins. Young fish are able to tolerate estuarine water (with its reduced salt component) better than adults. And so, while spawning takes place in the ocean during the summer months and the eggs and fry are distributed worldwide by ocean currents, it is not long before the fry migrate towards the coast and the comparative protection of river mouths.

Because snappers are very tasty game fish, they are much sought after by ski-boat anglers and spearfishermen. They are voracious and eagerly accept just about any live bait on offer.

The unusual generic name *Lutjanus* of this species is Malayan in origin.

Marine fishes

Spotted grunter

Gespikkelde knorder *(Pomadasys commersonnii)*

Size: Length averages 40 cm, but can reach 80 cm.
Colour: Bright silver, the upper flanks tinged with iridescent colours; paler underneath. Upper half of body (though not head) has irregular rows of dark brown spots, extending onto dorsal fin. A larger black blotch on each gill. Fins are dark. Juvenile fish have no spots.
Most like: Silver grunter, but the latter lacks the spotted grunter's rows of small, dark brown spots. The silver grunter has about five broken bars running down each flank.
Habitat: Shallow coastal waters, estuaries and lagoons (including freshwater lagoons).

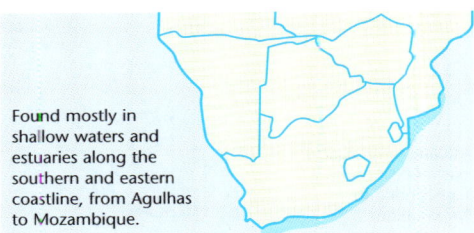

Found mostly in shallow waters and estuaries along the southern and eastern coastline, from Agulhas to Mozambique.

When a grunter is landed by an angler it emits a curious rasping 'croak' or 'grunt'. This is produced when the upper and lower pads of teeth in its gullet are ground together, the noise being amplified by the nearby air bladder. It has been proved that the fish 'grunts' in the same way under the water too.

Apart from its grunt, the spotted grunter is probably best known to anglers for its cunning habit of flushing out favoured food such as mud prawns, crabs and shrimps from their muddy shelters. First the grunter stands on its head, its tail fin often emerging above the surface in shallow water. Then, after taking in a large quantity of water through its gills, the grunter ejects the water forcibly through its mouth, 'blowing' the small marine creatures out of their holes.

The spotted species is the best-known local member of the grunter family. It has fleshy lips, a pointed snout, sharply receding forehead and a prominent, spiny dorsal fin. Anglers are wary of the exceedingly sharp edges to the front of its gill-covers.

This species cannot tolerate cold water. Sudden cold swells off the Cape coast have been known to kill grunters in large numbers. This fine game fish is especially sought-after by anglers during the summer 'grunter runs' in KwaZulu-Natal waters, and is very good to eat.

Spawning takes place in winter, mostly in the vicinity of river mouths.

White steenbras

Witsteenbras *(Lithognathus lithognathus)*

Size: Length averages up to 40 cm, but can reach 1 m.
Colour: Silvery grey, often with an iridescent sheen, and paler underneath. Between five and seven dark, vertical bars on each flank, distinct in young specimens but fading with age and often invisible in adults. Fins grey.
Most like: Westcoast steenbras but the white steenbras has a slightly longer head, and is not found north of the Gariep River mouth.
Habitat: Coastal waters, especially mud banks and shallow, sandy reaches, including river estuaries and lagoons.

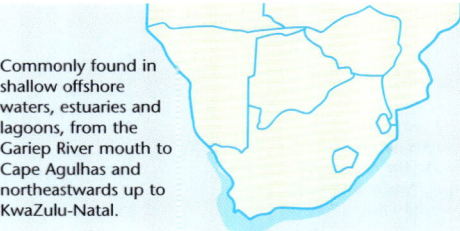

Commonly found in shallow offshore waters, estuaries and lagoons, from the Gariep River mouth to Cape Agulhas and northeastwards up to KwaZulu-Natal.

What brings this highly prized angling fish to shallow, sandy waters in great numbers are all the delicacies it likes best in its diet: prawns, shrimps, crabs, mussels, periwinkles and worms. It may patiently scour a single small area for minutes on end searching for these tiny creatures. And, like other 'grunters', it has a habit of blowing its prey out of their sea-bed burrows by forcing a strong jet of water through its mouth, its sharp snout well down in the sand and its waving tail sometimes visible above the surface. When hooked by an angler it may try the same blowing tactic on the bait, shooting it a metre or more up the line.

It is a vigorous fighter and when hooked will start off at speed with the hook in its mouth.

The thick, fleshy lips of this species—also known as the pig-nosed grunter—conceal rows of tiny front teeth and, further back, larger, powerful molars, hence the generic name *Lithognathus* meaning 'stone-jawed'. The word 'steenbras' derives from the Dutch *steenbrasem* or 'stone bream', a European freshwater fish that looks similar.

The firm, white flesh of the white steenbras makes an excellent meal. Spawning takes place from June to August in the sea along the east coast, and the young fish gather in river estuaries during spring.

Parasitic leeches are often found clinging to the bodies of these fish.

Marine fishes

CAPE MOONY

Kaapse maanskynvis *(Monodactylus falciformis)*

Size: Length up to 31 cm.

Colour: Bright silver, with iridescent sheen on dorsal and anal fins. Other fins grey. Young specimens duskier, with seven to ten dark, vertical bars on each flank.

Most like: Natal moony, but the Cape species (which is more common) is less high in proportion to body length. Juvenile Natal moonies have only two dark, vertical bars over the head.

Habitat: Shallow coastal waters, among reefs and around jetties and wharfs. Also in rivers.

Small shoals commonly found in shallow inshore waters from False Bay in the southwestern Cape to Mozambique.

Huge eyes and a large, brushlike tail fin emphasize the doll-like delicacy of the moony, so named because of its silvery sheen and silhouette—although in fact the body shape is more oval than circular and, with the addition of dorsal and anal fins, seems almost diamond-shaped (hence the alternative name 'kitefish').

These gregarious little fish frequent inshore reefs in small, dense shoals, and in clear water you may also see them from a jetty as they rise to the surface in search of plankton and other floating food.

Their compressed bodies are covered in fine scales that extend onto part of the fins; their mouths are small and downward-slanting, their teeth weak. In the gill membranes are special cells that can eliminate excess salts from the body—a useful adaptation enabling the moony to adjust to waters of differing salinity; it can live in fresh river water too.

The flesh of the Cape moony is edible and quite soft. This fish may be hooked with the lightest of tackle, and it will take the artificial fly as bait, like a trout; but there is so little of the fish that few are tempted by such a catch. (It is not a restricted species.) It makes an attractive addition to all aquariums, however.

Spawning takes place close to river mouths, the female fish producing relatively few eggs. The juveniles come into the estuaries in large numbers.

SOUTHERN MULLET

Suidelike harder *(Liza richardsonii)*

Size: Length up to 60 cm.

Colour: Entire body has silvery sheen, but darker on top and tinged white on flanks and belly. There is a yellow patch on each gill-cover.

Most like: The other 14 species of mullet in southern African waters, all of which are similar in shape and colour.

Habitat: Cool coastal waters, estuaries.

Frequently seen in shallow coastal waters off rocky coasts and sandy beaches from the Kunene River on the west coast to St Lucia in KwaZulu-Natal.

On the west coast many a southern mullet has ended up as *bokkems*, otherwise known as 'Cape biltong': fish that has been dried in the wind on long trestles, to be eaten with discriminating enjoyment by fishermen, local farmers and their labourers. The 15 species of mullet in southern African waters are very important to the commercial fishing industry, and many millions are caught locally each year, either in seine nets or, on the west coast, gill nets (which, as their name implies, trap the fish by their gills). Shoals of mullet are sighted from vantage points on high land and information about their movements is signalled to the fishing fleet.

The alternative name 'harder' aptly suggests this fish's firm flesh. The elongate body has a sharply pointed snout and a slightly forked tail fin. Two small and well-separated dorsal fins are other characteristics of all mullet. The scales are rather large and arranged in distinct rows. The lips are thin.

Though young southern mullet have pointed teeth, adults are toothless; food therefore is of the sort that is easily digested and consists of plant organisms such as algae. Sand, sometimes taken into the stomach as well, is thought to be an aid to digestion, which takes place not in the stomach but in a muscular crop.

Dense shoals of mullet are often seen off sandy beaches and rocky outcrops. Because they are able to tolerate water with low levels of salinity, large numbers of young mullet use estuaries and lagoons as nursery areas where they are preyed on by larger fish such as kabeljou and garrick.

Southern mullet are also sought after by fishermen for use as live bait.

Marine fishes

BARTAIL FLATHEAD
Balkstert-platkop *(Platycephalus indicus)*

Size: Length averages 50 cm, but can reach 1 m.
Colour: Brown or grey, with irregular dark patches, and whitish underneath. Fins yellowish with irregular spots, the tail fin with two or three horizontal black bars.
Most like: Half-spined flathead, but the latter lacks the distinctive horizontal bars which the bartail flathead has on its tail fin.
Habitat: Estuaries and shallow muddy coastal waters up to about 15 m deep.

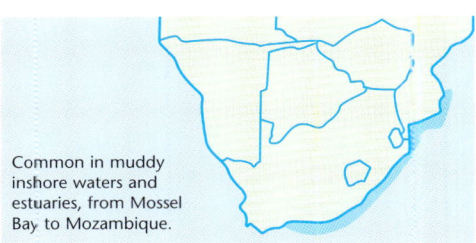

Common in muddy inshore waters and estuaries, from Mossel Bay to Mozambique.

There's nothing beautiful about the bartail flathead, but this long, thin, mud-coloured fish with small, close-set eyes at the top of its head is well equipped for foraging. It is a bottom-dweller, sometimes actually burying itself in the sand with only its eyes breaking the muddy surface; and in this camouflage it ambushes shrimps, mudhoppers, crabs, worms and other small marine creatures that make up its diet.

In its broad, flattened (but slightly ridged) head the lower jaw protrudes stubbornly beyond the upper one. The teeth are fine and threadlike.

The fins are large and spiny, and there is also an armoury of sharp spines on top of the head, which you should avoid when handling this fish. The black-and-white striped, squared-off tail fin at the end of the tapering body seems like a flag paraded by the cunning flathead.

It is not a particularly gregarious species but young specimens, which adapt well to differing levels of water salinity, may gather in estuaries, especially in mangrove areas, to feed and find shelter.

Despite its singular appearance the bartail flathead makes excellent eating. It is a fine angling fish as well, though its swampy habitat makes it difficult to locate. (Sometimes it is inadvertently caught up in fishing nets, trapped by its cranial spines.)

Bartail flatheads are found in warmish waters as far afield as Australia and Japan, and this particular species was first discovered off the coast of India—hence the *indicus* of the scientific name.

AFRICAN MUDHOPPER
Afrikaanse modderspringer
(Periopthalmus koelreuteri africanus)

Size: Length up to 15 cm.
Colour: Brownish to slate-grey, with irregular bluish white spots. The two dorsal fins are spotted with white and edged with a black, white-rimmed band.
Most like: The bigfin mudhopper, but the latter is larger, has more dorsal spines, and has a wider distribution than the African mudhopper.
Habitat: Estuaries and other muddy inshore waters; mud flats; rocks, roots and stems of mangrove plants.

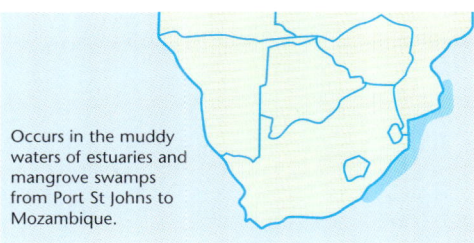

Occurs in the muddy waters of estuaries and mangrove swamps from Port St Johns to Mozambique.

The extraordinary, pop-eyed little mudhopper, known also as the African mudskipper, is one of the few amphibians of the fish world. Provided that its gills and at least a part of its body remain moist, it can stay out of water for long periods; oxygen is absorbed from this water and, in addition, the fish's surface blood vessels can take in oxygen directly from the air. Large pectoral fins with powerful muscular bases help the mudhopper to 'skip' over the mud flats and any slight obstacles in its path. A sucking disc, formed by the fusion of its pectoral fins, enables it to cling to solid objects.

The high, protruding eyes are close together at the very top of the large head. They provide virtually all-round vision and so give the mudhopper good advance warning of danger. Even on land it can make a surprisingly agile escape, hopping away more quickly than a man can pursue—a sudden jump followed by a series of smaller ones until it reaches the safety of water, or a mud hole.

Mudhoppers eat not only small marine creatures (shrimps, crabs, prawns and fish larvae) but also insects such as flies and mosquitoes.

Though obviously this fish is too small to be caught for food, it adapts well to life in an aquarium. In its natural state it is extremely territorial, and within the confines of a tank it is quite aggressive towards other members of the same species.

Before the breeding season, the male builds underground hideaways in estuaries, and the eggs are laid there.

Marine fishes

GALJOEN

Galjoen *(Dichistius capensis)*

Size: Length averages 35 cm, but can reach 80 cm.
Colour: Ranges from grey, silvery grey and silvery bronze to almost black, either uniform or blotched. Seven to nine dark, broad vertical bands may be visible on the flanks. The underside is lighter. Fins grey or blackish. Juveniles are unmistakeably banded.
Most like: Banded galjoen, Dichistius multifasciatus, which also has vertical bands, but is much smaller than the galjoen. The banded galjoen is found only off the east coast (occasionally as far south as Mossel Bay).
Habitat: Surf and rough waters along rocky shores.

Found in the vicinity of seaweed beds and rocky gullies in shallow coastal waters, from southern Angola southwards to Cape Agulhas and eastwards to Sodwana Bay.

South Africa's 'national fish' is a powerful swimmer much sought after by anglers because of its strong fighting ability when hooked. It is endemic to the waters off southern Africa.

The early Dutch settlers called it *galjoen* ('galleon') because of its resemblance to this lofty, sturdy sailing-ship. In silhouette the fish has a steeply arching 'forehead' and a high back which is surmounted by a dorsal fin in two parts: spiny in front, soft at the back. The undersurface is flat (except for the soft, tapering anal fin), and the large tail fin is very slightly forked.

The galjoen possesses a fine armoury of teeth inside its small, fleshy-lipped mouth, including bands of incisors and a set of crushing teeth in the gullet. It feeds on mussels, barnacles, redbait, seaweed and similar organisms associated with marine rocks.

Galjoen are not only very popular angling fish but are much sought-after table fish, although the taste of their white, black-veined flesh is too rich for some. In winter galjoen are much fatter, and consequently more desirable as table fish, than they are in summer.

The species was once much more common than it is today. However, the establishment of marine reserves has led to an increase in its numbers. To fishermen in the Eastern Cape this fish is known as 'highwater' or 'damba'.

HOTTENTOT

Hottentot *(Pachymetopon blochii)*

Size: Length averages 25 cm, but can reach 45 cm.
Colour: Bluish or brownish grey, sometimes with a bronze sheen, paler below. Fins dark.
Most like: The bronze bream, but the Hottentot is smaller and lacks the bream's iridescent blue colouring on the head. Hottentot also lack the bulge that forms between the eyes in older bronze bream specimens.
Habitat: Shallow and deep-water coastal reefs.

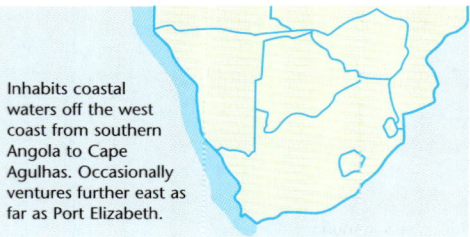

Inhabits coastal waters off the west coast from southern Angola to Cape Agulhas. Occasionally ventures further east as far as Port Elizabeth.

Khoekhoen (previously called Hottentot) beachcombers offered this fish in large numbers to the early Dutch settlers at the Cape, and so the fish were called Hottentot after the people who caught them. Today the species has a certain commercial value and is also quite popular as a game fish, being sought after both by anglers and spearfishermen (it can reach a weight of three kilograms).

It is the smallest of three members of the genus *Pachymetopon* ('thick forehead') found in southern African coastal waters: a trim creature with a plump, oval body, a large and rather forked tail fin, and a long, low dorsal fin.

Incisor teeth on the upper and lower jaws (but no molars) equip the Hottentot to tackle crabs and other small crustaceans, as well as redbait and worms, although seaweeds make up the major portion of its diet. As it grows older, the Hottentot eats mostly algae, which are more easily digested.

Hottentot are cunning and cautious when approaching a baited hook (redbait, shrimps and prawns are popular baits) but, once hooked, these strong swimmers will give anglers a good run for their money, darting off in all directions. The fish is a particular favourite of anglers on the shore or in small vessels, and with spearfishermen.

Bunches of small Hottentot are a common sight at fresh fish markets in Cape Town and along the west coast. The relative abundance of these fish, and their soft and juicy flesh, make them a popular choice among seafood lovers as table fish or at a braai.

Marine fishes

BLACKTAIL
Dassie *(Diplodus sargus capensis)*

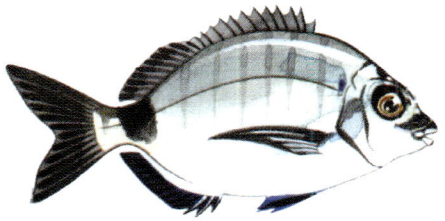

Size: *Length averages 25 cm, but can reach 45 cm.*

Colour: *Silver or greyish with dark fins, and with a black 'saddle' over the narrow section that connects the body and tail fin (the tail 'peduncle'). On each flank are four or five narrow, dark vertical bars that fade with growth and are hardly discernible in adults.*

Most like: *Zebra, Diplodus cervinus hottentotus, but the blacktail is smaller, has less fleshy lips and lacks the zebra's distinctive vertical bars.*

Habitat: *Rough inshore seas, especially off rocky coasts; it is also found around rock reefs deeper out to sea Blacktail rarely enter estuaries.*

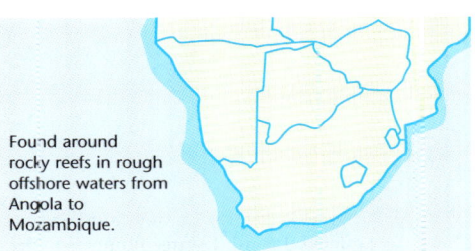

Found around rocky reefs in rough offshore waters from Angola to Mozambique.

Like galjoen, blacktail are popular game fish and are attracted to the same turbulent waters. (Their affinity to rock gullies and submerged ledges has earned them the name by which they are commonly known both in Afrikaans and English: 'dassie', that is rock rabbit.) Light-tackle anglers rate blacktail as great and plucky fighters, but they are generally regarded by spearfishermen as being too small a target. Attracted to drift baits of lobster, redbait or sardine cast into white-water gullies, they are described as both 'timid' and 'cunning'.

'Blacktail' refers to the so-called black saddle of this species and not to the forked tail fin itself. The body is oval, the snout sharp, and the bridge between the eyes is distinctly humped. A single, long dorsal fin is spiny in front, as is the much shorter anal fin. Inside the small, compact mouth are both big incisor teeth and rows of molars. The omnivorous diet of this species includes mussels, redbait, sponges and green and red seaweed.

In common with some other members of the seabream (Sparidae) family, blacktail change sex periodically. Spawning takes place throughout the year, though more commonly in winter and spring. Young blacktail find shelter in tidal rock pools.

This fish is good to eat although it is rather bony.

ZEBRA
Wildeperd *(Diplodus cervinus hottentotus)*

Size: *Length averages 30 cm, but can reach 50 cm.*

Colour: *Golden silver, with five broad, vertical black bars on each flank, and a sixth black bar on the head, passing through the eye. Fins dark. Juvenile specimens are often bright yellow between the bars.*

Most like: *Blacktail or dassie (Diplodus sargus capensis), but the zebra's stripes are strong and distinctive, and the zebra lacks the characteristic black saddle just in front of the blacktail's tail fin.*

Habitat: *Coastal waters up to 60 m deep; also in deep rock pools.*

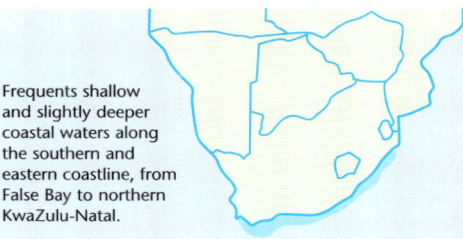

Frequents shallow and slightly deeper coastal waters along the southern and eastern coastline, from False Bay to northern KwaZulu-Natal.

The Afrikaans name *wildeperd* (wild horse) aptly describes this fish's fighting ability: when hooked in the turbulent, discoloured waters it enjoys, the fish runs this way and that, struggling to throw the hook as a wild horse might try to throw its rider. The fish is often caught in gullies by rock anglers, and offshore from ski-boats.

Closely related to the blacktail, the zebra shares many of its characteristics and habits, as well as being rather similar in general shape: oval with a pointed snout and a large forked tail fin.

It inhabits gullies and coves along rocky shores, coming in with the tide to feed on shrimps, crabs, redbait, mussels and, as it gets older, seaweed. The young are entirely carnivorous. It is also found less frequently in calm seas and off sandy beaches.

Zebra are less widely distributed than blacktail, rarely being found west of False Bay. They do not swim in large shoals, although small numbers may gather, especially during the breeding season in spring.

The species name *cervinus* means 'deerlike', a reference to the zebra's fleshy lips, which it uses to manoeuvre food into position for biting with its sharp incisor teeth.

The flesh of the zebra is generally thought to be good, although when landed from the sea it has a strong and unpleasant odour.

Marine fishes

WHITE STUMPNOSE

Witstompneus *(Rhabdosargus globiceps)*

Size: *Length averages 30 cm, but can reach 50 cm.*
Colour: *Silvery in general appearance but darker grey above, with usually six to seven dark, vertical bars on each flank. Fins dark.*
Most like: *Cape stumpnose, but the latter has a golden horizontal band along the middle of each flank, absent in the white stumpnose.*
Habitat: *Sandy sea beds of coastal waters, and often also near small rock reefs.*

Adults usually found over sandy sea beds, from southern Angola southwards to Cape Agulhas and eastwards to Eastern Cape.

Intrepid anglers of this popular game fish cast their lines on cold and moonless wintry evenings, for the white stumpnose prefers colder waters and will make for sheltered coastal areas such as estuaries when night falls.

Though the species is found from southern Angola to the Eastern Cape, it is most closely associated with the Western Cape; here the shoals gather regularly, to be culled by both net and line in great numbers, responding to almost any bait, but especially marine worms and shrimps thrown out to attract them. (Among anglers the fish has a reputation for cunning, however, in that it may take bait off the hook so gently that its presence is not felt at the end of the line.) It is a commercially important species.

The high, rounded head, large eyes and stubby nose of the white stumpnose are distinctive. The mouth contains four to eight rows of incisor teeth and several rows of strong molars that are well equipped to tackle a carnivorous diet of molluscs, crabs and other crustaceans. Young specimens try out their teeth on less tough fare such as prawns and other crustaceans, found in the estuaries where juveniles shelter, as well as on seaweeds, algae and sea grasses.

The white flesh of this species is soft and sweet, and is much in demand. (The fish should be well gutted before cooking: worms infest the intestines of rather a high proportion of white stumpnose.)

STREPIE

Strepie *(Sarpa salpa)*

Size: *Length averages 30 cm, but some may reach 40 cm; specimens from the colder waters in the western limits of its distribution range are apt to be larger.*
Colour: *Silvery, sometimes with a green or blue tinge; 8-10 narrow, yellow to orange horizontal stripes run from gill-covers to tail fin. Fins greyish.*
Most like: *Unlike any other fish.*
Habitat: *Shallow, rocky inshore coastal waters; also waters near harbours and piers; estuaries.*

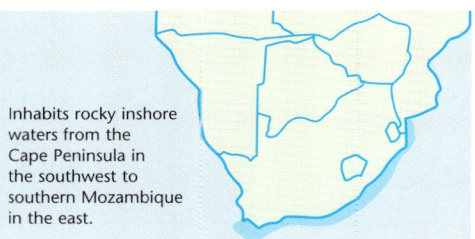

Inhabits rocky inshore waters from the Cape Peninsula in the southwest to southern Mozambique in the east.

Strepies, known also as karanteen, are beautiful, gregarious and extremely abundant little fish that irritate anglers by their eagerness to take the bait intended for more substantial victims. But vengeance is easily taken: strepies themselves make excellent bait, and to lure yellowtail and elf, for example, an angler may bait his hook with a live, not dead, strepie.

In silhouette the rather plump body of this fish is a shapely, elongated oval, with a strongly forked tail fin. Inside the small mouth are sharp incisors, used for cutting through the red seaweeds that make up the bulk of the adult strepie's diet. Young members of the species have different, pointed teeth; they feed on small crustaceans, plankton and other small marine organisms.

Juveniles tolerate low levels of salinity in water, and estuaries and shallow coastal waters serve as their nurseries. Adult strepies are powerful swimmers and commonly frequent gullies where the water surges strongly in and out between the rocks.

Freshly caught strepie can make a tasty meal, although the flesh soon softens and is not liked by all.

Because this fish is one of the most abundant plant-feeding species in southern Africa, it is considered an important link in the marine food chain. Spawning takes place from April to September, and the eggs and larvae are dispersed south of KwaZulu-Natal by the Agulhas Current.

The strepie also occurs in the Mediterranean Sea.

Marine fishes

NATAL STUMPNOSE

Natalse stompneus *(Rhabdosargus sarba)*

Size: Length averages 40 cm, but can reach 80 cm.
Colour: Bright silvery grey, with horizontal rows of gold (formed by the golden centres to each scale) covering the body. Belly and fins on underside of body a strong yellow, although the colour loses its brilliance with age.
Most like: White stumpnose and Cape stumpnose, but grows larger than these two species, and its yellow colouring is very distinctive.
Habitat: Mostly shallow water, especially surf near rock reefs and outcrops; also the brackish water of estuaries.

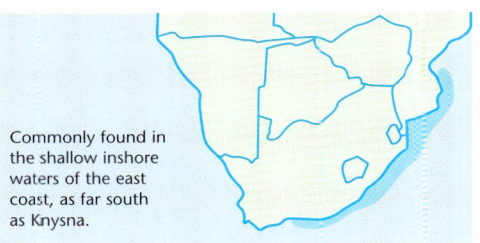

Commonly found in the shallow inshore waters of the east coast, as far south as Knysna.

The Natal stumpnose is the most beautiful of the stumpnose species swimming in southern African waters. Elsewhere in the world it is commercially trawled and netted; here it is only caught for sport—and a fine game fish it is too, being a robust and powerful fighter that will take most baits (although it prefers crustaceans such as the mussels, oysters and sea lice that make up its natural diet). It also falls prey occasionally to spearfishermen.

Rock anglers often fish for Natal stumpnose at night—and especially on an incoming tide—when they come close inshore. These stumpnose are most abundant in summer, but are not found in such plentiful shoals as white stumpnose. The fish become sexually mature at about 25 cm, and spawning takes place during winter near river mouths where the young take shelter for the first year of their lives.

In appearance this fish is deeper-bodied than the white stumpnose, its back arching high up from a rounded snout. It has a formidable array of teeth: in addition to the heavy, cone-shaped incisors and several rows of molars, there are grinding teeth in the gullet. The dentition of this fish enables it to make light work of the toughest molluscs and crustaceans.

Connoisseurs prize the flesh of Natal stumpnose, which can be prepared in a number of ways. It is particularly delicious smoked.

STONEBREAM

Stinkvis *(Neoscorpis lithophilus)*

Size: Length averages 35 cm, but can reach 50 cm.
Colour: Silvery grey, sometimes with about seven dark, vertical bands on the flanks. Fins dark grey.
Most like: Similar in colouring to the galjoen, but the latter is larger, has thicker lips, a more pronounced and rounded snout, and more prominent spines in the dorsal fin.
Habitat: Turbulent waters off rocky coastlines, and in rocky gullies.

Found in the shallow, turbulent waters of rocky shores from False Bay to Mozambique.

Fish that feed almost exclusively off seaweed, such as the stonebream, give off an unpleasant odour when they are gutted, hence the stonebream's Afrikaans name *stinkvis*. But, were it not for the black lining to its intestinal cavity, the stonebream might face a far more acute problem: light filtering through into the gut would act on the chlorophyll in the seaweed and, in the resulting chemical reaction (called photosynthesis), oxygen would be released, distending the belly and causing it to explode.

Stonebream, among the largest of the vegetarian fish in local waters, prefer red seaweed, but will eat green seaweed too.

This endemic species likes the same sort of rough waters as galjoen; and although it is not as good a fighter, it does provide sport for anglers. The young find sanctuary in tidal rock pools, where you can see them in summer.

Viewed sideways on, the stonebream is shaped rather like a rugby ball: a deep, full-bodied oval, with matching dorsal and anal fins towards the rear, and a large, slightly forked tail fin. (This symmetrical silhouette resembles that of the Cape moony, a much smaller fish, and this resemblance sometimes leads people to mistake it for a moony.) The body is covered in very small scales.

Scientifically the stonebream is very much on its own in southern African waters, being the only species representing the family Scorpididae.

In spite of its offputting smell when dissected, this fish is perfectly edible.

Marine fishes

SOUTH AFRICAN PILCHARD

Suid-Afrikaanse pelser *(Sardinops sagax)*

Size: Length up to 28 cm.
Colour: Silver, with a bluish tinge on the back; belly whitish. There is a horizontal row of small dark spots along each flank. Fins yellowish.
Most like: Round herring, white goldstripe or Madeiran sardinelle, but the South African pilchard is distinguished from these by its shallower body and the row of small spots along each flank.
Habitat: Cool, coastal waters, usually some kilometres from the shore.

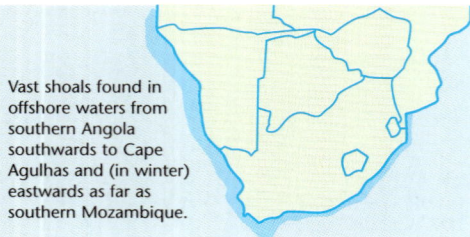

Vast shoals found in offshore waters from southern Angola southwards to Cape Agulhas and (in winter) eastwards as far as southern Mozambique.

Sardines—crammed into tins for consumption—are simply young pilchards; but in South Africa, at any rate, the word 'sardine' is often also used for the adult fish. This is especially true in KwaZulu-Natal, where the annual 'sardine run' is a famous phenomenon. It takes place in June and July, when huge, dense shoals of pilchards travel northeastwards up the coast in search of drifting planktonic food, and are driven towards the surf by a combination of ocean currents and hungry predators.

On these occasions the authorities remove most of the shark nets, which would otherwise be damaged by the predacious hordes. Swimming is then forbidden, but the sight of thousands of silvery pilchards churning in the shallow water tempts local residents to wade in up to their knees for a free haul. Seabirds have a field day too.

This annual migration is caused by the pilchards' need for warmer waters in which to spawn. When the shoals later return southwestwards, they include the juveniles—the true 'sardines'.

Pilchards are narrow, elongated fish with a sharply forked tail fin. They are filter-feeders: they have no teeth, but well-developed rakers in the gills sift out plankton from seawater that enters the mouth and exits through the gill slits.

These fish are of major commercial importance, and are caught extensively by trawlers off the west coast. Despite their great numbers, South African pilchards are vulnerable to over-exploitation.

CAPE ANCHOVY

Kaapse ansjovis *(Engraulis japonicus)*

Size: Length up to 13 cm.
Colour: Pale brown, with silvery belly and a silver, horizontal stripe along each flank in specimens more than 6 cm long.
Most like: Thorny anchovy (Stolephorus holodon), but the Cape anchovy is longer and rounder.
Habitat: In food-rich temperate coastal waters ranging to a depth of 200 m.

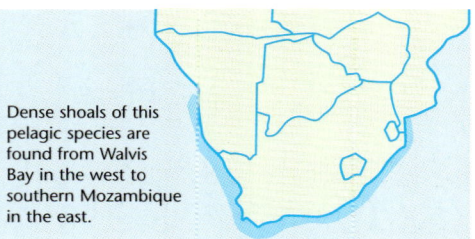

Dense shoals of this pelagic species are found from Walvis Bay in the west to southern Mozambique in the east.

You won't have any trouble identifying anchovies: with their projecting snouts and underslung mouths these little fish are the chinless wonders of the marine world.

The shoals of anchovies which abound in southern African waters have an amazing sense of community spirit: when leading members of a feeding shoal have had their fill of plankton, they turn to one side and move to the back, allowing those next in line to forage. When danger threatens, in the shape of predators such as tuna, for instance, the entire shoal will suddenly contract into a tight mass; and it is only the stragglers, and those with the least social discipline, that are likely to be picked off.

While there is a big demand for anchovies to be bottled as a savoury paste, or tinned as cocktail-snack adornments, the majority caught by purse-seine nets are destined to be dried and ground into fish meal. The drying process is made more complicated by the fish's high oil content.

The anchovy's body is elongated and almost cylindrical, the tail fin deeply forked, the single dorsal fin short and positioned in the centre of the back. The fins are without spines. Inside the mouth are very small teeth and, when the anchovy feeds, it swims with its mouth held open, allowing assorted plankton to drift inside. The numerous long and slender rakers on the gill act as traps for plankton too.

Anchovies are always found in schools, never singly, and they are probably the most numerous of all fish species.

Anchovies lay their eggs in estuaries, where they hatch about three days after fertilization.

Marine fishes

MACKEREL

Makriel *(Scomber japonicus)*

Size: Length averages 30-40 cm, but can reach 50 cm.
Colour: Upper body bright, metallic blue-green and marked with small, dark oblique streaks; lower body silvery white, often with small, dark spots. Fins yellowish, translucent.
Most like: A distinctive species, although somewhat similar to Rastrelliger kanagurta, which occurs northwards from Durban. The latter has golden-striped flanks and a black spot on the pectoral fin.
Habitat: Inshore coastal waters, mostly near the surface, though also found in depths of up to 300 m.

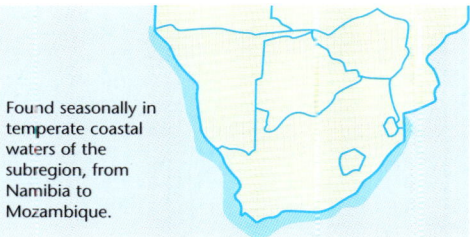

Found seasonally in temperate coastal waters of the subregion, from Namibia to Mozambique.

Mackerel travel in vast shoals and when, as sometimes happens, they make for shallow water, they are fair game for even the most amateur angler and are caught in their hundreds. Dedicated fishermen value fresh mackerel more than any other fish bait for catching bigger fish.

The mackerel's elongated body is a streamlined cylinder, even more torpedolike when the two dorsal fins and the anal fin are folded back. The tail fin is strongly forked. The eyes are partly covered by fatty tissue. Inside the mouth are rows of fine, conical teeth on each jaw, and there are more teeth on the palate. Mackerel live on a diet of plankton, filtered from surface water; the tiny planktonic organisms include shrimps, crab larvae and small, bony fish.

In calm weather members of a mackerel shoal may browse with the tops of their heads out of the water, and make a loud noise as they do so.

Spawning takes place during the winter months, and the fish's seasonal migrations are thought to be connected with its breeding habits.

Mackerel flesh makes good eating when fresh, but it goes soft rapidly after death. Although it is a commercially important species, and is protected by a 'closed season' from September to December, the mackerel is of little importance to spearfishermen.

This species is widely distributed elsewhere in the oceans. The first specimen to be described was found off Japan, hence the species name *japonicus*.

MAASBANKER

Maasbanker *(Trachurus trachurus capensis)*

Size: Length up to 70 cm.
Colour: Silver, but bluish green, olive-green, grey or nearly black above, paling to silvery white below. A black spot on each gill-cover. Fins are darkish.
Most like: African maasbanker which, however, is smaller and has dark blue rather than bluish green to grey colouring on its dorsal side. The African maasbanker also has a wider, thicker tail fin.
Habitat: Cold coastal waters, from the surface to depths of up to 400 m.

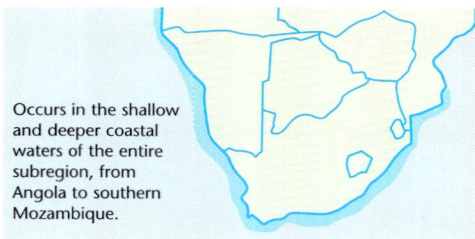

Occurs in the shallow and deeper coastal waters of the entire subregion, from Angola to southern Mozambique.

Wise anglers handle the maasbanker, or horse mackerel, with care, for a curving row of raised scales, hard and sharply spiked, extends along either flank of this fish from gill to tail fin. Hence the nickname *hakiesdraad* (barbed wire) applied to the species by Cape fishermen.

A protruding lower jaw and eyes partly covered by fatty tissue give the maasbanker a curious, almost surly expression. This is a well-streamlined, elongated fish, with a deeply forked tail fin, two dorsal fins (one situated immediately behind the other) and a long anal fin. The mouth is soft and papery, and the teeth in each jaw are small, fine and hairlike.

Maasbankers congregate in shoals that move to the surface at night to feed on krill (tiny phosphorescent shrimps) and other marine organisms, and descend to deep waters during daylight hours.

They are an important commercial species, especially on the west coast where they are caught in trawl nets.

Anglers regard maasbanker, like mackerel, as an excellent bait with which to tempt large game fish. As a fish for the table it has the advantage over mackerel of being firmer-fleshed and thus easier to preserve in good condition. Seals and dolphins also find its flesh to their liking.

The species owes its common English and Afrikaans name to the early Dutch settlers, who saw a resemblance between it and a freshwater fish frequenting the shallow banks of the Maas River in southern Holland.

Marine mammals

Marine mammals are the end-product of an extraordinary evolutionary journey—from the oceans, where all animal life originated, to dry land and then, in a second process of painstaking adaptation, back again to the sea. Like other mammals, they breathe air directly into the lungs and suckle their young, but they manage to do this in a watery environment. They are also warm-blooded, unlike fishes.

Some species of marine mammals have adapted more completely than others. Seals are perfectly able to exist temporarily ashore, but a whale stranded on the shoreline soon dies, suffocated by the weight of its own collapsed body. Only in the sea is its enormous bulk buoyed up and its breathing apparatus free to function normally.

The forelimbs of marine mammals have become flippers (with no visible sign of individual digits or fingers). So have the hindlimbs of seals. Whales have lost all outward trace of hindlimbs—and yet the degenerate remains of them survive in the form of isolated splints of bone embedded in the flesh.

In the sea otter (a marine mammal species not found in southern Africa) the furry mammalian tail survives intact. In whales it has been transformed into a powerful swimming and steering apparatus, consisting of two fleshy, horizontal 'flukes' or lobes.

All marine mammals must return regularly to the surface to expel stale air and take in a fresh supply. Probably their most remarkable characteristic, however, is the ability to remain under water for long periods and to reach great depths: some whales dive to 1 000 m in search of food. Nor do they suffer ill-effects on their rapid return to the surface—whereas when human divers are subject to such sudden decompression they risk the acutely painful and potentially lethal condition known as 'the bends'.

Whales, dolphins and porpoises belong to the mammalian order Cetacea. Some members of this order, including the killer whale—a well-known inhabitant of southern African waters, the sperm whale and all dolphins and porpoises, have teeth. Others are toothless; these are the 'baleen whales' that strain food particles from the sea by means of horny plates hanging down from the upper jaw. The southern right whale is a baleen whale, and so is the largest animal that has ever lived, the blue whale.

Seals are members of the order Pinnipedia ('wingfooted' creatures). The walrus, found only in the northern hemisphere, also belongs to this order.

Identifying marine mammals

Size
All whales are impressively large, but the southern right whale, at 14-18 m long, is noticeably larger than, for example, the killer whale (8 m).

By comparison the common dolphin is a mere 2,5 m from snout to tail.

Dorsal fin
The killer whale has a tall, prominent dorsal fin. Dolphins (with the exception of the southern right whale dolphin, a deep-sea species seldom seen close inshore, and the finless porpoise of Pakistan and India) have dorsal fins too. So do most whale species found in our waters.

Tail and flippers
Whales and dolphins have horizontal tails consisting of a pair of flukes.

All marine mammals have front flippers, those of the killer whale being especially large and paddlelike. Seals have rear flippers too. The Cape fur seal's flippers can be turned forwards under the body when the seal comes ashore, enabling it to 'walk' with relative ease and climb over rocks; the southern elephant seal is much clumsier on land as its hind flippers cannot bend forwards at all.

Ears
Whales and dolphins have no visible external ears, nor does the southern elephant seal. The fur seal has short but clearly visible ears.

Fur
Cetaceans are hairless except for a few bristles that may be present on the chin and snout of calves. Seals have a sleek covering of fur that is velvety on newborn pups. As their name implies, fur seals are distinguished by a thick, soft fur coat, hidden under coarser guard hairs.

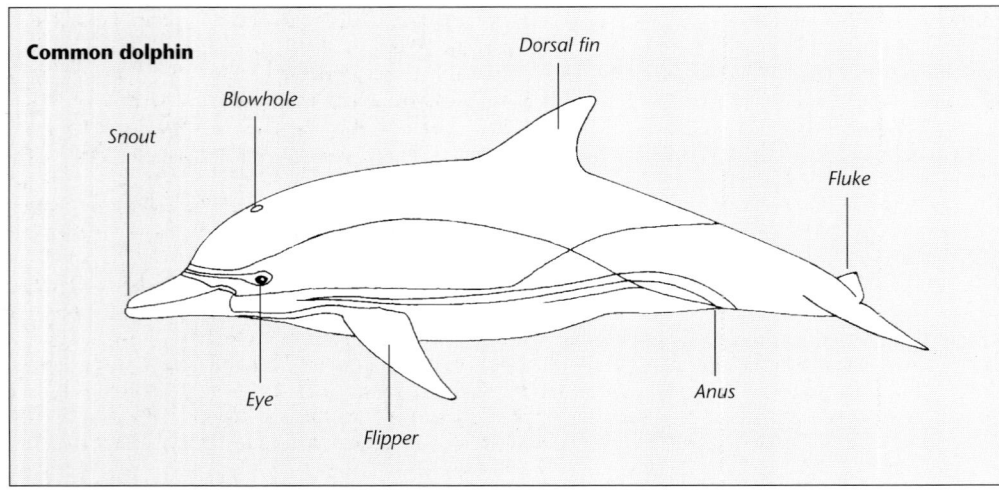

Marine mammals

SOUTHERN RIGHT WHALE

Suidelike noordkaper *(Eubalaena glacialis)*

Size: Length averages 15 m, but can reach 18 m.
Colour: Ranges from deep blue-black colour to pale brown, sometimes with irregular whitish markings on a portion or all of the upperparts, and sometimes also a whitish area towards the rear of the belly.
Most like: Humpback whale, which is about the same size but has distinctive scalloped flippers and a dorsal fin.
Habitat: Various sheltered bays along the southern African coast, from May to October, during which time the whales mate and calve.

Found in sheltered bays along the entire southern African coastline, but increasing numbers have been monitored in the sheltered bays of the southern and western coast.

Instead of teeth, southern right whales have a thick curtain of horny black plates, known as baleen, growing from the palate. (Baleen is the 'whale-bone' of commerce and, in the days when women wore corsets, it provided essential underpinning to the female figure.) The whale feeds by opening its mouth and using its hairy-fringed baleen plates to sieve huge quantities of plankton—krill and other small floating organisms—from the sea. It forces the water through the baleen plates by means of its enormous tongue.

Right whales were so called because, to the 18th century whalers, they were the 'right' species to hunt: they had a high oil content, their baleen plates were long, and they floated after being killed. The southern species is distinguished by its high, arching jaw and the 'bonnet' on the front of the upper jaw: crusty, cornlike outgrowths (called 'callosities') of skin that also occur in lesser amounts elsewhere on the head. (Their purpose is unknown, and they tend to be infested with parasites.)

Females of the species weigh close to 100 tons on average, males rather less. They plough through the water at a maximum speed of some nine kilometres per hour. Being mammals, they must regularly rise to the surface to take in air—this they do through a V-shaped blowhole at the top of the head. It is the expelled air, damp and foul-smelling, that forms the visible 'spout' shooting up at least five metres.

Southern right whales are usually found in pairs though they have also been sighted in small, usually family, groups.

KILLER WHALE

Moordvis *(Orcinus orca)*

Size: Length (m) averages 8 m, but can reach 9,75 m; (f) averages 7 m, but can reach 8,5 m.
Colour: Black back and sides, white belly. A lozenge-shaped white mark just above (and behind) each eye; large white ventral patch extending onto flanks; greyish 'saddle' over back, behind dorsal fin.
Most like: False killer whale (Pseudorca crassidens), but the latter is solid black, with a blaze of grey on the chest, is more slender, and has a more tapered head.
Habitat: Cooler marine waters wherever suitable prey abounds; sometimes enters shallow bays.

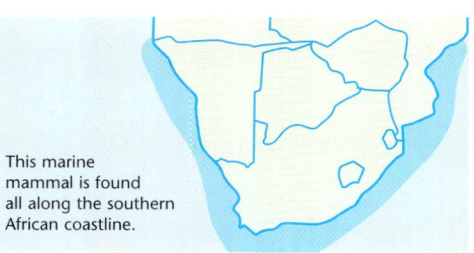

This marine mammal is found all along the southern African coastline.

Though there are no records of attacks on man by a killer whale, this formidable species is the terror of the high seas, for its victims include not only fish but seals, turtles, penguins and even other whale species. It may weigh as much as eight tons, is capable of speeds of 40 km per hour, it can stay under water for up to half an hour at a time, and it tends to travel, and often hunt, in packs of 4-50 individuals, the males swimming at a distance from the females and their young.

The body is beautifully streamlined, with a rounded snout and a prominent dorsal fin that is a distinctive feature. (A mature male's dorsal fin may be almost two metres high.) The 40-50 strong, sharp teeth inside the wide-angle mouth point backwards and inwards, meshing efficiently together to tear prey apart. As in other whales, the body ends in a pair of horizontal tail fins or 'flukes'.

In common with other mammals, female killer whales suckle their offspring. The mammary glands are enclosed in a pocket enabling the young to feed without the interference of seawater.

Killer whales are the largest members of the dolphin family and, like their smaller, friendlier cousins, use a sophisticated echolocation system—involving the use of supersonic vibrations—both to communicate with one another and to search out their prey. Like dolphins, too, they have proved highly receptive to training by man.

Marine mammals

COMMON DOLPHIN
Gewone dolfyn *(Delphinus delphis)*

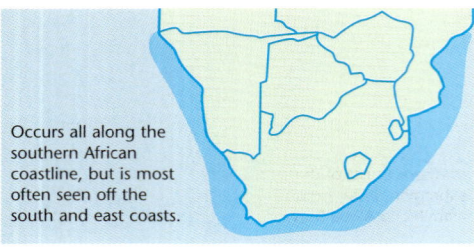

Size: Length averages 2,1 m, but can reach 2,6 m (males slightly larger than females).
Colour: Black or dark brown back, white belly; on each flank a horizontal figure-of-eight pattern formed by large, buffy grey or yellowish grey oval and, behind it, another such marking in grey. Assorted grey or buff stripes on sides and lower portion of body. Patterning variable from one specimen to another.
Most like: Striped dolphin, but the common dolphin is slightly smaller and lacks the striped dolphin's prominent dark stripe running along each flank.
Habitat: Warmer inshore and offshore waters.

Occurs all along the southern African coastline, but is most often seen off the south and east coasts.

DUSKY DOLPHIN
Vaaldolfyn *(Lagenorhynchus obscurus)*

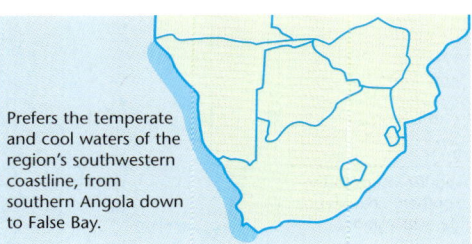

Size: Length averages 1,6 m, but can reach 2,1 m.
Colour: Snout, back, dorsal fin and tail flukes black; flippers grey; the slightly curved dorsal fin black with a narrow, white trailing edge. Flanks black with two greyish-white blazes at mid-flank pointing tailwards. A pale grey line runs from each eye to the front of the flipper. Underparts white except for the extreme rear, which is black.
Most like: Heavisides dolphin (Cephorynchus heavisidii), but the latter is much smaller and its dorsal fin is triangular, not curved like the dusky's.
Habitat: Temperate and cool waters.

Prefers the temperate and cool waters of the region's southwestern coastline, from southern Angola down to False Bay.

Common dolphins are not as popularly sought after for aquariums as bottlenosed dolphins are, largely because of their high mortality in captivity. They do, however, share the bottlenosed dolphins' ability to communicate with a wide 'vocabulary' of audible clicks and cries, squeaks and whistles.

The common dolphin's markings are beautiful and complex. The dorsal fin is a dark, backward-sloping triangle, often marked with a whitish inner triangle. The head tapers at the front of the elegantly streamlined body to form a long beak that seems set in a genial half-grin. Within it are about 200 regularly spaced teeth.

This dolphin feeds primarily on fish (pilchards and herrings), but also on squid and, more rarely, crustaceans. Although it has been recorded at a depth of 280 m, it routinely feeds at about 40 metres. The dive seldom lasts longer than five minutes; usually dolphins gambol at or near the surface, taking air in through their blowholes about twice a minute. They can accelerate to a maximum speed of about 50 km per hour.

Social animals, they live in schools numbering 20-200—even thousands—in which there is a distinct hierarchy: males dominate females, and within each sex a ranking order exists too. An injured member of the school will be helped and protected by colleagues; and a mother will tend her single offspring with devotion, always keeping it close by her. She gives birth to her young in the summer, after a gestation period of 10-11 months.

Like other dolphins, duskies are the acrobats of the oceans and, if you're lucky, you may see them accompanying a ship, riding the waves thrown up by the bow, or playfully leaping out of the water and turning somersaults.

Dusky dolphins cruise the waters off southern Africa, between Angola and False Bay, throughout the year, their movements often dictated by the availability of food and the water temperature.

The dusky is streamlined like other dolphins, and has a short snout that is distinctive of the genus *Lagenorhynchus*; this 'beak' is much smaller than that of the common dolphin (*Delphinus delphis*). The dusky's dorsal fin is lower and less broad than the common dolphin's, and it also has fewer teeth—between 100-128.

While the habits and social behaviour of dusky dolphins have not been fully studied, they are known to swim in schools ranging from a handful to several hundred. In southern African waters a school averages between four and five animals; however, schools of up to 300 have been recorded. The dolphins are thought to feed mainly on anchovies and squid.

The young are born in the summer months (tail-first, as are all dolphins), after a gestation period of about nine months.

Although not hunted commercially, dusky dolphins are sometimes caught inadvertently in fishing nets.

Marine mammals

SOUTHERN ELEPHANT SEAL

Suidelike olifantrob *(Mirounga leonina)*

Size: Length (m) 4,5-6,5 m, (f) 3-4 m; weight (m) 3 500 kg, (f) 350-800 kg.

Colour: Males vary from dark greyish brown in the spring breeding season to a rusty greyish brown by mid-January; females vary from grey-brown to reddish brown. The belly of both male and female is paler than the rest of the body.

Most like: Northern elephant seal, found only in the northern hemisphere. The southern species is slightly bigger, though the male's nose is shorter.

Habitat: In summer months, coastal stretches and offshore islands that have smooth, flat beaches.

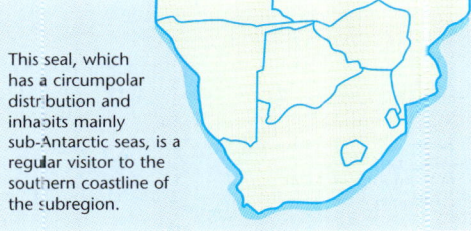

This seal, which has a circumpolar distribution and inhabits mainly sub-Antarctic seas, is a regular visitor to the southern coastline of the subregion.

In the breeding season it is not his heart on his sleeve that the enormous male elephant seal proudly wears, but his tumescent, air-filled proboscis on top of his head.

Biologists are unsure whether the elephant seal creates this balloonlike effect as a sexual display to impress the female, or merely to amplify his mating call—it is also used to threaten unwelcome opponents. When the mood is over, the wrinkled and deflated 'trunk' hangs down over the mouth. The female elephant seal lacks such an appendage.

True seals, of which the southern elephant seal is one, are distinguished from Otariidae ('sea lions' or fur seals, such as the Cape fur seal) by having no visible external ears. The rounded, whiskered head surmounts a body made shapeless by its ample padding of blubber, without which the seal could not withstand the sub-Antarctic seas where it lives for much of the year.

Both flippers are equipped with strong claws.

Southern elephant seals eat a prodigious amount of fish in inshore waters to fuel their huge bodies (fully grown males weigh as much as 3 500 kg, while their female counterparts weigh up to 800 kilograms).

These seals come ashore to moult, to mate and, among females, to give birth to pups. During the mating season a hierarchy is soon established among the males, though not before challenge and counter-challenge has taken place (with proboscises inflated).

CAPE FUR SEAL

Kaapse pelsrob *(Arctocephalus pusillus pusillus)*

Size: Length (m) 2,15 m, (f) 1,56 m; weight (m) 187 kg, (f) 75 kg.

Colour: Males dark brown; grey around neck; undersides lighter. Females vary from light brown to brownish grey.

Most like: Sub-Antarctic fur seal (Arctocephalus tropicalis), but the latter is much smaller and has a distinctive white 'bib' running from just above the eyes down to the chest.

Habitat: Sloping beaches and rocky headlands on the mainland; offshore islands and rocky islets.

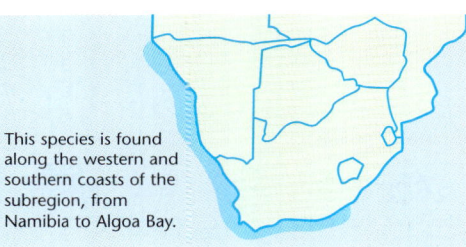

This species is found along the western and southern coasts of the subregion, from Namibia to Algoa Bay.

A visitor to Robben Island in 1608 reported the presence of Cape fur seals in 'unspeakable numbers'. In the years that followed, commercial exploitation (both for blubber and the valuable fur) vastly reduced the southern African population, and laws were introduced to stop indiscriminate sealing. Today, the population of these mammals stands at well over one million, and there are some 23 localities on or off the Namibian and South African coasts where the seals still breed.

The Cape fur seal spends about one third of its life ashore. It walks, albeit clumsily, on all four flippers; the undersides of the front pair of flippers have soles with 'prints' and these help it to cross wet rocks without slipping. The edges of the front flippers are scalloped, while the rear flippers are clearly divided into clawed digits.

A feature of the fur seal's head is the narrow, pointed ears, which extend for about two to three centimetres.

Squid, octopus and rock lobster form a small part of the fur seal's diet, but by far the largest intake is fish, including hake, anchovies, pilchards, mackerel and maasbanker.

The breeding season begins in late October. Males are fiercely territorial, establishing their terrain even before the females come ashore and mating takes place. The young pups learn to swim in safe rock pools; at seven months they are able to remain at sea for several days.

Marine invertebrates

When you are asked to name the creatures that inhabit the watery world of the oceans, your first thought is usually of fishes, dolphins and whales, but in reality these form no more than five per cent of the inhabitants of the seas. The dominant animals belong to a vast sub-kingdom scientifically known as the invertebrates.

The phrase 'as spineless as a jellyfish' accurately describes the basic characteristic of this sub-kingdom of marine animals, as all of them have no bony backbone or internal skeleton. While this single feature separates them from fishes, frogs, reptiles, birds and mammals, they nevertheless consist of many groups that differ radically one from another in body form.

Most invertebrates are mobile or free-swimming, yet many others are fixed permanently to rocks or buried in the sand. Some have obvious animal features such as head, trunk and tail, eyes and limbs, while others could easily be mistaken for plants or flowers. This incredible diversity of structures and features makes the task of describing the group far more difficult than describing fishes or marine mammals.

Within the invertebrates there are 27 major groupings known as phyla (phylum in the singular). These include single-celled animals, sponges, jellyfish and corals, flatworms, roundworms, segmented worms, insects and crabs, starfish and their allies, sea snails and sea squirts. All these groups are very different from one another and most contain many thousands of species.

How to recognize some major groups

Porifera *(sponges)*
Once thought to be plants, sponges appear mostly as flat, colourful, encrusting patches on intertidal rocks. These are rough to the touch and have a number of surface holes through which water filtered by the sponges flows out. The holes through which the sponge sucks the water in are too small to be seen by the naked eye.

Their skeletons are made of lime or silica and/or a fibrous material known as collagen or spongin, the latter serving duty as the familiar bath sponge. The porosity of these sponges enables them to hold water.

Some sponges look like delicate goblets; others resemble elaborate fans or branching trees.

Coelenterates *(corals, jellyfish and anemones)*
The members of this group can be subdivided into two major forms: the 'medusae'—free-swimming animals which carry tentacles with protective stinging cells, such as jellyfish and bluebottles, and polyps—organisms that remain fixed in one place, such as anemones. Corals are polyps surrounded by an external skeleton of a hard stony material into which the polyps retract for protection.

Still other forms within this group include the much-branched, bonsailike colonial gorgonians or sea fans found attached to deeper reefs and the colourful, featherlike sea pens seemingly planted in the sandy floor of the ocean.

Platyhelminths *(flatworms)*
You can easily recognize members of the platyhelminth group because they are very thin and flat. As they move they appear to flow or slide over the surface of the rock. Although they are related to rather nasty parasites such as tapeworms and liver flukes, marine flatworms tend to be exquisitely coloured with extravagant patterns.

Nematoda *(roundworms)*
The type of roundworms you are most likely to see are the parasitic variety, which are larger than their non-parasitic cousins; the latter, which usually live among the sand grains on beaches, are seldom seen because they are so small. They are, nevertheless, quite abundant and are very important inhabitants of wet sand. Typically they are unsegmented, long and slender, uniformly thick, and pointed at both ends.

Annelida *(segmented or bristle worms)*
Segmented worms of the sea are related to earthworms, and you can recognize them by the rings or segments into which their bodies are divided. Each segment has its own muscular system, reproductive and excretory organs.

Most of these marine worms have soft, lobelike limbs, often with long bristles. Some are free-moving, living among mussels and seaweed and in the sand. Others live in tubes constructed of sand grains, broken shells and debris. From an opening at the upper end of the tube, these worms often extend beautiful, featherlike structures, which they use to trap minute food particles suspended in the water.

Arthropods *(crabs, rock lobsters and prawns)*
This is the largest phylum in the animal kingdom. Marine arthropods, known as crustaceans, all have a hard shell or exoskeleton (external skeleton) and jointed legs. If you're trying to identify one, look to see if it has two pairs of antennae—most marine crustaceans do. The head and thorax are fused to form the cephalothorax, although the abdomen is distinct and consists of six segments. There are usually five pairs of walking legs, of which the first one, two or three pairs are modified to form nippers. In crabs the abdomen is bent under the cephalothorax.

Strangely enough, barnacles are also crustaceans. Each little animal sits in a protective box made of several hard plates permanently fixed to the rock. When covered with water, the barnacles extend feathery limbs to strain food particles from the water.

Molluscs *(snails, slugs, oysters, mussels and octopuses)*
All members of this group have very soft, smooth bodies, although the body is typically encased in a shell. The body is not segmented but is divided into a head, muscular foot and trunk, which contains the internal organs. Some molluscs have a spiral shell, while others have two concave shells encasing the whole animal.

Squid and cuttlefish have shells within their body. (The cuttlefish shell, often seen along the drift-line of a beach, is widely used in bird cages for pet birds to nibble on.) Some molluscs, such as sea slugs and

Marine invertebrates

Distribution of marine invertebrates

Tidal zone	Species (inner)	Species (outer)
High-water spring tide		Moue crab
		Common shore crab
		Sea louse
		Periwinkle
High-water neap tide		
		Common shore crab
		Long-spined limpet
		Sea anemone
		Cushion star
Mean sea level		
	Common octopus	Sea anemone
	Common shore crab	Sea cucumber
	Long-spined limpet	Common sea urchin
	Cape turban shell	Spiny starfish
	Brown mussel	Cushion star
	Black mussel	
Low-water neap tide		
	Common octopus	Black mussel
	Giant chiton	Sea anemone
	Long-spined limpet	Sea cucumber
	Cape turban shell	Common sea urchin
	Cape rock oyster	Spiny starfish
	Brown mussel	
Low-water spring tide		
	Common octopus	Black mussel
	West coast rock lobster	Redbait
	Giant chiton	Sea anemone
	Abalone	Sea cucumber
	Cape turban shell	Common sea urchin
	Cape rock oyster	Spiny starfish
	Brown mussel	

octopuses, are naked, having no shell. Sea slugs are often very brightly coloured and their bodies usually have fingerlike projections swaying in the water. These are the animal's gills.

The octopus and the oyster demonstrate the incredible diversity of forms found within this single group of invertebrates, for both are molluscs.

Echinoderms *(starfish, sea urchins, sea cucumbers)*
The members of this phylum are exclusively marine. They are all slow-moving creatures, with no head and therefore no front or back; they are divided into five equal sections. With the exception of the sea cucumber the bodies are covered in chalky plates located just under the skin. The mouth is usually on the undersurface of the body, and most forms are covered with spines of varying sizes and lengths.

Sea cucumbers are unusual members of the group as they have soft but rather warty skins and have evolved an elongate, cucumberlike body form. You won't have any problem identifying the five-armed brittle star as an echinoderm; but the only evidence to identify the pansy shell as part of this group is the five-petalled flower pattern on its shell.

The feather star is also a member of the group. It has five pairs of arms, which are very flexible, as they sway in the water or propel the animal about. You will usually see a feather star holding onto a rock with a fingerlike grasp.

Tunicates *(sea squirts)*
As the name implies, the internal organs of these creatures are enclosed in a shapeless 'tunic' or bag. There are two distinct openings, which in some are located at the top of turretlike protuberances. Some forms are colonial, appearing like smooth, slimy yet colourful patches on the undersides of rocks. The openings are usually paired, or sometimes a ring of smaller ones surrounds a larger pore. This feature immediately distinguishes the sea squirts from encrusting sponges.

Marine invertebrates

COMMON OCTOPUS
Seekat (Octopus vulgaris)

Size: From a few centimetres to 3,5 m between tips of outstretched tentacles.
Colour: Varies from pale cream to dark charcoal-grey. Rapid colour changes may occur uniformly over the whole body, or in regular or irregular patterns, depending on the mood of the animal.
Most like: The rarer southern Cape octopus (Eledone thysanophora), but the common octopus has a double row of suckers along the length of each arm, while the southern Cape octopus has only one row. Octopus species are difficult to tell apart.
Habitat: Under rocks and in crevices in tidal pools from mid-low spring tide level downwards.

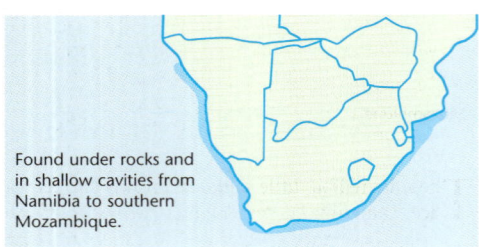

Found under rocks and in shallow cavities from Namibia to southern Mozambique.

The octopus is truly the wise man among animals without backbones. It has a very highly developed brain, which is protected by a case of soft, bonelike material. It has an incredible ability to learn, as well as a good memory.

Although the octopus has the texture of a jellyfish, it is actually closely related to shell-bearing invertebrates such as snails. The soft, bell-shaped body has eight long arms joined at the base by a web. The mouth, in the centre of its underside, is armed with a powerful, parrotlike beak.

Octopuses live in shallow grottoes sometimes camouflaged with small stones and shells; often they leave remnants of their favourite foods—shellfish, rock lobsters and crabs—outside their lairs.

These creatures have large, well-developed eyes similar in construction to the human eye, but with a 180-degree range of vision. Masters of the art of camouflage, they're able to change colour to blend in with the background and, when threatened, they may eject a smokescreen of black ink into the surrounding water.

For all their highly developed senses, they are cold-blooded 'lovers'. Mating pairs sit quietly apart. The only sign of emotion is when the male extends an arm as if to stroke the female. In the arm is a sac of sperm, which he slips into the female's respiratory siphon.

WEST COAST ROCK LOBSTER
Kaapse kreef (Jasus lalandii)

Size: Body length averages 25-30 cm, but can reach 46 cm.
Colour: Reddish brown, often with tinges of purple or violet, particularly on the tail fan. The antennae have a series of pale pink bands.
Most like: East coast rock lobster but, as the names suggest, the two species have distinct distributional ranges. The east coast rock lobster has a distinct groove across the top of each abdominal segment, absent in the west coast species.
Habitat: Under rocky ledges and in kelp beds from low spring tide level to a depth of about 30m.

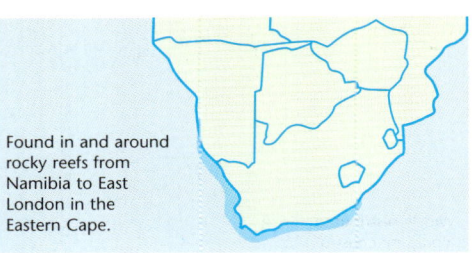

Found in and around rocky reefs from Namibia to East London in the Eastern Cape.

Mouth-watering west coast rock lobsters, much sought after by restaurateurs and seafood lovers throughout the world, have a particular delicacy of their own—black mussels. Such is this lobster's fondness for black mussels that it is the main force controlling the size of the mussel populations in our waters. However, these lobsters are fussy, selecting only those which they can open without too much effort. For this reason small lobsters will take small mussels, and large lobsters will take bigger ones.

In the cold Cape waters this species, known also as the Cape rock lobster, grows slowly, its carapace taking nine years to reach 80 mm—the minimum size at which it may be removed from the sea.

Rock lobsters reach sexual maturity at a carapace length of six to seven centimetres. Once mature, females grow much more slowly than males because they put most of their energy into producing eggs. As a result, more than 90 per cent of the commercial catch consists of males. Even these grow very slowly, taking 30 or more years to achieve a carapace length of 15 centimetres. This slow growth rate makes the rock lobster very vulnerable to overfishing.

Male rock lobsters are strongly attracted by moulting females, a fact some experts attribute to a chemical secretion from the female. While moulting, rock lobsters do not eat and therefore don't venture into lobster traps baited with food.

There is a definite hierarchy within communities of rock lobsters, with the largest members occupying the best crevices. So, if a diver removes the dominant individual from a crevice, it is likely to be occupied by a subordinate individual shortly afterwards.

Marine invertebrates

COMMON SHORE CRAB

Kuskrap *(Cyclograpsus punctatus)*

Size: Males up to 3,8 cm across the back, females up to 2,6 cm across.
Colour: Variable, usually reddish brown with white speckles, but ranging from buff, greyish, orange or salmon-red on rocks, to greenish brown, brown or violet in muddy areas.
Most like: Rock crabs, but smaller. Lacks the serrations found along the side of the shell of the Cape rock crab, and the mottled red, yellow and green coloration of the more active Natal rock crab.
Habitat: Under rocks and stones on the upper part of the shore, among matted weed on muddy sandbanks, or on mud flats near the mouth of estuaries.

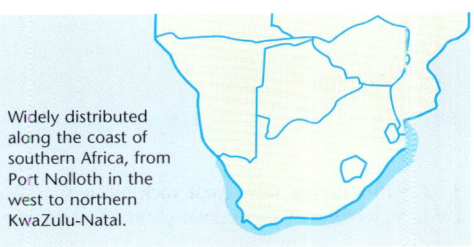

Widely distributed along the coast of southern Africa, from Port Nolloth in the west to northern KwaZulu-Natal.

An amazing characteristic of this shy little crab, probably the most common in southern Africa, is its ability to remain out of water for several days at a time. This does not mean that it is able to breathe air, but rather that it has developed an ingenious system which guarantees the essential supply of oxygen.

While submerged it breathes in typical crablike fashion, drawing oxygen-rich water through an opening at the base of each leg and circulating it over the gills and out through a hole at the base of the eyes.

When it is high and dry on *terra firma*, water from the gill chamber trickles from the exhalant opening and down the 'chest' of the crab to the inhalant pore at the base of the legs. A series of hairs and finely sculptured grooves increase the surface area of the chest region and guide the water to the base of the legs, resulting in its efficient re-oxygenation and re-absorption into the gill chamber.

To compensate for any water lost through evaporation, the inhalant openings are surrounded by a further dense fringe of hairs which can absorb water from the wet sand or mud surface and pass it to the gill chambers. To add to the ingenuity of the system the large nippers have small combs, which are skilfully used to clean both the hairs at the base of the legs and the 'hairy chest'.

MOLE CRAB

Molkrap *(Emerita austroafricana)*

Size: 2,5-3,5 cm long
Colour: Body almost uniform pink to grey; the antennae are bright pink.
Most like: Hippa adactyla, another type of mole crab, which occurs in the same area, but has a flatter, broader body and much shorter antennae.
Habitat: Along the water's edge of wave-washed sandy beaches in KwaZulu-Natal and Mozambique.

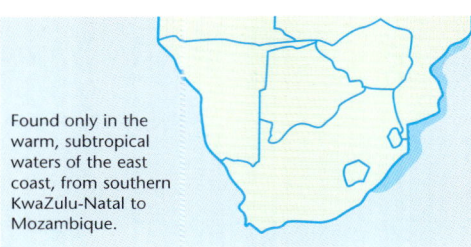

Found only in the warm, subtropical waters of the east coast, from southern KwaZulu-Natal to Mozambique.

These incredible little animals, known also as sea lice, can truly be described as the moles of the seashore. They bury themselves so well that they are seldom seen unless they are caught in a trap or net.

To ensure that they keep close to the water line and a continual supply of food, nature has equipped mole crabs with barrel-shaped bodies, which allow them to roll up and down the beach with incoming and outgoing waves. In this way they stay near the water's edge as the tide rises and falls. Having been 'dumped' by a wave, the mole crab digs itself into the sand so rapidly that when the wave recedes there is no sign of it.

The mole crab burrows into the sand with specially modified, spadelike legs that have become so adapted to digging that they are virtually useless for other activities such as walking or swimming.

An obvious threat to the mole crab is the sand around it, which could clog its gills, thus preventing adequate water circulation for breathing. However, nature has again come to this little burrower's aid, endowing it with a very long last tail segment that is fringed with long hairs and folded beneath the body to prevent sand from entering the gill chamber. As an extra measure of protection, the fifth pair of legs is long, thin and flexible and able to reach into the gill chamber to remove any sand particles which have managed to lodge within it.

The mole crab feeds by extending its long, hairy antennae across the sand surface to intercept food particles carried back by the retreating waves.

Marine invertebrates

MUD PRAWN
Moddergarnaal *(Upogebia africana)*

Size: Attains at least 5 cm in length.
Colour: Uniformly greenish brown.
Most like: Sand prawn, which occurs in cleaner sand, is off-white rather than greenish brown in colour, and has one greatly enlarged, shiny pink nipper.
Habitat: Mud flats and the muddy bottoms of estuaries, lagoons and tidal rivers.

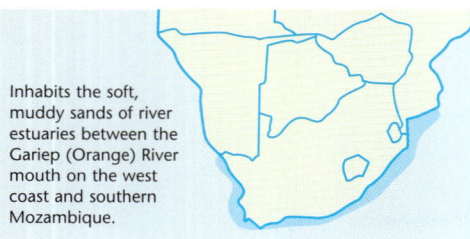

Inhabits the soft, muddy sands of river estuaries between the Gariep (Orange) River mouth on the west coast and southern Mozambique.

If you are a regular fisherman in southern African waters you will be quite familiar with mud prawns—a much sought-after bait collected by means of a prawn pump which is used to suck the creatures out of their U-shaped burrows in river estuaries.

The mud prawn is all but a prisoner of its dwelling and seldom leaves it because of its popularity as a potential meal to seabirds and fishes. In the comfort and safety of its home, the mud prawn continually beats its paddlelike swimmerettes (small, paired appendages on the underside of the abdomen) to create a current which draws water through the burrow. The water brings with it not only life-supporting oxygen, but also the mud prawn's sustenance—tiny particles of decomposing plants and animals, known as detritus.

In their usual estuarine habitat, mud prawns are sometimes exposed to flood waters with a very low salinity level. When this happens the prawns, unlike their sand prawn cousins, manage to survive by regulating their body fluids to maintain normal levels of salt in their blood.

Females mate immediately after they have moulted, a characteristic they share with all crabs, rock lobsters and prawns. Reproduction starts when the females are about 15 months old.

Although mud prawns have many natural enemies, the greatest threat to their survival is the wholesale destruction of their habitat by pollution, disturbance by bait collectors and the residential and recreational development which is taking place on an ever-increasing scale along the southern African coastline.

GIANT CHITON
Reuse chiton *(Dinoplax gigas)*

Size: Length up to 10 cm.
Colour: Shell plates eroded brown to grey and embedded in a tough, brown, leathery outer girdle tufted with brown hairs.
Most like: The other 26 or so chitons in the subregion, but giant chiton at least double the size of any other common species. The eroded shell segments and tolerance of sand are unusual features.
Habitat: Rock surfaces low on the shore, particularly in sandy crevices on flat reefs.

Distribution ranges from False Bay in the southwestern Cape to southern KwaZulu-Natal.

This armour-plated, limpetlike snail is a very slow-moving animal, capable of clinging very tightly to the surface of rocks and stones with its flat and muscular foot. Contrary to common belief, chitons do not hold firmly to a rock by means of suction. They do so rather by adhesion, which they accomplish by secreting slime, which forms a layer between the rock and the foot. To understand this force try to prise apart two sheets of glass that have a layer of water pressed between them.

The shell is made up of eight separate valves or plates which are articulated together in such a way that the animal can flex its body so as to fit snugly against the irregular surface of the rock.

This incredible characteristic, together with the slime, produces an efficient, airtight seal around the animal. If you are lucky enough to prise one off a rock it will immediately curl up like an armadillo in an effort to protect its soft vulnerable underside.

The body has a simple structure, but unlike most snails has no eyes or tentacles. To compensate for its lack of eyes, the chiton has developed a large number of simple, eyelike organs located in tiny pits on the plates; these can detect varying intensities of light.

Chitons are inactive by day, but at night they emerge from their hiding places and creep slowly over the rocks. They are herbivorous and feed by scraping a film of minute, encrusting algae off the rock surface with a long, filelike 'tongue'.

The giant chiton is sometimes used as bait, and even eaten, in spite of its tough, leathery flesh.

Marine invertebrates

ABALONE

Perlemoen *(Haliotis midae)*

Size: Up to 19 cm long.
Colour: Usually greyish or purplish brown, although west coast specimens are generally reddish pink. Ridged inner surface of shell iridescent.
Most like: Venus ear or siffie *(Haliotis spadicea),* but abalone are much bigger, and have distinct, wavy parallel configurations on the outer surface of the shell, absent in the Venus ear.
Habitat: Caverns and crevices on rocky shores, from extreme low spring tide level to a depth of about 22 m.

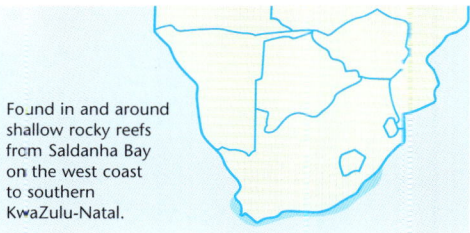

Found in and around shallow rocky reefs from Saldanha Bay on the west coast to southern KwaZulu-Natal.

In the evolution of this fascinating sea snail the opening of its shell has been greatly expanded. As a result the shell itself has become very flat, with only a slight hint of a spire, while the 'foot' of the abalone has grown extremely broad and muscular. Because of these two modifications the abalone, or perlemoen, is well adapted to resist the strong action of the waves that constantly beat on the rocks where it is found.

The abalone is a vegetarian, feeding largely on drifting seaweed, particularly the broad leaves of kelp. The way in which it succeeds in grasping its food is remarkable. It lifts up the front end of its shell and foot, and waits for the waves to sweep the seaweed under it. Finally, in a swift movement, the foot of the abalone clamps down and the meal is trapped.

Abalones sometimes form large, dense colonies on flat rocks or in forests of kelp, where communities of 15 to 20 per square metre may assemble. Sadly, however, concentrations of this size are extremely rare among the kelp beds of the Cape, thanks to the intense activity of commercial and recreational divers, and removal by poachers.

Quantities and sizes taken by harvesters are, in fact, controlled by legislation. Conservation-minded abalone collectors should remember that these animals are very slow-growing: they only start reproducing at eight years of age, and the minimum legal size of 11,4 cm is reached after 13 years. A permit is needed for recreational fishermen, who are limited to four per day.

LONG-SPINED LIMPET

Skerppuntige suigskulp *(Scutellastra longicosta)*

Size: Length averages 6-7 cm, but can reach 9 cm.
Colour: Upper surface dark brown to black (but often coated with algae); inner surface bluish white with a brownish centre and narrow black border.
Most like: The shells of several other limpets, such as the granite limpet *(Cymbula granatina)* and the eye limpet *(Cymbula oculus),* which are ridged and irregular in outline, but not nearly as jagged as the long-spined limpet.
Habitat: Rocky shores between low-water neap tide and low-water spring tide levels.

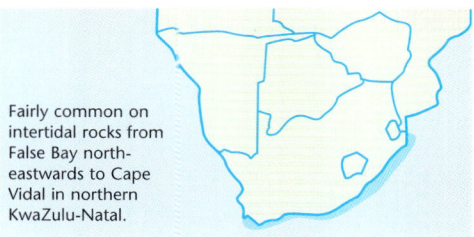

Fairly common on intertidal rocks from False Bay north-eastwards to Cape Vidal in northern KwaZulu-Natal.

Amazingly, the long-spined limpet protects and defends 'gardens' of a particular brown seaweed it favours, and will even drive off trespassers such as other limpets and small abalone (perlemoen) that stray onto its turf. The long-spined limpet will even go as far as to thrust its spines under the shell of the invading limpet and push vigorously until the encroacher backs off.

The sought-after alga *Ralfsia expansa* surrounds the long-spined limpet's home territory and flourishes under its 'gardener's' careful attention. The long-spined limpet removes other algae which try to grow in its garden. Incredibly, this limpet does not indiscriminately crop its garden, but rather cuts a path across it. As *Ralfsia expansa* grows from its edges the path creates many growth points, thus increasing the productivity of the garden.

Because this alga grows on the shells of other snails, juveniles of the long-spined limpet often ride 'piggy-back' on the snails' shells to feed on it.

When they are too large they then slide off onto a rocky surface and move about, feeding on tough, encrusting coralline algae which are low in nutritive value. During this time the limpets lose much weight and are unable to reproduce. Undaunted, they persevere and eventually manage to establish a garden of their own or, if they are lucky, find an abandoned garden to occupy and defend. Once their own gardens are productive, the limpets grow quickly and start to reproduce.

This star-shaped limpet is also called the duck's foot limpet on account of its long, projecting ribs which resemble a duck's webbed foot.

Marine invertebrates

Plough shell

Ploegskulp *(Bullia digitalis)*

Size: Length up to 6 cm.
Colour: Shell usually pale buff or cream, often tinged with violet or yellow. The large, oval foot is off-white.
Most like: Several similar-looking plough shells along the southern African coast, including Bullia rhodostoma on the south coast and Bullia natalensis on the KwaZulu-Natal coast. All the common plough shells along the coast are indistinguishable by colour alone.
Habitat: Wave-swept sandy beaches, from mid-tide level seawards, where the sand is not too coarse.

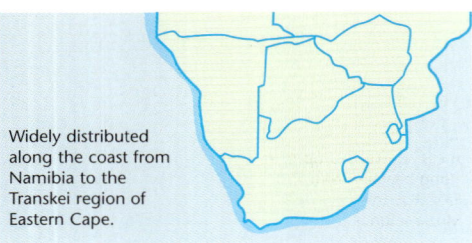

Widely distributed along the coast from Namibia to the Transkei region of Eastern Cape.

Like miniature ploughs pushed by invisible Lilliputian farmers, these snails creep along the sand at the water's edge. They are scavengers, emerging from the wet sand to crawl towards a stranded dead animal. Strangely enough, plough shells are blind, relying instead on their extremely acute sense of smell to constantly test the water for the scent of decaying flesh. When a dead fish or jellyfish is detected, dozens of the snails appear, as from nowhere, and converge on it. Each snail may eat as much as one third of its own mass in a single meal.

As soon as it has finished eating, the plough shell buries itself completely except for the tips of its single, long respiratory tube or siphon. In fact, these snails spend most of their time buried in the sand between mid- and low-tide levels. In this way they can conserve their energy so effectively that in order to survive they need to eat only one meal every 14 days.

How a plough shell knows that it has reached the mid-tide level of an incoming tide is a mystery. This sensible adaptation ensures that the snail is never stranded too high up the shore—for as the ebbing tide reaches the mid-tide level, the snail emerges and, with the aid of the waves, is taken seawards.

The plough shell has developed an ingenious means of transport. It rolls onto its back, expands its foot into an efficient 'sail' and, by using the wave as the wind, can be taken either up or down the shore.

Eggs are laid in oblong purses and are either carried by the female or buried in the sand. They hatch into crawling young.

Periwinkle

Alikreukeltjie *(Nodilittorina africana africana)*

Size: Up to 1,1 cm long.
Colour: Pale blue to bluish grey, with a narrow white band at the top of each whorl. Brown within and around the aperture.
Most like: The darker brown-to-black Nodilittorina africana knysnaensis, which ranges from Namibia to southern KwaZulu-Natal.
Habitat: Small hollows and crevices on rocks, at the high-water spring tide level.

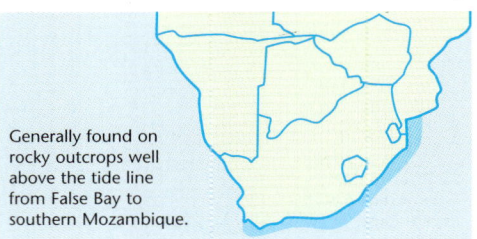

Generally found on rocky outcrops well above the tide line from False Bay to southern Mozambique.

This small, incredibly hardy marine snail lives at the perimeter of land and sea. It may be compared with the most efficiently adapted desert dweller as it can withstand extremes of desiccation and temperature.

Periwinkles live so high up the shore that they may spend several days without being submerged, or even sprayed, by water. Normally under these conditions animals lose a tremendous amount of water through evaporation. To prevent this the periwinkle produces a slimy substance from its foot, which it uses to glue its shell to the rock. It then withdraws into its shell completely and, tightly and efficiently, closes the aperture with its 'trapdoor' or operculum.

As an additional adaptation, periwinkles are able to survive the loss of their body water without experiencing apparent ill effects. During low spring tides, on sunny days, the rocks can become extremely hot. The periwinkle has developed a precarious, but astonishingly efficient, way of dealing with this problem: when things become uncomfortably hot, it attaches the lip of its shell to the rock with its sticky mucus and suspends the shell from this, minimizing contact with the hot rock.

Periwinkles are vegetarians. The smallest specimens are found high up the shore feeding on the sparse algae there. As they grow, and become able to withstand heavier wave action, they move lower down to richer algae harvests.

Marine invertebrates

CAPE TURBAN SHELL
Alikreukel *(Turbo sarmaticus)*

Size: Breadth up to 13,2 cm.
Colour: Generally greyish to olive green or even dull orange in smaller individuals. Large shells almost black. Inner lip white to bright orange.
Most like: The smooth and Natal turban shells, but the Cape turban shell is distinguished from the former by its large adult size and distinctive knobbly operculum, and from the latter by the absence of spiral ridges on the shell.
Habitat: Rock crevices of rocky shores, at low-tide level and below, to a depth of about eight metres. Adults are found lower down the shore than juveniles.

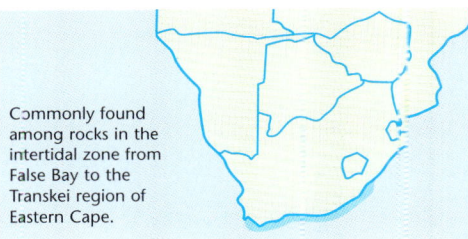

Commonly found among rocks in the intertidal zone from False Bay to the Transkei region of Eastern Cape.

VIOLET BUBBLE SHELL
Pers borrelskulp *(Janthina janthina)*

Size: Up to 3,4 cm across but usually smaller.
Colour: The thin shell may be purple, violet or lavender; the body inside is purple.
Most like: Other Janthina species, but *Janthina janthina* is larger and has a squarish, rather than rounded or oval, aperture.
Habitat: The sea's surface in warm waters. Dead or dying specimens of violet bubble shell may be found on the beaches of temperate seas, having been driven there by persistent onshore winds.

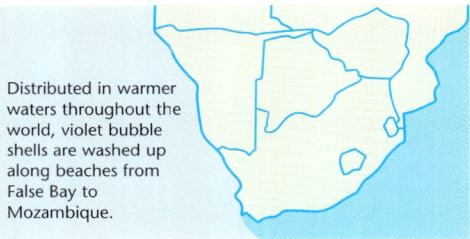

Distributed in warmer waters throughout the world, violet bubble shells are washed up along beaches from False Bay to Mozambique.

The Cape turban shell, or giant periwinkle, has a large, thick, heavy shell, sculptured with sizeable nodules that add to its cumbersome appearance. Little is known about its biology, in spite of the fact that it is exploited as bait, particularly in the Eastern and southwestern Cape where it is considered a seafood delicacy. The fact that these shells are found in relatively shallow water makes them easily accessible to skin-divers, who are limited to five specimens, each with a diameter of at least 63,5 mm, per person per day.

These snails are vegetarians, feeding on small, encrusting seaweeds. Such a diet is difficult to digest and, to cope with the problem, herbivorous snails have very long intestines, often more than eight times the length of the animal itself.

In addition, the Cape turban shell snail has developed an efficient system to sort out the more easily digestible small particles of food from the larger ones. Anyone who has removed an alikreukel from its shell will have seen, even through its skin, a long, white, tightly coiled, springlike tube. This structure forms part of the intestine. Along its length there are three internal grooves lined with fine hairs; food from the stomach enters the tube and is passed down the grooves by the beating hairs. Smaller food particles are gradually moved onto one particular groove and led directly to the digestive gland. The larger particles are returned to the intestine either for further processing or to be rejected as faeces.

This enterprising and attractive snail forms part of the floating oceanic community. Also called the bubble raft shell, it hangs upside down from a raft of bubbles, produced by a secretion of froth, which traps air; each bubble is covered with mucus, which hardens to a tough skin, and the bubble is then glued with more mucus to the raft. Such a raft may end up about three times the size of the snail.

Violet bubble shells feed on a number of fellow oceanic animals, particularly bluebottles (*Physalia utriculus*) and other jellyfishes such as the by-the-wind sailor (*Velella velella*). This organism is capable of using its stinging cells to protect itself, but the bubble shell retaliates by squirting out a violet dye, which is believed to anaesthetize its victim. The snail then holds onto the underside of the immobilized jellyfish and gradually devours it, tentacles, stinging cells and all. Eventually nothing is left but the victim's platelike float.

Janthina janthina has no eyes—it detects its prey by means of a black tentacle situated near its mouth.

Ironically, both the violet bubble shell and its favourite bluebottle and jellyfish prey are eaten with relish by young turtles.

Young individuals are males but change into females with age. Fertilization is internal and the eggs are incubated within the ovary. Eventually the larvae are expelled, with considerable violence, into the water. (Other *Janthina* species lay batches of eggs under the bubble raft.)

Marine invertebrates

Cape rock oyster

Kaapse rotsoester *(Striostrea margaritacea)*

Size: Length up to 18 cm.
Colour: Yellowish to violet-brown shell; the bowl-shaped lower shell sometimes has dark pink or purplish stripes. Interior surface white with a slight purple tinge.
Most like: Natal rock oyster, but distinguished from it by having a smooth white rather than a strongly undulating black margin, and by habitat—Natal rock oysters are restricted to a dense band near the top of the shore.
Habitat: Rocky outcrops at extreme low-tide level and just below, often where the surf is very rough.

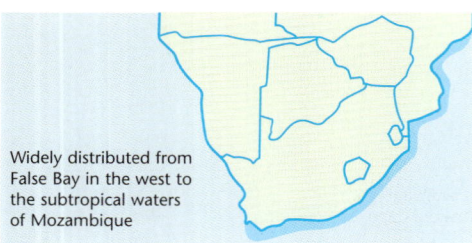

Widely distributed from False Bay in the west to the subtropical waters of Mozambique.

Cape rock oysters have large, thick, heavy shells in a variety of contorted shapes. Although these sought-after shellfish must cement themselves to rocks for survival, at times they are covered by sand. To prevent them from being totally buried, it is believed that the lower half of the shell grows vigorously and thus keeps the upper half above the sand surface. It is this growth reaction to sand that results in the long, beaklike appearance of some individual specimens.

Most oyster species can change sex—in fact a single oyster may alternate sexes several times in its life—but whether the Cape rock oyster shares this unusual faculty is not yet known. The biology of this species remains obscure, in spite of its economic importance. It reaches sexual maturity within a year and spawns during the spring and summer, when vast numbers of eggs and sperm are liberated into the water.

After a short free-swimming phase, the young oyster crawls over the rock surface, searching for a suitable spot to settle. As soon as the ideal position is found, it cements itself firmly to the rock and stays there.

Growth is very rapid in the first months, and the Cape rock oyster reaches an acceptable marketable size after a mere two years.

Oysters consume minute food particles which they filter from water that is pumped through their greatly enlarged, sievelike gills.

Brown mussel

Bruinmossel *(Perna perna)*

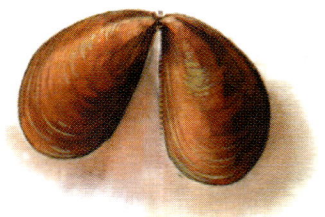

Size: Length averages 5-10 cm, but can reach 12 cm.
Colour: Ranges between yellowish brown to a rich rufous brown sometimes tinged with green.
Most like: Black mussel, but distinguished from it by the shell colour.
Habitat: Intertidal rocks and man-made structures below low-water neap tide level on wave-washed shores. Absent from the cooler waters of the west coast where black mussels replace it.

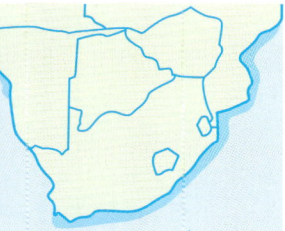

Abundant along the northern and central Namibian coast, and from False Bay to Mozambique. Absent from the western shores of the Western Cape, Namaqualand and southern Namibia.

The brown mussel is probably the most sought-after invertebrate found along the KwaZulu-Natal coast, for it is used both as bait and as a seafood delicacy. Gourmets may not like to know it, but the bulk of the mussel's flesh consists of reproductive organs, which are either creamy white (in males) or reddish orange (in females).

This species spawns between midwinter and spring. By late spring and summer the 'spat', as the spawn of shellfish are called, start settling. In some years settlement is so profuse that in certain areas every centimetre of exposed rock is covered by tiny mussels, and yet in other years settlement is hardly noticed.

By straining fine particles of organic matter from the water, mussels are extraordinarily efficient purifiers of water. In fact, a brown mussel that is a mere 10 cm long can filter as much as 15 litres of seawater an hour. This is such a substantial volume that the water that flows over a bed of mussels reaches the other side of the mussel belt significantly cleaner.

In cropping mussels you should not completely strip whole areas, but select the larger individuals of a bed, allowing space for the remaining individuals to grow to their full size.

If you look carefully at a mussel belt, you will see that those individuals on the edges which are more exposed to wave action tend to lie horizontally and are more firmly attached to the rock face than those mussels in the centre, which are attached more to one another than to the surface of the rock.

Marine invertebrates

BLACK MUSSEL
Swartmossel *(Choromytilus meridionalis)*

Size: *Length averages 6 cm, but can reach 15 cm.*

Colour: *The shell is black, but merges to violet or even white where it has been eroded.*

Most like: *Brown mussel, but the colour difference is quite distinctive. A second, introduced, species of black mussel, the Mediterranean mussel* Mytilus galloprovincialis, *is now the dominant species along the Atlantic coast of southern Africa.*

Habitat: *Lower mid-tidal zone of intertidal rocks, in colder waters, particularly adjacent to sand.*

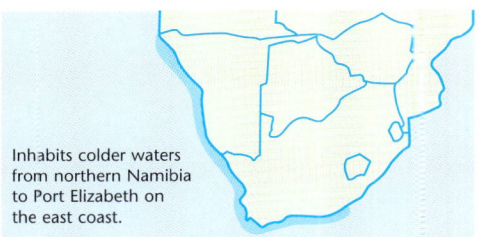

Inhabits colder waters from northern Namibia to Port Elizabeth on the east coast.

WHITE MUSSEL
Witmossel *(Donax serra)*

Size: *Averages 6-7 cm in length, but some specimens reach more than 8 cm.*

Colour: *Outer surface of shell white to pale purple. Inside of shell pale purple to salmon-pink.*

Most like: *The smaller* Donax sordidus *but distinguished by its much larger size and purple interior.*

Habitat: *Exposed beaches with clean, coarse sand where they occur in densities of several hundreds to the square metre.*

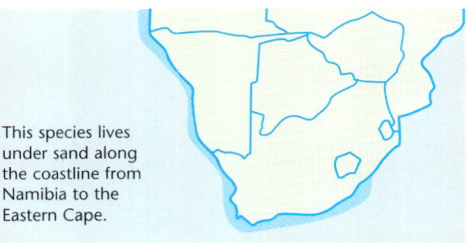

This species lives under sand along the coastline from Namibia to the Eastern Cape.

Black mussels form large, dense beds on rocks exposed at low spring and neap tides. They are firmly fixed to the rock by a 'beard' of tough threads. These are arranged in such a way as to best cope with the force of the waves, which constantly beat against them. If the wave force increases, additional threads are produced like extra guy ropes protecting a tent from being blown away by the wind.

Mussels may appear to be permanently fixed to the rocks, but this is not so. The juveniles, known as 'spat', settle on the rock when they are less than one millimetre long and, until they reach ten millimetres in length, move about quite freely seeking out the most suitable and best-protected position for final settlement. Although larger mussels do not voluntarily detach themselves, once removed they are capable of re-attaching themselves to the rock, although they take longer to do so than the juveniles.

Like efficient pumps, black mussels draw in large volumes of water, from which they filter out micro-organisms and other particles for food. However, under particular conditions along the west coast of southern Africa, certain marine micro-organisms may multiply excessively to produce a phenomenon known as the 'red tide', and black mussels may accumulate lethal quantities of the toxin contained in one such organism. Fortunately this is an infrequent phenomenon.

Black mussels are prolific breeders, spawning several times each year. In one year a single specimen releases eggs or sperm amounting to four times its own mass.

Anyone who digs in the sand at mid-tide level on a beach in the Western and Eastern Cape will be sure to unearth several white mussels. If you are a fisherman you will almost certainly use them as bait. If you appreciate seafood they will undoubtedly end up in the pot, as they make very good eating.

White mussels probably live for more than five years but only become sexually mature after two. Spawning takes place mainly during winter, although eggs continue to be produced until early summer. The 'spat' or juveniles settle just below extreme low-tide level where they remain for about two months.

As youngsters little more than 1,5 cm long they move into the beach's intertidal zone. Here they bury themselves with great efficiency, using their large, wedge-shaped foot, which they can distend or flatten by pumping fluid into the tissues.

White mussels spend most of their time buried a few centimetres beneath the sand surface, with just their two long, tubular siphons projecting into the water above. Water is sucked in through the shorter siphon, the entrance to which is protected by a grid of fleshy lobes to keep out sand grains. Food particles are sieved out by the gills, and waste water is squirted out of the longer siphon.

These mussels form an important part of the diet of many seabirds, crabs and fish. Some of these predators nip off just the projecting siphons, but the white mussels quickly regenerates them. Like their black counterparts, white mussels may accumulate dangerous quantities of toxin during a 'red tide', and should not be eaten then.

Marine invertebrates

REDBAIT

Rooiaas (*Pyura stolonifera*)

Size: Up to 10 cm wide and 25 cm high.
Colour: Olive-brown to blue-black, the name being derived from the colour of the flesh, which is bright orange-red.
Most like: Other solitary sea squirts, such as *Ciona intestinalis*, but redbait can be identified by its large size, wave-beaten habitat and red flesh.
Habitat: Rocks of wave-beaten shores, from the average low-water spring tide level to a depth of about 12 m.

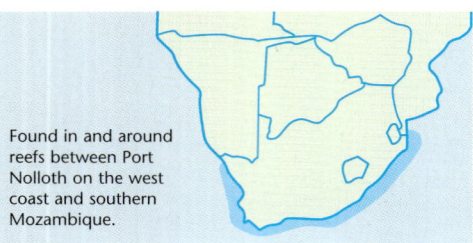

Found in and around reefs between Port Nolloth on the west coast and southern Mozambique.

Most fishermen slice open 'pods' of redbait unaware that this short, squat, baglike organism—an extremely popular bait—is actually closely related to the vertebrates. Don't be too quick to disregard the shapeless form of this sea squirt: it contains all the necessary organs of life. The outer protective 'skin' is tough, leatherlike and embedded with sand grains and bits of shell. Further camouflage is provided by a variety of small animals and plants that also inhabit the surface of its body.

The simple 'backbone' is found in the tail of the tadpolelike larvae, which hatch from eggs released into the water by the adult. The larvae are minute, no more than three millimetres, and after swimming freely for a while, they settle on a rock, attaching themselves by three small adhesive projections on the head. Soon the tail is absorbed, much like that of a real tadpole, and the creature is transformed into a baby sea squirt.

Although redbait are solitary individuals, they can form large, dense and tightly packed beds. Adults live permanently clamped to a rock and are well adapted to withstand strong wave action. To the untrained eye they are difficult to see, blending in well with the plant growth, which often surrounds them. They may, however, periodically betray their presence by contracting suddenly, squirting out thin jets of water.

Sea squirts are living pump stations, continuously pumping vast quantities of water through their bodies. The water is taken in through one of the two turretlike siphons at the upper end of the body. As it flows through the animal the food particles are filtered out and passed to the stomach and intestines.

SEA ANEMONE

Anemoon (*Pseudactinia flagellifera*)

Size: Diameter 5-10 cm.
Colour: Bright orange or red; tips of tentacles may be mauve.
Most like: Plum anemone (*Actinia equina*) in colour and habitat, but *Pseudactinia flagellifera* is distinguished by not being able to withdraw its tentacles when touched.
Habitat: Tidal pools in the intertidal and immediate subtidal zone.

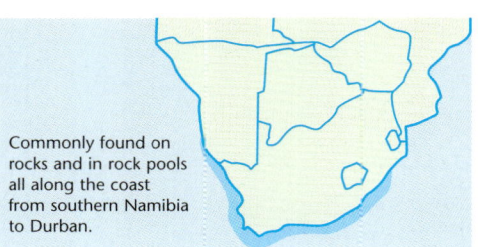

Commonly found on rocks and in rock pools all along the coast from southern Namibia to Durban.

Probably the most striking characteristic of these fleshy animals, which resemble flowers of the sea, is their brilliant orange or red colour. The sea anemone is a simple, solitary animal consisting of a cylindrical sac with a central mouth surrounded by numerous tentacles. Although it appears firmly fixed to the rock, it can move by either sliding on its base or by detaching itself, floating a distance, and re-attaching. In fact, *Pseudactinia* are surprisingly aggressive, and may move about a pool stinging to death other individuals that stray into their territory.

They are gluttonous feeders and will consume any creature that they can swallow, the most common food items consisting of shellfish and sea urchins dislodged from the rocks and swept into their clutches by the waves. The sea anemone can also survive for a long time without food, when it shrinks greatly in size. It's probably this mechanism that permits anemones to live for a very long time—they have been kept in aquariums for up to 100 years.

If an unsuspecting prey organism touches one of the tentacles, it is immediately paralysed by stinging cells. The immobilized prey is then gradually moved to the mouth, where it is engulfed. After digestion, the indigestible remains are eventually thrown out through the mouth.

This species has the most potent venom of all anemones, and can even cause a painful sting to a human who touches one of its stinging tentacles.

Reproduction takes place either by fertilization (the sperm and eggs being shed into the water) or in plantlike fashion as the body divides into two. Or small lobes of the fleshy 'foot' may break off and develop into tiny new anemones.

Marine invertebrates

Sea cucumber
Seekomkommer *(Pseudocnella sykion)*

Size: Maximum length 6,5 cm.
Colour: Uniformly deep black.
Most like: The red-chested sea cucumber (Pseudocnella insolens), but Pseudocnella sykion is about twice as long, and black rather than red. Similar to Stephenson's sea cucumber (Roweia stephensoni), but bands on Pseudocnella sykion's ventral surface each have up to four rows of tube-feet (Stephenson's sea cucumber has bands containing six rows each).
Habitat: Crevices of tidal pools and at, or just below, low-water neap tide level. Often found partially buried in sand, or under rocks.

Inhabits all rocky shores of southern Africa, but particularly the area between Cape Agulhas in the south and southern Mozambique.

The sea cucumber spends its indolent life lying on its side, the body slightly flattered so that three of its four bands of tube-feet are in contact with the ground. Progress is, predictably, very slow—and as a result, sea cucumbers cannot easily escape from their enemies. However, they have developed some ingenious ways of protecting themselves from attack.

Certain tropical species have a special internal organ packed full of long white threads, which are attached to the hindmost part of the gut. When threatened, these sea cucumbers forcibly eject the threads, which are extremely sticky and so tough that they are almost impossible to snap. They also contain a poison, which will kill most animals that dare to eat them.

More bizarre still, but in fact more common, is the phenomenon of voluntary evisceration in which many sea cucumber species, including *Pseudocnella sykion*, are able to disgorge part or all of their gut. By this means the threatened sea cucumber offers the predator a 'tasty morsel' in the hope that it will then be left alone to regenerate the sacrificed organ.

Unlikely as it seems, the soft, wormlike sea cucumber is a cousin of the starfish, brittle star and sea urchin. The only sign of their relationship is the bands of tube-feet symmetrically spaced around the body, the feet functioning in identical fashion to those of starfish.

A crown of ten sticky, branched tentacles, which are waved about in the water, surrounds the mouth of *Pseudocnella sykion*. They are used to capture a diet of tiny plants and animals as well as particles of decomposing plant and animal matter suspended in the water.

Paper nautilus
Papieragtige nautilusskulp *(Argonauta argo)*

Size: Up to 28 cm, including arms.
Colour: Shell white; body iridescent, ranging from reddish brown and green to blue and violet.
Most like: Pearly nautilus, but the paper nautilus is distinguished by its fragile, translucent, unchambered shell. The shell of the pearly nautilus is hard, opaque, brown striped and internally chambered.
Habitat: Floating on the surface of warm seas, although sometimes in deeper waters.

Although these delicate animals occur all along the southern African coast, their shells are usually found between False Bay and Mozambique.

If you enjoy walking along the drift-line of a sandy, rock-free beach you may be lucky enough to come across the shell of a paper nautilus, or argonaut. Remarkably, these beautiful, fluted and extremely fragile shells, which are much prized by collectors, are produced only by the female of this octopuslike creature. She constructs her shelter from a calcium carbonate secretion produced by two long, specially adapted, paddle-shaped arms. Each arm builds one half of the shell, and where the two halves are joined there is a ridge, with two rows of brown knobs corresponding to the suckers of the arms.

The female argonaut uses the shell to keep herself afloat by trapping some air in its apex. But the shell's primary purpose is as a 'perambulator' for several batches of stalked eggs, which are attached to its inner surface.

In total contrast to the female, the male is a minute, inconspicuous individual that resembles a tiny cuttlefish. The male is thought to float on the surface of the sea, but specimens have been found inside the shell of the female.

The mating procedure of this species is extraordinary. One of the male's arms is specially adapted to be a reservoir of sperm. It is enclosed in a membranous sac and, when full of sperm, the whole arm breaks away at its base and 'swims' to the female with the assistance of a whiplike device at one end. Then it clings to her with its suckers until all the sperm has been released.

Marine invertebrates

COMMON SEA URCHIN
Gewone see-eier (*Parechinus angulosus*)

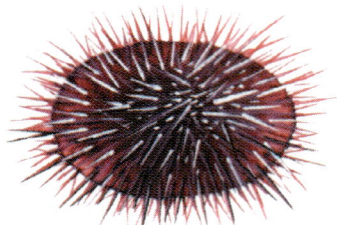

Size: *Diameter (including spines) usually about 6 cm.*
Colour: *The colour of the living sea urchin is given by the spines, which range from cream to bright red or purple. The shell is always green.*
Most like: *Other short-spined sea urchins, such as Stomopneustes variolaris or Echinometra mathaei, but these are usually dark purple to black.*
Habitat: *Rock pools and seaweed beds from mid-tide level down to depths of about 20 m.*

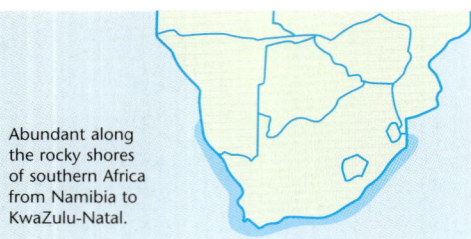

Abundant along the rocky shores of southern Africa from Namibia to KwaZulu-Natal.

SPINY STARFISH
Groot seester (*Marthasterias glacialis*)

Size: *Attains 25 cm between the tips of opposite arms.*
Colour: *Varies from salmon-pink to greyish blue.*
Most like: *Other starfish, but the spiny starfish is the only spiny species found in large numbers on rocky shores. The other common starfish are the much smaller cushion stars, or reticulated starfish (Henricia ornata) and the smooth orange or red starfish (Patiria granifera).*
Habitat: *Rocky shores around low-tide level.*

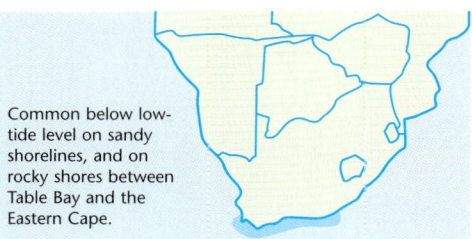

Common below low-tide level on sandy shorelines, and on rocky shores between Table Bay and the Eastern Cape.

The most striking and unmistakeable characteristic of sea urchins are the long pointed spines which cover their almost spherical bodies. These spines, which are movable, are often used for protection, and care should be taken when handling one—the spines may break off and pierce the skin, causing infection and discomfort.

Strange as it may seem, sea urchins are closely related to starfish. There is no front or back end, and so any direction is forward. They move by means of their tube-feet—fingerlike tubes tipped with suction pads which are controlled by an incredibly efficient hydraulic system of tubes, pipes and reservoirs. These tube-feet project through a series of holes situated in five bands equally spaced around the sea urchin's symmetrical body.

The common sea urchin is mainly a night prowler because it is sensitive to sunlight. During the day it hides under shady ledges and shallow grottoes, or covers itself with a sunshade of pieces of shell or weed, which it holds over its body with its tube-feet.

These sea urchins are common in the kelp beds of the Cape where they feed on broken pieces of kelp which fall to the sea floor. They also feed on the young, newly settled kelp plants—a habit which helps keep the kelp beds from becoming too dense.

The sea urchin devours the young kelp plants after scraping them off the rock surface with five massive teeth that are arranged in a circle around the mouth. The mouth is at the centre of the underside. Waste products are ejected through the smaller hole on top.

Much of the beauty of the spiny starfish, a species common also in Europe, lies in the perfect symmetry of its five radial arms. You will look in vain for this creature's eyes, for there are none, but at the tip of each arm is a cushion of light sensitive tissue which allows the animal to distinguish between light and dark.

Spiny starfish, unlike cushion stars, are predators feeding on a number of intertidal animals including limpets, winkles, barnacles and sea urchins, but especially mussels, which they detect chemically. A mussel enclosed in its double shell is notoriously difficult to prise open, but the cunning starfish has developed a feeding system to overcome this defence. Firstly it hunches up over the prey, attaching its tube-feet firmly to the two shells. Gradually and tenaciously it exerts force, pulling the shells apart. The tube-feet work relentlessly, some relaxing while others take up the strain.

The mussel may resist for a long time, but eventually—due, one could say, to muscle fatigue—it gives way just a little, allowing the shells to part by a fraction of a millimetre. That is all that is needed for the starfish to bring into operation its second line of attack. Amazingly, it can extrude its stomach out of its mouth and pour its digestive juices into the small gap. This juice contains a relaxant, and finally the mussel opens up completely. Once the flesh is fully digested it is absorbed by the starfish's stomach, which is then withdrawn.

Marine invertebrates

DWARF CUSHION STAR

Kussingseester *(Patiriella exigua)*

Size: Averages about 20 mm across.
Colour: Extremely variable, including pink, grey, blue, yellow, orange and red. Uniformly khaki-coloured on the west coast.
Most like: Other starfish, such as the spiny starfish but dwarf cushion star is much smaller and has very short, poorly developed arms, so that the body forms a pentagon rather than a star.
Habitat: Rocky shores in tidal pools at mid-tide level, and in shallow sea-grass beds in clean estuaries.

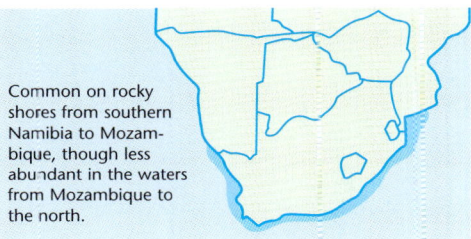

Common on rocky shores from southern Namibia to Mozambique, though less abundant in the waters from Mozambique to the north.

This starfish is undoubtedly a master of camouflage. It parades a startling variety of hues which at first-hand appear unusually bright, yet the mottled arrangement of the colours succeeds in breaking up the animal's outline. The colours usually conform to those of the background, with the result that the starfish blends in beautifully with the rocks on which it is found. In areas where the rocky background is uniform, these spiny starfish also take on a uniform coloration.

The cushion star feeds on the micro-algae which form a slimy covering on the rocks. Like other starfishes it feeds by extruding its stomach through its mouth onto the surface of the rock. Digestive juices are then secreted to digest the algal film. The digested material is directly absorbed by the stomach.

Cushion stars compete for their food with a species of limpet that inhabits the same environment. In fact the limpet has the upper hand as it can produce a substance which repels, and may even paralyse, the starfish.

Probably the most fascinating characteristic of this and other starfish is the possession of tube-feet. These are tiny fingerlike structures projecting from a groove running from the centre along the underside of each arm, and tipped by a large number of adhesive suckers. Hundreds of tube-feet, all working independently of one another, and powered by means of an intricate and efficient hydraulic system of pipes, tubes and small reservoirs, grip the rock and pull the starfish along.

BLUEBOTTLE

Bloublasie *(Physalia utriculus)*

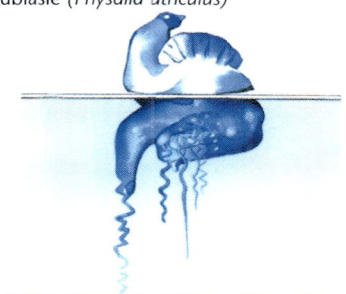

Size: Float length up to 50 mm; tentacles up to 10 m long, but contracting to about 30 cm.
Colour: Ranges from blue to purple and blue-green.
Most like: By-the-wind sailor (Velella velella) and porpita (Porpita pacifica) but distinguished from them by the bladderlike float and longer stinging tentacles.
Habitat: Surface of tropical and subtropical seas. Dead or dying specimens often found along the drift-line on beaches, where they have been cast by onshore winds.

Widely distributed in waters of the subregion. Often blown onto beaches by strong winds.

The bluebottle, a form of jellyfish, is actually a colony composed of four different types of organism—the most conspicuous of which forms the bladderlike float. This is not rigid, but will periodically twist and turn, partially deflate and flop into the water, first to one side, then the other, so that it is kept moist. The bladder is kept afloat by a mixture of gases secreted into it by a gland situated on one side. (The gas is essentially nitrogen, with some carbon monoxide and other rarer gases.) Pressure within the bladder is regulated by a thin layer of muscle in the membrane forming the walls.

Below the float, hanging down into the water, are strands of varying lengths which are formed by the remaining three types of organism in the colony. Some are feeding individuals that form tentacles up to ten metres long and possess stinging cells used to paralyse prey and for defence. These are the tentacles so troublesome to bathers.

Once caught in the tentacles the prey is lifted, and passed to shorter feeding organisms which start the digestive process. Closer to the float are branched organisms that are responsible for reproduction.

The bluebottle, or Portuguese man-of-war, feeds mainly on fishes, although one small fish, *Nomeus*, seems to be immune to the stings and actually shelters among the tentacles. The sea swallow and plough snails also seem immune to the bluebottle's venom, and regularly make a meal of it.

It is thought that the bluebottle common in local waters is a relative of the larger *Physalia physalia*, a more venomous species that occurs elsewhere.

Spiders, scorpions and others

Many people react with revulsion at the mere mention of the word spider; generally, the larger and hairier the specimen, the greater the aversion. Scorpions, too—notorious for their large pincers and potentially lethal sting—are not held in high esteem. In spite of their reputation, however, the 4 000 species of spider and 175 species and subspecies of scorpion in southern Africa play a vital role in maintaining the delicate balance of nature.

Spiders and scorpions are arachnids (class Arachnida), distinguished by their four pairs of legs (insects have three pairs). They lack antennae but have two appendages called pedipalps, one on either side of the mouth. In spiders these touching-and-feeling organs look like miniature legs; in scorpions they are much more prominent and end in pincers rather like those of a crab.

Folklore attributes all kinds of properties to spiders, from bringing good luck and money, to curing diseases (you could rid yourself of jaundice, it was alleged, by swallowing a large, live house spider rolled up in butter).

Spiders are also held up as examples of industry, a well-deserved description, as they take great pains to create their intricate silken webs, spun from their abdominal glands, to ensnare insects. Not all spider webs are of the classic circular pattern: hammocks, sheets, domes and funnels are the varied blueprints preferred by some species when they get weaving.

Almost all spiders secrete venom and have a pair of fangs for administering it; but of the southern African species very few are potentially harmful to man. Most dangerous is *Latrodectus indistinctus*, the black widow spider (or button spider), whose poison is neurotoxic. Young children are most at risk from the bite of this fortunately rarely encountered species.

Scorpions
Man's fear of scorpions is far greater than his aversion to spiders. There is something particularly menacing about the scorpion's defensive posture; its pincers held wide apart, ready to grab, its five-segmented tail curved over its back, the sharp-pointed tail segment poised to strike.

The 175 species indigenous to southern Africa are grouped into two easily distinguishable families. The Scorpionidae, chiefly found in the west of the subregion, have broad, strong pedipalps and a slender tail. Their venom is not nearly as toxic as that of the Buthidae, which have thick tails and thin pedipalps.

Ticks and mites
These are also arachnids, and belong to the order Acari. Many are parasitic, and their mouthparts and legs have become modified in response to their specialized methods of feeding.

Centipedes and millipedes
These two groups belong to the class Myriapoda ('many-footed'). Both lead sheltered lives in cracks and crevices, or underground; and the bodies of both are made up of a large number of similar segments; yet in looks they are quite distinctive.

Millipedes are wormlike, with two pairs of legs for each body segment (totalling perhaps 100 legs in all, not 1 000 as the name 'millipede' would suggest). They proceed at a slow, stately pace in a straight line and, if threatened, will curl up in a spiral or ball—their only defence, except for the unpleasant-smelling fluid that some species secrete. Some 380 species have been recorded in the subregion, all feeding on detritus.

Centipedes have flattened bodies, long antennae and relatively long legs, with only a single pair of legs per body segment. They can move much faster than millipedes, with a rather winding motion. The front pair of legs carries poison-bearing claws that can inflict a hurtful, but seldom harmful, bite. Unlike millipedes, centipedes are carnivorous. There are some 125 local species.

Earthworms
Although the earthworm—class Oligochaeta—has no legs, it is equipped with tiny bristles that help it to crawl along. Humble it may be, but by aerating and fertilizing the soil, it plays an invaluable role in nature, and Charles Darwin exalted its status among animals on this account.

Land snails
Land snails, some prized by gourmets, others cursed by gardeners, are molluscs. They are close cousins of the marine inhabitants of our seashells. Indeed they are at home in moist conditions, and you are most likely to encounter them after rain. In the dry season they retreat into their shells, seal the aperture with an epiphragm (from the Greek word *epiphragma*: a lid)—a 'front door' composed of lime and mucus—and sit out the heat, like tropical travellers in air-conditioned hotel comfort.

Identifying spiders and scorpions

Spiders
When you're trying to identify spiders, look carefully at these telltale features: body shape; shape, colour and articulation of the feeding structures (chelicerae); the size, number and arrangement of the eyes (particularly important); size and hairiness of the legs; and the number of breathing structures or book lungs.

Once you have positively identified a specimen as a true spider (order Araneae)—it must have eight legs—find out which of the two suborders it belongs to. If the chelicerae and fangs move up and down in the same plane as the long axis of the body, the spider is a member of the suborder Orthognatha; if the chelicerae move horizontally at right angles to the long axis of the body, the spider belongs to the suborder Labidognatha. Should you still be unsure about the creature's identity, look at the number of book lungs on the underside of the abdomen: the Orthognatha have four; the Labidognatha have two.

Further identification to family level is possible. In the suborder Orthognatha, the two most common families are the baboon spiders (Theraphosidae) and the trap-door spiders (Ctenizidae).

You can identify the baboon spider easily by its medium-long, hairy legs which differ from the stout, shiny, almost hairless legs of the trap-door spiders.

Spiders, scorpions and others

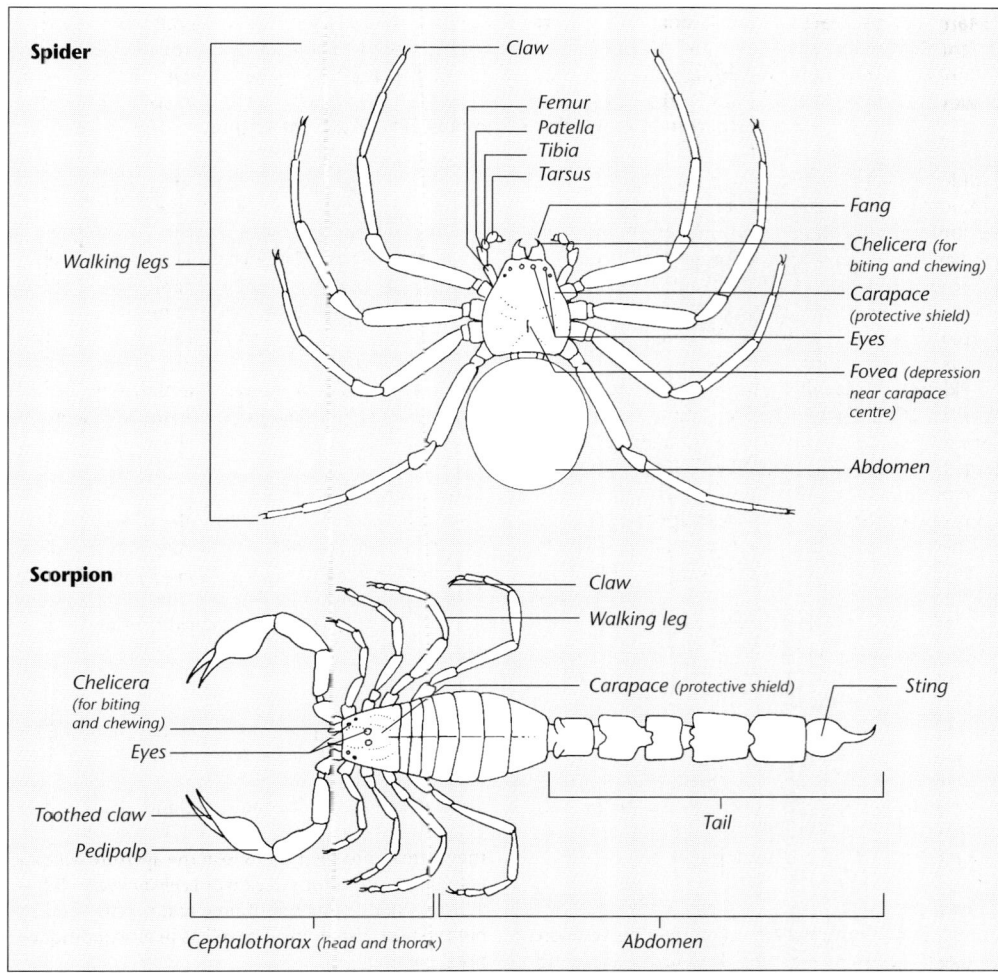

The suborder Labidognatha is a very heterogeneous group and contains many families, the largest of which are quite easy to identify. One of these is the family of sac spiders (Clubionidae), which you can identify by their yellow or cream-coloured bodies and large, pitch-black chelicerae. Above the base of the chelicerae you can see eight eyes in two parallel rows of four. Sac spiders move fast and don't spin webs.

If you see a spider with two exceptionally large eyes surrounded by smaller ones on the front of the head, it is probably a jumping spider (Salticidae). Brightly coloured spiders that spin large, circular webs are invariably orb-web spiders (Araneidae and Tetragnathidae). The crab spiders (Thomisidae) move and look like tiny crabs, and can easily be recognized by the first two pairs of legs, which are longer than the rest and have powerful spines to snap up prey.

Scorpions

When trying to identify scorpions (order Scorpiones) look carefully at the thickness of the tail and size of the pincers. Also observe the shape of the pedipalps and sting, the length of the tail, and the granulation and hairiness of the body.

Others

As clear-cut as these indicators may seem to be, a problem with identification does arise when you encounter specimens that are not typical spiders or scorpions, and belong to one of the other seven orders of southern African arachnida.

The most spiderlike of these are the so-called harvest spiders (order Opiliones), that live among the leaf litter in forests. They can easily be distinguished from true spiders by the fact that they have a segmented abdomen, long pedipalps, and lack a constriction between the head and the abdomen.

Other close relatives of the true spiders are the sun spiders (order Solifugae), which you can identify easily by their huge jaws, armed with sharp teeth.

The 'scorpion' without a tail would be a false or book scorpion (order Pseudoscorpiones). It has pedipalps with pincers, like the scorpions, but lacks a tail and is never more than seven or eight millimetres long. Another scorpionlike creature without a tail is a whip scorpion (order Amblypygi). This is a harmless little animal that usually hides under rocks and the floors of houses during the day. Instead of pincers it has spines at the end of the pedipalps, and the first pair of legs is extremely long and slender.

Even closer to the true scorpions are the whip scorpions with tails (order Uropygi), only here the tail does not end in a sting (instead of stinging, it ejects a repellent liquid when disturbed).

The other two orders of the Arachnida are the ticks and the mites, which are distinctly different.

Spiders, scorpions and others

EARTHWORMS
Erdwurms (Class Oligochaeta)

Size: Length up to 40 cm in many species, but the giant earthworm of the Eastern Cape grows to 3,5 m and even longer.
Colour: From pale pink or grey-pink to purple-red. Near the front end you can usually see a length of paler segments, referred to as the saddle or, more correctly, the clitellum.
Most like: Parasitic worms which, however, do not live in soil.
Habitat: In the soil. Also found in decaying vegetable matter and rotting logs.

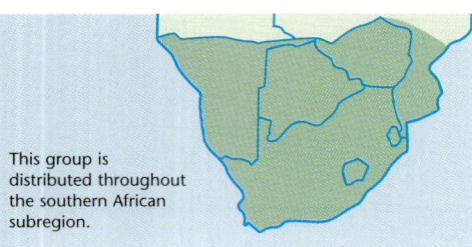

This group is distributed throughout the southern African subregion.

At first glance an earthworm does not appear to have any bristles, but look at it carefully and you will see that there are four pairs of tiny, transparent bristles growing on each segment of its body. If you are unable to see these bristles, try rubbing your finger along the length of the worm—you should be able to feel them quite easily.

The bristles serve to anchor the front or rear of the body to the walls of the worm's underground tunnel, so that by contraction the rest of the body can be pulled forward or retracted.

The earthworm 'eats' by swallowing soil. As it passes this through its tubelike body it draws nourishment from the decaying plant tissue and the numerous micro-organisms that the soil contains. The digested soil is then deposited above ground in ring-like castings.

It is widely recognized that earthworms help to aerate the soil and that they enrich it by drawing vegetable matter down into their burrows. But it was only in the 19th century that Charles Darwin speculated that earthworms also till the soil, serving as nature's plough, by moving all that they swallow from below ground to the surface. Modern scientists have proved him correct.

Each year, in every 4 000 or so square metres of soil they occupy, earthworms bring from below ground and spread over the surface between two and 100 tons of nutritious 'processed' soil—amounting in just a few years to many centimetres of topsoil.

LAND SNAILS
Landslakke (Class Gastropoda)

Size: Length from 3-20 cm.
Colour: Giant land snail's shell cream or pale mustard-yellow with irregular, dark brown, wavy stripes running across the whorls. Garden snail's shell olive-brown with stripes.
Most like: Marine snails, but different habitats distinguish the groups.
Habitat: All species like lush vegetation and moisture, but the Mediterranean snail can tolerate relatively dry conditions as on the Cape's west coast.

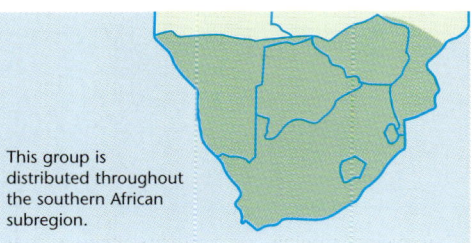

This group is distributed throughout the southern African subregion.

Giant land snails have an appetite to match their gigantic proportions. They will eat almost anything, making fast work of dead animals and all kinds of vegetable matter, rotten or fresh. They need calcium for the formation of their shells, and to get it they will go as far as to scour the whitewash off the walls of houses.

These enormous snails are native to the hotter parts of Africa, including Northern Province, Mpumalanga and KwaZulu-Natal. During the day, they shelter in a hideaway—a hollow tree trunk or a crevice under a stone. As night falls they emerge from their lairs to devour the tropical vegetation.

Although it eats man's crops, the giant land snail itself is edible, and in many parts of its African home it provides a regular and substantial source of protein-rich food.

The garden snail is an immigrant, having come here from western Europe, but it thrives along the southern and Eastern Cape coast. It is closely related to the much-prized edible snail of Europe, *Helix pomatia*, and is itself an edible species.

The Mediterranean land snail is also an immigrant, and has almost reached plague proportions in some coastal regions of the Cape. Like all snails it needs moisture, but it has a noted ability to thrive in regions where the days are extremely hot and dry.

The adult female lays up to 500 eggs per year. Resembling small yellow peas, the eggs hatch in just a few days.

Spiders, scorpions and others

BURROWING SCORPIONS

Grawende skerpioene (Genus *Opistopthalmus*)

Size: Length up to 10 cm.
Colour: Varies from olive to yellow or yellow-brown in some species to dark brown and almost black in others.
Most like: Bark scorpions, but burrowing scorpions grow larger, have thinner tails and much larger pincers.
Habitat: Burrows in sandy or hard soil; hides under stones, fallen tree trunks and large, dried cowpats. More common in arid regions.

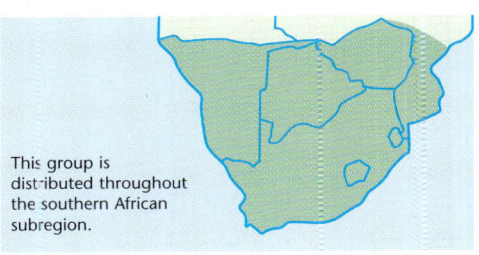

This group is distributed throughout the southern African subregion.

Burrowing scorpions are strictly carnivorous, as are all scorpions and spiders. They emerge from their hiding places at night to hunt down small prey such as beetles, grasshoppers, cockroaches and spiders. They rely mainly on their pincers to capture their prey but, if the victim is large and difficult to subdue, the scorpion then clamps the unlucky creature tightly with its pincers, arches its long tail over the full length of its body and, with unerring accuracy, delivers a deadly sting.

Most burrowing scorpions have thin tails with a sting at the tip. Often the tail accounts for more than the total body length. Although the scorpion's sting quickly kills the small creatures on which it preys, it is not normally dangerous to humans. In general, a scorpion with big pincers and a thin tail is unlikely to be particularly poisonous—it relies more on its pincers and less on its sting. However, small or thin pincers and a thick tail usually indicate a scorpion with a highly venomous sting.

When alarmed, burrowing scorpions emit a hisslike warning sound, which they produce by rubbing the outer surface of their jaws against the hard under-edge of their head capsule.

Scorpion eggs hatch as they are being laid. Between 20 and 40 young are born at a time, usually in early summer, and as soon as the young have hatched they climb onto the safety of their mother's back. They are almost perfect miniatures of the adult, except that they are pale.

Some 80 species of *Opistopthalmus* are endemic to southern Africa.

BARK SCORPIONS

Basskerpioene (Genus *Uroplectes*)

Size: Length up to 6 cm.
Colour: Predominantly yellow. Some species greyish yellow or brownish yellow with brown markings. Dorsal side frequently striped
Most like: Thick-tail scorpions, but bark scorpions are generally smaller and yellower, and have smaller pincers and longer tails.
Habitat: Under the peeling bark of trees, and often under stones; sometimes under layers of dry leaves.

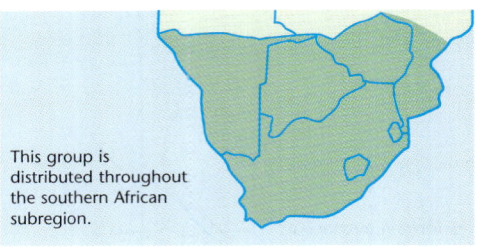

This group is distributed throughout the southern African subregion.

Bark scorpions belong to the thick-tailed and venomous Buthidae family and are more poisonous than burrowing scorpions, but they pose little serious threat to humans.

The sting is very painful and causes a local swelling, but seldom requires special medical treatment. However, do clean the sting area with an antiseptic to avoid the puncture turning septic. Aspirin or paracetamol will help reduce the pain.

As in all scorpions, the poison is held in the final segment of the tail, which ends in a needle-sharp sting. This last segment usually has a swollen look to it, for it contains two plump poison glands wrapped in a sheath of muscle. The instant the scorpion tenses this muscle, poison is squirted out through two minute holes near the tip of the sting.

Although bark scorpions are found in many parts of southern Africa, the various species are each restricted to particular geographical areas. The green bark scorpion (*U. olivaceus*) is a greenish-yellow colour and is found in Mpumalanga. The southern and south-western parts of the Cape are home to the four-lined bark scorpion (*U. lineatus*). This scorpion has a ground colour of greyish yellow with brown patches, and the brown patches join up to form four brown stripes on its back.

The desert regions of the northwestern Cape are the haunt of the carinated bark scorpion (*U. carinatus*) which is brighter yellow with orange-yellow legs. Like other *Uroplectes* species (there are some 40 in all), it conceals itself under stones and leaves.

Spiders, scorpions and others

THICK-TAIL SCORPIONS

Dikstert skerpioene (Genus *Parabuthus*)

Size: Length up to 14 cm, with most being longer than 7 cm.
Colour: Mostly yellow, but olive-yellow or yellow-brown in some species to dark brown and almost black in others.
Most like: Bark scorpions, which also have long tails. Most *Parabuthus* species, however, grow much larger, and have very thick tails.
Habitat: Under stones, in burrows and under dried cowpats. Sometimes you will see them in or near houses and outbuildings.

This group is distributed throughout the drier regions of southern Africa. Absent from the extreme Eastern Cape, KwaZulu-Natal, Lesotho, most of the Free State and the highveld.

Treat these scorpions with great respect. In some species the sting can kill, and small children are especially vulnerable. Several species are capable of blinding you by squirting poison into your eyes in much the same way as a spitting cobra does.

Many of the more serious stings in southern Africa can be attributed to the Cape thick-tail scorpion (*P. capensis*), the most commonly encountered member of this group.

The yellow-brown Cape thick-tail scorpion is much smaller than other *Parabuthus* species (there are some 20 endemic to southern Africa), seldom growing much more than five centimetres long. Its deadly relatives living in the drier regions to the north are much larger and usually dark brown or almost black. One of these big brown cousins is the granulated thick-tail scorpion (*P. granulatus*), so called because most of its body surface has a grainy texture. The best known, and certainly the most photographed, is the hairy thick-tail scorpion (*P. villosus*).

The latter is the largest of southern Africa's scorpions, growing up to 14 centimetres. It is also well known for its ability to squirt poison, so treat it with respect. This scorpion inhabits the deserts of the Northern Cape and Namibia. Tourists in these areas may see it roaming the countryside in search of prey, or dining on some small creature that it has caught. Its size enables it to tackle larger prey than its smaller relatives can handle, and it has been known to hunt and kill mice.

SAND-DWELLING THICK-TAIL SCORPIONS

Dikstert sandskerpioene (Genus *Hottentotta*)

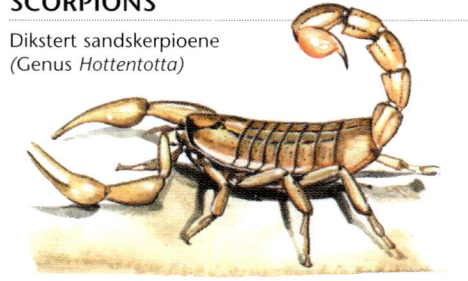

Size: Length 4-7 cm.
Colour: Yellow or yellow-orange to light brown with black markings on the front segments of the body.
Most like: Bark scorpions, but sand-dwelling thick-tail scorpions have large, short stings.
Habitat: Dry, sandy areas, where they make burrows underneath low-lying shrubs.

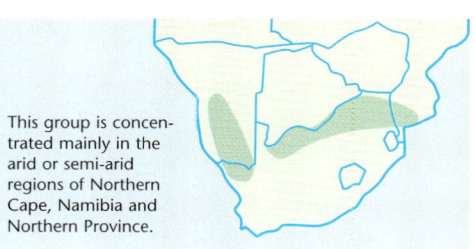

This group is concentrated mainly in the arid or semi-arid regions of Northern Cape, Namibia and Northern Province.

Although these scorpions are smaller than those belonging to the *Parabuthus* group, they must be treated with a similar degree of wariness. They have thin pincers and thick tails, with a noticeably large sting at the end of the tail—precisely the combination that spells danger.

Relatively few cases of serious injury have been attributed to sand-dwelling scorpions. This may indicate no more than the fact that they live in sparsely populated desert regions, such as Namaqualand and Bushmanland—dry, desolate expanses where man and scorpion seldom encounter each other.

The females of this group are home-lovers, tending to remain in or near their burrows, while the males are more inclined to roam the countryside in search of their dinner.

Like all scorpions, the male and female sand-dwelling thick-tail species tend to arouse a lot of popular interest because of the well-orchestrated and elaborate courtship ritual they perform prior to mating. Typically, the male will grasp the female's pincers in his own, then he will walk backwards and sideways quite deliberately, as if he were leading his lady in a dance.

In at least some of the *Hottentotta* (previously called *Buthotus*) species the two partners start their performance by straightening their backs, lowering their bodies to the ground, then entwining and disentwining their tails overhead. After this, the take-your-partner-by-the-hand routine begins. This ritual dance can continue for several hours, with the female meekly allowing herself to be led about, exactly as if she had been trained in ballroom etiquette.

Spiders, scorpions and others

SUN SPIDERS

Jagspinnekoppe (Order Solifugae)

Size: Body length 1,5-2 cm, but can reach 7 cm (16 cm with legs outstretched) in arid regions.
Colour: Light to dark brown.
Most like: Hunting spiders, but sun spiders have much bigger jaws and can run faster. Sun spiders also distinguished by the very long, fine hairs covering their bodies.
Habitat: Hot, dry country; often in the vicinity of houses and outbuildings.

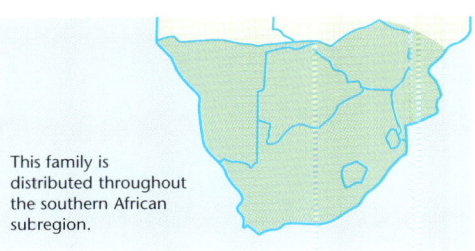

This family is distributed throughout the southern African subregion.

Sun spiders may look ungainly and bulky, but don't be deceived, they are among southern Africa's fastest terrestrial invertebrates. They need to be swift on their feet because they are hunters, preferring to actively hunt for their prey instead of building traps or webs. Their English name applies to their habit of dashing between patches of shade to escape from the sun. Other Afrikaans names for the species include *baardskeerders* ('beard shavers') or *haarskeerders* ('hair cutters')—a reference to their disturbing habit of cutting the hair of sleeping people or dogs to use as a soft lining for their nests. They are not true spiders.

Apart from having enlarged pedipalps, sun spiders are conspicuous for their huge, fearsome jaws, which account for almost a third of their total body length and make quick work of any prey. After seizing its victim, the sun spider crushes it, sucks out the body fluids, then discards the rest. Included on this species' menu are beetles, grasshoppers, scorpions, spiders and, occasionally, small lizards and mice. Formidable though the jaws are, they don't carry any poison, and therefore aren't a serious threat to humans.

Mating is a dangerous game for the males, which risk being attacked and eaten by their mates. In some species the male performs an elaborate courtship dance, and the rhythm of his movements appears to put the female into a motionless trance. While she remains in this state, the male uses his oral appendages to deposit a small drop of his sperm into her genital orifice—then he scuttles away to safety.

In due course the female lays her 20-200 eggs in a burrow, and for some time after the eggs have hatched she can be seen bringing prey back to the burrow for her young to feed on.

BABOON SPIDERS

Bobbejaanspinnekoppe (Family Theraphosidae)

Size: Average body length 2-5 cm, leg span up to 12 cm.
Colour: From light brown or grey in some species to dark brown or almost black in others.
Most like: Lesser baboon spiders (species Harpactirella), but the more common baboon spiders are larger. Often confused with the large hunting spider (Palystes natalius) which enters homes frequently. These, however, have a more slender build and are more agile.
Habitat: In the veld under stones and dungpats. They often build nests in clumps of grass. Sometimes found in houses and outbuildings.

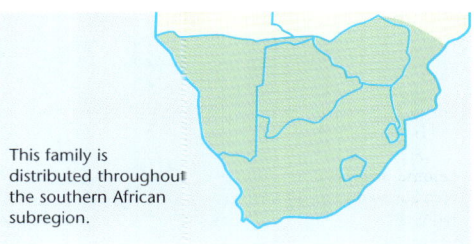

This family is distributed throughout the southern African subregion.

This is the kind of spider that nightmares are made of. They have large, fat bodies which, like the legs, are thickly covered in hair, making the spider seem even bulkier than it really is, and giving it the most frightening appearance.

By spider standards, baboon spiders are particularly long-lived. While most spiders live for only a year or so, baboon spiders have a lifespan of up to 25 years. They take from eight to ten years to reach maturity.

They spend most of their time inside or very near their nests, which are usually silk-lined holes in the ground, reaching down some 30-40 centimetres. If alarmed near its nest the spider may rear up on its hindlegs, with its front legs and fangs poised to strike downwards at its adversary.

When it adopts this formidable posture you can see its sharp, five-millimetre brown fangs, surrounded by reddish hairs. The fangs can inflict a painful bite, but the bite is not dangerously venomous and presents no serious threat to humans. (Some of the lesser baboon spiders in the Western Cape are thought to be dangerously poisonous, but no fatality has been recorded.)

Several closely related American spiders are often reared as household pets, but our African baboon spiders seem to be harder to 'domesticate'.

Spiders, scorpions and others

ORB-WEB SPIDERS

Wawielwebspinnekoppe (Families Tetragnathidae and Araneidae)

Size: Body length up to 3,5 cm; leg span up to 8 cm.
Colour: The common large garden orb-web spiders (species Argiope) often have bold stripes of bright yellow and black; in some species the stripes are yellow, black and silver. The golden orb-web spiders of the bushveld (genus Nephila) have patterned abdomens and banded legs. (The 'golden' in their name refers to the web's colour.)
Most like: Some species may be confused with crab spiders. The latter, however, are always found in flowers and do not construct webs.
Habitat: Bushy countryside where they can spin their webs between bushes, trees and tall shrubs.

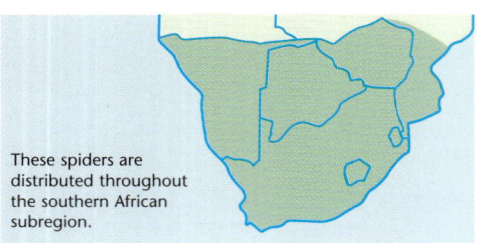

These spiders are distributed throughout the southern African subregion.

CRAB SPIDERS

Krapspinnekoppe (Family Thomisidae)

Size: Body length up to 6 mm; leg span up to 15 mm.
Colour: Brightly coloured, usually yellow, cream or white, sometimes with markings of pink, green or brown. These spiders are noted for their ability to change colour to some extent to match their surroundings.
Most like: In body form most like orb-web spiders, but crab spiders have no web, inhabit flowers and keep all four legs on each side parallel to one another, unlike orb-web spiders.
Habitat: Usually found inside flowers (particularly daisies), waiting to pounce on bee and other flower-visiting insects.

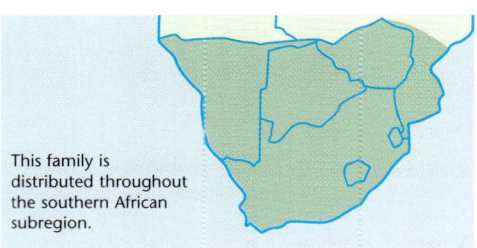

This family is distributed throughout the southern African subregion.

The Afrikaans name for these spiders, 'wagon-wheel-web spiders', is most appropriate. It accurately describes the large wheel-shaped webs that orb-web spiders spin across the gaps between bushes and trees.

You can usually see the spider in the centre of the web, hanging head-down, often with each pair of hindlegs, and also the forelegs, held close together on each side, so that it appears to have only four legs, instead of eight. This formidable creature is the female of the species.

In some species the male, which is far smaller and quite insignificant in comparison, is attracted by the scent of the female, and you will sometimes see him sitting in her web, just above her. When the female is eating, the male climbs down onto her abdomen and mates with her, then beats a hasty retreat to prevent her consuming him too.

Females of the larger species can inflict a painful bite but, as far as is known, none is venomous.

If you look closely at the wheel-like web you may be able to see a band of zigzag threads radiating outwards from the centre—this is known to arachnologists (spider scientists) as the stabilimentum. Its use is debated by the experts, with some believing it to be a stabilizing device, others that it serves as camouflage, as a warning to birds, or even acts as a lure for prey.

Crab spiders, known also as 'flower spiders', take their name from their crablike posture and their distinctive method of moving. While waiting inside a flower for its prey of butterflies, bees and other insects to arrive in search of nectar, the spider sits with its four front legs spread out wide—like the curving pincers of a crab.

When alarmed, the crab spider will bolt for the shelter of a leaf or petal, slipping away with a sudden, sideways movement (again reminiscent of a crab), and for this reason it may be difficult to spot.

One of the fascinating features of crab spiders is their chameleonlike ability to change colour to suit their surroundings. A bright yellow specimen, sitting in a yellow flower, when moved onto green-and-white foliage, may change its colour to a mixture of green and white.

As is the case with many spiders, the male is smaller than the female, and he has to go about the business of mating very carefully, lest his lady snatches him and eats him.

In both male and female crab spiders the front legs, which are used to capture prey, are armed with spines.

Although their bite is probably venomous for the small creatures on which they prey, it is quite harmless to man.

Spiders, scorpions and others

JUMPING SPIDERS

Springspinnekoppe (Family Salticidae)

Size: Body length up to 5 mm; leg span up to 20 mm.
Colour: Black and white, or grey and white, occasionally brown, or brown and white. In most species the male is far more brightly coloured than the female.
Most like: Similar to small hunting spiders, but combination of small size, squat body, large eyes and jumping locomotion distinctive.
Habitat: Dry leaves and wood; commonly found on the walls and ceilings of houses.

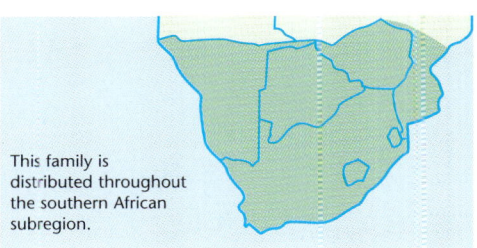

This family is distributed throughout the southern African subregion.

Jumping spiders are hunters. They build no webs or traps, but prowl about in search of flies and other small insects.

They have two prominent eyes, with excellent vision, which stand out like great headlamps in the middle of their flat faces. These are surrounded by three other, smaller pairs of eyes.

All these eyes scan nearby surfaces for a likely meal and, when they spot a fly or similar prey, the jumping spider stalks it just as a cat would. When it is within pouncing range of the victim, the spider jumps upon it so fast that the human eye isn't able to follow its movement.

The jumping spider may leap upon its prey from a wall or ceiling, to which it returns with the unfortunate victim in its grasp. It accomplishes the return journey by stringing out behind it a long, thin strand of silk that it uses as a lifeline to pull itself back.

Jumping spiders are very bold. While most spiders are decidedly wary of an approaching human hand and will quickly scurry away, the jumping spider often acts with brazen curiosity, and will run up towards one's hand as if eager to inspect it. Despite their small size and obvious vulnerability, these spiders seldom seem to show any fear.

Little is known about the jumping spider's bite but, although it may result in swelling and pain in humans, it is certainly not dangerous.

During courtship, the male approaches the female, waving his brightly coloured palps and front legs in front of her, until he is close enough to mate.

BUTTON SPIDERS

Knopiespinnekoppe (Genus *Latrodectus*)

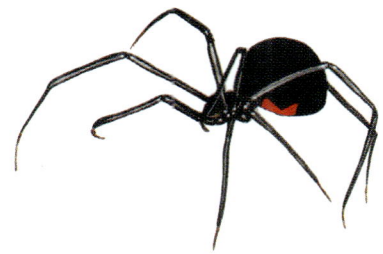

Size: Body length (f) up to 16 mm, (m) 2,5-5 mm; leg span of females up to 40 mm.
Colour: Mostly shiny brown or black, but sometimes grey or even cream. The brown button spider usually has a geometric pattern on its back and a large, hourglass-shaped, orange-red mark on the underside of its abdomen. The more poisonous black button spider has neither of these markings, although it often has a red spot or stripe on the top of its abdomen.
Most like: There are many other species in the same family (Theridiidae) which are quite harmless. Unfortunately it is almost impossible for an amateur to distinguish between some of these harmless species and their poisonous relatives. Though button spiders only bite when trapped, the best policy is to steer clear of any spider that is shiny and spherical—just like an old-fashioned shoe button.
Habitat: Black button spiders are found in the wheat fields of the Western Cape; brown button spiders in woods and forests, and in built-up city areas. Both build their nests in crevices in the bark of trees; sometimes under tables, windowsills or old boards.

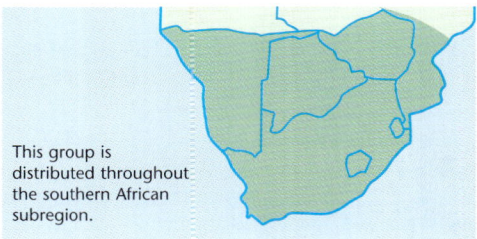

This group is distributed throughout the southern African subregion.

While a bite from a black button spider can be fatal, the brown button spider is regarded as less deadly. In common with many spiders, the male of both species is far smaller than the female—too small to be harmful.

The females build untidy nests of silky webs up to half a metre above the ground. They spend most of their day inside the nests, emerging at night to hunt nearby. The deadly lady captures her insect prey by quickly casting silk around it, closing in to kill with her poisonous bite only when the prey is thoroughly immobilized.

Sometimes the female hauls her catch, including large beetles and grasshoppers, up to her nest on a thin line of silk. In and around this nest she weaves spherical, silky egg sacs. The black button spider produces smooth-surfaced egg sacs; those of the brown button spider are covered evenly with small silky projections, rather resembling tiny pimples.

Spiders, scorpions and others

TICKS

Bosluise (Suborder Ixodida)

Size: Length up to 3 mm before engorging; up to 10 mm when fully engorged.
Colour: Usually brown, red-brown or red. The females of some species turn blue-grey when engorged.
Most like: Mites, to which they are related, but mites are smaller, and many are bright red.
Habitat: Shrubland and grassy areas; some species occur in sandy soil. They live on host animals during blood-sucking stages of their lives.

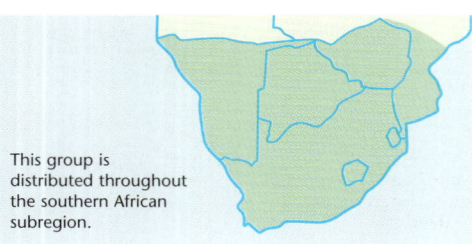

This group is distributed throughout the southern African subregion.

A tick's career starts out as a tiny, almost invisible egg laid on the ground. After a month, a little six-legged larva emerges from the egg, promptly climbs up a nearby grass stem, and hops aboard the first animal that brushes past. It pierces the animal's skin with a tiny, rasplike projection and spends perhaps two days sucking the animal's blood. It then drops off its host onto the ground again, where it moults, changes form and becomes an eight-legged nymph.

The nymph climbs another grass stem or shrub, latches onto another passing animal, engorges itself on the animal's blood, then drops off onto the ground—where it now changes into an adult tick. The adult then lays eggs to repeat the whole performance.

Following their engorgement, a marked difference between the adult sexes becomes apparent in hard ticks. The male's whole body becomes encased in a hard shell, which prevents it from expanding and so limits the amount of blood it can take on board. The female has a softer, more expandable body, and can become so bloated with its host's blood that it looks like a small balloon.

After mating, it is usual for the female to drop onto the ground where she lays up to 8 000 eggs.

Ticks commonly carry such human diseases as tick typhus (tick-bite fever) and Congo fever; also the cattle diseases red-water fever and heartwater disease, and the fatal dog disease biliary.

LAND CRUSTACEANS

Landskaaldiere (Orders Isopoda and Amphipoda)

Size: Length up to 2 cm.
Colour: Woodlice are pale to dark grey; sand-hoppers are a pale, sandy colour.
Most like: Unlike any other arthropods.
Habitat: Woodlice are found in moist, mossy places, often under stones and flowerpots in gardens. Sand-hoppers flourish on beaches littered with jetsam.

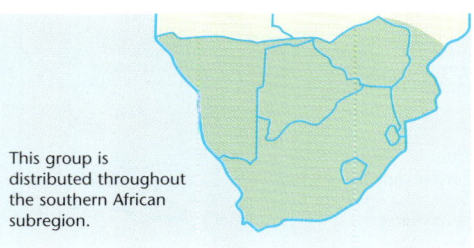

This group is distributed throughout the southern African subregion.

The class Crustacea includes many thousands of species grouped into several orders and suborders. Most crustaceans live in water, but there are a few that have evolved land-based lifestyles. In the garden you can scarcely move a flowerpot without disturbing an assortment of woodlice, and if you stroll along a beach strewn with jetsam you will see large colonies of sand-hoppers clustered about rotting clumps of seaweed.

Woodlice are particularly successful creatures, as much at home in equatorial jungles as they are in Arctic tundra. You will find them in a variety of habitats, from the seashore to the highest mountains. Their body shape gives them the lowest possible surface area in relation to their body mass, enabling them to conserve the moisture they depend on for survival. Some species can roll themselves into a perfect little armour-plated ball.

Woodlice are quite harmless, living entirely on decaying vegetable matter. However, when alarmed they can exude an unpleasant fluid, pungent enough to protect them from potential predators.

Sand-hoppers—you could regard them as shrimps that have ventured out of the shallows and settled into a new life as beachcombers—can walk and swim easily. Their great talent, however, is for jumping, which they do with great abandon. The lower part of their bodies has evolved in such a way that they can curl up, then suddenly spring straight out, jumping to heights of up to 30 cm and covering distances of up to one metre. This is an enormous leap for creatures so small.

Spiders, scorpions and others

MILLIPEDES
Duisendpote *(Class Diplopoda)*

Size: Length up to 20 cm.
Colour: Mostly glossy brown or black, but some species have red or orange stripes.
Most like: Centipedes, but millipedes are cylindrical while centipedes have flattened bodies. Millipedes also have many more legs than centipedes; the legs are tucked neatly under the body, whereas centipedes' legs are spread out sideways.
Habitat: Every type of habitat. Under stones in dry areas; among dead leaves and under the bark of trees in moist areas. Abundant in forests.

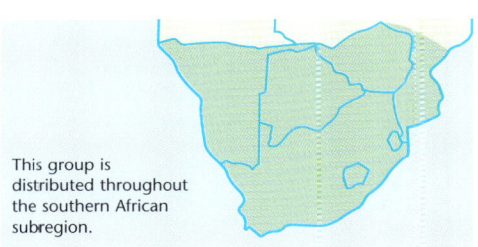

This group is distributed throughout the southern African subregion.

Millipedes, known commonly by their Zulu name, *shongololo*, live a lie. Their name means 'a thousand legs', but no millipede really has that many. The number, in fact, varies from one species to another—the highest count recorded so far is 710.

Nearly all millipedes are plant-eaters and most live on a strict diet of rotting leaves and dead wood. The one or two species that live on growing plants can damage crops and gardens, but mostly these creatures are harmless.

Millipedes don't have a poisonous bite or sting, but most species defend themselves by squirting out a foul-smelling fluid from special glands on the head. This fluid contains hydrogen cyanide, which makes the millipedes potentially toxic.

Southern Africa is home to several hundred species of millipede, ranging from shiny black giants of 20 cm, which you may see roaming the veld after rain in most of the northern parts of the region, to a small, delicate white species that lives only in the darkness of deep caves on Table Mountain.

When alarmed, a millipede usually rolls itself into a tight ball. One species, known as the pill-millipede, takes its name from the fact that it can roll itself up so neatly and tightly that it looks like a hard, round, shiny pill. In spite of their highly poisonous nature, millipedes are eaten by various animals.

CENTIPEDES
Honderdpote *(Class Chilopoda)*

Size: Length up to 18 cm.
Colour: Body usually dark olive-green, black or dark bluish, though sometimes red, yellow or brown.
Most like: Millipedes, but centipedes have a flattened body and fewer legs. The legs tend to spread out sideways, whereas a millipede has its many legs tucked neatly underneath its cylindrical body.
Habitat: All kinds of countryside. Found under stones in dry areas; amid decaying vegetation and even deep in the soil in moist areas.

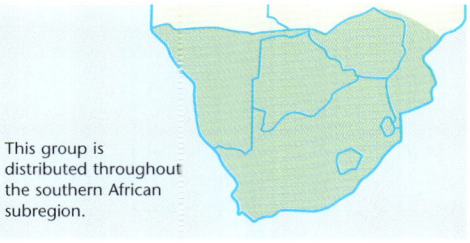

This group is distributed throughout the southern African subregion.

Centipedes are fast-moving predators. Unlike millipedes which amble slowly and purposefully among the rotting leaves, eating only the vegetable matter, centipedes are usually seen scurrying this way and that, searching impatiently for the small creatures on which they prey.

The southern African subregion is home to well over 100 different species of centipede, many differing widely in their forms and lifestyles.

In the eastern parts of southern Africa you'll find the brick red *Alipes*, whose flattened hindmost legs make it look like a tennis racquet. When alarmed the *Alipes* vibrates these flattened limbs to produce a hissing sound.

Another species, often found in areas of human settlement, and commonly called the house-centipede (*Scutigera*), has developed long legs with which it catches flies and other small prey. To equip it for this kind of hunting life the house-centipede has well-developed eyes, but most of its relatives, which are either active at night or live entirely underground, have ineffectual sight or are blind.

All centipede species have fangs and can inflict a poisonous bite. These fangs are in fact specially modified forelegs with sharp points, and have ducts leading back to venom glands. There is no record of a South African centipede inflicting a fatal bite on a human, but the more venomous individuals can deliver a painful wound.

Beetles

Majority rule in a parliament of insects would place beetles firmly in the seat of power, for at least three out of every five insect species in the world belong to the beetle order Coleoptera. Of the world total of more than 600 000 beetle species, about 30 000 are represented in southern Africa.

What singles out the Coleoptera is that their front pair of wings is not functional but has become a set of hard, horny shields protecting the delicate, transparent rear wings underneath, and also protecting the abdomen. The shields are known as 'elytra' (singular: 'elytrum' or 'elytron'). When the beetle is on the ground the elytra lie neatly folded together along the back, forming the case or sheath; but when the insect is in flight they are held forwards, allowing the true wings to beat.

In some species, such as the toktokkies, the rear wings are so attenuated that the beetle cannot fly. And in rare instances the female is altogether without elytra and rear wings; female glow-worms are of this kind, and they actually look much more like worms or larvae than beetles.

In their metamorphosis from egg to adult, beetles are twice transformed. All growth takes place during the first larval stage. As the larva or 'grub' outgrows its skin it moults, a process that is repeated several times; the form of the larva between each moult is known as an 'instar'. Then, when growth is complete and the larva has stored up enough energy for the next stage, it becomes a pupa. During pupation the insect tissues are rearranged to form the organs of the adult beetle.

Beetles have chewing mouthparts—hence the origin of their name, for the word beetle comes from the Old English *bitela*, 'to bite'. But as far as man is concerned their nip is mild, they have no sting, and the worst that a few species of predacious ground beetles can do is discharge a jet of acid liquid that is painful if it enters your eye.

However, the blood of certain beetles contains poisonous substances. The San of the Kalahari make a poison for their arrows from the pupae of the chrysomelid leaf beetle. And the blood of a blister beetle can be irritating to the skin because of the ingredient cantharidin.

Unfortunately a large number of beetle species can damage man's agricultural crops and garden plants. Such pests include many weevils and fruit beetles (among them, the so-called 'rose beetle'), and even one kind of ladybird, which is a vegetarian and partial to potato and bean plants in particular. On the plus side, dung beetles and toktokkies are beneficial scavengers; most ladybirds, too, help gardeners by eating aphids and scale insects.

Some beetles can live in the absence of free water, such as the larvae and adults of the flour beetles and the larvae of the furniture and powder post beetles. Others live in very dry environments such as the Namib Desert by using ingenious ways of procuring moisture. One species condenses water from fog by climbing to an exposed spot and lifting its abdomen. Water droplets collect near its mouth opening, and these are then swallowed by the beetle. In contrast, many families of beetles live closely associated with fresh water—the whirligig beetles on the water surface, and the predacious diving beetles below.

The 12 entries on beetles in this section of the book cover some of the most important groupings into which the Coleoptera are divided; illustrations are of particular species. To distinguish beetles from other insects, look for hard wing-cases, and allow for the enormous variations on this basic beetle format.

Identifying beetles

Shape
Body shape is often a reliable way of identifying beetle families, even if you have to resort to using a hand lens or microscope to detect physical characteristics not readily discernible to the naked eye.

Ladybirds (family Coccinellidae) can generally be recognized by being oval or highly convex; the rhinoceros beetles (Scarabaeidae) by being robust and having large horns on the head or thorax; the water beetles by their streamlined appearance; and the toktokkies (family Tenebrionidae) by their globular thorax and abdomen.

Most beetles are brown or black, but in some families the colour is distinctive: ladybirds, for instance, are often spotted; blister beetles (family Meloidae) usually have transverse yellow and black bands across the elytra; and most of the jewel of buprestid beetles (family Buprestidae) have bright, metallic colours.

Head
The shape of the head makes it easy to identify some of the families. In the weevils (family Curculionidae) the head tapers off into a shortish or longish snout (rostrum); the heads of shot-hole borers (family Bostrychidae) are directed downwards.

Antennae
The antennae of some insect families are good identification pointers. In the stag beetles (family Lucanidae) and most of the weevils the antennae are elbowed; in the longhorns, or longicorns (family Cerambycidae), they are usually as long as or longer than the body and directed backwards; in the dung beetles they end in a club consisting of three to seven movable plates. Ground beetles (family Carabidae) possess antennae, which are inserted between the eye and the base of the mandible, but the closely related tiger beetles (subfamily Cicindelinae) have antennae in front of the eye and above the base of the mandible.

Mouthparts and eyes
These are not very useful for identification purposes, but the carnivorous ground and tiger beetles have prominent and sharp mandibles that face forward. Similarly, the eyes are not very characteristic of families, but if you see a beetle whose eye is divided into an upper and lower half, then it can only be a whirligig beetle.

Legs and feet
If you are observant you can learn a great deal about the identity and behaviour of beetles by looking at

Beetles

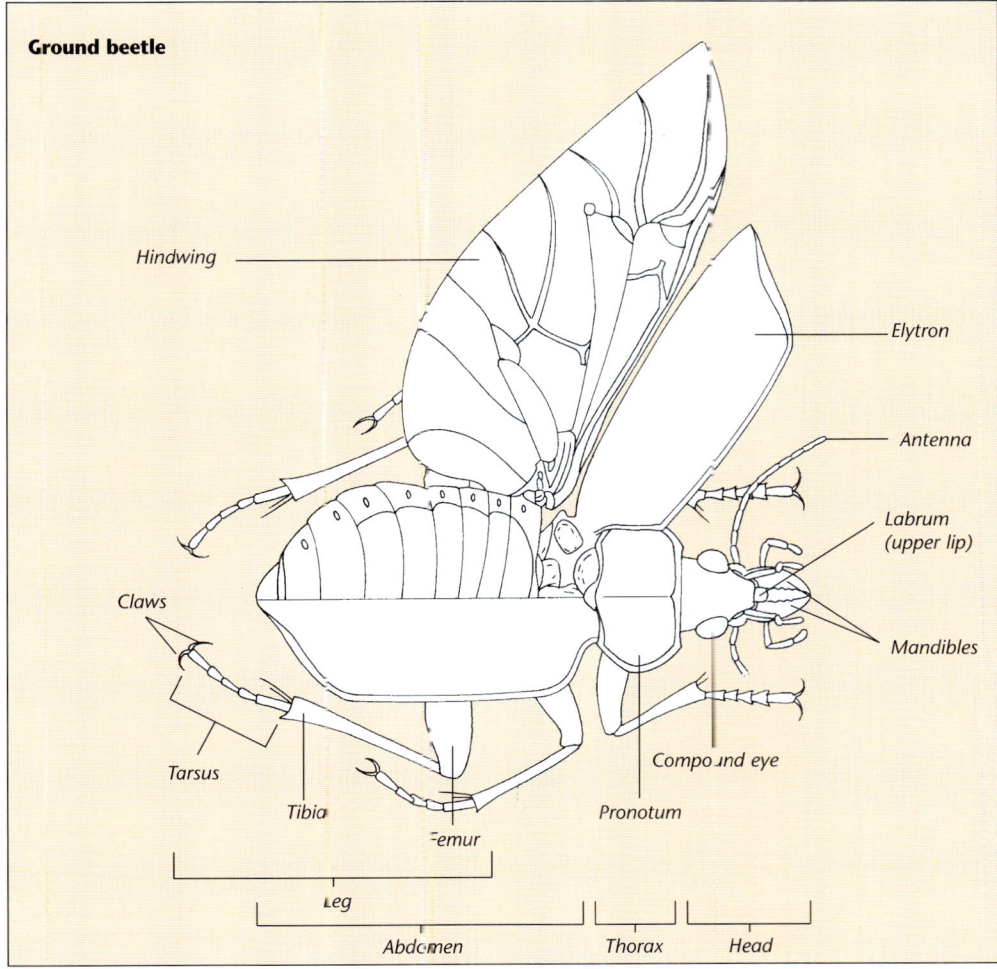

Ground beetle

their legs. Very long legs may point to a desert-dwelling member of the Tenebrionidae, which uses its legs to lift its body away from the hot sand during the day. A beetle which has its front legs ending in curved tibia with strong projections, and the feet (tarsi) apparently missing, is undoubtedly a dung beetle—the peculiar legs are used to manipulate the dung in which they lay their eggs. A small beetle with enlarged hindlegs that enable it to jump, is a flea beetle.

Experts very often look at the number of segments on the feet to classify beetles, and this approach will undoubtedly assist you too. Ladybirds and leaf beetles, which sometimes look superficially alike, have four and five segments respectively. Toktokkies and their various relatives have five segments on the front and middle legs but only four on the hindlegs.

One of the most important ways of classifying beetles is to examine the underside of the first visible abdominal segment. If this segment is ventrally divided in two by the base of the leg (coxa), the beetle belongs to the more primitive suborder Adephaga and, if it is complete, to the suborder Polyphaga.

Elytra

Some families can be recognized by the extent to which the elytra cover the abdomen. Normally the abdomen is completely covered, but in the rove beetles (family Staphylinidae) the elytra are usually very short and most of the abdominal segments are exposed, while in the sap or dried fruit beetles (family Nitidulidae) two or three segments are exposed.

Beetles

PREDACIOUS GROUND BEETLES
Oogpisters (Family Carabidae; *Anthia* and related genera)

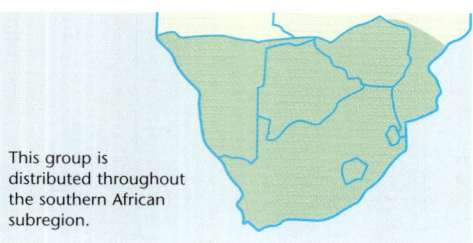

Size: Length 3-60mm.
Colour: Black, often with white, yellow and red patches on the thorax or elytra (wing-cases).
Most like: Certain darkling beetles (including toktokkies). Both are large, black, flightless beetles, but predacious ground beetles have prominent sabre-like mouthparts and are much more active than darkling beetles.
Habitat: Widespread, but most abundant in the drier parts (Namibia, Namaqualand and the Karoo). The large species are often seen crossing roads.

This group is distributed throughout the southern African subregion.

As their name implies, nearly all ground beetles are incapable of flight, but they are agile runners and, if threatened, rely mainly on their speed to escape. However, they have also developed a very effective form of chemical defence. Ground beetles of the genus *Anthia* and related genera secrete an abdominal substance of some organic acid, for example formic acid, which they are able to squirt out in a strong jet at an attacker. The jet has a range of up to 30cm and can blind a small domestic animal if it is not treated immediately. The substance can also harm the human eye, and causes severe pain if it touches human skin. The Afrikaans name for the beetle 'eye-shooter', draws attention to this defensive technique. Don't pick up this beetle with bare hands—it can give you a deep bite.

The wing-cases of the *Anthia* ground beetle are fused together, and the membranous wings that normally would lie underneath have disappeared. Light-coloured spots on the wing-cases advertise the fact that the beetle is unpalatable. They also alert potential predators to its vigorous defence mechanisms.

Ground beetles prey on insects, including such pests as grasshoppers and caterpillars. They are fierce hunters, searching for prey at random. Some species go as far as to defend their 'territory' against other beetles wishing to use the same hunting ground.

WHIRLIGIG BEETLES
Waterhondjies (Family Gyrinidae)

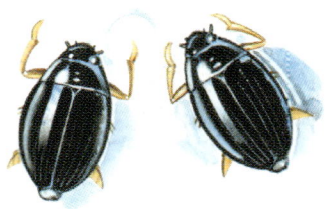

Size: Length 3-18mm.
Colour: Shiny black or grey, with a paler border to the wing-cases and back in some species.
Most like: Can only be confused with the other major group of aquatic beetles, the Dytiscidae. Whirligigs are mostly confined to the surface of the water, and only dive for brief spells. They are smaller than most diving beetles.
Habitat: Freshwater pools in gently flowing streams (in which the current bears the whirligig beetle's diet of dead or drowning insects).

This family is distributed throughout the southern African subregion.

Whirligig beetles are wonderfully equipped for their aquatic life. The body is smooth and streamlined; the four rearmost legs are fringed with bristles and act as efficient paddles; the front pair of legs is longer than the others and is used to catch prey or, when necessary, to cling to submerged objects. But the most remarkable adaptation is the whirligig's dual-vision eyes. Each eye is divided into two sections, an upper part for air vision and a lower part for underwater vision. The upper part is situated on top of the head, with the lower beneath it, giving the effect of four eyes.

Whirligigs swim in groups on the surface of the water, waiting for the current to deliver their dinner. Any insect trapped on the water film is seized and consumed with relish. When alarmed, the beetles will speed up their characteristic twirling locomotion and, as a last resort, will dive below the surface, still moving around in agitation. A small silver air bubble trapped under the wing-cases serves as the whirligigs life-support system, enabling it to breathe under water for some time.

There are about 53 species of whirligig beetles in southern Africa, most of which can fly well. Their occasional flights take them on expeditions to other pools.

The female lays eggs in neat rows on submerged vegetation. The centipedelike larvae that hatch breathe under water through 10 pairs of feathery gills, and feed on small insects on the bottom of the pool.

Beetles

WATER BEETLES

Waterkewers (Family Dytiscidae)

Size: *Length up to 40 mm.*
Colour: *Bodies pale yellow to black, or greenish black with yellow margins.*
Most like: *Whirligig beetles, but the latter are rarely found under water. Water beetles cannot be confused with terrestrial beetles, their bodies are distinctively streamlined and orange-pip-shaped, their legs flattened for swimming. They walk very feebly and clumsily.*
Habitat: *Freshwater pools and ponds where there is little or no current. The beetles are often attracted in large numbers to artificial lights.*

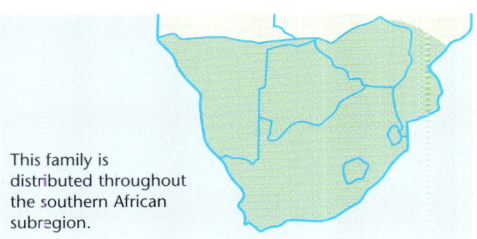

This family is distributed throughout the southern African subregion.

Water beetles swim below the surface and are beautifully streamlined for doing so. When they wish to breathe they swim to the surface. The beetle comes up end-first, and an air bubble is then trapped between the two elytra (wing-cases) and the abdomen. Equipped with this new aqualung, the beetle can dive again.

Among the water beetles, the large species of *Cybister* is very common. This fierce predator of aquatic insects, small fish and tadpoles owns a useful arsenal of defensive weapons, including a sharp, backward-projecting spine on its underside that can draw blood. Glands in its neck can emit a foul-smelling white fluid capable of temporarily stunning fishes and frogs, while two anal glands secrete an ammonialike fluid that is discharged with a tiny explosion.

To propel itself in the water *Cybister* uses its powerful hindlegs, which can carry stiff brown bristles. These legs can be 'operated' like oars: on the backward kick the bristles 'feather' out, offering a wide surface of resistance to the water, but when the legs are pulled back before the next stroke they are turned at an angle, so that the bristles lie flat.

Like other aquatic beetles, for example the whirligig beetle, *Cybister* flies well and covers large distances during the evening in search of other bodies of water. On land, however, it is awkward and ill-equipped.

DUNG BEETLES

Miskruiers (Family Scarabaeidae)

Size: *Length 5-50 mm.*
Colour: *Black, brown or metallic bronze, blue or green.*
Most like: *Certain fruit chafer beetles (Cetoniinae) but generally more oval and darker-hued. Dung beetles do not fly as readily, and are always terrestrial; they are not found in vegetation.*
Habitat: *From arid desert to tropical forest.*

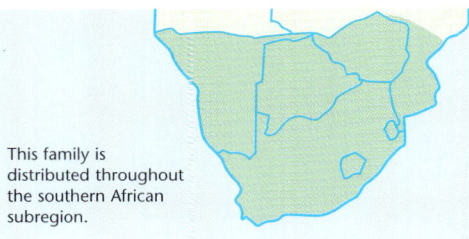

This family is distributed throughout the southern African subregion.

To the ancient Egyptians the scarab or dung beetle was sacred, and today it is certainly recognized as a beneficial scavenger. Southern Africa has a rich supply of these insects; there are about 300 species in the Scarabaeidae family, varying greatly in size, appearance and habits. The typical scarab beetle belongs to the subfamily Scarabaeinae.

Common to these species is the habit of rolling dung into a ball. The completed ball is often many times larger and heavier than the beetle, which may then roll this precious food store energetically for several metres before burying it in a hole it digs in the ground. Mating takes place in this bridal chamber, and in due course the female lays an egg in a hollow at the side of the ball of dung. When the white grub hatches, it begins feeding on the nutritious dung store.

Some species breed above ground within a dung pad. The female lays her egg inside a small piece of dung, then rolls this into a ball that remains within the dung pad while the larva hatches.

A third type of dung beetle excavates a nest beneath a dung heap, with a tunnel connecting the two.

Generally dung beetles transport their dung pellets by pushing them backwards with their hindlegs. But the flightless species of the Namib Desert grips the pellet with its hindlegs and drags it forwards.

There are dung beetles that augment their diet by eating carrion—the flesh of dead animals. Others feed on the fungus that develops on decaying vegetable matter, and some have a taste for wild mushrooms.

Beetles

Fruit beetles
Vrugtetorre *(Subfamily Cetoniinae)*

Size: Length 10-70 mm.
Colour: Most fruit beetles are brilliantly coloured. One common species (*Pachnoda*) is black, with rows of bright yellow patches on the wing-cases; another is green, with yellow bordering the wing-cases.
Most like: Blister beetles, as they have the same coloration and feed together on flowers. Fruit beetles, however, are flat, not round in cross-section as are blister beetles.
Habitat: Orchards, flowerbeds, beehives.

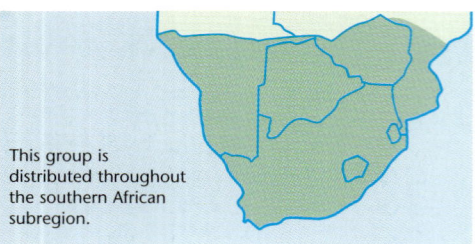

This group is distributed throughout the southern African subregion.

Rhinoceros beetles
Renosterkewers *(Subfamily Dynastinae)*

Size: Length 10-45 mm.
Colour: Black or brown.
Most like: Scarab beetles, to which they are related, but rhinoceros beetles have parallel-sided bodies which are more elongate than those of scarabs.
Habitat: Found generally on decaying wood and plant matter; compost heaps.

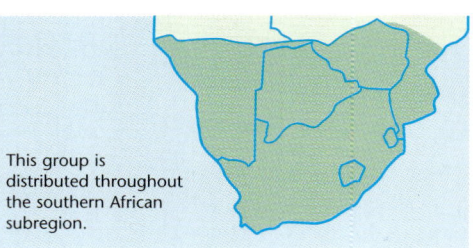

This group is distributed throughout the southern African subregion.

Fruit beetles are strong fliers and can cause fruit and flower mayhem during the course of their day's foraging. At night, they repair to special 'sleeping trees' or else bury themselves in the soil at the foot of the very plants they have been ravaging.

Roses are among the flowers most at risk, hence the name 'rose beetle' given to the genus *Pachnoda*. Almost any soft, ripe fruits, including apricots, peaches, plums and pawpaws, are also attacked—the beetle bores into the fruit to extract the juices. Some fruit beetles enjoy honey, fearlessly entering beehives in search of it—this species also destroys wasps' nests. And some beetles of this family feed on tree sap.

There are, however, some insect-eating species which are regarded as beneficial. One of these enjoys the poisonous yellow aphids found on milkweed plants; another makes a meal of the soft brown scale insects on citrus trees.

The larvae of fruit beetles feed on decaying vegetable debris and on plant roots. The female of *Pachnoda sinuata* takes a trick from the dung beetle: she makes several little balls of dung (or compost) and then lays an egg in each of them. The tiny larvae that hatch feed on the contents of these balls before transforming themselves into pupae. You may find up to a dozen of these little dung balls attached to one another within the warm, moist intimacy of an aromatic manure heap or pile of compost, or in a well-fertilized flowerbed.

An unmistakeable feature of the rhinoceros beetle is the rhinolike horn that adorns the head of the male, making him look so top-heavy that he seems in constant danger of toppling over. The species with the longest horns, *Oryctes boas*, uses horns as weapons when two males do battle. This species is the largest and most widely distributed of the 60 different species recorded in southern Africa. (The southern African rhinoceros beetle cannot compare in size to specimens found in Central and South America, where this unusual-looking insect can grow to a length of 17,5 cm.)

These insects have squat, lozenge-shaped bodies with protruding heads, although the bases of the antennae cannot be seen from above. They are nocturnal, and occasionally you may see one of them flying haphazardly towards a light source to which they are attracted. Beetles that have collided with a light, or a lighted window, may fall to the ground, where they lie stunned for some time before pursuing their flight again.

The larvae of rhinoceros beetles, which are white and very large, are usually found in manure heaps or piles of humus, where they develop into pupae without the protective covering of a cocoon. The larvae of some species feed on plant roots, while the adult beetles nip through the stems of young shoots just below ground-level. Because of these disconcerting habits, both larvae and beetles are regarded as serious pests on cultivated land and also on lawns—in particular the genus *Heteronychus*. *Heteronychus licas* damages sugar cane, while *H. arator*, the black maize beetle, attacks maize, potatoes and pineapples.

Beetles

GLOW-WORMS AND FIREFLIES

Glimwurms en vuurvliegies *(Family Lampyridae)*

Size: Length 5-25 mm.
Colour: Dark brown, tan or black.
Most like: Similar in shape to some ground beetles, but are small, elongate, parallel-sided; the head and huge eyes are covered by a shield.
Habitat: Woods, ditches, lawns; also in forests, bushy areas and near vleis.

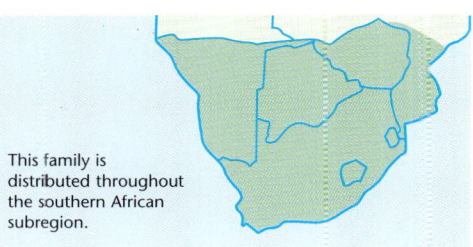

This family is distributed throughout the southern African subregion.

Neither worms nor flies, these fascinating insects are, in fact, beetles.

At night, the end of the abdomen lights up as a result of a chemical reaction between a luminous substance, luciferin, contained in the tail, and an oxidizing enzyme, luciferase, in the blood. Cells filled with tiny crystals act as reflectors. Since the light is confined to the visible part of the spectrum (that is, there is no infrared or ultraviolet), virtually no energy-wasting heat is generated.

The luminescence enables the sexes to locate each other. Among glow-worms it is the female who literally holds a torch for her mate as she radiates a steady glow. She is up to 25 mm long and wingless. She looks rather like a larva or a worm, although in the Luciolinae the females are winged. Male glow-worms have wings and resemble fireflies. Communication between the sexes is similar to that of toktokkies, and results in mating.

The family is represented by two main subfamilies: Lampyrinae and Luciolinae.

Both male and female Luciolinae are winged, and the male's light signals are brighter than the female's. He is a flasher—or, more accurately, a flickerer—as he flies through the dark, and can control the flash frequency of his signal.

Each firefly species emits its own, distinctive light signals—and these visual IDs are sufficient, it seems, to prevent crossbreeding among species (there are about 30 firefly species in southern Africa).

The larvae of these insects closely resemble the female glow-worm.

LADYBIRD BEETLES

Liewenheersbesies *(Family Coccinellidae)*

Size: Length 0,5-12 mm.
Colour: A bright, shiny yellow or red, with a pattern of black dots or crescent-shaped markings.
Most like: Leaf beetles, although these are flatter and rarely oval in shape.
Habitat: Plants that are infested with aphids, mealy bugs and other pests. Cultivated crops including cucumbers, potatoes and maize.

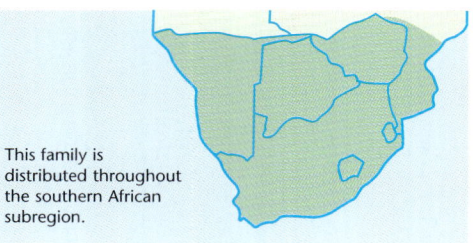

This family is distributed throughout the southern African subregion.

At an early age we are taught to admire this pretty little beetle, and most species are certainly worthy of our protection since they feed, both in the larval stage and as adults, on aphids, which are garden pests. Their bright colouring is, in fact, a warning to birds and other predators to keep clear. If you pick up a ladybird and manhandle it, it secretes a bitter, yellow, unpleasant-tasting liquid from between the joints of its legs.

The female lays her cluster of 20-30 yellow, elongated eggs on the underside of a leaf, conveniently close to an aphid colony. When the little, black six-legged larvae emerge they sink their sharp jaws into the aphids and suck out their vital juices. Prominent yellow or white markings develop on the growing larvae, which eventually leave their food source to pupate from a stone.

How the nursery rhyme about the ladybird originated is a mystery. She is exhorted to 'fly away home' because her house is on fire, but home for *Cheilomenes lunata* is likely to be a rock crevice where these insects hibernate. Most ladybird species can fly.

Without the action of predacious insects such as the red-and-black ladybird beetle, the aphid population would soon overrun gardens and cultivated crops. As it happens, most ladybirds are beneficial pest-controllers.

However, one subfamily, the Epilachninae, are regarded as pests themselves. They are vegetarians, and attack the leaves of a wide range of crops, especially those of the cucumber family.

Beetles

TOKTOKKIES

Toktokkies *(Family Tenebrionidae; Psammodes and related genera)*

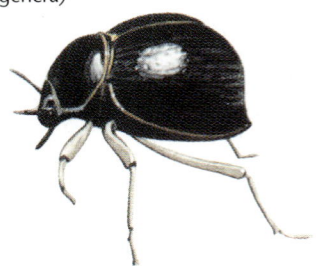

Size: *Length up to 65 mm.*
Colour: *Black or dark brown.*
Most like: *Toktokkies and their many relatives may be confused with predacious ground beetles, which occupy the same habitat. The latter, however, have large, sabrelike jaws, which are not present in toktokkies.*
Habitat: *More arid, warmer areas, with sandy soil and little ground cover.*

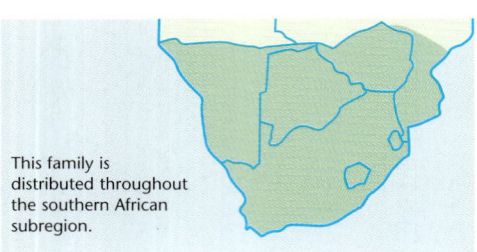

This family is distributed throughout the southern African subregion.

These conspicuous members of the large family of darkling beetles are stout, heavy-bodied and wingless, with a tough outer casing. Their habit of knocking loudly on the ground at intervals has given their name to a children's game (knocking on front doors and then running away). The beetle makes the noise by raising its abdomen and then bringing it down on the surface of the ground several times in quick succession.

The tapping is a form of communication between both sexes. The male initiates the tapping and is answered by a receptive female. After a prolonged exchange of signals, the pair finally makes contact and mates.

The females lay single eggs, each about six millimetres long, which they place in a shallow hollow in the ground. The long, yellow larvae that hatch live in the soil.

The mature toktokkie beetle scavenges on a variety of plant and animal debris.

The Tenebrionidae family to which this insect belongs is very large, with at least 3500 species in southern Africa. In the Namib Desert some species survive by collecting dew from specially excavated trenches that trap moisture from banks of fog rolling in from the Atlantic Ocean. Others in the same area drink by doing a 'headstand', thereby allowing condensed dew to trickle into their mouths. The Namib is also home to the fastest running beetle in the world, a Tenebrionid that scurries across the scorching sands at lightning speed. Another species boasts the longest beetle legs in the world.

BLISTER BEETLES

Blaartrektorre *(Family Meloidae)*

Size: *Length 5-50 mm.*
Colour: *Usually black with bright red, orange or yellow markings.*
Most like: *Mylabris species may be confused with Pachnoda fruit beetles as they have the same coloration.*
Habitat: *Found on flowering plants throughout the summer.*

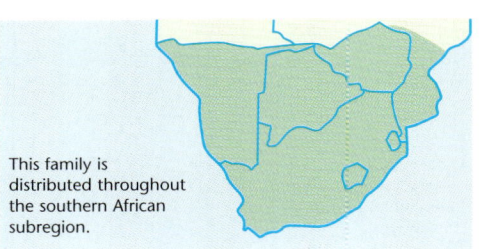

This family is distributed throughout the southern African subregion.

Among the brightly coloured blister beetles is the CMR beetle, so named because the black-and-yellow stripes across its wing-cases resemble the stripes on the uniforms of the Cape Mounted Rifles Brigade, a unit which no longer exists. The purpose of such bright markings is to advise predators to keep away, for the body fluid of these beetles contains a poison, cantharadin. On human skin it raises blisters, and it is used medicinally for this purpose. If taken internally, cantharadin can do much harm and even cause death.

For gardeners blister beetles are a mixed blessing. Their fondness for petals is bad news for flowerbeds; knowing that enemies such as lizards and birds are deterred by their warning semaphore of stripes, the beetles take their time in crawling, or noisily flying, from one blossom to another. But blister beetle larvae do sterling work by feeding on the eggs of locusts (including the notorious swarm locust) and grasshoppers.

The female is a model of motherhood. Having laboriously dug a shallow hole in the ground, she lays her eggs in it, carefully covers them and then repeats the process, day after day, until her ovaries are exhausted. Then, having fulfilled her duties, she dies.

Her offspring go through several metamorphoses: first from egg to tiny, six-legged larva that must find the underground egg pod of a locust or grasshopper if it is to survive. Once entrenched in this pod it becomes a fat white grub, which rests during the winter months. Then, with the advent of the warmer weather, it casts its skin and becomes a pupa. Finally it emerges in all its striking, striped beetle glory.

Beetles

LONG-HORNED BEETLES

Langhoringkewers (Family Cerambycidae)

Size: Length 8-75 mm.
Colour: A great variation, nocturnal species being grey, brown or black; flower-eaters are brightly coloured.
Most like: No other insect. The oversized antennae of these beetles make them quite distinctive.
Habitat: Trees, shrubs, herbaceous plants.

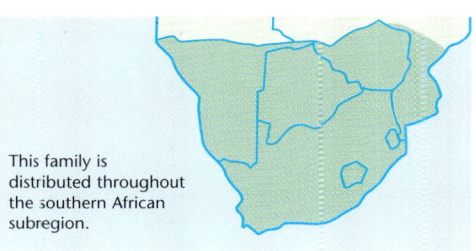

This family is distributed throughout the southern African subregion.

'Long-horned' refers to the long antennae (often longer than the body) of this large family of beetles, of which there are over 800 species in southern Africa alone. Most of them are woodborers, with enormously powerful jaws that can chomp through the hardest of woods. Fortunately, most species are interested only in weakened or dying branches and trees. By speeding up the breakdown of this wood and allowing the nutrients within it to be returned to the soil, the beetle actually performs a useful natural function.

But there are long-horned beetles that damage healthy trees and are regarded as pests. *Ceroplesis thunbergi* attacks wattles. Other trees at risk include willows, fig trees and orange trees. The larvae of many such long-horned beetles feed on freshly cut logs.

The long-horned beetle population is controlled in a macabre way, for the larvae are cannibals. After several of them have hatched from a group of eggs, they eat one another—until the survivors are so few and far apart that no further damage can be done. Even so, the surviving grubs take pains to avoid the burrows of their peers as they tunnel through the wood, turning away when approaching another burrow. It is thought that one of the ways by which they can detect another grub's presence is by means of microscopic sense organs, sensitive to airborne vibrations, that are scattered over their bodies.

If you hold a long-horned beetle between your fingers it is apt to emit a pathetic little creaky squeak. It is made when the back of the neck rubs against a roughened area between the bases of the wing-cases, but its purpose remains obscure.

WEEVILS

Kalanders (Family Curculionidae)

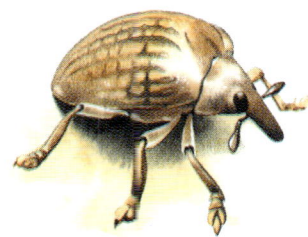

Size: Length 1-60 mm.
Colour: Usually brown or black, and often with a camouflage pattern of other colours. The largest weevils have pink or red spots
Most like: Ground beetles (Carabidae), but weevils are recognizable by their elongated snouts and 'elbowed' antennae.
Habitat: An extensive range of plants, including many cultivated crops such as citrus, vines, tobacco and maize, as well as stored grains.

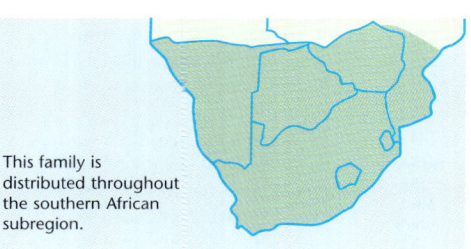

This family is distributed throughout the southern African subregion.

Weevils make up the largest beetle family in the world. There are more than 2 500 species in southern Africa alone, all of which are characterized by the family's distinctive snout or 'rostrum' at the front of the head. Among different species this snout varies enormously in shape and size, from short and squat to long and narrow. The female cycad weevil, *Antliarrhinus zamiae*, has a threadlike extension three times the length of her body; with it she bores into an ovule (seed) in a cycad cone, lays an egg, and shoves it to the end of the tunnel that she has made.

The leaf-rolling weevil has a short snout, and so the female resorts to other means to protect her egg. Like an origami enthusiast, she cuts out a portion of leaf and, using her legs, folds it into a neat little container into which she deposits her egg. The leaf is both protection and, in due course, food. The larvae of weevils have no legs and therefore cannot forage on the external surface of plants; invariably they develop within the plant tissue.

Weevils are commonly regarded as pests. They are perhaps most notorious for destroying stored grain. The dark red *Brachycerus obesus* is about 25 mm long and enjoys feeding on the newly emerged leaves of garden bulbs, including those of the gladiolus and lily.

Weevils are unusual in that they owe part of their colour to the presence of small scales which can be rubbed off.

Butterflies and moths

Was it really once thought that butterflies stole milk and butter? That explanation has been suggested for their unusual name, yet it is difficult to associate these beautiful, fragile insects with anything so down-to-earth—and it takes a real flight of the imagination to link them, and their closely related cousins, moths, with the unlovely caterpillars from which they have been transformed.

Butterflies and moths make up the large insect order Lepidoptera, a word that means 'scale-winged': the four wings of these creatures are covered in tiny, flat, powderlike scales that carry the wings' pattern and colouring. These scales rub off rather easily.

Lepidoptera share one characteristic with beetles and flies: they both have four distinct stages in their life cycle. The egg hatches into a larva, known as a caterpillar; the fully-grown caterpillar becomes an apparently inactive pupa (or 'chrysalis'); and from the husk of the chrysalis the adult emerges, its wings initially soft, damp and quite small. Fluid is pumped into the wings from the butterfly's body, gradually enlarging them, and they are held apart until dry.

Many Lepidoptera species are better known in their larval stage than as winged insects. An example is *Bombyx mori*, not an indigenous species, yet familiar to schoolchildren as the silkworm; the 'worm' (scientifically a wrong term) is the caterpillar of a moth. Similarly, that troublesome garden pest, the cutworm, is the larval stage of a moth of the genus *Agrotis*; 'army-worms', so named because they are apt to invade crops in large numbers, are caterpillars too.

Most adult butterflies and moths are equipped with a coiled proboscis that can be extended for feeding and drinking; nectar from flower blossoms is consumed in this fashion, and pollination is incidentally brought about as the insect moves from plant to plant. But in many moths, including the emperors, the proboscis has atrophied or disappeared altogether.

Lepidoptera use many different tricks to avoid being eaten in the larval or adult stage. Many larvae are camouflaged to look like part of a leaf or twig. Others carry spines or stinging hairs. The larvae of some hawk moths have a large, black spot surrounded by a yellow ring on the front part of the body. This looks like a glaring eye when the head is withdrawn into the thorax. Most moths avoid being eaten by birds by flying only at night, while butterflies ensure their survival by flying erratically, or through camouflage or poisonous substances in their body.

The order Lepidoptera contains more than 160 000 species of moths and butterflies around the world. Some 12 000 of these are found in southern Africa—about 830 butterfly species and more than 11 000 moths.

NOTE: The maps reflect butterfly distribution in South Africa only.

How to tell a butterfly from a moth

There are a number of good, though not infallible, guidelines, for distinguishing between moths and butterflies. Most butterflies are more brightly coloured than moths. They are mostly active in the daytime and have long, slender, smooth bodies, whereas most moths have relatively short, heavy, furry bodies and fly by night. At rest, butterflies hold their wings upwards or spread out beside them, while most moths fold their forewings over their hindwings, flat along the body.

Close inspection reveals that the antennae or feelers of butterflies thicken at the tips, like clubs, but those of moths are generally threadlike or feathery. It is this last distinction that has given butterflies their group name Rhopalocera ('horns like clubs'), and moths the group name Heterocera ('horns of different kinds').

Identifying butterflies and moths

Size

A butterfly's size, in combination with other physical characteristics or habits, can be a great help in identifying it. The largest of our butterflies are the swallowtails (family Papilionidae), which attain a total wingspan of up to 12 centimetres. The swallowtail's short, stubby hindwing tails, together with its characteristic habit of constantly fluttering its wings when feeding on flowers or laying its eggs, will probably enable you to identify it positively.

Other large butterflies (wingspan 7-8 cm) are the charaxes (family Nymphalidae), which you can distinguish by their short, sharply pointed tails on each hindwing. Medium-sized butterflies (wingspan 3,5-5 cm) include the acraeas (family Acraeidae), pansies (family Nymphalidae) and whites (family Pieridae), while among the very small butterflies are the blues and coppers of the family Lycaenidae, with wingspans of two to three centimetres.

Colour

The butterfly families of southern Africa come in a spectacular array of colours, some of which change according to whether the butterfly emerges from its pupa during the wet or the dry season. The fact that some of the butterflies mimic the colours and patterns of others doesn't always allow for easy identification. However, there are certain families that you can sometimes identify by colour alone. Members of the family Pieridae, for instance, which includes the whites and the African migrant, generally have white or yellow rings, sometimes with black markings. Other species of the same family are largely white, but have vivid red, purple or orange forewing tips.

Butterflies of the family Satyridae, which includes the Table Mountain beauty, are known as the 'browns' for the characteristic brown colour of most species, although they typically have one or more yellowish eye-spots along their wing margins. These butterflies are very common in meadows and in open glades in woodland. Milkweed butterflies (family Danaidae) may be brownish orange with black-and-white areas on their wing tips, or dark brown with whitish spots or blotches.

The largest, most diverse butterfly family is the Nymphalidae, which includes the pansies, commodores, charaxes and the mother-of-pearl. Most are intricately patterned and range in colour from whites and reds to browns and black.

Butterflies and moths

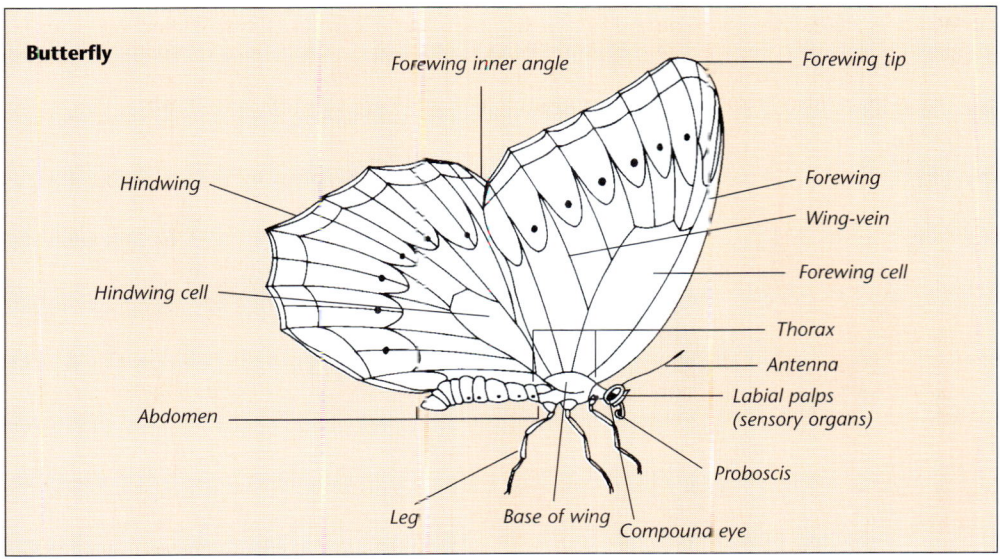

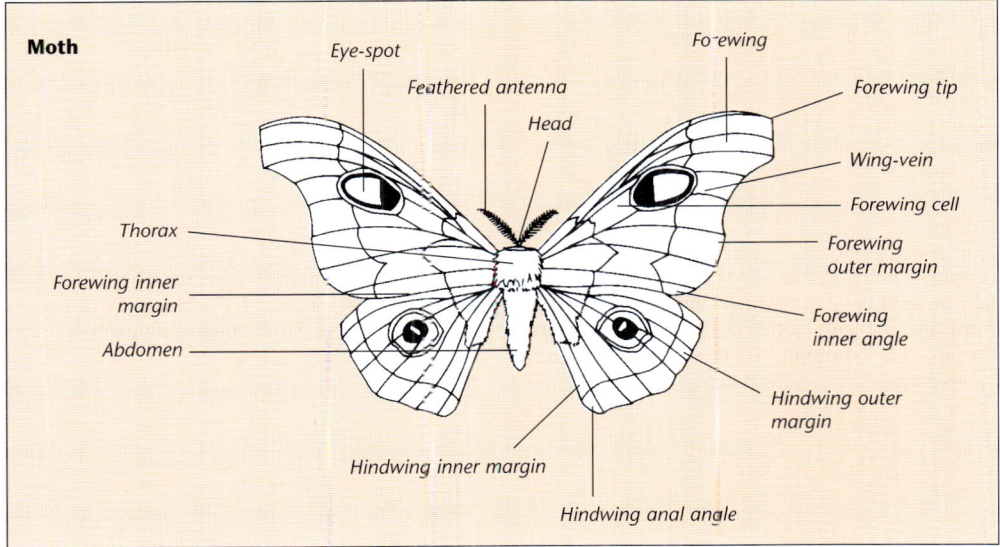

Movement

If you cannot positively identify a butterfly by its colour or markings, carefully observe how it flies. Poisonous or distasteful species (and their mimics) tend to fly slowly and deliberately. The milkweed butterfly, for instance, flies very slowly. So does the garden acraea—a common butterfly in many suburban gardens—which is characteristically red with black spots and transparent wing tips. Among the very rapid fliers are the Table Mountain beauty, the scarlet-tip and the diadem.

Overall impressions

If by size, colour or movement you are still unable to identify a butterfly, try to gain an overall impression of its physical characteristics, habits, any peculiarities and its habitat.

If, for instance, the butterfly is small, is found near ant nests, has delicate, hairlike tails on its hindwings and has iridescent blue or orange wings, it is quite likely a member of the family Lycaenidae—the blues or coppers. If you see a dull-brown, mothlike creature with a very large head and strongly developed antennae flying rapidly about during the day, it will most likely be a skipper (family Hesperiidae).

As in most moths, the males of the emperor moths (Saturniidae) have feathery antennae, while those of the females are threadlike. Their wingspan ranges from a few centimetres to over 30 cm in some species from Asia. Nearly all have a large, ringed eye-spot in each hindwing and a smaller one in each forewing.

Some hawk moths (family Sphingidae) are nearly as big as the emperors but have narrow, streamlined wings and usually very long tongues. Their larvae, which can grow to 14 cm long, are characterized by having a hornlike tail. The larvae of the tiger moths (Arctiidae) are covered in a thick brownish fur and for this reason are called 'woolly bears'. They are often very common in gardens. Loopers are larvae of the family Geometridae and move by bending and stretching their bodies—hence their other name, 'measuring worms'. Their adults are usually grey or blackish grey but with delicate patterns on their wings. This is one of the more common moth groups.

Butterflies and moths

Mocker swallowtail

Na-aperswaelstert *(Princeps dardanus cenea)*

Size: Wingspan (m) 8,0-9,0 cm, (f) 7,5-8,5 cm.
Colour: Males yellow, outer third of each forewing black; irregular black band across each hindwing which has a long, broad 'tail'. Females quite unlike males, existing in several colour forms; none in South Africa has hindwing tails, and all have black forewings and broad, black outer borders to the hindwings; markings orange-red, white or yellow, depending on the form.
Most like: Male similar to other swallowtails, none of which, however, has inner two-thirds of forewing yellow. Female may resemble the southern milkweed butterfly *(Danaus chrysippus aegyptius)*, the chief *(Amauris echeria)* or the friar *(Amauris niavius dominicanus)*.
Habitat: Rainforest, from Knysna to KwaZulu-Natal, Mpumalanga and Swaziland.

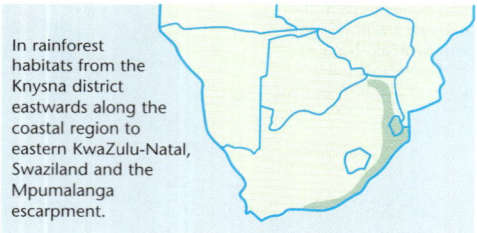

In rainforest habitats from the Knysna district eastwards along the coastal region to eastern KwaZulu-Natal, Swaziland and the Mpumalanga escarpment.

The mocker swallowtail exists in several colour forms and is one of the most confusing of butterflies. The tailed male is instantly recognizable and, although he is regarded as a tasty meal by many birds, he nevertheless appears to court danger by flying in a leisurely manner along paths and the edges of forests.

The tail-less females rarely venture from their woodland habitat, despite the protection they obtain from the fact that their markings closely mimic those of four or five other, unpalatable species of milkweed butterfly. Some of the females are so different from each other, and from the male, that they were once believed to be different species. Their relationship was confirmed, however, when it was established that one batch of eggs could give rise to butterflies of several different forms.

Interestingly, the females have not only dispensed with 'tails' and altered their colour patterns to copy other species—they have also adopted a similar slow and deliberate flight to reinforce the deception.

Citrus swallowtail

Lemoenskoenlapper
(Princeps demodocus demodocus)

Size: Wingspan (m) 8,0-9,0 cm, (f) 8,5-9,0 cm.
Colour: Black with a yellow band across each hindwing that continues, broken, across the middle of the forewing. Sexes similar. No 'tails' to hindwing despite the name 'swallowtail'. Two large blue, black and orange eye-spots occur on each hindwing.
Most like: Emperor swallowtail, but lacks the tails.
Habitat: Widely varied, from Karoo to the fringes of tropical forest; suburban gardens; citrus orchards.

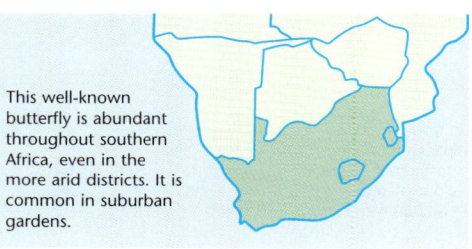

This well-known butterfly is abundant throughout southern Africa, even in the more arid districts. It is common in suburban gardens.

Also known as the Christmas butterfly, because it is particularly abundant in midsummer, the citrus swallowtail is certainly the most widespread of all our swallowtails. The female lays her eggs singly on the leaves of horsewood, small knobwood and white ironwood trees as well as on citrus trees; she also uses the leaves of shrubs and the garden herb, fennel, as egg-laying sites. The green caterpillars, which have dark brown and orange markings, are known as 'orange dogs', and in large enough numbers can cause damage to commercial citrus trees.

Although fat and helpless-looking, the orange dog is equipped with an extraordinary defence mechanism—the osmeterium. This fleshy, bright red, Y-shaped organ situated behind the head is normally hidden but, if the caterpillar is threatened, it shoots out the osmeterium suddenly, frightening predators off with its bright warning colour and pungent smell.

The male and female butterflies are similar, but you can tell them apart by looking at the eye-spot at the forward edge of each hindwing. On the outer edge of each spot is a half-moon of yellow in the male, or yellow flushed with orange-brown in the female.

Males of this species may often be found chasing other butterflies at the tops of small koppies at midday, a practice associated with mate selection.

Butterflies and moths

LARGE STRIPED SWORDTAIL

Jagswaardstert *(Graphium antheus)*

Size: Wingspan (m) 6-6,5 cm, (f) 6,5-7 cm.

Colour: Black with pale emerald-green spots, blotches and bars on forewings and hindwings. Each hindwing has a long, black, white-tipped, sabre-shaped 'tail'; there is a red spot on the inner edge of the wing, a short distance from the base of the curved tail.

Most like: Other species of green-and-black swordtails, but the three S-shaped (not straight) green bars at right angles to the front margin of the forewing are diagnostic; this butterfly also has a round, red-and-black eye-spot on the forward edge of the hindwing underside.

Habitat: Coastal bush and tropical and subtropical woodland along the coastline between the extreme Eastern Cape and Mozambique.

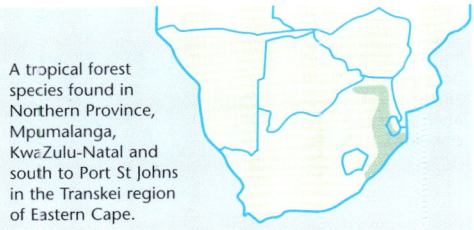

A tropical forest species found in Northern Province, Mpumalanga, KwaZulu-Natal and south to Port St Johns in the Transkei region of Eastern Cape.

Nature has endowed the male large striped swordtail with a special aphrodisiac that the females of the species find irresistible. This consists of a volatile chemical which the male disperses through a tuft of long hairs tucked under a flap on the inner edge of the hindwing. This aphrodisiac is lacking in the look-alike swallowtails, which are often mistaken for swordtails.

There is another difference between swallowtails and swordtails: while the caterpillars of swallowtails feed mainly on plants of the citrus family, the swordtails have a taste for plants of a different family, the Annonaceae, which include the indigenous hookberry and cluster-pear.

Predatory birds have to work hard to catch the fast and high-flying large striped swordtail. Like many other species, however, it is fond of settling on mud, apparently to suck moisture, but usually to obtain dissolved salts, and on flowers for nectar. At such times the butterfly presents an easy target for birds or butterfly collectors.

The blossoms of the noxious weed *Lantana camara* are particularly attractive to this species.

MOTHER-OF-PEARL

Perlemoenskoenlapper
(Protogoniomorpha parhassus aethiops)

Size: Wingspan (m) 6,5-7,5 cm, (f) 7,5-8,5 cm.

Colour: White above with a hint of green and violet. Uppersides have mother-of-pearl lustre and also carry several prominent eye-spots. The eye-spot nearest the outer corner of each hindwing has a black-and-purple centre, ringed by orange, yellow, then black. The tip of the forewing is bordered in black. Undersides of wing similar, more greenish, and eye-spots less developed.

Most like: Clouded mother-of-pearl which, however, is smaller and whose eye-spots are not as well-developed (except the one near the outer corner of the hindwing).

Habitat: KwaZulu-Natal coastal forests; rainforests of Mpumalanga.

Occurs in coastal and dune forests in the extreme Eastern Cape and KwaZulu-Natal and in well-wooded parts of Swaziland, Mpumalanga and Northern Province.

This spectacular and exotic-looking relative of the commodores and pansies shares with them the capacity to fool predators into thinking it is a leaf when it settles with its wings closed. The undersides of the wings have a pale false 'midrib' and, with the tail and forewing tip resembling a leaflike stalk and leaf-tip, the butterfly has an almost foolproof means of escaping the unwelcome attentions of predators. The eye-spots on the uppersides of the wings probably also serve to dissuade predators from attacking it.

This butterfly is a forest-loving species of the warmer and wetter eastern half of South Africa; it is easily recognizable by its backward-pointing tip to the forewing and the short but prominent tail on each hindwing. The females are larger than the males and are usually lighter in colour. Both males and females can fly sufficiently strongly to avoid predators. The typical flight pattern includes frequent gliding on wings held out at right angles to the body. These butterflies frequently settle on the underside of leaves, their own colours blending in with the pale green background.

Butterflies and moths

African migrant
Afrikaanse swerwer *(Catopsilia florella)*

Size: Wingspan (m) 5,5-6,0 cm, (f) 5,5-6,5 cm.
Colour: *Male creamy white above with slight greenish tinge; female usually yellow above with a narrow chestnut border to the tip of the forewing. Both sexes have a small black spot in the middle of the forewing.*
Most like: *Ant-heap white (Dixeia pigea), the male of which is white above but lacks green tinge and black spot in forewing, female ant-heap white usually has white forewings and yellow hindwings.*
Habitat: *Tolerates most environments from semi-desert and thornveld to the mountains of KwaZulu-Natal.*

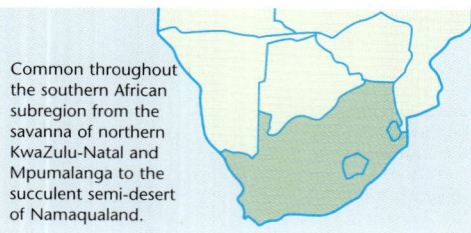

Common throughout the southern African subregion from the savanna of northern KwaZulu-Natal and Mpumalanga to the succulent semi-desert of Namaqualand.

This aptly named butterfly is one of the best known of the migratory butterflies of Africa. It is found from the Cape to Cairo in most habitats, except the wet tropical jungles of the equatorial regions.

One enormous migratory flight recorded in East Africa started at Christmas and was still continuing steadily in early April—against the seasonally prevailing winds. It was estimated that these butterflies were travelling at speeds of between 19 and 26 km per hour.

A similar migration, involving millions of butterflies, which took place in South Africa in 1966, was said to have advanced on a 640 km front through the Transkei region of Eastern Cape and KwaZulu-Natal. Holidaymakers saw hundreds of thousands of them flying over the beaches and out to sea.

The female African migrant ensures that an insect-eating bird cannot devour her entire brood of caterpillars at one fell swoop by laying her long, tapered eggs singly on separate plants.

Although African migrant caterpillars are known to eat the leaves of various species of cassia shrubs and trees, it is believed that they also eat other related species, perhaps acacias, to sustain them on their huge migrations.

Koppie charaxes
Koppiedubbelstert *(Charaxes jasius saturnus)*

Size: Wingspan (m) 6,5-7,0 cm, (f) 7,5-8,0 cm.
Colour: *Both sexes have a broad black band along the outer edges of their wings; this is followed by a light orange band across the middle area of each wing, while the bases of the wings are orange-red. The outer margins of the wings are chequered in orange and black and there are two long, slender tails to each hindwing.*
Most like: *Green-veined charaxes which has bright yellow, not orange-red, inner halves to its wings, and green veins in the forewings.*
Habitat: *Thornveld and bushveld.*

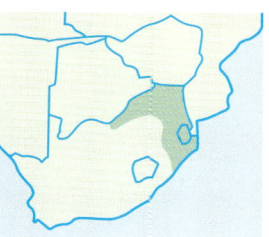

Favours thornveld and bushveld in northern KwaZulu-Natal, Swaziland, Mpumalanga, Northern Province and the North-West. Absent from the Gauteng and western Mpumalanga highveld.

Once it has established its 'post' or 'throne' on a twig or branch, the large and beautiful male koppie charaxes will defend it doggedly against all comers. Any other male of the species which strays into its territory will be harassed until it flees. This aggression is not confined to its own kind: koppie charaxes have also been known to attack intruding butterflies of other species, bees, beetles and small birds. One was observed chasing a hoopoe across its territory, while another repeatedly bumped the forehead of a visiting entomologist!

The butterfly, also known as the foxy charaxes, gets its name from the male's habit of spending the hotter hours of the day 'playing' at the tops of koppies—the sites they choose for territorial display and defence.

The females of the species are believed to visit the koppies only when they are ready for mating. They lay their eggs on hibiscus, fever-berry trees, boer-beans, pod mahogany, pride-of-De-Kaap and proteas.

Like other charaxes, the koppie charaxes is attracted to damp localities where it sucks up moisture. It has been observed feeding from the juices of hyaena droppings and at the bones of a leopard kill. It also congregates in areas where liquids contain dissolved salts or nitrogen.

Butterflies and moths

SMALL SPOTTED SAILOR
Spikkelswewer *(Neptis saclava marpessa)*

Size: Wingspan (m) 4,2-4,5 cm, (f) 4,5-4,8 cm.

Colour: Both sexes are dark brown with rows of black spots parallel to the outer edges of the wings. The forewing has three white spots near the tip and two larger white patches in mid-wing. There is a broad white band across the middle of the hindwing.

Most like: The friar which, however, is twice as large, is black rather than dark brown, and has a large white patch on the hindwing rather than a white cross-band.

Habitat: Rainforest and thick bushveld.

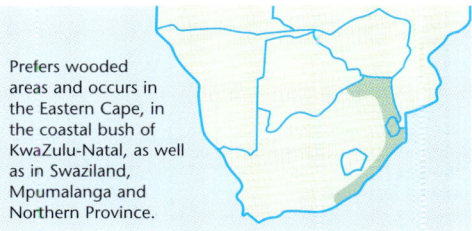

Prefers wooded areas and occurs in the Eastern Cape, in the coastal bush of KwaZulu-Natal, as well as in Swaziland, Mpumalanga and Northern Province.

FRIAR
Monnik *(Amauris niavius dominicanus)*

Size: Wingspan (m) 8,0-8,5 cm, (f) 8,0-8,5 cm.

Colour: Background black but with large white patch towards tip of forewing and a larger white patch over most of hindwing, extending also onto the forewing. Several white spots dotted around forewing edges. Veins in white patches outlined in black.

Most like: The novice, but the latter's white hindwing patch is not joined to the second of the two white forewing patches as it is in the friar.

Habitat: Coastal and inland forests.

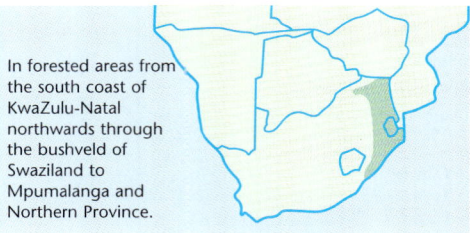

In forested areas from the south coast of KwaZulu-Natal northwards through the bushveld of Swaziland to Mpumalanga and Northern Province.

This neat little butterfly has a characteristic flight style, giving a few rapid flaps of its wings and then gliding along in leisurely fashion until it needs to pick up speed again. Like many other butterflies, the male appears to be territorial, as it has favourite perches on branches or twigs to which it returns between flights. It may patrol the same area for days at a stretch. Intruding butterflies or other insects are pursued until they leave the territory, although the small spotted sailor has no armament other than bluster to enforce his authority.

The females fly apparently at random through the bush and do not favour any particular locality above another. When mated, they lay their eggs on their caterpillars' food plants, the castor-oil plant, the forest false-nettle and the hiccup creeper.

Although it is edible and palatable to predators, the small spotted sailor does enjoy some measure of protection: its colours are close enough to the two poisonous or distasteful butterflies, the friar (*Amauris niavius dominicanus*) and the novice (*A. ochlea ochlea*), to fool predators into believing that it, too, is bitter and poisonous.

There are several look-alike species of *Neptis*, but you can recognize all of them by their bold white and black markings and slow, almost floating flight.

The old saying 'once bitten, twice shy' could be conveniently applied to the relationship between the friar and its potential enemies. For the friar is a close relative of the family of milkweed butterflies and, like them, is poisonous and unpalatable to birds and other predators. Numerous experiments have shown that birds are quick to learn which colour patterns to avoid. It is, therefore, to the friar's advantage to flaunt its bold and conspicuous colours openly. This it does by flying lazily, gently floating along forest tracks and through glades.

The extent of its immunity to attack by birds may be gauged from the number of palatable butterflies which mimic its appearance in order to escape predation. One of these is the form *hippocoonoides* of the mocker swallowtail which is an excellent mimic but is distinguishable by the row of white dots along the outer margin of the hindwing, lacking in the friar.

Another near-perfect palatable mimic is the form *wahlbergi* of the variable mimic (*Hypolimnas anthedon wahlbergi*). All three species—model and two mimics—are of a similar size and live in the same forested habitats.

The male friar can be distinguished from the female by his slightly smaller white hindwing patch and by the long, feather-shaped, dark brown 'scent-patch' next to it.

Butterflies and moths

CHIEF
Toordokter *(Amauris echeria)*

Size: Wingspan (m) 5,5-6,0 cm, (f) 6,5-7,5 cm.
Colour: Both sexes are black above with small, white (sometimes yellowish) spots on the forewing and a row of white spots near the outer edge of the hindwing. There is a large yellowish patch over most of the inner half of the hindwing against which the wing veins are outlined in black.
Most like: The friar, but the latter's hindwing patch is white, not yellow, and it has two large white patches in each forewing. Mimicked by the female mocker swallowtail.
Habitat: Rainforest and coastal bush.

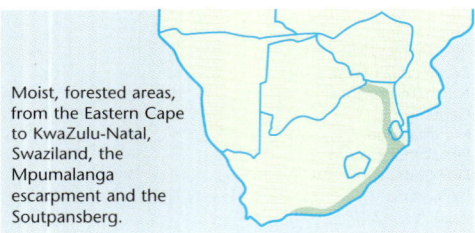

Moist, forested areas, from the Eastern Cape to KwaZulu-Natal, Swaziland, the Mpumalanga escarpment and the Soutpansberg.

Like the friar, the chief is a member of the monarch or milkweed butterfly group, all of whose caterpillars feed almost exclusively on milkweed plants (asclepiads). These plants protect themselves against grazing animals by producing toxic chemicals that are powerful enough to kill cattle and sheep. Monarch caterpillars, however, are not only immune to these poisons, but accumulate them in their tissues as a protection against predators. The poisons are passed on through the pupal stage to the adult butterfly, and woe betide the bird which is foolish enough to try to make a meal of the chief!

The object, however, is not to kill the predator, but to teach it to avoid butterflies with the chief's distinctive colour pattern. That this ploy works is clear from the fact that predators are extremely wary of other, palatable butterflies which mimic the chief's colour pattern closely.

The variable diadem (*Hypolimnas anthedon wahlbergi*) is one such mimic and one of the forms of the mocker swallowtail (*Princeps dardanus cenea*) is another.

An interesting feature of the poisonous butterflies is the fact that they are all very tough, presumably to withstand initial attacks by birds taking their first unpalatable bite.

DIADEM
Blougans *(Hypolimnas misippus)*

Size: Wingspan (m) 6,0-6,5 cm, (f) 7,0-7,5 cm.
Colour: Male velvet-black above with large white patch in mid-hindwing, another in mid-forewing, and small white patch near the tip of the forewing. Patches surrounded by deep violet—caused by diffraction of light on the wing-scales. Female completely unlike male, being orange above with black outer margins to both wings; she may or may not have a black outer half to the forewing containing white markings.
Most like: The male closely resembles the novice but the latter is slightly larger and has several white spots scattered over the black parts of the wings. The female is a mimic of the various forms of the southern milkweed butterfly.
Habitat: Woodland, grassland and forest habitats in the moister eastern half of southern Africa.

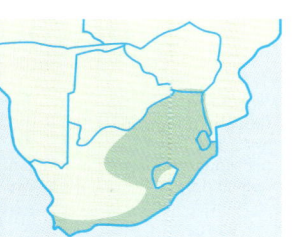

Widespread throughout South Africa but absent from the more arid regions of the Karoo, Namaqualand and the western half of the Northern Cape. Absent from eastern Lesotho.

Strictly speaking, the name 'diadem' is applied only to the male of this extraordinary butterfly; the female is called simply the 'mimic' in recognition of the fact that she provides one of the best-known examples of mimicry in the animal kingdom.

Her 'model' is the southern milkweed butterfly, a common species which discourages predators by storing poisonous chemicals in its tissues from the poisonous milkweed plants its caterpillars eat. If a bird swallows a mouthful of this butterfly it will vomit and may become quite ill. Having experienced the harsh effects of its ill-chosen meal, and having associated it with the southern milkweed's bright wings, the bird will take care to avoid insects with that distinctive colour pattern in the future.

This is very fortunate for the female diadem which has exactly the same coloration as the southern milkweed, although it is not at all poisonous and would make a tasty mouthful for any gourmet bird or lizard.

Male and female diadems are strong fliers, and are on the wing all year round, although they're most often spotted during early winter.

Butterflies and moths

SOUTHERN MILKWEED

Suidelike melkbosskoenlapper (*Danaus chrysippus aegyptius*)

Size: Wingspan: (m) 5,0-7,0 cm, (f) 5,0-7,0 cm.

Colour: Orange-brown wings with black margins that broaden over the tip of each forewing into a large triangular black patch enclosing a band of several large white spots. Male has four black spots in middle of hindwing, while the female has only three.

Most like: Female of the diadem butterfly. The female diadem is called the 'mimic', as she is almost indistinguishable from the southern milkweed butterfly. She has, however, only one black spot on each hindwing, and has scalloped edges to her wings.

Habitat: Open and bushy country, woodlands and gardens throughout southern Africa, always near milkweeds.

Widespread throughout southern Africa, and may even be encountered in the more arid parts of the Northern Cape and the Karoo.

This large and conspicuous butterfly almost seems to invite capture, with its slow, lazy and undulating flight. But although human butterfly collectors might find it easy to net, predatory birds have learned to leave it strictly alone. For this butterfly has evolved a fascinating strategy for survival—its caterpillars feed on various plants of the milkweed family which contain toxic chemicals. The toxins don't harm the caterpillar, but they make it positively unpalatable, and poisonous, to predators. In due course the toxins are passed on unchanged through the pupal stage to the body of the adult butterfly.

Both caterpillar and butterfly maintain a high profile during their lives. The caterpillar is brightly coloured in alternate bands of black, bluish white and yellow, and often has long, fleshy black tubercles growing from its head and back.

During its slow, deliberate flight the butterfly appears to flaunt its 'warning colours' to a host of potential enemies. A bird may attack a milkweed butterfly once—but will never make the same mistake again.

Palatable butterflies such as the mimic have cannily adopted the orange, black and white colours of the milkweed butterfly to escape being eaten.

EVENING BROWN

Skemerbruintjie (*Melanitis leda helena*)

Size: Wingspan (m) 6,0-6,5 cm, (f) 6,5-7,0 cm.

Colour: Mid-brown above with one, two or three small white-centred black eye-spots on each hindwing and a single, prominent eye-spot near the apex of each forewing which encloses two white spots and is surrounded by a patch of orange-brown. This eye-spot is shaped like a horizontal comma and is diagnostic for the species.

Most like: The marsh patroller, but the latter has two perfectly round and completely separate eye-spots on each forewing; the edges of its wings are smoothly rounded, not angular and 'tailed' as in the evening brown.

Habitat: Coastal forests, bushveld and other wooded areas.

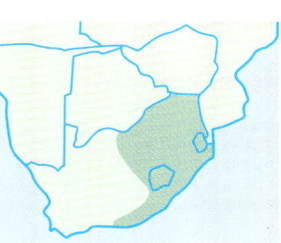

Occurs in forest and bushveld areas in the North-West, Northern Province, Gauteng, Mpumalanga, Swaziland, eastern Free State, KwaZulu-Natal, Lesotho and Eastern Cape.

This unusual butterfly has the peculiar habit of flying only at dusk and at dawn, hence its name. It avoids sunlight and spends the day well concealed amongst dead leaves on the forest floor, although on overcast days you may see it flapping heavily through open glades. Normally, however, it is reluctant to move by day and, when disturbed, will fly off erratically for only a few metres before dropping suddenly to the ground to blend again with its background of brown leaves.

As with many woodland butterflies, the undersides of its wings have a 'dry-leaf' camouflage. The evening brown, however, carries the deception a stage further by having separate winter and summer forms. In summer the undersides are uniformly finely mottled in various shades of brown and there are several small eye-spots resembling fungal leaf-spot. The winter form looks more like a dead leaf: the eye-spots almost disappear, a 'leaf mid-rib' appears, and the hindwing 'tails' increase in size and look more like leaf stalks.

The greenish caterpillars feed on various grasses, including rice and sugar cane, and have the forked tail segment characteristic of the 'browns'.

Although generally confined to rainforests and areas of dense bush, the evening brown has also been spotted in plantations of the alien bluegum tree.

Butterflies and moths

Table Mountain beauty
Bergnooientjie *(Aeropetes tulbaghia)*

Size: Wingspan (m) 7,0-7,5 cm, (f) 7,5-8,0 cm.
Colour: Both sexes dark brown with two broken orange bands parallel to the outer edge of the forewing and another on the hindwing. Between the hindwing band and the outer edge of the hindwing is a row of large, mauve eye-spots each with a white dotted centre and ringed with black. Female easily distinguished from male by having third (short) orange bar on forewing.
Most like: Koppie charaxes; the latter, however, has two tails to each hindwing and only one main orange band across the forewing. Its three blue hindwing spots are less conspicuous and are in a short row near the tails.
Habitat: High rocky and mountainous areas in wetter parts of South Africa.

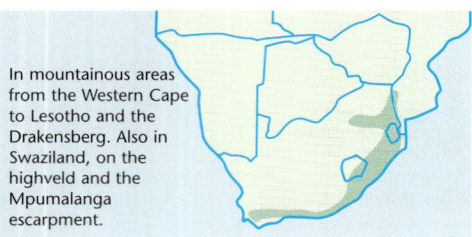

In mountainous areas from the Western Cape to Lesotho and the Drakensberg. Also in Swaziland, on the highveld and the Mpumalanga escarpment.

The Table Mountain beauty, or mountain pride, as it is also called, is the largest of the group of butterflies known as the 'browns' to occur in southern Africa. Although browns normally have a weak, fluttering flight, the Table Mountain beauty is a fast and strong flier and, once disturbed, is difficult to capture or approach.

These butterflies are normally only on the wing between December and April when you can see them around clumps of red or orange flowers such as red-hot pokers or watsonias to which they seem particularly attracted. They are also known to pollinate red disas in the southwestern Cape. While feeding they are less wary than usual and if you move quietly you can get close to them.

Table Mountain beauties prefer rocky terrain and, at midday, to avoid the heat of the sun, they seek out the shade of rocks or overhanging banks. Here they rest unseen, camouflaged by the wavy patterns under their wings.

The butterflies lay their eggs on the caterpillars' favourite food plants—various species of grass, including thatch-grass.

Adult butterflies are frequently spotted in suburbs in the Cape Town area.

Pearl charaxes
Pereldubbelstert *(Stonehamia varanes varanes)*

Size: Wingspan (m) 6,5-7,0 cm, (f) 7,5-8,0 cm.
Colour: Reddish brown outer half to the upperside of all four wings in both sexes. This area on forewing carries two rows of yellowish spots. The inner half of each wing, however, is bright pearly white, hence the butterfly's common name. The undersides are mottled in shades of light orange-brown to deep brown and have a false 'midrib'. There is a short 'tail' on each hindwing, almost halfway along the length of its outer edge.
Most like: Green-veined charaxes, which has bright yellow, not pearly white, inner halves to its wings, and two 'tails' to each hindwing.
Habitat: Forested areas and dense bush.

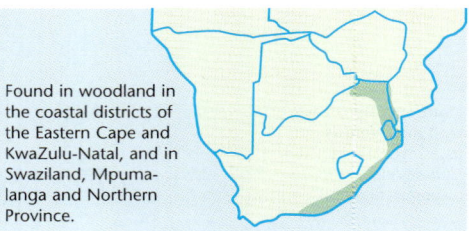

Found in woodland in the coastal districts of the Eastern Cape and KwaZulu-Natal, and in Swaziland, Mpumalanga and Northern Province.

Like many of our beautiful forest butterflies, the pearl charaxes has a somewhat disconcerting fondness for rotten fruit and meat, both of which are used by collectors to bait butterfly traps. The butterfly also has a taste for the sap of some trees and it can be attracted to mashed-banana bait and even to honey smeared on bark.

Although the males of most other Charaxes butterflies delight in frolicking about the tops of small koppies or trees at midday, the pearl charaxes is usually found lower down among the branches of trees or on the leaves and twigs of a bush.

When it settles, it closes its wings and presents its 'dead leaf' appearance to potential predators. If it is disturbed it will flutter only a short distance and settle down again—protected by interlaced twigs and branches. Females may be distinguished from the males by their hindwing tails, which are club-ended, not tapering. They lay their eggs on various species of wild currants.

Like other Charaxes these butterflies are powerful fliers. The wings are far stiffer than those of all other butterflies and the disproportionately large thorax houses large flight muscles.

Butterflies and moths

MARSH PATROLLER

Moeraswagter *(Henotesia perspicua)*

Size: Wingspan (m) 4,0-4,3 cm, (f) 4,5-4,8 cm.

Colour: Mid-brown above, sometimes with a reddish tinge. Two eye-spots on the forewing and three on the hindwing together form a line parallel to the outer edge of the wings. The spots resemble a bull's-eye target, with a white centre surrounded by a black ring and an orange ring. The underside of the hindwing has a row of six or seven of these eye-spots.

Most like: Common bush brown which, however, has no eye-spots on the hindwings.

Habitat: Along grassy river banks, around dams and in marshy localities in bushveld and coastal forest environments.

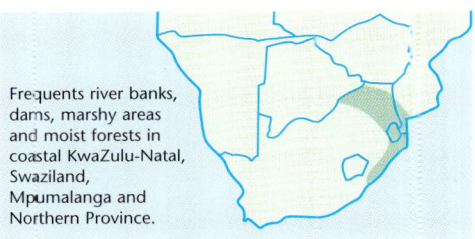

Frequents river banks, dams, marshy areas and moist forests in coastal KwaZulu-Natal, Swaziland, Mpumalanga and Northern Province.

The marsh patroller has a weak and wavering flight pattern that may fool predators into mistaking it for a dead leaf being tumbled along by the wind. As it flutters about in its preferred habitat of marshes (hence the name marsh patroller), or near river banks and dams, it drops to the ground every now and then to rest. This hopping flight enables the marsh patroller to manoeuvre between dense stalks of grass close to the ground.

On the ground it looks very much like a dead leaf with its very clear, brown-bordered, cream 'mid-rib' across both fore- and hindwings. Although the eye-spots on the underside may appear to make the 'dead-leaf' camouflage less effective, it is worth noting that these eye-spots are reduced to mere pinpoints on those marsh patrollers which emerge from their pupa in winter, when many trees shed their leaves.

The female marsh patroller lays her ribbed, melon-shaped eggs on various species of grass, and you can distinguish the smooth-skinned caterpillars, like those of other browns, by the sharply forked tail segments. This butterfly is not difficult to rear in captivity.

Like other members of the large family Satyridae—the 'browns'—the marsh patroller is a sombre-coloured butterfly with relatively short wings, and degenerate front legs which are covered with hairs.

JOKER

Tolliegrasvegter *(Byblia anvatara acheloia)*

Size: Wingspan (m) 4,0-4,5 cm, (f) 4,0-4,8 cm.

Colour: Bright orange above with two large, jagged-edged black patches extending from the middle of the wings to the body. There is a narrow black border along the margin of the forewing, and a broad black border along the margin of the hindwing which encloses a row of seven or eight orange spots.

Most like: The common joker, which is almost identical to the joker but has a row of small, black dots across the middle of each hindwing. The joker also resembles several species of acraea.

Habitat: Open savanna woodland or grassland.

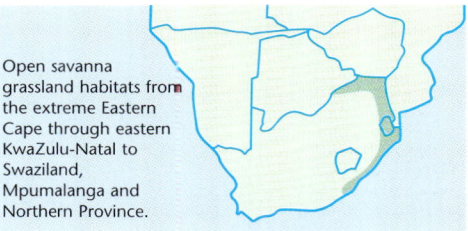

Open savanna grassland habitats from the extreme Eastern Cape through eastern KwaZulu-Natal to Swaziland, Mpumalanga and Northern Province.

The joker is not a particularly fast flier and usually flutters along sluggishly within a metre or so of the ground—easy prey, one would think, for a hungry bird, especially as it is quite edible and neither toxic nor distasteful.

It probably owes its survival to its resemblance to the toxic and unpleasant-tasting large spotted acraea (*Acraea zetes*) or other acraeas, the majority of which are red or orange-red with black markings. Most birds have learned through bitter experience to avoid the genuine acraeas and will, no doubt, view the provocatively slow flight of the joker with a healthy distrust.

The joker is a familiar and common orange butterfly often found in company with its close relative, the common joker. The latter, however, has a wider distribution in and and is the only one of the two found in the eastern Karoo, Free State and Northern Cape.

Both the joker and the common joker frequently feed on the juices of rotting fruits and animal dung, and butterfly collectors have learnt successfully to entice them to banana-baited traps.

Both species can be seen throughout the year in the warmer regions. Males are found occasionally on the tops of koppies.

Butterflies and moths

Painted lady

Sondagsrokkie (*Vanessa cardui*)

Size: Wingspan (m) 4,0-4,5 cm, (f) 4,5-5,0 cm.
Colour: Orange background colour; outer half of forewing black with white spots. There are three rows of small black spots parallel to the outer margin of the hindwing and an irregular, broken black band crosses the orange inner half of the forewing. Undersides beautifully marked in a mosaic of various shades of brown, orange and white.
Most like: Southern milkweed butterfly (*Danaus chrysippus aegyptius*) which, however, is deeper orange, has no broken black band across the inner half of the forewing, and has a solid black outer margin to the hindwing.
Habitat: Most South African environments, from suburban gardens in lush subtropical KwaZulu-Natal to the succulent veld of arid Namaqualand.

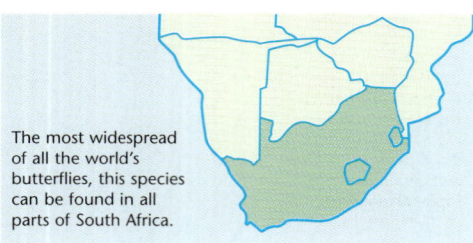

The most widespread of all the world's butterflies, this species can be found in all parts of South Africa.

Migratory swarms of painted ladies are said to number many hundreds of millions of butterflies—an unforgettable spectacle for those lucky enough to witness it. Astonished sailors once encountered these beautifully marked butterflies more than 1 600 km from land in the middle of the Atlantic Ocean.

Another migrating swarm was seen in 1900 in the North-West Frontier district of what is now Pakistan, travelling towards India at an altitude of 5 200 metres. Closer to home, migrations occur regularly in the Western Cape and KwaZulu-Natal, usually after a rapid population growth.

The secret of this lovely butterfly's breeding success is the adaptability of its caterpillars, which feed on a wide variety of plants from stinging nettles to members of the daisy and pea families. The female lays her eggs singly on separate leaves of the food plant, a strategy designed to make it difficult for insect-eating birds to find the vulnerable caterpillars.

Birds, lizards and frogs prey on the adult butterflies, but many of them escape detection simply by closing their wings, the undersides of which are cunningly patterned to blend in with the butterfly's background.

Garden acraea

Tuinrooitjie (*Acraea horta*)

Size: Wingspan (m) 4,5-5,0 cm, (f) 5,0-5,3 cm.
Colour: Largely red, but the outer third of each forewing is clear or translucent. Red inner part of forewing has two or three small black spots, while the hindwing is dotted all over with black spots. Female more orange-red than male.
Most like: Natal acraea (*Acraea natalica natalica*) which, however, does not have a translucent tip to the forewing and usually has more black spots on the forewing.
Habitat: Forested areas and suburban gardens in southern and eastern Africa wherever its larval food-plant, the wild peach, occurs.

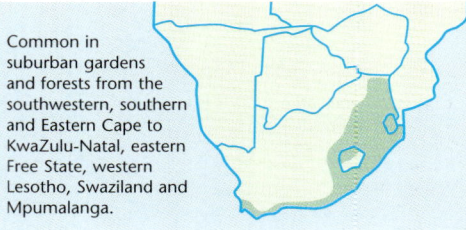

Common in suburban gardens and forests from the southwestern, southern and Eastern Cape to KwaZulu-Natal, eastern Free State, western Lesotho, Swaziland and Mpumalanga.

The first line of defence of the dark brown caterpillar of the garden acraea is its formidable armour of branched spines. However, should a bird or lizard be hungry enough or foolish enough to attempt to make a meal of this mobile minefield, it will certainly bite off more than it can chew, for the hollow spines are filled with a yellow fluid containing cyanide. Like the milkweed butterflies, garden acraeas acquire this poisonous protection from their food plants at the caterpillar stage, and retain the toxins in their bodies through to adulthood.

The bright colours and tantalizing flight of the garden acraea are its passport to safety. Potential predators soon learn to avoid both it and all other butterflies with similar 'warning coloration'. Not only do these include other poisonous species of acraea but also palatable mimics from other butterfly families such as Trimen's false acraea (*Pseudacraea boisduvalii trimenii*).

The pupa of the garden acraea is also poisonous; it is found on exposed positions such as garden walls, tree trunks and ferns and has its own warning colours of black and white with yellow dots.

Females deposit their eggs in neatly laid-out batches on the uppersides of the leaves of the wild peach. They also, however, use cultivated species of passion-flower in gardens for the same purpose.

Butterflies and moths

POLKA DOT

Polkastippel (*Pardopsis punctatissima*)

Size: Wingspan (m) 3,0-3,3 cm, (f) 3,2-3,5 cm.
Colour: Both male and female are light orange, with a narrow black border to the outer edges of both fore- and hindwings. The tip of each forewing is black. Both wings are evenly studded with numerous black spots. The undersides of the wings are similar to the uppersides.
Most like: Several species of acraea, such as the Natal acraea, which are often orange or red with black spots. None, however, has the uniform distribution or the evenly sized black spots of the polka dot.
Habitat: Grassy slopes often near rocks and along the edges of open woodland areas.

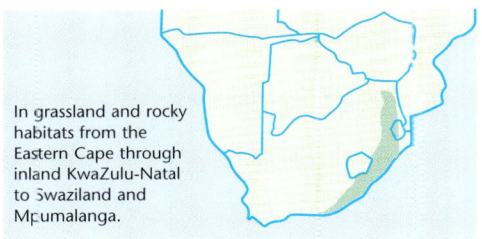

In grassland and rocky habitats from the Eastern Cape through inland KwaZulu-Natal to Swaziland and Mpumalanga.

A defenceless butterfly fluttering slowly over short grassland would normally entice a hungry bird into catching a quick and easy meal. However, if the butterfly is medium-sized, red or orange in colour and carries a scattering of black spots, the bird will leave it strictly alone. For these are the 'aposematic' or 'warning' colours typical of the family Acraeidae, all of whose members are poisonous or extremely distasteful to predators.

The appropriately named polka dot, which is closely related to other acraeas, shares not only their warning colours of orange with black dots, but also exudes from its thorax a yellow, acrid-smelling chemical composition which is intensely disagreeable to bird predators.

Protected as it is by its unpalatability, the polka dot flies slowly as the acraeas do, keeping low down in its grassy habitat, almost as if daring predators to attack it. You may, in fact, think it easy to catch, but it can put in an evasive spurt of speed when threatened. The polka dot may be seen flying in all months of the year, but it is more commonly seen in summer.

Acraeas normally lay their eggs in clusters. The polka dot, however, lays its eggs singly on the lady's slipper (*Hybanthus capensis*), a low-growing herbaceous perennial of the violet family with white or lilac flowers.

GAUDY COMMODORE

Rooi-en-bloublaarvlerk (*Junonia octavia sesamus*)

Size: Wingspan (m) 5,0-5,7 cm, (f) 5,5-6,0 cm.
Colour: Sexes similar but winter and summer forms totally different. Winter form is violet-blue above with a curving row of black-tipped red spots parallel to the outer edges of the wings. The summer form is red with a broad black margin to the outer edges of the wings.
Most like: In the case of the summer form, various species of acraea such as the garden acraea, but the outer edges of acraea wings are smoothly curving, while the gaudy commodore's are noticeably scalloped.
Habitat: Bushveld, forest fringes and in suburban gardens.

In natural habitats and suburban gardens from the coastal districts of the Eastern Cape and eastern Lesotho through KwaZulu-Natal and Swaziland to Mpumalanga and Northern Province.

Because gaudy commodores which hatch out in summer are very different in appearance to those which hatch out during the winter, they were once thought by entomologists to be two different species.

When the red summer form was seen to mate with the blue form, entomologists assumed that each butterfly belonged to different species, and it was just a case of hybridization in action. But when red specimens were reared from eggs laid by blue pairs and vice versa, the experts finally realized that only one species was involved.

This occurrence of two distinct types of individual in one species—known as 'dimorphism'—is common to many butterflies, but the gaudy commodore provides perhaps the best example of it in the insect world. The phenomenon is believed to be controlled by the humidity in the atmosphere.

Oddly enough, it is not only the colours but also the habits of the two forms that differ, the red form preferring more open, grassy areas while the blue form is usually found in shady habitats. The males of both forms, however, will play for hours on koppies and mountaintops during the heat of the day.

The eggs are laid on members of the nettle family, including the common painted nettle or *Coleus*, which is used as a decorative pot plant.

Butterflies and moths

Yellow pansy

Geelgesiggie (*Junonia hierta cebrene*)

Size: Wingspan (m) 4,0-4,5 cm, (f) 4,5-5,0 cm.
Colour: Black, with a bright orange-yellow patch on each fore- and hindwing, and a large, violet-blue spot on each hindwing where it meets the forewing. Small white blotch near apex of each forewing.
Most like: Blue pansy (*Junonia oenone oenone*), which is also black, with a large, rich blue spot on each hindwing where it meets the forewing. The blue pansy, however, lacks the orange-yellow patches and has instead a creamy-white fringe to its hindwings and a broken white band across its forewings.
Habitat: In moist open country, savanna, bush and suburban gardens.

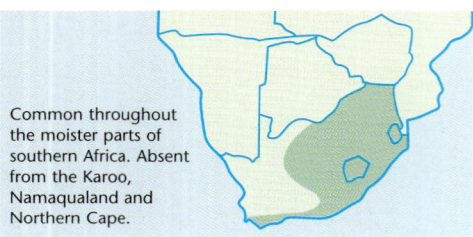

Common throughout the moister parts of southern Africa. Absent from the Karoo, Namaqualand and Northern Cape.

Although birds and other predators relish the taste of this attractive insect, catching and cornering it require extraordinary skill. In the face of danger, the yellow pansy (whose Afrikaans name means 'little yellow face') can protect itself from its enemies simply by closing its wings, the undersides of which are cryptically coloured in mottled grey-brown and blend perfectly with various backgrounds. If this ploy fails, this artful dodger will take to the air with startling speed.

The yellow pansy is not a sociable butterfly and prefers to fly alone, flitting from flower to flower where it feeds on nectar with its wings outspread. You may often, however, see a male chasing other butterflies around the garden, presumably defending its territory from the unwelcome attentions of other males intent on attracting a mate for themselves.

The spectacular markings of this butterfly make it easy to identify. The female is similar to the male, but has well-developed eye-spots on both fore- and hindwings, and a short, dark bar extending into the orange-yellow patch on each forewing. It lays its eggs singly on herbaceous plants and small shrubs belonging to the thistle family.

Blue pansy

Blougesiggie (*Junonia oenone oenone*)

Size: Wingspan (m) 4,0-4,8 cm, (f) 4,5-5,0 cm.
Colour: Black overall with a large iridescent blue spot in the middle of the front half of each hindwing. There is a broken white band across each forewing and a treble white band along the outer edge of each hindwing. Each wing has two blue-centred, orange-red eye-spots.
Most like: The yellow pansy, but lacks the large yellow patch on each wing characteristic of that species.
Habitat: Bushveld with koppies, savanna and open veld in rocky areas.

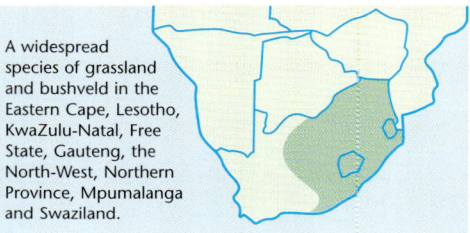

A widespread species of grassland and bushveld in the Eastern Cape, Lesotho, KwaZulu-Natal, Free State, Gauteng, the North-West, Northern Province, Mpumalanga and Swaziland.

This is one of the many butterflies that indulge in 'hilltopping' during which, on hot sunny days, the males gather on rocky knolls and ridges to set up territories and await the arrival of sexually receptive females—at the same time engaging in aerial battles with other males.

The male blue pansy usually chooses a resting-place on the ground where it opens and closes its wings, perhaps to draw attention to its iridescent blue wing-patches. Every time another male passes, the territory-holder takes off and chases it away, after which it returns to its 'patch'.

The blue pansy makes a palatable morsel for a number of birds and lizards. However when it is not deliberately flaunting its colours to others of its kind to gain advantage in the mating game, it can avoid the unwelcome attention of these predators simply by closing its wings. Like the yellow pansy, its underwings are cryptically coloured in shades of brown and are inconspicuous against a variety of backgrounds.

This handsome butterfly is one of the more common species in the eastern half of southern Africa and you can see it throughout the year, but more frequently in summer. It belongs to the Nymphalidae family of butterflies, the members of which have front legs that are too short for clinging or walking.

The eggs of the blue pansy, like those of other pansies, are round and generally lime-green in colour.

Butterflies and moths

BROWN-VEINED WHITE
Grasveldwitjie *(Belenois aurota aurota)*

Size: Wingspan (m) 4,0-4,5 cm, (f) 4,0-4,5 cm.
Colour: Male white above with a broad black tip to the forewing which encloses narrow streaks of white; black spots along the outer edge of the hindwing. Female similar but no white streaks in black forewing tip; black spots on hindwing join to form a black band. Both sexes, but especially the female, have a black bar in the middle of the forewing. The veins on the white undersides of both male and female are broadly outlined in brown.
Most like: Forest white, which, however, has yellowish undersides and veins, outlined in black.
Habitat: Open country throughout southern Africa.

This very common white butterfly can be found throughout southern Africa, from the moist coastal forests of KwaZulu-Natal to the succulent veld of Namaqualand.

This is perhaps the most common of the 'whites' of southern Africa and, indeed, of all Africa. It is familiar to all South Africans as *the* migratory white of the summer months, with uncounted millions taking to the wing, usually heading in a northeasterly direction, in KwaZulu-Natal and Mpumalanga. Farmers mistakenly believe that such migrations portend a plague of crop-eating caterpillars. This belief is quite false. The caterpillars of the brown-veined white do not eat agricultural crops but feed on two indigenous trees of no economic value, the bush-cherry and the bastard shepherd's tree.

The white eggs are laid in clusters on the food plant, and after seven weeks the life cycle is complete and the adult butterflies are on the wing. The eggs may be laid in vast numbers: after a brown-veined white migration in Kenya, a lepidopterist found 57 000 eggs on a small bush 80 cm high and 20 cm in diameter. The potential for a population explosion is clear.

The adult butterfly has a fast and regular flight as befits a migratory species, but you can easily observe or capture it as it frequently pauses to feed from the flowers of low-growing plants. It flies throughout the year in most parts of southern Africa.

SCARLET-TIP
Skarlakenpuntjie *(Colotis danae annae)*

Size: Wingspan (m) 4,0-5,0 cm, (f) 4,0-5,0 cm.
Colour: Males white with outer half of each forewing scarlet, bordered narrowly with black. Hindwing white with black-tipped edges. Females more heavily pigmented with black than males, with black dots across the scarlet of the forewing and the white of the hindwing; their wings are also blackish near their point of attachment to the body.
Most like: The red-tip, which, however, has an orange-red tip to the forewing. The red-tip has a broad black bar along the edge of the forewing nearest to the hindwing, a feature lacking in the scarlet-tip.
Habitat: Savanna and thornveld.

A savanna and thornveld butterfly occurring in the Eastern Cape, KwaZulu-Natal, Swaziland and in Mpumalanga and Northern Province.

The bright scarlet-and-white coloration of the scarlet-tip's uppersides is an open invitation to predators. However, like other *Colotis* species, it is an active, fast-flying butterfly which can easily evade the lunges of the butterfly collector's net or a bird's beak.

When it is at rest, the scarlet-tip resorts to camouflage, closing its wings to display the yellowish brown undersides finely speckled with darker brown. This pattern is a particularly effective camouflage against predators in the dry winter season.

Like many other 'whites', the scarlet-tip varies in colour according to both sex and season, with the female always being more heavily marked in black than the male; wet-season specimens of both sexes are blacker than their dry-season counterparts.

It is interesting to note that the lighter dry-season female lays eggs, which develop into darker wet-season butterflies; these in turn produce lighter offspring as winter approaches.

The yellowish eggs are laid singly on twigs of the bead-bean and Natal worm-bush, and exactly one month later a new generation of butterflies is on the wing. The adults are present at any time of the year.

Butterflies and moths

DOTTED BORDER
Voëlentwitjie *(Mylothris chloris agathina)*

Size: Wingspan 5,0-5,5 cm (both sexes).
Colour: *Male white above with black dots round outer edges of wings, joining to form a narrow black tip to the forewing. Females similar but light yellow, not white. In both sexes undersides of hindwings are yellow, spotted with black along the outer edge; the forewings are similar but lack the upperside's black tip, and they are flushed with a deep, vivid orange towards the body of the butterfly.*
Most like: *Twin-dotted border, which, however, possesses orange patches on both the uppersides and the undersides.*
Habitat: *Wooded and bush areas.*

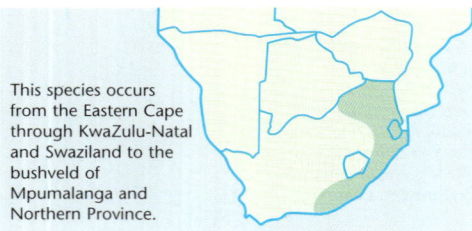

This species occurs from the Eastern Cape through KwaZulu-Natal and Swaziland to the bushveld of Mpumalanga and Northern Province.

This lovely, delicate-looking 'white' lays its 45-70 (sometimes more than 100) bright yellow eggs in clusters on the leaves of various species of mistletoe of the family *Loranthaceae*—in Afrikaans *voëlent* means mistletoe, hence the name *voëlentwitjie*. The caterpillars, which are green with small stripes down each flank, are gregarious and gather together between meals. They have the curious habit of marching off to feed in a processionary line. The short, fine hairs on their backs exude a liquid, which may serve to protect them from predators.

A very common butterfly in its distribution area, the dotted border is a slow flier that avoids predation to some extent by flying in amongst the branches of trees in its woodland habitat. When it feeds from flowers, however, it tends to lose its natural caution and can be caught by predators with ease.

The species breeds continuously in the warmer parts of the country, because of the availability of mistletoe throughout the year. The cycle of growth from egg to adult butterfly takes about two months, and somewhat longer in winter.

Dotted borders occur only in areas where trees are heavily festooned with mistletoe. The species have recently spread to the southeastern Cape where you can see them in great numbers at the end of summer, although they are on the wing throughout the year.

AFRICAN CLOUDED YELLOW
Lusernskoenlapper *(Colias electo electo)*

Size: Wingspan 3,5-4,0 cm.
Colour: *Male orange-yellow above with broad black or dark brown outer margins to both fore- and hindwings, a black spot in the middle of the forewing near the forward edge, and a yellow edge to the inner part of the hindwing. Female similar but the orange-yellow shading is partly obscured by brown and there are flecks of yellow in the dark wing borders. Undersides of both sexes golden yellow, spotted lightly with black.*
Most like: *Broad-bordered grass-yellow, which is yellow, not orange-yellow, has narrower black borders, and no black spot in the forewing.*
Habitat: *Most habitats, but especially grassveld and pastures, throughout southern Africa.*

Common throughout southern Africa and particularly abundant in agricultural areas where lucerne is grown.

The African clouded yellow, or lucerne butterfly, is one of the very few of the 800-odd southern African butterflies that feeds on man's agricultural crops. Flowering fields of lucerne are irresistible to these orange-yellow butterflies which descend on them in swarms to feed on the nectar and lay their eggs. Their larvae, known as 'lucerne caterpillars', can reach plague proportions if climatic conditions are right. The larval caterpillar stage lasts about a month.

Farmers often use a form of biological control to reduce this threat to their livelihoods: they collect some lucerne together with a large number of larvae, and keep them in overcrowded conditions in a closed container. When the caterpillars, overwhelmed by the bacteria-laden atmosphere, invariably succumb to disease, they are pulped and the resulting bacteria-laden 'soup' is diluted with water and sprayed over the lucerne fields to spread the pathogen to the free-living caterpillars.

The African clouded yellow flies the whole year round and its lifecycle takes around two months to complete. Besides lucerne, its caterpillars feed on clover, vetches and many other leguminous plants, including the alien false acacia, or locust-tree, *Robinia pseudo-acacia*.

Butterflies and moths

BROAD-BORDERED GRASS-YELLOW

Grasveldgeletjie *(Eurema brigitta brigitta)*

Size: Wingspan 3,0-3,5 cm.

Colour: Bright yellow above with a broad blackish brown outer border to the fore- and hindwings. This border is wider in summer specimens than in winter specimens. The undersides are yellowish with faint darker streaks on each hindwing. The winter form has a pink flush to the underside, especially near the tip of the forewing.

Most like: Angled grass-yellow. However the broad-bordered grass-yellow has a rounded outer edge to the hindwing, while the angled grass-yellow has a distinctly angular outer edge with three clear angles.

Habitat: Found in most habitats except the arid areas of the subregion.

Widely distributed in southern Africa and absent only from the Western Cape and the semi-desert regions of the Karoo, Namaqualand and western parts of the Northern Cape.

The conspicuous colours and leisurely flight of the broad-bordered grass-yellow would seem to make it a natural and easy victim for hungry predators but, like most butterflies, it has developed a remarkable adaptation to foil its enemies—when it settles to rest on low bushes it often hangs by one leg only. In this rather precarious position it trembles and sways to and fro with each passing breeze, closely resembling a yellowing leaf.

This butterfly's slow, somewhat lazy flight near the ground as it searches for nectar-bearing flowers makes it quite easy to spot. Groups may often be spotted clustered around roadside puddles.

Like most 'whites', the family to which this butterfly belongs, you can see the broad-bordered grass-yellow throughout the year, but in slightly different colour forms. In summer (the wet season) it has a broader black or dark brown marginal band to the wings, and the yellow of the upper surfaces of the female's wings may be dusted with black scales. The undersides of the wings are yellowish dusted with black streaks in summer, but turn yellow flushed with pinkish buff in winter.

The white eggs are laid on St John's wort or *boesmanstee* bushes.

GOLD-SPOTTED SYLPH

Reënboswalsertjie *(Metisella metis)*

Size: Wingspan 2,5-3,0 cm.

Colour: Both sexes are dark brown to black above with a scattering of golden spots and a dusting of golden scales at the wing bases. Undersides are similar but lack the gold dusting; the male's hindwing underside has no gold spots.

Most like: Macomo ranger, but gold spots of the latter tend to be rectangular and to touch each other on the hindwing.

Habitat: Woodland and forest.

A woodland species which occurs from Cape Town along the southern Cape coast to the Eastern Cape, southern KwaZulu-Natal, the KwaZulu-Natal midlands, the Mpumalanga escarpment and the Soutpansberg.

This attractive little insect is one of the 'skippers'; a group of butterflies characterized by their rapid, unpredictable, 'skipping' flight, quite unlike that of other butterfly families. Like that of its relatives, the distinctive low, erratic, zigzagging flight of the gold-spotted sylph is confusing not only to flycatchers and other insect-eating birds, but also to would-be butterfly collectors. Like other skippers, it settles frequently between bouts of darting flight and, with its dark coloration, is often very difficult to spot. This species has the peculiar habit of resting with its wings held vertically over its head, but a little apart (other butterflies usually fold their wings close against each other when at rest).

Although generally considered to be a woodland or forest species, the gold-spotted sylph is by no means confined to this habitat and large numbers can often be found flying together on moist, grassy mountain slopes or in suburban gardens, feeding from flowers.

The long, thin eggs are laid singly on grass stems. When the caterpillar hatches it crawls to the leaf tip and rolls the leaf blade into a cylindrical tube which it then binds together with silk, which is produced from a special gland in the head. It remains hidden and safe from predators in this shelter by day, emerging only at night to feed on Bushman grass and the coarser couch grass. Skippers often fly at dusk and are similar in so many ways to moths that they are considered to be a link between moths and butterflies.

Butterflies and moths

MOUNTAIN COPPER
Bergkopervlerkie *(Aloeides thyra)*

Size: Wingspan (m) 2,4-2,6 cm, (f) 2,8-3,0 cm.
Colour: Orange above with a broad black band along the outer margins of the wings, edged with a black-and-white chequered fringe of short hairs. The wing veins are outlined in black against the orange background. Undersides of hindwings are dark brown with irregular patches of grey and brown. Undersides of forewings have dark brown margins and orange central area with silver-centred black dots.
Most like: The streaked copper, which shares the mountain copper's geographical range but has light brown not dark brown hindwing undersides.
Habitat: Fynbos scrub ranging from sea level to mountain top in the Western Cape.

This species occurs only in the southwestern Cape, especially in the mountains, but also in the coastal lowlands from Lambert's Bay and Clanwilliam to Swellendam and, perhaps, Stilbaai.

Hill-walkers and mountain-climbers will be familiar with this little 'copper', or with any of a number of very similar close relatives in different parts of southern Africa—because of its erratic habit of flying along and settling on mountain paths. It sits tight until almost trodden upon, then takes off with a fast zigzagging flight, lands a few metres off and immediately closes its wings to expose the 'rock-surface' camouflage of its undersides. You need a keen and practised eye to detect this butterfly, which is most active between August and April.

In warm weather at midday, male mountain coppers may be seen in groups, flying and chasing each other. This is the territorial behaviour known as 'hilltopping' in which each male selects a special 'post' and defends it against his rivals while awaiting the arrival of females ready for mating.

Like many other coppers, the mountain copper caterpillar depends upon ants for its survival, and spends some of its life inside, or close to, the nests of the small black sugar ant. At night the caterpillar emerges to feed on its food plant, accompanied and protected from predators by a group of ants. As the caterpillar has no honey gland, it is believed to produce volatile chemicals which 'persuade' the ants to look after it.

THYSBE COPPER
Pragkopervlerkie *(Poecilmitis thysbe)*

Size: Wingspan (m) 2,3-2,7 cm, (f) 2,6-3,0 cm.
Colour: The outer halves of the male's wings are orange-red above with a black border to the outer edge of the forewing and a scattering of black spots. The inner halves of all four wings are a lustrous, almost iridescent blue-pink. The female is similar but the blue-pink area is less extensive.
Most like: The female of the blue jewel copper which, however, has a silver rather than blue inner half to each wing. The two species share the same geographical range.
Habitat: Fynbos habitats of the southwestern and southern Cape; sandy areas near the coast.

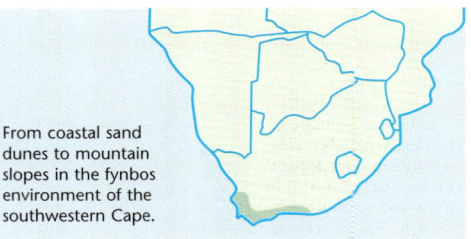

From coastal sand dunes to mountain slopes in the fynbos environment of the southwestern Cape.

The caterpillar of the beautiful Thysbe copper butterfly has an intriguing relationship with cocktail ants, without which it cannot survive. At an early stage of its development it crawls down the food plant to live in shelters made by the ants. Here, safe from predation, the caterpillar is a most welcome guest because a 'honey gland' on its back secretes a sugary substance the ants find quite irresistible.

The caterpillar stays in the ants' subterranean shelter during the day, coming out at night to feed. It also pupates in these shelters. In exchange for this protection, the ants are allowed to 'milk' the caterpillar of its sugary secretion.

The Thysbe copper larvae feed on a variety of indigenous plants, including the rooibos tea bush *Aspalathus*.

Southern Africa is particularly rich in butterflies of the family Lycaenidae, known as the 'blues' and 'coppers'. Some species are blue, some are copper, some are neither, but the Thysbe copper is both and is one of the loveliest of our smaller butterflies. The remarkable mother-of-pearl sheen of the blue-pink area of the wings is seen to its best advantage when the butterfly is at rest on the ground, basking in the sun with its wings half open. One famous butterfly expert has compared the sight to a 'brilliantly burnished jewel'.

Butterflies and moths

Fig tree blue
Vyeboombloutjie *(Myrina silenus)*

Size: Wingspan (m) 3,0-3,5 cm, (f) 3,2-3,8 cm.

Colour: Sexes similar. The inner halves of fore- and hindwings are a brilliant, deep metallic blue, bordered with blackish brown shading to chestnut. Undersides are orange-brown with a 'dead-leaf' appearance. At the end of each hindwing is a single, long, brown, slightly twisted 'tail'.

Most like: Sapphire (Iolaus silas) which, however, has sparkling white undersides and two thin tails at the tip of each hindwing.

Habitat: Varied, but mostly in areas where fig trees occur. Absent from the arid interior of southern Africa.

Three recognized subspecies exist in southern Africa: *M. penningtoni* (from Citrusdal to Springbok), *M. deserticola* (Namibia, not shown on map) and *M. ficedula* (eastwards from the Karoo through Eastern Cape to Northern Province).

The striking fig tree blue butterfly is aptly named, for its caterpillars feed only on the leaves of the many indigenous members of the fig tree family that are found in southern Africa.

The adult butterflies are on the wing in the warmer months from September to April or May, and are somewhat elusive. But if you lie in wait at a suitable fig tree, you will probably see the fast-flying males chasing one another and mating with receptive females. The eggs are laid singly on leaves or twigs of the food plant, and hatch in about a week.

The well-camouflaged caterpillar feeds on the edge of the leaf and is difficult to see, especially in its final stage before pupation when it can adopt any one of several schemes to avoid detection by birds or other predators. Its favourite trick, however, is to pinch in its eighth body segment, which makes it look like a bud or a young fig.

Pupae may often be found cleverly concealed at the bases of the tree on which they feed.

The brilliant coloration of the adult butterfly's upperside may seem to be an inviting target for a hungry predator. However, when the fig tree blue settles on a branch or twig and closes its wings, its orange-and-chestnut brown undersides closely resemble a dead leaf, an impression that is reinforced by the light brown false 'midrib' which bisects each wing. Predators are deceived and pass by.

Sapphire
Saffier *(Iolaus silas)*

Size: Wingspan (m) 3,0-3,4 cm, (f) 3,2-3,6 cm.

Colour: Male brilliant blue above with black borders and a black triangular patch at the tip of the forewing; two red spots at tip of each hindwing. Female similar but blue is violet-tinged and whitish in the middle of the forewing; orange band along outer edge of hindwing. Undersides of both sexes white with orange-red stripe across hindwing and a black-and-red spot near tip, where there are two 'hair-tails'.

Most like: Fig tree blue (Myrina silenus), but the latter has brown 'dead-leaf' undersides and only one 'tail' to each hindwing.

Habitat: Woodland and forest.

Savanna woodland environments in the Eastern Cape, KwaZulu-Natal, Swaziland, Mpumalanga and Northern Province.

When at rest, butterflies often close their wings over their heads to expose camouflaged undersides to the prying eyes of predators. So the sapphire, with its snow-white undersides, would seem at first glance to be too conspicuous for the insect's safety. However, careful observation has shown that this is not necessarily so, for when the butterfly sits on a shiny leaf of a tree in full sun, both the leaf and the wing reflect white light and the sapphire becomes almost indistinguishable from the leaf.

Should the sapphire be recognized for what it is, however, it has another card up its sleeve: the two hair-tails at the tip of each hindwing are false 'antennae' and 'mouthparts', and the red-and-black spot behind them is an 'eye'. The function of the orange-red line, which runs across the hindwing to this 'eye', becomes clear—it is there to lead the predator's eye to the false 'head'. Invariably, the hungry predator snaps hopefully at the butterfly—and obtains a mouthful of wing while the butterfly escapes to tell the tale.

The caterpillars feed exclusively on semi-parasitic mistletoes, and their pupae look like brown or green mistletoe berries. The adult butterfly generally flies alone or in small groups, and may be seen fluttering among the treetops.

Butterflies and moths

LUCERNE BLUE

Lusernbloutjie *(Lampides boeticus)*

Size: Wingspan (m) 2,8-3,2 cm, (f) 2,5-3,2 cm.
Colour: *Male violet-blue above with a narrow margin to outer edges of wings. Near tip of each hindwing are two tiny black spots; a fine, dark hair-tail projects from hindwing between these spots. Female is lighter blue, has a broader brown margin to the wings and the eye-spots behind the hair-tail are more conspicuous. Underwings are light brown streaked with off-white, the two eye-spots at the anal tip of hindwing are bordered in orange.*
Most like: Sapphire which, however, has broad black borders to the wings, two hair-tails at the base of each hindwing and white undersides.
Habitat: *From succulent semi-desert and grassland to fynbos, bushveld and forest. Also in cultivated lucerne fields.*

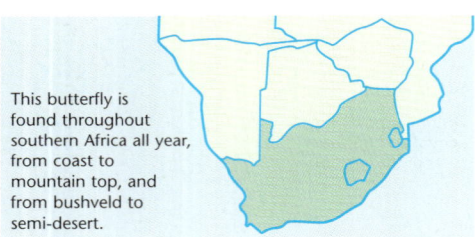

This butterfly is found throughout southern Africa all year, from coast to mountain top, and from bushveld to semi-desert.

The lucerne blue shares with the painted lady the honour of being one of the world's most widespread butterflies. A well-known migrant, it has been recorded far out at sea as well as crossing a Himalayan pass at 3 700 metres. The secret of its success lies in the ability of its caterpillars to thrive on almost any member of the widespread pea family (the legumes). The common agricultural crop, lucerne, is also a legume and adult lucerne blues drink happily from its flowers while their caterpillars feed on the leaves—occasionally reaching pest proportions.

Like the sapphire, the lucerne blue uses the hair-tail (the false 'antenna') projecting from its hindwing, and its bold underwing eye-spots (the false 'eyes') to deceive predators into seizing a mouthful of the 'wrong end', while the 'right end' flies off. The fact that this adaptation works successfully in saving the lives of lucerne blues, and other butterflies with similar physical characteristics, was shown by a study of a related South American butterfly. About a quarter of the specimens observed showed signs of having been unsuccessfully attacked, the predator mistakenly having gone for the false 'head'.

TAILED BLACK-EYE

Langstertswartogie *(Leptomyrina hirundo)*

Size: Wingspan (m) 1,8-2,1 cm, (f) 1,8-2,6 cm.
Colour: *Male upperside uniformly dark grey except for a white-edged black spot on the lower outer corner of the forewing and a series of up to five similar spots on the outer edge of the hindwing near its tip. Each hindwing has a single, long, twisted tail. Female more grey-brown. Undersides whitish, crossed by several broken golden-brown bars.*
Most like: Common black-eye; the latter, however, is brown above, not grey, has two white-edged black spots on the lower outer corner of the forewing and lacks the long tail on the hindwing.
Habitat: *Open thorn country.*

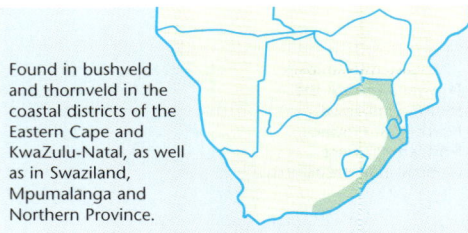

Found in bushveld and thornveld in the coastal districts of the Eastern Cape and KwaZulu-Natal, as well as in Swaziland, Mpumalanga and Northern Province.

The tailed black-eye is an enchanting butterfly that flies about slowly, its whitish underwings flashing like a firefly as its wings open and close. Its spectacularly long, somewhat hairy and twisted tails, in conjunction with the eye-spots, serve to deceive predators into seizing the wrong end of the butterfly.

Although this butterfly is a member of the family generally known as the 'blues' or 'coppers' (Lycaenidae), because of the colour of their wings, the tailed black-eye is one of the exceptions, having velvet-textured, uniform grey upperparts.

It breeds on several species of succulents, some of which, such as *Kalanchoe* and *Crassula* species, are popular garden plants. If you are patient and observant you can watch the tiny white eggs being laid singly on the undersides of the leaves. When the minute caterpillars emerge from the eggs a week later, they burrow into the leaf and spend their lives between its upper and lower surfaces. As with some other species of caterpillar, small ants are often in attendance to gather the honeylike excretion from a specialized gland on the caterpillar's back.

The common black-eye butterfly also inhabits cultivated succulent gardens.

Butterflies and moths

AFRICAN MOON MOTH

Afrikaanse maanmot *(Argema mimosae)*

Size: *Wingspan 10 cm.*

Colour: *Pale green wings, each containing one more or less centrally situated large eye-spot coloured in pink, yellow, grey and black. The very long tail on each hindwing is red-brown with a yellowish apex.*

Most like: *Unique amongst moths in southern Africa. Could perhaps be confused with tailed swallowtail butterflies but strictly nocturnal and has typically 'feathery' or comblike antennae unlike the slender, unbranched, club-tipped antennae of butterflies.*

Habitat: *Savanna bushveld.*

Occurs in northeastern Namibia, Botswana (except the south), Zimbabwe, North-West Province, Northern Province, Mpumalanga, Mozambique and the northern coastal regions of KwaZulu-Natal.

To protect itself during pupation, the African moon moth's caterpillar spins a silvery silk cocoon that bears a strong resemblance to a parasitic gall or swelling on the twig of its food plant, an illusion cleverly reinforced by small punctures 'built into' the cocoon while it is being spun. These punctures resemble the exit holes of the tiny mature gall wasp and probably help to persuade predators that the 'gall' is not worth eating and is best left alone.

The female lays her clusters of smooth white eggs on bushveld trees such as the marula and tamboti. The fully grown caterpillar is fat and green with a small head and rows of hair-tipped green protuberances on top of each of its 10 segments. When its growth is complete it settles on a twig and spins its cocoon.

The various moon (or luna) moths are so called simply because the first of the group to receive a name was an American species with eye-spots shaped like a crescent moon. Although the African moon moth has large round eye-spots, like most other members of the emperor moth family, close inspection reveals that each spot is made up of two clear half-circles in which the bands of colour do not match. This feature, together with the long tails on the hindwing, serves to distinguish the moon moth from other emperor moths.

MOPANE EMPEROR MOTH

Mopanie pouoogmot *(Imbrasia belina)*

Size: *Wingspan (m) 10-11 cm, (f) 11-13,5 cm.*

Colour: *Pale fawn to orange-brown above but inner half of each hindwing flushed with pink. Forewing divided into three parts by two straight white bands bordered with dark brown. Hindwing has one similar curved band and a large, round, orange eye-spot ringed with black, yellow and white. There is a similar but much smaller eye-spot in the mid-forewing.*

Most like: *Pine emperor which, however, is usually more mustard-coloured overall, has pink instead of white in its eye-spots and wing-bands, and has more wavy bands on the inner forewing.*

Habitat: *Semi-desert to thick bush and savanna.*

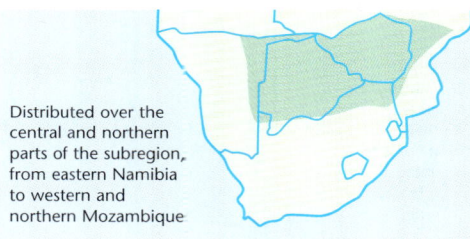

Distributed over the central and northern parts of the subregion, from eastern Namibia to western and northern Mozambique.

With a wingspan of up to 13,5 cm, the adult mopane emperor is a magnificent and conspicuously large moth that can cause consternation amongst the faint-hearted as it flaps batlike around a verandah. While some people try to catch and kill it as it flutters around outside lights, it would be better just to turn the lights off and let this harmless creature go free: its lifespan is numbered in days and it must not be distracted from its sole purpose in life—to find a mate.

To achieve this, the male is equipped with large, feathery antennae with which he can detect and trace to source over long distances the delicate perfume given off by a virgin female.

Many people are more familiar with the caterpillars of this species than with the adult moth itself; the caterpillars are the famous 'mopane worms', regarded as a delicacy by African people throughout a large part of southern Africa. When mature they are as thick as a man's finger and about seven succulent centimetres long. Villagers collect the protein-rich larvae by the sackful from mopane trees, and either roast them or squash them flat and leave them to dry. In this form they can be stored for months.

Butterflies and moths

CONVOLVULUS HAWK MOTH
Patatpylstertmot *(Agrius convolvuli)*

Size: Wingspan 10,5-12 cm.

Colour: Wings grey-brown in general appearance but cryptically patterned in grey, white, black and brown when viewed at close range. Abdomen marked with transverse bars of pink, brown and black.

Most like: Silver-haired hawk moth which, however, is smaller (wingspan 7,5 cm) and has a conspicuous silver-white band across the forewing.

Habitat: Widely distributed through southern Africa in woodland and more open habitats such as farmland and suburban gardens.

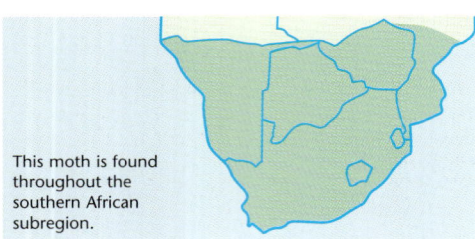

This moth is found throughout the southern African subregion.

This powerful moth is well worth watching, for it can hover, whirring like a hummingbird, in front of a flower which it delicately probes with its extremely long proboscis. This 'tongue' is some nine centimetres long—about twice the length of the moth's body—and must be proportionately one of the longest in the animal kingdom. When not being used, it is coiled up like a watch spring below the moth's head.

Feeding time for this moth is at dusk and dawn when it sallies forth to dine on the nectar of flowers with long corolla-tubes, such as the moonflower, clematis and even the petunia. During the day it rests, closely pressed against the bark of a tree or fence post, perfectly camouflaged against predators. The caterpillars feed on plants of the convolvulus family, such as the morning glory and sweet potato, on which they can reach pest proportions. The red-brown pupa is easily recognized by its long proboscis-case projection which is curved like the handle of a shepherd's crook.

Because of its wide distribution this species is perhaps the most often seen of the hawk moths in southern Africa. It also occurs throughout Europe, Africa and Asia, from Iceland to New Zealand, and periodically undertakes long migrations over land and sea. It has even been caught on a ship 560 km west of the Azores.

TRICOLOURED TIGER MOTH
Driekleur tiermot *(Rhodogastria amasis)*

Size: Wingspan 5,0-7,0 cm.

Colour: Forewings silvery-white above, with a scattering of small black spots, usually grouped towards the base of the wing, and sometimes with fine brown lines or streaks. Hindwings yellow above, with a crescent-shaped black mark in the middle of the edge nearest the forewing. Head and thorax covered in silvery hairs; abdomen carmine-red or orange, either with black cross-bands or a single row of black spots.

Most like: The blushing tiger (Seirarctia metaxantha), but the latter has a yellow forewing with no black spots and is not found south of Gauteng.

Habitat: A wide range of habitats from fynbos to bushveld; has adapted well to gardens.

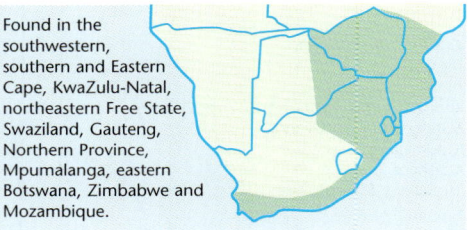

Found in the southwestern, southern and Eastern Cape, KwaZulu-Natal, northeastern Free State, Swaziland, Gauteng, Northern Province, Mpumalanga, eastern Botswana, Zimbabwe and Mozambique.

The tiger moth gets its name from the 'tigerlike' black stripes across the orange or red abdomen, a feature common to many members of the family Arctiidae—'the family of the Bear' (from the Greek *arktos*, meaning bear).

The hairs or bristles on the caterpillar are believed to help prevent parasitic wasps laying their eggs on its body and also to discourage birds from preying on it. However, this armoury of bristles is quite ineffective against cuckoos, which actually seem to prefer tiger moth caterpillars to smooth caterpillars.

The caterpillars of this species feed on most plants, but are particularly partial to the Cape honeysuckle.

Unlike some of its relatives in the same family, the tricoloured tiger moth is not a day-time flier, and you will most likely see it at night when it is attracted to lighted windows or verandahs.

If you pick the moth up, it usually feigns death. Held in your hand, it may resort to a warning display, folding its wings over its back to expose the 'warning' colours—bright red, yellow and black—on its abdomen, and the red flushes where the wings meet its body. It may also defend itself by exuding a foul-smelling froth from glands on its thorax.

Butterflies and moths

BEAUTIFUL TIGER

Pragtige tiermot *(Amphicallia bellatrix)*

Size: Wingspan 5,0–7,0 cm.

Colour: Wings yellow above, with broad, blue-black cross-bands—six or seven on the forewing and two or three on the hindwing. The thorax is yellow with a central brown spot; the yellow abdomen usually has brown cross-bands, but these are sometimes absent.

Most like: Cheetah tiger moth (Alytarchia amanda), but the markings on the beautiful tiger's forewings form well-defined bands across the wings. The cheetah tiger moth's body is not banded in brown, but has a series of brown dots running along the top.

Habitat: Mountain forest or bush in the warmer parts of southern Africa.

Occurs in the southern and Eastern Cape, coastal and central KwaZulu-Natal, eastern Swaziland, Mpumalanga, eastern Northern Province, Zimbabwe (except the west) and Mozambique.

There are about 200 species of tiger moths and their relatives in southern Africa. Their caterpillars, which are usually extremely hairy, are known as 'woolly bears'. The beautiful tiger's 'woolly bear' is very similar to that of the tricoloured tigermoth, but is not found in gardens.

All of these caterpillars are very active, and are often found running along the ground searching for a suitable site in which to pupate. Tiger moth caterpillars are not particularly choosy about what food plant they eat, but the beautiful tiger moth is particularly partial to wild peas.

Most tiger moths are active in the evening, but some are diurnal, and you may occasionally see them flying in the company of butterflies. While many butterflies are protected from bird predators by their bright colours (birds associate bright colours in butterflies with poison), moths are not as fortunate; being mostly night-time fliers, their chief predators are bats.

However, in the face of aerial assaults on them by bats, several unpalatable tiger moths have been shown to emit high-pitched squeaks of alarm which are sensibly interpreted as 'do not touch' signals by those bats which have previously preyed upon them and found them to be extremely distasteful.

PINK-LACED EMERALD LOOPER

Groen landmeter *(Comostolopsis stillata)*

Size: Wingspan 1,2–1,8 cm.

Colour: Wings and body emerald green. Wings bordered on the outer margins by a thin cream fringe. Each forewing crossed from top to bottom by two lines of tiny, blood-red dots: the outer line consists of three dots, and the inner of two. These lines of dots continue on to the hindwings, where the outer series continues as a row of three fainter dots, and the inner series as a single dot.

Most like: Many other small green moths, but the pink-laced emerald looper has distinctive dots on the wings, and a cream border to the outer edges of the wings.

Habitat: Disturbed lands; coastal bush.

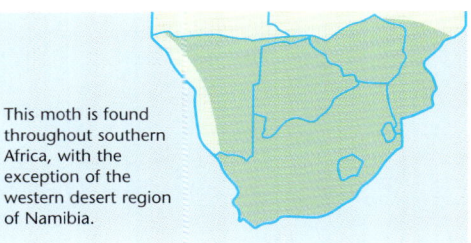

This moth is found throughout southern Africa, with the exception of the western desert region of Namibia.

'Looper' caterpillars give themselves away by their jerky locomotion and the extraordinary way in which they pull themselves along, bending the middle of the body into a vertical, upside-down U. The reason they move along in this fashion is that, unlike the caterpillars of most other moth groups, 'looper' caterpillars lack the five or so pairs of false legs or 'prolegs' along the length of the body; consequently for transport they rely only on three pairs of true legs towards the head, one pair of false legs near the end of the body and a pair of claspers at the rear.

When not in motion, the caterpillar manages to camouflage itself very well by adopting a 'twiglike' pose, the rear end of its body anchored to a branch or flower, the front half held erect and motionless. Because it appears to measure or 'inch' its way along, it is popularly known as a measuring worm or inchworm.

The pink-laced emerald looper, like other moths, has the habit of opening its wings and holding them flush to the surface on which it is resting.

This common, small-to-medium-sized green moth is one of a number of similar species in southern Africa—one which you are most likely to see resting on a wall in the vicinity of artificial lights.

Other insects

There's something breathtaking about the sheer number of insects on our planet. About a million species have been recorded worldwide—far more than all the animals put together—but it is quite possible that there may be 10 million more. Last century, a South African entomologist estimated that there were at least 40 000 identified species of insect on the southern tip of the continent. Today this number is, in fact, closer to 80 000.

In the great creepy-crawly cast of characters that make up our insect world, we think of some as villains—the ones that ravage our gardens, our crops and our possessions (aphids, locusts, fishmoths and termites)—or those that threaten our health (mosquitoes and tsetse flies). There are a few heroes, though, such as the cunning praying mantis that consumes garden pests.

About others we harbour mixed feelings: the honeybee stings but it also supplies us with delicious food in the form of honey; crickets chirp pleasantly but some species may damage our plants and lawns. And there are one or two eccentrics, such as the stick insect, that earn our admiration simply because of the wonderful way in which nature has disguised them.

Whatever our feelings about them, insects play an immensely important role in the natural cycle, their presence being essential to maintain a balance between the animal, vegetable and mineral kingdoms. (The remarkable way in which honeybees pollinate flowers is perhaps the best-known example of the mutual dependence that exists between plants and insects.)

Insects are the earth's most successful colonizers. Scarcely a single natural environment, however harsh, has not been invaded and settled by some kind of insect; the sea alone seems to have defeated their infinite adaptive ingenuity.

To protect themselves properly from their predators, insects are equipped with a variety of ingenious defences. Camouflage is one of them, stings and the emission of unpleasant-smelling liquids two others, while stick insects, for example, can 'play dead' in order to escape detection. Some insects, such as aphids, maximize their chances of survival simply by breeding at an enormously rapid rate—as gardeners know to their cost.

What is an insect?

Insects take their name from the Latin word *insectum*, meaning 'notched': their adult bodies are divided into three distinct sections (head, thorax, abdomen). They share this segmented appearance with the other arthropods, the large division of the animal kingdom to which they belong (also including spiders, centipedes and crabs), but they are distinctive in having three pairs of jointed legs.

In addition, most insects have a pair of antennae or two pairs of wings, although in some primitive species, such as springtails, the wings have never developed, and in other species they may have degenerated, as in the flea.

Legs and wings are attached to the insect's thorax, the middle section of its body.

In many species a conspicuous feature at the tip of the third section, the abdomen, is the female's 'ovipositor', a pointed structure with which she can lay her eggs in the earth, inside plant tissue or even inside the body of some other insect. Among bees and wasps this ovipositor has been modified for use as a sting.

In all insects the softer tissues are enclosed in a protective structure—a kind of body framework—known as an exoskeleton, composed of a carbohydrate called chitin. The exoskeleton may be hard and opaque (as in beetles, cockroaches, crickets) or delicate and transparent (dragonflies, crane flies). Sometimes its many, minutely thin layers refract the light, giving the insect a beautiful metallic sheen or iridescence.

On the road to adulthood most insects undergo a remarkable series of transformations or 'metamorphoses'. Out of the egg hatches a larva called a caterpillar in moths and butterflies, a grub in beetles, and a maggot in flies. The larva eats voraciously, becoming longer and fatter, and moults regularly. When fully grown it attaches itself to some convenient leaf or stem and turns into a pupa, sometimes surrounded by a cocoon of silken thread. In this so-called 'passive' stage the body tissues are recomposed to form the organs of the adult. And so, finally, the adult or 'imago', so called because it represents the completed 'image' of the species, emerges.

Dragonflies and grasshoppers are among the insects that have no pupal stage as they grow. Their young, looking like smaller versions of adults but without wings, are known as nymphs.

Identifying insects

Each entry in this section refers to a group of insects, not to a species. The descriptions are appropriate for all the species within the group—but a single sample species is illustrated alongside the entry.

Antennae

The length and shape of the antennae provide important clues. For example, locusts have short antennae, crickets long ones; but grasshoppers ('long-horned' and 'short-horned') may have either. The long, threadlike, backward-curving antennae of cockroaches easily distinguish them from beetles.

Mouthparts

These are of two basic kinds, adapted either for biting and chewing hard substances or for piercing and sucking fluids. Insects with typical biting mouthparts are dragonflies, grasshoppers, cockroaches, beetles and ants, while shield bugs, cicadas, aphids and scale insects have sucking mouthparts, which are used to extract plant fluids (beetles and shield bugs often look alike superficially, but the mouthparts are clearly different). The mouthparts of horseflies and female mosquitoes also consist of lancetlike structures which are efficiently used for piercing the skin of their victims to draw blood. In moths and butterflies the mouthparts are rolled up in a proboscis which is extended only during feeding.

Wings

Study the wings to see how many there are and which of them are functional. All true flies (order Diptera)

Other insects

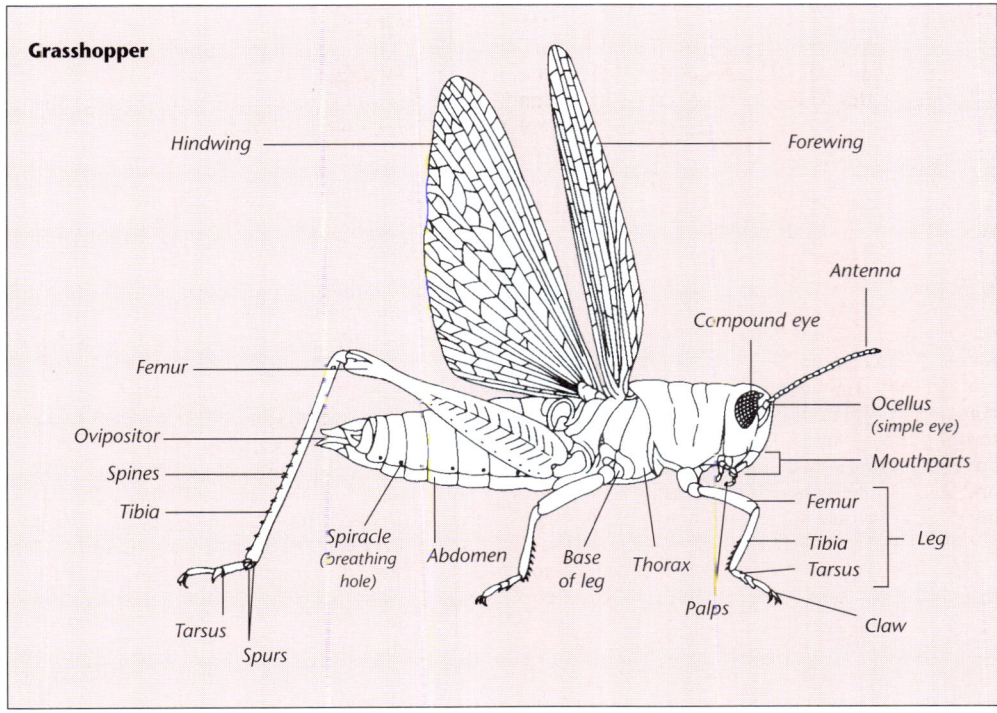

Grasshopper

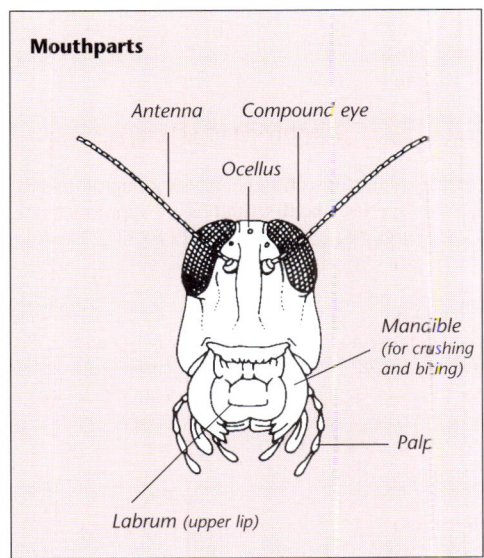

Mouthparts

have a single pair of wings, the fore pair, providing flight. (The rudimentary hindwings, shaped like drumsticks, vibrate in time with the forewings and control the insect's movements like a pair of gyroscopes). Despite their name, dragonflies, damselflies (order Odonata) and mayflies (order Ephemeroptera)—insects with two pairs of functioning wings—are not really flies at all. Bees and wasps also have two pairs of wings, as do winged ants.

Three orders of insect have hardened or partly hardened forewings: the Coleoptera (beetles), the Dermaptera (earwigs) and the Orthoptera (crickets, grasshoppers, locusts, cockroaches, stick insects and the mantids). Nature has carefully designed their forewings to serve as protective cases or shields for the hindwings.

Somewhat similar are the shield bugs (order Heteroptera), for the basal part of their forewings is harder and more leathery than that of the rear ones. Some bugs, such as common garden aphids (order Homoptera), have both winged and wingless phases.

Make a note of the texture, colour, markings and vein structure of wings. The wing venation is particularly important in identifying flies and distinguishing between the different families. A conspicuous, opaque spot near the wing tip is a characteristic feature of both pairs of wings in the dragonflies.

Legs

Notice any distinctive feature to the insect's legs? Locusts and grasshoppers have outsize hindlegs (modified for use as jumping organs), with tiny spines; but it is the front, 'praying' legs of a mantis that are spined, ready to catch an unsuspecting victim that approaches too close. Insects that live in association with water, such as water striders (family Gerridae), have long spindly legs that keep their bodies free of the water surface when they settle on a pool, while the back swimmers (family Notonectidae) and water boatmen (family Corixidae) have oarlike legs. The front legs of mole crickets end in pawlike feet that enable them to dig through the soil. Remember that all insects have six legs, although in the larval stage no legs may be apparent at all.

Abdomen

Watch for any appendages at the tip of the abdomen. The presence of an ovipositor means the insect is female. Earwigs (order Dermaptera) carry a prominent pair of pincers, used in defence. A forked springing organ, also at the tip but held underneath the abdomen, is characteristic of springtails (order Collembola). Some male insects bear a pair of claspers, used to grip the female during mating.

Other insects

FISHMOTHS

Vismotte (Order Thysanura)

Size: *Length 1,0-15 mm.*
Colour: *Silvery grey or brown.*
Most like: *The combination of a three-pronged tail and a permanent lack of wings make this insect unmistakeable.*
Habitat: *Bookshelves and linen cupboards; in the open, among leaf litter, in rotting wood or under stones.*

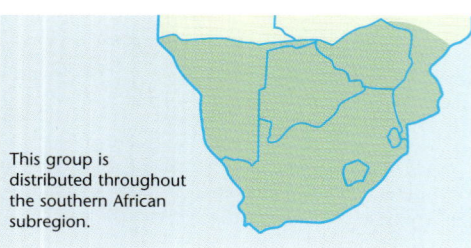

This group is distributed throughout the southern African subregion.

Fishmoths, like springtails, belong to a very ancient order of insects and were scuttling around in the age of the dinosaurs. They are dreaded by librarians and stamp collectors, among others, because of their partiality to starch and cellulose, which means they can damage papers, prints and photographs, as well as bookbindings. Wallpaper and starched clothes are also at risk, which is why the wise householder regularly airs cupboards and sprays them with a suitable spray to deter these creatures.

Members of the same insect order are the 'bristletails' (so called because of the three bristly tails these brown insects possess), which are found in the wild, among garden litter or under stones.

Close examination shows that the fishmoth is covered with overlapping rows of tiny plates which look like fish scales but are actually modified hairs. The head and sides of the body also have a covering of hairs, providing the insect with a keen sense of touch, on which it relies more heavily than its rather poor sight. They are agile, and can run very nimbly.

The most common species in southern Africa (one of about 60 in the region) is *Ctenolepisma longicaudata*, the domestic fishmoth, or silverfish. Another well-known species, *Lepisma saccharina*, occurs only in the south-western Cape. Both were introduced from Europe.

The mating of fishmoths takes place after a courtship dance in which the male deposits his sperm on the ground before the female. She then lifts it up with her ovipositor and tucks it into her reproductive tract. She lays batches of six to ten eggs at a time in crevices and cracks. The young hatch after a period of one to four months.

SPRINGTAILS

Springsterte (Order Collembola)

Size: *From less than 1,0 mm up to 5,0 mm.*
Colour: *White, grey, black, orange, red, green and other colours, sometimes mottled.*
Most like: *Could only be confused with fleas, but are never shiny brown or hard.*
Habitat: *Damp soil, decaying vegetable matter (including compost heaps), bark, the roots of over-watered pot plants, the surface of freshwater pools (including swimming pools) and stagnant ponds, the seashore and the surface of the sea.*

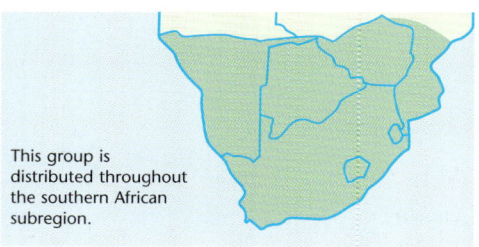

This group is distributed throughout the southern African subregion.

Some entomologists dispute that springtails are insects. If we give these creatures the benefit of the doubt, they are certainly the oldest order of insect in existence (a fossil insect more than 300-million years old is of the same order), and today they are the most numerous—tens of thousands have been recorded in a single square metre of soil. They are also quite small and insignificant to the layman: wingless creatures that live mostly out of sight and, for the most part, do no harm. Because of their superb jumping prowess they may be mistaken for fleas.

The diminutive springtail can jump anything up to 30 cm at a hop. It does so, in mechanical toy fashion, by virtue of its furcula (little fork). This structure, which is attached to the underside of the abdomen, usually lies clasped to the body. When released, however, it shoots suddenly downwards and backwards, propelling the insect forward.

Another unique feature of the springtail is a tube, a little higher up the abdomen than the furcula, that acts as a sucking organ, enabling the insect to grip on a smooth surface. (Again some experts dissent, seeing the tube as an organ for imbibing water.)

Among the 2 000 or more different springtail species, some live on land—in soil or vegetation, under bark and even on snow-capped mountains—while others are supported by the surface film on freshwater pools or on rock pools along the seashore.

They are scavengers: their diet may be decaying plant material, fungi, bacteria, faecal matter, algae or, in certain circumstances, dead (or even living) insects.

Other insects

DRAGONFLIES

Naaldekokers (Suborder Anisoptera)

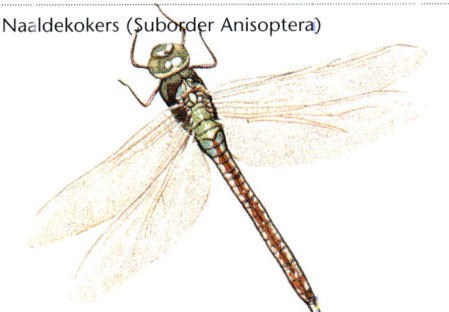

Size: Length of abdomen averages 1,5-8,5 cm; wingspan 4,5-14,0 cm.
Colour: A wide range of colours and colour combinations, including green, red, yellow, brown and black.
Most like: Damselflies (suborder Zygoptera). Dragonflies are more robust, more active fliers and more boldly coloured. Damselflies fold their wings over their bodies when at rest, while dragonflies hold theirs out at right angles to their bodies.
Habitat: The edges of quiet stretches of water, and on the leaves of plants growing in water.

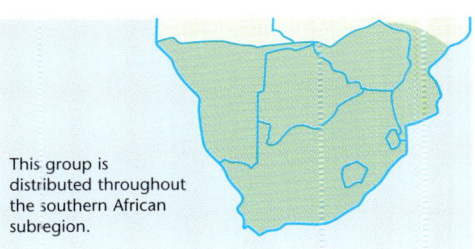

This group is distributed throughout the southern African subregion.

There are about 130 dragonfly species in southern Africa, many of which, such as the large green and sky-blue emperor dragonfly *Anax imperator*, are exceptionally beautiful. The vivid bodies and gossamer wings of these insects inspired the French jeweller René Lalique to fashion some of his most exquisite creations at the end of the 19th century.

In spite of its delicate appearance, the dragonfly is a fierce aerial predator. In a stylish mid-air manoeuvre it captures smaller insects by forming its six legs into a 'basket' into which it scoops its prey. And in defending its territory, the male engages rivals in airborne skirmishes that may lead to damaged wings and legs.

The female, which is less colourful than the male, traverses several male territories before finding her mate. Prior to mating, the male transfers semen to a small pouch on the underside of his abdomen. When mating, he grasps the female by the neck with his claspers and she, suspended below him, arches her body in order to collect the contents of the pouch.

In some species the female lays her eggs on the surface of the water while in flight. In others she settles on a water lily leaf or other aquatic plant and, once again curving her abdomen, uses her ovipositor (egg-laying tube) to pierce a hole in a submerged stem, where an egg is laid. The hatched 'nymph' lives under water until fully grown.

COCKROACHES

Kakkerlakke (Order Blattodea)

Size: Length 5,0-50 mm.
Colour: Reddish brown, greyish brown, black or yellow-brown. Often shiny.
Most like: The permanently wingless species of cockroach may be confused with woodlice, but the latter have 14 legs, while cockroaches have only six legs.
Habitat: Moist hiding places in human dwellings, among leaf litter and loose stones, or beneath bark.

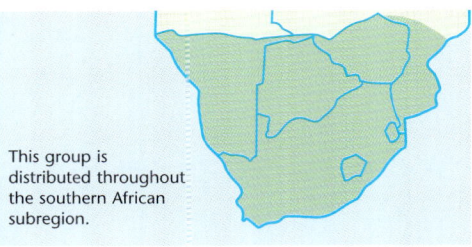

This group is distributed throughout the southern African subregion.

The two most common household cockroaches in southern Africa are immigrants. One of them, the large, reddish-brown *Periplaneta americana*, comes from America and is found all along our coast (the famous Durban cockroach). Smaller and paler is the German cockroach, *Blattella germanica*, a pest of inland towns. And there is a third imported species, *Blatta orientalis*, which is black and flightless. These insects associate closely with man and will scavenge on almost anything, from scraps of food left around the house to paper, glue and fabric.

Many indigenous species of cockroach are found in the wild. Especially interesting is the boldly marked Table Mountain cockroach, *Aptera fusca*, which is nocturnal and vegetarian: if disturbed, it will release an unpleasant-smelling liquid from glands on its back. The male is slender and has wings; the female is wingless, flat underneath but bulbous above. Unlike other cockroaches she does not lay her eggs in a neat package but carries them—from 18 to 24—around inside her until they hatch.

In late summer and autumn you may encounter family groups of Table Mountain cockroaches: a brood of black offspring, a wingless mother or two, and perhaps a few males, all living in some hidden crevice.

The female Table Mountain cockroach will squeak if you pick her up. This little distress signal is made as she rubs the rough edge of one segment of her body against another.

Some 3 500 to 4 000 species of cockroach occur globally, although most are not troublesome to man. In southern Africa approximately 175 species have been recorded.

Other insects

TERMITES

Termiete (Order Isoptera)

Size: Length: workers 2,0-8,0 mm; queen up to 25 mm.
Colour: Varies from brown-grey to reddish brown and pale yellow according to species.
Most like: The workers could be confused with ants, but are easily distinguished by their larger size, heavier bodies and large, reddish heads.
Habitat: The old wood of dead trees; veld and grassland, and the soil beneath. Abundant in arid regions.

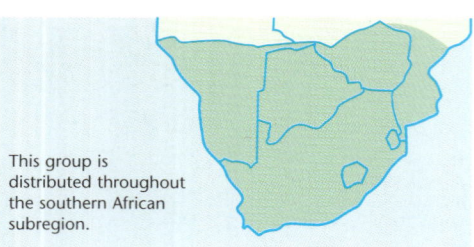

This group is distributed throughout the southern African subregion.

The popular alternative name for termites—'white ants'—is both confusing and erroneous since true ants (along with bees and wasps) belong to a different insect order, the Hymenoptera. And what are commonly known as 'ant hills', are really termitaria or termite heaps: the mounds thrown up by termites as they construct their nests. The mounds may be part of the insects' living quarters, or chimneys leading down to a subterranean chamber.

Termites live in large colonies that have a highly developed social structure. Up to 95 per cent of the members of any colony are workers (sterile males and females). They build the nest and keep it clean, gather and store food, tend the eggs and the young that hatch from them, and look after the king and queen termites. After mating, the king and queen settle in a small hole in the ground, bonded for life. They share the duty of looking after their first offspring; but as their progeny grows this task is left to the workers. The queen, meanwhile, becomes adjusted to a routine of almost nonstop reproduction. The queens of some species may lay as many as 30 000 eggs a day.

Completing the membership of the colony are the soldier termites; very much like the workers, they have larger heads and a pair of fearsome jaws perfectly capable of snapping other insects in two. The soldiers' task is to defend the colony, mainly against ants.

There are more than 150 termite species in the southern African subregion.

PRAYING MANTIDS

Hotnotsgotte (Order Mantodea)

Size: Length 2,0-8,5 cm.
Colour: Green, brown, yellow or pink. One yellow-and-green species, Pseudocreobotra wahlbergi, has eyelike markings (ocelli) on its forewings.
Most like: Many species, especially the more slender ones, resemble long-horned grasshoppers (family Tettigoniidae), but the mantids are easily distinguished by their enlarged, spiny, raptorial forelegs.
Habitat: Shrubs, trees, garden plants.

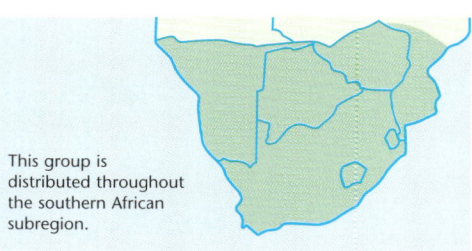

This group is distributed throughout the southern African subregion.

To the San the praying mantis was a god whose activities inspired whimsical legends. The ancient Greeks thought the insect looked like a prophet (which is what the Greek word *mantis* means). Certainly it spends much of its time sitting motionless with its forelegs held up in an attitude of prayer—but what this cunning carnivore is 'praying for' is simply that a fly, spider or beetle will settle within arm's reach. Then the powerful forelegs, fringed with spines and capable of the grasp of a pair of pliers, pounce into action. And the mantis's sturdy jaws soon reduce the prey to a mince. Even bees and wasps are consumed.

There are about 120 species in southern Africa. The large green mantis, *Sphodromantis gastrica*, is a regular visitor to gardens. Since it feeds on other insects it performs a useful horticultural service. It sometimes also feeds on its own kind.

The female's notorious habit of consuming the male immediately after copulation is well proven. She may even bite off his head during the act itself; indeed his successful sexual performance depends on his decapitation and will not cease since it is controlled by a nerve centre in his abdomen.

Before laying her eggs, the female climbs a twig or plant stem and extrudes from the end of her body a secretion that, with a special pair of plates, she whips up into a white froth. Into this meringue she delivers her eggs.

Other insects

GARDEN EARWIGS
Oorkruipers (Order Dermaptera)

Size: Length 8,0-25,0 mm.
Colour: Brown, tan, yellow or blackish.
Most like: Some resemble harvester termites, but are readily distinguished from them by the long pair of forceps at the end of the abdomen.
Habitat: Moist, dark places in gardens, such as under stones or rotting logs, or in compost heaps.

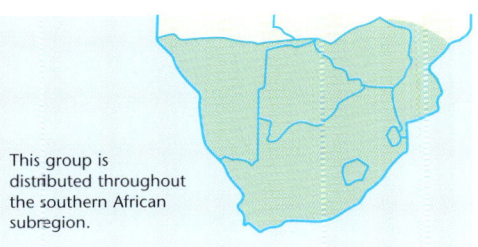

This group is distributed throughout the southern African subregion.

The 'wig' of this insect's curious name derives from an old English word meaning 'beetle'. In Europe, where the earwig is more common than in southern Africa, and is considered to be both a garden and a household pest, it has a gruesome reputation in folklore. It is said to enter a sleeping person's ear and even to burrow through the eardrum and lay its eggs in the brain. That's nonsense, of course.

In southern African gardens this harmless insect actually does good in that its diet includes fly maggots, aphids and decaying vegetable matter. For the rest, it scavenges on dead insects.

A curious feature of the earwig is the pair of crescent-shaped 'pincers' at the end of its abdomen, larger in the male than in the female. In some carnivorous species they are used to capture live insects and may also play a role in courtship. When the insect is threatened, it raises its pincers in self-defence. They are also used to fold its delicate hindwings under its leathery forewings—a uniquely complicated operation in the insect world, for the hindwings are first closed like a fan and then folded over twice into a compact package.

Garden earwigs are nocturnal. During the day they rest in damp, shady recesses. It is in such places that the female lays her white eggs, staying with them to defend and clean them and, if necessary, collect any that have rolled away. After hatching, the young stay with their mother for some time before dispersing.

Garden earwigs are among about 70 different earwig species in southern Africa.

KING CRICKETS
Koningkrieke (Family Stenopelmatidae)

Size: Length 2,5-7,0 cm.
Colour: Brown to red-brown, often banded.
Most like: Armoured crickets (subfamily Hetrodinae), but king crickets can be distinguished by their smooth bodies, which also lack the spines of armoured crickets.
Habitat: Moist, rich soils. Common in highveld gardens; montane forests in Northern Province and northern Mpumalanga.

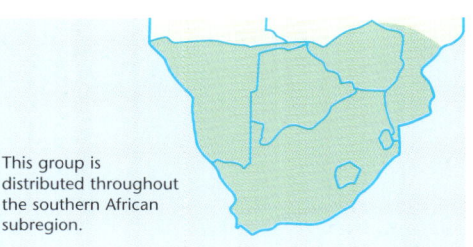

This group is distributed throughout the southern African subregion.

King crickets are a family of large, bizarre, wingless insects of which about 50 species occur in Africa, many of them in southern Africa. The best-known example is the 'Parkmore prawn', jokingly named after one of Johannesburg's northern suburbs—until its invasion of highveld gardens it was known only by its Latin species name. If its antennae and hindfeet are included, the Parkmore prawn's length is very impressive indeed: up to 160 millimetres.

Males and females are quite distinctive. The female possesses a long, scimitar-shaped ovipositor, or egg-laying organ, at the rear of the abdomen. The male has massive jaws, the function of which has not yet been identified.

The male Parkmore prawn produces a sound by rubbing its abdomen against its hindlegs—a noise of irritation when disturbed, it seems, rather than a mating call.

Like other king crickets, Parkmore prawns eat more animal than vegetable matter. Since their diet includes snails, they perform a useful pest-control service to gardeners in this respect. They also eat windfall fruit.

King crickets have a habit of wandering into houses where they bury themselves in all kinds of intimate nooks and crannies, including bedclothes. Their natural predators are in short supply in suburban gardens, so they are likely to become a well-established feature of Johannesburg's northern suburbs, and perhaps further afield.

They depend on moist, dank, compost-laden soils; gardens thus offer a most suitable habitat. In nature these crickets are found in humus on the forest floor.

Other insects

ARMOURED CRICKETS

Koringkrieke (Family Tettigoniidae, subfamily Hetrodinae)

Size: Length up to 4,0 cm.
Colour: Dark brown, grey or reddish brown, with two narrow yellow stripes along the back of the abdomen. A grey, spiky armour plate covers the neck.
Most like: King crickets, but spiky plate over the neck distinguishes armoured crickets.
Habitat: Occur mostly in dry country. Often found in maize fields.

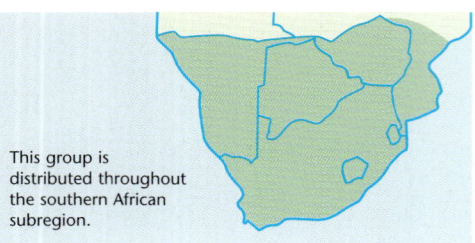

This group is distributed throughout the southern African subregion.

Armoured crickets occur only in Africa, where about 12 species have been described. The most common species found in southern Africa is *Hetrodes pupus*, which is often seen in drier regions such as Namaqualand.

In close-up the stoutly built armoured cricket or *koringkriek* is very ugly, resembling some prehistoric monster or science-fiction film extra. Five rows of spines protect the back of its abdomen; sharp spikes bristle from its pronotum (the tough plate protecting its neck and forebody); its jaws are strong enough to inflict a nasty nip, and its small, hemispherical eyes are out on stalks, giving it wide-angle vision and an expression of beady malevolence.

Though some people fear them, armoured crickets are not poisonous, and if left alone will not harm you. However, as a defensive measure when frightened, they will squirt a strong-smelling jet of blood from either side of the thorax.

The armoured cricket is not a true cricket, being biologically more closely related to the long-horned grasshoppers. All that remains of its wings is a pair of sturdy, membranous stumps underneath the armour plate of the male; and when a male rubs these together they produce a coarse, loud, rasping sound. The female has not even the vestige of wings and is silent.

Using her ovipositor, the female lays her huge eggs in clusters in the soil, and in due course the young armoured crickets appear, looking just like miniature adults, only darker, and some with green coloration.

LONG-HORNED GRASSHOPPERS

Langhoringsprinkane (Family Tettigoniidae)

Size: Length 2,0-7,0 cm including antennae.
Colour: In most cases green, either uniformly so or with wing markings.
Most like: Short-horned grasshoppers (Acrididae) but have long to very long, fine antennae.
Habitat: Gardens, cultivated land, grassland, forests.

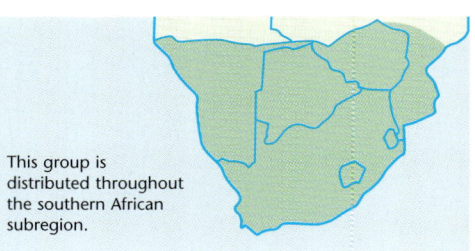

This group is distributed throughout the southern African subregion.

'Long-horned' refers simply to these grasshoppers' slender, jointed antennae, which are always longer than their bodies. (The formidable-looking armoured cricket or *koringkriek* belongs to the same family, *see left*.)

Long-horned grasshoppers, or katydids, are closely related to true crickets and, like them, the male is able to 'stridulate' or make a shrill chirping or scraping sound. This it does by rubbing one forewing against the other, the fine 'teeth' on the underside of the left wing coming into contact with a rough patch on the right wing. The sound is amplified by the grasshopper's 'mirror', a tiny, circular, resonating membrane on the right wing. The male katydid's song is a mating call and is a common nocturnal sound of the southern African outdoors.

The female, which is silent, is distinguished by the long, curved ovipositor at the end of her body. Some species lay eggs in plant tissue, others in the crevices of tree bark. And the females of the widespread bush variety of long-horned grasshopper (subfamily Phaneropterinae) often lay their eggs inside a leaf, first splitting the edge of it with their ovipositors.

Long-horned grasshoppers have their hearing organs on the tibia of their front legs. Close inspection will reveal their position, marked by tiny slits on the legs just below the insect's 'knees' or femoral joints.

Grasshoppers of this family are mostly nocturnal, resting in thick bush during the day. Most can fly although the shield-backed species (subfamily Decticinae) cannot.

Other insects

FIELD CRICKETS

Veldkrieke (Subfamily Gryllinae)

Size: Length 2,0-4,0 cm.
Colour: Black, brown or greyish brown.
Most like: Other grasshopper families. However, field crickets are never green, unlike long-horned grasshoppers and snowy tree crickets. Could be confused with mole crickets, but lack the latter's huge, digging front legs.
Habitat: In the veld under rocks or in gardens under heaps of vegetable refuse or loose stones.

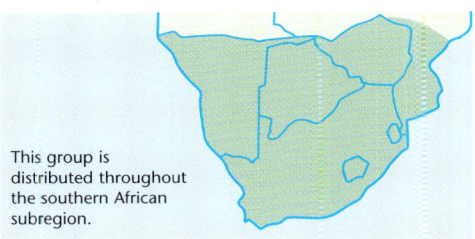

This group is distributed throughout the southern African subregion.

The most common member of this subfamily is the cheerful chirper *Gryllus bimaculatus* which you hear in your garden on a summer evening. Its repetitive noise, made only by the male, may sound less attractive—and amazingly loud—when the cricket is inside the house. Nor will it be easy to eradicate, for crickets are skilled ventriloquists and difficult to locate. In the garden they have a tendency to hide under stones or among rubbish.

Thousands of years ago, the Chinese and Greeks used to keep crickets in cages to sing in their homes. This mating call is made through a process called 'stridulation', in which the leatherlike (chitinous) forewings are rubbed one over the other at high speed to produce a sound of great intensity. Each forewing is modified with special scraper apparatus, which makes the distinctive sound. The speed and intensity of the chirping is affected by the temperature—the hotter it is, the faster the cricket trills.

The female and male have 'mirrors' (ears) on their front legs to detect the sound.

Field crickets, of which there are at least 30 species in southern Africa, are nocturnal. During the day they hole up in burrows dug in the soil, perhaps in a flowerbed or lawn. They feed on plants and insects.

In late autumn the female lays eggs singly in the ground, preferably in wet soil, and it is not until the following spring that they hatch. The young, or 'nymphs', resemble miniature, wingless adults and go through several moults before they emerge as adults.

TREE CRICKETS

Boomkrieke (Subfamily Oecanthinae, genus *Oecanthus*)

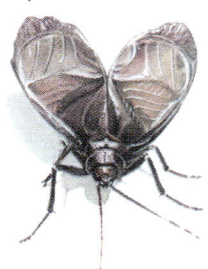

Tree cricket stridulating

Size: Length 2,0-3,0 cm.
Colour: Brownish, pale green or pale straw-yellow. Wings glassy and clear.
Most like: Long-horned grasshoppers (katydids), but forewings translucent and unpigmented.
Habitat: Trees, shrubs, grassland.

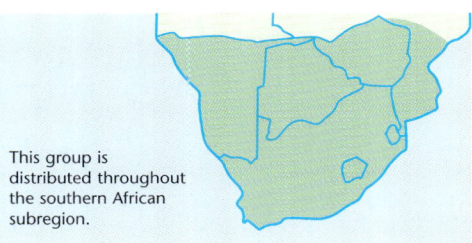

This group is distributed throughout the southern African subregion.

Tree crickets are slender and somewhat delicate, but they are robust singers. As with other crickets, only the male stridulates to produce a call. In this subfamily the apparatus for stridulation is highly advanced—there is a file and scraper on each forewing, and a sounding board which amplifies the call created as the base of the wings, which are held over the back at an angle of 45 degrees, are rubbed vigorously against each other.

While broadcasting his love song, the male often uses a leaf as an amplifier. After gnawing an appropriately sized hole in the leaf, he inserts his body halfway through it, and sings, gaining direction and amplification from his position.

These are night sounds, for tree crickets in general are nocturnal. Some species trill monotonously while others, including the snowy tree cricket, *Oecanthus fultoni*, chirp. The chirp rate is influenced by the temperature of the surroundings: when the temperature rises, the chirp rate increases. In fact, the one is so finely tuned to the other that you can quite reliably use a tree cricket's call as a kind of garden thermometer: count the number of chirps in 15 seconds, add 40, and you have the temperature in Fahrenheit!

In southern Africa the tree cricket subfamily is represented by only one genus, *Oecanthus*. Some species are plant-eaters, others feed on other small insects, including aphids and caterpillars. The female may damage fruit trees when she lays her eggs, for she deposits them in a slit her ovipositor carves into a twig, and the twig may die as a result.

Other insects

MOLE CRICKETS
Molkrieke (Family Gryllotalpidae)

Size: Length 3,0-3,6 cm.
Colour: Golden brown to black.
Most like: Field crickets, but mole crickets are unable to hop, have smaller wings and their forelegs are uniquely flattened with strong teeth for digging.
Habitat: Flowerbeds, vegetable beds, lawns where the soil is damp. Around vleis and marshes.

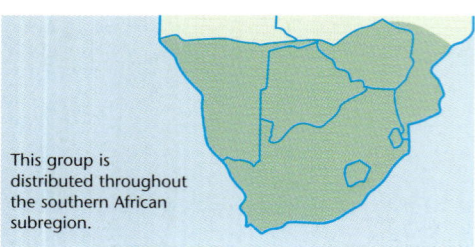

This group is distributed throughout the southern African subregion.

The awkward, blundering insect that flies into your house at night, attracted by the light, and then flops onto the floor and scuttles around is a mole cricket. There are only about 50 species of this unusual-looking creature in the world, four of which are found in southern Africa. *Gryllotalpa africana* is widespread and the most common.

Mole crickets are so named because of their burrowing prowess, especially in the damp soil they prefer, and their compact bodies are adapted for this purpose. The forewings are small and the front legs are powerful and armed with 'teeth'. As it burrows, this cricket throws up little mounds of earth, like diminutive molehills, to the detriment of immaculate lawns and bowling greens. The permanent burrow of a mole cricket may be as much as a metre deep.

Sometimes at night mole crickets feed on the surface (and may then be trapped with poison bait). But their foraging is mostly subterranean: they eat plant roots and other vegetable matter, and it is suspected that they may be carnivorous. Regarded as a pest when they indulge in crops of potatoes, carrots and other root crops, they also have a fondness for strawberries.

The 'stridulation' or chirruping of the male is a shrill buzzing or churring noise that may last for minutes on end, a sound quite unlike the merrier note of the common garden cricket. While emitting his call, the male often stands proprietorially at the entrance to his burrow, which acts as a kind of megaphone or resonator.

The female lays her oval eggs in groups in holes in the ground.

BLADDER GRASSHOPPERS
Blaasopsprinkane (Family Pneumoridae)

Size: Length 5,0-10 cm.
Colour: Green, sometimes tinged with pink and often dotted and striped with silver or red.
Most like: Large, green, short-horned grasshoppers, but male bladder grasshoppers have hollow, bladderlike abdomens. Females are wingless and lack bladder.
Habitat: Forests.

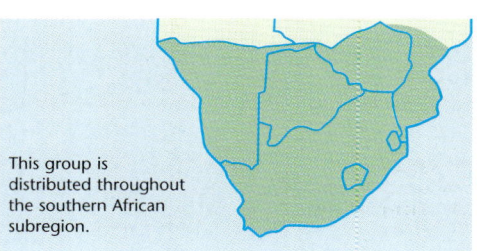

This group is distributed throughout the southern African subregion.

There are 17 species of bladder grasshopper in southern Africa, most of them beautifully camouflaged in their forest surroundings. It is the male's bloated appearance that gives the family its name. What looks like a bad case of indigestion is, in fact, nature's way of providing this insect with an extremely effective sounding box to amplify its deep, rasping call. Air-filled sacs inflate the abdomen, on each side of which is a horizontal row of raised, yellow bumps. Against these the male rubs the small, stiff-pointed 'comb' attached to the inside of each hindleg. The resultant noise could be mistaken by most people for the croaking of a large frog—particularly as it is broadcast at night. The call emitted by one species of bladder grasshopper, *Physophorina livingstoni*, has been differently described: as resembling the energetic shaking of a coin-filled collecting box.

The sound is made to attract the female. In contrast to her mate she is a plain creature: stout but bladderless, her wings reduced to stumps, her hindlegs not adapted to hopping, she can do no better than crawl among the forest undergrowth. Like the male, her antennae are short. It is thought that she lays her eggs in the ground.

Bladder grasshoppers are mostly confined to southern Africa, although two species are found in Uganda. Their excellent disguise means that they are not often spotted in the wild, but males, attracted by the light, often fly into homes at night. They are perfectly harmless.

Other insects

STINK LOCUSTS

Stinksprinkane (Family Pyrgomorphidae)

Size: Length up to 4,2 cm.

Colour: Green, brown or black, many species having bright markings in red, yellow, blue or green (or in a combination of some of these colours).

Most like: Their close relatives, the short-horned grasshoppers, but the latter are brownish yellow, and generally lack the brightly coloured markings of stink locusts.

Habitat: Bushes, gardens, agricultural crops.

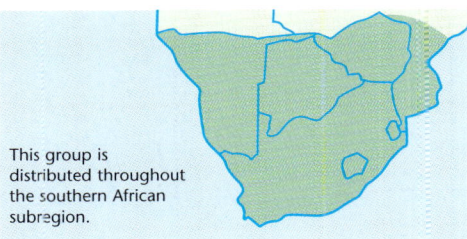

This group is distributed throughout the southern African subregion.

In the insect world, bright colours are 'aposematic', that is, they serve as a warning sign to possible predators. One of these stink locusts (which are also called, appropriately, gaudy grasshoppers) is *Zonocerus elegans*, an especially beautiful specimen which, when threatened, emits a repulsive smell produced by a yellow fluid. The popular Afrikaans name for this species, *stinksprinkaan*, sums it up well. The milkweed grasshopper or milkweed stink locust, *Phymateus morbillosus*, uses a similar defensive technique and it, too, has a startling appearance: black, with a bright red head, thorax and legs, yellow-spotted, purple wings, and purple and yellow abdomen.

Most of these species of locust have only short, nonfunctional wings and so, when in danger, they can do no better than hop away. They are generally slow-moving, being so well protected chemically as not to need any escape mechanisms.

More gregarious than most locusts, they are sometimes encountered in small swarms. They can be a serious pest of fruit (citrus, peaches), vegetables (tomatoes, pumpkins, beans) and a variety of other crops including cotton, sugar cane, coffee and tobacco. And they are extremely resistant to commercial poisons.

One other member of the stink locust family that may damage crops is *Phymateus leprosus*, the 'bush stink locust', which has an olive-green body and mottled wings in an assortment of greens and black; it is at its most destructive when its numbers, which fluctuate from year to year, are at their peak.

LOCUSTS

Sprinkane (Family Acrididae)

Size: Length 5,0-8,0 cm.

Colour: Brown, but with a number of colour variations depending on species and 'phase' of the locust. For example, the adult red locust, *Nomadacris septemfasciata*, changes from brown to reddish, with striped forewings. The immature brown locust, *Locustana pardalina*, may be green or grey in its solitary phase but is brightly patterned in orange and black when swarming.

Most like: Long-horned grasshoppers and stink locusts, but Acrididae locusts have short, thick antennae unlike long-horned grasshoppers, and are not brightly coloured as stink locusts are.

Habitat: Grassland and semi-desert.

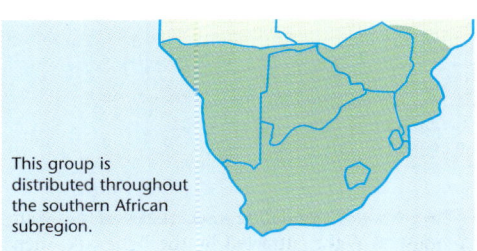

This group is distributed throughout the southern African subregion.

There is a Jekyll and Hyde element to the locust's existence. In the 1920s entomologists discovered that the insect leads two distinct lives, and that its character and coloration may change as it moves from the single phase, through an intermediate form, to the swarming phase. The trigger to these changes is overcrowding; when this happens, a small population builds up into a devastating swarm that flies in the direction of the prevailing wind, destroying all vegetation in its path.

Four locust species are found in southern Africa, the most important of which is the brown locust, found in parts of the Karoo and migrating to central Namibia, Botswana and Zimbabwe.

The brightly coloured 'hoppers' are known as *rooibaadjies* (red jackets)—a reference to the red-coated British troops who, before the advent of khaki, fought in South Africa. Like the soldiers, the hoppers march, because their wings are still only partially developed.

The red locust, a large species, of which the swarming hoppers are brown with orange, black and yellow markings, is a pest of the tropics; but when it migrates it may reach as far south as KwaZulu-Natal and the Eastern Cape. Huge swarms up to 60 km long have been reported.

By contrast swarms of large desert locusts are comparatively small and soon disperse.

Other insects

STICK INSECTS
Stokinsekte (Order Phasmida)

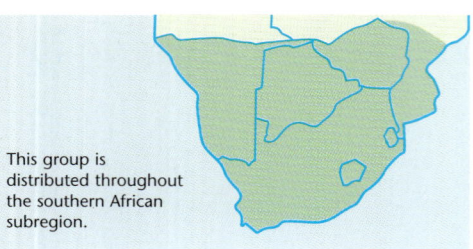

Size: Length 1,0-25 cm.
Colour: Green, brown or buff.
Most like: May be confused with some of the very slender praying mantids or grasshoppers. The mantids, however, have grasping forelegs, and grasshoppers have jumping hindlegs; stick insects have neither.
Habitat: Foliage, twigs, long grass.

This group is distributed throughout the southern African subregion.

There are about 50 species of stick insect in southern Africa, some tiny and some, such as *Bactrodema aculiferum*, very long indeed. All are plant-feeders, all have the same anorexic appearance and all are past masters at the art of camouflage, closely resembling the plant stems or grasses on which they lurk. Some, chameleonlike, can even alter their colour to improve their disguise.

The deception is essential, for stick insects have precious little in the way of defence—and they have many predators, including birds (especially the voracious red-winged starling), frogs, lizards, ants and flies. One fly actually lays her eggs on the stick insect, and the maggots that hatch feed on the living creature!

The normal gait of this unusual insect is a slow, jerky shuffle. This may change, at the hint of disturbance, to a rhythmic swaying on the spot. But if the danger is imminent, the stick insect feigns death, falling to the ground and remaining rigid as if in a fit.

Camouflage extends even to the stick insect's reproductive cycle, for the hard, tiny eggs are seed-shaped, often resembling the seeds of the plant on which the insect feeds.

The female simply lays them on the ground, or rather lets them drop to the ground from her perch above. The eggs lie there during the hot summer months, and when the nymphs emerge in the autumn they are tiny replicas of the adult.

In gardens one of the commonest species is *Macynia labiata*, the green stick insect of the Cape, growing to about 60 mm in length.

SPITTLE BUGS
Skuimbesies (Family Cercopidae)

Size: Length 6,0-15 mm.
Colour: Usually dark green or black, but sometimes more brightly coloured.
Most like: Spittle bugs bear a slight resemblance to small tree frogs; they can be distinguished from unrelated insect groups by their ability to jump. Nymphs are easy to recognize in their cuckoo-spit nests.
Habitat: Shrubs, trees, long grasses.

This group is distributed throughout the southern African subregion.

'Cuckoo-spit', the blobs of white froth you sometimes see on the twigs and stems of plants, is the product not of a bird but an insect. The nymph of the spittle bug, or froghopper, creates this viscous candyfloss possibly to hide itself from predators, or to protect itself from the sun's hot rays, which might otherwise soon kill it by desiccation. Scrape the white foam away and the vulnerable nymph is revealed, looking somewhat like a tiny, indistinctly patterned frog—hence this insect's alternative name.

Spittle bugs are sap-suckers. But whereas other sap-suckers excrete honeydew, the liquid excrement of the young spittle bug is mixed with a waxy secretion and then blown out into a froth by means of spiracles situated in a special chamber on the underside of the abdomen. The foam oozes out until the nymph is entirely surrounded by it, providing it with a temporary home that is impervious even to heavy rain.

Because of the waxy nature of this shelter, the bubbles that it consists of do not burst for some time—and in any case the shelter is constantly being renewed as the nymph feeds and excretes.

Once the spittle bug is fully grown it emerges from the foam, moults for the last time and grows wings.

The sap that provides the spittle bug with its daily meal has to be taken in large quantities to provide adequate nourishment. Some species imbibe and excrete so much of it that their host trees drip with the substance and are known as 'rain trees'.

Other insects

SHIELD BUGS

Stinkbesies (Family Pentatomidae)

Size: Length 1,0-2,0 cm.
Colour: Green, yellow, brown or black, sometimes with bright orange or yellow markings.
Most like: Spittle bugs, but flatter. Shield bugs, unlike spittle bugs, have hard forewings, with membrane-like tips.
Habitat: Vegetable gardens, fruits under cultivation, cotton and tobacco crops, wild plants in the veld.

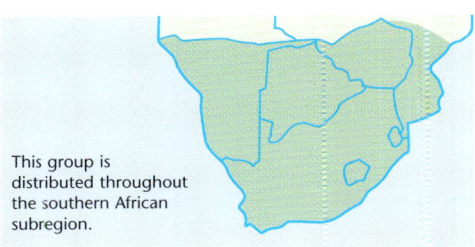

This group is distributed throughout the southern African subregion.

Shield bugs, or stink bugs, are pretty in shape and often in colour, but many of them are pests. They also emit an unpleasant smell if you squash or hold them, for they have well-developed stink glands. Best known of the family is the small, pale green *Nezara viridula*, which is very common in southern Africa and occurs worldwide in warm climates. Like other shield bugs it is active by day and feeds on plants by sucking out the vital juices; the long beak it uses for this purpose is folded back under the body when not in use.

It is fond of the kind of plants cultivated by man in vegetable gardens, especially tomatoes, attacking the aromatic, sappy stems.

In spring the female lays her eggs in large clusters on the underside of leaves. The brown, wingless hatchlings, born about a week later, eventually develop spots so that they resemble ladybirds. With successive moults they grow to look more like the adult bug, and also acquire the adult's characteristic stink.

The bagrada bug is smaller than *Nezara viridula*, and feeds on plants belonging to the cabbage family. The adult is black, with orange or yellow spots, while the nymphs are dark red, spotted and banded.

A third important shield bug pest is the antestia bug (*Antestiopsis variegata*), which is pale yellowish green, speckled with black and orange. In the wild, antestias feed on veld plants, but they are attracted to cultivated crops, especially soft fruits such as peaches and pears.

POND-SKATERS

Waterlopers (Family Gerridae)

Size: Length 5,0-10 mm.
Colour: Black or dark brown.
Most like: Distinctive. Pond-skaters are not easily confused with any other insect.
Habitat: Calm surfaces of freshwater ponds, swimming pools and streams. One species is marine and lives on the surface of the ocean.

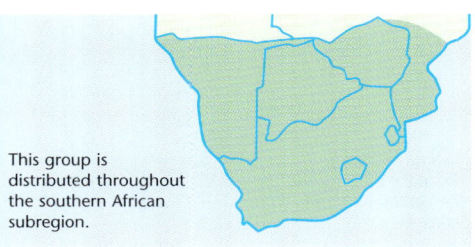

This group is distributed throughout the southern African subregion.

There are about ten southern African species of these ingenious long-legged insects, known also as water-striders. They are wonderfully adapted to make use of 'surface tension'—the property by which an untroubled water surface behaves like a stretched elastic membrane able to bear a delicate weight. Using their middle and hind pairs of legs, pond-skaters literally walk, or 'skate', on water. The lower parts of these legs are the only parts to make contact with the surface, and they are covered with fine, water-repellent hairs. The front pair of legs is shorter and is used for capturing food; when not in use they are kept tucked under the front of the body.

What happens if the back legs become wet? The pond-skater will sink and drown, unless it can quickly find a dry surface to cling to, hauling itself out of danger. If rain or wind breaks the water's surface tension, pond-skaters skim to the shore, where they seek shelter under some protective cover.

They feed mostly on drowning or dead insects, firmly grasping them by the forelegs and bringing them to the beak. The featherweight pond-skater is sensitive to vibrations on the water's surface and immediately detects the death-throes of an insect that has fallen into the pond.

That sensitivity is used also in courtship. Holding onto a floating object such as a leaf, the male instigates a Morse message of ripples by moving his long legs up and down in the water. The female, sensing these, responds in kind.

After mating, the female lays her eggs on a leaf that provided the opportunity for the happy introduction.

Other insects

CICADAS
Sonbesies (Family Cicadidae)

Size: Length 1,0-6,0 cm.
Colour: Mottled pale to dark green and/or brown. Wings usually clear in parts.
Most like: Most distinctive by virtue of large size, heavy body and translucent wings.
Habitat: Trees, forests, bushveld.

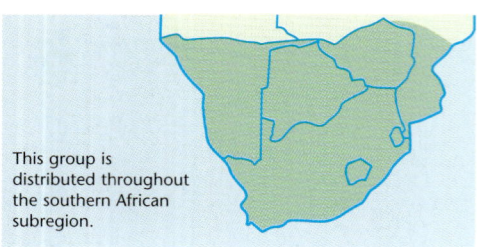

This group is distributed throughout the southern African subregion.

As is usual in the insect world, it is the male cicada that 'sings' and the silent female to whom this love-call is addressed. The piercing call is made by the muscular vibrations of two tight membranes called 'tymbals' or 'drums' covering cavities at the base of the male abdomen. Sound is detected by reflectors or 'mirrors' (ears) on the insect's underside. The whole remarkable apparatus may be sealed off by two semi-circular plates or 'opercula', one for each small abdominal cavity. The opercula can muffle the cicada's song or guide it in a particular direction.

Since the strong muscles activating the tymbals contract at the rate of about 400 times a second, the cicada's song has an extremely high frequency and sounds continuous. This sound is far more familiar to most people than the cicada's appearance, despite the fact that there are some 140 species, all sap-suckers, in southern Africa.

They have transparent or mottled wings which are held at an angle over the green or brown body when the insect is not in flight. There are five eyes on the head: two compound ones and, between them, three simple ones that cannot produce images. When cicadas see trouble, they fly swiftly away, leaving the predator a nasty parting gift—a foul-smelling droplet of half-digested plant sap expelled from the anus.

The female cicada lays her eggs in slits, which she makes in the bark of trees with her ovipositor. The nymphs emerge after about a month, and drop to the ground. With their strong forelegs they then burrow into the soil, tunnelling about until they encounter roots, whose sap provides them with food.

APHIDS
Plantluise (Family Aphididae)

Size: Length 1,0-6,0 mm.
Colour: Green, black or occasionally yellow. Some species have a covering of powdery wax that varies from white to blue-grey.
Most like: Aphids with a wax covering may resemble scale insects or mealy bugs.
Habitat: Gardens and a wide range of cultivated crops including peaches, apples, wheat and maize.

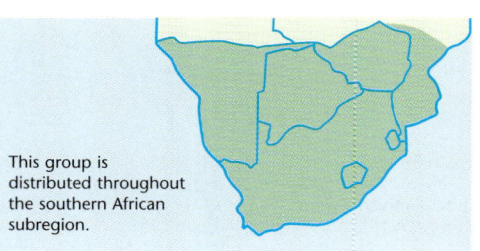

This group is distributed throughout the southern African subregion.

Aphids are small, soft-bodied, sap-sucking insects that can devastate garden plants and farm crops if they are not controlled. Their reproductive system and powers of procreation are remarkable. In many species the female does not need a male to produce young, which she may start doing when she's only a week to ten days old. Her eggs hatch inside her body, so that she gives birth to live nymphs—two or three of them a day if weather conditions are favourable. And so accelerated is the generative cycle that the embryo nymphs inside her may already contain developing embryos inside them!

Within quite a short time, an aphid-infested leaf becomes so crowded with these tiny pests that it can no longer provide them all with a meal. Up to this point the leaf colony has consisted of only wingless females, but now females with transparent wings appear, and they are able to fly away to establish new colonies.

There are more than 120 aphid species in southern Africa. Among the widely distributed species are the green peach aphid, *Myzus persicae*, which is a pest of potatoes, cabbages and other crops such as peaches; the black citrus aphid, *Toxoptera citricida*; and the woolly apple aphid, *Eriosoma lanigerum*, a North American import with bright red body fluid.

The copious amounts of honeydew excreted by aphids are greatly prized by ants, which are the aphids' natural protectors. But aphids also have many enemies, including ladybirds and parasitic wasps. One tiny wasp has successfully been imported to control the woolly apple aphid.

Other insects

MEALY BUGS

Witluise (Family Pseudococcidae)

Size: Length 2,0-5,0 mm.
Colour: The grey-white or pink body is covered with a layer of white, powdery wax.
Most like: The nymphs of certain leaf-hoppers, which also secrete wax. Mealy bugs, however, are unable to move fast like the leaf-hopper nymphs.
Habitat: Citrus orchards, vineyards, sugar cane fields and among many other cultivated crops. They are also found on thorn trees.

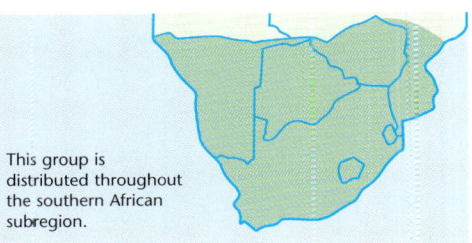

This group is distributed throughout the southern African subregion.

Mealy bugs are not pests found on maize: their name is derived from the waxy secretion that covers the body of the female in a white, meal-like powder. The behaviour pattern of these tiny bugs parallels that of the hard scale insects, for it is the squat, oval female that steals the limelight, feeding on sap by means of a long, hairlike beak that is custom-made to penetrate the fibrous stems of fruit trees and other plants. She is scarcely identifiable as an insect. The male, however, is recognizably one—a feeble, red, two-winged creature that, unlike the female, has pupated inside a cocoon.

The male lives for only a few days. He has no feeding apparatus, and his sole function is to find a mate and fertilize her.

There are about 110 species of mealy bug in southern Africa. All of them secrete a sticky honeydew through the anus; this covers the leaves and fruits of plants on which they feed. This honeydew is very attractive to ants, which feed on it, and at the same time protect the bugs from their natural enemies such as small wasps and ladybirds.

The citrus mealy bug, *Planococcus citri*, has done severe damage to citrus fruits, particularly navel oranges (the bugs finding shelter at the navel end of the fruit).

The female bug is enormously prolific in her egg-production, laying 1 000 or more in one stint. It is no wonder that at the end of this reproductive binge she shrivels up and dies.

HARD SCALE INSECTS

Gepantserde dopluise (Family Diaspididae)

Size: Up to 2,0 mm in diameter.
Colour: A wide colour range including light red, dark red, bluish brown, grey and black.
Most like: Soft scale insects in shape and size, but the hard scale insects are flatter and have a loose, hard scale covering their bodies.
Habitat: The fruit, leaves and branches of fruit trees. Other trees including oaks, pines and poplars. Also found on indigenous vegetation such as aloes, on rose bushes and other ornamental shrubs.

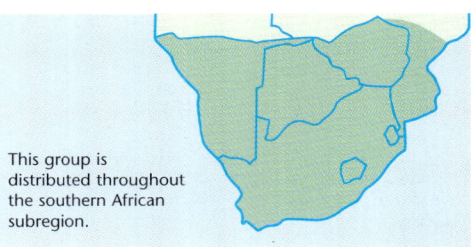

This group is distributed throughout the southern African subregion.

These diminutive insects, known also as armoured scale insects, can do severe damage to the host plants they feed on. About 220 species of armoured scale insects are known in southern Africa, about 30 of which are exotic.

Size, shape and colour depend on the species. The body of the female is fairly shapeless: a flat, eyeless, legless, wingless bag equipped with a long, threadlike beak. Once she has inserted her beak into the living plant it is never removed, and she stays in this position for the rest of her life. The protective scale over her incorporates the cast-off skins from her early moults and is reinforced by a waxy secretion which acts as a type of cement.

The male is more insectlike. Smaller than the female, he matures as a nymph under an elongated scale. He has a pink body with wings, antennae, eyes and six legs. He has no mouth, for feeding is not part of his destiny: his sole purpose is to crawl out from under his scale, find a female and mate with her. Then he dies, his adult life having lasted only a day or two.

The eggs hatch in the female's body. The blind hatchlings, or 'crawlers', are born singly, and roam about until they find a place of their own on the plants.

Without pest-control measures a fully grown tree can succumb to an incrustation of hard scale insects within two or three years.

A very common imported species is the red scale insect, *Aonidiella aurantii*, found on fruit trees and roses.

Other insects

ANTLIONS
Mierleeus (Family Myrmeleontidae)

Size: Wingspan 3,0-15 cm.
Colour: Transparent wings of the larger species are attractively patterned in brown, yellow, black and white. In smaller species the wings may also be transparent.
Most like: Damselflies and dragonflies, but the antlion is a comparatively slow, feeble flier, and is active mostly in the evening and at night. Its antennae are longer and stouter than either the damselfly's or dragonfly's.
Habitat: Shrubs and long grass, especially in sandy, more arid areas.

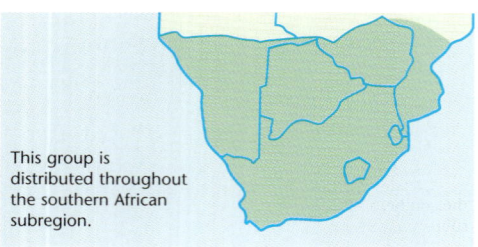

This group is distributed throughout the southern African subregion.

Adult antlions are delicate creatures, with long, slender bodies and gauzelike wings. During the day they shelter among vegetation or rest on the ground, where they are well camouflaged. They forage for small insects at night, flying clumsily on slowly flapping wings.

The layman does not readily associate the adults (often seen at lights on summer nights) with their cunning and voracious larvae: podgy, with short, bloated abdomens, large heads and long, curved jaws equipped with teeth. The larvae are, in fact, the 'lions' which prey on ants, as well as other insects.

The larvae of three genera of antlions ambush ants by constructing a conelike pit some 30 mm in diameter and 25 mm deep in the sand and then, hiding at the bottom with just the tips of their jaws visible, lying in wait for some unsuspecting prey (anything from an ant to a grasshopper) to fall in. Once in the pit, the prey is helpless. The larva's jaws close firmly on it, dragging it beneath the surface, and the creature's vital juices are sucked out. The husk is discarded.

The anatomy of the antlion larva is unusual in that there is no mouth as such, but channels on the inner edge of each jaw lead to the pharynx and direct juices into it. It also has no anus.

CRANE FLIES
Langpootmuskiete (Family Tipulidae)

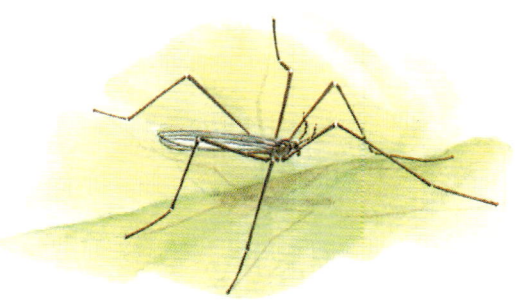

Size: Body length 1,0-2,5 cm.
Colour: Black, brown, grey, yellow or orange.
Most like: Mosquitoes, but crane flies are much larger. Wings usually smoky brown, whereas mosquitoes' wings are grey, some with black markings on them. Crane flies also have longer legs than mosquitoes do.
Habitat: Near water and among dense vegetation, out of sunlight. They often enter homes.

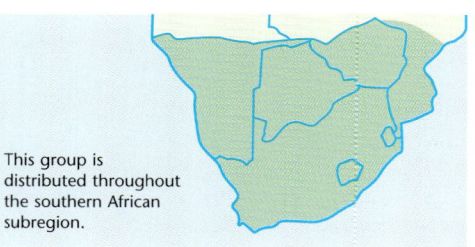

This group is distributed throughout the southern African subregion.

In flight the six long, threadlike legs of the crane fly dangle. Aground, the fly teeters along on them like an acrobat on stilts. The males of some species wave their legs—or wings—rhythmically as part of the courtship ritual; indeed, the whole body may sway, as if to some unheard insect rumba. These fragile legs easily break off if the insect is roughly handled.

Crane flies resemble long-legged mosquitoes. Like mosquitoes, these harmless insects are closely associated with water, and the female of many species lays her eggs in water: in other species the eggs are laid in damp soil or among decaying vegetable matter. Aquatic larvae are carnivorous, feeding on aquatic insects, worms and other larvae. Terrestrial larvae, also known as 'leatherjackets', eat mosses, grass roots, vegetable debris and subterranean parts of garden plants.

Adult crane flies draw their nourishment from the nectar of flowers, which they reach with their long proboscises. They are incapable of biting or chewing.

Among the simplest of flies, crane flies are found all over the world. In southern Africa there are about 360 species. While they shelter among vegetation out of the sunlight, they are often attracted to light, and you may see a whole swarm of males dancing in the sun's rays. This exhibition is also part of the mating dance, being designed to attract female crane flies. No sooner does a female appear on the scene than a member of the dancing team hustles her off to a nearby leaf, where copulation takes place.

Other insects

ANOPHELINE MOSQUITOES
Malariamuskiete (Genus *Anopheles*)

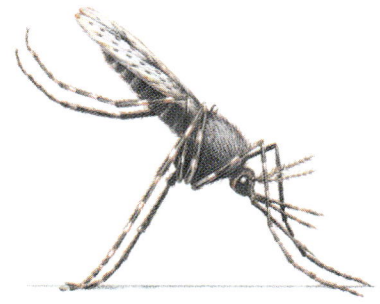

Size: Length 1,0 cm.
Colour: Grey-black body, with grey wings often spotted black.
Most like: Common household mosquito (genus *Culex*), but anopheline's spotted wings diagnostic. Also, when at rest, this genus holds itself at an angle of 45 degrees to the surface on which it stands, while the genus *Culex* stands parallel to the surface.
Habitat: The vicinity of natural vleis, with abundant vegetation nearby.

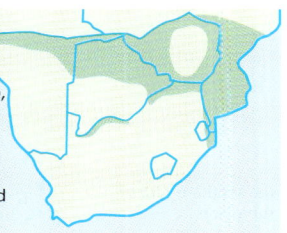

Northern Namibia, northern and eastern Botswana, Zimbabwe (except the central part), Mozambique, Northern Province, eastern Mpumalanga, eastern Swaziland, the northern KwaZulu-Natal coast and the Northern Cape.

Only the female mosquito sucks blood. The male is not equipped with the means to pierce human skin, and he feeds, beelike, on the nectar of flowers and the juice of fruits. (So does the female when no blood is available.)

The female's feeding equipment consists of a long, thin, grooved proboscis furnished with minute cutting devices or 'lancets'. A sheath covering the proboscis folds back as the female inserts her proboscis into the flesh. She then channels a stream of saliva, carrying the malaria-causing *Plasmodium* parasite, through the proboscis, which sets up a local irritation that draws blood to the surface. Her meal can then begin.

It is easy to understand how a female mosquito may be a malaria carrier. If she has fed on the blood of someone who is infected with the disease and moves on to another person within a short space of time, then that second person is at risk.

Fortunately, the number of mosquito species that transmit malaria is small. All of these species are of the genus *Anopheles*, and the most important transmitters belong to the so-called *Anopheles gambiae* group. But the *Anopheles* genus also includes several other species that are harmless.

Anophelines lay their eggs singly on water, each egg having two small air sacs to keep it afloat. The larvae—appropriately known as 'wrigglers'—rest horizontally just below the water surface, as do the pupae, which breathe via tubes on their backs.

HORSEFLIES
Blindevlieë (Family Tabanidae)

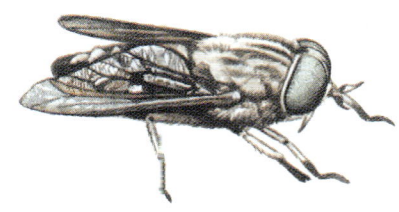

Size: Length 1,0-2,5 cm.
Colour: Brown or black. The large eyes are iridescent.
Most like: Tsetse flies and robber flies, but horseflies can be distinguished by their wings, which are held apart, not folded across one another.
Habitat: Larvae found in damp soil near streams or vleis; rotting organic matter, sometimes in tree holes. Adults common in forest, bushveld and on farmlands.

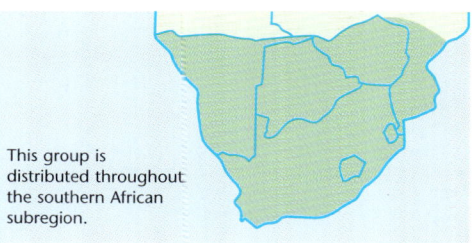

This group is distributed throughout the southern African subregion.

These large, squat flies have much in common with mosquitoes—the males feed on the nectar and pollen of flowers, but the females prefer a diet of blood, usually that of mammals, less often that of birds, reptiles or amphibians.

In the female's long proboscis are tiny grooves harbouring cutting lancets'. These enable her to pierce the skin of her victim before sucking out the blood. By ferrying infected blood, female horseflies may transmit a number of diseases, including anthrax, which is deadly to cattle and sheep. They also carry the trypanosomes, or tiny parasites, that cause the disease surra in horses and nagana in cattle. (Nagana is more often transmitted by tsetse flies.) The male horsefly is harmless.

By closely examining one of these flies you can quite easily tell its sex, for the large eyes of the male meet at the top, but there is a gap between those of the female.

Like mosquitoes, horseflies breed in association with water. The female lays a mass of eggs on the leaves of aquatic plants, on stones or grass adjacent to water, or in damp soil. The larvae, whose bodies are armed with tiny spines, thrive in a watery habitat, but have to come up to the surface regularly to 'breathe' through a tube at the rear of their bodies.

The larvae have sharp, curved jaws which are used to spear tadpoles, worms and water insects. Other larva species prefer a diet of vegetable debris.

Other insects

ROBBER FLIES
Roofvlieë (Family Asilidae)

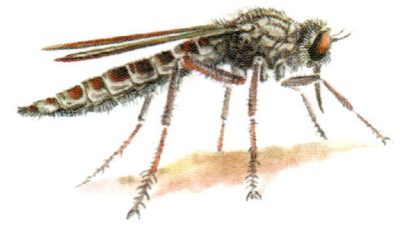

Size: Length 3,0-40 mm.
Colour: Grey or brown, sometimes with darker markings on the body.
Most like: Many species may be confused with sand and mud wasps, especially in flight. Robber flies, however, have only one pair of wings, whereas wasps have two pairs.
Habitat: A wide range of environments, from semi-desert to mountain forest. Open country—grassveld or bushveld—is the preferred habitat of most species.

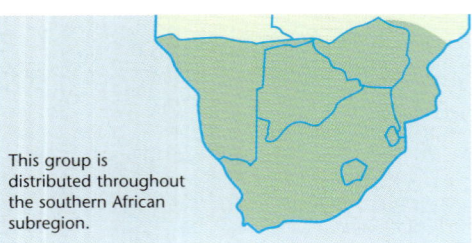

This group is distributed throughout the southern African subregion.

Robber flies are misnamed. 'Killer fly' or 'vampire fly' would be more appropriate, since these carnivorous insects feed exclusively on other insects, whose body fluids they suck out by means of a stout proboscis. The empty shell of their hapless victim is then discarded.

Usually the robber fly captures its prey in flight. Before this happens, it either patrols a particular 'air corridor' or else sits in wait on a grass stem, leaf or stone. Once it spots its victim, this species gives chase rapidly, and grabs the prey with its strong, spiny legs. A sharp stab with the proboscis is the *coup de grâce* (but whether the robber fly's salivary fluid acts as a poison or paralysing agent is as yet unknown).

There are some 500 southern African species, varying greatly in size. The distinctive eyes are large and bulging, with a deep furrow between them. The body is usually thickly bristled, and so is the mouth area—these whiskers being known as the fly's mystax. The bristles protect the fly's eyes when it closes in on potentially dangerous prey such as bees and wasps. It has no qualms about attacking insects larger than itself, but favours those that move at a leisurely pace.

In some species the female lays her eggs in the soil; in others the eggs are laid on plants or rotting wood. The cylindrical larvae are mostly vegetarian, though some feed on the larvae of other insects.

HOVER FLIES
Sweefvlieë (Family Syrphidae)

Size: Length up to 2,0 cm.
Colour: Brown, yellow or black, with bright yellow stripes or spots.
Most like: Honeybees or wasps, but hover flies have only a single pair of wings and no sting.
Habitat: A wide range of localities, wherever there are flowers to provide nectar for food.

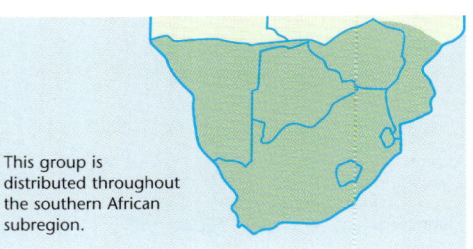

This group is distributed throughout the southern African subregion.

Rapidly vibrating wings enable hover flies to remain characteristically poised in the air where, with their distinctive black-and-yellow coloration, you could easily mistake them for bees and wasps. Like these insects they feed on the nectar and pollen of flowers. They don't carry stings, however, and are harmless to man.

The large and very common *Eristalis tenax*, a rather slow-moving species, closely resembles a drone bee and is therefore known as the 'drone fly'.

The larvae of this large insect family (226 species have been recorded in southern Africa) vary greatly in their appearance, diet and lifestyle. Syrphinae larvae feed on aphids, while *Microdon* larvae live in ant nests and consume dead or dying larvae and pupae. Some larvae make a meal of the decaying vegetation in which they live, while others feed on the sap of growing plants.

The larvae of many species, including *Eristalis tenax*, are aquatic, living on the muddy bottoms of polluted pools, blocked drains or the like. They are known as 'rat-tailed' maggots, a reference to the long, slender tube that each maggot has attached to its posterior. Using this telescopic device, equipped at its tip with two tiny spiracles or breathing vents, the maggot can make contact with the water surface and inhale life-giving air.

Confusion between hover flies and bees probably accounted for the ancient belief that swarms nested in rotting carcasses. However, hover flies do not feed on carrion at any stage of their life cycle.

Other insects

FRUIT FLIES
Vrugtevlieë (Family Tephritidae)

Size: Length 4,0-8,0 mm.
Colour: Yellow, brown or black, often with iridescent eyes and black-and-brown patterned wings.
Most like: Hover flies, but most fruit flies can be distinguished by their heavily marked wings.
Habitat: Orchards, vegetable crops including pumpkins and melons, and the flower heads of ornamental plants.

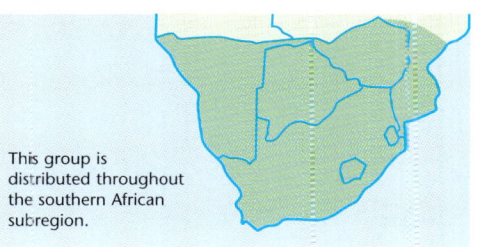

This group is distributed throughout the southern African subregion.

It is the fruit fly's larvae that are the villains, not the adult flies, which feed harmlessly on nectar. The larvae hatch from eggs that the female lays inside plant tissue, using her sharp ovipositor like a gimlet; they then feed on the juicy pulp that surrounds them. When fully grown, they drop to the ground. The fruit or vegetable that has served as a food source for these hungry creatures develops soft spots that decay.

The mature larva is typically about six millimetres long with a pointed head and a blunt tail to which two spiracles, or breathing holes, are attached. Place the larvae on a hard surface and it will wriggle about, then curl into a ring, head to tail, and finally straighten itself with a spasmodic movement that propels it centimetres into the air. This is how it moves about after falling from its host plant.

Finally the larva finds a place to burrow, hides itself away and pupates.

A little smaller than common houseflies, fruit flies have mottled or banded wings, and when they are at rest on a plant their wings droop characteristically. Nearly 400 different species exist in southern Africa. Among the species best known for their destructive role among cultivated fruit crops are the Mediterranean fruit fly, the Natal fruit fly and the marula fruit fly.

Some fruits, such as bananas and prickly pears, are immune to these pests. In pawpaws a resinous coating forms around the eggs and expels them.

HOUSEFLIES
Huisvlieë (Family Muscidae)

Size: Length 5,0-10 mm.
Colour: Brown to black.
Most like: Some houseflies look like blowflies (Calliphoridae), but are never metallic green or blue. The most common species of housefly, Musca domestica, is a familiar insect in the subregion.
Habitat: Garbage, manure, rotting vegetables, wood and other organic matter.

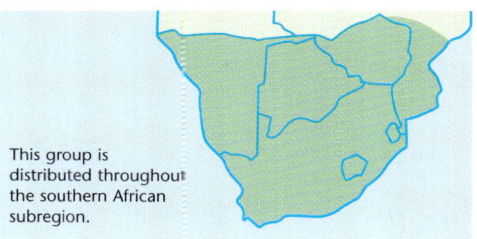

This group is distributed throughout the southern African subregion.

However accustomed we may be to common houseflies, we should not forget that they are a potential menace: major carriers of such diseases as dysentery and typhoid. They may fly straight from the domestic garbage bin (their diet includes excrement) to the diningroom table. The liquid food they suck up may later be regurgitated, hence the fly spots that are often found on windowpanes and elsewhere about the house. Houseflies cannot ingest solid food, but moisten it with their saliva until it can be sucked in as a liquid. This is how they deal with a grain of sugar, for example.

Houseflies breed prolifically in all varieties of decomposing organic matter. In a few days a female may lay up to 500 eggs which, in a suitably warm environment, can hatch in just eight hours. The maggots are fully grown three days later and, after only a further five days, the adult flies emerge from the shrivelled larval skins in which they have been pupating.

There are 364 different species of the family Muscidae in southern Africa, including one that sucks blood from nestling birds. The stable fly, *Stomoxys calcitrans*, is a blood-sucker that preys on horses and cattle. With its hard, black proboscis it easily penetrates the skin prior to feeding.

A fly often seen indoors is the lesser housefly, *Fannia canicularis*, which is smaller and has a different pattern of veins in the wings. This is the fly that circles in small groups endlessly under light bulbs or lamp fittings.

Other insects

Tsetse flies
Tsetsevlieë (Family Glossinidae)

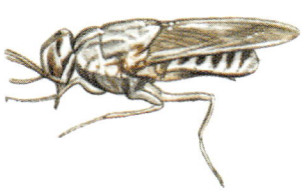

Size: Length 6,0-16 mm.
Colour: Yellowish brown or a darker brown, sometimes with black bands on the back.
Most like: Horseflies and robber flies, but the tsetse fly holds its wings folded over its back (the wings of horseflies are held apart), and the proboscis projects upwards (in robber flies it projects downwards).
Habitat: The shade of tropical forests, bush and woodland.

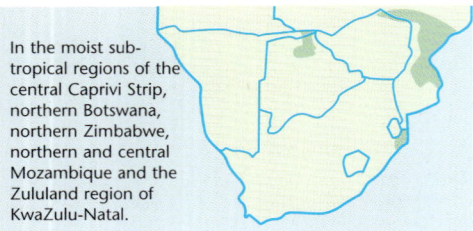

In the moist sub-tropical regions of the central Caprivi Strip, northern Botswana, northern Zimbabwe, northern and central Mozambique and the Zululand region of KwaZulu-Natal.

Tsetse flies are found only in sub-Saharan Africa, where for many years they provided a dreaded barrier to colonial advance. They are the main carriers of single-celled organisms called trypanosomes that cause sleeping sickness in man and a disease named nagana in horses and cattle. There are no medical prophylactic measures offering immunity to sleeping sickness (unlike malaria), and the drugs used in the treatment of the often fatal illness have unpleasant side effects.

The tsetse fly's pointed wings fold over each other like a pair of scissors (the common housefly's wings do not), and they protrude beyond the rear of the body.

Danger lies at the other end in the form of the insect's forward-projecting proboscis—the organ with which both male and female feed on blood. Warthogs, bushbuck, rhinoceros, elephants, buffalo and ostriches are among the favoured hosts (man features quite low down on the list). Infection is transmitted via the tsetse fly's saliva when it inserts its proboscis into the flesh.

The female is not oviparous (egg-laying). A single egg is fertilized at a time, and it hatches within the mother's uterus, growing to larval maturity in about a fortnight—during which time the mother must drink a large quantity of blood to feed it. She then deposits the fully grown larva in a moist and shady patch of soil, where the pupation process begins almost immediately. The larva takes about a month to develop into the adult fly.

Fortunately for man, a female tsetse fly produces only 8-12 offspring in her lifetime.

Blowflies
Brommers (Family Calliphoridae)

Size: Length 8,0 mm.
Colour: Metallic blue or green.
Most like: Closely resemble cuckoo wasps, which are brilliantly coloured green, blue and red, and may be confused with them in flight.
Habitat: Carrion, uncovered meat, or sheep that have either open wounds or soiled wool.

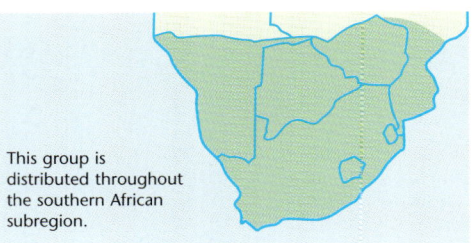

This group is distributed throughout the southern African subregion.

Blowflies, which include the flies commonly known as 'bluebottles' and 'greenbottles', could be called nature's undertakers. They breed in meat; and their larvae have a taste for carrion. In the wild they perform a useful service as they feed on decaying animal tissue and dispatch the body.

Unfortunately blowflies also lay their eggs on live animals, sheep in particular. They are attracted to areas of bacterial infections such as wounds, or where the wool has been stained with sweat or urine. The small white eggs are laid in groups of up to 200. In hot weather they can hatch in half a day, but may take up to three days when it is cooler. The little white maggots wriggle over the sheep's flesh, depositing a supply of meat-tenderizing saliva; when this has done its work, the maggots slurp up the soupy meat solution into their porelike mouths.

The fully grown maggot drops off the sheep and secretes itself either in the soil or under a stone, where it pupates—to emerge a week later in spring or summer as a fly.

During World War I, soldiers lying helplessly in no-man's land had an extra cross to bear: a blowfly species laid its eggs in their wounds, which were soon crawling with larvae. It was found, however, that such wounds often healed more quickly than conventionally treated ones, for the maggots had disposed of suppurating tissue. Inspired by the phenomenon, surgeons then actually used sterile blowfly larvae to treat certain bone-sores, a method of treatment that thankfully has been superseded.

Other insects

FLESH FLIES

Vleisvlieë (Family Sarcophagidae)

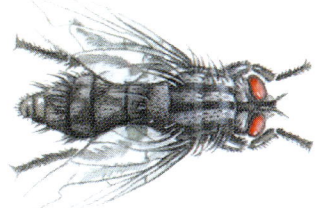

Size: Length 5,0-10 mm.
Colour: Silvery grey to blackish with black stripes on the thorax. Some common species have a reddish tip to the end of the abdomen.
Most like: Blowflies, but flesh flies are a duller colour and never have a metallic sheen.
Habitat: Excreta and other decomposing organic or vegetable matter; rarely nests of bees, wasps and other insects.

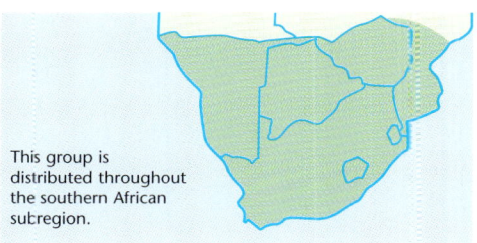

This group is distributed throughout the southern African subregion.

Flesh flies are those troublesome, loudly buzzing creatures which are apt to disturb you at a picnic, where their attentions among the food may be persistent. In southern Africa 157 different species have been recorded.

The adults feed on the nectar of flowers, sap fruit juices and other sweet substances including honeydew, an excretion of aphids and similar small insects. But the larvae of nearly all species digest animal matter of one kind or another.

In many species the female produces her young viviparously—that is, she gives birth to larvae that have hatched from eggs while still inside the body, dropping them where they're ensured plentiful food. Among flesh flies of the subfamily Sarcophaginae this food source could be excreta, decaying meat or other organic matter, or vegetable debris. Human food is sometimes contaminated by the presence of these larvae. If you are unlucky enough to digest the larvae of *Sarcophaga haemorrhoidalis*—the large, common flesh fly, grey with a red-tipped abdomen—you may experience painful intestinal disorders.

Larvae of the less commonly encountered subfamily Miltogramminae are parasites or predators of other insects, including caterpillars, earthworms, termites, cockroaches, bees and wasps. If the female fly deposits her newly hatched larvae in a bees' nest, they feed on the honey and pollen contained in it.

ICHNEUMON WASPS

Parasietwespes (Family Ichneumonidae)

Size: Length 0,2-60 mm.
Colour: Black or brown.
Most like: Social wasps and caterpillar wasps. Ichneumon wasps, however, have the ovipositor projecting from the end of the abdomen, whereas social wasps and caterpillar wasps have ovipositors that are always concealed.
Habitat: Wherever the ichneumon wasp's hosts, which include worms, caterpillars, spiders and many types of insects are to be found.

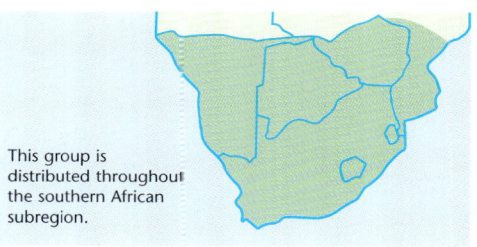

This group is distributed throughout the southern African subregion.

Females of this large, parasitic family of wasps lay their eggs on (or in) another living insect, or else among the eggs of an insect or spider. As a result, the hatched wasp larvae have a ready source of food.

By eventually destroying their assorted hosts, ichneumon wasps perform a useful service in preserving the balance of nature—for example, *Gelis latrodectiphagus* keeps the sinister little button spider under control. The female of the species, about five millimetres long, is wingless and closely resembles a black ant, except for her stinglike ovipositor.

With this egg-laying organ she deposits her own eggs in the sac of eggs that the spider has laid. The wasp larvae feed on the spider eggs and then, still within the sac, spin cocoons in which to pupate.

Sericopimpla sericata is a parasite of the wattle bagworm. In laying her large, yellow egg the black-and-red female thrusts her ovipositor right through the 'bag' of the bagworm and attaches the egg to the inside of the bag. By means of tiny spines on its back the larva can actually move about inside the bag and, with its sharp jaws, suck the bagworm caterpillar's juices. The deflated husk of the dead bagworm provides shelter in which the larva can pupate.

The wood-boring female ichneumon wasp locates a host for her eggs by boring through a branch with her long ovipositor; she then lays her egg within the host.

Other insects

SPIDER WASPS

Spinnekopjagters (Family Pompilidae)

Size: *Length 5,0-70 mm.*
Colour: *Usually black, black and orange or dark brown; sometimes grey. Wings of many species orange-brown, others dark metallic blue.*
Most like: *Ichneumon and paper wasps, but spider wasp has distinctively curled antennae and jerky movements when not in flight.*
Habitat: *Undergrowth that provides a home for spiders; dead leaves, fallen branches, loose stones.*

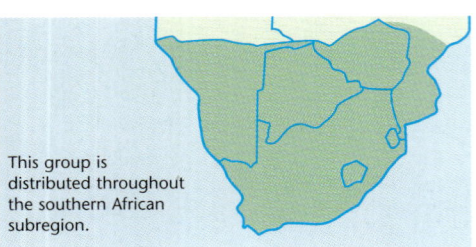

This group is distributed throughout the southern African subregion.

Spiders are the exclusive diet of the larvae of these wasps, of which there are more than 200 species in southern Africa. The female does the hunting, for her primary purpose is to find food for the larvae that will hatch from her eggs.

No spider is safe from these intrepid insects. Even the hairy, stout-bodied baboon spider is unable to escape being cornered by the relentless *Hemipepsis capensis*, a large, black spider wasp, which in flight makes a loud rattling sound.

Fighting can be quite dramatic. The wasp darts in and out until, gaining an advantage, she administers her powerful sting. This swiftly paralyses the spider and the fight is over. Then the wasp retreats to dig a hole large enough to accommodate the spider. She drags her prey into it, lays a single egg on the spider's abdomen and then covers it with soil, disguising the combined grave and nest with dried leaves until not a trace remains.

She repeats the same procedure for each egg she lays. Sometimes she conserves energy by using a ready-made hole rather than digging one herself.

The larva hatches from the egg in about ten days, and the food provided by the spider is enough to last until it is fully grown. At this stage it spins a thick silk cocoon in which it shelters all winter. Warmer spring weather sets in motion its metamorphosis into an adult wasp. The adults feed mainly on nectar.

The long legs of the spider wasp indicate that this insect spends much of its time on the ground in search of prey.

SOCIAL WASPS

Duiwelbye (Family Vespidae)

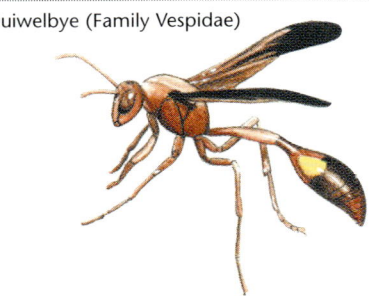

Size: *Length 7,0-35 mm.*
Colour: *Brownish, usually with black, grey, yellow or white markings. Vespula germanica is black and yellow.*
Most like: *Ichneumon wasp and caterpillar wasp. However, the social wasp has a concealed ovipositor, unlike the ichneumon's which projects from the end of its abdomen. The social wasp's waist (petiole) is shorter than the caterpillar wasp's.*
Habitat: *Beneath roofs and hanging rocks, in bushes.*

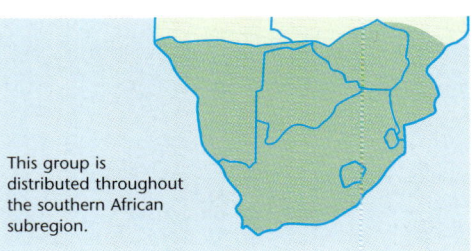

This group is distributed throughout the southern African subregion.

'Social' these wasps may be in their gregarious, nest-building behaviour, but if disturbed they are capable of giving you a painful sting. Fortunately its effect is short-lived.

Using tree bark and other finely chewed vegetable material, social (or paper) wasps build their paperlike nests in a sheltered position, suspended from a fibrous stalk. A single, fertilized female starts the work, though later she is usually helped by others. When this housing development of hexagonal cells in concentric circles is large enough, the females lay their eggs, one to a cell.

The cells normally have their openings at the bottom. Into each aperture the female thrusts pellets of chewed-up caterpillar to feed her larva. The hungry little grub tends to be very demanding, thrusting its head out into the open. For the female nurse there is a reward, because as soon as the larva has consumed its snack, a drop of clear saliva forms at its mouth—and the adult social wasp finds this most appetizing.

Once the larva is fully grown, the adult female closes its cell with the same papery material used to build the nest, and the imprisoned larva pupates.

In southern Africa there are three indigenous genera of social wasps. Large wasps of the genus *Belonogaster* are often called 'hornets'—wrongly, for the true hornet is a native of Europe and North America. The smaller *Polistes* species occurs throughout Africa. *Vespula germanica*, which belongs to the hornet genus of social wasps, has been introduced to southern Africa from Europe.

Other insects

SAND WASPS
Sandwespe (Subfamily Sphecinae)

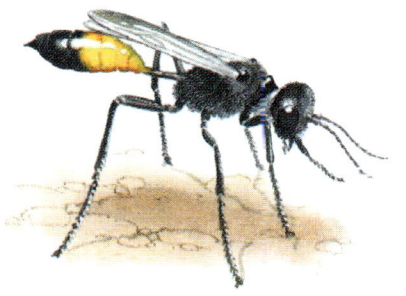

Size: Length 20-25 mm.
Colour: Head, thorax and tip of abdomen black; slender 'waist' (petiole) red.
Most like: Could be confused with other wasps, but none has the slender, long 'waist' of the sand wasp.
Habitat: Holes in the ground.

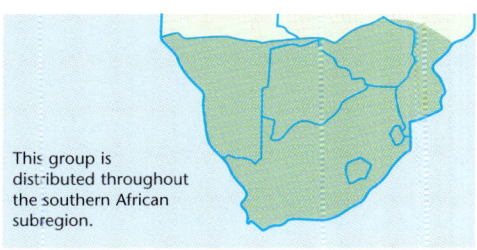

This group is distributed throughout the southern African subregion.

If you are a gardener you should be grateful for sand wasps—genus *Ammophila*—because they help to dispose of that horticultural pest, the cutworm.

Sand wasps are solitary, not social, insects. The female makes her nest by digging a hole in the ground: a 50 mm-long tunnel leading to a cavity some 20 mm across. She carries the soil backwards between her head and forelegs, then kicks it out of the tunnel with her hindlegs. She picks up small stones with her jaws, then flies a short distance away to dump them.

All this is rather exhausting, and the sand wasp will rest for a while in the sun, preening herself with her in-built toilet set: a 'brush' and 'comb' attached to each foreleg. Then she will fly off in search of a cutworm. The cutworm, though larger than her, is no match for her paralysing stings, and she drags her anaesthetized victim back to the burrow, placing it in the inner cavity. A single white, oval egg is laid on top of the cutworm, which will provide a meal for the larva when it emerges from the egg. Finally the female wasp fills the entrance tunnel with sand to disguise it. She won't return, but will repeat the entire process of nest-burrowing and egg-laying up to a dozen times.

Having provided for posterity, she dies. For several months her subterranean offspring sleep in silk cocoons before emerging as adults.

Sand wasps of the genus *Ammophila* are credited with being primitive tool-users, because when the female plugs the entrance to a nest she may use a piece of gravel to tamp the soil down. This behaviour is entirely instinctive.

CARPENTER BEES
Houtboorderbye (Subfamily Xylocopinae)

Size: Length 10-35 mm.
Colour: Shiny blue-black, or banded with white, yellow or orange-red hairs. Iridescent blue-black wings.
Most like: Quite distinctive by virtue of their large size and vigorous buzzing flight.
Habitat: Dry branches or bamboo stems.

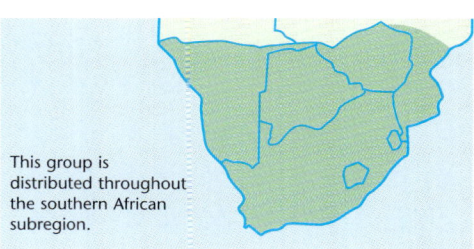

This group is distributed throughout the southern African subregion.

These large, hairy fliers are sometimes wrongly identified as bumblebees (no true bumblebees exist in southern Africa). Their 'carpentry' is of one kind and it is confined to the female: using her powerful jaws she tunnels into dry wood—a dead or partially rotted branch or plant stem, or occasionally the untreated pine timber of a house—to provide a nest in which to lay her eggs. (Damp wood encourages fungus, and fungus disease would kill the grubs.) The tunnel is anything up to 15 cm long.

The female carpenter smoothes its walls, then brings in a supply of pollen (attached to her hairy legs). A quantity of pollen and honey is mixed and placed at the end of the tunnel; a large, curved white egg is laid on top; and the small cell is sealed off with a plug of sawdust and saliva. The process is repeated several times. When the tunnel is nearly full, the female settles into the space at the end of it, somewhat exhausted, but with enough energy to put up a vigorous display of buzzing and wing-vibrating to ward off intruders. She will be dead before her young emerge.

The bee grubs greedily devour their pollen-and-honey rations, pupate in their cells and finally, as adults, break down the seals between the row of siblings. This family group cohabits amicably throughout the autumn and winter, but in spring the female bees cast the males out. A little later, one female will oust the others, claiming the tunnel for the rearing of her own young—the others must pursue their carpentry elsewhere.

There are about 24 species of carpenter bee in southern Africa, all of them of the genus *Xylocopa*.

Other insects

HONEYBEES
Heuningbye (Family Apidae)

Size: Length 2,0-15 mm.
Colour: Blackish brown, either uniform or with yellow abdominal bands.
Most like: Hover flies, but honeybees have two pairs of wings, while hover flies have one pair. Honeybees also have enlarged hindlegs for gathering pollen.
Habitat: Hollow trees, holes in rocks, caves.

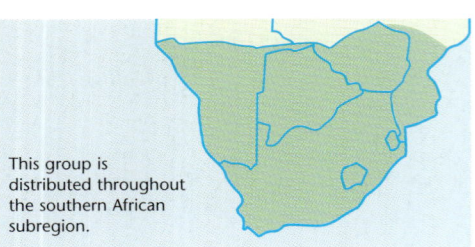

This group is distributed throughout the southern African subregion.

Most bee species are solitary, but bees of the family Apidae—including *Apis mellifera*, the common honeybee that has been transported by man to all parts of the globe—have a sophisticated social organization. A colony of honeybees consists of workers, drones and a queen. Workers (sterile females) are in the great majority and theirs is all the drudgery: building a comb, or aggregate, of waxen cells; gathering nectar and pollen; processing the nectar into honey and feeding the larvae; defending the hive against intruders.

Drone bees are males with but one purpose in life, to mate with a queen. This duty done, they may be killed by the workers without further ado, or allowed to live on in the colony while food remains in good supply.

The queen, after a single mating, retains enough male sperm on her to fertilize all the eggs she will ever lay. She has been born to privilege: from her first days as larva she has been fed on nothing other than 'royal jelly', a nutritious substance secreted by young adult worker bees.

In southern Africa the honeybee is represented by two subspecies. The black and yellow *Apis mellifera scutellata* has a reputation for aggression and its sting is severe. The all-black *Apis mellifera capensis*, the Cape bee, is less hostile, and its colonies are usually smaller.

Belonging to the same insect family as honeybees are the stingless mopane bees, which line a ready-made cavity (such as a tree hollow), with a mixture of wax and resin to form a nest.

DRIVER ANTS
Rooimiere (Subfamily Dorylinae)

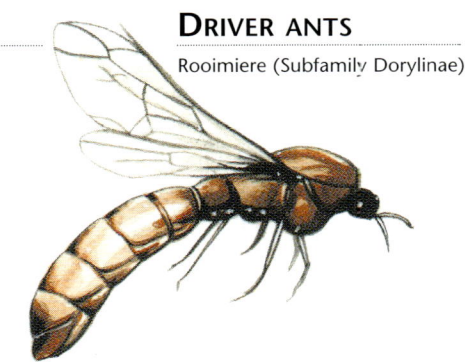

Size: Length 2,0-8,0 mm (worker ants); up to 30 mm (male ants); up to 50 mm (queen ants).
Colour: Reddish brown to brown.
Most like: Male driver ants resemble a common ichneumon wasp (Enicospilos), but the ants have a round abdomen, unlike the wasps' which is slender.
Habitat: A wide range of terrain, where beetles, grubs and other slow-moving insects provide a plentiful supply of food.

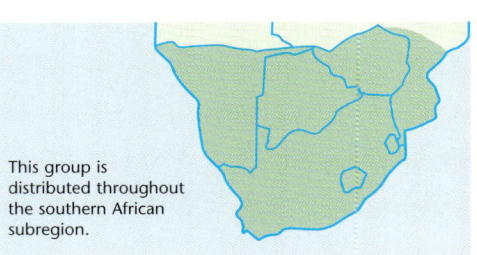

This group is distributed throughout the southern African subregion.

Driver (or army) ants are the stuff of tall stories and science fiction films in which remorseless battalions of these insects march on a town and devour several of its citizens before being repulsed with flame-throwers!

Indeed, they lead a nomadic life, travelling together in huge numbers in purposeful, disciplined ranks—but only to get from one nesting site to another, and at such a slow pace (a few metres an hour) that any healthy, unfettered large animal can easily avoid them. As they usually nest underground, they are seldom seen except on the migratory marches, which take place on dull, overcast days.

The three classes, or castes, of ant are quite distinctive. The usually sterile 'workers' form the bulk of a colony; there may be as many as 20 million of them.

Male ants, also known as 'sausage ants' or 'sausage flies', are much bigger, with furry heads, shiny bodies and large wings. They fly well, and at night are sometimes attracted to lights inside a house; they will then bumble around noisily but, although they look quite formidable, they are perfectly harmless. The blind, wingless 'queen' ant is a clumsy giant—the largest ant in the world. Inside her outsize abdomen are ovaries with the capacity to deliver 100 000 eggs a day.

The usual fare of driver ants consists of caterpillars, cutworms, beetles and other small insects, so they are useful pest controllers in a garden.

Other insects

COCKTAIL ANTS
Wipstertmiere (Genus *Crematogaster*)

Size: Length: males and worker ants 3,0-6,0 mm; queen ants 8,0-12 mm.
Colour: Most species are black; some are black and red.
Most like: Easily distinguished from other ants by the pear-shaped abdomen.
Habitat: Trees, bushes, reeds, flower stalks.

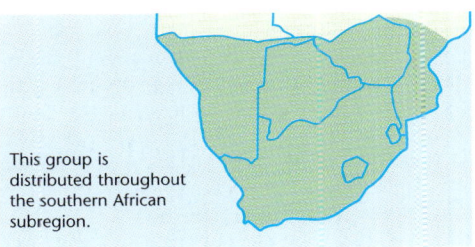

This group is distributed throughout the southern African subregion.

If alarmed or disturbed, cocktail ants raise their abdomens over their heads, and it is this gesture that gives the insects their name. The cocking of the tail may be a prelude to a more specific defensive technique: the ant emits a sticky, white, foul-smelling liquid from a gland at the tip of the abdomen, and with its broad sting it spreads the poisonous fluid over the creature, or person, that has caused the disturbance. As it does so, it waves its raised, flexible abdomen from side to side, and starts biting its unfortunate tormentor.

Cocktail ants belong to the very large subfamily Myrmicinae that includes the common brown house ant, *Pheidole megacephala*, and the larger harvester ant, *Messor barbarus*. All have stings but many, including cocktail ants, do not make use of them.

Cocktail ants are arboreal. Some species nest in hollow branches, others in crevices beneath the bark; and many make so-called carton nests, constructed of chewed vegetable matter mixed with a secretion from the jaw glands of the workers. The walls, blackened by the secretion, are paper-thin, and the inside is divided into many irregular, interconnecting cells.

These spherical nests may be hung among the branches or lie in a tree hollow.

Carton nests of *Crematogaster peringueyi*, a common cocktail ant, are often built in low bushes or among reeds, some of which pass right through the completed nest.

Cocktail ants are fond of sugary substances, which include the honeydew excreted by sap-sucking insects such as aphids.

SUGAR ANTS
Suikermiere (Subfamily Formicinae)

Size: Length 8,0-12 mm.
Colour: Brown, black, often with a whitish yellow abdomen.
Most like: Generally much larger and longer-limbed than other ants. Desert species are easily recognized by their black-and-yellow coloration and their aggressive and rapid movements.
Habitat: In soil under stones or logs, under the bark or in hollow branches of trees.

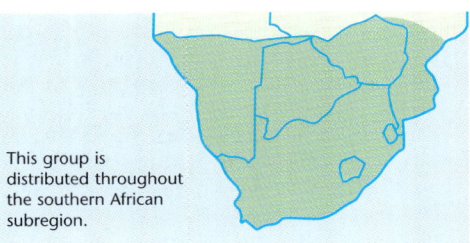

This group is distributed throughout the southern African subregion.

Best-known and most widespread of this subfamily of ants is *Camponotus maculatus*, the pale brown, spotted sugar ant with an uncanny ability to sniff out any sweet foodstuff in the kitchen or pantry, where it is an unwelcome visitor. In the presence of their favourite food, for instance in a sugar bowl, these long-limbed creatures rush about with great agitation, almost as if they had ants in their own pants.

In their greed for sweet things some species of this subfamily amass large amounts of 'honeydew', the liquid excretion of sap-sucking insects such as aphids and mealy bugs. Unlike bees they have no cells in which to store the precious substance, so some of the worker ants, called 'repletes', act as living storehouses instead. Their industrious colleagues regurgitate the honeydew, and the repletes then lap it up until their abdomens grow to an enormous size. As and when the ant colony requires food, the honeydew is again regurgitated.

The larger worker ants can be recognized by their black heads.

Camponotus maculatus nests in the soil, often under the protection of a large stone. A telltale indication of the nest is a ridge of excavated earth forming a craterlike ring on the surface.

Members of the genus *Camponotus* are highly advanced, specialized ants. They have no sting, but some larger species can inflict a painful bite, and all these ants secrete formic acid, which may be used as a spray against enemies.

Families of the wild

WHERE TO SEE OUR WILDLIFE

The story of southern Africa's great but vulnerable wildlife community is one of adaptation and survival: not only in the face of ever-increasing exploitation by man, but also in the face of a shrinking—and changing—natural environment. In this environment, whether it be the dim, green world of the Tsitsikamma Forest, or the sun-baked dunes of the Namib Desert, the different species of mammals, birds, snakes, lizards, insects, fishes and other creatures live their lives in strict compliance with the age-old law of the jungle: 'kill or be killed'.

To human eyes, animals of the wild may often seem astonishingly ruthless in their struggle for existence: the rock python that throws its coils around a young buck, stifling it of breath; the female praying mantis that, in the very act of copulation, bites off the head of her mate; the spider wasp that lays her egg on the abdomen of a paralysed spider so that the wasp larva may feed on the spider's flesh.

Different environments

In spite of man's encroachment, the wealth of animal life in southern Africa is made possible by a wide diversity in the natural environment—from the parched Skeleton Coast to KwaZulu-Natal's luxuriant coastal forests, from the rolling highveld grasslands to fragrant expanses of Western Cape fynbos, and from the flat Karoo to the steep Drakensberg escarpment.

There is a very close relationship between animal distribution and local environment. In any environment (itself the product of vegetation, climate and the land's physical features), the distinctive fauna and flora are part of an endless and infinitely varied energy cycle or 'food chain'. Plants absorb energy directly from the sun, and their food from nutrients in water and earth; this energy is transferred to plant-eating animals such as insects, birds and herbivores (antelope, buffalo, zebras); and these animals in turn provide food for the insect-eaters (aardvarks, pangolins) and the carnivores (lions, leopards).

When the carnivores die they, too, extend the energy chain—the cycle of eating and being eaten—for nature's refuse-disposal team immediately gets to work. These are the vultures, hyaenas and other, much tinier scavengers, from bacteria to beetles, that thrive on decaying organic matter. In the same way there are insects that eat decaying vegetable matter. Nothing in nature goes to waste.

Amazingly, even the most hostile or awkward environment is home to certain animal (and plant) species. In the Namib Desert are insects that quench their thirst from the mists that condense on their bodies; and the side-winding or Péringuey's adder, which has found a unique undulating method of traversing the shifting expanses of dry sand. In its mountain habitat the klipspringer bounds from rock to rock on its rubbery hoof-tips. The mudskipper, an amphibious fish species, uses its fins to scramble out of the water and negotiate the mud of a mangrove swamp to catch its insect prey as the tide recedes. And the lumbering female sea turtle, too, heaves herself laboriously from the Indian Ocean high onto dry land to dig a hole in which to lay her eggs.

Adaptations for survival take all kinds of forms. At its simplest it may merely be the colour of an animal's coat, a bird's plumage, or the camouflage of a snake's skin.

Or the adaptation may be one of physical shape. With their lithe, flattened bodies, rock-dwelling lizards can disappear almost instantly into the merest slit of a rock crevice. The hinged tortoise can fold down one end of its carapace (hard upper shell) to give complete protection to its rear—as safe as a castle with the drawbridge pulled up.

Extraordinary sense faculties are part of the survival kit too. To negotiate an obstacle-free path unerringly at night, and to communicate among themselves, bats make use of an echolocation 'radar' system far more sophisticated than anything that man has yet been able to invent.

Thus in the 'cruel' world in which the families of the wild exist, a huge repertoire of adaptive faculties give each creature its fair chance of survival.

And it is a solemn thought that man the hunter, not nature, must take the blame for the extinction of such southern African animals as the quagga and the blue antelope.

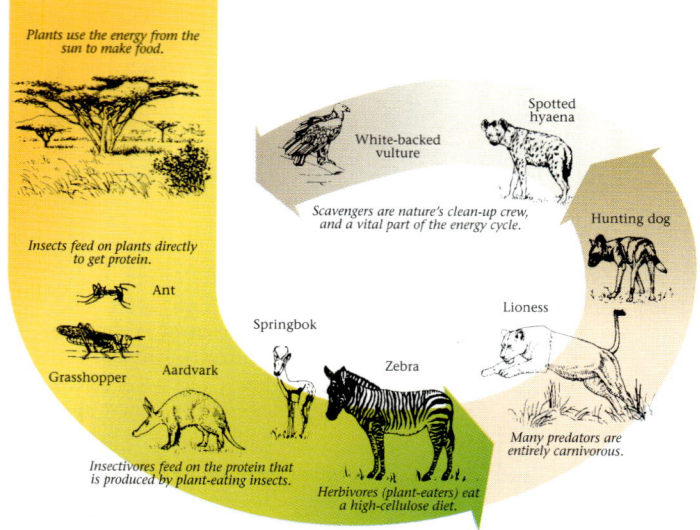

In this representation of an energy cycle (food chain), energy from the sun is absorbed by the plants and then transferred to many plant-eating animals. The various animal participants, from ant to vulture, eat, and in turn, are food for others. A number of species share particular levels of the food chain.

Families of the wild

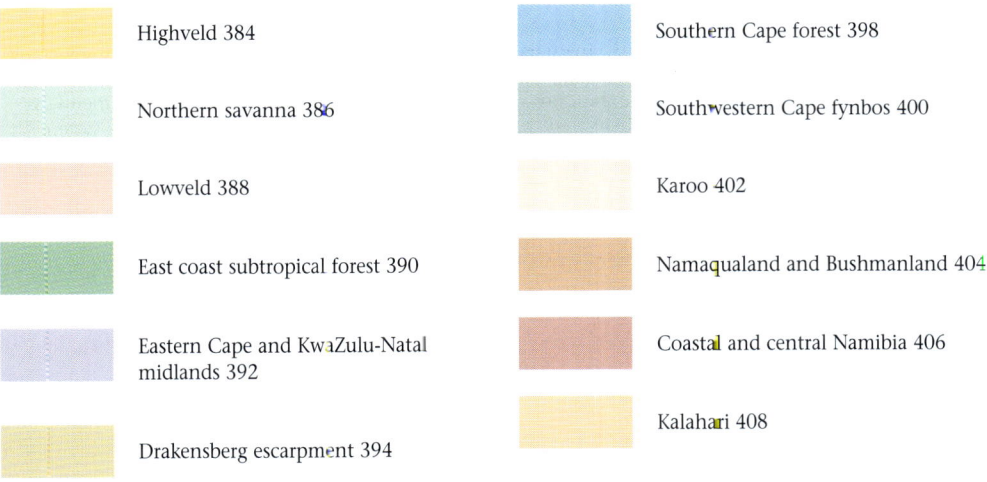

- Highveld 384
- Northern savanna 386
- Lowveld 388
- East coast subtropical forest 390
- Eastern Cape and KwaZulu-Natal midlands 392
- Drakensberg escarpment 394
- Cape fold mountains 396
- Southern Cape forest 398
- Southwestern Cape fynbos 400
- Karoo 402
- Namaqualand and Bushmanland 404
- Coastal and central Namibia 406
- Kalahari 408

How to use this section

In this section we have divided southern Africa into 13 natural or environmental zones. Of course there is really no sharp dividing line between one zone and the adjoining zone. For example, the Karoo merges imperceptibly along various stretches of its perimeter, into the highveld, the Kalahari and Bushmanland, while in the south it changes into mountain fynbos. But the division into zones is a convenience.

In the following pages each zone is described separately and illustrated on a map of the subregion. Alongside the description is a list of the more common animal species indigenous to this environment (the list includes the page numbers on which the species are described).

Bear in mind that very few animals are exclusive to a single zone; indeed there are species that are found in almost every one of the 13 zones (the porcupine and the African wild cat are just two examples). If you're planning a holiday along, say, the Garden Route, you will need to refer to at least three environments: southwestern Cape fynbos, Cape fold mountains and southern Cape forest. Reading these three spreads gives you a head-start by acquainting you with the area in advance; then for more detailed facts turn to the descriptions of particular species.

Families of the wild

HIGHVELD

The great sweep of the highveld, which includes southern Gauteng, the Free State, the eastern extremities of the Northern Cape and northwestern KwaZulu-Natal, forms a rolling, grassy plateau 1 200-1800m above sea level, with not many hills. It has a summer rainfall (and, incidentally, the highest hailstorm frequency in southern Africa); mists and fogs are rare. Indigenous trees, mostly the thorn-bearing acacias, are sparse, but where man has cultivated the land and planted crops he has also introduced willows and eucalyptus, among other species, to provide shade; while in the suburbs of towns and cities the fertile soil has enabled him to establish flourishing gardens and parks that attract fauna untypical of the highveld region.

To many large mammals this relatively treeless habitat is inhospitable, although black wildebeest are at home here, as are blesbok and the ubiquitous common duiker. Two smaller predators, the African wild cat and the black-backed jackal, skulk in the long grass—and, given the opportunity, the former will make a meal of domestic chickens, while the latter is regarded by farmers as a serious predator of lambs. Before the advent of fire-breaks, devastating grass fires were one of the hazards faced by the local highveld fauna; it is perhaps not surprising that many of the surviving mammals are digging or burrowing species such as the suricate, aardvark, yellow mongoose and various assorted small rodents.

Away from the towns, the wide-open spaces are home to birds whose plumage is streaked on top to camouflage them from the attentions of high-flying predators such as kites, eagles and common buzzards. By contrast the bellies of these camouflaged species are often brightly marked for visual communication among themselves. Trees and shrubs are the familiar and favoured territory of such well-known birds as the malachite sunbird and the African hoopoe (though the latter often descends to forage, a familiar crested visitor on suburban lawns).

The long grasses, some sweet, some sour, provide ideal cover for numerous ground birds, including game birds such as quail and guineafowl, and such prominent individuals as the secretarybird and the hadeda ibis. Watch out for the fluttering display of the rufous-naped lark as it calls for its mate in the crisp highveld air, or the loud wing-rattle of the aptly named clapper lark.

The grass also provides cover for many snakes (of which the most dangerous to man are the rinkhals and common puff adder), and to a profusion of spiders, scorpions and insects. Grasshoppers abound and occasionally swarm, with devastating results. Outstanding in size among the insects are the king crickets—none being larger than the formidable 'Parkmore prawn' well known to the gardeners of Johannesburg's northern suburbs.

Patrolling at low level over this lively theatre of activity among the highland grasses is a colourful array of butterflies and moths—the more common painted ladies, lucerne blues and African clouded yellows, as well as many other intriguing species dear to the heart of lepidopterist and casual admirer alike.

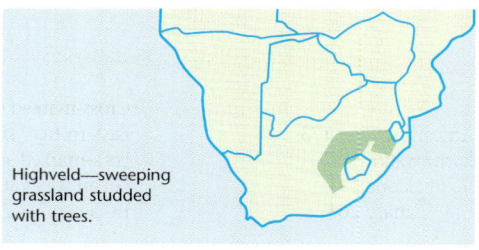

Highveld—sweeping grassland studded with trees.

Large mammals

Aardwolf 66
Black-backed jackal 67
Black wildebeest 50
Blesbok 55
Cape fox 68
Caracal 64
Chacma baboon 69
Grey rhebok 57
Leopard 62
Mountain reedbuck 57
Vervet monkey 69

Smaller mammals

Aardvark 76
African wild cat 86
Cape clawless otter 85
Cape hare 78
Common duiker 71
Common molerat 94
Common vlei rat 91
Egyptian free-tailed bat 97
Geoffroy's horseshoe bat 97
Ground squirrel 89
Honey badger 84
Klipspringer 74
Multimammate mouse 93
Porcupine 77
Rock dassie 79
Rock elephant-shrew 92
Slender mongoose 81
Small spotted cat 86
Small-spotted genet 87
Southern African hedgehog 77
Spotted-necked otter 85
Springhare 78
Steenbok 71
Striped mouse 93
Striped polecat 84
Suricate 83
Water mongoose 80
Woodland dormouse 90
Yellow mongoose 82

Ground birds

Abdim's stork 106
African pipit 121
African stonechat 120
Alpine swift 116
Black-headed heron 104
Blue crane 110
Blue korhaan 112
Burchell's courser 114
Cape bunting 124
Cape longclaw 121
Cattle egret 105
Common quail 109
Common waxbill 124
Crowned lapwing 113
Denham's bustard 112
Hadeda ibis 107
Helmeted guineafowl 110
Little swift 117
Long-tailed widowbird 123
Red-winged starling 122
Rock martin 118
Rufous-naped lark 118
Secretarybird 108
Southern black korhaan 113
Speckled pigeon 115
Spotted thick-knee 114
White stork 105

Waterbirds

African darter 128
African sacred ibis 131
African spoonbill 132

Families of the wild

Blacksmith lapwing 139
Cape wagtail 147
Common moorhen 136
Common sandpiper 139
Egyptian goose 133
Grey heron 129
Hamerkop 131
Little grebe 125
Malachite kingfisher 145
Pied avocet 141
Red-billed teal 134
Red-knobbed coot 136
Reed cormorant 128
South African shelduck 133
Southern red bishop 147
Spur-winged goose 135
Three-banded plover 138
White-breasted cormorant 127
Yellow-billed duck 134

Birds of prey

African marsh harrier 156
Barn owl 158
Black-chested snake eagle 153
Black-shouldered kite 150
Common buzzard 154
Common kestrel 157
Lanner falcon 157
Spotted eagle owl 159

Tree birds

African hoopoe 173
Barn swallow 177
Bokmakierie 191
Cape canary 205
Cape crow 180
Cape glossy starling 194
Cape robin-chat 184
Cape sparrow 199
Cape turtle dove 161
Cape white-eye 197
Cardinal woodpecker 177
Common fiscal 188
Diederik cuckoo 167
European bee-eater 171
Familiar chat 183
Greater honeyguide 176
Greater striped swallow 178
Malachite sunbird 195
Namaqua dove 162
Neddicky 186
Olive thrush 183
Pied crow 180

Pin-tailed whydah 203
Red-backed shrike 189
Red-billed quelea 200
Red-chested cuckoo 166
Red-eyed dove 161
Red-faced mousebird 169
Red-headed finch 202
Southern masked weaver 200
White-crowed sparrowweaver 198
Yellow canary 205

Turtles and tortoises

Helmeted terrapin 209
Mountain tortoise 209

Snakes and lizards

Aurora snake 223
Bibron's blind snake 234
Brown house snake 223
Cape centipede-eater 234
Cape cobra 218
Cape file snake 229
Cape gecko 241
Cape skink 243
Cape wolf snake 228
Common brown water snake 222
Common egg-eater 229
Common night adder 230
Common puff adder 231
Common slug-eater 233
Cross-marked grass snake 227
Eastern tiger snake 235
Fork-marked sand snake 226
Green water snake 221
Herald snake 222
Mole snake 216
Rinkhals 219
Rock leguaan 237
Southern burrowing asp 228
Southern rock agama 242
Spotted harlequin snake 224
Spotted skaapsteker 226
Sundevall's garter snake 224
Sundevall's shovel-snout 225
Sungazer 237
Water leguaan 236

Frogs and toads

Angolan river frog 250
Bullfrog 252
Common platanna 248
Guttural toad 249
Senegal kassina 252

Spiders, scorpions and others

Baboon spiders 323
Burrowing scorpions 321
Centipedes 327
Earthworms 320
Jumping spiders 325
Land snails 320
Millipedes 327
Thick-tail scorpions 322
Ticks 326

Beetles

Dung beetles 331
Fruit beetles 332
Ladybird beetles 333
Predacious ground beetles 330
Weevils 335

Butterflies and moths

African clouded yellow 350
Brown-veined white 349
Citrus swallowtail 338
Diadem 342
Lucerne blue 354
Marsh patroller 345
Painted lady 346
Southern milkweed 343
Yellow pansy 348

Other insects

Antlions 372
Aphids 370
Blowflies 376
Cockroaches 361
Dragonflies 361
Driver ants 380
Honeybees 380
Horseflies 373
Houseflies 375
King crickets 363
Long-horned grasshoppers 364
Mole crickets 366
Praying mantids 362
Robber flies 374
Sand wasps 379
Shield bugs 369
Spittle bugs 368
Sugar ants 381
Termites 362

Families of the wild

NORTHERN SAVANNA

'Savanna' is a term of Carib Indian origin imported via Spanish from Central America. In the African context it is often used loosely for all kinds of level grassland, but in this book we refer specifically to the environment typical of the Northern Province, North-West Province, eastern Botswana and much of Zimbabwe: open land covered in tall grasses and shrubs, with a discontinuous canopy mostly of assorted thorn tree species up to 15 m high. The vegetation is less dense and tangled than that of the Mpumalanga 'bushveld', and rather drier than that of the highveld.

It is a region watered mostly by tributaries of the Limpopo and Zambezi rivers, and characterized by summer rainfall and dry winters. To the west and south the savanna gradually merges into the harsher environment characteristic of the Kalahari.

In the natural state, undisturbed by man, his crops and his livestock, savanna conditions support a varied fauna as abundant as that of the lowveld, and very similar to it.

The birdlife in particular is extremely prolific. Typical of the area are the weavers and waxbills, whose neat, ball-like grass nests adorn the branches of countless thorn trees; the brilliantly coloured sunbirds with long, scimitar-shaped beaks (used for probing into aloe and acacia blossoms in search of nectar); and several species of shrike—highly vocal birds with a repertoire of harsh alarm calls.

A well-known inhabitant of the region is the ostrich, which cannot fly, but which, with wings outstretched for balance, can escape predators in a mad, ungainly gallop. Ironically the male's deep, booming call sounds rather like the distant roar of a lion, which happens to be the ostrich's most feared predator.

A feature of the savanna plains is the series of mountain ranges that break them up into smaller zones (and are suppliers of water, being the sources of the region's rivers). They include Zimbabwe's Matopo Hills, and the Northern Province's Soutpansberg and Blouberg. To the south the Magaliesberg marks the border with the highveld, while to the east lie the straggling remnants of the great Drakensberg chain.

The outcrops and kranses associated with these ranges provide a congenial home for a number of mammal species, such as the ubiquitous chacma baboon and rock dassie, the tiny rock elephant-shrew, the mountain tortoise (by far the largest tortoise species in the subcontinent) and, if the area is well-wooded, by the vervet monkey. A lone leopard will sometimes sun itself on an exposed rock, one of its favoured vantage points for surveying the surrounding flatlands stretching away to distant horizons. The southern African rock python and black mamba are also found in the vicinity of kranses.

More detailed inspection of the vegetation reveals a wealth of miniature life, including such insect curiosities as dung beetles, giant stick insects and carpenter bees. Unfortunately the savanna tends also to be the habitat of insects—including the tsetse fly—that bear diseases potentially fatal to livestock and man. The tick has the same unhealthy reputation.

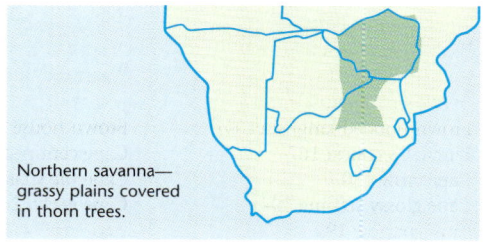

Northern savanna—grassy plains covered in thorn trees.

Large mammals

Black-backed jackal 67
Blue wildebeest 50
Buffalo 48
Burchell's zebra 49
Bushbuck 60
Bushpig 61
Chacma baboon 69
Civet 64
Elephant 46
Giraffe 48
Hippopotamus 46
Impala 54
Kudu 60
Leopard 62
Lion 62
Roan antelope 51
Sable antelope 51
Spotted hyaena 65
Tsessebe 54
Vervet monkey 69
Warthog 61
Waterbuck 58
Wild dog 66

Smaller mammals

Aardvark 76
African wild cat 86
Cape clawless otter 85
Common duiker 71
Egyptian fruit bat 96
Greater cane rat 94
Honey badger 84
Porcupine 77
Rock dassie 79
Rock elephant-shrew 92
Sharpe's grysbok 75
Southern African hedgehog 77
Southern lesser bushbaby 88
Springhare 78
Steenbok 71
Striped mouse 93
Striped polecat 84
Tree squirrel 90

Ground birds

Black-headed heron 104
Cattle egret 105
Crested francolin 108
Crowned lapwing 113
Fiery-necked nightjar 116
Hadeda ibis 107
Helmeted guineafowl 110
Kori bustard 111
Marabou stork 106
Ostrich 104
Rufous-naped lark 118
Secretarybird 108
Spotted thick-knee 114
Swainson's spurfowl 109

Waterbirds

African jacana 137
African pied wagtail 146
African purple swamphen 135
Black heron 130
Egyptian goose 133
Giant kingfisher 145
Grey heron 129
Hamerkop 131
Little grebe 125
Malachite kingfisher 145
Pied kingfisher 144
Red-billed teal 134
Reed cormorant 128
Three-banded plover 138

Families of the wild

Birds of prey

African fish eagle 154
African harrier hawk 156
Barn owl 158
Bateleur 153
Black kite 150
Black-chested snake eagle 153
Black-shouldered kite 150
Common kestrel 157
Lanner falcon 157
Lappet-faced vulture 149
Martial eagle 152
Pearl-spotted owlet 159
Spotted eagle owl 159
Tawny eagle 151
Verreaux's eagle owl 160
White-backed vulture 149

Tree birds

African dusky flycatcher 187
African green pigeon 163
African hoopoe 173
African house martin 178
African palm swift 168
Arrow-marked babbler 181
Black-backed puffback 190
Black-collared barbet 175
Black-headed oriole 179
Blue waxbill 201
Bronze mannikin 203
Brown-hooded kingfisher 170
Burchell's coucal 167
Cape crow 180
Cape glossy starling 194
Cape sparrow 199
Cape turtle dove 161
Cape white-eye 197
Cardinal woodpecker 177
Chinspot batis 187
Common fiscal 188
Crested barbet 176
Crimson-breasted shrike 190
Dark-capped bulbul 182
Diederik cuckoo 167
European bee-eater 171
Fork-tailed drongo 179
Greater honeyguide 176
Green woodhoopoe 173
Grey go-away bird 166
Laughing dove 162
Lilac-breasted roller 172
Little bee-eater 172
Long-tailed paradise whydah 204
Orange-breasted bush shrike 191
Pied crow 180
Pin-tailed whydah 203
Purple-crested turaco 165
Rattling cisticola 185
Red-backed shrike 189
Red-billed hornbill 174
Red-billed oxpecker 194
Red-billed quelea 200
Red-chested cuckoo 166
Red-eyed dove 161
Red-faced mousebird 169
Scarlet-chested sunbird 197
Southern black tit 181
Southern boubou 189
Southern masked weaver 200
Southern yellow-billed hornbill 174
Speckled mousebird 168
Village weaver 199
Violet-backed starling 193
Violet-eared waxbill 202
White-browed sparrowweaver 198
White-crested helmetshrike 192
Woodland kingfisher 170
Yellow-fronted canary 204

Turtles and tortoises

Bell's hinged tortoise 210
Helmeted terrapin 209
Mountain tortoise 209

Snakes and lizards

Bark snake 225
Bibron's blind snake 234
Bibron's gecko 239
Black mamba 217
Boomslang 220
Brown house snake 223
Cape centipede-eater 234
Cape file snake 229
Cape gecko 241
Cape wolf snake 228
Common brown water snake 222
Common egg-eater 229
Common night adder 230
Common puff adder 231
Common slug-eater 233
Eastern tiger snake 235
Egyptian cobra 217
Flap-neck chameleon 238
Fork-marked sand snake 226
Herald snake 222
Mole snake 216
Nile crocodile 236
Rock leguaan 237
Shield-nose snake 235
Southern African rock python 216
Southern burrowing asp 228
Sundevall's shovel-snout 225
Sundevall's writhing skink 244
Twig snake 221
Water leguaan 236

Frogs and toads

Bushveld rain frog 249
Cape river frog 250
Common platanna 248
Foam nest frog 251
Guttural toad 249

Spiders, scorpions and others

Baboon spiders 323
Burrowing scorpions 321
Centipedes 327
Jumping spiders 325
Land snails 320
Millipedes 327
Thick-tail scorpions 322
Ticks 326

Beetles

Blister beetles 334
Dung beetles 331
Fruit beetles 332
Ladybird beetles 333
Long-horned beetles 335
Predacious ground beetles 330
Weevils 335

Butterflies and moths

African migrant 340
African moon moth 355
Blue pansy 348
Broad-bordered grass yellow 351
Brown-veined white 349
Fig tree blue 353
Koppie charaxes 340
Mopane emperor moth 355
Painted lady 346
Sapphire 353
Scarlet-tip 349

Other insects

Anopheline mosquitoes 373
Antlions 372
Blowflies 376
Carpenter bees 379
Cicadas 370
Dragonflies 361
Driver ants 380
Honeybees 380
King crickets 363
Locusts 367
Long-horned grasshoppers 364
Praying mantids 362
Robber flies 374
Sand wasps 379
Shield bugs 369
Spittle bugs 368
Stick insects 368
Termites 362
Tsetse flies 376

Families of the wild

LOWVELD

Climate and natural vegetation, combined with man's efforts at wildlife conservation, conspire to make the lowveld a congenial home for an impressive roll call of the larger mammals, including elephant, lion, giraffe, hippo, rhinoceros, buffalo, Burchell's zebra and antelope species ranging from kudu and roan antelope down to bushbuck and the common duiker. A swathe of subtropical and tropical 'bushveld', the lowveld extends from Swaziland north through Mpumalanga to the Limpopo River and beyond, at altitudes ranging between 150 and 600 m above sea level. The Kruger National Park forms a substantial portion of this region rich in indigenous fauna.

Acacias, aloes and bushwillows are part of the tangle of natural vegetation, as well as mopane trees and baobabs ('cream-of-tartar' trees) in the parklike expanses to the north. Rocky outcrops, the home of baboon colonies and klipspringer, are also a feature of the landscape.

Daytime temperatures are high, and the predominantly summer rainfall is mostly in the form of thundershowers. Here, unlike on the highveld, frost is rare although winter nights can be chilly. Highveld and lowveld are separated by the northward extension of the great Drakensberg escarpment that forms the lowveld's western boundary.

Complementing the impressive array of mammals is an equally wide range of birdlife. Common southern African species such as the Cape glossy starling and the Cape turtle dove share the air with more truly subtropical ones: the crested barbet, with its alarm-clock trill, the bee-eaters and sunbirds, the parrots and kingfishers, the turkeylike southern ground hornbill... To complete the natural cycle are the various birds of prey—their kingdom dominated by three imposing giants, the martial eagle and the scavenging Cape and lappet-faced vultures. The smaller birds of the lowveld are also menaced by the boomslang and the common egg-eater, just two of the region's many snake species.

The lowveld is drained by eastward-flowing rivers (the major ones are the Limpopo, Olifants, Crocodile and Komati), and though the smaller streams may be reduced to dry gulleys by the end of winter, the region supports a thriving water-dependent fauna. This includes otters, terrapins (water tortoises), water snakes, water leguaans and Nile crocodiles—the only crocodile species indigenous to southern Africa. Dwarfed by all these is a miniature water world inhabited by a large variety of delicate creatures such as whirligig beetles and gossamer-winged dragonflies.

Bewhiskered catfish (barbels) are some of the indigenous fish species, while man, for his enjoyment, has stocked the rivers and pools with various imported species.

At one time the lowveld was infested by the tsetse fly. This is no longer a scourge, but the insect population includes the anopheline mosquitoes, some species of which are carriers of malaria. Ticks (which are not insects but acarids, related to spiders) are another of the area's less welcome residents.

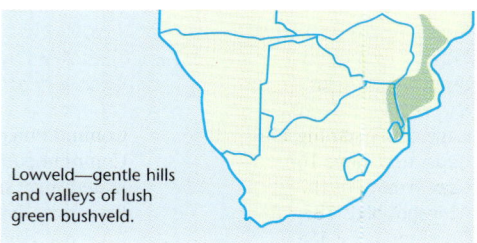

Lowveld—gentle hills and valleys of lush green bushveld.

Large mammals

Black-backed jackal 67
Black rhinoceros 47
Blue wildebeest 50
Buffalo 48
Burchell's zebra 49
Bushbuck 60
Bushpig 61
Chacma baboon 69
Cheetah 63
Eland 52
Elephant 46
Giraffe 48
Hippopotamus 46
Impala 54
Kudu 60
Leopard 62
Lion 62
Nyala 59
Roan antelope 51
Sable antelope 51
Spotted hyaena 65
Vervet monkey 69
Warthog 61
Waterbuck 58
White rhinoceros 47
Wild dog 66

Smaller mammals

Banded mongoose 82
Cape clawless otter 85
Common duiker 71
Dwarf mongoose 83
Honey badger 84
Multimammate mouse 93
Pangolin 76
Peters' epauletted fruit bat 96
Porcupine 77
Small-spotted genet 87
Southern lesser bushbaby 88
Steenbok 71
Tree squirrel 90

Ground birds

Common waxbill 124
Crested francolin 108
Crowned lapwing 113
Fiery-necked nightjar 116
Hadeda ibis 107
Helmeted guineafowl 110
Kori bustard 111
Marabou stork 106
Ostrich 104
Secretarybird 108
Southern ground hornbill 117
Spotted thick-knee 114
Swainson's spurfowl 109

Waterbirds

African darter 128
African pied wagtail 146
African purple swamphen 135
Black heron 130
Blacksmith lapwing 139
Egyptian goose 133
Giant kingfisher 145
Goliath heron 129
Great white pelican 126
Grey heron 129
Hamerkop 131
Lesser swamp warbler 146
Little egret 130
Little grebe 125
Pied kingfisher 144
Reed cormorant 128
Three-banded plover 138

Birds of prey

African fish eagle 154
African harrier hawk 156

Families of the wild

Bateleur 153
Black-chested snake eagle 153
Black kite 150
Black-shouldered kite 150
Lanner falcon 157
Lappet-faced vulture 149
Martial eagle 152
Pearl-spotted owlet 159
Pel's fishing owl 160
Spotted eagle owl 159
Tawny eagle 151
Verreaux's eagle owl 160
White-backed vulture 149

Tree birds

African dusky flycatcher 187
African firefinch 201
African green pigeon 163
African hoopoe 173
African palm swift 168
African paradise flycatcher 188
Arrow-marked babbler 181
Bar-throated apalis 185
Black-backed puffback 190
Black-collared barbet 175
Black-headed oriole 179
Blue waxbill 201
Bronze mannikin 203
Brown-headed parrot 163
Brown-hooded kingfisher 170
Burchell's coucal 167
Cape glossy starling 194
Cape turtle dove 161
Cape white-eye 197
Chinspot batis 187
Common fiscal 188
Crested barbet 176
Dark-capped bulbul 182
Diederik cuckoo 167
European bee-eater 171
Fork-tailed drongo 179
Green woodhoopoe 173
Grey go-away bird 166
Laughing dove 162
Lilac-breasted roller 172
Little bee-eater 172
Long-tailed paradise whydah 204
Meyer's parrot 164
Narina trogon 169
Natal robin-chat 184
Orange-breasted bush shrike 191
Pin-tailed whydah 203
Purple-crested turaco 165
Rattling cisticola 185
Red-billed hornbill 174
Red-billed oxpecker 194
Red-billed quelea 200
Red-chested cuckoo 166
Red-eyed dove 161

Scarlet-chested sunbird 197
Sombre greenbul 182
Southern black tit 181
Southern boubou 189
Southern carmine bee-eater 171
Southern yellow-billed hornbill 174
Speckled mousebird 168
Village weaver 199
Violet-backed starling 193
White-crested helmetshrike 192
Woodland kingfisher 170
Yellow-fronted canary 204

Turtles and tortoises

Bell's hinged tortoise 210
Helmeted terrapin 209
Mountain tortoise 209

Snakes and lizards

Bark snake 225
Bibron's gecko 239
Black mamba 217
Boomslang 220
Brown house snake 223
Cape centipede-eater 234
Cape file snake 229
Cape wolf snake 228
Common barking gecko 240
Common brown water snake 222
Common egg-eater 229
Common night adder 230
Common puff adder 231
Eastern tiger snake 235
Egyptian cobra 217
Flap-neck chameleon 238
Fork-marked sand snake 226
Green water snake 221
Herald snake 222
Mole snake 216
Nile crocodile 236
Rock leguaan 237
Shield-nose snake 235
Southern African rock python 216
Southern burrowing asp 228
Sundevall's garter snake 224
Sundevall's shovel-snout 225
Sundevall's writhing skink 244
Twig snake 221
Water leguaan 236

Frogs and toads

Bullfrog 252
Bushveld rain frog 249
Cape river frog 250
Foam nest frog 251
Guttural toad 249

Spiders, scorpions and others

Baboon spiders 323
Centipedes 327
Jumping spiders 325
Land snails 320
Millipedes 327
Thick-tail scorpions 322
Ticks 326

Beetles

Dung beetles 331
Fruit beetles 332
Ladybird beetles 333
Long-horned beetles 335
Predacious ground beetles 330
Rhinoceros beetles 332
Weevils 335
Whirligig beetles 330

Butterflies and moths

African migrant 340
African moon moth 355
Blue pansy 348
Brown-veined white 349
Citrus swallowtail 338
Diadem 342
Fig tree blue 353
Gaudy commodore 347
Koppie charaxes 340
Mother-of-pearl 339
Painted lady 346
Scarlet tip 349
Small spotted sailor 341
Yellow pansy 348

Other insects

Anopheline mosquitoes 373
Antlions 372
Blowflies 376
Carpenter bees 379
Cicadas 370
Cockroaches 361
Dragonflies 361
Honeybees 380
Houseflies 375
Hover flies 374
Long-horned grasshoppers 364
Praying mantids 362
Robber flies 374
Shield bugs 369
Social wasps 378
Spittle bugs 368
Stick insects 368
Termites 362

Families of the wild

EAST COAST SUBTROPICAL FOREST

Man's depredations have done away with large stretches of the forests that once lined KwaZulu-Natal, yet the extent of this wooded belt still remains impressive. The vegetation is enormously varied, and so is the fauna it supports.

In parts of northeastern KwaZulu-Natal dry, semi-deciduous 'sand forests' raise a high tree canopy over the flat, sandy soil. Alongside the shore, facing the Indian Ocean, are closely wooded, deciduous 'dune forests' which soon colonize—and stabilize—new sand dunes created by wind and tide, the salt-laden sea breezes 'pruning' the top of the forest in characteristic fashion. On the long, white beaches fringing the dunes of northern KwaZulu-Natal female loggerhead and leatherback turtles laboriously heave themselves out of the ocean at nesting time, flounder towards the sparse beach vegetation and lay their copious spherical eggs in holes they dig in the sand above the high-water mark.

Inland, lowland forests are dense tangles of evergreen vegetation among which lianas form contorted, ropelike branches; shrubs and low trees provide a forest 'under-storey', and in glades and clearings the ground is thick with grasses and sedges, the haunt of brilliantly coloured butterflies such as the swallowtails and swordtails. This is also ideal territory for playful troops of vervet monkeys—and for tree-loving snakes (boomslangs, twig snakes, green mambas, black mambas) that lie stealthily in wait for birds and lizards. It is also the home of the fearsome, though beautifully marked, Gaboon adder, by far the largest African adder and one of the most venomous.

There is yet another category of subtropical forest; the fern-strewn mangrove swamps where, in the words of the Noel Coward song, 'the python romps and there's peace from twelve to two'. Mangroves are trees that grow in the mud of tidal estuaries, surviving periodic flooding by salty seawater; there are five species in the subregion. Although each species differs in the details of its specialized root structure, all have some form of aerial or 'breathing' root which provides ventilation and usually support as well. Flourishing among this mesh of roots, mud and plant debris are fiddler crabs, herons and kingfishers, especially the mangrove kingfisher, which is only found in mangrove swamps, and, amazingly, the mud skipper, an amphibious fish.

Many mangrove swamps have been drained and cleared for cultivation or filled in for industrial use. However, they still exist in certain estuaries as far south as the Nahoon River in the Eastern Cape, and are prolific in the Richards Bay/St Lucia region in northern KwaZulu-Natal.

The lakes of this north coast belt provide a home to hippos and a small number of crocodiles; to the tiny little grebe (or dabchick) and to three large avian predators, the white-backed night heron, the African fish eagle and Pel's fishing owl (among over 200 bird species in the region); and to an abundance of frogs, amongst the noisiest of which are the male marbled reed frogs with their piercing whistles.

Elephants once roamed all of KwaZulu-Natal. Today they are confined mainly to the Tembe Elephant Reserve, north of Ingwavuma, and have also been reintroduced to the Greater St Lucia Wetland Park.

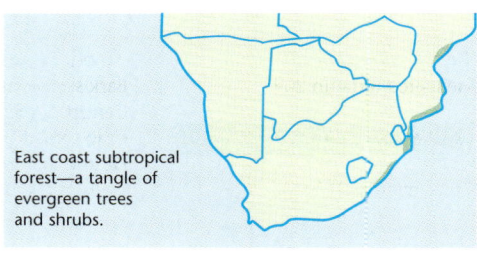

East coast subtropical forest—a tangle of evergreen trees and shrubs.

Large mammals

Aardwolf 66
Black-backed jackal 67
Black rhinoceros 47
Blue wildebeest 50
Buffalo 48
Burchell's zebra 49
Bushbuck 60
Bushpig 61
Caracal 64
Chacma baboon 69
Elephant 46
Hippopotamus 46
Impala 54
Kudu 60
Leopard 62
Lion 62
Nyala 59
Reedbuck 58
Serval 63
Side-striped jackal 67
Spotted hyaena 65
Vervet monkey 69
Warthog 61
Waterbuck 58
White rhinoceros 47

Smaller mammals

Aardvark 76
African wild cat 86
Blue duiker 72
Cape clawless otter 85
Common duiker 71
Large-spotted genet 87
Porcupine 77
Red duiker 72
Sharpe's grysbok 75
Spotted-necked otter 85
Steenbok 71
Striped polecat 84
Suni 73
Tree squirrel 90

Ground birds

Hadeda ibis 107
Red-winged starling 122

Waterbirds

Little grebe 125

Birds of prey

African crowned eagle 152
African fish eagle 154
African harrier hawk 156
Black kite 150
Lanner falcon 157
Pel's fishing owl 160
Spotted eagle owl 159

Tree birds

African dusky flycatcher 187
African green pigeon 163
African hoopoe 173
African palm swift 168
African paradise flycatcher 188
Barn swallow 177
Bar-throated apalis 185
Black-backed puffback 190
Black-collared barbet 175

Families of the wild

Black-headed oriole 179
Bronze mannikin 203
Brown-hooded kingfisher 170
Burchell's coucal 167
Cape glossy starling 194
Cape white-eye 197
Cardinal woodpecker 177
Crested barbet 176
Dark-capped bulbul 182
Fork-tailed drongo 179
Greater honeyguide 176
Knysna turaco 165
Lesser double-collared sunbird 196
Little bee-eater 172
Narina trogon 169
Natal robin-chat 184
Olive thrush 183
Purple-crested turaco 165
Red-chested cuckoo 166
Red-eyed dove 161
Red-faced mousebird 169
Red-fronted tinkerbird 175
Sombre greenbul 182
Southern black tit 181
Southern boubou 189
Speckled mousebird 168
Village weaver 199
Yellow-fronted canary 204

Turtles and tortoises

Bell's hinged tortoise 210
Helmeted terrapin 209

Snakes and lizards

Black mamba 217
Boomslang 220
Brown house snake 223
Cape centipede-eater 234
Cape file snake 229
Cape wolf snake 228
Common brown water snake 222
Common egg-eater 229
Common night adder 230
Common puff adder 231
Common slug-eater 233
Egyptian cobra 217
Flap-neck chameleon 238
Forest cobra 218
Gaboon adder 232
Green mamba 220
Green water snake 221
Herald snake 222
Mole snake 216
Natal black snake 227
Nile crocodile 236
Rock leguaan 237
Shield-nose snake 235
Southern African rock python 216
Southern burrowing asp 228
Spotted skaapsteker 226
Sundevall's garter snake 224
Twig snake 221
Water leguaan 236

Frogs and toads

Angolan river frog 250
Bushveld rain frog 249
Common platanna 248
Foam nest frog 251
Marbled reed frog 253

Spiders, scorpions and others

Baboon spiders 323
Bark scorpions 321
Centipedes 327
Crab spiders 324
Land crustaceans 326
Land snails 320
Millipedes 327
Ticks 326

Beetles

Dung beetles 331
Fruit beetles 332
Ladybird beetles 333
Long-horned beetles 335
Predacious ground beetles 330
Weevils 335
Whirligig beetles 330

Butterflies and moths

African moon moth 355
Blue pansy 348
Citrus swallowtail 338
Fig tree blue 353
Gaudy commodore 347
Large striped swordtail 339
Marsh patroller 345
Mocker swallowtail 338
Mother-of-pearl 339
Painted lady 346
Sapphire 353
Scarlet-tip 349
Yellow pansy 348

Other insects

Anopheline mosquitoes 373
Antlions 372
Blowfies 376
Carpenter bees 379
Cicadas 370
Cockroaches 361
Dragonflies 361
Driver ants 380
Flesh flies 377
Honeybees 380
Houseflies 375
Locusts 367
Long-horned grasshoppers 364
Praying mantids 362
Sand wasps 379
Shield bugs 369
Social wasps 378
Spider wasps 378
Stick insects 368
Termites 362
Tsetse flies 376

Families of the wild

EASTERN CAPE AND KWAZULU-NATAL MIDLANDS

This southeastern belt is a summer-rainfall zone characterized by great undulating sweeps of open grassland intersected by deep river valleys, from the Great Fish River all the way northeastwards to the Tugela River. Indigenous woodland thrives in sheltered places, while in some parts the valleys are clothed in a thick tangle of aloes and thorny undergrowth. In the northern half of KwaZulu-Natal the grassveld and open bush of the province's midlands merge gradually into thornveld.

This zone is bordered on its east side by coastal subtropical forest (of which the Transkei region's Wild Coast forms part). Flanking the KwaZulu-Natal midlands on the other side, at about the 1350 m level, are the foothills of the imposing Drakensberg range. The extreme southern outposts of this range are covered in dense forest and bush.

As man settled here and appropriated the rich soil for agriculture, the larger mammals were driven away or eliminated. Several antelope species survived, however, as did their most formidable natural enemy, the leopard. Today the nearest elephant and buffalo populations are those that live in the protection of the Addo National Park to the south, and in the game reserves of the Zululand region of KwaZulu-Natal to the north.

Oribi and mountain reedbuck are characteristic local antelope species, but the outstanding one is the stately kudu with its great corkscrew horns. Kudu thrive in the inland area between the Keiskamma and Great Fish rivers where rocky terrain, woodland (for shelter) and an ample water supply are found in combination.

Two monkey species, the agile vervet and the larger, darker samango, occur here. Their natural environment is the forest; like the bushpig, another forest-dweller, they are a potential menace to farmers as they have a taste for fruit, and are inclined to raid orchards.

The fauna of the region is abundant but not exclusive to it. Many tropical and subtropical species, such as the samango monkey, the water lily frog and the tree dassie, however, reach their southern distribution limits in the Eastern Cape.

Birdlife is especially prolific and ranges from species such as bush-shrikes and crested barbets, associated with the northern part of the subregion, to the well-known Cape turtle dove. An awe-inspiring enemy of birds—but especially of monkeys and even small antelope—is the majestic African crowned eagle. Most at home in dense, indigenous forests, it may venture further afield in search of food, dropping onto its unsuspecting prey like a stone, usually from a perch, but also from flight. With the razing of forests the African crowned eagle's numbers are on the decline; and it is sometimes killed by farmers who allege that it swoops down and takes lambs and goat-kids from fields bordering on forested areas.

One of the more unusual KwaZulu-Natal birds is the common myna (previously called the Indian myna), found also in Gauteng. This member of the starling family was introduced to Durban from India towards the end of the 19th century; it has become an abundant resident and boasts an extraordinary repertoire of loud, but not altogether melodious, calls.

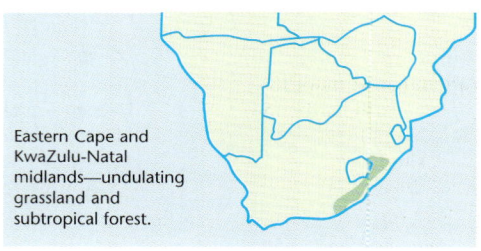

Eastern Cape and KwaZulu-Natal midlands—undulating grassland and subtropical forest.

Large mammals

Aardwolf 66
Bat-eared fox 68
Black-backed jackal 67
Bushbuck 60
Bushpig 61
Cape fox 68
Caracal 64
Chacma baboon 69
Kudu 60
Leopard 62
Mountain reedbuck 57
Reedbuck 58
Serval 63
Vervet monkey 69

Smaller mammals

Aardvark 76
African wild cat 86
Blue duiker 72
Cape clawless otter 85
Common duiker 71
Common vlei rat 91
Forest shrew 92
Geoffroy's horseshoe bat 97
Honey badger 84
Large grey mongoose 80
Large-spotted genet 87
Oribi 70
Porcupine 77
Red duiker 72
Rock dassie 79
Slender mongoose 81
Southern African hedgehog 77
Spotted-necked otter 85
Springhare 78
Steenbok 71
Striped polecat 84
Suricate 83
Tree dassie 79
Water mongoose 80
Yellow mongoose 82

Ground birds

African pipit 121
African stonechat 120
Alpine swift 116
Black-headed heron 104
Blue crane 110
Cape longclaw 121
Cape rock thrush 119
Cattle egret 105
Common quail 109
Common waxbill 124
Crowned lapwing 113
Denham's bustard 112
Fan-tailed widowbird 123
Grey crowned crane 111
Hadeda ibis 107
Helmeted guineafowl 110
Little swift 117
Long-tailed widowbird 123
Red-winged starling 122
Rock martin 118
Rufous-naped lark 118
Secretarybird 108
Southern bald ibis 107
Southern ground hornbill 117
Speckled pigeon 115
Spotted thick-knee 114
Swainson's spurfowl 109
White-necked raven 119
White stork 105

Families of the wild

Waterbirds

African darter 128
African purple swamphen 135
African sacred ibis 131
African spoonbill 132
Blacksmith lapwing 139
Cape wagtail 147
Common moorhen 136
Common sandpiper 139
Egyptian goose 133
Giant kingfisher 145
Grey heron 129
Hamerkop 131
Lesser swamp warbler 146
Little grebe 125
Malachite kingfisher 145
Pied kingfisher 144
Red-billed teal 134
Red-knobbed coot 136
Reed cormorant 128
South African shelduck 133
Southern red bishop 147
Spur-winged goose 135
Three-banded plover 138
White-breasted cormorant 127
Wood sandpiper 140
Yellow-billed duck 134

Birds of prey

African crowned eagle 152
African harrier hawk 156
African marsh harrier 156
Barn owl 158
Black kite 150
Black-shouldered kite 150
Cape vulture 148
Common buzzard 154
Common kestrel 157
Jackal buzzard 155
Lanner falcon 157
Martial eagle 152
Spotted eagle owl 159
Verreaux's eagle 151

Tree birds

African dusky flycatcher 187
African firefinch 201
African paradise flycatcher 188
Barn swallow 177
Black-backed puffback 190
Black-collared barbet 175
Black-headed oriole 179
Bokmakierie 191
Bronze mannikin 203
Brown-hooded kingfisher 170
Burchell's coucal 167
Cape canary 205
Cape crow 180
Cape glossy starling 194
Cape robin-chat 184
Cape sparrow 199
Cape turtle dove 161
Cape white-eye 197
Cardinal woodpecker 177
Common fiscal 188
Common myna 193
Crested barbet 176
Dark-capped bulbul 182
Diederik cuckoo 167
Fork-tailed drongo 179
Greater honeyguide 176
Greater striped swallow 178
Green woodhoopoe 173
Karoo prinia 186
Laughing dove 162
Narina trogon 169
Neddicky 186
Orange-breasted bush shrike 191
Pied crow 180
Pin-tailed whydah 203
Red-backed shrike 189
Red-chested cuckoo 166
Red-eyed dove 161
Red-faced mousebird 169
Sombre greenbul 182
Southern black tit 181
Southern boubou 189
Southern masked weaver 200
Speckled mousebird 168
Village weaver 199
Violet-backed starling 193
Yellow-fronted canary 204

Turtles and tortoises

Helmeted terrapin 209
Mountain tortoise 209

Snakes and lizards

Aurora snake 223
Bibron's blind snake 234
Black mamba 217
Black thread snake 233
Boomslang 220
Brown house snake 223
Cape centipede-eater 234
Cape cobra 218
Cape file snake 229
Cape legless skink 245
Cape skink 243
Cape wolf snake 228
Common brown water snake 222
Common egg-eater 229
Common night adder 230
Common puff adder 231
Common slug-eater 233
Cross-marked grass snake 227
Green water snake 221
Herald snake 222
Mole snake 216
Natal black snake 227
Rinkhals 219
Rock leguaan 237
Southern African rock python 216
Southern rock agama 242
Spotted harlequin snake 224
Spotted skaapsteker 226
Sundevall's garter snake 224
Water leguaan 236

Frogs and toads

Angolan river frog 250
Common platanna 248
Gray's frog 251
Guttural toad 249
Marbled reed frog 253

Spiders, scorpions and others

Baboon spiders 323
Centipedes 327
Earthworms 320
Land crustaceans 326
Land snails 320
Millipedes 327
Ticks 326

Beetles

Blister beetles 334
Dung beetles 331
Fruit beetles 332
Ladybird beetles 333
Predacious ground beetles 330

Butterflies and moths

Blue pansy 348
Citrus swallowtail 338
Convolvulus hawk moth 356
Diadem 342
Dotted border 350
Evening brown 343
Gaudy commodore 347
Mocker swallowtail 338
Painted lady 346
Polka dot 347
Scarlet-tip 349
Yellow pansy 348

Other insects

Antlions 372
Blowflies 376
Cicadas 370
Cockroaches 361
Dragonflies 361
Driver ants 380
Honeybees 380
Horseflies 373
Houseflies 375
Locusts 367
Mole crickets 366
Praying mantids 362
Robber flies 374
Sand wasps 379
Shield bugs 369
Spider wasps 378
Stink locusts 367
Termites 362

Families of the wild

DRAKENSBERG ESCARPMENT

Massive, fortresslike basalt, high plateaus, deep valleys sheltering evergreen forests, rolling grassy foothills—these are features of the majestic Drakensberg range and its immediate surroundings. The range, some 2000m above sea level, with peaks rising to more than 3400m, forms a natural barrier between the highveld to the west and, to the east, the KwaZulu-Natal midlands. Being subject to heavy rains and snows, it also contains the headwaters of the three most important and powerful river systems in South Africa: the Vaal, Gariep (Orange) and Tugela.

Temperatures in this montane environment are apt to be extreme, especially during the frosts and snows of winter, but a hardy fauna has made the Drakensberg escarpment its home. Mammal species well adapted to a life on the rocks, or on the grassy slopes between rocky areas, include the grey rhebok, the mountain reedbuck, the diminutive rock elephant-shrew and, of course, the common and well-known rock dassie.

The past master, however, is the little klipspringer: it leaps with ease from boulder to boulder on the tips of its curious rounded hooves, like a dancer on ballet pointes. The hollow, springy bristles of its unique coat insulate it from the worst of the cold and heat, and help to protect it, too, in the unlikely event of a heavy fall.

Birdlife in the mountains is dominated by magnificent birds of prey of awesome wingspan: the Verreaux's (or black) eagle (nemesis of many a rock dassie), the Cape vulture and, above all, the bearded vulture or lammergeier, with its golden body plumage and black wings. This rare and endangered species is now confined, in southern Africa, to the Drakensberg area alone, where its population is estimated at perhaps no more than 200 hunting pairs.

Mountain environments typically support a variety of different vegetation zones. The less precipitous slopes of the Drakensberg escarpment may be thickly wooded, covered in hardy shrubs, spread with low bushes and heaths, or cloaked in a luxuriant green carpet of resilient grasses.

As a result you will come across a wide variety of interesting birds—from weavers, sunbirds and white-eyes to doves and thrushes, and from secretarybirds to hadeda ibises—associated with many different southern African environments.

The same wide variety is seen in other categories of fauna, such as snakes and insects. Game reserves add to the sum total of local animal species. For example, black wildebeest and blesbok—mammals indigenous to highveld grasslands, and which declined drastically in the 19th century—have been reintroduced to Drakensberg reserves such as Coleford in the south and Giant's Castle in the north. The latter reserve also supports a thriving population of eland and some of the smaller antelopes.

Many of the mountain streams in this part of KwaZulu-Natal are well stocked with imported trout, for this is one of the premier trout-fishing areas of the subregion.

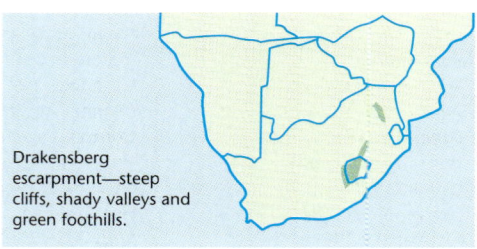

Drakensberg escarpment—steep cliffs, shady valleys and green foothills.

Large mammals

Aardwolf 66
Black-backed jackal 67
Black wildebeest 50
Blesbok 55
Cape fox 68
Caracal 64
Chacma baboon 69
Eland 52
Grey rhebok 57
Leopard 62
Mountain reedbuck 57
Reedbuck 58
Serval 63
Vervet monkey 69

Smaller mammals

Aardvark 76
African wild cat 86
Bushveld gerbil 91
Cape clawless otter 85
Cape hare 78
Common duiker 71
Common vlei rat 91
Forest shrew 92
Honey badger 84
Klipspringer 74
Oribi 70
Porcupine 77
Rock dassie 79
Rock elephant-shrew 92
Small grey mongoose 81
Small-spotted genet 87
Southern African hedgehog 77
Spotted-necked otter 85
Steenbok 71
Striped mouse 93
Striped polecat 84
Suricate 83
Tree dassie 79
Water mongoose 80
Woodland dormouse 90
Yellow mongoose 82

Ground birds

African pipit 121
African stonechat 120
Alpine swift 116
Black-headed heron 104
Blue crane 110
Cape bunting 124
Cape longclaw 121
Cape rock thrush 119
Cattle egret 105
Common quail 109
Common waxbill 124
Denham's bustard 112
Grey crowned crane 111
Hadeda ibis 107
Helmeted guineafowl 110
Little swift 117
Long-tailed widowbird 123
Red-winged starling 122
Rock martin 118
Secretarybird 108
Speckled pigeon 115
Southern bald ibis 107
Southern ground hornbill 117
Swainson's spurfowl 109
White-necked raven 119
White stork 105
Yellow bishop 122

Waterbirds

Cape wagtail 147
Common moorhen 136
Common sandpiper 139
Giant kingfisher 145
Grey heron 129
Hamerkop 131

Families of the wild

Little grebe 125
Malachite kingfisher 145
Red-knobbed coot 136
Reed cormorant 128
Southern red bishop 147
Yellow-billed duck 134

Birds of prey

African harrier hawk 156
Barn owl 158
Bearded vulture 148
Black-shouldered kite 150
Cape vulture 148
Common kestrel 157
Jackal buzzard 155
Lanner falcon 157
Martial eagle 152
Spotted eagle owl 159
Verreaux's eagle 151

Tree birds

African dusky flycatcher 187
African firefinch 201
African hoopoe 173
African paradise flycatcher 188
Barn swallow 177
Bar-throated apalis 185
Cape crow 180
Black-backed puffback 190
Black-headed oriole 179
Bokmakierie 191
Bronze mannikin 203
Cape canary 205
Cape robin-chat 184
Cape sparrow 199
Cape turtle dove 161
Cape white-eye 197
Cardinal woodpecker 177
Common fiscal 188
Dark-capped bulbul 182
Diederik cuckoo 167
Familiar chat 183
Fork-tailed drongo 179
Greater honeyguide 176
Greater striped swallow 178
Karoo prinia 186
Malachite sunbird 195
Narina trogon 169
Neddicky 186
Olive thrush 183
Pied crow 180

Pin-tailed whydah 203
Red-chested cuckoo 166
Red-eyed dove 161
Red-faced mousebird 169
Sombre greenbul 182
Southern boubou 189
Southern double-collared sunbird 196
Southern masked weaver 200
Spotted-backed weaver 199
Yellow canary 205

Turtles and tortoises

Helmeted terrapin 209

Snakes and lizards

Aurora snake 223
Berg adder 231
Bibron's blind snake 234
Boomslang 220
Brown house snake 223
Cape centipede-eater 234
Cape cobra 218
Cape gecko 241
Cape skink 243
Cape wolf snake 228
Common brown water snake 222
Common egg-eater 229
Common night adder 230
Common puff adder 231
Common slug-eater 233
Cross-marked grass snake 227
Green water snake 221
Herald snake 222
Mole snake 216
Rinkhals 219
Rock leguaan 237
Southern rock agama 242
Spotted harlequin snake 224
Spotted skaapsteker 226
Sundevall's garter snake 224
Sundevall's shovel-snout 225
Water leguaan 236

Frogs and toads

Angolan river frog 250
Common platanna 248
Gray's frog 251
Guttural toad 249
Karoo toad 248

Spiders, scorpions and others

Burrowing scorpions 321
Centipedes 327
Jumping spiders 325
Millipedes 327
Orb-web spiders 324
Ticks 326

Beetles

Blister beetles 334
Dung beetles 331
Ladybird beetles 333
Long-horned beetles 335
Predacious ground beetles 330
Weevils 335
Whirligig beetles 330

Butterflies and moths

Citrus swallowtail 338
Convolvulus hawk moth 356
Diadem 342
Evening brown 343
Lucerne blue 354
Painted lady 346
Table Mountain beauty 344

Other insects

Antlions 372
Blowflies 376
Carpenter bees 379
Cicadas 370
Cockroaches 361
Dragonflies 361
Field crickets 365
Flesh flies 377
Honeybees 380
Horseflies 373
Houseflies 375
Long-horned grasshoppers 364
Pond-skaters 369
Praying mantids 362
Robber flies 374
Sand wasps 379
Shield bugs 369
Spider wasps 378
Termites 362

Families of the wild

CAPE FOLD MOUNTAINS

Anyone who has observed them knows how appropriately named the Cape 'fold' mountains are. The immensely powerful movements of the earth's crust some 120 million years ago gave rise to a series of mountain chains whose buckled, convoluted rock strata were revealed when the softer outer shales eroded. A north-south chain runs from the Cederberg via the Hex River Mountains as far as the Hottentots Holland, and then runs 600km eastwards almost to Port Elizabeth.

The eastern extension is actually composed of two separate chains. Sandwiched between the Swartberge to the north, and the Langeberg and Outeniqua Mountains to the south, lies the Little Karoo.

Wildlife of this zone is typical of, firstly, a mountainous habitat; secondly, the distinctive 'mountain fynbos' vegetation that botanists distinguish from the 'renosterveld' of the lowland shales; and thirdly, in the case of the Little Karoo, the drier Karoo environment.

Be on the watch here for tortoises—but do not take them home as pets, for they are protected by law. No fewer than five species are found; they include the large mountain tortoise, often of venerable age, and the tiny, beautifully patterned tent tortoise, which looks like a cluster of miniature Bedouin tents.

Rarest among local mammals is the Cape mountain zebra. Only the proclamation of a Cradock farm as a national park, and the inaccessibility of three or four other mountain areas, saved this species from extinction in the 1930s. Today the zebras are found in small numbers in the wild elsewhere, grazing on mountain grasses and sheltering in secluded kloofs. The stripe pattern of the Cape subspecies of the mountain zebra is distinct from that of the more common Burchell's zebra (which, outside zoos and reserves, is found only in the north and northeast of the southern African subregion).

Among an abundant bird population, one of the small species confined to the Cape fold mountain belt is the protea canary, whose rich song is not matched by its dull brown plumage. More attractive is the Cape rockjumper, with its black throat and chestnut 'waistcoat'. You'll see it perched on a rock with its white-tipped tail cocked, or scrabbling on the ground for insects and lizards. Its curious descending call has been likened to the shrill peal of an alarm-clock running down.

Incidentally, the word 'Cape' (or Latin *capensis*—of the Cape) in a species name is no guarantee that the species inhabits this region alone. The Cape sparrow and Cape white-eye, for example, are as much at home throughout most of the subregion as in the Cape fold mountains, while the Cape clawless otter occurs from Cape Town to Ethiopia and Senegal.

This zone has a generous share of snakes, of which the berg (or mountain) adder is a particular hazard to climbers. Though it is moderately venomous, no deaths resulting from its bite have been recorded. The same cannot, unfortunately, be said of the common puff adder.

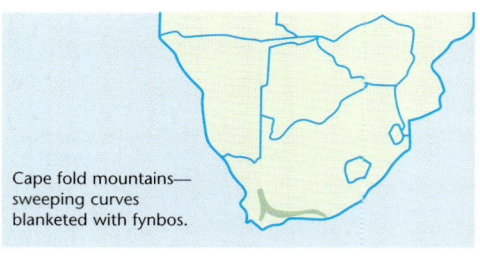

Cape fold mountains—sweeping curves blanketed with fynbos.

Large mammals

Aardwolf 66
Bat-eared fox 68
Black-backed jackal 67
Bushpig 61
Cape fox 68
Cape mountain zebra 49
Caracal 64
Chacma baboon 69
Grey rhebok 57
Kudu 60
Leopard 62
Mountain reedbuck 57
Vervet monkey 69

Smaller mammals

Aardvark 76
African wild cat 86
Cape clawless otter 85
Cape golden mole 95
Cape grysbok 75
Cape hare 78
Common duiker 71
Common molerat 94
Common vlei rat 91
Egyptian free-tailed bat 97
Egyptian fruit bat 96
Fallow deer 74
Geoffroy's horseshoe bat 97
Hottentot golden mole 95
Klipspringer 74
Large grey mongoose 80
Large-spotted genet 87
Porcupine 77
Rock dassie 79
Small grey mongoose 81
Small-spotted genet 87
Steenbok 71
Striped mouse 93
Striped polecat 84
Water mongoose 80
Woodland dormouse 90
Yellow mongoose 82

Ground birds

African pipit 121
African stonechat 120
Alpine swift 116
Blue crane 110
Cape bunting 124
Cape rockjumper 120
Cape rock thrush 119
Cattle egret 105
Common waxbill 124
Denham's bustard 112
Fiery-necked nightjar 116
Hadeda ibis 107
Little swift 117
Red-winged starling 122
Rock martin 118
Speckled pigeon 115
White-necked raven 119
White stork 105
Yellow-rumped widow 122

Waterbirds

African darter 128
Cape wagtail 147
Egyptian goose 133
Giant kingfisher 145
Grey heron 129
Hamerkop 131
Lesser swamp warbler 146
Malachite kingfisher 145
Reed cormorant 128
Southern red bishop 147
Three-banded plover 138
Yellow-billed duck 134

Families of the wild

Birds of prey

African harrier hawk 156
African marsh harrier 156
Barn owl 158
Common kestrel 157
Jackal buzzard 155
Lanner falcon 157
Martial eagle 152
Spotted eagle owl 159
Verreaux's eagle 151

Tree birds

African dusky flycatcher 187
African hoopoe 173
African house martin 178
African paradise flycatcher 188
Barn swallow 177
Bar-throated apalis 185
Bokmakierie 191
Cape canary 205
Cape crow 180
Cape robin-chat 184
Cape sparrow 199
Cape sugarbird 195
Cape turtle dove 161
Cape white-eye 197
Cardinal woodpecker 177
Common fiscal 188
Diederik cuckoo 167
Familiar chat 183
Fork-tailed drongo 179
Greater striped swallow 178
Karoo prinia 186
Laughing dove 162
Malachite sunbird 195
Namaqua dove 162
Natal robin-chat 184
Neddicky 186
Olive thrush 183
Pied crow 180
Pin-tailed whydah 203
Red-chested cuckoo 166
Red-eyed dove 161
Red-faced mousebird 169
Sombre greenbul 182
Southern double-collared sunbird 196
Southern masked weaver 200
Speckled mousebird 168
Yellow canary 205

Turtles and tortoises

Cape padloper 212
Helmeted terrapin 209
Karoo padloper 213
Mountain tortoise 209
Tent tortoise 211

Snakes and lizards

Armadillo girdled lizard 238
Aurora snake 223
Berg adder 231
Bibron's gecko 239
Black thread snake 233
Boomslang 220
Brown house snake 223
Cape cobra 218
Cape gecko 241
Cape legless skink 245
Cape skink 243
Common brown water snake 222
Common egg-eater 229
Common long-tailed seps 245
Common puff adder 231
Common slug-eater 233
Cross-marked grass snake 227
Herald snake 222
Mole snake 216
Rinkhals 219
Rock leguaan 237
Southern rock agama 242
Spotted harlequin snake 224
Spotted skaapsteker 226
Sundevall's shovel-snout 225

Frogs and toads

Angolan river frog 250
Cape river frog 250
Common platanna 248
Gray's frog 251
Karoo toad 248

Spiders, scorpions and others

Centipedes 327
Jumping spiders 325
Land snails 320
Millipedes 327
Thick-tail scorpions 322
Tick 326

Beetles

Blister beetles 334
Dung beetles 331
Ladybird beetles 333
Predacious ground beetles 330
Toktokkies 334
Weevils 335

Butterflies and moths

African clouded yellow 350
Brown-veined white 349
Citrus swallowtail 338
Convolvulus hawk moth 356
Lucerne blue 354
Mountain copper 352
Painted lady 346
Southern milkweed 343
Table Mountain beauty 344
Tricoloured tiger moth 356

Other insects

Antlions 372
Blowflies 376
Carpenter bees 379
Cockroaches 361
Cocktail ants 381
Dragonflies 361
Flesh flies 377
Honeybees 380
Horseflies 373
Houseflies 375
Praying mantids 362
Robber flies 374
Sand wasps 378
Shield bugs 369
Social wasps 378
Spider wasps 378
Termites 362

Families of the wild

SOUTHERN CAPE FOREST

The southern Cape boasts an irregular belt of indigenous forests stretching from Swellendam in the Western Cape to Humansdorp in the Eastern Cape, and reaching an altitude of no more than 1000 metres. Typically the forests are in sheltered valleys, river gorges and mountain kloofs; it is only in the east of this region that the belt has any continuity. The Knysna and Tsitsikamma forests are, in fact, the last large indigenous high forests surviving in the whole of South Africa (just 60 000 ha of an original 250 000 ha remain). Conservation-conscious bodies are justifiably indignant whenever a plan is mooted to drive a major road through this majestic natural heritage, or in any other way impair it.

Some of the subregion's most famous (and most valued) timber tree species are found here. They include the renowned stinkwood, and the Outeniqua and real yellowwoods—in size the most magnificent of trees, soaring up to 60 m in height. Other beautiful and widespread species include the Cape chestnut, with its large, dome-shaped clusters of pink or mauve blossoms; the red alder or rooiels, with sweet-scented white flowers; and the wild pomegranate, which forms part of the lower timber storey, and whose dense flowers are a bright orange-red. Festooning the crowns of the forest giants are old man's beard lichens; carpeting the forest floor are ferns and brightly coloured fungi.

Delicate bushbuck, blue duiker, vervet monkeys and the ubiquitous chacma baboons are among the inhabitants of this Garden-of-Eden setting, as well as two lithe nocturnal predators, the caracal and leopard (the latter mostly confined to the wooded mountains). There is little trace left of large mammals such as buffalo that were once so abundant here. In the depths of the forests just one elephant cow—the last of the original population—battles for survival (there were 12 or 13 in 1972). In 1994 three elephants were relocated to the forest from the Kruger National Park: one died, and the other two strayed onto adjacent farmlands, from where they were moved to a nearby reserve. The Knysna elephant could go the way of the extinct blue antelope or 'bloubok' that once roamed the open veld and lower mountain slopes fringing these southern forests.

The Eden has its inevitable serpents, most notably the timid, but potentially lethal, boomslang. Its slender build and usually green colouring camouflage it so well that you may approach to within less than a metre before seeing it.

In the leafy habitat a miniature wildlife kingdom thrives—a world that includes not only rare and radiant butterflies but also baboon spiders and bark scorpions. In the gloom, fireflies and glow-worms carry a torch for their mates; despite their names, both these insects are beetles.

Perhaps the most appealing wildlife category of the southern Cape forest belt is its birds. A green-and-blue Knysna turaco (lourie) in flight, its crimson wing-feathers revealed, is an unforgettable sight. Just as memorable is Burchell's coucal—not for its brown-and-white plumage, which is hardly out of the ordinary, but for its extraordinary call: a succession of clear, liquid notes imitating the sound of water being poured from a narrow-necked bottle.

Southern Cape forest—indigenous trees soaring skywards.

Large mammals

Aardwolf 66
Black-backed jackal 67
Buffalo 48
Bushbuck 60
Bushpig 61
Cape fox 68
Caracal 64
Chacma baboon 69
Elephant 46
Leopard 62
Vervet monkey 69

Smaller mammals

Aardvark 76
African wild cat 86
Blue duiker 72
Cape clawless otter 85
Cape grysbok 75
Common duiker 71
Common molerat 94
Common vlei rat 91
Egyptian free-tailed bat 97
Egyptian fruit bat 96
Forest shrew 92
Geoffroy's horseshoe bat 97
Honey badger 84
Hottentot golden mole 95
Large-spotted genet 87
Multimammate mouse 93
Porcupine 77
Rock dassie 79
Small grey mongoose 81
Small-spotted genet 87
Striped mouse 93
Striped polecat 84
Water mongoose 80
Woodland dormouse 90

Ground birds

Cape rock thrush 119
Fiery-necked nightjar 116
Hadeda ibis 107
Red-winged starling 122

Waterbirds

Cape wagtail 147
Giant kingfisher 145
Malachite kingfisher 145

Birds of prey

African crowned eagle 152
African harrier hawk 156
African marsh harrier 156
Spotted eagle owl 159

Tree birds

African dusky flycatcher 187
African paradise flycatcher 188
Bar-throated apalis 185
Black-headed oriole 179
Brown-hooded kingfisher 170
Burchell's coucal 167
Cape canary 205
Cape robin-chat 184
Cape turtle dove 161
Cape white-eye 197
Cardinal woodpecker 177
Fork-tailed drongo 179
Greater honeyguide 176
Karoo prinia 186
Knysna turaco 165

Families of the wild

Malachite sunbird 195
Narina trogon 169
Olive thrush 183
Red-chested cuckoo 166
Red-eyed dove 161
Red-faced mousebird 169
Red-fronted tinkerbird 175
Sombre greenbul 182
Southern boubou 189
Southern double-collared sunbird 196
Southern masked weaver 200
Speckled mousebird 168

Turtles and tortoises

Angulate tortoise 210
Cape padloper 212
Helmeted terrapin 209

Snakes and lizards

Aurora snake 223
Berg adder 231
Black thread snake 233
Boomslang 220
Brown house snake 223
Cape cobra 218
Cape legless skink 245
Cape skink 243
Cape wolf snake 228
Common brown water snake 222
Common egg-eater 229
Common long-tailed seps 245
Common night adder 230
Common puff adder 231
Common slug-eater 233
Cross-marked grass snake 227
Green water snake 221
Herald snake 222
Mole snake 216
Rinkhals 219
Southern rock agama 242
Spotted harlequin snake 224
Spotted skaapsteker 226
Sundevall's shovel-snout 225

Frogs and toads

Angolan river frog 250
Cape river frog 250
Common platanna 248
Gray's frog 251
Marbled reed frog 253

Spiders, scorpions and others

Baboon spiders 323
Bark scorpions 321
Centipedes 327
Crab spiders 324
Land crustaceans 326
Land snails 320
Millipedes 327
Orb-web spiders 324
Ticks 326

Beetles

Blister beetles 334
Dung beetles 331
Glow-worms and fireflies 333
Ladybird beetles 333
Long-horned beetles 335
Predacious ground beetles 330
Weevils 335

Butterflies and moths

African clouded yellow 350
Citrus swallowtail 338
Convolvulus hawk moth 356
Dotted border 350
Evening brown 343
Lucerne blue 354
Mocker swallowtail 338
Painted lady 346
Pink-laced emerald looper 357
Scarlet tip 349
Southern milkweed 343
Tricoloured tiger moth 356

Other insects

Antlions 372
Bladder grasshoppers 366
Carpenter bees 379
Cicadas 370
Dragonflies 361
Flesh flies 377
Honeybees 380
Houseflies 375
Praying mantids 362
Robber flies 374
Shield bugs 369
Social wasps 378
Spider wasps 378
Termites 362

Families of the wild

SOUTHWESTERN CAPE FYNBOS

No region of comparable size in the world is richer in plant species than the narrow zone bounded by the southwestern Cape's fold mountains and the sea. The Afrikaans word *fynbos*—literally 'delicate bush' or 'fine bush'—used of the indigenous vegetation seems inadequate to describe the wealth of flora that includes some 600 kinds of heath or erica, almost 70 proteas and over 50 disa species. To walk through fynbos (formerly known as Cape macchia) in spring can leave one with the impression of being not in the wild but in a prolific garden.

This winter-rainfall region has a 'Mediterranean'-type climate. Varying degrees of dryness are experienced in summer, which is why many of the evergreen shrubs that predominate among the fynbos have leathery, drought-resistant leaves; other species have subterranean bulbs serving as storage organs.

The local wildlife includes species that, like so many of the plants, are uniquely adapted to the fynbos region and occur nowhere else. Among birds of this kind are the Cape sugarbird, with its long tail, and the orange-breasted sunbird, which feeds largely on the nectar of proteas, ericas and other plants characteristic of the fynbos. Another is the Cape bulbul, a cheerful, noisy little brown bird that becomes quite tame in suburban gardens.

Gardeners are not necessarily pleased that the southwestern Cape boasts four mole-like mammals: two golden mole and two molerat species. The golden moles, however, are insectivorous and are the gardener's friend, even if their subsurface 'runs' are sometimes a nuisance; the molerats on the other hand are vegetarians and can destroy bulbs and tubers. Nature has provided the antidote, however, in the form of the mole snake, which is particularly abundant in the sandy ground favoured by molerats.

The familiar grey squirrel, another local resident, is in a class of its own. This American species was introduced from Europe to the southwestern Cape during the 1890s by Cecil John Rhodes; and in the intervening years it has spread into the hinterland wherever its diet of acorns and pine-seeds is available.

Of the southern African antelope, two have a particular association with the southwestern Cape. The handsome bontebok was once widespread but is now the least common antelope of the subregion and occurs only in the lowlands around Swellendam and Bredasdorp. The solitary Cape grysbok is much smaller and less rare. An inhabitant of thick scrub, it is inclined to venture out to nibble on vine shoots—much to the annoyance of the Cape's wine farmers.

The southwestern Cape fynbos is periodically damaged by fire, especially during the dry summer months. This risk is made all the more real because many indigenous shrubs contain inflammable oils and resins. However, while many species are severely damaged, others thrive after burning, and fires are, in the case of certain species, now regarded as essential for their survival.

But there is a more serious threat than fire to this natural vegetation and the wildlife it supports, and that is man himself. Some 90 per cent of the lowland region's fynbos has been replaced by towns, roads, farms, forests and similar man-inspired projects.

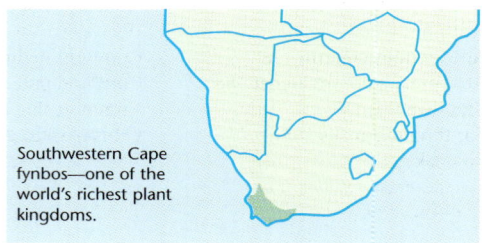

Southwestern Cape fynbos—one of the world's richest plant kingdoms.

Large mammals

Aardwolf 66
Bat-eared fox 68
Black-backed jackal 67
Bontebok 55
Cape fox 68
Cape mountain zebra 49
Caracal 64
Chacma baboon 69
Eland 52
Grey rhebok 57
Leopard 62
Mountain reedbuck 57
Red hartebeest 53

Smaller mammals

Aardvark 76
African wild cat 86
Cape clawless otter 85
Cape golden mole 95
Cape grysbok 75
Cape hare 78
Common duiker 71
Common molerat 94
Common vlei rat 91
Egyptian fruit bat 96
Geoffroy's horseshoe bat 97
Grey squirrel 89
Honey badger 84
Hottentot golden mole 95
Klipspringer 74
Large grey mongoose 80
Large-spotted genet 87
Peters' epauletted fruit bat 96
Porcupine 77
Rock dassie 79
Small grey mongoose 81
Small-spotted genet 87
Steenbok 71
Striped mouse 93
Striped polecat 84
Suricate 83
Water mongoose 80
Woodland dormouse 90
Yellow mongoose 82

Ground birds

African pipit 121
African stonechat 120
Alpine swift 116
Black-headed heron 104
Cape bunting 124
Cape longclaw 121
Cape rockjumper 120
Cape rock thrush 119
Cattle egret 105
Common quail 109
Common waxbill 124
Crowned lapwing 113
Denham's bustard 112
Helmeted guineafowl 110
Namaqua sandgrouse 115
Ostrich 104
Red-winged starling 122
Secretarybird 108
Southern black korhaan 113
Speckled pigeon 115
Spotted thick-knee 114
White-necked raven 119
White stork 105
Yellow-rumped widow 122

Waterbirds

African purple swamphen 135
African sacred ibis 131
African spoonbill 132
Blacksmith lapwing 139

Families of the wild

Cape wagtail 147
Common moorhen 136
Egyptian goose 133
Grey heron 129
Hamerkop 131
Lesser swamp warbler 146
Little grebe 125
Red-knobbed coot 136
Reed cormorant 128
Southern red bishop 147
Three-banded plover 138
Yellow-billed duck 134

Birds of prey

African harrier hawk 156
African marsh harrier 156
Barn owl 158
Black-shouldered kite 150
Cape vulture 148
Common buzzard 154
Lanner falcon 157
Spotted eagle owl 159
Verreaux's eagle 151
Verreaux's eagle owl 160

Tree birds

African dusky flycatcher 187
African hoopoe 173
African house martin 178
African paradise flycatcher 188
Barn swallow 177
Bar-throated apalis 185
Bokmakierie 191
Cape canary 205
Cape crow 180
Cape robin-chat 184
Cape sparrow 199
Cape sugarbird 195
Cape turtle dove 161
Cape white-eye 197
Common fiscal 188
Diederik cuckoo 167
Familiar chat 183
Greater striped swallow 178
Karoo prinia 186
Laughing dove 162
Malachite sunbird 195
Namaqua dove 162
Neddicky 186
Olive thrush 183
Orange-breasted sunbird 196
Pin-tailed whydah 203
Red-chested cuckoo 166
Red-eyed dove 161
Red-faced mousebird 169
Sombre greenbul 182
Southern boubou 189
Southern double-collared sunbird 196
Southern masked weaver 200
Speckled mousebird 168
Yellow canary 205

Turtles and tortoises

Angulate tortoise 210
Cape padloper 212
Geometric tortoise 211
Helmeted terrapin 209
Mountain tortoise 209

Snakes and lizards

Aurora snake 223
Berg adder 231
Bibron's gecko 239
Black thread snake 233
Boomslang 220
Brown house snake 223
Cape cobra 218
Cape dwarf chameleon 239
Cape legless skink 245
Cape skink 243
Cape wolf snake 228
Common brown water snake 222
Common egg-eater 229
Common long-tailed seps 245
Common night adder 230
Common puff adder 231
Common slug-eater 233
Cross-marked grass snake 227
Fork-marked sand snake 226
Green water snake 221
Herald snake 222
Knox's desert lizard 243
Mole snake 216
Rinkhals 219
Silvery dwarf burrowing skink 244
Southern rock agama 242
Spotted harlequin snake 224
Spotted skaapsteker 226
Sundevall's shovel-snout 225
Yellow-bellied sea snake 232

Frogs and toads

Angolan river frog 250
Cape river frog 250
Common platanna 248
Gray's frog 251
Karoo toad 248

Spiders, scorpions and others

Baboon spiders 323
Centipedes 327
Crab spiders 324
Earthworms 320
Land crustaceans 326
Land snails 320
Millipedes 327
Orb-web spiders 324
Thick-tail scorpions 322
Ticks 326

Beetles

Blister beetles 334
Dung beetles 331
Fruit beetles 332
Glow-worms and fireflies 333
Ladybird beetles 333
Toktokkies 334
Weevils 335
Whirligig beetles 330

Butterflies and moths

African migrant 340
Citrus swallowtail 338
Garden acraea 346
Lucerne blue 354
Painted lady 346
Southern milkweed 343
Table Mountain beauty 344

Other insects

Antlions 372
Aphids 370
Blowflies 376
Carpenter bees 379
Cicadas 370
Cockroaches 361
Cocktail ants 381
Crane flies 372
Dragonflies 361
Field crickets 365
Fruit flies 375
Hard scale insects 371
Honeybees 380
Houseflies 375
Hover flies 374
Long-horned grasshoppers 364
Mealy bugs 371
Mole crickets 366
Pond-skaters 369
Praying mantids 362
Robber flies 374
Shield bugs 369
Social wasps 378
Spittle bugs 368
Termites 362

Families of the wild

KAROO

The Karoo is uniquely evocative among the geographical regions of southern Africa. Its name conjures up a very specific crisp-aired, arid environment, flat but relieved by characteristic koppies, very hot during the day but with frost common on winter nights: a mosaic of dwarf shrubs, dusty bare soil, grasses, aloes and fleshy-leaved plants that have their moment of annual glory after spring rains, when they burst into bright bloom.

Atlases usually identify two Karoos. The Little Karoo lies between two parallel mountain chains of the southern Cape, the Witteberg-Swartberg mountain range and the Langeberg-Outeniqua range. North of the mountains, and rather higher in altitude, is the plateau of the Great Karoo, extending from Laingsburg east to Somerset East, and north to the Gariep (Orange) River, with Beaufort West and Graaff-Reinet two of its key towns.

But the full spread of the Karoo environment is much wider, covering parts of the Western, Northern and Eastern Cape and nearly one third of South Africa as a whole; it overlaps with Namaqualand and Bushmanland, with the southern extensions of both the Namib and the Kalahari, and with the grasslands of the Free State highveld.

In addition, certain farmers, through destructive agricultural techniques, have contributed to the slow but relentless spread of the Karoo eastwards—a movement that is still in progress.

If sheep are the livestock most readily identified with this enormous region, the springbok takes popular pride of place among the Karoo's wildlife. Actually many herds of this species have been reintroduced to the area by game farmers in quite recent times; in the truly natural state springbok are today most in abundance north and west of the Karoo proper. Precisely the same applies to the ostrich, which has been farmed with such success in the vicinity of Oudtshoorn that it has become a popular and well-known tourist attraction.

The quagga, a distinctive subspecies of Burchell's zebra, which lacked stripes on the rear half of its body, used to roam the region until it was hunted out of existence in the 19th century. In mountainous terrain at the southern boundary of the Karoo, and also in a national park near Cradock, the Cape mountain zebra thrives in limited numbers, having itself been rescued from the brink of extinction last century.

Another large mammal that once occupied the Karoo and adjoining grasslands in great abundance was the so-called black—but more usually buffy brown—wildebeest. (The characteristic loud *ge-nu* of this gregarious beast almost certainly accounts for the Khoisan word *gnu*, adopted into the English language.) Wildebeest, like gemsbok and springbok (when unhindered by farm fences), escape from the Karoo's drought by regular migration in search of seasonal rains. Sheep-farming, however, has led inevitably to the ruthless persecution and elimination of the large carnivores—lions, cheetahs, wild dogs, spotted hyaenas and brown hyaenas—although leopards survive precariously in rocky kloofs on the fringes of the Karoo.

Few wildlife species are unique to the region, but some of those very typical of it are hardy survivors like the aardvark (which feeds on termites), the small spotted cat, bat-eared fox and suricate.

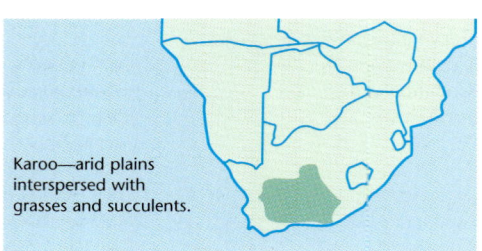

Karoo—arid plains interspersed with grasses and succulents.

Large mammals

Aardwolf 66
Bat-eared fox 68
Black-backed jackal 67
Black rhinoceros 47
Black wildebeest 50
Burchell's zebra 49
Cape fox 68
Cape mountain zebra 49
Caracal 64
Chacma baboon 69
Eland 52
Gemsbok 52
Grey rhebok 57
Kudu 60
Leopard 62
Red hartebeest 53
White rhinoceros 47

Smaller mammals

Aardvark 76
African wild cat 86
Cape clawless otter 85
Cape hare 78
Common duiker 71
Common vlei rat 91
Ground squirrel 89
Honey badger 84
Klipspringer 74
Porcupine 77
Rock dassie 79
Small grey mongoose 81
Small spotted cat 86
Small-spotted genet 87
Springbok 70
Springhare 78
Steenbok 71
Striped mouse 93
Striped polecat 84
Suricate 83
Water mongoose 80
Yellow mongoose 82

Ground birds

Abdim's stork 106
African pipit 121
African stonechat 120
Alpine swift 116
Black-headed heron 104
Blue crane 110
Blue korhaan 112
Burchell's courser 114
Cape bunting 124
Cattle egret 105
Common quail 109
Common waxbill 124
Crowned lapwing 113
Denham's bustard 112
Fiery-necked nightjar 116
Hadeda ibis 107
Helmeted guineafowl 110
Kori bustard 111
Little swift 117
Namaqua sandgrouse 115
Ostrich 104
Rock martin 118
Secretarybird 108
Southern black korhaan 113
Speckled pigeon 115
Spotted thick-knee 114
White-necked raven 119
White stork 105

Families of the wild

Waterbirds

African darter 128
African sacred ibis 131
African spoonbill 132
Blacksmith lapwing 139
Cape wagtail 147
Common moorhen 136
Egyptian goose 133
Giant kingfisher 145
Grey heron 129
Hamerkop 131
Lesser swamp warbler 146
Little grebe 125
Malachite kingfisher 145
Pied avocet 141
Red-billed teal 134
Red-knobbed coot 136
Reed cormorant 128
South African shelduck 133
Southern red bishop 147
Spur-winged goose 135
Three-banded plover 138
White-breasted cormorant 127
Yellow-billed duck 134

Birds of prey

Barn owl 158
Black kite 150
Black-shouldered kite 150
Cape vulture 148
Common buzzard 154
Common kestrel 157
Jackal buzzard 155
Lanner falcon 157
Martial eagle 152
Southern pale chanting goshawk 155
Spotted eagle owl 159
Verreaux's eagle 151

Tree birds

African hoopoe 173
African house martin 178
Barn swallow 177
Bokmakierie 191
Cape canary 205
Cape crow 180
Cape glossy starling 194
Cape robin-chat 184
Cape sparrow 199
Cape turtle dove 161
Cape white-eye 197
Cardinal woodpecker 177
Common fiscal 188
Diederik cuckoo 167
European starling 192
Familiar chat 183
Greater honeyguide 176
Greater striped swallow 178
Karoo prinia 186
Laughing dove 162
Malachite sunbird 195
Namaqua dove 162
Neddicky 186
Olive thrush 183
Pied crow 180
Pin-tailed whydah 203
Red-backed shrike 189
Red-chested cuckoo 166
Red-eyed dove 161
Red-faced mousebird 169
Red-headed finch 202
Southern double-collared sunbird 196
Southern masked weaver 200
White-browed sparrowweaver 198
Yellow canary 205

Turtles and tortoises

Angulate tortoise 210
Helmeted terrapin 209
Karoo padloper 213
Mountain tortoise 209
Tent tortoise 211

Snakes and lizards

Bibron's gecko 239
Boomslang 220
Brown house snake 223
Cape cobra 218
Cape gecko 241
Cape legless skink 245
Cape skink 243
Common barking gecko 240
Common egg-eater 229
Common puff adder 231
Cross-marked grass snake 227
Fork-marked sand snake 226
Giant ground gecko 240
Herald snake 222
Mole snake 216
Rinkhals 219
Rock leguaan 237
Southern rock agama 242
Spotted harlequin snake 224
Spotted skaapsteker 226
Sundevall's shovel-snout 225
Water leguaan 236

Frogs and toads

Bullfrog 252
Cape river frog 250
Common platanna 248
Gray's frog 251
Karoo toad 248

Spiders, scorpions and others

Baboon spiders 323
Burrowing scorpions 321
Centipedes 327
Millipedes 327
Orb-web spiders 324
Sun spiders 323
Thick-tail scorpions 322
Ticks 326

Beetles

Blister beetles 334
Dung beetles 331
Ladybird beetles 333
Predacious ground beetles 330
Toktokkies 334
Weevils 335

Butterflies and moths

African clouded yellow 350
Brown-veined white 349
Citrus swallowtail 338
Lucerne blue 354
Painted lady 346
Southern milkweed 343
Thysbe copper 352
Tricoloured tiger moth 356

Other insects

Antlions 372
Blowflies 376
Cockroaches 361
Cocktail ants 381
Dragonflies 361
Driver ants 380
Field crickets 365
Flesh flies 377
Honeybees 380
Horseflies 373
Houseflies 375
King crickets 363
Locusts 367
Mole crickets 366
Praying mantids 362
Robber flies 374
Sand wasps 379
Shield bugs 369
Stink locusts 367
Termites 362

Families of the wild

NAMAQUALAND AND BUSHMANLAND

The Namaqua (a Khoekhoen people) and San who gave their names to these adjoining regions of the Western and Northern Cape have long since disappeared from the vicinity as recognizable cultural entities. So, too, have the hippo, elephant, lion, buffalo, giraffe, ostriches and enormous herds of antelope that once, to judge from explorers' tales, roamed Namaqualand: they were eliminated with scant regard for the consequences by the murderous onslaught of well-armed white hunters in the 19th century.

Today, after good winter rains, it is the magnet of wild flowers that lures coachloads of visitors to Namaqualand for just a few weeks in the spring of each year. By contrast the flat, dry, sparsely populated expanses of Bushmanland, dotted with numerous shallow depressions or 'pans', and extending gradually down to the lower Gariep (Orange) River from the northern Karoo, remain off the tourist route.

The zone is bordered on the west by a 50 km-wide stretch of coastal sandveld. Eastwards for another 60 km runs a contrasting band of *hardeveld*: broken, mountainous country in which lies the district's major town, Springbok, as well as a considerable peak, the 1707-m Welcome Kop, further south. Further east again are the regions known commonly as Little Bushmanland and Great Bushmanland.

There are few trees here. Because of the meagre winter rainfall the vegetation is apt to be Spartan and stunted (except for the succulents and daisies that miraculously burst into bloom in September). Like the flora, various animal species have adapted to these harsh conditions; their colouring is often lighter than usual, blending in well with the parched landscape.

The larger mammals are confined to a handful of antelope species, and their inveterate enemy, the leopard, but there are plenty of smaller creatures. They include some species found nowhere else, such as the Namaqua dune molerat (which subsists on a diet of roots and bulbs) and two of the region's four species of golden mole. The quaint Brants' whistling rat, indigenous also to parts of the Karoo and the southern Kalahari, is a creation straight out of Walt Disney: if alarmed it will stamp its hindfeet in agitation, vocalize with a piercing whistle, and only then dive to the safety of its leaf-lined burrow.

Despite their names, neither the Namaqua sandgrouse nor the Namaqua dove are confined to Namaqualand, although these birds prefer a dry environment. You can readily distinguish the male of the little Namaqua dove from other doves by its black face and breast.

Geckos and sand lizards are very much at home in this sun-baked northwestern region, as are sand snakes and a complement of more dangerous snake species. The puff adder is among them—and yet the little town of Pofadder, situated in remote Great Bushmanland, was named after a Khoekhoen cattle rustler, Klaas Pofadder, and not after the reptile, as some may believe.

Note that the southern one-third of Namibia also used to bear the name 'Namaqualand' or 'Great Namaqualand', although the name is now generally used for the northwestern coastal districts of the Northern Cape.

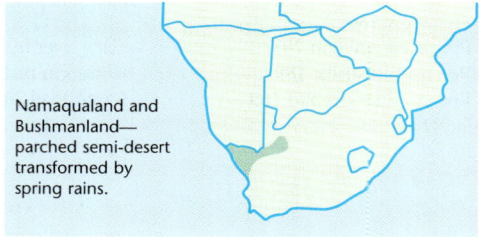

Namaqualand and Bushmanland—parched semi-desert transformed by spring rains.

Large mammals

Aardwolf 66
Bat-eared fox 68
Black-backed jackal 67
Cape fox 68
Caracal 64
Chacma baboon 69
Gemsbok 52
Grey rhebok 57
Leopard 62
Spotted hyaena 65
Vervet monkey 69

Smaller mammals

Aardvark 76
African wild cat 86
Cape clawless otter 85
Cape golden mole 95
Common molerat 94
Common vlei rat 91
Egyptian free-tailed bat 97
Geoffroy's horseshoe bat 97
Ground squirrel 89
Honey badger 84
Klipspringer 74
Porcupine 77
Rock dassie 79
Slender mongoose 81
Small grey mongoose 81
Small spotted cat 86
Small-spotted genet 87
Springbok 70
Springhare 78
Steenbok 71
Striped mouse 93
Striped polecat 84
Suricate 83
Water mongoose 80
Yellow mongoose 82

Ground birds

African pipit 121
Alpine swift 116
Black-headed heron 104
Burchell's courser 114
Cape bunting 124
Cape rock thrush 119
Common quail 109
Common waxbill 124
Crowned lapwing 113
Little swift 117
Namaqua sandgrouse 115
Ostrich 104
Rock martin 118
Secretarybird 108
Southern black korhaan 113
Speckled pigeon 115
Spotted thick-knee 114

Waterbirds

Blacksmith lapwing 139
Cape wagtail 147
Egyptian goose 133
Grey heron 129
Lesser swamp warbler 146
Little grebe 125
Malachite kingfisher 145
Pied avocet 141
Red-billed teal 134
Reed cormorant 128
South African shelduck 133
Three-banded plover 138

Families of the wild

Birds of prey

Common kestrel 157
Jackal buzzard 155
Lanner falcon 157
Southern pale chanting goshawk 155
Spotted eagle owl 159
Verreaux's eagle 151

Tree birds

African hoopoe 173
Barn swallow 177
Bokmakierie 191
Cape crow 180
Cape glossy starling 194
Cape robin-chat 184
Cape sparrow 199
Cape turtle dove 161
Cape white-eye 197
Cardinal woodpecker 177
Common fiscal 188
Diederik cuckoo 167
Familiar chat 183
Karoo prinia 186
Laughing dove 162
Malachite sunbird 195
Namaqua dove 162
Olive thrush 183
Pied crow 180
Pin-tailed whydah 203
Red-backed shrike 189
Red-faced mousebird 169
Southern double-collared sunbird 196
Southern masked weaver 200
Yellow canary 205

Turtles and tortoises

Angulate tortoise 210
Helmeted terrapin 209
Karoo padloper 213
Speckled padloper 213
Tent tortoise 211

Snakes and lizards

Armadillo girdled lizard 238
Bibron's gecko 239
Brown house snake 223
Cape cobra 218
Cape dwarf chameleon 239
Cape flat lizard 242
Cape skink 243
Common barking gecko 240
Common egg-eater 229
Common puff adder 231
Cross-marked grass snake 227
Eastern tiger snake 235
Fork-marked sand snake 226
Knox's desert lizard 243
Mole snake 216
Mozambique spitting cobra 219
Rinkhals 219
Southern rock agama 242
Spotted harlequin snake 224
Spotted skaapsteker 226
Sundevall's shovel-snout 225
Water leguaan 236
Web-footed gecko 241

Frogs and toads

Cape river frog 250
Common platanna 248
Karoo toad 248

Spiders, scorpions and others

Baboon spiders 323
Burrowing scorpions 321
Centipedes 327
Jumping spiders 325
Millipedes 327
Orb-web spiders 324
Sand-dwelling scorpions 322
Sun spiders 323
Thick-tail scorpions 322
Ticks 326

Beetles

Blister beetles 334
Dung beetles 331
Ladybird beetles 333
Predacious ground beetles 330
Toktokkies 334
Weevils 335

Butterflies and moths

Brown-veined white 349
Convolvulus hawk moth 356
Painted lady 346
Southern milkweed 343

Other insects

Antlions 372
Armoured crickets 364
Blowflies 376
Cicadas 370
Dragonflies 361
Flesh flies 377
Honeybees 380
Horseflies 373
Houseflies 375
King crickets 363
Locusts 367
Mole crickets 366
Praying mantids 362
Robber flies 374
Sand wasps 379
Shield bugs 369
Social wasps 378
Spider wasps 378
Stink locusts 367
Termites 362

Families of the wild

COASTAL AND CENTRAL NAMIBIA

The desert that gives its name to the whole of Namibia forms its western flank, a long coastal belt between 50 and 100 km wide. The southern half of this inhospitable terrain is an undulating sea of sand dunes whose contours are continually being reshaped by the wind. North of the Kuiseb River—its flow intermittent and largely subterranean—sand dunes give way to the gravel plains of the Skeleton Coast, notorious graveyard of ships and their stranded crews.

Namib vegetation is minimal and sometimes grotesquely adapted, like the huge, sprawling welwitschia, to cope with the arid environment. Such animals as exist have also developed ingenious behaviour patterns for survival. Here the web-footed gecko crosses the loose sand on webbed feet; and the side-winding or Péringuey's adder, a dwarf species, does so in a sequence of continuous lateral thrusts, leaving behind an unlikely but diagnostic trail of parallel lines at right angles to its path.

Thick fogs, created when the cold Benguela Current sweeps up the Atlantic coast, regularly drift inland from the sea, and the drops of dew they precipitate are life-saving thirst-quenchers for insects, spiders, scorpions and many other tiny creatures.

To the east of the coastal desert lies Namibia's central plateau. A feature of this region is a series of irregular mountain ranges that include some impressive peaks, although Namibia's highest mountain is the isolated granite mass of the 2 580 m Brandberg, at the fringe of the Namib north of Swakopmund. The plateau vegetation ranges from a cover of dwarf shrubs in the southern region (where the rainfall is lowest), to thornbush and mopane savanna further north.

Gemsbok and springbok are widely distributed here. Rocky areas provide a home for klipspringers and smaller fauna, of which some species are found nowhere else, such as Jameson's red rock rabbit (a true rabbit, not a hare, and certainly not a dassie) and the Kaokoveld rock dassie, a close relative of the common rock dassie. The unusual dassie rat, confined to Namibia and the northwestern Cape, looks more like a squirrel than anything else, though its hairy tail is not bushy. Like the squirrel, it follows an entirely vegetarian diet.

Hartmann's mountain zebra, which differs only subspecifically from the Cape mountain zebra, is entirely restricted to Namibia, and so is the shy little Damara dik-dik which can survive quite easily, without water, on the nourishment of the leaves, flowers and fruit of bushes, as well as on grasses.

Large game, including elephants, lions, giraffes and ostriches, are found in greatest abundance in the far north, the region that includes the Etosha Pan. These animals follow an age-old pattern in their regular migrations along the region's dried-up watercourses in search of food and water.

The black or hook-lipped rhinoceros is another indigenous species. Once it was so widespread in the subregion that it browsed on the slopes of Table Mountain; today it is restricted in its natural state to northern Zimbabwe, central Mozambique, the northern KwaZulu-Natal game reserves and to this part of Namibia.

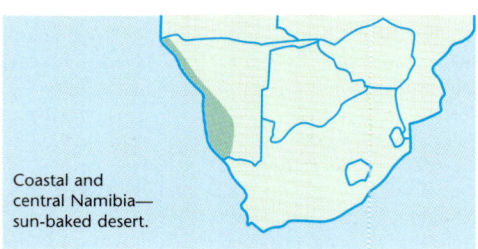

Coastal and central Namibia—sun-baked desert.

Large mammals

Bat-eared fox 68
Black-backed jackal 67
Black rhinoceros 47
Blue wildebeest 50
Brown hyaena 65
Burchell's zebra 49
Cape mountain zebra 49
Caracal 64
Cheetah 63
Eland 52
Elephant 46
Gemsbok 52
Giraffe 48
Impala 54
Kudu 60
Leopard 62
Lion 62
Red hartebeest 53
Warthog 61

Smaller mammals

African wild cat 86
Banded mongoose 82
Cape hare 78
Common duiker 71
Dwarf mongoose 83
Egyptian free-tailed bat 97
Geoffroy's horseshoe bat 97
Honey badger 84
Klipspringer 74
Porcupine 77
Rock dassie 79
Slender mongoose 81
Small-spotted genet 87
Springbok 70
Springhare 78
Steenbok 71
Striped polecat 84
Suricate 83
Yellow mongoose 82

Ground birds

Abdim's stork 106
Black-headed heron 104
Burchell's courser 114
Cape bunting 124
Crowned lapwing 113
Namaqua sandgrouse 115
Ostrich 104
Rock martin 118
Secretarybird 108
Southern black korhaan 113
Spotted thick-knee 114

Waterbirds

African black oystercatcher 137
Blacksmith lapwing 139
Cape cormorant 127
Cape gannet 126
Cape wagtail 147
Common tern 143
Egyptian goose 133
Great white pelican 126
Hartlaub's gull 142
Kelp gull 141
Pied avocet 141
Red-billed teal 134
South African shelduck 133
Swift tern 143
Three-banded plover 138
White-fronted plover 138

Birds of prey

Barn owl 158
Black-chested snake eagle 153

Families of the wild

Black kite 150
Common kestrel 157
Lanner falcon 157
Lappet-faced vulture 149
Martial eagle 152
Pygmy falcon 158
Southern pale chanting goshawk 155
Tawny eagle 151
Verreaux's eagle 151

Tree birds

African hoopoe 173
Bokmakierie 191
Cape crow 180
Cape glossy starling 194
Cape robin-chat 184
Cape sparrow 199
Cape turtle dove 161
Cape white-eye 197
Cardinal woodpecker 177
Common fiscal 188
Crimson-breasted shrike 190
European bee-eater 171
Familiar chat 183
Fork-tailed drongo 179
Greater striped swallow 178
Grey go-away bird 166
Namaqua dove 162
Red-backed shrike 189
Red-headed finch 202
Rosy-faced lovebird 164
Sociable weaver 198
Southern masked weaver 200
Southern yellow-billed hornbill 174
Violet-eared waxbill 202
White-browed sparrowweaver 198
Yellow canary 205

Turtles and tortoises

Angulate tortoise 210
Helmeted terrapin 209
Kalahari tent tortoise 212
Mountain tortoise 209
Tent tortoise 211

Snakes and lizards

Bark snake 225
Bibron's gecko 239
Black mamba 217
Boomslang 220
Cape cobra 218
Cape flat lizard 242
Cape gecko 241
Cape skink 243
Common egg-eater 229
Common puff adder 231
Eastern tiger snake 235
Fork-marked sand snake 226
Giant ground gecko 240
Knox's desert lizard 243
Mole snake 216
Mozambique spitting cobra 219
Péringuey's adder 230
Rock leguaan 237
Shield-nose snake 235
Southern burrowing asp 228
Southern rock agama 242
Spotted skaapsteker 226
Sundevall's garter snake 224
Sundevall's writhing skink 244

Frogs and toads

Angolan river frog 250
Bullfrog 252
Cape river frog 250
Common platanna 248
Senegal kassina 252

Spiders, scorpions and others

Baboon spiders 323
Burrowing scorpions 321
Centipedes 327
Jumping spiders 325
Millipedes 327
Sand-dwelling scorpions 322
Thick-tail scorpions 322
Ticks 326

Beetles

Blister beetles 334
Dung beetles 331
Long-horned beetles 335
Predacious ground beetles 330
Rhinoceros beetles 332
Toktokkies 334
Weevils 335

Butterflies and moths

African clouded yellow 350
Brown-veined white 349
Lucerne blue 354
Painted lady 346
Southern milkweed 343

Other insects

Antlions 372
Armoured crickets 364
Blowflies 376
Cicadas 370
Dragonflies 361
Driver ants 380
Flesh flies 377
Honeybees 380
Horseflies 373
Houseflies 375
Locusts 367
Praying mantids 362
Robber flies 374
Sand wasps 379
Shield bugs 369
Social wasps 378
Spider wasps 378
Stick insects 368
Termites 362
Tree crickets 365

Families of the wild

KALAHARI

The Kalahari is a vast expanse that defies easy definition, for it has many faces. It is mostly flat, but includes the Langeberge mountain range on its far southern borders near Kuruman in the Northern Cape. Permanently running streams are almost non-existent, yet after summer rains great shallow depressions or 'pans' start to fill up temporarily with water, and flood plains such as the Okavango Delta teem with a variety of wildlife.

The southwestern Kalahari has the least rain. Here the fine sand, swept up into low dunes by the wind, is covered only in sparse grasses. Further to the northeast the grass cover may be positively luxuriant, and the numerous mopanes (favourite browsing fare of elephants) range from low shrubs to medium-sized trees. Over much of the area the dense foliage of the camel thorn tree provides welcome shade, and in the southern Kalahari its stout branches offer a strong platform for sociable weavers to build their enormous communal stick-and-straw nests.

The grotesquely shaped baobab can hardly provide shade: its branches are puny in comparison with its outsize trunk, which may be up to eight metres in diameter. But its leaves and fruit are edible, and its bark, which has a high water content, is gratefully chewed by thirsty animals.

The boundaries of the Kalahari are ill-defined. The area includes the eastern half of Namibia, almost all of Botswana, part of the Northern Cape north of the Gariep (Orange) River, and even a western section of Zimbabwe. What these regions have in common is a dearth of surface water, the characteristic described by the Tswana word *kgalagadi* from which 'Kalahari' is derived.

For the San the Kalahari is a last refuge, and they have made this harsh land their home. Like the local wildlife, they have learnt ways of surviving in drought conditions. They search for water-bearing plants like the tsamma melon and the 'gemsbok cucumber'; store water in gourds and ostrich-egg shells which they bury underground; and dig for subsurface water that they suck out through carefully-made, grass-filtered reed pipes.

Some of the vast herds of game that once lived here still flourish in remoter parts and in reserves. Blue wildebeest, gemsbok, eland, red hartebeest and springbok—all species that can survive on little water—are among the fauna found in the southern Kalahari. These animals are apt to lead a nomadic lifestyle, roaming in search of what seasonal rain there is.

Several bird species in the Kalahari are similarly sensitive to the availability of water. Flocks of several hundreds or thousands of Namaqua sandgrouse will fly up to 60 km daily to waterholes. Vast numbers of red-billed queleas—reminiscent of locust swarms—'roll' over water surfaces, the lowest birds dipping into the water, and then flying up again.

In the moister wooded north the large variety of game includes elephant, hippopotamus, giraffe, kudu, sable, tsessebe, impala, buffalo, Burchell's zebra and many others.

One of the tinier creatures confined to the Kalahari region is Woosnam's desert rat, which survives on a diet of seeds and insects. Like the bushveld elephant-shrew, another local inhabitant, it has a very pale coat, a feature typical of small mammal species found in the drier parts of the subcontinent.

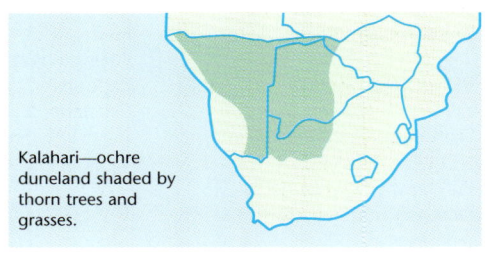

Kalahari—ochre duneland shaded by thorn trees and grasses.

Larger mammals

Black rhinoceros 47
Blue wildebeest 50
Buffalo 48
Burchell's zebra 49
Bushbuck 60
Caracal 64
Cheetah 63
Civet 64
Eland 52
Elephant 46
Gemsbok 52
Giraffe 48
Hippopotamus 46
Impala 54
Kudu 60
Leopard 62
Lion 62
Red hartebeest 53
Roan antelope 51
Sable antelope 51
Serval 63
Spotted hyaena 65
Tsessebe 54
Warthog 61

Smaller mammals

Aardvark 76
African wild cat 86
Banded mongoose 82
Common duiker 71
Honey badger 84
Klipspringer 74
Oribi 70
Porcupine 77
Rock dassie 79
Slender mongoose 81
Small spotted cat 86
Springbok 70
Springhare 78
Steenbok 71
Suricate 83
Yellow mongoose 82

Ground birds

Abdim's stork 106
Burchell's courser 114
Crowned lapwing 113
Kori bustard 111
Namaqua sandgrouse 115
Ostrich 104
Secretarybird 108
Southern black korhaan 113
Spotted thick-knee 114

Birds of prey

Barn owl 158
Bateleur 153
Black-chested snake eagle 153
Black kite 150
Black-shouldered kite 150
Common kestrel 157
Lanner falcon 157
Lappet-faced vulture 149
Martial eagle 152

Families of the wild

Pygmy falcon 158
Southern pale chanting goshawk 155
Spotted eagle owl 159
Tawny eagle 151
Verreaux's eagle owl 160
White-backed vulture 149

Tree birds

African hoopoe 173
Cape crow 180
Cape glossy starling 194
Cape sparrow 199
Cape turtle dove 161
Cardinal woodpecker 177
Common fiscal 188
Crimson-breasted shrike 190
Diederik cuckoo 167
Familiar chat 183
Fork-tailed drongo 179
Lilac-breasted roller 172
Namaqua dove 162
Red-backed shrike 189
Red-billed quelea 200
Red-headed finch 202
Sociable weaver 198
Southern masked weaver 200
Violet-eared waxbill 202
White-browed sparrowweaver 198
Yellow-billed hornbill 174
Yellow canary 205

Turtles and tortoises

Bell's hinged tortoise 210
Helmeted terrapin 209
Kalahari tent tortoise 212
Mountain tortoise 209

Snakes and lizards

Bark snake 225
Bibron's gecko 239
Black mamba 217
Boomslang 220
Brown house snake 223
Cape centipede-eater 234
Cape cobra 218
Cape file snake 229
Cape gecko 241
Cape wolf snake 228
Common barking gecko 240
Common egg-eater 229
Common night adder 230
Common puff adder 231
Eastern tiger snake 235
Egyptian cobra 217
Flap-neck chameleon 238
Fork-marked sand snake 226
Giant ground gecko 240
Herald snake 222
Mole snake 216
Mozambique spitting cobra 219
Rock leguaan 237
Shield-nose snake 235
Southern African rock python 216
Southern burrowing asp 228
Sundevall's garter snake 224
Sundevall's shovel-snout 225
Twig snake 221
Water leguaan 236

Frogs and toads

Bullfrog 252
Bushveld rain frog 249
Cape river frog 250
Common platanna 248
Senegal kassina 252

Spiders, scorpions and others

Baboon spiders 323
Burrowing scorpions 321
Centipedes 327
Jumping spiders 325
Millipedes 327
Sand-dwelling scorpions 322
Sun spiders 323
Thick-tail scorpions 322
Ticks 326

Beetles

Blister beetles 334
Dung beetles 334
Predacious ground beetles 330
Toktokkies 334
Weevils 335

Butterflies and moths

African clouded yellow 350
Brown-veined white 349
Convolvulus hawk moth 356
Lucerne blue 354
Painted lady 346
Southern milkweed 343
Tricoloured tiger moth 356

Other insects

Antlions 372
Armoured crickets 364
Blowflies 376
Dragonflies 361
Flesh flies 377
Honeybees 380
Horseflies 373
Houseflies 375
King crickets 363
Locusts 367
Mole crickets 366
Praying mantids 362
Robber flies 374
Sand wasps 379
Shield bugs 369
Social wasps 378
Spider wasps 378
Stink locusts 367
Termites 362

Glossary of terms

abdomen: the hindbody of an arthropod (for example, insect, spider, scorpion).
alarm (call): a call given in potentially or actually dangerous situations to warn other individuals of danger.
algae (singular 'alga'): unicellular or multicellular plants found in fresh or salt water or on moist ground.
amphibian: any member of a class of vertebrates that lives both on dry land and in water.
anal fin: a fin situated on the underside of a fish, between the anus and the tail fin.
angulate: having angles or an angular shape—used to describe a tortoise with triangular markings on its upper shell.
antenna: one of a pair of feelers or horns attached to the heads of insects, centipedes, millipedes and crustaceans.
aposematic: (of coloration) designed to warn potential predators of dangerous (for example, poisonous or distasteful) properties: common aposematic combinations of colours are black with white, red, yellow or green.
aquatic: living in or dependent on water.
arachnologist: one who studies the Arachnida (spiders, scorpions, ticks and mites).
arboreal: living in trees.
argonaut: another name for the paper nautilus. In Greek mythology the Argonauts were those who sailed in the ship *Argo* in search of the Golden Fleece.
arthropod: an invertebrate animal with a hard outside skeleton, a segmented body and jointed legs (for example, insects, arachnids, millipedes, centipedes, crustaceans).
back-fanged: having the fangs at the back of the mouth.
baleen: horny, black, fringed plates growing down from the palate of certain whales; these whales are without teeth and use the plates to sieve a diet of marine organisms from the sea.
barbel: a whiskerlike sensory organ trailing from the side of the mouth of certain fish species; there may be one or more pairs of barbels. The name 'barbel' also applies to a freshwater fish species of the carp family.
barred: marked with cross-stripes (bars) at right angles to the long axis of the body.
beak: the projecting jaws of a bird, covered with a horny sheath, or any beaklike mouthpart in other animals such as turtles and tortoises, and most dolphin species.
blaze: a mark, usually white, on an animal's face.
blotched: having large and untidy colour markings (*see* spotted).
blowhole: the nostril of a whale, situated at the top of the head. Air sharply expelled from the blowhole forms a visible 'spout'.
blubber: a thick, insulating layer of fat beneath the skin of whales and other aquatic mammals.
bonnet: hardened, cornlike outgrowths of skin on the front of the southern right whale's upper jaw.
brindled: marked with streaks or patches.
brood: the number of young hatching out of one clutch of eggs at a single breeding attempt.
brood parasite: a bird that lays its eggs in the nest of another species, the host or foster parent, which will then incubate the parasite's eggs and rear its nestlings as its own (for example, widowfinches, honeyguides and most cuckoos).
browser: an animal that feeds on the shoots and leaves of plants.
burrow: an underground hole used for shelter by an animal, and often excavated by that animal.
Cainism: the killing of the younger sibling by the older in a brood of birds, usually raptors.
camouflage: shape or coloration that conceals an organism by making it blend visually with its environment.
canines: sharp-pointed teeth on either side of the incisors.
canopy: the leafy crown of a tree or forest.
carapace: the upper shell of a tortoise or turtle.

cardiotoxic: (of poison) affecting the action of the heart.
carinated: having a 'keel' or ridge (as does one species of bark scorpion).
carnivore: a flesh-eating mammal.
carrion: the putrefying flesh of a dead animal.
cartilaginous: having a skeleton composed entirely of cartilage and not bone. Sharks, skates and rays are among the cartilaginous fishes.
carton nest: a boxlike nest, with paper-thin walls and interconnecting cells, of the sort made by cocktail ants.
casting: the coil of digested soil left above the ground by an earthworm.
caterpillar: the grub, or larva, of a butterfly or moth—the immature insect before metamorphosis into an adult.
caudal fin: *see* tail fin.
cere: a waxy swelling, containing the nostrils, at the base of the upper beak of certain birds, for example, parrots.
chelonian: any member of the reptile order Chelonia—that is, tortoises and turtles.
chevron: a V-shaped mark on an animal's coat.
clasper: one of a pair of clasping appendages at the rear end of a caterpillar.
clitellum: a thickened, saddlelike band round a worm, paler in colour than the rest of the body.
clutch: the number of eggs laid at a single breeding attempt.
cocoon: a protective covering of silk, spun by an insect when it pupates.
collar: a distinctive colour mark circling an animal's neck.
colony: a number of animals living together as a community; among birds, an aggregate of individuals in a fixed place for the purpose of breeding.
comb: (a) in a honeybee colony, a structure consisting of waxen cells in which honey is stored, eggs are laid by the queen, and larvae develop; (b) a stiff-pointed attachment on each inside hindleg of a grasshopper—when rubbed against a series of bumps on the abdomen the comb produces the grasshopper's call or 'stridulation'.
commensal: living in association with another species, as the household mouse does with man.
convergent (evolution): the process whereby unrelated organisms come to look and behave alike as a result of having been subjected to similar environmental pressures.
courtship: behaviour directed at establishing a pair bond between members of opposite sexes, usually initiated by the male.
crawler: the blind offspring of a scale insect.
crustacean: any arthropod of the class Crustacea, having a hard shell and being typically aquatic—including crabs, lobsters, shrimps and barnacles.
cryptic: concealed, usually by coloration or camouflage.
cuckoo-spit: the blobs of white froth produced by the nymph of the spittle bug as a protective covering.
cytotoxic: (of poison) attacking the body's cells, causing great pain and often leading to severe swelling and eventual cell death.
dead-leaf: the camouflaged appearance of some butterfly species when they close their wings, the colour and shape of which resemble a dead leaf.
decurved: curved downwards. Applied often to bill shapes, for example, the bill of a sunbird or an ibis.
diagnostic: able to be used as a feature on its own to identify (or 'diagnose') a species.
dimorphism: the occurrence of two distinct forms in a single species, for example, the red and blue forms of the gaudy commodore butterfly.
display: any behaviour that has signal function, i.e. that conveys a message, such as courtship display or distraction display.
distraction: behaviour intended to draw a potential predator's attention away from an animal's eggs, young or nest (for example, injury-feigning).
diurnal: active by day (as opposed to nocturnal).

Glossary of terms

dorsal: belonging to the back.
dorsal fin: a vertical fin on the back of a fish. Some fish species have two dorsal fins, arranged one behind the other.
drey: the shelter or 'nest' of a squirrel.
drone: in a honeybee colony, a male bee whose sole function is to mate with the queen.
dustbathe: to rub sand all over the body and then shake it off, probably in order to get rid of parasites.
echolocation: a system by which supersonic vibrations, bounced off objects, are used to determine the position of those objects—practised by bats to plot a free flight path in the dark. Aquatic mammals also use supersonic vibrations to communicate with one another and to locate objects.
eclipse (plumage): nonbreeding plumage, usually resembling female plumage; especially common among weavers, bishops and widowbirds.
elytrum (plural 'elytra'): a beetle's modified forewings, hardened to form a case or sheath for the hindwing.
emergent (vegetation): plants that stick out above the surface of the water (for example, reeds, rushes, sedges).
endemic: occurring in a given region and nowhere else in the world.
epaulette: a distinctively coloured patch of fur on the shoulder of certain bat species.
evolution: a biological process of structural and physiological change over time, that enables organisms to adapt to changing environmental conditions.
exotic: introduced to a region, i.e. not native or indigenous to that region.
eye-spot: a colourful marking like an eye (or target), on the wing of a butterfly or moth.
false midrib: a brown marking bisecting a butterfly's wing, and increasing the insect's resemblance to a dead leaf when it settles on a branch with its wings closed.
fang: one of the long, needle-sharp teeth through which certain snakes, spiders or insects inject venom; the fang is either hollow or deeply grooved. The 'fangs' of a centipede are modified forelegs.
fetlock: part of a horse's or antelope's leg, immediately above the hoof, where a tuft of hair grows.
filter-feeder: a fish that feeds by using its gill rakers to sift organisms from seawater, the water entering the mouth and exiting via the gill slits.
fingerling: a young fish, especially a trout or salmon, no bigger than a finger.
fledge: to acquire feathers; also taken to mean the act of leaving the nest.
fledgling: a young bird that has acquired its feathers; usually refers to the young bird after it has left the nest.
flipper: limb of a seal (or other aquatic mammal) adapted for use in swimming.
fluke: one of the two horizontal lobes that make up the tail of a whale or dolphin.
forage: to go about in search of food.
forest: a habitat dominated by trees with a continuous canopy, i.e. in which the canopies of adjacent trees touch each other (see woodland).
form: the shallow resting place of a hare—so named because it is formed or moulded by the animal's body.
foster parent: see host.
freeze: to become motionless—as an animal may do when confronted by danger.
front-fanged: having the fangs at the front of the mouth.
fry: young fishes newly hatched from the spawn.
furcula: a tiny, fork-shaped structure attached to the underside of a springtail's abdomen. Sudden release of this structure enables the insect to hop over long distances.
fynbos: a habitat characteristic of the winter-rainfall region of South Africa (mainly southwestern Cape), dominated by plants of the protea and heath families.
gape: the angle of the mouth formed by the meeting of the upper and lower jaws.
gill: one of a pair of breathing organs that enable fishes to breathe in water. The word is also used, loosely, of the visible gill-cover—a bony fold of skin—protecting each breathing organ.
glide: to fly without wingbeats, using the lift provided by moving air (wind), or by a horizontally moving body part with aerodynamic properties, such as a wing.
grazer: an animal that feeds on growing grass or pasture.
gregarious: living together in herds, colonies or other groups; not solitary.
grizzled: grey, or mixed with grey.
grub: the short, fleshy, legless larva of certain insects.
guano: the droppings of fish-eating seabirds; usually found in large accumulations, such as on the breeding islands of seabirds.
guard hair: thick, protective hair on the outer surface of an animal's coat.
habitat: any definable living place.
haemotoxic: (of poison) affecting the blood system, preventing clotting and causing bleeding. Adder venom is of this type.
hair-tail: a thin extension projecting from a butterfly's hindwing. Because hair-tails resemble antennae, a predator may be misled into taking a bite from the 'wrong end' of the butterfly, allowing it to escape relatively unharmed.
helper: a nonbreeding member of a group of birds that contributes to the parental care of a brood of young produced by the breeding pair (known as the alpha pair); helpers are usually the young of previous broods of the alpha pair.
herbivore: an animal that eats grass.
heronry: a colony of nesting herons and/or egrets.
hilltopping: territorial behaviour of male butterflies over rocky ridges on sunny days. Each male, having selected his territory, defends it against intruders while waiting for a sexually receptive female butterfly to arrive.
holt: the den of an otter.
honeydew: a sugary substance excreted by sap-sucking insects, and prized as food by other insects, including ants.
honey gland: the name given to a gland, secreting a sugary substance, on the backs of some caterpillars.
hood: a flattened expansion of the neck 'spread' by cobras and some other snake species when angered or threatened. The hood may be as much as three times the width of the body.
hopper: a locust at the earthbound, marching stage, when its wings are not yet fully developed.
host: a bird in whose nest a brood parasite lays its eggs for the host to incubate, and whose young it will then rear as its own; also known as a foster parent.
immature: not yet able to reproduce sexually, but no longer a juvenile.
incisors: cutting teeth at the forefront of an animal's mouth.
incubate: to warm the eggs with the body to enable the embryos to develop.
indigenous: occurring naturally in a region, i.e. native to that region.
injury-feigning: a distraction display in which an animal behaves as if wounded or physically disabled. Especially common among ground-nesting birds.
insectivore: a creature that feeds on insects.
intertidal: between the low-water and high-water marks. Used of animals that live within this area.
invertebrates: animals without backbones.
juvenile: a young animal not yet of adult size or coloration, usually still dependent on parental care.
keel: a longitudinal ridge on a fish's flank.
keeled: ridged, like the body scales of some snakes.
kelp: any large brown seaweed.
king: in a termite colony, the fertile, active male, which bonds with the termite 'queen' for life.
krill: tiny shrimplike marine animals drifting near the sea's surface.

Glossary of terms

lamellae (singular lamella): fine, toothlike projections along the sides of a bird's bill for filtering out small particles of food from water or mud.
lanceolate: (of a tooth), narrow and tapering towards the end, like a lance-head.
lancet: one of several cutting surfaces on the proboscis of a mosquito or horsefly, enabling the insect to pierce the skin of its victim before sucking blood.
larva: the immature form of an insect (and certain other creatures), from the time it leaves the egg (for example, a grub or a tadpole).
lateral line: a line of sensory organs (modified nerve endings) along each side of a fish's body, and corresponding to a line of scales. These organs detect vibrations and pressure changes.
latrine: a piece of land communally used by a herd (e.g. of buck) for urinating and defecating. At the edge of a territory a latrine may serve as a boundary signal.
leading edge: the front (anterior) edge of a wing (*see* trailing edge).
leatherjacket: a name for the larva of a crane fly.
litter: the young of any animal, collectively.
lobed: having movable flaps of tissue on either side of the toes as an adaptation for swimming, but not joining the toes as webs do (*see* webbed).
long-horned: having long antennae.
maggot: the grub of a fly.
mammae: milk-bearing glands, represented externally by the nipples, that are a characteristic of all mammals.
mermaid's purse (also known as a 'sea purse'): the leathery egg-case produced by the female of certain sharks and rays. By means of tendrils or hooks the mermaid's purse attaches itself to submerged vegetation.
metamorphosis: the changes in form and shape that take place as an insect develops from egg to adult.
migrate: to move seasonally from one place to another and back again.
mirror: one of a pair of surfaces on the base of a cicada's abdomen, reflecting or amplifying the insect's call.
mobbing: concerted action—for example, calling out harshly—by a community of animals in order to frighten a predator.
montane: inhabiting mountains.
moult: the process of replacing feathers or skin by loss and regrowth.
mouth-brooder: a female fish that protects her fertilized eggs by keeping them in her mouth until they hatch.
muzzle: the projecting part of an animal's head, including the jaws and nose.
neap tide: a tide of minimum height, occurring when the attractions of the sun and moon work against each other (*see* spring tide).
nestling: a bird in the nest, still being cared for by its parents.
neurotoxic: (of poison) attacking the nerve tissue, causing paralysis and affecting breathing, eyesight, speech or locomotion. Cobra venom is of this type.
nippers: the two grasping claws (or 'chelae') of a crab.
nocturnal: active at night (as opposed to diurnal).
nomadic: wandering from place to place in search of food and water; not confined to a single territory.
nursery: an expanse of quiet water, such as a tidal rock pool or a dam, in which young fish shelter.
nymph: an immature insect, similar to the adult but lacking wings, and with undeveloped sex organs.
ocellate: with circular, eyelike markings.
ocellus (plural 'ocelli'): any eyelike marking in animals, such as the eye-spots on the wings of some butterflies.
omnivorous: eating all kinds of food, both plant and animal.
operculum (plural 'opercula'): a covering or lid, for example, the hard plate covering the entrance to a sea shell when the animal retracts, or the semicircular plate closing the abdominal cavity in which a cicada produces its shrill call.

orange dog: a name given to the green-and-orange caterpillars of the citrus swallowtail butterfly.
organism: any living thing (for example, plant, animal, bacterium, fungus).
osmeterium: a forked, fleshy organ behind the head of certain caterpillars. Normally concealed, it can be shot out to frighten predators; and it emits an unpleasant smell.
ossuary: a firm, usually rocky, place on which bearded vultures (lammergeiers) drop bones to break them into pieces small enough to swallow.
oviduct: the tube through which eggs leave the ovary.
oviparous: egg-laying.
ovipositor: the long egg-laying organ at the end of a female insect's abdomen.
ovoviviparous: producing eggs that hatch inside the body.
palp: *see* pedipalp.
parasite, brood: *see* brood parasite.
pavement teeth: a surface of flat molar teeth possessed by some fish species, and used for crushing shellfish before consumption.
pectoral fin: one of a pair of fins on either flank of a fish, each situated just behind the head.
pedipalp: one of a pair of appendages on a spider's head, used for feeding and moving, and in the courtship ritual.
peduncle: the narrow part at the rear of a fish's body, just in front of the tail fin.
pelagic: living in the upper waters of the open sea.
pelvic fin: one of a pair of fins on the underside of a fish's body, behind the head.
petiole: the narrow 'waist' connecting the thorax and abdomen of wasps and ants.
pincers: the pair or pairs of jointed, grasping appendages in lobsters and certain other arthropods such as scorpions.
plankton: small, drifting marine organisms that live in the surface waters of oceans.
plastron: the undershell of a tortoise or turtle (*see* carapace). The word is derived from the French for 'breastplate'.
plumage: the covering of feathers on the body of a bird.
post: a special vantage point taken up by a male butterfly during the territorial behaviour known as 'hilltopping'.
predacious: (of an animal) predatory, that is, preying naturally on other animals.
predator: an animal that preys on others.
preen: to dress the plumage with the bill in order to keep it in good condition.
prehensile: capable of grasping (used, for example, of a tail, limb, lip).
primary (feathers): the flight feathers on the hand or outermost part of the wing of a bird.
proboscis: the long, tonguelike mouth-piece of some insects, used for sucking nectar, blood or other food.
prolegs: the 'false' legs arranged in pairs along the length of a caterpillar—as opposed to the caterpillar's three pairs of 'true' legs situated towards its head.
pronk: to prance high in the air—a term used of some buck species, and derived from the Dutch word meaning to 'strut' or 'show off'.
pronotum: the back of an insect's thorax, in armoured crickets a tough protective plate.
pup: the young of a seal or shark.
pupa: an insect at the intermediate stage (immobile and non-feeding) between larva and adult.
pupate: to become a pupa; to undergo the stage of passive development typical of a pupa.
quadrate bone: a bone attached to a projection at the back of a snake's skull, and from which the lower jaw is suspended.
queen: in colonies of social insects, the only fertile, sexually functioning female.
raptor: a bird of prey, usually one of the diurnal kinds, such as eagles, buzzards and goshawks.
ray: one of the bones—either soft or hard—that form part of a fish's fin and help to support it.

Glossary of terms

recurved: curved upwards. Used to describe bill shapes, for example, that of the pied avocet.

red tide: an uncommon phenomenon along the west coast of southern Africa, when certain marine microorganisms multiply excessively, staining the sea. One of these organisms contains a toxin that may accumulate in mussels, making them dangerous to eat.

regurgitate: to bring food up from the stomach to the mouth, usually for the purpose of feeding young.

repletes: the name given to certain worker ants, which act as food storehouses for their colleagues by swallowing large quantities of honeydew and later regurgitating it.

resident: an animal that does not migrate; one that usually stays in one place all year round.

ringing: placing on a bird's leg a ring of metal (with a number) or plastic (in a particular colour or colour combination) for individual identification.

roost: to retire to a resting place for the inactive part of the daily cycle.

rostral shield: the nose-scale of the shield-nose snake.

rostrum: a prominent beak or snout, such as the toothed snout of the sawfish, or an insect's beak or sniff snout.

royal jelly: a nutritious substance secreted by worker honeybees and fed to the larva of a queen bee.

rufous: reddish brown (includes rust, russet, chestnut).

rut: a period of sexual excitement experienced by male deer.

saddle: a distinctive colour marking on an animal's coat, across part of the back or, sometimes, running the full length of the back from neck to tail.

savanna: a habitat dominated by woodland with a grassy lower level; in southern Africa savanna trees are usually species of acacia, hence this habitat may be known as thornveld.

scat: an animal dropping.

scavenger: an animal that feeds on organic or vegetable debris.

scute: a horny plate that forms part of the exoskeleton in certain animals. Examples are the raised segments that make up a tortoise's upper shell, or the bony scales which form a fish's lateral line.

shield: (of a carapace) another word for 'scute'.

short-horned: having short antennae.

sibling: an animal of the same brood or litter (i.e. a brother or sister).

silk: the fine fibre produced by a spider to spin its web or nest.

slough: to cast off the skin.

soar: to fly without wingbeats, using upcurrents of warm air, or thermals.

soldier: a class of termites that defends the termite colony against invaders.

song: a vocalization made to advertise territory.

spat: the spawn of any shellfish.

spawn: (noun) the eggs laid by a fish; (verb) to deposit eggs.

speculum: literally a mirror—a conspicuously coloured area on a bird's wing, often shiny, as in many ducks

spine: a hard, pointed fin ray.

spiracle: a breathing-hole.

spit: (of snakes) to eject venom forcibly. The poison is aimed not specifically at the eyes but at any part of the victim that moves.

spotted: marked with small, rounded markings, or spots.

spring tide: a tide of maximum height, occurring when the sun and moon pull together (see neap tide).

stoop: to dive from the air at prey (refers to the hunting behaviour of raptors).

stot: another term for 'pronk'.

streaked: marked with short, elongate markings parallel to the long axis of the body.

stridulation: the chirping or scraping sound produced by grasshoppers or crickets. The sound is produced when one part of the body is rubbed against another.

sub-Antarctic: north of the antarctic convergence, i.e. not quite Antarctic.

swimmerets: small abdominal appendages, used for swimming, possessed by prawns, shrimps and other crustaceans.

tadpole: the larva of a frog or toad.

tail fin: (also known as 'caudal fin') the fin at the end of a fish's body—colloquially, the 'tail'. It may be forked, or have a straight or concave trailing edge.

tentacles: slender, flexible organs used for feeling, grasping and moving.

terrapin: a freshwater tortoise. The word is of American origin.

territorial: (of a fish or other animal) identified with a particular 'home' area, which may be protected against invasion by other animals.

territory: any area of land treated by an animal as its own, marked out (for example, with urine or glandular scent) and defended from invaders.

thermal: a bubble or column of warm air rising from a land surface, usually heated by the sun.

thorax: the part of an insect's body between the head and abdomen. The thorax carries the legs and wings.

throne: another term for 'post'.

toad: an amphibian distinguished from a frog by its relatively clumsy, 'warty' body. Toads are more terrestrial than frogs.

trailing edge: the hind (posterior) edge of a wing (see leading edge).

tube-feet: the fingerlike structures, tipped with suction pads, possessed by cushion stars, sea cucumbers, sea urchins and starfish.

tubercle: a small, wartlike protuberance of the sort found on the backs of some gecko species or those displayed by the southern milkweed caterpillar.

tundra: a treeless, boglike habitat at high northern latitudes, with short summers and long, freezing winters.

tymbal: one of two drumlike membranes vibrated at great speed—by cicadas, for example—to produce a call.

underslung: (of the lower jaw) extending beyond the upper jaw.

upending: a foraging method of ducks in which they tilt the head down under the water and the tail up.

urine-washing: behaviour in which mammals such as bushbabies wet the soles of their feet with their urine to mark out a territory and also as part of the mating ritual.

vegetarian: eating only plant matter.

vertebrates: animals with backbones.

viviparous: giving birth to live young that have developed from eggs within the female's body.

vocalize: to make a cry, call or other sound.

wader: a member of the suborder Charadrii, including the lapwings, plovers, oystercatchers, dikkops, avocets, jacanas, sandpipers and their relatives.

warren: a series of interconnecting burrows used as a shelter by rabbits, gerbils and other small mammals.

warts: popular (but erroneous) name for the small protuberances on a toad's skin, these being glands that secrete a sticky, white substance. It is a myth that by touching the skin of a toad a person will acquire warts.

wattle: bare, fleshy area around the eye, base of the bill, throat or other areas on the head of a bird.

webbed: joined by a web of skin, as, for example, the toes of swimming birds such as ducks and gulls (see lobed).

wing-case: see elytrum.

woodland: a habitat dominated by trees with a discontinuous canopy (see forest).

woolly bear: the hairy caterpillar of certain moth species, including tiger moths.

workers: among social insects, a class of individuals (usually sterile) that form the bulk of the colony and do all the work, including foraging for food and caring for the larvae.

wriggler: the larva of a mosquito.

Index

Page numbers in **bold** indicate a main reference that is illustrated.

A

aardvark **76**
aardwolf 3, **66**
aasvoëls **148-9**
abalone **309**
Abdim's stork 7, **106**
abdomen **319**, **329**, **337**, **359**, 410
Abudefduf vaigiensis **287**
Acanthopagrus berda **290**
Acanthurus leucosternon **287**
Acari **326**
Acinonyx jubatus **63**
Acontias meleagris **245**
acraea, garden 30, **346**
Acraea horta **346**
Acrididae **367**
Acridotheres tristis **193**
Acrocephalus gracilirostris **146**
Actitis hypoleucos **139**
Actophilornis africanus **137**
adaptations for survival 382
adders 20, 21, **230-2**
adipose fin **264**
Aepyceros melampus **54**
Aeropetes tulbaghia **344**
African
　black eagle 9, **151**
　black oystercatcher **137**
　clouded yellow (butterfly) 30, **350**
　crowned eagle 9, **152**
　darter 8, **128**
　dusky flycatcher **163**
　firefinch 18, **201**
　fish eagle 9, **154**
　green pigeon 15, **163**
　harrier hawk 11, **156**
　hoopoe **173**
　jacana 12, **137**
　luna moth **355**
　marsh harrier **156**
　migrant (*butterfly*) 30, **340**
　moon moth **355**
　mudhopper **293**
　palm swift 15, **168**
　paradise flycatcher **188**
　penguin **125**
　pied wagtail 16, **146**
　pipit **121**
　purple swamphen 12, **135**
　python, southern 20, **216**
　sacred ibis **131**
　skimmer **144**
　spoonbill **132**
　stonechat 16, **120**
　wild cat 5, **86**
Afrikaanse
　kwartel **109**
　maanmot **355**
　modderspringer **293**
　naguil **116**
　swerwer (*butterfly*) **340**
　vleivalk **156**
agama 215
　southern rock 22, **242**
Agapornis roseicollis **164**
Agrius convolvuli **356**
Agulhas Current 264
akkedisse **242-3**
albacore **275**
albakoor **275**

Alcedo cristata **145**
Alcelaphus buselaphus **53**
alikreukel **311**
alikreukeltjie **310**
Alipes spp. 327
Aloeides thyra **352**
Alopochen aegyptiacus **133**
Alpine swift 15, **116**
alula **100**
Amadina erythrocephala **202**
Amauris echeria **342**
Amauris niavius dominicanus **341**
Amblypygi 319
Amblysomus hottentotus **95**
amethyst starling **193**
Ammophila spp. 379
Amphibia 246
Amphicallia bellatrix **357**
Amphipoda 326
anal fin **255**, **264**, **265**, 410
Anas erythrorhyncha **134**
Anas undulata **134**
anatomical features
　birds **100-3**
　butterflies **337**
　freshwater fish **254-5**
　frogs & toads **247**
　grasshopper 358-9
　ground beetle **329**
　insects 358-9
　lizards **215**
　mammals 43, 44
　marine fishes **264-5**
　marine mammals **300**
　moths **337**
　scorpions **319**
　snakes **214**
　spiders **319**
　tortoises & turtles **207**
Anax imperator 361
anchovy, Cape **298**
Andropadus importunus **182**
anemone, sea 304, **314**
anemoon **314**
angelfish 286
Angolan river frog 23, **250**
Angolese rivier-padda 23, **250**
angulate tortoise 19, **210**
Anhinga melanogaster **128**
Anisoptera 361
Annelida 304
Anopheles spp. 373
Anopheles gambiae 373
anopheline mosquitoes 373
ansjovis, Kaapse **298**
anteater, scaly **76**
antelope
　anatomy **43**
　roan I, **51**
　sable I, **51**
antennae 328, **329**, **337**, 358, **359**, **377**, 410
antestia bug 369
Antestia variegata 369
Anthia 330
Anthobaphes violacea **196**
Anthropoides paradisea **110**
Anthus cinnamomeus **121**
Antidorcas marsupialis **70**
Antliarrhinus zamiae 335
antlions 32, **372**
ants 32, 33, 362, **380-1**
Anura 246
Aonidiella aurantii 371

Aonyx capensis **85**
apalis, bar-throated **185**
Apalis thoracica **185**
Apaloderma narina **169**
Aparallactus capensis **234**
Aphididae 370
aphids **370**
Apidae 380
Apis mellifera 380
Aptera cingulata 361
Apus affinis **117**
Aquila rapax **151**
Aquila verreauxii **151**
Arachnida 318
Araneidae 319, 324
arboreal birds *see* tree birds
Arctic tern **143**
Arctiidae 337, 356
Arctocephalus pusillus pusillus **303**
Ardea cinerea **129**
Ardea goliath **129**
Ardea melanocephala **104**
Ardeotis kori **111-12**
arende **151-3**, **154**
arendrog **272**
Argema mimosae **355**
argonaut **315**, 410
Argyrosomus inodorus **279**
Argyrosomus japonicus 279
Argyrozona argyrozona **281**
arid areas, wildlife 402-3, 406-7
armadillo girdled lizard 22, **238**
armoured crickets 32, **364**
armoured scale insects **371**
army ants **380**
arrow-marked babbler **181**
Arthropods 304
Asilidae 374
asp, southern burrowing 20, **228**
Aspidelaps scutatus **235**
aspis, suidelike grawende **228**
Atelerix frontalis **77**
Atilax paludinosus **80**
Atlas Project, Bird 103
Atractaspis bibronii **228**
Atractoscion aequidens **279**
aurora snake 20, **223**
avocet, pied **141**
axillaries **101**

B

baardaasvoël **148**
baars (*fish*) **261**
babbler, arrow-marked **181**
baber, skerptand **256**
baboons 59
　chacma **69**
　savanna **69**
baboon spiders 318, **323**
Bactrodema aculiferum 368
badger, honey **84**, 155
bagrada bug 369
bagworm, wattle 377
bakoorjakkals **68**
bald ibis 9, **107**
Balearica regulorum **111**
baleen 301
balkstert-platkop (*fish*) **293**
banded mongoose 5, **82**
banded tilapia 24, **259**
bandkeelkleinjantjie **185**

414

baro, chubbyhead **257**
barbel (*sensory organ*) **264**, 410
barbets 17, **175-6**
Barbus andrewi **257**
Barbus anoplus **257**
Barbus kimberleyensis **256**
barking gecko, common 22, **240**
bark scorpions 27, **321**
bark snake 20, **225**
barn owl 13, **158**
barn swallow 15, **177**
barracuda, great **276**
bartail flathead (*fish*) **293**
bar-throated apalis **185**
bass 24, **261**
basskerpioene **321**
basslang **225**
bastergemsbok **51**
bat-eared fox 3, **68**
bateleur 11, **153**, 155
batis, chinspot **187**
Batis molitor **187**
Bats 6, **96-7**
　anatomy **44**
beak/bill 101, **102**, 207, 412
bearded vulture **148**
beautiful tiger (*moth*) **357**
bee-eaters 14, **171-2**
bees **379-80**
beetles 328-9, **328-35**
　Cape fold mountain region 397
　Drakensberg escarpment 395
　east coast subtropical forest region 391
　Eastern Cape & KwaZulu-Natal midlands region 393
　highveld region 385
　Kalahari region 409
　Karoo region 403
　lowveld region 389
　Namaqualand & Bushmanland 405
　Namib Desert region 407
　northern savanna region 387
　southern Cape forest region 399
　southwestern Cape fynbos region 401
Belenois aurota aurota **349**
Bell's hinged tortoise 19, **210**
Belonogaster spp. 378
Benguela current 264
berg adder 21, **231**
berghaan **153**
bergkopervlerkie (*butterfly*) **352**
berglyster, Kaapse **120**
bergnooientjie (*butterfly*) **344**
bergsebra, Kaapse **49**
bergskilpad **209**
Bibron's blind snake 21, **234**
Bibron's gecko 22, **239**
bill/beak 101, **102**, 412
binoculars 98, **99**
bird calls 101
birds 98-103
　Cape fold mountain region 396-7
　Drakensberg escarpment 394-5
　east coast subtropical forest region 390
　Eastern Cape & KwaZulu-Natal midlands region 392-3
　ground *see* ground birds
　highveld region 384-5
　Kalahari region 408-9
　Karoo region 402-3

lowveld region 388-9
　Namaqualand & Bushmanland 404-5
　Namib Desert region 406-7
　northern savanna region 386-7
　southern Cape forest region 398
　southwestern Cape fynbos region 400-1
　tree *see* tree birds
　waterbirds *see* waterbirds
birds of prey **148-60**
　Cape fold mountain region 397
　Drakensberg escarpment 395
　east coast subtropical forest region 390
　Eastern Cape & KwaZulu-Natal midlands region 393
　highveld region 385
　Kalahari region 408
　Karoo region 403
　lowveld region 388-9
　Namaqualand & Bushmanland 404-5
　Namib Desert region 407
　northern savanna region 387
　southern Cape forest region 398
　southwestern Cape fynbos region 401
birdwatching 98, 100-1, 103
bishop, southern red (*bird*) **147**
bishop, yellow (*bird*) 18, **122**
biskops/musselcrackers **283**
Bitis arietans **231**
Bitis atropos **232**
Bitis gabonica **232**
Bitis peringueyi **230**
blaartrektorre **334**
blaasop (*frog*) *see* bosveldblaasop
blaasopsprinkane **366**
black
　button spider 325
　citrus aphid 370
　crow **180**
　eagle **151**
　heron 10, **130**
　kite **150**
　korhaan **113**
　maize beetle 332
　mamba 21, **217**
　marlin **274**
　mussel **313**
　musselcracker **283**
　porgy **290**
　rhinoceros 47
　snake, Natal 20, **227**
　steenbras **283**
　thread snake 21, **233**
　tit, southern **181**
　wildebeest I, **50**
　worm snake **233**
black-backed jackal 3, **67**
black-backed puffback 17, **190**
black-chested snake eagle 9, **153**
black-collared barbet 17, **175**
black-eyed bulbul **182**
black-eye, tailed (*butterfly*) 31, **354**
black-footed cat **86**
blackhead (*snake*) **234**
black-headed heron 8, **104**
black-headed oriole **179**
blacksaddle goatfish **289**
black-shouldered kite **150**
blacksmith lapwing 13, **139**
blacksmith plover **139**

blacktail (*fish*) 27, **295**
black widow spider 318
bladder grasshoppers 32, **366**
blafgeitjie, gewone **240**
Blatta orientalis 361
Blattella germanica 361
Blattodea 361
bleeksingvalk **155**
blesbok II, **55**
bleshoender **136**
blindeslang, Bibron se **234**
blindevlieë **373**
blind snake, Bibron's 21, **234**
blinkogie **238**
blister beetles 29, **334**
blommetjie **241**
blouaap **69**
bloublasie **317**
blouduiker **72**
blougesiggie (*butterfly*) **348**
blouglans (*butterfly*) **342**
bloukopdrawwertjie **114**
bloukorhaan **112**
bloukraanvoël **110**
bloukuifloerie **165**
blou-kurper **258**
blou pylstert **272**
information reier **129**
blousysies **201-2**
bloutjies (*butterflies*) **353**, **354**
blouvalk **150**
blouwang-sonvis **259**
blouwildebees **50**
blowflies 33, **376**
blowhole **300**, 410
blue
　bream **258**
　crane 7, **110**
　duiker 4, **72**
　jay **172**
　korhaan 10, **112**
　kurper **258**
　musselcracker **283**
　pansy (*butterfly*) 31, **348**
　pointer (*shark*) **266**
　stingray 25, **272**
　waxbill 18, **201**
　wildebeest I, **50**
　see also blues
blue-billed firefinch 18, **201**
bluebottle (*invertebrate*) **317**
bluebottles (*flies*) 376
bluegill sunfish 24, **259**
blues (*butterflies*) 31, 337, **348**, **353**, **354**
bobbejaanspinnekoppe **323**
bobbejane 59
　Kaapse **69**
body shape
　beetles 328, **329**
　freshwater fishes 254, **255**
　frogs & toads 246-7
　marine fishes 264, **265**
　tortoises & turtles 206, **207**
bokmakierie 17, **191**
bokvis, swartsaal **289**
bontebok II, **55**
bontelsie **141**
bontkiewiet **139**
bontkwikkie **146**
bontpaling, heuningkoek **289**
bontrietpadda **253**
bontrokkie, gewone **120**
bontrugwewer **199**

bontsebra **49**
bontvisvanger **144**
bony fish, anatomy **264**
book/false scorpion 319
boomdas **79**
boomeekhoring **90**
boomkrieke **365**
boomslang 20, **220**
borrelpadda **252**
borrelskulp, pers **311**
bosbok **60**
boskobra **218**
bosloerie **169**
bosluise **326**
bosluisvoël **105**
bosnagaap **88**
bospatrys **108**
bosruiter **140**
bosskeerbek **92**
Bostrychia hagedash **107**
bosvark **61**
bosveldblaasop **249**
bosveldfisant **109**
bosveldnagmuis **91**
bosveldpapegaai **164**
bosveldtinktinkie **185**
bosveldvisvanger **170**
boswaaierstertmuis **90**
bottergat **182**
boubou, southern 17, **189**
Brachycerus obesus 335
Bradypodion pumilum **239**
bream
 blue **258**
 river 26, **290**
breathing, tortoises & turtles 206
breëkoparend **152**
bridle triggerfish **288**
brilpikkewyn **125**
bristletails 360
bristle worms 304
broad-bordered grass-yellow
 (*butterfly*) 30, **351**
broadnose sevengill shark **269**
brommers **376-7**
bromvoël **117**
bronze mannikin (*bird*) 18, **203**
brown
 button spider 325
 house snake 20, **223**
 hyaena 3, **65**
 locust 367
 mussel **312**
 trout 24, **262**
 water snake, common 20, **222**
 see also browns
brown-headed parrot 16, **163**
brown-hooded kingfisher 14, **170**
browns (*butterflies*) 31, **343**, 344,
 345
brown-veined white (*butterfly*) 30,
 349
bruinforel **262**
bruin huisslang **223**
bruinjakkalsvoël **154**
bruinkoppapegaai **163**
bruinkopvisvanger **170**
bruinmossel **312**
bruin waterslang **222**
brulpadda **252**
brusher (*fish*) **283**
bubble raft shell **311**
bubble shell, violet **311**
bubbling kassina **252**

Bubo africanus **159**
Bubo lacteus **160**
Bubulcus ibis **105**
Bucorvus leadbeateri **117**
buffalo **48**
buffel **48**
Bufo gariepensis **248**
Bufo gutturalis **249**
bulbuls **182**
bullfrog **252**
Bullia digitalis **310**
bumblebees 379
bunting, Cape **124**
Buphagus erythrorhynchus **194**
Burchell's
 coucal 13, **167**
 courser 13, **114**
 zebra I, **49**
Burhinus capensis **114**
burrowing
 asp, southern 20, **228**
 scorpions 28, **321**
 skink, silvery dwarf 22, **244**
bush
 shrike, orange-breasted 17, **191**
 squirrel **90**
 stink locust 367
bushbabies 5, **88**
bushbuck 1, **60**
Bushmanland, wildlife 404-5
bushpig 2, **61**
bushveld
 gerbil **91**
 rain frog **249**
 wildlife 388-9
bustards 7, **111-12**
Buteo buteo **154**
Buteo rufofuscus **155**
Buthidae 318
Buthotis spp. **322**
butterflies **336-337**, **338-54**
 and moths, comparison 336
 Cape fold mountain region 397
 Drakensberg escarpment 395
 east coast subtropical forest region
  391
 Eastern Cape & KwaZulu-Natal
  midlands region 393
 highveld region 385
 Kalahari region 409
 Karoo region 403
 lowveld region 389
 Namaqualand & Bushmanland
  405
 Namib Desert region 407
 northern savanna region 387
 southern Cape forest region 399
 southwestern Cape fynbos region
  401
butterflyfish, limespot **286**
button spiders 318, **325**
buzzards 11, **154-5**
Byblia anvatara acheloia **345**
bye/bees **379-80**
byvanger *see* mikstertbyvanger
byvreters **171-2**

C

Calidris ferruginea **140**
Calliphoridae 376
calls
 of birds 101

 of frogs & toads 246, 247
 of mammals 45
camouflage 42, 410
Camponotus maculatus 381
canaries 18, **204-5**
cane rat, greater **94**
Canis adustus **67**
Canis mesomelas **67**
Cape
 anchovy **298**
 bunting **124**
 canary 18, **205**
 centipede-eater 21, **234**
 clawless otter 5, **85**
 cobra 21, **218**
 cormorant 8, **127**
 crow 11, **180**
 dassie **79**
 dikkop **114**
 dwarf chameleon 22, **239**
 file snake **229**
 flat lizard 22, **242**
 fox 3, **68**
 fur seal 300, **303**
 gannet **126**
 gecko 22, **241**
 glossy starling 14, **194**
 golden mole 6, **95**
 grey mongoose **81**
 ground squirrel **89**
 grysbok 4, **75**
 hare **78**
 hunting dog **66**
 kurper **260**
 legless skink 21, **245**
 longclaw **121**
 moony **292**
 mountain adder **231**
 mountain zebra I, **49**, 396
 padloper 19, **212**
 reed warbler **146**
 river frog 23, **250**
 robin-chat **184**
 rockjumper **120**
 rock lobster **306**
 rock oyster **312**
 rock thrush 16, **119**
 salmon **279**
 skink 22, **243**
 snake-lizard **245**
 sparrow 16, **199**
 sugarbird **195**
 terrapin **209**
 thick-tail scorpion 322
 turban shell **311**
 turtle dove 15, **161**
 vulture 8, **148**
 wagtail 16, **147**
 white-eye **197**
 wolf snake 20, **228**
 yellowtail (*fish*) 25, **277**
Cape fold mountains, wildlife 396-7
Caprimulgus pectoralis **116**
Carabidae 330
caracal 2, **64**
Caracal caracal **64**
Caranx ignobilis **277**
carapace 206, **207**, 319, 410
Carcharhinus leucas **268**
Carcharhinus obscurus **268**
Carcharias taurus **267**
Carcharodon carcharias **266**
cardinal woodpecker **177**
Caretta caretta **208**

carinated bark scorpion 321
carmine bee-eater, southern 14, **171**
carp **260**
carpenter (*fish*) 26, **281**
carpenter bees **379**
cartilaginous fish, anatomy **265**
caterpillars 336, 410
catfish, sharptooth **256**
Catopsilia florella **340**
cats 5, **86**
catshark, striped **270**
cattle egret 10, **105**
caudal peduncle **264**
caudal/tail fin **255, 264, 265,** 413
Causus rhombeatus **230**
centipede-eater, Cape 21, **234**
centipedes 28, 318, **327**
Centropus burchellii **167**
Cephalophus monticola **72**
Cephalophus natalensis **72**
cephalothorax **319**
Cerambycidae 335
Ceratotherium simum **47**
Cercomela familiaris **183**
Cercopidae 368
Ceroplesis thunbergi 335
Cervus dama **74**
Ceryle rudis **144**
Cetacea 300
Cetoniinae 332
chacma baboon **69**
Chaetodon unimaculatus **286**
Chaetops frenatus **120**
Chalcomitra senegalensis **197**
Chamaeleo dilepis **238**
chameleons 22, 215, **238-9**
chanting goshawk, southern pale 11, **155**
Charadrius marginatus **138**
Charadrius tricollaris **138**
charaxes 336
 koppie 30, **340**
 pearl 30, **344**
Charaxes jasius saturnus **340**
chat, familiar 16, **183**
cheetah 2, **63**
Cheimerius nufar **284**
chelicera **319**
Chersina angulata **210**
chevron **43**, 410
chief (*butterfly*) 30, **342**
Chilomenes lunata **333**
Chilopoda 327
chinspot batis **187**
Chiromantis xerampelina **251**
chiton, giant **308**
Chlorocebus aethiops **69**
Chondrodactylus angulifer **240**
Choromytilus meridionalis **313**
Christmas butterfly **338**
Chrysoblephus anglicus **285**
Chrysoblephus cristiceps **281**
Chrysoblephus gibbiceps **280**
Chrysoblephus laticeps **280**
Chrysoblephus puniceus **284**
Chrysochloris asiatica **95**
Chrysococcyx caprius **167**
chubbyhead minnow/barb **257**
cicadas **370**
Cicadidae 370
Cicoria abdimii **106**
Cicoria ciconia **105**
Cinnyricinclus leucogaster **193**
Cinnyris chalybea **196**

Ciraetus pectoralis **153**
cisticola, rattling 17, **185**
Cisticola chinianus **185**
Cisticola fulvicapillus **186**
citrus mealy bug 371
citrus swallowtail 31, **338**
civet **64**
Civettictis civetta **64**
Clarias gariepinus **256**
clasper **265**, 410
classification, of birds 98-9
clawless otter, Cape 5, **85**
clicking grass frog **251**
clouded yellow (*butterfly*), African 30, **350**
Clubionidae 318-19
CMR beetle 334
coastal and central Namibian wildlife 406-7
cobras 21, **217-19**
Coccinellidae 333
cockroaches **361**
cocktail ants 33, **381**
Coelenterates 304
Coleoptera 328
Colias electo electo **350**
Colius striatus **168**
Collembola 360
Colotis danae annae **349**
colour
 butterflies & moths 336
 freshwater fishes 254
 frogs 247
 marine fishes 265
 tortoises & turtles 206
Columba guinea **115**
'comic' tern 143
commodore (*butterfly*), gaudy 31, **347**
common
 barking gecko 22, **240**
 brown water snake 20, **222**
 buzzard, 11, **154**
 dolphin **302**
 duiker 4, **71**
 fiscal 17, **188**
 house martin 15, **178**
 egg-eater 20, **229**
 joker **345**
 kestrel **157**
 long-tailed seps 22, **245**
 molerat **94,** 95
 moorhen 12, **136**
 myna 14, **193**
 night adder 20, **230**
 octopus **306**
 platanna **248**
 puff adder 21, **231**
 quail **109**
 river frog **250**
 sandpiper 17, **139**
 sea urchin **316**
 shore crab **307**
 slug-eater 21, **233**
 starling **192**
 tern 10, **143**
 vlei rat **91**
 waxbill 18, **124**
Comostolopsis stillata **357**
compound eye **329, 337, 359**
Connochaetes gnou **50**
Connochaetes taurinus **50**
convulvulus hawk moth **356**
coot, red-knobbed 12, **136**

coppers (*butterflies*) 30, 31, 337, **352**
Coracias caudata **172**
corals 304
Cordylus cataphractus **238**
Cordylus giganteus **237**
cormorants 8, **127-8**
Corvus albicollis **119**
Corvus albus **180**
Corvus capensis **180**
Coryphaena hippurus **276**
Corythaixoides concolor **166**
Cossypha caffra **184**
Cossypha natalensis **184**
costal shield **207**
Coturnix coturnix **109**
coucal, Burchell's **167**
courser, Burchell's 13, **114**
couta **274**
coverts
 greater primary **100**
 greater under primary **101**
crabs 304
 mole **307**
 shore **307**
crab spiders 28, 319, **324**
crane flies **372**
cranes 7, **110-11**
crayfish 304
Crematogaster spp. 381
Crematogaster peringueyi 381
crested barbet **176**
crested francolin 12, **108**
crickets 32, **363-6**
crimson-breasted shrike 17, **190**
crocodile, Nile 215, **236**
Crocodylia 215
Crocodylus niloticus **236**
Crocuta crocuta **65**
cross-marked grass snake 20, **227**
Crotaphopeltis hotamboeia **222**
crown **100**
crowned
 crane 7, **111**
 eagle, African 9, **152**
 lapwing 13, **113**
 plover (lapwing) **113**
crows 11, **180**
Crustacea 326, 410
Cryptomys hottentotus **94**
Ctenizidae 318
ctenoid scale **255**
Ctenolepisma longicaudata 360
cuckoos 13, **166-7**
cuckoo-spit 368
Cuculus solitarius **166**
cuda **274**
Curculionidae 335
curlew sandpiper 17, **140**
currents, ocean, and marine fishes 264
Cursorius rufus **114**
Cursus ranivorus **156**
cushion star **317**
Cybister spp. 331
cycad weevil 335
Cyciograpsus punctatus **307**
cycloid scale **255**
Cymatoceps nasutus **283**
Cynictis penicillata **82**
Cyprinus carpi **260**
Cypsiurus parvis **168**

D

dabchick **125**
dageraad 26, **281**
Damaliscus dorcas dorcas **55**
Damaliscus dorcas phillipsi **55**
Damaliscus lunatus **54**
Damara dik-dik 4, **73**
damba (*fish*) **294**
damselfish 287
Danaidae 336
Danaus chrysippus aegyptius **343**
dark-capped bulbul **182**
darter, African 8, **128**
dassie (*fish*) **295**
dassies (*mammals*) 4, **79**
Dasyatis chrysonota chrysonota **272**
Dasypeltis scabra **229**
deer, fallow 1, **74**
Delichon urbica **178**
Delphinus delphis **302**
Dendroaspis angusticeps **220**
Dendroaspis polylepis **217**
Dendrohyrax arboreus **79**
Dendropicos fuscescens **177**
Denham's bustard 7, **112**
Dermaptera 363
Dermochelys coriacea **208**
desert gecko, palmate **241**
desert lizard, Knox's 22, **243**
desert wildlife 406-7
diadem (*butterfly*) 30, **342**
Diaspididae 371
Diceros bicornis **47**
Dichistius capensis **294**
Dicrurus adsimilis **179**
diederik cuckoo/diederikkie 13, **167**
diet and habitat, freshwater fishes 254
digits **44**
dik-dik, Damara 4, **73**
dikkop (*bird*), Cape **114**
dikkop-ghieliemientjie (*fish*) **257**
dikstert-skerpione **322**
Dinoplax gigas **308**
Diplodus cervinus hottentotus **295**
Diplodus sargus capensis **295**
Diplopoda 327
Dispholidus typus **220**
distribution, marine invertebrates 305
dog, wild **66**
doktervis, poeierblou **287**
dolfyne **302**
dolphinfish **276**
dolphins **300**, **302**
Donax serra **313**
donkerhaai **268**
donkervlieëvanger **187**
dopluise, gepantserde **371**
doppies (*fish*) **281**
dorado/dorade **276**
dormouse, woodland 90
dorsal
  fin **255**, **264**, **265**, **300**, 410-11
  fringe **43**
  scales **214**
Dorylinae 380
dotted border (*butterfly*) 30, **350**
double-collared sunbird, southern 15, **196**
doves 15, **161-3**
draadslang, swart **233**
draaijakkals **68**

dragonflies 32, **361**
Drakensberg escarpment, wildlife 394-5
driebandstrandkiewiet **138**
driekleur tiermot **356**
drilvis, marmer **273**
driver ants 32, **380**
drongo, fork-tailed **179**
Dryoscopus cubla **190**
dubbelsterte (*butterflies*) **340**, **344**
duck, yellow-billed 9, **134**
duikers (*birds*) **127-8**
duikers (*mammals*) 4, **71-2**
duinadder, Namib **230**
duisendpote **327**
duiwe **161-3**
duiwelbye **378**
duneland, wildlife 408-9
dung beetles 29, **331**
duskies **268**
dusky
  dolphin **302**
  flycatcher, African **187**
  shark 25, **268**
dwarf
  burrowing skink, silvery 22, **244**
  chameleon, Cape 22, **239**
  cushion star **317**
  garter snake, spotted **224**
  mongoose 5, **82**
dwerg-grawende skink, silwergrys **244**
dwergmuishond **83**
dwergvalk **158**
dwergverkleurmannetjie, Kaapse **239**
Dynastinae 332
Dytiscidae 331

E

eagle owls 11, **159-60**
eagleray 25, **272**
eagles 9, **151-3**, **154**
ear coverts **100**
ear-shield **44**
ears, marine mammals 300
earthworms 318, **320**
earwigs, garden 33, **363**
east coast tropical forest, wildlife 390-1
Eastern Cape, wildlife 392-393
eastern tiger snake 21, **235**
Echinoderms 305
edelvalk **157**
edible snail 320
eekhorings **89-90**
eel, moray, honeycomb **289**
eels, freshwater 254
eende **133-4**
eenkol-vlindervis **286**
egg-eater, common 20, **229**
eggs, tortoises & turtles 206, 207
Egiptiese
  kobra **217**
  losstertvlermuis **97**
  vrugtevlermuis **96**
egrets 10, **105**, **130**
Egretta ardesiaca **130**
Egretta garzetta **130**
Egyptian
  cobra 21, **217**
  free-tailed bat 6, **97**

  fruit bat 6, **96**
  goose 9, **133**
  mongoose **80**
eiervreter, gewone **229**
eland **52**
Elanus caeruleus **150**
Elapsoidea sundevallii **224**
electric ray, marbled 25, **273**
elephant **46**
elephant seal, southern **303**
elephant shrew, rock **92**
Elephantulus myurus **92**
elf (*fish*) 25, **278**
elytra/elytron/elytrum 328, **329**, 411
Emberiza capensis **124**
Emerita austroafricana **307**
emperor dragonfly 361
emperor moth, mopane **355**
energy cycle 382
Englishman/Engelsman (*fish*) 26, **285**
environment and wildlife distribution 382-409
epauletted fruit bat, Peters' 6, **96**
Epinephelus marginatus **285**
Epomophorus crytyrus **96**
Equus burchellii **49**
Equus zebra zebra **49**
erdvark **76**
erdwurms **320**
Eriosoma lanigerum 370
Eristalis tenax 374
Estrilda astrild **124**
Eubalaena glacialis **301**
Euplectes axillaris **123**
Euplectes capensis **122-3**
Euplectes orix **147**
Euplectes progne **123**
Eupodotis afra **113**
Eupodotis caerulescens **112**
Eurema brigitta brigitta **351**
European
  bee-eater 14, **171**
  fallow deer **74**
  starling 14, **192**
  swallow 15, **177**
Europese
  byvreter **171**
  spreeu **192**
  swael **177**
  takbok **74**
evening brown (*butterfly*) 31, **343**
eyes, beetles 328
eye-spot **337**, 411

F

Falco biarmicus **157**
falcons **157**, **158**
Falco tinnunculus **157**
fallow deer 1, **74**
false/book scorpion 319
familiar chat 16, **183**
families of the wild 382-409
fangs 214, **319**, 411
Fannia canicularis 375
fan-tailed widowbird 18, **123**
feet
  beetles 328-9
  tortoises & turtles 207
Felis nigripes **86**
Felis sylvestris lybica **86**

femur **247, 319, 329, 359**
fetlock **43,** 411
field crickets 32, **365**
fiery-necked nightjar **116**
fig tree blue (*butterfly*) 31, **353**
file snake, Cape **229**
fin
 anal **255, 264,** 410
 dorsal **255, 264, 265, 300,**
  410-11
 pectoral 2**55, 264, 265,** 412
 tail **255, 264, 265,** 413
finch, red-headed 18, **202**
fins
 freshwater fishes 254-**5**
 marine fishes **265**
firefinch, African 18, **201**
firefinch, blue-billed **201**
fireflies 29, 333
fisant *see* bosveldfisant
fiscal, common 17, **188**
fiscal shrike **188**
fish eagle, African 9, **154**
fishes
 freshwater 254-**5,** 254-63
 marine **264-**99
fishing owl, Pel's 13, **160**
fishmoths **360**
fiskaallaksman **188**
flamingo, lesser **132**
flamink *see* kleinflamink
flap-neck chameleon 22, **238**
flappie **122-3**
flathead (*fish*), bartail **293**
flat lizard, Cape 22, **242**
flatworms 304
flesh flies 377
flies 33, **373-7**
flippers, marine mammals **300,** 411
flower spiders **324**
fluke **300,** 411
flycatchers **187, 188**
flying fox **96**
foam nest frog **251**
fold mountains, Cape, wildlife 396-7
folklore, and spiders 318
food and habitat, freshwater fishes
 254
food chain 382
forelle **262**
forest
 cobra 21, **218**
 shrew **92**
forest wildlife
 east coast subtropical 390-1
 southern Cape 398-9
forewing
 cell **337**
 inner angle **337**
 inner margin **337**
 outer margin **337**
fork-marked sand snake 20, **226**
fork-tailed drongo **179**
Formicinae 381
four-lined bark scorpion 321
fovea 319
foxes 3, **68**
foxy charaxes **340**
francolins 12, **108-9**
free-tailed bat, Egyptian 6, **97**
freshwater eels 254
freshwater fishes **254-63**
fret, gewone **203**
friar (*butterfly*) 30, **341**

frogs 246-**7,** 249-53
 and toads, compared 246
  Cape fold mountain region 397
  Drakensberg escarpment 395
  east coast subtropical forest region
   391
  Eastern Cape & KwaZulu-Natal
   midlands region 393
  highveld region 385
  Kalahari region 409
  Karoo region 403
  lowveld region 389
  Namaqualand & Bushmanland
   405
  Namib Desert region 407
  northern savanna region 387
  southern Cape forest region 399
  southwestern Cape fynbos region
   401
fruit
 bats 6, **96**
 beetles 29, **332**
 flies 33, **375**
Fulica cristata **136**
fur, marine mammals 300
fur seal, Cape 300, **303**
fynbos, wildlife 396-7, 400-1

G

Gaboon adder 21, **232**
Galago crassicaudatus **88**
Galago moholi **88**
Galeocerdo cuvier **267**
Galerella pulverulenta **81**
Galerella sanguinea **81**
galjoen 27, **294**
Gallinula chloropus **136**
gallinule, purple 135
game viewing 42
gannet, Cape **126**
gans *see* kolgans
garden
 acraea 30, **346**
 earwigs 33, **363**
 snail 320
garnaal *see* moddergarnaal
garrick 25, **278**
garter snake
 spotted dwarf **224**
 Sundevall's 20, **224**
Gastropoda 320
gaudy commodore (*butterfly*) 31,
 347
gebande muishond **82**
geckos 22, 215, **239-41**
geelbek (*fish*) 26, **279**
geelbekeend **134**
geelbek reushoringvoël **174**
geelbeksterretjie **143**
geelbekvou **150**
geelgat (*bird*) **182**
geelgesiggie (*butterfly*) **348**
geelkanarie **205**
geeloogkanarie **204**
geelpens-klipkabeljou **285**
geelstert (*fish*), Kaapse **277**
geelvis, grootbek **256**
geese *see* goose
geitjies **239-41**
Gelis latrodectiphagus 377
gemsbok 1, **52**
genets 3, **87**

Genetta genetta **87**
Genetta tigrina **87**
Geochelone pardalis **209**
Geoffroy's horseshoe bat 6, **97**
geometric tortoise 19, **211**
Geometridae 337
geometriese skilpad **211**
gepantserde dopluise **371**
gerbil, bushveld **91**
Geronticus calvus **107**
Gerridae 369
gespikkelde knorder **291**
gespikkelde padloper **213**
gevlekte
 hiëna **65**
 kousbandjie **224**
 muisvoël **168**
 ooruil **159**
 skaapsteker **226**
gewone
 blafgeitjie **240**
 blousysie **201**
 bontrokkie **120**
 dikkop **114**
 dolfyn **302**
 duiker **71**
 eiervreter **229**
 fret **203**
 janfrederik **184**
 koester **121**
 kwikkie **147**
 langstertseps **245**
 luislang **216**
 mossie **199**
 nagadder **230**
 paradysvink **204**
 platanna **248**
 rivierpadda **250**
 ruiter **139**
 see-eier **316**
 slakvreter **233**
 spekvreter **183**
 spreeu **192**
 sterretjie **143**
 swartmees **181**
 tarentaal **110**
 tortelduif **161**
 troupant **172**
 vleiloerie **167**
 willie **182**
giant
 chiton **308**
 eagle owl 11, **160**
 girdled lizard **237**
 ground gecko 22, **240**
 kingfish **277**
 kingfisher **145**
 land snails **320**
 leatherback turtle 206
 periwinkle **311**
gill (*cover*) **255, 264, 265,** 411
Giraffa camelopardalis **48**
giraffe **48**
girdled lizards 22, **237-8**
Glaucidium perlatum **159**
glimwurms **333**
Glossina 376
glossy starling 14, **194**
glow-worms 29, **333**
gnu **50**
goatfish, blacksaddle **289**
go-away bird, grey 12, **166**
goldbar wrasse **288**
golden moles 6, **95**

golden sand lizard **245**
gold-spotted sylph (*butterfly*) 30, **351**
Goliath heron 8, **129**
gompou **111-12**
goose
　Egyptian 9, **133**
　spur-winged **135**
goshawk, southern pale chanting 11, **155**
goudstaaf-lipvis 288
gouemol
　Hottentot **95**
　Kaapse 95
graafneusslang, Sundevall's **225**
granulated thick-tail scorpion 322
Graphium antheus **339**
Graphiurus murinus **90**
grass frog, clicking **251**
grasshoppers
　anatomy 358-**9**
　bladder 32, **366**
　long-horned **364**
grasslands, wildlife 384-7, 392-3
grass snake, cross-marked 20, **227**
grass-yellow (*butterfly*), broad-bordered 30, **351**
grasveldgeletjie **351**
grasveldwitjie (*butterfly*) **349**
grawende aspis, suidelike **228**
grawende skerpioene **321**
Gray se klikpadda **251**
Gray's frog 23, **251**
great
　barracuda **276**
　hammerhead shark **269**
　white shark **266**
greater
　cane rat **94**
　honeyguide **176**
　striped swallow 15, **178**
grebe, little **125**
green
　bark scorpion 321
　mamba 20, **220**
　peach aphid 370
　pigeon, African 15, **163**
　stick insect 368
　water snake 20, **221**
　woodhoopoe **173**
greenbottles (*flies*) 376
grey
　crowned crane 7, **111**
　duiker **71**
　go-away bird 12, **166**
　heron 8, **129**
　lourie **166**
　mongoose
　　large 5, **80**
　　small 5, **81**
　nurse shark **267**
　rhebok 1, **57**
　squirrel 6, **89**, 400
grey-headed gull 10, **142**
groen landmeter **357**
groenmamba **220**
groen waterslang **221**
groot
　barrakuda **276**
　hamerkop **269**
　seester **316**
grootbek-baars **261**
grootbek-geelvis **256**
grootgrondgeitjie **240**

grootgrysmuishond **80**
grootheuningwyser **176**
grootkoningriethaan **135**
grootkop-seeskilpad **208**
grootlangtoon **137**
groototter **85**
grootrietrot **94**
grootstreepswael **178**
ground beetles
　anatomy **329**
　predacious 29, **330**
ground birds **104-24**
　Cape fold mountain region 396
　Drakensberg escarpment 394
　east coast subtropical forest region 390
　Eastern Cape & KwaZulu-Natal midlands region 392
　highveld region 384
　Kalahari region 408
　Karoo region 402
　lowveld region 388
　Namaqualand & Bushmanland 404
　Namib Desert region 406
　northern savanna region 386
　southern Cape forest region 398
　southwestern Cape fynbos region 400
ground gecko, giant 22, **240**
ground hornbill, southern **117**
ground squirrel 6, **89**
grunters (*fish*) 27, **291**
Gryllinae 365
Gryllotalpa africana 366
Gryllotalpidae 366
Gryllus bimaculatus 365
grysbok 4, **75**
grysbok, Sharpe's 4, **75**
gryseekhoring **89**
gryskopmeeu **142**
grysmuishond
　groot **80**
　klein **80**
guineafowl, helmeted 12, **110**
guitarfish, lesser **271**
gulls 10, **141-2**
guttural toad 23, **249**
gutturale skurwepadda **249**
gymnogene 11, **156**
Gymnothorax favagineus **289**
Gypaetus barbatus **148**
Gyps africanus **149**
Gyps coprotheres **148**
Gyrinidae 330

H

haaie **266-70**
habitat and diet, freshwater fishes 254
hadeda ibis 9, **107**
Haematopus moquini **137**
hairy thick-tail scorpion 322
hakiesdraad *see* maasbanker
Halcyon albiventris **170**
Halcyon senegalensis **170**
Haliaeetus vocifer **154**
Haliotis midae **309**
hamerkop (*bird*) **131**
hamerkop (*shark*), groot **269**
hammerhead shark, great **269**
harder, suidelike **292**

hardneus-hondhaai **270**
hardnosed smooth-hound **270**
hard scale insects **371**
hare, Cape **78**
hares **78**
harlequin snake, spotted 20, **224**
harrier, African marsh **156**
harrier hawk, African 11, **156**
hartebeest/hartbees II, **53**
Hartlaubse meeu **142**
Hartlaub's gull 10, **142**
harvester ant 381
harvest spiders 319
hase **78**
hawk moths 337
　convolvulus **356**
head
　beetles 328
　freshwater fishes 255
　tortoises & turtles 206
hedgehog, southern African 4, **77**
Helix pomatia 320
helmeted guineafowl 12, **110**
helmeted terrapin **209**
helmetshrike, white-crested 17, **192**
helm-waterskilpad **209**
Helogale parvula **83**
Hemachatus haemachatus **219**
Hemipepsis capensis 378
Hemirhagerrhis nototaenia **225**
Henotesia perspicua **345**
herald snake 20, **222**
herons 8, **104**, **129-30**
Herpestes ichneumon **80**
Hesperiidae 337
Heteronychus spp. 332
Hetrodes pupus 364
Hetrodinae 364
heuningbye **380**
heuningkoek-bontpaling **289**
heuningwyser *see* grootheuningwyser
hiëna, gevlekte **65**
highveld, wildlife 384-5
highwater (*fish*) **294**
hindwing
　anal angle 337
　cell 337
　inner margin 337
　outer margin 337
hinged tortoise, Bell's 18, **210**
hippopotamus **46**
Hippopotamus amphibius **46**
Hippotragus equinus **51**
Hippotragus niger **51**
Hirundo cucullata **178**
Hirundo fuligula **118**
Hirundo rustica **177**
hoephoep **173**
Homopus areolatus **212**
Homopus boulengeri **213**
Homopus signatus **213**
Homoroselaps lacteus **224**
honderdpootvreter, Kaapse **234**
honderdpote **327**
hondhaai, hardneus **270**
honey badger **84**, 155
honeybees 33, **380**
honeycomb moray eel **289**
honeyguide, greater 155, **176**
hook-lipped rhino **47**
hoopoe, African **173**
horingvoëls **174**
hornbills 12, **117**, **174**

hornets 378
horseflies 33, **373**
horse mackerel **299**
horseshoe bat, Geoffroy's 6, **97**
Hotnotsgotte **362**
Hottentot (fish) **294**
Hottentot golden mole 6, **95**
Hottentotta spp. **322**
house
   ant 381
   martin, common 15, **178**
   snake, brown 20, **223**
house-centipede 327
houseflies 33, **375**
houtboorderbye **379**
houtkappers (birds) **175, 176**
hover flies 33, **374**
huisslang **223**
   bruin **223**
huisswael **178**
huisvlieë **375**
hunting dog, Cape **66**
Hyaena brunnea **65**
hyaenas 3, **65**
Hydrocynus vittatus **263**
Hyperolius marmoratus **253**
Hyperolius pusillus **253**
Hypolimnas misippus **342**
Hystrix africaeaustralis **77**

I

ibises 9, **107, 131**
Ichneumonidae 377
ichneumon wasps 32, **377**
Ictonyx striatus **84**
identifying
   beetles **328-9**
   birds **100-3**
   butterflies & moths **336-7**
   freshwater fishes **254-5**
   frogs & toads **246-7**
   insects **358-9**
   lizards 215
   mammals **43-5**
   marine fishes **264-5**
   marine mammals **300**
   scorpions **319**
   snakes 215
   spiders **318-19**
   tortoises & turtles **206-7**
ietermagog **76**
impala 11, **54**
inchworm 357
Indicator indicator **176**
Inciese spreeu **193**
inhlekabafazi **173**
insects 358-9
   Cape fold mountain region 397
   Drakensberg escarpment 395
   east coast subtropical forest region 391
   Eastern Cape & KwaZulu-Natal midlands region 393
   highveld region 385
   Kalahari region 409
   Karoo region 403
   lowveld region 389
   Namaqualand & Bushmanland 405
   Namib Desert region 407
   northern savanna region 387
   southern Cape forest region 399
   south-western Cape fynbos region 401
invertebrates, marine **304-17**
Iolaus silas **353**
Isopoda 326
Isoptera 362
Ixodida **326**

J

jacana, African 12, **137**
jackal buzzard 11, **155**
jackals 3, **67**
jackass (African) penguin **125**
jagluiperd **63**
jagspinnekoppe **323**
jagswaardstert **339**
jakkalsvoëls **154-5**
Janfrederiks **184**
Jangroentjie **195**
Janthina janthina **311**
Jasus lalandii **306**
jellyfish 304
joker (butterfly) 31, **345**
jumping spiders 28, 319, **325**
Junonia hierta cebrene **348**
Junonia octavia sesamus **347**
Junonia oenone oenone **348**

K

kaalwangvalk **156**
Kaapse
   ansjovis **298**
   berglyster **120**
   bergsebra **49**
   bobbejaan **69**
   dwergverkleurmannetjie **239**
   flap **122**
   geelstert **277**
   geitjie **241**
   glasogie **197**
   gouemol **95**
   honderdpootvreter **234**
   kanarie **205**
   kliplyster **119**
   kobra **218**
   kreef **306**
   kurper **260**
   maanskynvis **292**
   padloper **212**
   pelsrob **303**
   platakkedis **242**
   pootlose skink **245**
   rietsanger **146**
   riviercadda **250**
   rotsoester **312**
   skink **243**
   suikervoël **195**
   vuurvinkie **201**
   vylslang **229**
   wolfslang **228**
kabeljou **279**
kaiservoël **190**
kakelaar, gewone **173**
kakkerlakke **361**
Kalahari-tentskilpad **212**
Kalahari tent tortoise 19, **212**
kalanders **335**
kalkoeribis **107**
kameelperd **48**

kanaries **204-5**
Kapenaar (fish) **281**
karanteen **296**
kardinaalspeg **177**
karet **208**
Karoo
   padloper 19, **213**
   prinia **186**
   toad 23, **248**
   wildlife **402-3**
karoolangstertjie **186**
karp **260**
kassina, Senegal **252**
Kassina senegalensis **252**
kathaai, streep **270**
katonkel **274**
katydids **364**
keel **264**, 411
kelkiewyn **115**
kelp gull 10, **141**
kestrel, common **157**
kestrel, rock **157**
kiewiets **113, 138-9**
killer whale **301**
king crickets **363**
kingfish, giant **277**
kingfishers 14, **144-5, 170**
king mackerel 25, **274**
king-of-six (bird) **203**
Kinixys belliana **210**
Kirk's dik-dik **73**
kitefish **292**
kites **150-1**
kleinbek-baars **261**
kleinbyvreter **172**
kleindobbertjie **125**
kleiner sandkruiper **271**
kleinflamink **132**
kleinglansspreeu **194**
kleingrysmuishond **81**
kleinkolmuskejaatkat **87**
kleinotter **85**
klein-rooibandsuikerbekkie **196**
kleinswartooievaar **106**
kleintand saagvis **271**
kleinwindswael **117**
kleinwitreier **130**
klkpadda **251**
klipdas **79**
klipkabeljou, geelpens **285**
klipklaasneus **92**
klplyster, Kaapse **119**
klipspringer 4, **74**
knopiespinnekoppe **325**
knoppiesdopskilpad **211**
knorder, gespikkelde **291**
Knox's desert lizard 22, **243**
Knysna lourie **165**
Knysna turaco 12, **165**
kob 26, **279**
kobras **217-19**
Kobus ellipsiprymnus **58**
Kobus leche **56**
Kobus vardonii **56**
koedoe **60**
koester, gewone **121**
koggelmander *see* rotskoggelmander
kolgans **133**
kommetjiegatmuishond **80**
koningblousysie **202**
koningkrieke **363**
koningrooibekkie **203**
koningvis, reuse **277**
kopereend **133**

kopervlerkies (*butterflies*) **352**
koppie charaxes 30, **340**
koppiedubbelstert **340**
korhaans 10, **112-13**
kori bustard 7, **111**
koringkrieke **364**
koringvoël **198**
kortstertflap **123**
kousbandjie, gevlekte **224**
kousbandslang, Sundevall se **224**
kraaie **119**, **180**
kraanvoël *see* bloukraanvoël
kransaasvoël **148**
kransduif **115**
kransswael **118**
kransvalk **157**
krappe **307**
krapspinnekoppe **324**
kreef, Kaapse **306**
krieke **363-6**
krimpvark, Suider-Afrikaanse **77**
krombekstrandloper **140**
kroonarend **152**
kroonkiewiet **113**
kruismerkgrasslang **227**
kudu 1, **60**
kuifkophoutkapper **176**
kuifkopvisvanger **145**
kurpers **258-9**, **260**
  blue **258**
kuskrap **307**
kussingseester **317**
kwartel, Afrikaanse **109**
kwelea *see* rooibekkewelea
kwevoël **166**
kwikkies **146-7**

L

Labeo umbratus **263**
labial palps **337**
Labidognatha 318
labrum **329**, **359**
ladybird beetles **333**
Lagenorhynchus obscurus **302**
Lagonosticta rubricata **201**
laksmanne **188-9**, 190, **191**, **192**
lammergeier 9, **148**
Lampides boeticus **354**
Lamprophis aurora **223**
Lamprophis fuliginosus **223**
Lamprotornis nitens **194**
Lampyridae 333
Lampyrinae 333
Lanarius atrococcineus **190**
land crustaceans 326
landmeter, groen **357**
landskaaldiere 326
landslakke **320**
land snails 318, **320**
langhoringkewers **335**
langhoringsprinkane **364**
langpootmuskiete **372**
langstertflap **123**
langstertseps, gewone **245**
langstertswartogie (*butterfly*) **354**
Laniarius ferrugineus **189**
Lanius collaris **188**
Lanius collurio **189**
lanner falcon **157**
lappet-faced vulture 8, **149**
lapwings 13, **113**, **139**
large grey mongoose 5, **80**

large mammals **46-69**
  Cape fold mountain region 396
  Drakensberg escarpment 394
  east coast subtropical forest region 390
  Eastern Cape & KwaZulu-Natal midlands region 392
  highveld region 384
  Kalahari region 408
  Karoo region 402
  lowveld region 388
  Namaqualand & Bushmanland 404
  Namib Desert region 406
  northern savanna region 386
  southern Cape forest region 398
  southwestern Cape fynbos region 400
largemouth bass 24, **261**
largemouth yellowfish 24, **256**
large-spotted genet 3, **87**
large striped swordtail **339**
lark, rufous-naped **118**
Larus cirrocephalus **142**
Larus dominicanus **141**
Larus hartlaubii **142**
larvae 336, 337, 412
lateral line **255**, **265**, 412
Latrodectus spp. 325
Latrodectus indistinctus 318
laughing dove 15, **162**
leaf-rolling weevil 335
leatherback turtle 206, **208**
lechwe 1, **56**
leerrug **208**
leervis **278**
leeu **62**
legless skink, Cape 21, **245**
legs
  beetles 328-9
  insects **359**
  tortoises & turtles 207
leguaans **236-7**
lemoenskoenlapper **338**
leopard 2, **62**
leopard tortoise 19, **209**
lepelaar **132**
Lepidoptera 336
Lepisma saccharina 360
Lepomis macrochirus **259**
Leptailurus serval **63**
Leptomyrina hirundo **354**
Leptoptilos crumeniferus **106**
Leptotyphlops nigricans **233**
Lepus capensis **78**
lesser
  bushbaby 5, **88**
  flamingo **132**
  guitarfish **271**
  housefly 375
  sandshark 271
  swamp warbler **146**
Lichia amia **278**
Lichtenstein's hartebeest ll, **53**
liewenheersbesies **333**
life cycle
  beetles 328
  butterflies & moths 336
  frogs & toads 246
life span, tortoises 206
likkewane **236-7**
lilac-breasted roller **172**
limespot butterflyfish **286**
limpet, long-spined **309**

lion **62**
lipvis, goudstaaf **288**
Lithognathus lithognathus **291**
little
  bee-eater 14, **172**
  egret 10, **130**
  grebe **125**
  swift 15, **117**
lizards **215**, **236-45**
  Cape fold mountain region 397
  Drakensberg escarpment 395
  east coast subtropical forest region 391
  Eastern Cape & KwaZulu-Natal midlands region 393
  highveld region 385
  Kalahari region 409
  Karoo region 403
  lowveld region 389
  Namaqualand & Bushmanland 405
  Namib Desert region 407
  northern savanna region 387
  southern Cape forest region 399
  southwestern Cape fynbos region 401
Liza richardsonii **292**
lobster, rock, west coast **306**
locusts 32, **367**
loeries **165-6**, **167**, **169**
loggerhead turtle **208**
Lonchura cucullata **203**
longclaw, Cape **121**
longfin tuna **275**
long-horned beetles **335**
long-horned grasshoppers **364**
long-spined limpet **309**
long-tailed seps, common 22, **245**
long-tailed widowbird 18, **123**
looper, pink-laced emerald **357**
loopers 337
losstertvlermuis, Egiptiese **97**
louries **165-6**
louse, sea **307**
lovebird, rosy-faced 16, **164**
lowveld, wildlife 388-9
Loxodonta africana **46**
lucerne blue (*butterfly*) 31, **354**
lucerne butterfly **350**
Luciolinae 333
Ludwig's bustard **112**
luiperd **62**
luislang, gewone **216**
luna moth, African **355**
lusernbloutjie (*butterfly*) **354**
lusernskoenlapper **350**
Lutjanus argentimaculatus **290**
Lutra maculicollis **85**
Lybius torquatus **175**
Lycaenidae 337, 352
Lycaon pictus **66**
Lycodonomorphus rufulus **222**
Lycophidion capense **228**
Lygosoma sundevallii **244**
lysters **119**, **120**

M

maanmot, Afrikaanse **355**
maanskynvis, Kaapse **292**
maasbanker **299**
Mabuya capensis **243**
mackerel 27, **299**

horse **299**
king 25, **274**
Macrelaps microlepidotus **227**
Macronyx capensis **121**
Macynia labiata 368
Madoqua kirkii **73**
mahem **111**
maize beetle, black 332
Makaira indica **274**
makou *see* wildemakou
makriel **299**
malachite kingfisher 14, **145**
malachite sunbird 15, **195**
malariamuskiete **373**
mamba
  black 21, **217**
  green 20, **220**
mammals 42-5
  Cape fold mountain region 396
  Drakensberg escarpment 394
  east coast subtropical forest region 390
  Eastern Cape & KwaZulu-Natal midlands region 392
  highveld region 384
  Kalahari region 408
  Karoo region 402
  large *see* large mammals
  lowveld region 388
  marine **300-3**
  Namaqualand & Bushmanland 404
  Namib Desert region 406
  northern savanna region 386
  small *see* smaller mammals
  southern Cape forest region 398
  southwestern Cape fynbos region 400
mangrove swamps 390
Manis temminckii **76**
mannikin, bronze (*bird*) 18, **203**
mantids **362**
mantle **100**
Mantodea 362
maraboe **106**
marabou stork 7, **106**
marbled electric ray 25, **273**
marbled reed frog 23, **253**
marginal shield **207**
marine
  fishes **264-99**
  invertebrates **304-17**
  mammals **300-3**
marlin, black **274**
marlyn, swart **274**
marmer-drilvis **273**
marmerrietpadda **253**
marsh
  harrier, African **156**
  mongoose **80**
  patroller (*butterfly*) 30, **345**
Marthasterias glacialis **316**
martial eagle 9, **152**
martin
  house 15, **178**
  rock **118**
masked weaver, southern 16, **200**
Mastomys coucha **93**
mealy bugs **371**
measuring worm 337, 357
Mediterranean land snail 320
Mediterranean type climate 400
meerkat **83**
meeue **141-2**

Megaceryle maxima **145**
Mehelya capensis capensis **229**
Melantis leda helena **343**
Melierax canorus **155**
melkbosskoenlapper, suidelike **343**
Mellivora capensis **84**, 155
Meloidae 334
mermaid's purse 270, 273, 412
Meroles knoxii **243**
Merops apiaster **171**
Merops nubicoides **171**
Merops pusillus **172**
Messor barbarus 381
metacarpal bones **44**
metamorphosis
  beetles 328
  butterflies & moths 336
  frogs & toads 246
Metisella metis **351**
Meyer's parrot 16, **164**
mice 6, **93**
Micropterus dolomieui **261**
Micropterus salmoides **261**
miere **380-1**
mierleeus **372**
miershooptier **86**
migrant, African (*butterfly*) 30, **340**
migration, freshwater fishes 254
mikstertbyvanger **179**
milkweed
  butterflies 30, 342, **343**
  grasshopper **367**
millipedes 28, 318, **327**
Miltogramminae 377
Milvis migrans aegyptius **150**
mimic (*butterfly*) 342, 343
minnow, chubbyhead **257**
Mirafra africana **118**
Mirounga leonina **303**
miskruiers **331**
Miss Lucy (*fish*) **280**
mites 318
mocker swallowtail 30, **338**
moddergarnaal **308**
modderspringer, Afrikaanse **293**
moeraswagter (*butterfly*) **345**
moeraswaterskilpad **209**
moggel **263**
mole
  crab **307**
  crickets 32, **366**
  snake 20, **216**
molerat, common **94**, 95
moles 95, 400
molkrap **307**
molkrieke **366**
molluscs 304
molslang **216**
monarch butterflies 342
mongooses 5, **80-83**
  anatomy 44
monitor, Nile **236**
monkey, vervet **69**
monrik (*butterfly*) **341**
Monodactylus falciformis **292**
Montazilla aguimp **146**
Montazilla capensis **147**
montane wildlife 394-5, 396-7
Monticola rupestris **119**
moor moth, African **355**
moorvy, Cape **292**
moorvis **301**
moorhen 12, **136**
mopane emperor moth **355**

mopane worms 355
mopaniepouoogmot **355**
moray eel, honeycomb **289**
Morus capensis **126**
Mosambiekse spoegkobra **219**
mosquitoes, anopheline **373**
mossels **312-13**
mossie, gewone **199**
mother-of-pearl (*butterfly*) 31, **339**
moths **336-7, 355-7**
  and butterflies, compared 336
  Cape fold mountain region 397
  Drakensberg escarpment 395
  east coast subtropical forest region 391
  Eastern Cape & KwaZulu-Natal midlands region 393
  highveld region 385
  Kalahari region 409
  Karoo region 403
  lowveld region 389
  Namaqualand & Bushmanland 405
  northern savanna region 387
  southern Cape forest region 399
mountain
  adder, Cape **231**
  copper (*butterfly*) 30, **352**
  reedbuck 1, **57**
  tortoise 19, **209**
  zebra, Cape I, **49,** 396
mountain pride (*butterfly*) **344**
mouse *see* mice
mousebirds 13, **168-9**
mouth, marine fishes 265
mouthparts
  beetles 328
  insects 358, **359**
movement
  butterflies & moths 336
  mammals 45
Mozambique
  Current 264
  spitting cobra 21, **219**
  tilapia 24, **258**
mud
  bream **290**
  mullet **263**
  prawn **308**
mudhopper, African **293**
mudskipper **293**
muise **93**
muishonde **80-3**
muisvoëls **168-9**
mullet
  mud **263**
  southern **292**
multimammate mouse 6, **93**
Mungos mungo **82**
Muscicapa adusta **187**
Muscidae 375
muskejaatkatte **87**
Musophaga porphyreolopha **165**
musselcrackers **283**
musselcrushers 26, **283**
mussels 304, **312-13**
Mustelus mosis **270**
muzzle **43, 44,** 412
Myliobatus aquila **272**
Mylothris chloris agathina **350**
myna, common 14, **193**
Myosorex varius **92**
Myriapoda 318
Myrina silenus **353**

Myrmeleontidae 372
Myrmicinae 381
Myzus persicae **370**

N

naaldekokers **361**
na-aperswaelstert **338**
nagadder, gewone **230**
nagapie **88**
naguil, Afrikaanse **116**
Naja annulifera **217**
Naja melanoleuca **218**
Naja mossambica **219**
Naja nivea **218**
Namakwaduifie **162**
Namaqua dove 15, **162**
Namaqualand, wildlife 404-5
Namaqua sandgrouse 15, **115**
Namib-duinadder **230**
Namibia, coastal & central, wildlife 406-7
nape **100**
Narina trogon **169**
Natal
 black snake 20, **227**
 red duiker **72**
 robin-chat 14, **184**
 stumpnose **297**
Natal midlands, wildlife 392-3
Natalse swartslang **227**
national fish 294
nautilus, paper **315**, 410
near-passerines 98, 99
 bills 101
neck fringe **43**
Nectarinia famosa **195**
neddicky 17, **186**
Nematoda 304
Neoscorpis lithophilus **297**
Neotis denhami **112**
Neotragus moschatus **73**
Neptis saclava marpessa **341**
nest record cards 103
Nezara viridula 369
night adder, common 20, **230**
nightjar, fiery-necked **116**
Nile crocodile 215, **236**
Nile monitor **236**
njala 59
Nodilittorina africana africana **310**
Nomeus spp. **317**
nonnetjie-uil **158-60**
non-passerines 98, 99
 bills 101
noordkaper, suidelike **301**
Northern Cape, wildlife 404-5
northern savanna, wildlife 386-7
Notorynchus cepedianus **269**
NRC scheme 103
nuchal shield **207**
Numida meleagris **110**
nyala 1, **59**
Nylkrokodil **236**
Nymphalidae 336

O

ocean currents, and marine fishes 264
ocellated sand lizard **243**

ocelli/ocellus **359**, 412
octopuses 304
 common **306**
Octopus vulgaris **306**
Oecanthinae 365
Oecanthus spp. 365
Oecanthus fultoni 365
Oena capensis **162**
old woman (*fish*) **286**
olifant **46**
olifantrob, suidelike **303**
Oligochaeta 318, 320
olive thrush 16, **183**
olyflyster **183**
Oncorhynchus mykiss **263**
onweerskilpad **213**
Onychognathus morio **122**
oogpisters **330**
ooievaars **105-6**
oorbietjie **70**
oorkruipers **363**
oostelike tierslang **235**
Opiliones 319
Opistopthalmus spp. **321**
orange-breasted bush shrike 17, **191**
orange-breasted sunbird 15, **196**
orange dogs (*caterpillars*) **338**, 412
oranjeborslaksman **191**
oranjeborssuikerbekkie **196**
oranjekeelkalkoentjie **121**
orb-web spiders 28, 319, **324**
Orcinus orca **301**
Oreochromis mossambicus **258**
Oreotragus oreotragus **74**
oribi 3, **70**
oriole, black-headed **179**
Oriolus larvatus **179**
Orthognatha 318
Orycteropus afer **76**
Oryctes boas 332
Oryx gazella **52**
ostrich **104**
Otocyon megalotis **68**
Otomys irroratus **91**
otters 5, **85**
Ourebia ourebi **70**
ou vrou (*fish*) **286**
ovipositor 359, 412
owls 11, 13, **158-60**
oxpecker
 red-billed 47, **194**
 yellow-billed 47
oystercatcher, African black **137**
oysters 304
 rock, Cape **312**

P

Pachnoda spp. 332
Pachydactylus bibronii **239**
Pachydactylus capensis **241**
Pachymetopon blochii **294**
paddavreter, Afrikaanse **156**
padlopers 19, **212-13**
painted
 lady (*butterfly*) 31, **346**
 reed frog 23, **253**
 surgeon (*fish*) **287**
pale chanting goshawk 11, **155**
palmate desert gecko **241**
Palmatogecko rangeri **241**
palm swift 15, **168**
palmwindswael **168**

palps/pedipalps **359**
pangolin **76**
pansies (*butterflies*) 31, **348**
Panthera leo **62**
Panthera pardus **62**
papegaaiduif **163**
papegaaie **163-4**
paper nautilus **315**, 410
papieragtige nautilusskulp **315**
Papilionidae 336
Papio cynocephalus ursinus **69**
Parabuthus spp. **322**
Parabuthus capensis 322
Parabuthus granulatus 322
Parabuthus villosus 322
paradise flycatcher **188**
paradise whydah 18, **204**
paradysvink, gewone **204**
paradysvlieëvanger **188**
parasietwespes **377**
Paraxerus cepapi **90**
Pardopsis punctatissima **347**
Parechinus angulosus **316**
Parkmore prawns 363
parotid gland **247**
parrots 16, **163-4**
Parupeneus rubescens **289**
Parus niger **181**
passerines 98, 99
 bills 101
Passer melanurus **199**
patatpylstertmot **356**
patella **319**
Patiriella exigua **317**
patroller, marsh (*butterfly*) 30, **345**
patrys *see* bospatrys
pearl charaxes 30, **344**
pearl-spotted owlet 13, **159**
pectoral fin **255**, **264**, **265**, 412
Pedetes capensis **78**
Pedipalps/palps **319**, **359**, 412
pelagic fishes 264
Pelamis platurus **232**
Pelea capreolus **57**
Pelecanus onocrotalus **126**
pelican, great white **126**
Peliperdix sephaena **108**
Pelomedusa subrufa **209**
Pel's fishing owl 13, **160**
pelser, Suid-Afrikaanse **298**
pelsrob, Kaapse **303**
pelvic fin **255**, **264**, **265**, 412
penguin, African **125**
penguin, jackass **125**
Pentatomidae 369
pêreldubbelstert **344**
Péringuey's adder 21, **230**
Periopthalmus koelreuteri africanus **293**
Periplaneta americana 361
periwinkle **310**
periwinkle, giant **311**
perlemoen **309**
perlemoenskoenlapper **339**
Perna perna **312**
pers borrelskulp **311**
Peters' epauletted fruit bat 6, **96**
Petrus rupestris **282**
Phacochoerus aethiopicus **61**
Phalacrocorax africanus **128**
Phalacrocorax capensis **127**
Phalacrocorax carbo lucidus **127**
'Pharaoh's rat' **80**
Phasmatodea 368

Pheidole megacephala 381
Philetairus socius **198**
Philothamnus hoplogaster **221**
Phoenicopterus minor **132**
Phoeniculus purpureus **173**
Phymateus leprosus 367
Phymateus morbillosus 367
Physalia physalis **317**
Physophorina livingstoni 366
pied
    avocet **141**
    crow 11, **180**
    kingfisher 14, **144**
    wagtail, African 16, **146**
Pieridae 336
Piet-my-vrou **166**
pigeon
    African green 15, **163**
    rock **115**
    speckled 15, **115**
pig-nosed grunter **291**
pikkewyn see brilpikkewyn
pilchard, South African 27, **298**
pink-laced emerald looper **357**
Pinnipedia 300
pin-tailed whydah 18, **203**
pipit, African **121**
Planococcus citri 371
plantluise **370**
plastron **207**, 412
platakkedis, Kaapse **242**
Platalea alba **132**
platanna, common **248**
platkop (fish), balkstert **293**
platneus-sewekiefhaai **269**
Platycephalus indicus **293**
Platyhelmintha 304
Platysaurus capensis **242**
Plectropterus gambensis **135**
Plocepasser mahali **198**
Ploceus cucullatus **199**
Ploceus velatus **200**
ploegskulp **310**
plough shell **310**
plovers 13, **113**, **138-9**
plum-coloured starling **193**
Pneumoridae 366
Poecilmitis thysbe **352**
poeierblou-doktervis **287**
poekoe **56**
poenskop **283**
pofadder **231**
Pogoniulus pusillus **175**
Poicephalus cryptoxanthus **163**
Poicephalus meyeri **164**
poisonous
    beetles 328
    frogs 246
    snakes 214-15
polecat, striped **84**
Polemaetus belicosus **152**
Polihierax semitorquatus **158**
polka dot (butterfly) 30, **347**
polkastippel (butterfly) **347**
Polyboroides typus **156**
Polysteganus undulosus **282**
Pomacanthus striatus **286**
Pomadasys commersonnii **291**
Pomatomus saltatrix **278**
Pompilidae 378
pond-skaters **369**
pootlose skink, Kaapse **245**
porcupine 4, **77**
Porifera 304

Poroderma africanum **270**
Porphyrio porphyrio madagascariensis **135**
Portuguese man-of-war **317**
Potamochoerus larvatus **61**
poue **111-12**
powder-blue surgeon **287**
pragkopervlerkie (butterfly) **352**
pragtige tiermot **357**
prawns 304
    mud **308**
praying mantids **362**
predacious ground beetles 29, **330**
primary (feathers) **101**, 412
Princeps dardanus cenea **338**
Princeps demodocus **338**
prinia, Karoo **186**
Prinia maculosa **186**
Prionops plumatus **192**
Pristis microdon **271**
proboscis **337**, 412
Procavia capensis **79**
Promerops cafer **195**
pronotum **329**, 412
Prosymna sundevallii **225**
Proteles cristatus **66**
Protogoniomorpha parhassus aethiops **339**
Psammobates geometricus **211**
Psammobates oculifer **212**
Psammobates tentorius **211**
Psammodes 334
Psammophis crucifer **227**
Psammophis leightoni **226**
Psammophylax rhombeatus **226**
Pseudactinia flagellifera **314**
Pseudaspis cana **216**
Pseudocrenella sykion **315**
Pseudococcidae 371
Pseudoscorpiones 319
Ptenopus garrulus **240**
Pternistes swainsonii **109**
Pterocles namaqua **115**
puff adder, common 21, **231**
puffback, black-backed (bird) 17, **190**
puku 1, **56**
purple-crested lourie **165**
purple-crested turaco 12, **165**
purple gallinule **135**
Pycnonotus tricolor **182**
pygmy falcon **158**
pyjama shark **270**
pylstert, blou **272**
pylvlekkaïlagter **181**
Pyrgomorphidae 367
python, southern African 20, **216**
Python sebae natalensis **216**
Pyura stolonifera **314**
Pyxicephalus adspersus **252**

Q

quail, common **109**
quelea, red-billed 18, **200**
Quelea quelea **200**

R

raft shell, bubble **311**
ragged-tooth shark, spotted **267**

rainbird **167**
rainbow trout 24, **262**
rain frog, bushveld **249**
Raja alba **273**
Ralfsia expansa 309
Rana fuscigula **250**
Raphicerus campestris **71**
Raphicerus melanotis **75**
Raphicerus sharpei **75**
raptors see birds of prey
rat
    cane **94**
    vlei **91**
ratel **84**, 155
rattling cisticola 17, **185**
raven, white-necked 11, **119**
rays (fin) **255**, 412-13
rays (fish) 25, **272**, **273**
Recurvirostra avosetta **141**
red
    bishop, southern **147**
    duiker 4, **72**
    hartebeest II, **53**
    locust 367
    roman **281**
    scale insect 371
    steenbras 26, **282**
    stumpnose 26, **280**
red-backed shrike 17, **189**
redbait **314**
red-billed
    hornbill 12, **174**
    oxpecker 47, **194**
    quelea 17, **200**
    teal **134**
    woodhoopoe **173**
redbills **134**
redbreast tilapia 24, **258**
red-capped robin-chat **184**
red-chested cuckoo 13, **166**
red-eyed dove 15, **161**
red-faced mousebird 13, **169**
red-fronted tinkerbird 17, **175**
red-headed finch 18, **202**
red-knobbed coot 12, **136**
red-shouldered widow **123**
red-tailed lizard **242**
Redunca arundinum **58**
Redunca fulvorufula **57**
red-winged starling 14, **122**
reed
    cormorant 8, **128**
    frog, marbled 23, **253**
    warbler, Cape **146**
reedbuck 1, **58**
    mountain 1, **57**
reënboogforel **262**
reënboswalsertjie (butterfly) **351**
reënskilpad **213**
Reichsvogel **190**
reiers **104**, **129-30**
renosterkewers **332**
reproduction, frogs 246
reptiles **214-45**
reuse chiton **308**
reuse koningvis **277**
reuse-ooruil **160**
reuse-reier **129**
reuse-seeskilpad **208**
reuse visvanger **145**
Rhabdomys pumilio **93**
Rhabdosargus globiceps **296**
Rhabdosargus sarba **297**
rhebok, grey 1, **57**

Rhincodon typus **266**
Rhinobatos annulatus **271**
rhinoceros **47**
rhinoceros beetles **332**
Rhinolophus clivosus **97**
Rhodogastria amasis **356**
Rhynchops flavirostris **144**
Richard's pipit **121**
ridgeback grey shark **268**
rietbok **58**
rietduiker **128**
riethaan *see* grootkoningriethaan
rietpadda *see* bontrietpadda
rietsanger, Kaapse **146**
right whale, southern **301**
rinkhals 21, **219**
river
 bream 26, **290**
 frogs 23, **250**
 roman **290**
 snapper **290**
rivierpaddas **250**
rivier-snapper **290**
roan antelope l, **51**
robbe/seals **303**
robber flies 33, **374**
robin-chats 14, **184**
rock
 agama, southern 22, **242**
 dassie 4, **79**
 elephant shrew **92**
 kestrel **157**
 leguaan **237**
 lobster, Cape **306**
 lobster, west coast **306**
 martin **118**
 oyster, Cape **312**
 pigeon **115**
 thrush, Cape 16, **119**
rockcod, yellowbelly **285**
rockjumper, Cape **120**
rogge/rays **272**, **273**
roller, lilac-breasted **172**
roman (*fish*) 26, **280**
 river **290**
roofarend **151**
roofvlieë **374**
rooiaas **314**
rooibaadjies (*locusts*) 367
rooibekeend **134**
rooibekkakelaar **173**
rooibekkwelea **200**
rooibekneushoringvoël **174**
rooibekrenostervoël **194**
rooibeksysie **124**
rooiblestinker **175**
rooibok **54**
rooiborsbyvreter **171**
rooiborsduifie **162**
rooiborsjakkalsvoël **155**
rooibors-kurper **258**
rooiborslaksman **190**
rooiborssuikerbekkie **197**
rooiduiker **72**
rooi-en-bloublaarvlerk (*butterfly*) **347**
rooihartbees **53**
rooijakkals **67**
rooikat **64**
rooikolmuskejaatkat **87**
rooikophoutkapper **175**
rooikopvink **202**
rooilipslang **222**
rooimiere **380**
rooineklewerik **118**

rooioogtortelduif **161**
rooipens **210**
rooiribbok **57**
rooiruglaksman **189**
rooisteenbras **282**
rooistompneus **280**
rooivink **147**
rooivlerkspreeu **122**
rooivlerkstreepkoppie **124**
rooiwangmuisvoël **169**
rooiwangparkiet **164**
roseate tern 143
rose beetle 332
rosy-face lovebird 16, **164**
rotskoggelmander, suidelike **242**
rotsoester, Kaapse **312**
roundworms 304
Rousettus aegyptiacus **96**
rufous-naped lark **118**
ruiters **139-40**
running frog **252**
russet garden snake **233**
rusty-spotted genet **87**

S

saagvis, kleintand **271**
saalneusvlermuis, Geoffroy se **97**
SABAP 103
sable antelope l, **51**
sacred ibis **131**
sac spiders 318-19
saffier (*butterfly*) **353**
Sagittarius serpentarius **108**
sailor (*butterfly*), small spotted 30, **341**
sakabula **123**
Salientia 246
salinity of sea water 264
salmon, Cape **279**
Salmo trutta **262**
Salticidae 319, 325
sand-dwelling thick-tail scorpions 28, **322**
Sandelia capensis **260**
sandgrouse, Namaqua 15, **115**
sand-hoppers 326
sandkruiper, kleiner **271**
sand lizard
 golden **245**
 silver **244**
sandpipers 17, **139-40**
sandshark, lesser **271**
sandskerpioene **322**
sand snake, fork-marked 20, **226**
sand wasps 32, **379**
sandwespe **379**
santer 26, **284**
SAOS 103
sapphire (*butterfly*) 31, **353**
Sarcophaga haemorrhoidalis 377
Sarcophagidae 377
sardine **298**
Sardinops sagax **298**
Sarpa salpa **296**
Satyridae 336, 345
Sauria 214
sausage ants/flies **380**
savanna baboon **69**
savanna, wildlife 386-7
sawfish, smalltooth **271**
Saxicola torquata **120**
scale insects, hard **371**

scales
 freshwater fishes **255**
 marine fishes 265
 snake **214**
scaly anteater **76**
scapulars **100**
scarab **331**
Scarabaeidae 331
scarlet-chested sunbird 15, **197**
scarlet-tip (*butterfly*) 30, **349**
Scelotes bipes **244**
Sciurus carolinensis **89**
Scomber japonicus **299**
Scomberomorus commerson **274**
Scopus umbretta **131**
Scorpionidae 318
scorpions 27, 318, **319**, **321-2**
 Cape fold mountain region 397
 Drakensberg escarpment 395
 east coast subtropical forest region 391
 highveld region 385
 Kalahari region 409
 Karoo region 403
 lowveld region 389
 Namaqualand & Bushmanland 405
 Namib Desert region 407
 northern savanna region 387
 southern Cape forest region 399
 southwestern Cape fynbos region 401
Scotopelia peli **160**
Scutellastra longicosta **309**
scute/shield 206, **207**, 413
Scutigera spp. 327
sea
 anemone **314**
 cucumber **315**
 cucumbers 305
 louse **307**
 salinity 264
 snake, yellow-bellied **232**
 squirt **314**
 squirts 305
 temperature, and marine fishes 264
 urchins 305
 common **316**
seabreams 282, 283, 295
seagulls **141-2**
seals 300, **303**
seasonal migration, freshwater fishes 254
sebras **49**
secondaries, wing **100**, **101**
secretarybird 7, **108**
see-eier, gewone **316**
seekat **306**
seekoei **46**
seekomkommer **315**
seeskilpaaie **208**
seeslang, swart-en-geel **232**
seesterre **316-17**
seeswaels **143**
segmented worms 304
sekretarisvoël **108**
semidesert, wildlife 404-5
Senegalese kassina **252**
Senegal kassina **252**
sensory organ, snake 214
seps, common long-tailed 22, **245**
sergeant-major (*fish*) **287**
Sericopimpla sericata 377

Serinus canicollis **205**
Serinus flaviventris **205**
Serinus mozambicus **204**
Seriola lalandi **277**
Serpentes 214
sersant-majoor *(fish)* **287**
serval 2, **63**
sevengill shark, broadnose **269**
seventyfour *(fish)* 26, **282**
sewekiefhaai, platneus **269**
shape *see* body shape
sharks 25, **266-70**
Sharpe's grysbok 4, **75**
sharptooth catfish 256
shelduck, South African 9, **133**
shield/scute 206, **207**, 413
shield bugs 33, **369**
shield-nose snake 21, **235**
shongololos **327**
shore crab, common **307**
shovel-snout, Sundevall's 20, **225**
shrews **92**
shrikes 17, **188-9, 190, 191, 192**
side-striped jackal 3, **67**
sidewinding adder **230**
Sigmoceros lichtensteinii **53**
silverfish *(fish)* 281
silverfish *(insects)* **360**
silver sand lizard **244**
silver steenbras 283
silvery dwarf burrowing skink 22, **244**
silwergrys dwerg-grawende skink **244**
silwerjakkals **68**
simple eye/ocellus **359**, 412
sitatunga 1, **59**
siwet **64**
size
  birds 100-1
  butterflies & moths 336
  frogs & toads 246
  marine mammals 300
skaapsteker, spotted 20, **226**
skarakenpuntjie *(butterfly)* **349**
skarnierskilpad, Bell se **210**
skate, spearnose 25, **273**
Skeleton Coast, wildlife 406-7
skemerbruintjie *(butterfly)* **343**
skerpione **321-2**
skerppuntige suigskulp **309**
skerptand-baber **256**
skeurtandhaai, spikkel **267**
skildneusslang **235**
skilpaaie **209-13**
skimmer, African **144**
skinks 21, 22, 215, **243-5**
skippers *(butterflies)* 337, 351
skoorsteenveër **131**
skuimbesies **368**
skuimnespadda **251**
skurwepadda **248-9**
slakke *see* landslakke
slakvreter, gewone **233**
slanghalsvoël **128**
slaty egret **130**
slender mongoose 5, **81**
slimjannie *(fish)* **290**
slinger *(fish)* 26, **284**
slug-eater, common 21, **233**
slugs 304
small
  grey mongoose 5, **81**
  spotted cat 5, **86**

spotted sailor *(butterfly)* 30, **341**
smaller mammals **70-97**
  Cape fold mountain region 396
  Drakensberg escarpment 394
  east coast subtropical forest region 390
  Eastern Cape & KwaZulu-Natal midlands region 392
  highveld region 384
  Kalahari region 408
  Karoo region 402
  lowveld region 388
  Namaqualand & Bushmanland 404
  Namib Desert region 406
  northern savanna region 386
  southern Cape forest region 398
  southwestern Cape fynbos region 400
smallmouth bass 24, **261**
small-spotted genet 3, **87**
smalltooth sawfish **271**
smooth-hound, hardnosed **270**
snails 304
  land 318, **320**
snake eagle, black-chested 9, **153**
snake-lizard, Cape **245**
snakes **214-15, 216-35**
  Cape fold mountain region 396, 397
  Drakensberg escarpment 395
  east coast subtropical forest region 391
  Eastern Cape & KwaZulu-Natal midlands region 393
  highveld region 385
  Kalahari region 409
  Karoo region 403
  lowveld region 389
  Namaqualand & Bushmanland 405
  Namib Desert region 407
  northern savanna region 387
  southern Cape forest region 399
  southwestern Cape fynbos region 401
snapper, river **290**
sneeubal *(bird)* **190**
snellervis, toom **288**
snoek 25, **275**
snowy tree cricket **365**
sociable weaver 16, **198**
social wasps 32, **378**
soenie **73**
soldier *(fish)* **284**
Solifugae 319, **323**
sombre bulbul **182**
sombre greenbul **182**
sonbesies **370**
Sondagsrokkie *(butterfly)* **346**
sonkyker **237**
sonvis, bouwang **259**
South African
  pilchard 27, **298**
  shelduck 9, **133**
southern
  bald ibis 9, **107**
  black korhaan 10, **113**
  black tit **181**
  boubou 17, **189**
  burrowing asp 20, **228**
  carmine bee-eater 14, **171**
  double-collared sunbird 15, **196**
  elephant seal **303**

lesser bushbaby 5, **88**
masked weaver 16, **200**
milkweed *(butterfly)* 30, 342, **343**
mullet **292**
pale chanting goshawk 11, **155**
red bishop **147**
right whale **301**
rock agama 22, **242**
yellow-billed hornbill 12, **174**
southern African
  hedgehog **77**
  rock python 20, **216**
Southern African Bird Atlas Project 103
Southern African Ornithological Society 103
southern Cape forest wildlife 398-9
southwestern Cape fynbos, wildlife 400-1
Sparodon durbanensis **283**
Sparrman's tilapia **259**
sparrow, Cape 16, **199**
sparrowweaver, white-browed 16, **198**
spat 313
spearnose skate 25, **273**
speckled mousebird 13, **168**
speckled padloper 19, **213**
speckled pigeon 15, **115**
spekvreter, gewone **183**
Sphecinae 379
Spheniscus demersus **125**
Sphingidae 337
Sphodromantis gastrica 362
Sphyraena barracuda **276**
Sphyrna mokarran **269**
spider wasps 32, **378**
spiders 318-**19, 323-5**
  Cape fold mountain region 397
  Drakensberg escarpment 395
  east coast subtropical forest region 391
  Eastern Cape & KwaZulu-Natal midlands region 393
  highveld region 385
  Kalahari region 409
  Karoo region 403
  lowveld region 389
  Namaqualand & Bushmanland 405
  Namib Desert region 407
  northern savanna region 387
  southern Cape forest region 399
  southwestern Cape fynbos region 401
spiesneus-rog **273**
spikkel-skeurtandhaai **267**
spikkelswewer **341**
spines 255, 264, **359**, 413
spinnekopjagters **378**
spinnekoppe **323-5**
spiny starfish **316**
spiracle 265, **359**, 413
spitting cobra, Mozambique 21, **219**
spittle bugs 33, **368**
spoegkobra, Mosambiekse **219**
sponges 304
spoonbill, African **132**
spotted
  cat, small 5, **86**
  cikkop **114**
  dwarf garter snake **224**
  eagle owl 11, **159**

grunter 27, **291**
harlequin snake 20, **224**
hyaena 3, **65**
prinia **186**
ragged-tooth shark **267**
sailor (*butterfly*), small 30, **341**
skaapsteker 20, **226**
sugar ant **381**
thick-knee **114**
spotted-backed weaver 16, **199**
spotted-necked otter 5, **85**
spreeus **122, 192, 193-4**
springbok II, **70**
springhaas/springhare **78**
springspinnekoppe **325**
springsterte **360**
springtails **360**
sprinkane **364, 366-7**
spurfowl, Swainson's **109**
spurs **359**
spur-winged goose **135**
Squamata 214
square-lipped rhino **47**
squirrels 6, **89-90**
  grey 400
stable fly 375
Stanley's bustard **112**
starfish 305, **316-17**
starlings 14, **122, 192, 193-4**
steenbok 3, **71**
steenbras
  black **283**
  red 26, **282**
  silver **283**
  white 27, **283, 291**
Stenopelmatidae 363
Stephanoaetus coronatus **152**
steppe buzzard **154**
Sterna bergii **143**
Sterna hirundo **143**
stick insects **368**
stingray, blue 25, **272**
stinkbesies **369**
stink bugs **369**
stink locusts 32, **367**
stinkmuishond **84**
stinksprinkane **367**
stinkvis **297**
stokinsekte **368**
stokstertmeerkat **83**
Stomoxys calcitrans 375
stompneus *see* rooistompneus
stonebream 27, **297**
stonechat **120**
Stonehamia varanes varanes **344**
storks 7, **105-6**
strandjut **65**
streep-kathaai **270**
streepmuis **93**
strepie (*fish*) **296**
Streptopelia capicola **161**
Streptopelia semitorquata **161**
Streptopelia senegalensis **162**
Striostrea margaritacea **312**
striped
  catshark **270**
  mouse 6, **93**
  polecat **84**
  swallow, greater 15, **178**
  swordtail, large **339**
Strongylopus grayii **251**
Struthio camelus **104**
stumpnose/stompneus 26, **280, 296, 297**

Sturnus vulgaris **192**
subtropical forest, wildlife 392-3
Sufflamen fraenatus **288**
sugar ant 33, **381**
sugarbird, Cape **195**
Suid-Afrikaanse pelser **298**
suidelike
  grawende aspis **228**
  harder **292**
  melkbosskoenlapper **343**
  noordkaper **301**
  olifantrob **303**
  rotskoggelmander **242**
  waterfiskaal **189**
Suider-Afrikaanse krimpvark **77**
suigskulp, skerppuntige **309**
suikerbekkies **196-7**
suikermiere **381**
suikervoël, Kaapse **195**
sunbirds 15, **195-7**
Sundevall's
  garter snake 20, **224**
  shovel-snout 20, **225**
  writhing skink 22, **244**
sunfish, bluegill 24, **259**
sungazer 22, **237**
suni 4, **73**
sun spiders 28, 319, **323**
supra caudal shield **207**
surgeon, painted (*fish*) **287**
Suricata suricatta **83**
suricate 5, **83**
survival of wildlife 382
suurpoortjieskilpad **211**
swaarweerskilpad **213**
swaels **118, 177-8**
Swainson's francolin **109**
Swainson's spurfowl 12, **109**
swallows 15, **177-8**
swallowtails (*butterflies*) 30, 31, 336, **338**
swamp rat **91**
swartaasvoël **149**
swartborsslangarend **153**
swart draadslang **233**
swart-en-geel seeslang **232**
swartkeelgeelvink **200**
swartkopreier **104**
swartkopwielewaal **179**
swartkraai **180**
swartmamba **217**
swart marlyn **274**
swartmossel **313**
swartoogtiptol **182**
swartpootkat **86**
swartreier **130**
swartrenoster **47**
swartrugmeeu **141**
swartsaal-bokvis **289**
swartslang, Natalse **227**
swarttobie **137**
swartvlerkkorhaan **113**
swartwasmuishond **81**
swartwildebees **50**
swartwitpens **51**
swartwou **150**
sweefvlieë **374**
swerwer, Afrikaanse (*butterfly*) **340**
swifts 15, **116-17, 168**
swift tern 10, **143**
swordtail (*butterfly*), striped, large **339**
sylph (*butterfly*), gold-spotted 30, **351**

Sylvicapra grimmia **71**
Syncerus caffer **48**
Syrphidae 374

T

tabakrolletjie (*snake*) **233**
Tabanidae 373
Table Mountain
  beauty (*butterfly*) 31, **344**
  cockroach 361
Tachybaptus ruficollis **125**
Tachymarptis melba **116**
Tadarida aegyptiaca **97**
Tadorna cana **133-4**
tail
  bird 101, **103**
  marine mammals 300
tailed black-eye (*butterfly*) 31, **354**
tail fin **255, 264, 265,** 413
takbok, Europese **74**
takslang **221**
tarentaal, gewone **110**
tarsus **100, 247, 319, 329, 359**
Tatera leucogaster **91**
Tauraco corythaix **165**
Taurotragus oryx **52**
tawny eagle 9, **151**
teal, red-billed **134**
teardrop butterflyfish **286**
teeth
  freshwater fishes 255
  marine fishes 265
Telescopus semiannulatus **235**
Telophorus sulfureopectus **191**
Telophorus zeylonus **191**
temperature, sea, and marine fishes 264
Tenebrionidae 334
tent tortoises 19, **211, 212**
Tephritidae 375
Terathopius ecaudatus **153**
termites 33, **362**
terns 10, **143**
Terpsiphone viridis **188**
terrapins 206, **207,** 413
  Cape fold mountain region 397
  Drakensberg escarpment 395
  east coast subtropical forest region 391
  Eastern Cape & KwaZulu-Natal midlands region 393
  helmeted **209**
  Kalahari region 409
  Karoo region 403
  highveld region 385
  lowveld region 389
  Namaqualand & Bushmanland 405
  Namib Desert region 407
  northern savanna region 387
  southern Cape forest region 399
  southwestern Cape fynbos region 401
tertials, wing **100, 101**
Tetragnathidae **324**
Tettigoniidae 364
Thalassoma hebraicum **288**
Thelotornis capensis **221**
Theraphosidae 318, 323
thick-knee, spotted **114**
thick-tailed bushbaby 5, **88**
thick-tail scorpions 28, **322**

Thomisidae 319, 324
thorax **377, 359,** 413
thread snake, black 21, **233**
three-banded plover 13, **138**
three-striped skink **243**
Threskiornis aethiopicus **131**
thrush
  Cape rock 16, **119**
  olive 16, **183**
Thryonomys swinderianus **94**
Thunnus alalunga **275**
Thyrsites atun **275**
Thysanura 360
Thysbe copper (*butterfly*) 31, **352**
tibia **100, 247, 319, 329, 359**
tickbird **105**
ticks 318, **326**
tide levels, and marine invertebrates 305
tierboskat **63**
tiermotte **356, 357**
tierslang, oostelike **235**
tiervis **263**
tiger
  moths 337, **356, 357**
  shark **267**
  snake, eastern 21, **235**
tigerfish **263**
Tilapia rendalli **258**
tilapias 24, **258-9**
Tilapia sparrmanii **259**
tinkerbird, red-fronted 17, **175**
tiptol **182**
Tipulidae 372
tit, southern black **181**
toads 23, 246-7, **248-9,** 413
  and frogs, compared 246
  Cape fold mountain region 397
  Drakensberg escarpment 395
  east coast subtropical forest region 391
  Eastern Cape & KwaZulu-Natal midlands region 393
  highveld region 385
  Kalahari region 409
  Karoo region 403
  lowveld region 389
  Namaqualand & Bushmanland 405
  Namib Desert region 407
  northern savanna region 387
  southern Cape forest region 399
  southwestern Cape fynbos region 401
Tockus erythrorhynchus **174**
Tockus leucomelas **174**
toktokkies 29, **334**
tolliegrasvegter (*butterfly*) **345**
toom-snellervis **288**
toordokter (*butterfly*) **342**
toppie **182**
Torgos tracheliotus **149**
Torpedo sinuspersici **273**
tortelduif, gewone **161**
tortoises 19, 206-7, **209-13**
  Cape fold mountain region 396, 397
  east coast subtropical forest region 391
  Eastern Cape & KwaZulu-Natal midlands region 393
  highveld region 385
  Kalahari region 409
  Karoo region 403

lowveld region 389
Namaqualand & Bushmanland 405
Namib Desert region 407
northern savanna region 387
southern Cape forest region 399
southwestern Cape fynbos region 401
toxic *see* poisonous
Toxoptera citricidus 370
Trachurus trachurus capensis **299**
Trachyphonus vaillantii **176**
Tragelaphus angasii **59**
Tragelaphus scriptus **60**
Tragelaphus spekei **59**
Tragelaphus strepsiceros **60**
Transkei, wildlife 392-3
trap-door spiders **318**
tree
  crickets 32, **365**
  dassie 4, **79**
  squirrel 6, **90**
tree birds 98, **161-205**
  Cape fold mountain region 397
  Drakensberg escarpment 395
  east coast subtropical forest region 390-1
  Eastern Cape and KwaZulu-Natal midlands region 393
  highveld region 385
  Kalahari region 409
  Karoo region 403
  lowveld region 389
  Namaqualand & Bushmanland 405
  Namib Desert region 407
  northern savanna region 387
  southern Cape forest region 398
  southwestern Cape fynbos region 401
trekduiker **127**
Treron calva **163**
tricoloured tiger moth **356**
triggerfish, bridle **288**
Tringa glareola **140**
trogon, Narina **169**
tropical forest, wildlife 390-1
tropiese grysbok **75**
troupant, gewone **172**
trout 24, **262**
tsessebe 11, **54**
tsetse flies 33, **376**
tuinrooitjie (*butterfly*) **346**
tuna, longfin **275**
Tunicates 305
turban shell, Cape **311**
Turbo sarmaticus **311**
Turdoides jardineii **181**
Turdus olivaceus **183**
turtle dove, Cape 15, **161**
turtles 206-7, **208**
twig snake 20, **221**
Typhlops bibronii **234**
Tyto alba **158**

U

uile **158-60**
under tail-coverts **100**
Upogebia africana **308**
upper tail-coverts **100**
Upupa africana **173**
Uraeginthus angolensis **201**

Uraeginthus granatina **202**
urchin, sea **316**
Urocolius indicus **169**
Uroplectes carinatus 321
Uroplectes lineatus 321
Uroplectes olivaceus 321
Uroplectes spp. **321**
Uropygi 319

V

vaalboskat **86**
vaaldolfyn **302**
vaalmol **94**
vaalribbok **57**
vaalstrandkiewiet **138**
vaalveldmuis **93**
valke **155, 156-8**
Vanellus armatus **139**
Vanellus coronatus **113**
Vanessa cardui **346**
Varanus exanthematicus **237**
Varanus niloticus **236**
veereier **105**
veldkrieke **365**
veldlikkewaan **237**
veldpou **112**
venom, snake 214-15
ventral scales **214**
verkleurmannetjies **238-9**
Verreaux's eagle 9, **151**
Verreaux's eagle owl 11, **160**
versamelvoël **198**
vertebral shield **207**
vervet monkey **69**
Vespidae 378
Vespula germanica 378
Vidua macroura **203**
Vidua paradisaea **204**
vier-en-sewentig (*fish*) **282**
village weaver 16, **199**
vinke **147, 200, 202, 204**
violet-backed starling 14, **193**
violet bubble shell **311**
violet-eared waxbill 18, **202**
visarend **154**
vismotte **360**
visuil **160**
visvangers **144-5, 170**
vlakhaas **78**
vlakvark **61**
vleiloerie, gewone **167**
vlei rat, common **91**
vleirot **91**
vlei-tilapia **259**
vleimuise **96-7**
vlieë **373-7**
vlieëvangers **187, 188**
vliedervis, eenkol **286**
voëlentwitjie (*butterfly*) **350**
volstruis **104**
vrugtetorre **332**
vrugtevlermuise **96**
vrugtevlieë **375**
Vulpes chama **68**
vultures 8, **148-9**
vurkmerksandslang **226**
vuurvinkie, Kaapse **201**
vuurvliegies 333
vyeboombloutjie (*butterfly*) **353**
vylslang, Kaapse **229**

W

waaierstertgrondeekhoring **89**
wagtails 16, **146-7**
walvishaai **266**
warbler, Cape reed **146**
warbler, lesser swamp **146**
warthog 2, **61**
warts **247**, 413
wasps 32, **377-9**
water
  beetles 29, **331**
  leguaan **236**
  mongoose 5, **80**
  snakes 20, **221, 222**
  tortoises/terrapins 206, **207**
waterbirds 98, **125-47**
  Cape fold mountain region 396
  Drakensberg escarpment 394-5
  east coast subtropical forest region 390
  Eastern Cape & KwaZulu-Natal midlands region 392-3
  highveld region 384-5
  Karoo region 403
  lowveld region 388
  Namaqualand & Bushmanland 404
  Namib Desert region 406
  northern savanna region 386
  southern Cape forest region 398
  southwestern Cape fynbos region 400-1
waterbuck/waterbok 1, **58**
waterfiskaal, suidelike **189**
waterhoender **136**
waterhondjies (*beetles*) **330**
waterkewers **331**
waterkoedoe **59**
waterleliepadda **253**
waterlikkewaan **236**
water lily frog 23, **253**
waterlopers **369**
waterploeër **144**
waterskilpad *see* helmwaterskilpad
waterslange **221, 222**
wattle bagworm 377
wawielwebspinnekoppe **324**
waxbills 18, **124, 201-2**
weavers 16, **198, 199-200**
web-footed gecko 22, **241**
webvoetgeitjie **241**
weevils 29, **335**
wespes **377-9**
west coast rock lobster **306**
wewer **199**
whales 300, **301**
whale shark **266**
whip scorpions 319
whirligig beetles 29, **330**
white
  ants **362**
  biskop **283**
  helmetshrike **192**
  mussel **313**
  musselcracker 26, **283**
  pelican **126**
  rhinoceros **47**
  steenbras 27, **283, 291**
  stork 7, **105**
  stumpnose 26, **296**
  see also whites
white-backed vulture 8, **149**
white-breasted cormorant 8, **127**
white-browed sparrowweaver 16, **198**
white-crested helmetshrike 17, **192**
white-eye, Cape **197**
whitefish 24, **257**
white-fronted plover 13, **138**
white-necked raven 11, **119**
whites (*butterflies*) 30, **349-50, 351**
whydahs 18, **203-4**
widowbirds **122-3**
widow-finch 201
wielewaal *see* swartkopwielewaal
wild cat, African 5, **86**
wild dog **66**
wildebeest l, **50**
wildehond **66**
wildemakou **135**
wildeperd (*fish*) **295**
willie, gewone **182**
windswaels **116-17, 168**
wing-cases *see* elytra
wing-coverts
  greater under **101**
  lesser upper **100, 101**
  marginal under **101**
  marginal upper **101**
  median **100**
  median under **101**
  median upper **101**
wing membrane **44**
wings
  bird **101**
  insects 358, **359**
wing-vein **337**
wipstertmiere **381**
witbiskop **283**
witborsduiker **127**
witborskraai **180**
witborsspreeu **193**
witdoodshaai **266**
withalskraai **119**
withelmlaksman **192**
witkoluil **159**
witkolvrugtevlermuis, Peters se **96**
witkruisarend **151**
witkwasjakkals **67**
witkwasmuishond **82**
witliesbosbontrokkie **187**
witluise **371**
witmalgas **126**
witmossel **313**
witooievaar **105**
witpelikaan **126**
witpenswindswael **116**
witrenoster **47**
witrugaasvoël **149**
witsteenbras **291**
witstompneus **296**
witvis **257, 284**
woestynakkedis, Knox se **243**
wolfslang, Kaapse **228**
wolf snake, Cape 20, **228**
woodhoopoe **173**
woodland dormouse **90**
woodland kingfisher 14, **170**
woodlice 326
woodpecker, cardinal **177**
wood sandpiper 17, **140**
woolly apple aphid 370
woolly bears (*caterpillars*) 337, 357, 413
worm snake, black **233**
worms, segmented/bristle 304
wrasse, goldbar **288**
wriemelskink, Sundevall se **244**
writhing skink, Sundeval's 22, **244**

X

Xenopus laevis **248**
Xerus inauris **89**
Xylocopinae 379

Y

yellow
  bishop (*bird*) 18, **122**
  canary 18, **205**
  mongoose 5, **82**
  see also yellows
yellow-bellied sea snake **232**
yellowbelly rockcod **285**
yellow-billed
  duck 9, **134**
  hornbill, southern **174**
  kite **150**
  oxpecker 47
yellow-eyed canary 18, **204**
yellowfish, largemouth 24, **256**
yellow-fronted canary **204**
yellow-rumped widow (*bird*) **122**
yellows (*butterflies*) 30, 31, **348, 350-1**
yellowtail, Cape 25, **277**
ystervark **77**

Z

Zambezi shark 25, **268**
zebra (*fish*) 27, **295**
zebra (*mammal*) l, **49**
  mountain, Cape 396
Zonocerus elegans 367
Zosterops pallidus **197**

Bibliography

The publishers gratefully acknowledge the following publications, which were referred to in the production of this book:

African insect life, SH Skaife (Struik 1979); *The amphibia of South Africa*, JC Poynton (Natal Museum 1964); *Amphibians of Malawi*, MM Stewart (State University of New York Press 1967); *Angling fishes of the Transvaal*, T Babich and P Mulder (Department of Nature Conservation 1977); *Animal life encyclopedia*, Dr HB Grzimek (Van Nostrand Reinhold 1972); *Animal life in southern Africa*, DJ Potgieter, PC du Plessis and SH Skaife (NASOU 1971); *Atlas of insects*, Michael Tweedie (Heinemann 1974); *Atlas of southern Africa* (Reader's Digest 1984); *Atlas of wildlife*, Jacqueline Nayman (Heinemann 1972); *The batoid fishes of the east coast of southern Africa*, John H Wallace (South African Association for Marine Biological Research 1967); *The bats of West Africa*, DR Rosevear (Trustees of the British Museum 1965); *Biogeography and ecology of southern Africa*, MJA Werger (Dr W Junk Publishers 1978); *Biogeography and ecosystems of South Africa*, ME Meadows (Juta 1985); *Birdlife in southern Africa*, ed by K Newman (Macmillan 1979); *Birds*, Dr C Perrins and Dr CJO Harrison (Reader's Digest 1980); *Birds of prey*, I Sinclair and D Goode (Struik 1986); *A book of beetles*, Dr J Winkler and V Bohac (Spring Books 1964); *Britain's wildlife, plants and flowers* (Reader's Digest 1987); *Butterflies of southern Africa*, Hugo Germishuys (Chris van Rensburg Publications 1982); *Classification of the animal kingdom* (Hodder and Stoughton 1979); *Collins guide to wild life in home and home*, H Mourier and O Winding (Collins 1975); *The common dog tick Haemophysalis leachi as a vector of the tick typhus*, J Gear and B de Meillon (SA Medical Journal 1939); *The common sea fishes of southern Africa*, R van der Elst (Struik 1981); *Did you know that?* M and G Purcell (Van Schaik 1945); *The Drakensberg of Natal*, DP Liebenberg (TV Bulpin 1982); *East African mammals*, J Kingdon (Academic Press 1971-1982); *Ecology of tropical savannas*, BJ Huntley and BH Walker (Springer-Verlag 1987); *Emperor moths of south and central Africa*, Elliot Pinhey (Struik 1971); *The encyclopedia of sea mammals*, DJ Coffey (Hart-Davis, MacGibbon 1977); *Explore the seashore of South Africa*, Margo Branch (Struik 1987); *The fascination of reptiles*, Maurice Richardson (Andre Deutsch 1972); *The fauna and flora of southern Africa*, Douglas Hey (Department of Nature and Environmental Conservation 1982); *A field guide to the birds of southern Africa*, OPM Prozesky (Collins 1980); *Field guide to the birds of southern Africa*, I Sinclair (Struik 1987); *A field guide to the butterflies of Africa*, JG Williams (Collins 1978); *Field guide to the butterflies of southern Africa*, Ivor Migdoll (Struik 1994); *A field guide to the insects of America north of Mexico*, Donald J Borror and Richard E White (Houghton Mifflin 1970); *A field guide to the larger mammals of Africa*, J Dorst and P Dandelot (Collins 1980); *A field guide to the mammals of Africa*, T Haltenorth and H Diller (Collins 1980); *Field guide to the mammals of southern Africa*, Chris and Tilde Stuart (Struik 2001); *A field guide to the seabirds of southern Africa*, Gerald Tuck and Hermann Heinzel (Collins 1979); *A field guide to the snakes of southern Africa*, VFM FitzSimons (Collins 1970); *The fishes*, FD Ommanney (Time-Life International 1964); *FitzSimons' snakes of southern Africa*, ed by DG Broadley (Delta Books 1983); *Focus on fauna*, J Clarke and J Pitts (Keartland 1972); *Freshwater fish and fishing in Africa*, AC Harrison et al (Nelson 1963); *Freshwater fishes of Natal*, RS Crass (Shuter and Shooter 1964); *Freshwater fishes of southern Africa*, RA Jubb (Balkema 1967); *The freshwater fishes of the Kruger National Park*, U de V Pienaar (National Parks Board 1978); *Freshwater fishes of the world*, G Sterba (Vista Books 1962); *The frogs of South Africa*, VA Wager (Purnell 1965); *The frogs of the Kruger National Park*, U de V Pienaar, NI Passmore and VC Carruthers (National Parks Board 1976); *Garden pests and diseases in South Africa*, WM de Villiers and AS Schoeman (Struik 1988); *Guide to the common sea fishes of southern Africa*, R van der Elst (Struik 1981); *Guide to the rats and mice of Rhodesia*, RHN Smithers (Trustees of the National Museums and Monuments of Rhodesia 1975); *The Hamlyn all-colour animal encyclopedia*, C Kilpatrick and J Hard (Hamlyn 1981); *Illustrated guide to the game parks and nature reserves of southern Africa* (Reader's Digest 1983); *Illustrated guide to the southern African coast* (AA The Motorist Publications 1988); *Insects*, Erik Holm and Elbie de Meillon (Struik 1986); *Insects* (Hamlyn 1979); *The insects of southern Africa*, Margaret Bevis (Thomas Nelson and Sons 1964); *Insects of southern Africa*, H Scholtz Clarke and E Holm (Butterworths 1986); *Insects: review of insect life in Rhodesia* Alan Weaving (Regal Publishers 1977); *The international wildlife encyclopedia*, ed by Dr M Burton and R Burton (BPC Publishing 1970); *An introduction to animal ecology in southern Africa*, JM Winterbottom (Maskew Miller 1971); *Introduction to insect study in Africa*, ECG Pinhey (Oxford University Press 1968); *An introduction to the study of insects*, DJ Borror and DM De Long (Rineholt and Winston 1972); *The invertebrata*, LA Borrada le and FA Potts (Cambridge University Press 1961); *Land mammals of southern Africa*, RHN Smithers (Macmillan 1986); *Life in the oceans*, FR de la Fuente (Orbis 1974); *The life of the chameleon*, VA Wager (Wildlife Society of Southern Africa 1984); *The lives of wasps and bees*, C Andrews (Chatto and Windus 1969); *Living fishes of the world*, ES Herald (Doubleday 1971); *Living insects of the world*, AB Klots and EB Klots (Hamish Hamilton 1959); *Living invertebrates of the world*, R Buchsbaum and LJ Milne (Hamish Hamilton 1960); *Living reptiles of the world*, KP Schmidt and RF Inger (Hamish Hamilton 1957); *The living shores of southern Africa*, G Branch and M Branch (Struik 1981); *The lizards of South Africa*, VF FitzSimons (Trustees of the Transvaal Museum 1946); *Illustrated animal encyclopedia*, ed by Dr P Whitfield (Longman 1984); *The Low-veld: its wild life and its people*, J Stevenson-Hamilton (Cassell 1934); *Maberly's mammals of southern Africa revised*, R Goss (Delta Books 1986); *The mammals*, D Morris (Hodder and Stoughton 1965); *The mammals of southern Africa*, A Roberts (Trustees of 'The Mammals of Southern Africa' Book Fund 1951); *The mammals of the southern African sub-region*, RHN Smithers (University of Pretoria 1983); *Mammals of the world*, EP Walker (John Hopkins Press 1964); *Marine life along our shores*, Pauline Harding (Tafelberg 1987); *Marvels and mysteries of our animal world* (Reader's Digest 1979); *Moths of southern Africa*, ECG Pinhey (Tafelberg 1975); *Mountain environments* (Council for the Habitat 1976); *Mountain odyssey in southern Africa*, David Coulson (Macmillan 1983); *Mountains of southern Africa*, David Bristow and Gerald Cubitt (Struik 1985); *The Natal bushveld* (Natal Parks Board 1981); *The natural history of southern Africa*, David Bristow and Gerald Cubitt (Struik 1988); *New Larousse encyclopedia of animal life*, ed by L Bertin et al (Hamlyn 1980); *North American wildlife* (Reader's Digest 1982); *Official place names in the Republic of South Africa and South-West Africa* (Place Names Committee 1978); *Ons eie insekte*, E Holm en M de Villiers (Tafelberg 1983); *Oxford book of insects*, John Burton (Oxford University Press 1968); *Pennington's butterflies of southern Africa*, ed by CGC Dickson and Dr DM Kroon (AD Donker 1978); *A pictorial guide to South African fishes*, KH Barnard (Maskew Miller 1947); *Pocket guide to the freshwater fishes of southern Africa*, MN Bruton, PBN Jackson and PH Skelton (Centaur 1982); *The population explosion and its effect on entomology in South Africa* (Department of Agricultural and Technical Services 1974); *Pretoria to Beit Bridge*, TV Bulpin (TV Bulpin for Mobil 1974); *Reptile fauna of the Kruger National Park*, U de V Pienaar (National Parks Board 1978); *The reptiles and amphibians of southern Africa*, W Rose (Maskew Miller 1962); *Reptiles and amphibians of the world*, H Hvass (Methuen 1964); *Reptiles of southern Africa*, R Patterson (Struik 1987); *The reptile world*, CH Pope (Routledge, Kegan Paul 1956); *Roberts' birds of southern Africa*, ed by Gordon Lindsay Maclean (The Trustees of the John Voelcker Book Fund 1985); *The rodents of southern Africa*, G de Graaff (Butterworth 1981); *Seashore life*, Charles and Roberta Griffiths (Struik 1988); *Sea turtles: a guide*, GR Hughes (Natal Parks Board 1978); *Sea turtles of south-east Africa*, GR Hughes (South African Association for Marine Biological Research 1974); *Sharks* (Reader's Digest 1986); *Sharks and stingrays*, R van der Elst and R Vermeulen (Struik 1986); *The small mammals of the Kruger National Park*, U de V Pienaar, IL Rautenbach and G Graaff (National Parks Board 1980); *Smith's sea fishes*, ed by Margaret M Smith and Phillip C Heemstra (Macmillan 1986); *Snails of land and sea*, Hilda Simon (Vanguard Press 1976); *Snakes and snakebite*, J Visser (Purnell 1978); *Some well-known African moths*, Elliot Pinhey (Longman Rhodesia 1975); *South African and Rhodesian freshwater fishing guide*, Len Jones (The author 1971); *South African frogs*, NI Passmore and VC Carruthers (Witwatersrand University Press 1979); *South African nature notes*, SH Skaife (Maskew Miller 1961); *South African shells*, Deidre Richards (Struik 1984); *South African spiders and scorpions*, A Prins and V Leroux (Anubis Press 1986); *South African wild flower guide 2: Outeniqua, Tsitsikamma and eastern Little Karoo*, Audrey Moriarty (Botanical Society of South Africa 1982); *South African wild flower guide 4. Transvaal lowveld and escarpment*, Jo Onderstal (Botanical Society of South Africa 1984); *South African wild flower guide 5: Hottentots Holland to Hermanus*, Lee Burman and Anne Bean (Botanical Society of South Africa 1985); *Spiders*, G Newlands and E de Meillon (Struik 1986) *Spiders of southern Africa*, JH Yates (Books of Africa 1968); *Strike!*, S Schoeman (Balkema 1982); *Studies on the land molluscs of Zululand*, AC van Bruggen (EJ Brill 1969); *The study of ants*, SH Skaife (Longmans 1961); *A systematic revision of the shrew genus Crocidura in southern Africa*, J Meester (Transvaal Museum 1963); *Transkei: the 50th state in Africa* (Department of Information 1976); *Tsitsikamma shore*, RM Tietz and Dr GA Robinson (Natal Parks Board 1980); *Two oceans: a guide to the marine life of southern Africa*, GM Branch, CL Griffiths et al (David Philip 1994); *Veld and vlei*, W Rose (Specialty Press of South Africa 1929); *Venomous animals and their venoms*, ed by W Bucherl and EE Buckley (Academic Press 1971); *Venomous creatures*, Gerry Newlands and Elbie de Meillon (Struik 1987); *What antelope is that?* Paul Rose (Purnell 1967); *Wildlife heritage of South Africa*, Douglas Hey (Oxford University Press 1966); *The world of amphibians and reptiles*, R Mertens (George G Harrap 1969).

Periodicals: *African wildlife*; *Custos*; *Outspan*; *Sedgewick's Old Brown rock and surf angling guides*; *Vagabond*. Thanks also to the South African Museum's website, www.museums.org.za

Reproduction by Imvakalelo Repro cc
Printed and Bound by CTP Book Printers (Pty) Ltd Cape Town.